Herman Melville, 1851–1891

Herman Melville

A Biography
Volume 2, 1851–1891

❦

Hershel Parker

THE JOHNS HOPKINS UNIVERSITY PRESS
BALTIMORE AND LONDON

Copyright © 2002 Hershel Parker
All rights reserved. Published 2002
Printed in the United States of America on acid-free paper
2 4 6 8 9 7 5 3 1

The Johns Hopkins University Press
2715 North Charles Street
Baltimore, Maryland 21218-4363
www.press.jhu.edu

Library of Congress Cataloging-in-Publication Data will
be found at the end of this book.
A catalog record for this book is available from the
British Library.

ISBN 0-8018-6892-0

Frontispiece: *Herman Melville*
Copyright © 2002 Maurice Sendak

FOR HEDDY-ANN RICHTER

Contents

	LIST OF ILLUSTRATIONS	*xi*
	PREFACE	*xiii*
	ACKNOWLEDGMENTS	*xv*
[1]	Crowned and Blindsided: November–December 1851	*1*
[2]	"Mad Christmas": December 1851	*31*
[3]	The Kraken Version of *Pierre:* November–December 1851	*53*
[4]	Melville Crosses the Rubicon: January 1852	*70*
[5]	Richard Bentley: *The Whale* and *Pierre*, January–May 1852	*90*
[6]	Fool's Paradise and the Furies Unleashed: June–September 1852	*111*
[7]	*The Isle of the Cross:* September 1852–June 1853	*136*
[8]	The Magazinist: Idealist Turned Would-Be Stoic, July 1853–January 1854	*162*
[9]	The Shift Away from Herman and Arrowhead: January–March 1854	*190*
[10]	Tortoises and *Israel Potter:* 1854	*207*
[11]	"Benito Cereno": Early 1855	*235*
[12]	The Confidence Man's Masquerade: Melville as National Satirist, June 1855–January 1856	*255*
[13]	Foreclosing on Friendship: Confession and Shame, February–October 1856	*275*
[14]	Liverpool and the Levant: Late 1856–February 1857	*295*
[15]	Rome to Liverpool, and Home: February–April 1857	*321*
[16]	"Statues in Rome": May 1857–February 1858	*349*

Contents

[17]	"The South Seas": March 1858–Spring 1859	*374*
[18]	The Poet and the Last Lecture, "Travel": Summer 1859–Early 1860	*402*
[19]	An Epic Poet on the *Meteor*: May–October 1860	*428*
[20]	The Dream of Florence, a State Funeral, and War: November 1860–December 1861	*454*
[21]	A Humble Quest for an Aesthetic Credo: January–April 1862	*482*
[22]	Farewell to Arrowhead and the Overthrow of Jehu: April–December 1862	*506*
[23]	Displacements: January–June 1863	*525*
[24]	Wartime Second Honeymoon and Manhattan: Summer–Fall 1863	*544*
[25]	The War Poet's Scout toward Aldie: 1864	*558*
[26]	Two Years — of War and Dubious Peace: 1865–1866	*585*
[27]	*Battle-Pieces*: Poet, Poems, Reviewers, 1866	*606*
[28]	The Deputy Inspector amid Domestic Maelstroms: 1867	*626*
[29]	A Snug Harbor for the Melvilles: Late 1867–1868	*651*
[30]	The Man Who Had Known Hawthorne: 1869	*673*
[31]	West Street, and "Jerusalem": 1870	*690*
[32]	The Last Mustering of the Clan, and "The Wilderness": 1871	*712*
[33]	Death, Death, and Flight to a Snug Harbor: 1872	*734*
[34]	A Family in Disarray, and "Mar Saba": 1873	*754*
[35]	The New Generation, and "Bethlehem": 1874–1875	*773*
[36]	*Clarel*: Melville's Centennial Epic, 1876	*790*
[37]	"Old Fogy" and Imaginary Companions: 1877–1879	*815*
[38]	The Shadow at the Feasts: 1880–1885	*845*

Contents

| [39] | Fragments in a Writing Desk: 1886–1891 | *878* |
| [40] | In and Out of the House of the Tragic Poet: 1886–1891 | *905* |

GENEALOGICAL CHARTS	*925*
DOCUMENTATION	*931*
INDEX	*969*

Illustrations

Following page 268

1. Tupai Cupa
2. Herman Melville, 1861
3. "Pittsfield Village, 1851"
4. Arrowhead Farm from the North Meadow, ca. 1862
5. "Winyah. The Residence of Colonel Richard Lathers."
6. Sarah Morewood, ca. 1862
7. Broadhall with J. R. Morewood, ca. 1873
8. Crane Paper Mills in Dalton, Massachusetts: Red Mill and Old Stone Mill, ca. 1867
9. John C. Hoadley, ca. 1867
10. "Locomotive Engine 'Irvington' Coal Burner," ca. 1855
11. Herman and Thomas Melville, 1860
12. "Clipper Ship 'Meteor' passing Cape Horn, January 3rd 1860"
13. "Arrowhead In the Olden Time, A. D. 1860"
14. *Holy Palm of Mar Saba*
15. 49 Mount Vernon Street, Boston, Massachusetts
16. Chief Justice Lemuel Shaw, 1859
17. John Oakes Shaw, ca. 1900
18. Lemuel Shaw Jr.
19. Samuel Savage Shaw, 1887
20. Malcolm, Elizabeth, Frances, and Stanwix Melville, ca. 1861
21. Melville Home (1862–63), Pittsfield, ca. 1902
22. Chaplain Charles A. Humphreys, ca. 1864
23. Colonel John Singleton Mosby, ca. 1865
24. Allan Melville, 1865
25. Jane Dempsey Randolph Melville, 1871
26. Chimney Room at Arrowhead, 1870
27. Susan Gansevoort
28. Peter Gansevoort, ca. 1863
29. Henry Sanford Gansevoort

Illustrations

Following page 620

30 Richard Lathers
31 George Long Duyckinck, 1861
32 Sailors' Snug Harbor
33 Catherine (Katie) Bogart Melville, ca. 1868
34 Thomas Melville, 1884
35 "Admission of an Old Sailor to the Harbor"
36 "Governor's Residence, Sailors' Snug Harbor, S. I.," ca. 1905
37 Dr. John W. Francis
38 Henry T. Tuckerman
39 Orville Dewey
40 Henry W. Bellows, ca. 1870
41 All Souls Unitarian Church, ca. 1855
42 Elizabeth Shaw Melville, 1872
43 Herman Melville, 1870
44 Maria Gansevoort Melville, ca. 1870
45 Gansevoort Mansion, 1880
46 Helen Melville Griggs, 1879
47 Augusta Melville, ca. 1855
48 Catherine (Kate) Melville Hoadley, after 1880
49 Frances (Fanny) Priscilla Melville, 1879
50 "Along the Docks, New York City — View from West Street"
51 Malcolm Melville, ca. 1866
52 Stanwix Melville, ca. 1880
53 Elizabeth (Bessie) Melville, 1884
54 Frances Melville, 1870
55 Library of Colonel Richard Lathers
56 Catherine Gansevoort Lansing, 1916
57 Hand and Torch of the Statue of Liberty, displayed in Madison Square Park, 1876
58 "A Brisk Gale," 1763
59 "Beatrix Cenci," ca. 1838
60 "House of the Tragic Poet at Pompeii," ca. 1888
61 Elizabeth Shaw Melville, 1885
62 Herman Melville, 1885
63 Elizabeth Shaw Melville, 1905

xii

Preface

> Forty — forty — forty years ago! — ago! Forty years of continual whaling! forty years of privation, and peril, and storm-time! forty years on the pitiless sea! for forty years has Ahab forsaken the peaceful land, for forty years to make war on the horrors of the deep!
>
> *Moby-Dick*, ch. 132, "The Symphony"

This volume covers forty years of Melville's life ("fourty," he sometimes wrote). "What? a thousand-page second volume on four decades when nothing happened?" After all, Raymond Weaver in 1921 had hurtled from *Pierre* (1852) through *The Confidence-Man* (1857) then entitled the last thirty-four pages "The Long Quietus." And Lewis Mumford (1929) had glided over the decades: "The days pass and one day is like another: there is comfort in monotony" — a pronouncement I kept affixed to my computer monitors for several years, during which I took no comfort in monotony but lived intensely in rediscovering Melville's life. Weaver and Mumford had acknowledged that in his last years Melville wrote some poetry, and they even quoted some of it, but their complacency toward what they saw as failure and prolonged silence pervaded the New York literary establishment throughout the century. In 1997, at a forum on my first volume, Alfred Kazin brusquely instructed an audience at Barnes and Noble on Union Square: "You have to remember that poetry was just a sideline with Melville; it was never important to him and he was never good at it." As a fellow-participant at that forum along with Paul Metcalf, one of Melville's great-grandsons, I pointed out that whatever we think of the poetry, it was hardly a sideline: it was what Melville wrote for some thirty-three years. This soon afterward, I only survive from that forum, and although, toward the end of the book, I track the effects of age and overexertion on Melville after the late 1870s, I do not think of this packed, dramatic narrative as "The Long Quietus."

Herman Melville: A Biography emerges from my own forty years of research on Melville, beginning in 1962, when, for my Northwestern University dissertation on Melville and politics (the director, Harrison Hayford, having sailed for Florence), I transcribed manuscripts and took notes on old newspapers in eastern libraries. (Some of those tidy young 1962 transcriptions are printed in this 2002 volume.) Once, my forte had been the plain tan penny postcard, and then, decades later, the thirty-some-page metatextual article on *Pudd'nhead Wilson, The Red Badge of Courage,* Henry James's prefaces, *An American Dream*—pieces too long for most academic journals yet wangled into print somehow, taut, hefty, satisfying, all but "definitive." In the mid-1980s, when I set out, already half a century old, to write a biography of Herman Melville, I did not plan two volumes and two thousand pages. The biography is long because (as I explain in the preface to the first volume) in the process of expanding Jay Leyda's *The Melville Log* I discovered documents that threw crosslights on dozens of old stories. Furthermore, I discovered dozens of new episodes, some of which sprang full-size out of darkness; others pecked or clawed their way out, requiring serious preliminary head-scratching on my part, hearty yanking, and then tender ministrations. A test of mental agility, I saw up close and often, was the willingness and the ability to accommodate new episodes into a pre-existing view of Melville's life; an even stricter test was the willingness and ability to modify stories that we thought we already knew and to integrate them into larger narratives. Of the readers of this book, those who already know something about Melville will be more sharply challenged than new hands. All the way through, this is a new portrait of Melville, drawn from the original manuscripts, rigorously, strenuously condensed into a mere thousand pages—forty years of human life, forty chapters.

Acknowledgments

My greatest debt is to Heddy-Ann Richter, in-house critic, picture editor, and indexer. Several of Melville's great- and great-great-grandchildren helped: Priscilla Ambrose, Kitty Howe, Melville and Lizanne Chapin, Barton Chapin, Jamie Whittemore. Elizabeth B. Osborne corralled all the names and dates of the descendants of Herman and Elizabeth Melville; from that information Colin Dewey helped design the genealogical chart. Several friends criticized the long version of this volume: Chris Coughlin, Frederick J. Kennedy and Joyce Deveau Kennedy, Dennis Marnon, Mark Niemeyer, and Maurice Sendak. David Syracuse read several chapters of that version. Alma MacDougall Reising read thoughtfully as she copyedited. As I emphasize in "Documentation," this volume owes very much to Dennis Marnon, Administrative Officer at the Houghton Library, and to Ruth Degenhardt, former Local History Librarian at the Berkshire Athenaeum. Kathleen Reilly, the new Local History Librarian, and others at the Berkshire Athenaeum were unfailingly helpful. Years ago, Richard Colles Johnson of the Newberry Library supplied valuable information for this volume. Chris Coughlin made research trips to libraries in eastern Massachusetts for information I needed—and discovered some unsought items I used. Several of my research assistants at the University of Delaware helped, among them Kevin Hayes, Joseph Coulombe, Thomas Osborne, Steven Olsen-Smith, Todd Richardson, and especially Dan Lane. Dan Lane and I used monthly Amtrak commuter tickets for intensive research at the New York Public Library when it seemed possible that I might retire abruptly in order to complete this volume.

Among the encouragers, foremost was William S. Reese, magnanimous Melville collector, book dealer, and patron of old and young researchers. So that I could work in the British Museum and the Colindale branch of the British Library, Cormac McCarthy persuaded Roger Payne and Lisa Harrow to welcome us to London, where on our one afternoon out of the library Harrow gave us and Paul Watson an unforgettable gift, a hard-hat tour of the uncompleted Globe Theatre. Paul Seydor and David Morrell helped keep me clear on strategies and tactics. Alden and Rosamond Gifford introduced me to one of my major characters, the grandest house on Beacon Hill; Arthur and Sylvia Stein showed us Holmesdale. Enduring cheer came from Katherina von Fraunhofer-Kosinski, Robert and Roslyn Haber, Tony Kushner, and Edwin Shneidman. Toward the end much-appreciated cheer came from

Acknowledgments

Tobias Wolff and Patrick Stewart. I am grateful to Warner Berthoff, Elaine Boies, Steven E. Bonham, Thomas Bowen, R. Bruce Bickley Jr., Stephen Crump, Shirley Dettlaff, Bethany Dumas, Mary K. Bercaw Edwards, A. Eugene Gibson, Thomas Heffernan, Lloyd Holden, Lottie Cain Honea, Walter D. Kring and Sage Kring, Robert Madison, Joseph McElrath, John Munroe, Robert Newman, Helen Plunkett, Robert Schaefer, Haskell Springer, Dan Troilo, and Louis Zara. I owe special thanks to Phoebe-Lou Adams, Edwin T. Arnold, Jonathan A. Cook, Robert Faggen, Gregory Feeley, William Foltz, Philip Horne, Randall Howe, Hillel Itale, Robert D. Kaplan, Martin C. Langeveld, Elizabeth Lowry, Richard Nunley, Brian Phillips, David Scribner, Douglas Sealy, William W. Starr, Welford D. Taylor, and Philip Weiss.

Thanks are due to librarians besides those named above. At the Albany Institute of History and Art, Mary Alice Mackay. At the American Antiquarian Society, Thomas Knoles, Dennis Laurie, Marie Lamoureux, and Ellen Dunlap. At the Bancroft Library, Robert H. Hirst. At the Boston Athenæum, Stephen Nonack. At the Essex County Law Library, Richard Adamo. At the Luce Library, State University of New York Maritime College, Richard Corson, Constantia Constantinou, and John Lee. At the Massachusetts Historical Society, Peter Drummey and Virginia Smith. At the Morris Library of the University of Delaware, John D. Broderick and Timothy D. Murray. At the Nantucket Athenaeum, Charlotte Maison. At the Nantucket Historical Association, Jacqueline Haring, Betsy Tyler, and Elizabeth Oldham. At the New Bedford Free Public Library, Paul Cyr, Curator of Special Collections. At the New York State Library, Frederick Bassett, Warren Broderick, James Corsaro, and Charles Gehring. At Pennsylvania State University, Sandra Stelts. At the Railroad Museum of Pennsylvania, Kurt Bell. At the Rensselaer County Historical Society, Donna Hassler. At Sailors' Snug Harbor, F. Patrick Ausband and Pam Morris. At Stanford University, Roberto G. Trujillo, William McPheron, and Stephan Potchatek. At the Staten Island Institute of Arts and Sciences, Dorothy D'Eletto.

These benefactors shared their expertise or undertook specific library research missions for me: James Alexander Jr., Virginia Barden, Harriet Bergmann and Johannes D. Bergmann, Dennis Berthold, Kent Bicknell, Frances Broderick, John Bryant, Carl Randall Cluff, Margaret M. Dardis, Colin Dewey, Frank Doble, Mort Engstrom, Jay Fliegelman, Ed Folsom, Stanton Garner, John Gretchko, Frank Gruber, Philippe Jaworski, James C. Keil, Greg Lennes, Alex Liddie, Murray MacQuarrie, Irwin Marks, Rich Mauro, Lion G. Miles, Peter Norberg, Scott Norsworthy, Hilton Obenzinger, Steven Olsen-Smith, Robert Pepper, Fred Pinnegar, Gordon Poole, John B. Putnam, Dr. John Rainer, Jay Rainey, Todd Richardson, Douglas J. Robillard, Captain J. Michael Rodgers, U.S.N., James Emmett Ryan, Clare

Acknowledgments

Spark, David Syracuse, Martin Torodash, Mandy Victor, Robert K. Wallace, Ronald Webb, John Wenke, Richard E. Winslow III, Mark Wojnar, George Worth, James N. Yates, and Don Zochert. At the Johns Hopkins University Press, I thank especially Juliana McCarthy, MaryKatherine Callaway, Glen Burris, and the director, James D. Jordan.

Too many people who held volume 1 have died, among them Merton M. Sealts Jr. and Harrison Hayford; two of Melville's great-grandsons, Barton Chapin and Paul Metcalf; Richard Colles Johnson, Walter D. Kring, and Louis Zara. Sealts read several semifinal chapters and told me to condense them, so I shortened the volume by a sixth or so; Hayford read only a very early version of several chapters, in the early 1990s. My last half-Indian aunt, whose Irish father said grace in Choctaw, died in 2001, having lived in three centuries, but not very long in two of them. My mother, a white woman, as we said, who was born in Oklahoma Territory, died in 1998, having lived longer, as it turned out later, than any of her brothers and sisters. When I asked her in the late 1970s how she had survived extreme deprivations, she replied, "I guess it must be that old Costner drive." That drive was her legacy to me.

I could not have finished the volume in Morro Bay without the Internet. In the last stages of composition, after research was supposed to be all but finished, I was able to buy, from home, several dozen books essential to my work. I paid high prices, a few times, but for ten or twelve dollars apiece I bought priceless marmalade-smeared sermons of Orville Dewey and water-sogged Ticknor & Fields reprints of Tennyson and Browning: no one else wanted them and I could not go on without them. For all the flaws of the Internet, to call up, say, an image of the William Worth monument the moment I wanted to see what Melville was talking about—this was riches running wild, and unimagined a few years earlier, when I wanted something better than my own snapshots of the Nelson Monument in Liverpool. From the Internet, also, came Doris Lane, who generously mailed Heddy Richter her postcard of the Governor's House at Sailors' Snug Harbor. Riches could run wilder still: if there were free Internet access to a few dozen nineteenth-century American newspapers from a few dozen cities, the resourceful troop of amateur genealogists and local history buffs, along with a handful of scholars, could revolutionize American historical research.

Herman Melville, 1851–1891

[1]
Crowned and Blindsided
November–December 1851

Thrice unlucky Herman Melville!

London *Literary Gazette*, 6 December 1851

THE FIRST VOLUME of this biography ends with Herman Melville and Nathaniel Hawthorne in the dining room of the Little Red Inn at Lenox, Massachusetts, on an afternoon in mid-November 1851. There Melville had been holding his publication party for *Moby-Dick*, to which he had invited a single guest. The two authors had shocked Lenox by dining in public in a village where by custom the hotel was for guests only, and the indigenous yokels (according to a new resident) had taken turns peeking in at them, sure that the two most notoriously reclusive literary men in the county had perversely chosen this indecorous way of meeting each other instead of going to Melville's Arrowhead outside Pittsfield or Hawthorne's rented little red cottage outside Lenox. The local belles and beaux, the newcomer wrote some weeks later, had found long-lasting amusement in this peculiar attempt at acquaintanceship between such dissimilar men, the dour author of the Puritanic *The Scarlet Letter* and the free-and-easy Melville, author of *Typee* and *Omoo*, books which had made him the first American literary sex symbol. There, alone in the dining room after the hotel guests had dined, the two had lingered with the first presentation copy of *Moby-Dick* while Hawthorne accustomed himself to the astounding dedication: "In token of my admiration for his genius, This Book is Inscribed to Nathaniel Hawthorne." Afterward they had made their farewells, for Hawthorne, unknown to most of the townspeople, was leaving the Berkshires.

The hours in the dining room had been sacred, but the day itself was miserable. The weather had been "of the most dreary sort" (as Melville's neighbor Sarah Morewood wrote on 21 November to their New York friend George Duyckinck). Sleet, hail, and snow squalls, varied by "high winds leaden skies," had battered the county for weeks. The year before, the glorious Berkshire autumn had seemed endless. This year, ice on the limbs had already been so heavy as to uproot trees. Deep mud on the roads alternated with patches of frozen snow and ice that made it "really unsafe for a horse to travel," Sarah had decided the day before, when she abandoned a drive and returned "to the mud and slush of the Lenox road," which ran by the Morewood estate, previously the farm of Melville's uncle Thomas Melvill. In front of the storm, across the state in eastern Massachusetts, rumors were swirling like wind-whipped snowflakes. The Lynn *News* gossiped that Hawthorne intended to move among its shoemakers "and to build a house on the beautiful range of hills in the western part of that city" (a report the *Evening Commonwealth* spread throughout Boston on 22 November). The truth was more prosaic, for the Hawthornes were taking temporary occupancy of the house of Horace Mann during his term in Congress, Mary Mann being Sophia Hawthorne's sister.

This second volume opens a day or two after the meeting in the Little Red Inn, around 14 November (the official publication date of *Moby-Dick*) or the fifteenth, and it begins not with the author but with the dedicatee, and with the book. Nathaniel Hawthorne sat with his copy of *Moby-Dick* in his study in the little red cottage above Stockbridge Bowl where he had written *The House of the Seven Gables* under the gaze of Emerson's gift, a print of Raphael's transfigured Jesus. Now the inside of the little red cottage was as bleak as the winter landscape. Honored by Melville's dedicating the book to him, Hawthorne was determined to respond fittingly, even in a chaotic household, by reading it at once and writing Melville about it. Despite his views on equal parenting, he left Sophia to take care of the baby while she packed their possessions with the dubious intermittent assistance of the obstreperous older children, Una and Julian. She was already putting away smaller household items, perhaps including Emerson's gift. A few days earlier, the transfigured Jesus would have scrutinized the pages of *Moby-Dick* over Hawthorne's shoulder all the hours he read; as it was, the book would have scrutiny enough from human critics.

In his inexperience with intellectual women, Herman Melville admired Sophia Peabody Hawthorne uncritically and idealized her relationship with her husband. In the same household where Ellery Channing weeks before had witnessed mismanagement, bad parenting, and misanthropy, Melville saw a mutually supportive marriage beyond any ideal he could hope to attain. For her part, Sophia had looked forward to the publication of what her husband called *The White Whale* in his *A Wonder-Book*, itself published in early November. She admired Melville, she revelled in the honor he bestowed upon her husband by his uncharacteristic openness, and she identified with the exotic eroticism of *Typee*—to the point of visualizing the naked Fayaway when she first looked upon Melville. In the middle of November 1851, however, and not for the first time, Melville had inconvenienced

Sophia. She was far from a competent and gracious hostess, and Melville could be less than an ideal guest. He had a way of showing up unexpectedly, as he had just done when he hauled Hawthorne off to the Little Red Inn for several hours. Accustomed to his mother's Dutch bounty, he ate too much without assessing the total number of available tea-cakes before he enjoyed them. He gestured too much and talked too much, exhausting Sophia even while exhilarating her. No matter how much she liked having him there once she had adjusted to his arrival, she never regretted when it came time for him to leave. Now *Moby-Dick*, his latest cargo of "rare and costly merchandise" (one of her phrases about Melville's writings, from 1852), with its exalting dedication, made her a martyr, for she could not stop to read it herself and her husband perforce *must* stop to read it, or at least to read enough to write a proper letter about it. All the time her husband was putting everything aside to turn the pages of *Moby-Dick*, Sophia was doing all the packing and all the child-minding herself.

Under the circumstances, Hawthorne must have shared with Sophia the private joke put there for them at the end of "The Street" (ch. 6), where Melville reported that the girls of Salem exhaled such strong musk that their sailor sweethearts could smell them miles off shore, but he did not dawdle to reread all the striking passages or to identify teasing language that echoed many different books of the Bible and a throng of British writers, foremost and midmost of whom was Shakespeare. No earlier than 15 November, and more likely the sixteenth, Hawthorne wrote Melville a long letter of heartfelt praise. When Melville wrote to Sophia Hawthorne several weeks later, after she had read the book herself, he claimed that her husband's letter about *Moby-Dick* had taught him how to read some parts of his own book: "I had some vague idea while writing it, that the whole book was susceptible of an allegoric construction, & also that *parts* of it were—but the speciality of many of the particular subordinate allegories, were first revealed to me, after reading Mr Hawthorne's letter, which, without citing any particular examples, yet intimated the part-&-parcel allegoricalness of the whole." Unwontedly reckless in his emotional and intellectual response to the power of the book, which gave the dedication its true significance, Hawthorne had offered in his letter to review *Moby-Dick*, repayment in kind for Melville's momentous two-part essay on *Mosses from an Old Manse* in late August 1850 in the New York *Literary World*, edited by Evert and George Duyckinck. The Hawthornes, like the poet Henry Wadsworth Longfellow, Hawthorne's college friend, were sure that the essay, signed "By a Virginian Spending July in Vermont," had marked a turning point in Hawthorne's national recognition.

After his day's stint of writing, Melville's habit was to drive from Arrowhead, his farm on the middle road to Lenox, to pick up his mail at the post office in the village of Pittsfield. On 16 November, a Sunday, someone handed Hawthorne's letter to him as he was driving with his sisters Helen, Kate, and Fanny to visit Rowland and Sarah Morewood, the new owners of the farm that had been Herman's "first love," a cousin said in 1848. Melville's next-younger sister, Augusta, was in New York City and the matriarch, Maria Gansevoort Melville, was left at Arrowhead to care for his son Malcolm, almost two, and for his very sick wife, Elizabeth (Lizzie) Shaw Melville, who despite a breast infection was still nursing the three-week-old Stanwix, the Melvilles' second child. Melville read Hawthorne's letter "there," as he put it, leaving uncertain whether enough daylight had remained for him to read it on the road or whether he waited until he had light at the Morewoods' house, where he had written a little of *Moby-Dick* the year before. Wherever he read Hawthorne's letter, he had to stifle his joy throughout the evening. He would have suppressed his feelings even in a small family group, but at the Morewood house there were other guests besides the Melvilles, so he pocketed the letter and said nothing about it.

Through November, Sarah and the English-born Rowland Morewood had been "living in the midst of confusion," as she wrote to George Duyckinck on 21 November, moving doorways and taking down an enormous chimney so as to gain a large dining room, the one room where Sarah most required spaciousness. Neither household confusion nor early pregnancy checked her compulsion to entertain, and on this occasion the host, hostess, and guests amused themselves by drawing lots for names of the Morewood house and cows. Long afterward, the Morewoods' daughter Annie, not yet born in 1851, pasted into a scrapbook a newspaper clipping from the 1880s on "The Name of Broadhall": "it was decided that each person present should drop a name in a box and the first drawn out should be accepted. Herman Melville, the famous author of 'Omoo,' 'Typee,' etc., wrote the name of Broadhall on his slip and it was drawn out and accepted with applause." Melville as the namer of "Broadhall" was the small stuff of local literary legend, the sort that had begun to stick to his Berkshire behavior like lichens. Sarah's account to George Duyckinck on 21 November credits him with the rhyming bovine names but not the name of the house: "A party of friends were spending the evening with us — Mr Melville and three of his sisters among the number — we agreed by way of amusement to write names for our cows and house — and to decide by drawing lots — I drew for the house Broadhall — for the three cows — Molly Polly & Dolly. Miss Kate Melville had the naming of the house — Herman Melville the cows." Kate's suggestion of "Broadhall" was not original, for the poet and novelist Cornelius Mathews had celebrated "the great rooms of Broad Hall" in the *Literary World* the year before. One of the guests who had been in Pittsfield then, while Kate was in New York, may have prompted her—perhaps Melville, perhaps the local manufacturer John C. Hoadley, who was courting her by this time.

Melville, the new master of Shakespearean prose, had outdone himself with the simplicity of Molly, Polly, and Dolly (whatever complication lurked in the fact that "Dolly" was one of his pet names for his wife). During the evening his repressed joy broke out in the form of irreverent salvoes which disturbed and perplexed his Anglican-bred host. Later, upon reflection, Rowland decided that he liked his neighbor better the more he saw of him, except that his "opinions and religious views" were expressed too frequently in "irreverent language" (as his wife wrote to George Duyckinck, 28 December). Between such outbursts, Melville sat in an inward rapture, Hawthorne's letter in his pocket, in the old parlor where he had sat with his father and uncle, and with his older brother, now dead, and with cousins now dead. Later, suffused with triumph, he sat in the strangely enlarged dining room. Molly, Polly, and Dolly named, he lived those hours as one of "God's true princes of the Empire" (*Moby-Dick*, ch. 33). The setting was not inappropriate for such a conqueror, for his Grandfather Melvill had bought the house for the residence of Melville's Uncle Thomas, who held the contracts for feeding and clothing the British prisoners in the cantonment during the second war of independence; in Melville's youth his uncle pointed with pride to the miniature ship made by men his uncle called "my Prisoners in the last war" (in a letter to Judge Lemuel Shaw, 14 January 1842). The farm, strongly associated with the defeat of the British, was also strangely associated with the French empire (the "Tuileries and the Taghconics," Melville wrote), because Thomas Melvill had so often reminisced, there in Broadhall, of "martial displays and spectacles of state which he had witnessed in Paris in the time of the first Napoleon" ("Sketch of Major Thomas Melville Junior by a Nephew").

Melville himself had witnessed later, and contrasting, phases of British and French imperialism with his own eyes. He was on the spot in 1842 when the French seized the Marquesas Islands and, later, Tahiti. During his whaling years the Pacific islands had been there for the taking, he knew. The British had taken control of the Sandwich Islands to forestall the French, and he had been in Honolulu in 1843, once again an eyewitness to history, on the day the British formally relinquished the islands, under pressure from President John Tyler, who five years later, in 1848, had sat in the same Broadhall parlor and eaten in the old, smaller dining room. Melville had witnessed American imperialism, also, for he had returned home in time to hear the last of his brother Gansevoort's orations advocating the election of James K. Polk and the immediate annexation of Texas. Melville had written *Omoo* (1847) and started *Mardi* (1849) during the war with Mexico, which gained the United States vast tracts of what he called in "Loomings" the "great American desert" (*Moby-Dick*, ch. 1). In 1848 Melville had read accounts of the gold fever in California and had written the start of the Gold Rush into *Mardi*. By 1849 thousands of gold-seekers had been making the dangerous voyage around the Horn or chancing the terrifying passage over the Isthmus of Panama, before a railroad was built, and all the while Melville wrote *Moby-Dick*, and even as he sat there with Hawthorne's letter in his pocket, ordinary Americans were crossing the continent to California in wagons, on horseback, and on foot. While he wrote *Moby-Dick*, California became a state. After California, what then? In *Moby-Dick* (ch. 89), Melville had just defined imperialism in whaling terms: "What to that apostolic lancer, Brother Jonathan, is Texas but a Fast-Fish?" What was Mexico to the United States? A Loose-Fish, as yet, except for the territories already seized or purchased. He had foreseen (ch. 14) the time when America would "add Mexico to Texas, and pile Cuba upon Canada" in its piratical acquisitiveness. Better than any other American of his generation, Melville knew geopolitics as a humble but reflective observer and as a pondering autodidact. This man who now saw the world in terms of "linked analogies" (*Moby-Dick*, ch. 70) had known, as early as 1848, and believed passionately in 1850 and 1851, that literary greatness was there for the seizing as much as the Marquesas Islands and California had been just a few years earlier. American literary greatness had been a Loose-Fish that Melville in his whaling book had made a Fast-Fish forever.

Such a book would create a great sensation and allow him to pay off the $2050 he had secretly borrowed from a Lansingburgh friend the previous May and make him a free man, financially—if he did not take account of what he owed Harper & Brothers, his American publisher, and Dr. John Brewster, the former owner of his house, Arrowhead. (He never counted what did not need to be repaid—what his father-in-law, Lemuel Shaw, the chief justice of the Supreme Court of Massachusetts, had advanced for the purchase of a lease on a house on Fourth Avenue in 1847 and toward the purchase of Arrowhead in 1850, or what his current British publisher, Richard Bentley, had lost on *Mardi*, *Redburn*, and *White-Jacket*, Melville's most recent books, before *Moby-Dick*.)

Broadhall was named, the cows were named, and the world went partly round before Melville sat down to write to Hawthorne the next day, 17 November. Had he been at Arrowhead when he read the letter, he would have replied at once, Melville said, even though he almost never wrote by candlelight because of his weak eyes. As it was, he was not able to write precisely what he would have written then, but he remembered something of what he had felt the night before: "I felt pantheistic then—your heart beat in my ribs

& mine in yours, and both in God's." This last letter to Hawthorne in Lenox is known only by a transcription made long afterward by Rose Hawthorne, then a baby. Hawthorne's letter, which Melville later destroyed, is known by what can be inferred from Melville's reply and from his later comments to Sophia. It was, Melville said in his reply, "joy-giving and exultation-breeding," and we know that it had been unwontedly enthusiastic or even emotional because Melville's characterization of it has to be ironic: "What a pity, that, for your plain, bluff letter, you should get such gibberish!" For once, Hawthorne had not been diffident and restrained—he had given Melville "the crown of India":

> People think that if a man has undergone any hardship, he should have a reward; but for my part, if I have done the hardest possible day's work, and then come to sit down in a corner and eat my supper comfortably—why, then I don't think I deserve any reward for my hard day's work—for am I not now at peace? Is not my supper good? My peace and my supper are my reward, my dear Hawthorne. So your joy-giving and exultation-breeding letter is not my reward for my ditcher's work with that book, but is the good goddess's bonus over and above what was stipulated for—for not one man in five cycles, who is wise, will expect appreciative recognition from his fellows, or any one of them. Appreciation! Recognition! Is Jove appreciated? Why, ever since Adam, who has got to the meaning of his great allegory—the world? Then we pigmies must be content to have our paper allegories but ill comprehended. I say your appreciation is my glorious gratuity. In my proud, humble way,—a shepherd-king,—I was lord of a little vale in the solitary Crimea; but you have now given me the crown of India. But on trying it on my head, I found it fell down on my ears, notwithstanding their asinine length—for it's only such ears that sustain such crowns.

Melville isolated one moment to stand on record as a mood a great artist experiences after triumphant creativity, one of absolute distance from the created object and absolute security in the knowledge that the one ideal reader had understood it: "A sense of unspeakable security is in me this moment, on account of your having understood the book. I have written a wicked book, and feel spotless as the lamb. Ineffable socialities are in me. I would sit down and dine with you and all the gods in old Rome's Pantheon. It is a strange feeling—no hopefulness is in it, no despair. Content—that is it; and irresponsibility; but without licentious inclination." He added, freezing the onrush of thoughts: "I speak now of my profoundest sense of being, not of an incidental feeling." To the dining room of the Little Red Inn, or the Parker House in Boston, or Hawthorne's own Hall of Fantasy, the next time he held a new great book of his in his hands (*Pierre*, already well in progress), he would invite not just his friend alone but Hawthorne and all the gods of pagan Rome. As it turned out, he did not hold that publication party.

Hawthorne had come into Melville's life in August 1850, just when he was awakening to the conviction that he was becoming, or had become, a very great writer—so great a writer that to admit his self-appraisal would have been accounted madness. Excited by Hawthorne's glamorous presence and by reading the first book by the older writer he could lay hands on, Melville in his essay "Hawthorne and His Mosses," only belatedly disguising himself as a Virginian in Vermont, had made Hawthorne a godlike embodiment of the greatness an American writer might achieve. Revisiting the Berkshires, re-experiencing episodes of his early life there, then encountering Hawthorne there had overwhelmed Melville, drawing him away from New York City to settle near Pittsfield in October 1850. Many weeks had passed thereafter without their seeing each other, although only six miles apart, but the men had met several times for sympathetic talk on "time and eternity, things of this world and of the next, and books, and publishers, and all possible and impossible matters," as Hawthorne wrote in his journal on 2 August 1851, after Melville came as a birthday gift to himself the day before and stayed into the early hours (while Sophia was away with the two daughters). Now Melville wrote: "Whence come you, Hawthorne? By what right do you drink from my flagon of life? And when I put it to my lips—lo, they are yours and not mine. I feel that the Godhead is broken up like the bread at the Supper, and that we are the pieces. Hence this infinite fraternity of feeling." In this letter Melville declared that, as Hawthorne had read *Moby-Dick*, he had "understood the pervading thought that impelled the book," and that it was the impelling thought that Hawthorne praised: "You were archangel enough to despise the imperfect body, and embrace the soul." Melville's tone is that of a benediction, delivered not from a secure vantage point like his rocky outjutting of land nearby but from fluid states of pell-mell emotional, intellectual, and aesthetic change, where (he said) "the very fingers that now guide this pen are not precisely the same that just took it up and put it on this paper." In his exaltation he asked Hawthorne not to rob him of his "miserly delight" by reviewing *Moby-Dick* (an action that ranks high among the worst mistakes Melville ever made) and declared his again-expanded ambition: "Lord, when shall we be done growing? As long as we have anything more to do, we have done nothing. So, now, let us add Moby Dick to our blessing, and step from that. Leviathan is not the biggest fish;—I have heard of Krakens."

The book in progress, *Pierre*, was to be a Kraken book, more ambitious, more profound, if not longer than *Moby-Dick*. In *Pierre* Melville was writing the story of an adventure he had been witnessing first hand—his own interior growth, especially as he wrote *Moby-Dick*. He had never written about anything except his own experiences, if one takes *Mardi* as his current intellectual autobiography; and his interior development, after all, was his wildest adventure, not killing whales in the Pacific. In a letter to Hawthorne in early May 1851, Melville had dated his life as having begun in his twenty-fifth year. Technically, that was when he was serving in the frigate *United States*, from 1 August 1843 until his twenty-fifth birthday in 1844; but he meant the year beginning on his twenty-fifth birthday, during which he arrived home from the Pacific and wrote *Typee*. Melville himself thought of *Mardi* (written 1847–48) and then *Moby-Dick* (written 1850–51) as the chief evidence of his growth as a writer. But his aesthetic and psychological life had burgeoned most precipitously because of *Redburn*, which he dashed off in two months, June and July of 1849. A consequence of his writing *Redburn* so swiftly was that, after a few years, he may not have remembered much about writing it, but the aftereffects were profound.

Writing *Redburn* had been an act of unwitting bravado. In the late spring of 1849, after it was clear that *Mardi* had failed in London and in the United States, Melville had realized that he must set to work and write, fast, an unambitious popular book to make up for the self-indulgently drawn-out "voyage thither" to *Mardi*. Just at that time, his youngest brother, Tom, signed on the *Navigator*, bound for China. Herman went aboard Tom's ship in New York Harbor and saw him off, reenacting the scene ten years earlier when the oldest brother, Gansevoort, had seen him off on his first voyage, to Liverpool. In those ten years Melville had gone to the Pacific and returned and become a published writer with the help of Gansevoort—who had died while launching *Typee*. In 1849, Tom, ten years his junior, looked uncannily like Herman in 1839, and Herman himself was playing the role of older brother. In Melville's mind at the end of May 1849, two New York wharf scenes fused, and the bewilderingly similar pairs of brothers fused in his mind, Gansevoort merging into Herman even as he himself merged into Tom, and Tom into him. Within a very few days, Melville was writing *Redburn*, much of it an autobiographical account of his boyhood and his first voyage. The intensity of Melville's psychological life in 1850 and 1851 derives from the collision of sets of brothers and times at Tom's sailing in 1849 and Herman's thereafter composing a book too close to the truth to bear thinking about while he was dashing it off.

Seeing Tom as himself, himself as Tom, in 1849 was not the first such hallucinatory experience Melville had experienced. In *Omoo* Melville had described the sensations of seeing on the stern of a beached whaler in the harbor at Tahiti the name of a town on the Hudson: "In an instant, palm-trees and elms—canoes and skiffs—church spires and bamboos—all mingled in one vision of the present and the past" (ch. 27). This sort of experience may be a universal characteristic of the creative process. Albert Rothenberg in *The Emerging Goddess* (1979) describes "homospatial thinking," in which two disparate images become superimposed and fused, "a conception leading to the articulation of new identities." What distinguishes Melville's imagination is not the process itself, which may be one every creative artist experiences in order to "overcome repression," as Rothenberg says, and "to unearth unconscious material." Rather, what is special about homospatial thinking in Melville is his becoming highly conscious of it and his exploiting it as a tool for the intense, prolonged self-psychoanalysis he put himself through after writing *Redburn*.

Melville used "metamorphosis" (the word and the concept) overtly a few years later in *The Confidence-Man,* but the modern term "morphing" more nearly fits Melville's experience of the psychological and physiological phenomenon of blending and separating identities. What might normally have been all but unconscious became subject matter in his literary works, in part because of the sheer range of his experiences: how many men of his time could see a ship from their own Hudson River stranded, like them, on the beach at Tahiti? The way he experienced the merging and separating of identities also owed something to his being from a family where names were routinely reused, where Priscilla was grandmother and aunt and sister and where Kate was grandmother, aunt, sister, and cousin and other cousin and where Thomas, Allan, Herman — where one's very name was not only one's own. Any "Herman" in the family in the nineteenth century was one of the present re-embodiments of Harmes and Harmans and Hermans past. In this large family, brothers resembled brothers (some more than others), but also there were enough cousins so that some of them inevitably resembled other cousins. At different times Guert and Henry Gansevoort, first cousins themselves, reminded family members of their first cousin Herman. In faces of brothers and sisters and cousins the observer could see not only the person being looked directly at but also bone structure, coloring, and subtler expressions "strangely translated, and intermarryingly blended" (to misapply a phrase from *Pierre*, bk. 6, ch. 2).

In Melville's society and particularly in his family, identity could be obliterated and then supplanted. Herman had been fond of his cousin Allan Cargill Melvill who died in 1832, and he became fond of the little Allan Cargill Melvill who had taken over his name before Herman next visited the farm south of Pittsfield. At that time of high infant mortality, the concept and the actual fact of "replacement children" was a casual challenge to personal identity, and Melville became profoundly concerned with the basic contradiction between the fragility of life and the rage for identity (which manifested itself in what he called in *Moby-Dick* the "queenly personality" [ch. 119]). In *Typee* (ch. 10), by having "Mehevi" address the narrator as "Tom" (which the chieftain pronounces as Tommo, Tomma, Tommee, "every thing but plain 'Tom' "), was Herman Melville appropriating something from the history of his once-fiery alcoholic cousin Thomas Melvill, who had died on a whaleship and been buried at Lahaina just before Herman arrived home in 1844? Still worse than having your name or your history appropriated was actually being incorporated into another person. When a man was devoured by cannibals, all sailors knew, he surrendered his qualities to the cannibals who ate him, so that a Hawaiian after digesting the big toe of Captain James Cook might swagger in seamanlike fashion. At some point (perhaps in the Pacific, after reading Owen Chase's cannibalistic narrative) Melville came to sense, if not yet to articulate to himself, that his father, Allan Melvill, by wasting his children's inheritances, had been eating their futures, eating *them*—even eating them alive, in the technique perfected by the Battas of Sumatra, according to sensational popular accounts. For Melville it was as if Chronos, the god he introduced into *Pierre* late in his work on it, had metamorphosized into an American dry-goods importer and back again to Chronos. The hallucinatory merging of Tom into young Herman was powerful enough to threaten the release of more horrific childhood memories than Melville was ready to confront in the summer of 1849.

Then, in late May 1849, hurtled back ten years to 1839, Melville thought that fictionalizing his own first voyage would be a safe way of spinning out a little story fast and making up for the critical and financial failure of *Mardi*. The family situation Melville depicted in *Redburn*—early death of father, impoverishment of widow and children—was autobiographical. He wrote so fast that nothing was too close for comfort for very long. He kept a jocular, rueful stance as he depicted Redburn's youthful self-pitying feelings of bewildered injustice after he had been left impoverished by the death of his beloved father. Melville was still too simple-hearted then, to use Thomas L. Nichols's term, to know how dangerous it was to fish in the well of childhood, even with a hook held tentatively. For a time Melville seemed to escape unscathed from his excursion into terrain so psychologically dangerous—the terrain in which he confronted his memories of his father's life and death and all he had subsequently remembered and had suppressed. There was no time for self-indulgent and possibly catastrophic introspection. After all, he had yet another book to write in the next two months of 1849, August and September—*White-Jacket*, which was written in a "score of sittings," Oakey Hall, the young friend of the Duyckincks, reported in the New Orleans *Commercial Bulletin*. Melville's use of his childhood made for rapid writing in 1849, then made for tumultuous self-psychoanalysis in the next year and more, during and after several intense weeks in England and the Continent and a prolonged voyage home.

Melville spoke contemptuously of *Redburn*, but that seemingly innocuous book had laid open the floodgates to his unconscious. The effects of having dipped into his unconscious in *Redburn* enriched *White-Jacket* (always one of Melville's most underrated books) and came home to him during the months he planned and worked on *Moby-Dick*, when he at last focused his full attention on what was emerging from that "wonder-world" (*Moby-Dick*, ch. 1). Melville implied in *Moby-Dick* that he, like his narrator, had been haunted by the image of the white whale. What first took recognizable shape, perhaps on the voyage home from England at the start of 1850, may indeed have been a grand hooded phantom, like a snow-hill in the air. By the time the shape of the white whale emerged, Melville had become extraordinarily aware of his states of being, so acutely aware of his self that to talk of bodily states and mental states is to set up falsely distinct categories. Recurrently in *Moby-Dick*, Melville described the separation of the mind from the body, when the body becomes absent-minded, absent of mind. Shifting moods of mind and thought, linked to bodily moods, states of mind-body, are characteristically Melvillean, especially those states which cannot be simplified, cannot be classified. The Washington *National Era* (19 August 1852) had it wrong in saying Melville was at home "in the manifold intricacies of a ship's rigging" but not "amid the subtleties of psychological phenomena."

Melville's gliding, sliding imagery for thought processes and the phenomenon of dissolving and merging identities was at least as old as *Omoo*. Then early in 1849, two years after that book was published, had come Melville's overwhelming experience of reading Shakespeare. During the subsequent months of his burgeoning psychological growth, Melville had responded deeply to this passage in *The Tempest* (4.1):

> These our actors,
> (As I foretold you) were all Spirits, and
> Are melted into Ayre, into thin Ayre,
> And like the baselesse fabricke of this vision
> The Clowd-capt Towres, the gorgeous Pallaces,
> The solemne Temples, the great Globe it selfe,
> Yea, all which it inherit, shall dissolve,
> And like this insubstantiall Pageant faded
> Leave not a racke behinde: we are such stuffe
> As dreames are made on; and our little life
> Is rounded with a sleepe.

Shakespeare did not inspire in Melville a tendency to imagine one figure merging into another and perhaps re-forming into the original shape, but at some time soon after his intense engagement with Shakespeare's plays, Melville seized on Prospero's imagery to describe the peculiar phenomenon he had long been aware of.

Attracted by the imagery, not by Prospero's renunciation of his magic powers, in *Pierre* Melville appropriated Prospero's "melted" when the mysterious dark Isabel says that for her "the solidest things melt into dreams" (bk. 6, ch. 3); in a late addition to the book, Melville combined "baseless vision" with "airy spectacle" (bk. 25, ch. 4). Other words and images from Prospero's speech (melted, air, baseless, vision, temples, dissolve, rack, dreams) figured complexly in Melville's depictions of sliding, gliding psychological states and evanescent perceptual states in *Pierre*, as in this passage:

> And now, by irresistible intuitions, all that had been inexplicably mysterious to him in the portrait, and all that had been inexplicably familiar in the face, most magically these now coincided; the merriness of the one not inharmonious with the mournfulness of the other, but by some ineffable correlativeness, they reciprocally identified each other, and, as it were, melted into each other, and thus interpenetratingly uniting, presented lineaments of an added supernaturalness.
>
> On all sides, the physical world of solid objects now slidingly displaced itself from around him, and he floated into an ether of visions. (bk. 4, ch. 5)

A more specific literary parallel for the psychological phenomenon is Dante's depiction in the *Inferno* (canto 25) of the way the bodies of two Florentine thieves fuse together: "Agnello! See! thou art not double now, / Nor only one!" — what Melville calls the "two mutually absorbing shapes" (*Pierre*, bk. 4, ch. 5). In Dante, Melville had literary precedent for the psychological phenomenon and its literary use, and Shakespeare gave him words and imagery which nevertheless seemed to have been anticipated in his own strange South Sea experiences (where Tahiti and the town of Hudson merged into each other and then separated again) and his hallucinatory confusion of self and brothers. From the Shakespearean set piece in *The Tempest* more than anywhere else Melville had developed the vocabulary and imagery with which he conveyed his new understanding of conscious and unconscious psychological processes.

Melville's Kraken book would not look like a companion book to *Moby-Dick*, but the imagery for psychological processes in book 4 of *Pierre* continues directly from passages in *Moby-Dick* such as chapter 35, "The Mast-Head," where "absent-minded young men" make poor watchers for whales.

Lulled into "an opium-like listlessness of vacant, unconscious reverie," such a youth "loses his identity; takes the mystic ocean at his feet for the visible image of that deep, blue, bottomless soul, pervading mankind and nature; and every strange, half-seen, gliding, beautiful thing that eludes him; every dimly-discovered, uprising fin of some undiscernible form, seems to him the embodiment of those elusive thoughts that only people the soul by continually flitting through it." The imagery in *Pierre* also continues from chapter 111, "The Pacific" ("When gliding by the Bashee isles we emerged at last upon the great South Sea"), where Melville has his narrator, Ishmael, depict what would later be called the collective subconscious, if not collective unconscious, a serene Pacific in which "millions of mixed shades and shadows, drowned dreams, somnambulisms, reveries; all that we call lives and souls, lie dreaming, dreaming, still; tossing like slumberers in their beds; the ever-rolling waves but made so by their restlessness."

Most strange and powerful is the way in which Isabel reenacts the role Fedallah had just played. In *Moby-Dick* Fedallah and his boat's crew are "five dusky phantoms that seemed fresh formed out of air" (ch. 47), manifestations of the encroachment of the unconscious upon conscious life (ch. 50):

> that hair-turbaned Fedallah remained a muffled mystery to the last. . . . He was such a creature as civilized, domestic people in the temperate zone only see in their dreams, and that but dimly; but the like of whom now and then glide among the unchanging Asiatic communities, especially the Oriental isles to the east of the continent—those insulated, immemorial, unalterable countries, which even in these modern days still preserve much of the ghostly aboriginalness of earth's primal generations, when the memory of the first man was a distinct recollection, and all men his descendants, unknowing whence he came, eyed each other as real phantoms.

Any doubt that high psychological purposefulness underlies this gothic mood-stuff is banished by comparing the recasting of this passage in *Pierre*, where Melville portrays the stirrings of Pierre's unconscious from which those armies of hooded phantoms disembark and attack his conscious mind: "But now!—now!—and again he would lose himself in the most surprising and preternatural ponderings, which baffled all the introspective cunning of his mind. Himself was too much for himself. He felt that what he had always before considered the solid land of veritable reality, was now being audaciously encroached upon by bannered armies of hooded phantoms, disembarking in his soul, as from flotillas of specter-boats" (bk. 3, ch. 2). The imagery is recurrent in Melville, in *Mardi*, in "Benito Cereno," derived from tales of Asiatic crews reported to have boarded and ravaged ships at sea. In *Pierre* Melville was working directly forward from his analysis of psychological processes in *Moby-Dick*, the dark mysterious Isabel a new manifestation of the encroachment of the unconscious upon the conscious, as Fedallah had been.

Hawthorne had recognized how much greater *Moby-Dick* was than Melville's earlier books, otherwise Melville could not have exclaimed, on the basis of the older man's praise, "Lord, when shall we be done growing?" Melville also trusted Hawthorne to guess at what he meant by calling the whaling book "wicked," or to remember specific conversations that would make clear what he meant. Melville had been called degraded, immoral, and irreligious for writing *Typee* and *Omoo*, but in calling *Moby-Dick* "wicked" he was thinking of a book on the Berkshires he had bought the year before, D. D. Field's *History of the County of Berkshire* (Pittsfield, 1829). In Field's book, Melville had marked the paragraph stating that Jonathan Edwards was living in Stockbridge when he "completed his greatest work, 'The Inquiry concerning the Freedom of the Will,'" and that he also composed there "his treatise on Original Sin, and carried forward the 'History of Redemption,' and probably some other works." Field congratulated himself on progress in the Berkshires: "Works on infidelity, or of an irreligious and immoral tendency, which were once abundant, have become very rare among the people." The nature of these "works" went unspecified (were they deistic?), but Melville took the description as applying to him as he worked on his whaling book. He underlined "which were once abundant" and checked that line in the left margin. He had been warned, early in 1850 by his friend Evert Duyckinck in the *Literary World* review of *White-Jacket*, and again in what he read in Field's book that summer, yet he had written what he called to Hawthorne a "wicked book," wicked because it challenged conventional American piety and because much of it was composed near where a great and saintly book had been written on Original Sin.

Melville also said "wicked" because he was thinking of "Superstition and Knowledge," an old essay (1823) in the *Quarterly Review* that he had recently encountered in some American reprint. The essay was anonymous, so Melville would not have known that the writer was Francis Palgrave, who had some personal interest in religious persecution, being born a Jew. Melville had been transfixed by the lessons "both in psychology and in jurisprudence" afforded by the history of witchcraft. Trials of witches, Palgrave wrote, "furnish the most painful proofs of the fallibility of human testimony and the infirmity of human judgment." Rather than condemning, Palgrave sought to comprehend the witch-hunters, some of whom were, by normal standards, on other topics, "very humane and learned": "Without seeking to enter into the dread question of moral responsibility, we may in some degree extenuate, without excusing, the crimes of the persecutors, by ascribing them to virtual insanity. In considering the actions of the mind, it should never be forgotten, that its affections pass into each other like the tints of the rainbow: though we can easily distinguish them when they have assumed a decided colour, yet we can never determine where each hue begins." Madness, Palgrave continued, "is almost undefinable." Unable to mark up whatever copy he was reading, Melville jotted down notes on "Superstition and Knowledge" in a back flyleaf of his Shakespeare, determined to preserve this insight of Palgrave's: "Right reason and insanity are merely the extreme terms of a series of mental action, which need not be very long." Those persecuted as witches, however wise, could be driven into madness, and equal madness was manifested in the persecutors. (The passage on insanity and the tints of the rainbow was fresh in Melville's mind decades later, when he worked on his story of Billy Budd: "Who in the rainbow can draw the line where the violet tint ends and the orange tint begins?" [ch. 21].)

Palgrave drew parallels between the violence of witch persecution and later kinds of violence, locating a persistent "mysterious love of destruction which is always lurking in human nature," so that the individuals making up a nation "may be exalted into a paroxysm of moral frenzy, possessing as little countroul over their actions as the raving maniac." In Palgrave, Melville read of six hundred women executed in the bishopric of Bamberg, where priests "were convicted of baptising in the following form:—Ego non baptizo te in nomine Patris et Filii et Spiritus Sancti—sed in nomine Diaboli." Melville noted in his Shakespeare: "Ego non baptizo te in nominee Patris et Filii et Spiritus Sancti—sed in nomine Diaboli." On 29 June 1851, Melville had written Hawthorne, just as he was completing his book (not yet retitled *Moby-Dick*): "Shall I send you a fin of the *Whale* by way of a specimen mouthful? The tail is not yet cooked—though the hell-fire in which the whole book is broiled might not unreasonably have cooked it all ere this. This is the book's motto (the secret one),—Ego non baptiso te in nomine—but make out the rest yourself." The "moral frenzy" of reviewers of *Typee* and *Omoo*, George Washington Peck, W. O. Bourne, and a mob of other self-righteous witch-hunters, had left Melville damaged but defiant, so that (following Palgrave) at the end of June he had implied to Hawthorne that the book was baptized in the name of the Devil, and later he may have talked to Hawthorne about the source of the motto. Now in November he called *Moby-Dick* a wicked book, trusting Hawthorne to know what he meant. Hawthorne's letter buffered him against the likelihood that the new book, *Moby-Dick*, would make him, once again, the victim of a witch-hunt, but Melville's retrospective view of his career is plain in something he jotted down five years later, the idea that he might dedicate *The Confidence-Man* to "victims of Auto da Fe" like himself.

A lifetime earlier—a year and a half—Melville had fantasized about Richard Henry Dana Jr. as his ideal reader: "I almost think, I should hereafter—in the case of a sea book—get my M.S.S. neatly & legibly copied by a scrivener—send you that one copy—& deem such a procedure the best publication." The obstacle, he had explained in this letter to Dana, was that he wrote his books "almost entirely for 'lucre'" and therefore had to publish them. The whaling work in progress was a "strange sort of a book," he had forewarned Dana, defining the challenge in terms of needing to let blubber be blubber, to press the oil of realistic description out of it, but also to press out poetry, and to throw in a little fancy while cooking it up, so as to end with something telling the physical and metaphysical truth of whaling. Now, Melville added this to his letter to Hawthorne: "I can't stop yet. If the world was entirely made up of Magians, I'll tell you what I should do. I should have a paper-mill established at one end of the house, and so have an endless riband of foolscap rolling in upon my desk; and upon that endless riband I should write a thousand—a million—billion thoughts, all under the form of a letter to you. The divine magnet is in you, and my magnet responds. Which is the biggest? A foolish question—they are *One*." By understanding *Moby-Dick* as a great truth-telling allegory, Hawthorne had proved himself the ideal audience of one.

Hawthorne received Melville's letter on the eighteenth or the nineteenth, in time to pack it safely away. On Friday the twenty-first he and his family boarded the train in Pittsfield ("in a storm of snow and sleet," he wrote in his journal). He made no record of Melville's or anyone else's seeing them off. The day was fierce even for western Massachusetts, "one of the severest storms we have ever known," according to the Springfield *Republican* (22 November). This was the last Hawthorne saw of the Berkshires. He left behind a friend whose ecstatic state of emotional security was already disintegrating, for it did not survive the first barrage of commentary on *Moby-Dick*.

In Great Britain cadres of brilliant literary people reviewed for the daily London newspapers as well as the weeklies, monthlies, and the still majestic London and Edinburgh quarterlies. In the United States only a handful of reviewers were fit to be called critics, and most American editors and reviewers obsequiously, and justifiably, deferred to British opinion. British displeasure could damn an American book in America, or could make it a success, the way London praise of *Typee* had made it a sensation at home. A few brief American notices of *Moby-Dick* appeared as early as 12 November, but not more than a couple of serious American reviewers had the chance to express their opinions unaffected by news of the British reception. The first word of the British reception of *The Whale* (for the change of title had reached London too late to be used) reached all of Boston and much of New England in the Boston *Post* of 20 November (the day before the Hawthornes took the train at Pittsfield). Although still owned by Melville's brother Gansevoort's old Democratic ally Charles Gordon Greene, the *Post* had gone out of its way to denounce *Mardi* two and a half years earlier, and now was going out of its way to vilify Melville, justified by the ultimate authority of the London *Athenæum*. The *Post* began: "We have read nearly one half of this book, and are satisfied that the London Athenæum is right in calling it 'an ill-compounded mixture of romance and matter-of-fact.'" The *Post* thereafter interposed its own judgment: "It is a crazy sort of affair, stuffed with conceits and oddities of all kinds, put in artificially, deliberately and affectedly, by the side of strong, terse and brilliant passages of incident and description."

Then the reviewer in the *Post* gloatingly quoted "the greater portion" of the 25 October review in the *Athenæum*, giving it currency in ample time to influence many reviews in Boston and elsewhere:

> The style of his tale is in places disfigured by mad (rather than bad) English; and its catastrophe is hastily, weakly, and obscurely managed. The second title — "Moby Dick" — is the name given to a particular sperm whale, or white sea monster, more malignant and diabolical even than the sperm whale in general is known to be. This ocean fiend is invested with especial horrors for our ship's crew; — because, once upon a time, a conflict with him cost their Captain a limb. Captain Ahab had an ivory leg made, — took an oath of retribution, — grew crazy, — lashed himself up into a purpose of cruising in quest of his adversary, — and bound all who sailed with him to stand by him in his wrath. With this cheerful Captain, on such a wise and Christian voyage of discovery, went to sea Ishmael, the imaginary writer of this narrative.
>
> Frantic though such an invention seems to be, it might possibly have been accepted as the motive and purpose of an *extravaganza* had its author been consistent with himself. Nay, in such a terrible cause — when Krakens and Typhoons and the wonders of Mid-Ocean, &c. &c. were the topics and toys to be arranged and manoeuvred — we might have stretched a point in admission of electrical verbs and adjectives as hoarse as the hurricane. There is a time for everything in imaginative literature; — and, according to its order, a place — for rant as well as for reserve; but the rant must be good, honest, shameless rant, without flaw or misgiving. The voice of "the storm wind Euroclydon" must not be interrupted by the facts of Scoresby and the figures of Cocker. Ravings and scraps of useful knowledge flung together salad-wise make a dish in which there may be much surprise, but in which there is little savour. The real secret of this patchiness in the present case is disclosed in Mr. Melville's appendix; which contains such an assortment of curious quotations

as Southey might have wrought up into a whale-chapter for "The Doctor," — suggesting the idea that a substantial work on the subject may have been originally contemplated.

In this last sentence, the "appendix" was not Melville's in any sense, except that he was the author of the words that had been moved from the start of the book to the end; but the reviewer was right about the influence of the late laureate's *The Doctor*, where Melville had found the model for his "Extracts." The reviewer raged on about the "patchiness":

> Either Mr. Melville's purpose must have changed, or his power must have fallen short. The result is, at all events, a most provoking book, — neither so utterly extravagant as to be entirely comfortable, nor so instructively complete as to take place among documents on the subject of the Great Fish, his capabilities, his home and his capture. Our author must be henceforth numbered in the company of the incorrigibles who occasionally tantalize us with indications of genius, while they constantly summon us to endure monstrosities, carelessnesses, and other such harassing manifestations of bad taste as daring or disordered ingenuity can devise.

The *Post* omitted "an interesting and powerfully written extract" quoted and condensed from chapters 2 and 3 (thereby depriving its readers of a sample of Melville's prose), but including some more denunciation, ending with this, still quoted from the *Athenæum*:

> We have little more to say in reprobation or in recommendation of this absurd book, — having detailed its leading incident. Mr. Melville has been on former occasions characterized by us as one who thoroughly understands the tone of sea superstition. There is a wild humorous poetry in some of his terrors which distinguishes him from the vulgar herd of fustian-weavers. For instance, his interchapter on "The Whiteness of the Whale" is full of ghostly suggestions for which a Maturin or a Monk Lewis would have been thankful. Mr. Melville has to thank himself only if his horrors and his heroics are flung aside by the general reader, as so much trash belonging to the worst school of Bedlam literature, — since he seems not so much unable to learn as disdainful of learning the craft of an artist.

The strangely vicious conclusion by the writer in the *Post* focused on the exorbitant price being asked for *Moby-Dick*: "The production under notice is now issued by the Harpers in a handsome bound volume for *one dollar and fifty cents* — no mean sum, in these days. It seems to us that our publishers have gone from one extreme to the other, and that instead of publishing good books in too cheap a form, they are issuing poor books, in far too costly apparel. 'The Whale' is not worth the money asked for it, either as a literary work or as a mass of printed paper. Few people would read it more than once, and yet it is issued at the usual cost of a standard volume." At *"twenty five cents,"* Moby-Dick "might do to buy," but at any higher price it was "a poor speculation."

There was no keeping this onslaught from Lemuel Shaw and his family in Boston — particularly not Hope Savage Shaw (Lizzie's stepmother) and her son Lemuel Jr., both of whom had written Melville's career off when *Mardi* was contemptuously reviewed in 1849 and were alert for anything that reinforced their disdain for him. Anyone unlucky enough not to see the *Post* had another chance to read the entire review on 22 November, when it was reprinted in full in the Boston *Statesman*, the sister paper of the *Post*. There was no keeping the *Post* (or the *Statesman*) from the Melvilles at Arrowhead for long, either. Melville found the condemnation in the *Athenæum* utterly inexplicable. How could any reviewer, however hostile, have called the ending "hastily, weakly, and obscurely managed"? What could be more masterfully paced than the three days of the chase? All his books were botches, Melville could say, but he knew he had elaborately and subtly prepared for Ishmael's surviving the disaster in still earlier chapters, before the chase chapters, and had brought all the preparations together in the "Epilogue" — recalling to the reader the scene in which one man (now identified as Ishmael) had fallen from a boat and been left behind, making high dramatic use of Queequeg's coffin, bringing back onto the scene the *Rachel* (which of course *would* have been circling still, looking for the captain's son), and at the very end making magnificent use of the messengers' words from Job. This was no huddled together ending. Whatever complaint the London reviewer had about the ending of *The Whale*, that objection simply did not apply to the book he had written, Melville knew, and it patently did not apply to *Moby-Dick*, copies of which he had held. Whoever wrote the review in the *Post* may have read nearly half of *Moby-Dick*, as he said, but he had not looked to the back of the book so as to form an independent judgment of the ending. The reviewer in the *Athenæum* had read all the way through and had saved him the trouble.

What Melville learned about the British reception is what any American who scanned the papers would have learned, for he got no weekly or monthly kit of reviews from Richard Bentley, the English publisher. The *Athenæum* surfaced yet again when the New York *Eclectic Magazine* for December (available in late November) reported that it had given the book "a severe handling," and not with "its accustomed candor" ("candor" meaning "fairness"). The brief comment did not mention the specific objection to the ending, but offered this defense, probably not from a full reading of the book: "Faulty as the book may be, it bears the marks of such unquestionable genius, and displays graphic powers of so rare an order, that it cannot fail to add to the popular author's reputation." The New York *North American Miscellany* (December) simply spread the bad report: "Melville's new work, 'The Whale, or Moby Dick,' is pronounced by the Athenaeum an absurd book. Its catastrophe, it says, is hastily, weakly, and obscurely managed, and the style in places disfigured by mad (rather than bad) English."

At the same time, about the end of November, the December New York *International Magazine*, without malice but too short of time to commission an original review of *Moby-Dick*, reprinted the attack on *The Whale* in the London *Spectator* (25 October), thereby spreading the influence of a second hostile English review:

> It is a canon with some critics that nothing should be introduced into a novel which it is physically impossible for the writer to have known: thus, he must not describe the conversation of miners in a pit if they *all* perish. Mr. Melville hardly steers clear of this rule, and he continually violates another, by beginning in the autobiographical form and changing ad libitum into the narrative. His catastrophe overrides all rule: not only is Ahab, with his boat's-crew, destroyed in his last desperate attack upon the white whale, but the Pequod herself sinks with all on board into the depths of the illimitable ocean. Such is the go-ahead method.

The *Spectator* was specific about there being nothing in *The Whale* to account for the survival of the narrator—that is, no "Epilogue," but no American commentator focused on the accusation sharply enough to see that it did not apply to *Moby-Dick*. Now Melville at least knew that he was being condemned for a fault he had not committed. The *Athenæum* review as quoted in the *Post* had been more insidious in that it never spelled out precisely what was wrong with the "catastrophe." Melville could only assume that other British reviewers, perhaps all of them, were condemning him because they had not read the ending he had taken profound satisfaction in setting up.

Quite against the pattern that had prevailed with Melville's earliest books, and simply through bad luck, American readers never got to see a wide sampling of British opinion on *The Whale*, and got to see only the *Athenæum* and *Spectator* reviews before the end of November. Other papers with highly favorable reviews could have arrived on the same ship or the next one, but did not, or else were not quoted in the American press, and the *Athenæum* and the *Spectator* (and *only* those two) were reprinted, and not belatedly, but just in time to keep some reviewers from having to make up their own minds about *Moby-Dick*. On the basis of the early chance arrival of these two periodicals in the United States, American readers all through the crucial first weeks after the publication of *Moby-Dick* had every reason to assume that the British reception was uniformly hostile. So did Herman Melville. Furthermore, no American reader of *Moby-Dick* ever pointed out in public that there was no discernible problem with the ending: no one asked what in the world the *Athenæum* and especially the *Spectator* were talking about.

Melville himself would have seen from the *Athenæum* and the *Spectator* that Bentley had not been able to make the last-minute substitution of *Moby-Dick* as the title and that the "Extracts" had been moved somewhere as an "appendix." Even after reading what the *Spectator* said and knowing for sure that the "Epilogue" was not in *The Whale*, for many weeks Melville remained in baffled uncertainty on some points. What he realized by early December was that he had been condemned by some reviewers in England for a literary sin of which he as author was innocent. Then, all vulnerable, he had been punished again for that sin in the United States, where reviewers sycophantically echoed British condemnation even though they had in hand a book guiltless of that heinous sin against all the expectations of storytelling. Having proudly rejected, months earlier, the sort of publicity tactics Evert Duyckinck thought were necessary for promoting and sustaining a reputation, Melville would have scorned the thought of trying to get on record a public correction in either country. In London it would have been a strangely tardy protest at best, if he waited to dispatch it in January 1852, after he had his copies of *The Whale*, by which time the book was old news. Apparently Melville never made any complaint at all to Bentley about anything that had been done to *The Whale*.

Uninfluenced by the news from England, Evert Duyckinck in the *Literary World* (15 and 22 November) wrote the single most influential American review, judging by borrowings from it or allusions to it. This patron and close friend of Melville's, in the journal that only a year before had rushed into print Melville's essay on Hawthorne, now displayed his enduring myopia. Melville had begun as a sea-writer and in Duyckinck's mind Melville stayed a sea-writer. Yes, Duyckinck had been surprised when Melville had begun to borrow and read "old Books" from his library a few years before — a quaint thing for an adventurer to do, even one from such a good family, and he had been further surprised when Melville had begun to say extraordinary things — sayings Duyckinck perceived as extraordinary not in themselves but because the speaker was a sailor. Melville's assigned role in Duyckinck's mind was that of his in-basement expert on nautical affairs (his "Bunsby"), just the man to ask to review a book like *The California and Oregon Trail* by the sailor's second cousin Catherine Bigelow's then-fiancé Francis Parkman or *The Red Rover* by his uncle Peter Gansevoort's boyhood friend James Fenimore

Cooper, or to contribute a salt-water piece to one of Duyckinck's editorial ventures like the *Dollar Magazine.*

Duyckinck commenced the first installment of his review of *Moby-Dick* with avid interest—but *not* interest in what his friend had spent the better part of two years creating. Possibly Duyckinck had not read the book yet, just as not having read *The Prelude* in 1850 had not deterred him from faking a review of it while vacationing in the Berkshires as Melville's guest. Instead, he evinced inordinate interest in the startling news making the rounds of the papers that the *Ann Alexander,* a New Bedford whaler, had been sunk by a whale off Chile, a report of which he had mailed to Melville early in the month. Now, Duyckinck retold her story in fascinated detail, relating it to the book under review only when almost halfway through this installment (the part that he did not fill up with extracts from ch. 91, headed "The Rose Bud," and ch. 81, headed "Death Scenes of the Whale"). The news of the *Ann Alexander* could have worked to Melville's advantage. After all, in 1846 the resurrection of his companion Toby Greene just when the authenticity of *Typee* was fiercely debated in the press had been a publicity bonanza; if there was any challenge to the new book's authenticity, the sinking of the *Ann Alexander* might become another such publicity boon. As it was, the news detracted from Melville's achievement, for every line Duyckinck devoted to the timely coincidence was a line not devoted to the book under review, and the effect was to reduce *Moby-Dick* to yet another story about the hazardous industry of whaling. At least the news in the 17 November Nantucket *Inquirer* of "A Ship Struck by a Whale" (the *Bella Vascongoda,* supposedly struck by a sleeping whale on 31 July 1851) was not mentioned in any known review of *Moby-Dick.* Duyckinck's conclusion was a polite cliché, no better or worse than what a dozen or two small papers around the Northeast were saying: "This is no everyday writing, and in Herman Melville's best manner." For a crucial week in the reception of *Moby-Dick,* including several days before the poison from the Boston *Post* spread unchallenged, this banality was the final word of criticism from the bellwether *Literary World.*

On 19 November, between the *Literary World* installments, the younger Duyckinck brother, George, sent a copy of *Moby-Dick* to his Long Island friend Joann Miller with a comment on Melville's "failings" as a matter they had already had discussions about: "Melville's book is not entirely what I hoped it would be, but you know his failings and will make allowance for them. There is enough of it at any rate. He seems to have had an idea of giving so complete a view of whaling as to convey the feeling and length of a three years voyage as well as its incidents (perhaps I might say its tedium) to his readers. It will be I suppose of general interest to your family circle, and I am curious to hear what you all think of it." With no disparagement at all, he sent for her little nephew a copy of *Wonder-Book* (published a week or so before *Moby-Dick*) — a children's book which contained Hawthorne's proud pre-publication announcement of *The White Whale*, the "gigantic conception" of which his friend Melville had been "shaping out" in his study the previous summer, while "the gigantic shape of Graylock" loomed upon him.

Evert Duyckinck's second installment, on 22 November, was both more respectfully attentive and more damning. Nothing he wrote should have been a surprise to Melville, for it was of a piece with the man's constant character. Duyckinck had given Melville a discreet warning in his review of *White-Jacket* that his humor could be "a most dangerous" weapon, leading him into "a bewildering, barren, and void scepticism," precisely what Duyckinck thought had happened in *Moby-Dick* (where he used the word "dangerous" again). The duty of a Christian was to dissociate himself from the recklessness of his friend in matters of the immortal soul. Duyckinck tried to soften some of his criticisms by acknowledging that the irreverence in the volume was "to be taken as in some sense dramatic; the narrator throughout among the personages of the Pequod being one Ishmael, whose wit may be allowed to be against everything on land, as his hand is against everything at sea." Yet Melville was the creator of disrespectful Ishmael, and the "piratical running down of creeds and opinions, the conceited indifferentism of Emerson, or the run-a-muck style of Carlyle" was (if not downright "dangerous" to belief) at least "out of place and uncomfortable": "We do not like to see what, under any view, must be to the world the most sacred associations of life violated and defaced." Duyckinck singled out Ishmael's worshiping Yojo with Queequeg in the New Bedford tavern: "why dislodge from heaven, with contumely, 'long-pampered Gabriel, Michael and Raphael'"? or inveigh "against the religious melancholy of priestcraft"? Yet he reminded himself again that the speaker of the book was a fictional narrator, not his host in the Berkshires: "So much for the consistency of Ishmael—who, if it is the author's object to exhibit the painful contradictions of this self-dependent, self-torturing agency of a mind driven hither and thither as a flame in a whirlwind, is, in a degree, a successful embodiment of opinions, without securing from us, however, much admiration for the result." The tone was that of a righteous but determinedly fair-minded man, who in the last short paragraph takes genial relief in making an end of what he had been "reluctantly compelled to object to in this volume." Melville might have expected Duyckinck to see that it was, in all equity, his turn to be promoted in the *Literary World* as he had generously and extravagantly promoted Hawthorne the year before. But Duyckinck was righteous, as well as fair minded, and Melville simply did not deserve praise such as Hawthorne had merited and belatedly received. With the publication of Duyckinck's second installment, the damage to

Moby-Dick in the United States was done. No wonder Hawthorne took the unusually aggressive step of reproving Duyckinck on the first of December, saying bluntly that he hardly thought the *Literary World* had done justice to the best features of Melville's book.

On 20 November, like Duyckinck uninfluenced by the news from England, "H" reviewed *Moby-Dick* in the Congregationalist organ, the New York *Independent*. "H" was not a regular reviewer but someone who had special qualifications for writing about *Moby-Dick*, possibly a former missionary to the South Seas, possibly Henry T. Cheever, the author of the attack on *Typee* in the *Evangelist* and the author of a whaling book Melville had used in writing *Moby-Dick*. Borrowing from Melville's own favorite, Robert Burton, "H" gibed at the "fantastical title" and at "harlequin writers" like Melville, "as ready as in Burton's time to make themselves Merry-andrews and Zanies, in order to raise the wind of curiosity about their literary wares." In Melville "H" saw talent that was misused because of something foul inherent in his nature: "there is a primitive formation of profanity and indecency that is ever and anon shooting up through all the strata of his writings; and it is this which makes it impossible for a religious journal heartily to commend any of the works of this author which we have ever perused." Melville and the four Harper brothers were all risking eternal damnation: "The Judgment day will hold him liable for not turning his talents to better account, when, too, both authors and publishers of injurious books will be conjointly answerable for the influence of those books upon the wide circle of immortal minds on which they have written their mark. The book-maker and the book-publisher had better do their work with a view to the trial it must undergo at the bar of God." This widely distributed paper was unavoidable in Pittsfield, where there were many Congregationalists and where all the Protestant sects were conservative in doctrinal matters. In the absence of a Dutch Reformed church, Melville's mother was comfortable at the Episcopal St. Stephen's, where she did not have to see anyone crossing himself (as she might see in Manhattan's Episcopalian Church of the Ascension, where her son Allan and his wife, Sophia, worshiped). In Pittsfield, alerted by the *Independent*, the religious gossips set to work on *Moby-Dick* without reading the book, which did not go on sale at Phineas Allen's bookstore until 18 December.

Promptly enough, after the shocks of the *Post* (and the *Statesman*, the *Independent*, and the *Literary World*), Melville saw at least a few favorable American reviews — those in the New York *Tribune* (written by George Ripley, the Transcendental socialist, a veteran of the Brook Farm experiment) and the *Albion* (both 22 November), the *Home Journal* (29 November), *Harper's* (December, apparently also by Ripley), and the *Spirit of the Times* (6 December); later he probably saw a remarkable review by William Allen

Butler, George Duyckinck's friend, in a Washington paper widely read in New York City and Albany, the *National Intelligencer* (16 December). In the *Tribune* on 10 May 1849, Ripley had wearied of the "huge allegory," bits of which peeped out "here and there" through *Mardi*, and had deplored the "mystic speculation and wizard fancies" ungrounded in "graphic, poetical narration." Now he wrote: "We have occasional touches of the subtle mysticism, which is carried to such an inconvenient excess in Mardi, but it is here mixed up with so many tangible and odorous realities, that we always safely alight from the excursions through mid-air upon the solid deck of the whaler. We are recalled to this world by the fumes of 'oil and blubber,' and are made to think more of the contents of barrels than of allegories." After quoting extensively, Ripley parted reluctantly with "the adventurous philosophical Ishmael" (whom he blurred with Melville): "We think it the best production which has yet come from that seething brain, and in spite of its lawless flights, which put all regular criticism at defiance, it gives us a higher opinion of the author's originality and power than even the favorite and fragrant first-fruits of his genius, the never-to-be-forgotten Typee." Ripley's praise of *Moby-Dick* was spread throughout the East and beyond, thanks to Horace Greeley's superb distribution system, swamping what Duyckinck had to say, at least for the day.

On the same day (22 November) the New York *Albion*, edited for British expatriates by the English-born William Young, published a substantial review. The *Albion* reviewer found that *Moby-Dick* was "not lacking much of being a great work," and he was the man to show just how "it falls short of this." The "*dramatis personae*" were "all vivid sketches done in the author's best style," and it was "only when Mr. Melville puts words into the mouths of these living and moving beings, that his cunning fails him, and the illusion passes away," for from "the Captain to the Cabin-boy, not a soul amongst them talks pure seaman's lingo." He substantiated that charge by quotations from Starbuck, Stubb, and Flask before concluding: "But there is no pleasure in making these extracts; still less would there be in quoting anything of the stuff and nonsense spouted forth by the crazy Captain; for so indeed must nine-tenths of his dialogue be considered, even though one bears in mind that it has been compounded in a maniac's brain from the queer mixture of New England conventicle phraseology with the devilish profanity too common on board South-Sea Whalers." Despite the reviewer's irritation, this was a clear attempt to acknowledge a dramatic justification for Ahab's speech, and he revealed throughout a genuine delight in aspects of the book, such as a passage from "The Hyena" that he offered as a "peep into a particular mood of mind" in which Melville had blended truth and satire.

Melville's friend Nathaniel Parker Willis was embroiled in scandal still, the aftermath of his reckless intimacy with the wife of the actor Edwin Forrest, so what he wrote in the *Home Journal* was very brief, but focused shrewdly on Melville's likely motives. Willis guessed that in *Moby-Dick* Melville, "conscious of the vivid expectation excited in the reading public by his previous books," had "resolved to combine in the present all his popular characteristics, and so fully justify his fame." "Accordingly," Melville had "chosen a subject which affords the greatest scope for adventure and the most striking phases of sea-life, and at the same time, by its relation to commerce and natural history, is associated with the most matter-of-fact interests." Aiming at broadest popularity, Melville had "treated of the Whale under three points of view—as the nucleus of maritime adventure, as a subject of scientific curiosity, and as a kind of hero of romance." The result, Willis concluded, was "a very racy, spirited, curious and entertaining book, which affords quite an amount of information, while it enlists the curiosity, excites the sympathies, and often charms the fancy." This was not Willis at his best, but it was based on intimate, if now interrupted, personal acquaintance with Melville, who from London had written him about the lack of money that was forcing him to relinquish his hopes for more extensive travel, and the gossipy *Home Journal* every week reached an audience far beyond New York and Boston.

As Melville might have expected, the review in the December *Harper's* was favorable (pretty clearly by Ripley, writing not only for the *Tribune* but the magazine he was helping to edit):

> On this slight framework [of Ahab's pursuit of Moby Dick], the author has constructed a romance, a tragedy, and a natural history, not without numerous gratuitous suggestions on psychology, ethics, and theology. Beneath the whole story, the subtle, imaginative reader may perhaps find a pregnant allegory, intended to illustrate the mystery of human life. Certain it is that the rapid, pointed hints which are often thrown out, with the keenness and velocity of a harpoon, penetrate deep into the heart of things, showing that the genius of the author for moral analysis is scarcely surpassed by his wizard power of description.

Seeing that the processes of procuring oil contrasted "strangely with the weird, phantom-like character of the plot, and of some of the leading personages, who present a no less unearthly appearance than the witches in Macbeth," the reviewer declared his admiration: "These sudden and decided transitions form a striking feature of the volume. Difficult of management, in the highest degree, they are wrought with consummate skill. To a less gifted author, they would inevitably have proved fatal. He has not only deftly avoided their dangers, but made them an element of great power." The reviewer observed shrewdly that many readers would be most interested in the "succession of portraitures, in which the lineaments of nature shine forth, through a good deal of perverse, intentional exaggeration," and then pursued the topic to the point of declaring that the members of the ship's company "all stand before us in the strongest individual relief, presenting a unique picture gallery, which every artist must despair of rivaling."

The reviewer of *Moby-Dick* in the 6 December *Spirit of the Times* may have been the editor, William T. Porter, the indefatigable encourager of the Big Bear school of literature. His paper had long evinced a fondness for Melville's works, and indeed the opening sentence of this review ("Our friend Melville's books begin to accumulate") may not be formulaic but may indicate personal acquaintanceship, since in the tiny publishing center in lower Manhattan Melville would have had opportunities aplenty to get to know Porter or members of his staff. The reviewer called all five of Melville's earlier books the "results of the youthful experience on the ocean of a man who is at once philosopher, painter, and poet." He went on to make the remarkable point that Melville's painful early experiences had become "infinitely valuable to the world" simply because "the humanities of the world" had been quickened by his first five books: "it is only now and then when genius, by some lucky chance of youth, ploughs deeper into the soil of humanity and nature, that fresher experiences — perhaps at the cost of much individual pain and sorrow — are obtained; and the results are books, such as those of Herman Melville and Charles Dickens. Books which are living pictures, at once of the practical truth, and the ideal amendment: books which mark epochs in literature and art." As for the title (which the *Independent* scorned on 20 November), "*Moby-Dick*" was one of the "taking titles" at which no man was more felicitous than Melville — "taking" being one of the many references to Melville as a writer with a magician's or witch's power to allure and spirit the reader away.

Melville's brother Allan may well have seen the review in the Washington *National Intelligencer* (16 December) and forwarded it to Pittsfield right away. The family would have known the reviewer was William Allen Butler, who had written an account of the literary doings in the Berkshires a year earlier, after visiting there. Butler found in the book at hand an example of Melville's blatant sexuality which he could talk about without revealing that his own sexual security had been threatened by the man who had abducted his bride from the railroad cars on 9 August 1850: "Neither good taste nor good morals can approve the 'forecastle scene,' with its maudlin and ribald orgies, as contained in the 40th chapter of 'Moby Dick.' It has all that is disgusting in Goethe's 'Witches' Kitchen,' without its genius." Still, Butler thought that

Melville's "delineation of character" was "actually Shakespearean" and that the "humor of Mr. Melville is of that subdued yet unquenchable nature which spreads such a charm over the pages of Sterne," while the "wild imagining" was reminiscent of Coleridge's "Ancient Mariner." Butler was after all too good a critic not to say some words that needed saying: "Language in the hands of this master becomes like a magician's wand, evoking at will 'thick-coming fancies,' and peopling the 'chambers of imagery' with hideous shapes of terror or winning forms of beauty and loveliness."

In this handful of reviews in the *Tribune*, the *Albion*, the *Home Journal*, *Harper's*, the *Spirit of the Times*, and the *National Intelligencer* most of the right words had been said about *Moby-Dick* before wide audiences, but what reached Melville, day by day, was trivial and demeaning. A few American papers merely listed the publication of *Moby-Dick*, sometimes identifying the local bookstore that had copies for sale, sometimes making an offhand comment about it. Two dozen or so of the notices that ran to several lines of a newspaper column were based on a predisposition toward Melville (normally favorable) but not on more than a glance at some pages of the book. Several items were more or less openly based on other reviews. A couple of dozen papers around New England printed lengthy extracts from *Moby-Dick*, usually deriving them from the first installment of the *Literary World* review (ch. 81, "Death Scene of the Whale") or the 22 November New York *Tribune* (part of ch. 61, usually entitled "Killing a Whale" or "Stubb Kills a Whale"), or third or fourth hand, from other papers that had already copied from one or the other of these convenient sources (it being easier to hand these papers to the printer than a copy of the book itself). The publicity these extracts gave the book can only have helped sales and was undoubtedly good for Melville's reputation: better a column and more of Melville's prose, noncommittally or favorably offered, than a perfunctory review.

Yet, exasperatingly, most reviewers who made an effort to read *Moby-Dick* could not rise to many of its challenges, as this brief review in the New Haven *Daily Palladium* (17 November) suggests:

> Herman Melville has long ago made his name current among men of taste and letters. His "Typee," "Omoo," and "White Jacket," have all afforded pleasure to thousands of readers, and his lively, roving story of Moby-Dick, we presume will be as popular as any other work that bears his name. It has numerous thrilling sketches of sea life, whale captures, shark massacres, &c. — but in some of the colloquies between old weatherbeaten Jacks, there is a little more irreverence and profane jesting than was needful to publish, however true to the life the conversation may be. The work possesses all the

interest of the most exciting fiction, while, at the same time, it conveys much valuable information in regard to things pertaining to natural history, commerce, life on ship board, &c.

Give or take a point or two of emphasis, this is almost interchangeable with what reviewers said in the Albany *Argus* (14 November), the Boston *Daily Evening Traveller* (15 November), the Springfield *Republican* (17 November), the Utica *Daily Gazette* (19 November), and later ones in the St. John (New Brunswick) *News* (10 December), the New York *Methodist Quarterly Review* (January), and the Philadelphia *Peterson's Magazine* (January). The evidence is clear that many reviewers had made their minds up about Melville: they enjoyed him, despite some reservations, but they certainly did not expect him to write great works of literature. Several authors of moderate-sized reviews, two or three times as long as the one quoted in this paragraph, took much the same line as the perfunctory reviewers, with only an occasional intensity or individuality of response to set them apart. Lurking in the minds of many of the reviewers was what the New York *Parker's Journal* (22 November) made explicit: Melville had run "into the grave error of giving us altogether too much for our money" when he changed his formula and added fiction to the information which had made *Typee* "just perfect."

On 25 November Harper & Brothers sent its seventh account to Melville, showing 1535 copies of *Moby-Dick* sold and, counting sales of other books, a balance of $422.82 due. The figures showed that Melville's reputation and any new praise for *Moby-Dick* had not stimulated sales to equal those of *Redburn* and *White-Jacket*. Melville had prepared himself to add *Moby-Dick* to his blessings and step from that, but there was nothing to step from. By December, scarcely two weeks after his hours with Hawthorne at the Little Red Inn and their exchange of exultant letters, Melville found it harder, day by day, to see himself as the author of a great Shakespearean whaling book in hand and a great work in progress, one still more ambitious and profound—a Kraken to stand on his shelf beside *Moby-Dick*.

[2]

"Mad Christmas"
December 1851

In his *Poetical Works of John Milton* Melville marks a passage on Milton's not attending any church and believing that any church fit to attend was to be "unconnected with the state," its ministers preferably unpaid; instead, true worship was "to dwell alone in . . . holy meditations, cloistered from public gaze, and secluded within the humbler sanctuary of the adoring heart." Melville comments: "A singular coincidence."

AFTER STANWIX'S BIRTH on 22 October 1851, Elizabeth Shaw Melville had been slow to recover her strength. The baby boy was "small and thin" but "very little trouble, sleeping a good deal & having a famous appetite," his Grandmother Melville wrote on 5 November to Augusta, who was visiting Allan and Sophia in New York. But Stanwix's appetite was difficult to satisfy once Lizzie developed a breast infection. A local woman, Mrs. Proctor, who was attending Lizzie, had reported to Maria that day her fear that there might be "a gathering" in one breast, "if it could not be scattered." Maria's report to Augusta drew on her intimate knowledge of Lizzie, going back almost a decade: "She is very nervous being constitutionally so, and now being so weak, with loss of appetite, that a sheet had to be placed on the wall to cover the paper the figures of which seem'd to her in motion." There is an edge of intolerance in this, for Maria would never have said that one of her daughters was constitutionally nervous, the most anxious, Kate, having been made so by events in childhood, not by nature. Maria could not help thinking that lack of firm character was involved in Lizzie's problems. Therefore, perhaps, no one in the family had let Lizzie's painful condition interfere with an exhilarating invitation from Charles and Elizabeth Sedgwick to meet the Hawthornes and the English novelist G. P. R. James and his wife on 4 November. Leaving Lizzie and the boys with Fanny (and perhaps one servant as well as the man, David), Maria, Helen, and Kate had wrapped themselves up in buffalo robes and Herman had cheerfully driven them off to Lenox (where Hawthorne arrived without his wife and Mrs. James without her husband). Hawthorne and Melville had been happy to see each other but more than a little frustrated: the one would have his *Wonder-Book* to give to Malcolm Melville any day now, and the other would have his whaling book to proffer to Hawthorne any day now — with any luck while the Hawthornes were still in Lenox.

Around mid-November, the time of the publication of *Moby-Dick*, Lizzie "dried the milk" in the right breast, but a little later, apparently just before Thanksgiving, the twenty-seventh, that breast "gathere'd & broke" (as Maria wrote Augusta on 30 December). A large lump formed under Lizzie's left arm but since it did not interfere with the production of milk the local physician, Dr. O. S. Root, advised her to continue nursing Stanwix from the left breast, despite the pain. The pain grew so severe that she decided she had to go to Boston to seek the help of the Shaw family physician, her uncle by marriage, Dr. George Hayward. She could hardly have imagined herself sitting at the table with her family for the high New England holiday, but she knew she would feel safer in her own house with her own family, cared for by the housekeeper, Mrs. Sullivan, visited by her own doctor, so she most likely decided to brave the terrible weather in order to be home before Thanksgiving rather than later. Even in perfect health and good weather, Melville women almost never traveled unescorted; so under the circumstances Herman was obliged to accompany her and the baby. He must have gone grudgingly. It had been bad enough to have to stop work on *Moby-Dick* to drive his sister Helen or his mother to the depot. Now he had to interrupt a book that again required intense concentration for long periods, and to do so when the last thing he wanted was to go to the city where the *Post* and the *Statesman* had just shamed him.

Those contemptuous quotations from the London *Athenæum*, augmented with the Bostonian's ferocious hostility for Melville, hung in the air, justifying Lem Jr. and Hope Savage Shaw in their opinion of Herman and his writings. After such annihilating news about the reception of the book in London, after the savaging in the New York *Independent* and other papers, the Shaws (even the judge) could only assume that *Moby-Dick* was a failure, like *Mardi*, and wonder what Herman hoped to achieve by involving himself already in yet another book at the cost of neglecting Lizzie's health for weeks. Herman had to face the hostility of Hope and her older son at a time when he was still baffled by the complaint about the ending of the book and when any protestation of bewilderment he made would have struck the Shaws as specious. As far as we know, Melville had not yet received sets of *The Whale* (in three volumes) from Bentley, and no copies are known to have arrived in the United States, as might have happened if someone had purchased the volumes soon after publication for shipboard reading. Why should anyone believe there was nothing wrong with the ending of *The Whale*, or should have been nothing wrong if Bentley had printed what he had been sent? Nothing had been left out of *Mardi* in the English edition, had it? The *Athenæum* had been contemptuous then, too (24 March 1849): "Matters become crazier and crazier — more and more foggy — page by page — until the end — which is no more an end than the last line of Coleridge's 'Kubla Kahn' — is felt to be a happy release. Few besides ourselves will take the pains of reaching it." Now, new book, same fault with the ending. Worse still for his state of mind, Melville carried the secret of his debt to T. D. Stewart, for money to repay the loan was not flooding in from *Moby-Dick*. Inexplicably, two or three weeks after its American publication, *Moby-Dick* was already a failure, comparatively speaking, in its sales as well as in reviews.

In Boston the most likely topic for polite intellectual conversation was pleasant for everyone else and exacerbating for Herman. All of Unitarian Boston had been enthralled with the lecture series at the Lowell Institute by Lemuel Shaw's friend Orville Dewey on successive Tuesday and Friday nights between 21 October and 28 November, the day after Thanksgiving. The crowds for Dewey's lectures had been immense and reporters had attended the lectures and written enthusiastically about them. In extending the invitation early in 1850, John A. Lowell had suggested "a subject connected with Natural Theology." The final title, "The Problem of Human Destiny, considered in its bearings on Human Life and Welfare," was one Melville could hardly speak neutrally about, since it epitomized for him pseudo-Christian piety passing for true biblical religion. Dewey's triumphs were particularly unpleasant to hear about while his own absolutist yearnings toward New Testament Christianity were being denounced as flings at revealed religion. Melville dealt as best he could with the hostility of the Shaws (always excepting the judge), said good-bye to his wife and the undernourished baby, and turned around and caught one of the next trains back, just possibly after being dragooned into hearing Dewey's lecture on Tuesday the twenty-fifth or Friday the twenty-eighth.

Since Augusta temporarily was not in the same house with Lizzie, her correspondence log ought to help date Lizzie's trip to Boston, but it lists not a single letter to or from Lizzie in November or December 1851, nothing until she wrote Lizzie (still in Boston) on 2 January 1852. Then she received a six-page reply from Lizzie on 8 January, wrote Lizzie in Boston on 13 January, and then wrote jointly to her mother and Lizzie on 28 February, knowing they were both at Arrowhead. In the 29 December part of her long year's-end letter to Augusta, Maria gave medical details. When Lizzie went to Boston "her left breast[,] rather under the arm had a large lump, which kept increasing in size. This lump did not interfere at all with the milk vessels, but she suffered a great deal of pain when nursing him which kept increasing." She continued: "Dr Heyward commenced poulticing this after Lizzie's arrival at Boston, but the pain when nursing increased to such a degree that it seems she has been urged by it to do that which from the begin[n]ing I told her would have to be the final result but to which she was very averse, that was, to wean Stanwix." As late as that same day, 29 December, Herman received a letter in which Lizzie reported that she was "suffering a good deal of pain," even after starting to wean Stanwix. Maria's refusal to take Lizzie's plight seriously is clear in her phrasing to Augusta: "Otherwise Lizzie is well or rather would be well[.] I hope this week will bring this matter to a crisis and enable her to retrieve her strength, and give her an opportunity to enjoy the society of her friends and cheer her spirits a little, she has had a long tedious confinement, which all our care and tenderness could not prevent." Malcolm, Maria added coolly, was "apparently not at all troubled at his mothers absence."

Melville had to stifle his anger at the reviews and deny their financial implications for *Moby-Dick* if he were to preserve his aesthetic control over his dangerous psychological material. To concentrate on his manuscript after late November, by which time he had written much or perhaps most of the rural opening section of *Pierre*, which takes place in a series of carefully delineated days and parts of days, five in all, he also had to convince himself that *Pierre* might be a financial success as well as a Kraken book. He had written scornfully to Richard Bentley on 5 June 1849 of books merely calculated "to please the general reader" and not to "provoke attack." Now he meant to write a great book which would look like a book "in the ordinary novel form" (as he said in that letter) and would please readers as a piece of modern gothic fiction, the first of many new ventures. As much as he could, he had to put out of mind the sufferings of his wife (easier once she was away in Boston). He had to make the best he could of the thwarting of the expectation he had naturally cherished during the summer—that he might have been able to resume marital relations with his wife reasonably soon after the birth of the child she had been carrying since late January. Also, he had to try to avoid distractions in the household, among which was his son Malcolm, almost three. Instead of devouring him with kisses, as Augusta thought he might do at the New Year, Melville was devouring Malcolm's future, and the baby's, by going into debt and by writing yet another new book that might be great but would be "said to 'fail,'" as he wrote to Shaw on 6 October 1849, in the wake of *Mardi*. At whatever cost to his family and to his own feelings toward them, Melville absorbed himself in his manuscript in early December, toiling onward with the brief tragic life of his hero, Pierre. Around 3 December he put in a request to Augusta—to bring home with her the copy of Machiavelli's Florentine history which Allan had borrowed ("Don't forget.") — an indication that he had progressed to or beyond the "Book" called "The Cousins" (15), where he alludes to some "ulterior refinements of cool Tuscan policy" that Pierre had not yet become initiated into. It also means he then expected Augusta home well before he finished the book. He may have planned to construct the city section as transpiring in a limited number of days, perhaps another five days altogether before heaping up a Shakespearean pile of corpses at the end. For weeks he worked through the morning into the early afternoon before breaking, and sometimes worked past his usual stopping point till it was almost dark — that is, three or even four o'clock. Neither his subject nor his work schedule was such as to make Melville a fit companion at the end of the day, and whatever complexities of guilt he felt about his behavior to his family at Arrowhead, he knew, all the time, that his paramount duty as a great writer was to shut out every human or inhuman concern that might threaten the sacred perfection of the emerging book.

During these weeks, in consciously turning away from events which threatened to impinge on him, Melville was enacting a personal variation on the national frenzy of self-delusion. In Melville's childhood the Compromise of 1820 had let liberal-minded Americans put the issue of slavery out of their minds so they could bask in feel-good sympathy for distant causes such as Greek independence that would cost them nothing in money or lives. The last year, respectable Whigs and Democrats alike had determined that the Compromise of 1850 would solve the slavery crisis for their time (if only a few incorrigible slaves and a handful of fanatical abolitionists would settle down). The Boston enthusiasm over Orville Dewey's Lowell Institute lectures was proof enough that all responsible people wanted to put the issue of slavery behind them, or far in abeyance, and think instead of serious American moral issues such as the problem of human destiny and the purpose of Providence in the world and in man. Then in early December 1851 a new feel-good escapist media sensation monopolized the newspapers in New York and other cities — the triumphal (and ultimately futile) tour of Lajos Kossuth to raise support for a Hungarian revolt against the oppressive Austrians. Kossuth's progress seemed one of the great events of the century to many infatuated Americans, including the young William Dean Howells, who in his mature wisdom recalled that the only effect that lasted very long was the fad for a black slouch hat like the great Hungarian's. Many an ostrich died so feathers could bedeck those hats in tribute to the great, remote cause of Hungarian independence.

Then for New Yorkers, especially, and anyone like Melville in reach of the *Herald* and the *Tribune*, in mid-December the preoccupation with Kossuth was replaced by collective fascination (lasting through three weeks of

January) with the lurid details of the actor Edwin Forrest's divorce suit against his wife, in which Melville's friend Nathaniel Parker Willis was named as an adulterous partner of Mrs. Forrest. Willis was tall, two or three inches taller than Melville, and admittedly a sensualist. He had come "very near being very handsome," old Oliver Wendell Holmes recalled in another era, when he could characterize Willis as "something between a remembrance of Count D'Orsay and an anticipation of Oscar Wilde" ("Introduction" to *A Mortal Antipathy*, 1885). Stars of the bar outshone the stars of the stage, for Forrest's lawyer was Martin Van Buren's son, Prince John, and his opponent, the lawyer for Mrs. Forrest, was Charles O'Conor, the Hunker lawyer, a member of the Albany Regency in Melville's youth. It was a duel of high-priced and stagy advocates. Almost two years earlier Evert Duyckinck's young friend Oakey Hall in his "Croton" letter in the New Orleans *Commercial Bulletin* (13 February 1850) had described O'Conor as a man with "soulless eyes, but piercing glance, who sees a point in a case as an Indian sees a scalp-lock in a dense forest." O'Conor was famous, Prince John was still glamorous, Forrest was magnificent (even Fanny Kemble said he had the best calves she ever saw on a man), and the sexual details were unprecedentedly graphic. Many Americans yielded themselves to these two media sensations, the one supplanting the other, but Melville pushed them out of his consciousness through most of this month, however much he rued the public allegations of sexual impropriety against Nat Willis. The cases provided him, later, with fodder for his reflections on the insignificance of most public events. A bloody battle in "Affghanistan" and a grand contested election in the United States had overshadowed news of a whaling voyage by one Ishmael. Now, whatever the papers said about Hungarian freedom fighters and cuckolded actors, what counted in the study looking out at Greylock was the new aesthetic-psychological voyage by one Melville.

In the middle of December Melville interrupted his work to indite a private letter as a public statement. He had heard the news of the death at Cooperstown of James Fenimore Cooper in mid-September, and soon afterward had received from Rufus W. Griswold, whom Melville had met often at Dr. John W. Francis's house in Bond Street, an invitation to attend a memorial service for Cooper in New York City. Nothing suggests that Cooper's death was remarkably meaningful to Melville. In his letter to Griswold on 19 December, Melville testified to Cooper's early influence: "his works are among the earliest I remember, as in my boyhood producing a vivid, and awakning power upon my mind." This probably occurred in the 1830s, perhaps as late as the time Gansevoort was making notes in his *Index Rerum* of his reading of some of the novels, among them *The Pioneers*, *The Red Rover* ("Pirate's cabin Red Rover Vol 1 chap 6 page 84 description of, good"), and

The Spy. "Boyhood," however, may indicate an earlier reading. Cooper in his known letters does not mention the young American writer Melville, though he knew who Melville was. Melville's mother remembered Cooper as a big boy who played with her brother Peter when he stayed over at the Gansevoort house waiting for the breakup of the ice on the Hudson so he could go south. For his part, Melville had manifested no sense of competitiveness in moving into a literary genre, the sea novel, hitherto dominated by Cooper. He sincerely regarded Cooper as "a great, robust-souled man, all whose merits are not even yet fully appreciated," as he wrote to Griswold. Melville declined the invitation to the meeting, which was set for 24 December (but subsequently postponed till 27 February 1852): "My very considerable distance from the city, connected with other reasons, will prevent my compliance." Cooper simply was not significant to him once Melville began his career. Washington Irving had been his literary model and obstacle, the literary parent he had to surpass and repudiate, not Cooper. The "other reasons" for not accepting the invitation included his obsessive work on his manuscript.

For Melville, the past year and several weeks, it had sufficed to have Hawthorne only an hour or so away by horseback, although weeks and even months had passed without the men's seeing each other. Melville had known that, if he needed to, he could ride or drive down to see the one friend with whom he could talk of almost all matters, books and publishers, but also Providence, Free Will, Fate, all the topics of discussion among the fallen angels of *Paradise Lost* that Hawthorne later identified as Melville's persistent themes. Now he was more isolated than he had ever been, and, far from being a sure bet, his great gamble on the whaling book had failed, whether he could admit it to himself yet or not. In the foreseeable future Melville would have interest payments to John Brewster, interest payments to T. D. Stewart, but, with caution, his debt to the Harpers would slowly diminish and he would begin to receive a little income from them. The money the Melvilles received that December was Lizzie's $180 from her trust fund (earned up through 4 August 1851, her fourth wedding anniversary), not thousands of dollars in profits from the whaling book—not money with which Melville could pay off Stewart and Brewster and start construction on that towered house he had been sure he would build, to replace the old farmhouse. And with every indication that *Moby-Dick* would do, at best, about as well as *White-Jacket,* Melville knew that *Pierre* had to sell phenomenally more than *Moby-Dick* if he were to be able to pay off Stewart and support his family. Yet in what he wrote he was casting off familial responsibility as surely as his deluded young hero had done, and was with equal certainty, in following his artistic impulses in the face of all practical behavior, bringing down upon himself the same sort of opprobrium Pierre was bringing down upon himself. Herman Melville was his irresponsible father's son, but with an ugly twist to the paternal failing. Allan Melvill had made desperate, profligate financial decisions while seeing himself as the model of fiscal probity; Herman Melville, certain of his literary genius, could take pride in his recklessness, as when he wrote Richard Bentley (5 June 1849):"some of us scribblers, My Dear Sir, always have a certain something unmanageable in us, that bids us do this or that, and be done it must — hit or miss."

During these weeks Melville cringed intermittently under well-meant perfunctory comments on his whaling book almost as much as under lacerating personal assaults. High praise abounded in many reviews, but unjust, obtuse, libelous, and barely endurable and exceedingly memorable phrases were strewn thickly in highly accessible reviews. The word "blasphemy" had not occurred in the review in the *Literary World*, but Duyckinck's challenge had been read everywhere: "Surely Ishmael, who is a scholar, might have spoken respectfully of the Archangel Gabriel, out of consideration, if not for the Bible (which might be asking too much of the school), at least for one John Milton, who wrote Paradise Lost." Duyckinck's puritanical convictions were damaging the possibility that *Moby-Dick* might sell unusually well, and any such comments on irreverence fueled the local outrage against Melville's writing such a book in their Christian part of the world.

It was 18 December before copies of *Moby-Dick* went on sale in the Pittsfield bookstore of Phineas Allen, but before then, on the basis of reviews (more likely than on copies acquired elsewhere), there was village gossip that the book was "more than Blasphemous." In his years away from the Berkshires, Melville could put out of his mind how his Aunt Mary and his cousins had suffered from their neighbors' gossip about Uncle Thomas's prolonged stays in a jail cell in Lenox, but now he could not ignore the old Berkshire relish of malicious gossip. At any time, knowing that the village was gossiping about him would have distracted and perturbed Melville, increasing the likelihood that he would flail out recklessly in his manuscript and behave rudely to the women in his household, as he had behaved to Helen and his mother months earlier, during the composition of *Moby-Dick*. Just as well that Lizzie was away now, for an accusation of blasphemy was painful to the women in Melville's household and would have been especially painful to the daughter of Lemuel Shaw, who in 1838 had become the last judge in America to sentence a man to jail for blasphemy (legally defined as "speaking evil of the Deity with an impious purpose to derogate from the divine majesty," and "a wilful and malicious attempt to lessen men's reverence of God"). Accusations that he was irreligious were particularly painful for Melville because living in the Berkshires had encouraged his mother to move into one of her more evangelical phases, exacerbated by her being in intimate contact, day by day, with the only one of her children whose immortal soul seemed to be in imminent danger. For his part, the accusation of committing a sin *worse* than blasphemy was in itself strong enough to shake Melville's briefly cherished emotional security, frightening and enraging him.

Since the start of October 1850, Melville had endured a strong dose of his mother in his home. The situation in New York City had been very different, for there Maria's attention had been diffused not only by the household of six children (occasionally seven, when Tom was home from sea), two daughters-in-law, and two babies but also by four live-in Irish servants (according to the 1850 census), as well as the responsibility of making calls and receiving callers, some of whom were old friends from the 1820s. At Arrowhead she could supervise only a cook, a man, and perhaps one houseservant, and it was difficult for her to travel from house to village. Once she was back in a small circle where religion was the tie that held the neighborhood together (where everyone counted noses at church services and those present had to apologize for those absent), once Herman was the only male offspring in the house, and the one with the greatest power to embarrass her publicly by (for instance) making himself a local scandal for not attending church, it was her duty to focus on the state of his soul. From the previous December, if not earlier, his mother and sisters had (they thought subtly) begun pressuring him to take part in religious services in the village — and when he did, on rare occasions, go to church with them, they promptly relayed the news to any absent sister even while enjoining her not to mention to him that she had heard the news, lest he resent their talking about it, and refuse to go again. Now Melville was the stiff-necked, sinful man who refused the importunities of his mother that he attend church with her and his sisters.

In private, and even in public, Herman routinely let himself be provoked into sallies or outbursts that people — Rowland Morewood, for one — took as disturbingly irreverent. Maria never knew what he would say next. In the close confines of Arrowhead, she could walk into his private study needing to consult a certain scriptural verse (although Bibles were to be found in other rooms) and see a Bible (say the one Herman dated 23 March 1850) marked up in so frivolous a way as to be downright sacrilegious. What heretical relativistic spirit could have caused her son to write that if Christ had been born in Tartary he would have been a Tartar? Why would he put in the margins the impudent theory that some of the divinely dictated books were written by Egyptian Jews contaminated by Greek Platonism? From *Typee* onward Herman had taken a relativist view of religion, in which the gods of the ancients might have been very good gods, in which the god most like Jesus might have appeared to the Mardians under different titles, Brami (like

Bramin) and Manko (as in Manco Capac), as well as Alma (*Mardi*, ch. 113), and in which a clumsy fat old Marquesan god might be upbraided and beaten with a stick (*Typee*, ch. 24). Reviewers of the early books had denounced Melville not so much for lashing out against Christian doctrines as for implying that Christianity was only one of many equally valid religions.

Further, Melville's bent of mind was perversely relativistic in ways not obvious from a glance at such marginalia as that on Jesus and Tartary. In *Moby-Dick*, for example, he had taken the history of Queequeg from George Lillie Craik's account of Tupai Cupa in *The New Zealanders* (London, 1830). (This book he encountered in 1850 after writing Bulkington into his manuscript as Ishmael's companion; once Melville read about Tupai Cupa he brushed his tall Virginian aside.) Melville had deliberately inverted the true account of Tupai Cupa's drinking the water from finger-glasses, once, but never falling into that social error again. In the story Queequeg tells Ishmael, Melville makes a European captain the blundering violator of the polite social codes of Kokovoko — deliberately altering a source so as to upset the unthinking cultural chauvinism of his American and British readers. Cultural chauvinism and religious chauvinism were inseparable, so that Ishmael in his courtesy toward Queequeg facilely reasons himself into worshiping Yojo with his new friend — a scene Melville had precisely calculated to enrage his old enemies at the *Evangelist*. By Melville's absolute standards, conventional, worldly Christians such as he had been around recently in Boston were not true Christians: how many residents of Beacon Hill would leave all and follow Jesus? Maria would have rejoiced in Herman's being a nominal Christian as long as he had been conventionally Christian. As indicated by her excessive adulation of Martin Farquhar Tupper (in March of 1851) and the Hungarian revolutionary Kossuth (her recorded comments date from late December 1851), she was casting about for manly religious leaders whom she could pronounce men after her own heart, as her oldest living son was conspicuously not. She lavished expressions of respect on anyone else she assumed held both high literary reputation and unimpeachable Christian principles (such as G. P. R. James, in her phrase the "great novelist"). It never entered her mind that her own son's hostile reviewers could be wrong.

Resisting his mother's evangelizing, Melville had reason to recall from Field's *History of the County of Berkshire* a section on "General Character of the People, — Improvement in Manners — Amusements." The "present time" of the following passage is the late 1820s, but religious attitudes had changed very slowly in the county. Under the category "amusements" Field explained that the county was "composed of a very intelligent and moral, and, relatively considered, religious population." The "literary and pious institutions and customs" of the earlier settlers had "sent down a blessed influence" on their descendants to the present. Repeated revivals, affecting not just the lower classes but "many of the influential men & families, and very many of the substantial yeomanry," had benefited "the whole community." No matter how humble, anyone could do good works and receive benefits from the efforts of other Christians: "The distribution of tracts, and various literary and religious publications, is producing great improvement among persons of all ages; while sabbath schools, with their libraries, are accomplishing the greatest blessings for the young." Amusements indeed. This self-congratulation about handing out tracts came home to Herman because Augusta had made her earnest pedestrian rounds in the Irish area of Lansingburgh, trying to pass out among the hostile Romists the pious tracts embellished with what Helen described as luridly hallucinatory covers (the later word "surreal" would have fit), and because Augusta still retained the proselytizing impulse and would act on it once she had the opportunity again.

This year, while gossiping Christians enraged Melville, Christmas itself loomed as an indefinite threat against his time and concentration. The Massachusetts Puritans had fined anyone caught celebrating the pagan holiday of Christmas, and, as the *History of the County of Berkshire* made clear, even well into the nineteenth century Christmas was "rarely observed" in western Massachusetts, except by Episcopalians. New Year's Day, as in Dutch New York, received "some attention," but all holidays were tinged with paganism and the people of Berkshire were "more in the habit of extending their '*compliments*' through the several seasons than of confining them to any particular one." Sarah Morewood, an Episcopalian fresh from spending the previous Christmas with Rowland's Anglican family in England, was determined to educate the Dutch Maria and her children into the mysteries of the holiday. For weeks she pressed on them an invitation ("so often & so earnestly given") to come to Broadhall for "a real old fashion'd english Christmas, with Holly & Mistletoe, & bobbing apples & a thousand odd & new things to us Arrowheads" (Maria to Augusta, 29 December). (This is the first known use of "Arrowheads," perhaps Maria's invention.) But as the holiday neared Sarah was off in New York City and seemed to have forgotten about her promises, so the inhabitants of Arrowhead decided that they would have to make do with their own pitiable Dutch Christmas and that they might even need, in charity, to invite Sarah's sister Ellen Brittain over from Broadhall so she would not be all alone with the servants on the holiday.

Knowing pretty much what was making Sarah break her word, Maria and her daughters conspired to leave Herman and Allan ignorant of it or at least to make them satisfied with whatever limited knowledge they already possessed. In *Pierre* Herman was writing about falsity in family relationships, in which mother-son flirtations were followed by intense, sexually charged scenes between the son and a young woman who may be his half-sister. Whatever sexual behavior Herman had seen or participated in at sea and in English or South American ports or in the Pacific islands (surely he had done nothing reprehensible in the United States), whatever he had written about or hinted at in his books, it was understood in the Melville family that domestic sexual practices were something women could discuss but that men were better off not knowing about. In the most glaring recent family scandal, Maria's cousin Catherine Van Vechten knew the details of what their cousin John De Peyster Douw wanted to do with, or to, his cousin-wife, their cousin Maggie Van Rensselaer Douw, and the details were not gross enough to keep Catherine from telling the story to her young cousin Helen Melville, who alluded to her knowledge in a letter to Augusta. Whatever it was, Maggie's sister Cornelia (Nilly) Van Rensselaer Thayer, wife and mother herself, knew all about it and did not consider it grounds for breaking up a marriage. Herman may have known almost nothing of the details of that case, although Allan had been consulted on points of marriage law.

As uncertainty grew about how they would spend Christmas 1851, Maria and her daughters grew more upset themselves, knowing that the present strange behavior of Sarah Morewood had to do with the fact that she was a married woman who permitted herself reckless friendships with men other than her husband. Even if Augusta, one midnight that fall, had not been forced to become Sarah's confidante, Maria could see for herself, especially since in 1850 she had received excellent information about a previous infatuation. In the summer of 1849 when Sarah Morewood visited the Berkshires, she had boarded with a family named Chapman (not the minister Dr. George Chapman), where the family of the robustly progenitive ex-president Tyler was also staying (the Tylers having boarded the previous year with Robert Melvill, Herman's cousin). Alexander Gardiner (of the feudal Gardiner's Island family), the young brother-in-law of Tyler, unmarried and something of a lady's man, arrived in the Berkshires well before the former president himself. Gardiner may have stayed at Robert and Susan Melvill's boardinghouse, since they had occasion to make observations of his behavior. Gardiner met and became acquainted with Sarah Morewood. Equestrianship may have facilitated the progress of the intimacy, for the Morewoods were avid appreciators of horseflesh, and Alexander proudly reported (to his brother David, in California) that the horses his mother and their sister Margaret Gardiner Beeckman had with them were attracting "a great deal of notice in the neighborhood of Pittsfield, and at Lebanon Springs some six miles distant." Alexander Gardiner and Sarah Morewood were attracting less admiring attention.

Toward the end of September 1849, after a period back in New York,

Alexander Gardiner went up the river to the town of Hudson to meet his mother and Margaret Gardiner Beeckman and accompany them on the passage down the river. The next day, the twenty-eighth, having heard the women out on a scandal all abubble in Pittsfield, he drafted a letter in a state of extreme perturbation. Robert and Susan Melvill had been gossiping:

> That servants should indulge in all sorts of slander and suspicion is not to be wondered at; but I cannot conceive what else than a morbid or malicious feeling could prompt Mr & Mrs Melvill to sow mischief or do injustice to either party by such a system as they seem to have pursued of espionage, of misconstruction of trivial and innocent circumstances, and of suspicion attaching to alleged acts of which I am ignorant or to transactions of which the most that could be said is that they were very indiscreet and imprudent.

Sarah Morewood had behaved with a familiarity so out of bounds that Gardiner himself, for all his experience with modern women, was disturbed and, even when it was happening, had tried to dampen her ardor. Servants had gossiped to Robert and Susan (Gardiner was not referring to the Melvills as servants), and Robert and Susan had promptly spread the gossip. The fault, according to Gardiner, was first Sarah Morewood's then the Melvills'. In the end, Gardiner most likely kept silent, and, after all, the gossip may not have spread farther than Lebanon Springs, or Lee, or North Adams, or Sheffield, or thereabouts.

When Maria arrived at the Melvill house in June 1850, ahead of other members of her New York City household, she heard whatever Robert and Susan had to say about the Morewoods, who were to spend the summer there and who by then were buying the house and lands, though they were not to take occupancy for many months. A little later Herman Melville on his crop-viewing excursion with Robert had a chance to hear the gossip at first hand, or at most second hand, from a startled servant to Robert to Herman; just possibly, Robert's excessive relish of local gossip might have been a factor in Herman's jumping wagon, abandoning his country cousin to his appointed agricultural task. As far as the Berkshire gossips were concerned, Sarah Morewood may as well have committed adultery with Alexander Gardiner. In the summer of 1850, as far as we know, Sarah Morewood's intense emotionality was not focused on any strange man in particular, and soon afterward she and Rowland departed for their several-month visit to England.

By December 1851 Melville's mother and his sister Augusta, at least, knew that Sarah had bestowed her obsessive affections on George Duyckinck, the innocuous, self-effacing younger brother of Evert. This was the man they ironically called "the Saint" in a specimen of Melville family humor — because his first name was George, because he was a most unlikely dragon-slayer and rescuer of Andromeda, because he was a devout Episcopalian, and because he was interested in some of the peculiar religious English poets later known as the Metaphysicals. Maria's phrasing after Christmas (her reference to Sarah's "present friend") makes it clear that the male favorites would change but Sarah's need for such an intense intimacy with a courtier would remain. The wonder was that Sarah had not focused her attention on Herman in 1850. Nothing survives to indicate that she had done so, and the question arises sharply, for the first time in Herman's history: just how alert was he to alarm signals in social intercourse? He had been alert to the more or less blatant sexual nature of responses to his first two books, where Ellen Oxenham and other robust and forward idolaters of the author of *Typee* had become excited by the book and strongly desirous of meeting the man who wrote it, and where Ellery Channing on reading *Typee* or a woman on the *Southampton* reading *Omoo* might confuse aesthetic with sexual responses. Melville's friend Willis, a genteel libertine, after sauntering through a crowded parlor might later infallibly identify three current and two incipient liaisons among the company; unlike his experienced friend, Melville may have been oblivious to signs of unlawful sexual attraction not emanating from him or being overtly directed toward him. Perhaps Herman and Allan had missed what happened on Greylock the previous August.

Herman had become a heterosexual sex symbol and had remained so. "Maherbal," the new resident of Lenox who had begun collecting information to send home to the Windsor (Vermont) *Journal*, after recording the gossip about Melville and Hawthorne's "solemn time" alone "in the dining-room of a hotel," relayed a story about Melville in 1837 or early 1838:

> I hope it will not turn the heads of any unfortunate pedagogues who may read the Journal, and set them madly to quill-driving, if I tell them that not many years ago in a neighboring town, Herman Melville had the misfortune to exasperate to such a degree the republican spirit of two very wicked pupils in the district school of which he was teacher, as to make it incompatible with his safe continuance in the room! Tell it to those despairing, crest-fallen, jilted beings, who have experienced a similar fate in Vermont, that one whose name often lingers now in terms of adulation upon many rosy lips, was thought by the independent youth of Mount Washington, utterly unfit to hold the reins of government in a district school. But whisper it cautiously, lest the indignation of his admirers wax hot against Maherbal for giving publicity to the scandal!

In this version of the story, perhaps the first one about Melville's schoolteaching to reach print, the pedagogue who could not keep discipline had lived to become a famous writer who was spoken of in adulation by rosy-lipped belles, or perhaps even matrons. Sophia Hawthorne saw Fayaway, beautiful, naked, and available, when she looked in Melville's face for the first time. How sexually alert was the sex symbol in daily life?

Sarah Morewood had become infatuated with George Duyckinck during (or just before) the grand Morewood-Melville excursion to Greylock in August 1851. Since her English coachman had brought writing material and her traveling desk, Sarah had written some "Greylock Thoughts" frenetically by the light of that wild campfire, beginning: "Are we not more happy far more happy when we throw off the restraints of conventional life?" Back in "drawing room circles" she might reproach herself or be reproached, but was it really "wrong to throw off the yoke of civilised life as it is called"? She badgered poor George, on paper: "why when we return to the forms of society are we reproached for our former forgetfulness of forms? Can you? Will you answer me Why?" She wrote on in this vein, by moonlight and firelight, while rats ran across their covers and Allan Melville snored, he, at least, being oblivious to her frenzy.

On the descent from Greylock, Sarah had managed to be alone with George for a time. Innocently Evert had described the scene to his wife (13 August): "I go ahead, Mrs Morewood and George straggling along to gather the mosses and wild flowers and pick the strawberries (which she only can find) and yellow raspberries by the way — the rest of the party waiting for the horses to ascend to them.... How fragrant these fields of raspberries up here and how exquisite this slender stem of strawberries brought in by Mrs Morewood, each berry firm and polished with a curious varnish of the mountain mist." Herman and Allan may have been missed the signs also, and George Duyckinck may as yet have been merely uneasy, not yet in a state of mortal terror at being the subject of Sarah's reckless, ferocious infatuation. For she proved to be terrifying, the formidable sort of flirt who with seemingly casual persistence extracts promises from men (to call on her, to drive her to a scenic locality) and later, all inappropriately, reminds them of their promises and ruthlessly holds them to their word.

Sarah managed to keep her "Greylock Thoughts" to herself for several weeks. That allowed George to send her some religious books on 18 August, in proper thanks for her hospitality. In her response to his letter that accompanied the books, Sarah went so far that George drew "a line and limit" for her, words she threw back at him in a letter written on 2 and 3 September. Sarah made it all but impossible for George to evade her pursuit. Outwardly Sarah Morewood seemed to control herself better for a few weeks, the early weeks of her new pregnancy, during which she saw Melville several times in natural settings related to *Pierre*. On 26 September she drove with Melville and others to Lake Pontoosuc. They were shocked to see a new settlement of cottages for laborers being built "near a large brick mill which for some years has been going to ruin in an unfinished state," but "now repaired and ready to be set at work" (as she wrote to George on 8 October). Power was readily available: "the beautiful stream of the Housatonic has been turned off to supply the mill with power." The "once pleasant roadside" was damaged, but Sarah had been through this in the 1840s, on the Hudson, and now said ruefully: "as this is a 'growing country' and money must be made, who has time to admire nature? Who at least of the operators will stop to consider that they are placing a bar & ban upon her?" She rationalized the "marring of the river" as she had to do: "We can spare that if the Lake be left to us wild & free." After all, the day was "charming," as Joseph Edward Adams (J. E. A.) Smith recalled in his memoir of Melville, remembering that the "accustomed party of merry ladies and gentlemen, over smooth roads" had come to Balance Rock, "and there had their usual picnic." This outing, Smith recalled, was the occasion when Sarah hid her music box deep in the crevasse, so that the stone seemed to speak like the temple of Memnon. Sarah recorded in her 8 October letter: "The strong wind had whipped the surface" into "white crested waves giving it a miniature sea look," and Herman Melville had declared that "each time he came there he found the place possessing new charms for him."

Even in her letters to George Duyckinck, Sarah for a time kept decorum. On 27 September she recalled the excursion to Greylock, and reminded him of wonders yet unknown to him: "You have not yet seen our autumn sun shine, so you know nothing about the halo of the haze (if I may so express it) which hangs over the mountains and melts as you approach them." A month later she let him know that the excursion was "often recalled in an amusing way, by Mr Herman" or herself, and that in some of their longer walks they had carried a spyglass so as to bring nearer "the Tower and its associations." Augusta learned Sarah's deeper feelings during a "midnight confidence" at Arrowhead that made her "inexpressibly sad" for Sarah, as she wrote her (in a surviving draft, undated): "Did you ever think Mrs Morewood of the mighty influence for good which might be yours. You are one of God's brightest creatures gifted with powers of mind & a fascination that wins love & confidence, that attracts & interests. . . . May the . . . beautiful stars upon which you gazed during your woodland drive home, ever as then be associated with thoughts of me, charged with peaceful admonitions from the heart." Sarah's "poetry—that heart poetry" evoked hours too dark to live in anyone's memory, for then there could be "no trust in Heaven." At Broadhall in mid-November, Hawthorne's letter praising *Moby-Dick* stowed in a pocket, Melville had been suffused with inexpressible feelings of kinship with the older writer, had seethed with his exalted thoughts through the banter of the long evening. His hostess, at the same time, had been suffused with highly physical thoughts of the man the Melville womenfolk called "Saint George."

In December Augusta and Sarah were both in New York City, but apparently did not meet, although Augusta called and left a card. Sarah, however, managed, with or without her husband, to accompany the Duyckincks to Tripler Hall on 20 December to hear the speech by the Hungarian Kossuth, then hounded George even as he pleaded the need to dress a Christmas tree. Sarah wildly asked him to read her "Greylock Thoughts" again, and then made impossible demands for meetings, threatening to call on him with her husband in tow. Rebuffed, frantic, febrile, hormonally confused by her pregnancy, Sarah had run roughshod over the limits poor George had tried to set for her. Having aroused everyone's anticipation for her first Christmas at Broadhall, Sarah had suddenly seemed to forget the invitation. Before Christmas she wrote her sister Mrs. Brittain at Broadhall telling her to pack up her mittens and come on to New York, "for she was not thinking of returning in some time." Then Sarah and Rowland arrived at Pittsfield on Christmas Eve, on the train that brought the letter. Up to the last moment the Arrowheads were puzzled as to the seriousness of Sarah's plans for the holidays, as Maria reported to Augusta on 29 December:

> On Christmas Eve it was frightfully cold, the wind & snow together blinded every thing. Herman who loves to go out in such wild weather had the Sleigh brought to the door, & David who had ask'd permission to go to town two hours before, declined going if Mr Melville did not particularly want him to go. At the post office Mr Taylor told him that Mr Morewood had gone last Tuesday to New York for Mrs Morewood they had just come in with the Cars, & they would expect us next day to dinner, as we did not think proper to notice so informal an invitation we made arrangements to stay at home.

In a letter to George on Christmas Eve Sarah announced her decision to "make it all up" to the Melvilles, even to the extent of inviting "friends to meet them at dinner tomorrow"—under the Episcopalian assumption that none of the low-church local inhabitants had made plans for Christmas dinner. She concluded the letter after midnight, saying that the Melvilles had sent her "tokens which silently reproached" her for her "intended neglect" of her promise to them. Sarah was playing a dangerous game. George had told her that he would cease writing to her whenever Rowland Morewood objected. Now she declared that she would be the first to tell him when her husband did object, but his objections would be the less likely since she was not "always" showing him her letters to George. In her wiles she sought

George's verdict: "he [Rowland] would object no doubt do you therefore wish me no longer to write to you?" All this, and many notes to be carried by servants the next morning, occupied the early minutes of the twenty-fifth.

A few hours later, early on Christmas Day, a servant arrived at Arrowhead: "a note from her ladyship announce'd her return from New York, & her invitation to us to pass the day, also her regrets that we had not come over to pass Christmas Eve there," this last a piece of effrontery. "What a strange woman she is," Maria said when she described all this to Augusta on 29 December. Yet Maria professed herself as glad that Sarah had returned because they "had reason to expect much amusement & novelty from the length of the invitation & the lady's agreeable powers." Sarah found a large number of people willing to put in abeyance whatever plans they had made in order to dine with her and Rowland at Broadhall. Dr. Root, who had failed in his treatment of Lizzie's infection, came, with his wife and daughter (named Love). Joe Smith came, and Captain Taylor, a veteran of the masquerade of the day Melville started writing his essay on Hawthorne. A Miss Dillingham was there, and Miss Taylor.

Sarah wrote George that Maria was "looking better in health" than she had "ever yet seen her look," despite her simmering indignation at being so discourteously treated. Herman reacted to the intrusion into his work schedule by withdrawing into himself; always, whatever the circumstances, Broadhall was thronged with memories of the dead: his father, Cousin Allan Cargill (the first of that name), Cousin Julia, Uncle Thomas, and Gansevoort. Sarah noticed his periods of silence, and ruminated on the matter to George on 28 December: "Mr Herman was more quiet than usual—still he is a pleasant companion at all times and I like him very much—Mr Morewood now that he knows him better likes him the more—still he dislikes many of Mr Hermans opinions and religious views—It is a pity that Mr Melville so often in conversation uses irreverent language—he will not be popular in society here on that very account—but this will not trouble him—I think he cares very little as to what others may think of him or his books so long as they sell well." Helen may have stayed home with Malcolm; the younger Fanny and Kate "expected many games & much Frolic," but Sarah was for once unprovided ("she had not the material to work with, & besides must have been weary riding in the Cars all the day before").

Sarah explained to Maria that she had not returned either Augusta's or Sophia's visit, not being well, having gone out only "with the Duyckincks to hear Kossuths address to the Ladies at Tripler Hall," where she was "charmed with Kossuths appearance & manner." Maria noted what Sarah said and conflated it with newspaper reports before she wrote Augusta about the Hungarian: "It is said his manner together with his appearance" revealed "the

Humility of a great & good man not, the mean, servile, humility of a Uriah Heap." (They had read *David Copperfield* aloud at Arrowhead.) Rather than the false humility of Uriah Heep, Kossuth's was "the Godlike humility of a great soul, full of good, great, magnanimous, self denying works, supported by a high trust in God, and the sacred Principle he embodies." Maria had sat through Christmas dinner making hostile judgments against her hostess and drawing painful comparisons between her son and the Christian patriot. Conscious of such contrasts between the Hungarian's "high trust in God" and her son's mockery of faith, which was scandalizing her local acquaintances, Maria would have been untrue to herself and her Christian duty if she had not determined to find an early opportunity to express to Herman the results of her maternal broodings.

One or another of the Arrowheads confided to Sarah that Herman was "now so engaged in a new work as frequently not to leave his room till quite dark in the evening—when he for the first time during the whole day partakes of solid food" (as she reported in the 28 December letter to George). Sarah decided that "he must therefore write under a state of morbid excitement which will soon injure his health," and made no scruple to tell him so, laughing at him "somewhat" and declaring "that the recluse life he was leading made his city friends think that he was slightly insane—he replied that long ago he came to the same conclusion himself—but if he left home to look after Hungary the cause in hunger would suffer." In her raillery about his city friends (the Duyckinck brothers) she was oblivious of the wounds inflicted by the review of *Moby-Dick* in the *Literary World* (hearing anyone say "Duyckinck" or "*Literary World*" was now painful), and Melville was philosophically defending his decision not to participate in the empty national triumphal tour of the Hungarian.

Sarah slighted some of her other guests in making up to the author, so that Maria in her 29 December letter to Augusta concluded that her current gallant, "Mister George," would have been jealous at her attentions. When Herman led Sarah into the dining room—the new spacious room—she did something extraordinary, something which showed that despite her haste she had possessed herself of some material to work her magic with: "she stopt before a plate on which lay a beautiful Laurel Wreath, which she gently lifted & quickly placed upon his brow, he as quickly removed it to her head saying he would not be crowned it was place'd on a table." This was high drama for the older Melvilles in the room, for Gansevoort had been crowned at this season in 1826, a quarter century and two days earlier, at the High School in the presence of Chancellor James Kent. In November 1851, from Hawthorne, Melville had been ready to accept the crown of India. Now he could not tolerate his hostess's gesture, and "would not be crowned." Unwilling to let the incident pass, Sarah made sure that the wreath accompanied the Melvilles home to Arrowhead ("when we were seated in the Sleigh it was handed to Herman"). (Years later he sent a funeral wreath for her on the train from New York to Pittsfield. Did he remember then this attempt to crown him?)

Unperturbed by the storm that had swirled about the now-spacious dining room, Sarah congratulated herself in the letter to George: "I am very glad that I returned to Berkshire to pass my first Christmas day in our house, for I feel sure that my presence here gave pleasure to my friends." She gave an account of infantile sexuality involving her son, Willie, that would not be so perturbing if she had not written it to the man she was pursuing: "No one of the party seemed to enjoy themselves so well as my little boy, he had Love in to dinner and sat next to her talking to her in a very amusing manner. Some of his remarks led to roars of laughter, and one request of his[,] simple beautiful in childhood[,] was the wish expressed to Love that she would stop all night and sleep in his little bed with him." Sarah had behaved strangely at Christmas. She behaved even more strangely when the Broadhalls called on the Melvilles on the twenty-ninth, so much so that Maria (perhaps not realizing Sarah was pregnant) reproved her, as she told Augusta in an account to be kept from Allan ("*Read the fourth page to Sophia*, alone"):

> Madame betrayed many traits of character which I was really concerned to observe. She has written her present friend George an account of the Christmas festivities, it seems at his request. Her mind was in an excited state & from all accounts must have been so all day, she express'd ungrateful feelings towards Mrs Brittan, who has done more to make Broadhall comfortable in the past two weeks than the lady has done in the past year. She said many things to her "liege lord" which even his long patient forbearance could not let pass. Altogether so much more was said that I requested her to take some thing to quiet her nerves, as She did not seem to like this, I at last told her that her conversation affected her.

Maria's advice, as usual, was extremely sensible, more so than she knew (although the "thing" Sarah might have taken is dubious). Furthermore, Maria generously unfolded her expert character analysis of her febrile neighbor, thereby putting Sarah under new stresses, as Sarah wrote to George on 4 January 1852: "I wish you had known me longer and better and then you would understand me now—Mrs [Maria] Melville tells me 'that I have some good in me—She also says that my real character is not yet formed—that I have in fact no fixed purpose in life—' So she judges me—little knowing my real feelings—So you must not judge me—for I mean to acquire a *real decided* character." Sarah meant, also, not to lose the child she was carrying, although modifying her behavior (by avoiding the mob at Kossuth's "Ladies Day" speech, for instance, or by avoiding repetitive ordeals of eight hours in the jostling cars) was a sacrifice she was not prepared to make. By the thirtieth the snow had rapidly melted, so that there was no prospect of decent sleighing. Melville remained absorbed with his manuscript.

Maria was tense — concerned about and a little impatient with Lizzie (although perfectly satisfied that Malcolm was not missing her at all), irritated at Sarah Morewood's rude and erratic behavior, lonely for Allan, annoyed at captivity when the roads did not allow good sleighing, depressed by the dullness of winter ("everything looks so desolate"). On the twenty-ninth Maria received Augusta's account of the New York festivities, and then could make (in what she added to her letter on the thirtieth) another contrasting judgment on the basis of a letter she had received from Lizzie before Christmas: "you write something about a castle in the air, she writes anniversaryies are very depressing, make one low spirited, and keep one at home." Being of a superior character (as well as physique, character seeming to her the more important), Maria had nursed eight children with never a problem, and she had molded her daughters' characters into satisfactory replicas of her own; anyone could see that she truly had, except possibly with the nervous Kate. As always, Maria was worried about her son the writer: "Herman is perfectly absorb'd by this book he is now writing, and he is moreover very angry at the opinion the serious part of the community about here have loudly spoken of the book saying it is more than Blasphemous"—that is, the latest book, *Moby-Dick*. Augusta was to "say nothing of all this, however." After Christmas, Maria had been "reading the great Magyar's speeches," brooding about the contrast between Kossuth's trust in God and her son's lack of faith, which had led to such scandal among her local acquaintances. Maria concluded her eulogy of Kossuth with an emphatic one-sentence paragraph: "He is the man after my own heart." This was to say that the great Magyar was a Christian, as her oldest surviving son was not.

In the midst of this miserable time, apparently to the astonishment of everyone but Helen, who was sacrificing her winter as copyist, Herman announced that he had finished his book and was going to New York to sell it to the Harpers. At once, around 27 December, Helen fled to her friend Mrs. Ives in Lansingburgh, and Herman left for New York on 31 December or New Year's Day. By leaving, he missed, as Sarah wrote to George (4 January 1852), "some of the most beautiful winter changes I ever saw—and a view from his house which he may never have again—the river has overflowed all the Marsh below his land—forming a Hudson as it were out of the Housatonic." That's how his luck was running.

Melville left behind a small household of stirred-up sociable women. The twenty-eighth was the day "when M^r & Mrs Morewood & Mrs Britton called work in hand to pass the Eveg," as Maria told Augusta the next day. While Herman was gone, Maria seized her opportunities for calling on her neighbors, thereby giving the young widower John C. Hoadley greater access to Kate. Hoadley may have met Kate months before, soon after her arrival from New York with Maria on 9 April, and he must have been captivated by her from the start, to judge from what followed. Maria deserved to have such a man in the family. Whether Kate was the most deserving of the unmarried girls is another matter: Helen or even Augusta might have been more of a match for Hoadley intellectually and emotionally. Sarah returned to New York soon after Herman went there, and she pursued George relentlessly, but gradually George's silence and her own advancing pregnancy saved her from further recklessness. In January 1852, the reckless one was the man who would not be crowned.

[3]
The Kraken Version of *Pierre*
November–December 1851

> He who thinks for himself never can remain of the same mind. I doubt not that darker doubts crossed Milton's soul, than ever disturbed Voltair. And he was more of what is called an Infidel.
>
> Melville's annotation to a passage on Milton's "wanderings in religious belief"

AND WHAT, Hawthorne might have asked himself on the train to Boston on 21 November 1851, could the plot of the book bigger than *Moby-Dick* look like? Here is the summary in the Boston *Post* on 4 August 1852 of *Pierre; or, The Ambiguities*, just after its publication:

> Pierre Glendinning and his proud but loving mother are living together, surrounded by everything the world, intellect, health and affection can bestow. The son is betrothed to a beautiful girl of equal position and fortune, and everything looks brightly as a summer morning. All at once, Pierre learns that his father has left an illegitimate daughter, who is in poverty and obscurity. His conscience calls upon him to befriend and acknowledge her — although, by the way, his proof of the fact that the girl is his father's offspring is just nothing at all. On the other hand, he will not discover to the world or to his mother the error of his (supposed) sainted father, and he adopts the novel expedient of carrying off the girl, and giving out that he has married her. His mother discards him and soon dies of wounded love and pride, and his betrothed is brought to the brink of the grave. She finally recovers somewhat, and strange to say, invites herself to reside with Pierre and his sister, who, as far as the world and herself were concerned, are living as husband and wife. The relatives of Lucy, as a matter of course, try to regain her, and brand Pierre with every bad name possible. The latter finally shoots his cousin who had become the possessor of the family estate and a pretender to the hand of Lucy — is arrested and taken to prison. There he is visited by the two ladies, the sister and the betrothed. Lucy falls dead of a broken heart and Pierre and his sister take poison and also give up the ghost. This tissue of unnatural

horrors is diversified a little, by the attempts of the hero to earn his living by authorship, and by the "ambiguous" love between Pierre and his natural sister.

In November 1851, and even in December, the manuscript contained nothing about Pierre's attempts to earn his living by authorship, but the "unnatural horrors," undiversified, were very much present then. Otherwise, this irony-laced summary is accurate enough for the work Melville referred to in his letter to Hawthorne.

Melville had written strange books before (*Mardi*, above all), but *Pierre* struck all its reviewers as not only strange but as a wholly new departure for Melville. The Boston *Advertiser* (7 August 1852) exclaimed: "The author has taken the Hero of this story from the very highest aristocracy of the country, so high one hardly knows where to look for it, and the scene of it is entirely on land" (all on land, not counting a brief scene in New York Harbor). *Pierre* looked like nothing so much as a belated late-gothic romance, more akin to sensational books from the turn of the century than the latest novels. The New York *Herald* reported on 29 July 1852, just before publication: "In fiction, Herman Melville has a new book, 'Pierre, or the Ambiguities,' in which it is understood that he has dressed up and exhibited in Berkshire, where he is living, some of the ancient and most repulsive inventions of the George Walker and Anne Radcliffe sort — desperate passion at first sight, for a young woman who turns out to be the hero's sister, &c., &c., &c. It is conceded that Mr. Melville has written himself out." This gossipmonger was right about Melville's knowledge of *The Mysteries of Udolpho* (1794) and other lurid novels by Anne Radcliffe. In a January 1857 journal entry Melville noted with easy familiarity that "the sight of haunted Haddon Hall suggested to Mrs Radcliffe her curdling romances." In *Moby-Dick* (ch. 73) he knowingly referred to George Walker's melodramatic novel *The Three Spaniards* (1800). Among the gothic dramas and novels condemned as depraved by moralists of the previous generation, he knew Horace Walpole's *The Mysterious Mother* (1768), which he darkly alluded to in *White-Jacket* as dealing with the theme of incest, and probably Matthew Gregory Lewis's piece of pornographic cruelty ("sadism" before there was a word for it), *The Monk* (1796). As a youngster Melville read not only Sir Walter Scott's poetry but also his historical novels. Gansevoort Melville's *Index Rerum* shows a fascination both with Scott's writings and with John Gibson Lockhart's biography of him. (Some of Gansevoort's copies of the Parker edition — one of many American editions — survive in the Berkshire Athenaeum.) In his youth Herman Melville had absorbed Scott to the point where all his life he could echo him or allude to his characters casually, from *Waverley* (1814) in *Moby-Dick* (ch. 72) or from *The Talisman* (1825) in *Clarel* (pt. 2, canto 16). Melville had kept up, however unsystematically, with more recent British novels, such as Edward George Bulwer-Lytton's *Ernest Maltravers*, which was in his mother's house in 1837, when Gansevoort read through it for hints on authorship as a means of earning a living. Mrs. Morewood's recent gift, Bulwer-Lytton's *Zanoni*, was at hand, when he could manage to overcome the difficulty of the small print. (*Zanoni* was so popular that the Savannah *Republican* on 15 May 1850 noted but did not review the new Harper edition: "It is unnecessary to speak of *Zanoni*, as it is well known to every reader of romance.") Melville knew the novels of Benjamin Disraeli. He knew Dickens's novels, as every literate American and many illiterate Americans did. In the Melville household, reading aloud was the principal form of evening entertainment. Early in 1851 the book read aloud was *David Copperfield*, which Lizzie had brought back from Boston on New Year's Day. Envious, perhaps, of Dickens's great success, Melville tended to regard his plotting with disdain (to judge from later allusions) and it was just that excessive over-plotting that he now set out to incorporate into his manuscript.

Melville knew that the Duyckincks in the *Literary World*, despite their prejudices against sensationalism, had come to admire the Bell brothers, whose books had been more popular than even his own best-known book, *Typee*. While Melville as Evert's protégé was writing *Mardi*, on 29 January 1848, the *Literary World* had said this of the Harper edition of Currer Bell's *Jane Eyre*: "The machinery that carries on the story may have been invented, but the actual suffering, the sad experience, the sorrowing existence of the heroine, these are no cunning devices, and the story of these is the outpouring of the over-charged soul speaking in tones that find an echo in the reader's heart." (A copy of *Jane Eyre* had been in the Melville house since early 1848, a gift from young Lemuel Jr. to Augusta.) On 29 April of the same year, the *Literary World* had decried the Harper *Wuthering Heights* ("By the Author of 'Jane Eyre'") as unworthy of its predecessor, "for, although possessing far more strength and power in its darker portions, yet it lacks the relief necessary to make it as pleasing as 'Jane Eyre'": "It is 'a dark tale darkly told;' a book that seizes upon us with an iron grasp, and makes us read its story of passions and wrongs whether we will or no. Fascinated by strange magic we read what we dislike, we become interested in characters which are most revolting to our feelings, and are made subject to the immense power, of the book, — a rough, shaggy, uncouth power that turns up the dark side of human nature, and deals with unbridled passions and hideous inhumanities." Duyckinck's "hideous inhumanities" was so striking a phrase that Melville may have recalled it in the "horrible and inscrutable inhumanities" of Isabel's dark tale of her childhood (*Pierre*, bk. 6, ch. 5). On 12 August 1848, in reviewing the Harper edition of *The Tenant of Wildfell Hall* by Acton Bell (identified as the author of *Wuthering Heights*), the *Literary World* had made claims for the aesthetic freedom of the artist: "while we hold the writer responsible at the bar of criticism for painting life and manners as they really exist — yet as to the correctness of his characters in the abstract, we assuredly do not mean to hold him or any other author responsible. We consider him here solely as an artist. Who holds Moses [the author of Exodus] accountable for the conduct of the children of Korah?" Duyckinck had not been willing to grant the sailor-author such aesthetic freedom in *Moby-Dick*, but Melville might now, in *Pierre*, deal with his own versions of unbridled passions and hideous inhumanities and might hope to convert skeptics into admirers, as the Bell brothers had done, even before they emerged transformed in sex and disentangled from each other as the Brontë sisters. In hoping that he could write a great book that would sell like the most popular sensational romances, Melville had not needed to gather and assimilate British fiction the way he had assembled his whaling sources early in 1850. One way or another, he knew before starting just the sort of novelistic conventions he would imitate to such deliberately extreme excess in *Pierre*.

Important as British fiction writers of the previous seventy-five years were to *Pierre*, Shakespeare saturated it even more, and not only the most popular plays. Melville himself knew, and consciously reminded himself and others in the essay on Hawthorne's *Mosses*, that American writers who tried to imitate Elizabethan tragedy were doomed to failure, since a great writer would always appear dressed in the garb of his own day. Nevertheless, Melville was overmastered to the point of not being able to think in tragic terms without thinking in Shakespearean language. *Macbeth* and *King Lear* had been strongly in his mind in mid-1851, when he wrote the ending of his whaling book. Referring to *Pierre* on 8 January 1852, Melville told Sophia Hawthorne that the "next chalice" he would commend to her would be "a rural bowl of milk" — not so *Macbeth*-like a chalice as *Moby-Dick* had proved. In writing *Pierre* in November and December 1851 Melville explicitly portrayed his hero as an American Hamlet, and his depiction of the young lovers, Pierre and Lucy, was thick with allusions to Shakespeare's late romances, particularly to *The Winter's Tale*. He made Mrs. Glendinning in some speeches sound very like Volumnia in *Coriolanus*, to the point that a listener might have the momentary illusion that Pierre's mother was speaking unfamiliar speeches that Shakespeare had written for his Roman matron, the way Ahab almost seemed to speak hitherto unpublished speeches Shakespeare had written for Lear or Timon. When it worked, the illusion Melville achieved was that he was extending Shakespeare rather than merely imitating him. Such speculation about Melville's Shakespearean language quickly turns specious, and the high-flown language of *Moby-Dick* and *Pierre* has always struck many readers as abhorrent bombast. Melville, if overmastered, nevertheless was struggling on the same terrain where Shakespeare had wrestled with tragic forces. The mightiest of the influences on the language of *Pierre* is Shakespeare, and even the mother-son relationship may owe more to Shakespeare than to modern fiction, but Melville wanted his plot and even his language to be taken as highly saleable Americanized gothic romanticism.

One modern poet influenced *Pierre* strongly, for Melville had begun to identify himself with aspects of William Wordsworth's experiences and attitudes. He had known some of Wordsworth's poems from his youth, and he knew many others well from the 1840s or the time of *Moby-Dick*. He marked his copy of *The Excursion* (Philadelphia: James Kay, Jun. & Brother, 1839) throughout, obviously identifying with the author who (according to the preface) "retired to his native Mountains, with the hope of being enabled to construct a literary Work that might live." Melville probably read only excerpts of *The Prelude* (1850), but he read much about it, including the London *Examiner* review reprinted in the September 1850 *Harper's New Monthly Magazine:* "This ambiguous conception has been doomed to share the fate of so many other colossal undertakings. Of the three parts of his *Recluse*, thus planned, only the second (the *Excursion*, published in 1814), has been completed. Of the other two there exists only the first book of the first, and the plan of the third. The *Recluse* will remain in fragmentary greatness, a poetical Cathedral of Cologne." Melville had been to Cologne in 1849 and seen the crane atop the unfinished cathedral for himself, but this passage influenced the image he worked into chapter 32 of *Moby-Dick* as a type of ambition which aimed too high for a man or a generation to finish in a lifetime. In that essay from the *Examiner* Melville saw comments on a mind like his own, nurtured in isolation, amid the grandeur of nature, so that the "conversation and writings of contemporaries trained among books, and with the faculty of speech more fully developed than that of thought, seemed colorless and empty to one with whom natural objects and grandeurs were always present in such overpowering force." In New York, he had known many a man — Evert Duyckinck, Cornelius Mathews, Thomas Powell, too many to count — whose faculty of speech was more fully developed than that of thought.

On a page of *The Excursion* (bk. 3) Melville wrote out two lines of Spenser he was reminded of, and on the facing page saw a passage he recalled in *Pierre*, on the naming of rocks:

> The shapes before our eyes
> And their arrangement, doubtless must be deemed
> The sport of Nature, aided by blind Chance
> Rudely to mock the works of toiling Man.
> And hence, this upright Shaft of unhewn stone,
> From Fancy, willing to set off her store
> By sounding Titles, hath acquired the name
> Of Pompey's Pillar; that I gravely style
> My Theban Obelisk; and, there, behold
> A Druid Chromlech!

The Berkshires had their own Balance Rock near Lanesboro, and Melville had known other powerful rock formations since his youth. Being himself now in the American Lake District had made Melville more closely attuned to Wordsworth, to the point that the late laureate helped humanize the Berkshires for him. Wordsworth helped lead him to associate the natural grandeur not merely with solitary Byronic posturing but with striving, suffering men and women, himself now among them.

Melville had projected his hero Pierre Glendinning into a fictional world of wealth and privilege like that of his New York Van Rensselaer cousins and his Gansevoort ancestors, particularly his grandfather, General Peter Gansevoort, whose physique and martial history he had appropriated for Pierre's grandfather, along with other family paraphernalia. Herman had seated himself in the titanic phaeton—high aloft in his Uncle Herman's carriage house in Gansevoort, New York, if not on perilous Adirondack roads. Then Melville had transported his fictional aristocratic Glendinnings across the Hudson into a grand house in a mountainous American landscape, where Saddle Meadows is based on Greylock, also called Saddleback. He had appropriated various Berkshire locales, some of them visited in excursions as recent as that summer and fall of 1851, from the Balance Rock to the Little Red Cottage above Stockbridge Bowl. When he planned *Pierre* in September and October 1851 and began writing it, the mountains surrounding him (the Catskills far to the west, the Taconics to the west and south, Greylock to the north) still formed a magic circle containing the disparate fragments of his life from childhood to the present—rich boy arriving at Broadhall with his father in a carriage or stagecoach; poor boy working the farm when his Uncle Thomas left for frontier Illinois; half-educated youth doing his best to teach in a rough country school where the biggest Yankee ruffians were determined to cow him; famous author visiting country cousins, in 1848; and at last in 1850 famous author (married and a father) finding high literary society in nearby Lenox. Sorrow at Hawthorne's leaving for eastern Massachusetts, bafflement and anguish at the early reviews of *Moby-Dick*, distress over Lizzie's prolonged illness, the persistence of wretched weather, and word of new venomousness in the local inhabitants, all shook him, cracking the charmed serenity of the Berkshires long before he finished *Pierre* at the end of the year.

Melville was, as always, starting from close to home. What he first pulled up from the recesses of his memory, as he fashioned the story of his hero's encountering a young woman who may be an older child of his own father, may have had something to do with an experience of his Uncle Thomas soon after the death of his brother, Herman's father, in the few months between that death and the death of Herman's grandfather, old Thomas Melvill, the hero of the Boston Tea Party. At that time two women, perhaps aunt and niece, had called at the family house in Green Street hoping to obtain some money from the estate of Melville's father, and had been turned away after being told that he had died deeply in debt. It was unfortunate, Melville's uncle had later observed to Lemuel Shaw, that the junior of the two "had not been brought up different," especially since he thought her an interesting young person. Something about the episode—Melville's Uncle Thomas's insistence that no one else alive knew about the visit but his sister Helen (Herman's aunt, later Helen Souther)—suggests that the purpose was graver than an ordinary attempt to collect a business debt. Evidence is strongly against the younger woman being an illegitimate daughter of Allan Melvill's, but something about the situation was made a matter of mystification by the elders and was a mystery to any younger members of the family who caught hints of it. Melville may have heard that story years before at the Melvill farm, now called Broadhall. In recent months, in the close confines of Arrowhead, Maria may have said "a sainted man like your father" once too often in Herman's ears—or even more pointedly something like, "Why can't you be a Christian such as your sainted father was?" Something of that sort may have prompted Melville to create a plot that could only bring opprobrium to the family, either because there was some truth in it or because people would assume there was truth in it. Adding injury to insult, Herman, in among innocuous family paraphernalia, had appropriated the highly recognizable "chair portrait" of his father and made it the subject of disturbing sexual speculations. Readers of *Pierre* who knew the Melville family would think the worst of Allan Melvill, regardless of what was true and what was fiction.

Whether or not Thomas Melvill's peculiar experiences with the female callers at Green Street had anything to do with the plot of *Pierre*, one of his daughters, the French-born Cousin Priscilla, demonstrably did. Priscilla may have faded from Herman's mind during his years in the Pacific and of his early success, but since he encountered her again in Pittsfield in April 1848 she, as part and parcel of his Berkshire associations, had figured in his emotional life, particularly now that her work in Canandaigua, New York, was aggravating her tuberculosis. French-speaking in childhood, four when her French mother died in the backwoods Massachusetts military outpost of Pittsfield in 1814, she pursued, year after year, into the 1850s, her "French claims," asking Judge Shaw to depute travelers to seek out her unknown kindred and establish her right to some inheritance. In her correspondence with the inhabitants of Arrowhead, and in her talks with them in the summer of 1852, and probably earlier, Priscilla speculated about the possibility of buying or renting a tiny place of her own in Pittsfield. The surviving documentation dates from just after the publication of *Pierre*, but some of the conversations must have preceded it: coincidence cannot account for the similarities of situation and language between Priscilla and Isabel, and Priscilla did not remake herself in the image of the strange character in her cousin's book. This is from Priscilla's letter from Canandaigua to Augusta at Arrowhead on 7 October 1852:

> I often dream of blissful solitude — freedom from care — & a *crust* & *water*, in the "Brown Cottage" — which quiet retreat from some of the vexations & anxieties of Life, Helen assures me looks as *"enticing as ever"* — "Gus" dear! supposing I presume a little (& not a very little either) on the affectionate kindness of your heart — (not but what I feel assur'd that any one of my cousins could do the same or anything else to serve me) & request you to act as my man of business in this matter — merely for the present to make some *careless* inquiries — as to the *terms* that the present proprietress would be willing to dispose of her coveted property at — perhaps it would be no loss to me to possess the little paradise — & rent it until I finally conclude to sacrifice my present enjoyment of abundance & the accompanying responsibilities — perhaps again I could bargain with a respectable family to furnish two of the rooms myself & *board* for the rent.

Here Melville had a female relative deeply sensitized to what it was like for one "in the station to which by birth & taste" she felt herself to belong to be "cast upon the world, to depend upon their own exertions, with a less galling sense of the yoke." This is Priscilla, not the fictional Isabel: "It is *more this* circumstance of *birth* & *taste* that causes my spirit to chafe *thus* under the burden than ought else — & doubtless I should consider my lot a most admirable one — did not my *native* aristocracy rebel."

This passionate woman was reduced to the hope of finding constant employment for her needle, as an alternative to dragging along an existence in Canandaigua far from any of her blood. Priscilla wrote from Arrowhead on 19 November 1853 to Lemuel Shaw: "I . . . ask if you will send it [the interest due from her father's estate] at your *earliest* convenience, as I have finally left, *very much* wearied, the situation that I have so long occupied, at that school in Canandaigua, and intend to try boarding, for the present, in Pittsfield, and if *possible* make my *needle* profitable." Since she had to "furnish" the rented room, her request was urgent: "I wish to make use of the money, *whatever* the amount may be, *at once*—please forward to Hermans care, at *this* place." On 15 February 1855 she inserted an advertisement in the Pittsfield *Sun:* "Miss Melville will devote herself to EMBROIDERY and the making of the nicer articles pertaining to Ladies', Gentlemen's, or Children's wardrobes—at her room, opposite the Methodist Church in Fenn Street, up stairs."

In *Pierre*, Isabel is not a realistic portrait of Cousin Priscilla or of anyone, but she is suffused with pride at least as strong as Priscilla's: "I began to feel an increasing longing in me; but side by side with it, a new-born and competing pride,—yes, pride, Pierre. Do my eyes flash? They belie me, if they do not. But it is no common pride, Pierre; for what has Isabel to be proud of in this world? It is the pride of—of—a too, too longing, loving heart, Pierre—the pride of lasting suffering and grief, my brother! Yes, I conquered the great longing with the still more powerful pride, Pierre" (bk. 8, ch. 4). Melville portrays her almost as feral, repeatedly traumatized, one who knows for a time "two childish languages" then retreats into self-protective silence before acquiring a late-learned, self-taught speech which is daringly conveyed through peculiarities of syntax and vocabulary. She has dim memories of "an old, half-ruinous house" since recalled to her mind by seeing "plates of the outside of French chateaux" (bk. 6, ch. 3). Her history emerges as a gothic story of abandonment and abuse, but Melville's chief concern in it is to recount the halting process of awakening to a sense of a self separate from other things and people, then a realization of her unique identity through a conscious analysis of memories.

At some early period Isabel seems to recall being in America, in a poorhouse or madhouse, then a farmhouse where she first could distinguish between nonhuman and human creatures. At the farmhouse (bk. 6, ch. 5) she concludes that "all good, harmless men and women were human things, placed at cross-purposes, in a world of snakes and lightnings, in a world of horrible and inscrutable inhumanities." There she expands in mind and hears the word "beautiful" spoken of her, and there she is visited by a "new being" who is not a farmer: "they called him gentleman." He whispers in her ear "Father" and comes every month or two until he does not come at all. She hears a word, "*Dead,*" and learns that the gentleman had sent money and that no more money was coming: "I felt that something was miserably wrong; I said to myself, I am one too many; I must go away from the pleasant house."

By chance she associates the gentleman with the "grand house" where Pierre lives, and sends a message to him, and presents herself to Pierre as his half-sister, the daughter of his father. Nothing is simple in this depiction, for the place where Pierre visits her is not a little brown cottage such as Priscilla Melvill may already have longed to live in. Instead, sited on the shore of a lake, it is a "small and low red farm-house," the roof of which is "a bed of brightest mosses" on the southern side, nearest the lake, and is "moss-incrusted" on the north side (bk. 6, ch.1). It has not seven but only two gables, but it is recognizably a Hawthornesque dwelling place, based on the little red cottage above Stockbridge Bowl where the "Man of Mosses" had lived. Isabel, the embodiment of Pierre's awakening unconscious, was linked in Melville's mind with Hawthorne, the man who more than any other person had triggered in Melville his newest unfoldings within himself during the completion of *Moby-Dick* and the planning of *Pierre*.

Fascinating as Melville made her, the focus of his book was not on Isabel but on Pierre's responses to her as she awakens in him a sense of tragedy. Melville was writing the story of a youthful idealist whose "infinite magnanimities" are inextricably linked with appalling self-delusion, as Brian Higgins and I said in "The Flawed Grandeur of Melville's *Pierre*" (1978), an essay I draw on in this paragraph and the next. From the opening pages Melville set forth the artifice underlying Pierre Glendinning's chivalric ideals and tingeing his intimate relationships, including the ambiguous relationship with his mother. Even the Christianity that Pierre has insensibly absorbed is tainted by falsity, involved as it is with the un-Christlike glorification of militarism. That ambiguous idealism, it becomes clear, makes him uniquely vulnerable to the particular appeal that the mysterious Isabel will make. Pierre "is woefully ill-equipped to set out as a Christian Knight-Champion, most obviously because the pattern of chivalric, romantic idealization has developed simultaneously with—and at the cost of—dangerous sublimation of his sexual feelings." In his securely naive youth, Pierre has had, Melville tells us, unbidden inklings of a tragic side of life, but he is reluctant to awaken fully to a tragic sense of life. By book 3, Melville began to develop Pierre's darker side, portraying the stirrings of Pierre's unconscious from which "bannered armies of hooded phantoms" disembark and attack his conscious mind, much as Fedallah erupts from the hold of the *Pequod*.

Melville began his book 4, "Retrospective," with this disclaimer: "In their precise tracings-out and subtle causations, the strongest and fieriest emotions of life defy all analytical insight." Nothing daunted, he proceeds there and elsewhere to attempt just such precise tracings out, and later in "Retrospective," announces the supersubtle complexity of psychological motivations and indeed of all psychological processes. After this book, as Higgins and I said, "treatment of Pierre's inward development is inseparable from the theme of the shadowiness of all human motivation," impulses which lurk in what Melville called the "ever-elastic regions of evanescent invention" through which the mind roams up and down. By the end of book 4, Melville had "gone beyond the supersubtlety of all human psychology to assert the *autonomy* of those subtler elements of man," including what he referred to as those "ineffable hints and ambiguities, and undefined half-suggestions, which now and then people the soul's atmosphere, as thickly as in a soft, steady snow-storm, the snow-flakes people the air." The imagery "suggests an evanescence of thought which the individual no more controls than he does the snow-storm, and Melville distinguished these 'reveries and trances' from the 'assured element of consciously bidden and self-propelled thought.' " As he traces the processes of Pierre's mental growth, Melville makes the reader privy to the seemingly "boundless expansion" of Pierre's life. In one of the most complex passages of book 5, "Misgivings and Preparatives," Melville portrays a rapidly expanded mental terrain glimpsed by his hero, but still a chaotic and uncontrollable one. Thus even before Pierre encounters the girl who claims to be his half-sister (in bk. 6, "Isabel, and the First Part of the Story of Isabel"), the reader understands that Isabel is identified either as Pierre's unconscious or a product of it. Nourished on tainted idealisms which coexist with an unworldly Christian absolutism, Pierre is just the youth to mistake an intense expansion of consciousness for the attainment of true wisdom, just the youth, suffused with acknowledged idealism and ambiguously unacknowledged sexual desires, to dare to apply Jesus' words to actual earthly life. Melville had converted the clichés of gothic sensationalism into profound psychological exploration.

Everything about this new book was dangerous to its author, particularly the pattern of dubious, falsified family relationships. Melville had observed at close range a falsity in family relationship when Gansevoort was forced to become the man of the family; now he could be grateful that Gansevoort had borne the brunt of any excessive emotional demands of his widowed mother. At midcentury, readers of popular fiction knew their *Typee*, knew that for Melville the two greatest words in the English language, the very words any worthy young man would first teach to a beautiful naked woman at the ends of the earth, were "home" and "Mother." Now Melville's joking about every good boy's sentimental love for his mother had caught up with him just as he was enduring very strong doses of his mother's religiosity at home. In *Pierre* mother and son in play call each other brother and sister, and a young man and woman who might be half-brother and sister enter into a pretense of marriage which may involve sexual intercourse. Melville's sister Helen copied all this, day by day, confiding or choosing not to confide the content of the book to her mother.

Just as his mother's recent phase of religious fervor emerged in the themes of *Pierre*, so did Melville's fresh saturation with human pettiness in a majestic natural setting. In the Berkshires an avid appetite for vicious gossip was coupled with extreme religious intolerance. Among his poorer neighbors Melville was capable of identifying, now and then, some "gem" of a character, but he had ample reason to think of many of them as ignorant but arrogantly opinionated yokels, irredeemably malicious. He may have encountered members of the subhuman Yankee family he had boarded with in 1837 ("they all burrow together in the woods—like so many foxes," he had written his Uncle Peter), perhaps passing on the roads the hulking louts who had tried to drive him from the school. Nor did he idealize the long-established Berkshire families with famous names, Sedgwick, Dewey, Field, some of whose members had made great careers for themselves in Boston or New York. Successful, these people treated themselves to prolonged visits to their Berkshire homes, and brought back their friends, as Catharine Sedgwick, by then a famous novelist, had brought the English actress Fanny Kemble in the mid-1830s. Encouraged by the miraculous improvements in transportation, the returning natives and their friends, then friends of friends, and at last mere acquaintances and strangers, beginning in the late 1830s and accelerating in the late 1840s, had made the Berkshires a summer resort. As the local squireocracy was augmented by city relations and associates, the chasm widened between the wealthier families and their poorer neighbors, who, especially in hard times, might feel like peasants, or feel treated like peasants.

Melville knew these better families, especially the Sedgwicks. His mother, along with his Uncle Thomas's wife, had called on Elizabeth Sedgwick in the 1830s, and Helen had been granted the privilege of attending Mrs. Sedgwick's school for one year—a privilege she cherished all her life. Elizabeth's husband was Charles Sedgwick, Judge Shaw's clerk when he held court at Lenox, and it was Charles and Elizabeth who had summoned the Melvilles to a party early in November so they could say good-bye to the Hawthornes and meet the Jameses. At such gatherings Melville witnessed from close up the views of the novelist Catharine Sedgwick and other Sedgwicks on the issues of the day. Miss Sedgwick, a daughter of Federalism, protected by her inheritances and by the prosperity of her brothers, never had to do battle in the literary marketplace. Her career owed much to her religion, for her first novel, *A New-England Tale* (1822), began as a Unitarian tract. Inspired, like James Fenimore Cooper, by the new novels not yet acknowledged as written by Sir Walter Scott, she determined to add to "the scanty stock of native American literature," as she said in the preface. Miss Sedgwick as a Unitarian was not required to make any embarrassing profession of personal salvation. Repelled by the emphasis on eternal damnation in the frontier Calvinism of the lower classes, disgusted by the vulgarity of camp meetings during periods of revivalism in the Berkshires, she distanced herself from reform movements, preferring to address the aspirations and insecurities of the rising middle class in such bestselling didactic books as *Home: Scenes and Character Illustrating Christian Truth* (1835) and *The Poor Rich Man, and the Rich Poor Man* (1836), where she suggested that despite some legitimate complaints about "the low rates of women's wages," most women were "paid according to their capacity." She was certain that in New England, and even in New York City, poverty was almost always the result of vice or disease. A woman competent as a seamstress could always support herself and live decently, if frugally. In *Pierre* Melville introduced his Isabel with a needle in her hand, sewing.

The Sedgwicks' views on poverty were repugnant to Melville, but, perhaps dating from his youthful months in the Berkshires, he nursed still stronger moral grievances against his older Berkshire neighbor, Orville Dewey, the Sheffield-born Unitarian, close friend of Lemuel Shaw and the Sedgwicks. In Boston, on his return from the South Seas, Melville may have seen William Lloyd Garrison's "Spasmodic Philanthropy" in the 11 October 1844 *Liberator*, an attack on Daniel Webster, Rufus Choate, and Orville Dewey, all intimates of Judge Shaw: "It would be amusing, were it not for the meanness and hollowness of the trick, to see how eager certain time-serving politicians and pseudo ministers of Christ are to make an anti-slavery reputation for themselves, and to hide their odious pro-slavery position and conduct, by affecting to be overwhelmed with indignation and horror at the proposal to annex Texas to the United States." Garrison singled out Dewey: "Among the anti-abolition clergy, who are trying to retrieve their character by the same ruse, is 'Orville Dewey, pastor of the Church of the Messiah in New-York' — who has recently preached and printed 'A Discourse on Slavery and the Annexation of Texas,' the perusal of which has, if possible, increased my abhorrence of the moral philosophy of its author, and deepened my displeasure at his lack of manly courage." In 1844 and thereafter Melville, emotionally an absolutist, was more akin to Garrison the abolitionist than to Dewey, whatever either Melville or Dewey thought about practical ways of ending slavery.

Melville had had ample opportunity to learn more about this "pseudo minister of Christ," Orville Dewey, who was preaching at the Church of the Messiah in New York City during Melville's early career, until the spring of 1848, when he retired to Sheffield, occasionally going back to the city to preach or lecture. That was only two years before Melville enrolled with his

Unitarian wife in the other Unitarian church, All Souls, in February 1850, just after returning from London. (In volume 1 this was misdated 1849, following Walter Kring's 1975 essay rather than his 1981 revision, which has the correct date, 1850.) It was common knowledge that Dewey hated the beggary he witnessed in New York City and held that great evil and mischief lay in indiscriminate charity to the almost invariably undeserving poor. Melville could have encountered these ideas of Dewey's in an occasional visit to his church, or elsewhere, as in the 1846 *Discourses on Human Nature, Human Life, and the Nature of Religion*, especially the third part, "On the Nature of Religion," in chapter 24, "Spiritual Interests, Real and Supreme": "What is it that distresses the poor man, and makes poverty, in the ordinary condition of it, the burden that it is? It is not, in this country, — it is not, usually, hunger, nor cold, nor nakedness. It is some artificial want, created by the wrong state of society. It is something nearer yet to us, and yet more unnecessary. It is mortification, discontent, peevish complaining, or envy of a better condition; and all these are evils of the mind." This denial of evil and suffering in prosperous America, this intellectualizing about charity, this smug aloofness from real suffering, outraged Melville, who in *Pierre* (bk. 2, ch. 2) called attention to those in "the humbler walks of life" who were physically deformed by "unequal toil and poverty," and he went out of his way (bk. 6, ch. 1) to say that "in other climes many a pauper was that moment perishing" from cold, and rued "the wretched rush-lights of poverty and woe." The novel analyzed the luxurious self-delusions of the rich, scrutinizing attitudes toward poverty, particularly un-Christlike ways of dealing with Jesus' words on what he would have his would-be followers do, either sell all they had and give it to the poor and follow him, or, a sophist could argue, put other exigencies first, like your own comfort, since the poor would always be with you. Unlike Orville Dewey, Jesus had not said that the poor really lacked only artificial wants, not real necessities.

Dewey had delivered a notable oration at Pittsfield on 27 December 1850, two and a half months after Melville had moved there. The occasion was the North American Union meeting which John C. Hoadley had helped organize, and the point of the speech might have been that slavery was regrettable but disunion was deplorable. It was quoted at length in the Pittsfield *Sun* on 2 January 1851, the day after Elizabeth Shaw Melville returned from her long visit to Boston, so the words are known, if not the meaning. Later Dewey claimed that his speech had been misunderstood, though being misunderstood was all but inevitable, since he always tried to see everything from every possible angle so as to offend no possible listener. In this he habitually left his own position in question, blurred by a mass of judicious, noncommittal, excruciatingly inoffensive verbiage. Dewey complained: "I did not discuss the present fugitive slave law, though I was immediately represented as a violent advocate for it, but rather addressed myself to the question whether we at the North could, in conscience, yield our assent to *any* such bill—to *any* bill that should give the Southern master the power to reclaim one of his slaves that had fled to us for refuge." This seemingly soulless minister, this cold-hearted mealy-mouthed pontificator on "human nature" and "human life," pushed Melville into insisting in *Pierre* that some poor people were hungry and cold. Later, in January 1852, Melville exploded at the fatuous pomposity and impious arrogance of Dewey's lecture series in the fall of 1851 at the Lowell Institute in Boston, "The Problem of Human Destiny, considered in its bearings on Human Life and Welfare," and wrote the lecture title "Human Destiny" into his book as the *ne plus ultra* of fatuousness.

The figure Melville first created as Christian minister with un-Christlike deference to the opinions of the rich and un-Christlike concern for the poor was Mrs. Glendinning's minister, Mr. Falsgrave, a name Bunyan or Hawthorne might have invented. As he heightened his examination of absolutism versus expediency, Melville required a more intellectual embodiment of nominal Christianity than Falsgrave—Plotinus Plinlimmon, whose lecture on the "Chronometricals and Horologicals" (preserved however imperfectly in a pamphlet that Pierre finds but does not wholly read and does not understand) Melville made the centerpiece of the novel (bk. 14, ch. 3). Pierre takes shelter in the city at the Church of the Apostles, a collection of hand-to-mouth "artists of various sorts; painters, or sculptors, or indigent students, or teachers of languages, or poets, or fugitive French politicians, or German philosophers" (bk. 19, ch. 1), a range of crackpot reformers, all idealistic, all ill equipped to live in the real world. This structure is a deconsecrated church, suggested to Melville by the fate of buildings like the old Grace Church at Broadway and Rector, sold in 1845 to be converted into stores below and, in the upper part, a museum of Chinese curiosities—fit emblem of the fate of Christianity in a commercial society where the better people were retreating farther and farther uptown. Abiding at the Church of the Apostles is Plotinus Plinlimmon, the worldly philosopher crowding in wherever New Testament Christianity is expelled. In the pamphlet (bk. 14, ch. 3) Plinlimmon advocates "virtuous expediency" as "the highest desirable or attainable earthly excellence for the mass of men." In coolly rational arguments Plinlimmon demonstrates to his satisfaction that while Jesus may have lived on earth by heavenly rules, keeping God's perfect chronometrical time, anyone who attempts to imitate Jesus' example will fail, since the horological will creep in, despite all attempts to live absolutely. The man who attempts to obey Jesus will find that the experiment has terrible consequences: "in his despair, he is too apt to run clean away into all manner of moral abandonment, self-deceit, and hypocrisy (cloaked, however, mostly under an aspect of the most respectable devotion); or else he openly runs, like a mad dog, into atheism." Just as well the rich young man had gone sorrowfully away after hearing Jesus' words: "almost invariably, with inferior beings, the absolute effort to live in this world according to the strict letter of the chronometricals is, somehow, apt to involve those inferior beings eventually in strange, *unique* follies and sins, unimagined before."

Persistently aggrieved at the Boston and New York Unitarians, Melville had long nursed a similar disgust toward English Utilitarians, judging them by Jesus' standards for what one had to do to become one of his followers. He had taken an extract in *Moby-Dick* from *Natural Theology* (1802) by William Paley, the man who systematized the arguments of the early Utilitarian Abraham Tucker. Years later in *Germany*, by Madame de Staël-Holstein (New York: Derby & Jackson, 1859), he marked a passage on one man, "regarded in a religious light," being "as much as the entire human race"; then he commented: "This was an early and innate conviction of mine, suggested by my revulsion from the counting-room philosophy of Paley." Early and innate was his revulsion against the Utilitarians. Now he had at hand William Hazlitt's lengthy condensation of the diffuse, redundant work by Tucker, the 1807 edition entitled *An Abridgement of "The Light of Nature Pursued,"* a coolly rational textbook on human psychology, including the psychology of social behavior and the psychology of religion. In "Benevolence," Tucker had satisfied himself it was not necessarily selfish to act out of sensible self-interest: "What, if a man agreeable and obliging in company, should happen to desire another lump of sugar in his tea to please his own palate, would they pronounce him a whit the more selfish upon that account? So that selfishness is not having a regard for oneself, but having no regard for anything else. Therefore, the moralist may exhort men to a prudent concern for their own interests, and at the same time dissuade them from selfishness, without inconsistency." That example of the lump of sugar in "Benevolence" lies behind Plinlimmon's smooth way of counteracting the impractical and impracticable advice of Jesus (bk. 14, ch. 3):

> To turn the left cheek if the right be smitten, is chronometrical; hence, no average son of man ever did such a thing. To give *all* that thou hast to the poor, this too is chronometrical; hence no average son of man ever did such a thing. Nevertheless, if a man gives with a certain self-considerate generosity to the poor; abstains from doing downright ill to any man; does his convenient best in a general way to do good to his whole race; takes watchful loving care of his wife and children, relatives, and friends; is perfectly tolerant to all

other men's opinions, whatever they may be; is an honest dealer, an honest citizen, and all that; and more especially if he believe that there is a God for infidels, as well as for believers, and acts upon that belief; then, though such a man falls infinitely short of the chronometrical standard, though all his actions are entirely horologic; — yet such a man need never lastingly despond, because he is sometimes guilty of some minor offense: — hasty words, impulsively returning a blow, fits of domestic petulance, selfish enjoyment of a glass of wine while he knows there are those around him who lack a loaf of bread.

"Benevolence" to Melville was a finely ironic title. In book 21 Plinlimmon rejects, unopened, a gift of books, among which is a handsome edition of Abraham Tucker. Why open it? Plinlimmon has already learned all there is to learn from Tucker.

British Utilitarianism and American Unitarianism, sound-alike philosophy and religious denomination, overlapped in Melville's mind because of their similar countinghouse mentality toward all things moral. Very likely he knew that all the famous British Utilitarians were, in fact, leading Unitarians. "Utilitarians, — the every-day world's people themselves, far transcend those inferior Transcendentalists by their own incomprehensible worldly maxims," Melville declared (*Pierre*, bk. 18, ch. 2). Transcendentalists, being "theoretic and inactive," were harmless, while Utilitarians put their selfish morality into practice in "living deeds." Yet American Transcendentalists could not be trusted to remain theoretic and inactive, for some innocent reader or auditor might take seriously their heartless views on human relationships: Melville, reading Ralph Waldo Emerson's "Friendship" in the Hawthornes' boudoir in 1850, remembered that the essayist and lecturer had been a Unitarian minister and still retained essentially Unitarian attitudes. In a further twist, American Unitarian attitudes toward slavery, poverty, and charity coalesced in Melville's mind with Shakespeare's time-servers, from the nurse in *Romeo and Juliet* (whose advice Juliet meets with the cool "thou has comforted me marvelous much") to Polonius in *Hamlet*. What Melville wrote, during that trancelike period of concentration in November and December 1851, was the tragic story of a youthful idealist who tried to put Christian principles into practice and came to the tragic knowledge that Christianity as Jesus taught it was, however alluring, also impracticable. The reader would learn along the way, if he did not know already, that what passed for Christianity in midcentury America, especially among socially prominent and wealthy Unitarians, was very far from Christlike.

[4]

Melville Crosses the Rubicon

January 1852

>   Remember that composure of mind is every thing.
>
>   Herman Melville to Gansevoort Melville,
>   29 May 1846

HERMAN ARRIVED AT Allan and Sophia's house on Thirty-first Street in New York City about the last day of 1851 or the first day of 1852. Probably he took himself to the third-story room where he had written some of the last sections of his *Whale* the previous late spring and early summer—a room frigid now, rather than sweltering. He carried with him baffled grief about the reception of *Moby-Dick* and his new fearful letdown from the prolonged creative process on *Pierre*, all heightened by some of the Christmas hysteria caught from Sarah Morewood's intensity of emotion over George Duyckinck, hysteria that reverberated in Allan's household as Augusta shared her mother's letter with her sister-in-law. Sophia was several months pregnant, and despite cook, nurse, and maids, she had her hands full with little Maria (Milie) and Florence. Allan was uneasy about having Augusta there if it meant not having Kate. He kowtowed to his mother about Sophia's imperiousness, aware that Kate had left for Arrowhead feeling aggrieved. Augusta was good to have in any house—especially with Milie not yet three, and Florence not yet one and a half. When Augusta wrote Nilly Van Rensselaer Thayer that she was passing a pleasant winter there, Nilly responded realistically: "Sophia must enjoy having you with her for I suppose the distance [uptown] she is from her family must in a measure separate them much, particularly when a Mother is most at leisure in the evenings." Sophia was always hospitable, to Herman and everyone else, although her liking her own ways could put her at odds with Maria and Kate, especially. Melville had not intended to stay for long and had not intended to need a copyist, but he did stay, through the third week of the month, and did require Augusta's devoted service before he went home.

What Melville brought to New York was a manuscript he and Allan estimated would make about 360 pages—his shortest book since *Omoo*. A scrap of a draft passage of the contract in the lawyer-brother's hand shows that Allan was thinking that the book would be apt to come out even *shorter* than 360 pages; only as an afterthought did he caret in language to cover the possibility that it might run *longer* than that. This short version of *Pierre* was in all essentials complete. Melville had not been in the habit of approaching the Harpers for a contract before he had a book in hand—most recently, a book already plated, in his awkward, hapless hope of peddling the whaling book to the highest bidder. Chances are that the essentials of the plot were just what was published, except that the manuscript contained no passages on Pierre as an author and lacked the bit of late fiddling required to fit those passages in. Reviewers who summarized the story upon its publication at the end of July 1852 barely mentioned the section on authorship, treating it, as did the reviewer in the Boston *Post* quoted in chapter 2 above, as outside the main plot, a divagation. Ironically, the section of *Pierre* now most widely known was not in the manuscript that Melville initially took to the Harpers at Cliff Street, most likely on 2 January 1852.

From a later comment it is clear that about this time Melville offered the short book to Richard Bentley. Anything he said about *Pierre* (other than the estimate of its length) and anything he said about *The Whale* (such as a question about the "Epilogue") is unknown. As Melville had been taught late in 1849, according to the British courts a London publisher might pay an American author anything his generous nature inspired him to do, but that payment bought no copyright on the book. If a London publisher got a book out before a rival publisher could print and bind it, then he had priority of publication, first chance with the more eager buyers, but he could not prevent another publisher from resetting the book from his text or from a copy of an American printing. Under the circumstances, Bentley had been extraordinarily generous to Melville—overpaying for *Mardi* and publishing it despite the best advice of the professional reader he hired, then also losing money on *Redburn* and *White-Jacket* in due course, and just now realizing how much he was apt to lose on *The Whale*. Dealing with the Harpers had reinforced in Melville his conviction, common among authors, that any publisher of his must be profiting from his books: why else would Bentley keep giving him large advances?

Since Wall Street was near Newspaper Row, Allan could scan many of the three dozen or so Manhattan dailies that Herman would not see in the course of his day of literary work. For *Moby-Dick*, Herman's first book printed after he moved away from the city, where friends could hand him reviews and where he could see them himself in the reading rooms in the evening, the actual or metaphorical bushel basket Allan had used for Gansevoort's notices came back into service, and he accumulated dozens of reviews of *Moby-Dick*, ready for display to the author, among them some that modern scholars have never seen, for several contemporary newspapers with good literary sections have disappeared with barely a trace, surviving only in stray issues, random clippings in scrapbooks, or items reprinted in other papers, with credit to the now-lost source. Herman had to take a moment for a social obligation, writing a friendly note to Evert Duyckinck on Friday the second. He thanked Duyckinck for his New Year's gift of nutcrackers and explained that he could not call at 20 Clinton Place the next day, but that he would be glad to call on him "at some other time — not very remote in the future, either." Melville's urgent need was to form a strategy for getting the best deal for the new manuscript, so the brothers must have sat down with the bushel to familiarize themselves with the reception of *Moby-Dick* in the United States. Melville needed good news in New York City, but there was little good in the fresh news. The worst, until January, had been the 20 November review in the influential new Congregationalist magazine, the New York *Independent*, where "H." declared that the "book-maker and the book-publisher had better do their work with a view to the trial it must undergo at the bar of God." None so cruel as the righteous, Melville knew; and this was carefully worded so as to devastate him and intimidate the Harpers. On 6 December the New York *Churchman* had concluded: "it is pitiable to see so much talent perverted to sneers at revealed religion and the burlesquing of sacred passages of Holy Writ." As he surveyed the worst that had been said, Melville suddenly had to repress not merely one grievance at a time but, all at once, a hoard of grievances — too many to keep locked silently away as he dealt with the Harpers.

Now in his luckless timing Melville was confronted with January magazines, most of which had appeared, as usual, at the end of the previous month, just after Christmas, and were lying in wait for him. The New York *United States Magazine and Democratic Review* began in full fury: "Mr. Melville is evidently trying to ascertain how far the public will consent to be imposed upon. He is gauging, at once, our gullibility and our patience." The savagery went on unabated: Melville had "survived his reputation," *White-Jacket* was "such a very bad book, that, until the appearance of 'Moby-Dick,' we had set it down as the very ultimatum of weakness to which its author could attain." *Moby-Dick* had proved them wrong: "For, in sober truth, Mr. Melville's vanity is immeasurable. He will either be first among the bookmaking tribe, or he will be nowhere. He will centre all attention upon himself, or he will abandon the field of literature at once. From this morbid self-esteem, coupled with a most unbounded love of notoriety, spring all Mr. Melville's efforts, all his rhetorical contortions, all his declamatory abuse of society, all his inflated sentiment, and all his insinuating licentiousness." The review was laced with phrases that the Harpers could use in the next days to identify faults in the manuscript Melville was offering them. Other American magazines for January contained harsh condemnations. The New York *Methodist Quarterly Review* said *Moby-Dick* contained "a number of flings at religion, and even of vulgar immoralities that render it unfit for general circulation." (Some of the worst was delayed; it was the middle of the month before copies of William Gilmore Simms's January *Southern Quarterly Review* arrived from Charleston with the accusation that Ahab's "ravings, and the ravings of some of the tributary characters, and the ravings of Mr. Melville himself, meant for eloquent declamation, are such as would justify a writ *de lunatico* against all the parties.")

The Melville brothers saw that, too late to do much good, the Harpers in the January *Harper's New Monthly Magazine* had announced, without indicating how many British reviews had reached them, that Melville's latest work "has excited a general interest among the critical journals of London." Admitting that the "bold and impulsive style of some portions of the book" seemed "to shock John Bull's fastidious sense of propriety," *Harper's* quoted a passage from the London *Atlas*, one of the "most discriminating reviewals":

> In some respects we hold it to be his (Mr. Melville's) greatest effort. In none of his previous works are finer or more highly-soaring imaginative powers put forth. In none of them are so many profound and fertile and thoroughly original veins of philosophic speculation, or rather, perhaps, philosophic fancy struck.... Upon the whale, its mysteries, and its terrors, he revels as if the subject had enchantment for him. He pours into multitudinous chapters a mass of knowledge touching the whale—its habits and its history—the minutest details of its feeding or sporting, or swimming, strangely mixed with ingenious and daring speculations on the mysterious habits and peculiarities of the great brute—the whole written in a tone of exaltation and poetic sentiment, which has a strange effect upon the reader's mind, in refining and elevating the subject of discourse, and, at last, making him look upon the whale as a sort of awful and unsoluble mystery—the most strange and the most terrible of the wonders of the deep. That Herman Melville knows more about whales than any man from Jonah down, we do really believe.

Here the Harpers said nothing about the mysterious textual flaw that lay behind the hostility of the two British reviews that had been reprinted in the United States; perhaps they never understood what had happened. The publishers may have been trying to put the best face on word from England, but Melville was not appeased.

Melville kept a long row of mental oubliettes. In one of them there still rankled the memory that the Harper brothers sitting in council had rejected the manuscript of *Typee* in 1845 because "it was impossible that it could be true and therefore was without real value." Melville's niece Charlotte Hoadley, an attentive listener to her aunts in later years, declared a century afterward, in 1944: "One thing I do know, the Harpers refusing it calling it [*Typee*] a second 'Robinson Crusoe' embittered his [Melville's] whole life." The Harpers' rejection of that manuscript may have driven Melville to compose an "Appendix" to *Typee* in which he railed against the missionary schemers in Hawaii as "a junto of ignorant and designing Methodist elders in the councils of a half-civilized king." John Wiley saw to it that the "Appendix" was dropped from the expurgated edition, which appeared at the end of July 1846, and it was the expurgated edition that the Methodist Harpers had been printing and selling since 1849. Melville never felt at ease with the Harpers, although he had been a Harper author since 1847, when he took *Omoo* to the brothers, more furious at Wiley than at them, and although the Harpers since 1849 had been the only American publisher of his books, and had given him the benefit of their incomparable distribution system. Melville was intolerant of intolerant evangelical denominations like Methodism and prone to see all shrewd business dealings by such religious people as manifestations of religious hypocrisy. After the Harpers' refusal to make him an advance the previous spring and after the mediocre early sales of *Moby-Dick*, Melville was more tense about working with the Harpers than he had been for years. The Harpers were not the publishers Melville would have chosen, if he had been granted a choice; and only a few months had passed since he had tried, however ineptly or briefly, to avoid giving the whaling book to them. Because of his acknowledged debts to Shaw and Brewster and his unacknowledged debt to Stewart, it was essential that he get good terms for the manuscript of *Pierre* and that the book sell far more copies than any of his earlier works.

Presumably having already left the manuscript with the Harpers, on 5 January Melville saw his friend Dr. Robert Tomes and presented him with a copy of *Moby-Dick*. That was the day the newspapers blanketed New York City with lewd testimony about Edwin Forrest and the actress Josephine Clinton's behavior at the Eagle Hotel in Albany in 1842. Melville seems to have passed a night or two "out of town" (judging from his letter to Evert Duyckinck on 2 January) — with Richard and Abby Thurston Lathers in New Rochelle, where their plain country house was being replaced by a grand Italian villa. Alexander Jackson Davis, the architect who was making a great reputation for luxurious country villas, had created the prizewinning design, and Lathers was intent on furnishing it opulently, on a scale that must have astonished Melville. Born in Ireland, Lathers was reared in the South near Charleston (where he found the name for the villa, Winyah). Lacking a circle of blood relations outside his own house, Lathers, strongly familial in his attachments, treated Abby's sister Sophia's husband Allan as his brother, not brother-in-law, and drew Herman Melville into a similar intimacy. Some of the Bond Street Thurstons may have been out there for a New Year's visit when Melville was, and Allan may have accompanied him. In his innocence Melville may have passed the entire visit without realizing that there would be any problem with the Harpers.

In New York again (forty-five minutes from New Rochelle behind Lathers's fine horses on a dry day), Melville found, forwarded from Arrowhead, what he called in his reply a "highly flattering letter" from Sophia Hawthorne about *Moby-Dick*. Slow to have her chance at her husband's presentation copy what with packing in Lenox and then settling in at the Mann house in West Newton, she broke decorum by writing him, justified by her greater age, by her private conversations with him about her husband, and by her pride in the dedication to the man whose "genius" she revered more even than Melville did. On Thursday, 8 January, probably already under intense new stress about the fate of *Pierre* and with it his career, Melville replied to her:

> It really amazed me that you should find any satisfaction in that book. It is true that some *men* have said they were pleased with it, but you are the only *woman* — for as a general thing, women have small taste for the sea. But, then, since you, with your spiritualizing nature, see more things than other people, and by the same process, refine all you see, so that they are not the same things that other people see, but things which while you think you but humbly discover them, you do in fact create them for yourself — therefore, upon the whole, I do not so much marvel at your expressions concerning Moby Dick. At any rate, your allusion for example to the "Spirit Spout["] first showed to me that there was a subtile significance in that thing — but I did not, in that case, *mean* it.

This is where Melville went on to say that her husband's letter had revealed to him some of the "particular subordinate allegories" in the book. Characteristically, he alluded to nothing distressing in his present circumstances. The letter remains elusive, since he wrote from his private knowledge of what one particular man, her husband, had written to him in praise of the book, knowing that she had read what Hawthorne wrote to him as well as his own ecstatic reply. Melville would not again send her "a bowl of salt water"; the next chalice he would commend would be "a rural bowl of milk." Then into this letter he worked an amusing fantasy of the reclusive Hawthorne: "And does Mr Hawthorne continue his series of calls upon all his neighbors within a radius of ten miles? Shall I send him ten packs of visiting cards? And a box of kid gloves? and the latest style of Parisian handkerchief? — He goes into society too much altogether — seven evenings out, a week, should content any reasonable man." This intimate, affectionate jocularity hardly conceals the pride Melville felt in having been welcomed into the Hawthornes' little red cottage. He added that his sister Augusta sent her sincerest regards to both Sophia and Mr. Hawthorne—an indication that Augusta had met Sophia at one of the unknown Melville-Hawthorne encounters which Harrison Hayford first numbered in the 1940s and to which we are still making additions.

When the Harpers took a skeptical look at the new manuscript, they saw not a crowd-pleasing, loosely strung together story of knocking about in the South Seas (the sort of story that had gained Melville an instant international reputation), not even (what they might have expected) a charming account of the several-month trip to England and the Continent Melville had made late in 1849 (a trip ballyhooed in the papers as an opportunity for gathering literary material). Instead, the sea-author had packaged a psychological novel, a meticulous case history of an ignorant idealist, in the guise of an American gothic romance. What they saw was the book they later published —with one enormous difference: there were no passages on Pierre as an author interspersed through the last two-thirds of the book (and, consequently, no attack on Pierre's malicious publishers). When Melville showed up on Cliff Street again, the Harpers were armed with their sales figures showing that *Moby-Dick* was doing much worse than *White-Jacket* and *Redburn* had done in their first weeks. They were also armed with their evidence about the damage *Moby-Dick* had done to their reputation among their many particular friends in the Methodist ministry as well as to their general reputation for publishing Christian books. The Harpers were not only good Methodists, and well known to be good Methodists, they were also transplanted Yankees who drove hardfisted bargains (a "regular Yankee," Melville called Joseph Harper when he encountered him in London in November 1849). They were merciless when they could get away with being merciless. What other publishers charged interest on advances? Even if his friend Richard Henry Dana Jr. did not tell him, everyone in Melville's Boston circle knew the story of how, in 1839 and 1840, the Harpers had haggled with the genteel elder Richard Henry Dana and William Cullen Bryant over the manuscript of young Dana's *Two Years before the Mast* until they got the book outright for $250 and made a fortune from it, fair and square.

The Harpers were nervous around Melville, having scooped him up after rebuffing him, having profited by him, but having been slurred in the press because of him. He had lost his reputation, and they did not any longer regard him as valuable. They could afford to lose anything new by Melville, the author whose first book was still acknowledged as his best and still, as they knew, had sold better than any of his subsequent books. They owned both his good books, *Typee* and *Omoo*, and everyone said he would never surpass them or even equal them. They decided that they did not want to publish *Pierre* but that they would turn Melville away with the smooth strategy of offering him a contract he would have to refuse. Their standard terms had been to split the profits with him fifty-fifty after publishing costs had been recouped, and even on those terms Melville had run up his considerable debt to the firm. Now they offered him not fifty cents but twenty cents on the dollar after costs, which meant, even the older and unmathematical Melville brother would have seen at once, that *Pierre* would have to sell two and a half times as many copies in order to earn him the same share that had already proved inadequate. Feelings on both sides of the table (Allan probably flanking his brother and one or more of the Harpers representing the firm) must have run high. Neither Melville brother liked to confront other men, although Allan the lawyer, as when he was deprived of creature comforts by an excursion to Greylock, was a better man to turn loose on any local extortionist than Herman. Here, the surface calm was preserved, and they all behaved like gentlemen.

Melville seems to have asked for a little time to make his decision about the terms of the contract, perhaps planning to try other publishers, but something deterred him from hawking the manuscript along Publishers' Row at the tip of Manhattan. Once, he had hawked the proofs of *White-Jacket* "from Piccadilly to Whitechapel, calling upon every publisher in his way" (the *Times* of London, 22 January 1850); and in mid-1851 he had paid for the stereotyping of his whaling book and had fantasized of peddling it to the highest bidder. Something, very early in January, made him decide to accept the terms the Harpers had offered, maybe within a day or two of his discussing the contract with them. Melville had not let his resentment over Duyckinck's sanctimonious criticism of *Moby-Dick* in the *Literary World* alter his polite behavior toward his friend, so he was free to consult him. What happened in the day or two or three (hardly more) between Melville's initial negotiations with the Harpers and the conclusion of those negotiations involved Duyckinck.

Melville had been vague about the day he could see Duyckinck because he wanted to be free to meet with the Harpers at their convenience on or after Monday the fifth. Meanwhile, the 3 January issue of the *Literary World* contained a bit of gossip salted with a private message written before Melville came to town: "Nathaniel Hawthorne, who has just drawn off a third or fourth series of his Twice Told Tales from his nutty old vintage, has exchanged the ice and snows of Lenox for a village shelter near Boston, at

Newton; while Herman Melville, close-reefed in his library at Pittsfield, is doubling old Saddleback and winter, with a thermometer below zero, it is rumored on a new literary tack for the public when he next emerges in Cliff street." The thermometer was Duyckinck's own bread-and-butter gift for the previous summer's hospitality, as few but Melville would know, a hospitality repaid by a review that helped to destroy his career. (Subscribers would know the Harpers' establishment was on Cliff Street.) Mrs. Morewood was presumably the one who, most likely in person, had passed along the accurate rumor about Melville's "new literary tack" to the Duyckinck brothers. Melville would have found in this genial personal mention a painful reminder of the discrepancy between his own generosity as a host, two years running, and Evert's Christian rectitude and literary dogmatism as a reviewer, but he would have borne it with his usual attempt at stoicism.

After the Harpers had offered him only twenty cents on every dollar of profits instead of fifty, the natural thing for Melville to do was to walk directly from Cliff Street to Clinton Place to see the friend who had acted as his literary adviser since the spring of 1846, and who only a few months before had been pressing him to consider letting J. S. Redfield, not the Harpers, publish the whaling book. The Duyckincks were tense and awkward around anyone who might know of Sarah Morewood's pursuit of George, and had no way of knowing that the Melville women knew a good deal more than Herman did. For his part, Melville may have known enough to be edgy around George. Embarrassed or not, Evert Duyckinck was still the earnest Christian who in the *Literary World* had condemned *Moby-Dick* as irreligious. We know what he thought of *Pierre* in the expanded form that the Harpers published, for in the *Literary World* for 21 August 1852 he denounced the book for violating the "holy relations of the family" and for hinting at, if not depicting, "the horrors of an incestuous relation between Pierre and Isabel." In early January 1852, in person, after looking at the manuscript, with Melville waiting for his judgment, or with a day or so to look it over, Duyckinck was even more direct than he was in the review, and with good reason: in January Duyckinck could hope that his strong advice would prevent Melville from publishing the manuscript at all. Then Duyckinck would have saved the world from a corrupting book. Duyckinck regarded himself as Melville's friend still, but he had a Christian duty to be rigorously honest to a friend about a manuscript dangerously inculcating "the impracticability of virtue." In "every respect a thoroughly genial man," as recorded by a memorialist (and quoted by Lathers), Duyckinck's reputation for self-control was such that it was said "that no one ever saw him affected by ill temper." He would not have been ill tempered in what he said about *Pierre*, but he would have been forthright, and his religious convictions may have impelled him past his usual "slight hesitation in speech." Melville heard him out, and more than four and a half years passed before he again entered the hallowed basement library of 20 Clinton Place.

Only a dramatic, if subdued, personal confrontation just at this time, a meeting in which Duyckinck told Melville that he could not recommend the work to any publisher, can account for the fury Melville displayed toward his friend in what he wrote into his manuscript at once, not much more than a week or so into January. Duyckinck's opinion had been so conclusive that despite his agony and fear Melville did not even consider trying to find another publisher for his manuscript, any one of whom would have asked Duyckinck's opinion on any manuscript his protégé submitted to them. In his profound misery at the contract, Melville probably let Allan convey his acceptance of it, since Allan went down to Wall Street every day and could walk over to Cliff Street. Once he agreed to the contract and it was all drawn up, although not signed, there was no reason for Melville to stay in town. He was sexually frustrated, angry in several directions, guilty (for endangering Shaw's money laid out to secure Lizzie's happiness), and with idle hands. He had paid Lizzie little attention during her sufferings at Arrowhead, but now he could go to Boston to bring her and their baby son home, or he could go directly to Pittsfield and start another nautical book, which he might sell on better terms than twenty cents on the dollar.

Instead, he stayed on at Allan and Sophia's house, and no sooner had he accepted the contract than he fell to expanding the manuscript. Never, from the fall of 1846 when he sent chapters and parts of chapters to London after Gansevoort left with the manuscript of *Typee*, had Melville been content to finish up a book without last-minute enlargements. He kept the finished manuscript of *Mardi* for several *months* to write into it his responses to news of the revolutions in Europe. Whatever he had felt or made himself feel as he read the first installment of Duyckinck's review of *Moby-Dick*, and during the week of waiting for the second part and then responding to it, Melville's feelings had undergone further changes. As he made up his mind to accept the ruinous contract, he focused on Duyckinck, not just on the Harpers, as working to destroy his career. He began writing his anger into new pages for the completed manuscript. Chances are that he did not set out to write many new pages, certainly not anything like the 160 he later estimated that he added. He probably thought he would write only long enough to free himself of his anger at Duyckinck and the other reviewers and of his contempt for the publishing world as he had come to know it. Not a journalist like his beleaguered friend Willis, he could hardly write an attack on Duyckinck for publication in a magazine, but he could do what he had so often done before — he could work something new into his manuscript. He always wanted to be a stoic but sometimes he hurt too much to be one.

Melville retained or retrieved the manuscript, and by the first few days of the second week of the month he turned his fear and rage into a new episode for insertion into it. On the eighth Melville's comment to Sophia Hawthorne on what he had "heard" about *Moby-Dick* was restrained, but about the time he wrote her he began to express elsewhere his agonized reactions to the reviews — in the manuscript of *Pierre*. What he first wrote for interpolation into his Kraken book was "Young America in Literature" (bk. 17), an insertion which violates the compact he had scrupulously kept between author and reader: "Among the various conflicting modes of writing history, there would seem to be two grand practical distinctions, under which all the rest must subordinately range. By the one mode, all contemporaneous circumstances, facts, and events must be set down contemporaneously; by the other, they are only to be set down as the general stream of the narrative shall dictate; for matters which are kindred in time, may be very irrelative in themselves. I elect neither of these; I am careless of either; both are well enough in their way; I write precisely as I please." This cavalier declaration precedes the news, outrageous to every reader who has patiently followed the meticulously timed revelations about the hero, that Pierre had in his adolescence been an author, and a published author at that, sought out by editors of "magazines and other polite periodicals" and acclaimed by literary reviewers. Worse still, Pierre, Melville now announced, had been importuned from "various quarters of the land, both town and country," to lecture before "Lyceums, Young Men's Associations, and other Literary and Scientific Societies." The chairman of the Zadockprattsville "Urquhartian Club for the Immediate Extension of the Limits of all Knowledge, both Human and Divine," had gone so far as to suggest a lecture title for the young Pierre, "Human Destiny." Why pass up a chance to flail out at Orville Dewey? Even after basing parts of his portrait of Plotinus Plinlimmon on Dewey, Melville was aghast at the way all of Unitarian Boston had knelt at the feet of the lecturer on "The Problem of Human Destiny" — a topic Dewey and the Shaws and their friends did not realize was fit only for God, not mortal man.

To snipe at Dewey was bad enough, for it was to risk offending his father-in-law, but that was incidental. Melville's purpose in "Young America in Literature" was to attack Evert Duyckinck, the joint editor of the *Literary World*, which like most American magazines reprinted items from British sheets without paying for them, there being no international copyright law. In what Melville now wrote, the joint editor of the piratical "Captain Kidd Monthly" badgers Pierre for his daguerreotype (to be engraved for the magazine) just as Duyckinck had badgered Melville himself in letters (and Maria in person) early in 1851 for a daguerreotype which could be engraved for a portrait of Melville in *Holden's Monthly Magazine*. To write his personal correspondence with Duyckinck into what became book 17 was to repudiate all pretense at a friendship, though months would pass before Duyckinck would see what Melville had written about him. It is simply not possible that Melville could have written book 17 before he wrote the friendly note to Duyckinck on 2 January 1852, and the timing makes it all but certain that Melville had written that "book" of *Pierre* no later than the first days of the second week of January. By 21 January 1852, when Allan informed the Harpers that *Pierre* already exceeded the agreed-upon length, Melville had written not only book 17 but a great deal more having to do with Pierre as an author. (In reviewing *Pierre* the next summer Duyckinck of course refrained from mentioning the fact that he had recognized himself in the officious joint editor of the *Captain Kidd Monthly*.)

If the causes of his rage had been slighter, Melville might have contented himself with writing this little satirical passage and not putting it into his manuscript. The pages might have passed in Manhattan as "Rabelaisian" amusement if shown in manuscript to some of Melville's more sophisticated city acquaintances such as Dr. Francis or Dr. Tomes (there was no chatting with Nat Willis, not during his month in the pillory). Some of Melville's artistic and literary acquaintances in London might have prized "Young America in Literature" as pungent satire on literary fame in America and the pretensions of literary reviewers in the land where their own writings could be stolen or mangled at will by anyone with access to a printing press. Even published in a magazine in New York, the piece could have amused some and done little harm, except to distress the Duyckincks and their intimates, such as Cornelius Mathews (who already, after Christmas of 1850, a whole year earlier, had dropped out of Melville's life, as far as anyone knows). But although often importuned to write for magazines, Melville was a bookman still.

If Melville had stopped there, as he probably meant to do, he would have done little new harm to himself. But Melville's rage was complicated. Into these pages he also worked in his anger at the reviews that had led people in Pittsfield to gossip about him self-righteously and had laid him open to the Harpers' punitive contract. Here Melville sardonically quoted from imaginary reviewers who had lavished fatuous praise upon the juvenile inanities of his hero. The last thing Melville would have wanted, in good times, was for a clerical reviewer to decide that "the predominant end and aim" of a book of Melville's "was evangelical piety." In quoting such fictional reviews, Melville was recalling that his first book had been expurgated after the ferocious onslaught (by the Reverend Henry T. Cheever) in the New York *Evangelist* and that *Omoo* had also occasioned vicious attacks on him (by G. W. Peck and others) as irreligious.

In book 17 Melville was reacting specifically to the reviews of *Moby-Dick*, more than to his past reviews in general. Where Pierre was commended for "his euphonious construction of sentences," a reviewer had just condemned Melville for his "involved syntax" (the *Democratic Review*). While Pierre's writings were praised for "highly judicious smoothness and genteelness of the sentiments and fancies," Melville had just been condemned for his "forced," "inflated," and "stilted" sentiment (the *Democratic Review*). Where Pierre was "characterized throughout by Perfect Taste," Melville had just been condemned for "harassing manifestations of bad taste" (the *Athenæum* — twice reprinted in Boston) and for "many violations of good taste and delicacy" (the New York *Churchman*) and called (by Duyckinck) "reckless at times of taste and propriety" and called also the author of scenes which neither "good taste nor good morals can approve" (by William Butler in the Washington *National Intelligencer*). A reviewer said that Pierre "never permits himself to astonish; is never betrayed into any thing coarse or new; as assured that whatever astonishes is vulgar, and whatever is new must be crude." Reviewers had just pointed to Melville's "lawless flights, which put all regular criticism at defiance" (the New York *Tribune*). Reviewers had just praised Melville for "vigor of style" (the *National Intelligencer*), even while condemning him for "vulgar immoralities" (the New York *Methodist Quarterly Review*); one of Melville's fictional critics declared that "vulgarity and vigor — two inseparable adjuncts" — were "equally removed" from Pierre. A clerical reviewer declared that Pierre was "blameless in morals, and harmless throughout," while real critics had just condemned Melville's "irreverence" (the Albany *Argus*), his "irreverence and profane jesting" (the Worcester *Palladium*), his frequent "profaneness" and his occasional "indelicacies" (the Boston *Evening Traveller*), and his "insinuating licentiousness" (the *Democratic Review*), or else deplored his "primitive formation of profanity and indecency" (the New York *Independent*). Rather than being praised for "evangelical piety" like young Pierre, Melville had just been denounced by clerical critics or pious lay reviewers for "sneering at the truths of revealed religion" (New York *Commercial Advertiser*), for "a number of flings at religion" (the *Methodist Quarterly Review*), and for "irreligion and profanity" and "sneers at revealed religion and the burlesquing of sacred passages of Holy Writ" (the *Churchman*). Similar parallels are abundant. Melville was making reviews of *Moby-Dick* into literary source material, cannibalizing them, in a way.

Melville still may have thought he could stop his additions there, having expressed his wrath at Duyckinck for playing first the domineering, then the betraying patron, and having less obviously gibed at the Harpers for taking away what he had counted on, half-profits. These passages on Pierre's surprising authorship and on the American publishing scene would have made a relatively small bulge in the outline of the book as it stood, and Melville could still have told himself, however speciously, that he was enriching his manuscript with spicy truth-telling satire and sober meditations on what constitutes literary originality. Having written these satirical pages, in which fictional reviewers praise his hero for the very qualities that reviewers were condemning Melville himself for lacking, he was unwilling to admit that his history of Pierre as a juvenile author, impulsively stuck into the manuscript at the likeliest spot he could see, could only damage the coherent book he had written. Now, not earlier, he was writing precisely as he pleased.

Writing what was later numbered book 17 had left Melville purged of some of his rage but in a new, retrospective mood. Led into a look back at the cramped labor of the seven years since the London publisher John Murray accepted his first book, most recently the dark frigid winter days in his study at Arrowhead, Melville wrote a new addition which became book 18, "Pierre, as a Juvenile Author, Reconsidered." No longer heavily facetious about his reviewers, he moved into a non-satirical, non-humorous, retrospective analysis of his own literary career: "And in the inferior instances of an immediate literary success, in very young writers, it will be almost invariably observable, that for that instant success they were chiefly indebted to some rich and peculiar experience in life, embodied in a book, which because, for that cause, containing original matter, the author himself, forsooth, is to be considered original; in this way, many very original books, being the product of very unoriginal minds." Here Melville rightly attributed the success of a work (obviously like his own *Typee*) to "some rich and peculiar experience in life, embodied in a book," rather than genuine originality.

Melville may have been recalling from Francis Jeffrey's essay on Victor Alfieri in his set of *Modern British Essayists* (1847–49) the passage on the men who become writers after an early life spent in non-intellectual lassitude then achieve success by a "confident and fortunate audacity." That reckless impulsiveness had led Alfieri to dash off a tragedy without knowing anything of the rules and models he should have been following. Rather than failing, "he found himself suddenly embarked in an unexpected undertaking, and in sight of unexpected distinction." Then, not contenting himself with unmerited success, Alfieri had set out to educate himself, so that he might deserve his success, much as Melville had embarked upon a rigorous course of self-education as he wrote *Mardi*. In what became book 18, Melville also traced Pierre's delusive notion that he "could live on himself" by becoming a writer, while ignorant that the world operates on the system "of giving unto him who already hath more than enough, still more of the superfluous article, and taking away from him who hath nothing at all, even that which he hath." Even before he wrote the first of the additions, any lingering exultation at Hawthorne's understanding of *Moby-Dick* was dissipated, for the prospect of drastic reduction in his already insufficient earnings meant that his career was ending — ending, he knew, just as he had become a great writer. In six weeks Melville had passed from "unspeakable security" to helpless vulnerability.

By the middle of the second week or the beginning of the third week of January, Melville had thrown himself into the composition of sections in which Pierre immaturely attempts to write a mature book. Melville wrote on, putting on paper something like a melodramatic version of his own immature attempt to write a mature book, *Mardi*, as well as his later attempts to write still greater books, *Moby-Dick* and the Kraken version of *Pierre*. These sections explored his struggles (perhaps recollected from writing *Mardi*, and surely from phases of writing *Moby-Dick* and *Pierre*) to transform himself (to "force" himself, as one would force a plant) into a great writer and thinker — a struggle that had brought him, momentarily, the crown of India from Hawthorne's hands but had left him publicly flayed and deprived of the future royalties he needed if he were to pay the interest on his debts and support his family.

Melville was writing at his top speed, the rate at which he had written *White-Jacket* in a score of sittings. Toward the end of the third week of January he had written much more than the Harpers had contracted to publish. Quite aside from the chance he was taking that he might wreck any success the book might have had, expanding the book was against his immediate financial interests, since under the terms of the contract if the book ran, say, half again longer than estimated, then the Harpers would be entitled to sell 1785 copies before declaring that the costs had been met and it was time to start paying him his pittance per copy. Upon departing for Boston or Pittsfield, Herman instructed Allan to convey the news to the Harpers. Accordingly, on 21 January Allan wrote the Harpers to tell them that the book already exceeded the estimate, so that they could adjust their plans accordingly:

> My brother would like to have his account with your house to the 1st Feby made up and ready to render to me, as near that date as will be convenient to you.
>
> Respecting "Pierre" the contract provides that if the book exceeded 360 pages a corresponding addition should be made to the number of copies required to liquidate the cost of the stereotype plates &c for a book of that

size. As the book exceeds that number of pages it will of course be necessary to ascertain how many more copies are to be allowed than provided by the contract for a book of 360 pages. The retail price of the book has been also raised beyond the price fixed by the agreement, which was one dollar & of course a corresponding increase per copy should be made to the author.

Allan would have realized that provisions already agreed to covered the eventuality that the book was shorter or longer than planned, so his letter was perhaps more a courtesy than a legal necessity. (That day, 21 January 1852, the papers reported in full John Van Buren's claim that he had established beyond doubt the adultery of Mrs. Forrest with Nathaniel Parker Willis — horrid reading for friends of Willis like Melville.)

When Melville got home to snowy Arrowhead late in January 1852 he pushed on with the story of the immature Pierre's attempt to write a mature book — which is to say that in anger, bitterness, and blind panic Melville was writing his own apologia for a career that he knew might have ended a few days into the year, however he was managing to deny that knowledge. His work could not have been as obsessive, by this stage, as it had been in December, or in mid-January, for most of the Pierre-as-author section must have been written in the city, judging by what Allan wrote to the Harpers on the twenty-first. Melville had work to do, still, aside from finishing the sections on authorship in America as he had experienced it — a career in which his most amateurish book was accounted his best and in which his greatest originality, genius, and his ferocious industry had gone unappreciated. Given his temperament, it is not likely that Melville worked the Pierre-as-author section into the city part of his original manuscript as he wrote. At home, with Helen just returned from her own visits to copy whatever Augusta had not copied in New York, he managed to assemble a full copy of his added pages. After that, however cavalier he could be about novelistic niceties, Melville had his hands full (for a day or two, or three — not long) shuffling manuscript pages, renumbering, making some transitions. Aside from the obvious affront to the reader at the start of "Young America in Literature," his declaration that he wrote precisely as he pleased, he left some passages in confusing form. With the first additions on Young America in literature he had already wrecked the next best crafted thing he had yet written, so nothing he went on to do could weigh heavily upon his aesthetic conscience. According to his own later estimate, the book as published was longer by 150 pages or more than the work he had completed at the end of December.

It has seemed obvious to everyone who has looked at *Pierre*, from reviewers to modern critics, that the pages Melville added to his completed manuscript must be those dealing with Pierre as an author. G. W. Peck in the

November 1852 *American Whig Review* knew what to say when he came to this section: "Just in this part of the book it comes out suddenly that Pierre is an author, a fact not even once hinted at in the preceding pages." All this, Peck announced, "is told in a manner that proves it very clearly to be nothing more than an afterthought of Mr. Melville's, and not contemplated in the original plan of the book, that is, if it ever had a plan. It is dragged in merely for the purpose of making Pierre a literary man, when the author had just brought him to such a stage that he did not know what else to do with him." Peck was wrong in assuming he was encountering the sections of the book in the order of composition, rather than encountering a whole new Pierre-as-author plot stuck down into a book in which Melville had not only known what else he was going to do with Pierre but had done it. However, his basic judgment is palpably true: Pierre's early literary career was "nothing more than an afterthought of Mr. Melville's." It can't be the other way around: the proportion of 360 to 150 roughly fits the proportion of non-author hero to Pierre-as-author, not the proportion of Pierre-as-author to the rest of the plot.

At Pittsfield, probably from the last week or week and a half of January, Melville toiled on under a compulsion which probably had little to do, day by day, with Duyckinck and the Harpers. Among the pages Melville wrote were some that suggest how Melville felt as he rushed to finish *Moby-Dick* the year before: "the first pages must go to the printer; and thus was added still another tribulation; because the printed pages now dictated to the following manuscript, and said to all subsequent thoughts and inventions of Pierre — *Thus and thus; so and so; else an ill match*. Therefore, was his book already limited, bound over, and committed to imperfection, even before it had come to any confirmed form or conclusion at all. Oh, who shall reveal the horrors of poverty in authorship that is high?" (bk. 25, ch. 3). Now his concern was to write new sections, not to integrate those into the original manuscript, although he would have discarded some little passages and recast others in order to splice the new sections in. There are some telltale signs of haste and carelessness, as in "The Church of the Apostles" (bk. 19), and in later passages where Pierre writes on a wide board laid on flour-barrels instead of putting to good use the portable writing desk he had taken from Saddle Meadows: when he made Pierre an author, Melville forgot that Pierre had packed his writing desk as part of his gentleman's equipment. Melville has Pierre and Isabel settle at the Church of the Apostles in book 19, then at the start of book 20 he accounts for their being there; and Charles Millthorpe is introduced and seemingly reintroduced.

Much of what Melville added to *Pierre* was bitter, overwrought, and even suicidal, yet some of it must rank among the most splendid prose passages he ever wrote. In the later phases of his depiction of his reconceived hero's attempt to write a "great, deep book" (bk. 25), Melville gave Pierre a dream or vision of Enceladus, the Titan thwarted in his attempt to scale heaven—a ruined figure, an armless trunk, who at the end wears, Pierre seems to see, Pierre's own head and features. The vision began realistically: "On the north side, where it" (the Mount of the Titans) "fronted the old Manor-house, some fifteen miles distant, the height, viewed from the piazza of a soft haze-canopied summer's noon, presented a long and beautiful, but not entirely inaccessible-looking purple precipice, some two thousand feet in air, and on each hand sideways sloping down to lofty terraces of pastures." Down the slopes was "the repulsed group of heaven-assaulters, with Enceladus in their midst shamefully recumbent":

> No more now you sideways followed the sad pasture's skirt, but took your way adown the long declivity, fronting the mystic height. In mid field again you paused among the recumbent sphinx-like shapes thrown off from the rocky steep. You paused; fixed by a form defiant, a form of awfulness. You saw Enceladus the Titan, the most potent of all the giants, writhing from out the imprisoning earth;—turbaned with upborne moss he writhed; still, though armless, resisting with his whole striving trunk, the Pelion and the Ossa hurled back at him;—turbaned with upborne moss he writhed; still turning his unconquerable front toward that majestic mount eternally in vain assailed by him, and which, when it had stormed him off, had heaved his undoffable incubus upon him, and deridingly left him there to bay out his ineffectual howl. (bk. 25, ch. 4)

In these magnificent pages the Berkshire topography plays the role it had played in Melville's composition of *Moby-Dick*, providing him an equivalent of Milton's plains of heaven, a vantage point from which he could hurl himself toward heaven. It forms a powerful, isolated commentary on the way he saw both his creation of *Moby-Dick* and his creation of his Kraken book, the short version of *Pierre*. But in a book as carefully crafted as *Pierre* had been, the Enceladus passage should have provided a complex reminder of, and variation on, a magnificent, and perfectly integrated, passage early in the book, Pierre's visit to the Memnon Stone. Instead, it is a great afterthought, unintegrated but awe-inspiring, great, but not as great as it should have been. For readers of *Pierre* as published but not as originally completed, the aesthetic lesson of the evidence is that it is folly to look for ways of seeing the Pierre-as-author pages as unified with the rest of the book. To find unity in the mixed product of ecstatic confidence and reckless defiance after failure is to trivialize Melville's aspiration, his achievement, and his wrecking of that achievement — to dehumanize Melville as man and artist while exalting a false image of a perfect verbal icon.

Before he was done with his additions, probably around the middle of February, Melville wrote the Harpers into the manuscript in an accusatory and self-accusatory fantasy: in book 26 Pierre receives this letter from his publishers:

> SIR: — You are a swindler. Upon the pretense of writing a popular novel for us, you have been receiving cash advances from us, while passing through our press the sheets of a blasphemous rhapsody, filched from the vile Atheists, Lucian and Voltaire. Our great press of publication has hitherto prevented our slightest inspection of our reader's proofs of your book. Send not another sheet to us. Our bill for printing thus far, and also for our cash advances, swindled out of us by you, is now in the hands of our lawyer, who is instructed to proceed with instant rigor.
>
> (Signed) STEEL, FLINT & ASBESTOS.

What the Harpers thought when they encountered this addition is not known; did they try to assign identities, betting on which one was Asbestos, and therefore equipped to survive even in Hell-fire? They had been unhappy even with the shorter manuscript and must have been appalled by the larger one. The wonder is that they honored the contract. By the time they published *Pierre* they were dropping the news into literary circles that they thought Melville was a little crazy, and they found reason to reject the next book Melville offered them, in June 1853. On 24 November 1853, when Melville offered the Harpers yet another book, he specified that his willingness to have them publish it was contingent on their writing a contract "on the old basis — half-profits" — not, he did not have to spell out, twenty cents on the dollar.

At the end, most likely, in a moment of calm at Arrowhead, Melville dedicated the book to "Greylock's Most Excellent Majesty," in gratitude for the mountain's "most bounteous and unstinted fertilizations." This was a fitting acknowledgment for the provocatives and preparatives instilled in him during the climbs and walks of a few months before. More than that, he could still work himself momentarily into the turbulent, exalted, boundlessly ambitious state that had exploded in him in the summer of 1850. Then past and present had collided, his childhood memories overlaid by his new experiences with Nathaniel Hawthorne, his futureless childhood replaced by international fame and a burgeoning awareness that he was attaining literary greatness such as no American, not Irving, the godfather of *Typee*, not even his new friend Hawthorne, had ever achieved. In December 1850 his head had been so full of literary projects that he appealed to Duyckinck to send him fifty fast-copying youthful scriveners to keep up with him: he had planned "about that number of future works" and could not "find enough time to think about them separately." Thirteen or fourteen months later, he was not ready to admit that his literary career was all but finished.

[5]

Richard Bentley
The Whale and *Pierre*, January–May 1852

      Misfortune's advantageous.

      In all Misfortunes this Advantage lies,
      They make us humble, & they make us wise;
      And he than can acquire such Virtues, gains
      An ample Recompence for all his pains.

"Allan Melvills Book," 1796 (William S. Reese Collection)

MELVILLE'S AUTHOR'S COPIES of *The Whale* arrived from England in January, judging from the timing of his gift of a set of *The Whale* (now at the Rosenbach Museum) to "Chief Justice Shaw / from H Melville / Jany: 1852." Nothing about the inscription shows whether Melville wrote it in New York or in Pittsfield, or, for that matter, Boston. Late in the month, perhaps on the birthday of Thomas Melville, twenty-two years old on the twenty-fourth, he inscribed a set of the two-volume Bentley edition of *Redburn* (now in the Berg Collection of the New York Public Library) to "Maria G. Melville / from Her Affectionate Son / Herman / Pittsfield, January, 1852" — thoughtfully writing on the page of the first volume which bore the dedication to Maria's baby, now in China or near that part of the world. Perhaps Bentley at Melville's request had sent an extra set of *Redburn* along with the sets of *The Whale*, directed either to Allan's office or to Pittsfield. When he unwrapped the books, Melville saw at a glance that Bentley had served the book well physically, for instead of the ugly binding and crowded pages of the American edition Bentley had offered the British public three volumes beautiful to see and to hold, although the author must have been bemused at the whale on the spines of the volumes, handsome, but no spermaceti whale. The London *Literary Gazette* (6 December 1851) had already had fun with the three spines: "Thrice unlucky Herman Melville! Three goodly volumes has he written, with the main purpose of honouring the Cachalot, and disparaging the *Mysticete*, and his publisher has sent them into the world in brilliant covers of blue and white, with three Greenland whales stamped in gold on their binding. How they spout! Three unmistakeable Mysticeti, sloping heads, and jaws fringed with long combs of baleen. Shade of extinguished spermaceti, how thy light has been put out by the bookbinders!" Like so much that was sparkling in the British reviews, this was something Melville probably never saw. And any pleasure in the books as physical objects was undercut by his rush to examine them and see for sure that the "Epilogue" was nowhere in the three volumes. Now at least he knew just what had happened to the "Etymology" and the "Extracts." Indeed, "Thrice unlucky Herman Melville!"

Meantime, Melville was still in close contact with the Hawthornes, who displayed their affection (and probably their dismay at the reviews of *Moby-Dick*) by encouraging Julian, aged six, to print a letter to Melville in which he conveyed his affection, not much diminished from its startling rank the previous August, when he had declared that he loved Mr. Melville as well as his father, his mamma, and Una (Rose not yet having taken human status in his consciousness). On 9 February Melville replied: "I am very happy that I have a place in the heart of so fine a little fellow as you." Julian had mentioned the snow in West Newton and in reply Melville wrote him that he had been in the woods "the other day," deep in "the drifts among the big hemlocks & maples"—the only known record of Melville's exerting himself physically for many weeks. The snow had been so deep that he thought he might "stick fast there till Spring came, a Snow Image"—a charming allusion to Hawthorne's collection of tales published in December 1851 (a book that "parents will love to give and children to receive," said the *Christian Register* two days after Christmas). Melville's affection for the Hawthorne children had been apparent in his letter to Sophia the month before ("Are all domestic affairs regulated? Is Miss Una content? And Master Julian satisfied with the landscape in general?"). The irony is that from this point forward there is no surviving record of Melville's behaving toward his own son Malcolm in the exuberantly tactile way of the year before, as if the failure of *Moby-Dick* and the impossible contract for *Pierre* had made Melville feel unworthy to show the same affection to Malcolm as before. In his absorption with his early work on *Pierre*, his worries about Lizzie's health, and his fears about his debts, he may never have felt for Stanwix anything like the joyous love he had felt and openly displayed toward Malcolm. It was as if having failed as a provider (and failed more profoundly than anyone but Allan knew) he had no right to any joys of fatherhood.

Whatever inner turmoil Melville was experiencing, his return signaled the regathering of the family at Arrowhead and a resumption of tensions specific to that household. It had taken time for the Melvilles and for the wider circle of aunts and uncles and cousins to realize just how sick Lizzie had been after Stanwix's birth. After hearing of her illness from Augusta, Nilly Thayer called at the Shaw house in January 1852 and was not admitted to see Lizzie but was told by a servant that "she had almost entirely recovered and was much benefitted by the change of air." Caroline Shaw, the wife of Lizzie's older brother, John Oakes Shaw, stopped by at Mt. Vernon Street with their children (the lame Josephine and John Oakes Jr.) while Lizzie was there in January. Caroline, apparently without seeing Lizzie, went away thinking she had both Malcolm and Stanwix with her. A garbled account of the events reached Bath, Maine, where Melville's Aunt Lucy and her husband, Dr. Amos Nourse, were specially concerned, having loved Lizzie ever since her vacations with them in her girlhood. Dr. Nourse wrote Shaw on 18 February: "We have heard indirectly from time to time of Elizabeth, that she was feeble, & did not regain her strength after confinement as at the birth of her first child — that some weeks, perhaps months ago, she went to Boston in the hope of being able to avail herself there of more auspicious agencies in the work of restoration." They had heard, also, that Melville had gone to Boston to bring her home. Judging from Hope Savage Shaw's diary, Lizzie returned from Boston on 12 February on the railroad, with only a maid to help her care for Stanwix, with no male escort, but Hope may simply not have listed her son-in-law as a member of the party. Panicked about money, deeply engaged in his last expansions and patching the whole book together, Melville may have avoided going to Boston and bringing his wife home — an evasion of his simple duty far worse than dumping his mother and her trunk at the Pittsfield depot early in 1851. On 1 March Dr. Nourse expressed their gratification at "the good tidings of Elizabeth's restoration," but offered a professional concern: "Her husband I fear is devoting himself to writing with an assiduity that will cost him dear by & by." Lizzie may have been distressed at arriving home to find Helen (newly returned from Lansingburgh and Albany) at work, copying behind Melville, a reenactment of 1848, when she had gone to Boston thinking *Mardi* was completed and it was safe to leave him.

Melville would not have admitted to Lizzie the full story of the ruinous terms of the Harper contract: at least he had a contract and could hope for greater sales from a wider market than his sea-books had attained. Melville had borrowed $2050 from Stewart without telling her and had counted on repaying it fast, out of profits from *Moby-Dick*, without her or her father's knowing. He had put himself on false footing with his wife and with her father, his benefactor. It is inconceivable that Melville told his wife but demanded she keep the secret from her family, a situation which would have created, in the months since May 1851, terrible tensions between "Typee" and his "Dolly." Therefore any manifestations of his guilt — deflected into excessive irritation or bursts of anger—must have seemed to Lizzie and other members of the household abnormal or outright inexplicable. Very angry, his mother described his reaction to the local gossip about *Moby-Dick* as blasphemous. Very angry, anyone would have said, seeing him make Evert Duyckinck the object of satire in pages he wrote in New York. His letters to Sophia Hawthorne and to Julian sound normal—a coolness achieved at the price of intense denial of what had happened to him since the week the Hawthornes left Lenox. One way or another, however, Melville's having borrowed the money from Stewart created tensions at Arrowhead. Those tensions lie behind the fact that two days after Lizzie's return Melville wrote one of the more abrupt messages of his life, not to Evert and George Duyckinck but coldly to the nameless "Editors" of the *Literary World:* "You will please discontinue the two copies of your paper sent to J. M. Fly at Brattleboro' (or Greenbush), and to H Melville at Pittsfield. Whatever charges there may be outstanding for either or both copies, please send them to me, & they will receive attention." Melville had realized that picking up his copy of the *Literary World* at the post office every week was too painful to bear. Perhaps he simply was near enough to the end of the book to face the consequences of publishing his satire on Duyckinck. This was the end, Melville thought, of his career-long involvement with the Duyckincks and their ephemeral self-serving (or Mathews-promoting!) periodicals. Insultingly, it seemed to him, the Duyckinck brothers kept sending the paper.

Melville finished his enlargement of *Pierre* in mid-February and shipped the now-expanded manuscript to Allan, who met with the Harpers on Friday, 20 February, to sign the contract. The original contingency clause about the number of pages being "much less or much more than 360" adequately covered the increased length of the manuscript, so the contract was copied out and signed as it had stood in early January: "It is understood that the said work will contain about 360 pages 12mo and it is agreed that the publishing price of said work is to be fixed at one dollar per copy, and that the proceeds of 1190 copies will be required to liquidate the cost of the stereotype plates." The Harpers raised the price to $1.25 to help pay the costs of a longer book (making Melville's share a quarter a book), but they let 1190 stand as the number of copies to be sold to cover their expenses. The Harpers had been prompt with their accounting, as Melville had requested, and they now paid Melville $500, partly earnings from earlier books, partly an advance on *Pierre*. The only holdup now was for Melville to fulfill his part of the eighth clause of the contract: "The said Harper & Brothers agree to furnish the said Herman Melville with a corrected proof of the said work as soon as it can be struck off and to defer the publication thereof until after the time fixed for its publication in England; Provided they shall be at liberty to publish said book at any time after the expiration of three months from the delivery of perfect proof as aforesaid." Richard Bentley, who had always been prompt and courteous, had not replied to Melville's "Note" mailed to him from New York early in January. Now Melville had reason to mark time: if he did not hear from London, he would have a fresh excuse to write Bentley when he had a set of the Harper proofs.

During Melville's absence in New York, Maria's church attendance had been regular and, weather permitting, she had socialized more than usual while her recalcitrant son was away. Because Helen and Augusta were also away, Maria had been able to focus on her younger daughters and their prospects. Since 1848 John C. Hoadley had lived in Pittsfield, associated with Gordon McKay in the firm of McKay & Hoadley, "designing and constructing steam engines, water wheels, and other machinery." Hoadley was a known quantity, since he was a professed Christian and a member of the congregation at St. Stephen's, the Episcopal church Uncle Thomas had attended and which Maria placidly attended in the absence of a Dutch church, tolerant of doctrinal differences. (She may not have taken communion there, for while living in Lansingburgh she had made a point of observing that sacrament with her Van Rensselaer cousins at the Dutch church in Albany.) A young widower, a self-made man, Hoadley had smoothed off the rough edges year by year until he was remarkably polished, polite, and conciliatory in Pittsfield society, for all the independence and non-confrontational strength of some of his unconventional views. Politically active, he had helped organize the great union meeting Orville Dewey had addressed just after Christmas 1850. A man with literary attainments, Hoadley had declaimed some of his unexceptionable verse with aplomb at the dedication of the new cemetery in August 1850 (when he shared the stage with Sarah Morewood and others). He read one of his poems to the Library Association at West's Hall on 5 February 1852, his last public appearance in Pittsfield before leaving, that month, to take charge of the Lawrence Machine Shop, a large concern, employing at times as many as 750 men. There in the next years he designed and constructed "woolen, cotton, and paper machinery, water wheels, stationary steam engines, and locomotives," according to the *Transactions of the American Society of Mechanical Engineers* (vol. 8); by the mid-1850s he was advertising a fine printing press. If Sophia had kept Kate with her through more of 1851, he might have gotten away from Pittsfield unentangled.

Up to this point, and considerably afterward, nothing survives to show that any of the Melville family knew of Hoadley's existence, and Kate, the Melville sister he married in 1853, had not even been at Arrowhead until the previous April, when *Moby-Dick* was nearing completion. But Hoadley had met the women, at least, at church and surely at tea at one house or another, very likely Broadhall, since he and Sarah were acquainted. The women were immensely taken with him, and he with Kate. In Herman's absence, with Helen and Augusta both away, Hoadley took his chance to pay serious court to Kate Melville. Maria welcomed him: he was successful in business as well as an amateur literary-man (the only safe kind, given the economics of being a writer in America), he was a Christian, and he was refreshingly and perhaps reassuringly unlike the Melville men in his personal manner. That manner took some getting used to, for unlike Gansevoort, unlike Herman when aroused, Hoadley was "a slow, low talker, rhetorical, poetical, philosophical" (according to a paper called the *Ledger*, sometime after February 1861). From Lawrence on 22 March 1852 Hoadley wrote the piece called "Berry Pond" for J. E. A. Smith's Berkshire collection, *Taghconic*. There he recalled the "heaven-clad hills" with an "ennobling majesty" which stood round about Pittsfield " 'as the mountains are round about Jerusalem' " in order to contrast them with the "dead sand plains, or faintly swelling hills" of northeastern Massachusetts — fine writing, a touch pantheistic or religiose, but never approaching blasphemy, unlike Herman. The Berkshires, he wrote, loomed "over the length of a state in the soft mirage of memory," looking "lovelier, holier than ever." In the soft mirage of Hoadley's memory Kate Melville also looked lovelier. By character she was the least desirable of the Melville "girls," but Helen was already being wooed, in lethargic fashion, by a Boston lawyer she had met long before while staying at the Shaw house; Augusta had broken two engagements in her early maturity and was a bad risk; and Fanny was pathologically shy. Hoadley was a matrimonial prize. The opinion the Melville women held of Hoadley rose later that year, when he revisited the Berkshires to receive the honorary degree of A.M. from Williams College. Herman, family legend had it, disapproved on the grounds that Kate deserved a man who had not been married before — curious if true, coming from the inventor or describer of Fayaway.

Fayaway's historian was now a struggling family man in need of patient copyists, and apt to frustrate his copyists by his erratic behavior. Helen had agreed to be copyist, and had labored through Christmas before taking herself off to Lansingburgh. Augusta, in New York for a change of scene and to assist Sophia during the middle months of her third pregnancy, had been pressed into service there as copyist, to Sophia's astringent amusement, although Herman may have carried some manuscript pages with him back to Arrowhead for Helen to copy. After that, Augusta spent February with the Blatchfords in New York, as a mourning duty to the family of her friend Mary, who had died the previous year about the same time as Aunt Mary Chandonette Gansevoort, when Augusta had been at the Manor House. Maria wrote Augusta about "Poor Mary Blatchford" on 6 March 1852: "How vividly must you have brought to mind our similar bereavement." Gansevoort, Maria's noble and ever-lamented son, who had never expressed an irreverent thought, was as much as ever the family ideal by which Herman was measured and found lacking. Augusta received her mother's letter at the Manor House of the Van Rensselaers. Sophia wrote her there: "I suppose you are congratulating yourself on being nicely rid of assisting Herman with his book." Herman's shifting demands had confused Augusta and Helen both. Although the Bond Street sister-in-law had her crotchets, she was genuinely hospitable; but at the great Manor House "Gus's room" was kept unoccupied, ready for her — the purest evidence of her value to any household.

Augusta had delighted Maria by writing her that a spirit of revival was sweeping Albany, and had awakened her mother's hopes that "that an interest in this greatest of all concerns would come in our midst," into the village of Pittsfield in general and Arrowhead in particular. Maria's religious fervor, fanned all the previous year, was unabated. In her 6 March letter to Augusta she included a mildly worded but charged account of what she had gotten Herman to do:

> We that is Herman, Lizzie, Helen & I took tea at Dr Chapman's this week, pass'd a pleasant Eveg — The Do^r has taken a great fancy to Herman. The majority of the congregation or I should say to my knowledge but one of the members object to him, all wish the Doc^r to remain among us ... his whole heart & soul is with his church, & he would be willing to do any thing for its welfare. This very feeling operates to remove our Doctor, because he thinks a younger man would visit more & that the congregation would increase more rapidly with an energetic young Clergyman who would mix more generally with the families of the congregation.

The most ominous element in all this was the assertion that the minister of St. Stephen's, Dr. George T. Chapman, had taken a great fancy to Herman, the mildest reading of which means that he was determined to bring him into regular attendance in his congregation and save his soul.

Temporarily placated by Herman's new docility, Maria expressed herself less agitatedly than she had done in December when contrasting the great Hungarian Kossuth with her irreverent son. She sounded, as she said, sanguine: "But I am sanguine & hope to see the day when all my belove'd children will in truth & sincerity openly come forward before the world and proclaim themselves on the side of God, feeling in their hearts their own unworthiness, trusting in the atonement of their blessed Redeemer Jesus Christ, believing fully in his promises. May God in his great mercy thus guide & direct them." She had been listening to gossip in Pittsfield for many months, had recently been reading and hearing about reviews of *Moby-Dick*, and was rarely sanguine for long. In these weeks Herman lived every day in her fervid evangelical glow, however banked. Arrowhead was a tense house.

The 6 March letter Maria wrote Augusta testifies to other tensions in the family. Augusta had apparently relayed an expression of warm feelings from Sophia to Kate, who, "wonder struck" at the information, said, "why last summer I thought Sophia had taken a positive dislike to me, she is a strange woman." Because the winter had begun ferociously in November, shortly after Stanwix's birth, Maria despite her freedom to drive out with Charlie, the old safe horse, was feeling confined at Arrowhead by March, what with the presence of Herman and Lizzie, the small boys, her other three daughters, and at least a cook and David, the hired man, besides Lizzie's "nurse" or maid. Everyone else except Kate and Fanny had gotten away on visits, even Lizzie and Stanwix, although the Boston trip could not be called a pure vacation except by a mother-in-law. Maria was annoyed with what Sophia (six months pregnant) had written her: she had kindly urged Maria "to make them a visit now, & remain until they are ready to move" — but *only* until then. Restless like her second son, ambivalent, and obscurely discontent, Maria remembered her vow the year before not to go back to New York in the bad weather of March. She could remind herself how wretched the city was in March and still be annoyed that Sophia was not entreating her to visit them and *stay on* to direct the move. Maria groused: "Sophia is peculiar in some things . . . but she is good in her way altho a little Aunt 'Catherineness'; as Allan often jestingly tells her." "Often" and "jestingly" are ominous indications of tensions between Allan and Sophia, and especially ominous because they may fit a family pattern in which Herman also at times jested about Lizzie's failings, challenging her, his oldest granddaughter thought. And Allan made this jest often in his mother's presence. It would never do for one of Maria's daughters-in-law to be her equal in every way.

Caught between two strong women, Allan found it easier to criticize his wife than to rebuke his mother. To accuse someone of Aunt Catherineness, in this family, was to evoke the tyrannical wife of poor Uncle Herman, the woman who had unforgivably refused to let sweet docile ten-year-old Herman spend his vacation at the Mansion House in Gansevoort — and incidentally the aging woman who now stood between Maria and a home of her own. It was also to confess himself henpecked. The fact that Allan criticized his wife in what passed as jest conveys the edginess of the boy who had lived in rented rooms before he married the girl from Bond Street. Sophia, seven months pregnant, was proving herself a young woman who had learned early that if you had enough money you could pretty much get your own way except in matters of health. Once again she politely declined Maria's "offered assistance" in moving, accommodating herself to Allan's upward and uptown strivings. Among Sophia's peculiarities was that she regarded moving "as a sort of 'pleasing excitement' " instead of the chaotic horror reasonable people considered it. (Seeing that there was no hope of establishing immediate "beautiful order," Augusta had sensibly taken to her bed after the move to Arrowhead in October 1850.) Maria's letter is elliptical on some points, so we do not know quite what Sophia did to release Augusta "from considerable care & responsibility"; perhaps she just did not insist that she come back to her after visiting the Blatchfords. Peculiarly, Sophia wanted a little time in her own house with her husband and her children and her servants. She did not get it.

A woman with two small children, invaded intermittently by her writer brother-in-law who demanded space, service, and her husband's attention, and until the previous April housing a young unmarried woman whose compulsive behavior had become very hard to bear, Sophia may well have expressed some impatience during the previous summer. Only someone obligated to love Kate, one would have thought, or only a besotted young widower in need of a wife from a distinguished family, could endure a woman who became high strung if she had to eat off a tablecloth that was infinitesimally awry, or had to sit at dinner in front of a castor in which a cruet was not in the proper geometrical position. By contrast, Sophia could live easily even if the vinegar cruet did not face the Church of the Ascension. In her last letter Sophia had said nothing about Kate's returning to New York and nothing about Augusta's plans to leave for Albany. Kate was, nevertheless, "expecting a note from Sophia next week." Offended now by Sophia's casual refusal to kowtow or even to put herself out when she did not want to, Maria restlessly raked over Sophia's sayings and doings not only with Augusta but with Kate, and very likely with the others.

On 6 March, while the Morewoods were making a winter visit, Herman, Lizzie, and Helen went to spend the evening at Broadhall, but they had little time to settle into the old routines, for Herman decided to go to New York. Word from England precipitated Melville's decision. Bentley, appalled at the prospect of trying to market a new book of Melville's while *The Whale* was still being reviewed, put the early January letter aside until he could bring his accounts up to date. Then on 3 March by mistake a clerk sent Melville a half-finished letter and an account of the publisher's losses on his editions of Melville. The next day Bentley wrote to apologize for the "most ridiculous Blunder." He was conciliatory but wary, in the surviving letterbook copy, thanking Melville for the offer of his new work, but telling him frankly that by *Mardi* he had lost £68.7.6, by *Redburn* £76.7.6, by *White-Jacket* £173.9.6, and by *The Whale* £135.9.6, for a total of £453.4.6. The books were still selling, so that he had hope of making another £100 from sales, leaving a loss of some £350. Multiply by five for the dollar equivalent and that was enough to support many American households comfortably for two years. Bentley nevertheless made an offer: "Your books, I fear, are produced in too rapid succession. It was not long ago since The Whale was published—not time sufficient has yet been given to it, before another is ready! Under the circumstances, I put the matter to you whether your new book should not be put into my hands to publish on our joint account; I yielding to you half the profits as they arise. For my sake I shall do the best for it—in fact no publisher can do more for it than I can." This offer of half-profits was magnanimous, given not only the state of the copyright law but also the enormous sums Melville had cost Bentley. The letter probably reached Melville well before the end of March. Up to that time, he was hoping that although he had accepted a punitive contract from his New York publisher at least he might do as well as ever with his English publisher. If he accepted Bentley's terms, no advance for *Pierre* would be forthcoming from London and it would be a long time before any profits could be expected. In May, an interest payment to Stewart was due. The letter was friendly but devastating; no wonder Melville could not bear to keep it in his file of business letters.

Melville's decision to go to New York again was unexpected, but not the most surprising part of the news. Sophia wrote Augusta on 16 March: "But just think of Lizzie's coming to New York." Before mailing Sophia's letter on 18 March, Allan added that "Herman was expected" that day, although Allan was "fearful the storm will detain him." He careted in "& Lizzie" after Herman, but left the verb "was"; maybe they could hardly believe that Lizzie would actually leave both children, although she had been forced to wean the baby in December. What Herman expected to do in New York was to read proofs and make his necessary trips back and forth to the compositors from Allan and Sophia's new place at 47 East Twenty-fourth Street rather than trying to supervise corrections from Pittsfield. Lizzie's role may have been to help with the proofreading, so that they would make at least twice the speed. The early proofs were probably waiting when Herman and Lizzie got to town, since they finished the proofreading by the middle of April.

About the time Herman and Elizabeth arrived in the city, the April issue of *Harper's New Monthly Magazine* appeared with a welcome item quoting the review of *The Whale* in the London *Leader* (8 November 1851): "Want of originality has long been the just and standing reproach to American literature; the best of its writers were but second-hand Englishmen. Of late some have given evidence of originality; not *absolute* originality, but such genuine outcoming of the American intellect as can be safely called national. Edgar Poe, Nathaniel Hawthorne, Herman Melville are assuredly no British offshoots; nor is Emerson—the *German* American that he is!" These writers had in common the power to "move a horror skilfully, with something of the earnest faith in the Unseen, and with weird imagery to shape these phantasms so vividly that the most incredulous mind is hushed, absorbed—to do this no European pen has apparently any longer the power—to do this American literature is without a rival." The reviewer (perhaps George Lewes) asked, "What *romance* writer can be named with Hawthorne? Who knows the horrors of the seas like Herman Melville?" After the Harpers were through with this issue of the *Leader*, they may have given it to Allan, for at some time he transcribed a different passage into his copy of *Moby-Dick*, at the beginning of chapter 42: "There is a chapter on the 'Whiteness of the Whale' which should be read at midnight alone with nothing heard but the sounds of the wind moaning without, and the embers falling into the grate within. London *Leader.*" This may have been as much as the family ever knew of the best that was said about *The Whale* in London.

Buoyed a little by this public report, Melville consulted Allan about the implications of his recent news from Bentley. Maybe he hoped Allan could see some loophole that he did not see, some way of saving his career. At other times he might have tried to find another English publisher, but now he did not. On 5 April Melville wrote a letter to his first publisher, John Murray, introducing his brother-in-law Lemuel, who was taking the grand tour. Melville hoped it might lie in the publisher's power "to extend his views of life in your metropolis." He concluded with this assurance: "You will find Mr Shaw —as a New-Englander and Bostonian—peculiarly ready to appreciate & admire all that you can show him of what is admirable and enjoyable in England"—something of a covert dig, given his disdain of Bostonian flunkeyness. At the same time he wrote the same sort of note for Lemuel to Bentley, probably making no reference in it to business matters, although he by then had received Bentley's offer. On 2 May, Lemuel Shaw wrote to his son and namesake in London, giving news some two weeks old: "Elizabeth & her husband have returned to Pittsfield, she was glad to get home, & still more to find her children well & improving." On 30 May, Amos Nourse wrote Lemuel Shaw, grateful for $210.89 from old Thomas Melvill's estate: "We were rejoiced to hear of Elizabeth's well-being & well-doing. Hope she will not this time get so enfeebled as before" (that is, during the approaching allergy season).

As it happened, Sophia was not only hospitable to Herman and Lizzie, she also asked Kate to return, and paid her a remarkable compliment. Augusta went there as well, as Maria wrote to her sister-in-law Susan Gansevoort on 18 May, from Arrowhead: "Sophia has another daughter [on 30 April] & she has named it 'Catherine,' after Kate, who is also to be godmother. Kate is much flatter'd by the compliment." Fatigued from the move to Twenty-fourth Street, Sophia had been lying down when the earth caved in on workmen digging a drain outside, "carrying with it a large tree & almost burying them, their heads were only visible they swear'd most lustily, & some men came with their spades & fell to, to extricate them, in five minutes a great crowd had assembled and with the aid of ropes they were drawn out uninjured, as far as anything serious was concerned, But the excitement had been sufficient to throw Sophia into a most violent agitation, and the Doctor & nurse had to be summon'd." At one time Sophia's pulse was gone, and Augusta thought she was dying. Maria remembered her *Macbeth*, a little inexactly: "Troubles & accidents it is said never come alone, but in battalions." At least she had good news from Arrowhead: "The trees[?] & flowering ash & the shrubs are growing finely their leaves have opened and they are doing well. Herman & Lizzie send much love in which the girls join." Herman, she added, hoped that they all were coming to Arrowhead to see them—a pretty clear indication that Herman was not even brooding about a new writing project.

Herman had two old projects, *Moby-Dick* and *Pierre*, still not quite off his mind. What Melville knew and what Richard Bentley knew about *The Whale* were an ocean apart. Bentley knew that the opening of the Crystal Palace the week of the publication of *The Whale* had crowded it from the columns of papers and magazines that would ordinarily have reviewed the new Melville book, and some periodicals were simply erratic, as when the London *Globe* chose to review *The Cow* by M. M. Milburn (6 November) but never found space for *The Whale*. Bentley saw some reviews that no biographer of Melville has seen, for when he gathered some of the best phrases from the early ones in a large advertisement in the London *Morning Post* (14 November) he quoted the *Athenæum*, *John Bull*, the *Spectator*, the *Morning Advertiser*, and the *Britannia*, as well as an unidentified "Evening paper" that called the work "the raciest thing of the kind that was ever produced." He knew, as Melville did not, that *The Whale* had received two dozen or so extraordinary reviews in London.

Yet Bentley may have been as confused as Melville in one particular. Having delegated the expurgation of the book and presumably the handling of what had been the prefatory material, Bentley may never have realized that there had been an "Epilogue" which had been lost either in the process of unpacking the proofs (perhaps stuck with wax to the wrapping paper), or in the later process of moving the "Etymology" and "Extracts" from the start of volume 1 to the back of volume 3 (where it may have been crumpled at the bottom of the pile of "sheets" the way the last piece in a tall stack of paper always gets crumpled after the pile has been moved about a few times). If he had realized that the fault was not Melville's, he could have made a humorous apology, taking the blame on himself in manly fashion, thereby gaining more publicity for the book even while guaranteeing a fairer evaluation of it. He could have quickly printed up a page with the "Epilogue" to tip into unsold volumes and to give to the press and early buyers of the book, much as Murray had printed "The Story of Toby" in the same format as his *Marquesas*. Nothing like that happened—an indication that Bentley had not learned what went wrong, and therefore was the less disposed to go out of his way to take yet another chance on Melville.

Even if the ending had not been lost, *The Whale* would have posed problems for London reviewers, all of whom approached a Bentley triple-decker with specific expectations. The *New Quarterly Review* (First Quarter, 1852) threw up the matter: "Many, doubtless, will cavil at the application of the term 'novel' to such a production as this, seeing that no tale of love is interwoven with the strange ana of which it is compounded. Still we cannot trouble ourselves to devise for it a happier term." There was striking agreement that the book was (in the phrase in the *Morning Chronicle* on 20 December) *sui generis*. The uniqueness was a problem, but few reviewers denied out of hand Melville's right to mix genres, if only he had managed the mixture tactfully. Several London reviewers applauded Melville's triumph in bringing unlikely and recalcitrant materials and dangerous styles under firm literary control. *John Bull* (25 October) said that praise was "the more abundantly due" because the artist had succeeded "in investing objects apparently the most unattractive with an absorbing fascination." Observing that if "Captain Ahab was bewitched by Moby Dick, Mr. Melville is not the less spell-bound by Leviathan in general," the *Atlas* (1 November) declared that the "mass of knowledge touching the whale" was all "written in a tone of exaltation and poetic sentiment which has a strange effect upon the reader's mind in refining and elevating the subject of discourse, and at last making him look upon the whale as a sort of awful and unsoluble mystery." The *Morning Post* (14 November) triumphed over its uneasiness: "Judgment is occasionally shocked by the improbable character of the incidents narrated—and even reason is not always treated with the punctilious deference she has a right to expect—but imagination is banqueted on celestial fare, and delight, top-gallant delight, is the sensation with which the reader is most frequently familiar." Others besides *John Bull* cheerfully acknowledged the charm of what "may not fall within the ordinary canons of beauty." As the *Leader* said, "Criticism may pick many holes in this work; but no criticism will thwart its fascination."

Because what Bentley later referred to as a "judicious literary friend" had expurgated the text expertly, in the reviews of *The Whale* there was only one known complaint about "heathenish talk" and "thrusts against revealed religion," and that a restrained remark in *John Bull*. The "friend" had also taken out some needlessly inflammatory republican references to royalty and had made the book more palatable by altering some of the Americanisms. *John Bull* defended all "that is idiomatically American" in the tone of Melville's sentiments and "in the slang which runs through his discourse," as if what was left was just enough to spice the book. Nevertheless, the *Britannia* (8 November) thought that "a few Americanisms" sometimes marred "the perspicuity and purity of the style," in which the language was otherwise "appropriate and impressive." Despite being spared some of the worst affronts to good taste, some London reviewers found it hard to deal with Melville's mixture of styles, particularly his indulging in rhapsodic writing appropriate perhaps for one inferior sort of work, an "extravaganza," but not for a novel. The *Spectator* (25 October) sorted out some varieties: "The rhapsody belongs to wordmongering where ideas are the staple, where it takes the shape of narrative or dramatic fiction, it is phantasmal—an attempted description of what is impossible in nature and without probability in art." Though praising Melville for showing in *The Whale* his most thorough "command over the strength and the beauties of our language," the *Atlas* (1 November) lamented his "besetting sin of extravagance": "Extravagance is the bane of the book, and the stumbling block of the author. He allows his fancy not only to run riot, but absolutely to run amuck, in which poor defenceless Common Sense is hustled and belaboured in a manner melancholy to contemplate. Mr. Melville is endowed with a fatal facility for the writing of rhapsodies. Once embarked on a flourishing topic, he knows not when or how to stop." As a random example of Melville's "maundering with the pen in the hand," the reviewer cited Stubb's long soliloquy in "The Doubloon" (ch. 99).

The omission of the "Epilogue" from *The Whale* forced British reviewers to read a book in which the first-person narrator seemed to perish at the end, so they could only assume that Melville was either ignorant of basic narrative conventions or else willfully reckless of literary proprieties. The reviewer in the *Spectator* certainly did, in his indictment of the catastrophe, which overrode all rule in destroying the narrator with the rest of the crew and the ship. In a tone of baffled fascination John Francis Waller in the *Dublin University Magazine* (February 1852) complained that all "the rules which have been hitherto understood to regulate the composition of works of fiction are despised and set at naught"; one of those rules was that narrators should survive to tell the tale: "he [Ishmael] was present at those scenes which he so vividly described, or else he could not have described them at all; he must also necessarily have been present, too, at the final catastrophe, or how could he have known anything about it?—and if he was present when the whale smashed the ship to pieces, capsized the boats, and drowned every mother's son among the crew, how does it happen that the author is alive to tell the story? Eh! Mr. Melville, answer that question, if you please." Other British critics made sport of the situation, as the *Literary Gazette* did on 6 December: "How the imaginary writer, who appears to have been drowned with the rest, communicated his notes for publication to Mr. Bentley is not explained." The damage caused by the loss of the "Epilogue" was insidious, for some critics who did not specifically condemn the defective catastrophe seem to have had it in mind when pointing out violations of rules of fiction elsewhere in *The Whale*. Melville's characterization, for instance, was not a topic easy to treat with comprehensive sympathy when the narrator seemed to perish with the rest of the crew, especially not for the few reviewers who talked of the narrator as if he were Melville himself.

British reviewers were concerned with *The Whale* as a phenomenal literary work, a philosophical, metaphysical, and poetic romance, not primarily as a source of practical information about the whale fisheries, which was a high concern with many American reviewers. (An exception is the only known Scottish review, in the Edinburgh *Evening Courant* [25 November], which said the information about "a fishing voyage in the South Seas" was "the only redeeming point in the work, for assuredly both the story and the style are sufficiently absurd.") The *Morning Advertiser* (24 October) praised Melville's learning (as evinced in "Cetology"), his "dramatic ability for producing a prose poem" (evinced in "The Whiteness of the Whale" and "The Quarter-Deck") as well as the "whale adventures wild as dreams, and powerful in their cumulated horrors." The *Morning Post* declared: "There is a wild and wonderful fascination in the story against which no man may hope to secure himself into whose intellectual composition the faculty called fancy has in any degree entered." Reviewers said that no work had been "more honourable to American literature" (*Morning Advertiser*), that *The Whale* was "far beyond the level of an ordinary work of fiction" (*John Bull*), that it was "a book of extraordinary merit, and one which will do great things for the literary reputations of its author" and was "one of the cleverest, wittiest, and most amusing of modern books" (*Morning Post*), and that it was "certainly one of the most remarkable books that has appeared many years past" (*Bentley's*, January 1852).

Wasting no time on comparisons to writers of nautical fiction, the London reviewers described the affinities of *The Whale* to works by masters of English style. The *Morning Advertiser* said that the "whalers' hostelrie and its inmates" in chapter 3 were "pencilled with the mastery and minuteness of Washington Irving" (by then accounted almost an English writer). Furthermore, Ishmael's reflection that a "good laugh is a mighty good thing, and rather too scarce a good thing" (ch. 5) was reminiscent of Charles Lamb, while through the middle of the book one could find now "a Carlylism of phrase," then a quaintness suggestive of Sir Thomas Browne, "and anon a heap of curious out-of-the-way learning after the fashion of the Burton who 'anatomised' melancholy." The reviewer in the *Athenæum* (25 October), for all his hostility, identified "a wild humorous poetry in some of his terrors which distinguishes him from the vulgar herd of fustian-weavers. For instance, his interchapter on 'The Whiteness of the Whale' is full of ghostly suggestions for which a Maturin or a Monk Lewis would have been thankful." As "a fit prelude to the thrilling pages of Melville's *Whale*," the reviewer in the *Leader* printed "a splendid passage from our greatest prose writer, descriptive of the superstitious nature of sailors—(you divine that we are to quote from De Quincey)." The reviewer did not spell out what he felt was obvious—that the passage from the greatest prose writer of contemporary England could well have been lifted from *The Whale*, not only because of the coincidence of subject matter but also because some of Melville's greatest prose was patently—and brilliantly—De Quinceyan. The writer in the *Leader* and his fellow London reviewers most often acted as if *The Whale*, whatever its faults, belonged in the finest literary company.

Some of the London reviews revealed unrestrained joy in Melville's special qualities. *Bell's New Weekly Messenger* and the *News of the World* (both 2 November) ran the same review, a remarkable identification of what constitutes a lover of Melville: "There are people who delight in mulligatawny. They love curry at its warmest point. Ginger cannot be too hot in the mouth for them. Such people, we should think, constitute the admirers of Herman Melville." There was, all in all, a feeling of delight manifested toward *The Whale*, as in *Reynolds's Newspaper: A Weekly Journal of Politics, History, Literature, and General Intelligence* (21 December): "This is a most agreeable and exciting work, in three volumes, quaintly told, but full of life and anecdote." Part of it was simply the exotic experiences Melville purveyed, as the *Weekly Times* (2 November) indicated by saying that Melville stood "alone in his peculiar celebrity, that of enabling the public to obtain glimpses of the private life and confidential transactions of seamen and their companions." "Top-gallant delight," the *Morning Post* had said. That *The Whale* was one of the notable works of the London publishing season in 1851 is proved by several explicit comments, such as the willingness of the *Morning Advertiser* to put "Loomings" (ch. 1) "against the same amount of prose in any book of fiction for the last dozen years, with a couple of exceptions, which we shall keep to ourselves." For so many of the London reviewers to praise the work offered to them in truncated form was a triumph of their own—a triumph of acute literary sensibility and human decency over a masterpiece slightly botched by the author and then mangled in being sent to England and published there. Testimony from decades later suggests that it occasioned much ardent discussion, but neither the initial printed commentary nor whatever conversations the volumes inspired among literary-minded Londoners was sufficient to establish it in public record as a book of *more* than one season. And Bentley lost money on it.

Melville lived out his life without knowing that many London papers late in 1851 told their readers that the prolific and interesting young American sea-writer had now written his most ambitious and most successful book. If he had known just how respectful many of the British reviewers were, as early as October and November 1851, he would have been better armed against the self-righteous provinciality of Evert Duyckinck and the personal savagery of other reviewers, then better equipped to abandon the original *Pierre* to its fate as a little book and go on to write something different. Instead, what he knew was that British reviewers (all of them? most of them?) had denounced his catastrophe as impossible, and time may have passed between his seeing what the Boston *Post* quoted from the *Athenæum* before he saw the reprint of the *Spectator* review and fully accepted that they were denouncing him for a real literary sin, although not one that he was guilty of. How could a reviewer give the benefit of the doubt to Melville and say, "Something must have gone wrong in the printing of this volume?" After all, the publisher was the respected Bentley and the author was the man who had blithely violated cardinal rules of genre-purity in *Mardi*. Melville was in no position to speculate that other reviewers might have praised the book despite the baffling ending: he could only go by what was reprinted in the United States.

On 16 April Allan Melville sent Richard Bentley a set of proofs of *Pierre* along with a letter from his brother written earlier on the same day, Herman's reply to Bentley's proposition of 4 March. What Melville wrote was a long, maundering, specious, self-justifying, begging, try-anything letter. He had deferred replying, he explained, until he could send the book before reconsidering the terms of half-profits which Bentley had laid down. Melville could not put the poor sales of his earlier books in a good light, yet tentatively suggested that "by subsequent sales the balance-sheet may yet be made to wear a different aspect." He still dared to hope that "the success, (in a business point of view) of any subsequent work" of his would carry off some of "those previous books" along with it. Now he could not possibly bring himself "to accede to the overtures" Bentley had made, since he insisted on seeing the damning figures of costs and losses as likely to be corrected by future sales of his books. Then he moved to an argument concerning *Pierre* itself, which now Bentley would have a chance to read:

> And more especially am I impelled to decline those overtures upon the ground that my new book possessing unquestionable novelty, as regards my former

ones,—treating of utterly new scenes & characters;—and, as I beleive, very much more calculated for popularity than anything you have yet published of mine—being a regular romance, with a mysterious plot to it, & stirring passions at work, and withall, representing a new & elevated aspect of American life—all these considerations warrant me strongly in not closing with terms greatly inferior to those upon which our previous negotiations have proceeded.—Besides,—if you please, Mr Bentley—let bygones be bygones; let those previous books, for the present, take care of themselves. For here now we have a *new book*, and what shall we say about *this?*

It was "a larger book, by 150 pages & more," he pleaded, than when he first wrote in January, and therefore Bentley might more readily visualize it as one of his customary triple-deckers: "Other things being equal, this circumstance,—in your mode of publication—must of course augment its value to you." In calculatingly calling attention to the total length of the book, Melville, wittingly or not, seems to have exaggerated the number of pages he had added. He urged Bentley to take the book outright for one hundred pounds ("for England"), and laid out his vision of "the new feild of productions" upon which he had embarked in *Pierre*, and where he and Bentley would "hereafter participate in many not unprofitable business adventures" (meaning something close to "ventures," the way "avocation" still meant "vocation," as he used in "Bartleby" the next year).

Melville added a postscript telling Bentley to publish without further correspondence if he agreed to pay Melville a hundred pounds for the copyright, and that Bentley need not worry about some other English publisher getting a copy of the book: Melville had sent him proofs made even before the book was plated, and he would "suspend the publication" at Harper's until he had "concluded some satisfactory negotiation in London"—with Bentley or someone else, apparently. Desperate, he tried to meet Bentley's objection about the speed in which his books were following each other: he suggested that Bentley publish *Pierre*, if he thought best, "*By a Vermonter*" or, perhaps, "*By Guy Winthrop.*" Having finished the proofs for Harper's, apparently, and tinkered a little with the set for Bentley (any changes he made were lost when Bentley disposed of the proofs), and at last written his reply to the letter he had received two or three weeks earlier, Melville and Lizzie took a train for Pittsfield. Late that same day, perhaps after finding the new issue of the *Literary World* waiting for him, Melville wrote an urgent note reminding the Duyckincks (still addressing them as the editors, not by name) to discontinue his subscription. Then he had to await the arrival of the first of May, when despite the $500 from the Harpers he knew he would default on the $92.25 interest due to T. D. Stewart.

Bentley received the sheets of *Pierre* speedily, and on 5 May wrote Melville a long open and respectful letter asserting that the only two of his books profitable in England were those Murray had published. Speaking in a friendly spirit, Bentley told Melville bluntly that all four books of his he had published had been flawed: "if you had revised your work 'Mardi', to the latest, the 'Whale', and restrained your imagination somewhat, and had written in a style to be understood by the great mass of readers—nay if you had not sometimes offended the feelings of many sensitive readers you would have succeeded in England." Bentley had seen the tributes to Melville's genius, but he had also seen the references to offended sensibilities, and he had fresh in mind the record of his enormous losses on Melville's books. He continued: "Everybody must admit the genius displayed in your writings; but it would have been impossible for any publisher with any prudent regard to his own interests to have put out your books here without revisal, & occasional omission." This was an allusion to something that may not have been mentioned between the two men before, the fact that Bentley himself or someone in his employ had pruned Melville's more reckless passages from *The Whale*, expurgating it slightly but pervasively, and wisely so, from Bentley's point of view, since the alterations had prevented needless outrage on the score of disrespect for royalty and disrespect for deity, as well as preventing annoyance at an excess of unpalatable Americanisms.

In pained sincerity, Bentley now continued with a frank statement of his intent to do the same thing, if Melville were after all to agree to half-profits, this time asking "permission to make or have made by a judicious literary friend such alterations as are absolutely necessary to 'Pierre' being properly appreciated here." Genuinely respectful of Melville's genius, he refused again to risk advancing money on *Pierre*, although he added that someone "ignorant of the absolute failure" of *Mardi, Redburn, White-Jacket*, and *The Whale* "might be tempted to make a trifling advance on the chance of success." Whether or not he thought for a moment that, as Melville had assured him, *Pierre* was really "calculated for popularity" or that it could be accepted as "a regular romance," we do not know, but Bentley saw what the full Harper version was like, was neither shocked nor outraged, and apparently decided that even in its swollen form it could be made publishable, and perhaps even profitable as an American gothic romance. In any case, he was willing to take his chances on the book because of his respect for Melville's genius and for Melville personally. Under the circumstances Melville surely did not try another English publisher, but, by late May, when he received the letter (after he had defaulted on his interest payment to Stewart), he simply retreated into his stance of stoicism, and did not even give Bentley the courtesy of a reply.

Apparently after the proofs of *Pierre* had arrived in London, Lemuel Shaw Jr. paid a visit to Bentley's establishment, where he delivered his letter of introduction from Melville and talked to an "assistant," probably Edmund Morgan, one of the very few people in the world who knew anything about *Pierre*, and who was more chatty than he should have been, judging by what Lem wrote his parents on 9 May: "I did not see him [Mr. Bentley]. I saw his assistant & had some conversation about Herman's books & was sorry to hear that Mr. Bentley is unwilling to take Herman's new work on the terms Herman wishes. I was told what I knew before that he is losing *the prestige of his name which he gained by his first books*, by writing so many books that nobody can read. I wish very much he could be persuaded to leave off writing books for a few years & that is what his friends here say." The implication is that Murray and perhaps others had said the same thing Bentley's assistant had said. Lem reported honestly, not saying that Bentley had refused to publish the book but that he would not take it on Herman's terms. Lem knew the worst before his father did: Shaw's letter of 12 May saying he had "no notice, yet, of Herman's new book" crossed Lem's on the Atlantic.

Hope Savage Shaw added a message to Lem on the back of her husband's letter: "Where [were] you not interested with Uncle Tom's Cabin? — That & Kos[s]uth is the constant topic." (What survives from Lem's book-buying in London is an English edition of *The Scarlet Letter*.) Hope continued: "This paper is so thin, that I thought that this sheet was a part of my letter. As I have written it you must excuse it. May every blessing be granted to my son Lemuel — Oakes family are much better . . . Elizabeth is at Pittsfield, remarkably well &c." However momentous Lem's news about Melville's failure with Bentley should have been, Hope had weightier matters on her mind, as is clear in the instructions she gave Lem on 25 May: "I wish you to write me how the English ladies walk, you know I am apt to swing my arms — do write how they place theirs to prevent motion that is visible." To glide through life without visible motion — like an English lady, not a denizen of the deep! By about that time, thanks to Lem, the judge and Hope knew, without being told by Herman, what had been going on between Melville and Bentley, put into the ugliest possible light by Lemuel.

Except for Judge Shaw, and to some extent his youngest son, Sam, the Shaws had been hostile to Melville at least since the publication of *Mardi* in 1849. Hope and her son Lem had begun maligning Melville that year. Following a visit to Hope Savage Shaw, J. C. Sharp wrote Samuel H. Savage, Hope's nephew, on 30 November 1849 that if the new book, *Redburn*, were not better than *Mardi*, Melville "had better have saved his ink and paper." About that time Lem Jr. wrote Sam Savage, then in Guatemala, that Melville had lost "his reputation as a writer" (as Sam wrote back to Lem on 21 January

1850); Allan, by contrast, was writing Sam Savage (29 April 1850), "Herman still continues to write books which are well received." Neither Melville nor the Shaws had seen recent extravagant praise of *The Whale*. Instead, Hope and the other Shaws read the Boston *Post* (20 November 1851), where they were assured that *Moby-Dick* was "not worth the money asked for it," and that it was worth twenty-five cents at most. They would have seen also the repetition of these words in the *Statesman* and would have seen this flat statement in the Boston *Evening Gazette* (6 December 1851): "Had Mr. Melville retired from the literary field after the production of 'Typee' and 'Omoo' he would have possessed an enviable reputation; but like many other authors he has spun the golden web so very fine in each succeeding work that it is almost valueless." The writer had read "portions" of the book without finding "any marks of freshness, any traces of originality." They would have seen the *United States Magazine and Democratic Review* (January 1852), where the critic had begun: "Mr. Melville is evidently trying to ascertain how far the public will consent to be imposed upon," and then had concluded: "The truth is, Mr. Melville has survived his reputation."

Neither Lem Jr., Oakes, nor Hope was saying anything against Melville that professional journalists were not saying. The Shaws (always excepting the judge) had no way of defending the books against these critics; and not even those who genuinely loved Melville were able to challenge such evidence that Melville had lost what reputation he had gained with *Typee* and *Omoo*. From the moment she read the first hostile review of *Mardi*, Lizzie had been bewildered, certain that she had no judgment of her own that was worth putting forward, eager to know from her stepmother whatever the family was hearing about *Mardi*. Perhaps having bitten her tongue for two years, having accepted as fact that *Redburn* and *White-Jacket* had done much to restore Herman's reputation, Hope from this time forward felt no need to restrain herself around her sons and her stepson, with whom she could be overtly contemptuous of Herman and with whom she could commiserate about the damage he had done to their own respectability. The horror is that she felt, from this time forward, no need to restrain her opinions around Lizzie, or, as the years passed, around Oakes's or Lizzie's children. What with Maria's daily reproaches for his religious lapses, Hope's and the younger Shaws' carping criticism of his lost reputation, what with his enormous debts and his defaulting on a payment on 1 May, what with the failure of *The Whale* and *Moby-Dick* after publication and the humiliating American contract for *Pierre* and no English contract for it at all, Melville chose to escape as best he could: he went outdoors into the Berkshire spring.

[6]

Fool's Paradise
and the Furies Unleashed
June–September 1852

In *The Faerie Queene* (bk. 4, canto 1, stanza 45), Melville marks the lines about Scudamour, after Blandamour has denounced him, then closes the volume, turns it around so the spine faces him and copies the words out across the back flyleaf: "He little answered, but in manly heart / His mighty indignation did forbear" (Priscilla Ambrose Collection)

FROM EARLY IN MAY through the middle of July, with *Pierre* in press with the Harpers and no prospect of its publication in London, Melville became, as he wrote Hawthorne on 17 July, "an utter idler and a savage — out of doors all the time." In the "Report of the Committee" that he ghostwrote for his Cousin Robert in 1850, Melville had noted with satisfaction "the extensive embellishments of our road-sides with forest trees." He had trusted that "at no distant day" those "embellishments" might be "continuous from one end of the County to the other, — that the shades that beautify our villages, extend over hills that are now bleak with the winter's wind, or arid with the summer's sun." This desirable result could be attained, Melville had said sanguinely, with only "a few days' attention annually, by each landholder." The spring of 1852 may well have been the time Melville took his own advice and set out a row of saplings along the road that had grown into mature trees by 1892, when Lizzie recalled his planting them.

Augusta came home from the Manor House in time to take part in and record a series of spring outings, on a sheet of paper she labeled "The Excursions of '52." On 22 May, a Saturday, the family took a long drive: "vehicle — carriage — party — The Author, his mother, & wife & sister Augusta. time of starting — 2 P.M. hour of returning 6 P.M. distance — 20 miles in four hours. Went over the Lenox mountain & reached Mrs Morewoods by the way of Richmond hill & the village of Pittsfield. Decorated the carriage with the blossoms of the wild cherry. Took tea at Broadhall & reached home at 10." Ironically, Augusta had begun to refer to Herman as the Author just as his career as an international writer had ended. Five days later they were off again:

No 2. vehicle — wagon — party — The Author, his wife, & sisters Helen & Augusta. time of starting 9 A.M. hour of return 8 P.M. distance 28 miles in eleven hours. Drove North towards the Hancock Mountain, visited the old house of Jessee Potter built as a white tablet in the chimney informed us in 1807 [1817?] which is situated on the very summit, & descending the other side spite of its steepness, lunched at the old fashioned town of Hancock, & returned home by the way of Lebanon & Hancock Shakers.

In early June, recalling "Spring" in James Thomson's *Seasons* ("Delightful task! to rear the tender thought / To teach the young idea how to shoot"), Augusta recorded: "*No. 3.* vehicle — carriage — party, The Author, his wife & sisters Helen & Fanny. time of starting 2 P.M. hour of return 7 P.M. distance 16 miles in five hours. Visited the old school house of Washington Mountain where the Author once taught the young idea how to shoot." (The precise location of this schoolhouse has never been identified.) The next excursion was on 7 June: "*No 4.* vehicle — wagon — party — the Author, his wife & sisters Fanny & Augusta. time of starting 9 A.M. hour of return 7½. Drove to Cheshire, & Lanesborough, & Constitution Hill from whence we had a magnificent view. (distance — 29 [27?] miles 10½ hours. Carried our dinner with us, & refreshed ourselves between the showers which were frequent." In the next days Tom materialized in the Berkshires.

As recently as 12 March Augusta had received a two-page letter from Tom in Shanghai, but he was one of the party on the excursion Augusta recorded on 12 June, another Saturday: "*No 5.* vehicle — wagon — party, the Author his wife brother Tom & sister Fanny. Time of starting 8½ — hour of return 7½. 16 miles Berry pond & Taconic Gorge." Tom's presence regularly meant that everyone in the family became invigorated and happy, so he may have made it easier for Herman to pretend he was still what Augusta was innocently calling him, the Author. With Tom there to help, the family made its most ambitious excursion yet, on 14 to 16 June: "No 6. Saddle Back, South Adams ascent, & on foot after leaving the cars. absent from Monday 10 A M until Wednesday 4 P.M. Slept two nights on the Mountain. party. The Author, his brother Tom, wife, & sisters Helen & Fanny." Augusta wrote "No. 7" down, ready for seventh excursion that never happened. Everyone gathered at Arrowhead, Kate coming with Allan and his two older girls (and perhaps even Sophia and the month-and-a-half-old baby) so they could all rejoice at the sight of Tom. Sam Shaw may have arrived at Arrowhead already, since he was there during some if not all of the next two weeks.

On 3 July Herman bade Tom farewell and went alone to Boston, for Judge Shaw had followed through on the plans he had written to Lem about on 7 June: "I am expecting to hold the court at Nantucket, & Herman has promised to go with me. I wish him to see some of the gents at New Bedford & Nantucket connected with whaling. If he goes, I propose after getting through with the business of the court, to visit Martha's Vineyard then Elizabeth Islands I think we can make it a pleasant excursion for July." Having heard from Lem the gossip from Bentley's establishment, Shaw was demonstrating the depth of his love for Herman and for long-dead Melvills, and acting out of deep decency and generosity. On Saturday, 3 July, Herman met Shaw at 49 Mt. Vernon Street, which looked more splendid than ever in contrast with Arrowhead, of which the kindest adjective was "quaint." No one could celebrate on the Glorious Fourth because it fell on a Sunday. Shaw wrote Lem: "Independence was celebrated on Monday & on Tuesday morning we left in the Cars for New Bed[ford]. Mr John H. Clifford met us by appointment at Cars, & after riding about the town a little, visiting Mr Arnolds beautiful garden, we dined with Mr. Clifford." As far as we know, this was Melville's first visit to New Bedford since that bleak winter when Gansevoort had arrived with him from Manhattan to see him off to the Pacific.

Compulsive about contrasting two or more experiences in the same place, Melville must have reflected on his situation at the end of 1840 and now, 6 July 1852, when he was met by a prominent lawyer and driven about the town before being taken to James Arnold's famous botanical garden. (The garden is gone, but some of the Arnold mansion survives as the Wamsutta Club.) Judge Shaw and John H. Clifford, currently the attorney general, and soon to be governor, shared a powerful intellectual and emotional bond as judge and prosecutor in the sensational Harvard murder case of two years before, in which Clifford won the conviction of Professor John W. Webster for the murder of Professor George Parkman and Shaw sentenced Webster to be hanged. To be in each other's company was to remember the hate mail both men had received during the course of the investigation and trial and after the sentencing, when the coolness with which both had behaved had become legendary in the family. Melville's head must also have been peopled again with the fictional characters he had put into motion at that place in *Moby-Dick*. The three men dined, perhaps with Mr. Arnold or others, then went down to the docks to catch the steamer for Nantucket, which Melville had never boarded before, but which he had celebrated in *Moby-Dick*, making it the scene of Queequeg's heroism, adapted from an account of Tupai Cupa's actions in Craik's *The New Zealanders*.

The 5 July Nantucket *Inquirer* had advised its readers that "The Supreme Judicial Court will be opened in this town to-morrow morning at 9 o'clock, and adjourn till the afternoon, to await the arrival of Chief Justice Shaw, who will come in the steamer from New Bedford." Shaw arrived on the *Massachu-

setts about sunset, as he wrote Lem, with both Herman and Attorney General Clifford in tow. It was, as already understood, "too late to open the court that day," but it was just time enough for the men to get settled into their quarters and find a quiet public room where they could settle down for a long evening of smoking and talking. Most likely they stayed in the Ocean House, built on Broad and Center in 1845 by Jared Coffin as the island's first three-story brick house. Only seven years old, it had survived the Great Fire of 1846 (its brick walls and slate roof retarding the flames), and then had been sold to the Nantucket Steamship Company for use as a hotel. Chances are that Shaw and his companions took possession of the gentlemen's smoking room in the converted basement, where from the high windows one could see glimpses of newer structures built after the fire—a suitable place for nicotian philosophical meditations.

Herman would have had tact enough to avoid asking any questions about the trial of Professor Webster, but he availed himself of the opportunity to ask Clifford questions on other topics, and later (on 13 August) wrote Hawthorne that the lawyer gave him "considerable information upon several matters" concerning which he was curious. There was much marvelous desultory, intermittently intense talk—talk among these three extraordinary men, and perhaps some notable Nantucketers as well. Thomas Macy may have been there, for at some point on the visit he presented to Melville a copy of Obed Macy's *The History of Nantucket* (Boston, 1835), a valuable gift, Melville was well aware. Not since precious hours on the *United States* with Jack Chase, or not since London, perhaps never before in his life had Melville participated in such talk among men of such powerful and varied experiences. At some point the conversation turned to the "great patience, & endurance, & resignedness of the women of the island in submitting so uncomplainingly to the long, long absences of their sailor husbands." Accepting Melville as an intimate, Clifford, "by way of anecdote," gave him "a leaf from his professional experience," a story he had learned a decade before—a story of shipwreck, love, desertion, patience, endurance, and bigamy. Long ago, a sailor named Robertson had been wrecked "on the coast of Pembroke" (by Duxbury, the home, Melville may already have known, of Captain Amasa Delano). A girl named Agatha Hatch cared for him, and they married, the sailor signed on short voyages, then, leaving her pregnant, he disappeared. Removing to Falmouth, she supported herself and managed to give her daughter a good education. After seventeen years Robertson returned and gave his wife and daughter money, and again returned to give a bridal present to his daughter. After his death it became clear that he had married twice more, to a woman who had died and another who had survived him, as Agatha did. Although suspecting that her husband had committed bigamy, Agatha had done nothing, not wanting to make his second family unhappy and not wanting to drive him away from their own daughter. Clifford had grown vague on the details ("items," in Melville's vocabulary, as in Shakespeare's), but he told his auditors that he had made a record in his books at the time, and what he remembered was significant enough to arouse lively interest in Melville.

Melville's response during the narration of the story was, he later wrote Hawthorne, "heightened by the emotion of the gentleman who told it, who evinced the most unaffected sympathy in it, tho' now a matter of his past." With characteristic discretion, he did not name the famous Clifford, even to Hawthorne. Melville added deprecatingly, "But perhaps this great interest of mine may have been largely helped by some accidental circumstances or other" — perhaps simply because it struck him as a poignant human story, perhaps because it struck some more complicated chord in him, such as the contrast between the God-defying ways in which his last heroes had reacted to disaster (by attempting to seize lightning bolts and hurl them against the deity as returning-strokes) and the way the Pembroke woman had responded. After the series of self-destructive decisions he had made in the previous winter and spring, Melville may have been seeing himself in a new role of passive acceptor of his fate. He may have been stirred by thoughts he could never name to anyone — feelings of sympathy and envy toward the sailor, caught off guard and married, who soon fled from his wife. In the letter to Hawthorne he said of this sailor: "he was a weak man, & his temptations (tho' we know little of them) were strong." Melville may have thought of the way he had recently portrayed a woman repudiated by her father in his beautiful, tragic Isabel (and thought as well of whatever elements, literary or personal, went into that portrayal). The theme of the disappearing and reappearing father could not help stirring up intense feelings in Melville. Even given a vagueness in the telling, the story as Clifford knew it was richly suggestive. Whatever the causes, the intensity of Melville's response that night at Nantucket is revealed by his echoing the language of the great narrative within a narrative he had put into *Moby-Dick*, "The Town-Ho's Story" (ch. 54), about the human and cosmic power that can inhere not only in biblical or classical or Shakespearean stories but in stories current in the modern democratic, technological world of the mid-nineteenth century. Ishmael's story, as he told it on the thick-gilt tiled piazza of the Golden Inn in Lima one saint's eve, to a lounging circle of his Spanish friends, was "wildly heightened" by certain circumstances. Melville's response to Clifford was also "heightened," so that he "begged" the teller to be sure to send him a fuller account, the way the Spanish dons had begged Ishmael to assure them that the story was true. Melville was so manifestly intrigued that Clifford thought he was thinking of the story as literary material, and on that basis soon mailed him the copy of his journal account of the story.

The next morning, 7 July, Shaw held court, and on 9 July Edward W. Cobb, the editor of the *Inquirer*, made a point of letting everyone know the state of his health: "The Supreme Court has been in session here this week; Chief Justice Shaw presiding. The venerable chief, though fleshy and ponderous in body, still retains the same clear head that he had thirty years ago when he was a young and leading member of the Bar. Wo to the poor barrister who undertakes any more flourish of words where he presides, or hopes to win attention from the Court by a collocation of 'Grimgribber.'" Drawing on *Bleak House*, the Dickens serial everyone was reading in newspaper and magazine piratings, Cobb amused himself in describing the process by which Shaw dispatched his business, something Melville most likely witnessed:

> The cases on the Docket disappeared one by one without the Intervention of a Jury. — "Continued" seemed to be a very common and conclusive and satisfactory word about the clerk's desk and we suspect that most of the cases are put off to await the decision in Jarndyce vs. Jarndyce. . . . There were one or two equity cases, as they are called. — These, as we understand, are the progeny generally of those who lose their way in the Law and go groping about the chair of the chancellor in hopes light enough will be shed by him, to extricate them from their dubious dilemmas. Sometimes this happens and the solicitor on the winning side swells up with all the pomp and circumstance of a root beer war. Verily we live in the heart of a wonderful country.

By dint of such continuing (and some discontinuing, the *Weekly Mirror* reported on 10 July), Shaw, as he wrote Lem, "dispatched all the business there was to be done, in about two hours." The *Weekly Mirror* also assured its readers that the "venerable Judge seemed in good health, and unimpaired in the discharge of his official duties." Notorious for ugliness of face and form, Judge Shaw possessed such force that those who knew him well suspended their aesthetic judgments. Herman Melville was seeing his father-in-law as a man among men, even as a great man among great men, and as a revered public figure, not a mere literary celebrity.

Venerable but expeditious in court, the judge was unimpaired in appetite and interest in life on the island. He and Herman dined with a friend, who then rode with them in a carriage "to Siasconset, & various parts of the island." Near Siasconset they saw the Sankaty lighthouse with a remarkable French reflecting device, the Fresnel lens. They "passed the evening with Mr. Mitchell the astronomer, & his celebrated daughter, the discoverer of comets" (Shaw to Lem, 20 July). This would have been in the Mitchell quarters above the Pacific Bank, looking down to the harbor. Melville may have made little impression on Maria Mitchell, but she became important to him, either from the power of her personal presence, or what she represented to him as a female in what had been a masculine field. Later she had some adventures in Europe with the Hawthornes, but Sophia Hawthorne identified her only as "Miss M———" in the few mentions of her she retained in the 1871 *Passages from the French and Italian Note-Books*, so Melville may never have known Maria Mitchell had met his old friends; he certainly would not have learned how hapless she had discovered Hawthorne to be. On considering Maria Mitchell's status as an intellectual woman, single, living at home, Melville may have been struck by a latent strength of sexuality that could not be repressed indefinitely. Whatever he thought at the time, she figured, later, by occupation at least, in the portrait of the narrator of one of his best poems, "After the Pleasure Party."

On 8 July the men "made various calls & visits," Shaw wrote to Lem: "Amongst others he [Melville] met with Capt Pollard" (easy enough if they were staying at the Ocean House, a stone's throw from George Pollard's own house) "who was master of the whale ship Essex, which was designedly destroyed by a whale nearly thirty years ago." Long afterward, Melville made this record: "I—sometime about 1850–3—saw Capt. Pollard on the island of Nantucket, and exchanged some words with him. To the islanders he was a nobody—to me, the most impressive man, tho' wholly unassuming, even humble—that I ever encountered." The fate of the *Essex* was old news, which everyone there now saw in relation to the plot of *Moby-Dick*, even Pollard, who had probably seen at least the extract of *Moby-Dick* that the *Inquirer* had printed on 29 November. Melville's reaction to Pollard, hard to define, apparently had little to do with pleasure at confirmation of his literary device of having a whale sink a whaleship. It had more to do, however subtly, with Pollard's being alive because he had eaten human flesh during the long period between the wreck of the *Essex* and his rescue. In the Marquesas Herman Melville had experienced moments of real fear that he might be killed and eaten; perhaps he had experienced terrors as intense as those with which he later enthralled his shipmates and the readers of *Typee*. Older than that memory was the knowledge that Allan Melvill had survived, however briefly, his devouring of his children's fortunes. By now, after his introducing Chronos into *Pierre*, Melville may have faced up to his sense that Allan Melvill might have proclaimed himself as "cannibal old me," the words given to Ahab. In any case, Pollard remained powerful in Melville's memory, and may even have provided him with a model for his own humble behavior, in some circumstances, long afterward.

On Friday morning, 9 July, Shaw and Melville took the steamer to Martha's Vineyard, late enough, probably, to read Cobb's account of the session and thereby catch up on the news of their own activities. There was time also for Melville to focus on the splendor of the term "Grimgribber" to denote the extreme overuse of technical legal jargon, a word that would have appealed to the man who a few years later began his first lecture by disclaiming any knowledge of technical aesthetic terminology. At the Vineyard once again there were people eager to show the visitors about: "We visited various parts of the island including that celebrated promontory of the west end called Gayhead, through a tract of indian territory." On Monday morning they sailed off for what Melville described to Hawthorne a few days later as "the solitary Crusoish island of Naushon (one of the Elisabeth group)." The judge wrote to Lem: "We visited Mr [William] Swain there, by previous invitation. He is the sole proprietor of the island lives there during the summer in quite a Baronial style, & receives a good deal of company. Mr. Peabody of the King's chapel, with his wife & family, and several ladies were there as visitors. We rode over a considerable part of the island, much of which is well wooded; there are many deer that live quite wild in the woods & coverts, some of the party started a fine buck." Shaw was well acquainted with the Reverend Mr. Ephraim Peabody, and Melville had seen, many times, the King's Chapel at the corner of Tremont and School in Boston, known as the oldest stone building in New England and the bastion of royal tyranny in his Grandfather Melvill's early years. After the Revolution, it had been transformed from Anglican church to Unitarian, the earliest Unitarian church in the country. On Swain's "stately piazza" — Melville was a connoisseur of piazzas — he saw the words *The Blithedale Romance* gilded "on the back of a very new book and in the hands of a clergyman." In his thoughts at the time, connecting a beautiful piazza with gilding on a book, or on 17 July, when he wrote this to Hawthorne, he may have been self-consciously remembering "The Town-Ho's Story."

His rich imaginative life of the recent past newly fueled by a series of remarkable experiences, Melville made this inscription in the guest register before they left the next morning: "Sweet shall be the memory of Naushon, / Herman Melville / Tuesday July 13, 1852 / Blue sky — blue sea — & almost every thing blue / but our spirits." Shaw and Melville then "crossed Wood's hole, to Falmouth, returned by way of Sandwich, & the Cape Cod R. to Boston, on Tuesday evening," completing the whole of their proposed route except going to Cutty Hunk, the westernmost of the Elizabeth Islands. And while Boston had sweltered, in the islands they had enjoyed "comfortably cool weather especially during the nights." Shaw reported that Herman had "expressed himself extremely well pleased with the excursion, he saw many things & met with many people, whom he was extremely glad to see"—among them the "most impressive" man he ever met, Pollard.

On the trip Melville said nothing to Shaw about the subject of *Pierre*. His father-in-law knew from his second son that *Pierre* had been declined by Richard Bentley—all during this excursion knew more than Herman knew about the state of his reputation in London—and said not a word of reproach during these days and nights of intimacy. Blue skies, blue sea, and almost every thing blue but their spirits. Later, many years later (to Uncle Peter's daughter Kate and her husband, 27 August 1876), Melville could say sardonically, "I myself am ever hilarious," but this was the last week he would ever convince himself or anyone else that he was happy. He was thirty-two years old, just short of thirty-three.

When Melville got home on 16 July, Lizzie said to him, "there is Mr *Hawthorne's* new book, come by mail," and the next day Melville in a letter to Hawthorne made a charming story of his successive encounters with *The Blithedale Romance* being read and sold and happily handed to people. For the first time, he may have sensed what would become a recurrent phenomenon for the rest of his life, that he was being eclipsed by Hawthorne; but the publication of *Pierre* was two weeks away, and Melville could still pretend that nothing was wrong. A young man who had achieved instant fame and an older man who had inched his way out of anonymity, Melville and Hawthorne had met as equals, only months after the simultaneous laudatory reviewing of *The Scarlet Letter* and *White-Jacket* (published two or three days apart in March 1850). In the natural course of things they had been reviewed cheek-by-jowl in the same papers, but the diversity of their literary works had discouraged reviewers from making comparisons. Now *The Blithedale Romance* was published, a book with a voyeuristic, sexually ambivalent narrator which deals with psychological violation and betrayal and contains a particularly lurid suicide; *Pierre*, a few weeks from publication, contained an even more detailed psychological analysis of a sexual-psychological awakening in the context of a plot involving incest and culminating in a modestly Shakespearean pile of corpses.

Early critics were intrigued by what they recognized as the Brook Farm setting of *The Blithedale Romance* and the likelihood that Zenobia was modeled on Margaret Fuller (who had behaved scandalously in Italy, Boston gossips said, and been punished by death off Fire Island with her child and its Italian father), but they were not comfortable with the plot. The Boston *Post* on 16 July said Hawthorne had "wasted his fine powers upon a theme and personages utterly unworthy his genius," in a book "not worth naming" along with *The Scarlet Letter.* In the *Literary World* (24 July) the Duyckincks, chastened by Hawthorne's rebuke of the review of *Moby-Dick* and smarting from Melville's brusque little notes canceling and recanceling his subscription, offered restrained comments on Hawthorne as "a delicate spiritual anatomist, with scalpel and probe in hand," dissecting the human heart. The reviewers did not like *Blithedale Romance*, but they did not denounce it as, say, sexually prurient. The reviews of Hawthorne's and Melville's new books continued to appear side by side for months, but no reviewers made any overt comparisons about the directions of their careers. The writers and their friends and families would inevitably have marked the tempered praise of the older man and the near-universal condemnation of the younger.

The morning after Melville reached home he received a note from Hawthorne inviting him to make a visit, and not to West Newton. The Hawthornes had done something extraordinary: they had bought a house in Concord, Bronson Alcott's Wayside. In his reply, Melville complimented *The Blithedale Romance* on the basis of his first moments with it: "As I am only just home, I have not yet got far into the book but enough to see that you have most admirably employed materials which are richer than I had fancied them. Especially at this day, the volume is welcome, as an antidote to the mooniness of some dreamers—who are merely dreamers—Yet who the devel aint a dreamer?" In Melville's polite caginess, the fact emerges that he had known for some time that Brook Farm was the subject of Hawthorne's new book and that he had been skeptical about how it could bear literary treatment. Much as he would like to see the Hawthornes, the hour had come for him "to sit down again." He could not think of doing anything else with his life besides writing. Besides, a literary subject had been thrust upon him. Mailed on the fourteenth, and probably lying in wait with Hawthorne's book on his return, was a letter from John Clifford. True to his promise, the attorney general had sent Melville a clerk's copy of his journal entry about the case of the Pembroke girl and a sailor. The story had begun around 1806, with Robertson's shipwreck; he had married Agatha Hatch in 1807. As Clifford had remembered, after Robertson's reappearance and subsequent visits, it had emerged that he had remarried not once but twice. When these facts came to light after Robertson's death, the rival families had settled his estate out of court, Agatha asking for little. The document intriguingly dated the denouement of the tragedy to the end of May 1842, when Clifford was a young New Bedford lawyer, and just before Herman Melville jumped ship in the Marquesas. Clifford took for granted that Melville intended to make literary use of the story. In the light of what happened later, it is significant that the attorney general of Massachusetts saw nothing potentially libelous or otherwise actionable in Melville's using actual events in any narrative he might write.

Nevertheless, from the rest of July 1852 to the middle of August, Melville was much out of doors, still, caught up in the family routines, which were complicated by the presence of Sophia and her three daughters and (intermittently) Allan, as well as, for the first half of August, Sam Shaw, who expected to go home and then go to Maine. Tom seems to have accompanied him to Boston in mid-August, to look for a ship. In late July, Nilly Thayer wrote to Augusta from Newport, where she was living "about a mile from the town in a quiet little cottage with green fields all around," and "the Ocean on every side," a "glorious place for the children." Nilly expanded on her vision of life in the Berkshires: "I can picture happiness & contentment glowing upon each feature. How much after all our happiness depends upon ourselves & cultivating the spirit of love & contentment where ever our lot may be." Augusta, at least, shared those last sentiments, with a more religious tinge. Nilly had heard of the temporary expansion of the Arrowhead household: "With Allan's children you must have quite a party of little ones & make your house resound with their merry pranks, for they are always so happy together provided their play things do not disturb their equanimity. Mrs. Herman I think is getting quite weaned from Boston, as I hear of her being there very seldom, does she like the country?" Arrowhead was indeed full. All the daughters and Maria were there all summer, and at some point Cousin Priscilla Melvill also visited at Arrowhead (according to her letter to Shaw on 31 March 1853). Allan and Sophia and the three girls (with one or more servants) seem to have stayed into September, Allan commuting as usual. For some of the "Arrowheads," life that summer may have been as idyllic as Nilly's own. Toward the end of August or early September, Augusta went on a number of rides with Mrs. Brittain and perhaps others, making use of the good weather. Writing to Augusta on 12 September, after he had a berth on the *Gem of the Ocean*, bound for San Francisco, Tom professed to be concerned that Mrs. Brittain would catch all the fish out of the "Tear of Heaven" before he returned—that being Longfellow's poetic name for Melville Lake, or now in the early 1850s, sometimes called Morewood Lake.

Happiness and contentment did not glow upon Herman's features during the last days of July, just before the publication of *Pierre*, but tense stoicism might have reflected from them. During the last two weeks of July Melville agonized over how *Pierre* would be received, for the phenomenal sales he hoped for depended on favorable reviewing—depended on the critics' eager acceptance of him as a regular novelist. He knew that Evert Duyckinck would hale *Pierre* to the bar of judgment, as a matter of duty, and that he would discover in the printed book a personal attack on him that had not been in the manuscript half a year earlier. As he prepared to stand before that earthly bar of judgment, not to speak of the Higher Assizes before which he as the writer and the Harper brothers as the publisher of *Moby-Dick* would be arraigned, Melville could hardly have denied to himself any longer that at stake was not only his career. At stake was his home, which two different men thought they held as collateral for their loans to him, while the bulk of the money he had laid out on the property had come from a third, his father-in-law.

Around 28 July, Melville rode down to call on G. P. R. James at his three-hundred-acre estate, which included part of Monument Mountain. James had erected what the New York *Herald* (18 September) called a "picturesque farm house" on an eminence east of the Housatonic railroad, on the high road about a mile and a half past Stockbridge on the way to Great Barrington. James's popularity was great, for he was already known throughout the English-reading world as the "solitary horseman" author, from the opening of *Barbazure:* "It was upon one of those balmy evenings of November which are only known in the valleys of Languedoc and among the mountains of Alsace, that two cavaliers might have been perceived by the naked eye." Thackeray had parodied this all too memorably, reducing James's many volumes in the public mind to this one image. Just before he came into Melville's terrain, in the story *Fate* (1851), James managed to have some fun of his own about his famous horseman, and he remained ready to acknowledge his inveterate fondness for any story about a white horse and rider.

The Lenox locals were predictably less enthusiastic about the Englishman. "Maherbal," the correspondent of the Windsor (Vermont) *Journal*, had vented his scorn in a letter dated 10 January 1852 and published six days later. If one of James's "transatlantic friends" who saw him as the emissary of international copyright or one of "those Americans who look upon him with a suspicion of his intermeddling designs" — if one of either class should come to Berkshire, Maherbal said, "they would find him peaceably at work in his study on some half-finished chapter of a love story, or else industriously superintending the clearing up and draining of his newly purchased farm on Negro Pond." He had purchased "a parcel of mud," and should build "a wall or a barn before his house to hide the view which now opens upon the only dirty pond in Berkshire county." When Melville arrived at Negro Pond, he was thwarted by the hostile stolidity of the tight-mouthed Yankee servants, who turned him away without a tidbit of information. On learning this James was indignant, as he wrote Melville on 28 July: "Few things could have vexed me more than to find, on my return from a little open air dinner at my farm, that you had been at my house and gone away again. Why did not my people send you over? it is but a mile across." Promising to return the call, James added clues to keep them from passing each other on the road: "I will come to see you as soon as I can; but pray do not let me pass you if we ever meet on the road. I should not know you of course by sight; nor you me. But I will tell you how you can recognize me: by a great rough pair of nearly white mustachoes very like those of a wiry haired terrier dog. There is not such a pair in the county." Melville may never have had a chance to test either his discrimination among moustaches or his resistance to the snuff that permeated James's clothing, hair, and moustaches so thoroughly that it set people close to him into sneezing fits: no record survives of any meeting between the two. Perhaps the two would have celebrated their addictions to tobacco together, but James's addiction was indeed notorious. He may have been the only celebrity of his generation, when tobacco (Melville's "herba santa") was accounted beneficial by many, to have taken snuff so incessantly that when he died everyone agreed that it had killed him.

The first public word about *Pierre*, on 29 July, Melville may have attributed to Thomas Powell (the "English egotist," Sophia had called him), since this lurid pre-publication gossip was in the sensationalistic New York *Herald*, where James Gordon Bennett had previously given Powell free rein for his convoluted machinations. This was the news that Melville had "dressed up and exhibited in Berkshire, where he is living, some of the ancient and most repulsive inventions of the George Walker and Anne Radcliffe sort," and that it was "conceded" in literary circles that Melville had "written himself out." On 4 August the Boston *Post* denounced *Pierre* as perhaps "the craziest fiction extant." The *only* book of Melville's that the *Post* approved of was *Typee*, and a "thousand times better" if Melville had "dropped authorship" after it: "The author of one good book more than offsets the amusement derived from it by the reading public, when he produces a score of trashy and crazy volumes; and in the present case, and after the delivery of such stuff as 'Mardi' and the 'White Whale,' are not disposed to stand upon much ceremony." The reviewer ranted about *Pierre:* "What the book means, we know not. To save it from almost utter worthlessness, it must be called a prose poem, and even then, it might be supposed to emanate from a lunatic hospital rather than from the quiet retreats of Berkshire." Melville had "produced more and sadder trash than any other man of undoubted ability among us, and the most provoking fact is, that in his bushels of chaff, the 'two grains of wheat' are clearly discernible."

Melville did not see all the reviews of *Pierre* we now know of, but he probably saw many of them, as well as some equally harsh ones that we have not located, so that the known reviews from the major periodicals constitute a fair sample of what he and all his family and friends saw. On 5 August Charles Creighton Hazewell denounced Melville personally in the Boston

Daily Times, calling him a would-be reformer thwarted in his goals by lack of personal experience with suffering:

> What *he* has to grumble about we are at a loss to know. We have always been under the impression that he was rather a fortunate person, and had as little to complain of as a man well could have — an impression which his works have by no means reversed, for men who have any thing [like] real causes of complaint do not resort to the imagination for troubles, as Mr. Melville does. To get up any thing like a grievance he has to locate his characters in some *Chateau en Espagne*, and it is even then so thin and shadowy and unsubstantial, — so wholly unlike what rational men consider evils, — that we have no patience with him or his characters. He has to expressly erect walls against which his heroes and heroines can dash out such small amount of brains as it has pleased heaven (through the agency of the author) to endow them.

This is so uncalled for, so seemingly inapplicable to *Pierre*, that one wonders if Hazewell were specifically refuting someone's comment on Melville's early hardships. It is as if he were retorting to William T. Porter's praise of Melville in the *Spirit of the Times* the year before, comparing him and Dickens as kindred geniuses who had plowed deep "into the soil of humanity and nature" and obtained fresh experiences, "perhaps at the cost of much individual pain and sorrow."

In a smugly knowledgeable tone Hazewell made some good artistic connections for wrong reasons: "Of that deep tragedy, growing out of natural causes, which is so formidable an element of the higher class of works of fiction, and the best illustrations of which are to be found in the Greek drama, in *Hamlet*, *The Bride of Lammermoor*, *The Scarlet Letter*, and *Kreutzer*, Mr. Melville has no conception, and when he attempts to create it he falls into something that would be sufficient to damn a farce writer." In the revival of interest in Melville that came three-quarters of a century later, critics would make comparable lists, and with passionate conviction place *Moby-Dick* and even *Pierre* among other great works. Not now. Hazewell followed this with language that could only recall to the Shaws the language of some of the reviewers of *Moby-Dick*, specifically the unforgettable "writ de lunatico" of the *Southern Quarterly Review*, a publication respected among the Cotton Whigs of Boston:

> The motives for the conduct of any of the parties are such as would consign the best of them to the madhouse; and there is a wonderful harmony between the motives and the actions of them all. The annals of Bedlam might be defied to produce such another collection of lunatics as the hero, his mother, his sister, and the heroine. Were there no mad doctors in that part of the country

where they lived? Were the asylums all full? Was there nobody to swear out a commission *de lunatico inquirendo*, out of regard to the common safety?

If Hope Savage Shaw had been a man, if Oakes Shaw had not feared his father, one or the other might have sworn out the commission; in New York City the Harpers did the next best thing. The brothers decided that the literati should know that the author was at fault and that the Harpers had been forced, by legal contract, by their perhaps reprehensible loyalty to the young author, or by their always overly-generous natures, whatever, to publish this novel of Melville's—something they would never do again, you could be sure. On 23 August 1852 Hawthorne's distant cousin Elizabeth Barstow Stoddard (married to the young poet Richard Henry Stoddard) wrote to Margaret Jane Muzzey Sweat that "the Harpers think Melville is a little crazy."

In Boston not only the chief justice but even Hope Savage Shaw worked to keep the best face on the disaster of *Pierre*, despite the disdain toward Herman that Lem and Oakes both were now openly displaying. Lucy Nourse was in the Shaw house from July through August. As a girl and young woman she had watched the long dying of her beloved sister Nancy, Shaw's fiancée. As a widowed and remarried woman she had cared for Elizabeth during long vacations in Hallowell, Maine, in the late 1830s, when Judge Shaw's mother was still alive. Dr. Nourse's letter to Shaw in August 1839 expresses his and his wife's strong feelings for the girl: "Elizabeth's visit has given us a great deal of pleasure, *unmingled* pleasure, for such has been her whole deportment as to leave us nothing to regret but her too early departure." These strong ties, joined to her memories and emotions as Herman's aunt, made Lucy a restraining factor, especially after Tom joined the household, assuming, rightly, that he would be welcome there for an indefinite stay.

Judge Shaw in mid-August was full of his part in "a celebration of the C. Cod Association," a "great occasion for the people of Provincetown, who rarely have any thing like a holiday"—conditions very gradually rectified over the next century and a half. To his son Lem, who had reported on Bentley's refusal to give Melville his old terms, Shaw wrote cautiously on 17 August: "Herman has just published his new work, the title of which is 'Pierre, or The Ambiguities.' I have not read it, & do not know, how it is received; it does not I believe relate to incidents, or characters, connected with the sea. I hope it will have a run & succeed well, & realize his hopes & expectations." It is a little hard to think that Shaw did not know how *Pierre* had been received, since the *Post* review, at least, would have come before his eyes everywhere he went. About Tom, there was no vagueness at all in what Judge Shaw reported to Lem: "I think he is quite an accomplished mariner,

& I have little doubt, will in due time have the Command of a ship." On 18 August Tom reported to Augusta in detail, first describing, winningly, the effect of her letter: "I . . . was perfectly happy while reading it but it brought Arrowhead so vividly before me that I have been home sick ever since." On Saturday the fourteenth, after squiring Aunt Lucy and Mrs. Shaw about, he had gone "down town read the papers, and smoked a segar," before going to the docks to survey the ships and look out "for a good chance." Sunday he went to Brattle Street church where "Grand papa used to go," old Thomas Melvill of the Tea Party, on whom Tom had laid eyes only when a toddler. Tom found it "a fine old church," but a little old woman crowded him, and the shape of the pew backs was so awkward that he sat stiff and went away with a backache. Ashore, Tom needed all the creature comforts he could arrange for. He had conscientiously called on his maiden aunt Priscilla Melvill, who asked to be taken riding the next day. Knowing his aunt, Tom reported that she had commenced writing Augusta a letter the week before and that Augusta would probably receive it in September. Moreover, Aunt Priss proposed to visit Arrowhead in the fall.

In his search for a ship Tom succeeded admirably, if provisionally, with the help of a man he had introduced Herman to in 1849:

> I met Captain Magoun who was first mate of the ship Navigator when I was in her before the mast I was in his watch and we were good friends. He is now Captain of the A. No 1 ship "Capitol," and has just returned from San Francisco by the way of Manilla. Learning in the course of Conversation that I was looking for a ship he told me that if I would wait a week or two he would give me the *F I R S T* mates berth on board his ship. I of course accepted his kind offer. Which is just the thing, could not be better. Having sailed togeather he knows what I am, and I know how he likes to have things done and will be able to get along with him much better than with a stranger.

This was quintessential Tom, making his way on his own, encountering a man whose friendship he had earned years earlier his own good behavior, now looking forward in his manly way to performing his duties in an atmosphere of mutual understanding and respect. None of the other Melville brothers could have taken any satisfaction in saying, "he knows what I am, and I know how he likes things done." It was pure Tom to send greetings to the nag Charley (named for Sophia's brother Charles Thurston, that appreciator of fine horseflesh) and the Major (the Newfoundland dog, named for Uncle Thomas), and like him to sign himself as a reasonable optimist, "your loving brother, Captain Melville that is to be." Shaw wrote to Lem on 17 August that Tom had "just engaged as chief mate of a ship called the Capitol, bound to Australia, & thence to China." Delighted with his companionship, Sam, whose Maine plans had fallen through, took Tom out to Milton one night during the week of the twenty-third of August, where even Oakes formed a good opinion of Tom and his prospects. On 12 September Tom took Sam down to his ship, and the younger man was so much pleased with it that he told Tom he "would like to go himself as passenger."

At Mt. Vernon Street Hope Savage Shaw in a letter to Lem on 29 August managed to keep Lizzie's problems in proportion. The sneezing part of her husband's annual catarrh had started, leaving the judge "very sound in mind, but slightly debilitated in body," and they were trying a new "medicine highly recommended by a person situated as he is." There was news from Milton: "Oakes's family are tolerable well. Josephine runs about though in a clumsy manner. Oakes understands every word but does not talk. Caroline's health is much improved from last summer." She gave a good report of Thomas Melville, her houseguest: "I think he is very promising—he will sail in a few weeks as first Mate, for the Indies. There is nothing extravagant in his views—he is rational." That was to say that Herman was both irrational and extravagant in his irrational views, but Hope for the moment took a positive view, knowing that Lem accepted her own deep-seated opinions on her son-in-law: "Herman's farm, they say is improving—he only needs money—I like him much." If Herman were to give up writing and work the farm, with the help of his man, David, it might prosper. Perhaps some of this unwonted benignity came from the fact that "Mrs. Nourse from Bath" was still, after some weeks, proving to be a surprisingly charming guest: "I never knew her more agreeable." Hope in a Plinlimmon-like version of Christian ethics wrote sententiously to her son, specifying that she was offering him fruits of her own observations: "The more I see of the world the more I value the New Testament where we read Christianity is what *all must do* — and *what all can* do & what can be more encouraging for one who wishes to be elevated in moral character than to read that *if a cup* of cold water is given with a spirit to *oblige* it is *rewarded*." Such a view of one's social responsibility her son-in-law had just found worthy of extravagantly satirical treatment in the pamphlet of *Pierre*. This reasoning could justify her giving cold water and good wishes rather than beef-broth to the hungry and cold cash to any man who needed "only" money. All one had to have to get away with giving only a cup of cold water was the right spirit, and an enterprising Boston Unitarian, advised by sages like Orville Dewey, could work that sort of spirit up, readily and cheaply enough.

On 31 August, from Milton, John Oakes Shaw, who had never taken the grand tour, indeed, who had been no farther than Chicago when it was an outpost on the western shore of Lake Michigan (far enough away, to be sure, that a little office thievery should have gone unnoticed) wrote to the half-brother who had been enjoying his grand tour for many months. Oakes was still plodding along in the old fashion at the Custom House in Boston, and disappointed that General Winfield Scott had elbowed their father's old friend Daniel Webster away from "the regular Nomination for President," for Webster would have favored Oakes: "I am Certain I Could have Managed My Cards to better advantage." He reported that his daughter, Josephine (Joe), was improving but not as fast as he had hoped: "She has been at different places at the Sea Shore for the benefit of Sea Air & bathing With I think Marked effect." Oakes continued: "they Came up from Barnstable last Week Where they had been for a fortnight With Calvin ... Crocker & family Who have been at our house a good deal this Summer & are there yet, they bring along With them a pair of Horses, Carriage & Driver Which is a great addition to the Comfort of Country life, Oakey is Stout & Well grown but although over two years old Cannot Speak the first Word." Oakes had not seen Lizzie all summer, but from Sam he had heard that "She & the Children are Well." The next news Oakes knew would please his half-brother, whose disdain for their brother-in-law had been overt since 1849: "Herman has published another book Some *high faluting* romance Which is Spoken of with anything but praise at least So far as I have heard." So far as anyone had heard, the reviews of *Pierre* were in fact all disdainful.

During these weeks, while Hawthorne was trying to get his campaign biography of his friend Franklin Pierce off to press, Melville endured one blow after another, any one of which must have been for the moment all but annihilating. On 21 August the New York *Albion* began an extremely long review with the pronouncement that *Pierre* was "a dead failure, seeing that neither in design or execution does it merit praise." This "crazy rigmarole" and "incoherent hodge-podge" was imperiling Melville's "literary standing." On the same day in the *Literary World* Duyckinck denounced the erring former protégé. Melville had entertained him bounteously in the dog days of the two previous summers, but this man was not to be swayed by such demonstrations of friendship:

> The most immoral *moral* of the story, if it has any moral at all, seems to be the impracticability of virtue; a leering demoniacal spectre of an idea seems to be speering [that is, querying] at us through the dim obscure of this dark book, and mocking us with this dismal falsehood. Mr. Melville's chapter on "Chronometricals and Horologicals," if it has any meaning at all, simply means that virtue and religion are only for gods and not to be attempted by man. But ordinary novel readers will never unkennel this loathsome suggestion. The

stagnant pool at the bottom of which it lies, is not too deep for their penetration, but too muddy, foul, and corrupt. If truth is hid in a well, falsehood lies in a quagmire.

Duyckinck could not pass "without remark" what he rightly saw as a depiction of unnatural family relationships, "the supersensuousness with which the holy relations of the family are described," Pierre's relationship with his mother as well as that with Isabel, in which "the horrors of an incestuous relation" seemed "to be vaguely hinted at." Duyckinck graciously allowed, at various points, for the possibility that Melville was going through a phase of psychological change which the young author misjudged as development, and that he might yet redeem himself by telling a brisk and sturdy "traveller's tale, in which he has few equals in power and felicity," but he was not the sort of Christian who let friendship cloud his sense of duty to the public.

All the reviewers saw Melville as having fallen away from the originality and beauty of *Typee* and *Omoo*. The Troy *Budget* on 9 August pointed to the "sort of gloomy complaining philosophy pervading his later writings," something deeply regretted by "his best friends, and those who have been his warmest admirers." Old acquaintances from Lansingburgh and Troy, admirers of "his lofty capacity" and "his acknowledged genius," were now "compelled to withhold their commendation from honest doubts as to the tendency of his writing." With no such old loyalties to inhibit, the reviewer in the Richmond *Semi-Weekly Examiner* (13 August) recalled *Typee* and *Redburn* as original books but, a little off in chronology, called *Mardi* and everything after that "unintelligible," while *Pierre* was still worse, "execrable." The Springfield *Republican* (16 August) played with Melville's stylistic excesses in its lament: "Genteel hifalutin, painful, though ingenious involutions of language, and high-flown incidental detail, characterize the work, to the uprooting of our affection for the graceful and simple writer of Omoo and Typee. Melville has changed his style entirely, and is to be judged of as a new author.—We regret the change." The Washington *National Era* (19 August) declared: "Truly is there 'but one step from the sublime to the ridiculous,' and as truly hath Mr. Melville herein accomplished it" (*Typee* and *Omoo* being the "sublime"). Duyckinck called the author of *Pierre* "but a spectre of the substantial author of 'Omoo' and 'Typee,' the jovial and hearty narrator of the traveller's tale of incident and adventure." While echoing Duyckinck's "outline," the New York *Evening Mirror* (27 August) said, "Mr. Melville should feel almost as much ashamed of the authorship of 'Pierre,' as he has a right to be proud of his 'Typee.'" The Richmond *Southern Literary Messenger* (September) was sure that from the time *Typee* "came from Mr. Melville's portfolio, he seems to have been writing under an unlucky star."

The *Southern Quarterly Review* (October) professed astonishment, for it "was not surely to be predicted or anticipated" that "'Typee,' 'Omoo,' and other clever books, should be followed by such a farrago as this of 'Pierre.'"

Melville resolutely tried to ignore the reviews, brooding instead over the memorable oral narrative and later over the formal clerk's copy made from Clifford's original diary account. Reflecting to Hawthorne on 13 August about what had happened in Nantucket the month before and how he now responded to Clifford's letter and data, Melville carefully explained that he had not, in Nantucket, hinted at all to Clifford that he saw the story as literary raw material. Instead, he said, his "first spontaneous interest in it arose from very different considerations" — including, perhaps, a sense that his own god-defying phase might have worn itself out the previous winter, and that it might be time for him to explore the way of passive endurance. Once the document arrived, it exerted its own power. During the next weeks, with his memory of the striking oral account in Nantucket still fresh in his mind and with Clifford's written account confirming and supplementing his first impressions, Melville began to regard the story as literary material, just as Clifford had assumed he had done from the start. Melville's 13 August letter to Hawthorne makes this clear: "I confess . . . that since then [since receiving the packet from Clifford] I have a little turned the subject over in my mind with a view to a regular story to be founded on these striking incidents." Try as he might to carry on as usual, Melville had to acknowledge that early August 1852 was not the very best time for planning a new work of any kind, even one on the theme of remorse and patient suffering.

On 13 August, while Arrowhead was still bustling (Sam was still there, and Allan's family, at least), Melville sent a copy of *Pierre* inscribed to both the Hawthornes, and to Hawthorne he sent the scrivener's copy of the Robertson story. He had decided that the whole story (including his own reflections) lay "very much in a vein" with which Hawthorne was "peculiarly familiar," so much so that the enhanced story now seemed "naturally to gravitate" to the older romancer. His long letter to Hawthorne contains the most extended explicit evidence that survives to show how his mind played over a written document he was planning to rework into a story of his own. At the outset, Melville allowed for the possibility that "some accidental circumstances or other" in his own mind or the situation in which he heard the story might have invested it with more pathos and depth than Hawthorne would find in it, but he confidently laid down some guidelines. (From these it seems clear that twentieth-century scholars were misled in referring to "The Story of Agatha": it was at this stage, at least, the story of Robertson — or Robinson — and Agatha.) Clifford had been too sternly judgmental toward the bigamous sailor Robertson; as a sailor himself, Melville was sure that charity "should be allowed a liberal play." As he speculated about the stages in which Robertson (whom he was calling Robinson) deserted his wife, Melville recalled the abrupt departure of Hawthorne's *"London husband"* (in "Wakefield") and backed away to let Hawthorne find out the "suggestiveness" for himself. Melville offered him some "tributary items" which he had collected by chance during his strolls through Nantucket. These were partly atmospheric effects — the value of portraying a calm before the opening story, the need for a "strange & beautiful contrast" between the innocence of the land and the "malignity of the sea." Hawthorne should make Agatha resolve never to marry a sailor, so that her doing so ("overborne by the omnipotence of Love") was the more dramatic. She should herself in some way be Robertson's (or Robinson's) rescuer from the shipwreck, and the beached ship should decay and sink partly into the sand, leaving the stem projecting above low water to be a "melancoly monument," reminding her of the rescue and her subsequent loss and pain. For seventeen years the patient Agatha would go daily to the rude mailbox on a post, and the post would become symbolic: "As her hopes gradually decay in her, so does the post itself & the little box decay." A few other items Melville also offered to Hawthorne, items that seemed to him "legitimately to belong to the story" because they were visibly suggested to him by scenes he "actually beheld while on the very coast where the story of Agatha occurred." These items he did not actually write down, but he did direct Hawthorne to the "skeleton of actual reality" in Clifford's account, the skeleton Hawthorne could build about, emphasizing that the diary was "instinct with significance," as in the noncommittal but (to a writer) all but overtly symbolic mention of handsome shawls (which had belonged to the inland wife). Melville's deciding Hawthorne should write the story of Robertson and Agatha Hatch was natural enough. He must known that Hawthorne himself had given the story of exiled Arcadians to his college friend Longfellow, who then enhanced his international reputation with *Evangeline*. Besides, Hawthorne had laid himself open to a suggested literary project by rejoicing that he could see his way, already, to having the biography of his classmate Franklin Pierce off his hands. Melville was not being officious — he was simply incapable of telling anyone that he could not pursue this darkly fascinating topic while in such pain from the reviews.

And the reviews came, relentlessly. The reviewer in the September issue of the Richmond *Southern Literary Messenger* began by confessing not to know "what evil genius delights in attending the literary movements of all those who have achieved great success in the publication of their first book" and ended by saying that "badly as we think of the book as a work of art, we think infinitely worse of it as to its moral tendency." On the seventh, the New

York *Day Book* ran a straight-faced news item: "HERMAN MELVILLE CRAZY. — A critical friend, who read Melville's last book, 'Ambiguities,' between two steamboat accidents, told us that it appeared to be composed of the ravings and reveries of a madman. We were somewhat startled at the remark; but still more at learning, a few days after, that Melville was really supposed to be deranged, and that his friends were taking measure to place him under treatment. We hope one of the earliest precautions will be to keep him stringently secluded from pen and ink." (In one of those steamboat accidents so flippantly alluded to, Hawthorne's sister Louisa had been killed.) The *Herald* on 18 September printed a very long, brilliant denunciation of *Pierre* — probably not by Powell, because it was full of verbal pyrotechnics not common in Powell's writings. Focusing on stylistic excesses rather than offenses against morality, the writer denounced Melville as "the copyist of Carlyle," and, worse, of Martin Farquhar Tupper, "a man who has done no good to our literature." Yet he did not utterly write Melville off:

> Why did Mr. Melville desert "that bright little isle of his own," in the blue waters of the Pacific? Is Polynesia used up? Has the vulgar herd of authors penetrated the fastnesses of those primitive tribes, whose taboo has become naturalized among us, and whose aquatic nymphs have fired the imagination of many a future Bouganville or Cook? Is there not a solitary whale left, whose cetacious biography might have added another stone to the monumental fame of the author of *Moby-Dick?* If our senses do not deceive us, Mr. Melville will rue his desertion of the forecastle and the virgin forest, for the drawing room and modest boarding-house chamber. . . . Mere analytical description of sentiment, mere wordy anatomy of the heart is not enough for a novel today. Modern readers wish to exercise some little judgment of their own; deeds they will have, not characters painted in cold colors, to a hairbreadth or a shade. We are past the age when an artist superscribed his *chef d'oeuvre* with the judicious explanation, "this is a horse." Mr. Melville longs for the good old times when the chorus filled the gaps between the acts with a well-timed commentary on the past, and a shrewd guess at the future.

The scandal of *Pierre* was such that some October reviewers commented approvingly on the severity of earlier reviews, taking for granted that every newspaper and magazine reader had been warned away from the book already.

One charming tribute to *Pierre* made no difference to anyone at the time, for the family could hardly have seen what young Oakey Hall wrote in New York on 13 August and shipped off for the New Orleans *Commercial Bulletin* (23 August):

It is a land story, and barring the air of a seventh heaven of rhetoric, not only interesting, but engrossing. In one great point, it is my *beau ideal* of a novel — at its conclusion, you do not draw a deep sigh, and say, "Ah, it's all over;" but the book gradually falls from the hand, while in reverie your own imagination upon the author's steed — late rider being dismounted — travels farther and farther on in the regions of speculation. A novel, which, like a dog cart, stops the moment the original impetus is withdrawn, is no novel for me.

Hall took the book to be bound in half-sheepskin to match his *Shirley* and kept it through his years as district attorney and mayor of New York City (years during which he had occasion to do business with Thomas Melville). No one in a New York or Boston paper except Nathaniel Parker Willis wrote so sympathetically as Hall did in this comment for a New Orleans audience.

A very few tolerant reviewers of *Pierre* talked about Melville's dubious advances in subtlety, not in relation to *Moby-Dick* but in relation to his previous works in general. The Springfield *Republican*, regretting the change in style, explained the gain and loss: "while the new Melville displays more subtleness of thought, more elaborateness of manner, (or mannerism), and a higher range of imagination, he has done it at a sad sacrifice of simplicity and popular appreciation." The Washington *National Era* came up with the vivid analysis cited in chapter 1 above of just what complications it expected Melville to deal with: "He is more at home in the manifold intricacies of a ship's rigging than amid the subtleties of psychological phenomena." Duyckinck in the *Literary World* sternly concluded: "Nor, if it be a true psychological development, are we sufficiently advanced in transcendentalism to lift ourselves skywards and see clearly the coming light with our heads above the clouds." Melville's old friend Willis, battered by Edwin Forrest's cane and fists and the ugliest divorce case New York had yet seen, and suffering from tuberculosis already, knew he was in the minority when he published this in his New York *Home Journal* (4 September): "The story is not artistically contrived, but it is psychologically suggestive. It is subtle, metaphysical, often profound, and has passages of bewildering intensity." The Philadelphia *Graham's Magazine* (October) used its tardiness to make a retrospective judgment: "This work is generally considered a failure. The cause of its ill-success is certainly not to be sought in its lack of power. None of Melville's novels equals the present in force and subtlety of thinking and unity of purpose. Many of the scenes are wrought out with great splendor and vigor, and a capacity is evinced of holding with a firm grasp, and describing with a masterly distinctness, some of the most evanescent phenomena of morbid emotions." This handful of reviewers recognized that Melville was evidencing a concern, however inept, for psychological phenomena. All of them thought it was new, not a further outgrowth of something present in *Moby-Dick*.

Some reviewers had recognized in *The Whale* a concern with psychological phenomena, although the word "psychology" did not appear in any known review of *The Whale*. The London *Morning Advertiser* (24 October 1851) got at Melville's fascination with motives in itemizing "High philosophy, liberal feeling, abstruse metaphysics popularly phrased, soaring speculation" and in calling him "philosophically playful," before concluding: "we will back his opening chapter, descriptive of New York, with its disquisitions on men's motives, the sea, nay water in the abstract as well as the concrete, against the same amount of prose in any book of fiction for the last dozen years, with a couple of exceptions, which we shall keep to ourselves." The London *John Bull* (25 October 1851) asked happily: "Who would have looked for philosophy in whales, or for poetry in blubber? Yet few books which professedly deal in metaphysics, or claim the parentage of the muses, contain as much true philosophy and as much genuine poetry as the tale of the *Pequod*'s whaling expedition." The London *Atlas* in its first notice (1 November 1851) said: "In none of his previous works are finer or more highly soaring imaginative powers put forth. In none of them are so many profound, and fertile, and thoroughly original veins of philosophic speculation, or rather perhaps philosophic fancy, struck." A. B. R. in the *Illustrated London News* (1 November 1851) said: "Mr. Melville's romance will worthily support his reputation for singularly vivid and reckless imaginative power — great aptitude for quaint and original philosophical speculation, degenerating, however, too often into rhapsody and purposeless extravagance — an almost unparalleled power over the capabilities of the language."

The former Brook Farm Transcendentalist George Ripley in the New York *Tribune* (22 November 1851) is the only reviewer known to have used the specific word "psychology" in a review of *Moby-Dick* (in referring to the "numerous gratuitous suggestions on psychology, ethics, and theology"). The reviewer in the New York weekly journal for expatriates, the *Albion* (22 November 1851), was probably British. Irritated by unlike elements being thrown together, he admitted that *Moby-Dick* was "not lacking much of being a great work," and quoted the section on the hyena mood in chapter 49 as a "peep into a particular mood of mind." Just possibly, Melville himself may have picked up the striking words "mood of mind" from the *Albion* (although Mary Shelley had used it in *Frankenstein*, a copy of which Bentley had given Melville in 1849). George Duyckinck's companion on the grand tour, William A. Butler, in the Washington *National Intelligencer* (16 December 1851) paid the most eloquent tribute to Melville's power in pursuing mental intricacies in *Moby-Dick:* "Mr. Melville has a strange power to reach the sinuosities of a thought, if we may so express ourselves." In 1852 no one questioned that *Pierre* was a psychological novel, albeit a study of morbid psychology, but only a handful of reviewers of *The Whale* or *Moby-Dick* had specified that part of the fascination of Melville came from his interest in motives, moods of mind, or "sinuosities of a thought" (that remarkably arresting phrase that Butler did not reuse in the *National Intelligencer* for four years, when he summoned it up again for his review of Walt Whitman's *Leaves of Grass*).

Melville meant for *Pierre,* like *Moby-Dick,* to appeal to readers as an exploration of physical and psychological states. In that it failed, partly because *Moby-Dick* had not been read that way in the United States and partly because *Pierre* did not have a chance to be widely read in England. Apparently almost no one who picked up *Pierre* and began to read it in 1852 thought of it as being very much like *Moby-Dick* except for the shared ugly Harper's binding, but the two books were continuous. *Typee* and *Omoo* were the Chang and Eng, the "Siamese Twins" of American literature, throughout Melville's lifetime and even through most of the twentieth century. Perhaps in the twenty-first century *Moby-Dick* and *Pierre* will be known as the *Typee* and *Omoo* of depth psychology—the former a whaling epic, the latter, to all appearances, a nineteenth-century novel such as Bulwer-Lytton or one of the Bell brothers (or Brontë sisters) might have written.

[7]

The Isle of the Cross
September 1852–June 1853

For thee, for thee, is left the sense
Of trial past without offence
To God or Man; — such innocence,
Such consolation, and the excess
Of an unmerited distress;
In that thy very strength must lie.

Marked by Melville in Wordsworth's
The White Doe of Rylstone, canto 2

ON THE SAME DAY that Melville mailed the copy of *Pierre* to the Hawthornes, 13 August, Sophia Hawthorne wrote her mother about reluctantly putting up at the Wayside a visiting English artist who talked incessantly, almost putting Hawthorne to sleep. He "talks like the Cataract of Lodore," Sophia told her mother, referring to the poem by Robert Southey. The chattering painter had kept his face turned to Hawthorne "as the sunflower to the sun" so that when Sophia spoke and he tried to turn to her, his "head whirled back again like a toy-witch." Reflecting on how "the mighty heart" and "the grand intellect" (made visible in her husband's eyes and head) had the power to open "the bosoms of men," she thought of their Pittsfield friend: "So Mr Melville, generally silent & incommunicative, pours out the rich floods of his mind & experience to him, so sure of apprehension, so sure of a large & generous interpretation, & of the most delicate and fine judgment."

Melville's packet on the sailor Robertson and Agatha Hatch reached Wayside just as Hawthorne was making sure his *Life of Franklin Pierce* would be published in time to be a true campaign biography, so he could not give full attention to the merits or demerits either of *Pierre* or of the suggested literary topic. On 3 September, after a hasty and frustrating trip to Bowdoin which could hardly have allowed him to unwind from the tensions of finishing the biography, Hawthorne vacationed at the Isles of Shoals, where he kept up his journal with unwonted regularity for two weeks — just possibly with the view of writing the Robertson and Agatha story and setting it there instead of Nantucket. (The sibilant-heavy name of the islands being unpleasing to pronounce, Hawthorne regularly referred to the Isle of Shoals; so did others, as young Dana made clear in his diary for 15 August 1843 in referring to "the Isle of Shoals, so called, although they are a group of seven high, rocky islands.") On the sixth Pierce and his party came to spend the night at Laighton's Hotel on Appledore Island, where Hawthorne was staying, and political sugarplums danced in the head of the writer long inured to poverty. Yet he continued to talk as if his career were going to continue in its course. On 13 October he wrote his old friend Horatio Bridge (then in the Pacific): "In a day or two, I intend to begin a new romance, which, if possible, I mean to make more genial than the last"—that is, more genial than the baffling look at Brook Farm Transcendentalism through the eyes of a prissy voyeur, *The Blithedale Romance*. Already, however, he was wavering from his earlier scruple that if he wrote the campaign biography he could hardly accept a political appointment from Pierce. Hawthorne did not begin a new romance, genial like his hypothetical one or gloomy like the one Melville had sent him: for the first time in his life, real money was in sight.

Real money was nowhere in sight for Melville, but on 14 September he paid John M. Brewster ninety dollars, one year's interest on his mortgage against Arrowhead. Stunned by the reviews and what they meant for his future, he was too upset to write to Tom, who complained to Augusta on 12 September, as he instructed her to direct mail to "Thomas Melvill[e], ship Gem of the Ocean, San Francisco." Tom was still passing his nights at Mt. Vernon Street, but was on board his ship from early morning until evening. He bought one of the first copies of Hawthorne's *Life of Franklin Pierce*, wanting to take something by Herman's friend along on the voyage and thinking it might be just as well to have information on shipboard about the unknown Yankee who had at least a fifty-fifty chance of becoming the next president. On 16 September, probably leaving Tom with the housekeeper, Mrs. Sullivan, and the servants, Judge Shaw and Hope Savage Shaw went to Pittsfield for the regular term arguments in the court at Lenox.

The judge reported to Lem that he and his wife had arrived at Arrowhead in time for dinner: "Elizabeth & her children are very well and also Herman, Mrs Melville & the rest of the family. The daughters are all at home. Allan & his family, who have been passing part of the summer there, have recently returned to N. York." Herman took the Shaws for a long ride the next day, Friday, and Saturday they walked. Hope wrote Lem on 4 October: "Elizabeth was in health & the two children very promising—Lizzy says that Malcolm has picked up three barrels of potatoes,—David their boy is a particular *friend of his*—He is training Malcolm & the old lady Mrs Melville is educating David—as I think no one more capable;—the farm in time will yet flourish." (David was the Irish servant, there almost a year already.) No one had any faith in Melville's literary productions, but they allowed themselves to believe that with the help of the hired "boy" or man, under Maria's expert direction, the farm might produce enough food for the household and the animals. After the spring of 1851 no one expected Herman to run the farm himself. The Shaws went to Lenox on the twentieth, and the next day a troupe came over to dine with them at the Little Red Inn: "Tuesday 21, Mrs Melville & daughter [Helen]—Elizabeth Herman & Mr & Mrs Morewood dined here." Then on Friday the twenty-fourth Hope recorded: "Elizabeth Miss [Helen] Melville Mr Morewood came over here on horseback." Life looked almost normal.

Just at this time, on 23 September, the Albany *Daily State Register* printed an original essay about the Dead Letter Office in the General Post Office in Washington: "Dead Letters—By a Resurrectionist" (that is, one who digs up corpses to sell to surgeons and others needing to improve their dissecting skills). Dead Letter Office items were having a vogue, but this journalist had a real voice, one could hear from the start: "Piled in the halls, outside the doors of these melancholy vaults, are great sacks, locked and sealed and labelled 'DEAD LETTERS,' and ever and anon, appears a grim, sexton-like old negro, who seizing a bag disappears with it into one or other of the tombs." In one of several passages of heightened rhetoric the writer gave some dramatic examples of items found in dead letters by the inspectors: "Here is one contains a lock of hair—nothing more; valueless in the hard, unromantic judgment of the law. . . . Money, bills of exchange, Daguerreotypes, notes of hand, receipts, emigrant passage tickets, lottery tickets, an old wallet, health, fire and life assurance policies, a bunch of keys, a specimen of wheat, bottles, sugar samples, hanks of yarn, a bed quilt, a rattlesnake skin, two diamond ornaments, an old hat, a draft for ten thousand dollars, a paving stone." The New York *Times* of 24 September reprinted a slightly altered version of this article, and on 9 October the Washington *National Intelligencer* reprinted it, slightly abbreviated. Melville saw it, in one place or another, and put it at least figuratively "on the file," a phrase that suggests that he had a standard piece of office hardware fastened to the wall, a flat brass plate with a spike protruding out two or three inches and then upwards, for spearing a sheet of paper and pulling it down flat for easy viewing. On the file may have gone invitations he received in the next months, one from George P. Putnam dated 1 October to contribute to a new "original periodical of a character different from any now in existence," and one from Bentley dated December to contribute to *Bentley's Miscellany*.

On 30 September, just after the Shaws left the Berkshires, Melville attended the anniversary celebration of the Pittsfield Young Ladies' Institute, where his Uncle Peter's townsman Alfred Billings Street read a poem about the blessings of married love ("Though harsh cares pursue him through the day / Her hand of comfort drives them all away"). Augusta was a friend of Street's, and Melville apparently greeted the poet politely enough, but confronted with such successful inanity just when he was such a failure as a husband and just when his own work of genius was being heaped with opprobrium, he could not bring himself to go through all the proper social forms. Peter protested to his sister (9 October) that Street had complained to him "with great earnestness & much feeling" that Herman had not called on him and had not invited him to Arrowhead, thereby (such were the social codes) preventing him from visiting Augusta. Peter lamented to Maria: "Alas — Herman, thou art a sorry boy — Thou might have tipped thy beaver, kissed thy hand & last tho not least dropped thy Card, but tho' Hat & Hand & Card were thine, all those were withheld by thee Typee from Alfreds anxious hopes — no, no the Poet sings, no, no — he took no friendly token from his quiver, and locked up 'Arrowhead.' " He concluded: "Oh Herman, Herman, Herman truly thou art an 'Ambiguity.' "

In the first week of October the locals were titillated by the publication of *Taghconic; or Letters and Legends about Our Summer Home*, edited by Godfrey Greylock (J. E. A. Smith). On 6 October, before she received his protest about Herman's treatment of Street, Maria Melville sent a copy to Peter, calling it a "sort of guide book of our beautiful County of Berkshire," and adding: "Mr John C Hoadley wrote 'Berry Pond,' Mrs Morewood wrote 'That excursion to Greylock,['] & some of the gifted ones around us wrote a few other chapters." Her phrasing indicates that Peter already knew who Hoadley was, as well as Mrs. Morewood. Maria continued: "After writing the above I shou[l]d add that Herman has not contributed one line, tho often requested to do so." She could rely on Peter to interpret her correctly and understand that during the previous winter and spring her recalcitrant son had rebuffed a series of perfectly reasonable requests from a polite, deferential member of Mrs. Morewood's set. Herman had acted out of the peculiar vanity that had made him behave so rudely and shortsightedly in the matter of the daguerreotype for Mr. Duyckinck a year and a half earlier. She had done her best, again, but her son again had been stubborn, to the detriment of his reputation in Pittsfield. Eager to get away from the tensions at Arrowhead, in mid-October Maria took herself off, in the company of Helen and Fanny, for a visit with Allan and Sophia, where she could talk freely about the reception of *Pierre* and obtain Allan's advice on what could be done to save Herman from himself. Peter had been humiliated, Maria was exasperated: the front the family had put up was beginning to crack.

Melville's Cousin Priscilla, after visiting Arrowhead in the summer, became piteously importunate about her fantasy of moving into a cottage near her cousins. In October Augusta made inquiries and reported back, evoking this response from Canandaigua on the first of November: "You make a *sober* reality — *indeed* — of my little pleasant romance connected with the 'Brown' Cottage — & your affectionate solicitude for my *greatest* happiness has penetrated *deep* into the *shadows* of its quiet seclusion, & discover'd a grim array of frightful spectres, enough to daunt the courage of any *helpless* woman who was indulging faint dreams of attempting to seek comfort & content unaided & alone." She resigned herself to two possibilities: "I *would* like very much to find constant employment for my needle — in *that* case, I *could board* as you suggest — *If not* — *I can* drag along an existence *here*." His Pierre had sworn to be Isabel's "leapingly-acknowledging brother," and Melville felt Priscilla's situation deeply, but he was unable to help her. She was grateful for the love shown in "the *grave* consultations" held about her at Arrowhead, while he exercised a man's privilege of resenting any such consultations held about *him*, whether safely away in New York City or Albany, or in Arrowhead itself.

Melville's troubles had been accumulating week by week. William Gilmore Simms in the October Charleston *Southern Quarterly Review* lamented that Melville had "gone 'clean daft'" in "a very mad book." Melville's "dramatis personae" were "all mad as March hares, every mother's son of them, and every father's daughter of them," and the sooner Melville was "put in ward the better." The New York humorous paper the *Lantern* for 2 October touted a "FATAL OCCURRENCE": an intelligent young man had deliberately bought a copy of *Pierre*, with predictable results: "He has, of course, not since been heard of." The fake Diogenes bearing aloft his lantern in search of an honest man was the English scoundrel Thomas Powell, making sure that *Pierre* would become a national laughingstock as well as a scandal.

Hawthorne and his wife may not have read *Pierre* at once, for a long disquisition on Melville which Sophia wrote to her mother on 24 October seems wholly untainted by concern about the direction of his career:

> I received last evening your long letter. I am very glad you have enjoyed Typee and Omoo so much. Mr Melville shall know your pleasure when I see or write to him again. He is a very rich person, & grasps his subjects in superb India shawls. By & by I think we shall receive from him still rarer & more costly merchandize; for he cruises in far off, golden seas & ships treasures of moon shells and sunfishes & snatches at star-dust as his prow grazes against remote orbits at either pole. He is an incalculable person, full of daring & questions, & with all momentous considerations afloat in the crucible of his mind. He tosses them in, & heats his furnace sevenfold & burns & stirs, &

waits for the crystalization with a royal indifference as to what may turn up, only eager for truth, without previous prejudice. His ocean-experience has given sea-room to his intellect, & he is in the mere boyhood of his possibilities. Meantime he is his own Captain & goes on his own adventure & what he discovers will be told in his own words. He is as graphic in his speech as in his writings, & when he describes any thing with the living voice, it is there, it is here, just as he says it, & he himself is each several person of the tale. You know I told you once how this magic power of his created Allan Cunningham with a stout oak cudgel in his hand, in our boudoir at Lenox, & how I looked round for the stick after he retired for the night, & could not find any.

Sophia dated this letter 1851, clearly wrong because she was in Concord, though a year before she might well have been waiting for the cargo he would bring home from his cruises in far-off golden seas and ships. This analysis is powerful and curious for many reasons, not least the furnace imagery, in the light of Hawthorne's decision not to make the forge of his Robert Danforth in "The Artist of the Beautiful" a symbol of the creative process.

Generally so diffident, Melville may have received a now-lost response in which Hawthorne expressed some degree of interest in writing the story, for on 25 October he sent more suggestions for the Robertson and Agatha story, in case his friend should already "be engaged upon it." The new "little idea" Melville had been cogitating about was this:

> The probable facility with which Robinson first leaves his wife & then takes another, may, possibly, be ascribed to the peculiarly latitudinarian notions, which most sailors have of all tender obligations of that sort. In his previous sailor life Robinson had found a wife (for a night) in every port. The sense of the obligation of the marriage-vow to Agatha had little weight with him at first. It was only when some years of life ashore had passed that his moral sense on that point became develloped. And hence his subsequent conduct— Remorse &c. Turn this over in your mind & see if it is right. If not—make it so yourself.

Still brooding upon the psychological motivations of the characters (the name of the real Robertson tightening down to Robinson, perhaps with some slight allusion to Daniel Defoe's castaway), Melville had fixed upon a particularly inward emotion, the one that turns and feeds upon itself. (Powell in 1856 claimed that Melville had told him, in 1849, it would have been, that he was planning a work on the theme of remorse; this may be true.) The most Melville allowed himself to show his own feelings was in a cryptic postscript play on the sand used to blot his ink: "If you find any *sand* in this letter, regard it as so many sands of my life, which run out as I was writing this." Hawthorne may have renewed the invitation he had given Melville to visit him in Concord, for the younger man promised to lay eyes on him "one of these days" and told him to keep some "Champagne or Gin" for him. He would need it.

On the first of November, Melville defaulted on the semiannual interest payment of $92.25 due to T. D. Stewart—the second time in a row. Outwardly he may have seemed calm enough during these days. Half a century later, on 20 September 1901, Lizzie critiqued an article by Mary Lanman Douw Ferris, a distant cousin of Melville's, a granddaughter of John De Peyster Douw, objecting to the statement that the reception of *Pierre* had caused Melville "to lead 'a recluse life.'" Not at all, she said: "in fact it was a subject of joke with him, declaring that it was but just, and I know that however it might have affected his literary reputation, it concerned him personally but very little." His "seclusion from the bustling outer world was but the outcome of a naturally retiring disposition, and the desire of repose after what would now-a-days be called the 'strenuous life' of his boyhood and youth and had been his habit from the beginning of his home life long years before 'Pierre' was thought of." Melville may have made such a would-be stoical dismissal of the reviews, but Lizzie's declaration papered over the reality of Melville's agony. The horror about the marriage would be if Lizzie in 1852 blandly accepted her husband's assurances that the reviews were only fair, only what he deserved, and had been oblivious either of the grandeur of the undertaking or of the splendor Melville had actually achieved.

Herman was in New York on election day, 2 November, having come to escort his mother home. In the November *American Whig Review* (published in late October) was one of the longest reviews of any Melville's books and one of the harshest reviews ever published about a serious American work of fiction. The writer was Melville's perverse alcoholic nemesis, G. W. Peck, who lurked with his jug in one squalid cock-loft or another in lower Manhattan until he could review the newest book by the genius he hated. Now he exulted: "A bad book! Affected in dialect, unnatural in conception, repulsive in plot, and inartistic in construction. Such is Mr. Melville's worst and latest work." Much of the endless essay consisted of condemnation of the immorality of *Pierre*, but toward the end Peck elaborated a fierce denunciation of Melville's language. Then he mustered his charges together: "Mr. Melville is a man wholly unfitted for the task of writing wholesome fictions"; he "possesses none of the faculties necessary for such work"; and "his fancy is diseased, his morality vitiated, his style nonsensical and ungrammatical, and his characters as far removed from our sympathies as they are from nature." Peck's few remaining acquaintances realized what a pathetic wreck of a man he had become. In February 1853, Richard Henry Dana Jr. and others,

The Isle of the Cross: September 1852–June 1853

deciding that all had "been done for him that can be done," took up a subscription among his friends, "nearly all of whom he had sponged & worried out of all patience" and sent him off to Australia where he could drink himself to death — Botany Bay or another hellhole being a fit place for a once meritorious man now "so wofully impaired & disgraced." In 1852 no mental health standards for reviewers had yet been enacted.

However Herman and Lizzie behaved, the rest of the family was near hysteria. According to the account given by Maria Melville several months later (20 April 1853), soon after the election of Franklin Pierce, Herman had been eager to be given a foreign consulship. To her brother Peter she gave this circumstantially detailed history of discussions held in November 1852, perhaps in New York City: "we talked the matter over again & again, arranged that the girls [Helen, Augusta, and Fanny] & myself, & the children should stay at Arrowhead & Lizzie accompany Herman." This must contain some literal truth, although another view would be that she had urged the matter on her son over and over again, and in her own mind had worked out the arrangements for distributing the family. By election day 1852 Lizzie must have known she was pregnant and therefore should have been less than receptive to any plan which would involve her leaving her small sons, Malcolm and Stanwix, and traveling abroad with an infant, especially since her previous (and normal) pregnancy had been followed by a breast infection so prolonged and so severe that she had been forced to flee to the only city in the civilized world where a Mt. Vernon Street girl could hope to find adequate medical attention. By the spring of 1853, Lizzie was willing to go abroad, but nothing shows that in the early weeks of her third pregnancy she had any notion of leaving her sons and going across one or two oceans with Herman. During all of the discussions the secret loan loomed large in Melville's own mind: if he went abroad would Stewart seize Arrowhead from under the family he had left there?

And during this crisis Melville went to the Manhattan bookstores as if he had all the money he needed. Dr. John W. Francis, Mrs. Thurston's neighbor, was now Sophia's doctor, and for Herman he was forever associated with the wonderful evenings at Bond Street when Tuckerman, Duyckinck, Griswold, and others had talked and smoked together. For decades Dr. Francis had been intrigued by reports of fair-skinned pygmies said to be living in the interior of Madagascar. Two years earlier, while he was appropriating his portrait of Queequeg in *Moby-Dick* from Craik's *The New Zealanders*, Melville had noticed there a citation of Rochon's 1791 "account of his own voyages to Madagascar and the East Indies, which was reprinted in 1802, with the addition of two other volumes." Somehow, extravagantly, he procured the Rochon as a gift for Dr. Francis, who on 3 November, addressing him at Allan's new house on Twenty-fourth Street, thanked him for "the curious volume Rochon's Voyage to Madagascar." The last day Augusta addressed her mother in New York City was 4 November, so Herman and Maria left for Pittsfield soon after that. For Herman the ride home, trapped in the railway car, was fraught with wild thoughts of escape—but where could he escape to? Making good *their* escape from the Berkshire winter, Helen and Fanny both stayed on at Allan and Sophia's. By the first of December Helen was in New Rochelle at Winyah before going to stay with George and Kate Gansevoort Curtis in Brooklyn, and she was not in residence at Arrowhead until March. Fanny stayed with Allan and Sophia until late spring or summer of 1853 (Maria joined her in late March, despite all her concern about the discomforts of that month in the city). The family was fearful for Sophia, who had been near death earlier in the year, anxious about Herman, planning for new lives for Kate and perhaps Helen.

Before Thanksgiving it was arranged that, through December, Maria, Augusta, and Kate would hold down the farmhouse, with the help of the cook, the man David, and any other temporary servant. On 22 November (as Lemuel Shaw wrote to Lem, in Rome) "Elizabeth with her husband & children arrived this evening from Pittsfield, well, but tired & all gone to bed." Oakes and his family were due the next day or two. Sam was home, so all the family was there but Lem. Shaw said the obvious: "We always look to this annual family meeting with great pleasure," Thanksgiving remaining the great New England holiday. In making sure that Herman and Lizzie were there with their children, Shaw was demonstrating that the family was united and that Herman was part of it, regardless of the public accusations of insanity and depravity. Nilly Thayer, on Mt. Vernon Street like the Shaws, reported to Augusta: "I saw Mrs Herman soon after her arrival here & the children, the eldest is a nice boy & grown much since I last saw him. She seems very happy with her country home & says you pass your time very pleasantly which I can readily imagine with all your fondness for a rural life." Everyone was behaving more normally now, after the intense conferences at Arrowhead and in New York City, as well as the smaller and darker ones Hope Savage Shaw held in Boston.

Before this Melville had probably visited the new Boston Athenæum, on the southerly side of Beacon, between Bowdoin and Somerset streets, notable for its magnificent second-story library. There he charged to Shaw's membership *Notes and Lectures upon Shakespeare and Some of the Old Poets and Dramatists; with Other Literary Remains of Samuel Taylor Coleridge* (London, 1849), sufficient reading for a few days. In view of Maria's later account of the grand consultations, Lizzie must have confided to her father and stepmother the family's anxiety about Herman's state of mind and their speculations

The Isle of the Cross: September 1852–June 1853

about separating the family in the case he did receive a foreign appointment. Foremost on her mind was the news she may have told them in person after she arrived — that she was pregnant again. On 2 December Melville made a day-trip to Concord to see Hawthorne, who had purchased the "miserable little house of two peaked gables" which Bronson Alcott had improved without belying "the innate sobriety of a venerable New England farm-house" (G. W. Curtis's description in *Homes of American Authors*). Melville would have seen, out back, the ruins of Alcott's rustifications, "terraces, and arbors, and pavilions, of boughs and rough stems of trees," the whole "terraced hillside" in a state of decay. He would have examined the familiar art works, now gathered in a western room, where at sunset (as Sophia wrote her mother) "Apollo's 'beautiful disdain' seemed kindled anew — Endymion smiled richly in his dream of Diana — Lake Como was wrapt in a golden mist — The divine form in the Transfiguration floated in light." The Transfiguration, for sure, Melville remembered from the study in Lenox.

In Concord the men seem to have kept themselves closeted to discuss the story of "Robinson" and Agatha rather than seeking out any literary society the village might have to offer. They considered the possibility (suggested by Hawthorne?) of changing the setting from Nantucket (already chosen over the real Pembroke) to the Isles of Shoals, on which Hawthorne had a trove of fresh notes in his journal. Hawthorne told Melville he was uncertain that he would undertake the story and, before they parted, urged Melville to write it himself. Anxious not to embarrass the president-elect, Hawthorne was not entirely candid with Melville about the degree of certainty with which he regarded the prospect of a political appointment. About 12 December Melville wrote Hawthorne from Boston that he had decided to take Hawthorne's advice and write the story himself "immediately upon reaching home." Recalling their conversations, Melville wanted, with Hawthorne's permission, to "make use of the 'Isle of Shoals,' as far as the name goes at least." The "at least" is ambiguous, perhaps indicating that all Melville was sure he wanted was the name, the "Isle of Shoals," not the notes Hawthorne had made there.

On 13 December Melville departed for Pittsfield with Malcolm, leaving Lizzie and Stanwix to stay a few weeks longer. The mild December of 1852 was followed by a cold January. Before 10 January 1853, Lizzie returned to Arrowhead with Stanwix, more than halfway through her new pregnancy. She carried a portrait of her father drawn or commissioned by her cousin Elizabeth Dow, and she left behind a family concerned about her health, but bustling with visiting young women, as Hope Savage Shaw liked it. While his wife and children were in New York at her sister's, Oakes had settled into residence, making himself at home in Lem's study and bedroom (news which Hope blandly transmitted to her traveling firstborn), and appearing "as happy as he can be situated as he is." Hope's view of her stepson (expressed on 25 July) was that Oakes was extremely "sensitive" and even downright " 'peculiar' " in his feelings. Mainly, he was dissatisfied with himself, jealous of Lem and Sam (Hope decided), and was "thinking if he had gone to College he would have been more successful in life." Sam was in the house, and also miserable, facing graduating without any distinction. On 23 January Hope explained to Lem that Sam had "a decided taste" for "Literature" but had not devoted himself to study. Herman, it would have been granted, possessed or had formerly possessed a taste for "Literature" himself, imperfectly controlled. Now the youngish and young males were a pair—Oakes paying lifelong for the marriage made in unseemly haste, with a minister picked by the obliging Gansevoort Melville, reason enough to despise Gansevoort's literary brother; Sam in academic disgrace, both of them envious of the arrogant, triumphant Lem. In February, Hope invited Helen Melville to join the lively household. Helen had not been to Boston in five years, but she was making a full winter's visit to her Brooklyn cousins. On 14 February 1853, Helen wrote Hope Shaw that she and Kate Curtis had both made their way to Arrowhead briefly, in early February, so Helen could see the children, especially "little Stan" ("my especial pet I am afraid that I love him more than all my nephews and neices put together"). She added: "I know that you will be glad to hear from an eye witness that they were all well. Lizzie is remarkably active and cheerful, and the little ones have improved very much since I saw them in the Autumn."

According to what Maria wrote to Peter on 20 April 1853, Herman out of his dislike of asking "favors from any one" had postponed writing to influential politicians "from time to time," week to week. Once back at Arrowhead, Melville soon became "so completely absorbed" by his new work that he could not think of breaking away from it in order to write the necessary letters seeking a consular appointment. The postponing took place in November 1852 through December 1852 and the total absorption came by January 1853. By the early spring of 1853 Melville had settled on the title *The Isle of the Cross*, a title so like the common misnomer Hawthorne and Melville had been using, "the Isle of Shoals," as to confirm the subject of the story. The title indicated that on the now-fictionalized island Melville had erected some tangible cross, perhaps one which (during the lonely wait of the woman) slanted toward the ground (he would memorably address a "slanted" cross in *Clarel*) or fell, the way in his early broodings on Clifford's documents he had visualized Agatha's mail box decaying and falling. The title also showed how profoundly Melville was treating the sufferings of the woman based on Agatha Hatch. The isle was the site where one or more characters suffered something like a crucifixion, the Agatha character because of her abandonment and her struggles to educate her child alone, the Robertson character because in the slow gnawings of conscience he was eating himself alive with his remorse (a word of which Melville knew the Latin root). As a man abandoned by his public, Melville may have been disposed to be sympathetic toward another loving, responsive young person wrongly abandoned. At the same time, the sort of shame Melville was suffering for in effect mortgaging Arrowhead to a second creditor may have disposed him toward the young sailor who came ashore and took on a commitment which he was not prepared to honor, only to suffer remorse when he came to understand the significance of the rules he had violated. Some such raw psychological material went into the book, lacerated as Melville was by the opprobrium from the critics and by his own self-accusations. Under the circumstances, *The Isle of the Cross* may have become a story of such unrelieved gloom as to make *The Scarlet Letter* look almost sunny. Long before I discovered the title *The Isle of the Cross* in Cousin Priscilla's letters to Augusta, the subject of the proposed story was known by biographers as "The Story of Agatha"; as I suggested in the previous chapter, it may have been equally the story of Robertson (or Robinson) and Agatha (under another name), remorse and modern, un-Griselda-like long-suffering.

In early 1853 something astonishing began to be bruited about the Shaw household, relief from the onslaught of scathing comments on Herman's *Pierre*. In a letter received in January, Lem suggested that his father join him for the last months of his grand tour. Friend of a great traveler, Allan Melvill, and that friend's son the professional travel-writer and other son the first mate, friend also of innumerable connections from Harvard College who had gone abroad and written him and later regaled him with their adventures, father of a son whom he was sending on a grand tour such as he had denied himself, the aging Lemuel Shaw, chief justice of the Supreme Court of the Commonwealth of Massachusetts, yielded to temptation. He too would go to Europe. Consternation shook at Mt. Vernon Street like nothing since the great Beacon Hill earthquake of 1846. Hope succumbed to a highly public declaration of what would happen if she attempted to accompany the judge: "I should *die — crossing the Atlantic —*." The decision thus made to preserve her life, she determined that her husband could not depart without being in the charge of a reliable manservant. Canning, his longtime valet, had amassed what they all considered a "competence" and retired. The new Irish manservant was a "well *intentioned man*," but he lacked "in education," and had "much to learn." For weeks Lem and Hope conducted a duel of wills across the Atlantic, she determined that her husband would not travel without a manservant, Lem insisting that an elderly servant would amount to an additional useless set of bones for him (Lem) to drag around. It was 5 March before Shaw himself wrote to Lem, with unwonted elation, and glossing over any knowledge he had of the recent transatlantic correspondence between his wife and son: "I hardly know how to introduce the subject of this letter, which I am sure will greatly surprize you.... I have now a purpose of joining you in England, before you return, if all things can be brought to concur in promoting such a meeting." Hope worked frantically to draw Canning back into service, meanwhile writing Lem, briefly relaying the latest bad news about Sam's performance at Harvard but emphasizing that her husband required watching: "So dependant as he is, how can he get along without some one to take that care of him that he requires. Remember *Lemuel, he is seventy two* in years—I am aware that he is remarkably active but he needs much care."

On 23 May Lem wrote from Paris: "In my last letter I so fully stated my opinion that to bring a sick servant, would only be to have the care of an additional & expensive useless piece of luggage, that I will not recur to the subject again." (Selfish as always, Lem had not delivered to M. Fleury, Priscilla's uncle, the miniature of Françoise Fleury Melvill, Priscilla's mother, that Hope had sent after Lem by Dr. Jacob Bigelow, with whom the judge had made the excursion in the White Mountains in 1816.) In Liverpool he stayed at the best place, the Adelphi Hotel, on a hill looking down toward the Mersey, where Evert Duyckinck had stayed in 1839. There Lem could watch in comfort for the appearance of his father and an unknown number of elderly retainers, none capable of carrying his own carpetbag. Hope was not worried so much about her husband's ability to move his own set of bones as she was about his ability to take care of matters of intimate personal hygiene. The judge had "always" had her to take great care of his person: "I beg my dear Son, that this will be a care of faithfulness, and that in a most delicate & friendly manner *give him the attention of a daughter*. Pay great attention to his person—we always give much credit to age advancing when we see them very *neat*.... Do not oppose it I shall never consent his going without Canning." On 12 June Hope spelled out the grounds of her anxiety as explicitly as she could bring herself to do. She begged Lem, "be very particular respecting your father's external appearance." He should watch, "for if his ears are not particularly & daily seen to, the external part is a disadvantage to him." He needed to be inspected before being seen by anyone outside the family. Herman had traveled happily with Shaw the previous summer: in his years at sea he had witnessed worse sights than rheumy eyes, leaky noses, waxy ears, and septuagenarian mouths that oozed a little liquid at a corner.

While Augusta was at the Manor House, Maria and Kate were at Arrowhead from December through March. In March Maria went to New York, and Helen and Kate were both at Arrowhead with Lizzie and Herman. In April Maria and Kate went to Lansingburgh; Kate, at least, was there late in

June, where she could revel in sharing with her relatives and girlhood friends the news of her engagement to John Hoadley (the widower who had moved to Lawrence). Augusta came home in early May so she could be with Lizzie during her confinement. The constants at Arrowhead were the little boys, Lizzie and her growing child within, and Herman with his growing manuscript. When Herman drove to the village for mail he took the long way round, at times, so as to keep a neighborly eye on the Morewood property, and he wrote Rowland a caution about something that needed attention while the Morewoods were stuck in the city. Maria and Fanny paid a call at the place the Morewoods were boarding on 18 March, walking from Allan's on Twenty-fourth Street. The women suffered "innumerable disagreeables" as they tried to avoid accidents on the broken-up parts of Fourteenth Street where new houses were being built. In that street Maria found the squalid place where the Morewoods were boarding. Sarah, of course, was out. Maria was appalled at the general filth and the inattention of Mrs. Brittain to the feeble little Alfred Morewood. When the baby awoke hungry, someone stuck "a bottle of cold mutton soup" in his mouth, but he rejected it and Maria repeatedly rang for the nurse to come up and warm the bottle, and at last dispatched "a dirty fat girl about 12 years old" to carry the message below, but no one returned. Mrs. Brittain's excuse was that they were only living there until Alfred was better, when they would go to the Berkshires. This was the woman Maria had credited with making Broadhall habitable. The visit had one good consequence, Maria's writing Augusta a masterfully Dickensian account.

The location of Allan and Sophia's new house was an improvement over the Thirty-fifth Street misadventure, but still so far uptown as to make Maria's stay difficult. As she wrote to Kate on 21 March, she suffered merely from taking her sewing down to Mrs. Thurston's in Bond Street: "the dust blew enough to blind me, every one was trying to keep their eyes shut, to see their way without opening them." The month of March in the city was so unpleasant that Fanny fled with Abby and Richard Lathers for an indefinite stay at Winyah. Maria gave up on Allan and Sophia and moved down to Bond Street with Mrs. Thurston, so as to be more convenient to the daily church services during "Passion week," and after that she went to Brooklyn for a week with the Curtises, who were full of praise for Helen's ministrations in a household where someone was always ailing. Maria then joined up with Fanny for their return to Arrowhead. Maria's wish for Lizzie, before Easter, was characteristic: "she must keep up her spirits" — must actively work at keeping herself cheerful rather than giving in to her naturally nervous constitution.

All indication is that Melville hibernated, aside from driving into town for the mail — not a pleasure he would willingly relegate to David, boy or man. The end of January brought the initial (February) issue of a new journal, *Putnam's Monthly*, which had solicited him as a contributor. It contained the young Irish immigrant Fitz-James O'Brien's summary of Melville's career from *Typee* through *Pierre* ("with its inexcusable insanity"), and some advice. Melville was tottering "on the edge of a precipice, over which all his hard-earned fame may tumble" if he cumbered himself with another dead weight like *Pierre:* "Let him diet himself for a year or two on Addison, and avoid Sir Thomas Browne, and there is little doubt but that he will make a notch on the American Pine." This stern warning ended the article, the first retrospective survey of Melville's career anyone had ever published. Some newspapers from New York still arrived at Arrowhead, besides *Harper's New Monthly Magazine*. On 18 February the *Tribune* (and the new rival, the *Times*) contained an advertisement for a new book called *The Lawyer's Story* — including the entire first chapter, which opened this way: "In the summer of 1843, having an extraordinary quantity of deeds to copy, I engaged, temporarily, an extra copying clerk, who interested me considerably, in consequence of his modest, quiet, gentlemanly demeanor, and his intense application to his duties." Nothing in the rest of the chapter was notable, and, as far as we know, Melville never saw the book, but that remarkably evocative sentence went onto his "file."

While Maria and Fanny were away, Herman had a visitor, perhaps one who arrived at the door in late March with no warning at all — his shipmate Henry F. Hubbard, who had stayed on the *Acushnet* while Melville and others deserted, and had returned home on her after a voyage lasting more than four years. Hubbard may have been at Arrowhead when Harper's 21 March account came, showing 2310 copies of *Pierre* printed, 150 review copies sent out, and 283 copies sold, leaving Melville with a balance due the Harpers of $298.71. In any case, what Hubbard had read about his friend for years, and everything that he saw at Arrowhead, must have conveyed an impression at odds with Herman's actual financial status — a situation just as well, since it allowed Herman to play one of his best roles, that of Lord of Arrowhead, feasting a friend. There was recent news to mull over, for one or both would have heard that the *Acushnet* had been wrecked in August 1851 (as the New Bedford *Whalemen's Shipping List* had reported just before Christmas 1851). They talked over old times in great detail. The captain whom Melville had maligned in *Typee*, Valentine Pease, had "retired & lives ashore at the Vineyard," Melville recorded in a memorandum on what had become of the men who had shipped with him. Fewer than ten came home on the *Acushnet*, Hubbard had reported. One "had a fight with the Captain & went ashore at Payta"; one "went ashore at Payta"; another either ran away or was "killed at

Ropo one of the Marquesas"; one "went ashore at Santa coast of Peru, afterwards committed suicide at Mobile"; two "went ashore at Mowee half dead with disreputable disease," and one or both of them died there; two had "run away at St: Francisco," one being Backus, the "little black"; one had "run away at Salango coast of Columbia"; one other "went ashore half dead at the Marquesas"; one had "run away aboard of a Sydney ship"; one "went ashore half dead, spitting blood, at Oahu"; one "went ashore, shunning fight, at Rio Janeiro." Melville left some men out of his list. Hubbard came home and went west. Richard T. (Toby) Greene jumped ship in the Marquesas but came home. Herman Melville ran away in the Marquesas and came home and wrote about living among the cannibals.

For a man like Melville, one whose mind could be suffusingly invaded by the dead and missing people from the past, the visit from Hubbard was an intensely moving experience, particularly coming as it did as an interruption of his obsessive work on his manuscript, and near the end of his wife's pregnancy. He gave Hubbard what he knew was an extraordinary gift — perhaps his next-to-last set of *The Whale*, not bothering to copy out the "Epilogue" into it, as he might have done if he was confident Hubbard would actually read the volumes. Hubbard carried the volumes to California, where they remained in his family until the 1970s. Then it was revealed that Hubbard had annotated page 58 of the third volume, in "The Castaway," where Stubb, the second mate, orders the whaleline cut in order to save Pip's life: "Pip — Backus — his real name. I was in the boat at the time he made the leap overboard — Stubs = J Hall real name," Hall being the second mate. Melville was so far along with *The Isle of the Cross* that it is unlikely that memories evoked by the visit or stories Hubbard told had much effect on the manuscript, except to interrupt it, and to draw his thoughts back toward the Pacific, and the possibility of gaining the consulship at Honolulu.

If he had ever agreed, the previous fall, that a consulship would be a good thing to have, Melville had committed his old sin of procrastination in a case where the stakes were high. One of Herman's character flaws, Gansevoort had realized, was that peculiar form of procrastination which most thoroughly sabotages what should have been the specific result most to be desired; and now this constitutional weakness was compounded by another, Herman's ingrained dislike of "asking favors from any one." Working so hard and so single-mindedly at *The Isle of the Cross*, something which was not likely to benefit him, he had repeatedly refused to divert his attention long enough to make small timely efforts to set in train the forces that might benefit him enormously. On 26 March, about the time Hubbard left, Hawthorne's appointment as consul to Liverpool was confirmed by the Senate — at a time when the Melville-Gansevoort-Shaw family had not yet bestirred itself in any efforts on behalf of Herman. Indeed, anyone in the family who remembered the serious consultations the previous fall remained quiescent through the next three crucial weeks. Instead of mobilizing politicians himself, from the Pittsfield party regulars up to the president-elect, instead of appealing to his Uncle Peter and his father-in-law and other influential people, Melville had kept writing his book, which was, as of 20 April, nearly ready for the press.

Hawthorne was ready to help. On the way to Washington City he stopped off in New York City from midnight Thursday, 14 April, till early afternoon on Monday the eighteenth. During that time he called on Allan on Wall Street, and promised to personally deliver to the president any letters Allan could have sent to him, in Washington. Allan at once wrote his mother, perhaps to Pittsfield, where she had gotten the grit of the Manhattan streets out of her eyes and had taken fresh stock of the situation, but the letter was, as it turned out, handed to her by her brother Peter in Albany on 20 April as she got into a stagecoach (there were still stagecoach routes) for a visit to Lansingburgh. From her cousin Maria Peebles's house she wrote a long, anxious letter to Peter late that night. At this point, very late for office-seeking, Maria Melville's concern for her son was intense enough to drive her to importunities likely to distress the recipient but not likely to have any positive results: "The constant in-door confinement with little intermission to which Hermans occupation as author compels him, does not agree with him. This constant working of the brain, & excitement of the imagination, is wearing Herman out, & you will my dear Peter be doing him a lasting benefit if by your added exertions you can procure for him a foreign Consulship." She was frantic to find some way to stop Herman from writing any more, at least from writing the sort of works that caused him such mental and physical strain in the composition (and which brought him so little money and such opprobrium once they were published).

Maria was frantic with good reason. She had been a wife whose still youngish husband (father of her two-year-old child) had died with horrible mental distress and terrifying suddenness, and she was a mother whose gallant oldest son had battled shoulder to shoulder with her to regain the family fortunes then had died with equally terrifying suddenness in a foreign capital, with no one of his blood to attend him and with no one of his blood even having any notion that he was gravely ill until the news of his death arrived. If her husband and her first son could have been struck dead in what seemed their prime, then her less sensitive second son, after the reviews of *Mardi*, *Moby-Dick*, and *Pierre*, and oppressed by the psychological burdens of his sad new work, might die just as suddenly. (Augusta, and then Kate, apparently, then Helen as copyists could not keep the contents of the new work secret, even if Herman for any reason wanted them to.) Furthermore, Maria was intensely conscious of a recent literary precedent in New York City. She knew that Gansevoort and Herman had become well acquainted with the famous writer Charles Fenno Hoffman, and she may very well have known from her own reading that Hoffman had been a student of the period of New York history in which her father had played so conspicuous a role. In 1849 the widely printed news reports of Hoffman's insanity had been quite explicit as to what had broken his physical and mental health. This was Greeley's account in the *Tribune* for 21 April 1849: "C. F. HOFFMAN, whose health had become impaired by too close confinement and incessant application to literary labors, being threatened with a serious affection of the brain, sometime since very judiciously determined to place himself in a position where, with sufficient seclusion, entire avoidance of literary pursuits, and judicious medical treatment, he was likely most speedily and certainly to be restored to his wonted good health." Four years had passed, and after a brief period of experimenting with freedom, Hoffman was still locked up (and remained so till his death in 1884). Four years was no time at all to Maria. She was a supremely officious woman, but her fears about Herman were based on bitter experience, not merely selfish concern that slurs against him were reflecting on her and other members of the family. Wise in the twists of human psychology, Maria now saw, in Hoffman's situation, the specter of Herman's own fate.

Maria's appeal reached her brother early the twenty-first, the next day after she wrote, and he went to work at once rounding up letters from his intimate friend Amasa J. Parker, a justice on the New York Supreme Court; from his close connection through his second wife, Garret Yates Lansing (the chancellor of New York University); and from Edwin L. Croswell (still editor of the Albany *Argus*, as he had been in Gansevoort's and Herman's young manhood), men who in Peter's judgment were "the only persons here whose opinions & wishes could most aid us in the application." Parker's letter to Pierce was direct and personal: "Mr Melville has contributed to our Literature much that is instructive and delightful, and gives ample promise, with proper encouragement, of a most brilliant career as a writer. But he is toiling early & late at his literary labors & hazarding his health to an extent greatly to be regretted." The letters from Lansing and Parker, Uncle Peter received personally and forwarded to Allan, promising to write to Washington (presumably to the president) himself. He assured Allan, "I think these letters, with the kind influence of Mr. Hawthorne with the President will be sufficient," but he suggested "the propriety of obtaining a letter from Boston," meaning Chief Justice Shaw.

On 21 April Allan wrote to Hawthorne, by this time staying across from the White House at Willard's Hotel, an urgent long letter which suggests (in the absence of any surviving letter of Hawthorne's from this period) just how much and how little effort the romancer was willing to put forward for his friend. He enclosed the letters to Pierce that Peter Gansevoort had solicited as well as one "from *Charles O'Conor* (now United States District Attorney (a very strong one) . . . and one from Edward C. West." (O'Conor, Mrs. Forrest's attorney in 1851–52, was still a celebrity-lawyer and celebrity himself; West was a New York lawyer with an office near Allan's on Wall Street.) He continued: "I beg of you Mr Hawthorne to do what you can and what I know you are willing to do to aid in the selection of my brother for the Consulate at Honolulu—Should it in your opinion be *impossible* to secure to him this post, I would mention *Antwerp* as a consulate of which I have certain information. I suppose my brother would prefer a post in Great Britain." General John A. Dix had told him no more consulates would be filled from New York, and therefore Melville should stress his residence in Massachusetts. After this Allan did his best to move heaven and earth, which might have been easier than winning a lucrative appointment in 1853 for the non-voting author of *Pierre*.

Hawthorne was back in New York on 4 May, saying that the new attorney general, Caleb Cushing, was "warmly in favor of Herman's appointment," but that Pierce was making "no promises." This Allan repeated to Peter Gansevoort that day, adding that he inferred from what Hawthorne said that Pierce would "favor Herman" when the matter came up "in Cabinet Council." Up until the day he sailed, Shaw was trying to help Herman, and incidentally was soliciting help with Oakes's application to become a purser in the navy. It transpired later that Hawthorne had succeeded in getting Pierce to appoint the pale Keatsling poet Richard H. Stoddard to the New York Custom House, and the young man "entered the granite temple in Wall Street," where he stayed until ousted in 1870. One of Melville's young admirers (an imitator of Irving, as Melville had been), Donald G. Mitchell (Ik Marvel), got the Venice consulship.

When Maria wrote Peter on 20 April that Herman had composed a "new work, now nearly ready for the press," she was, as usual, speaking the exact truth. On 6 April from Arrowhead Augusta had written to her Cousin Priscilla, still slaving in the female academy in Canandaigua—the first letter she had written to her since the previous October, when she had sent bad news about the little "Brown Cottage." Now she told her cousin the title of Melville's manuscript: "The Isle of the Cross." Not thinking of the necessary lag in time between the near-completion of a manuscript and its publication, Priscilla Melvill in late April through part of May kept watch for any public mention of the new story. (Melville had his eye on a date that approached and passed—1 May, when a third installment of interest on the loan from Stewart went unpaid.) At Arrowhead, Elizabeth (Bessie) Melville was born on 22 May, and on the same day, from Canandaigua, Priscilla Melvill coincidentally wrote to Augusta: "When will the 'Isle of the Cross' make its appearance? I am constantly looking in the journals & magazines that come in my way, for notices of it." The letter arrived at Arrowhead on 26 May, and four days later Augusta replied to Priscilla, telling her of the birth of Bessie and also that Melville had completed *The Isle of the Cross* (on or about the day Bessie was born).

Two years before, in 1851, May had been the month for Melville to stop writing and do his multitude of chores "all accumulating upon this one particular season," as he wrote Hawthorne. Melville could not have been so confident of a consular appointment that he did not plant his crops; even if he expected to be abroad, he would have planted potatoes and corn, knowing that his mother was more than competent to supervise the care and harvesting. But David or another "boy" must have done the vigorous farming in 1853, as in 1852, while Melville devoted his own labors to the manuscript. That, he could tell himself, was his way of caring for the new baby and the two little boys. On 12 June Priscilla wrote to Augusta: "I am glad to hear such a favorable report of *Lizzie*—she is really gathering quite a little family around her & Arrowhead Mansion will hardly be spacious enough—the 'Isle of the Cross' is almost a twin sister of the little one & I think she should be nam'd for the heroine—if there *is* such a personage—the advent of the two are singularly near together." Perhaps Melville helped with some of the farm chores while he waited for Augusta to finish the last copying, but he did not wait at Arrowhead until the crops were properly laid by. David must have been entrusted the remaining work, under Maria's eye.

Melville did not have to worry about Lizzie this time. The day she had the baby, she was so much better than she had been at Stanwix's birth that Herman assured the Shaws (in a letter they received 23 May) that she was very well ("very well," Shaw qualified the phrasing to his son Lemuel, "compared with her situation on the last similar occasion"). Apparently she gained strength steadily, and in any case Melville had rarely been needed inside Arrowhead, once the furniture had been put into place late in 1850. Around 6 or 7 June he left for New York City, carrying the completed manuscript of *The Isle of the Cross* to the Harpers. He also may have decided that since the book was finished and Lizzie and Bessie were doing well he could now take some time to assist in Allan's efforts to gain him a political appointment. An air of unreality pervades the belated frantic efforts. More than two months after Hawthorne had received his appointment (and then devoted much time to fending off or placating supplicants who wanted him to approach Pierce for them), after hundreds of office-seekers had pushed forward their carefully plotted campaigns to gain one of the few lucrative consulships, Melville deigned to interest himself slightly in the efforts belatedly set in motion, however erratically, on his behalf.

In fact, Melville's office-seeking was all over except for admitting that it was over. On 10 June Allan received a letter from Shaw which relayed Cushing's offer of one of the honorific consulates in Italy, and the next day Allan wrote Shaw that there could "be no consulship in Italy, not even Rome, where the fees would amount to sufficient to make it an object for Herman to accept a position there." Antwerp, however, he had heard was worth from $2500 to $3000, and Herman should accept it if it were offered. Accepting the facts of the situation, Allan apprised Shaw that Herman was in town and would be there when Shaw arrived to take a ship to England. In the intensity of these plans, Lizzie's uneventful pregnancy and the routine birth of her daughter seemed simply incidental. Shaw did not even find it necessary to plan on going to New York by way of Pittsfield so as to see the new child before he left.

When he reached New York, probably on Monday, 6 June, Melville may have taken the manuscript straight to the Harpers to be free of it. At 47 East Twenty-fourth Street Herman found that Sophia had taken the children to the Hippodrome, which he at once determined to take in during his trip. This was Franconi's Hippodrome, installed before Christmas near Reservoir Square (later Bryant Square, behind the New York Public Library), close to the American version of the Crystal Palace. It seated several thousand spectators and featured two dozen thoroughbred steeplechase horses, half a dozen ring horses, ponies, chariots, and special attractions such as racing ostriches and Lapland and English deer. It was contrived "to create a sensation of no ordinary character" (so said the impressionable Philadelphia *Dispatch*). One could look elsewhere, in literary woodlands, for Truth fleeing like a sacred white doe. Happy to have another male in the house, Allan "had the impertinence to tell Herman that when the fourth corner of the table was filled, it would be well balanced." Not having recovered from the birth of Catherine the year before, Sophia was not amused. She wrote to Augusta around 8 June: "For my part I am not anxious, and thank God, no present prospects of such a thing." She sent a message to Lizzie: "Give my best love to her, and tell her I am glad to hear she is coming on so well, so much better than I." Sophia expressed her astonishment that Herman and Lizzie had chosen the name Bessie and not Lucy, for that name would have won the gift of a porringer from the none-too-subtle Aunt Lucy.

Herman made himself unavailable for any last-minute political activity by going at once to New Rochelle, to visit Lathers, who on 7 June inscribed to him a set of Washington Irving. Despite the fact that Abby was not at her hospitable best (Agnes was born at Winyah on 10 June), Melville felt so perfectly at home in the huge and well-staffed house that he went out there again in a week or two, this time staying three days, keeping Richard company while the women looked after the children and the new baby. Over the next week or so Melville made himself available in New York City to the new great voyagers in the family, not Shaw first of all but Uncle Peter, for the men of the family were converging on Manhattan, two of them bound across the Atlantic for the first time. Before 11 June Melville made a list of things and places for Peter Gansevoort to see and do, entitling it "London." They reveal his best guesses at his uncle's interests as well as some aspects of London that had proved delightful in his own memory: "Covent-Garden — before breakfast. / A sail in the Penny steamers on the river. / A Lounge on the bridges. / Go to Greenwich Hospital in the *morning* so as to see the pensioners at dinner. (An American negro is among them) / Greenwich Park, for the view. / Leicester Square—the French emigrants. Good breakfast there. / Seven Dials—Gin shops. / Judge & Jury—Drury Lane / The Temple—Go to the Church on Sunday (Templar's tombs) / —Dining Halls & Desert Room & Kitchen on week days. / Lincoln's Inn Kitchen. Reform Club / 'Blue Posts' Cork Street near the Arcade—fine punch & dinners. / For fine ale—Edinborough Castle Strand." He knew his uncle would find his way to the great public government buildings and museums on his own, so this list deals with good reasonably priced food, places for great views, and special treats more or less out of the way but sure to appeal to a traveler about the age of Washington Irving, that great lover of nooks and corners of London. Herman also wrote letters introducing his uncle to friends in London, including Robert Cooke. At ten o'clock on the morning of 11 June, a Saturday, Herman, Allan, Edward Sanford (Peter's first wife's brother), and young Henry Sanford Gansevoort (Peter's son by that wife) all bade good-bye to Peter Gansevoort at the foot of Canal Street, and he boarded the steamship *Atlantic*—"Weather calm, wind adverse," Peter noted.

Over the last weeks Judge Shaw had made his own plans. On 31 May, preparing himself for a trip from which he might not return, he had made a will, leaving his daughter, Elizabeth S. Melville, "one fifth part of the said residue & remainder" of his real and personal estate. All money he had lent to Herman was to be treated as advances to her, so that he relieved and discharged Melville "from the payment thereof, from all debts, dues and demands." Further, he directed his executors to turn Elizabeth's $3000 wedding fund over to Benjamin R. Curtis so he could invest it for her. Curtis was not only a distinguished lawyer but had been the husband of one of Herman's second cousins, and now was a new resident of a fine house in the northeast of Pittsfield. Shaw took care of routine business, such as the acquisition of a passport signed in Washington on 7 June by William Marcy. Someone filled in a personal description: "Stature 5 Feet 6 Inches Eng[lish measure]; Forehead low; Eyes blue; Nose common; Mouth common; Chin short; Hair brown; Complexion fair; Face Round"—so much for the outward appearance of a most uncommon man.

Some of Shaw's plans were such as a former president might have envied. George S. Hillard, writing to the judge on 12 April, took it for granted he would see the artistic colony in Rome, especially "the Storys and the Crawfords." Jared Sparks (the historian, president of Harvard, 1849–52) sent him on 8 June "a letter for Mr. Guizot, & another for Mr. Tocqueville"—a respectable list of contacts for a Barnstable boy. Herman dined with his father-in-law at least once, on the fourteenth, at the home of a connection of Shaw's traveling companion Thomas W. Ward, head of the American branch of the great Baring Brothers' bank. With Herman there to see him off, as he had just done his Uncle Peter, Shaw sailed from New York for England in the *Arabia* on the fourteenth or fifteenth, accompanied by Ward and his mother, who would take their own way after arriving in Liverpool. Having taken prudent care of his earthly family before leaving Boston, Shaw in his private cabin on the twentieth reflected on his love for each member of that family: "In being made to realize that the crowning and pervading joy of life is love, and that without it imagination, learning, powers of mind are all in vain, we are made wise, and taught the true source of all happiness." He wrote out a supplication to "Almighty God, maker alike of the vast Ocean, and of the solid land, author & creator of all worlds," thankful that he was not beyond God's reach. This was the prayer of the patriarch, at peace, ignorant that his son-in-law had more than $2050 in a secret debt and had toiled for months on a manuscript that would not be published.

From the Morley Hotel in London on 26 June Peter Gansevoort wrote to his wife enough to show that he was taking Herman's advice whenever it was convenient, but otherwise following his own interests. He had left Herman's letter of introduction to Robert Cooke, who wrote him on 28 June: "I regret being out when you called upon me & left your card & a letter from my friend Hermann Melville." The next day Cooke wrote again, more urgently: "What will Typee say, if we dont put our legs under the same Mahogany together.?!!!" The Cookes had been fast friends of Herman's, on the basis of the intense intimacy of great food, and drink, and brilliant conversation in rooms in the "Temple" and at the Erechtheum Club. Lem had invaded the Paradise of Bachelors and tried his best to take Melville's place, but he had not effaced the Englishmen's memories of the good fellow Typee. Lem had taken care of matters at Liverpool, as the judge wrote his wife on

1 July: "We have an excellent courier, or an attendant & servant, who was recommended by Mr [Joshua] Bates & sent down to Liverpool, to meet us on arrival.... Thus far, he appears to be all that could be wished." Shaw had been treated with all possible deference, notably when Baron Alderson, introduced by the former minister Abbott Lawrence, invited him and Lem to the House of Lords, where they saw "many of the distinguished personages of the kingdom, and were introduced to several of them." That evening they attended a party at Baron Alderson's, on which he reported reassuringly: "The house and arrangements in all respects, and the conduct of all parties, were very much the same as we might expect at the house of a respectable family in our own place." George Peabody, who had been kind to Herman, put himself out to welcome both Peter Gansevoort and Lemuel Shaw.

The Americans in London got the jump on those celebrating the Glorious Fourth at home, for the two Lemuel Shaws and Uncle Peter rendezvoused with the three brothers Cooke in London, the British men graciously making a Fourth of July party. Later Melville learned enough of the Fourth of July party to have his imagination beguiled. (Melville spent the Fourth as an honored guest of Julius Rockwell at the Pittsfield celebration, having declined to speak on the occasion.) The judge wrote to his wife on 5 July: "Yesterday Monday we visited a collection of pictures & works of art, at 4 o'clock went to the H of Commons, passed some time there. Dined with Mr Cooke's, three bachelor brothers friends of Lemuel . . . then met Judge Parker & Mr Peter Gansevoort of Albany." Amasa J. Parker recognized Shaw from a meeting "at Capt Wyman's at the Navy Yard Portsmouth." Peter Gansevoort wrote his wife the next day: "dined with Rob. Fr. Cooke Esq & a large party — There I met Judge Shaw & Son. We had a charming party — we left them at 12 and went home." All in all, the best of London society was not noticeably inferior to the best of Washington Street in Albany and Beacon Hill in Boston.

During the second week of June the Harpers had possession of the manuscript, and after they had a chance to read it they declined to publish it. From what is known of Melville's subsequent relationship with the Harpers, it seems unlikely that anything overtly unpleasant occurred during the interviews over *The Isle of the Cross*, no matter how painful the circumstances were to Melville. In a 24 November letter to the Harpers, Melville used phrasing that implied that the firm had not simply rejected *The Isle of the Cross* but that he somehow had been "prevented" from publishing it, as if it were somehow not simply a matter of their not liking it. How was Melville "prevented" from publishing the story? The most obvious guess is that the Harpers feared that their firm would be criminally liable if anyone recognized any surviving originals of the characters in *The Isle of the Cross*. Yet Melville seems to have taken some pains to alter the facts, changing the setting to something similar to (if not specified as) one of the Isles of Shoals. And the question remains: if the Harpers saw the story as possibly actionable on the part of the families of the parties involved, why did Clifford, the attorney general of Massachusetts, fail to recognize danger in any literary use Melville might make of the material? Nothing indicates that this was like the case of *Cape Cod Folks*, which Helen described decades later, 21 February 1882, when the publisher, Williams & Co., was sued by people "whom the authoress drew from the life *too* plainly to be mistaken — the real *names even*, having been printed in the first edition, but altered in the later ones, so that copies of the former now command any price that the fortunate holders may desire." Melville's word "prevented," after all, may be like the word "induced" he used of Stewart's persuading him to take a loan: masterful as he could be, he had a way now, after the failure of *Moby-Dick* and *Pierre*, of seeing himself as passive victim to whom things were done.

If the Harpers had simply not liked the story or had thought it was not in their line, Melville ought to have sought some other publisher for the story. Only two years before, Evert Duyckinck had pressured him to let the firm of Redfield publish *The Whale* (as his whaling book was still called), but since then he had become estranged from Duyckinck, and we have no evidence that he went the rounds of New York publishers in June 1853 as he had gone the rounds of London publishers in November 1849. The possibility of publishing in magazines had been held out to him by Bentley and by Putnam, yet as far as we know Melville did not seek serial publication for *The Isle of the Cross*. He had left off negotiations with Bentley, apparently, with the publisher holding a set of the Harper proofs of *Pierre* and awaiting a response to his offer to publish on half-profits. Perhaps now, certainly over the next three or four years, Melville reflected on the aesthetic theory proclaimed in his friend Hawthorne's "The Artist of the Beautiful," the "art for artists" theory that what is important is not the created work of art but the artist's feelings: "When the artist rose high enough to achieve the Beautiful, the symbol by which he made it perceptible to mortal senses became of little value in his eyes, while his spirit possessed itself in the enjoyment of the Reality." By this theory, it would not have mattered whether or not Shakespeare's plays had been preserved. What mattered was that Shakespeare had thought of them. What was important was that Melville had possessed the "bright conception" of *The Isle of the Cross* then, most lamentably, had chased "the flitting mystery beyond the verge of his ethereal domain," and crushed "its frail being in seizing it with a material grasp," and holding that grasp between December or January and about the twenty-second of May. Was Melville to feel that since he had created the beautiful, it would not matter that no

The Isle of the Cross: September 1852–June 1853

earthly transcription of *The Isle of the Cross* survived? For years Melville had been an artist who created the beautiful without knowing how to talk about literary theory, and as he began to think about such rarefied matters in the following years he did so clumsily, at first, and gradually realized that he had to think beyond Hawthorne, whose theory had not, after all, comforted him marvelous much. At intervals in the next decades Melville may have reflected that he had devoted more time to writing *The Isle of the Cross* than to, say, *Redburn* and *White-Jacket* both — a large segment of his creative life.

Around the last week of June Melville went home to his wife and three children and mother and three sisters, a man who had failed to get a political job (while his friend had seized the greatest plum of all), a man who (after *Pierre* had demonstrated that his career was over) had demanded for months that everyone defer to his schedule for the sake of the important book he was writing, only to have to confess to them that he could not get the Harpers to publish it. In the memoranda made after his death Melville's widow recalled: "We all felt anxious about the strain on his health in Spring of 1853" — perhaps in April when Maria was so concerned, perhaps in the late spring and early summer, when Melville was about as beaten as a man can be. On 16 June Lem wrote his mother from the Bath Hotel in Piccadilly. The next day he — not Herman — was going to dine with John Murray. He was mildly curious about the baby ("What are they going to name my new neice?") but downright "astonished" that Herman wanted to go as consul to the Sandwich Islands. "I suppose he knows best," he added; Herman had "certainly written more than enough books for his reputation." That was the death croak for Herman's career, as far as all the Shaws were concerned — all except the judge. But Melville had a plan for holding on to it.

[8]

The Magazinist
Idealist Turned Would-Be Stoic, July 1853–January 1854

> the childhood shows the man,
> As morning shows the day.

In Milton's *Paradise Regained* (4.220–21) Melville underlines these words and comments: "True, if all fair dawnings were followed by high noons & blazoned sunsets. But as many a merry morn precedes a dull & rainy day; so, often, unpromising mornings have glorious middays & eves. The greatest, grandest things are unpredicted."

MELVILLE STILL HAD an international reputation, although there was a gap in it because (for good or ill) very few copies of *Pierre* had circulated in England. "Sir Nathaniel" (Francis Jacox) turned some memorable phrases in "American Authorship," in the London *New Monthly Magazine* for July 1853:

> For so successful a trader in "marine stores" as Mr. Melville, "The Whale" seemed a speculation every way big with promise.... And his three volumes entitled "The Whale" undoubtedly contain much vigorous description, much wild power, many striking details. But the effect is distressingly marred throughout by an extravagant treatment of the subject. The style is maniacal — mad as a March hare — mowing, gibbering, screaming, like an incurable Bedlamite, reckless of keeper or strait-waistcoat.

What Jacox wanted was the return of Melville's better literary self: "O author of 'Typee' and 'Omoo,' we admire so cordially the proven capacity of your pen, that we entreat you to doff the 'non-natural sense' of your late lucubrations — to put off your worser self — and to do your better, real self, that justice which its 'potentiality' deserves." Such sympathetic criticism in what was, after all, a place of honor — inclusion in a series on American authors, and only the second time anyone had published a retrospective article on him as an author with an ongoing career — this criticism could only seem authoritative to the family. The Boston family got to read it in full on 20 August in the popular reprint magazine, *Littell's Living Age*, and anyone who missed that could read it in the frankly titled New York *Eclectic Magazine* for September.

No member of the family was capable of the independent act of aesthetic and historical judgment that would allow him or her to appreciate Herman's achievement. They knew he was reckless, impulsive, knew he committed acts all but blatantly designed to bring down the wrath of reviewers and neighbors, knew how cavalierly he treated his manuscripts, knew how restless he was—and they also knew the correlation between pleasing the public and selling books. Lem and Oakes took the most scathing critical pronouncements as infallible, amply justifying them in not trying to read what Herman wrote. Even Melville's own brothers and sisters and his mother had no means of responding to or arguing with such criticisms; they were bewildered and hurt for themselves and for Herman, but none of them could have mustered a defense for him.

Rather than behaving with characteristic recklessness after the Harpers refused *The Isle of the Cross*, Melville picked himself up stoutly. The Harpers must have told him that the best way of working off his debt to them and getting ahead would be to write for their magazine, where *Pierre* would not be an obvious liability, for stories were published anonymously and a reader would not have to get past the barrier of the devalued name of Herman Melville. Newspapers regularly noticed the publication of the new month's magazines and commented on the contents, but the writers of these columns would not necessarily know who the magazine contributors were, though in practice names were often leaked to the press. On 27 July in a burst of unwonted optimism Melville's mother-in-law reported to her nephew Sam Savage: "Between us the Harpers have persuaded Herman to write for him [them]; and he is admirably paid." Melville had received invitations from Putnam and Bentley the previous year, but he never, so far as we know, sent anything to *Bentley's Miscellany*, though he soon began contributing to *Putnam's*. Why he did not send *The Isle of the Cross* is a mystery. The family had reason for rejoicing that Melville would not continue to risk denunciation as a novelist of American high life but instead be an anonymous contributor of magazine pieces. (The Harper brothers presumably had not paid him for his first contribution to the magazine, the printing of "The Town-Ho's Story" in the October 1851 issue. They would thriftily have defined that story as pre-publication publicity for *Moby-Dick*, for which Melville ought to have paid them, if anything.) The policy of anonymity meant notoriety might be avoided, and writing short stories was good news for those interested in Herman's health, since it meant his periods of intense concentration would be shorter, and might readily be broken up by farm work (which always seemed bracingly wholesome to those not performing it themselves) or outdoor recreation.

Melville had declined an invitation to speak at the Fourth of July 1853 celebration in Pittsfield, but he attended it, and heard Julius Rockwell make a charming complimentary allusion "to the fact in revolutionary history, that the ancestor of Mr. Melvill was one of the celebrated party who threw overboard the tea into Boston harbor; and to the other fact, well known to the present generation, that the grandson had drawn from the sea rich and various materials for the entertainment and instruction of the world." Not yet thirty-four, he felt sure that his literary life was not over. At once he sat down again to work, in the summer, just the time that he, like Hawthorne, preferred not to write. He may have managed to write outdoors, on the piazza, at least a little while, for in his *Pontoosuc Lake* (1890), Joe Smith declared that "the" *Piazza Tales* (the magazine pieces collected under that title in 1856) were "written on a piazza which commands a grand view northward to Greylock." On the piazza or, more likely, in his study (which after all had cross-ventilation for warmer days, a window on the north and the east), Melville achieved a remarkable amount of intermittent work, relishing the new literary form which allowed him to throw his energies into a piece for a few days then put it behind him. He may have exercised his fingers with the short "The Happy Failure" and "The Fiddler" first, but if so he rapidly proceeded to the much longer "Cock-A-Doodle-Doo!" and "Bartleby, the Scrivener" as well. The stories take on a new light now that we know that Melville wrote an entire book between *Pierre* and the first of the stories, a book he had been prevented from publishing, for we have to allow for his honing his craft as a regular storyteller, not as a writer of South Sea adventure books. The evidence is lost with *The Isle of the Cross*, but never before had he written a book without learning something significant from it. The challenge for readers, given the story of the lost book, is to imagine how writing it allowed Melville to grow from *Pierre* to "Bartleby." Furthermore, new evidence about Melville's indebtedness, his defaulting on payments, and in particular about Stewart's holding, in effect, a second mortgage on Arrowhead forces us to take the autobiographical elements in some of the stories as more stark than scholars used to do.

One of the mysteries about Melville is how, in these years, he found daylight hours for reading while he was writing so industriously, for he did read, obsessively, despite the weakness of his eyes. Since 1850, if not earlier, he had been reading Wordsworth's poems along with criticism on the late poet laureate, for *Pierre*, and presumably for the *Isle of the Cross*, also, and stories he wrote starting in the summer of 1853 were marked by a new, and specifically Wordsworthian, way of thinking about himself, nature, and humanity — a way of thinking that manifested itself in his subdued moods in the next years. Melville said of Pierre that Nature had planted him in the country because she "intended a rare and original development" in him: "Never mind if she proved ambiguous to him in the end; nevertheless, in the beginning she did bravely" (bk. 1, ch. 4). In the beginning, counting afresh from July 1850, the Berkshires had done bravely for Melville, offering him an early ecstatic period when he felt he was drawing some of the best parts of his diverse life together in one charmed circle of memory-charged and newly inspiring terrain. Months later he confronted poignant memories in the Berkshires, a setting where he might have known that he would inevitably dip his angle deeper into the well of his own childhood.

Wordsworth helped teach Melville "To look on nature, not as in the hour / Of thoughtless youth; but hearing oftentimes / The still, sad music of humanity." Starting in *Pierre*, and still strongly in 1853, Melville often described landscapes which derive a haunting part of their power from human associations with them, a familiar Wordsworthian situation, as in this passage from *The Excursion* (bk. 1), in a page Melville marked in his copy:

> Beside yon Spring I stood,
> And eyed its waters till we seemed to feel
> One sadness, they and I. For them a bond
> Of brotherhood is broken; time has been
> When, every day, the touch of human hand
> Dislodged the natural sleep that binds them up
> In mortal stillness; and they ministered
> To human comfort. Stooping down to drink,
> Upon the slimy foot-stone I espied
> The useless fragment of a wooden bowl,
> Green with the moss of years, and subject only
> To the soft handling of the Elements.

There suddenly appear in Melville's works humble, resolute, suffering Wordsworthian characters, from "Agatha" (whatever name he finally gave her), to the Merrymusk family in "Cock-A-Doodle-Doo!" to the Coulters in the first half of "Poor Man's Pudding and Rich Man's Crumbs." (Being self-reliant Americans, the Coulters find themselves worse off than Wordsworth's poor, who can, at the worst, always beg.) In Sketch 8 of "The Encantadas" (written early in 1854), because of Hunilla's sufferings Norfolk Isle becomes a "spot made sacred by the strongest trials of humanity." Again and again Melville was to write of relics of "vanishing humanity" in the islands, such as (in Sketch 10) "small rude basins in the rocks" which "reveal plain tokens of artificial instruments employed in hollowing them out," the basins serving to catch drops of dew exuding from the upper crevices. The first chapter of *Israel Potter* (serialized in *Putnam's*, 1854–55) makes more boldly picturesque use of a Titanic region of decay and desertion on which "the tokens of ancient industry" are seen on all sides. In his own wanderings in the Berkshires Melville had found deserted homesites and other evidence of older human occupancy (starting with the aboriginal artifacts for which he named his house), but to some degree, as a poetic writer in the American Lake District, he came to see the region and himself, in his thwarted impoverished state, through Wordsworth's eyes.

The character of the narrator's elderly uncle in "The Happy Failure: A Story of the River Hudson" recalls Melville's endlessly projecting Uncle Thomas, who in his old age had left the penal region of the Berkshires to follow a will-o'-the-wisp to ague-ridden Galena. The fictional uncle's last invention, the "Great Hydraulic-Hydrostatic Apparatus for draining swamps and marshes, and converting them, at the rate of one acre the hour, into fields more fertile than those of the Genessee," reflected a pattern among the Melville men—a yielding to seductive hopes for fortune. Herman himself had recently written a great Shakespearean-Romantic apparatus for establishing the grandeur of American literature and himself as an American genius, and had followed that with what he was sure, during the first intensity of composition, was an even greater contrivance, a psychological Kraken novel. The narrator of "The Happy Failure" claims that his uncle's failure made him a wise man, the uncle's example keeping him from having to experience the overweening aspiration himself. Melville had learned nothing from the consequences of his uncle's and his father's overextending themselves, but recent bitter experience was putting him through what their example might have saved him from.

"The Fiddler" also requires an autobiographical reading. The story records the transformation of an attitude—by example, after hard experience has failed to work the change. Melville managed a tone of rueful mockery toward his narrator, Helmstone, a poet distraught at the reception of his great work: "So my poem is damned, and immortal fame is not for me! I am nobody forever and ever. Intolerable fate! Snatching my hat, I dashed down the criticism, and rushed out into Broadway, where enthusiastic throngs were crowding into a circus in a side-street near by, very recently started, and famous for a capital clown." Helmstone (the name may derive from Caroline Helstone, whose drawn-out agony is described in Currer Bell's, or Charlotte Brontë's, *Shirley*) is accosted in his flight by a friend, Standard: "Haven't been committing murder? Ain't flying justice?" Standard hauls him into the circus along with Hautboy, a short, round fellow who seems at first only a child but then is revealed to be forty or older. Full of his own tragedy, Helmstone recites to himself "that sublime passage" in his poem, "in which Cleothemes the Argive vindicates the justice of the war," a passage no doubt equal in sublimity to Ahab's much-mocked soliloquies. Helmstone fantasizes that he will leap into the ring to recite the whole tragic poem, which deserves the applause being showered upon the mere clown. Then the unaffected but not innocent delight of Hautboy at the clown sets in motion the transformation in the attitudes of the narrator:

> It was plain that while Hautboy saw the world pretty much as it was, yet he did not theoretically espouse its bright side nor its dark side. Rejecting all solutions, he but acknowledged facts. What was sad in the world he did not superficially gainsay; what was glad in it he did not cynically slur; and all which was to him personally enjoyable, he gratefully took to his heart. It was plain, then . . . that his extraordinary cheerfulness did not arise either from deficiency of feeling or thought.

Pressed for the secret of Hautboy's life, Standard reminds the narrator of Master Betty, the "great genius and prodigy," who as a twelve-year-old actor had astonished audiences in England and the United States. Hautboy is not Master Betty incognito: the mystery about Hautboy is that he had been in boyhood an extraordinary violinist, a prodigy like Master Betty.

Betty was real, and had been in the news in recent years. The London correspondent of the Philadelphia *Sunday Dispatch* (22 June 1851), for instance, had written:

> We met what was *once* "Master Betty," commonly known as the "Roscius". . . . He was, perhaps, the first of those precocious theatrical geniuses upon the English boards. . . . But *such* a "Master Betty" as we beheld now! Instead of the childish boy, light, lithe, graceful, a model of beauty, and a picture of hot-housed intellect, just imagine a man tall, with the rotundity of a punc[h]eon, his chin lost in the folds of his capacious neck. . . . "Master Betty" indeed! The prodigy!

Like Betty, Hautboy had been a genius who "drained the whole flagon of glory; whose going from city to city was a going from triumph to triumph," but who now walked a Broadway where no man knew him. He had been "crowned with laurels" (Herman wisely had put Sarah's wreath off his own head at Christmas 1851) and now wore a bunged beaver hat, but in Standard's eyes he was more a prodigy than ever, happier than a king, *with* genius and *without* fame. Helmstone's defiance of fortune is over: " 'If Cicero, traveling in the East, found sympathetic solace for his grief in beholding the arid overthrow of a once gorgeous city, shall not my petty affair be as nothing, when I behold in Hautboy the vine and the rose climbing the shattered shafts of his tumbled temple of Fame?' Next day I tore all my manuscripts, bought me a fiddle, and went to take regular lessons of Hautboy." Deeply and secretly in debt, his career in shreds, Melville was changing. An ironic footnote: Betty's death, long years afterward, was so well chronicled that Melville may have seen various accounts. For one example, in Boston the *Saturday Post* of 22 September 1874 in "A Forgotten Celebrity" commented in words very similar to some printed after Melville's own death: "there were very few people in England, I imagine, who remembered who and what Mr. William Henry Betty was." "Ourselves are Fate" — so Melville had written in *White-Jacket* (ch. 75). He had a way of anticipating his fate far ahead of time.

What may have been Melville's third story, "Cock-A-Doodle-Doo! Or, The Crowing of the Noble Cock Beneventano," certainly written that summer of 1853, was another lesson in readjustment of vision. The narrator is a wry self-portrait of what Melville had been perilously close to becoming that season, a man too full of the hypos to sleep, a man looking at the bludgeoning events of the world (despots around the world knocking on the head idealistic revolts such as that led by Kossuth; railroads and steamboats knocking high-spirited travelers on the head) and drawing dismal analogies with his "own private affairs," also "full of despotisms, casualties, and knockings on the head." Into the narrator's outrageous comic rants, in which doleful dumps are brought to new miasmic lows, Melville dropped clues to his own situation as the sort of man who claps new mortgages on his estate to pay old debts. In writing this way Melville was living dangerously, hinting at horrific truths about himself under the guise of jocular fiction. In one evocative passage, the narrator describes the local man who had sawed his wood amid the snows of March, displaying a "wondrous intensity of application at his saw," such as Melville himself had displayed in the summer of 1849, when he had written two books as other men might saw wood — and such industry as Bartleby the scrivener was shortly to display (assuming that "Bartleby" was written later than "Cock-A-Doodle-Doo!"). Another passage hinted at the inexplicable appearance of genius. The woodsawyer Merrymusk had raised the magnificent cock himself: "It chipped the shell here" (rather than being an imported Shanghai bird). The transformation in the narrator's attitude is effected by the cock, whose crow strangely inspires him, to the point that at the end (after witnessing strange multiple transcendent deaths) he is able to banish the encroaching dumps with a continual crow of triumph, although he still labors under mortgages on his estate. It was in his new mood that Melville said what his wife quoted decades later, that the criticism of *Pierre* was "but just."

On 5 July 1853 Hope wrote her husband that "Lizzie keeps her strength & so far, all is doing well." Carefully casting her thoughts abroad, she imagined her husband as spending the Glorious Fourth in London with "a large gathering of American society" (having sought each other out amid hoards of foreigners), and she professed to want him to make the most of his chances: "Enjoy yourself I beg; that is unnecessary to say, but do not think you cannot *afford* it [—] every indulgence you have granted to every branch of us, now's your time for a little self indulgence — See every thing but a Theatre on the Sabbath day. You are on a Pinnacle and every eye is *on you* all are rejoicing that one of your respectability is a Representative from America." It was not in her nature to let Shaw enjoy his fine tour without being burdened by the complaint that she had been left deprived and anxious. Three weeks later, as Sam Shaw was preparing to escort Elizabeth Dow to Arrowhead, Hope wrote her husband about the trouble Oakes was giving her, now that he had made himself at home in Lem's bedroom and study and was often underfoot even when he was nominally living back at Milton. Oakes's behavior was forcing her to pay attention to his peculiarities, but her most pressing problem, she emphasized, was financial:

> I am short of money — Shall I take the Coal in before you return or wait untill you return. Write Mr Bartlett & tell him that you are willing for me [to] have money as I wish; I have not been out of town a day since you left I am a fixture but money I must have. Economically "I live" as I can[.] I have sent Elizabeth's $90 by Samuel — I have paid Samuel's College bills and the others ... be assured that I take no advantage of *confidence in* me. I live cheaper than *you could live* — but every article is very high.

Shaw knew that he had left her amply provided for, and dealt in his own benign way with her feelings about his granting himself a little, or a lot, of self-indulgence. Never subtle, never able to be disingenuous or to appear guileless, Hope flew her mixed signals, urging her husband to indulge himself while confiding piteously how frugally she was living and how precariously ill-funded he had so thoughtlessly left her.

Pittsfield and Arrowhead were abuzz that summer (a beehive, Hope reported Lizzie as saying). Sam Shaw (carrying the welcome ninety dollars) and Elizabeth Dow made a short visit, giving Lizzie's cousin the chance to approve the placement of her gift, the portrait of the judge. Sam as usual got Herman outdoors. The Arrowheads saw less than usual of the Broadhallers, for Alfie's illnesses and Sarah's pregnancy kept the Morewoods subdued. (Sarah had been pregnant since February, and gave birth to Anne Rachel on 10 November — the Annie Morewood who grew up and married Richard Lathers Jr.) The Thurstons (apparently including not only the matriarch but also Charlie Thurston and Rachel Thurston Barrington and their families, as well as their brother Henry, the boy who had idolized Tom just a few years earlier, and now was a medical student) betook themselves in overlapping shifts to the village of Pittsfield, where they boarded; at times, Abby Thurston Lathers was there with her family (the baby, Agnes, younger than Bessie). Sophia and her three daughters stayed all summer. As always, Allan came up intermittently, probably at times in the company of Richard Lathers or another of the Thurston clan. This meant there was a good deal of stopping by Arrowhead for one or another of the daughters or Herman, or of course to call on Maria or take her for a drive. Charles Thurston (three weeks older than Herman) and his wife, Caroline, were childless, but there were children and new babies on the scene. Rachel Thurston and Charles Connor Barrington had Rachel (1844); Richard and Abby Lathers had Abby Caroline (1848) and Agnes (the new baby, born 10 June 1853); Allan Melville and Sophia Thurston Melville had Maria Gansevoort (1849), Florence (1850), and Katherine (or Catherine) Gansevoort (1852); Herman and Lizzie had Malcolm (1849), Stanwix (1851), and Bessie (22 May 1853); Sarah and Rowland Morewood had William (1847), Alfred (1852), and were soon to have Anne. The Melvilles, Thurstons, and Latherses were still-young parents with young children.

We know little about Melville's relationship with Charlie Thurston, but they probably rode or drove out together, since the Thurstons came equipped with steeds, even if they rented a carriage instead of bringing their own. Like Thurston, Richard Lathers could not vacation without his own horses. There was no shortage of horses to pull carriages, even discounting Herman's slow old Charlie. For Lathers (in his *Reminiscences*), visiting Herman in his second-floor study was one of the highlights of the vacation: "I visited him often in his well-stocked library, where I listened with intense pleasure to his highly individual views of society and politics. He always provided a bountiful supply of good cider—the product of his own orchard—and of tobacco, in the virtues of which he was a firm believer." This August Herman got Richard aside long enough to present him with Hazlitt's 1807 abridgment of Abraham Tucker's *The Light of Nature Pursued*, that early Utilitarian dissertation he had consulted in elaborating his characterization of Plotinus Plinlimmon.

On 23 September 1853, Maria told her brother Peter about a lawyer named George Griggs, who had visited them often since their "removal to this place." He had "an office at Boston & one in Brookline," where he lived. Judge Shaw had known him for many years and Helen had met him at Shaw's house eight years or so earlier, about the time of Herman's return from the Pacific. He had at least two sisters (a Mrs. Dearborn is mentioned in an 1855 letter and a Mrs. Coolidge in one from 1863). He had a brother who later lived in St. Paul, Minnesota, and at some point the brother had a son called Willie. In 1888 Griggs was described in a Boston paper as born on 8 September 1813 in Brookline, a graduate of Brown University in 1837 and of Harvard Law School in 1839. He had studied law in the office of a man with a Nantucket-sounding name, Judge Peleg Sprague. That is almost all we know of this man except what emerges in family letters. He too liked to drive when he got the chance, as he did later with Hoadley's fine horses; later, perhaps gradually, he became gruff and stingy. Now he was putting in appearances at Arrowhead.

From Lawrence, John C. Hoadley managed to be extremely attentive. He was there at Arrowhead the second week of July, and there again in the fourth week, pushing his advantages. On 14 June Augusta received a four-page letter from him, apparently his first formal overtures to her as prospective sister-in-law. Situated as he was with his mother and his sister Hetty in Clinton, Massachusetts, he wanted Augusta to visit them: "Cannot you be prevailed upon to make us a visit during the Summer? — If not earlier, say on my return from Pittsfield, after going to Lansingburgh for Kate. It would be highly agreeable to us all, and I am sure we could make your stay pleasant to you. — We have beautiful winding, wooded roads for riding; — saddle horses are to be obtained, if not equal to yours, at least tolerable, and good company will not be wanting." Saddle horses equal to any at Arrowhead would be easy to find, but the implication was that the visiting Thurstons and Latherses were supplying any deficiency. Hoadley continued:

> We can do no less than discuss this proposition in our correspondence; for, if Kate refuses to write me, I shall appoint you her secretary. — I wrote her last night, — a mere rhapsody, I fear, — for I felt just in the mood, — and I always write "right on" — just as I feel. — I am quite sure that if my mood were to fall upon her, she would find pen and paper in a trice, and give utterance to her emotions. —
>
> In serious truth, I feel a deep contentment, a thorough satisfaction in the step I have taken; and life and its purposes and hopes have all a new significance.

Augusta cannot have failed to recognize a dangerous quality in this confession. Her brother Herman's impulse to write "right on" had been proclaimed in *Mardi* and in *Pierre*, but Hoadley was not a reckless man, even in making her an invitation which became a topic of aghast reproaches.

On 30 January 1854, when he was safely remarried, to Kate, and had a houseful of delights in Lawrence, Hoadley recurred to this letter in a new one to Augusta. The "delights" ("Kate, — Mamma; Fanny, Tom, and — Kate, — first and last Kate! — ") had been talking about his old invitation to Augusta, and they all had declared "it was shocking, that it would have been highly improper for you to come, that it was hardly less so for me to ask you."

Shrugging off their objections, he allowed: "Doubtless they are right; but it only makes me respect proprieties less than ever." He went on to say something Herman would have been proud to have said, though he would have been uneasy at the intruder Hoadley's saying it: "Propriety, as distinguished from right, is little worthy of the attention of those who can think for themselves, and discern the requirements of duty." This was a man who knew himself as much as Lathers did. Having money did not guarantee that, but it allowed it to flourish.

During this time, through much or all of June, Kate lingered on in Lansingburgh among her girlhood friends. On 11 July from Pittsfield Hoadley wrote to Alfred B. Street, whom Herman had so offended, asking that Street send to him from Albany, fast, his "little Ms. volume, 'Destiny,'" since his friends the Melvilles desired to have it: "and as with one of them, (Miss Kate,) I hope to form a 'strict alliance' — a true *entente cordiale*, — I should like to gratify their curiosity." On 25 July Hoadley gave Helen a copy of John Greenleaf Whittier's new book, *The Chapel of the Hermits*. Nilly got the news in Newport, from Augusta, that the engagement was pleasing to everyone "and so excellent a match." Experienced in such things, Nilly replied (28 July): "the Ice broken I dare say you will soon follow in her footsteps, so I shall be prepared to hear another announcement soon."

Hoadley was a new force in the family, like Herman an autodidact (but systematically self-schooled, as Gansevoort had been and as most observers thought Herman was not), now a poet-technocrat, a widower only eight months older than Herman, and a man who had applied himself with dedication even beyond that of the revered Gansevoort: "Mr. Hoadley was indeed a self-made man. From early years an orphan boy obliged to support a widowed mother and others of the family, he obtained a thorough knowledge of practical matters in engineering work, while his evenings were passed in studies which enabled him to master French, German, Latin and Greek, a thorough knowledge of the higher mathematics, and a wide range of literary culture treasured up in a retentive memory and apparently always at command." Thus said C. J. H. W. in an obituary in the *American Machinist* in 1887. It was hard not to admire this man, especially since his personal qualities were so captivating. Hoadley drew people to him as a forceful public speaker but also in conversation, without having to be thawed into mellowness, as Herman did. Reports are that he spoke slowly, in a confidential whisper that encouraged his companion to lean toward him. He had lost some hearing already, spending his days as he did around the heaviest of machinery, and compensated by speaking in a low tone (since he could not gauge the volume of his own voice) and moving closer to his interlocutor. His intimate letters, the written equivalent of confidential conversations, could be powerfully winsome, even seductive. When he wanted to do so, he brought people into intimacy with him—and he wanted to be on intimate terms with all his in-laws and their connections. George Griggs might have been pleased if Helen came to him without her family, but Hoadley wanted Kate and he wanted the family to come with her. Almost everyone succumbed to Hoadley's vitality and charm; only Herman, who ought to have welcomed him, held back for some time from what can only have been some form of jealousy.

Hoadley had met Kate, as far as we know, only because Sophia had released her in April 1851 for what turned out to be a permanent removal to Arrowhead, nearly a year before Hoadley moved to Lawrence, where he was paid a phenomenal salary as manager of the Lawrence Machine Shop—three thousand dollars was the figure whispered in the family. Herman, according to family legend, disapproved of Kate's being wooed by a widower, and it may have been a long time before he realized what was plain to everyone from Maria to the Latherses and the Shaws—that Hoadley was the best thing that had happened to the family in anybody's memory—maybe the best until Tom took his position as the man of the family in the late 1860s. Any of Hoadley's poetry which Herman read would have struck him as being about as good as that of the Albany poet Alfred F. Street, or a notch above that of J. E. A. Smith. The question is whether Herman ever looked beyond the much-admired third-rate poetry and saw that Hoadley possessed an aesthetic sensibility akin to his own—one which emerged only faintly in his conventional verse but emerged dazzlingly in his beautiful and powerful machines. As one admirer said of a Hoadley locomotive a few years later, "on the road, where the work is to be done, this elegant locomotive will tell of thorough workmanship and a masterly adaptation of means to ends." Whether or not Melville ever recognized the fact, Hoadley's best machines embodied principles of architectonics such as he had mastered in *Moby-Dick* (for all his professing that it was botched) and would master again in *Clarel*.

By early August, Melville and Rowland Morewood had belatedly cemented their friendship by ascending Greylock on foot, apparently unattended (although Sam might have gone along without Lizzie's mentioning it in her letter to her father on 10 August)—an outing of at least two or three days, strangely contrasting with the boisterous outings of two and three years previous, notably the one in which Rowland's wife had become enamored of George Duyckinck. Early in August the artist Felix Darley left his charming Owl's Nest in Claymont (just south of the Pennsylvania-Delaware arc, carefully sited for unobstructed views of the Delaware River to the east), and made it out to the Berkshires to see his friend Herman Melville. Allan possessed Darley's illustrations of "Rip Van Winkle," which he had received in mid-September 1848 as a member of the American Art-Union, and Darley's fame was such that Herman could not have been ignorant of him, but no earlier record has been found of their friendship, which was firm enough to make Darley brave the hazards of getting from Pittsfield to Arrowhead, a perilous trek that gave Darley an anecdote he told and retold. Two years later, through Henry Dwight, one of the Sedgwick connections, Helen heard a version of Darley's quest for Arrowhead: "He said he met an Irishman on the road and asked Herman's direction. The man went off in a most lofty panegyric upon Herman & the family, the more especially upon the young ladies — 'Ah! is it the *young ladies* you're going to see! There's the fine young ladies! &c &c.' *Who* could it have been? He told him that he lived near us." The thing to do with an artist in the Berkshires was to get him outdoors as fast as possible, so in company of several other men Melville and Darley set off for the Taconic Dome, what Melville in *Israel Potter* called the "great purple dome of Taconic — the St. Peter's of these hills" (ch. 1), below Great Barrington, on the New York border, near Bash Bish.

There had been at Arrowhead, Lizzie said, "a good deal of transient company," but she was left much in the company of her three children, as she wrote her father, in London, on 10 August:

> Three little ones to look after and "do for," takes up no little portion of the day, and my baby is as restless a little mortal, as ever crawled — She is very well and healthy in every respect, but not very fat, as she sleeps very little comparatively and is very active. A few weeks since, Malcolm made his debut as a scholar at the white school-house by Dr. Holmes' — I was afraid he would lose the little that he already know[s] "of letters," and as I could not find the time to give him regular instruction, I sent him to school rather earlier than I should have done otherwise.

Neighbors' children stopped by for Malcolm every morning, and the family relished watching him go off, the morning sunlight behind him, his pail of dinner in one hand and his primer in the other, and enjoyed asking him what he did at school, knowing that his invariable answer would be that he ate "his dinner under the trees," the high point of his day. At twenty-two months Stannie was talking a great deal, and seemed "to be uncommonly forward for his age," although he had a severe cough which Lizzie thought could be the "hooping-cough," which was prevalent just then.

Lizzie herself had been "very quiet that summer," scarcely out at all, and she felt more isolated than usual. Herman was either at his desk or out of doors away from Lizzie and the children, and away from his mother and his sisters. On 13 August, just returned from that memorable outing to the Dome of the Taconic, Melville sent to the Harpers "three articles which perhaps may be found suitable for your Magazine." He asked: "Be so good as to give them your early attention, and apprise me of the result." These were probably "The Happy Failure," "The Fiddler," and "Cock-A-Doodle-Doo!" While Herman was involved, outside or at his desk, Lizzie's mother-in-law and her sisters-in-law were, a little thoughtlessly, leaving her too much with her children while they prepared for Kate's wedding. Helen was preoccupied, having her own imminent decision to make. In the midst of everything Augusta had to copy for Herman — which may explain why her correspondence record for July was left blank. On 27 August Hope sent the sort of word a traveling father did not need to hear. Elizabeth was full of care, "and Mr Melvilles family a beehive, as this marriage has brought forth every kind of talent." Hope's words seem cryptic, but versifiers may have enlivened the parlor with dueling prothalamia (perhaps with only Kate and John as the subjects), and the sisters may have outdone themselves and each other with feats of needlework. Augusta may have put herself into gypsy mode and told fortunes with the help of her oracular book. All summer the grapevines grew wonderfully, boding an abundance of grapes for preserves and perhaps for wine, appropriate for a household where the "fine young ladies" could think of themselves as desirable still, rather than unmarriageable because they had been so poor when they were in their first youth.

 Herman by the summer's end may still have retained his surly distrust of Hoadley, but Lizzie pleasantly reminded her father of what Herman had probably told him in New York, the connection between Hoadley's first wife and one of Shaw's classmates, and the charming coincidence of Hoadley's marrying the same day she and Herman did (although Hoadley's first wedding day is elsewhere reported as 24 August, not the fourth). Hope, worried about her winter coal, kept her eye on the essentials when she wrote Sam Savage on 27 July: "a manufacturer — or one that sees to it, salary three thousand — A man of worth all say — and of much cultivation of mind." Hoadley himself, experienced in dealing with in-laws, was determined to keep affectionate ties with his first set even as he established his ties with the new set. A manufacturer might have been easy to welcome, but Herman had to accept another literary man, a true modern American poet, into the family. Brought face to face with successful poets, Herman could be a snob, and a jealous one, since he had long despaired of getting anyone in the family to realize that he himself might not be immeasurably inferior as a wordsmith to, say, Martin Farquhar Tupper, Victoria's favorite. Now the family was pressing him to acknowledge the true geniality and decency — as well as formidable intelligence — of Kate's choice. Whatever tensions persisted in some form for years, Melville ultimately came to value Hoadley as a kindred reader of literature, and he had never been so rarefied a reader himself that he could not talk about Wordsworth or Spenser, two of his recent favorites, with another intelligent reader.

Melville apparently wrote "Bartleby, the Scrivener" between mid-August and the week of Kate's wedding in mid-September. Augusta recorded no letters written between 6 and 24 August, a possible indication that she was copying furiously as well as making her preparations for the festivities. Melville elaborated his story from the February advertisements for *The Lawyer's Story*, which included that suggestive opening of the first chapter about the hiring of a temporary copying clerk. Other newspaper reading, from far back, may still have been in Melville's head, such as the anonymous item in the *Broadway Journal* of 2 August 1845, "The Business Man," which had this epigram: "Method is the soul of business. — *Old Saying.*" The story began: "I am a business man. I am a methodical man. Method is *the* thing, after all." If Melville missed this in the paper in 1845, he could have seen it, on his return from England in 1850, in the new posthumous edition of Edgar Allan Poe's writings. The tone of voice of the narrator in "Bartleby" (whose grand points John Jacob Astor had declared to be first "prudence" and next "method") was an accumulation of influences, not least that of the lamented Gansevoort. Here he lectures Allan, from Galway, New York, 25 September 1840: "You have acquired habits of attention to business, & have already passed nearly half the requisite legal time of preparation, in the study of a profession in which I feel confident that you will succeed." Melville did not have to go far to find the stuffy pomposity he gave his lawyer in "Bartleby," the man of rich experiences whose avocations had brought him into more than ordinary contact with law-copyists or scriveners ("avocation" in Melville's time still being used where we would say "vocation").

Melville was not finished with his critique of his Unitarian acquaintances. In his empty office, after comprehending something of Bartleby's isolation, the narrator experiences "a not-unpleasing sadness." During these feelings a "fraternal melancholy" arises to link him with the woeful scrivener: "Ah, happiness courts the light, so we deem the world is gay; but misery hides aloof, so we deem that misery there is none." The lawyer dismisses these thoughts as "sad fancyings-chimeras, doubtless, of a sick and silly brain" and the next moment is rifling Bartleby's desk. What he finds leads him not to profound, disturbing melancholy, not to a tragic sense of the world, but to prudential feelings:

> My first emotions had been those of pure melancholy and sincerest pity; but just in proportion as the forlornness of Bartleby grew and grew to my imagination, did that same melancholy merge into fear, that pity into repulsion. So true it is, and so terrible too, that up to a certain point the thought or sight of

misery enlists our best affections; but, in certain special cases, beyond that point it does now. They err who would assert that invariably this is owing to the inherent selfishness of the human heart. It rather proceeds from a certain hopelessness of remedying excessive and organic ill. To a sensitive being, pity is not seldom pain. And when at last it is perceived that such pity cannot lead to effectual succor, common sense bids the soul be rid of it.

Somehow, the narrator feels "disqualified" for church-going, and abandons his intention of going to Trinity Church — not a place to bring deep sorrows to.

The rationality is akin to that of Plinlimmon, and derives from the same source, the public controversy in the 1840s in New York City over Unitarian attitudes toward the sufferings of the poor. At some point Melville learned at least the gist of the argument the Unitarian Joseph Curtis and the Pantheist gadfly Horace Greeley had waged in the columns of the *Tribune* and elsewhere, and understood just how firmly the family friend Orville Dewey stood on Curtis's side. This is Dewey long afterward, in his *Autobiography*:

> The upshot was, that, in his [Curtis's] opinion, the miseries of the poor in New York were not owing to the rich, but mainly to themselves; that there was ordinarily remunerative labor enough for them; and that, but in exceptional cases of sickness and especial misfortune, those who fell into utter destitution and beggary came to that pass through their idleness, their recklessness, or their vices. That was always my opinion. They besieged our door from morning till night, and I was obliged to help them, to look after them, to go to their houses; my family was worn out with these offices. But I looked upon beggary as, in all ordinary cases, *prima facie* evidence that there was something wrong behind it.

Dewey's own father "never could bear the sight of sickness or distress: it made him faint." Dewey, sharing that sensibility, lamented that clergymen were expected to go to their parishioners and express sympathy with affliction: "to take into one's heart, more or less, the personal and domestic sorrows of two or three hundred families, is a burden which no man who has not borne it can conceive of." Besides, respectable parishioners would not want a clergyman intruding in their house of mourning; better he should wait to make his consolatory call, after the "suffering of sickness or of bereavement" has passed. Melville knew enough of this sticking-point for Unitarians, first hand and second hand, to embody New York Unitarian prudentialness in his respectable narrator. The lawyer even finds a fine utility in Jesus' commandment that men love one another: "charity often operates as a vastly wise and prudent principle — a great safeguard to its possessor." Jesus is the ideal against whom the narrator is judged, but any superiority the reader feels is undercut by the narrator's willingness to go very far indeed to accommodate himself to Bartleby — farther than most readers would go.

In her papers Augusta retained a scrap of the original (or at least an early) portion of "Bartleby," perhaps what then stood as the conclusion:

> Some few days after my last recorded visit, I again obtained admission to the Tombs & went through the yard in quest of Bartleby, but without finding him.
> "I saw him standing by the wall there some few hours ago," said a turnkey maybe he's gone to his cell.
> So saying he led the way a few steps, & pointed out the direction of the cell.
> It was clean, well lighted & scrupulously whitewashed. The head-stone was standing up against the wall, & stretched on a blanket at its base, his head touching the cold marble, & his feet upon the threshold lay the wasted form of Bartleby.

Here is the version printed in *Putnam's:*

> "I saw him coming from his cell not long ago," said a turnkey, "may be he's gone to loiter in the yards."
> So I went in that direction.
> "Are you looking for the silent man?" said another turnkey passing me. "Yonder he lies — sleeping in the yard there. 'Tis not twenty minutes since I saw him lie down."
> The yard was entirely quiet. It was not accessible to the common prisoners. The surrounding walls, of amazing thickness, kept off all sounds behind them. The Egyptian character of the masonry weighed upon me with its gloom. But a soft imprisoned turf grew under foot. The heart of the eternal pyramids, it seemed, wherein, by some strange magic, through the clefts, grass-seed, dropped by birds, had sprung.
> Strangely huddled at the base of the wall, his knees drawn up, and lying on his side, his head touching the cold stones, I saw the wasted Bartleby.

Melville did not revise on the surviving scrap, but he reworked the passage before it appeared in *Putnam's* in the now familiar form, lacking a portable tombstone but enriched with the Egyptian massiveness, the architecture of the Tombs having been suggested by a drawing in John Lloyd Stephens's *Incidents of Travel in Egypt, Arabia Petræa, and the Holy Land* (1837).

This is to say that Melville may have written a version of the story as an elaboration of the opening words of a story he had seen in a newspaper advertisement and ended it with Bartleby's death, with the narrator taking Job's challenging words and converting them to comfortable melancholy:

"With kings and counsellors." If that happened, before very long the narration he had built on the copying clerk in *The Lawyer's Story* collided in Melville's memory with the evocative prose of the "Resurrectionist" of the previous fall, the author of the article on the Dead Letter Office in the Albany *State Register*, and he appended a "sequel" based on melancholy reports of the Dead Letter Office. In those last two paragraphs of the story as published, the narrator mentions a mere rumor that connected Bartleby with a job in the Dead Letter Office, then avidly seizes on that rumor as the truth that explains everything to him, that plucks the heart out of Bartleby's mystery. The lawyer needs the explanation, needs that his story convey a not-unpleasing sadness.

Just before 20 September — that is to say, just after Kate's wedding to John Hoadley — Melville wrote someone at *Putnam's* about something he was submitting to the new magazine, already prestigious because it aimed at promoting American writers rather than recycling British literature for American readers, as *Harper's* and many other magazines were content to do. Handling the correspondence at *Putnam's*, Charles F. Briggs looked in vain for the packet from Melville then asked the Harpers on 20 September if Melville had misdirected it to them. Without much trouble "Bartleby, the Scrivener" ended in Briggs's hands, and he rapidly readied it for publication in the November and December issues. The elder Richard Henry Dana, the poet, learned from the 3 December 1853 *Literary World* that Melville was the author of the story, and several weeks later wrote to Evert a formal critique: "It touches the nicer strings of our complicated nature, & finely blends the pathetic & ludicrous. The secret power of such an inefficient & harmless creature over his employer, who all the while has a misgiving of it, shows no common insight. — The two other clerks relieve the picture, at the same time that they are skilfully & humorously set off against each other." No one had the evidence that in the first version of *Pierre* Melville had achieved an astonishing new control of point of view, in comparison with either *Redburn* or *Moby-Dick*. Nor could anyone know that in *The Isle of the Cross* he had consolidated what he had been learning about basic literary techniques and had made new advances. As the elder Dana could not have known, "Bartleby" is a masterpiece partly because it was *not* the next thing Melville wrote after *Pierre:* he had learned more about literary techniques as he wrote the book now lost — sustained Dickensian characterization, for example; control of narrative point of view; and control of a difficult aesthetic device, that of a narrator who is reliable as to facts but unreliable as to attitude toward them. From the beginning, as Dana's comments suggest, "Bartleby" was praised, and it remained hauntingly in some readers' minds for decades, mentioned in print in unpredictable contexts.

In her intervals of copying for Herman, Augusta had written the necessary letters about the wedding. On 27 August she wrote Aunt Susan Gansevoort in Albany and Aunt Mary Melvill in Galena, then at a coup she did four Melvill aunts—writing to Aunt Priscilla in Boston, to Aunt Mary D'Wolf and Aunt Jean Wright in Dorchester, and Aunt Helen Souther in Hingham—plainly rephrasing a basic announcement of Kate's wedding and perhaps an invitation, two pages to each aunt, treating them equally lest the Melvill aunts compare their documents. She must have left the task of writing to Aunt Lucy Nourse to Lizzie, who had spent vacations with her, while Augusta probably barely knew her, her own aunt though she was. Augusta surely spared Kate the trouble of keeping a meticulous inventory of wedding gifts: Augusta would keep the list, as she did a few months later for Helen, and Kate would know just which donors to thank for which thoughtful presents. The Melvilles may have had to put some of the aunts up at Arrowhead, for Lizzie wrote her father on 10 August that they would not have any company on Kate's wedding day, 15 September, "excepting some of the relatives who will unavoidably be here for a day or two." (If Aunt Lucy had been coming, she would have said so; probably Lucy was too weakened by the neuralgic pain that tormented her at night.) The day before the wedding, 14 September, Melville's interest payment to Dr. Brewster came due, and the day passed without his paying it. He went into St. Stephen's Church the next day with that fresh secret knowledge of a double defaulting, to Stewart and to Dr. Brewster. The Reverend Mr. R. J. Parvin performed the ceremony, and John whisked Kate off on a traditional upper-class honeymoon, to Niagara Falls.

The journey was well chosen to recapitulate a heroic period of Hoadley's life. In 1836, at seventeen and a half, he had been hired as a chainman on an enlargement of the Erie Canal. "Successively rodman, leveler, surveyor, and draughtsman," according to the *Transactions of the American Society of Mechanical Engineers* (1887), he worked right through the period when Melville's studied surveying at the Lansingburgh Academy. In 1840 Hoadley was put in charge of the party locating the enlargement between Utica and Rome; afterward he worked on the Black River Canal, the Chenango Canal, and the enlargement of the Erie Canal between Little Falls and Syracuse. He survived the layoffs of the summer of 1842: "when work on the canal was nearly suspended, and the assistants were generally discharged, it was found that he had performed his work with so much foresight, and had represented, in his notes and upon his plans, the old work, as well as the new, with such thoroughness and completeness, that in the settlement of claims he was indispensable, and he was retained and transferred to other sections of the canal, to apply as far as possible the methods which he had instituted." Kate had been old enough to know that Herman had offered himself, under the cool patronage of his Uncle Peter, as a prospective worker on the Erie Canal, but had been rejected. The Melville women understood just how strongly Hoadley's career contrasted with Herman's. For all his sense of the fame he had gained by going to sea and becoming a writer instead of attempting to refurbish the tempestuous canal, Melville had to feel stabs of jealousy, now that he, not to mention the Shaws, knew that his literary career had crumbled from under him.

Herman had been hopeless—imagine a bridegroom who could write to his father-in-law that he would bring his bride back refreshed from her rambles. Brother John was all Augusta could have wished as a romantic lover for her sister. From the International Hotel, during his honeymoon, John wrote to Augusta in his new intimacy: "Kate is asleep on the bed; I have been dozing in an arm chair . . . It has been a happy day for us, both, — happy and memorable . . . for to-day we have our first letters from home!" Kate had never aspired to mastery of correspondence (Allan did not call Augusta the princess of correspondence without an invidious glance at the next younger sister), but John willingly accepted the master's role, and for his sister-in-law Augusta (who had been to Bath, New York, but would probably never see Niagara) he described the great natural wonder (in abominable handwriting — the worst in the family except the judge's):

> Why attempt to describe the indescribable? . . . The spray leapt to heaven, like a martyr's soul, as if it should never descend in tearful rain. — . . . And two fond, foolish lovers looked and listened, and turned from all to gaze into each other's eyes, as if their life, and love, and joy, were emblemed by the ceaseless stream, and steadfast rock, and ever rising spray, — and not by the bubble glittering an instant on the crest of the fall . . . Two fond, foolish lovers . . . and at their feet God's rainbow lay like the promise of a path of joy, — significant promise, — born of the marriage of the light of heaven and the mists of Earth.

The author of *Typee* was enough of a prude where his sisters were concerned to be uncomfortable around any of the romanticism that reached his ears, but Hoadley won everyone over, even Herman, at last.

Lemuel Shaw just missed the festivities, and Hope had gladly martyred herself by declining to attend without him. Shaw's ship arrived in Boston on 16 September, and on the nineteenth he and Hope took the new "express train," arriving at Arrowhead in time for dinner, the midday (or early afternoon) meal. They got their first glimpse of Bessie, still healthy and restless — Lizzie's way of saying the baby was Herman all over again. They were in time for wedding cake and other delectable leftovers, as well as fresh grapes from the vineyard. On Tuesday, 20 September, Herman and Lizzie accompanied the Shaws to Lenox for his court session, probably seeing the Sedgwicks, at least Charles, Shaw's clerk.

At this time, and probably for some days, even before the wedding, Shaw's acquaintance George Griggs (a middle-aged suitor, not a youngish beau) was at the village, for on the day the Shaws arrived Augusta performed a tender ritual. Inside the front cover of her commonplace book, *Orient Pearls at Random Strung*, she pasted a newspaper printing of Longfellow's "Endymion," and noted the date, 19 September, at the top, and the initials "GG"—the date Griggs became officially engaged to Helen Maria Melville.

> Like Dian's kiss unasked, unsought,
> Love gives itself, but is not bought,
> No voice, nor sound betrays
> Its deep, impassioned gaze.
>
> . . .
>
> No one so accursed by fate,
> No one so utterly desolate,
> But some heart, though unknown,
> Responds unto his own.
>
> Responds—as if with unseen wings,
> An angel touched its quivering strings;
> And whispers, in its song,
> "Where has thou strayed so long?"

No one should be so "utterly desolate," and Augusta had thrown away two chances, in her youth. We know almost nothing of her second cousin John Van Schaick except that he was a master of self-deprecation who could manage to be humorously alert to Maria's imperiousness without showing anything but the most profound respect—a charming fellow. Perhaps for reasons utterly frivolous in the world's eyes, such as the perception of a dangerous relation between personal grooming (how one clipped one's fingernails, for instance) and moral fastidiousness, Augusta had not married her purse-proud cousin Augustus Peebles, the Lord of the Isle. The irony was that as the decades passed Augustus's faults fell away and he behaved decently to everyone in the family. When Helen's successful suitor gracelessly fell ill, presumably in the village, Augusta gave him her best medical advice until he managed to go home. Romantic to the core, as Sarah Morewood realized, Augusta lived vicariously for a time through Helen, as through Kate, as she did through the "author."

In this family you could go round two oceans, as Herman had done, and return to Allan's description of how little had really changed (Uncle Peter's sick wife had died, Uncle Peter had remarried, Gansevoort had become a famous orator), but any traveler had to be aware of how fast changes *could* come. Having greeted the Shaws, Maria on 23 September wrote to her brother Peter, whose return from abroad, like his departure, almost coincided with the judge's: "Permit me to express to you, my dear brother, my sincere pleasure at your safe return home . . . Some changes have taken place in my family. Kate is married & gone on her wedding tour. Helen is engaged to be married to a Mr George Griggs." Herman, she said, was "looking remarkably well" and joined her in good wishes. Finally, the Shaws were to return from Lenox to Arrowhead before going to Boston.

In Lenox or at Arrowhead everyone got to decide whether to dwell on yet another *Herald* article on the Berkshires, a year after the last one, which the Great Barrington *Courier* excerpted on 22 September. The writer enumerated "some very great people" who had been drawn to the locale, starting with Fanny Kemble but progressing to notable men:

> Berkshire has produced her full share of eminent men, and seems to be especially favored by distinguished persons from abroad. . . . Among them are Herman Melville, who if he would understand to write about the things of this world, would be as popular as Dickens, but whose later works are such as neither gods nor men, nor columns can tolerate. He lives at Pittsfield, and has a beautiful place there. Dr. Holmes, the poet and wit, is another Pittsfield landed proprietor; and Nathan Appleton has a place there. It [is] scarcely necessary to say that Gov. Briggs is a Pittsfield man, or that Mr. Rockwell, who succeeded him in Congress, and who was his colleague in the Constitutional Convention, also resides there.

Herman could at least mention in his defense that the articles he had been writing were about "the things of this world," and he may even have suspected that the last of them, "Bartleby," would soon be identified as Dickensian in its characterizations. (On 3 June 1856, the Boston *Daily Evening Traveller* said that "for originality of invention and grotesqueness of humor" "Bartleby" was "equal to anything from the pen of Dickens, whose writings it closely resembles, both as to the character of the sketch and the peculiarity of the style.")

All the Arrowheads would have their chance to hear tales of ocean travel and European touring rather than reading more about the writer whose *Moby-Dick* and *Pierre* neither gods nor men nor newspaper column-stuffers could tolerate. The Shaws could assure the Melvilles, on the basis of their long knowledge of Griggs, that Helen had made a safe choice, and they could in turn hear about the new three-thousand-dollars-a-year manufacturer who happened to be a romantic lover such as the family had not previously encountered. For the month of October Augusta decamped to Winyah, deserving the welcome she received. At the end of the honeymoon Hoadley took Kate for an early October visit to Winyah, while Augusta was still there. The Hoadleys had to cut short their stay before the household was stirring ("'Time and *trains* wait for no man'"), but Winyah had been glorious, as John wrote Augusta on 10 November:

> I have often recalled the pleasant hours of that bright day spent in the enjoyment of Mr. Lathers' generous and refined hospitality . . . as the French say, — "plus heureux les un que les autres" — happier than one another! — That ramble in the woods, gathering faded [?] leaves, — the panorama from the tower, the ride through shady lanes[?], and by the borders of the shimmering Bay [Long Island Sound], — the stroll through the grounds at the [Pelham] Priory, and the interesting call upon its inmates: — and better than all, the quiet hours of cheerful conversation in his peaceful house; — all things and more, — making me feel a sense of grateful obligation, not bad to bear, — but impossible to repay.

Richard had left John appreciative of his and Abby's "generous and delicate hospitality," and Kate and John had seen enough of the New York Melvilles for John to send his "brotherly love to Allan and Sophia." Now Augusta listed his letter as being from "brother John," and on 21 October, while she was still at Winyah, she received her formal fraternal note from Mr. Griggs in Boston.

No description has been found of the house Hoadley had rented in Lawrence, but for several months in 1854 the Lawrence *Courier* ran an advertisement for a house next to it: "For Sale. A 'DWELLING HOUSE, pleasantly situated in Summer street, adjoining the premises occupied by J. C. HOADLEY, Esq. Said House contains 13 rooms. . . . marble chimney pieces, cemented cellar . . . stables." The Hoadley house was comparable, not a hovel next to the mansion. As for the manufacturing capital, Hoadley in late March 1852 in his anonymous contribution to *Taghconic* (discreetly writing from "L——"), compared it unfavorably to Pittsfield: "But here, with nothing in all the tame horizon but dead sand plains, or faintly swelling hills, still more lifeless in their weak aspiring; here, where nothing, not even the church spires, are so near heaven as the manufactory chimnies, — the awe-inspiring spell of the mountains is broken, while their blue and cloud-like summits, looming over the length of a state in the soft mirage of memory, look lovelier, holier than ever." By 22 October 1853 through his generosity and downright genius for the right psychological stroke, Hoadley was looking forward to having Maria ensconced with him and Kate at Lawrence, where she could give her daughter and her daughter's staff the benefit of her incomparable Dutch training and her vast and varied experience in domestic management.

Herman on 1 November had again defaulted on the $92.25 semiannual interest due to T. D. Stewart. This time his failure to meet the obligation was exacerbated by his earlier failure in September to pay Dr. Brewster the interest he owed him. On 8 November Putnam's sent Allan a check for the first installment of "Bartleby," $55 for eleven closely-printed pages. Lizzie and Maria made preparations to leave for Boston on 21 November, and a visitor at Arrowhead, Cousin Priscilla, entrusted Lizzie with a "petition" in addition to her own letter to Shaw on the nineteenth ("*she* will explain the circumstances better than I can possibly do, upon paper"):

> I . . . ask if you will send it [the interest due] at your *earliest* convenience, as I have finally left, *very much* wearied, the situation that I have so long occupied, at that school in Canandaigua, and intend to try boarding, for the present, in Pittsfield, and if *possible* make my *needle* profitable — but, as I furnish my own room, I wish to make use of the money, *whatever* the amount may be, *at once* — please forward to *Hermans* care, at *this* place —
>
> — My aunt & Lizzie are making busy preparations for their departure on Monday — and anticipate spending the joyous season of Thanksgiving most delightfully with near and dear friends, in Boston and vicinity.

Priscilla's tragic situation weighed upon the overburdened household at Arrowhead. Shaw was being importuned by other heirs of old Thomas Melvill, Amos Nourse (8 November) writing from Bath to Shaw hoping that the banks had even a small dividend: "My quarter's rent & housekeeping become due next week, & I am ashamed to say that I have not the means of meeting them." Anything Maria heard about Shaw's disbursements as trustee of her father-in-law's estate enforced upon her that, irresponsible as her brother-in-law Thomas had been, he had not squandered all of his share of his inheritance before he died.

Meanwhile, Griggs had been paying court to the family. He wrote Augusta on 19 October (a month to the day since his engagement to Helen), identified himself as her "Pittsfield patient," and credited her prescription and "the fine indian-summer-October-weather" for his being able to declare, "I am in good health and hope you are enjoying the same blessing." He thanked her for her sympathetic pleasure in the success of his suit: "Should you ever permit yourself to gladden the heart of one of The Sons of Men may he prize you as highly and deserve you even more than does your dear Sister's happy lover prize and deserve her." John would never have been so gauche as to claim to deserve Kate, and Helen in everyone's eyes was a pearl above price, a second mother to all of the other children, and Augusta did not need to be reminded that she was unmarried. Nevertheless, Griggs kept trying to be gallant, as on 22 November, when he sent a "Private" note to Maria Melville, who was at the Shaws: "I had a little plan which involved the loss of a dinner to you, viz. to jump into a chaise and go out to Brookline and look at an unfurnished house about which I wished the benefit of your good judgment but as I am afraid there will not be time today perhaps you will oblige me by going next week." On 15 December he wrote her in regard to matters Helen should have been consulted on: "I have been trying this morning to match the dining room carpet in vain — If you are not otherwise engaged will you select some other pattern for it. If you would like to have me go with you, I will call at ½ past three this afternoon — If you prefer to select it, this morning, by calling at Judkins 75 Hanover Street, New England Carpet Store — where I went with you yesterday, they will wait on you, and put it in my bill." (Did they pass Henry Delano, nephew of Amasa Delano, on Hanover Street? He had been living there.) It was hard to fault so attentive a man as Griggs had suddenly become, and Maria may not have noticed much that he lacked Hoadley's finesse as well as much of Hoadley's innate generosity of spirit and decisiveness as a suitor. At least Griggs understood that a man who wanted a Melville daughter had to court her whole family as best he could.

Thanksgiving always compelled the Shaws to gather at the Mt. Vernon Street house, but Maria Melville as a New Yorker had never made a great to-do over it. This year Herman stayed at home to work. Although he had mastered the art of magazine writing, he had not stopped thinking of himself as a man who wrote books. On 24 November Melville wrote the Harpers offering them a new book, this time a work in progress, but using the occasion to itemize his literary stockpile in a way that makes clear that he had not destroyed *The Isle of the Cross* and had not abandoned hope of publishing it:

> In addition to the work which I took to New York last Spring, but which I was prevented from printing at that time; I have now in hand, and pretty well on towards completion, another book — 300 pages, say — partly of nautical adventure, and partly — or, rather, chiefly, of Tortoise Hunting Adventure. It will be ready for press some time in the coming January. Meanwhile, it would be convenient, to have advanced to me upon it $300. — My acct: with you, at present, can not be very far from square. For the abovenamed advance — if remitted me now — you will have security in my former works, as well as security prospective, in the one to come, (The Tortoise-Hunters).

Anxious to make the payment to Brewster (which plainly bothered him more than the payments he owed Stewart), Melville was temporizing when he claimed to have a three-hundred-page book "pretty well on towards completion."

At the end of his letter Melville carefully specified that he was offering the book "on the old basis—half-profits," not the ruinous basis they had insisted on for *Pierre*. Perhaps swayed by the promise of "nautical adventure" more than the wishful suggestion that their account with Melville could not be very far from square, the Harpers responded promptly enough, on 7 December, with what Melville had asked for, an advance of three hundred dollars. The day before, Putnam's sent Allan a check for the second installment of "Bartleby," thirty dollars for six pages. On 8 December Melville paid Brewster the interest he owed him, three months late; Brewster's notation does not indicate that he charged interest on the overdue interest.

By blocking out of his mind the thought of his debt to Stewart and his repeated defaultings on the interest, Melville must have hoped to face Christmas and New Year's then Helen's wedding with something like equanimity, but headlines in the *Herald* of 11 December proclaimed what had happened the day before (which happened to be Hoadley's thirty-fifth birthday): "ANOTHER AWFUL CONFLAGRATION: Harper's Establishment in Ruins. At an early hour in the evening the appearance of the ruins on Cliff street was beautifully terrific. The entire establishment of the Messrs. Harpers was one mass of rubbish, comprising six houses on Cliff street, running through to Pearl." This Sunday edition may have reached Melville before the day was over, throwing himself into agony over the loss of the plates of his books. To have brought down the wrath of the critics with *Pierre* and to have failed to persuade the Harpers to publish *The Isle of the Cross* at all was to experience misery beyond calculation, but to lose all the plates of his books—even the plates of *Typee*, which the Harpers had bought from Wiley & Putnam, was to have his career wiped out abruptly and absolutely.

Then an article on the twelfth made the correction: "The most valuable property of the establishment, the stereotyped plates, we understand, are in a good state of preservation. . . . This property was stowed away in vaults extending under the sidewalk." The fire destroyed none of the plates of Melville's books, but it did destroy many of his unsold books (bound or in sheets). Melville then experienced the slow realization that although he was not wiped out he was terribly damaged—ultimately, it became clear to him, to the tune of about a thousand dollars, for in 1856 he explained to his father-in-law: "Before the fire, the books (not including any new publication) were a nominal resource to me of some two or three hundred dollars a year; though less was realised, owing to my obtaining, from time to time, considerable advances, upon which interest had to be paid." After the fire, the Harpers made "extra charges" against him, "consequent upon the fire, in making new impressions, ahead of the immediate demand, of the books." As the defeated Melville came to see, the coolly avaricious Harpers in effect blamed him for the fire, charging him all over again for their new costs, costs which they had already deducted from his account before paying him any royalties. Honest men would have cut their losses and not charged Melville double. Income from the Harpers would be very slow in coming, since sales would be slow: people who wanted their copy of *Mardi* or *Moby-Dick* or the other books had bought copies as they came out. For Melville the fire was less than catastrophic only because his books were already selling very slowly and much of his income, for the last months, had been from stories, which he could continue to sell to the Harpers for their magazine as well as to Putnam's.

Even as he took the advance for *The Tortoise-Hunters*, Melville was beginning to be known as a magazinist. "Cock-A-Doodle-Doo! Or, The Crowing of the Noble Cock Beneventano," was out in *Harper's New Monthly Magazine* a few days before its December date, as was the second installment of "Bartleby." *Putnam's* leaked the authorship, so that on 1 December even Charleston, South Carolina, could read in the *Courier* that "Bartleby" was by Melville. Duyckinck in the 3 December *Literary World* acted as if nothing had happened between him and Melville (and, indeed, he had kept up his correspondence with Augusta): "Putnam's Monthly for December closes its first year.... The corps of contributors who have defeated the anonymous system of the magazine, by writing such clever articles that they have become perfectly well known, were never in better force than on this occasion.... Mr. Melville's 'Bartleby, the Scrivener,' a Poeish tale, with an infusion of more natural sentiment, is concluded." "Poeish" was coolly chosen; "Dickensian" would have been truer and clearly complimentary. On 27 December John wrote Augusta: "Tell Herman I thank him with all my heart for that noble, spiritual lesson of hope,—enduring, triumphant,—never-desponding,—in the 'Crowing of the noble Cock Beneventano.'" This man, who knew by heart that noble, spiritual lesson of hope, was a blessing to the Melville family.

Christmas is poorly recorded that year. Lizzie may have stayed on in Boston (leaving the boys at Arrowhead?), Maria had returned from Lawrence, Helen, Augusta, and Fanny were probably all at home at Arrowhead getting ready for Helen's wedding on 5 January. Cousin Priscilla stayed on through the holidays before going to see Allan and Sophia. It was Sarah Morewood who aspired to celebrate Christmas elaborately in imitation of her English in-laws and who "had" that holiday in a way that spared Arrowhead the effort. This year Sarah left her invitation so open that Melville specified which of the possibilities he (and presumably his household) would be delighted to attend: Christmas Dinner—that is to say, the "Day Dinner," starting in mid-afternoon and lasting some hours. Sarah was "your Ladyship of Southmount" and Herman was "the humble Knight on the Hill," his hyperbolic courtliness undampened by the Doleful Dumps. The family celebration would start with the Dutch holiday, New Year's, and John and Kate made their plans accordingly (still having to go south in order to get a train west, there being no suitable way to get from Lawrence to Pittsfield through Worcester). He wrote to Augusta on 27 December: "Your note, under cover to Kate, was received to-day.—I answer thus early to tell you that we intend to start from home at noon on Saturday [31 December],—from Boston at 4½ (dining at Judge Shaw's) and hope to reach Arrowhead about midnight. I write to Burlingham to meet us at the Dépôt and take us out to the house.—Kate and I rival each other in anticipation for the arrival of the hour of meeting around that cavernous fire place." A severe snowstorm struck on the twenty-ninth, completely blocking up the railroads, and delaying them until Monday, 2 January. A girl had become exhausted and died in the snow, Hoadley reported. Kate added a note without a thought of the human snow-image: "It is too, *TOO BAD for I had set my heart upon starting to-morrow.*" Kate felt heartsick to be left out of some of the preparations for Helen's wedding. The year ended in suspense and frustration, the New Year's Day celebration delayed twenty-four hours (John Hoadley had pre-inscribed New Year's Day before wrapping his gift for Malcolm, Hawthorne's new *Tanglewood Tales*), and pushed almost to the wedding day.

[9]

The Shift Away from Herman and Arrowhead

January–March 1854

❦

> These widowers, are generally *well read*, they cannot, *well deceive*. Not, that I would say *a word against single men*, to discourage you. — Oh, no, after my visit at Helen's, I could not find it in my heart to do so. How pleasantly she is situated, surrounded by so many kind friends.... Then I visited Kate in her new home. What, has she to wish for? The dear girls, did everything in their power, to make my visits agreeable.
>
> Aunt Lucy Melvill Nourse to Augusta Melville, 25 July 1854

MELVILLE WAS ABLE to work through much of December 1853, but after Christmas Arrowhead was no place for a man wanting to concentrate on the adventures of tortoise hunting in the Galapágos Islands. Helen's wedding preoccupied everyone. The Hoadleys arrived on 2 January 1854, by which time Griggs must have been hovering in the village or at Broadhall, and gifts were arriving regularly at the post office and the express office. The inventory of gifts that Augusta kept includes some belated offerings, such as second cousin Augustus Peebles's unexpectedly generous gift of remarkably handsome spoons and the magnificent sugar bowl which Nilly Thayer carried out to Helen's house in Longwood, near Boston (a gift that must have cost twenty-five dollars, Tom judged, which means, quality considered, that you simply could not buy its like today, new, even for fifty or a hundred times that amount). Some of the best items were not new, since both the Melville and Gansevoort families already had mastered the grand habit of passing on cherished items of old family silver at special occasions. In fact, they possessed so many pieces of plate that they could discriminate to the point of reserving certain pieces for certain occasions; one descendant has a tea service best rebestowed only on a silver wedding anniversary. Some relatives were hopelessly stingy. Aunt Priscilla was full of promises about the gifts she was going to present, but as Helen said, "When? When? When?" Augusta's inventory demonstrates which family members and friends were closest to the Melvilles, outlay of money being an all but infallible test of loyalty. The list also suggests the sort of gifts Kate must have received a few months before.

Even allowing for the fact that some gifts arrived late, this trove for Helen and George occasioned much disruption, some members of the family perhaps spelling Herman on the trips to the village. Keeping the gifts in a controlled display area must have been difficult, despite their recent practice with Kate's gifts. The house may have been occupied by "transient company," in Lizzie's phrase (though the Nourses did not come, and they would more likely have made the effort than any of the other Melvills). Sophia was newly pregnant, but that had never stopped her traveling before, so she and Allan were probably there. Once Hoadley and Kate arrived, everyone, including Herman, had to get used to the fact that they now slept in the same bed at Arrowhead, which altered sleeping arrangements for Fanny if not for Augusta as well. The wedding day, 5 January, was a Thursday, so Rowland may not have come up from the city, but Sarah and Ellen Brittain were spending the winter at Broadhall instead of boarding in New York City, so they attended. The Reverend R. J. Parvin, who had married Kate and John, now performed the Episcopal ceremony for Griggs and Helen at St. Stephen's (the church full of memories for the older Melvilles, as well as recent memories for Hoadley and Kate). Afterward, the wedding guests were welcomed to partake of a collation at Arrowhead, which must have been by that time buzzing like a hive, again, despite the season.

Instead of leaving on a honeymoon, Helen and Griggs may have taken a train to Boston and gone directly to their new rented house in Longwood. Kate and John stayed on at Arrowhead, and the next day everyone looked on and criticized as Herman and John engaged in some delicate familial negotiations. Once again passing up a chance to copy out the "Epilogue" at the end of volume 3, Herman inscribed one (perhaps the last) of his gorgeous and precious sets of *The Whale*, blue boards with white whale-like creatures swimming down the spines, to "John C Hoadley / from his friend / Herman Melville / Pittsfield Jan: 6th 1853" (a slip for 1854), and inscribed this on the flyleaf, from Lorenz Oken's *Elements of Physiophilosophy:* "'All life' says Oken 'is from the sea; none from the continent. Man also is a child of the warm and shallow parts of the sea in the neighborhood of the land.'" A little contretemps followed, with most likely Maria and Kate, if not also Augusta and Fanny, reproaching Herman for not accepting John into the family. Herman could have argued that in family usage "friend" could still mean "relative," but he fell into an acquiescent mood in which, to propitiate everyone, he then inscribed to Hoadley the volumes of Thomas Chatterton he had bought in London: "To My Brother / John C. Hoadley / Pittsfield, Jan' 6th 1854," and added a footnote to "Brother": "Presented in earnest token of my disclaimer as to the criticism of the word 'friend' used on the fly-leaf of the 'Whale.'" He also reinscribed *The Whale* with a footnote to "friend": "If my good brother John take exception to the use of the word *friend* here, thinking there is a *nearer* word; I beg him to remember that saying in the Good Book, which hints there is a *friend* that sticketh CLOSER than a *brother.*" (He underlined "closer" two times in this citing of Proverbs 18:24.) This was public diplomacy, urged on by a teasing and perhaps exasperated family (not least by the September bride), but it had better consequences than most rapprochements sealed under duress: it pushed Herman toward taking John into the family, whatever qualms he had felt about giving Kate into the hands of a widower, and whatever hostility might, at times, flash out against the successful brother-in-law.

After the extravagance of the second wedding Herman cast about for ways to economize and on 7 January canceled his subscription to the New York *Herald*. By that day, the Arrowheads had some news to feel happy about, but also wistful that it had not come two or three days earlier. Tom had docked in Boston on the *Townsend* on Helen's wedding day — one frustrating day too late for him to be in Pittsfield, for a telegraphic dispatch would have delayed her wedding as effectively as John De Peyster Douw's telegram had halted his wife's attempt to remarry illegally. Tom arrived at Arrowhead some days after the bride and groom had flown, and stayed until 16 January, when he escorted Cousin Priscilla Melvill to New York for a visit to Allan and Sophia. Tom wrote Augusta on 19 January: "We arrived hear safe and sound on monday night at 11 O'clock found the supper table waiting for us Sophia had received Pris's letter that evening. They gave us a hearty welcome. After supper we had a long talk a *smile* and a segar, and went to bed about one O'clock. Sophia is looking very well, better than I have seen he[r] look for some time. Allan has been troubled with a bad tooth but is gettin better." The health report was not worrisome: Sophia looked good early in her pregnancy, and Allan had only a specific localized ailment.

In letters from New York later in January 1854 Tom brought the Arrowhead contingent up to date on the wonders of the Crystal Palace at the New York World's Fair, to which he had taken Priscilla. He had been "most pleased with the painting, Statuary, and Naval departments." The whole Thurston family put themselves out to welcome Priscilla. Tom and Sophia took her out to Winyah and left her there for a rare treat, perhaps the only chance she ever had to luxuriate in surroundings befitting a woman so conscious of her *"native* aristocracy." (The "fam'd" Winyah, she called it on 10 February, when she reported that Mr. Lathers was at home, sick, but that Abby nevertheless had urgently invited her to return.) When Tom went with Allan to Brooklyn to see Cousin Kate Curtis he found that Kate's brother Leonard Gansevoort had been sick for a month and a half — ominous news, it turned out. Tom returned to Arrowhead on 24 January "by the Bridgeport route," probably with the gingerbread horses he had hoped to find for "Stany and Malcom." Herman continued the pattern he had begun on the sixth, plundering his own library for gifts rather than making new purchases. Because Tom was going east, escorting his mother, Herman gave him an early birthday present on 26 January, his copy of Seneca's *Morals by Way of Abstract* (London, 1746), inscribing it: "My Dear Tom, This is a round-of-beef where all hands may cut & come again." The joke may have crossed his mind that having absorbed Seneca on stoicism as he read the reviews of *Pierre* he did not need the book any more himself, but he probably had his copy of the 1614 edition of Seneca's *Workes . . . Both Morall and Naturall* to fall back on. Herman's odd stoic levity may lie behind a cryptic comment in a letter his mother soon wrote to Augusta from Lawrence: "Kate, Fanny, and Mr Hoadley are well & 'happy,' as Herman says."

As long as Tom was ashore the family revolved around him, wherever he was. All but ignored, Herman at the end of January settled back down to write, but Lizzie, even with three children to care for, was ready to drop everything to knit Tom a proper scarf until he told her that Priscilla had already given him one, and everyone kept track of his peregrinations and hoped to see him more than once before he sailed. On 28 January Tom explored Helen's house in Brookline ("and was delighted with it, especially with the dining room"), then went into town with Griggs and went to see "L. John De Woolf," his cousin named for Uncle John D'Wolf's companion, the great G. H. von Langsdorff. At three, after Helen had served him dinner, Tom took Maria into Boston, where he hired a carriage so as to get the trunks to the Lawrence depot for the five o'clock cars, and arrived at Kate's near seven, finding that the sisters had been worrying themselves all afternoon and that Hoadley was still at work.

Tom had been content enough in Pittsfield, since he could drive up past the depot on North Street to Dodge and Hubbard and buy the New York *Tribune* and the *Herald* and their new rival, the *Times*, among others. Lawrence was uncivilized, by his standards, for no dealer stocked the same day's New York papers with their up-to-date shipping notices. Nevertheless, the family pampered Tom as best they could. He suffered during these winter homecomings, his blood thinned by the warmth of the tropics; he hovered near the fire with Maria while the sisters and Hoadley went to church. This was the three-year-old Grace Church (Episcopal), an elegant slate-roofed building, with pews, pulpit, reading-desk, and doors all in undressed black walnut; the congregation had rejected the idea of stained glass in favor of an experimental brown enameled glass (according to the *Semi-Weekly Courier* of 16 May 1854). Hoadley, any mother-in-law's dream, was a vestryman. At Lawrence for the first time in family memory two perfect men could occupy the same room, Hoadley and Tom. Hoadley was irreproachable, and anything Tom did—even staying home from church—was all right with every member of the family. In his letters he regularly wrote, with no self-consciousness, that this or that person had been happy to see him, and sometimes he mentioned what was also always true, that he had been happy to see them. It simply never occurred to him that not everyone possessed his total —and absolutely correct—assurance that he was welcome wherever he went. On 10 February Priscilla reported that she and Sophia were "passing the time *very* pleasantly," although they had lost "*one* principal ingredient in our happiness" when Tom left them. Better than anyone except Maria, Cousin Priscilla could remember the times when Tom was the joy of the Melvill farm, so adorable as to be all but edible. The reduced Arrowhead contingent hoped in vain to see Tom a third time before he sailed.

Tom was well placed to judge the new brothers-in-law and their households. He was, after all, the best judge of household comfort as well as the man of his generation most comfortable for everyone to be around, as Herman Gansevoort had been, according to Gansevoort Melville, the man of *his* generation. Tom decided that Kate had "a very fine house and very tastefully furnished," but he "would rather have Helens, to live in." This has to do with Kate's obsessive tidiness as well as the fact that Helen's household training was superior to Kate's (as were her education and social experiences): the older the Melville children, the better educated they were. Helen had conscientiously settled into her new house in the burgeoning subdivision of Longwood (an early upper-middle-class "development"). In late May, long after Tom had taken his first view, she reported on community improvements, including three new houses in progress: "all the unswarded earth has been harrowed, sewed with oats & grass seed, & rolled. The oats are up, three inches, green & bright, and what with the numerous young trees that have been set out in all directions, & the old apple trees in one sheet of white blossoms, we look verdant & rural just now, despite the *new* look of this new suburb." Within, Helen made the house comfortable. She respectfully reframed an oil portrait of Maria at considerable expense (eight dollars) to preside benignly from the parlor wall. While it was unframed, the shrewdly ingratiating George took advantage of new technology to have two daguerreotypes made from it, one for Kate and one for Fanny. A few months later, after Maria had returned, the Arrowheads shipped to Helen an awkward "wardrobe," at the cost of breaking the neck of a bust of Demosthenes (the Greek Gansevoort), but Helen cheerfully promised they should have "a marble bust of Judge George Griggs on the same pedestal one of these days," not a mere plaster one. Her account around 20 June of the placement of the wardrobe at Longwood conveys a good deal about the family's attitude toward alcohol at this period—the time when Cousin Priscilla was so concerned about Shaw's vulnerability: "two able-bodied, but by no means Samsonic looking men, carried it up stairs, without much apparent effort; but I thought it my duty to restore their expended strength by a glass of wine after the feat was performed. Tell Herman (for Mama's edification) that they gulped it down at one swallow, and did not stop 'to sip and taste the flavor as gentlemen do who are accustomed to drink wine daily,'—I quote from the maternal—perhaps they did wisely, considering the quality of the liquid, our vintner cheated us in that last pipe." Whatever Helen meant by "Tell Herman (for Mama's edification)," she was sharing a loving joke with Herman, not reproaching him. Only Helen and Herman were old enough to recall and recite at will all the sage maxims drilled into them by the "paternal" as well as the "maternal," and by the semi-paternal but maxim-laden Gansevoort. Herman could hurt Helen's feelings, as when he grumped at her once in November 1850, but they rejoiced in each other's ways. Now at last Helen could luxuriate in placing her maiden treasures in her own home: "I spent one day very happily in placing upon its dear old shelves, and nice long drawers my valuables of various kinds." She had pronounced herself "as happy as a queen" whenever she looked at the portrait of her mother, and by summer she was settled.

During her first visit to her married daughters, Maria for her part could feel that she was at last treated like a queen in the houses of her sons-in-law, if not always in the house of her oldest living son. In February while the Hoadleys visited Longwood Maria got a foretaste of the way life should be for her. On the fifth she wrote Augusta: "Shall not we have a merry party at Longwood. I wish you dear Gus could be with us, Herman, Allan & all their wives & little ones. What a numerous party & the Mother of all present, happy in their midst." In this lightening of mood as she took on the responsibility of guiding two new households and familiarizing herself with both a new and a renewed Boston circle of acquaintances, Maria lost some of her religious intensity. Her church-going did not slacken noticeably (although she would willingly stay home with Tom as he cowered close to the fire), but a grievous theological burden was lifted from her: the responsibility of brooding obsessively over the state of her son Herman's soul. When she had other things to think about, Maria gave him a little respite about his immortal soul.

Yet rather than ceasing to offer timely guidance to her second son altogether, Maria shifted her terrain from theological exhortation to occupational guidance. At Boston and Lawrence she was exposed to one lecturer after another. On 30 January Fanny reported on two. E. P. Whipple had disgraced himself with a talk on "Eccentric Character" while Josiah Quincy, who had been president of Harvard from 1829 to 1846, had delivered a very fine lecture on the Mormons. Revolving these matters in her heart, Maria on 10 February commissioned Augusta to convey her message to Herman: "*one Lecture* prepared by himself can be repeated seventy times with success." Lecturers "prepare one lecture & travel the rounds with this one for the whole season, are feasted made much of," and seldom paid less than fifty dollars. This, she pronounced, "is the present style of enlightening the many who have no time to devote to reading & research." Here Maria broke out in a direct address to her stubborn son: "& now my dear darling Herman all your friends, relatives & admirers, say that you are the very man to carry an audience, to create a sensation, to do wonders, to close this subject I will only request you to think over this *not* new subject, when in a happy hopeful state of mind, and there is a chance of your coming to the wise conclusion, to do that thing, which at once, and by the same agreeable act, will bring us fame & fortune." Herman ignored her, but the seed of the idea had been planted, as Maria knew.

In her rosy view of the future possibilities of the more recent son-in-law, Maria, in 1854, may have overvalued Griggs — "George is a treasure, simple, gentle, unaffected & withal sensible & manly." Tom, a better judge, was quickly taken with John. Tom was just the man to comprehend the merits of the Parker Water Wheels which Hoadley was perfecting (to the prideful notice of the editor of the *Semi-Weekly Courier* on 16 May: "Cheaper than the turbine, and not more expensive than the breast wheel; simple and easy of access for inspection or adjustment; free from all liability to wear or accident, and almost always exempt from the possibility of interruption"). Hoadley winningly attached one of Tom's gorgeous shells (drawn up from the warm waters of the South Seas) to the end of his watch chain so that (until he died?) he thought of Tom when he looked to see what time it was. Used to hiring and firing men, Hoadley understood Tom's value (as he wrote Augusta on 30 January): "I like him much, — a noble, manly fellow, — capable of acting a man's part in any sphere of life."

In mid-February 1854 Tom and Mr. Hoadley, as he still called him, walked into town from Helen and George's house in Longwood and went all over his present ship, the *Townsend*, and then to his new ship, the *Meteor*, which Hoadley much admired. This was in fact a splendid clipper ship, launched only in 1852 in South Boston and meant to cash in on the California trade. Built for speed rather than tonnage, she carried a slightly inapt figurehead on her sharp bow, Atalanta breaking her stride to pick up the golden apples. The next morning Tom heard someone asking for the first mate — the first day Tom held that position — and stepping out of the cabin on the *Meteor* found Hoadley. After this new contact, Tom pronounced to Augusta on

15 February: "He is a fine fellow from the top of his graceful head, down to the extream point of his V-toe." This was before Tom saw his going-away gift from Hoadley, a superb marlinespike forged at his own factory in Lawrence! How John won Allan over is not documented, but any man who in a few weeks received an inscribed set of *The Whale* from Herman and fabricated a marlinespike for Tom was sensitive, imaginative — in short, irresistible. George could not compete with Hoadley's assurance and grace, but no one complained about him for a long time: he had finally married Helen.

Both Hoadley and Griggs wisely consulted Maria on domestic matters, and during the transitional months early in 1854 Maria continued to luxuriate in two new households where she could be treated as she deserved. Maria had trained her daughters to do fine needlework and to supervise households — literally to carry the keys and the purse of the office of chatelaine. She had tried to teach Helen, Augusta, Kate, and Fanny all there was to know about domestic economy, but Kate may have missed some of the lessons, and in Lawrence during these months the youngest daughter, Fanny, carried the purse and keys of the housekeeper instead of Kate. Hope Shaw had never given Lizzie the requisite training — perhaps because the judge controlled so many aspects of the household himself, while Mrs. Sullivan did the rest. Maria had of course not taught her daughters to cook. To Augusta on 2 February, Helen amusingly described her own descent to the "the sober *practicals* of life," in which George performed "the arduous duties of *chief Stoker* in the several departments of furnace, kitchen-range, and parlor fire." Helen's own "attempts at actual culinary triumphs, went no farther than boiling the tea-kettle, and making tea or coffee," or frying a few previously boiled potatoes for breakfast, the servant Anne having left her "a substantial peice of cold corned-beef, and an abundant supply of the staff of life": "George by my advice dined in town, and we had a 'real tea' when he came home, a thing which ordinarily is precluded by our late dinner." None of this was a confession of inadequacy.

Ever since the middle of the twentieth century it has proven hard for students of Melville to understand why Melville ran advertisements in the local papers seeking a cook, highest wages paid, or put such knowing passages in *The Confidence-Man* about the search for an honest "boy" to help with the outdoor work. In volume 1 of this biography I underestimated the number of live-in servants at the Melville house on Fourth Avenue. The census-taker on 19 July 1850 among the "free inhabitants" at 103 Fourth Avenue in New York City listed four Irish servants, Eliza Brown, age thirty-two; Mary Lynch, twenty-six; Margaret McGuire, twenty-five; and Eliza Whittendale, twenty. The census report, taken 8 June 1855, at the brick house on Twenty-sixth Street (valued at nine thousand dollars) owned by

"Allen Mellville," thirty-year-old (actually thirty-two) lawyer, born in New York City, listed (besides his twenty-seven-year-old wife, a native of Rhode Island, and their three living children), two servants born in Ireland, Joana, age twenty-nine, eight years a resident of New York City (listed as "Joana D[itt]o"—i.e., "Joana Mellville") and Ellen Carlise, three years a resident of New York City. At this time, people of Melville's class, even those who lived in rough old farmhouses like Arrowhead, always had a staff of servants, at least one man for outdoor work and driving, a cook, a nursemaid when there was a child, and a woman to do the cleaning.

At the beginning of the third millennium it is hard to convey the severity of the servant problem as it was experienced by characters in this biography. Youthful Irish had tumbled off the Liverpool ships in the 1840s and early 1850s. Passenger lists show that they were heartbreakingly young, exiled alone so that they might survive, almost never arriving in united family groups as the Scandinavians and Germans often did. By the 1850s the worst famine years were past. Some of the Irish immigrants were moving into the general American workforce and fewer of their younger brothers and sisters and cousins were arriving. In the Melville family, almost no one had good help any more, year after year, except the extremely lucky and financially stable, like the Van Rensselaers at the Manor House, who for years had their Ashbul as a personal postal and expressman, or the Shaws, who kept Mrs. Sullivan after Lizzie was married, although they loaned her to Lizzie at times. Their recent loss of Canning had devastated the Shaw household, and any replacement, like the current Stewart, lacked the knowledge of the minutiae of services Canning had performed and lacked the will to perform all the tasks that he let himself become aware of. At a party in 1854, the Shaws painfully had to make do with a new lady's maid, though happily not a stranger to them. Even Nilly, with her fine Dutch training and wealth, was vulnerable: one time Maria and Helen found her huddled in the cold in her Mt. Vernon Street mansion because her waiter had gone off without starting the morning fires.

Being away in Boston did not deter Maria from offering good advice to Augusta at Arrowhead on 10 February: "Why do you not enquire about a cook, give Mrs Welsh notice. No more green hands for me in the kitchen department. I hope Lizzie by this time is suited and comfortable in the possession of an efficient woman to take charge & assist her in her maternal duties." Judge Shaw relayed to Maria *"a fine story"* Lizzie had written him about the last cook, who had left abruptly. Maria and Helen were both anxious that Augusta "not wait longer, but make *earnest* enquiries about getting a cook," and relief floods a note from Helen to Augusta on 5 April: "I am charmed to hear that you have the Cook in good training, remember me to William, Lizzie likes her nursery maid, I hope." At Arrowhead so many of the Catholic cooks had the same name that "Mary" became the generic term, and the family invested progressively less effort in getting to know the servants as individuals, since they tended to disappear abruptly. The worst of it was trying to remember that the new Mary rarely started work with her head full of everything that had been inculcated so carefully into the previous Mary. In Manhattan, Allan and Sophia had fewer servant problems than most members of the family, partly because Sophia through the Thurstons had access to an established network of employers, partly because it was easy to waylay a ship from Liverpool and pick out a likely servant. Decade after decade, the Melvilles faced the problem of getting and training new servants (which, in Melville's case, in later years, meant speaking brusquely to them through the basement pass-through). In 1892, the year after Herman died, Lizzie gave as one reason for moving out of her house her desire to live a life which was not "servant-ridden" — the management of the apartment house, the Florence, doing all the hiring and firing of servants.

In the nature of things the eastern sisters and their guests from Arrowhead came into renewed contact with the Melvill family, of whom (except for Helen's contact with them in the early 1840s and Herman's in the mid-1840s) they had seen very little after Allan Melvill's failure in 1830. Seeing them aroused tensions still, since all of these relatives had banded together in a lawsuit against Maria and her eight children so as to protect their own inheritances and since all of them continued to receive checks from old Thomas Melvill's estate (through Judge Shaw, the active trustee). In February Tom took Hoadley to call on Aunt Priscilla, then walked the two and a half miles back to Longwood with a great appetite for the oysters that Helen had promised them for supper. That evening "Lang[s]do[r]ff de Wolf" called and stayed four hours (as Tom wrote Augusta on 15 February), and he later went on board the *Meteor* to say good-bye. On 4 March Maria settled into a room with the Shaws on Mt. Vernon Street and since the weather looked "ominous," at once paid a call on her sister-in-law Priscilla, living at 31 Green Street (not the old Melvill house but the Winslow Wright house into which Jean had moved at her marriage). As she wrote Augusta that day, Maria found Priscilla looking "as usual" but skeptical as to Maria's intention to bring Tom to call on her. Priscilla was a gadabout ("out as usual," Helen reported on 15 January 1855) and Jean always held forth about her miserable condition (Helen said in the same letter: "I sat down with Aunt Jean, and heard all about all her ailments, and how well Aunt Priscilla was, and how she never went out, but Aunt Priscilla went out every day &c &c"). Priscilla, as

Allan said in 1854, rarely wrote letters and was irresponsible when she did write, leaving the recipient to guess as to what the handwriting was meant to signify. The Melvill aunts did not endear themselves to the Melvilles.

Widening her swath, Maria called on her late husband's first cousin Mary Scollay, since 1817 the wife of Lemuel Shaw's old friend Dr. Jacob Bigelow; there she saw Catherine Scollay, another cousin of Allan Melvill. Then Sam Shaw took Maria to the Hingham cars, where a young friend of the Shaws escorted her to Helen Souther's "very door" (as Maria wrote Augusta on 5 March): "She was very happy to see me. Threw her arms around me & burst into tears. Your aunt never looked better. Her hair is black & she wears it as she did when I first knew her, falling in easy ringlets about her cheeks. She is far from well having a large tumor in her right side which prevents her taking much exercise ... Mr Souther was very kind called me Maria, his daughters called me Aunt Maria." Helen Souther's wedding gift for her namesake was such as to excuse its tardiness: "Your Aunt Helen gave me a magnificent Oyster spoon for Helen, nearly as large as a Soup spoon of solid silver very heavy, the bowl in the form of a shell." She also gave a special gift to Bessie: "Now Lizzie & Herman Listen, — your Aunt drew me one side & gave me for little Bessie a silver tumbler marked with her sister Nancys name, has never been in use, and was given to Bessie as a delicate compliment to her Grandfathers engagement with her sister." That is, Aunt Helen was delicately giving her late sister Nancy's tumbler to Nancy's grandniece, Herman's daughter, in remembrance of the fact that had she lived Nancy would have married Lemuel Shaw, now, strangely enough, the grandfather of little Bessie — almost as if the child were his and Nancy Melvill Shaw's granddaughter.

The Griggses took Maria to Dorchester, and in her account to Augusta on 14 March Helen displayed her satirical bent:

> We called at Nancy's [Nancy D'Wolf Downer's], but she was out, and little Miss Gertrude escorted us to Aunt Jean's, and then to Aunt De Wolf. The latter had something like an appoplectic fit, and looks wretchedly. Aunt Jean talks as fast as ever, about her "terrible bad back." and "good for nothing eyes," and told me seventeen times in as many minutes that Mr Hought[?] had been "confined-to-the-house-for-a-week-with-his-old-complaint-the-catarrh," pronouncing the name of the malady, as if it were a musical instrument which caused his torment; and filled up all pauses with lamentations about the unbecomingnesss of the "dirty cap" she wore, and her never-to-be-sufficiently-expressed sorrow, that her "beautiful-new-one-trimmed-with-pink-had-not-happened-to be-on-when-Mr Griggs-came."

The D'Wolfs politely called on Helen, with *their* Nancy, niece of Shaw's late fiancée, and in May Aunt Priscilla made a spectacular call, as Helen wrote Augusta: "she stayed about an hour, with a grand carriage at the door, price of the trip $5. She said to me, 'Well I have never given you and Kate anything, but it is coming!' When? When? When?" Priscilla could put her money down at the livery stable, not in gifts for the newly married daughters of her late brother Allan. Helen was well brought up, and knew her Christian duty to forgive those who had trespassed against her, but none of the Melville children forgot their early grievances, whether toward Peter Gansevoort or the Melvills.

After years of being a poor relation, Maria revelled in her close connection with good Boston families and intimacy with her young Van Rensselaer cousin, Nilly Thayer, the Shaws' neighbor on Mt. Vernon Street. The Griggses also had contacts with old connections from the Berkshires. Helen had known Kate Sedgwick in the late 1830s, when she had the privilege of studying at Eliza Sedgwick's school in Lenox, and now this daughter of Eliza and Charles (the clerk at court when Judge Shaw made his circuit) was Mrs. William Minot and lived on the great estate of Woodbourne. In February, invited by Mrs. Minot, Maria, Helen, and George dressed elegantly and took a comfortable carriage with large windows, even in front, and drove in the very bright moonlight past "numerous splendid houses" which "spoke loudly of great wealth taste & luxury," as Maria wrote Augusta on the tenth. At Woodbourne they saw the great novelist Catharine Sedgwick, who "seemed very happy" to see them, having perhaps not seen them since early November of 1851, when several of the Arrowheads drove to Lenox for the party at which only the female member of the James pair and the male member of the Hawthorne pair showed up. Kate Hoadley did not have the experience and assurance of Helen, and could not have moved so easily into Boston society, but she may, with Hoadley's guidance, have fitted into the Lawrence setting admirably.

The Melville women had to master the schedules of the horse-drawn omnibuses (the last of which left Boston for Brookline at six) and the train of cars that ran from Boston to Brookline, and all the family, western and eastern, tried out each latest innovation. On 27 January Tom read Charlotte Brontë's recent *Villette* on the way from Pittsfield to Boston, and arrived just in time for George to hustle him (and Maria?) on the last "carrs" for Longwood. Railroad travel remained problematical, but by the fall the Shaws were able again to take the express train from Boston to Pittsfield, as they had done in 1853. People who had grown up with stagecoaches and river boats — the judge and Maria were man and woman before they saw a steamboat —

accommodated themselves to the latest forms of transportation, but the Melvilles also kept their independence as lifelong pedestrians. In mid-March Helen and George missed "the last train of cars," so (as Helen wrote Augusta on 14 March) they "crossed over from the foot of Boy[l]ston Street along the outer edge of the Public Gardens, turned onto the Mill Dam, and walked home through a magnificent mild moonlight." Even in February Maria (who wisely recommended discreet jumping practice for adolescent girls to loosen and stimulate all the internal organs) was capable of walking the two and a half miles into the city then coming back on "the 'bus' as they say here."

The presence of Helen in Longwood (even more than the presence of Kate in Lawrence) effected a series of shifts in family relationships. Maria and her family in due course came into more or less intimate contact with the relations and acquaintances of John Hoadley and George Griggs, but at the center of the social world of Boston were Judge Shaw and Hope in their capacious house on Mt. Vernon Street. The proximity of Longwood, conjoined by the great convenience of access to the Shaw house, made Helen's location almost ideal. During the March thaw, the Shaws gave a large party for Governor Clifford (who had told Melville the story that he made into *The Isle of the Cross*) and his "lady." There was drizzle and fog, but Maria had remodeled her silk dress and had "'stuck a feather in her cap'" (literally or metaphorically) and Helen had trimmed her white dress and had laid everything out on the bed, "from head dress of feather flowers, down to silk stockings and satin slippers" (Helen wrote Augusta on 14 March), so they took the closed carriage George had ordered from the city and went out, safely and pleasantly. After the party Maria stayed the night at the Shaws' so she would not have to make a useless trip before making a call on Nilly Thayer the next day. The Griggses returned in the carriage, and the next day Helen took the 1:30 train in, went to "the Judge's," where she "put the finishing touches of best collar, undersleeves, gloves &c," then, joined by George, the three of them walked down Mt. Vernon Street to Nilly's. They had tea in her beautiful room, then went to Judge Shaw's "until time to take the half after nine cars for the Longwood Station." After three years at Arrowhead, where the womenfolk had been dependent on Herman except when they were, rather grudgingly, allowed to drive out themselves, this was personal liberation.

The pattern set, it became customary for Maria, Helen, or the other Melville daughters to treat the Shaw house as a pied-à-terre, a convenient staging place between Brookline and Boston, not to mention Pittsfield and Lawrence. Helen, after all, had *lived* there months at a time, and felt perfectly at home. They dropped in at the Shaws, left bags there for the day, outfitted themselves less heavily, and made their forays into stores or paid their social calls unencumbered. When Allan's daughter Maria (Milie) spent the summer that year with the Griggses, the first of two or three summers, Helen could leave her there for hours at a time, confident that Mrs. Sullivan would keep an eye on her. Sam Shaw was sometimes available for escort duties, as when he took Fanny on the cars to Lawrence to prevent her having to go alone. Beyond this, the Shaws included Maria and her children in intimate family gatherings as well as in large formal entertainments. Ultimately, Griggs's and Helen's old intimacy with the Shaws and the progressive new intimacies drew some of Herman's brothers and sisters into another orbit, so that by the mid-1860s they could seem to side with the Shaw household in internecine struggles.

Renewed contact with Nilly Van Rensselaer Thayer put Maria close to new tragedy on top of old scandal. John De Peyster Douw and his cousin-wife, Margaret Van Rensselaer Douw, both of them Maria's cousins two or more ways, the couple whose entertainments on Clinton Square in 1842 had so impressed Gansevoort Melville, now paid the price for their marital estrangement. Whatever unacceptable demand De Peyster had made on her, sexual or otherwise, Maggie had exercised the prerogative of a rich and very spoiled aristocrat in leaving him and determining to remarry in defiance of family, church, and state. On 23 February, at his school in Chatham, New York, near Poughkeepsie, De Peyster and Maggie's son Henry Augustus Douw died at fourteen of typhoid fever. De Peyster generously held the funeral in Albany, from the Episcopalian St. Peter's Church, so the Van Rensselaers could attend, although they would have preferred their Dutch church. Nilly Thayer told Maria that Henry was to be buried from Volkert Douw's house at Greenbush. Henry, Maria reported to Augusta on 5 March, had been a "remarkably bright & a very promising boy." Paying the price of her "remarriage," Margaret had not seen him in three years. De Peyster "was nearly frantic, his whole soul was wraped up in him," Mrs. Abbe (a Douw-Cuyler connection) told Maria.

Calling at the Shaws, Nilly (wearing deep mourning for her Grand-mother Bayard) found Maria, and fell into a long, intimate talk which made Maria like her better than ever before (she told Augusta on 5 March), both for her deep feelings "for poor Margaret" and for her attitude toward her sister's behavior: "Said separation of parents was an awful thing. That Margaret & dePeyster could not sympathise together at the death of their child, as was so natural at this time, that she had always been averse to Margarets second marriage, &c. Cornelia talked with so much real feeling and her beautiful eyes filled with tears & she look'd so sympathising & sisterly that I could have kiss'd her." Mrs. Van Rensselaer had written Nilly details which Maria relayed to Augusta, Maggie's special friend. On 16 March, in Norwich, Connecticut, with Margaret Schuyler Van Rensselaer Douw still alive, John De Peyster Douw married again, Marianne Chandler Lanman of the family of the art historian who admired Melville's essay on Hawthorne. (One of their descendants, Mrs. Ferris, asked Lizzie's help with an article on Melville, half a century later, apparently not knowing the secret history of De Peyster Douw's dubious second marriage, to which she owed her existence.) Augusta's pain over old Mrs. Bayard and young Henry Douw was compounded by her inability to be with the Van Rensselaers during their losses in these months.

Both Kate and Allan had serious dental work that year (Kate going to Boston for hers), but the more ominous change involved Allan and Sophia. Having earlier suffered from his teeth, in June Allan failed to keep to his expected schedule in visiting his "eastern" sisters, leading Helen to write to Augusta around 20 June: "Perhaps the weather was so warm, he did not feel strong enough for such hurried traveling. Sophia was to be here some day this week. That is all I know about them, but doubtless you have heard from some of the Lawrenceites by this time." Sophia was bringing Milie to stay with Helen—not as a pleasant treat but because she and Allan were unwell. Milie remembered, always judging herself harshly: "In the summers I used to go to Longwood near Boston to visit Aunt Helen and Uncle George. They had a cat named Jorkins that I was very fond of. I was a very passionate child, and many were the times that Aunt Helen had to put me in my room for being naughty." Increasingly unable to care for her oldest daughter, Sophia turned to Helen rather than her own sisters or mother as the woman in the family best able to care for Milie properly. From New York there was other bad news, which, after a few years, had consequences for Maria, Augusta, and Fanny, in particular. Allan kept contact with Cousin Kate Curtis in Brooklyn, although, he reported to Augusta on 1 March, she "does not trouble us with calling." Kate's brother Leonard Gansevoort had been ill for some weeks, as Allan and Tom had learned, then had been "removed from the Custom House after about 13 years enjoyment of the berth he held there," in Manhattan. The firing eventually (around 1861) led to the Curtises and Gansevoorts uniting in Glens Falls, near Uncle Herman's place at Gansevoort, where Maria saw them frequently, as she had done in the late 1830s.

Even as they dealt with physical problems, Allan and Sophia had been moving far too often for the comfort of most couples, but Allan thought of each house as an advance in his financial condition and Sophia (strangely, Maria thought) took actual pleasure in the excitement of moving. Mrs. Thurston at last decided that Bond Street (that short street of marble-fronted houses that Maria as a young mother had envied in the years she lived in rented houses downtown) was being left behind by areas farther north, and decided to take the $23,000 or so that the house would bring and move to the new Irving Place, where she found a house which, with repairs, would be suitable. This was the street Samuel Ruggles had laid out through his lands in 1833 and cannily named in honor of Washington Irving, soon after Scottish Americans had renamed Sixth Street, north of Washington Square, "Waverly Place" (so spelled) in honor of Sir Walter Scott.

Allan and Charles (if not other Thurstons) decided they could use some of the money that would be left over from the sale of the Bond Street house. Allan told Augusta in the 1 March letter: "I have some idea of building a basement house in connection with others on a fine location 22nd street near 4th Avenue — the next street above Calvary Church." Allan continued: "Charles falls in with this notion. I propose to buy two lots and cut them up into three and sell two to a builder he contracting to build me a house for a specified sum and undertaking the other two on his own account. I *am* to get an answer from a builder tomorrow. A house in this street, and one of the row in which the Westerlo's live, is to be sold at auction tomorrow. Should this go at a reasonable price it may be bought. By purchasing a house one gets a much cheaper rent." The two did not pursue this plan, but within a few months Allan had bought a house at 60 East Twenty-sixth Street (later renumbered 104) and fitted it for him and Sophia. The two youngest Melville brothers took their supervisory responsibilities differently. Tom as first mate was on top of everything (as he wrote Augusta on 15 February): "I have been very busy all day seeing the carpets put down having the cabin put in order, and looking out for the painters, carpenters, joiners, riggers, caulkers, and shipkeepers." Allan had never liked getting dirty, and plainly did not want to know all the details that went into the fitting up of a house. On 27 March he wrote Augusta: "We expect to get possession of the 26th street house in a few days at all event by Saturday when the carpenter, the plumber, the gas fitter, the plasterer, the mason, the painter, the roofmender, the flager, the bell hanger, and the drain builder are expected to commence operations."

Sophia might well have done more actual supervising than Allan did for this — her and Allan's last Manhattan house — but Allan was always ready to consult on real estate. The next year, 1 March 1855, while sitting "on the sofa with a pipe in mouth," Allan wrote to Augusta about recently visiting Lizzie's aunt and uncle, the Maretts, "in their comfortable apartments," and about a call he had made that evening on "Mrs Charles Thurston," his mother-in-law, where he "had a pleasant chat with Carrie": "She and Charles have lately been building castles in the air about going to housekeeping so I assisted them in selecting the furniture for some of the imaginary apartments of their house." The boy who had been stuck in a tiny room at Maggey Wynkoop's in Albany was always ready to play house.

Through the long winter and early spring of 1854 Herman at Arrowhead was regaled with news and advice from the East, through Augusta's correspondence more than Lizzie's or his own. The most perturbing news of all, for Herman, came in an offhand comment from Tom in late January, from Boston, in a letter to Augusta: "By the way tell Herman that *Mr Fly is dead*" — the friend Cousin Priscilla had called his insect companion. In some little things Herman had continued to do Eli James Murdock Fly service, buying him a subscription to the *Literary World* for a time, escorting him on the cars, perhaps as far as Springfield, once. Maria learned more, as she wrote on 4 March 1854, after a talkative Miss Titmarsh had called at the Shaws (while Lizzie was there, on an otherwise unrecorded visit):

> In one of the pauses I enquired if she knew Mr Fly. Oh yes the most interesting man she had ever seen. She did not wonder, that notwithstanding his bad health Miss Hinkley had married him. I then enquired about his death. Mr Fly had left a message to Herman said Mrs Titmarsh, looking at the Judge & something about a Cloake, Sir, I believe which Mr Melville had given him? A post mortem examination had taken place, one lung was entirely gone, of the other but half remained. The widow was inconsolable. No man is a prophet in his own country. I wish I could remember more. His sister was at the funeral. He died in Boston where they were passing the winter.

Conceivably, Herman may have loaned Fly a cloak in recent years, but more likely, dying, Fly's memory flashed back to the "parting souvenir" of Herman's "shore toggery" that Gansevoort had brought back to New York City in January 1841. On departing for his voyage to the South Seas, one that had by 1854 already changed the course of literature in the United States, Herman had sent Fly his "vest & pantaloons" (as Gansevoort wrote Allan on 14 January 1841). The news of Fly's death put finish to a youthful adventure in which the two young men had set out to make their fortunes in the West, only to return, defeated by the hard times. From his mother's report from Boston, Herman knew that his shrunken, twisted friend had died remembering his strangely intimate contact with a great literary genius, when both the friends had been healthy and young, and the same size. Dying, he tried to communicate "something about a Cloake," or some article of clothing, that Herman had (Miss Titmarsh supplied a question mark by her voice) once given him. Gansevoort, the bearer of the garments, was dead, and Fly was dead, but Herman remembered, and understood that, defeated as he was by the failure of *Moby-Dick* and *Pierre* and by the suppression of *The Isle of the Cross*, and overwhelmed by debts, he had been the one figure of power and glamour in Fly's obscure and pain-filled life.

[10]

Tortoises and *Israel Potter*
1854

❦

> But the continual happiness, which so far as I was able to judge appeared to prevail in the valley, sprung principally from that all-pervading sensation which Rousseau has told us he at one time experienced, the mere buoyant sense of a healthful physical existence.
>
> *Typee*, ch. 17

AS EARLY AS JANUARY 1854, even before the eastern sisters were settled into their new patterns of living, it was clear that Augusta was seriously overworked at Arrowhead. Being chatelaine of the old house, now proven to be nearer ramshackle than quaint, was a tiring responsibility, and it was wholly Augusta's. A decade later, in a letter to Augusta on 16 April 1863, Lizzie alluded to "S'liny," a daughter of one of the Marys. S'liny had kept house three years at Arrowhead, where (in her impudent words to Lizzie in 1863) "'Miss Gusty' did'nt find no fault, when she was here." Augusta had been in charge of servants while being Herman's sole copyist, with no sister in the house to relieve her, for, even when she was home, Fanny seems not to have copied for Herman. What with using daytime for copying and perhaps for necessary sewing, Augusta had no time for reading and for her essential correspondence unless she stayed up far into the night with her candle. Julia Blatchford innocently wrote her on 18 January 1854: "I suppose you have plenty of time for reading, now that the bustle of two weddings is over, or perhaps you occupy yourself in copying for Herman. Do not write too steadily — break off sometimes to scribble a letter to me." By 30 January Fanny was concerned: "Augusta, I hope you have done with staying up late at night."

By 2 February 1854, Helen was also anxious. Helen had shaken Dickens's hand, in 1842, and thereafter had threatened not to wash it. Now she encouraged Augusta by reference to the new Dickens novel, which the family was passing around: "When Fanny goes back to Arrowhead, Gus dear, you must come and make me a visit, to recruit your exhausted energies, which will be loudly called upon for exertion as Sole dame Durden of the house on the hill.

You shall have a nice lazy time here, and read as much as you wish to." Tom became so engrossed in *Bleak House* that he postponed answering a letter from Augusta until 5 February, then in masculine innocence hoped that the future "Mrs Tom Melville will resemble 'Dame Durden'"—his imagination having been excited by his cousin Cuyler Van Vechten's urgent invitation to him to come to Albany and meet his wife, "a 'perfect angel of sweet sixteen.'" All three other sisters had time for literature. Fanny was reading Thackeray's *Newcomes* as it was serialized in *Harper's*, and reading and hearing other works, as she wrote to Augusta on 5 February: "I have been reading several interesting books lately, one called 'Up Country Letters' I liked very much, it is written in Ike Marvel's style, quiet, soothing! Mr Hoadley has just finished reading aloud for us Longfellow's 'Golden Legend.' I was delighted with it, have you ever read it?" Augusta had less and less time to read, and on 10 February, after Maria and Tom were back at Longwood, Helen added a note to her mother's letter: "You must not make a martyr of yourself." The sisters gradually learned not to be infinitely obliging at all times. In the bleak months of early 1854, Augusta was lonely as well as exhausted. Fanny wrote her on 5 February that although she was having "a nice, a very nice time" away she wanted to see her much "and talk over matters & things for really we have not had time to talk quietly since last fall a year ago!!"—since the frantic consultations over reviews of *Pierre* and the hope that Herman might gain a consulship and be able to give up writing.

Augusta was reduced to reading little except what she copied for Herman, and some of that copying was done under great pressure of time, unlike three years before, when she had had the luxury of copying the whaling book at her own pace, well behind Herman because he was writing slowly, by his standards. On 20 March she took up an interrupted letter to Fanny: "Thus far I had written, dear Fanny, when Herman came in with another batch of copying which he was most anxious to have as soon as possible. That has occupied my every spare moment until the present one in which I resume the sheet which on Friday I laid aside." Augusta, who never complained, moaned to Fanny on 30 March: "Poor Kate, I have sadly neglected her last kind letters, but I have had so much copying to do for Herman, that I really have not had an opportunity of writing her.... My hand is so weary of holding a pen, the fingers relaxed their grasp upon it, without my will." She asked Fanny to tell Maria that she was "taking a motherly care of the chicken's—Herman has put a padlock upon the door for me, & I am in the receipt of nine or ten eggs a day." Herman would help with simple farm maintenance when he had to, but he was focused on his own exigencies, not on how onerous his demands upon Augusta had become.

Repeatedly, hard tasks fell on Augusta that a man ought to have handled.

When Tom gained a berth as first mate on the *Meteor* (a great advance for him), he saw he could not visit Arrowhead a third time, and made an earnest request on 15 February: "Dont forget to forward those trunks immediately, Dear Gus as I am in want of many things." Not only did Augusta have to miss saying good-bye again to the baby of the family, she had to manhandle the trunks (after washing and mending the clothes inside them). She had at hand the envelope that had contained the letter she had received from Howard Townsend in December, announcing that his wife, Justine (Augusta's Cousin Teny), had given birth to their first child and, good Van Rensselaer son-in-law, assuring her that a room in his house was always set aside for her. She noted on the envelope: "roped black trunk— / big square yellow / Charles Grandison— / desk—sewed up— / STRAP SIR CHARLES." (Had they been reading Richardson at Arrowhead and did she send Tom a book quite long enough for a voyage round the world and a famous rarity, just what a sailor needed in the Pacific, a Christian novel?) Tom responded on 19 February that he was "very, very, glad to get" the two trunks and a bale: "you showed your indefatigable zeal in getting them down to the depot, as you did in getting them ready to go." Augusta, fingers already hurting from copying, did this service for Tom with no help from Herman, who could have strapped a trunk to travel the few hours from Pittsfield to Boston. He was not just busy writing but also seriously unwell. Just at this time, judging from Allan's letter to Augusta on 1 March, Herman endured a "Horrid week" of pain in his eyes. If he was crowding Augusta with pages to copy in February, then he was overworking himself as well as her, and if ever an illness was psychosomatic, it was this pain in the eyes, brought on not only by overstraining under weak lights but also by the lurid intermixture of secret guilt and resolute denial of the looming threat of exposure to humiliation in the family and even in the public press, if T. D. Stewart ever went to court against him.

When Melville wrote to the Harpers in late November 1853 that he had "in hand, and pretty well on towards completion," a book "partly of nautical adventure," he had qualified himself: "or rather, chiefly, of Tortoise Hunting Adventure." At that time, promising the manuscript for "some time in the coming January" (1854), he had asked for and received the advance—a dollar for each of the three hundred estimated pages. And he had specified that he was expecting "the old basis—half-profits"—not the ruinous terms he had accepted for *Pierre*. Enthusiast to truth as he was, Melville had never held himself to strict veracity in letters to his publishers. To a high degree he shared the over-optimism endemic among authors describing their progress on a manuscript to publishers from whom they hope to receive an advance, but he also brought to his negotiations now some personal adversarial quirk, grounded in the bitterness that had rankled in him toward the

Harpers since the summer of 1845 and exacerbated by the punitive contract they had given him for *Pierre* and by their rejection of *The Isle of the Cross*. If in mid-December 1853 Melville had concluded that after the fire the Harpers could not possibly publish any book right away, then the straightforward thing would have been to write them and ask in so many words if they would be able to publish the book they had just given him the advance for. If they had said they could not be back in business for six months, he could not have returned their advance since he had already spent much or most of it, but he could have asked their permission to try to place the tortoise manuscript elsewhere and to turn over to them three hundred dollars if he got that sum from another source, or, more reasonably, turn over to them for their magazine some new articles worth that sum. What he did was not quite as culpable as it looks, perhaps, but it manifested no tortoise-like impulse toward straightforwardness: Melville made an expedient, emotional decision that does not look wholly honest. The man who had taken a loan of $2050 from Stewart with no collateral except the already mortgaged Arrowhead now decided to get more money from another publisher for the tortoise story— or at least for some prose about tortoises.

On 6 February 1854, Melville wrote George P. Putnam: "Herewith I send you 75. pages adapted for a magazine. Should they suit your's, please write me how much in present cash you will give for them." "Adapted" may indicate that Melville had altered material meant for his book so that it would be suitable for a magazine, but by using that word he may have meant merely that the material was in his opinion suited to magazine use. The batch of pages seems to be what was published in the March issue of *Putnam's* as the first four sketches of "The Encantadas." No one has identified any other possible subject matter Melville could have been referring to, although the wonder is that he was not trying, still, to sell *The Isle of the Cross* to Putnam and Bentley, from whose magazines he had received overtures. Putnam and his staff must have been enthusiastic about the seventy-five pages, for they sent them to the compositor at once, apparently at the cost of displacing some of the contents planned for the issue, which always came out well before the month whose date it bore.

This was unusual prose, Putnam recognized, and on a fascinating topic. Individual sentences, such as this one from the first sketch, are touchstones: "But the special curse, as one may call it, of the Encantadas, that which exalts them in desolation above Idumea and the Pole, is that to them change never comes; neither the change of seasons nor of sorrows." In Sketch 2, describing the "hopeless toil" of the tortoises, the way they "ram themselves heroically against rocks, and long abide there, nudging, wriggling, wedging, in order to displace them, and so hold on their inflexible path," Melville concluded:

"Their crowning curse is their drudging impulse to straightforwardness in a belittered world." Readers do not need to test themselves on ginger hot in the mouth, as the reviewer in the *News of the World* said in 1851; if they love such sentences as these, they are Melvilleans.

At the end of Sketch 1, after playing off a scene in the Adirondack Mountains against a scene in the Galápagos, Melville confided, "I can hardly resist the feeling that in my time I have indeed slept upon evilly enchanted ground." He followed this contrast of scenes with a remarkable example of his characteristic habit of blurring one vision into another, the sliding, displacing phenomenon he had made such powerful use of in *Pierre*:

> such is the vividness of my memory, or the magic of my fancy, that I know not whether I am not the occasional victim of optical delusion concerning the Gallipagos. For often in scenes of social merriment, and especially at revels held by candle-light in old-fashioned mansions, so that shadows are thrown into the further recesses of an angular and spacious room, making them put on a look of haunted undergrowth of lonely woods, I have drawn the attention of my comrades by my fixed gaze and sudden change of air, as I have seemed to see, slowly emerging from those imagined solitudes, and heavily crawling along the floor, the ghost of a gigantic tortoise, with "Memento ****" burning in live letters upon his back.

Incidentally a compliment to the hospitality at Broadhall, this was evocative prose to serve up to late winter readers, American gothic juxtaposing the Galápagos and the Adirondacks, or the Berkshires. Putnam paid handsomely, fifty dollars for the eight finely-printed pages the sketches took up in the March issue. Instead of being printed with no ascription, the usual practice, the name "Salvator R. Tarnmoor" was given as the author of "The Encantadas," a flourish simultaneously reminding readers of Salvator Rosa's wild Calabrian scenes and Poe's gothic tarns and woodlands.

When someone from Putnam's office leaked the news of the forthcoming serial, William Cullen Bryant announced in the 14 February *Evening Post* that Melville had "awakened from that uneasy sleep, during which his genius was disturbed by such distempered dreams as Mardi, and frightful nightmares like the ambiguous Pierre." Under Melville's "pilotage," readers would be "sure of falling in with refreshing fountains of pleasure and delight." Allan spotted this item and at once sent word through his "dear darling dark eyed Augusta": "Say to Herman that he ought to reserve to himself the right to publish his magazine matter in book form. It might be desirable & could probably be secured by agreement made at the beginning." In New York, also, the Harpers would have encountered the item with surprise, but they may have concluded from the *Post* item only that Melville was not giving their "Tortoise Hunting" manuscript top priority—not that he was diverting all or part of it to *Putnam's*.

In placing any of his tortoise material with a publisher other than the Harpers, Melville was being paid twice by different people for substantially the same product. Knowing the Harpers were going to see the start of "The Encantadas" that week in *Putnam's*, Melville wrote them on or about 20 February: "When I procured the advance of $300 from you upon the 'Tortoises' or 'Tortoise Hunting', I intimated that the work would be ready for press some time in January. I have now to express my concern, that, owing to a variety of causes, the work, unavoidably, was not ready in that month, & still requires additional work to it, ere completion. But in no sense can you loose [lose] by the delay." In the last paragraph he assured them that he would be "in New York in the course of a few weeks" and would then call upon them and inform them "when these proverbially slow 'Tortoises' will be ready to crawl into market." This sounds like nothing so much as a disingenuous effort to assure the Harpers, in advance of their seeing the March *Putnam's*, that their proprietorial rights were not being violated, although when the issue came out they must have known at once that Melville was either serializing in their rival's magazine what they had given him an advance for, or else that he was giving Putnam a different but similar account of tortoise hunting, one which would inevitably diminish the freshness of whatever version they might ultimately receive. Little wonder he had a horrid week with pain in his eyes.

Herman apprised Allan and Sophia that he would arrive within a ten-day period, 15–25 March or thereabouts, but did not go. On 20 March Augusta reported to Fanny: "He is making preparations to go down to New York, that is he is getting his MS ready (not *the book*, for the Harpers owing to the two fires, are not in a situation to publish it now) but Magazine articles &c; & has written Allan that he will probably leave here within a fortnight." (The second fire has not been dated.) Herman was postponing his trip because he was still writing or revising and Augusta was still copying, but this letter raises questions. Perhaps in response to her obvious puzzlement at seeing tortoise material go to Mr. Putnam, Herman had told her that the Harpers were not in a situation to publish his book on "Tortoise Hunting." That can hardly have been the truth, given the content of his 20 February letter to the Harpers. Augusta—like Herman—did not talk of "The Encantadas" as wholly replacing the tortoise book. In June 1853 Melville had gone down with the manuscript of *The Isle of the Cross*. Now he may have carried down some later (and more laxly written) sketches of "The Encantadas," which he could just as well have shipped by express. Most likely he carried to the Harpers a number of "articles" for their magazine, probably "The Paradise of Bachelors and the Tartarus of Maids," "Poor Man's Pudding and Rich Man's Crumbs," "The Happy Failure," and "The Fiddler," of which the last two or possibly three were probably left over from his initial "article" writing of the year before. He apparently left the manuscript of *The Isle of the Cross* at home, if he still had it: no definite evidence survives about its fate after November of 1853. His strongest motive in making the trip may have been to appease the Harpers, for, unquestionably, he also carried down to them a sample from the ongoing tortoise book, a "no fudge" and "bona fide" sample, to borrow a phrase he used in April, to Lathers.

Fueling Melville's desire to go to New York just then may have been a severe case of cabin fever. He had been locked up in his second-floor study, toiling incessantly until midafternoon, then sharing the parlor with a cruelly overworked and anxious Augusta; a sickly, perennially overwrought, and homeless Priscilla (as much an outcast, in her way, as the wretched and brave Hunilla, the abandoned and violated Chola woman whom he may have worked into his serial while Priscilla was back in his house early in March); and a wife with three active small children to amuse and instruct day after day in weather so miserable there was no thought of putting the boys out to play, even briefly, so that they stayed in, vying in restlessness with the notoriously "restless" baby. This situation is clear in a letter Priscilla wrote to Lemuel Shaw on 27 March, after one of Melville's self-imposed deadlines for leaving had come and gone: "*We — that is —* Lizzie, Augusta, Herman, the little folks, & myself are driven to the necessity of being *very* amiable, and *obliged* to play the agreeable for mutual entertainment *within* doors — for the weather continues very severe, gales, and snow storms prevail, *even yet*, with *no* promise of Spring — and we are becoming rather weary of winter quarters — But we are all in the enjoyment of very robust health." In a palliating "postscript to *Grandpapa*" she assured the judge that "Lizzie's little ones have made *wonderful* advances physically and mentally during the winter."

Sophia and Allan, under the circumstances, were likely to be significantly more amiable, or at least refreshing company, and Herman's letter to Sophia announcing his plans had been jocularly affectionate (somewhat in the vein he used with Sarah Morewood). Sophia's letter to Augusta on 26 March reveals some of the family tensions centering on Lizzie's perturbation at what was left of Melville's free-and-easy ways: "What has become of Herman we have been expecting for several days. His room is ready for him. I received a comical letter from him, advising me of his proposed visit. I suppose he did not expect any answer, for it would never do to have the 'Argus eyes' of *that Lizzie* scanning the contents, for of course I should write in the same affectionate strain, and I should fear the indignation of the 'Lamb.'" This is less hostile than it sounds to outsiders, and may indeed have been written with the knowledge that Lizzie would as a matter of course have ample chance to scan the contents, but it does underline a continuing struggle between Herman and Lizzie over what some saw as insignificant points of propriety. She was concerned that he refrain from high-flown epistolary rhetoric which drew any recipient — Sarah Morewood, Sophia Melville — into reading his letters as intimate documents. Far from being pathological, her jealousy was grounded in good maxims from conduct books and in personal knowledge of the possible effects of such flights as Herman's winsome, comical letters. By good Beacon Hill standards, Hoadley had been wrong to flout proprieties as he did in that much-analyzed invitation to Augusta, and Herman was wrong in writing with comical intimacy to anyone but her, or perhaps her and his sisters.

On 5 April, still delaying with the eastern sisters, Maria wrote Augusta about more man's work that would befall her, arranging for the slaughter of an unspecified animal. The season was wrong for pork, which would be hard to preserve with spring coming; perhaps it was a calf or a cow: "Oh Augusta, about the *animal* so soon to be slain — by all means wait until my return, more care than usual care is needed on account of the season. It will make but a week or more difference, & will be all the heavier for that. You had better let the owner know, Herman being absent. Suppose you engage to receive the 'defunct' *two weeks from to day*, we shall be at home early in the week . . . See to this at once." Maria went on to praise her daughter: "Gus you are a dear good girl from all accounts, your house keeping must be a model, for all." It *was* a model, but Augusta was more and more strained. The not yet "defunct" animal became the focus of considerable attention. On 16 April, after a week's absence in Stockbridge, and just before her departure for Galena, Priscilla wrote: "*What* has been the order of the day? Did Herman return in the afternoon from the city invigorated in mind & body? — & did the *half* of *that defunct animal* require your attention — & did Lizzie surprise her husband with the new wrapper all completed[?]" This period made it clear to everyone that Lizzie was of no help in running a household, however competent she might be to care for her three children and however charming a mantle or shawl she might sew for herself. Even with a cook and a man, newly trained to her own standards, Augusta found new heavy burdens in the slaughter and salting down and whatever else was required.

The eastern contingent of the family understood very well Augusta's subtle revelation in her letters that she was drawing on her reserves of "self denial and devotion" (not her words but Hoadley's shrewd interpretation of her letters). The inhabitants of Arrowhead were increasingly tense at their enforced confinement with each other. Hoadley allowed to Augusta on 28 March that the bad weather was making it less delightful to have Maria in

Lawrence than it could have been otherwise, but he was infinitely tactful: "It is delightful to see Mother here again; but I should like a little pleasant weather for her." He continued with a deeply sensitive vision of what was going on at Arrowhead (not visualizing Priscilla there — perhaps because he did not know her):

> —Then too I should enjoy her [Maria's] stay more, if I could dismiss the thought of your solitude in the deserted mansion at Arrowhead, which you and Lizzie, and Herman & the children must have enough to do to keep blue devils out of; — which with Mother's and Fanny's help it was easier to make a paradise. — Yet I err, the noble, generous spirit of self denial and devotion which breathing in your letters, would bathe in hues of heaven's own splendor, a duller scene than your group around the wide-distended, laughing jaws of that cavernous chimney ever can present. —
>
> I can see you now, your face, shaded by your hand, — glowing in the ruddy light, and full of changeful expression, as the flickering fire burns brighter or subsides; — changeful, yet continuous, like the notes of an Irish melody; while Lizzie looks up at intervals from her sewing or her book, to recall by a tone and look of love, the musing wanderer from his enchanted Isles.

This last paragraph, delicate in its allusion to Herman's meditations about the work being serialized in *Putnam's*, is precious as almost the only surviving depiction of Herman and Lizzie as loving husband and wife. John was not one to indulge in a fantasy that, if baseless, would inflict pain, so we may take his vision of life at Arrowhead as a realistic depiction of it at something like its best. Winter confinement, all of them knew, could create intense strains.

There came to the frigid, isolated Arrowhead occasional blessings from the press, like the balmy "little breezes" and "little zephyrs" Herman kept talking about. These tags from poetry stuck in his head just then, when the Berkshire winds were blasting the porous old house — perhaps a memory of Tennyson's "The Lady of Shalott": "Willows whiten, aspens quiver, / Little breezes dusk and shiver / Through the wave that runs for ever / By the island in the river / Flowing down to Camelot." Newspaper reviewers were being kind toward "The Encantadas," ostentatiously showing a willingness to forgive and forget Melville's earlier excesses if only he would henceforth write only such reasonable prose. If he proved himself properly chastened, they would accept him. Locally, Joe Smith on 10 March in the *Berkshire County Eagle* was able to see improvement in Melville rather than deterioration from *Typee* and *Omoo:* "the four chapters contained in the present number of Putnam, are distinguished by the same simplicity of diction, vividness of description and power of narrative, which made *Omoo* and *Typee* two of the most charming books ever written. Mr. Melville's style is however no longer quite the same. It is matured by the experience, the study, and the labors of years." Subtly making a point with his neighbors who had gossiped so cruelly about *Moby-Dick* without reading it, Smith declared that not only in "The Encantadas" but also in "other late articles in Harper and Putnam" Melville had combined "the excellencies of his early and later style, to the advantage of both."

On Monday, 27 March, Allan urged Augusta to hurry Herman along (although it was "as cold as Greenland" there), and explained that they were moving from 47 East Twenty-fourth Street to 60 East Twenty-sixth when they got possession — by Saturday, April Fools' Day, at latest. That was the official publication day for the April *Putnam's*, with its second installment of "The Encantadas," for which Putnam's sent a check for fifty dollars. Herman's timing, as the days passed, made it more and more likely that he would discommode Allan and his pregnant wife, but Sophia peculiarly always found a tonic in a planned move, and Allan loved trading up, this time with the hearty advantage of a loan of some of the cash from the Bond Street house — a prideful achievement for the boy who had rented a room on the cheap at Mrs. Garahan's boardinghouse only a decade earlier. Rather distractingly, as Augusta wrote Fanny on 20 March, Herman had begun "to talk about the pleasures in anticipation of a visit to Lawrence & another to Longwood," so that Augusta thought there was a possibility that he would "make out to travel thither before August." Herman wanted to see how his sisters were settled, but on 30 March Augusta reported that he had decided he could not go east until June, "as he must return home from New York" — that is, directly home. For once he was not writing nonstop as he prepared to leave the house for a few days: "He is full of business superintending the piling up of the split wood. It would rejoice Mamma's heart to see him." He wasn't cutting the wood this year, he was supervising. Out of the April payment from *Putnam's* Herman sent some money to Fanny and his mother, but as usual not enough for the latter, as she astringently informed Augusta on 5 April: "Fanny & I received your two letters with enclosures, much obliged to Herman, but I wanted to get a few necessary articles for myself, & should have been glad to have had sufficient to do so." Still, Maria hoped he would be at home when they arrived ("it seems a great while since I saw him, indeed I feel as if it would do me good to see your dear loved faces").

Melville went to New York around the first of April. In town he may not have conducted business with Putnam, or he may have left off some magazine pieces, perhaps the little Berkshire salesman story (a fear-instilling religionist playing the role of the peddler) "The Lightning-Rod Man," for which he was paid in June. He kept his promise to call on the Harpers, and left off at their temporary offices a batch of pages on tortoises which must not have duplicated anything in "The Encantadas." He also left off some magazine articles. That was probably 7 April, a Friday, the day he browsed in the Harper bookstore long enough to pick out Tom Taylor's biography of the painter Benjamin Haydon ($1.31) and charge it. As far as we know he made no effort to interest any publisher in *The Isle of the Cross*, and he made no recorded attempt to sell any of his wares to *Godey's*, the Philadelphia magazine which had recently listed him among prospective contributors. He came home on 10 April, judging from what he said in a letter he wrote to the "Lord of Winyah" on the ninth. He had purposed inviting himself out to Winyah, he told Lathers, but had been "prevented" (that vague word he used about not publishing *The Isle of the Cross*). He had brought into town some books (including a Coleridge volume) which he had apparently borrowed the June previous, and Allan would carry them out to Lathers on his next visit. He was confused: "By the way — did I get *two* or *three* volumes? I made a Mem: at the time, but have mislaid it. I return 'The Friend' & the Essays of Combe &c. When I get home I will look particularly among my books, and see if my impression is correct about having had *three* volumes." He urgently invited Lathers to bring his wife for a visit that summer: "Come & *stay with us* a few days. You & Mrs: Lathers. We shall all be delighted to see you. No fudge — but bona fide."

Melville was home to greet Fanny and Maria on 18 April, but probably too late to say good-bye to Priscilla, for she had gone to make a visit in Stockbridge with the woman who would later accompany her to the West. Apparently Augusta had gotten the new man, William, to harness Charlie and had driven Priscilla to Stockbridge and then driven home alone. She got this tense warning from Priscilla, who must have seen Shaw there or in Lenox before she wrote on 16 April: " — *By the way* — you remember what I mention'd to you about *Judge S____'s* former habits — he *appears* to have *reform'd now*, & my request is, that if at any time, you offer them the generous hospitalities of 'Arrowhead' that *Herman* will bear in mind the *infirmity* of his guest, & considerately refrain from placing the *least* temptation in his way — even *innocent wine* may arouse a taste for something *stronger.*" She went on to ask if Herman had returned "invigorated in mind & body." This specific advice on dealing with Shaw as an alcoholic is the only such comment known, unless Hope Savage Shaw's concern about leakage from his ears, the year before, had masked an unmentionable concern that he might drink too much. In New York, Allan escorted Priscilla and her Stockbridge friend and little son to the Erie station. Augusta still had the letters the long-dead Julia Maria Melvill had written from western outposts on the weeks-long family trek to Galena in 1838, so she could at least guess at the mix of memories that filled Priscilla's mind at the thought of leaving Manhattan on Monday evening with her "'*through* Ticket' to *Chicago*," expecting to arrive at Galena on Wednesday evening of the same week!

Melville may have attempted a little touristic church-going in the metropolis, for soon after getting home he wrote "The Two Temples," one of his three diptychs (as Jay Leyda felicitously called them) dating from about this time. Melville submitted the diptych to Putnam around the end of April, about the time the third and last installment of "The Encantadas" appeared, and about the time he received a third fifty dollars from Putnam for the sketches. There was no problem with the second "temple," which depicted the narrator's welcome into a shrine of the arts, a London playhouse. The problem was the first half, which satirically depicted the narrator's expulsion from a fashionable church in Manhattan, plainly Grace Church, near the old Fourth Avenue Melville house. The officious usher who expels the narrator was plainly the egregious sexton of Grace Church, Brown, a "huge fellow, coarse in his features, resembling a dressed-up carman," and notorious for keeping out the ineligible. On Sundays, "very red" of face, Brown liked to pass "up and down the aisles of Grace Church with a peculiar swagger"—a born bully exulting in the use and misuse of his institutional power, like many men Melville had despised at sea and on shore. "The Two Temples" caused such consternation in the office that the editor, Charles F. Briggs, and Putnam himself decided to orchestrate their handling of the situation so as not to offend Melville. Briggs rejected the piece on 12 May with this diplomatic letter: "I am very loth to reject the Two Temples as the article contains some exquisitely fine description, and some pungent satire, but my editorial experience compels me to be very cautious in offending the religious sensibilities of the public, and the moral of the Two Temples would array against us the whole power of the pulpit, to say nothing of Brown, and the congregation of Grace Church."

Briggs used the occasion to apologize for making "a slight alteration in the Encantadas, in the last paragraph of the Choula Widow," which he had thought "would be improved by the omission of a few words." This had to do with Melville's comparison of the ass Jesus rode into Jerusalem and the ass the Chola widow rode into Payta, a passage Briggs left reading this way: "The last seen of lone Hunilla she was passing into Payta town, riding upon a small gray ass; and before her on the ass's shoulders, she eyed the jointed workings of the beast's armorial cross." The "alteration" was a bit of censorship: "That I did not injure the idea, or mutilate the touching figure you introduced, by the slight excision I made, I receive good evidence of, in a letter from James R Lowell, who said that the figure of the cross in the ass' neck, brought tears into his eyes, and he thought it the finest touch of genius he had seen in prose." Probably all that is lost is an explicit mention of Jesus as riding an ass in a similar way, or His eyeing the premonitory workings of the "armorial cross" on the ass He rode.

Melville must have been mollified by this secondhand praise from James Russell Lowell, who had satirized Duyckinck and Mathews in his *Fable for Critics* a few seasons earlier, and Putnam himself wrote the next day to express his regret at "the *point*" of the offending part of "The Two Temples" and, all sweet disingenuousness, to wonder if this point could somehow be avoided. More practically, and flatteringly, he offered to reimburse Melville for his expenses if would have his daguerreotype taken in Pittsfield so they could publish an engraving of his "head" in *Putnam's*. If in the height of his success, in early 1851, Melville had come to think so differently about Fame that he would not let Duyckinck immortalize him in *Holden's*, now after the unappreciated *Moby-Dick*, the infamous *Pierre*, and the wholly suppressed *The Isle of the Cross*, in his impoverished state, he was still more unwilling to have his portrait in a magazine. Putnam's final comment reflected the universal praise of "The Encantadas": "We hope you will give us some more of your good things." Briggs had said, "The only complaint that I have heard about the Encantadas was that it might have been longer." Curiously, Melville kept Augusta's fair copy of "The Two Temples" all his life, although he let *The Isle of the Cross* disappear without a trace.

On 16 May Melville first replied to Briggs in a lost letter, then he wrote to Putnam, dismissing the request for a daguerreotype by claiming not to know of "a good artist in this rural neighborhood," and promising before long to "send down some other things, to which, I think, no objections will be made on the score of tender consciences of the public." Nine days later he wrote the Harpers acknowledging their "letter enclosing $100 on acct: of the 'Paradise of Batchelors &c.'"—a construction which leaves it unclear whether they were paying a hundred dollars for the diptych "The Paradise of Bachelors and the Tartarus of Maids" or whether the "&c." covered the diptych and still other stories. The "Paradise" part paid homage to Irving's "London Antiques" in the *Sketch Book*, and in "Tartarus" Melville made highly conscious use of homospatial perception in the hallucinatory merging and separating of the Wren arch at Temple Bar and the Black Notch. He kept up the claim that the tortoise book was still active: "When you write me concerning the 'Tortoises' extract, you may, if you choose, inform me at about what time you would be prepared to commence the publication of another Serial in your Magazine—supposing you had one, in prospect, that suited you." What was he doing? the Harpers would have thought. Was he proposing a new serial when he had not produced an entire manuscript for *The Tortoise-*

Hunters? They would have understood better than we do, since they had possession of something to do with "Tortoises" which is presumably no longer extant.

In the June issue of their magazine the Harpers published Melville's social commentary grounded in bitter experience, "Poor Man's Pudding and Rich Man's Crumbs." He had been thinking of Catharine Sedgwick's old book *The Poor Rich Man and the Rich Poor Man.* Even more directly, Melville was responding to what he was continuing to see or hear about his Berkshire neighbor, Orville Dewey. Before writing *Pierre,* Melville had encountered Dewey's ideas on poverty in America, in the 1846 *Discourses on Human Nature, Human Life, and the Nature of Religion* or elsewhere. In "this country," the poor were not hungry, cold, or unclothed: they had access to all necessities and merely envied "artificial wants," some luxury or another. Dewey and the Sedgwicks, like their fellow Unitarian Joseph Curtis, had long lamented that begging was permitted on the streets of New York, knowing full well that any misery felt by the poor was "not owing to the rich, but mainly to themselves." Granted, Jesus had said that rich people would always have the poor around them, but He had not said that Unitarians should have to see them begging in the streets of Manhattan. There was "remunerative labor enough" for the poor, if only you could get them to work. Having studied the matter, Dewey had ascertained that beggary was, "in all ordinary cases, *prima facie* evidence that there was something wrong behind it. The great evil and mischief lay in indiscriminate charity." Reflecting in his "Poor Man's Pudding and Rich Man's Crumbs" on his childhood experiences as well as his present indebtedness, Melville came to a different conclusion about what it was to be poor in America: "The native American poor never lose their delicacy or pride; hence, though unreduced to the physical degradation of the European pauper, they yet suffer more in mind than the poor of any other people in the world." They suffered bodily, and they endured peculiarly painful sufferings in mind, and there were real bodily evils and real "evils of the mind" created by American ideologies, not merely imaginary evils whipped up by the individual mind.

As always, Melville could not be relied upon to excite himself about whatever cause the nation was exciting itself about, whether it was a grand contested election for president or adulation for a traveling Hungarian. Just as he went his own way during the slavery crisis of 1850–51, now he went his own way during the new crisis in Boston in early June 1854 over the arrest and remanding of the fugitive slave Anthony Burns to slavery. Once again he was a galley-slave himself, in the grim pun, and a slave to secret debt. "Who aint a slave?" he had asked in "Loomings"; now Augusta in her way was a slave, yoked to him. Helen, the only one who knew what her sister was enduring, assured her in late June, "I can sympathise in your state of entire employment" — effectively a form of enslavement. Like poverty, slavery was not an imaginary evil, but it was not the evil Melville was focused on, even when a Boston mob stormed his father-in-law's bastion, the courthouse. In Boston the papers held to the positions they had taken during the last period of intense public dispute, 1850–51, Whig and Democratic papers united again. The Whig Boston *Courier* condemned the incendiary speech by Theodore Parker at Faneuil Hall on 25 May that had preceded the attack on the courthouse: "Mr. Parker advocated the higher law doctrine, and said 'there is a means and an end; liberty is the end; sometimes peace is not the means to obtain the end.'" The Democratic *Post* declared that "the eyes of the whole country are looking to see how Boston will come out of the struggle between law and anarchy," and denounced Parker and Wendell Phillips as murderers and the meeting at Faneuil Hall as treasonable. The weekly Pittsfield *Sun* on 1 June devoted three columns to attacking the "mischief-making 'philanthropists'" like Phillips, Parker, and Francis W. Bird, who on 25 May had made "treasonable" speeches at Faneuil Hall, and on 8 June it carried the full story of the deportation of Anthony Burns and ran Judge Edward G. Loring's decision on the case for a column and a half.

The Boston *Daily Evening Transcript* on 2 June gave this appalled description of the actual enforcement of the Fugitive Slave Law: "An immense concourse gathered upon the wharves adjacent to the scene of embarkation, and at every possible point where the slightest view could be had. Thousands upon thousands of people gazed upon this strange spectacle at high noon on a brilliant day, and under all the lights of civilization, liberty, law and religion." At those docks where Melville's grandfather had thrown bales of tea overboard, a chained man was sent back into slavery. The Boston *Investigator* declared (7 June) that the remanding of Burns was "perhaps unparalleled by any event since the revolutionary war." The Burns case was not uppermost in the minds of the Hoadley and Griggs families: it was on 29 May that Helen described the hoisting of her wardrobe and wished that Herman could come to visit her at Brookline, "this nice quiet corner of the Commonwealth," several stones' throws from Boston. If he wanted to see history in the making, of course, he would have "the privilege of visiting the noisy, busy, bustling, & now excited and tumultuous city" as often as he pleased. Melville's way of responding to the Burns case was to reflect more deeply on the American national character rather than on the specific issue of slavery.

Melville may well have been uncertain as to how he would react if the Harpers were to respond enthusiastically to their "Extract," now lost, and were to set an early date for him to produce more extracts and the complete manuscript. Had they done so, they would have put a kink in his line, for he had already started the quite unrelated serial he had hinted at in his letter to the Harpers on 25 May. Their lack of enthusiasm led to his reversion to *Putnam's* in a letter (accompanying a package) which someone later misread as dated 7 July—an error for 7 June:

> I send you prepaid by Express, to-day, some sixty and odd pages of MSS. The manuscript is part of a story called "Israel Potter," concerning which a more particular understanding need be had....
>
> This story when finished will embrace some 300 or more MS. pages. I propose to publish it in your Magazine at the rate of five dollars per printed page, the copyright to be retained by me. Upon the acceptation of this proposition (if accepted) $100. to be remitted to me as an advance. After that advance shall have been cancelled in the course of publication of the numbers, the price of the subsequent numbers to be remitted to me upon each issue of the Magazine as long as the story lasts....
>
> On my side, I guarantee to provide you with matter for at least ten printed pages in ample time for each issue.

Melville's concern for control over the copyright reflects Allan's advice the previous winter about "The Encantadas." He continued with a discreet allusion to the contretemps over "The Two Temples," engaging "that the story shall contain nothing of any sort to shock the fastidious." He emphasized, redundantly: "There will be very little reflective writing in it; nothing weighty. It is adventure." He concluded with an assurance that he would try to sustain the interest as well as he could.

Putnam demurred only about paying all the one hundred dollars at once, and Melville wrote back on 12 June: "Yours of the 10th is received. Tho' I should have preferred receiving the $100 at once, yet I am willing to consider the arrangement as closed, conceding to you the refusal of the privilege of subsequent publication of the thing [*Israel Potter*] in book form. For 12½% however, I should prefer half-profits. There may be no difference; but 12½% does not seem much." He closed by acknowledging receipt of payment for his story "The Lightning-Rod Man." In Longwood, Helen, enthusiastic about the news from Herman that the serial was a Fourth of July story, responded through Augusta around 20 June: "I shall be quite wild to make the acquaintance of 'Israel Potter,' and to have the Fourth of July come. I shall make George procure me *my* Independence namely—a new novel, & a paper of candy." What with Hoadley's messages and Helen's eagerness, the east winds were buoying.

His satire of barring Christians from Christian churches, "The Two Temples," now suppressed, but "Poor Man's Pudding and Rich Man's Crumbs" now in print in the latest *Harper's*, on 22 June Melville pursued the matter of the tortoise book, writing aggressively to the Harpers:

> You have not as yet favored me with your views as to the Extract from the *Tortoise Hunters* I sent you.
>
> I am desirous to learn your views with regard to that Extract, so as to know whether it be worth while to prepare further Extracts for you, at present.
>
> Though it would be difficult, if not impossible, for me to get the entire Tortoise Book ready for publication before Spring [of 1855], yet I can pick out & finish parts, here & there, for prior use. But even this is not unattended with labor; which labor, of course, I do not care to undergo while remaining in doubt as to its recompence.

He requested an early reply to relieve his "uncertainty." For their part, the Harpers must have been under no uncertainty at all that they had recompensed him in advance for the tortoise book, the previous December, under the impression that it would be completed in January 1854.

The course of life at Arrowhead the next months was affected by Lizzie's pregnancy, which began in early June and therefore seemed to parallel Melville's progress on the serialization in *Putnam's* of his *Israel Potter*, his long-planned adaptation and expansion of Henry Trumbull's *Life and Remarkable Adventures of Israel R. Potter* (Providence, 1824). He continued to write other pieces, such as the "brace of fowl — wild fowl" which he sent down to Harper's on 18 September, perhaps "Jimmy Rose" and "The 'Gees," perhaps the unaccounted-for piece called "October Mountain." J. E. A. Smith in *The History of Pittsfield (Berkshire County), Mass., from the Year 1800 to the Year 1876* said this about Melville at Arrowhead: "'My Chimney and I,' a quaintly humorous essay, of which the cumbersome old chimney — overbearing tyrant of the home — is the hero, was also written here, as well as 'October Mountain,' a sketch of mingled philosophy and word-painted landscape, which found its inspiration in the massy and brilliant autumnal tints presented by a prominent and thickly-wooded spur of the Hoosac mountains, as seen from the south-eastern windows, at Arrow-Head, on a fine day after the early frosts." This story has never been located, but Joe Smith knew much that no one knows today. The title *The Isle of the Cross* remained unknown until I found it in 1988, so we should be slow to say "October Mountain" never existed.

Melville's main efforts for the next months went into rewriting and greatly expanding the story of Israel Potter, which Trumbull had ghostwritten in the first person, as if it were entirely written by Potter. "Remarkable Adventures" was not an exaggeration, for the Rhode Island native (born in

1744), after brief periods of farming and going to sea, had marched to battle at Bunker Hill, where he was wounded, the first of many adventures. (Melville moved his birthplace to western Massachusetts.) Potter's hospital ship was captured and he was taken to England, where he escaped at Spithead. Twice seized and handcuffed, he escaped and found work as a gardener, for a time at "Quew," in King George's own famous gardens, where he on one occasion conversed briefly with the man who wanted to be his sovereign. American sympathizers, including Horne Tooke and James Bridges, sent him twice to Paris with secret letters to Benjamin Franklin. Stranded in London, he survived in abject poverty decade after decade, as a brickmaker and then as a mender of old chairs. He married, and fathered many children who died early. After the death of his wife, he managed at last to see the American consul, who in 1823 sent him to New York, from whence he sailed to Boston to join his son, his only living child, who had been sent there to await him. At Providence, in his extreme old age, he relied on the publication of his story to gain him what had been denied, a pension as a veteran of the Revolution. It was a story of brief early adventure followed by a long life of all but unbelievable misery.

Melville had owned the little Trumbull book and had been thinking about rewriting it for several years. The story may have appealed to him during his misery over the reviews of *Mardi* in 1849, about the time he decided to write *Redburn* and then *White-Jacket* as popular works, full of cakes and ale rather than conic sections. In the fall of 1849 he had done some anticipatory antiquarian researches in London and Paris. It presumably figured in his thronging imagination still in December 1850, when he wrote to Duyckinck about the infinite number of future works he was planning and how much he would be aided by fifty fast-copying youths. The story of Israel Potter seems so anomalously unambitious in the light of *Moby-Dick* and *Pierre* that it would be easy to attribute Melville's interest in it to his defeated mood as a man deeply and secretly in debt. Yet indisputably the story had appealed to him during his young, robust, and exuberant years, and the fact that he had seized on it so early and so eagerly as a story he might retell speaks poignantly about the way Melville could envision his future, even in 1849. In the seemingly enterprising Yankee who proves to have little flexibility, little resilience (after a series of defeats), but an almost infinite capacity for suffering and enduring, Melville found something recognizable and perhaps even comforting, however grotesquely unlike his new hero he would have looked to an objective observer in 1849.

On the surface there was little reflective or "weighty" in most of the pages of *Israel Potter*, but implicit in the portrayal of Potter's later life is Melville's anticipation of the ultimate loss of his own career. In the years during which he had brooded intermittently about the story, he had written the single most vehemently scorned novel in American literature, *Pierre*, he had lost his second British publisher, and he had failed to get into print a book on which he had lavished months of thought and some five months of labor, *The Isle of the Cross*. He may have worked an allusion to that wasted effort into the July installment of *Israel Potter* in *Putnam's:* "Farming weans man from his sorrows. That tranquil pursuit tolerates nothing but tranquil meditations. There, too, in mother earth, you may plant and reap; not, as in other things, plant and see the planting torn up by the roots." During the months he worked on the Revolutionary story, he was unable to meet the November payment of interest due to Stewart, and knew that the day was coming closer when he would not only have to pay the overdue interest (and probably the interest on the interest) but also the entire principal, a sum utterly out of his reach.

Keeping his promise, Melville sustained the attention of his readers month by month while avoiding anything "weighty," but he wrote some powerful scenes. Early enough, in chapter 12, "The Squire's Abode," he invented a terrifying account of Israel's "being masoned up in the wall" at Squire Woodcock's house in Brentford, in an ancient "coffin-cell of the Templars," where "in this very darkness, centuries ago, hearts, human as his, had mildewed in despair; limbs, robust as his own, had stiffened in immovable torpor." Escaping at last, Israel understands from the funeral aspect of the squire's room that his friend had not visited him and released him for the best of reasons: he had died. Israel escapes the house by exchanging his clothes for those of the squire, the complete suit he had last seen on the living man, down to the silver-headed cane and cocked hat. Feeling "almost as unreal and shadowy as the shade whose part he intended to enact," he terrifies the mourners as he walks out the house with slow and stately tread, passing for Squire Woodcock's "genuine phantom" (ch. 13). Having turned into another person, Israel undergoes a hallucinatory experience in the moonlight: "The whole scene magically reproduced to our adventurer the aspect of Bunker Hill, Charles River, and Boston town, on the well-remembered night of the 16th of June. The same season; the same moon; the same new-mown hay on the shaven sward; hay which was scraped together during the night to help pack into the redoubt so hurriedly thrown up." As always in Melville, such a scene of overlapping persons and places signaled an intensity of psychological involvement with his material.

Among the more memorable passages in the avowedly unreflective *Israel Potter* were those on Benjamin Franklin. Drawing on extensive knowledge of Franklin's writings and life (although portions of the autobiography remained unpublished), Melville summed up the great man authoritatively in chapter 8: "Printer, postmaster, almanac maker, essayist, chemist, orator, tinker, statesman, humorist, philosopher, parlor-man, political economist, professor of housewifery, ambassador, projector, maxim-monger, herb-doctor, wit: — Jack of all trades, master of each and mastered by none — the type and genius of his land, Franklin was everything but a poet." The real Israel Potter had been a courier to the real Franklin, but John Paul Jones is not in Trumbull's book; Melville brought them together, so that "across the otherwise blue-jean career of Israel, Paul Jones flits and re-flits like a crimson thread" (ch. 20). From Robert Charles Sands's *Life and Correspondence of John Paul Jones, including his Narrative of the Campaign of the Liman* (New York, 1830), Melville seized on many passages, almost verbatim, for his wholly invented scenes involving Israel and Jones, who is introduced in Franklin's rooms in Paris as "a rather small, elastic, swarthy man, with an aspect as of a disinherited Indian Chief in European clothes" (ch. 10). Unlike Franklin, Jones has "a bit of the poet as well as the outlaw in him."

For his set piece on the nocturnal battle between Jones's *Bon Homme Richard* (the translation of Franklin's Poor Richard) and the British *Serapis*, waged in full moonlight off the coast of Yorkshire (ch. 19), Melville plundered James Fenimore Cooper's *History of the Navy of the United States of America* (the posthumous Putnam edition of 1853). At the outset of that chapter, "They Fight the Serapis," Melville made Jones emblematic: "There would seem to be something singularly indicatory in this engagement. It may involve at once a type, a parallel, and a prophecy. Sharing the same blood with England, and yet her proved foe in two wars; not wholly inclined at bottom to forget an old grudge: intrepid, unprincipled, reckless, predatory, with boundless ambition, civilized in externals but a savage at heart, America is, or may yet be, the Paul Jones of nations." Later Melville used *A Narrative of Colonel Ethan Allen's Captivity* (1779 or a later edition) to bring the "Titanic Vermonter" into fictitious contact with Potter, having them thrown together as prisoners in England. In chapter 22, Melville makes Allen emblematic, as he had done Franklin and Jones:

> Allen seems to have been a curious combination of a Hercules, a Joe Miller, a Bayard, and a Tom Hyer; had a person like the Belgian giants; mountain music in him like a Swiss; a heart plump as Cœur de Lion's. Though born in New England, he exhibited no trace of her character. He was frank; bluff; companionable as a Pagan; convivial; a Roman; hearty as a harvest. His spirit was essentially western; and herein is his peculiar Americanism; for the western spirit is, or will yet be (for no other is, or can be) the true American one.

Hercules, the Bayard (chevalier sans fear and sans reproach), Coeur de Lion — all are recognizable; Joseph Miller is remembered as the English comic actor whose name was attached to a joke-book so famous that he became known as the Father of Jests. Tom Hyer was a Manhattan butcher and bareknuckles fighter who in mid-1838 became one of the first inmates at the newly opened Tombs, arrested after cutting off a friend's nose in a tavern at Chatham and Pearl streets, one stone's throw from Melville's birthplace. Once in the Tombs, Hyer beat the jailor insensible. Melville was fascinated by the Tombs, partly because the building was modeled on an engraving in Stephens's 1837 *Incidents of Travel*, and was a connoisseur of stories about the jail. Hyer's exploits may have been described in some of the papers Gansevoort Melville sent home from Manhattan in 1838. Running through the characterizations of these three archetypal Americans—Franklin, Jones, and Allen—was the theme that would resurface in "Benito Cereno" and take high place in *The Confidence-Man*, not the moral and political American national crisis of the mid-1850s but the American national character.

Besides his major sources, Melville put his incidental reading to good use, as always. The work he had charged to his Harper's account on 7 April, Taylor's *Life of Haydon* (New York, 1853), contains a passage on the smoke of London as "the sublime canopy that shrouds the City of the World," not an offensive pall: " 'Be Gode,' said Fuseli, to me one day, 'it's like de smoke of de Israelites making bricks.' 'It is grander,' said I, 'for it is the smoke of a people who would have made the Egyptians make bricks for them.' 'Well done, John Bull,' replied Fuseli." This Melville used in chapter 23, in the description of Israel Potter's labors as a brickmaker in London.

After being the sole Dame Durden of the Hill, Augusta yielded the household responsibilities to Maria and Fanny while she continued to copy Herman's manuscripts. The writing was steadily paced, the copying uninterrupted, for the monthly installments of *Israel Potter* were regularly composed and published. Nevertheless, there was some enforced respite. Maria's return had signaled a genuine Dutch housecleaning, a May first ritual, and one that (according to a letter Herman wrote to Helen) drove him utterly out of the house to take refuge in a barrel. (He had amused the eastern sisters by sending Helen's letter to Kate and Kate's to Helen—a deliberate joke, Kate was sure.) Helen, anxious to see Herman, was all sympathy in her 29 May reply: "Why did you not come and stay with me while they were suffering under the house-cleaning dispensation? I could have made you very comfortable, and you need not have been driven to such a strait as sleeping in a barrel. I hope the children were not crowded, but had a *keg* apeice to themselves. Bessie might have occupied the *mortar*, if the pestle were taken out." She was also full of affection, rallying with him over the rarity of his letters, and depicting his behavior in a little drama based on many scenes such as she had witnessed:

I should have sent one of my numerous epistles to your particular address ere now, if I had not been so well acquainted with your usual mode of treating such documents — "Any letters? Herman?" cries Gus, or Lizzie, or Fanny, as you are reining up old Charlie in gallant style at the pump-room door. "Y-e-s-s" — "one from Helen I guess — for some of you — here 'tis." "Why Herman, it's directed to you!" — "Is it? let me see — why so it is! Well, take it along, I'll be in presently, and then some of you can read it to me."

Helen visualized this scene so lovingly because she was genuinely homesick, despite the pleasures of Longwood. When Maria and Fanny left she had joked transparently, asking if Herman thought she should leave George and return to Arrowhead herself, and Kate had made similar motions. Now Helen revealed that George had "allowed the lower part of his face, to be clothed upon with a full and abundant continuation of whisker, which change is becoming in the extreme," since it kept him from looking so "much like Uncle Peter." She concluded that "the alteration for the better, (as Dickens says) 'the imagination can scarcely depicture.'" (This was Mr. Weller in the 1844 *Master Humphrey's Clock*, thinking how son Samuel would be transformed if taken out of petticoats; Dickens still held on to Helen's hand.) Helen was arranging for Sophia and Allan to visit, knowing that it would be better for Sophia to travel before she was as big as in 1850, when she felt like an elephant, and urging Herman to come. She had promised that George would be "delighted" to have him, and that he "could be as happy as a king" in her quiet house, and go into tumultuous Boston whenever he wanted. Not too much should be made of her not specifically inviting Lizzie, who of course would stay on Mt. Vernon Street whenever she was in Boston.

Herman did go to see Helen, perhaps making one of his flying visits. While there, Herman inscribed a book to Lizzie, giving the place as Boston and the date as July 1854, *The Modern Housewife's Receipt Book: A Guide to All Matters Connected with Household Economy*, by Mrs. Pullan (London, 1854). The book got hard use before being given to Harvard in 1945 by one of the Melvilles' granddaughters, Mrs. Binnian. Lizzie had probably asked Herman to find such a book, since with two of his sisters gone they all had to face the prospect that the remaining family unit might further break apart. Perhaps he was there in Boston during the record heat on 4 July, a Tuesday: one hundred degrees in the shade in Boston, according to the Lawrence *Courier* of the seventh. It was so hot in Lawrence, the *Courier* indicated, that the local Fourth of July celebration was truncated, after Hoadley gave a response to the toast, "*The Mechanic's Arm.* It gives the age its progress." A Writer's Hand, anyone would have known, had nothing to do with giving an age its progress, although writing poetry gave a man like Hoadley innocent aesthetic pleasure and a heightened social cachet.

When she wrote Augusta on 29 May, Helen was concerned that Allan had been "quite sick," the reason Allan and Sophia had accepted Kate's invitation so eagerly, change of air being thought a good thing for poor Ally. They were to visit Helen after staying at Lawrence. Allan's health and Sophia's pregnancy complicated their itinerary, but the plan was that Allan was to leave Lawrence for New York via Pittsfield, on 15 June, staying a day at Arrowhead. Helen wrote Augusta around 20 June the news from Aunt Lucy: Allan was so unwell he was trying to avoid "hurried traveling." Meanwhile, Sophia and the girls would leave Lawrence for Longwood, where Allan would meet her and escort them home; as it turned out, they probably left Milie with Helen. The real family vacation was planned, long in advance, for Arrowhead in August, when Maria's fantasy could come true, and all the children and four spouses and grandchildren should be "all gathered once more, under the Parents wing." Those words were from Aunt Lucy, who having heard from the eastern sisters all about "the family meeting in August," on 25 July cautioned Augusta of the dangers of a raucous celebration ("I hope the roof of the house will be secured"); they would certainly have to lash the roof down, if Dr. Nourse "was to be of the party." In one letter Augusta mentioned the Balance Rock, perhaps, or some other topographical feature of the Berkshires, enough to set Helen in a fever in her response (about 20 June): "The mere mention of the big rock, makes me long for August. Won't we have a lovely time!" The Hoadleys, the Griggses, and probably the Twenty-sixth Street family were all to come, as Helen assured Herman: "We are quite longing for August to come that we may be all gathered once more under one roof-tree. That excursion to Bash-Bish is just the thing for a family party, and if George's health continues to be progressive & his morning attacks of lethargy wear off, he will no doubt be well enough to join us in our excursions, and bear the consequent fatigue as well as any of the party." The grand Berkshire excursions of 1851, 1852, and 1853 had included some family outings, women included, but nothing so ambitious as this proposed journey to Bash Bish, where the divided waterfalls were already one of the scenes most favored by painters of the Hudson River School. The likelihood is that the excursion took place, and that it fulfilled its purpose in uniting the family, the blood members and the in-laws as well, under one roof-tree and under one Parent's wing. To all outward appearances Herman was doing well, despite *Pierre* and its aftermath, but the more people who were at Arrowhead the more people from whom he had to hide the secret of his debt to Stewart and his inability to pay the interest on the loan. A smoker must have tobacco, a writer must acquire books, but what he spent, he could tell himself, was a pittance weighed against what he owed Stewart. He dissembled in matters great and small a dozen times each day as Hoadley and Griggs in all innocence made remarks that stung—remarks as simple as compliments on the size and beauty of Herman's estate.

There survives what may be the equivalent of a candid photograph of the gathering, a depiction by "Beta" in the Springfield *Daily Republican* on 24 August (the day Augusta turned thirty-three) of the family gathered on the stoop facing the quiet Holmes Road. The piece ("Lenox and Its Attractions") may indicate that "Beta" had passed by Arrowhead in the middle of August, when the family gathering was in progress. The writer got some history wrong, accusing Melville of not showing "his taste in selling the fine old ancestral place," Broadhall, "and retiring hither" to "this ordinary looking house," Arrowhead: "There he sits now in the front 'stoop' with a party of friends around him. He presents outwardly no very salient point which you can seize to describe him by." Beta missed a chance to immortalize himself with a pen portrait, but perhaps it would have been hard to single out Melville, especially if the similarly bearded Allan was there (he may have stayed in New York, since Sophia was in her ninth month), along with the bearded Hoadley and the more extensively bearded Griggs. Lizzie's pregnancy—in its third month—would not have been evident to the passing Beta.

There survives also a mention of Melville on the front porch, rather than his piazza, in a hard-to-date passage in Maunsell B. Field's chaotic *Memories of Many Men and Some Women* (1874), an account that seems likely to describe an occasion in this summer, a "little excursion which Darley, the artist," and Field "once made together from Stockbridge":

> We started in a buggy to call upon Melville, intending to go from there to Dr. Holmes's, then to the hotel at Pittsfield to dine, and thence home. We found Melville, whom I had always known as the most silent man of my acquaintance, sitting on the porch in front of his door. He took us to a particular spot on his place to show us some superb trees. He told me that he spent much time there *patting them upon the back*. When we were about to start for Dr. Holmes's, we invited Melville to accompany us, and he accepted.

Theodore F. Wolfe in the 1895 edition of his *Literary Shrines* offered a late-century view of what had been Holmes's estate: "On a near knoll, commanding a view of the circle of mountains and the winding river, stands the sometime summer residence of Holmes among his ancestral acres.... His 'den,' in which he did much literary work, overlooks the beautiful meadows, and is now expanded into a large library, while the trees he planted are grown to be the crowning beauty of the place." Maunsell Field's account continues:

> We found the poet-physician, to whom I was presented for the first time, at home, and he took us into a room at the back of his house, which overlooked the mountains. For some time the talk, in which we all tried to participate, dragged. . . . At length, somehow, the conversation drifted to East India religions and mythologies, and soon there arose a discussion between Holmes and Melville, which was conducted with the most amazing skill and brilliancy on both sides. It lasted for hours, and Darley and I had nothing to do but listen. I never chanced to hear better talking in my life. It was so absorbing that we took no note of time, and the Doctor lost his dinner, as we lost ours.

Field offers unique but believable information. "Taconic" in the September 1852 *Norton's Literary Gazette* had noted that "Maunsell B. Field, Esq." was then occupying his "summer residence" (he lived much of his life abroad), so he might well have been there in 1854. Darley had first puzzled out the location of Arrowhead in 1853, so he would have known the way in 1854 or 1855. Melville's saying that he spent much time patting his superb trees upon the back parallels Duyckinck's saying that he knew every tree on the old Melvill property. As for his knowledge of East India religions and mythologies at this stage of his life rather than decades later, it must be accepted, if for no other reason than that Holmes stopped summering in Pittsfield in 1855 (making seven summers there, as he said), and was trying to sell the place as early as February 1856 (a year later he was consoling himself with the thought that he had planted there seven hundred trees for others to sit under). As with Melville's extensive knowledge of British poetry displayed in his markings in his father's Spenser, many of which markings antedate "The Encantadas," we have to assume a breadth of ongoing reading not possible to account for by the books Melville is known to have had access to. He may have gained much of it from his cyclopedias.

During the last half of 1854 Melville concentrated on *Israel Potter*. Augusta got away at least briefly—she was with Kate in Lawrence in the middle of September—but she copied behind him efficiently. The ailing Sarah Morewood wrote to Augusta and Kate (in September?), admitting to old frailties and new fears: "My poor brain never has been quite free from shadows—but of late it has become clouded and dark—and dearly as I love my friends Kate and Augusta I find that even a quiet talk with them does not lessen the task—does not clear the clouded brain. So you must take my misty letter and let your warm affection excuse the fog I write in." Sarah offered a fanciful picture of just how Augusta and Kate were occupied that dull day, a portrait based on long close knowledge of the sisters: "Kate as usual . . . [keeps] a careful look out about her house—and seeing to the pleasure and comfort of others—You with needle work in hand but mind intent upon some poetic dreaming or castle building of rare John Ruskin style—While in your work basket and on your chair-table near you, and every other available place—books are piled." (Keeping "a careful look out" meant Kate was making sure books were shelved according to height and that throw pillows sat stiffly, top corners checked by plumb-line.) In her weakened condition Sarah the omnivorous reader was reverting to Puritanic distrust of books that might deny the existence of the "holy, blessed, and glorious Trinity, three persons and one God," especially books by "such authors as Ware and the other writers whose books you have." She pleaded, "Dont meddle with strange doctrines dear Augusta." Sarah meant the strange doctrines of the Unitarian William Ware, the first minister of Dr. Bellows's All Souls Church in Manhattan, whose twenty-odd-year-old Roman novels, *Zenobia* and *Aurelian*, were still read, and whose *Julian* (1849) was a sort of early *Ben Hur*, where the Roman Julian goes to Palestine and meets Jesus. In New York Sarah had seen a doctor and repeated his opinion, as Augusta had requested: "It was more favourable than I had expected and very encouraging if I did not feel from constant pain and weakness how little I may hope. He says that no actual disease has as yet begun in the lungs." The doctor was wholly wrong, if he told her what he believed.

Melville's account with the Harpers as of 6 October showed him $319.74 in their debt, but he was receiving money from Putnam every month. On 7 July Putnam sent him $50 for the first installment of 9½ printed pages; in August Putnam paid $18 for "The Lightning-Rod Man" (3 pages) and $55 for 11½ pages of *Israel Potter*; in September Putnam paid him $67.50 for the third installment, 13½ pages; in October $35 for 7 pages; in November $52.50 for the fifth installment (10½ pages); in December $50 for the sixth installment (10 pages). (The January–March 1855 installments were 8¾ pages for $44; 7 pages for $35; and 6½ pages for $32.50.) Some correspondence survives or can be inferred. On 22 October Putnam wrote Melville to confirm some point about the terms for publishing *Israel Potter* in book form. In his reply on 31 October, Melville said the story would be completed in about thirty more manuscript pages, which he would send "in a week or so." Melville confirmed Putnam's memory of their agreement, and now asked only to be told when the book was put to press, so he could supply "title-page, preface &c"; finally, he pronounced that there seemed "no errors of the press (in the Magazine) worth correcting." Melville followed this up on 3 November with a correction—there would be nearer forty-five more pages of manuscript. (Between the days he wrote these letters he again defaulted on the payment of $92.25 due to T. D. Stewart.) In one of their communications about the first of November, *Putnam's* returned a manuscript that Melville in a letter of 3 November noncommittally acknowledged receiving. Throughout this period Melville sent his installments of *Israel Potter* on time and Putnam paid for them promptly; the only problem came in at the end. On 7 November Putnam sent Melville a request to rush them the promised conclusion, and with an apology Melville sent "the affair to the Finis" on 9 November. Perhaps the delay occurred because Augusta had not been able to keep pace with his rapid windup of the story. Otherwise, all went smoothly — and by the ninth or so of November Augusta was safely in Boston for a second visit to her married sisters and her new brothers.

Putnam had no reason to complain about the many comments that appeared in newspapers and magazines during the months Melville was serializing *Israel Potter*. On 29 July the *Morning Courier and New-York Enquirer* saw a transformation in Melville, if the rumor about his authorship of *Israel Potter* were true, for the story was told "quite as if De Foe had undertaken to tell it, albeit it is more enlivened with dialogue than it would be in that case." On 27 August the *Herald* printed a long extract and commented that Melville seemed to intend "to bring all the contemporaneous celebrities of the epoch at which the story is laid before his readers." Melville had no reason to feel anything but manly pride in his workmanship.

The final push on *Israel Potter* was the signal for scattering. Maria went to Albany, and probably to Lansingburgh as well. On 28 November she regaled her brother Peter with a dramatic account of her nocturnal journey in the cars from Greenbush on 24 November, in a fierce rainstorm during which the car's lamps went out. With relief she heard the stop at Pittsfield announced:

> I rose up at once, and slowly left my seat, being near the door I was soon on the platform, & there to my great delight, as I was stepping down, Herman received me in his arms — by the light of a lantern I saw him, for it was pitch dark, and the rain falling heavily. We had to walk across rails innumerable, to reach the Housatonic-Depot, every now & then a gleam from a lantern would light the surface of a puddle of water. Herman soon placed the Luggage in the Carriage and to my great joy we drove off, & reached home in safety.

Herman and Lizzie with all three children had a more frustrating experience on 27 November, when they set out to enjoy Thanksgiving in Boston (on the thirtieth that year). They all returned to Arrowhead, disappointed, as Maria told Peter:

> They arrived in time to see the cars steam off for Boston, leaving them behind. It was too bad, an early breakfast, and a regular departure. The mistake arose in the difference of our time from the Boston time. For accord-

ing to our time, more than an hour was left to drive to town in. They were all very good humoured about it, the day was fine & pleasant, they had a ride to town & the children said the Cars ran away from them. So in a few minutes after their return home, Herman went up to his library as usual Lizzie took a book and seated herself before the fire, Bessie was put to bed, & the boys went out to play.

The next day, the Melvilles succeeded in reaching Boston. Herman, short of money for the trip, had taken the liberty of cashing a draft of sixty dollars against Putnam — ten dollars more than they actually owed him — and writing to let them know not to send him a check for the installment of *Israel Potter* in the December issue. Nervous at being so short of money, he probably returned soon after Thanksgiving and began a new serial, "Benito Cereno." Lizzie and Augusta stayed on, and were still at the Shaws' house on 18 December, when Aunt Lucy wrote Augusta a letter which revealed her knowledge of how hospitable the eastern sisters and their other connections, not least Mary Nourse, had been toward Augusta, who was able, most rewardingly, to renew her intimacy with Nilly Thayer, after being long separated. Augusta stayed on into January.

The year ended sorrowfully. In the new Twenty-sixth Street house Sophia had given birth on 5 or 6 September to her fourth daughter, whom Allan named Julia — in compliment to his cousin Julia Maria Melvill, three years his elder, who had died young in Galena; Aunt Jean Melvill Wright also may have had a child named Julia Maria. The name brought no fortune, although (as Allan wrote Augusta on 13 September) an Irish nursemaid had performed an elaborate ritual before she would take the baby down to see Richard Lathers: "she trotted the little body up stairs to the third story before bringing her down to the parlor as she says no child will have *luck* unless it is taken up stairs before it is taken down stairs. So Miss Julia is ensured high life above stairs." But on 20 December Allan wrote his mother that he and Sophia had spent the last four days "expecting that our dear little Julia would breath[e] her last every moment." She died at half past three in the morning of 26 December, after the nurse had given her the "half hourly nourishment of wine whey." Allan and Sophia together "witnessed the departure of the little spirit." Milie, almost six, wrote this account a few years later: "We kissed her little hand, and one or two days after I stood at the front door, seeing two men carr[y]ing the little coffin on their shoulders." Julia was the first of four members of the family to die in that house. Carrying Julia upstairs was folly. Instead, the nursemaid should have spit in her face — the Irish custom for assuring good luck (according to the New York *Times*, 23 January 1856).

[11]

"Benito Cereno"

Early 1855

> I know not when I am to repay you. — experience tells me, more & more, every day, that, a farmer indebted, can but live. —
>
> Thomas Melvill Jr., in Pittsfield, to his father, 27 November 1822

For "Benito Cereno," as for *Israel Potter*, Melville took an actual printed account for his rewriting: chapter 18 ("Particulars of the Capture of the Spanish Ship Tryal, at the island of St. Maria; with the Documents relating to that affair") in Captain Amasa Delano's *A Narrative of Voyages and Travels, in the Northern and Southern Hemispheres: Comprising Three Voyages Round the World, Together with a Voyage of Survey and Discovery in the Pacific Ocean and Oriental Islands* (Boston, 1817); E. G. House was the printer, for Delano. No copy belonging to Melville has been located. Delano's book, still not excessively rare in Melville's time, might have been around one or another of the family houses (Herman's uncle John D'Wolf's, for instance, or his Grandfather Melvill's), and was the sort of book that in the course of things would gravitate to a writer about Pacific voyages. It might even have come to his attention by 1847 or so, when in chapter 19 of *Mardi* he described a seemingly abandoned brigantine in language fairly close to a similar passage in "Benito Cereno." His shipmate Henry Hubbard, who had visited him in 1853, was connected by marriage to the Delanos (also the family of the mother of President Franklin Roosevelt). Conceivably Hubbard might have brought him a copy as a gift.

In chapter 18 (pp. 318–53) Delano told, first, a great sea-story, in fourteen short pages, beginning with a two-page summary account written just after the events by the officer in charge of the log book of his ship, the *Perseverance*. This passage from that account shows just how closely Melville followed his source:

> "Wednesday, February 20th [1805], commenced with light airs from the north east, and thick foggy weather. At six A. M. observed a sail opening round the south head of St. Maria, coming into the bay. It proved to be a ship.

> The captain took the whale boat and crew, and went on board her. As the wind was very light, so that a vessel would not have much more than steerage way at the time; observed that the ship acted very awkwardly. At ten A. M. the boat returned. Mr. Luther [a midshipman] informed that Captain Delano had remained on board her, and that she was a Spaniard from Buenos Ayres, four months and twenty six days out of port, with slaves on board, and that the ship was in great want of water, had buried many white men and slaves on her passage, and that captain Delano had sent for a large boat load of water, some fresh fish, sugar, bread, pumpkins, and bottled cider, all of which articles were immediately sent. At twelve o'clock (Meridian) calm. At two P. M. the large boat returned from the Spaniards, had left our water casks on board her. At four P. M. a breeze sprung up from the southern quarter, which brought the Spanish ship into the roads. She anchored about two cables length to the south east of our ship. Immediately after she anchored, our captain with his boat was shoving off from along side the Spanish ship; when to his great surprise the Spanish captain leaped into the boat, and called out in Spanish, that the slaves on board had risen and murdered many of the people; and that he did not then command her; on which manœuvre, several of the Spaniards who remained on board jumped overboard, and swam for our boat, and were picked up by our people. The Spaniards, who remained on board, hurried up the rigging, as high aloft as they could possibly get, and called out repeatedly for help — that they should be murdered by the slaves."

The account continued through the taking of the Spanish ship by the Americans, after which the writer of the log gave the real story:

> "The Spanish captain then informed us that he was compelled by the slaves to say, that he was from Buenos Ayres, bound to Lima; that he was not from Buenos Ayres, but sailed on the 20th of December last from Valparaiso for Lima, with upwards of seventy slaves on board; that on the 26th of December, the slaves rose upon the ship, and took possession of her, and put to death eighteen white men, and threw overboard at different periods after, seven more; that the slaves had commanded him to go to Senegal; that he had kept to sea until his water was expended, and had made this port to get it; and also with a view to save his own and the remainder of his people's lives if possible, by run[n]ing away from his ship with his boat."

After this quotation from the ship's log, Captain Delano proceeded with his own account.

Delano was at pains to set out the handicaps under which he had been laboring, worst of which was that many of his crew had deserted at Botany Bay and their replacements had turned out to be convicts. He had made the best of the "peculiar situation," for the unquestioning obedience of the men during the taking of the *Tryal* demonstrated "the great utility of good discipline." Near the start of his account of his hours on the Spanish ship he noted also the good luck associated with his temperament on the day of the events: "They all looked up to me as a benefactor; and as I was deceived in them, I did them every possible kindness. Had it been otherwise there is no doubt I should have fallen a victim to their power. It was to my great advantage, that, on this occasion, the temperament of my mind was unusually pleasant. The apparent sufferings of those about me had softened my feelings into sympathy; or, doubtless my interference with some of their transactions would have cost me my life." Delano's narrative did not end with the taking of the ship and the restoration of as much order as could be established. Rather, musing over the fact that this was not the only time he was ever "treated with ingratitude, injustice, or want of compassion," he proceeded to tell the details of the perverse behavior toward him of the Spanish captain, Bonito Sereno, who, once safe in the port of Talcahuane, Chile, determined to find grounds to deny him any compensation for his rescue of the ship. After lengthy judicial procedures, the viceroy ordered Don Bonito to pay to Delano eight thousand dollars "for services rendered him." Neither the officer in his account in the log nor Delano in his subsequent account made any attempt to create suspense or mystery, and Delano's last pages were devoted not to narration of bloody revolt and heroic retaliation but to the Spaniard's ingratitude, which provoked this surly philosophical conclusion: "When I take a retrospective view of my life, I cannot find in my soul, that I ever have done any thing to deserve such misery and ingratitude as I have suffered at different periods, and in general, from the very persons to whom I have rendered the greatest services." Then Delano devoted the bulk of the chapter to a set of translations of depositions taken in the port of Talcahuane several months after the incidents at St. Maria (of which the longest deposition by far was that of the Spaniard, at this point spelled "Benito Cereno"). These were followed by the judicial sentence against the Negro slaves which was rendered in Concepción; then by the confirmation of the sentence rendered in Santiago, all in March of 1805. Delano appended an affidavit as to the accuracy of the translation, signed in Boston in 1808, then some comments introducing the final items, among which were grateful letters from the king of Spain's minister plenipotentiary to the United States and the Spanish consul at Boston.

Ignoring the petulance which marked parts of Delano's account, Melville, in accordance with his current preoccupation with the American national character, seized on Delano's finer aspects and from them fashioned his own Amasa Delano into an American type—one very different from

Benjamin Franklin, Paul Jones, and Ethan Allen. Melville's Delano was a man bluffly good-natured, practical, and resourceful but intellectually obtuse, naively optimistic, impervious to evil, a man who had gone through life as if he possessed no unconscious, and who, after having confronted what some would have found overwhelming evil, still tried to reduce evil to tales one might hear told but not tales that must be believed. Delano's American Protestant mind is quick to suspect Catholic Spaniards of being murderous, and from his own whaling months Melville would have known confirming stories of horrible events in these forsaken waters. An English whaler, *The Coquette*, for example (according to the ship's log in the Nantucket Historical Association), on 15 May 1821 spoke the *Offley* of London and learned that the Captain Hales who came as master of the ship from London "was with his Boats crew murdered on the Island of St Mary's on the coast of Chili, by some spaniards." The "Armorer was taken of[f] the beach the next day morning having 27 wounds in his body, he informed them of the murder" — before dying. Spaniards, being Catholic, in the minds of New England whalemen and sealers were treacherous, vengeful, and merciless, outdone in ferocity only by the Portuguese. Any sailor like Melville knew shocking true tales, true tales heightened into tall tales, true tales rejected as impossible.

In his most anxious moments, Melville's Delano held to the concept of a Providence above, but in his cosmology there was no devil below. Melville seized on the real Delano's comments on his temperament to warn the reader at the outset of his version of the story:

> Considering the lawlessness and loneliness of the spot, and the sort of stories, at that day, associated with those seas, Captain Delano's surprise might have deepened into some uneasiness had he not been a person of a singularly undistrustful good nature, not liable, except on extraordinary and repeated incentives, and hardly then, to indulge in personal alarms, any way involving the imputation of malign evil in man. Whether, in view of what humanity is capable, such a trait implies, along with a benevolent heart, more than ordinary quickness and accuracy of intellectual perception, may be left to the wise to determine.

This fictional Delano was a man who might blunder through evils where a more acute man would have been slaughtered when he perceived the truth of the situation quickly and betrayed his perception. The basic narrative, short but suggestive, proved easy for Melville to expand upon.

The New York *Herald* of 6 December 1847 had printed a story about Malay pirates who hid in the bottoms of their boats so approaching ships would think them unmanned and board them, only to be massacred. Knowing such reports, Melville made the narrator in *Mardi* suspicious of an apparently deserted craft: "I could not but distrust the silence that prevailed. It conjured up the idea of miscreants concealed below, and meditating treachery; unscrupulous mutineers—Lascars, or Manilla-men; who, having murdered the Europeans of the crew, might not be willing to let strangers depart unmolested" (ch. 19). In December 1854 or January 1855, Melville used his memory of stories about Malay pirates to show how the mysterious events on the fictional *San Dominick* had forced Amasa Delano to a limited acknowledgment: not that evil deeds were committed in a world governed by Providence, but that such deeds, at least, had been reported:

> On heart-broken pretense of entreating a cup of cold water, fiends in human form had got into lonely dwellings, nor retired until a dark deed had been done. And among the Malay pirates, it was no unusual thing to lure ships after them into their treacherous harbors, or entice boarders from a declared enemy at sea, by the spectacle of thinly manned or vacant decks, beneath which prowled a hundred spears with yellow arms ready to upthrust them through the mats. Not that Captain Delano had entirely credited such things. He had heard of them—and now, as stories, they recurred.

One can measure three stages of Melville's growth between the spring of 1847 and the end of 1854—roughly, since his marriage—in the gothic chill of the passage in *Mardi;* then in *Moby-Dick* the evocative imagery of yellow peoples of the immemorial East and in *Pierre* the image of hooded phantoms from the unconscious disembarking in Pierre's soul; and now the gothic revisited as an illustration of the psychological and metaphysical problem of evil in the universe.

The reader of Delano's *Voyages* encountered the straightforward two-page account, next Delano's longer account rhetorically focused to demonstrate his exemplary prudence and foresighted discipline, then the documents, which Delano despaired of summarizing and yet needed to include if he were to justify his grievances against the real Benito Cereno. There was no great tonal shock in going from the log to Delano to the documents. Melville's bold decision was to create a clash of tones by presenting two narratives, followed by a coda. The first narrative, greatly expanded from the accounts by the officer of the log and by Delano, held closely to the fictional Delano's mystification through his hours on the *San Dominick*, during which he repeats a pattern of suspicions-followed-by-reassurance, with progressively shorter periods in which suspicions can be allayed. A writer who had learned his craft as an oral storyteller, as the readers of *Typee* and *Omoo* always knew, Melville saw grand narrative possibility in the chance to follow a long narrative of all but unbearably ambiguous strangeness with the story told over again in a single deposition by Benito Cereno, in a voice that strove to be dispassionate, as befitted a legal statement. The reader would hear with great satisfaction what had really been going on at many of the most baffling moments in the first section, and learn the true history of the *San Dominick* before her appearance in the February fog at St. Maria. The date of Delano's experience, 1805, was the year of Admiral Horatio Nelson's victory and death at Trafalgar. Melville moved the story to February of 1799, so as to have it in the previous century, in the presidency of the first Adams, nearer the time of the building of great American frigates, including his own ship, the *United States* (1797), and, he might have remembered, not quite two years after the mutinies in the British navy at Spithead and the Nore.

For his work Melville needed a copy of Benito Cereno's deposition in pieces, for what he did with the deposition was to separate it into sections and double its length with his own fictional elaborations, making slight adjustments in the original to fit his additions. Cutting the pages from the bound volume would have made no sense, since he needed free use of the words on both sides of every leaf. Melville may have made it easy on himself by having Augusta copy out all of Benito Cereno's deposition from the end of Delano's chapter, perhaps after he had thoughtfully marked for her to skip some passages he was sure he would not need. Some marks in Melville's copy of *Mosses from an Old Manse* suggest that he was identifying passages there in August 1850 for Lizzie to copy into his essay on Hawthorne, rather than taking time to copy them out himself as he wrote, in which case she would have to copy them over anyway. Now, with the deposition, his process may have been to mark his short revisions directly in his copy of *Voyages*, so that Augusta could copy from the pages of the book. For his long additions, he most likely signaled in the book whenever Augusta was to stop copying from *Voyages* and to start copying from his new handwritten sheets, perhaps pinned to the page where a section was to be inserted.

The deposition section in "Benito Cereno," then, is a complicated and highly deliberate artifact, about half of it Melville's original composition, fused with the half copied and rather slightly adapted from the *Voyages*. Melville made great contributions: the image of Christopher Colon (Columbus) he added, cannibalism he added, the skeleton figurehead he added. Such contributions are not distinguishable without collation of the real depositions against Melville's deposition, for the Delano chapter provided dazzlingly evocative material for Melville to work from. In the original, for instance, the boatswain, Juan Robles, thrown overboard, keeps himself above water for a time, making acts of contrition, in his last words charging the Captain Cereno "to cause mass to be said for his soul, to our Lady of Succour" — reality, reported in Delano, and a touch of genius, we would think, if Melville had invented it.

Melville began his quiet coda with a portentous "If": "If the Deposition have served as the key to fit into the lock of the complications which precede it, then, as a vault whose door has been flung back, the San Dominick's hull lies open to-day." The Pauline mystery of iniquity was not opened to daylight, and Melville let the implications grow in the brief conclusion, pointing the moral that the American, confronted with evil in unescapable form, wanted only to turn over a new leaf, to deny and to forget the lesson he ought to have learned. Such an American might survive horrors (such as what Melville later said he had always thought of as the "atheistical iniquity" of slavery), but survive by being less than fully human, while — the persistent image patterns indicated — Europeans (including South American whites) might be broken by the weight of their knowledge of and complicity in human evil. The story was not only a commentary on the shallow cosmology and the rapid forgetting that characterized the emerging American type, but also upon Melville's own experiences in the last four years, when to survive and to function, day by day, required that he live in a state approximating absolute denial — denial of his missed payments to Stewart, at times also of his missed payments to Brewster, denial of the approaching deadline for repayment of principal and interest, denial of the impossibility of taking a consulship his family was trying to obtain for him, denial that he saw no way of becoming able to support his growing family. Melville knew something about surviving by denial, but (unlike his Captain Delano) he survived maimed, because his denial could never be, after all, absolute.

An ambiguous image of oppression has proved to be one of the most memorable parts of the story. The shield-like stern-piece, carved with the royal Spanish arms, is "medallioned about by groups of mythological or symbolical devices; uppermost and central of which was a dark satyr in a mask, holding his foot on the prostrate neck of a writhing figure, likewise masked." This image is enacted at the end of Amasa Delano's day on the *San Dominick*, just before the revelation: "the left hand of Captain Delano, on one side, again clutched the half-reclined Don Benito, heedless that he was in a speechless faint, while his right foot, on the other side, ground the prostrate negro." Oddly, the image had suggested itself to more than one thoughtful observer of the cruel irony at the heart of the American Republic. The British commentator "Mrs. Felton" in her 1843 *American Life* had seized on something similar as the appropriate motto and device for the United States: "Let this device be, the representation of a man wearing the cap of liberty, and brandishing a slave whip in his right hand, while his left displays the *Declaration of Independence;* his right foot at the same time resting on the naked back of a prostrate negro. — With this motto: 'All men are born free and equal.' Negro slavery is the foulest blot on the character of the American government." This similarity could be coincidental, even the foot on the back of the prostrate negro, but Melville may have seen it long before and carried in his mind Mrs. Felton's image of the great American moral conundrum.

This was an intensely controlled work, formally one of the most nearly perfect things Melville ever did (unlike "The Encantadas," which had trailed off after a dazzling start). To write it, he most likely left Lizzie and the children—and Augusta—in Boston as soon after Thanksgiving as he decently could and returned to Pittsfield to work through the isolation of December, as he had done with *Moby-Dick* in 1850, four years before, with *Pierre* in 1852, and with *The Isle of the Cross* in late December of 1853. Christmas was probably quiet, since Sarah Morewood had gone south—to Florida, as a few sick people already had learned to do. Melville had a long stretch for writing without serious interruption, but he went back for his family a few days into 1855, since he could not let a very pregnant woman with three small children travel unescorted home in the cars across Massachusetts. Back at Arrowhead, ebullient, in part because of a happy visit at Longwood, Melville ended a letter to Helen with a "spirited etching as a vignette," a lost piece of his artistry, a comical depiction of some denizen of the darker recesses of the depot where he caught the train to Pittsfield, perhaps the proprietor of a booth where traveling essentials such as a land version of hardtack were peddled. Helen in writing to Augusta on 14 January (about the week she became pregnant) exuberantly described Herman's letter and passed on an amusing account of George's eagerness to be a good sport. Her husband, "looking upon him (Herman) as a glorious leader," she wrote, had "followed his illustrious footsteps even to the counter of the Ship-Bread-Baker, where he purchased a half-barrel of the self same flinty abomination." Her description of the processes of breaking and chewing these adamantine biscuits is one of the best examples of her pyrotechnical style and must have given delight to her younger brother the writer, as her company had always given delight to her frequent escort, her older brother the orator. Helen, the queen of her own little parlor, had long forgiven Herman his rudeness when she broke into his writing time that day in November of 1850. Augusta copied "Benito Cereno" in late January and into February, before leaving for Boston, the first of three stops in a round of visits. Late January brought grimmer news from New York City. The *Herald*, before 25 January, printed a letter from Richard Bentley defending his behavior toward his current American authors—not including Melville. And about that time dear old Dr. Francis's twenty-two-year-old son and namesake died suddenly, just before qualifying as a doctor himself.

In February 1855 the question of lecturing came home to Melville, for

Richard Tobias (Toby) Greene was stealing his thunder by lecturing on "Typee; or Life in the South Pacific." The Toledo *Blade* said he delivered this "master piece" to "an overflowing house." Several Ohio papers praised his lectures, and on 9 March the Sandusky *Register* said he had "now gone East on a lecturing tour," giving "the people of Elyria his 'Typee' on Tuesday evening," the sixth. If Toby stole the topic that so far had been only Herman's, Herman would once again have been guilty of suicidal procrastination and Maria would in all reasonable minds stand vindicated in all matters for all time. While Toby was lecturing, Melville was writing, and passing some anxious moments about a copyist, for Augusta was visiting in Boston, then with Allan and Sophia in New York City, then in Albany, with Teny Van Rensselaer Townsend and Howard Townsend. There Allan wrote her on 1 March: "Hermans book (Potter) will not be out for a week yet. I was in at Putnam yesterday to get a copy but none were ready. He has sent a dedication to Bunker Hill Monument." Melville had seen the early construction work on the Bunker Hill Monument in his childhood, but it was completed only in 1842, a conspicuous new landmark, visible from afar when he arrived on the *United States*. This dedication was clearly a surprise to Allan, and he assumed that Augusta did not know about it, so the implication is that Melville had provided it for the book recently. (Although the dedication is dated 17 June 1854, that date had not appeared in the serial.) On 13 March Helen wrote Augusta: "What a fine time you have had in New York and Albany," such "a round of recieving and returning visits, dinner parties, evening parties"; she professed to be afraid Augusta would "never be able to sit down contentedly in the chimney corner at Pittsfield." By then, there was a new inhabitant of Arrowhead, Frances Melville, born 2 March; from the first she was called Fanny, like her aunt.

In her letter of 13 March Helen kept silent about her pregnancy but reported that she had declined an invitation to visit Sophia and Allan with her husband because she had promised Kate "to stay with her while John was at Pittsfield." Hoadley was to be gone for weeks to go over some plans with his old partner Gordon McKay. By now it was clear that John was not a man who cut clear of his moorings, whether his first wife's relations or his former business associates; good people stayed in his life much the way he accumulated and preserved beautiful books and works of art. Helen could count on seeing Sophia and Allan in the summer, when "no doubt they would come East on purpose, to see 'what sort of an angelic specimen of humanity would be entered for the prize of the silver porringer, in June'"—a reward Aunt Lucy was holding out for a next child named for her, since it was monogrammed. Lizzie had lost her chance for it again, by naming the baby Frances. Kate would "no doubt" win the porringer: "she has a weakness for silver that has 'come down from our ancient posterity,' and if it is a *boy*, will call it *Luci-fer*, rather than lose a choice peice of family plate." The best news, about her own pregnancy, she kept to herself, but passed on good word of Tom: "A ship which left the last *speaking* point from Calcutta, some days before Tom's, arrived last week, and judging from that he may be certainly expected from the 10th to the 20th of next month." John's stay in Pittsfield was a matter of some weeks, so he probably took a room in the village, but he must have been much at Arrowhead during the last weeks of winter, and therefore available as a prospective escort for Maria. In a postscript Helen asked, on behalf of herself and Kate, what "little Miss Fanny" preferred from the eastern aunts — a silver fork and spoon, or two dessert forks? Truth was, the whole family had a weakness for the spiritual benefits of ancestral silver, cherished for the original monograms and for the new monograms that asserted the links between the generations at salient occasions in their lives and deaths.

Priscilla was back, after less than a year in Galena, but her excessively mannered handwriting would have thwarted any compositor, so there was no thought of conscripting her as a copyist for Herman, and in any case she set about trying to support herself, advertising in the *Sun* her availability as a seamstress. Priscilla could not afford even the little brown cottage, but she owed nothing to anyone and in addition to her small income from her grandfather's estate she was earning a little interest on several hundred dollars she had loaned to her former employer in Canandaigua. Her presence was a reminder of the truth of Herman's own financial situation, and it did nothing to help his literary situation. Gansevoort, the whole family knew, would never have *needed* a copyist, and Gansevoort had heroically forced Allan to imitate his hand, so that despite a tendency to slur through his letters the younger brother could, at a need, still write like his oldest brother; by now everyone had accepted Herman's defective handwriting as incorrigible, not a personal tic but, because of its consequences, a family problem, although it was becoming clear that Augusta could not be enslaved forever as she had been in much of 1854.

After Bessie's birth Melville had failed to get *The Isle of the Cross* into print and had failed to obtain a consulship; what would he have done if he had received one — sell Arrowhead out from under his mother, his sisters, and his sons, in order to repay his loan to Stewart and to pay off the mortgage to Brewster? Before Frances's birth he had become helpless from rheumatism — and from guilt. With "Benito Cereno" far along, if not quite finished, Melville collapsed. In her memoir of him Lizzie recorded: "In Feb 1855 he had his first attack of severe rheumatism in his back — so that he was helpless." How long he was helpless is not clear. The timing of the attack suggests the possibility of *couvade;* perhaps increasing the possibility is the fact that

Kate also was pregnant, and bore her daughter on 30 May. Melville did not know Helen's secret—which indeed she did not confide to her sisters until May. Cousin Priscilla had remarked on the timing of the completion of *The Isle of the Cross* and Bessie's birth—but another close parallel is the composition and serialization of *Israel Potter* (the last installment in March) and its publication in book form about the time Fanny was born. In an allegory of the gestation process in "The Tartarus of Maids" (the second part of the diptych that he had submitted to *Harper's* the previous spring), Melville had made the narrator say: "But what made the thing I saw so specially terrible to me was the metallic necessity, the unbudging fatality which governed it." The burgeoning fetation was a reminder to him of the passing of months, including all the Mays and Novembers in which he missed interest payments to Stewart and the one September in which he had so far missed a payment to Brewster (paid three months late). The day of reckoning was approaching remorselessly—1 May 1856—and he was progressively less able to avert the disaster.

Herman made plans to go to New York but they fell through, for reasons which Augusta spelled out to Allan. On 30 March Allan replied, scant on details: "The explanation you make of Hermans non-appearance here is quite satisfactory though I could well wish it for some other less troublesome cause—We hope the new nurse answers fully well and that Mrs Johnson's not missed *too* much—& that Herman may be able to make his visit soon. Tell him we shall expect him till he comes." Presumably Herman did not come to town because he could not get out of bed, but Allan's paragraphing may indicate some relation between the "non-appearance" and the servant situation (as always a matter of entrances and fast exits), although Herman had not in the past been much hindered by such turmoil. At some point Allan had been deputed to do what Maria did best—go down to the docks, literally, and snag the likeliest Irish man or woman ("I am not at all sorry to have the matter of looking up servants pos[t]poned until Herman comes down"). Herman may have been delayed by a more "troublesome cause" than Lizzie's loss of the competent Mrs. Johnson (of course at the time she was most needed): he may still have been, at intervals, "helpless" from the rheumatism in his back. Perhaps the delay came because Augusta finished the copying of "Benito Cereno" after her peregrinations. In this letter Allan also promised to inform Elizabeth's aunt Martha Knapp Marett and her husband, Philip: "As to the Marets I shall endeavour to get Sophia to go down with me some evening before long, when the news of the new niece shall be duly announced." Such careful keeping up of this family tie was to prove of astonishing benefit to Herman and Lizzie's old age.

Also in the long term, it was personally important to Herman that Allan kept up his acquaintance with Sophia's old Bond Street neighbor, Dr. Francis, now her obstetrician, and with the Duyckinck brothers. The Duyckincks were absorbed in a gigantic enterprise which eventuated in the *Cyclopædia of American Literature* (1855) in two volumes, 676 pages in the first volume, 781 in the second. They wanted Herman Melville in it, and they needed the family's participation since no information could be gained directly from the subject. They allotted him three and a half pages. Avoiding *Moby-Dick* and *Pierre*, they gave one long sample of Melville's prose, "Redburn Contemplates Making a Social Call on the Captain in His Cabin," thereby saving them work, since they took it from the old file of their *Literary World*, but thereby immeasurably retarding among the users of the *Cyclopædia* Melville's recognition as a great prose writer. Allan cooperated with them, and during his visits to Clinton Place experienced an astonishing spectacle, one which various visitors saw. Henry T. Tuckerman described both the scene and the help Dr. Francis gave the workers: "They were in the habit of assorting the crude material of their work in large envelopes, and these were arranged in a long box divided into compartments. To examine, from time to time, add to, and discuss these memoranda, historical, biographical, and critical, was a friendly pastime to the Doctor." The raw materials of this almost all-absorbing three years' work of the Duyckinck brothers survive, in large part, in the Duyckinck Collection of the New York Public Library—correspondence with living writers of incalculable value. Included in Melville's folder is the opening of Allan's sketch: "Herman Melville was born at 55 Courtlandt street"—how like Allan, to attribute his own birth address to Herman: the world began in 1823, when he was born; if he drew you a map, it would start with where he was seated and ray out from there. Luckily, the Duyckincks simplified his sketch and gave no street address for Herman's birth.

If Melville came to New York in the spring it was to see his one or both of his publishers about new articles or a new book. Melville's hope, always, was for a bigger advance and reasonable terms (the "old terms" with the Harpers, which looked so good after the new terms for *Pierre*, and a higher percentage from Putnam). In March of 1855 things were changing for the worse, not better, though Melville may not have known it right away. At the center of the change was George W. Curtis, once a student at Brook Farm, now an artistic-looking fellow, luxuriant hair parted on the left, luxuriant sideburns before "sideburns" was a word, cleft chin. On 9 March Curtis told a friend "some secrets." Putnam had sold his magazine "to Dix & Edwards, or J. A. Dix & Co.," and Curtis had been offered "the exclusive Editorship" upon "the most flattering and advantageous" terms. He had declined, but remained "the friend of the Mag." He continued with a claim not justified by Melville's experience, that the magazine "under the new regime" would pay "better, nearly twice as well as before." What this meant for Melville, immediately, was the loss of an old acquaintance as publisher. The new proprietors of *Putnam's* (they kept the name) had no such link to Melville, and much as Curtis admired "Bartleby" (he wrote it into his *Prue and I*, in a passage serialized in *Putnam's*, July 1854), he was a young opportunist who had started a career by imitating Melville's travel-writing, and now was indifferent as to whether Melville would be consigned to the literary dustbin.

Israel Potter had been off Melville's hands since November, but *Putnam's* parceled the last big bundle out, so that the January 1855 issue contained the seventh installment, which earned Melville $44 ($10 of which he had drawn in advance, in November), and short February and March installments earned him $35 and $32.50. The book edition of *Israel Potter* was published by G. P. Putnam on or about 10 March, and the reviews were as kind as most comments on the monthly installments had been, but even favorably disposed reviewers could not get excited about the book when they had already read the serial. The strongest emotional reaction came from the writer in the New York *Norton's Literary Gazette and Publishers' Circular* (15 March), who read the book version through at one sitting, and found the interest to be "*intense*": "The reader is carried along from page to page, now admiring the quiet beauty of some bit of description, and owning, it may be, its truthfulness; now laughing at the Yankee shrewdness that is never outwitted, now filled with horror at the mad passions of fighting men, and taking as *real* each shifting scene that comes before him." On 17 March the *Morning Courier and New-York Enquirer* praised the style of *Israel Potter* as "remarkably manly and direct," in "pleasant contrast to that of Mr. Melville's last book," *Pierre*; it groused, nevertheless, that the book was "occasionally somewhat coarse for the refinement of our day; but so are *Robinson Crusoe* and *The Pilgrim's Progress*." The Boston *Post* in reviewing Charles Kingsley's *Westward Ho!* on 5 April made an extended comparison of that book to *Israel Potter* ("the American book, after making every proper deduction, is more truthlike, pithy, vigorous and readable than the English. But on the other hand, 'Amyas Leigh' is far superior to 'Israel Potter,' in scope, in brilliancy, in tone and in character"). The *Post* recognized the Kingsley book as "a much more elaborate production in every way" — close enough to what Melville himself had promised Putnam, but unkind in view of what it had said of Melville's more extended and ambitious efforts, *Mardi*, *Moby-Dick*, and *Pierre*.

For most reviewers, the appeal of *Israel Potter* lay in Melville's portraits of real Revolutionary figures. The Boston *Saturday Evening Gazette* (10 March) linked those portraits to Melville's improvement over his recent works: "Melville has recovered much of the vantage ground which he has lost since 'Omoo' and 'Typee.' Ethan Allen, Paul Jones and Benjamin Franklin are repictured with a master's hand, and the whole ground work is very able and skilfully wrought up." The New Bedford *Mercury* (12 March) declared: "Among the famous, Benjamin Franklin, and Capt. John Paul Jones, have a great part to play in this veritable history, which is a mixture of fun, gravity, romance and reality very taking from beginning to end." Melville's old enemy the Boston *Post* (15 March) was temperate in its remarks: "Mr Melville has made an interesting book from the facts at his command—a book, not great, not remarkable for any particular in it, but of a curt, manly, independent tone, dealing with truth honestly, and telling it feelingly. Its *Paul Jones* and *Benjamin Franklin*, to be sure, are not without a spice of Melville's former 'humors,' as they used to be called; but upon the whole, its style, sentiment and construction are so far above those of 'Pierre' and some of its predecessors, that we dislike to say one word against it." (The *Post* called for Melville's next book to be "quite as sensible, but be of wider scope and a larger subject"—an interesting observation about a book Melville had deliberately planned as non-weighty.) William Cullen Bryant's New York *Evening Post* (17 March) echoed the praise of the Revolutionary portraits. Only the May Boston *Christian Examiner and Religious Miscellany* dissented: "Dr. Franklin's homely wisdom and shrewd philosophy degenerate into ridiculous cant and officious imbecility; and the portraiture of Paul Jones seems almost equally infelicitous."

The review in the 17 March *Albion* (the New York paper for expatriate Britishers) liked Franklin and Paul Jones as "admirable sketches of character" but reserved its highest praise for Melville "on his own special element," the sea, and pronounced the "fight between *Serapis* and the *Bonhomme Richard*" as "a master-piece of writing; albeit some may deem its imagery too fanciful and far-fetched. Perhaps it is—but it helps the description wonderfully." (The *Christian Examiner and Religious Miscellany* on the contrary declared that a "battle so sanguinary and brutal in its whole character cannot form an attractive episode in a work of high art; and it is to be regretted that Mr. Melville should have dwelt so minutely upon its details.") The *Albion* warned its readers that Melville had not touched up his details about the Revolutionary War "to the exact taste of some British readers," but praised his "plain way of speaking" as it quoted a passage (from ch. 19): "Sharing the same blood with England, and yet her proved foe in two wars—not wholly inclined at bottom to forget an old grudge—intrepid, unprincipled, reckless, predatory, with boundless ambition, civilized in externals but a savage at heart, America is, or may yet be, the Paul Jones of nations." The *Albion* recommended "this short but expressive passage" as an antidote to "the terms wherein the famous 'Ostend Conference' recently heralded a scheme of spoliation, with a set of fine phrases about 'conscious rectitude' and 'approbation of the world.' Mr. Melville comes to the point."

Several reviewers recognized that Melville had based his "semi-romance" on "a bona fide autobiography, published years ago by the veritable Potter" *(Saturday Evening Gazette)*. Suspecting that *Typee* and *Omoo* had been more fictional than Melville confessed, the reviewer in *Norton's Literary Gazette and Publishers' Circular* decided that the story was not especially close to the source: "we believe that we are more indebted to him for this eager interest than to Israel's autobiography, which, he tells us, has been preserved almost as in a reprint." In May the reviewer in *Putnam's* suggested that the original was "not so rare as Mr. Melville seems to think." Writing with a copy before him, the reviewer disclosed that Melville had departed "considerably from his original," giving him a Berkshire birth and making him "acquainted with Paul Jones, as he was not." This reviewer was the only one to raise a question of literary ethics about Melville: "How far he is justified in the historical liberties he has taken, would be a curious case of literary casuistry."

A few London reviewers obtained copies of a pirated edition by George Routledge. On 5 May the *Economist* disparaged the book offhandedly: "It contains many wild adventures, some of them graphically told, and will amuse adventurous youth; but it is far from being a model of good taste or good writing. Mr Melville's talents for narration, particularly for the narration of sea adventures, are well-known; but in the present book his talents hurry him into excessive exaggeration." On 13 May *Lloyd's Weekly* disliked Melville's "extravagance, nay violence of expression," but recognized "a book of considerable merit, a story that fixes the reader at the first page and holds him to the end." That was enough: "What higher praise can be awarded to a story-teller? It is not so romantic as the lovely tale of Typee, with all its fascinating fiction; so fascinating that we are fain to think it as true, as real as *terra firma*." The 2 June *Athenæum* disparaged *Israel Potter* casually: "Mr. Melville tries for power and commands rhetoric,—but he becomes wilder and wilder, and more and more turgid in each successive book," as in a passage from "In the City of Dis" (ch. 24). The *Weekly Chronicle* of the same day observed keenly: "The book leaves the impression of having been carefully and purposely rendered common-place. You feel that the author is capable of something much better, but for a freak is resolved to curb his fancy and adhere to the dustiest routine." None of the English reviews yet found made any mention of Melville's *The Whale* or *Pierre*, and none treated him as seriously as many of the reviewers of *The Whale* had done. The English reviews had no measurable effect on Melville's rapidly fading reputation. In July, in Paris, the *Revue des deux mondes* gave fifty-one pages to

Emile Montégut's extended review and summary, "Israel Potter, une légende démocratique américaine" — with unknown consequences for Melville's reputation there.

Amid the American reviewing of *Israel Potter*, Melville's diptych "The Paradise of Bachelors and the Tartarus of Maids" at last appeared in the April *Harper's*, to which, on the twelfth, Melville renewed his subscription for three years. Nothing about the initial comments on that story or in the American reception of *Israel Potter* impressed on G. W. Curtis the need to be respectful toward Melville after he submitted the manuscript of "Benito Cereno" in early April. On 17 April, in a letter written in Providence to Joshua A. Dix, the new owner, Curtis professed himself "anxious to see Melville's story, which is in his best style of subject," an adventure story set in the Pacific. On the nineteenth he reported: "Melville's story is very good. It is a great pity he did not work it up as a connected tale instead of putting in the dreary documents at the end. — They should have made part of the substance of the story. It is a little spun out, — but it is very striking & well done: and I agree with Mr Law [Frederick Law Olmsted] that it ought not to be lost." Curtis's snap judgment on the documents ("dreary") may have been conditioned by the great number of handwritten pages they occupied, but it proved to be a common reaction. The fallacious assumption that the deposition section was the product of a fatigued imagination passed into Melville scholarship, with no one pointing out that half of the deposition was Melville's own prose, brilliantly interspersed into parts of the original. Feeling his oats at the outset of a brilliant career as a magazinist, Curtis made another comment as he returned the manuscript the next day to Dix in New York: "He does everything too hurriedly now." Bentley had said the same thing.

"Tombo First Officer of the 'Meteor' " (as Helen called him) docked in Boston Harbor in late April. He had onerous duties on board the *Meteor* even when he stayed at Helen and George's, so that Helen, in writing to Augusta around 20 April, said she felt she barely saw him. Remembering the saga of Augusta's washing, mending, packing, and strapping of trunks, Helen assured her that this time she had taken care of Tom's " 'shore traps' " and would mend any of "his white shirts" and other parts of his "citizen's wardrobe." But for once the world did not stop at Tom's arrival: Herman had been very sick; Lizzie was having trouble keeping a reliable nurse for the new baby; Kate was in her eighth month of pregnancy; Helen was concerned about Kate even while keeping the secret of her own pregnancy; Allan and Sophia were subdued, recovering from the loss of a daughter whom Tom never got to see; and even "Winyar" (as Tom spelled Winyah) was preoccupied with the presence of Richard Jr., born 23 April (later the husband of Annie Morewood, born the previous year). Tom brought great gifts — a muslin shawl, a feather boa, collars, square mats, pots of ginger, down muffs, coral, shells—many things for particular recipients, many to be shared. Helen asked to keep Augusta's and Fanny's coral and shells until they had a place of their own: "The parlor at Arrowhead is well stocked with knick knacks, and they would only be in the way." A realist, Helen added that she was not writing to "Mother dear herself" for the best possible reason: "when her baby-boy is at Arrowhead, she wont think of anybody else." She would keep her secret until Maria could focus for a moment on the eldest daughter she tended to take for granted, the one who had unselfishly helped to mother the fatherless younger Melville children in the 1830s.

Tom stayed at Arrowhead only briefly before going to New York by the beginning of May—the day Herman defaulted on yet another payment to Stewart. Maria could not go with him because she needed to be with Kate during the last month of her pregnancy, and around the end of April Lizzie suddenly asserted herself and asked John to escort her as far as Boston on his return to Lawrence, where Helen was keeping up Kate's spirits as best she could. Maybe Lizzie thought of Allan and Sophia's Julia Maria, dead before any of the Arrowheads saw her, and wanted to present her Frances to her parents sooner than she usually did. Helen shows how sudden Lizzie's decision was: "I was exceedingly surprised to hear of Lizzie's intended journey, but have no doubt it will be of great service to her." This is from Helen's letter to Augusta and Fanny on 2 May: "Tomorrow it seems there is to be a precious freight of Melville's [John Hoadley, Lizzie, and baby Frances] consigned to the tender mercies of the dilapidated Pittsfield Rail Road—poor Kate—she killed, maimed, bruized, mangled, and otherwise injured John several times between his departure and the arrival of his letter dated Arrowhead. And now I suppose she will inflict the same tortures upon him and herself when she thinks he is on the way home. She is sure some accident will happen unto him." The conclusion of her letter was private, to be kept from Maria, whom she meant to tell in person:

> {Private} Kate has almost done sewing, all but her two best dresses which she has wisely left for the last, and the wee things look sweetly. And now what do you think?—I have not told you before, because I did not want Mama to know it before she left Pittsfield—for I think of—beginning such a wardrobe for myself, as it will be wanted perhaps about the middle of October, and for your shares, dears, I think of sending you two small sized dresses, Augusta's to be worked the pattern she has for Kate, and yours Miss Fanny I will draw for you.
>
> I dont know darlings whether you will be glad or sorry of this bit of news; but I am beginning to be glad, for George seems to be so much pleased with

the prospect, and takes such care of my diet, exercise, employments, & recreations, that he bothers me to death. Expect an infant Hercules, or a goddess Diana, nothing less strong and active, to view for the first time the change of the leaf this autumn.

You must have your hands more than full now, sweet ones, so there is no hurry for your contributions to my little collection, I will send you the dresses (all cut out, and you can take a stitch a day) when Lizzie goes back.

This was characteristically Helen, biding her time, thinking of others, and possessor, like her older brother, Gansevoort, and her younger brother Herman, of her own prose voice. Reliable as always, Helen was back in Boston to see to Tombo before he sailed on 12 May for San Francisco and the East Indies. Maria stayed a while with her before going on to face the suffering in Lawrence which Helen described to Augusta around 22 May: "Poor Kate writes in the doleful dumps, such an excruciating tooth ache, and pain in her back almost all the time, and her feet & hands are so swollen she can take no comfort—I wish it were well over with, and she were dandling the little Hoadley on her knee."

Summer was coming, but Maria's blood was as thin as the much-missed Tom's ever was, and there had been only two days when they could do without fires ("Mama sits bending over the grate with her book, as if it were January instead of almost June.") Four months pregnant, Helen did not feel she could visit her sisters. Since George worked so hard, he needed her to be there when he came home: "If he ever went a pleasuring or even spoke cross or even short to me, I could find it in my heart to leave him for a while and let him feel my loss, but he never does; and so unless the hot weather is more than I can *safely* bear, I shall feel it my *duty* as well as pleasure to remain here, unless he can take a holiday himself & accompany me to Arrowhead." Fanny responded to this subtle plea and went to stay with Helen in the hottest weather, and meantime the long wait at Lawrence came to an end with the birth of Maria Gansevoort Hoadley on 30 May. This was plainly too imposing a name, and the family began calling the girl Minnie, just as Allan and Sophia's firstborn (resoundingly named in full for her grandmother, Maria Gansevoort Melville) was rarely called anything but Milie.

John was immoderately pleased with Minnie ("Mr Hoadley is quite in raptures with his daughter," Maria reported to Augusta on 7 June), but in early June the baby and Kate were subjected to a siege of medical practice, or malpractice, the doctor being of the opinion that the baby was not taking enough milk and prescribing the borrowing of the child of the neighbor Mr. Storrow's gardener to drain the excess milk. This overgrown five-month-old, a prodigy born with four teeth, was horrifying to the delicate Kate. By the twenty-third Maria reported a new disease ("I never heard of the '*red canker*' in all my baby experience") and a new treatment, fresh goat's milk, while the doctor insisted on keeping Kate's own milk fresh by heroic measures ("Mary the Cook, comes up *five times* a day to draw her breasts"). Despite all this, Kate and the baby survived, and in the midst of these problems Maria remained concerned about life at Arrowhead, which Kate began looking forward to visiting, with her baby. Maria was surprised at news from home that young Catherine Gansevoort (Uncle Peter's daughter, born in 1838) had been enrolled at Eliza Sedgwick's school, and was pleased that Peter and Susan had visited Arrowhead when they were depositing her at Lenox. (Now called Kitty, this cousin became the great family archivist, Kate Gansevoort Lansing.) Maria in writing Augusta on 16 June wanted to know just how far her brother had unbent from his stiffness toward them all: "Did your uncle or aunt desire you to call upon her or express a wish that she should visit you at Arrowhead?" Soon "Fanny Augusta Herman & the children" (the boys?) came to see her, according to Kitty's diary, and on hearing of the visit Maria wanted a detailed account. This seemingly excessive concern reveals just how estranged from her brother Maria had felt, and in fact Kitty's going to Lenox was the start of the Melville family's relationship with her as her own person (at this point, something of a snobbish chit) and as the unwitting instrument of their rapprochement with Uncle Peter. The rapprochement came not by openhearted admissions of wrongdoing and generous expressions of love but simply by default: no one was willing to tell the girl why they were estranged or to enlighten her when she expressed naive wonder, now and then, that she was not well acquainted with her long-dead Uncle Leonard's children, either.

From Lawrence on 7 June Maria was full of other commentary: she was glad Lizzie was "much benefitted by her stay at Boston" and that "miss Fanny" was growing fast; she wished she had some of the fish Augusta had caught in Melville Lake; she thought the family should have awakened Bessie and Stannie so they could meet their Grand-uncle Peter; she hoped the garden seeds had not been "planted in vain" ("a few warm days will bring forth those that have kept their peace"); "Herman should get half a (½) dozen lb of Halibut once a week it is much cheaper than meat, & is delicious when cold dressed like Lobster"; she worried about how "dear Herman" was and about how much Augusta was copying for him; she wanted to know who if anyone Lizzie had found "to assist her, with the care of the children"; she was titillated at Sarah's return ("I suppose Mrs Morewood has infused new life to you all both at Broadhall & Arrowhead") and supercilious about her flirtatiousness ("How like M^{rs} M — the cinder in the eye — &c — The Doc^t attentive — ").

This compulsive commentary was symptomatic, for Maria in the 7 June letter was deeply concerned that life go better at Arrowhead. Hoadley's sister Hattie was marrying a Mr. Wayne: "his father gave him one quarter of the store, their, or rather his share of the proceeds have been $5,000, hitherto, & their idea is, that will support them comfortably." Maria continued: "I think it may, I should like no less myself, & would we not have a nice Rockaway, & a pair of lively horses at Arrowhead, and a useful trim looking man, & I am affraid to think any more in this pleasant way, for I fear it may be vain thinking, but this I must add—that our dear Herman, would be not so dependant upon his pen—but go abroad if he wished to, & then come home to be at leisure to write all about his travels." Tired of giving sensible advice, tired of worrying about asparagus that once planted would spring up again every year, tired of worrying about the cost of meat, tired of worrying about newspaper aspersions on her son, tired of being the strong "only Parent" (as she signed herself to Allan on 20 August 1838 and 21 December 1840), Maria let herself melt for a moment into fantasy. Who had a better right?

[12]

The Confidence Man's Masquerade
Melville as National Satirist, June 1855–January 1856

Mortgage is certain to prove in the general, what the word signifies, a *death-gage* to the property upon which it is fastened, and to the prosperity of the man who allows it to be fastened upon his estate.

Melville draws a curved line along this sentence in his copy of
A History of the County of Berkshire

JUST AFTER MELVILLE got "Benito Cereno" off his hands, the Albany *Evening Journal* (28 April) printed "The Original Confidence Man in Town. — A Short Chapter on Misplaced Confidence." Anybody who brooded about Augustine on Original Sin might have been caught, as Melville was, by this headline, perhaps used quite innocently in reminding readers of the rogue who after his arrest in Manhattan in the summer of 1849 had been dubbed "the confidence man" from his ploy of asking not just for a watch or money but for the victim's trust. Americans had seized on the neologism and overnight had made it part of the language. Now, out of jail, and nowhere near as old as Satan, the rascal was up to his former trick, this time in Albany:

> He called into a jewelry store on Broadway and said to the proprietor: "How do you do, Mr. Myers?" Receiving no reply, he added "Don't you know me?" to which Mr. M. replied that he did not. "My name is Samuel Willis. You are mistaken, for I have met you three or four times." . . . "I guess you are a Mason," — to which Myers replied that he was — when Willis asked him if he would not give a brother a shilling if he needed it. By some shrewd management, Myers was induced to give him six or seven dollars.

On 5 May the Springfield *Republican* reprinted the item, and on the same day the Albany *Evening Journal* reported that the files of the *National Police Gazette* had been searched to complete a "Brief History of the Confidence Man." To assure that the man who had robbed Mr. Myers was indeed the Original Confidence Man, "William Stokely, a New York policeman," had been taken to the Albany Jail to identify "Samuel Willis." Stokely thereupon had spoken authoritatively: "Here is No. 1, the Original Confidence Man. I arrested him the first time in New-York, and afterward in New-Orleans." This was suggestive wording for anyone with a close knowledge of the Bible and an ironical cast of mind, and Melville began speculating on the varieties of confidence men at work in the modern world, ranging from the Father of Lies (who had asked Eve to have confidence that the apple was good, and who still walked to and fro upon the earth) to the wealthy gregarious admirer from Lansingburgh who had "induced" him to accept a friendly loan to further his ambitions for his whaling book.

Melville's attention had been elsewhere during the flurry of publicity about the confidence man in 1849, that hot New York summer when he wrote two long books. Forced, these last years, to put into abeyance his grand and grandiose literary aspirations, Melville was now ready to undertake some specifically national criticism. He would place some peculiarly American fools on a Mississippi steamship (the setting of the book he would write about the Confidence Man) making the voyage down the Father of Waters from St. Louis toward New Orleans. To gull his shipload of fools Melville assembled a notable gallery of rogues who had been going to and fro on the face of America — "Samuel Willis," P. T. Barnum (who displayed live Yankees and stuffed mermaids at the American Museum on Broadway in Manhattan), Ralph Waldo Emerson (the man who denied the existence of evil or even pain as well as the man who preached a high-minded notion of friendship that precluded "rash personal relations"); and other representative men of his time — not omitting Tertullus D. Stewart. What united them was that they all required confidence from their victims. Melville's purpose becomes clearer if the phrase is pronounced "the *confidence* man," as it had been pronounced in 1849 when the term was new — the swindler whose distinctive ploy is the demand that the victim place confidence in him.

Just as T. B. Thorpe had done in "The Big Bear of Arkansas," and Dickens and others had done, Melville could revel in the heterogeneity of the cast of characters assembled on a floating theater of a Mississippi steamboat. In chapter 2 Melville summarized the passengers as "an Anacharsis Cloots congress of all kinds of that multiform pilgrim species, man," leaving unspecific what tribunal they thought they could bare their grievances before. His interblended varieties of mortals possessed a "Tartar-like picturesqueness; a sort of pagan abandonment and assurance" like that of Ethan Allen: "Here reigned the dashing and all-fusing spirit of the West, whose type is the Mississippi itself, which, uniting the streams of the most distant and opposite zones, pours them along, helter-skelter, in one cosmopolitan and confident tide." Among the books that had celebrated that tide was Timothy Flint's *The History and Geography of the Mississippi Valley* (1828). Melville may have seen it in one edition or another, or may have seen only a reprint of portions of it in the *Description of Banvard's Panorama of the Mississippi River*, a pamphlet published in Boston in 1847, when the seemingly endless canvas was being unscrolled before astonished theater audiences—the panorama proving a truly American art form (big, none-too-subtle, and alluring the general public), and this particular panorama celebrating the greatest river in the greatest country in the world. Another of the books was by Judge James Hall, whose *The Wilderness and the War-Path* had been in the same Wiley & Putnam series as *Typee*. In Hall's *Sketches of History, Life, and Manners in the West*, Melville found a sober account of how John Moredock of Illinois, his family slain by red men, had become a dedicated Indian-hater, pledged to the eradication of any Indians he encountered. From 1840 Melville remembered the diabolical names of points on the Mississippi (such as the Devil's Bake-Oven) and was reminded of more by his small store of books on the West. His own memories of the Mississippi by this time may have been mingled with other images, such as those in the great panorama that he may have seen when it played in Boston in 1846.

For his satire Melville adopted a self-consciously literary mode. The title as it appears in the Dix & Edwards contract is "The Confidence-Man: His Masquerade," the "His" the old attempt at representing the possessive, as in *Purchas His Pilgrimage* (1613), one of the great travel books—in other words, *Samuel Purchas's Pilgrimage*. Any lover of old books would understand that the title meant "The Confidence-Man's Masquerade." Rather than relying solely on contemporary accounts of American life, Melville infused his tour of the American character with the spirit of British satires of the previous century such as Swift's *Gulliver's Travels* and Goldsmith's *Citizen of the World*. Melville modeled his ironically over-explicit chapter titles (e.g., "In Which a Variety of Characters Appear") on those in eighteenth-century novels such as *Tom Jones* and *Amelia*. The full title and the chapter titles constituted strong warning that this was no mere set of sketches of Mississippi roguery. Melville's twist on the hyperbole of journalists who possessed (like his Captain Delano) characteristically short historical memories was to cast the quotidian trickster into the oldest mode, the serpent who had beguiled Eve into woman's and man's first disobedience that brought about the Fall of Man. Instead of writing a modern sermon on the text of what Jesus would do if he came into the world again, he would write an old-fashioned allegory on what was happening every day as the Father of Lies moved about in confident America. As Hawthorne had done in several of his tales, Melville would rely on serpent imagery to hint at the identity of his shape-changing hero, and he would infuse thickly through his account biblical echoes which might still resonate even in modern ears, although business talk was drowning out the sound of biblical texts. As the Mississippi steamboat ironically named the

Fidèle passed some of the diabolically named terrain, the Devil would move about the ship of fools, spreading confidence, the Father of Lies making himself at home on the Father of Waters.

What happens on the *Fidèle* is relentless chicanery, quotidian and cosmic. A mysterious mute in cream-colors has his "advent" at the waterside in St. Louis on the morning of an April Fools' Day. Garbed to suggest Jesus, and traversing the deck with mottoes from 1 Corinthians 13 placarded on his slate, he is the Devil, who in the course of the book playfully saunters on the deck of the American ship of fools. He assumes eight disguises which are linked by a series of double entendres (the second, a Negro cripple, insists [ch. 3] that the "others" know him "as well as dis poor old darkie knows hisself," as they do, since they are the same) and by an array of serpent imagery and biblical allusions which project the most trivial conversations into a metaphysical realm. Except for his role as the unfortunate man with the mourning weed, in which he sets up a victim for later plying, the Devil comes preaching confidence in man, nature, universe, and God, knowing that the most tranquilized are the most vulnerable. In a series of conversations, some pungently colloquial, some abstractly formal, he explores among the passengers varieties of gulls, skeptics, and even lowercase confidence men (such as the Alabama swindler Charles Arnold Noble or the philosophical crook Mark Winsome). His object is not only to procure a little money and enter a few souls in his satanic transfer-book, it is to demonstrate in fair play that Christianity is not alive in America. Only two of the passengers are at all worthy to oppose his blandishments — the "invalid Titan" (ch. 17), who exhausts his energy in a single physical attack on the Devil in the role of the herb-doctor, and Pitch, the Missouri bachelor, who except for one softheaded moment *sticks* to his theological convictions despite the blandishments of the Devil as representative of an employment agency. True Christians may just possibly exist, however; Charlie Noble tells of "the Indian-hater *par excellence*" (ch. 26), a soul peeping out but once in an age, and John Moredock stands as an Indian-hater (or Devil-hater) *manqué*. At the end, in his guise as the Cosmopolitan, the Devil extinguishes a lamp that symbolizes the Old and the New Testaments, relegating Christianity to the row of religions that once burned but now swing in darkness. Midnight being past, the playfulness is over, and the Cosmopolitan ominously leads an old man out of the gentleman's cabin into the darkness of the deck.

Now ready to write a truth-telling national criticism to be infused month by month into the body politic, as a serialized series of boluses, Melville reckoned without G. W. Curtis, who had full authority at *Putnam's* as Briggs had never had. The letter is missing, but Melville wrote proposing to Dix & Edwards that they serialize *The Confidence-Man* in *Putnam's*, hoping to enter into another period of several months in which he could have a small regular income then afterward a little more money from book publication. It is not clear that he sent a sample. From Providence on 29 June 1855 Curtis wrote to Joshua A. Dix: "I should decline any novel from Melville that is not extremely good." Curtis was basing his rejection partly on his recent doubts about whether to accept Melville's "The Bell-Tower." On 18 June he had told Dix he was rejecting the story: "Melville & Cozzens have *not* passed muster. I'll send them tomorrow with Clark's Birds, with reasons." The next day he had second thoughts: "'The Bell Tower' is, after all, too good to lose. — It is picturesque & of a profound morality." He had "meant to say no," and had so written to Dix, but he had been converted. He would, however, make "some erasures." He reminded Dix, and himself: "In reading 'The Bell Tower' you must remember that the style is *consistently* picturesque. It isn't Addisonian nor is it Johnsonese. — Neither is Malmsey wine, Springwater." Having overcome his resistance to this story, Curtis still was as exasperated as ever with the deposition section of "Benito Cereno," as he showed when he advised on scheduling from Newport on 31 July. *Putnam's* should start running it, since they had already paid for it, but — he lamented — "I should alter all the dreadful statistics at the end. Oh! dear, why can't Americans write good stories. They tell good lies enough, & plenty of 'em." Curtis was ready to praise what he liked and welcome it into *Putnam's*, but he had other contributors in hand, and did not like clogging the magazine with pieces from a man who did "everything too hurriedly now."

Putnam's scheduled "The Bell-Tower" for the August issue and promptly paid Melville $37.50 for it. Hoadley wrote a shrewd appreciation on 29 July to Maria: "Herman's story of 'the Bell Tower,' I read night before last, by the dim lamp light of our chamber, with frequent reminding from Kate that it was time to go to bed, — that I should spoil my eyes, — that she was tired and wanted to get to sleep, — Strangely fascinating! — The first words betrayed the Author, but the wild, mysterious narrative, and the stately, solemn, *almost* strutting, character of the style, would lure to the end any who read the first lines." For all Dix's rejection of the chance to serialize *The Confidence-Man*, Melville sent his "I and My Chimney" on to *Putnam's*, and it seems to have been part of a pile of manuscripts that reached Curtis in Newport on 31 July. If so, he was slow in rendering judgment, but on 7 September he called it "a capital, genial, humorous sketch," and "thoroughly magazinish." He added: "If you can squeeze Melville into Oct. it would be great" — meaning "Benito Cereno," which was serialized in the October, November, and December issues. On 14 September he wrote when returning "the *Mss*": "The Benito Cereno is ghastly & interesting. How much will it make?" (that is, how many pages in *Putnam's*).

As the months passed in 1855 and early 1856, Melville made *The Confidence-Man* into a dazzlingly comprehensive indictment of American confidence. He turned on its head Dickens's premise in the "Concluding Remarks" of his *American Notes for General Circulation* (1842): "One great blemish in the popular mind of America, and the prolific parent of an innumerable brood of evils, is Universal Distrust." On the contrary, Melville saw Americans as cheerily confident. The book turns on the American willingness to accept satanic reassurance that all is well—amid such signs to the contrary as Bleeding Kansas. Melville's purpose can be clarified by rephrasing some of his topics in the light of the formula "nothing is amiss." The Devil's purpose is best served if he can persuade his victims that there is nothing amiss in an America where Wall Street is a model for solving problems such as world hunger. Nothing is amiss when America's wars (especially unconstitutional ones, undeclared Executives' Wars like Polk's against Mexico) are waged only against distant nations of smaller, browner peoples, and are always gloriously successful. Nothing is amiss when America's legal system doles out evenhanded justice to poor and rich alike, and when the nation's press is devoted to searching out and publishing the Truth, misled neither by mobs nor presidential messages. Nothing could be wrong with a country where all fiction is designed to reassure American readers that there are no dangerous depths and ambiguities either in human nature or in the universe (instead, the Devil recommends "serene and cheery books, fitted to inspire love and trust"—ch. 5); where all physical ills (which are probably only imagined, in any case) can be cured by a stroll in a park or a patented pill (organic, of course, Nature's own), or a few moments in the all-soothing Protean easy chair; where moralists assure every citizen that Truth can be felt intuitively by anyone without a strenuous exposure to ethically ambiguous choices; where the virtue most in demand in society is amenability, geniality, and where self-help and group-help programs devoted to revealing human nature on fixed principles (palmistry, physiognomy, phrenology, psychology) can expeditiously alleviate anything apparently anomalous or bothersome in human behavior; where popular philosophy (including Transcendentalism) will at all costs avoid being too sober; and where adherents of the more up-to-date religious sects, like the "Come-Outers," in the interests of free development of personal consciousness will let their inmost secrets hang out for public scrutiny. Melville himself, offering the norm of skepticism and holding up the Bible and the Greek and Roman classics against popular culture, was just the sort of man the Devil did not want on the scene, one of the fellows "who, whether in stocks, politics, bread-stuffs, morals, metaphysics, religion—be it what it may—trump up their black panics in the naturally-quiet brightness" (ch. 9). Melville was at last ready for the role of

American prophet, and had no doubt decided that as far as the interest of the story was concerned, Dix & Edwards (like Putnam before them) could leave that to him, the author of *Typee*. He would tell truth and shame the Devil, as Hotspur had demanded in *Henry IV, Part 1*. Hotspur is relevant, for during Melville's years at Pittsfield a lover of literature arrived at Arrowhead on a curious pilgrimage. Lured by journalistic testimony as to the high density of authors in the Berkshires, the enterprising seeker carried an album through the region confidently gathering autographs from celebrities. Melville signed the autograph book with a resolute determination not to surrender, not (as in the "capital" story of his awaiting publication) to allow his chimney to be razed: "Tell Truth, and shame the Devel."

No documents survive to chart Melville's progress on *The Confidence-Man* or to show whether Augusta had any relief from her duties as copyist. Arrowhead was hospitable as usual — Sophia was there, presumably with her daughters, in late July, if not at other times. Melville wrote, more or less steadily, despite pain, or in intervals between the worst pain, first from rheumatism in the back, which rendered him helpless in February 1855, then in June from an attack of sciatica (around the time he wrote that "genial, humorous sketch" "I and My Chimney"). "Our neighbor in Pittsfield Dr O. W. Holmes attended & prescribed for him," Elizabeth Melville wrote in her memoir of her husband. Joe Smith said the same in his little biography written for the Pittsfield *Evening Journal* (the 16 December 1891 installment), just after Melville's death: "Dr. Holmes visited him with fraternal tenderness, incidentally of course giving him his best medical advice, without — that also, of course — intruding upon the province of the local practitioner." Melville suffered months from excruciating, paroxysmal attacks of pain along the course of the branches of the sciatic nerve through the hips and down the back of the thighs. Joe Smith described Melville as late as 7 September as just recovering from a severe illness — of three months or so, apparently. Small wonder that he seemed to be what Dr. Holmes's son the jurist recalled in the 1920s as having seen in his father's study about this time — a "rather gruff taciturn man." Whether Holmes helped or not, Melville got a little better, and went about his work, knowing that the secret of his debt to Stewart could not be kept many months longer.

In an effort to escape his annual catarrh, Lemuel Shaw made his way to the wilds of Hyannis the last day of July, shepherded by his son Sam. After suffering a night at the primitive hotel (no soap or looking-glass, no way of washing thoroughly), they went on to the judge's home town, Barnstable, where Sam reported (on Herman's birthday) that it was cool, "with sea breezes." The family was still gathering at Arrowhead. Maria was home from the East for Sophia's stay there, and Allan's visits (these were true week-end visits, before, thanks to the railway system, that useful word was invented in England). Probably Cousin Kate Gansevoort Curtis from Brooklyn was there with Sophia, for one of the Kates was at Saratoga Springs with Allan and Sophia on 12 August. At Saratoga Springs Allan and Sophia got their money's worth by staying in a private house, as Sophia wrote her sister Rachel Barrington on 12 August, repeating Allan's judgment that "it is as good as we should get at the United States [Hotel], where we should be unable to get anything to eat unless we bribed the waiters." Then the next day they rode the train a few miles to Gansevoort where they paid a duty call on Uncle Herman and Aunt Catherine, the strong-minded woman to whom Allan frequently compared Sophia. Augusta had already made an affectionate gesture that year with her valentine "To Mr. & Mrs. H. Gansevoort," the "dearest friends," at "Cottage Home, and Manor Hall." Apparently Augusta had been received at the "Manor Hall" during her years at Lansingburgh, long before. Milie, young as she was, later recalled the scene at the Manor House in 1855: "One summer we went up to Saratoga and while there we went to Gansevoort to see Uncle Herman and Aunt Catherine. I remember how her hand shook as she handed me a plate of biscuit, and how I thought she must be very old." Catherine was not only very old, she was dying. Allan's reports must have stirred his mother to change her plans.

Cousin Priscilla was much at Arrowhead, judging from John Hoadley's greeting in a letter he wrote to Maria on 5 August. In that letter Hoadley issued to Maria and the household this travel advisory: "And now I have to say, that we intend to start for Arrowhead, on friday of this week [10 August], to pass friday night at Clinton, and to reach your hospitable mansion, D[ieu]. V[olant]. on saturday. — Until then, Adieu! — Kate sends love, — Mother & Hatty unite in it, — Love to Augusta, Lizzie, Fanny, — Helen, — Sophia, if still with you, — Herman, and the children. — Remember me to Priscilla." Kate and John arrived as Allan and Sophia went back to the city. Herman may have visited Allan and Sophia soon after they returned to New York, for on 28 August 1855 his Harper account was charged for two books about the Isthmus of Panama, his old friend Robert Tomes's *Panama in 1855. An Account of the Panama Railroad, of the Cities of Panama and Aspinwall, with Sketches of Life and Character on the Isthmus* and Ephraim George Squier's *Waikna: or, Adventures on the Mosquito Shore*, with sixty illustrations. The Panama Railroad had been completed, after five years and thousands of lost lives of cheap labor from the Orient, Europe, and the Caribbean.

On Friday, 7 September 1855, a magnificent day, the Morewoods held a fancy dress picnic ("a startling novelty in this region") at Melville Lake (that "exquisite little gem of a lake," Joe Smith called it in his account in the *Berkshire County Eagle* of the fourteenth). On the east side of the lake the

Morewoods had set up tables and laid a platform for dancing. Guests began arriving at ten in the morning, and by noon most of the guests were there, as was the popular Hodge's band. In his desire to please his readers, Smith itemized dozens of costumes. He punned his way through his description of Lizzie: "Mrs. H[erman] M[elville] as Cypherina Donothing, in a costume of cyphers was no cypher, and although continually adding up cyphers to get at a sum of cyphers, found naught to amuse her; and was one of the most successful characters of the day, although she did nothing well." Smith identified "Miss A[ugusta] M[elville] as a market woman of the olden time, in a red cloak and hood," a sight which led impudent young Kitty Gansevoort to hoot to her stepmother that her maiden-lady cousin had gone as the juvenile Little Red Riding Hood. Smith continued: "Master M[alcolm] M[elville], about eight years old, as Jack the Giant Killer, with sword and buckler, marched about bravely." On Malcolm's wide belt was an inscription, "I am the gallant Cornishman, / Who slew the giant Cormogan." (Malcolm was six and a half.) Herman Melville was there, as was Catharine Sedgwick: "During the day we were pleased to see on the ground, and apparently greatly enjoying the scene, the authoress of Hope Leslie and the author of Typee—the latter just recovering from a severe illness." Some of Melville's ruminations about the party went into the proposed novel Curtis had rejected: "Life is a pic-nic *en costume;* one must take a part, assume a character, stand ready in a sensible way to play the fool. To come in plain clothes, with a long face, as a wiseacre, only makes one a discomfort to himself, and a blot upon the scene" (ch. 24). Melville came in plain clothes, but he must have been careful not to be a blot upon the scene.

Smith was something of an unpaid flack of Sarah's and therefore liable to flatter, and he was not a great traveler, but he managed to convey his awed certainty that the affair was little short of phenomenal: "It was more like those scenes of Italy, France and Spain, which charm us in painting and poetry than our more sombre pleasures, and it was more fit to be described in poetry and painting than in the hurried columns of a newspaper." Smith modestly admitted that any incident he described would lose its charm in the telling, but he caught the wonder of one remarkable tableau: at the sound of a whoop, "a canoe was seen emerging from the opposite shore of the lake; as it approached, the tall and stalwart form of Ah-ne-wil-li-plunt-et-unk was discovered standing erect in the prow, while the squaws, Pontoosuc and Housatonic, rowed the skiff, and the boy Hoosac stood by the chief's side." When the Indians "sprang ashore, and with the true Indian gait and imperturbable gravity," ran to their lodge, the illusion was remarkable, requiring "but little aid from the imagination to bring back the Indian of olden time." The effect of this and another tableau on the water was, Smith said, magical. Whether or not the tableaux were performed in daylight or dark, they were breathtaking. Dazzled, excited, the hardier guests late in the evening left the lake to dance indoors at Broadhall. Sarah had happily seized on all the advantages of the magnificent natural setting and the splendor of the particular day as well as the heightening effects of costume, food, drink, lights, music, and dancing. Despite her own physical fragility, she was capable of creating moments when her guests could have the illusion of escaping out of a mundane world (though nothing was mundane in that season in the Berkshires) into a painting by Watteau or Claude (even though comparatively few of the American guests had actually seen such a painting). Like all great hostesses, Sarah was at her best an obsessive planner, a spendthrift, a brilliant illusionist — a mistress of magic, or "glamour," in Sir Walter Scott's sense of the word.

It was Maria who invited the Sedgwicks to the picnic when, taking seriously her duties toward her niece at Lenox, she called at the Sedgwick school along with Augusta and "the children" (the boys?) on 5 September, just before the picnic. There she told Kitty news that Kitty relayed to her father: "Cousin Herman had been very sick, but is now very much better." Allan's news of her brother Herman had stirred Maria into action, and now that her son Herman was better, mother and son were planning to start for Lansingburgh on Tuesday next, young Kitty reported, and on his way home Herman was thinking of making his Uncle Peter "a short visit." On 10 or 11 September Herman and his mother left for Lansingburgh, where they stayed with the Peebles overnight, or at most two nights. Maria was already having trouble with Herman: he "would not have staid so long at Lansingburgh if I had not been with him," she wrote to Augusta. In good times quick to play past off against present, to relish the collision and displacement of images of different epochs of his life, Herman now hated being in that once-pleasant village on the Hudson: still a village, not yet absorbed into the endless stretches of north Troy, it was a place where he could count on encountering T. D. Stewart or other members of the Stewart family. Chances are that by this time the Peebles family had heard rumors of Stewart's ever-growing and wholly justified grievance against their irresponsible kinsman. Stewart may have caught Melville for a little private chat in which he impressed on the defaulter the necessity of making good on the interest (and the interest on the interest? was he anywhere near as ruthless as the Harpers?) and repaying the entire principal on the upcoming first of May — or else Stewart would initiate legal action to seize Arrowhead. Stewart, a later reference shows, had begun to press Melville hard for repayment, and now he had his best chance, for there was no concealing Maria and Herman's presence.

Melville could not let down his guard for a moment's nostalgia in the humble village where he had finished the first book of his once flourishing literary career. Besides, however graciously Maria Peebles behaved, her son, although mellowing into responsible middle age, was still the Augustus who had flaunted his wealth around his destitute cousins who had dubbed him the Lord of the Isle, and who had offered Augusta marriage but had not behaved long enough in a way pleasing enough to have her join him at the altar. On 12 September Herman got his mother off with him for Gansevoort at seven in the morning, by way of Waterford, and arrived before ten. Maria reported that her brother Herman had been on the platform ready to receive them "with the warmest of welcomes," and that Catherine was "more than cordial." Any time Aunt Catherine was more than cordial was a day to mark with a white stone, but there was no repairing that woman's chance to establish an intimacy with Herman, a chance forfeited twenty-six years earlier when she had so cruelly rejected the charming companionship of the ten-year-old boy.

What Herman and his mother saw now was referred to in the family as the Mansion House or as the Manor House (although the last was usually reserved for the Van Rensselaers' splendid edifice just north of Albany). With much cellar or basement space, two full floors, and an attic, old Peter Gansevoort's Manor House was the grandest in the village, now belonging to his son, the feudal lord Herman Gansevoort, owner of the saw mill, the grist mill, and much of the surrounding land. Uncle Herman had remodeled it in Herman Melville's youth, in 1835, lifting the house four feet from its foundations and lowering it onto a new foundation. In the cellar (wrote Marian Chitty, a local historian in 1935, a century later), the original masonry was still visible, fieldstone and small boulders embedded in the plaster below the new (century-old) masonry. Uncle Herman had taken down the big chimney at the north end of the house, keeping the south one, and had left the old kitchen fireplace with its brick oven for baking. He had put up awkward partitions, stranding a stretch of the kitchen's brick hearth off in the back room known as the little sitting room.

The house, as it was before or after its renovations in 1835, had as yet no powerful associations for Herman Melville. He may not have seen it until after his return from the Pacific. Despite the view of distant Adirondacks and despite the charm of little Snook Kil, the stream which powered Uncle Herman's grist mill on its way to the Hudson, Melville was quickly bored with the flat crossroads village with at this time two churches, a hotel, two stores, a woolen factory, Uncle Herman's grist mill, several mechanics' shops, and about two hundred inhabitants. Now there was a railroad for a fast way out, north or south. Melville was never good about knowing precisely what day of the month it was, but he was particularly edgy around 14 September, the day he defaulted anew on the ninety dollars of interest due to John M. Brewster, as he had done two years before. He received a letter from

Lizzie on the fifteenth and answered it the same afternoon; it probably dealt with the arrival of Judge Shaw and his wife at Arrowhead on the fourteenth.

By the sixteenth Herman was upsetting his mother, as she wrote to Augusta, "getting homesick" and manifesting "his usual restlessness." Her brother Herman and his wife were both "growing old," and Catherine was subject to "frequent faint turns." The problem was Maria's son: "Every thing is so quiet here, that Herman is on the 'go-off' again, & on Tuesday morng [the eighteenth] we shall leave here for Albany where Herman proposes to remain until the next day, and take the afternoon train for Pittsfield." Therefore Augusta was "to bring up Charlie to the Depot, 19th Sept—*afternoon-train*, Wednesday." But then Maria added a bulletin dated "six O Clock A.M. Monday": "Herman has changed his mind. We are to leave here tomorrow, dine at Albany, take the *afternoon train & be with you in the Eveg*—I fear you may not get this letter, after this change of plans." This letter provides a vivid description of Melville in one of his characteristic moods, as well as a great family phrase, his being "on the 'go-off.'"

Meanwhile Fanny was staying with Helen to help keep her in good cheer, and consolation was needed during the "decidedly *hot*" days in the second week of September. She reported on the twelfth that Helen was "pretty well, but feels the heat very much 'pants' at times." On a recent cool morning George had driven them both several hours, despite Helen's condition, as far as Nathaniel and Nilly Thayer's country seat in Lancaster ("splendid place I should think," judged Fanny, from what was visible from the road). On 17 September, in ironic possession of the quietest room at Arrowhead, "Herman's study," where her son-in-law had written such highfalutin books, Hope wrote her son Lem:

> As expected, Mrs Melville & Herman are away and, when they return is uncertain. Elizabeth & her children are remarkably well, The children are bright & noisy.
>
> Miss Augusta is *all* energy, united with much kindness—anticipates wishes—You know that is my *idol*, to have a thing done—without a hint when my friend knows, exactly what I wish . . .
>
> Your father is making a Kite for Malcolm to day—I cannot imagine, it will be like the one for twenty years to my knowledge he has been wishing to make—as it would be larger than Lizzy & her four children all together.

Cousin Priscilla was still much at Arrowhead, though probably already living in the village. She recalled later how badly Shaw had suffered from his annual catarrh, "the uncomfortable malady, that interfer'd so distressingly," with the pleasure of his visit. Ashamed of himself, perhaps, or able, after all, to find ways of chatting quietly with his uncle, Herman reversed his change of plans, and stayed over at Gansevoort until the eighteenth, when he and his mother stopped at Washington Avenue in Albany, thinking they might stay overnight, only to find Peter and Susan gone. The servants gave them lunch, nevertheless, in the charming black-and-white-tiled breakfast room, since it was too stormy to eat in the garden. Herman penciled a note of thanks, then they caught the afternoon train for Pittsfield, in spite of the rain—having quite confused the family as to their whereabouts, which under normal circumstances should have been a matter of no great moment.

This once, it mattered that Maria's whereabouts were not known. In a letter dated Tuesday morning but not postmarked until Thursday, 20 September, Fanny sent tragic news to Augusta:

> Not knowing where Mamma is now, I write to you my dear Augusta. Helen was taken sick last evening, very soon after she, and we all, had retired for the night—leaving me with her, George went for Mrs Griggs [his mother?], brought her here and then went to the village for Dr Whild. . . . At daylight Mrs Dearborn (George's sister) was sent for, she came and between 8 & 9 oclock the child was born—a boy—*but alas! dead* poor Helen, who had suffered very, very much, saw something was the matter, so she had to be told, upon hearing it, she became very much excited but is now quiet.

Later she added that, purely by accident, John Hoadley, having missed the last train to Lawrence, had come over to spend the night and found her "*alone in the house,*" in "the midst of the confusion," so he had remained long enough to carry a note home to Kate. She had also written to Sophia. She had one question: "Where is Mamma?" For those in the Griggs household horror was piled on horror when they were favored by one of those offhand medical pronouncements that no one in a family can ever forget: "The Doctor said, that the child had been *dead three weeks.*" Three of the most poignant words any of the family ever wrote or spoke were Fanny's "*Where is Mamma?*"

Maria was by then at Arrowhead, and on 21 September, frantic to be with her oldest daughter, she left for Boston. Perhaps now she was summoned by one of the modern wonders, a telegraphic dispatch, and freshly appreciative of the railway cars—she who had made this trip by stagecoach less than a quarter century before, then as now bowed down with sorrows. Kate came down to Longwood, and four Melville women and George consoled each other in the presence of Kate's little Maria, who had begun to sleep at night "like any christian" (as Hoadley had described her to Maria on 6 August). After a few days, as Helen began to get on "famously," sitting "in her easy chair and regaling herself with boiled chicken and mashed potatoes!," Fanny in her 30 September letter to Augusta could even laugh about Sarah Morewood, who had spent a fortune on her last blowout (to use a term in Priscilla's vocabulary this year) and then two or three weeks later was talking about taking in boarders: "What an idea that is of Mrs Morewood's taking people in her house. I never heard such a silly thing, why she will never get along in the world."

Maria decided that she could trust Helen to Fanny, and finished her blue dress and fixed her hat for fall and made ready to visit the Nourses in Bath, after refusing so many invitations. Dr. Nourse wrote Shaw on 6 October: "Mrs Allan Melville arrived this morning to make us the visit so long talked of" — a rare reminder during these years of her status as the wife and widow of Allan Melvill (whom Nourse had never met). Even before her visit to Maine, Maria had begun to put her mind back to routine affairs, asking Augusta on 30 September: "Did Herman write an apology to the Publishers [Putnam], — 'Fruit Festival' " — the 27 September party to which many literary notables, including Herman, had been invited. Her question was not whether he had responded as politeness required, but whether he had gone down to New York. No evidence has been found either way.

On 8 October G. P. Putnam & Co. submitted a statement to Melville for three printings of *Israel Potter*, a large total of 3700 copies, of which 2577 had been sold at 75 cents a copy, making $1932.75. Melville's share was computed as $193.27, only 10 percent; this was corrected on the sheet to $241.58. After deducting the advances, $48.31 was now due to him, half what he owed Brewster. On that day, 8 October, Melville sent the Harpers something accompanied by this short, awkward note: "Herewith is an article, which, if it suit, will you, according to what you have said to me, send me the money for, without further trouble to yourselves or me." If this was "Jimmy Rose," the Harpers rushed it into print. Melville continued to be mobile, calling to see Priscilla in the village in the afternoon of 24 October, for instance — probably finding it convenient enough to stop occasionally after picking up mail and papers. He was able to drop everything and hurry to Gansevoort three days later, to be with Uncle Herman while Aunt Catherine was dying. On 29 October Herman Gansevoort wrote in his remembrancer: "The faithful and beloved Catherine S. Gansevoort wife of Herman Gansevoort, departed this life on the 29th day of October 1855 at 7 o'clock and 30 minutes in the evening." The death of the woman for whom the term "Aunt Catherineness" was coined altered the life of the family irrevocably.

Maria and her children had never felt estranged from Uncle Herman. In her mind it was her brother Peter's fault, not her brother Herman's, that their mother's estate had not been settled promptly, when she most needed her share. Everyone long ago had accepted that Herman Gansevoort would bear his cross silently as long as God meant him to, and that when he survived his

1 "Portrait of Tupai Cupa," from *The New Zealanders*, by George L. Craik (London, 1830).

2 Herman Melville, 1861. Carte de visite by R. H. Dewey. Berkshire Athenaeum, Pittsfield, Massachusetts.

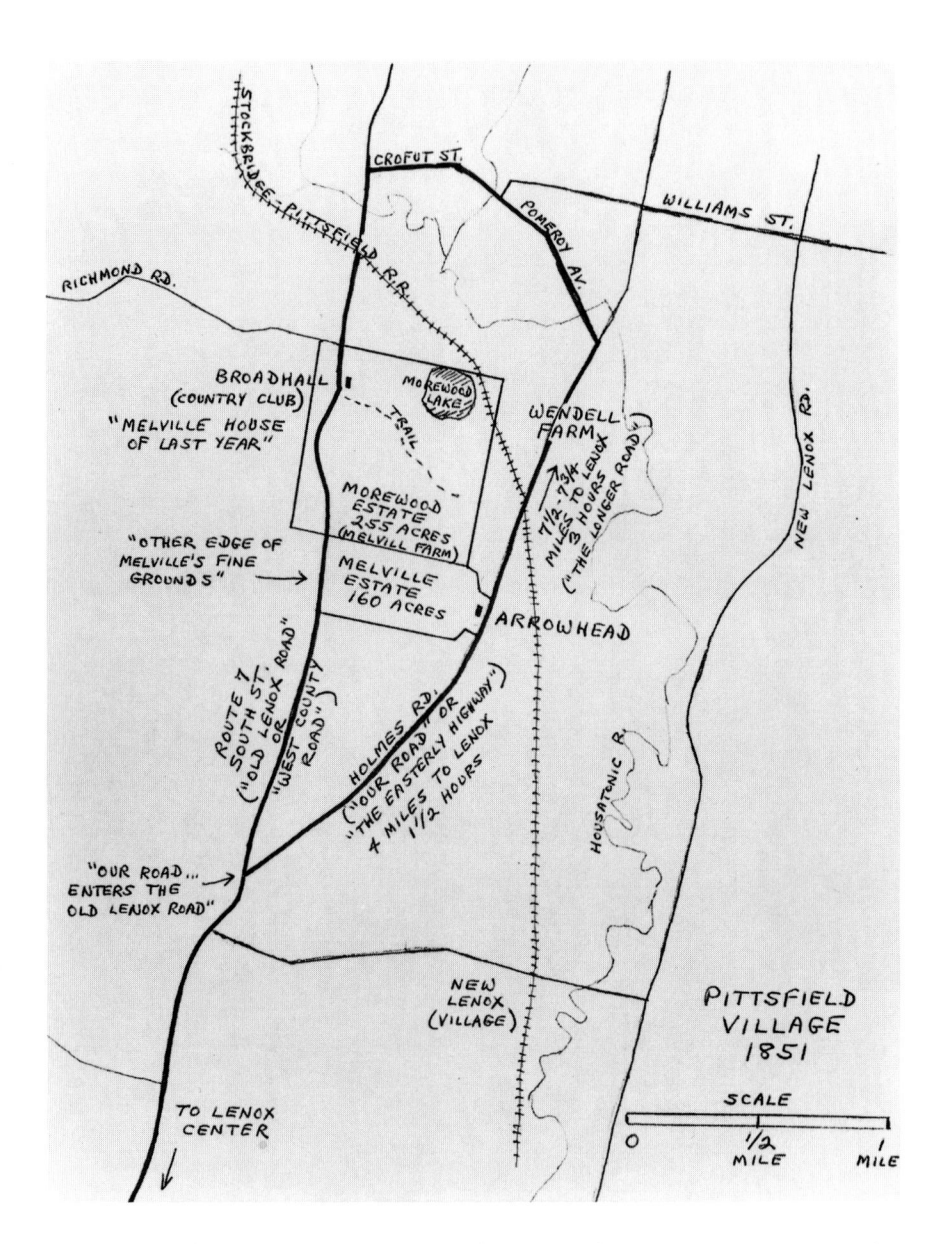

3 "Pittsfield Village, 1851." Manuscript map by Lion Miles, 1997. Courtesy Lion Miles.

4 Arrowhead Farm from the North Meadow, ca. 1862. Photograph. Berkshire Athenaeum, Pittsfield, Massachusetts.

5 "Winyah. The Residence of Colonel Richard Lathers. New Rochelle, New York," from *This Discursive Biographical Sketch of Colonel Richard Lathers, 1841–1902* (Philadelphia, 1902).

6 Sarah Morewood, ca. 1862. Carte de visite by R. H. Dewey. Berkshire Athenaeum, Pittsfield, Massachusetts.

7 Broadhall with J. R. Morewood, ca. 1873. Cabinet card by R. H. Dewey. Berkshire Athenaeum, Pittsfield, Massachusetts.

8 Crane Paper Mills in Dalton, Massachusetts: Red Mill and Old Stone Mill, ca. 1867. Photograph. Courtesy Crane & Company.

9 John C. Hoadley, ca. 1867. Carte de visite. Berkshire Athenaeum, Pittsfield, Massachusetts.

10 "Locomotive Engine 'Irvington' Coal Burner," ca. 1855. Lithograph by C. Van Benthuysen. Photograph courtesy of Railroad Museum of Pennsylvania, PHMC.

11 Herman and Thomas Melville, 1860. Ambrotype by Davis.
Berkshire Athenaeum, Pittsfield, Massachusetts.

12 "Clipper Ship 'Meteor' passing Cape Horn, January 3rd 1860," 1860. Pencil drawing by Thomas Melville. Berkshire Athenaeum, Pittsfield, Massachusetts.

13 "Arrowhead In the Olden Time, A. D. 1860," 1860. Drawing by Herman Melville now lost; reproduced from *Herman Melville: Mariner and Mystic*, by Raymond Weaver (New York, 1921).

14 *Holy Palm of Mar Saba*, by Peter Toft, 1882. Watercolor inscribed to Herman Melville by the artist. Berkshire Athenaeum, Pittsfield, Massachusetts.

15 49 Mount Vernon Street, Boston, Massachusetts, late nineteenth century. Photograph by A. H. Folsom. Courtesy of the Society for the Preservation of New England Antiquities. Negative #50428-A.

16 *Portrait of Chief Justice Lemuel Shaw*, by William Morris Hunt.
Oil on canvas, 1859. Courtesy of Pamela L. Surette, Essex County Bar Association
and Essex County Law Library.

17 John Oakes Shaw, ca. 1900. Photograph. Courtesy of the Society
for the Preservation of New England Antiquities.

18 *(left)* Lemuel Shaw Jr. Photograph by John Adams Whipple. Courtesy
of the Society for the Preservation of New England Antiquities. Negative #50426-A.
19 *(right)* Samuel Savage Shaw, 1887. Photograph by the Notman Photo Company.
Courtesy of the Society for the Preservation of New England Antiquities.
Negative #50427-A.

20 Malcolm, Elizabeth, Frances, and Stanwix Melville, ca. 1861. Photograph by R. H. Dewey. Berkshire Athenaeum, Pittsfield, Massachusetts.

21 Melville Home (1862–63), Pittsfield, ca. 1902. Photograph. Berkshire Athenaeum, Pittsfield, Massachusetts.

22 Chaplain Charles A. Humphreys, Second Massachusetts Volunteers, Cavalry Regiment, ca. 1864. U.S. Army Military History Institute.

23 Colonel John Singleton Mosby, Forty-third Virginia Partisan Ranger Battalion, ca. 1865. U.S. Army Military History Institute.

24 Allan Melville, 1865. Carte de visite. Berkshire Athenaeum, Pittsfield, Massachusetts.

25 Jane Dempsey Randolph Melville, 1871. Carte de visite by A. Sonrel. Berkshire Athenaeum, Pittsfield, Massachusetts.

26 Chimney Room at Arrowhead, 1870. Carte de visite by Chandler Seaver. Berkshire Athenaeum, Pittsfield, Massachusetts.

27 Susan Gansevoort, engraving by A. H. Ritchie,
in *Memorial of Henry Sanford Gansevoort*, edited by J. C. Hoadley
(Boston, 1875).

28 *(left)* Peter Gansevoort, ca. 1863. Carte de visite by C. D. Fredricks.
Berkshire Athenaeum, Pittsfield, Massachusetts. 29 *(right)* Henry Sanford Gansevoort,
engraving by A. H. Ritchie, in *Memorial of Henry Sanford Gansevoort*, edited by
J. C. Hoadley (Boston, 1875).

wife, five years or so his elder, he would then be free to express his affection for his blood kin. After the funeral Maria Melville and her youngest daughter, Frances Priscilla, remained at Gansevoort to keep house for him. The house, which Fanny, for one, called the Mansion House, became home first for Maria and Fanny, then for Augusta as well. It gradually rivaled and at last replaced Arrowhead as the favored summer gathering place of the family. Maria and her unmarried daughters took some of their possessions to Gansevoort, and in time Augusta and Fanny reclaimed odds and ends that Helen had been saving for them, but they knew in advance that they would be entering a house already as stuffed with grand old furniture as Baltus Van Tassel's house in "The Legend of Sleepy Hollow." They would not leave Arrowhead denuded. There was no blizzard of correspondence, so far as is known, no hasty consultations among the parties at New York, Pittsfield, Lawrence, and Brookline, and no competition among surviving nieces and nephews—say Leonard's children—for who would go to stay with the widower. Herman Gansevoort settled any question by making a will that left Maria his estate except for the contents of the house, which he left to Augusta and Fanny, with the request that they allow their mother "the use thereof during her natural life." A codicil to the will was drawn up (and signed on 25 May 1857) in which Herman left his sister Maria everything, lands and furnishings, if she survived him, as long as she was free from debt. Determined to keep the estate in the family, he would let it pass on to the nieces if his sister were in danger of losing the property to her creditors. At Gansevoort that autumn, especially on 6 December (the day Gansevoort Melville would have been forty), Maria had ample time to reflect on the vicissitudes of her life, and particularly on the likelihood that in due course she might have a home of her own, all paid for.

The November issue of *Putnam's* had the second installment of "Benito Cereno" and *Harper's* had something of Melville's also, "Jimmy Rose." Suggested by the way warehouses and factories were intruding into the grand downtown streets of his childhood in New York City, this was the pathetic yet stoical sketch of Jimmy Rose, a man who had suffered, as they said, reverses: "Though at the first onset of his calamity, when creditors, once fast friends, pursued him as carrion for jails; though then, to avoid their hunt, as well as the human eye, he had gone and denned in the old abandoned house; and there, in his loneliness, had been driven half mad, yet time and tide had soothed him down to sanity. Perhaps at bottom Jimmy was too thoroughly good and kind to be made from any cause a man-hater. And doubtless it at last seemed irreligious to Jimmy even to shun mankind." Timonism was not a useful philosophical stance for Melville, not with the exposure of his debt to Stewart so close. November was the month Melville missed yet another payment to Stewart. At least Stewart was not on the scene in Pittsfield; Brewster was, so *that* missed payment was direct cause of local humiliation. The December *Putnam's* was out by 24 November, a little early, and a literary item in the *Evening Post* commented that the "conclusion of Melville's singular and well-wrought tale," "Benito Cereno," would "be looked for with interest." Melville's control of his material was now being acknowledged, just as he was devoting intense concentration, days and weeks at a time, to his new book, where he was intermixing low comedy with metaphysical satire.

In *The Confidence-Man* Melville was examining literary concepts he had once taken for granted. Chapter 14, "Worth the consideration of those to whom it may prove worth considering" (one of his Fieldingesque titles), was his reflection on consistency in fiction. Chapter 33, "Which may pass for whatever it may prove to be worth," was a rejection of the demand for realism in fiction. Chapter 44, "In which the last three words of the last chapter are made the text of discourse, which will be sure of receiving more or less attention from those readers who do not skip it," was a dissent from the common claim that popular novelists were creating original characters. Many characters, Melville argued, are "novel, or singular, or striking, or captivating, or all four at once," but not original — not "in the sense that Hamlet is, or Don Quixote, or Milton's Satan." What are taken as original characters do not illuminate the other characters or the plot of a novel, in contrast to genuinely original creations: "the original character, essentially such, is like a revolving Drummond light, raying away from itself all round it — everything is lit by it, everything starts up to it (mark how it is with Hamlet), so that, in certain minds, there follows upon the adequate conception of such a character, an effect, in its way, akin to that which in Genesis attends upon the beginning of things." (Melville remembered the sensation when Barnum first illuminated Broadway with a Drummond light to advertise his American Museum.) Melville may have thought in 1850 and 1851 that he was achieving an original character in Ahab; he may have realized, then or later, that he had actually achieved such a character in Ishmael. Now a practitioner of fiction beginning to speculate about the theory of fiction, character depiction was a suitable place to start, an edge into the still more ambiguous matter gnawing at him, the relation of truth and fiction.

Like all Melville's other books except *Clarel*, this one bears traces of disruptions or shifts of direction during its prolonged composition. Interrupting his work on *The Confidence-Man* around mid-December, for example, Melville went to New York. There, almost four years after his last and disastrous end-of-year trip there, Melville was confronted with the Duyckinck brothers' lavish two-volume *Cyclopædia of American Literature*, dated 1856, but available in December 1855, the first volume early in the month, the second on the fifteenth, when Allan and other subscribers completed their sets. Allan had subscribed so as to possess the work toward which he had contributed a manuscript sketch, and other members of the family must have looked through the *Cyclopædia* with complicated emotions. Uncle Peter's brother-in-law Edward Sanford, like many another writer, had been given considerably more space than Herman Melville. Freshly written for the *Cyclopædia* (amid much that was reused without being rethought) was a pat little piece of psychoanalysis: "In the fields and in his study, looking out upon the mountains, and in the hearty society of his family and friends, he finds congenial nourishment for his faculties, without looking much to cities, or troubling himself with the exactions of artificial life. In this comparative retirement will be found the secret of much of the speculative character engrafted upon his writings." ("Retirement" meant withdrawal from the city.)

A pondering man, Melville had called himself in 1849. He could only take the Duyckincks' comment as superficial and unwittingly demeaning, as if he had never pondered or speculated before the summer of 1850. The biographical sketch concluded with a comment on *Pierre:* "Its conception and execution were both literary mistakes. The author was off the track of his true genius." The whole sketch could only have caused Melville pain, however well he controlled it. The article was accompanied by an engraving by W. Roberts of "Melville's Residence," the earliest known depiction of Arrowhead, and, as time passed, an irritant to Allan's covetousness. Allan, who had arranged for the making of the engraving, was the first person to focus on the fact that although the house and outbuildings were running down, year by year, Arrowhead was a historic property.

Before leaving Arrowhead Melville had tried to clear one item off his file by writing to the Harpers (10 December): "Some time ago I sent you an Article called the 'Apple Tree Table', from which I have not yet heard." He got the manuscript back, which freed him to carry it down to offer to *Putnam's* while he was talking to Joshua A. Dix about republishing "Benito Cereno" and some other stories in book form. For this book Melville was not selecting his private choices for the best short stories he had written since 1853. He had to rule out all those published in *Harper's*, and therefore subject to awkward negotiations if he wanted to reprint them, and apparently he did not even try to include the two which he was about to publish in *Putnam's*, "I and My Chimney" (March 1856) and "The Apple-Tree Table" (May 1856). During their talk, Melville as an inducement "volunteered something about supplying some sort of prefatory matter" which would be given a title that would be used for the book, thereby giving the impression of freshness. Nothing could be decided at the meeting, since Curtis was still away and Dix had to write asking his advice on the wisdom of publishing a volume of Melville's stories.

Curtis, rather surprisingly, approved the idea of publishing Melville's book of stories when he reported in from West New Brighton on 2 January 1856: "I don't think Melville's book will sell a great deal, but he is a good name upon your list. He has lost his prestige, — & I don't believe the Putnam stories will bring it up." He added, " I suppose you can't lose by it," and emphasized that he liked "The Encantadas" and "Bartleby" "very much." This was enough for Dix, who wrote Melville on 3 January 1856, offering to publish the collection. On the seventh Melville responded. He tried hard to be businesslike, consulting his copy of the contract for *Israel Potter* in an effort to repair a misstatement he had made in New York: "Since you are disposed to undertake the book, were it not well to have a written Agreement? Such, if you please, you may prepare & send me for signature. I am ready to sign one of the same sort made concerning 'I. Potter' with Mr Putnam. In your note you state *12 per cent* as the terms I mentioned. But I meant to say *12 & ½ per cent;* that is, the same terms as I had for 'I Potter'; which was *12 & ½* as I now find *by reference to the Agreement.* Pray, understand me so now." Having laid out his copies of *Putnam's,* he found himself lacking the December 1853 number (the conclusion of "Bartleby") and the April 1854 number (an installment of "The Encantadas") and asked Dix to send them on, so he could do his "share of the work without delay."

On 19 January 1856 Melville sent to Dix & Edwards the corrected tearsheets of *Putnam's,* renumbered sequentially to correspond with the order of the pieces in what he was calling *Benito Cereno & Other Sketches,* where the title story was followed by "Bartleby," "The Bell-Tower," "The Encantadas," and "The Lightning-Rod Man." On 9 October 1855, "Pictor," the officious Boston correspondent of the *Evening Post,* had made sure that all New York knew that "Benito Cereno" was founded on an incident in Amasa Delano's *Voyages and Travels* and also knew just how the story was going to end. Mindful of "Pictor," Melville wrote a note to be appended to the title of "Benito Cereno"—that is, a note that would come before the first paragraph (presumably in small type, or indented distinctively) or else would appear as a footnote at the bottom of the first page of text. This public acknowledgment of his source was not printed in the book and probably does not survive. Having put himself forward a little in person by volunteering to write a preface from which the book could be titled, Melville now did not even try to be optimistic: "upon less immature consideration," he judged that "both those steps" (writing a new preface and using it for a new title) "are not only unnecessary, but might prove unsuitable." Melville said glumly: "About having the author's name on the title-page, you may do as you deem best; but any appending of titles of former works is hardly worth while." This was a gesture of professional suicide (almost guaranteed to deter the publisher from launching a large-scale advertising campaign, especially since Curtis had been so discouraging about the book).

Dix insisted on having something new in the book, and also seems to have suggested that the popular "Bartleby" should come before any of the other pieces that had already been published. Early in February, most likely, Melville wrote "The Piazza," a piece brilliantly contrived for a book which would be recommended many times as ideal summer reading. In this sketch, incidentally a celebration of Melville's own piazza, the narrator, retired from an adventurous life and profoundly subdued after early defiant aggressiveness, makes a brief, inland voyage to fairyland, to locate the glinting surface that catches his eye far up the slopes of Mount Greylock—an internal, mental, philosophic, aesthetic adventuring. At issue was how an artist arrives at the right vantage point from which he can create great art. One answer was that the way lay "where path was none, and none might go but by himself, and only go by daring," even if instead of a laurel crown all the striver found were "fruitless growths of mountain-laurel." After such Hawthornesque mountain-climbing, in what the speaker had deluded himself to be fairyland, "in a pass between two worlds," he finds human reality, the lonely impoverished New England girl whom he calls, after Shakespeare and Tennyson, Marianna.

In the process of turning the sketch into a meditation on illusion and truth Melville rethought Hawthorne's "The Artist of the Beautiful," which once had pleased him as a treatise on aesthetics. Now, having reread some of Hawthorne's tales, including some early ones such as "The Three Vagabonds" and probably some familiar ones such as "The Artist of the Beautiful," he was groping past the simplicity of Hawthorne's doctrine of art for artist's sake. Indeed, what had pleased him in 1850 was shockingly inadequate in early 1856. Hawthorne had been wrong in "The Artist of the Beautiful": what counted was not, for instance, Shakespeare's having "thought" of *Macbeth* but his having written it and its having survived. What counted was having *Moby-Dick* published, not Melville's having glorified himself by experiencing *Moby-Dick* as a bright conception or as a work that did not need to survive — and to survive in a sufficient number of printed copies "perceptible to mortal senses." If Hawthorne had been right, Melville could have gone cheerfully on his way, telling himself that *The Isle of the Cross* was "of little value in his eyes, while his spirit possessed itself in the enjoyment of the Reality." At the end of "The Piazza," the narrator settles, in the daytime, for the illusion spread out before him in the amphitheater stretching down from the mountains, but reality comes in later: "every night, when the curtain falls, truth comes in with darkness." The last sentence is a compressed, evocative rumination on the truth of great fiction: "To and fro I walk the piazza deck, haunted by Marianna's face, and many as real a story" — among them "The Town-Ho's Story," the lost *The Isle of the Cross*, "Bartleby," "The Encantadas," "Benito Cereno," and other stories from 1853–56, not least that of the Revolutionary beggar Israel Potter. To Dix alone, or to the wily Curtis, operating behind him, we owe the existence of this sketch.

[13]

Foreclosing on Friendship
Confession and Shame, February–October 1856

❧

FRIENDSHIP.

A gen[er]ous Friendship no cold medium knows,
Burns with one Love, with one Resentment glows;
One should our Interest and our passions be;
My Friend must slight the man who injures me.

"Allan Melvills Book," 1796

ON 16 FEBRUARY 1856 Melville sent Dix & Edwards the new introductory piece, "The Piazza," and informed them that the title of the collection would be *The Piazza Tales*. There had been some discussion already about the order of the contents, and now Melville expressed his agreement with what Dix or Curtis had suggested: "I think, with you, that *'Bartleby'* had best come next," after the introduction, making the amended order "The Piazza," "Bartleby," "Benito Cereno," "The Lightning-Rod Man," "The Encantadas," and "The Bell-Tower." In view of the new title, the note Melville had written on the source of "Benito Cereno" was anomalous, so he took the easy way out: "as the book is now to be published as a collection of *'Tales'*, that note is unsuitable & had better be omitted." He requested proof of "The Piazza," the only part of the collection that had not yet appeared in print. As far as he was concerned, *The Piazza Tales* was ready for the printer, but Dix & Edwards did not have a contract ready until 7 March. It specified, as Melville had requested, that his royalties would be "12 ½ per cent, per copy on each copy sold." Proofs may have accompanied the contract. In any case, Melville returned the signed agreement and the corrected proofs along with a philosophical note: "There seems to have been a surprising profusion of commas in these proofs. I have struck them out pretty much; but hope that some one who understands punctuation better than I do, will give the final hand to it." No one seems to have bothered. On April Fools' Day Melville returned "the proof last sent" and added: "It may be well to send the whole as made up in page form." *The Piazza Tales* was ready for sale several days before the end of May 1856.

Meantime Melville's tales continued to appear, "I and My Chimney" in the March *Putnam's*, "The 'Gees" in the March *Harper's*, "The Apple-Tree Table, or Original Spiritual Manifestations," in the May *Putnam's*. He kept track of the status of *Israel Potter*, reminding Putnam on 18 February that the month for rendering their next account had come. The Harper's account on 6 March showed his debt to them as $348.51, but there were, besides his new publications, other signs of what looked like an ongoing literary career. In the January issue of the *University Magazine* (Dublin) an anonymous article (by William Hurton) compared "A Trio of American Sailor-Authors" — Cooper, Dana, and Melville. Hurton was doubtful about Melville's very identity: "A friend has informed us that 'Herman Melville' is merely a *nom de plume*, and if so, it is only of a piece with the mystification which this remarkable author dearly loves to indulge in from the first page to the last of his works." He deplored *The Whale* ("quite as eccentric and monstrously extravagant in many of its incidents as even 'Mardi' "). Yet Melville was "a man of whom America has reason to be proud, with all his faults; and if he does not eventually rank as one of her greatest giants in literature, it will be owing not to any lack of innate genius, but solely to his own incorrigible perversion of his rare and lofty gifts." This judgment resounded down Melville criticism far into the next century, quoted and plagiarized over and over again.

The Boston *Littell's Living Age* (a magazine made of previously published pieces, largely British) reprinted the *University Magazine* piece at the end of February, in its March issue. Melville was no longer positioned so as to see almost everything that was published about him, but he read this particular reprinting (or a reprinting of *it*) in Pittsfield, with Joe Smith watching him, if not looking over his shoulder (according to his *Biographical Sketch*): "We have Mr. Melville's own authority for saying that he was sensitive to the criticism of foreign reviews, for once when reading one of them he looked up to say, 'Well, it is pleasant to read what those fellows over the water say about us!' And he was greatly amused when he found the critic, thinking that his name was altogether too fine for common use in America, concluded it was a pseudonym." This was attention, flattering and insulting at once, the sort of notice that only people with viable careers could expect to receive, and in little ways the illusion persisted that Melville still had a career, as in the advertisements that Dix & Edwards began to run in the New York papers in the first week of April, announcing that *The Piazza Tales* was in press.

The English scoundrel Thomas Powell, still eking out a living as a part-time journalist and a full-time cadger, had formed one of his intense temporary connections with the New York *Daily News* (a valuable paper which frustratingly is known only in partial, broken runs). Taking advantage of the early publicity about *The Piazza Tales*, on 14 April, Powell put Melville first in his *Daily News* "Ambrotypes," which he described as "a series of Pictures of our leading authors, dramatists, &c., written in an impartial spirit, and with a gentle and appreciative pen, selecting those whom we personally know, in order to make the likeness more faithful." These articles did contain personal information, however distorted, about their subjects, particularly Robert Browning, whom Powell had known. As always, Powell reused some of his old material, still calling Melville a "Romancist," as he had done in his *Figaro!* piece in 1850. Few authors had become "more suddenly popular than Herman Melville," Powell wrote in 1855, since even Dickens had "served a sort of appren[ti]ceship as a reporter before he burst upon the world." He summed up the trajectory of Melville's career: "Ten years ago Melville was unknown to the public; he is now one of our most successful writers, although his *prestige* has been considerably damaged by his unfortunate attempt to load his graceful narrative with metaphysical speculations."

What Powell relayed as authentic biographical information was slapdash, as usual, personal knowledge intermixed with errors and fabrications, as in what he said of Melville's reading (a passage not in the 1850 version): "Had Melville been thoroughly acquainted with his own powers, he would have confined himself to his gambols with his immaculate nudities; but unfortunately stumbling over a copy of Sir Thomas Browne's works, he formed the idea of becoming a Psychological Cerberus, and consequently set to work to stuff himself with Swift, Rabelais and Browne." The "result" was *Mardi*, he now asserted, not wholly from his own observations but surely in part from what Evert Duyckinck had said to him about his own shock at Melville's declaring Browne to be a cracked archangel. Duyckinck had been in a position, also, to know just what works by Jonathan Swift Melville had read while he was writing *Mardi*. A three-headed dog, one head Swift, another Rabelais, the other Browne, with a shaggy mane and a snaky tail, admitting the dead to Hades and keeping them there? "Psychological Cerberus" is one of those off-the-cuff formulations that teases, since Powell knew Melville and may have perceived something about him that other witnesses missed.

Powell included in the "Ambrotype" a physical description of Melville as he had looked in 1849, one of the few such portraits: "He is a handsome, gentlemanly man: very kind and courteous, and a most agreeable companion — having more of the ease of the traveler than the dogmatism of the author. In person he is a little above the medium hight, and dresses very carefully." (The spelling "hight" was a passing fad in the New York publishing scene.) Melville as careful dresser is a surprise, but the implication is that Lizzie had kept him decorous in New York City; certainly he had been well dressed when Powell saw him at the Melville house after Milie's christening in 1849. The article is most interesting for a claim Powell makes for personal knowledge of a literary plan of Melville's, presumably in 1849:

> It may seem impertinent to reflect upon an author's undeveloped powers, but we are afraid that he has laid the brightest of his gifts at the footstool of that great tyrant—the world—who insatiably craves more, and of a better qua[l]ity. We conclude our rough, but we hope candid, ambrotype by mentioning that he once named to us the plan of a work which he has not yet carried out. It was intended to illustrate the *principle* of *remorse*, and to demonstrate that there is, very often, less real virtue in moral respectability than in accidental crime. Some men save their conventional reputation by living up to a decent average of legalized vice, always simmering up to that point but never boiling over; while some are entirely virtuous and truthful all their life, until some sudden and uncontrollable impulse carries them at one bound over the hight, and they perish eternally.

This may be simple truth or Powell's invention or something in-between, but he had the opportunity to hear Melville talking familiarly.

Gossipy surveys of his faltering career meant little, even the offhand comment that since Melville was "still a young man—somewhere about 37" he might "yet recover his lost popularity." The success or failure of the newest book, Melville knew, was all but irrelevant. Tertullus D. Stewart for some time had been pressing Melville for the interest and (probably) the interest on the interest, and had let him know baldly that he intended to collect the entire principal on the date agreed upon, 1 May 1856, a date that had seemed immeasurably far away to the young man finishing his whaling book five years earlier. Furthermore, Stewart was threatening to seize the farm in repayment or at least to force its sale so he could be repaid from the proceeds. Melville had to confess to his wife what he had done, for he involved her in his next steps, little as he had thought of involving her in his financial plans in 1850 and 1851. Much as he loved his trees, as much time as he had spent patting their mortgaged backs, and much as he loved having property that fronted on both roads to Lenox (a wide handle of it running south of the Morewood property all the way west to the county road), Melville on 14 April inserted an advertisement in the Pittsfield *Sun*, offering for sale: "PART of the FARM now occupied by the subscriber, being 80 acres, more than half well wooded, within a mile and a half of Pittsfield village by the County road. HERMAN MELVILLE." This advertisement, which began running on 17 April, reflected Melville's still irrepressible optimism and a shrewd sense that the market value of Berkshire property had been rising. He later described the eighty acres as having comprised the "western" half of the property, although "southwestern," as the *Sun* later said, would have been more exact.

About this time, Melville composed one of the strangest sections of *The Confidence-Man*, "The Story of China Aster" (ch. 40). The story is an experiment in maudlinism, imitative of woeful tales of gamblers and drunkards, the genre of the center section of chapter 112 of *Moby-Dick*, "The Blacksmith." The character Egbert, the disciple of Mark Winsome, is loosely based on what Melville knew of Henry David Thoreau, partly from his writings, but also from gossip by Duyckinck (who had rejected *A Week on the Concord and Merrimack Rivers* at a time he was much around Melville) and Hawthorne (who had joked with Melville at Arrowhead in 1851 about their spending a week on a work-bench in a barn). Where Egbert as imitator of Winsome comes closest to Thoreau is on the subject of friendship, a reminder of how Thoreau's inhuman ideal of friendship in *A Week* could sound slavishly imitative of Emerson's own cold ideas on the subject: you never have to assist a friend because no friend would ever betray friendship by asking for help. This section of *The Confidence-Man* is particularly convoluted: while Egbert is play-acting the role of another character (a Mississippi swindler who takes the name Charlie Noble), he warns the Cosmopolitan (the Devil) that he cannot repeat China Aster's story without "sliding" into the style of "the original story-teller" (ch. 39). The humor comes from the Transcendentalist's not recognizing the Father of Evil. Egbert (in the assumed role of Charlie) eludes responsibility for the tone of the story he repeats: "I forewarn you of this, that you may not think me so maudlin as, in some parts, the story would seem to make its narrator." The story, thus elaborately orphaned from the outset (with a satiric portrait of the real American writer, Thoreau, lurking somewhere behind the putative storyteller), concerns China Aster, a candlemaker from Marietta, Ohio, a man in the business of enlightening the world, much as an author is. His candles sell slowly, yet he has supplies enough of them to light up a whole street. Pierre had bought cigars by selling his sonnets then had lighted his cigars by the flames of printed copies of those sonnets. Melville could have outdone Pierre — could have lighted Broadway brighter than Barnum with copies of *Moby-Dick* and *Pierre*, before the fire of 1853, or with the manuscript of *The Isle of the Cross*. China Aster's friend Orchis, a shoemaker, is in the business of keeping men from contact with reality. As Melville explains in low puns from Shakespeare's *Julius Caesar*, Orchis has a "calling . . . to defend the understandings of men from naked contact with the substance of things." This cheery rich friend seduces poor China Aster into expanding his business with the help of a loan: "Orchis dashed off a check on his bank, and off-handedly presenting it, said: 'There, friend China Aster, is your one thousand dollars; when you make it ten thousand, as you soon enough will (for experience, the only true knowledge, teaches me that, for every one, good luck is in store), then, China Aster, why, then you can return me the money or not, just as you please. But, in any event, give yourself no concern, for I shall never demand payment.'" For all his offhandedness, Orchis does, subsequently, casually suggest that China Aster make a little memorandum of the loan, "at four years." Orchis's agent collects both interest and, in due course, principal, even to the point of seizing an inheritance of China Aster's wife.

Having become a workaday American version of Job in his miserable sufferings, China Aster dies; then his impoverished widow dies, and their children go to the poorhouse. China Aster leaves his own epitaph, the gist of which is that he had been ruined by allowing himself to be persuaded "into the free indulgence of confidence, and an ardently bright view of life." Plain Talk and Old Prudence, his comforters, arrange to have the epitaph chiseled upon his tombstone. Later, they decide something else has to be added "at the left-hand corner of the stone, and pretty low down": "The root of all was a friendly loan." Seeing himself as, like China Aster, a light-giver in poverty, Melville had worked into the story oblique, distorted, and perversely hilarious versions of incidents from his own life, relying on his ability to make the parallels remote enough that the public would scent no self-revelation. Yet for all the aesthetic objectivity Melville could achieve, he still thought of himself as having been victimized by his confident friend, having been "induced" to accept the loan from Stewart.

Herman had probably consulted Allan before inserting the advertisement for half the property, and in early May he went to Allan and Sophia's on Twenty-sixth Street. Sophia was eight months pregnant and occupied with three living daughters. She bore her fifth child and fifth daughter on 14 June, winning the porringer by naming her Lucy. Something was wrong with Lucy, although it is not clear how soon it became apparent. The brothers talked business out of Sophia's hearing and decided on a course of action. Having advertised the main wooded area of his farm in the local paper, Herman put the entire farm and farmhouse in "the hands of a broker" in New York City, hoping to profit on the new vogue among wealthy New Yorkers for acquiring or building summer houses. The way the brothers figured it, by the sale of the whole farm Herman might realize "through its enhanced value" a sum "sufficient to pay off Dr Brewster's mortgage," to pay off a mortgage (to be drawn up) to Judge Shaw for the amount he had advanced toward the purchase of the farm, and also enough to repay what Melville owed Stewart (what he would do if there was not money to repay *all* of what he owed Stewart is not clear: ask Shaw for the balance?). What were they going to do, postdate the mortgage to Shaw?—at best a transparent stratagem for protecting the property. It is doubtful that either of the brothers thought of actually *paying* anything back to Shaw. In confessing this all to Shaw on 12 May, Herman explained that the money from Stewart had been "expended in building the new kitchen, wood-house, piazza, making alterations, painting, — and, in short, all those improvements made upon these premises during the first year of occupancy; and likewise a part went towards making up the deficiency in the sum received from the sale of the New York house, which sum fell short of the amount expected to have been realized and paid over to Dr. Brewster as part of the purchase-money for the farm; and the residue went for current expences" — which had included paying for the plating of *The Whale*, as it was then called. He went on to state his hopes for what he might achieve by "the sale of the wooded part (reserving two or three acres of wood)": "to obtain such a sum as that Mr Stewart can, in whole or in part, be paid out of it, and yet leave a balance, which, added to the value of the remaining portion of the farm, will nearly equal the original price of the whole." Astoundingly, this turned out not to be merely wishful thinking.

By far the trickiest legal fancy work which Allan undertook was helping Herman try, all belatedly, to protect Lizzie's "dowry." By now the husband and wife had faced the consequences of Melville's indebtedness, as Melville wrote on 12 May in his confessional letter to Shaw: "Lizzie & I have concluded that it may be best for us to remove into some suitable house in the village, that is, if the whole farm can be advantageously sold." He accompanied the letter with the mortgage Allan had drawn up: "To the extent of the amount you advanced towards the purchase of this farm, I have always considered the farm to that extent, but nominally mine, (my real ownership at present being in its enhanced value) and my notes, given you at the time, as representing, less an ordinary debt, than a sort of trust, or both together. Agreeably to this, my view of the matter from the beginning, I have executed to you a mortgage for the sum." The after-the-fact mortgage, like a postdated deed, was pretty clearly improper if not illegal, an expedient, Stewart would have argued, had the matter come to trial, to defraud him of his just prior claims against Melville's assets. Herman's letter came as a shock to Shaw, and of course he refused to participate in anything so dubious as the mortgage ploy. Just the month before, Richard Henry Dana Jr. had written in his journal: "The truth is, Judge Shaw is a man of intense & doating biasses, in religious, political & social matters. Unitarianism, Harvard College, the social and political respectabilities of Boston are his idola specus & fori." Neither intense and doting biases such as Dana detailed nor intense scrupulosity in financial and legal matters prevented Shaw from being also a generous and loving father, hardly more so to his own three sons than to Herman.

Rather than reproaching Herman in his reply on 14 May, Shaw gave him at least general "assurances" but warned him not to put the mortgage "on record &c." and advised against telling Stewart of its existence. Perhaps dreading what he might find, and withholding comment until he knew the worst, he asked Herman for a detailed statement of his debts and his assets. On 22 May, Bessie's third birthday, Melville toted up his debts:

> Omitting Mr Stewart's claim there is nothing payable by me except $90 being last year's interest on the $1500 mortgage [held by Brewster], and perhaps $50 on inconsiderable bills. I know not whether I ought to include (as a present indebtedness) a balance of some $400 against me in the last Acct: from the Harpers; a balance which would not have been against me but for my loss of about $1000 in their fire, and the extra charges against me, consequent upon the fire, in making new impressions, ahead of the immediate demand, of the books. The acct: will gradually be squared (as the original balance has already been lessened) by sales. Before the fire, the books (not including any new publication) were a nominal resource to me of some two or three hundred dollars a year; though less was realised, owing to my obtaining, from time to time, considerable advances, upon which interest had to be paid.

(This bears emphasizing: the all but unbelievably mercenary Harpers had charged him twice for printing and binding, and were charging him interest on their advances to him.) Melville's assets were easily listed:

> After the present acct: is squared, the books will very likely be a moderate resource to me again. I have certain books [*The Confidence-Man*, perhaps *The Isle of the Cross*, perhaps parts of *The Tortoise Hunters*] in hand which may or may not fetch in money. My immediate resources are what I can get for articles sent to magazines....
>
> [P.S.] I should have mentioned above a book to be published this week [*The Piazza Tales*], from which some returns will ere long be had. Likewise some further returns, not much, may be looked for from a book [*Israel Potter*] published about a year ago by Mr Putnam. — The articles in Harpers Magazine are paid for without respect to my book acct: with them.

In response to Shaw's inquiries about the house they might rent in the village, Melville informed him: "I have learned (without more special inquiry) that a suitable house might be had for about $150 a year." He was not quite throwing himself, Lizzie, and the four children upon Shaw's tender mercies; he was, after all, trying, however tardily, to protect Shaw's advances of money on Lizzie's behalf and he was taking active measures to sell part or all of the farm in order to meet his most pressing obligations. And now he was being cautious about what he could expect from his "books" in hand. *The Confidence-Man* in fact did not "fetch in money." As early as *Omoo* and *Mardi*, what he spent on sourcebooks cut into his eventual profits, and for *The Confidence-Man* he was out of pocket what he had spent on paper and ink, and Augusta out her time and effort in copying it.

While Melville waited for Shaw to advise him, Dix & Edwards published *The Piazza Tales*. They seemed to have padded out the book, leaving such excessive white space that the book ran 431 pages, feeling as bulky as a brick, a needlessly annoying fault in a book published just in time for the burgeoning summer market, when volumes should feel light in the hand and attractive to the eye (think of *The Berber*, that orange sensation of 1850!). The reviewers of *The Piazza Tales* were kind—no one said Melville should stop writing—but irrelevant, since his career was winding down whatever they said. In New York on 25 May the *Atlas* welcomed the chance to meet Melville "on his 'piazza,'" and quoted the wonderful sentence from "The Encantadas" on the special curse being that to the islands "change never comes." Thomas Powell in the *Daily News* on 26 May (in one of his characteristic changes of face) elaborately defended Melville against an unnamed critic's allegations that his brilliance as a writer had declined (a critic he may have invented, for the charge is not in any criticism yet discovered). The new *Piazza Tales* would "effectually correct the acidity" of this real or imagined critic: "we are inclined to think that the source of discontent is only the altered mood of the reader to whom we have referred, as we can nowhere find in any of Mr. Melville's writings the slightest rational symptom of deterioration." He called the introduction "one of the most charming sketches in our language"; he saw reminders "of Poe in his strangest mood" in "The Lightning-Rod Man" and "The Bell-Tower"; he sagely compared the "indefinable but irresistible sway over the imagination" in "The Encantadas" to the effects of a "gorgeous poem":

> In fact, if we may use such a comparison and be understood, Mr. Melville's prose, particularly in his magnificent descriptions of scenery, sea and cloudland, resembles the Tennysonian verse. It possesses all the glowing richness, exquisite coloring and rapid, unexpected turn of phrase that distinguishes the Poet Laureate of our day—Marianna of the Piazza, "the lonely girl, sewing at a lonely window; the pale-cheeked girl and fly-specked window, with wasps about the mended upper panes"—has a distinct and yet not traceable relationship to "Marianna in the Moated Grange." The very cadence of the thought—the same heart melody—fills both.

This was Powell at his most perceptive and least self-serving, and it was not unique. The praise in the *Daily News* did no long-term good, nor did the comment in the 31 May *American Publishers' Circular and Literary Gazette* that these tales of Melville's had been "in no small degree" instrumental in making *Putnam's* "the best of all American *Monthlies.*"

Dix advertised *The Piazza Tales* in the 4 June New York *Tribune* as one of "TWO GOOD SUMMER BOOKS" — the other being an anonymous New England tale, *Twice Married.* The advertisement quoted the *Daily News* ("Buy this Book and take it into the country with you, where its hearty, healthy vivacity will gratify and excite as much as its deep undertone of native poetry, inspired by rural scenes, will soothe") then paraphrased from the New York *Criterion* of 31 May: "For a companion under the broad branches of an old elm in the hot Summer days, keeping company with us to the very borders of dream-land, and soothing the senses into repose, as with the sighings of distant music, we recommend these 'Piazza Tales.'" Yet another advertisement proclaimed: "In the Cars, on the Steamboats, at all Bookstores in city and country, and for / SALE EVERYWHERE, / MELVILLE'S PIAZZA TALES." The publisher sensibly was capitalizing on the timing and content that made *The Piazza Tales* ideal summer reading. More precisely, the New York *Criterion* recommended *The Piazza Tales* for "a companion under the broad branches of an old elm in the hot summer days, when the light breeze ripples the dank hair, and just flutters the end of the white handkerchief hanging over the knee, or for an after-dinner hour, keeping company with us to the borders of dream-land, and soothing the senses into repose, as with the sighings of distant music, or for any other odd corner of time into which a book, but only a first-rate one, will exactly fit." On 7 June the *Tribune* listed the Duyckincks and Tuckerman among the sponsors of the *Criterion,* a new attempt at "an able and independent Literary and Critical Journal." Chances are that this review of *The Piazza Tales* was Evert A. Duyckinck's way of forgiving Melville for *Pierre.*

The Boston *Daily Evening Traveller* on 3 June shrewdly declared that "Bartleby" was "equal to anything from the pen of Dickens, whose writings it closely resembles, both as to the character of the sketch and the peculiarity of the style." The most remarkable American review besides Powell's was by William Ellery Channing (Thoreau's friend who had poeticized *Typee*), who in the New Bedford *Daily Mercury* on 4 June declared that in "copiousness of fancy and gentility of imagination" Melville resembled Charles Brockden Brown more than he did Hawthorne and Irving: "Hawthorne is more dry, prosaic and detailed, Irving more elegant, careful and popular, but Melville is a kind of wizard; he writes strange and mysterious things that belong to other worlds beyond this tame and everyday place we live in." Summer book, summer book, the reviewers echoed. The Philadelphia *Daily Evening Bulletin* on 4 June declared that *The Piazza Tales* would "doubtless have an extensive sale as a summer book." The New York *Churchman* on 5 June predicted that the tales were "destined to be read in many a pleasant country house, at watering-places, by the seashore, and among the mountains, during the coming summer heats. Scarcely a pleasanter book for summer reading could be recommended." The reviewer reasonably seized the occasion to complain that *The Piazza Tales* like several other recent books had not been issued "in a more easily portable form," pocket companions being "proverbially the best read books." So it went, tributes to Melville's charming style, repeated tributes to his "gorgeous" prose passages, repeated comparisons of "The Bell-Tower," at least, to Poe, all offered almost invariably in a tone of affection and respect, without a single known mention of *Moby-Dick* and only one brief mention of *Pierre*. Not one of the reviewers understood that the book was the product of a dying career.

This summer for the first time in many years something involving money turned out better than could have been expected, and faster than anyone would have dared to hope, even Melville at his most optimistic. Within three months Melville succeeded in selling eighty acres, half of the land he had bought. In the Pittsfield Valuation Book the entry for "Herman Melvill" was made on 28 June. Later someone, in pencil, made an annotation: "Sold $5,500 to Geo S Willis"; still later, in pencil, someone made another annotation: "80 Acrs Set to Geo. S Willis / 1857." (This was the Col. George S. Willis who figured so conspicuously in the dedication of the new cemetery on 9 September 1850, just as Melville was purchasing Arrowhead.) About the first or second week of July 1856 Melville wrote Shaw that he had "sold the western half of his farm at Pittsfield — upon pretty good terms," so the always hostile Lem relayed to his brother Samuel, then on *his* grand tour. The Pittsfield *Sun* on 17 July proudly took credit for its part in the sale, even while satisfying the local appetite for specifics about any and all property transfers: "SALE. — Herman Melville, Esq., has sold a part of his Farm, which has been advertised in our columns, to Col. Geo. S. Willis. The portion sold comprises the fine growth of wood on the County Road to Lenox. The price paid was about $60 per acre." The price was in fact nearer $70 per acre, a boon to a desperate man.

The hitch was that the money was not paid over at once. As a result, Melville had to become party to a complicated set of mortgages designed to keep Willis from being liable to Dr. Brewster for the mortgage he held on the whole of Arrowhead as Melville had bought it, and designed to protect Dr. Brewster from having half the property sold away while he held a mortgage on it. Willis obligated himself to pay Melville $1000 on 1 January 1857; $2000 with unspecified interest on 1 April 1858; and $2000 with unspecified interest on 1 April 1859. From the sale Melville got no cash money at all. This must mean that Shaw intervened and paid T. D. Stewart directly, $2050 plus

$830.25 in interest (Melville having made the 1 November 1851 semiannual interest payment), plus, knowing Stewart, some indeterminate amount of interest on the overdue interest. This means, at best, that the first two payments, totaling $3000, went all or almost all to Shaw to repay him for paying off Stewart. Not until the third payment, in 1859, was there anything left for Melville. This fits with the history Shaw made in 1860 of Melville's debts to him. The fact that Melville got no money from the sale accounts for his waiting until 14 September 1856 to pay the interest due to Dr. Brewster on that day and the interest overdue since that day in 1855 (with no additional interest on the overdue $90). Nothing came of the advertisements of the farm in New York papers, but Augusta said (on 7 April 1857) that before October—probably some months before—her brother "was convinced that a residence in the country was not the thing for him, & could he have met with an opportunity of disposing of his place he would have done so." The village was something he and Lizzie were considering only for the interim, before returning to New York. Life went on at Arrowhead almost normally, despite the reduced population (Maria and Fanny being indefinitely removed to Gansevoort) and despite Herman's continued infirmities. In June or early July, Sam Shaw, in Europe, had received word that Herman was suffering very much "from ill health." A month or more before 27 August, Sam Savage in Guatemala, having heard of some of the troubles, wrote the Shaws: "Lizzy no doubt alone has had many of life's real trials to conflict with, but she's one of those who bear up well, & it shows her character—Herman I hope has had no more of those ugly attacks." What these "ugly attacks" were is not known, but they were apparently recent, perhaps recurrences of the rheumatism and sciatica of the year before. By mid-July Kate and Helen were both at Arrowhead, and on 18 July Lem Shaw was thinking of condescending to "pass a day or two" there "this summer." At the end of July or early August, Hope Shaw arrived from an unaccustomed direction, having visited at Red Hook before going to Albany, where Lem put her "in the cars for Pittsfield."

In his 18 July letter to Sam, Lem passed on the news about their literary brother-in-law (not intending any play on the title of the new book): "I believe [Herman] is now preparing another book for the press, of which Augusta is making a fair copy for the printer & which will be published before long—I know nothing about it; but I have no great confidence in the success of his productions." From June or July on through August or September Melville labored over his final additions and his revisions of *The Confidence-Man* and Augusta toiled behind him in preparing the fair copy of it. At some point in this period Melville discarded a rhetorically powerful but out-of-place tribute to "The River," the Father of Waters, and composed, laboriously, an essay on consistency and inconsistency in fiction in the light of the complications of human nature (ch. 14).

At this stage Melville drafted the titles and added the chapter numbers. A scrap of manuscript reads "First Part," suggesting that he had planned a two-part (or greater) division. At some point, also, in this final period he recklessly wrote down an idea, perhaps only a sardonic private joke, perhaps with the thought of actually using it: "Dedicated to victims of Auto da Fe" — that is, to the victims of the Spanish Inquisition and, by extension, to all who had suffered from religious persecution, as he had done at the hands of the reviewers of *Typee, Omoo, Moby-Dick,* and *Pierre,* at the tongues of his neighbors in Pittsfield, and at the tongue of his well-meaning Christian mother. In his Shakespeare, any day, he could see his notes on the article in the *Quarterly Review* which had supplied him with the secret motto of *Moby-Dick* and revealed him to himself as a modern victim of ferocious persecution by religious zealots. *The Confidence-Man* as published had no dedication at all, and in keeping with his suppression of the provocative impulse to give away the game with such a bitter dedication, Melville worked his way through his whole manuscript (as one can deduce from the direction of the revisions in the surviving fragments), muting the more plangent ironies where he applied Scripture in ways the genteelly pious would have called blasphemous, concealing some of his satire of the nominal practice of Christianity. In this progressive muting, the "narrative" was retarded by multiple examples of litotes, where constructions like "not unlikely," "not wholly without self-reproach," "less unrefined," or "not unsusceptible" almost but not quite turn a double negative into a positive, and the style at times relies on elaborately qualified "assertions" which may be hedgingly offered and ambiguously retracted. The style forged in private agonies was finally used to communicate, not to conceal — but only the rarest of readers in Melville's own time (a couple of the London reviewers) understood it.

On his thirty-seventh birthday Herman arrived, alone, at Gansevoort to see his mother and his Uncle Herman, bringing a gift for his mother to present to his uncle, *The Piazza Tales.* He was welcomed, but his being there reminded everyone that the beloved Tom had been away on the *Meteor* since May of 1855. Herman was still there on his wedding anniversary, 4 August; Lizzie apparently marked the ninth anniversary with her four children. (In Cologne, Sam, now a twenty-two-year-old, newly a traveler, in a letter to Lizzie that day recollected his blue jacket worn on the solemn occasion in 1847, "and how disgusting wedding cake got to be!") Allan joined Herman at Gansevoort, and on 7 August went off with him to Lake George, expecting to meet "in the Carrs" (according to Uncle Herman's "Remembrancer") their mutual friend Daniel Shepherd, who had just that year published a post-Revolutionary novel, *Saratoga: A Story of 1787* (1856). In the preface Shepherd claimed that "local peculiarities" of "various races" of settlers, their differing relations "to the Aborigines," and the variations in the topography and climate were such as to "afford an inexhaustible field for the historian and novelist." Since he also claimed to be basing his story on incidents "handed down by tradition as veritable facts," the family at Gansevoort would have found the book more interesting than Herman would have.

No description of Melville's visit to Lake George this year is known, but he held it as his standard of comparison for beauty until he had seen Lake Como, which gradually supplanted it as his ideal lake. After two nights at the lake, Melville left Allan and Shepherd there and returned to Gansevoort on the first train on 9 August. By that time the family at Gansevoort had bad news from Lenox: Charles Sedgwick had died on 3 August. Maria and Helen had known him better than Herman, probably, and Judge Shaw had been a friend of his for many years. Remarkably subdued, Herman resisted any outbreaks of the "go-off" until the twelfth, when he made a day-trip to Saratoga Springs. Back in Boston after his own excursion to Saratoga Springs, a little before Herman's, Lem went out to Oakes's "a good deal" (as he wrote Sam on 12 August), thereby concentrating ill will toward Herman in one spot. With the difficult Catherine Quackenboss Gansevoort gone and the hospitable Maria and the genial Herman Gansevoort holding forth, Gansevoort, New York, underwent a boom in familial tourism. Augustus Peebles, who had money and could vacation anywhere, came on the thirteenth, and on the fourteenth went with Herman for another day at Saratoga Springs, returning in the evening. Finally, Herman left on the first train on 16 August, stopping off in Albany to dine with his Uncle Peter on his way to Arrowhead. Charmed with this look at his nephew, Peter announced that he was reserving his "whole house" for Herman, Lizzie, and the children, during the Albany meeting of the American Association for the Advancement of Science (as he reminded Herman on 9 October); to his disappointment, none of the Melvilles came. Sarah Morewood invited Melville and his household to a party at the end of August. If this was the invitation Melville accepted "with the most boisterous pleasure," he was forced to decline after all, perhaps because of his health. Herman by this time had translated Dr. Holmes's medical opinion into a recommendation of an ocean voyage culminating in a extensive tour of the Mediterranean region.

Herman had stayed so long at Gansevoort partly because he wanted to work out some arrangements with his mother and uncle for leaving Stanwix with them (that is, Maria and her brother and not just Fanny but both her unmarried daughters) for a prolonged period. Allan was there partly to see his mother but partly to get his instructions or deliver his messages, one of which was that he would try to impress upon Lemuel Shaw the seriousness of Herman's illness and to lay forth the benefits a prolonged trip to the Mediterranean would have for Herman's health and for his literary career, since he could expect to return with adventure stories that could be written up without excessively taxing his mind and damaging his body. Allan was acting as the broker, as Shaw made clear in May 1860, when he recapitulated the financial situation between him and Herman. In 1856 Shaw advanced through Allan about $1400 or $1500 for Herman's "outfit" and for the expenses of his tour, as he recalled in 1860: "In my own mind, though I took no note or obligation for it, I treated it like the other advances, to be regarded as advance by way of loan or a gift according to some future arrangement." On 1 September 1856 Judge Shaw wrote to his son Samuel:

> I suppose you have been informed by some of the family, how very ill, Herman has been. It is manifest to me from Elizabeth's letters, that she has felt great anxiety about him. When he is deeply engaged in one of his literary works, he confines him to hard study many hours in the day, — with little or no exercise, & this especially in winter for a great many days together. He probably thus overworks himself & brings on severe nervous affections. He has been advised strongly to break off this labor for some time, & take a voyage or a journey, & endeavor to recruit. No definite plan is arranged, but I think it may result, in this that in the autumn, he will go away for four or five months, Elizabeth will come here with her younger children, Mrs Griggs & Augusta will each take one of the boys, their house at Pittsfield will be shut up. I think he needs such a change & that it would be highly beneficial to him & probably restore him.

Shaw's generosity is the more notable since by late August he had begun to feel "the coming on of the annual cold," as Lem informed Sam. Concern over the annual catarrh, like concern over Herman's ill health, stretched across the Atlantic to kind young Sam.

In preparation for his departure Melville continued to try to keep track of his assets. In response to his query of 25 August, Dix & Edwards on 30 August explained that the copies sold of *The Piazza Tales* had not yet paid the costs, so nothing was due him: "We published late in May, and business has been dull since that time, but is reviving with the opening of fall trade, and we feel the good influence upon sales of all our books." Furthermore, their "statement of Cost" would have to be revised to include their "advertising" and "incidental expenses." They professed, nevertheless, to hope that the next statement would "show a handsome return." In August Melville probably also asked Putnam for an accounting on *Israel Potter*, as he had done the previous year, but no such letter has been found.

While Arrowhead was preparing for a dispersal of its inhabitants, Sarah Morewood once again gathered onto the Broadhall property "a brilliant party" for her second annual "fancy-dress pic-nic in the open air," again held on the east side of Melville Lake, and lasting on 3 September from noon till midnight. Ellen Brittain led the way with a gypsy cart filled with costumed friends, apparently the houseguests of Broadhall, and their tent became "the centre of attraction through the day" (as chronicled by Joe Smith for the *Berkshire County Eagle* of the fifth): "Hardly was the gypsy tent pitched when the sound of a post-horn was heard echoing down the road, and soon an old English post chaise appeared, with Mr. M[orewood] as post-boy, in silvery livery, with about the most dilapidated old vehicle, and the most venerable trunks possible to conceive. In it was an old lady, (Mrs. M[orewood]) in a costume which did no discredit to the carriage." Hodge's band returned to produce "rich strains of the silver instruments," and "livelier notes for the dance," with a bugle solo by Mr. Hodge himself receiving the highest praises. At six o'clock, as the day began to darken, the band led the guests in a procession to "a beautiful tent which had been erected on the hill west of the lake," a great coup for Sarah:

> This was a portion of the large tent under which Hon. Edward Everett last week delivered his great oration at Albany on the uses of Astronomy. That portion used here was circular, over one hundred feet in diameter, made of red, white and blue canvas, and, when brilliantly lighted, made an appropriate canopy for the gaily dressed and many colored party assembled in it on Wednesday evening. — It was made and put up by the owner, Mr. John Moakly of Albany, to whose taste and workmanship it does great credit. Here supper was served and the dance resumed and continued until past ten o'clock.

Again Smith was dazzled by "the beauty of the kaleidoscope groupings of characters in the grove during the day and in the mazes of the evening dance," scenes in which "the rich costumes of picturesque nations and ages" gained glamour from "the natural beauties" of a charming September day in the Berkshires, the whole effect "not easily described." Again some of the Arrowheads participated: "Mrs. H M, as the Genius of Greylock, was original and unique, her head being shrouded in nests and her dress decorated with leaves, pine cones, and other mountain trophies. Miss A M originated a new style of Berkshire fashions, the material being the leaves of the grove and the flowers of the field. Miss B M, a miss of three years, as Little Bo-Peep." Herman Melville probably looked on, once again, this time with the consciousness that he might soon test the authenticity of European dress against his sight of the real thing.

In the next weeks there was much bustle. After an early morning farewell scene (Lizzie parting with both Herman and Stanwix, Melville parting from his wife, Malcolm, his daughters, and his sister Augusta), Melville and his five-year-old left on the early train to Albany on 27 September, a Saturday. Herman Gansevoort recorded their arrival in his remembrancer: "Herman Melville brot his little son Stanwix to remain with us to stay untill his father returns from Europe." The next day the two Hermans stayed at the Manor House while Maria, Fanny, Stanwix, and Kate (Kate Hoadley or possibly Kate Curtis) went to church. On Monday Melville "left here for New York, to take passage from there to Europe." Herman Gansevoort accompanied him as far as Saratoga Springs. In New York Melville put the manuscript of *The Confidence-Man* in Allan's hands, trusting him to see to its publication, and he renewed his friendship with Evert Duyckinck as if they had never been estranged. Allan once again may have been middleman, for he, and Augusta, had never given up their contact with Duyckinck. Possibly the friendship had been renewed during one of Melville's earlier trips to town. Duyckinck's diary for 1 October records the visit: "Herman Melville passed the evening with me — fresh from his mountain charged to the muzzle with his sailor metaphysics and jargon of things unknowable." Duyckinck's labeling of Melville as sailor metaphysician rather than simply metaphysician shows that he had not changed his way of limiting his expectations from Melville on the basis of his origins as the author of *Typee*. But he gave Melville hospitable scope, and recorded that it was "a good stirring evening — ploughing deep and bringing to the surface some rich fruits of thought and experience" — that is, an evening when Melville ploughed deep and brought such fruits to the surface.

Duyckinck listed four topics of Melville's conversation, each of which has affinities with passages in *The Confidence-Man:* covert atheism in literature, the conniving of an unfaithful young wife, secret blasphemy among the lower social orders, and the bitter contrasts between a life destined for disaster and one destined for triumph:

> Melville instanced old Burton as atheistical — in the exquisite irony of his passages on some sacred matters; cited a good story from the Decameron the *Enchantment* of the husband in the tree; a story from judge Edmonds of a prayer meeting of female convicts at Sing Sing which the Judge was invited to witness and agreed to, provided he was introduced where he could not be seen. It was an orgie of indecency and blasphemy. Said of Bayard Taylor that as some augur predicted the misfortunes of Charles I from the infelicity of his countenance so Taylor's prosperity "borne up by the Gods" was written in his face.

Taylor, the versifier who had written Melville a valentine at Anne Lynch's party less than a decade before, had solidified a career as a travel-writer in the years that Melville's was crumbling under him. On 6 October Evert wrote to George, who was in London: "Herman Melville starts on another European pilgrimage in a few days by one of the Glasgow steamers—I think the 'Glasgow' on the 12th. He passed an Evening with me last week. He goes to Italy—for a sensation I suppose." "Sensation" sounds like a condescending or even slightly contemptuous word for someone who had enjoyed the "good stirring evening" a few days before, but Duyckinck was satirizing not just his friend but also the line of literary pilgrims who had made and written about their Italian trips, from Goethe onward. He hoped Melville would meet George in London.

On 29 September Melville had been too pressed to stop to see Uncle Peter and Aunt Susan, but on 7 October he wrote his "adieus" along with his plans: "I think of sailing for the other side of the ocean on Saturday next, to be gone an uncertain time." From the panicky little episode in 1849, when he barely got a passport in time to take the *Southampton* to England, Melville might have learned to overcome his "disinclination to perform the special duty of the hour," but he once again waited until the last days to request a passport, writing from New York on 6 October to William L. Marcy, a comic butt in Melville's 1847 "Authentic Anecdotes of 'Old Zack,' " now secretary of state: "I am about to visit Europe. Will you be good enough to supply me with a passport? I sail four days hence." This letter was received in the State Department on 7 October. Someone wrote "Mr Reddall" at the top, as in 1849, and someone assigned Melville passport number 14,786 near the top of the letter. Someone also meticulously wrote "Herman Melville" under Melville's signature, so the letters of the name would all be clear for anyone who copied it, as a clerk had to do for the "Register of Passports." A clerk noted at the bottom: "Blank sent, to be filled with description—"; at the top of the "Blank" the clerk instructed Melville: "Please fill up blanks in Passport, with description of person, and return this, a copy of the same, to Department of State." Making it easy, the clerk wrote "Herman Melville." in his neat hand after the first printed line of the form, "Description of Mr.   "; Melville promptly received both the "Blank" and the passport, already signed by Marcy, both designated "N°. 14.786."

Doing as he was told, Melville filled in the printed form and returned it for the State Department files. He had written carefully, in his best hand, but when he finished he folded it over before all the ink had dried, thereby creating a small smudge. He was thirty-seven years old. He had listed his height as five feet eight and some fraction of an inch, but the smudge obliterated whatever fraction he had put down. Melville said his forehead was medium, his eyes blue, his nose straight, his mouth medium, his chin round, his hair dark brown, his complexion fair, his face oval. In the actual passport

Melville put his height at 5' 8¾", presumably what he wrote on the State Department copy where the fraction was smudged. Melville retained this passport after his return to the United States in 1857.

The long persistence of Melville's character flaw of procrastination may be less curious than the odd discrepancy in how tall he said he was. The earliest record of his mature height, at almost twenty, is in the crew list of the *St. Lawrence*, which he signed on 3 June 1839. There he gave his height as 5' 8½". The height Melville listed on his passport in 1849 (5' 10⅛") is curious on two grounds. First, the difference between 8½ and 10⅛ is unusual, since it is somewhat infrequent for a man to grow 1⅝ inches after the age of twenty. Second, while a man will say he is 5' 10½", or even 5' 10¼", a man will not ordinarily give his height in eighths of an inch. Something more than an urge for accuracy seems involved in Melville's calling himself 5' 10⅛" tall. For the perfunctory purpose of obtaining a passport, surely 5' 10" would have sufficed, or 5' 10¼". As evident from the personal descriptions in the crew list of the *Acushnet*, for instance, it was common to measure by the quarter inch, but not a smaller unit. Melville's hyper-precision in this matter is poignant in retrospect because it magnifies the discrepancy between how tall he said he was in 1849 and how short he said he was in 1856. If it is unusual for a man to grow 1⅝ inches between twenty and thirty, it is still more unusual for a man to shrink 1⅜ inches between the ages of thirty and thirty-seven. The height Melville gave in 1856 may be his honest acknowledgment that sciatica and other physical ailments of the past several years had literally reduced his stature — an example of the same honesty that had earlier led him to acknowledge procrastination to be a "sad failing."

On 8 October Allan sent a copy of Daniel Shepherd's *Saratoga* to Duyckinck and with the author in tow called on Duyckinck that night, without Herman, who may have been taking a last look at his manuscript, for conviviality was being mixed with work. The next night, Duyckinck went to Shepherd's on Fourteenth Street for a session with both Herman and Allan Melville and Dr. Robert Tomes, back from Japan: "Good talk — Herman warming like an old sailor over the supper — He is going to Italy for the winter." The stages of the negotiations with Dix & Edwards are not documented, but a contract was drafted on 10 October, and the next day specified for delivery of the manuscript. That day, the eleventh, Melville sailed, leaving Allan to finish the negotiations. (A substituted "Memorandum of Agreement," spelling out several routine provisions, basically those in the contract for *The Piazza Tales*, was signed by Allan on 28 October; it specified the delivery date of "a certain manuscript book entitled 'The Confidence Man his Masquerade' " as on or before 1 November.) The eleventh was, Duyckinck recorded, "Another, yet another of the series of extraordinary fine days;

sunny, mellow, quiescent" (as he wrote to George two days later, they had been having "a rare autumn — the mellowed perfection of the year, day after day of heavenly calm and beauty"). After seeing the voyager off in the propeller steamer *Glasgow* for Glasgow, Duyckinck recorded: "Melville right hearty — Pleasant fates to him on his Neapolitan way." It was seven years to the day since Melville's last voyage to Europe.

[14]

Liverpool and the Levant
Late 1856–February 1857

> Who life doth loath, and longs death to behold
> Before he die, already dead with fear,
> And yet would live with heart half stony cold,
> Let him to sea, and he shall see it there.

In his Spenser Melville brackets these lines (204–7) in "Colin Clout's Come Home Again"; at the foot he writes: "Absolute coincidence here between Spenser's conceit and another person's, in connection with a very singular thought" (Priscilla Ambrose Collection)

MELVILLE SAILED FROM New York on 11 October 1856. During the two-week voyage he avoided "some six or seven 'commercial travellers', a hard set who did little but drink and gamble the whole way over," as he wrote Allan, after he reached Liverpool. On the *Glasgow* was Colonel George Campbell Rankin, the author of *What Is Truth?* (1854, expanded 1856); the title, Melville immediately recognized, was the last thing Pilate said to Jesus before asking the Jews if they wanted him to be released for Passover. Francis Bacon had added a Melvillean twist with his expansion of John 18:38: "What is truth? said jesting Pilate, and would not stay for an answer." Rankin's book was a skeptic's challenge against the internal contradictions of the New Testament and the tyranny of conventional Christianity. Taken with Rankin as he was, Melville avoided naming him to Allan, out of some innate delicacy about putting down another man's name in ink: "there was one man, who interested me considerably, one who had been an officer of the native troops in India, and besides was a good deal of a philosopher and had been all over the world. With him I had many long talks, and we so managed to kill time." These talks were "on fixed fate &c." — once again, as with George Adler and with Nathaniel Hawthorne, the topics discussed in Hell by Milton's fallen angels in *Paradise Lost*.

When the *Glasgow* anchored at Greenock on 25 October, Melville acted out of old impulse, with disastrous results: "A sailor was lowering a boat by one of the tackles; the rope got foul; I jumped to clear it for him, when suddenly the tackle started, and a coil of the rope (new Manilla) flew up in my face with great violence, and for the moment, I thought my nose was ruined for life." For the next week, during the whole of his time in Scotland, he "presented the aspect of one who had been in a bar-room fight." The next morning, Sunday the twenty-sixth, the *Glasgow* went some twenty miles up the Clyde between banks that reminded Melville of towpaths on the Erie Canal and past people so pleased by the sight that Melville felt the ship was "received by acclamation" (a description he recorded in his journal of this trip, using, at first, the same notebook he had during his 1849–50 travels). His first goal in Glasgow was the cathedral, which had been despoiled by Calvinists. Then he climbed into the adjacent Necropolis to watch "John Knox in Geneva cap frowning down on the cathedral" rather than applauding the new arrival. He made an excursion on the twenty-eighth to Loch Lomond and on the way back explored Dumbarton Castle, magnificently situated on the promontory above the confluence of the Clyde and the Levern. He carried away images: William Wallace's six-foot broadsword (like a "great cleaver" — this before it was removed to Stirling); "soldiers in red coats about the Rock like flamingoes among the cliffs"; and rams with "smoky fleeces."

Melville had asked some Scots on the steamer about his Great-grandfather Melvill's ancestral home, Scoonie, and did some research ashore (checking lists of the clergy) before giving up, partly because he was embarrassed by the "ugly hurt" on the bridge of his nose. Between 29 October and 8 November he made a jagged tour from Glasgow. In tribute to his Melvill ancestors and to Sir Walter Scott, the great poet and novelist of his youth, he went straight to Stirling, where he could ascend to the castle on the volcanic crag above the town and look down toward the flat valley of the River Forth. He knew enough Scottish history to envision Wallace entrapping the English at Stirling Bridge in 1297, and to appreciate the city's strategic location for north-south as well as east-west traffic in Scotland. He left no mention of going to Bannockburn, but it would have been like him to walk out to the place where Robert the Bruce secured Scottish independence in 1314. There he could pay homage not only to the military heroes but to Robert Burns, who had memorably challenged those "Scots, Wha Hae wi' Wallace bled, / Scots wham Bruce has aften led." He stopped at Perth, farther down the River Forth (probably not lured by Scott's "Fair Maid" of that town), then made Edinburgh his base for a few days. From there he made his literary pilgrimage to see Scott's Abbotsford on the Tweed, the sort of home any great writer ought to have been able to build for himself. He toured the grand old-looking castle-like structure with its vast library where the bookshelves extended so high that the upper rows were reached from a railed-off balcony running around the room. Armories he was always interested in, especially where he could see Rob Roy's gun, and the high wall on the eastern side of Abbotsford stuck in his memory. Melville had dined with Scott's cold-fish son-in-law John Gibson Lockhart and knew Scott had worked himself to death to save Abbotsford for his heirs, a perturbing story for a tourist whose Scottish father had squandered a fortune but had not heroically recovered it before dying.

The Shaws had assumed that Melville's mission was to find Sam Shaw and travel with him. The best way for Melville to find Sam was to inquire at Baring Brothers in London, and at the outset Melville seemed to fall in with the plans for him to go directly to London and do his best to communicate with Sam. Even after he landed in Glasgow, according to Judge Shaw's letter to Samuel on 23 November, Melville "expected after a few days in Scotland to proceed to Liverpool & thence to London, where he would inquire for you at Baring Bro. Co. & thus probably be enabled to put himself in communication with you." Shaw added, "I hope you will meet him, and so make your arrangements, as to travel together." During some of his tour of Scotland, and down to Newcastle-upon-Tyne and York (where he took a day to walk the Wall and see the Minster), Melville did have a traveling companion, a young Mr. Willard of Troy, "a theological student, very uninteresting, but better than nobody," as he told Allan — a way of putting things that casually revealed how deep his gregarious impulse still was, despite all talk of Timonism. At some point Melville determined to go to Liverpool before going to London and trying to locate Sam Shaw. He could see Hawthorne and broach the subject of his forthcoming book, ascertaining whether he could then write Allan that Hawthorne would act as his agent in placing *The Confidence-Man* in London, rather than going himself and trying to sell it to a publisher without manuscript or proofs in hand. (Much later Lizzie recalled that he had taken "manuscript books" with him for publication, but he did not have a duplicate manuscript, and could not have had proofs.) He could leave with Hawthorne the trunk which the women had packed for him and which he taken aboard the *Glasgow*, easier than arguing with them about it. Most important, at the great port of Liverpool he could shop for the cheapest tolerable steamer for the Mediterranean.

After York, whenever possible taking the cheapest but miserably inconvenient Parliamentary trains, and practicing the "strictest economy" in lodging and eating, Melville went by way of Lancaster to Liverpool, where he wrote Allan on 10 November, two days after he arriving there. The strictest economy in 1856 contrasted sharply enough with his experiences in the squalor of the dock area in 1839, for he stayed now in a decent hotel, the White Bear, several blocks from the docks, although not up the slope at the Adelphi where wealthier travelers like Evert Duyckinck and Lem Shaw stayed. At his first meal at the White Bear he was amused at the farcical pretense that he was a guest, not a customer, and remembered Thomas Powell's old advice about asking prices. He paid a pilgrimage to the Exchange and "Looked at Nelson's statue, with peculiar emotion, mindful of 20 years ago." "Peculiar" was a guarded word for the emotions he felt standing there, remembering himself as an unknown young sailor in 1839, later a famous author, now a failure as author and husband. At the moment of Nelson's triumph Death had reached through his clothing to clutch his heart. Ourselves are Fate, Melville had decided (*White-Jacket*, ch. 75), and the scene depicted before him bore some resemblance to the way Fate had groped for his heart at the moment he had expected to gain literary immortality with *Moby-Dick*.

Later it rained, and it rained the next morning, a Sunday, when, thinking to find Hawthorne at home, Melville took a steamboat across the Mersey to Rock Ferry. He learned there that Hawthorne "had removed thence 18 months previous, & was residing out of town," in Southport—a sharp reminder of how completely he had lost touch with his friend during his personal miseries of the past years. The consulate itself was convenient. He could stop by the Nelson statue, then half a block south he could cross Dale and another block to Brunswick and the street where the consulate stood. When Melville showed up, unannounced, on 10 November, Hawthorne wrote in his journal that he looked "much as he used to do (a little paler, and perhaps a little sadder), in a rough outside coat, and with his characteristic gravity and reserve of manner." Melville felt uneasy after his frustrating ride to Rock Ferry, as Hawthorne did, for different reasons: "I felt rather awkward at first; because this is the first time I have met him since my ineffectual attempt to get him a consular appointment from General Pierce. However, I failed only from real lack of power to serve him; so there was no reason to be ashamed." Melville accounted for his presence not by laying out literary plans but by a selective medical history: he had "not been well, of late"; he had been "affected with neuralgic complaints in his head and limbs." Hawthorne concluded sensibly that Melville "no doubt" had "suffered from too constant literary occupation, pursued without much success, latterly." His writings, Hawthorne noted, "for a long while past, have indicated a morbid state of mind." Hawthorne's evidence for this was *Pierre*, as far as we know, although he may have read some of Melville's stories in imported copies of *Putnam's Magazine* and *Harper's New Monthly Magazine*, the sort of thing Atlantic passengers would carry for shipboard reading and then happily leave off with the literary-man at the consulate. Perhaps neither man mentioned the story Melville had tried to persuade Hawthorne to write, so that Hawthorne never knew that Melville, in a morbid state of mind or not, had actually completed *The Isle of the Cross*.

Taking up his letter to Allan after seeing Hawthorne, Melville outlined his plans for taking a steamer directly to Constantinople for a hundred dollars. He calculated that he could visit Alexandria, Cairo, Trieste, Venice, and Rome ("for a considerable stay"), then return to the United States by "March at the furthest." He did not mention the Holy Land in this sketch of his proposed itinerary. For whatever reason, he did not mention anything about *The Confidence-Man* to Allan in this letter, although Hawthorne subsequently acted as Melville's agent, after Allan asked him to do so. Melville spent the morning of 11 November looking at the available steamers, then went with Hawthorne up to Southport, a vacation spot, already slightly seedy, on the shore north of Liverpool. On the way, Hawthorne told him that George L. Duyckinck was lying in a London hospital, his leg broken in a collision on the Greenwich Railway on 30 October. Typically, while Melville had been traveling at the cheapest rates, George had kept better company, for the *Times* of London described him as "an American gentleman, travelling first-class." Hawthorne had inquired and been told that visitors were not permitted to see the injured American, so Melville assuaged his conscience, the more readily because Hawthorne heard further that George "was getting on well, and had friends about him." To Allan, later, Herman explained his motives cautiously: "as matters have turned out, I could not have gone to London without the utmost disarrangement of my plans. Nevertheless, did I suppose that my prescence would be particularly welcome to Mr Duyckinck, or give him ease, I would go on to see him as it is. But the extent of my acquaintance with him hardly justifies me in supposing that such would be the case." The coolly measured "extent of my acquaintance" was phrasing Allan could understand, with his own more intimate knowledge of the Duyckincks in recent years. Evert, before he learned of the accident, wrote George that he had heard of Melville "at Glasgow on his way to London" and assumed that by then, 18 November, Melville would have called on him. Thinking so carefully about money, having spent only about thirty-five dollars during his first two weeks ashore, Melville was not willing to undertake the expense of a trip to London, and had no desire to revive still-bitter associations under new and awkward circumstances, however genial he had managed to be in the presence of Evert before his departure.

For his visit to Southport, Melville carried "the least little bit of a bundle," which he told Hawthorne "contained a night shirt and a tooth-brush." At that time no gentleman thought of changing shirts every day, but when Melville wore the same shirt and other clothing from Tuesday to Thursday one could suspect that he might be capable of going still longer without changing shirts, socks, and drawers—a thought that prompted Hawthorne to this reflection: "He is a person of very gentlemanly instincts in every respect, save that he is a little heterodox in the matter of clean linen." Melville saw that Sophia was not in good health. In his journal Melville did not mention Rose, whom he did not recollect as a person in her own right, but noted that Una was taller than her mother and that Julian had "grown into a fine lad." There was nothing to see in Southport the town. On 12 November the men took a "pretty long walk" (Hawthorne noted) along the Irish Sea. "Sands & grass. Wild & desolate. A strong wind. Good talk" was Melville's description. Hawthorne recorded that they "sat down in a hollow among the sand hills (sheltering ourselves from the high, cool wind) and smoked a cigar." The men could no longer talk quite freely (as they had done on Melville's thirty-second birthday) of "time and eternity, things of this world and of the next, and books, and publishers, and all possible and impossible matters," for books and publishers was a topic best left unexplored, beyond, possibly, Melville's sounding out his friend to act as intermediary in offering *The Confidence-Man* to an English publisher. Here the subject of Melville's monologue was safely cosmic:

> Melville, as he always does, began to reason of Providence and futurity, and of everything that lies beyond human ken, and informed me that he had "pretty much made up his mind to be annihilated"; but still he does not seem to rest in that anticipation; and, I think, will never rest until he gets hold of a definite belief. It is strange how he persists—and has persisted ever since I knew him, and probably long before—in wandering to-and fro over these deserts, as dismal and monotonous as the sand hills amid which we were sitting. He can neither believe, nor be comfortable in his unbelief; and he is too honest and courageous not to try to do one or the other. If he were a religious man, he would be one of the most truly religious and reverential; he has a very high and noble nature, and better worth immortality than most of us.

That they were talking about Melville's loss of belief in the theological concept of immortality is clear from Hawthorne's use of "futurity" and his comment that Melville's noble nature makes him "better worth immortality than most of us." This is the only known testimony that Melville was obsessed with the problem of his own immortality, although ample evidence suggests that he was obsessed with the cluster of philosophical and theological concepts conveyed by the "Fixed Fate, Free-will, foreknowledge absolute," as he spelled the Miltonic words in his 13 October 1849 journal entry, after hearing the expoundings of his new acquaintance George Adler. His interest there, in 1849, was intellectual, and he had been at great pains to get down just what Adler thought.

If Melville actually used the "annihilated," Hawthorne, like Melville steeped in Milton, would have heard an echo of *Paradise Lost*. Hawthorne's attribution of "pretty much" to Melville may be verbatim (Melville had used the idiom as recently as his 24 March 1856 letter to Dix & Edwards), but he had just used it in his notebooks in his own voice, and it was an idiom he favored. As both men knew, in book 6 of *Paradise Lost* Milton explains that spirits like Satan cannot be killed piecemeal — "Vital in every part," they "Cannot but by annihilating die." Gansevoort had used this passage in a fiery speech. In his copy of *Paradise Lost* Melville underlined "Cannot but by annihilating die" and put a vertical mark in the margin by the line. His alluding to it to Hawthorne may have indicated that there was still a defiant edge to his resignation: being annihilated at once was better than slow death. Hawthorne's comment about Melville's reverential nature also sprang from a specific context, his knowledge of reviewers (Duyckinck among them) who had denounced *Typee* and *Omoo* and even *Moby-Dick* as not just irreverent but downright irreligious.

After dinner Melville and Hawthorne walked out again and found themselves at the Fox & Geese, where they drank stout as best they could, considering the lack of elbow room. On 13 November the two rode down to Liverpool together at noon, and Melville spent the rest of the day "pressing inquiries among steamers, & writing letters, & addressing papers &c." Hawthorne's young acquaintance Henry A. Bright, a Unitarian minister, son of a wealthy manufacturer, showed Melville around town the next day (reminiscing about his visiting Hawthorne in Concord and the American Unitarian Catharine Maria Sedgwick in Lenox). On 30 November Una wrote to her aunt, Elizabeth Peabody, that the visit had been a burden on the hostess: "Mr. Melville was here a day or two, and Mamma overtired herself during his visit, and was quite unwell for a day or two afterwards." Melville's visits had always worn her out, but in the past they had exhilarated her as well.

On Saturday, 15 November, Hawthorne and Melville went to Chester together for a packed day of systematic vagabondizing which Hawthorne recorded in his journal in great detail and which Melville wholly omitted from his own journal, merely listing his activities as riding in the omnibus, going "out to Toxhete Park &c" and seeing the great organ at St. George's Hall. Melville and Hawthorne did everything tourists do in Chester — walked the wall, admired the Roudee (a race course since Roman times), enjoyed the river (the Dee), ate in a confectioner's shop in the Rows (little veal-pies, damson tarts, washed down with Bass's ale), and toured the Cathedral and the Refectory. Best of all, they spent a good deal of time in a small snuggery behind the bar of the Yacht Inn, smoking cigars and drinking stout while conversing with the landlord, who then took them up to a room to show them the little windowpane where Jonathan Swift had etched with a diamond a bitter comment on the local clergymen who had left him waiting to sup with them. (Melville must have known a great deal more about Swift than we can prove; we have an offhand reference to the "Dean" but no copy of anything by Swift that had been in Melville's library.) The men parted just at dark on a street-corner in Liverpool, in the rainy evening, thinking they would not see each other again until Melville came back through to pick up the trunk he had left at the consulate. It was five years — perhaps five years to the day — from another parting, the time Melville had hired the dining room of the Little Red Inn in Lenox for his publication party for *Moby-Dick* and invited a single guest, the man to whom he had dedicated the book.

From Liverpool Melville spelled the situation out to Allan after he had all but decided to sail in the *Egyptian*, a screw-steamer: "I think this voyage is the best thing I can do — it is certainly the cheapest way in which I can spend the coming 26 days." On 17 November the departure of the *Egyptian* was put off a day ("Great disappointment. Tired of Liverpool."), which meant that Melville was able to see Hawthorne again. Out of his immediate disappointment, but perhaps also out of his deepest sense of being, Melville confided that "he already felt much better than in America," but that "he did not anticipate much pleasure in his rambles, for that the spirit of adventure is gone out of him." Hawthorne confirmed Melville's explicit statement: "He certainly is much overshadowed since I saw him last; but I hope he will brighten as he goes onward." At least Melville still knew how to travel light, for he had stowed all the gear he wanted in one carpetbag: "This is the next best thing to going naked; and as he wears his beard and moustache, and so needs no dressing-case — nothing but a tooth-brush — I do not know a more independent personage. He learned his travelling habits by drifting about, all over the South Sea, with no other clothes or equipage than a red flannel shirt and a pair of duck trowsers. Yet we seldom see men of less criticizable manners than he." Hawthorne was still uneasy about how long Melville could stay in the same clothes, but he admired the freedom Melville took as his right. And in fact Melville had his clothes washed whenever he could — at Edinburgh, for example, where he sent to the laundry "9 Shirts / 1 Night shirt / 7 Hankerchiefs / 2 Pair Stockings / Draw[er]s & undershirts."

When Hawthorne caught up on his journal-writing he decided that he and Melville after some initial awkwardness had soon been "pretty much" on their "former terms of sociability and confidence." "Pretty much" seems to be a quotation from Melville, but in fact it was formulaic with Hawthorne, something he said of himself and other men, not just Melville, so it must not be taken as something Melville in fact spoke. Hawthorne himself had secrets that obstructed real intimacy, Melville was later certain, and Melville (who in his exuberant confidence had written Hawthorne frankly that dollars damned him) could now say nothing about the horrors of his years of indebtedness any more than he could promise to make good literary use of his present voyaging. The men could still be sociable with each other, and, for his part, Melville could be confidential about anything beyond human ken easier than he could talk about what he faced on his return to the United States. During the rest of this voyage Melville seems to have encountered no one else to participate in his metaphysical speculations as Rankin had done on the *Glasgow* or listen to them as Hawthorne would do. The people Melville passed time with on shipboard tended to be the ship's captain or engineer rather than fellow passengers, and ashore he spent more time with drivers and guides than other tourists. He called on some British and American artists and sculptors. He spent time with a few new acquaintances, mainly Americans, some of whom might have been expected to make a record of their meeting the author of *Typee*, but no such documents have been found, and henceforth for this trip the only record is Melville's journal or what is known from reports of his letters home: no one is known to have preserved a record of meeting him, with the single exception of his brother-in-law Sam, who saw him for perhaps an hour in Rome. Melville's most profound historical, theological, philosophical, and aesthetic experiences during the trip occurred when he was quite alone.

Soon after the *Egyptian* left Liverpool on 18 November Melville made friends with the captain, Robert Taitt. Fine weather and increasing warmth combined with his sense of recent history to prompt Melville's reflection that from the lighthouse on Cape St. Vincent the "Great procession of ships bound to Crimea" could have been descried. His symbolic imagination revived at Gibraltar ("Rock strongly lit, all the rest in shade. England throwing the rest of the world in shade."), and once well into the Mediterranean he burst out: "Beautiful morning. Blue sea & sky. Warm as May. Spanish coast in sight. Mountains, snow capped, always so Captain says. Mate comes out with straw hat. Shirt sleeves. Threw open my coat.—Such weather as one might have in Paridise. Pacific. November too! Like sailing on a lake." Glimpses of the African coast recalled the story of the Moor in *Don Quixote*, as well as stirring episodes in the naval history of the young American republic, and the height of some of the mountains caught his interest. The weather continued glorious in the Mediterranean while Lizzie had her Boston Thanksgiving; and even after Malta, when the weather worsened and he had to secure himself in his berth to keep from being rolled out, he kept his stomach while other passengers suffered.

On 2 December the *Egyptian* arrived in Syra, the port of the Greek archipelago. There Melville made notes suitable for elaborating into a set piece, characteristically using the imperative—"Take all the actors" (as he had done in "The Encantadas" with his recipe for a true desert island):

> Animated appearance of the quay. Take all the actors of operas in a night from the theaters of London, & set them to work in their fancy dresses, weighing bales, counting codfish, sitting at tables on the dock, smoking, talking, sauntering,—sitting in boats &c—picking up rags, carrying water casks, bemired &c—will give some notion of Greek port. Picturesqueness of the whole. Variety of it. Greek trousers, sort of cross between petticoat & pantaloons. Some with white petticoats & embroidered jackets. Fine forms, noble faces. Mustache &c.—

The man who had written "Poor Man's Pudding" and knew just how little the picturesque meant to someone in poverty nevertheless was struck by this very un-American sort of poverty: "Poor people live here. Picturesque. Some old men looked like Pericles reduced to a chiffonier—such a union of picturesque & poverty stricken." The lack of sanitation made this a terrible "nest for the plague," but there was no denying the charm of the wharf:

> In December tables & chairs out of doors, coffee & water pipes.—Carpenters & blacksmiths working in the theatrical costumes—Scavenger in his opera costume going about with dust pan & brush through the streets, & emptying his pan into panniers of an ass.—No horses or carriages—streets merely made for footpassengers.—The crowds on the quays all with red caps, looking like flamingos. Long tassells—laborers wear them, & carry great bundles of codfish on their heads.—Few seem to have anything to do. All lounge. Greek signs over a pieman's.

In order to gain his impressions, he had engaged in strenuous exercise, for the best views in Syra always required that he climb, and climb some more. "Up & up, only guide was *to mount*," he wrote; at the top in the court of a church he at last had his "fine view of archilpago & islands" (which he made a note to get the names of). From that height, the wharf was "a kind of semicircle, coinciding with the ampitheater of hills," and from there he could make the observations which would go into his journal.

Recognizing how seriously his American passenger took the duty of seeing the best views, the captain roused Melville before dawn on 6 December during their passage to Salonica and asked him to come on deck: "Did so.

Saw Mount Olympus, covered with snow at the summit, & looking most magestic in the dawn. Ossa & Pelion to the South. Olympus 10,000 feet high, according to the Captain's chart. O & P about 4 or 5000. Long ranges of hills along the Thessalain shore. Mount Athos (rather conical) on the opposite shore." Once anchored at Salonica he could see "Olympus over against the town far across the water, in plain sight." At Salonica Melville's historical sensibility came into play as he looked at the minarets rising above walls built by the Genoese. For the first time, he saw mosques, which were "formerly Greek churches, but upon the conquest of the Turks turned into their present character." Beyond this comparatively recent history he was struck by "Roman remains of a triumphal arch across a street," with battle scenes sculpted at the base. Melville's ironic eye noted the tawdry or mundane present uses of parts of the glorious past, miserable wooden buildings about the arch, a Turkish café near one pier, three columns of a noble Greek edifice "used as gateway & support to outhouse of a Jew's abode."

The next day Melville had an outrageous encounter with "Duckworth, the English resident": "Said he had been *a day's shooting in the Vale of Tempe* — Ye Gods! whortleberrying on Olympus, &c." The "&c" suggests that Melville was leaving room for an elaboration of unconscious sacrileges by a modern man absolutely oblivious to historical associations. Such ignorance was all the more astonishing in a man born in Europe, not in the New World. Here Melville began moving into double or triple consciousness, playing off his immediate observations against one or more periods of the past. After this encounter he went on horseback with guide and guard to the house of John (Djékis) Abbot, or Abbott, a ship's agent of a Greek-English family, three miles inland. Abbott lived regally behind a "high thick stone wall" and buffered by armed guards, but on Melville's presenting his letter "a handsome, polite Greek" led him through the grounds: "Oriental style. Very beautiful. Hot houses & fountains & trellises & arbors innumerable. Old sycamores. Served with sweetmeats & liqueurs & coffee. Bath rooms Thick dome perforated — light but no heat." It was a glimpse of fabulous and exotic wealth. That evening Melville socialized with the captain, who "told a story about the heap of arms affecting the compass," something he remembered.

On 8 December after watching the tumult at the dock when an Austrian steamer arrived from Constantinople, Melville made a note (again using the imperative) which he could develop when he needed to: "Imagine an immense accumulation of the rags of all nations, & all colors rained down on a dense mob, all struguling for huge bales & bundles of rags, gesturing with all gestures & wrangling in all tongues. Splashing into the water from the grounded boats." Upon this modern scene "Olympus looked from afar cold & snowy." Melville commented with mild ruefulness: "Surprising the Gods took no interest in the thing. Might at least have moved their sympathy." The next day, remaining on board, waiting for the ship to sail, he observed the boarding of deck passengers for Constantinople, among whom were "two 'beys effendi' in long furred robes of yellow, looking like Tom cats," and accompanied by their harems. Melville left Salonica on the ninth for Constantinople, the moonlit night giving him a magical sight: "Passed Olympus glittering at top with ice. When it was far astern, its snow line showed in the moonlight like a strip of white cloud. Looked unreal — but still was there."

When the steamer entered the Hellespont on 10 December he compared the new castles on the European and the Asiatic sides and commented: "Little difference in the aspect of the continents. Only Asia looked a sort of used up — superannuated." He noted conventionally how long a swim Leander and Byron had made, then at Gallipoli recalled that he was "where the French & English first landed during the War" — the Crimean War, just concluded in March. He was not quite ready to come fully to life, but the life-affirming tug grew stronger: "I could not get up much enthusiasm; though passing Xerxes' bridge-piers (or the site of them) & the mouth of the Granicus, &c &c &c. Still, I thought what a sublime approach has the Sultan to his capital. Antichambers of seas & lakes & corridors of glorious straits." And he reminded himself that he had to rise betimes the next day to behold Constantinople. They arrived near Pera, the port of Constantinople, in a thick fog which trapped them all day close enough to the invisible capital to hear the dogs bark. The second noon the fog began to lift: "The fog only lifted from about the skirts of the city, which being built upon a promontory, left the crown of it hidden wrapped in vapor. Could see the base & wall of St. Sophia but not the dome. It was a coy disclosure, a kind of coquetting, leaving room for imagination & heigthing the scene. Constantinople, like her Sultanas, was thus seen veiled in her 'ashmack'. Magic effect of the lifting up of the fog disclosing such a city." That evening Melville made his way to the Hotel du Globe in Pera, then wandered around a little before dark, wary of "footpads & assassins."

The next day, 13 December, Melville explored, walking all the way into Constantinople, wearying himself and becoming lost:

> Intricacy of the streets. Started alone for Constan^ple and after a terrible long walk, found myself back where I started. Just like getting lost in a wood. No plan to streets. Pocket-compass. Perfect labryth. Narrow. Close, shut in. If one could but get *up* aloft, it would be easy to see one's way out. If you could get up into tree. Soar out of the maze. But no. No names to the streets no more than to natural allies among the groves. No numbers. No anything.

After a priest-dogged exploration of the interior of St. Sophia, he made his way to the Roman Hippodrome, near which stood "the six towered mosque of Sultan Achmet; soaring up with its snowy spires into the pure blue sky." Nothing was finer, Melville thought. He studied an obelisk with Roman inscription upon the base and "a broken monument of bronze, representing three twisted serpents erect upon the tails," the heads broken off, and examined other bits of ancient monuments. Still more impressive was the "Burnt Column" of Constantine, surviving on the site of Constantine's Forum on the hill west of St. Sophia. From there he went to "the Cistern of 1001 columns," a "palatial sort of Tartarus" once used as a reservoir, now full of boys operating spinning jennies, twisting silk. Going down was like going into a ship's hold, endangered from the invisible skeins of silk. He was frightened ("Terrible place to be robbed or murdered in"), feeling emotions very like those he had attributed to his Amasa Delano. At last he found his way out of the labyrinth and had his reward for climbing the Watch Tower: "From the top, my God, what a view! Surpasses everything. The Propontis, the Bosphorous, the Golden Horn, the domes the minarets, the bridges, the men of war, the cypruss. — Indescribable." From there he went to the Pigeon Mosque, then the Mosque of Sultan Suleiman, and at last down to the Golden Horn. Every time he got back into the crowds he was afraid he would be robbed (his guide set the example of walking with his hands on his pockets) and felt he would "suffocate for room."

The next day Melville's historic sense had freer play as he escaped the throngs to examine the wall where Constantinople "was taken by the Turks & the last of the Constantines fell in their defence." Beguiled rather than terrified, he wandered on through the gay — but not suffocatingly dense — Sunday crowds (one of three Sundays celebrated every week, he noted), making his way to "the wall-end at Sea of Marmora," where the water dashed "up against the foundation here for 6 miles to the Seraglio." From the walls of the Seven Towers he gained a "Superb view of the city & sea." After he passed "under an arch of the acqueduct of Valens" he saw a sight that prompted a grandiloquent reflection in the journal: "In these lofty arches, ivied & weatherbeaten, & still grand, the ghost of Rome seems to stride with disdain of the hovels of this part of Stamboul." Recrossing to Pera, the Franks' city, where only Europeans were allowed to reside (so said William Furniss in *Landvoieglee: or, Views Across the Sea* [New York: Appleton, 1850]), he watched the crowds on the bank of the Bosphorus ("like Brooklyn heights"), then gained "a superb view of Sea of Marmora & Prince Isles & Scutari." "Utterly used up" was the way he felt at night, back on the steamer.

The next morning, 15 December, Melville felt "as if broken on the wheel," but he roused himself to climb the prodigious Genoese Tower: "From the gallery without, all round, another glorious view. (Three great views of Consto^{ple}) All important to one desirous to learn something of the bearings of Pera &c. After much study succeeded in understanding the way to the two great bridges." Looking down on the throngs he saw a telling image, the street that seemed paved with tiles because so many "Fez caps" hid it from view. Incited by some literary precedents (from the forbidden *Anastasius* he had known the magnificence of the sea view of Constantinople), he was preyed upon by other literary memories. When he saw an Armenian funeral in the crowded streets of Constantinople and felt dogged by importunate Greeks, he remembered, with mounting nervousness, a passage from Johann Schiller's *Ghost-Seer*, and recorded his fear: "The mere mysterious, persistant, silent following. At last escaped them." He kept making comparisons: seeing the Burnt Column again, he thought of great "Croton water pipes on end," remembering the great civic improvement that awaited him on his return from the Pacific.

On 16 December on a steamer up the Bosphorus to Buyukdereh Melville felt safe, and enthusiastic: "Magnificent! The whole scene one pomp of art & Nature. Europe & Asia here show their best. A challenge of contrasts, where by the successively alternate sweeps of the shores both sides seem to retire from every new proffer of beauty, again in some grand prudery to advance with a bolder bid, and thereupon again & again retiring, neither willing to retreat from the contest of beauty. — Myrtle, Cyprus, Cedar — evergreens." His comparisons continued. The water was "clear as Ontario"; the alternation of promontories and bays was like "the Highlands of the Hudson, magnified"; the Euxine in sight from Buyukdereh was like a "chain of Lake Georges" ("No wonder the Czars have always coveted the capital of the Sultans"). He decided the cypress trees were green minarets, and that minarets may have been made in imitation of the shape of the tree. Back after his excursion, he wandered, watched, and entered into his journal a mass of detail ready to be worked up into a verbal panorama ("Banvard should paint a few hundred miles of this pageant of moving procession"). Knowing the *Arabian Nights* so well, he was startled at hearing literary names like Yusef, Hassan, and Hamet "bandied on all sides." Wandering near the Hippodrome till nearly dusk, he came out at a gate on the Sea of Marmara and took a "kayack" to "Tophanna" (Top-Khaneh, a northern suburb), fascinated at the height of the walls on the waterside (Abbotsford walls as seen from the east, "only, on a grand scale").

Melville continued to seek out observation points, on 17 December gaining the "Grand view from Seraglio Point — Marmora, Bospherous, Scutari." He took a caique across to the great barracks at Scutari on 18 December for a

"Noble view of Constantinople & up Bospherous." That afternoon in the steamer *Acadia*, bound for Alexandria, he rounded Seraglio Point at sunset: "Glorious sight. Scutari & its heights, glowed like sapphire. Wonderful clearness of air. As a promontory is covered with trees, terraced up clear to its top, so Consa^(tople) with houses. Long line of walls. — Out into Sea of Marmora." He was, despite his early expectations, taking great pleasure in his traveling, for all the inconveniences, stretches of boredom, and moments of dread or even outright panic. On the nineteenth they passed through the Dardanelles at daybreak, then passed the Plain of Troy with Mount Ida beyond, keeping close to the shore of Asia Minor. When they anchored in the bay of Mytelene, the captain let Melville examine his chart of "Mouth of Dardanelles & Plain of Troy," where he could see "that the whole coast hereabouts & for some ways inland is covered with ruins of great antiquity." Homer's war collided with Tennyson's war, for as he sailed through Besika Bay he envisioned the English and French fleets joining there, four years earlier. As the ship entered the bay of Smyrna on 20 December Melville saw ("conspicuous from the sea") an old castle on Mount Pagus. The steamer *Egyptian* was in port, so he paid his respects to Captain Taitt. There was a calamity interesting to any sailor, a steamer grounded and another towing her off. He went ashore and talked to the American consul, Edward S. Offley, born in Greece, and did his sightseeing with a guide ("a grave ceremonious man with a frogged coat carrying a silver mounted sword in a velvet scabbard in one hand, and a heavy silver mounted cowhide in the other"). Still game to gain the best views, he "Went up Mt Pagus" until he gained "a supurb view of bay & town." On the twenty-first he spent hours with Captain Taitt, culminating with dinner on the *Arcadia* with himself and three captains, Orpheus, Taitt, and Eustace, where there was much "talk of India voyages."

Melville had been shocked by Duckworth's ignorant irreverence for the past, but on the passage from Smyrna back to Syra on 23 December he found it hard to be reverent himself when he saw that Delos had "a most barren aspect, however flowery in fable." Worse, for one saturated in the book of Revelation, Patmos was "another disenchanting isle." In his ruminations on Christmas Day, Melville developed his notions about the Greeks, echoing his phrasing in "Benito Cereno" about the way an article of clothing may be contrived for utility then be continued merely as ornament:

> The Greek, of any class, seems a natural dandy. His dress, though a laborer, is that of a gentleman of leisure. This flowing & graceful costume, with so much of pure ornament about it & so little fitted for labor, must needs have been devised in some Golden Age. But surviving in the present, is most picturesquely out of keeping with the utilities. — Some of the poorest sort present

curious examples of what may be called the decayed picturesque. The Greeks have a great partiality for the tassel. This seems emblematic. You see one going about the quay displaying in every tempting mode, a long graceful tassel, — holding it up admiringly. —

This was to say that the Greeks were beings to be envied by a man of his recent experiences, yet they were living in a less than enviable world. Thinking the matter over the day after Christmas, Melville elaborated a distinction: the Greek isles had "lost their virginity," while the isles he had seen in the Polynesian archipelago were still "fresh as at their first creation." The Greek isles looked "worn" and were meager, "like life after enthusiasm is gone": "The aspect of all of them is sterile & dry. Even Delos whose flowers rose by miracle in the sea, is now a barren moor, & to look upon the bleak yellow of Patmos, who would ever think that a god had been there." He may have remembered his own state of mind and body a few days before, when he had been unable to muster much enthusiasm for the Hellespont.

At Alexandria on 28 December Melville described Pompey's Pillar as looking "like huge stick of candy after having been long sucked" (an echo of what he and Hawthorne had observed of the Cathedral in Chester, that it looked "as if it were a sugar toy, and had been sucked in a child's mouth," so much was it worn away). He saw Cleopatra's Needles, one of them upright, "one of them down & covered over," abraded on one side by siroccos over the millennia. (After 1880, he saw one of these Needles often, upright, in his walks through Central Park.) The next day he picked up his passport from the consul, an American his own age, Edwin De Leon ("formerly political literary man at Washington"), then managed to meet some congenial Americans, the officers of the U.S. frigate *Constellation* (which had been much modified since he had known her in the Pacific). He struck up a friendship at once with Dr. John Alexander Lockwood, ship's surgeon, brother to the professor of mathematics on the *United States* whom he had put into *White-Jacket*, and they became companions briefly, as Fate had it, in more than one country.

On his arrival at Cairo late in the afternoon of 30 December Melville checked into Shepherd's Hotel:

Life at hotel. Magnitude of Shepherds, lofty ceilings, stone floors, iron beds, no carpets, thin mattress, no feathers, blinds, moscho curtain. — All showing the tropics. And that you are in the East is shown by fresh dates on table for desert, water in stone jars — (cool) waited on by Arabs — dragomen — clap your hands for servants. — Brilliant scene at late dinner — hard to beleive you are near the pyramids. Yet some repose in fastidiousness.

These observations were written down later: as soon as he had registered, Melville left to walk about the square with Dr. Lockwood — the most congenial companion he had found since he left Hawthorne. (He may have traveled from Alexandria with Lockwood.) In his diary he made a note only a dozen and a half words long; the next day, when he went to the Pyramids and back to the hotel, he wrote fewer than three dozen words, racked that he could spend only that one full day in Cairo, the last day of 1856, because of the schedule of the steamer.

Later, on 3 January 1857, in Alexandria awaiting the delayed steamer, he made fuller notes on Cairo, which seemed to him "one booth and Bartholomew Fair — a grand masquerade of mortality." He jotted down his impressions of Cairo "without any order," rushing to get them down "ere they grow dim":

> Several of the thoroughfare covered at vast heigth with old planks & matting, so that the street has the light of a closed verandah. . . . Some of the streets of private houses are like tunnels from meeting overhead of projecting windows &c. Like night at noon. Sometimes high blank walls — mysterious passages, — dim peeps at courts & wells in shadow. . . . Great number of uninhabited houses in the lonelier parts of the city. Their dusty, cadaverous ogerish look. Ghostly, & suggestive of all that is weird. Haunted houses & Cock Lanes. Ruined mosques, domes knocked in like stoven boats. Others, upper part empty & desolate with broken rafters & dismantled windows; (rubbish) below, the dirty rites of religion. Aspect of the thoroughfares like London streets on Saturday night. All the world gossipping & marketing, — but in picturesque costumes. Crookedness of the streets — multitudes of blind men — worst city in the world for them. [Flies on the eyes at noon. Nature feeding on man. Contiguity of desert & verdure, splendor & squalor, gloom & gayety; numerous blind men going about led. Children opthalmick. Too much light & no defence against it. — Animated appearance of the population. Turks in carriages, with Osmanli drivers & footmen; sitting back proudly & gazing round on the people still with the air of conquerors. Footmen running ahead with silver tipped bamboos. Rapid driving, shouts of the driver. Camels carrying water in panniers of leather, carrying straw in bags — donkey loads of green grass, — of stones — of pottery — of garden stuff — of chickens in wicker panniers — of babies in panniers — Long strings of them. Turk on donkey, resting his pipe vertically before him on pommel. Grave & tranquil. — The antiquity of Egypt stamped upon individuals.

This was pell-mell writing from a man still overwhelmed by his sight of the Pyramids. Other parts of this entry emphasized the strangeness of the streets.

Characteristically, he had ascended the Citadel ("Built by Saladin") for the view: "Cairo nipped between two deserts — the one leading to Suez & the Red Sea, the other the Lybian Desert. — Dust colored city. The dust of ages. The Nile — the green — desert — pyramids." Melville had been wholly unprepared for the effect the Pyramids had on him. From the distance they were "purple like mountains" — like any mountains, accountable, describable. That confidence diminished:

> Seem high & pointed, but flatten & depress as you approach. Vapors below summits. Kites sweeping & soaring around, hovering right over apex. At angles, like broken cliffs. Table-rock overhanging, adhering solely by morter. Sidelong look when midway up. Pyramids on a great ridge of sand. You leave the angle, and ascend hillock of sand & ashes & broken morter & pottery to a point, & then go along a ledge to a path &c. Zig-zag routes. As many routes as to cross the Alps — The Simplon, Great St: Bernard &c. Mules on Andes. Caves — platforms. Looks larger midway than from top or bottom. Precipice on precipice, cliff on cliff.

One would need, Melville decided, a balloon to ascend them, in order to gain a full sense of their grandeur. In his imagination the Arab guides in their flowing white mantles became phantasmagorical, like angels conducting the tourists up to heaven.

In writing the journal he recaptured both his racing imagination and his racing heartbeats in these fevered notations:

> Resting. Pain in the chest. Exhaustion. Must hurry. None but the phlegmatic go deliberately. Old man with the spirits of youth — long looked for this chance — tried the ascent, half way — fainted — brought down. Tried to go into the interior — fainted — brought out — leaned against the pyramid by the entrance — pale as death. Nothing so pathetic. Too much for him; oppressed by the massiveness & mystery of the pyramids. I myself too. A feeling of awe & terror came over me.

The dread that had struck Melville in Constantinople returned, heightened. Part of it was due to his fear of strange peoples: "Dread of the Arabs. Offering to lead me into a side-hole"; it was a "Horrible place for assassination." More of the dread was from the place: "When I was at top, thought it not so high — sat down on edge, looked below — gradual nervousness & final giddiness & terror."

In his awestruck state Melville declared that "Nothing in Nature gives such an idea of vastness" as the Pyramids. Fascinated by the problem of their scale, he declared them unlike any other buildings. After reflection, he tried to account for the effect of the Pyramids on him by defining their uniqueness. First, the lines of stones were not like "courses of masonry, but like strata of rocks," like a natural "long slope of crags & precipices." In other buildings, "however vast," there was relief: "the eye is gradually innured to the sense of magnitude, by passing from part to part." Here there was "no stay or stage," no escaping from the power:

> It is all or nothing. It is not the sense of heigth but the sense of immensity, that is stirred. After seeing the pyramid, all other architecture seems but pastry. Though I had but so short a time to view the pyramid, yet I doubt whether any time spent upon it, would tend to a more precise impression of it. As with the ocean, you learn as much of its vastness by the first five minutes glance as you would in a month, so with the pyramid. Its simplicity confounds you.

The Pyramids loomed in his imagination, "dim & indefinite." In 1850 he had praised Hawthorne's "Artist of the Beautiful," in which the narrator seems to endorse a bluff character's comment that a work of art beats all nature, and in the intervening years he had not gone much beyond that in exploring Platonic problems of imitation. Now the Pyramids provoked him to ransack his memory for aesthetic terminology:

> It has been said in panegyric of some extraordinary works of man, that they affect the imagination like the works of Nature. But the pyramid affects one in neither way exactly. Man seems to have had as little to do with it as Nature. It was that supernatural creature, the priest. They must needs have been terrible inventors, those Egyptian wise men. And one seems to see that as out of the crude forms of the natural earth they could evoke by art the transcendent mass & symmetry & unity of the pyramid so out of the rude elements of the insignificant thoughts that are in all men, they could rear the transcendent conception of a God. But for no holy purpose was the pyramid founded.

Jehovah, he decided, was the product of these priests. Moses had been "learned in all the lore of the Egyptians. The idea of Jehovah born here." The Pyramids overwhelmed him, physically and psychically, then forced him into grappling with the basis of their effect. On this trip he saw no other monuments (and no sculptures or paintings) that so propelled him toward new aesthetic formulations as well as theological insights.

Melville's hours at Cairo were all the more precious because, as it turned out, he had torn himself away from it needlessly. On the first day of 1857 he arrived back in Alexandria, putting up at the Victoria Hotel in order to sail the next day for Jaffa (the biblical Joppa). The steamer was late, so that he burst out: "I am wearied to death with two days in Alexandria which might have been delightfully spent in Cairo. But travellers must expect these things." The enforced delay at least gave him time, on the third, to write up his impressions of Cairo and the Pyramids. He sailed on 4 January, and on the sixth arrived in Jaffa, where he employed a "Jew dragoman" to take him on horseback to Jerusalem. They put up at an "alleged" hotel in Ramleh, where he contended a few hours with "moschits & fleas" before getting back in the saddle at two in the morning for a ride unnerving because they were stalked by three riders whose shadows were visible as long as the moonlight lasted. In the afternoon of 7 January he reached Jerusalem and put up at the Mediterranean Hotel, overlooking the Pool of Hezekiah. A platform in front of his room commanded a view "of battered dome of Church of Sepulchre & Mount Olivet." He walked out to the north, but his eyes were so damaged "by the long days ride in the glare of the light of arid hills" that he returned to the hotel.

Melville did not write up his initial impressions of Jerusalem, and he lost track of days as he prowled about the sites familiar to him by name and biblical contexts since childhood. When he finally began writing in the journal, he attempted only a few dated notations: 7 January (actually the eighth), "All day with dragoman roaming over the hills"; the eighth (ninth), "The same"; the ninth (tenth), a "very prepossessing young man" from Boston arrived from Jaffa, Frederick Cunningham, "who seemed rejoiced to meet a companion & countryman." For his part, Melville had thought he "should have been the only stranger in Jerusalem." For the tenth (actually the eleventh) he admitted that he had some mistake in his dates which he could not rectify, and merely said: "Spent the remaining days till Jan. 18th in roaming about city & visiting Jordan & Dead Sea."

The consequence is that Melville for the first time divided his journal by topics rather than by sequence. Part way through, he tried to give his daily pattern: "In pursuance of my object, the saturation of my mind with the atmosphere of Jerusalem, offering myself up a passive subject, and no unwilling one, to its weird impressions, I always rose at dawn & walked without the walls." Repeatedly, he "would stroll to Mount Zion," look along the hillside of Gihon, see the sunlight strike "the reddish soil of Aceldema," and climb to the "Hill of Evil Counsel." In the afternoon, typically, he "would stand out by St: Stephen's Gate," where the first Christian martyr was stoned, and "watch the shadows slowly sliding (sled-like) down the hills of Bezetha & Zion into the valley of Jehosaphat" before creeping "up the opposite side of Olivet." Under the rubric "*From Jerusalem to Dead Sea &c*" he depicted his journey out of Jerusalem through the plain of Jericho to the Dead Sea, not in conventional narrative form but in a series of juxtaposed images and terse descriptive phrases like this sample: "Where Kedron opens into Plain of Jericho looks like Gate of Hell.—Tower with sheiks smoking & huts on top—thick walls—village of Jericho—ruins on hill-side—tent—fine dinner

—jolly time—sitting at door of tent looking at mountains of Moab.—tent the charmed circle, keeping off the curse."

The next section, *"Barrenness of Judea,"* contained his notes on his three-day trip, made somewhere between 10 and 16 January, to the Jordan and the Dead Sea, going as far as Mar Saba and returning by Bethlehem:

> —Monastery (Greek) rode on with letter—hauled up in basket into hole—small door of massive iron in high wall—knocking—opened—salaam of monks—Place for pilgrims—divans—St Saba wine—*"racka"*—comfortable.—At dusk went down by many stone steps & through mysterious passages to cave & trap doors & hole in wall—ladder—ledge after ledge—winding—to bottom of Brook Kedron—sides of ravine all caves of recluses—Monastery a congregation of stone eyries, enclosed with wall—Good bed & night's rest—Went into chapel &c—little hermitages in rock—balustrade of iron—lonely monks. black-birds—feeding with bread—numerous terraces, balconies—solitary Date Palm mid-way in precipice—Good bye—Over lofty hills to Bethalem.

These notes he used long afterward in *Clarel*. The concluding lines are nearer to conventional narrative: "Ride to Jerusalem—pressing forward to save the rain.—On way to Bethelam saw Jerusalem from distance—unless knew it, could not have recognized it—looked exactly like arid rocks." (The Melvilles used "save" to mean "get there before" or "anticipate.") Melville started the next section, *"Jerusalem,"* as brief notes under particular headings: *"Village of Lepers," "Ghostliness of the names," "Thoughts in the Via Dolorosa," "Wandering among the tombs," "Variety of the tombs," "Church of Holy Sepulchre."* He abandoned the system, but in the next notes included some other comments on locations: "Hill-side view of Zion," "South East angle of wall. Mosque of Omar—Solomon's Temple," "Siloam—pool, hill, village," "The Beautiful, or Golden, Gate," "The Holy Sepulchre," "Interior of Jerusalem."

Everywhere Melville encountered startling evidence that the Holy Land was territory under Muslim occupation: "Passed over Bethalem hills—where shepherds were watching their flocks, (as of old) but a Moslem with back to Jerusalem (face to Mecca) praying." In Jerusalem, as he wrote in one of his grandiloquent moods, the Mosque of Omar rose "upon the foundation stones of Solomon, triumphing over that which sustains it, an emblem of the Moslem religion, which at once spurns that deeper faith which fathered it & preceded it. &c." His sententiousness was strong in his ruminations on the Beautiful Gate:

> The Beautiful, or Golden, Gate—two arches, highly ornamental sculpture, undoubtedly old, Herod's Time—the Gate from which Christ would go to

Bethany & Olivet — & also that in which he made his entry (with palms) into the city. Turks walled it up because of tradition that through this Gate the city would be taken. — One of the most interesting things in Jerusalem — seems expressive of the finality of Christianity, as if this was the last religion of the world, — no other, possible.

Walling up the gate was an act of caution (reasonable enough, whether the fear was historically grounded or not). Turkish control of Jewish and Christian sites in some cases had led to desecrations reminiscent of the Babylonian conquest.

The climax of desecration (by Christians — specifically Roman Catholics — as well as Moslems) was at what purported to be the tomb of Jesus:

> The Holy Sepulchre — ruined dome — confused & half-ruinous pile. — Laberithys & terraces of mouldy grottos, tombs, & shrines. Smells like a deadhouse, dingy light. — At the entrance, in a sort of grotto in the wall a divan for Turkish policemen, where they sit crosslegged & smoking, scornfully observing the continuous troops of pilgrims entering & prostrating themselves before the anointing-stone of Christ, which veined with streaks of a mouldy red looks like a butcher's slab. — Near by is a blind stair of worn marble, ascending to the reputed Calvary where among other things the showman point you by the smoky light of old pawnbrokers lamps of dirty gold, the hole in which the cross was fixed and through a narrow grating as over a colecellar, point out the rent in the rock!

Inside the Church of the Holy Sepulchre Melville located an upper gallery, railed with marble. There "almost every day," also, he "would hang, looking down upon the spectacle of the scornful Turks on the divan, & the scorned pilgrims kissing the stone of the anointing." He already was using an ambiguous "you," both himself and his audience: "First passing a wee vestibule where is shown the stone on which the angel sat, you enter the tomb. It is like entering a lighted lanthorn. Wedged & half-dazzled, you stare for a moment on the ineloquence of the bedizened slab, and glad to come out, wipe your brow glad to escape as from the heat & jam of a show-box. All is glitter & nothing is gold. A sickening cheat." And he elaborated on the spot specific satirical comparisons and reminded himself of the kinds of elaborations he could later make. For anyone steeped in the New Testament, the Church of the Sepulchre cried out for Jesus to return and drive away the money-changers again. Wherever Melville went, from one holy place to another, touristtrade varieties of Duckworth's desecrating ignorance pursued him. He aped the successive comments of the guides: "Here is the stone Christ leaned against, & here is the English Hotel." As always when his imagination was engaged, he topped himself, reaching for an ultimate, clinching example: "Yonder is the arch where Christ was shown to the people, & just by that open window is sold the best coffee in Jerusalem. &c &c &c" — enough etceteras to cover his experiences all over the Holy Land.

On his return trip to Jaffa, Melville stayed overnight at the Greek convent at Ramleh on 18 January ("No sleep. Old monk like rat. Scurvy treatment."). He rode the next day to Lydda "in train of the Governor's son," protected from an Arab robbing party by a "mounted escort of some 30 men, all armed." They showed off:

> Fine riding. Musket-shooting. Curvetting & caracoling of the horsemen. Outriders. Horsemen riding to one side, scorning the perils. Riding up to hedges of cactus, interrogating & firing their pistols into them. Entering Lydda, Governor's son discharged all his barrel (Revolver) into a puddle — & we went to see the ruined church of Lydda. Evidently of the time of the Crusaders. A delightful ride across Plain of Sharon to Jaffa. Quan[t]ities of red poppies. (Rose of Sharon?)

At the hotel in Jaffa he found "the *Petra Party*" — just back from visiting the superb recently discovered ruins of Petra, described with high excitement in a book he had known since its publication in 1837, John Lloyd Stephens's *Incidents of Travel in Egypt, Arabia Petræa, and the Holy Land*. Heterodox in the matter of clean linen or not, Melville rushed to bathe in the Mediterranean before he set out to inspect "some old ruins of walls, by & in, the sea." On 20 January he described the house where he was staying as crowning the summit of the hill on which Jaffa was situated, rising steeply from the sea: "From the top of it, I see the Mediterranean, the Plain, the mountains of Ephraim. A lovely landscape. To the North the nearest spot is Beyroot; to the South, Gaza — that Philistine city the gates of which Sampson shouldered." After the Petra party left, he was "the only traveller sojourning in Joppa" — a description that he forcibly reiterated: "I am emphatically alone, & begin to feel like Jonah." Unable to sleep because of the fleas, he rose early and, realizing it was too stormy for a boat to get off, wrote up his Jerusalem experiences.

Later he went outside the wall to call on Charles Saunders, a missionary from Rhode Island, "a man feeble by Nature, & feebler by sickness; but worthy," and Mrs. Saunders, "an interesting woman, not without beauty, and of the heroine stamp, or desires to be." He gave their history: "They were sent out to found an Agricultural School for the Jews. They tried it but miserably failed. The Jews would come, pretend to be touched & all that, get clothing & then — vanish. Mrs S. said they were very 'deceitful'. Mr S. now does nothing — health gone by climate. . . . Their little girl looks sickly &

pines for home — but the Lord's work must be done." Saunders took Melville to meet "Deacon [Walter] Dickson," who sold his farm in Groton, Massachusetts, and "came out with wife, son & three daughters, about two years ago." Melville reflected: "Be it said, that all these movements combining Agriculture & Religion in reference to Palestine, are based upon the impression... that the time for the prophetic return of the Jews to Judea is at hand, and therefore the way must be prepared for them by Christians, both in setting them right in their faith & their farming — in other words, preparing the soil literally & figuratively. — " Melville found "Mr Dickson a thorough Yankee, about 60, with long oriental beard, blue Yankee coat, & Shaker waistcoat," his wife "a respectable looking elderly woman."

Melville recorded their conversation, curiously so, since he did not record Hawthorne's, or Lockwood's. Dickson was convinced that "Gentile Christians" could teach the lazy Jews to become farmers, and thus bring about "the restoration of the Jews." Asked if most people in America shared their beliefs, Melville quoted himself as saying, "Not unlikely," about the safest thing to say. Old Dickson, Melville decided, was "a man of Puritanic energy, and being inoculated with this preposterous Jew mania, is resolved to carry his Quixotism through to the end. Mrs D. dont seem to like it, but submits. The whole thing is half melancholy, half farcical — like all the rest of the world." Melville concluded firmly that the "idea of making farmers of the Jews is vain," since Judea was a desert and the Jews, greatly outnumbered by Arabs, hated farming and dared not live outside their walled towns or villages. How were the hosts of Jews "scattered in other lands to be brought here? Only by a miracle." Idealistic crackpots always fascinated him, and never more than these American millennialists in the hostile deserts of Zion.

The compatriots did little to mitigate the sense of isolation that almost overwhelmed him: "I have such a feeling in this lonely old Joppa, with the prospect of a prolonged detention here, owing to the surf — that it is only by stern self-control & grim defiance that I contrive to keep cool & patient." His stoicism, as always, was the resort of a man who could never stop suffering deeply. As he had implied in the description of his climbing the pyramid, he could never be classed as phlegmatic. With escape available to him in an Austrian steamer on 24 January ("Bravo!"), he let himself be amused at "the autographs & confessions" inscribed in the hotel register: " 'I have *existed* at this hotel &c &c'. Something comical could be made out of all this. Let the confessions being of a religious, penitential resigned & ambiguous turn, apparently flattering to the host, but really derogatory to the place." Here as elsewhere Melville focused his observations by planning how he would work up certain experiences, perhaps for articles, perhaps for delivery in lectures;

again his strategy was to use the imperative, to himself ("Let the confessions") and perhaps to an imaginary audience.

On 25 January from his Austrian steamer Melville saw "Leabonon mountains — snow-topped" but had to acknowledge a disappointment: "Mt Hermon not in sight — inland." He explored Beirut from the honestly named Hotel Belle Vue with the help of a dragoman (allegedly the same who had served the traveler Eliot Warburton): "Town occupies tongue of land projecting from base of Leabonon. Lofty mountains all round. Walled town. Old ruins of castles of crusaders. Town between desert & sea — both eating at it — buried trees & houses — Rich gardens. — Pier washed by surf — like walking on reef." He made friends with the consul, the Reverend Henry Wood of Concord, New Hampshire, from whom he heard an eyewitness account of "Mr Dickson going about Jerusalem with open Bible, looking for the opening asunder of Mount Olivet and the preparing of the highway for the Jews. &c." Melville had several "Quiet days" at Beirut during which he strolled on the seashore and watched and listened to the dashing billows say to him, "what is all this fuss about? &c." — for he abbreviated with his "&c." even what the billows said. After the terrors of the streets of Constantinople, after the awe of the Pyramids, and after the bitter lessons of the unholy land of the Bible — after his decade and more of laborious literary efforts, after his money-dealings with Stewart and Brewster, he was ready to try a different tack than stoic self-control. What had all that fuss been about?

The cheer of fine philosophy and a fine first day of February could not survive the passage on a wretched Austrian-Lloyd's steamer to Smyrna. In Beirut Melville had seen "ruins of castles of crusaders," ravaged monuments of ravaging Christian rescuers of early modern times. Before the ship anchored late the next day at Larnaca, Cyprus, he was merging Greek and Roman myth with biblical accounts: "From these waters rose Venus from the foam. Found it as hard to realize such a thing as to realize on Mt Olivet that from there Christ rose." He saw what there was to be seen from the ship. The next day during a violent squall the old sailor watched the "Poor devels of pilgrims" writhing in their seasickness. He had his own miseries on that ship ("Not a wink of sleep now for four nights, & expect none till I get to Smyrna. This affliction of bugs & fleas & moschitos fully counterbalances to me all the satisfactions of Eastern travel"). Those miseries counterbalanced the wonder of sailing by bright moonlight "through intricate part of the Sporades," past Rhodes. The engineer, a hard-drinking Cornishman in love with his engine, lured Melville down to supper in the hopes of sharing that emotion, if not some alcohol. Melville suffered, detained on deck by the beautiful moonlight and by the dread of his populous berth. When he saw

Patmos a second time he was struck by its isolation and lack of inhabitants, and by his own reaction:

> Was here again afflicted with the great curse of modern travel — skepticism. Could no more realize that St: John had ever had revelations here, than when off Juan Fernandez, could beleive in Robinson Crusoe according to De Foe. When my eye rested on arid heigth, spirit partook of the barreness. — Heartily wish Niebuhr & Strauss to the dogs. — The deuce take their penetration & acumen. They have robbed us of the bloom. If they have undeceived any one — no thanks to them. — Pity that ecclesiastical countries so little attractive by nature. —

He tried to get himself in a serious mood about St. John but from his standpoint the "figure of Santon a Arab holy man" came between him and the island; he knew from Stephens's accounts all about the Santons, but this one, "almost naked — ludicrous," chased away his own characteristic gravity. By 6 February, when they put in at Smyrna (two months after Melville's first visit), the nights on "The Scratching ship" had taken their toll: "While at breakfast felt very bad neuralgic pain top of head — owing to utter sleepless of last five nights." That night, in the paddle-steamer *Italia*, bound for Pireus, he got a good night's rest at last, and felt a little better by the time they reached Syra (for his third time) on the seventh. He left the next day. On 8 February Melville caught sight of the Acropolis, by bright moonlight as he traveled in an old hack on a macadamized road from the harbor at Pireus toward Athens.

From 8 February through the eleventh, when he took a steamer for Messina at the port, Pireus, he bestirred himself, getting a guide (Alexander), and visiting ruins and shops. He met an American named Marshall who was in the ice business ("Cut ice at Black Sea"). This man evoked a strong response from Melville: "I imagined his story of life." Seeing the Acropolis pushed Melville into a distinction between it and Stirling. Art and Nature corresponded at Stirling, where ruggedness of the crag and the mountains behind matched the ruggedness of the castle, but not at the Acropolis, where the plateau was rugged and the marble of the temples highly polished. Even the seams between blocks of marble seemed imperceptible, setting up for him a "Strange contrast of rugged rock with polished temple." The pavement of the Parthenon struck him in a similar way: "blocks of ice. (frozen together.) — No morter: — Delicacy of frost-work." He talked all his last evening in Athens with a young English officer, and after a lovely climb saw the sunset from "Lyccabacus" (Lycabettus). The next day, 11 February, he rode "on box" (outside the carriage) to Pireus, "Acropolis in sight nearly whole way." That was the last of the Levant for Melville.

[15]

Rome to Liverpool, and Home
February–April 1857

He doubtless was never by nature intended for a family man — a rover by inclination — but he played his part faithfully — there can be no doubt cast on that.

The response of Charlotte Hoadley — born 1858 —
to "myths" about Melville, in a letter to V. H. Paltsits,
8 September 1929

ON 11 FEBRUARY 1857 Melville reached Pireus, where he took a French steamer, the *Cydnus*. He found young Englishmen on board to talk to, and later chatted with Mysseri, famous as the dragoman of Alexander Kinglake, the author of *Eöthen; or, Traces of Travel Brought Home from the East* (1844), with whom he had dined at Samuel Rogers's house in 1849. Melville slept well in a good bed. The steamer was fast, and at daybreak on the thirteenth the coasts of Calabria and Sicily were in sight, both "very high & broken — picturesque"; "Calabrian" was already in Melville's vocabulary from his knowledge of Salvator Rosa's wild landscapes. At Messina among many American vessels in port to take on fruit he recognized the *Constellation*. After he had cleared customs and registered at a hotel in a "noble street" he went to a café near the opera house hoping to find Lockwood, but did not. The next day he went aboard one of the American ships, then he went out to the frigate where Captain Charles H. Bell, who as a midshipman had served under Stephen Decatur in the 1815 resumption of the Barbary wars, directed him to Lockwood. Melville promptly spirited the doctor away "on donkeys to a high hill four miles distant," from whence they seem to have observed the stringing of a telegraph before dining with the other officers in the wardroom of the frigate. ("Passed off pleasantly.") Afterward Melville "walked through the town with the Dr, and in evening went to the opera of Macbeth with him"; Giuseppe Verdi conducted. Happy with his day, Melville retired late, at eleven. The next day, Sunday, Lockwood "called at hotel, sat, and then proposed long walk": "Walked out in long suburbs skirting the sea. Calabria's mountains in sight. Salvator Rosa look of them. Met masquers on the road. Carnival. Walked 7 or 8 miles. sat on stones, much talk. Fine day.

Enjoyed it considerably. Back to dinner at hotel by 6 P.M. Streets very lively in evening. Walked about with Dr. till 10 o'clock. Cafe — habitue's." Melville and Lockwood made their farewells, but there was a sequel to this pleasant interlude (on 15 April). No record at all has been found of their conversations, but anyone Melville was so impatient to see in Messina and so happy to see in Bellinzona was, in his word, a trump.

On 16 February Melville took a steamer for Naples, saving money by going second class; the miserable accommodations caused him to suffer horribly again from sleeplessness, so that seeing Etna from Reggio was small consolation. On the eighteenth the steamer passed between Capri and the mainland, and soon Melville recognized Vesuvius from pictures and shortly afterward he "*smelt*" Naples. With some fellow passengers he went to the Hotel de Genève then joined a party going to Pompeii, but sleeplessness had taken its toll:

> Pompeii like any other town. Same old humanity. All the same whether one be dead or alive. Pompeii comfortable sermon. Like Pompeii better than Paris. — Guards there. Silent as Dead Sea. — To Vesuvius on horseback. Vineyards about the base. Ashy climb. Hanging on to guide. Haggling. Old crater of Pompeii. Modern crater like old abandoned quarry — burning slagmass — Red & yellow. Bellowing. Bellows. flare of flame. Went into crater. Frozen liquorice. —

They came down "with a rush," and rode to Torre dell'Annunziata in the dark, then took a *vettura* to Naples. He arrived back at midnight, coatless and chilled through.

In Naples on 19 February Melville first walked out in the "noble" Strada di Toledo, which reminded him of Broadway, except for the show of military might, for he was startled by the "clang of arms all over city" and the burst "of troops from archway," but struck even more strongly by the silent cannons, "posted inwards." He took a cab to Capo di Monte and saw "Supurb palace, roads, grounds, & view," and went into the Catacombs, his old guide holding a lantern. Mindful of the night before, the man who liked to travel light bought a good coat for an enormous portion of his remaining money, nine dollars. Back in the city Vesuvius was "in sight from square," smoke rising from it. The next day he "took voiture for eastern part of bay. Posilipo — beautiful promontory of villas — along the sea — new road — till came in sight of bay of Pozzuoli." Later he saw Baia ("the end of the bay") and the semi-dormant volcano Solfatara ("smoke — landscape not so very beautiful. — Sulphurous & aridity, the end of the walk"). He returned to Naples by the Grotto of Posilipo ("Very high. Scene of thoroughfare in Grotto. Smacking of whips, goats, twilight. — Sun streams through at sunset."). He saw what passed as Virgil's tomb ("mere ruin"). From there, high up, he had a "great view of bay & Naples & Vomero Mount & Castle of Elmo"; then he drove to Elmo Castle and from a "balcony over garden of Church of San Martino got glorious view of bay & town. Sunset. White friars." After dinner he walked in the great crowds in the Strada di Toledo, now void of any military show. He felt at home, as he had never felt in the crowds in eastern cities such as Constantinople or Cairo: "Could hardly tell it from Broadway. Thought I was there."

Having gained a sense of the terrain, on 21 February Melville went to the Museo Borbonico, where he examined "*Bronze utensils from Pompeii & Herculaneum*" and "*Terra cotta collection* — mythological delineations." At the "*Hall of bronze statuary*" he saw "Plato (hair & beard & imperial) Nero (villianous) Seneca (caricature.) Drunken faun on wine skin, Augustus. horse — colossal head of horse — &c &c." Among the "*Paintings*" were two small Correggios ("Could not see anything so wonderful in these last)"; he thought the "face of Raffael's Madonna touchingly maternal." He saw some "*Frescoes*" (fruit pictures from the dining room of Diomed's house) and "*Marbles*" (great things: "Hercules Farnese — colossal. gravely benevolent face. The group of the bull; glorious. — Tomb stones &c with inscriptions, identical with ours"). Oversaturated, wanting to see more of the town, he left reluctantly ("Had to quit Museum ere through with it"). He hired a *vettura* for "a promiscuous drive through the older & less elegant part of town," where the arched lanes were narrow and crowded, and there had an experience which he later wrote into "Naples in the Time of Bomba" (Bomba was the nickname for Ferdinand II, Bourbon king of the Two Sicilies, 1830–59). His way blocked by tumblers, who then cleared a passage for him, Melville rose to the occasion with "the most grateful & graceful bow" he could manage, and felt "prouder than an Emperor" when the people waved handkerchiefs from balconies and cried out their approval.

The next day Melville managed to get to Sorrento, pulled by three horses, abreast, with cock feathers in their harness: "Grand drive. Road. Windings broad sweeps & curves — ravines — bridge — terrace — rocks — inclined plain — heigth — sea — Sorrento" — and there was shown Tasso's house. He went back to the museum early on 23 February, but found it closed, so he took a hack to the Posilipo road for Lake Avernus, not a plausible hell, he decided. He descended, nevertheless, and even allowed a guide to take him on his shoulders across to the "bath & bed of Sybil." He was struck by the perversity of mankind, who would dive into the bowels of the earth instead of "building up towards the sky": "How clear an indication that he sought darkness rather than light." Inveterate cultural relativist that he was, Melville began a comparison-contrast of hells from two mythologies, Avernus and Hinnom. In his journal he wrote a "to do later" passage on the bay of Pozzuoli. He might "enumerate" the mementos "of the remorselessness of Nature" and reflect on the soberness of any city built there; "But no. Gayest city in the world." The moral would be simple: "Apt representation of that heedlessness, benignly ordained, of man which prevents him one generation from learning from a past," the beauty of place "in connection with its perilousness."

On 24 February Melville rode all day for Rome, sharing a diligence with only one other passenger, a Frenchman, and thanks to his new coat found it a great way to travel (like a "balcony overlooking horses. Snug"). He had another sleepless night, but in Rome on 25 February, after settling into the Hotel de Minerva, the first order of business, as it had been in the East, was to find the best views. After the intense experiences of the past weeks, even the Eternal City looked merely European: "Whether it is having come from the East, or chafed mood, or what, but Rome fell flat on me. Oppressively flat," so that the Tiber was merely "a ditch, yellow as saffron," and even St. Peter's looked small when viewed "from Tower of Capitol." He walked there, only to find the front view disappointing, despite the grand approach; he gave and he took away: "Interior comes up to expectations. But dome not so wonderful as St: Sophia's."

On 26 February, responsibly, he went to "Torloni's, banker, to find out about S. Shaw or letters," and learned nothing. Then he walked for many hours, first to "Capitol & Coliseum," and the Capitoline Museum, where he saw the Dying Gladiator ("shows that humanity existed amid the barberousness of the Roman time, as it now among Christian barberousness"). Later he walked to the Pincian Hill overlooking the Piazza del Popolo, and to the Piazza di Spagna. On the twenty-seventh he failed in attempts to find the American consul, then failed to see the American painter William Page. Misinformed, he looked for James Jackson Jarves, the Bostonian who had founded the Hawaiian newspaper *Polynesia* in 1840 but had left before Melville arrived in 1843; Jarves was living in Florence, not Rome. Then Melville went to the ruins of the Baths of Caracalla, impressed at last, partly by the massiveness of the ruins, partly by the way the ruins had decayed into "natural bridges of thousands of arches." Often accompanied in Rome by thoughts of the historical Goethe and his pioneering aesthetic pilgrimage, as well as the travels of the fictional Wilhelm Meister, Melville was governed, in the ruins of the baths, by the image of Shelley brooding, stirred by the same ruins, only a few decades earlier, into writing *Prometheus Unbound* — an image already famous from engravings of a painting. Melville simply could not see the ruins of the Baths of Caracalla without thinking of the young radical poet. So saturated in Shelley was he that without even thinking what he was doing (merely by an insensible process, he said), he consulted his maps and, alone, made his arduous way down the narrow streets until he found the Protestant Cemetery, where he could stand before the plot that contained Shelley's heart. He visited Keats's grave too, and read the epitaph Shelley said Keats had requested on his deathbed—"Here lies one whose name is writ in water." Keats had not been a powerful early influence on him, and the Romans had not yet realized the value of publicizing his association with the city. (Tourists in Melville's time could go up and down the Spanish Steps without looking toward the room where Keats had died.) Later, on the trace of Shelley's *The Cenci*, that closet drama of incest and murder, Melville went to one of the palaces of the Cenci. That was enough Shelley for one day, but five days later, on 3 March, he went to the Palazzo Barberini to see the portrait of Beatrice Cenci. There he looked not with originality but with the sentimentalizing that subdued the horrors for many of his generation: "Expression of suffering about the mouth—(appealing look of innocence) not caught in any copy or engraving."

The twenty-eighth of February he again lost time "going after Consul &c" but got to the Villa Borghese at noon, then the Villa Albani, various fountains, churches, tombs, and by Trajan's Forum back to his hotel. The most memorable image of the day was at Monte Cavallo, "colossal horses from ruins of baths—like finding the bones of the mastadon—gigantic figures emblematic of gigantic Rome." On Sunday, 1 March, he went back to Monte Cavallo to see the colossal equestrian group, "most imposing group of antiques in Rome." He made technical notes on how to work this up, using the imperative voice: "People those Caracalla baths anew with these colossal figures—Gigantic Rome.—St. Peters in its magnitude & colossal statuary seems an imitation of these fragments." He roamed: the Porta Maggiore; the basilica of St. John Lateran; the Porta San Giovanni, on the Naples side, where he had a fine prospect; the Porta San Sebastiano; the Cloaca Maxima. He lost his way getting back. From noon the next day he stayed in the Vatican until it closed: "Fagged out completely, & sat long time by the obelisk, recovering from the stunning effect of a first visit to the Vatican.—Went to Piazza di Espagna, & home." He visited awhile in the hotel with the Rousses, brother and sister originally from New Jersey, whom he had met in Naples. The brother, Peter Warren Rousse, had become a New York City lawyer; his sister, Anna M., was older, born around 1825. We know almost nothing of them, but Melville spent time with them several days, off and on.

Many days Melville crisscrossed Rome. He returned to St. Peter's, to the Coliseum, to the Capitol, to the Borghese gallery, back again for a "Vatican day" on 9 March, and to many other galleries (the Sciarra gallery and the Rospigliosi gallery on the seventh, for example). At the Sciarra gallery he moralized over a painting that probably reminded him of T. D. Stewart and himself: "The Cheating Gamblers (Honesty & Knavery—the self-possession & confidence of knavery—the irresolution & perplexity of honesty)." He made notes on some Claudes that drew on Scottish vocabulary (calling a "scene between dusk & dark" a "Gloaming" picture), but his labeling other Claudes as being in the painter's first manner and his comment on their effect smack of a guidebook ("All their effect is of atmosphere. He paints the air"). The Hall of Animals in the Vatican caught him off guard, unprepared for the greatness of such small realistic classical sculptures: "Wolf & lamb, paw uplifted, tongue—fleece. Dog on stag, eying him. Lion on horse.—But Playing goats—the goat & kid—show a Wordsworthian appreciation of the gentle in Nature." Other statues, of course, showed a non-Romantic awareness of the ferocity in Nature.

For the most part Melville was alone, and he was not well. The third of March had been such a "cold, raw, windy, dirty & horribly disagreeable day" that he became ill, and on the fifth his eye was so bad that he had to go to his room and take to his bed at five without dinner. The next day his eye (or eyes) still prevented him from doing or seeing much (merely St. Peter's, the Borghese gallery, and the Pincian, where he caught a glimpse of the pope in his carriage). Because of the trouble with vision and his "general incapacity" he did not write up his journal for over a week, not until the tenth. On Sunday, 8 March, he went to Il Gesù, the Jesuits' church, near the Capitol, which he called "Gibbon's church," knowing that Edward Gibbon claimed to have been meditating there when the idea of writing his *Decline and Fall of the Roman Empire* occurred to him. Melville was literary man enough to honor such a story but not vain enough to leave his own records of such moments (precisely where and how he thought of writing *Mardi* or *Moby-Dick*).

Then on 10 March he found the area where the American and English artists kept their studios. He had a talk with the English sculptor John Gibson, who in his studio near the Piazza del Popolo showed him his "colored Venus" and probably gave him a lesson on misimpressions about the chaste rigor of classical sculpture and architecture, telling him that the Greek temples and Greek sculptures had originally been painted, as Gibson's own Venus was. Gibson seems to have lectured him on Grecian art as acknowledging a "Limit to human power" while paradoxically making "perfection" an achievable goal for art although possibly not for Nature, a view of art antithetical to Melville's practice and out of line with his final attitude toward "finish." Melville saw Edward Bartholomew and made notes about his *Eve Repentant* and a bust of young Augustus. He talked twice to the portrait painter William Page in his studio near the Piazza di Spagna, perhaps already knowing that Page had painted many Bostonian acquaintances of his father-in-law, among them John Quincy Adams, Charles Sumner, and James Russell Lowell (son of a beloved classmate of Shaw's). At both visits Melville became the reluctant audience to the artist's monologues, first on the difficulty of representing flesh in paint: "Titian — kneading of flesh — Middle tint. Long lecture"; on the next occasion, "Long lecture. Swedenburgh. Spiritualist." Both times he noted what has been transcribed as "Thin Socks" — perhaps an exemplification of artistic tinting, perhaps a reference to a peculiarity in the artist's dress. Melville may have known all this already, from an installment of Page's treatise on the use of color in painting printed in the 8 February 1845 *Broadway Journal*, while he was working on *Typee*. He may have known, also, that Evert Duyckinck owned a much admired painting by Page, of a child (possibly one of Evert's two sons), good enough to be mentioned later by their friend Tuckerman in *American Artist Life*.

Health permitting, Melville continued his conscientious study of Rome, day by day, looking at architecture, paintings, sculpture, landscape, and observing daily life. On 15 March, a Sunday, he was attacked "by singular pain across chest & in back," and that day "saw nothing, learned nothing, enjoyed nothing, but suffered something." On 17 March he took the railway cars across the Campagna to the Villa Aldrobrandini at Frascati, where he had a "View of Tusculum (Cicero) from top of hill, at end of long avenue of olives." On the eighteenth he missed seeing the American sculptor Thomas Crawford, who was near death, but he looked around his studio on the grounds of the Baths of Diocletian and was impressed by the "colossal America," and the oddity of going to Rome to sculpt figures of American Indians and backwoodsmen. On 19 March he took a *vettura* to Città Vecchia and the Villa Doria Pamfili, then back through the Ghetto. Later he made a judgment: "View from piazza of San Pietro in Montorio. Best in Rome." On 20 March he went to Tivoli, a chilly ride across the Campagna which took him past evocative terrain: "Lake Tartarus. Travetine. — Villa of Hadrian — Solemn scene & solemn guide — Extent of ruin, — fine site. Guide philosophising. — Tivoli on heigth. Temple of the Nymph overhanging — paths — gallery in rock — Claude — Not to Paradise, but Tivoli. — shading — middle tint — Villa of Mecanas. — Chill ride home in the evening.." "Not to Paradise, but Tivoli" is cryptic, but he was something of a connoisseur of Paradises, and may have decided that Tivoli was heaven on earth.

Sam Shaw showed up on 21 March, the day Melville was leaving, but they had half an hour or so together, Sam able to share good news from home in a letter he had received the twentieth: "All well." In Melville's phrase, they "met to part." Sam wrote his father: "He has been almost entirely alone but has found traveling companions. . . . Although his general health is much improved, yet at Rome, the climate and the dampness have affected him somewhat. He is considerably sunburnt and is stout as usual." Melville had hoped to get a seat in a diligence to Florence, since he had enjoyed the drive from Naples so much, but he had to go by ship from Cività Vecchia, taking a *vettura* there for an all-night drive in company with the Rousses. In midafternoon they took a small new French steamer, *Aventine*, for the night trip to Leghorn. Melville escaped the New Jersey pair and talked happily with the Turkish envoy to Sardinia, getting his "views of Mahomattism &c" and learning that unlike in America it was socially acceptable for upper classes in Turkey to be indulgent about "philosophical opinions upon religion &." Having no berth, Melville slept on a settee. On 23 March he took the cars from Leghorn to Pisa, and at once got his bearings by the Tower (the Campanile) and set out for it, the Duomo, and the Baptistery. At the Campanile he thought of Wordsworth's "Resolution and Independence": "Campanile like pine poised just ere snapping. You wait to hear crash. Like Wordsworth's moore cloud, it will move all together if it move at all, for Pillars all lean with it. About 150 of 'em. There are houses in wake of fall." His timing was just right — a few hours of intense attention and appreciation, then the cars again for Florence and a bed at the Hotel du Nord ("no sleep for 2 nights past").

In Florence on 24 March Melville ate breakfast at the Caffè Doney, where high interior arches divided the eating area into separate spaces and created the illusion that separate tents were pitched together at a caravansary — his kind of place. He set out in the rain for the Pitti Palace, then went back to the Uffizi Palace. He saw the *Perseus* of Cellini in the Loggia outside (but did not mention Michelangelo's *David*), then wandered about so that he came "unexpectedly" upon the Duomo and Campanile. On 25 March, he crossed the Arno and climbed in the Boboli gardens until he had "Noble views of Florence & country," and strolled to churches and piazzas until he found Santa Croce and saw "tombs of Dante, M. Angelo, Alfieri, and Machiavelli." Later he walked out the Porta Romana to Bellosguardo: "Striking view from this hill of city & Vale d'Arno. Roundabout walk to get to it. Abruptly came upon it, by a narrow lane between high walls of gardens. The tower on the Vecchio palace the grand feature. — Came on violent rain; & walked home in it." On 26 March, Melville had a "Grand view of tower of Vechio palace from head of gallery. View of covered way that crosses the Vechio bridge." He went slowly round the Tribuno, "astonished at the Wrestlers" and "charmed with Titian's Venus." (His response to the wrestlers, like his response to the animals at St. Peter's, shows that he was not prepared to encounter such minute realism in Roman figures.) From there he went to the Accademia delle Belle Arti, where he saw enough Giottos to confirm the guidebook's assurance that here were "predecessors of the Peruginos & Raphaels," but by now he was so saturated with Italian painting that he could make his own observations: "Saw a large painting, not referred to in my hand book, which contained many faces, attitudes, expressions & groupings I had noted at Rome in Raphael. Undoubtedly Raphael took from this, or some yet older painting. But still more, the *whole spirit* was the same." He also saw the statues there ("such as they are").

Later Melville had a vivid encounter: "At dinner table accosted by singular young man who speaks 6 or 8 languages. He presented me with a flower, and talked like one to whom the world was delightful. May it prove so." The young man had not approached with flower in hand; rather, he had engaged Melville in conversation, then when flower girls came by he had bought a flower which he presented to him. The encounter affected Melville's mood the next morning, 27 March, at the Doney, where he "sat musing upon caffes in general, & the young men frequenting them," deciding that something good "might be written on the 'Caffe Doney', including that 'Henry' & the flower-girls." After breakfast Melville crossed the river to the Pitti Palace and then strolled on to the Museum of Natural History. To judge by the length of his journal entry, the most impressive moments of his museum-going in Florence took place not at the Uffizi or the Accademia or across the river in the Pitti Palace but a little farther on, at the Museum of Natural History. There he was transfixed by the immense collection of wax figures of the eighteenth-century Sicilian Zummo (or Zumbo). The man who had sought out the anatomical freaks at the Dupuytren Museum in Paris now was overwhelmed by the figures used by medical students for studying the human anatomy. "Terrible cases & wilderness of rooms of them," Melville noted — rooms of life-size or nearly full-scale male and female bodies showing musculature; cutaway female torsos showing pregnancies (especially twin pregnancies); and penises attached or unattached, erect or at rest.

Melville was particularly taken with some small cases on tables containing graphic scenes of Naples in the time of the plague:

> — The Sicilian's work. Nº 1. Interior of case, broken arches, skeleton thrown under arch — head of statue — dead expression — crown & scepter among bones — medallion — Death & scythe — pointing — tossed skeletons & tools. horrible humiliation. Cleft shows more temples & pyramid. Nº 2. Vault — heaps — all colors from deep green to buff — all ruins — detached bones — Mothers children old men, intricacy of heaps. Man with cloth over face bringing down another body whose buff contrasts with the putrid green. Nº 3. In a cavernous ruin. Superb mausoleum like Pope's, lid removed shows skeleton & putridity. Roman sarcophagus — joyous triumphal procession — putrid corpse thrown over it. — grating — rats, vampires — insects. slime & ooze of corruption. — Moralist, this Sicilian.

Having saturated himself in Zummo's view of the human body and the horrors of human experience, Melville walked back to the Pitti Palace and looked at the "3 Fates," a painting he thought was by Michelangelo. He focused on revelations of character: "The way the one Fate looks at other—Shall I?—The expectancy of the 3^d." The effect of the Michelangelesque painting (in fact assigned to Francesco Salviati) was heightened by the Michelangelesque poses of some of Zummo's wax figures ("Transition from splendid humanity of gallery to the Sicilian").

Then Melville called the Vermont-born sculptor Hiram Powers: "To Powers' studio. His America. Il Penseroso, Fisher Boy.—Saw him. Apron, plain man. Fine specimen of an American." With no mustache but a closely cropped gray chin beard, a fez-like cap protecting his hair from the dust, Powers kept his work-apron on as he talked—a practical habit that pleased Melville. The next year, Hawthorne was charmed with him also, noting that he had "hardly ever before felt an impulse to write down a man's conversation," as he felt when listening to Powers: "The chief reason is, probably, that it is so possible to do it, his ideas being square, solid, and tangible, and therefore readily grasped and retained"—squarer and more solid than Melville's, say. For his part, Melville was always more willing and able than Hawthorne to try to make solid and tangible notes on complex and elusive ideas (as he had done in summarizing George Adler's arguments in his journal in 1849), but equally willing to admire square ideas squarely stated. If Melville learned anything about the possibility that American sculptors could create great modern art in classical forms in the middle of the century, it was from Powers, a man of his own mental and creative kind, and a man who, unlike Melville, already had a tight grip on his aesthetic credo. This was fitting; in Melville's youth Vermont had seemed to shoulder up behind Lansingburgh.

The tough old Sicilian Zummo and the tough American sculptor satisfied a profound need in Melville to face the "weighty" in art and life, and put him in a fine mood for dining "at the Luna with the young Polyglot" that night and walking with him along the Arno. A young Florentine polyglot who accosts a middle-aged male tourist whose linen is no cleaner than it should be and presents him with a flower may be suspected of being willing to accept pay for sexual favors. For his part, Melville had known a tropical Paradise where all sex was freely offered, but he had no knowledge at all of a world in which a young man could grow up speaking several languages, accost an older stranger, present him with a flower, and talk (volubly) as if in his experience the world had always been delightful, as if he had inhabited a European Paradise before the Fall. A "batchelor," surely, "that 'Henry,'" and well worth musing on. Sarah had tried to crown Melville with a wreath that hellish Christmas of 1851. How long since anyone had held out a flower to him?

On 28 March early, on an empty stomach, Melville ascended the Duomo and entered the dome: "Fine morning & noble view." After breakfast at the Doney, he went "to Ufizzi gallery for last look," and then up to Fiesole, and "Boccaccio's villa — Medicis villa. Franscican convent." In the convent, he had a "View from windows." He packed his carpetbag and wrote up his journal without a final walk along the Arno. The porter failed to wake him ("us," he wrote in his journal) at three in the morning, and the diligence started off for Bologna, so that Melville and perhaps another passenger or two had to run around the Duomo to catch it at the gate. His reward was a day-long drive across the Apennines: "Grand scenery. Long reaches of streams through solitary vallies. No woods. No heartiness of scenery as in New England." At four thousand feet oxen were substituted for horses. In the coupé there was not much talk (perhaps because of linguistic differences) but "much smoking."

In Bologna he put up at the "Three Moors," and the next morning did his duty by the local food: "First thing at Bologna, tried Bologna sausage, on the principle that at Rome you first go to St. Peters." Then he toured the picture gallery, the Reale Pinacoteca, near the university, and the monastery that had been converted to a cemetery (Campo Santo) by Napoleon. The monastery and the church of the Madonna di San Luca were connected by an arcade with several hundred arches ("Arcade winding up the hill to church — three miles"). He walked through the university, seeing the "learned lady" statue, one of two or more. On 31 March he took the diligence for Padua "alone," except for a polite "elderly gentleman," and was surprised by the "dead level country," which was in such "strong contrast" to his previous drive, between Florence and Bologna. There was a two-hour stop at Ferrara, enough time for him to see the cathedral, where he noted the grotesquerie of the portico "sustained by pillars resting on old hunchbacks" and looked warily at the Last Judgment sculpted overhead, knowing his own place when he looked at any such depiction of the elect on the right hand of God and the reprobate on the left. He saw Tasso's prison (nothing fancy, a mere "cider-cellar") and found Byron's name and other graffiti on a grated window. The next stage of the drive to Padua was in a small old Austrian vehicle that apparently reminded him of coaches in gothic fiction: "Old fashioned vehicle. Mysterious window & face. Secret recesses. Hide. Old fashioned feeling." The broad Po was "Yellow as Missipi." It was midnight before they reached Padua and he got to bed at the "Star of Gold."

At Padua he went to "the famous caffe of Pedrocci" ("Worthy of its fame, being of great size and well furnished"). He hired a guide, donned his nine-dollar greatcoat, put up an umbrella, and saw the sights for a few hours, plainly delighted with everything despite the rain, especially "Satan & his host" (a large sculpture of the Fall of Lucifer, sixty figures carved from a single block of marble) and Santa Maria dell'Arena, designed and painted by Giotto. At two in the afternoon he took the railway cars for Venice in a hard rain across level terrain. At last it seemed very familiar: "Approaching Venice like approaching Boston from the West." (In Melville's boyhood the top of Beacon Hill had been dumped into the bay, tipcart load by tipcart load, but all his life there had been swampy areas along the Charles River; entrepreneurs were about to begin filling in the Back Bay in earnest.) From the station he took a gondola to the Hotel Luna in time to sally out to the Piazza of San Marco, where he wandered about till late. On 2 April he had a roll for breakfast at Florian's, at a little table like those on which the management now places neatly printed cards naming some of their eminent clients, among them Goethe, Byron, and Melville. He was disappointed in the dark, oily looking interior of San Marco's, but cheered up as he went to the Rialto and took a gondola "to Grand Canal & round by Guidecca."

In his few days in Venice, Melville as always did his duty as a tourist, making the best possible use of his time. He went to a glass bead manufactory and saw the church of Santi Giovanni e Paolo, which contained Titian's *Martyrdom of St. Peter* (burned a few years later). He toured the Arsenal, making some comparisons to the one at Abbotsford. He took a gondola to Murano, and on his return visited the Jesuit church, which charmed him with its lesson in just how plastic the plastic arts could be: "Marble drapery of pulpit. Astonishing what can be done with marble." On 3 April Melville located, unsurprisingly, a "Fine view of G. Canal," and on the fifth took a gondola to Napoleon's garden at the end of Venice "(Like Battery at N. York)," where he enjoyed "Fine view of lagoon & isles on two sides of Venice." He crossed to the Lido: "fine view of Venice, particularly the Ducal palace &c. Walked across the sand to the Adriatic shore." He went to Santa Maria della Salute and then to San Giorgio Maggiore, admiring the wood carvings, then landed "at steps of Ducal palace under Bridge of Sighs." Melville hired a guide, Antonio, who was sufficient of a character that he wrote him up in his journal, recording his rich anecdote of Byron "swimming over every morning to wake a lady in palace opposite." Melville reflected on the way he was spending time: "Floating about philosophizing with Antonio the Merry. Ah, it was Pausillippo" — meaning it was a space without pain. He enjoyed Antonio without trusting anything he said, and concluded that the guide was "good character for Con. Man." For the most part, he made his observations and reflections alone, and ate alone, watching the life of Venice.

Inevitably, the intensity of Melville's responses to city scenes had diminished as he moved into cultures nearer his own, and nearer to scenes he remembered from London, Paris, and Cologne in 1849. Nothing in the streets of Rome, Pisa, Florence, Bologna, Ferrara, or Padua had stirred him as the scenes in Constantinople and Cairo had done. In Venice he began to celebrate the throngs and the public space for the throngs: "Walk in St. Mark's. To bed. — No place like the St. M.s Square for enjoyment. Public ball room — no hours. Lights. Ladies taking refreshments outside (In morning they breakfast on sunny side). Musicians. singers. soldiers &c &c &c. Perfect decorum." He went back time and again, watching crowds of people promenading, seeing flocks of pigeons, walking "by moonlight & gaslight in piazza," and adding more description:

> St: Mark's at sunset, gilt mosaics, pinacles, looks like holyday affair. As if the Grand Turk had pitched his pavilion here for a summers day. 800 years! Inside the precious marbles, from extreme age, look like a mosaic of rare old soaps. — have an unctuous look. Fairly steamed with old devotions as refectories with old dinners. — In Venice nothing to see for the Venetian. — Rather be in Venice on rainy day, than in other capital on fine one. —

"Great gorgeousness of effect," he observed while visiting the Armenian convent in Venice: "Supurb vestments, blended with supurb light streaming in from shining lagoon through windows draped with rosy silks. chaunting, swinging silver censers — puff of incense at each worshipper." Venice, historically more akin to Constantinople than to Rome, entranced him with its puffs of incense, fantastic Byzantine architecture, old pictures in many of the galleries, great Titians, casual reminders of Byron.

On 6 April Melville left Venice before dawn, crossing to Milan, delighted at the show: "Between Verona & Brescia had noble views of Lago di Garda, with Mount Baldus in distance. Villages upon its shore & on an island. Long vista of the lake between great overlapping mountains whose snows insensibly melted into the purples. Passed on the north continually by the first tiers of the Alps. R.R. over dead level of Lombardy plain." Remembering that the region was "the scene of Napoleon's campaigns," he was stuck by the fertility apparent everywhere, by the farmhouses ("so unlike ours") and by the farmland: "No signs of hard work as with us." Arriving at dark, he took an omnibus to the "Hotel de le Ville" then walked out to see the cathedral of Milan by night.

Next day Melville went to the picture gallery of the Brera, and later to Santa Maria delle Grazie, where Leonardo's *Last Supper* was in the refectory of the adjoining monastery. The French had used the room as a granary and a stable six decades earlier. Now it was cleared except for a great stage always occupied by copyists of the remnants of the great painting ("Whole picture faded & half gone"). He knew that the French had only accelerated the constant degradation of the painting, Leonardo having tried a new technique of tempera on the dry wall. Melville mused on the significance of the painting, giving it a twist in which Judas looks a little like T. D. Stewart or Orchis ("One shall betray me, one of you — man so false — the glow of sociality is so evanescent, selfishness so lasting"). He also mused on the impracticality of the painter: "Leonardo & his oil, case of a great man (Wordsworth) & his theory." Here Melville was expressing one of his several ambivalences about Wordsworth. He admired Wordsworth as a great poet, rejected him for his later political conservatism, and was dismayed at his leveler's theories about the appropriateness of unpoetic language for poetry, theory that filled up many prosy pages in the appendix to his edition of Wordsworth's poems. (Melville marked in "Observations, &c.," now known as the preface to the second edition of *Lyrical Ballads*, the assertion "there neither is, nor can be, any essential difference between the language of prose and metrical composition.") Then Melville went back to the cathedral, which he decided was glorious, more "satisfactory" to him than St. Peter's: "A wonderful grandure. Effect of burning window at end of aisle. Ascended, — From below people in the turrets of open tracery look like flies caught in cobweb. — The groups of angels on points of pinacles & everywhere. Not the conception but execution. View from summit. Might write book of travel upon top of Milan Cathedral." Early on 8 April, Melville took the cars for Lake Como, and then took a steamer on the lake ("Like going to Lake George"). He went all the way to Bellagio, stunned by the views of the mountains ("rolled together in watery blue. Snow upon summits") and the "Wonderful populousness of shores of lake." The next morning he caught a diligence for Novara, on the way to Turin.

Once again, he remarked on the "dead flat Lombardy plain," now with Alps in sight to the north. He had a four-hour layover at Novara, waiting for his train, time enough to see the "Old duomo" with Bertel Thorwaldsen's angels. At Turin, at nine in the evening, he had an "adventure" with the omnibus and the porters before getting to the "Hotel d la Europe." The tenth of April was rainy, so he walked as much as possible "under the great arcades" before going to the Gallery, where he saw paintings by Titian, Rubens (a Mary Magdalen), children by Van Dyke, and particularly admired four allegorical paintings by Francesco Albani ("Earth, Air, Fire, Water"). A number of tavern scenes by David Teniers the Younger ("The remarkable Teniers effect is produced by first dwarfing, then deforming humanity") persisted in his memory. There were several Breughels ("always pleasing"). He noted the different behavior of the working classes in Italy and the United States: "Many caffes & fine ones — Laboring people & poor women taking their frugal breakfast in fine caffes. Their decorum, so different from corresponding class at home." The rain had thwarted him, but he managed a last-minute view, noting the "Singular effect of standing in arch of castle, & looking down vista of Via di Grossa to Mount Rosa & her snows. — Caught it unobscured by clouds early on the morning I left Turin."

On 11 April Melville left for Genoa on the cars, toward the end passing through a series of tunnels in the hills, the last two miles long. He arrived in the rain at three in the afternoon, to trouble: "Carpet bag fell from shoulder of clumsy porter. Afraid to look at Kate's affairs." He noticed at once the inferiority of the palaces in Genoa and the peculiarity that instead of grand, complex architecture the city was conspicuous for "*paintings of architecture instead of the reality*"—elaborate architectural detail represented on flat walls in fresco. He remembered Machiavelli's saying, "that the appearances of a virtue may be advantageous, when the reality would be otherwise." Melville found the streets "like those of Edinburgh; only still more steep & crooked." He ascended one for the view then in the evening "walked on pavilion nigh port" and from the "Tower of the Cross of Malta" attained his view "of hills in distance."

Seeing armed troops of occupation, Austrians, on 12 April he reacted with disgust ("Unhandsome set of men"), but went straight to the Cathedral. He took an omnibus to the end of the harbor and climbed the lighthouse (three hundred feet high):

> Superb view. Sea coast to south. Promontory. All Genoa & her forts before you. The heigth & distances of these forts, their outlying loneliness. The bleakness, the savageness of glens between, seem to make Genoa rather the capital and fortified camp of Satan: fortified against the Archangels. Clouds rolling round ramparts aerial. &c. Took the East side of harbor, and began circuit of the 3^d line of defences. Ramparts overhang the open sea, arches thrown over ravines. Fine views of sections of town. Up & up. Galley-slave prison. Gratings commanding view of sea — infinite liberty. Followed round & round. Nonplussed. Got to Public Promenade. Struck up steep lane to little church (fine view of sea from porch) Thence higher, and came to ramparts. Magnificent views of deep valley other side — & of Genoa & sea. Up & up. Finer & finer, till I got to the apex fort. Saw the two encircling vallies, and the ridge in which their heads unite to form the site of the highest forts. Great populousness of these vallies. Loneliness of some of the higher forts. Grounds enclosed by 3^d circuit. Deep, woodless glens. Solitary powder magazines. Lonesome as glen in Scotch highlands.

"With great fatigue" he "descended by irregular path, coming out by Doria palace." Unprepossessing Genoa, by virtue of its physical setting, had caught him off guard and worn him out. The next day he gave the palaces short shrift and returned to the hotel early, where he met the purser of the *Constellation* at dinner.

On 14 April Melville took the cars for Arona on Lake Maggiore at dawn, encountering Lieutenant Charles M. Fauntleroy from the *Constellation* at the station. He sailed (a cold passage) from Arona to Magadino, at dark, then took a diligence to Bellinzona, making a "Shadowy & vague approach among the roots of Alps." From another diligence, just arriving from Simplon, "out jumped Dr Lockwood," so Melville had an unexpected boon companion for dinner, although he dragged himself out two hours after midnight to board another diligence for crossing the San Gotthard Pass: "Bow window. Silence, mystery. Steady roll of wheel. Dawn, zig-zags, Gorge, precipice, Snow." While he was breakfasting at Airolo on 15 April another acquaintance greeted him — "Abbot" — probably Dr. Henry Abbott, an English physician in Cairo, the man who had for years displayed his collection of Egyptian antiquities in New York (to the great benefit of Walt Whitman, among many others). A cryptic notation about discussion of the gods during the wild crossing of the Alps may indicate that Melville recurred to his favorite themes with Abbott. The circumstances would have ruled out any sustained comparisons between Egyptian and Hebraic deities, but Melville may have had a chance to try out his new theory that dark Jehovah was an invention of Egyptian priests. Abbott (who had a daughter with him) became his companion during a harrowing journey and a ramble about Lucerne. On 17 April in a diligence for Berne, alone in the coupé with Abbott, he enjoyed the "Charming day & charming country. Swiss cottages. Thrift neatness &c.," and later went "to terrace of cathedral for view of Bernese Alps. There they were — seen over the green." The next day with "Mr Fay & Abbot & daughter" he explored and rode, enjoying the "Noble views of Alps." "Mr Fay" was Theodore Sedgwick Fay, the U.S. minister to Switzerland, and famous as an essayist and novelist; like Melville, he was a good friend of Nathaniel Parker Willis.

Melville's last significant new encounter on record was brief: on 19 April he rode inside a diligence (rather than his favored seat outside) on the way to Basle, and while dining at Soleure he encountered "a Mr Smyth merchant of N.Y.," Henry A. Smythe, the man who would approve his hiring at the New York Custom House at the end of 1866. Melville was as sociable as he could be while watching what passed his window: "Supurb views of the Bernese Alps & Jura ranges all morning. Beyond Solure drew near Jura, — palisades — About high as Saddle Back. 4000 feet. Old castles. Entered by a remarkable defile. View of white Alps through defile. Ride across." In Basle (perhaps with Smythe) he crossed the Rhine ("Deep, broad, rapid") by a bridge of boats, and before dawn on the twentieth set off in the cars for Strasbourg.

The view from the cathedral at Strasbourg disappointed him ("Not fine as Milan"). He enjoyed the lovely afternoon on the ride to Heidelberg ("Level country bounded by hills") and got up at five on the twenty-first in order to "mount" the Castle and enjoy the "View of Necker" (the Neckar River). At the station he met Dr. Abbott, both of them going to Frankfurt. Smythe had traveled with him or else encountered him again, for he invited both Melville and Abbott for a drive about town: "Goethe's statue. Faust's. Cathedral. Luther's preaching place. River side. Park. Jews quarter. Rothschilds home. &c &c &c."

On 22 April Melville took the wrong train and ended up not in Wiesbaden but in Mainz, from which he took a boat for Cologne, still vivid in his memory from 1849. Good thing it was: this time he arrived late at night and left before dawn, taking a train for Amsterdam. The Low Countries offered no such Romantic views as he had been recording, but there was an unspecified "adventure" after arriving at the hotel, perhaps a change of hotel, for he put up "at last" at the " 'Old Bible', upon which something good might be written in the ironical way." In Amsterdam he renewed his pleasure in "Dutch convivial scenes. Teniers & Breughel," and saw many great Rembrandts, but what most struck him was the "Wonderful picture of Paul Potter — The Bear." At Rotterdam on the twenty-fourth he went slumming, with the help of a guide: "went to Dance Houses. Into three of them. Striking & pathetic sight. The promenading girls—music—their expression & decorum.—Villiany of the guide." Early on the twenty-sixth his steamer entered the Thames, at the Isle of Dogs passing the "mammoth ship 'Great Eastern' " — so large it had to be launched sideways when it was finished. By seven at night he was settled in Tavistock Hotel, ready for a dreary Sunday, when he walked to Hyde Park and in Kensington Gardens, to get an idea of them, having not explored them in his rushed visit in 1849.

Monday morning, 27 April, having learned along the way (through a letter from Allan, perhaps, or indirectly through Sam Shaw in Rome) what firm would publish *The Confidence-Man*, he proceeded to Longmans, where he found it had been on sale for three weeks, already. Melville's reputation had suffered much less from *Pierre* in England than at home, since only a few copies had crossed the Atlantic and only one review had been published, as far as we know. Longmans had printed a thousand copies of *The Confidence-Man* and could show Melville that they had sent out a good number of review copies—twenty-nine. They had expended £17.1.19 in announcing it rather lavishly for a few days before they published it on 3 or 4 April ("Friday next"—3 April—was the usual date given). Most of the announcements identified Melville as the author of *Typee* and *Omoo* (on 4 April the *Sun* added *The Piazza Tales* to those two titles). Someone at Longmans had a sample of the earliest London reviews on hand when Melville showed up unexpectedly, and may have guided him through them, commenting on the biases and influence of the particular papers and perhaps identifying some of the reviewers. Chances are that Melville saw still other notices in reading rooms during his days in London.

There was only a fair return in reviews for the twenty-nine copies, but just then London reviewers were more swamped than usual, to the point that the *Daily News* on 22 April groaned, "Novels! our library table is groaning under their weight, our floor is covered with them." Aside from installments of *Little Dorrit* that every paper had to summarize every month, editors were dealing with important fiction and a classic biography. Among others, the *Daily News*, the *Globe*, the *Sun*, and the *News of the World* all printed long reviews of Elizabeth Gaskell's *Life of Charlotte Brontë*. Nothing pushed *The Confidence-Man* out of sight the way the opening of the Crystal Palace had eaten up space that ought to have been lavished on *The Whale*, but the competition for space in the columns for reviews was fierce. Whoever Melville talked to at Longmans may have been extremely polite, but nothing in the initial reception could have led anyone in the company to importune him to let the firm publish the next manuscript he produced, or one he might have left in a desk at home. Traveling light, worried about heavy and fragile items he was carrying, and knowing he had to buy last-minute gifts and get possession of his trunk once he reached Liverpool, Melville may not have carried away the three author's copies he was owed.

London reviews kept appearing, during Melville's voyage and after he arrived home. Once again, he never got a sense of the range or depth of the reviews, and the importance of the London reviews is not for anything they did to his career, such as it was, but for what they may have meant long afterward in the revival of his reputation. These men and women, as Melville's British reviewers had been from the beginning, were professional critics — witty, sophisticated, and well educated, whatever their personal peculiarities. While some of them retained warm affection for Melville's earlier work, most of them, unlike the American reviewers — were quite prepared to assume that Melville's change was development rather than deterioration. (Probably none of them had read *Pierre*.) Sharp though they were, the English critics did not find *The Confidence-Man* easy to read, but they made shrewd observations about their experiences of reading it as well as about its genre, its meaning, and its style. The *Literary Gazette* (11 April) began with this caveat: "We notice this book at length for much the same reason as Dr. Livingston describes his travels in Monomotapa, holding that its perusal has constituted a feat which few will attempt, and fewer still accomplish." The *Illustrated Times* (25 April) claimed to have been stymied in its attempt at forging straightway through: "After reading the work forwards for twelve chapters and backwards for five, we attacked it in the middle, gnawing at it like Rabelais's dog at the bone, in the hope of extracting something from it at last. But the book is without form and void." Bewildered as some of the English reviewers were, they responded to the challenges of the book with verve and humor.

The London reviewers had fidgeted over the genre of *The Whale* and now they stewed over the genre of *The Confidence-Man*. They saw it as "a morality enacted by masqued players," a "moral miracle-play" (the *Athenæum*, 11 April); as not a novel, "unless a novel means forty-five conversations held on board a steamer, conducted by personages who might pass for the errata of creation, and so far resembling the Dialogues of Plato as to be undoubted Greek to ordinary men" (the *Literary Gazette*); as "novel, comedy, collection of dialogues, repertory of anecdotes, or whatever it is" (the *Illustrated Times*); as "in fact, a puppet-show" (the *Westminster Review*, July); and as a "comedy" (the *Saturday Review*, 23 May). The *Illustrated Times* had an ultimate afterthought: "We said that the book belonged to no particular class, but we are almost justified in affirming that its *génre* is the *génre ennuyeux*." The reviewers knew well enough where to look for literary ancestry. Presumably recalling Coleridge's marginal glosses, the *Athenæum* thought the synoptic titles in the "Contents" were "like a reflection of 'The Ancient Mariner,' interspersed with some touches vaguely derived from the dialecticians of the eighteenth century." The *Spectator* (11 April) even more knowingly declared that the "spirit of the satire seems drawn from the European writers of the seventeenth and eighteenth centuries, with some of Mr. Melville's own Old World observations superadded." Several fretted aloud that they might be missing the meaning. The reviewer in the *Critic* (15 April) called it "the hardest nut to crack" of all Melville's books, of which he named the first six, excepting only *Redburn*. He was very near a major insight: "there are some parts of the story in which we feel half inclined to doubt whether this apostle of geniality is not, after all, an arch-impostor of the deepest dye." More than a century passed before this perception was rivaled in print.

A couple of the reviewers made perceptive comments on style on the basis of fairly close knowledge of Melville's earlier works. The *Leader* (11 April) declared that "festoons of exuberant fancy decorate the discussion of abstract problems," then defined a shift in Melville's style: "In his Pacific stories Mr. Melville wrote as with an Indian pencil, steeping the entire relation in colours almost too brilliant for reality; his books were all stars, twinkles, flashes, vistas of green and crimson, diamond and crystal; he has now tempered himself, and studied the effect of neutral tints." The *Athenæum* was also scrupulous in its analysis: "Mr. Melville is lavish in aphorism, epigram, and metaphor. When he is not didactic, he is luxuriously picturesque; and, although his style is one, from its peculiarities, difficult to manage, he has now obtained a mastery over it, and pours his colours over the narration with discretion as well as prodigality." Melville's tempering himself, his "muting" or subduing of his meaning so as to prevent reviewers from denouncing the book as irreligious was not wholly successful, for the reviewer in the *Saturday Review* complained about "his occasionally irreverent use of Scriptural phrases." Quite tardily, on 14 June, *Reynolds's Newspaper* noticed this "book of fragmentary sketches and anecdotes by an American author of celebrity," finding only John Moredock interesting and printing a long extract, "A Sanguinary Revenge," and a shorter one, "Anecdote of the Colonel," about Moredock's afterlife as a retired Indian-killer.

Longmans reported a sale of 343 copies in the first three months, but only 34 more over the next year, leaving Melville's account still £24.8.0 short of making up expenses in June 1858, when 516 copies in foolscap octavo quires were wasted (sold as scrap paper), bringing in £3.16.2. By June 1859 66 copies had been disposed of at a trade sale and 9 more sold. In all, 386 copies were sold, 32 presented (including the three sent to Melville), 66 disposed of at a trade sale, and 516 "wasted," making a loss over the two years of £20.14.9. These figures account for the full 1000, but after the Longmans buildings in Paternoster Row burned down in 1861 someone added a memorandum to the closed-out ledger: "6 Copies c[loth] Burnt." If these were not phantom copies, they had at least an apter fate than the wasted quires — six heretical volumes consumed in flames, like victims in autos-da-fé.

Worn out after facing Longmans and the preliminary report on *The Confidence-Man*, Melville bestirred himself enough on 28 April to visit Madame Tussaud's (the nearest he could get to the Sicilian moralist Zummo). He lay "a sort of waterlogged" for the rest of the week, indulging in an Irvingesque reverie at the "Cock," the topic being, inevitably, the difference between the way he felt there in 1849, deprived of his grand tour but assured of a great career, and now, having gained the one but lost the other. He took a train south to Sydenham to see the reconstructed Crystal Palace, moved there two years after its original opening when *The Whale* was published. He skeptically surveyed the reconstructions meant to convey the beauty and power of ancient and more recent Mediterranean architecture (the Alhambra Court, the Pompeian Court, and the Egyptian Court), and protested at the boasting he had seen about the size of the Crystal Palace and the size of the *Great Eastern:* "Comparison with the pyramid. — Overdone. If smaller would look larger. The Great Eastern. Pyramid. — Vast toy. No substance. Such an appropriation of space as is made by a rail fence. Durable materials, but perishable structure. Cant exist 100 years hence." But he admired the views from the terraces of the Crystal Palace, and when the train left him at London Bridge he took another look at the Thames Tunnel, which had enthralled him in 1849. Waterlogged or not, he got himself out to Richmond, and watched "the equestrians" in Hyde Park at evening ("Fine & bold riding of the ladies"); was he himself the "Poor devel looking over the rail"? He satisfied a profound aesthetic craving: "Visited the Vernon & Turner galleries.—Sunset scenes of Turner. 'Burial of Wilkie.' The Shipwreck. 'The Fighting —— taken to her last birth.'" (Later he learned the name of the *Temeraire* and used it in a poem.) Francis Jacox as Sir Nathaniel in 1852 had made a memorable comparison about the ending of *The Whale:* "The climax of the three days' chase after Moby Dick is highly wrought and sternly exciting—but the catastrophe, in its whirl of waters and fancies, resembles one of Turner's later nebulous transgressions in gamboge." Seeing that comparison in a Boston or New York reprinting in 1853, Melville rued again the loss of the "Epilogue" but revelled wryly in the public linking of him and J. M. W. Turner as kindred sinners. Melville made no effort to let his acquaintances from 1849 know he was in town. He might have done so, even in his defeated state, if the marplot Lem Jr. had not slithered his flunkeyish way into the Paradise of Bachelors.

On 3 May Melville took the train to Oxford. As a young man in Liverpool Melville had felt shut out of British life, and particularly he had felt that his cultural heritage was being denied, if he experienced anything at all like Redburn's being rebuffed from a reading room. As an educationally deprived American autodidact, Melville might understandably enough have seen Oxford as the home of privileged exclusivity hostile to him. Instead, magnanimous rather than defensive, he felt utterly at home:

> Most interesting spot I have seen in England. Made tour of all colleges. It was here I first confessed with gratitude my mother land, & hailed her with pride. Oxford to American as well worth visiting as Paris, tho' in a very different way.—Pulpit in corner of quadrangle. Deer. Garden girdled by river.—Meadows beyond. Oxen & sheep. Pastoral & collegiate life blended.—Christ Church Meadow. Avenue of trees.—Old reef washed by waves & showing detached parts—so Oxford. Ivy branch over portal of St. John intertwining with sculpture. Amity of art & nature. Accord. Grotesque figures. Catching rhuematism in Oxford cloisters different from catching it in Rome. Contagion in Pamfili Doria but wholesome beauty in Oxford. Learning lodged like a faun. Garden to every college. Lands for centuries never molested by labor. Sacred to beauty & tranquility. Fell's avenue. Has beheld unstirred all the violence of revolutions. &c.—Steep roof. Spanish chestnut. Dining halls.

He loved everything he saw:

> Each college has dining room & chapel — on a par — large windows. Soul & body equally cared for. — Grass smooth as green baize of billiard table. — The picturesque never goes beyond this. — I know nothing more fitted by mild & beautiful rebuke to chastise the ranting of Yankees. — In such a retreat Old Burton sedately smiled at men. — Improvement upon the monkish. As knights templars were mixture of monk & soldier, so these of monk & gentleman.

In an earlier note from which this entry was developed, he wrote: "I know nothing more fitted by a mild & beautiful rebuke to chastise the sophomorean pride of America as a new & prosperous country." He took Oxford as his own ideal place, the birthright of every lover of the English language and English literature. Oddly, he seems not to have sought a "view," not even from Carfax Tower.

A good second-generation Romantic, Melville had paid homage to Scott at Abbotsford. He had consciously followed in the footsteps of Byron, for no one of his time could see Athens, Rome, and Venice without thinking of him; indeed, anyone of his age could hear, as he did, unpublished if perhaps apocryphal stories of Byron. (Captain Bell, whom he met at Messina, had met the poet in May 1822.) He had paid homage to Shelley and Keats in the Protestant Cemetery. Now he could not leave England without paying his tribute to Irving and Shakespeare. Irving had told Americans what emotions best befitted a visit to Shakespeare's birthplace, and Melville had absorbed Irving long before he read Shakespeare as an adult modern writer reading a great genius from three and a half centuries earlier. From Oxford on 4 May Melville went to Stratford-upon-Avon, experiencing the oddity of a ride part way on a "horse rail road," such as he had ridden twenty-three years earlier, doing New York State Bank business. He saw what he needed to see, bare evidence: "Shakspere's home — little old groggery abandoned. — cheerless, melancholly. Scrawl of names. — The church. Tomb stones before Altar, wife, daughter son-in-law. — New Place. — Walk to Hathaway cottage at Shottery. Level country." He continued on to Warwick, having time to walk about before taking the train to Birmingham, where the "Mob of chimnies" reminded him of Newcastle-upon-Tyne. The railroad ride to Liverpool the next day exposed him to more than he needed of industrial pollution, for it was like "riding through burnt district." The chimneys looked tree-like, but "smoking or with shoots of flame from top."

In Liverpool Melville secured his berth on the steamer *City of Manchester*, picked up his mail, saw Hawthorne, called on young Henry A. Bright, who had shown him around the previous November, bought his final presents, got his trunk, and on 6 May got aboard the steamer and was "off for home."

Julian Hawthorne in the Dearborn *Independent* (24 September 1927) recorded or invented witnessing Melville sitting and talking for an hour at the consulate, possible on 5 May 1857, not the previous November: "But his talk was not in the improvisatorial style of the red-cottage days, it was for the most part unintelligible to me, a boy of eight or nine, and he seemed depressed and aimless. He said goodbye at last, and wandered away." As much as anyone, with passages like this one, Julian Hawthorne set the image of Melville in 1856–57 as a broken traveler.

In late 1856 and early 1857 Melville's family, in two states and in Europe, had tried to keep up with him — strong evidence against a rumor spread by Oakes's daughter, Josephine Shaw, in the 1920s that *all* the Shaws hoped he would never make it back home. Sam in Berlin on 2 November 1856 wrote his brother Lem that he had three pleasant letters that week ("your own, mother's and Elizabeth's") but nothing from Herman, although he expected a letter "every day." Maria on 11 November received two newspapers Herman had sent from Glasgow, then received a letter from Liverpool reporting that (in Uncle Peter's paraphrase of what Maria had written him) "his health is improving & that he is aware of the necessity of cessation from writing — & is convinced that by travelling he is renovating his system." There is no reason to doubt this report that by early November 1856 Melville had agreed with his mother that he should stop writing, despite journal entries he made about likely topics to be worked up. In Boston Elizabeth settled into old routines, with the faithful Mrs. Sullivan to help care for her two daughters. The Shaws expected Maria for Thanksgiving, but she changed her mind about leaving Gansevoort. On 23 November 1856 the judge wrote Sam that they would regret to see his seat vacant at Thanksgiving, adding: "We expect Oakes his wife & family . . . Elizabeth is here with her two youngest children, girls, they are very healthy & quiet & of course make themselves quite agreeable. Elizabeth has received but one letter from her husband, written soon after his arrival at Glasgow." They had heard that Sam Savage had arrived at Savannah, so they expected one Sam to be at the table, and Helen and George Griggs also went to the Shaws for Thanksgiving, bringing Malcolm. From Berlin on 23 November Sam Shaw wrote Lem of his plans (Dresden, Prague, Munich, Vienna, Venice, Rome) and said: "If by any method I could find Herman it would assist me perhaps in my arrangements." From Boston just before Thanksgiving Helen wrote to her mother, Maria reported to Peter: "Lizzie & the children are well and most agreeably & comfortably accommodated at her Fathers for the winter or until Hermans return from abroad."

Maria had not been in the habit of writing to Peter about Herman's family, the desperate letter in April 1853 being an exception. Her writing to him now was a natural outgrowth of her living with their brother Herman at Gansevoort. On 28 November 1856, having sent Herman's letter from Liverpool to Peter for him to read and return, which he promptly did, she wrote again: "I hope Herman will feel content to remain away for six months at least for he has sad[ly] overworked his strength—& requires recreation, freedom from care, from writing, & the little petty cares, & annoyances, of the farm which are ever recurring & are so distasteful to him." She was making, on Herman's behalf, two major renunciations: he would stop writing and he would stop any active supervision of farm work. She was not specifying any means of supporting his family if he did not write and did not farm; perhaps she had in mind still that he would turn to lecturing, work that would allow him to keep his family at Arrowhead without actively farming. Early in December Sam, still in Berlin, received "Herman's direction" from Elizabeth and wrote his mother: "I have a letter ready for him & hope to get some news from him."

The judge was sick early in December, but well enough by the thirteenth "to eat a small piece of roasted chicken" and to sip "a little champagne," Hope wrote to Sam; on the fifteenth she added: "Elizabeth's little Fanny has had a severe cold, but is now recovering.... Samuel Savage is with us." On the sixteenth she had good news of the judge: "the Doctor pronounces your father out of danger—. He sleeps much better than he has for nights past and I am in hopes that all will succeed as pleasantly as it has been painful. Your father is sitting by me dozing—time begins to hang heavy on him as he cannot read much or hear reading." She added: "Elizabeth is here as industrious as a bee her children are very interesting." By children she meant the daughters: Malcolm was with Helen and Stanwix in Gansevoort. As for duties, Lizzie continued to see members of her family, especially her cousin Maria H. Dow Wales, the daughter of Dorothy Knapp and Samuel Dow Jr., who had married George Wales in 1838, and she made time to visit her aunt Lucretia Knapp so as to "do up some fine sewing that she has ready for me, as I always do when in Boston" (as she said in 1863). A full life always awaited Elizabeth in Boston. There were many cases of scarlet fever in Boston at Christmas, but (as Hope wrote her son Sam) Elizabeth's children had been "much blessed with health." A few days after Christmas Lizzie had still "not heard one word from Herman since her husband left Liverpool, for Constantinople." Lem wrote Sam on the twenty-ninth to the same effect: "We have heard nothing from Herman since I last wrote you, when he was on the point of leaving Liverpool for Constantinople—we do not know whether he will go from there to Trieste & Venice or Naples or Ancona & cannot put you in the way of meeting him, when we do hear from him we will let you know—Lizzie & her two youngest children are still with us." Melville's mother knew better how to deal with her son's way of dropping out of sight than his wife and in-laws did. Judge Shaw still could not go out in the mid-January blasts, but on 12 January Lizzie "took little Bessey and went to Mr George Whitney's children's birthday party." Being just over three and a half, Bessie had to leave early, but before she left the fifty guests had devoured all the "luxuries such as Ice cream, cake and confectionary." Lizzie was giving her daughter a glimpse of the life she had led in the 1820s.

Christmas was not a great holiday for the Shaws, but as Episcopalians Allan and Sophia celebrated it. Milie recalled: "What lovely Christmases we used to have. We each had a table covered with presents, such as we have never had since. Toys of all kinds and books too." That month Evert Duyckinck kept up his Saturday night's men's club, reporting to George on the 27 December meeting. William Sidney Mount had begun joining them for Saturday evenings, along with John Milton Mackie, Henry T. Tuckerman, Edward S. Gould, Mr. Boyd, Robert Tomes, Mr. Waldrow, and Allan Melville. Washington Irving had been dropping in some Saturdays. He concluded: "We are upon the whole and in detail too very quiet—My dress coat hangs undisturbed on its ancient peg. Books are my world." Some of these men were good acquaintances of Herman's. He had delighted in Mount when they met in 1848; of the others, at least Tuckerman and Tomes were close friends of his. Allan was becoming part of the Duyckinck circle. If he did not contribute much at least he was appreciative, and he never sought to elbow Herman out, as Lem Shaw would have done.

In February 1857 Maria or Peter passed the word to the editor of the Albany *Atlas & Argus* that in new letters from Egypt Melville spoke "of being so much restored in health and strength that he 'climbed Cheops the other day, an enterprise of prodigious exertion.'" The paper continued: "He was to go to Jerusalem, and expected to be in Rome in the course of a few days"; someone misread or miscopied "days," for Melville must have said "weeks." In Pittsfield the *Sun* reprinted this item. Well before 6 April the family at Gansevoort had received a letter from Melville "dated Rome Feb 27th, announcing his return home next month." On 20 March, Hope wrote to Samuel: "I am afraid that you will miss Herman as his last date was the 19 of Feby in Naples—from there he was going to Rome—he did not say how long he would be in Rome, but from there he intended going to England and then after arriving in Liverpool to America." She added: "His health is improving much,—if he could only be absent one whole year, I think it would restore his health." This sounds sympathetic, and may indicate that she tried hard not to judge her son-in-law harshly. In April the judge wrote Sam in a way that showed how the family had been plotting the locations of the two travelers, waiting for the lines to intersect and merge: "We are strongly in hope that you will meet Herman in Rome. It appears by letters received from him, that he was in Rome, about the same time that you was at Genoa."

It was early April before any of the family received an eyewitness report on Herman abroad — in the form of Sam's letter from Rome on 25 March 1857 to his father about their brief meeting and Herman's being "considerably sunburnt" and as "stout as usual." Sam was greatly disappointed that he had not been able to travel with his brother-in-law, but pleased to have glimpsed him, and to have found him in better health. A letter from Rome which Herman wrote on 27 February to his mother and the others at Gansevoort decided the family upon action, with Augusta taking the role of organizer. If Herman was coming home in a few weeks, they had to be ready. On 7 April from Gansevoort Augusta wrote Uncle Peter about a plan she had already brought up with him in person in Albany. It was "of the utmost importance that something should be done to prevent the necessity of Herman's writing." To "return to the sedentary life which that of an author writing for his support necessitates, he would risk the loss of all the benefit to his health which he has gained by his tour, & possibly become a confirmed invalid. Of this his physicians have warned him." Earlier Maria had stressed only that Herman should neither write nor farm, but had not specified what he should do instead. Augusta emphasized the need "to secure to him some position which would give him occupation, & to some extent, means of support." The "only quarter" they knew was the Custom House. Here Uncle Peter's friends might help, Erastus Corning, and particularly Amasa J. Parker, "since from his position as Candidate for Governor, he commands influence with the Collector in New York in securing some appointments." A hitch was Herman's political record: "To be sure Herman has never been a politician, but he belongs to a Democratic family, & one which has done much for its party, & receive little from it. Then aside from these facts, Herman is just one of those persons who should be considered in filling these places, for he has done honor to, & reflected credit upon his country." She confided her "deep anxiety for the future well-being of a beloved brother" and conveyed a message: "Mamma desires me to say, dear Uncle, that her heart echoes all have said about Herman."

On 9 April Peter Gansevoort replied to Augusta assuring her that he concurred with her that a place in the New York Custom House would be good for Herman, but he or someone he consulted had raised "a serious obstacle viz, that he is not a Citizen of this State, but resides in the State of Mass^{ts}." This objection Augusta had to seek advice about; someone, probably

Allan, assured her, before she wrote her uncle on the fifteenth, that "there exists no necessity that the person applying for office should be a citizen of the state where the post is located." Furthermore, there was a recent decision in New York "which holds that a person doing business in New York who only sleeps out of the state is not a non-resident within the attachment laws." Herman could make a stronger claim than that: "Now Herman by birth & from his residence in the city of New York is known as a New Yorker; all his books are published in that city; all his interests are there except the land in Massachusetts. Then it is well known that he has never voted in Mass., or taken any part in state matters." Herman was acquainted with the collector, Augustus Schell, who already knew some of this information. On 17 April Peter Gansevoort called on Judge Amasa Parker and apparently waited on the spot while his friend wrote the letter to Schell urging Melville's appointment. Uncle Peter also saw Corning, who was "friendly" on the subject. Peter added warningly: "Hermans numerous friends in N.Y. ought without delay to write in a recommendation." In other words, Allan ought to be coordinating the campaign from Manhattan, not Augusta from Gansevoort. Later the same day Parker wrote to Shaw, judge to judge, expressing bland certainty that "considerations in the case of Mr Melville" would have "great weight," but keeping realistic: "I am told there is a very large number of applicants." There was no realistic hope that such a campaign for such a candidate could succeed, and, after the closest friends had done what they were asked to do, the matter faded away.

On 17 April, without having heard from Sam in Rome, the judge wrote him that they had had "a large family all winter," the full-time residents (the judge, Hope, and Lem) as well as Elizabeth and her daughters, and also Oakes—the longest time Lizzie had spent with her older brother in many years. Caroline and the children had been in New York much of the winter, but were all now in Mt. Vernon Street, and would not leave for Milton until the end of the month. Having been "industrious" in her father's house all winter, now Lizzie was being more resourceful than she had ever shown herself before. On the seventeenth she left the girls with the Shaws and went to Pittsfield alone to set Arrowhead in order. This took time. On the twenty-first Lem reported: "Elizabeth has now gone to Pittsfield to set her house in readiness to receive her husband whom she expects sometime in May." She returned to Boston, knowing that Arrowhead would be ready for them on Herman's arrival. From Bath on 1 May Amos Nourse wrote to Shaw: "I was glad to hear so good accounts of Herman & Elizabeth. The latter seems to have become quite a business character—She always proves just equal to the emergency whatever it may be. Her residence in our family when a girl so established her in our affections that we can never cease to be interested in whatever concerns her well-being." He went on to hope for a visit from Herman and Lizzie, a pleasure once "fairly in prospect" but which they now feared they had to give up. The wanderer would be home at Arrowhead soon, and he might want to stay close to home.

[16]

"Statues in Rome"
May 1857–February 1858

❦

> Agony — Physical — the expression of the highest degree of in the Laocoon — with a very just remark of the poet Rogers — Diary of an Ennuyee.
>
> Entry in Gansevoort Melville's *Index Rerum*

IN NEW YORK CITY, Dix, Edwards, & Co. published *The Confidence-Man* on 1 April, apparently only a coincidence, since the firm made no known effort to capitalize in its advertising on the special appropriateness of April Fools' Day to the book. Before publication, the company supplied the book to Fitz-James O'Brien so he could include it in his survey of Melville's career for the April *Putnam's*, still owned by Dix & Edwards, and distributed in late March. No other American periodical of a stature comparable to *Putnam's* reviewed *The Confidence-Man*, and most of the three dozen or so known American notices are only one or two sentences long. O'Brien's comments are atypical only by being longer than most and better expressed. After discussing *Israel Potter* as a "comparatively reasonable narrative" and a "coherent story" told with "considerable clearness and force," he categorized *The Confidence-Man* as belonging "to the metaphysical and Rabelaistical class of Mr. Melville's works," though he granted that "Melville, in this book, is more reasonable, and more respectful of probabilities, possibilities, and the weak perceptions of the ordinary mind than he usually is when he wraps his prophetic mantle about him." O'Brien bade Melville to "give up metaphysics and take to nature and the study of mankind" — that is, return to books like *Typee* and *Omoo* and refrain from writing books like *Mardi*, *Moby-Dick*, *Pierre* — and *The Confidence-Man*, with its unfulfilled but "occult object."

The American reviewers gave the book only a passing glance, hardly more than enough to offer it as a possible cure for dyspeptics (as the Boston *Puritan Recorder* did on 16 April) or to suggest that Melville himself had dyspepsia when he wrote it (as the Newark *Daily Advertiser* did on 23 May), or to express disappointment that "you read on and on" only to be "choked off at the end of the book like the audience of a Turkish story teller, without getting the end of the story" (Philadelphia *North American*, 4 April). The

Boston *Evening Transcript* (10 April) called Melville "an author who deals equally well in the material description and the metaphysical insight of human life." The New York *Daily Times* (11 April), echoing O'Brien, thought it full of "book learning," but as "essentially Western" and as "Indianesque" as one of Cooper's Leatherstocking Tales; furthermore, it was "a Rabelaisian piece of patch-work without any of the Rabelaisian indecency," mentioning in passing that this trait of "perfect decency" was a distinguishing mark of "Young American" literature. The Philadelphia *Daily Evening Bulletin* on 11 April was tersely ambivalent: "An eccentric, somewhat amusing and of course a rather more than somewhat indifferently digested novel. Like all of Melville's works, it contains material for suggesting thought to intelligent minds—and like all his works, too, its artistic or mechanical execution is wretched. Yet with all this it is curious, spirited, and well worth reading." The 17 April New York *Day Book* (which had reported "Herman Melville Crazy" five years before) said *The Confidence-Man* was "a clever delineation of western characteristics" that gave "considerable insight into the springs of human action." A copy reached Columbus, Ohio, and was noticed in the *Ohio State Journal* on 23 April: "To say the book is well written—that the agents employed talk well, theorize well, and indulge in fine touches of criticism and reasoning, (though some of it is of the inverse order,) is saying only what every one is prepared to admit who has ever read Mr. Melville." No American reviewer saw much structure in *The Confidence-Man*. The New York *Daily Times* said there was "no attempt at a novel, or a romance" in the pages; Melville "has not the slightest qualification for a novelist, and therefore he appears to much better advantage here than in his attempts at story books." The reviewer for *Mrs. Stephens' Illustrated New Monthly* (June) declared: "The book ends where it begins. You might, without sensible inconvenience, read it backwards." Some American commentaries, taking at face value the closing sentence ("Something further may follow of this Masquerade"), mentioned the possibility of a sequel. O'Brien, new to the United States, recognized only that the Confidence Man "comes and goes very mysteriously, and assumes new shapes, though he always betrays himself by a certain uniformity in the style of his thoughts and his machinations."

The family began to comment on the new book soon after it appeared, before Melville arrived home. On 15 April Augusta informed Uncle Peter cheerfully that "To-day's mail brought us several highly complimentary notices of Herman's new book 'The Confidence Man'"—a group probably composed mainly of the short notices by optimistic editors who had not read the book. On 17 April Judge Shaw wrote his son Sam: "A new work of Herman's has just been published at N. York entitled the 'Confidence Man.' He left the M.S. ready for publication, when he went out, last autumn, but it was not issued untill within a week or two. I have it but have not yet read it." It was Lem, on 21 April, writing his brother on the first anniversary of his setting out on his travels, who put the matter openly:

> A new book by Herman called "The Confidence Man" has recently been published. I have not yet read it; but have looked at it & dipped into it, & fear it belongs [to] that horribly uninteresting class of nonsensical books he is given to writing — where there are pages of crude theory & speculation to every line of narritive — & interspersed with strained & ineffectual attempts to be humorous. I wish he could or would do better, when he went away he was dispirited & ill — & this book was left completed in the publisher's hands.

Chances are that the judge would not allow Lem to express such opinions around him, and Hope at this period on occasion sounded sympathetic to Herman, but Oakes already shared Lem's hostility toward their brother-in-law, and Lem plainly felt no inhibition in expressing his true feelings to Sam in private. In the house in Mt. Vernon Street there were more topics every year that could not be brought to the surface until after the judge's death, and, after that, until Lizzie's view of her husband tilted even more toward that of the rest of the Boston household.

Herman's ship, the *City of Manchester*, docked in New York City on 20 May, a Wednesday. He greeted Allan and Sophia, conferred with his brother about the possibilities of getting into the New York Custom House, and collected the reviews of *The Confidence-Man* from Allan's basket. Allan and Sophia's baby had been christened at the end of April, before Melville returned: "Lucy was very cunning, how well I remember the first time she crept around the parlor! She was baptised at home by Dr Tyng. It was near Kitty's birthday, the last day of April, and both were celebrated at the same time." So wrote Milie in a schoolgirl autobiography. Evert Duyckinck's sixteen-year-old son and namesake had died on 10 February 1857, so Melville must have called on him to offer condolences before leaving to join Lizzie and his daughters in Boston, then to see Malcolm, close by at Helen's. At some point during his stay in Boston he said (as Lem reported to Sam on 2 June) that he was "not going to write any more at present & wishes to get a place in the N. Y. Custom House." On Monday, 25 May, Lem and Herman went over to Cambridge to look up Uncle Peter's son, Henry Sanford Gansevoort, who walked with them out to "Fresh Pond etc." — far enough to help Melville get his shore legs back. He said to Lem or in Lem's hearing that he was "better than at any time while absent," but still not perfectly well.

In his letter to Sam on 2 June, Lem Jr. said that he (not his father) "gave a dinner-party for him [Melville] & had a very pleasant one, Dr Holmes & the two Danas &c." Henry Gansevoort was included. Young Henry had been among politicians back in New York, but he had never seen a real Bostonian literary-political men's dinner, and his usual cheeky post-adolescent contempt melted away as he wrote his diary:

> Dined at 6 P.M. with Chief Justice Shaw and his son. There were present Dr Holmes, the poet, Herman Melville the author, R H Dana the jurist, and several others, including Dr Inches of Boston—After a short conversation in the parlor we were seated at a sumtuous repast, presided over by the Chief Justice. First Course Salmon in French style Mock Turtle soup, Spring chicken, squabs, broiled turkey, mutton chop sweetbread, Canvass back duck and too many other things to enumerate. Every kind of dessert, useless to name and Bergundy Hock Claret, Madara Heidsick Sherry Ancette and other wines cordials, etc Seltzer water etc. Wit circled the board, repartee flashed and humor, thundered until 11 P.M. when the joyous company seperated. This is a memorable day for me—Holmes remarked in the course of the conversation that a lecturer was a literary strumpet subject for a greater than whore's fee to prostitute himself.

Confident in his mental powers, Henry wrote: "Many good things were said which I shall ever treasure in my memory and therefore need not transcribe to paper." These good things, of course, are irretrievably lost, like all the experiences covered by Herman's "&c" in his journals.

It was late May before Melville escorted Lizzie and the girls to Pittsfield (leaving Malcolm behind?), where he got his first sight of the new depot of the Western Railroad, one hundred by twenty-five feet, wood painted to resemble red sandstone, with a forty-five-by-twenty-five-foot refreshment saloon (according to the Lee *Valley Gleaner* for 15 January 1857). At Arrowhead Melville also saw just how thoroughly Lizzie had prepared the house for his homecoming. Most likely he then left alone for Gansevoort to greet his mother, his Uncle Herman, Augusta, and Fanny, and to retrieve Stanwix (five and a half). Augusta had been most in charge of Stanwix, but now Maria felt free to make the trip east which she had projected in November. She was missing her baby acutely, Tom having been away more than two years. Her nephew Henry was no substitute, but in a temporarily benignant mood he took dinner at Longwood on 21 June, then reported to his sister Kitty that he had never seen "Aunt Melville" look better: "She seems to have renewed her youth and to have quaffed the elixier of life." She told him that Herman would be going with her to visit at Washington Avenue "sometime this week." Herman made the call with his mother but found that Uncle Peter "had gone west."

There was business to take care of immediately, for at this time Allan Melville gave his mother "a statement respecting the Gansevoort property as it is called at Gansevoort." According to George Griggs's letter to Peter Gansevoort on 12 September 1857, in this statement Allan affirmed that "the homestead was conveyed to him (Allan) and his brother Herman by a deed from you [Peter Gansevoort] in Dec. 1848 — And that there was at the same time a declaration of trust executed by them which has not been recorded." George Curtis's old lawsuit on behalf of Cousin Kate Gansevoort Curtis and her brothers had led Herman Gansevoort to assign his rights in the Manor House and land to Peter in 1847, and in turn Peter had assigned it to Allan and Herman in 1848. After Catherine Quackenboss Gansevoort's death in 1855 the claims of George F. Munro, a grandson of the original Tory owner of the property (which had been confiscated and awarded to the Hero of Fort Stanwix), came to trial after being pursued for several years, keeping Uncle Herman in profound distress. The ruling in December 1855 was against the Gansevoorts, and not until 1863, after Herman Gansevoort's death, was the property safe. When the interim strategies were all played out, the final decision was that after Uncle Herman's death the title to the property would go to Augusta and Fanny, who could be trusted to care for their mother until her death. On 9 September Herman Melville was in Albany on this matter, for Uncle Peter wrote to Henry that "Herman" (his nephew Herman) "is to dine with us, & I am to see him on Business at the house before Dinner" — the business being the matter of Maria's being made heir to Herman Gansevoort. There proved to be more to do than Herman Melville could handle in Albany. He consulted with Julius Rockwell in Pittsfield, then on 14 September went to Lenox, the shire town, to take care of what still needed to be done, although he could not conveniently do precisely what Allan had suggested, since the nearest "Commissioner" (according to Rockwell) was twenty-five miles from Pittsfield. That day Herman wrote Allan that he had done what Rockwell recommended ("& which he says he has known followed in many cases, and without difficulty"). Maria would be provided for.

Three weeks after Herman and Lizzie resumed their life at Arrowhead, Melville placed a running advertisement in the *Berkshire County Eagle* (starting in the issue of 26 June), offering for sale the "place now occupied by the subscriber (two miles and a half from Pittsfield village by the east road to Lenox,) being about seventy acres, embracing meadow, pasture, wood, and orchard, with a roomy and comfortable house. For situation and prospect, this place is among the pleasantest in Berkshire, and has other natural advantages desirable in a country residence." That Melville had abandoned the idea of moving into the village of Pittsfield seems clear from the fact that about this time he commissioned Allan to find him a suitable house, perhaps specifying Brooklyn, where Cousin Kate Curtis lived and where property was considerably cheaper than in Manhattan. In any case, on 3 July Allan

Melville used his power of attorney to sign a contract for Herman to buy the house on St. Felix Street at the southeast corner of Lafayette Avenue. This was a block from Flatbush Avenue, where Melville could catch a streetcar to the ferry, and it was only six blocks or so from the Brooklyn Navy Yard, where Guert Gansevoort was then stationed. The house was brownstone, three stories high, on a tiny lot, fifteen by eighty-five feet; gas fixtures, range, boiler, carpets, shades, and oil cloths went with the house, for a price of $4250, of which $2200 was to be put down on 1 August, Melville's thirty-eighth birthday. Melville apparently hoped that he would sell Arrowhead even faster than he had sold half of the acreage the year before, since the house and buildings went with it this time, but no offers came through the last week of June and the successive weeks of July. As 1 August approached, George Griggs called on Allan and gave him to understand (as Allan repeated to Judge Shaw on 11 August) that "there might be reasons why Herman had better get released from the contract." Thereupon Allan let the deadline for down payment lapse and on 11 August persuaded the owner of the building, John Holmes, to cancel the sale. That day Allan sent the canceled contract to Shaw, without specifying why the sale had not gone through. Shortly thereafter, Melville "forbade" the ad that had been running in the *Eagle* "tf" (till forbidden) and also the one that had been running in the *Sun* since 16 July. By mid-July Melville would have heard of T. D. Stewart's death in Lansingburgh on 11 July "after a short illness." The friend who had tempted him and then, as it seemed, terrorized him had not lived long to enjoy the return of the $2050 plus another $1000 or so of interest—a pittance to a man who died wealthy. On 22 July Emma was born at New Rochelle to Abby Pitman Thurston Lathers and her husband, Richard. About that time Rowland Morewood was seriously ill, according to a letter from his recently widowed mother, and he probably stayed at Broadhall through the summer. There may have been family gatherings at Arrowhead.

 Allan must have known before Herman returned that on 27 April, Dix, Edwards & Co. had dissolved and a new firm had been formed, Miller & Company, the entity which had deposited a bound copy of *The Confidence-Man* for copyright. G. W. Curtis was officially a partner by June, and around two months later the firm failed. On 4 September Curtis informed Allan that the stereotype plates of *The Piazza Tales* and *The Confidence-Man*, which it owned, would be sold—a necessary warning, since the contract gave Herman Melville joint ownership and the right to purchase the plates at a quarter of their original cost if the firm failed. Melville wanted a little time to consider what to do (specifically, whether to raise money somehow to buy the plates for one book which had brought him only a few dollars and another which had brought him not a cent). On 15 September Melville wrote to

Curtis that he could "not at present conveniently make arrangements" to buy the plates, but that later he might be able to; but he did not "wish to suggest anything in the way of a prompt settling up of the affairs of the late firm." When the stereotype plates of "Miller & Curtis" were put up for sale at the Leavitt auction house on 19 September, the plates for their two books by Melville were withheld in deference to Melville's suggestion. By 26 September Melville was frustrated and agitated when he wrote to the insistent Curtis: "I will try and do something about the plates as soon as I can. Meantime if they bother you, sell them without remorse. To pot with them, & melt them down." With this authorization and no buyer in sight, Curtis probably sent the plates of *The Piazza Tales* and *The Confidence-Man* to a cauldron right away, leaving Melville as a Harper author still (although $352.11 in debt to them at the last accounting), and with the Putnam plates of *Israel Potter* stored somewhere (and sold in late September to the Philadelphia publisher T. B. Peterson & Bros. for $218.66). Melville's career as a prose writer thus symbolically concluded, Curtis might help him start a new career.

After his hopes for a job at the New York Custom House fell through, along with the possibility of buying a house in Brooklyn and selling what was left of Arrowhead, Melville had two ways of earning money, realistically speaking. He could go back to writing for magazines, in a year of hard times. (The year 1857 was not as bad as the disastrous year 1837, but, in the present Panic, *Putnam's*, the most reliable market for his stories, was failing.) In Massachusetts, the Anthony Burns case of 1854 had led to a shift in public opinion and the passage of a personal liberty law, an unconstitutional feel-good gesture, and in the new climate the *Atlantic Monthly* was planned as a Boston magazine that would feature a now-safe intermixture of Harvard professors and formerly shunned abolitionists. Melville agreed to contribute, without specifying when, and the *Atlantic* advertised him on the back of the first (November) issue as a prospective contributor. (He never did contribute to it.) There was one alternative. Everyone thought lecturing might be the best thing—it would get him out of the house, it would give him some outlet for his restless nature, it would require little toll on his imagination, it might afford him some pleasant experiences with interesting people and places, and it would prove very profitable. Melville was at last ready to think about lecturing.

Accordingly, around 8 September Melville wrote G. W. Curtis for advice, since his handsome young follower as a travel-writer had proceeded him, and profitably so, onto the lecture stage. Melville ambivalently described himself as both thief and victim, according to what Curtis relayed to Allan in the process of negotiating over the Dix & Edwards plates: "He thinks well of lecturing, and wants to be hung for the whole sheep, and go the entire swine. His animal tastes can easily be gratified, I presume." If he was going to do it, in short, Melville might as well try for a regular season of lecturing about the country, not just locally—might as well be hung for a whole sheep as for part of a lamb. Curtis befriended Melville, probably passing his name on to organizations planning their seasons, giving Melville names of people in charge of various associations, and perhaps alerting him to professional tricks, such as getting his name in the annual list of available lecturers printed in the New York *Tribune*.

For his part, the idea of lecturing threw Melville beyond the invitations that had poured in unsolicited at the start of his career and back to the lectures and debates of his youth, particularly to the time he returned to Albany from teaching near Pittsfield (when the 27 January 1838 *Microscope* announced a spoof series by "the Young Men's Optimist Association For the Perfection of the Human Race," to be followed by a lecture "On the science of 'bowing.' P. G-nse——t"). Melville wrote Curtis on 15 September that he had been trying to scratch his brains for a lecture. He had scratched down as far as 1838 by the time he continued: "What is a good, earnest subject? *'Daily progress of man towards a state of intellectual & moral perfection, as evidenced in history of 5th Avenue & 5 Points'*"—that area being notorious as the most squalid in the city, where the lowest forms of prostitution were commonplace, an area worse than the most debased slums in the Liverpool of 1837. This was plainly not the attitude of a man who had cheerfully determined to do everything he had to do to charm culture-hungry crowds, but soon he was announced as a man ready to travel and talk for pay.

Melville's timing was bad: he announced his availability as lecturer in public forums across the country just at the start of the Panic of 1857, the first week of September, when stocks fell 8 or 10 percent in a day on the New York Stock Board. On 12 September 1857 *Harper's Weekly* took an appalled look at the catastrophe as a result of an epidemic of day-trading: "Merchants, lawyers, men of property, doctors, editors, clerks, and even clergymen and ladies, are constant customers of the brokers.... Every body supposes that he will be wise enough to retire at the right time, and to be content with what he has got. Nobody ever is." On 13 September 1857 all the banks of New York City, except the Chemical Bank, suspended specie payments, a third of them closing their doors. *Harper's Weekly* on 7 November laid out the situation of railroad stocks: "A few weeks ago there were at least a score of popular railway stocks in which it was considered safe to invest money; at present the most sanguine operators do not venture to enumerate over three in which a prudent man would be justified in placing his means." Hoadley was hit hard—orders for locomotives stopped coming, and in the next months the noisy Lawrence Machine Shop fell silent.

Nevertheless, the lecture committees had been in place before the Panic, and for a time lecture halls functioned almost as usual. In September 1857, as invitations began to reach him in Pittsfield, Melville worked up a lecture calculated to please himself rather than to please the elite citizens of American cities who might throng to see him disport himself on the tricky stage. He wrote out "Statues in Rome" and read it to audiences throughout the season. He never memorized it, never delivered it without his text before him, and to judge from the newspaper summaries of what he said, and from the sometimes substantial paraphrases or near quotations of what he said, he seldom deviated from the text before him. Probably he read from a manuscript in his own handwriting, but Lizzie may have helped him make a copy clearer than he could have made himself. Nothing suggests that he had the money or means to hire a job printer to set the speech in large type for easy reading, even though in Lawrence, where he first delivered the lecture, Hoadley would have had instant access to the product he manufactured, the "Gurrnsey Power Printing Press," advertised as excellent for "*all kinds of work*, such as Jobs, Pamphlets, Newspapers, &c.," work which would have included large-type printing for weak-eyed lecturers to read from. Melville or other members of the family preserved some clippings from newspapers reviews, but no manuscript of any lecture he gave survives among his papers. "Statues in Rome," perforce reconstructed from quotations in a number of newspapers, is now known in an undeniably faulty text that was never captured by a top-notch speed-writing "phonologist," the then-current term for shorthand recorder. There is enough agreement on the text to show that even some awkward transitions in the lecture, preserved by different reporters, must be Melville's own.

At the outset Melville justified his talking on "Statues in Rome," since everyone knew he was "neither critic nor connoisseur." He was not ready to say so from the stage, but his encounters with the art and architectural treasures of the Mediterranean had left him defensive about his ignorance of what he called the dilettante's "technical terms" for discussing the plastic arts. Whether or not he had quite articulated it to himself, he was almost ready to begin a self-conscious study of critics with the aim of mastering a vocabulary of aesthetic concepts, although never "grimgribber" terminology such as the Nantucket *Inquirer* had deplored in 1852. He wanted to be able to talk like Francis Jeffrey or Sydney Smith, talk in a professional way about what he had already achieved in *Moby-Dick* and other works without the benefit of training in aesthetics. In the next years as he studied critics, thinkers who aspired to be practical aestheticians, he realized that he needed more than vocabulary — he needed to think through aesthetic issues for himself. In this first lecture he was content to enunciate a rudimentary democratic theory of art appreciation: "the creations of Art" may be appreciated "by those ignorant of its critical science, or indifferent to it." Robert Burns's "poetical description of the daisy, 'wee, modest, crimson-tipped flower,' is rightly set above the technical definition of the Swedish professor" Linnaeus, he declared. This was gauged to please the public at a time when Americans were preparing to celebrate the centennial of Burns's birth as if he were the American national poet, but it was not the theory of art Melville had enunciated in the essay on Hawthorne, where he passionately identified with dark, obscure writers, not with pellucid writers, and with the class of eagle-eyed readers, not the superficial skimmers of pages. So far, the most interesting aesthetic comment he had made in his life had blazed forth in that essay fueled by the secret months of achievement in the manuscript of *Moby-Dick* and his sense of the distance between his achievement in *Typee* and the grandeur of his whaling book. Then, torn between his determination to regain his early popularity and the conviction that he was becoming a great writer, what emerged, in the essay on Hawthorne, was a theory of artist and audience extravagant and shaky, but at least his own.

No such immediate tension drove Melville in 1857 as he moved from his casual apologia into an evocation of the thousands of statues in and around Rome, and elsewhere in Italy, envisioned as "representatives of the mighty past" who hold out their hands to the present (those with hands still intact) and "make the connecting link of centuries." The ancient sculptors who had portrayed contemporary personages or figures from *their* past (Demosthenes, Titus Vespasian, Socrates, Julius Caesar, Seneca, Nero, Plato, and others) had supplied the deficiencies in ancient historians. Where the historian portrayed the public man, the sculptor went beyond the "outward seeming" to reveal the enduring complexity of human nature, a complexity in which the ancients as well as the moderns might appear one way and behave another. The ancients, Melville held, looked just like a modern crowd on the Corso: "the aspect of the human countenance is the same in all ages." He was hovering near the fatuous banalities of popular lecturers like Orville Dewey, who in his 1840 address to the Apollo Association (later the American Art-Union) on "The Identity of all Art" had declared that the "human heart is forever the same; the same now as it was in the days of Vinci and Raphael." Asserting more riskily that the moderns had lost "a heroic tone peculiar to ancient life," Melville made a dangerous point: that the admirable tone of the ancients had been lost under Christianity, which attempts to inculcate notions of "earthly vanity" rather than "natural majesty." Melville muted his criticisms of Christianity, as he had done in *The Confidence-Man*, but the Cleveland *Ohio Farmer* on 23 January 1858 identified his "affection for heathenism" as "profound and sincere": "He speaks of the heathenism of Rome as if the world were little indebted to christianity; indeed, as if it had introduced in the place of the old Roman heroism, a sort of trusting pusillanimity." The reviewer felt that this "under-current of regret" pervaded the whole lecture. Melville was living near the edge, once again, risking offense for his irreverence toward Christianity.

Melville then announced a three-part scheme. The Apollo in the Belvedere court of the Vatican, the world's most admired statue, belonged to the kind of art that "signally lifts the imaginations of men," giving a foretaste of heavenly perfection. By contrast, the Venus de' Medici at Florence represented natural perfection, human nature—not, like the Apollo, divine nature. Finally, the Laocoön, at the Vatican, gained "half its significance from its symbolism": "If the Apollo gives the perfect, and the Venus equally shows the beautiful, the Laocoön represents the tragic side of humanity and is the symbol of human misfortune." This playing with the perfect, the beautiful, and the tragic was just the sort of frothy pseudo-distinction other speakers got away with routinely, but it was not Melvillean. Some genuine personal notions emerged in the discussion of the Apollo and the Venus, however, when Melville elaborated the theory that during Milton's stay in Italy he saw the paintings (and statues, Melville also meant) from which, long afterward, the poet developed his images of the noble forms of the fallen angels in his English epic. Melville wrote that theory into his own copy of *Paradise Lost* in the passage in book 3 where Satan is seeking paradise, "the happy seat of man":

> he soon
> Saw within ken a glorious angel stand,
> The same whom John saw also in the sun:
> His back was turn'd, but not his brightness hid;
> Of beaming sunny rays, a golden tiar
> Circl'd his head, nor less his locks behind
> Illustrious on his shoulders fledge with wings
> Law waving round.

Along the words "His back was turn'd . . . a golden tiar" Melville commented, perhaps around this time: "The Italian paintin[gs] he saw in Rome." His marginalia was a notation for himself, cryptic to others, but in the lecture Melville elaborated his theory with ironic understatement: the circumstance of Milton's "having passed a year in Italy might not be deemed unfortunate for England's great epic." Warming to the point, Melville summed up: "the whole of that immortal poem, 'Paradise Lost,' is but a great Vatican done into verse."

From the gentler sculptures in the Hall of Animals in the Vatican, those so peaceful as to suggest "that best of all pastoral poets, Wordsworth," Melville argued that "the flame of kindness" had never been entirely stamped out in the breasts of the conquering Romans: Christian-like "tenderness and compassion" existed in the Romans before Christianity triumphed—not the aptest observation for leading into a passage on repeopling the Coliseum with bloodthirsty spectators, but his focus was in part on the sculptor who created the Dying Gladiator:

> Thus, when I stood in the Coliseum . . . the solitude was great and vast like that of savage nature. . . . But the imagination must rebuild it as it was of old; it must be repeopled with the terrific games of the gladiators, with the frantic leaps and dismal howls of the wild, bounding beasts, with the shrieks and cries of the excited spectators. Unless this is done, how can we appreciate the Gladiator? It was such a feeling of the artist that created it, and there must be such a feeling on the part of the visitor to view it and view it aright. And so, restoring the shattered arches and terraces, I repeopled them with all the statues from the Vatican, and in the turfy glen of the arena below I placed the Fighting Gladiator from the Louvre, confronting him with the dying one from the Capitol. And as in fancy I heard the ruffian huzzas for the first rebounded from the pitiless hiss for the last, I felt that more than one in that host I had evoked shared not its passions, and looked not coldly on the dying gladiator whose eyes gazed far away to
>
> > "where his rude hut by the Danube lay,
> > *There* were his young barbarians all at play."
>
> Some hearts were there that felt the horror as keenly as any of us would have felt it. None but a gentle heart could have conceived the idea of the Dying Gladiator, and he was a Christian in all but the name.

The verse, his readers knew, was from Byron's *Childe Harold's Pilgrimage* (canto 4, stanza 141). Melville had not delivered a sustained crowd-pleasing purple passage. Instead, he had interrupted the scene by a comment on the sensitive feelings of the sculptor of the Dying Gladiator and had concluded with a bland homily on that artist as a Christian-like pagan.

The comment on Christianity was enough to deflect Melville back to the topic of the change in tone between Roman and modern times: at first the triumph of Christianity had been joyous, but, once it became triumphant, Christianity had changed, so that now its mementos were "somber." Melville moved from that point to a tribute to "the sculptured horses of Monte

Cavallo, riderless and rearing, seeming like those of Elijah to soar to heaven" —sculptures which allowed him to deduce "the enlarged humanity of that elder day, when man gave himself none of those upstart airs of superiority over the brute creation which he now assumes." Tacitly, he was rejecting the tenet in Genesis, according to the King James wording, that man was to hold "dominion" over nature. Jumping again, he discussed the Moses of Michelangelo and the Perseus of Cellini (at Florence, not Rome) and the Farnese Hercules in elaborating a contextual theory according to which such statues can be understood only by knowing the circumstances under which they were formed and the places where they were meant to be placed. Fully to understand the statues of the Vatican, one would have to see them in their original placements. Melville apparently did not push the argument into the claim that only a person possessed of historical knowledge and profound imagination could hope even to approximate an understanding of the statues: this was not designedly an elitist lecture, however it would be perceived. Melville's explanation that some statues now gathered in the Vatican were once scattered in villas around the city led him to a passage on the irony that villas built to preserve works of art have crumbled, while some of the statues have survived. Gathering the statues together in his mind, Melville generalized that they displayed a "tranquil, subdued air such as men have when under the influence of no passion." Tired, inattentive, Melville contented himself with commonplaces: "They were formed by those who had yearnings for something better, and strove to attain it by embodiments in cold stone." He asked a tricky question ("Can art, not life, make the ideal?"), implying that the answer was yes, that "in the Apollo is expressed the idea of the perfect man." Having spoken earlier of Cellini's Perseus as a work of art "conceived in the fiery brain of the intense artist and brought to perfection as a bronze cast in the midst of flames," here he downplayed the artist in favor of the art.

Melville then juxtaposed the Vatican as "the index of the ancient world" with the Patent Office in Washington as the index of the modern world: "What comparison could be instituted between a locomotive and the Apollo? Is it as grand an object as the Laocoön? To undervalue art is perhaps somewhat the custom now. The world has taken a practical turn, and we boast much of our progress, of our energy, of our scientific achievements—though science is beneath art, just as the instinct is beneath the reason. Do all our modern triumphs equal those of the heroes and divinities that stand there silent, the incarnation of grandeur and of beauty?" The Boston *Evening Traveller* was probably accurate in quoting Melville as asserting that "science is beneath art, just as the instinct is beneath the reason." Melville was playing with Lysander's speech in act 2 of *A Midsummer Night's Dream*—"The will of man is by his reason swayed" — just as he had done in *The Confidence-Man* (ch. 3). The problem is not so much to establish what Melville said but what he thought he meant by it, for the context in *The Confidence-Man* is suffused with ironies — the Black Guinea's face is turned in passively hopeless appeal, "as if" instinct told it something; and Lysander's words rejecting one lover for another are described as "grave" words, "after Puck has made a sage of him with his spell."

In his conclusion Melville further exalted the achievements of the ancients: "We did invent the printing press, but from the ancients have we not all the best thought which it circulates, whether it be law, physics, or philosophy?" The scheme of Charles Fourier would supplant the code of Justinian only when the novels of Dickens would silence the satires of Juvenal. Melville's clincher derived from his days in London the previous April: "If the Coliseum expresses the durability of Roman ideas," what does the Crystal Palace of modern London merchants express? Will glass endure as well as travertine? The words of Roman historians and poets keep alive their deeds; and the memory of Roman arts is kept alive by "the careful preservation of their noble statuary." He ended by quoting *Childe Harold's Pilgrimage* again (canto 4, stanza 145): "While stands the Coliseum, Rome shall stand; / When falls the Coliseum, Rome shall fall; / And when Rome falls, the world." The most Byronic of American writers, the most profoundly pondering of American writers, was displaying himself in the guise of a superficial tour guide. Judging from the newspaper accounts, it was not a lecture that pleased anyone who took his or her contentment in the present state of the American experiment. Nor could it have sparked excited aesthetic exploration in anyone discontented with the state of art and aesthetics in the country.

The first lecture associations that booked Melville did not know what they were going to hear, only that they were going to get to see the author of *Typee* and *Omoo*, an author who had been for several years a national sex symbol through his first books but a man otherwise featureless, the only author of any note whose painted portrait or daguerreotype had never yet been engraved for reproduction in a magazine. Autograph collectors among the secretaries of lecture associations had reason for delight, since Melville handled the initial negotiations himself, now that Augusta was no longer living at Arrowhead. Yet Melville proved unwilling or unable to continue handling all the negotiations and scheduling, so within a very few weeks Lizzie began helping him — she having decided that henceforth she would rise to any occasion. In a surviving notebook of "Lecture Engagements 1857-8-9-60," she was the one who wrote *"Fixed"* by 16 February when that date was confirmed for Melville's lecture in New Bedford, and she who later canceled all of her earlier notions and inserted the date Melville in fact lectured there, 23 February, with a new "*Fixed.*" She also seems to have begun drafting his letters and writing summaries of them so she would have a copy of their side of the correspondence. In his absence, she routinely opened his mail and answered letters for him.

In October and November 1857 invitations came steadily—two or three by 26 September all prompted by Curtis, as Melville acknowledged to him. On 3 October, Melville accepted an invitation from New Bedford, and by 20 October he had an invitation from the Clarksville, Tennessee, Literary Association. On 31 October Aunt Mary in Galena had already heard the news from Shaw and replied: "I hope with you that Herman may succeed in lecturing his arrangements are probably fixed for the season, so that we can not expect to see him so far west, which we should rejoice to do." On 18 November the *New Hampshire Patriot and State Gazette* was announcing a lecture "on Tuesday evening next, November 24th—Subject, 'Roman Statuary.'" By Thanksgiving, which the Melvilles spent with the Shaws, apparently taking all four children with them, the itinerary was largely blocked out, though there would be some late changes.

The September collapse of stock prices had turned into a veritable new Panic, and around this time Hoadley, in support of the Lawrence Provident Association, printed in a local paper a poem he had delivered at the "Pond Festival" in Lawrence, "A Sermon in Rhyme" (with an epigraph from Mark 10:9: "Go sell whatever thou hast, and give to the poor, and thou shalt have treasure in heaven"). Hoadley, in the words Melville used of a fellow American in London in 1849, had shown a heart: "Winter is the dreadful season! / Heightened wants, and lessened means; / Hunger, ravening like the werewolf, / Cold as cruel as the fiends." Then he exclaimed: "O with what a different aspect / Winter comes to rich and poor!" This poem was preserved without date or name of newspaper (the *Courier*? the *Journal*?) in a scrapbook now at the Lawrence Public Library. The keeper of the scrapbook made a number of corrections on the clipping, some if not all from Hoadley himself. Hoadley's "sermon" on poverty wore the trappings of Victorian sentimentality, but Melville rightly would have perceived it as staking out a position commonly challenged by leading Unitarians. Hoadley and Melville were both drawn to New Testament absolutism, although their attitudes toward the impracticability of such idealism differed. Both men were setting themselves up against the very vocal campaign by national religious figures to deter any undue attention to undeserving people who might claim to be suffering from cold, hunger, or other spurious woes.

Hoadley set up a trial lecture at Lawrence for 23 November 1857, a Monday, two days after Herman and Lizzie had arrived in Boston for Thanksgiving. The writer of the promotional announcement in the Lawrence *Courier* (23 November) had not received the title or subject of the lecture, and wavered in the spelling of the speaker's name, but not in its connotations:

> HERMAN MELLVILLE, whose name suggests all gorgeous images of tropic groves, of fragrant, palm-shaded islands in the shining summer seas; of savages, in all the wild beauty of uncontaminated nature; and of adventures beside which the stories of Robinson Crusoe and Paul and Virginia seem prosie; — H. Melville, the Traveller, Renowned Philosopher, and Prose Poet; is to lecture in this city, at the City Hall, on Monday Evening, the 23d inst., for the benefit of the Provident Association.
>
> Need we say more than that the man and the object should fill the Hall to the utmost limit of its capacity.

Hoadley may well have supplied this item, all but the misspelling.

Kate and Hoadley must have received Melville in their house, and in Hoadley's grand library Melville saw that his brother-in-law had begun assembling a Melville collection around the set of *The Whale* that he had received after Helen's wedding and the set of *Putnam's Magazine* he had been accumulating (and having bound in morocco). Hoadley owned an 1855 Harper *Typee;* an 1855 Harper *Omoo,* which he inscribed with his name and "Lawrence 1857"; he had the 1855 Harper *Mardi, White-Jacket,* and *Pierre;* the 1855 Putnam *Israel Potter* ("Third Edition"); the 1856 Dix & Edwards *The Piazza Tales;* and the 1857 Dix & Edwards *The Confidence-Man.* All these volumes Hoadley at some time had bound in half-calf. As a bibliophile Hoadley might have sought out first printings, all of which were readily obtainable, but instead he seems to have placed an order with the Harpers in 1855 for all of Melville's books and cheerfully accepted what came. In his library Hoadley already had another trophy from his book-buying in 1855, the first edition of Walt Whitman's *Leaves of Grass.*

Melville read the lecture in Lawrence without pay, as a benefit at City Hall for the Lawrence Provident Association — that is, in a nice irony, impoverished author lectured for free to raise money for the poor of the city. The Lawrence *Courier,* two days after Melville's talk, was polite, though cautionary, about Melville's style — the style of his sentences, not his delivery of them: "Of the style, nervous and vigorous, yet easy and flowing, and falling constantly into the most melodious cadences; it can only be said in dispraise that it was perhaps too highly wrought, and too uniformly excellent." Much of what Melville said "was spoken so low that a large part of the audience could not hear it," yet the lecture "was a delightful entertainment to those who were more favorably placed or endowed with a keener sense of hearing." Hoadley's good friend John A. Godwin, the editor, tried to excuse Melville's difficulties with projecting his voice by saying that "like many others unacquainted, with our City Hall," Melville had been "baffled by its echoes": "Though endowed with a voice which could shake the roof, he feared to speak too loud, lest he should be out-shouted by the mocking wall, and the consequence was that he spoke so low, in general, as to be heard with difficulty except by those on the front seats." Worse, the torrential rain "detained" many, and "many who came got thoroughly wet." The poor received only thirty dollars from Melville's attempted munificence. Hoadley, ever alert, marked some obvious errors in the report so that Godwin could print a better text in the *Semi-Weekly Courier*, and say the rain had "deterred" people instead of detaining them, for instance.

Although Godwin's report in the *Courier* did not quote the conclusion of the lecture in any detail, nothing suggests that the lecture Melville read in Lawrence was different from what he read in Boston on 2 December. With the wind whipping the rain against the walls of Lawrence's City Hall, Melville read what he had written about the printing press not being as significant as the thought of the ancients (whether on "law, physics, or philosophy") which is circulated by the modern printing press. The doughty, rain-drenched auditors were asked to agree that it was ludicrous to institute a comparison "between a locomotive and the Apollo" and that a locomotive was hardly "as grand an object as the Laocoön." The fine machines Hoadley built were precisely the machines Melville seized on for his examples of scientific modernity arrogantly challenging the classics. Hoadley's admiration for Melville is clear, but nothing is pellucid about Melville's attitude toward Kate's husband. No one could innocently speak words like these in Lawrence, a capital of American manufacturing, especially when the city was already feeling the Panic — feeling it fast, in the loss of orders for just that modern Behemoth, the locomotive. No one could speak such words innocently while he was there under the auspices of Hoadley, the superintendent of the Lawrence Machine Shop, the maker of a fine printing press and the preeminent maker of locomotives, such as the 1855 Irvington. Hoadley probably had on display, in his library, a copy of the beautiful lithograph *The Irvington*, produced by C. van Benthuysen in Albany, which showed the engine and part of the coal car emerging from a tunnel in a tamed but still rugged Hudson River landscape. Most people in the audience knew that Hoadley was responsible for Melville's presence in Lawrence, and made their way to City Hall because of the sponsor and his cause as well as their admiration of the celebrity brother-in-law. Just possibly, something in the delivery of this portion of the talk could have made it seem deliciously arch, an in-joke between the brothers-in-law, a strong hint that Melville appreciated the architectonic grandeur Hoadley had achieved in his best locomotives. Possibly, but not likely. Years later, in 1871, Melville set himself up as Western critic and exploded in his markings in a volume of Matthew Arnold's poems: "What could a sage of the nineteenth century teach Socrates? Why, nothing more than something about Cyrus Feilds [Field] and the ocean telegraph, and the Sewing Machine &c." By that time, Hoadley had been manager of the McKay Sewing Machine Association. If Melville wrote the locomotive and the printing press into his lecture as a deliberate dig at the Lawrence manufacturer, then he kept it in every time he gave the lecture elsewhere.

Before Thanksgiving Melville went up to Concord, New Hampshire, to read in the Phenix Hall for the Pennacook Lyceum, at a fee of thirty dollars. There he learned that the next lecturer, set for 28 November, was Horace Greeley, who was visiting Boston and vicinity on Thanksgiving week on a lecturing tour. Greeley probably was more bemused by his occupying the same stage with Melville, a few days apart, than Melville was, since he would have recalled being on the same program in Boston with Gansevoort in the cause of Repeal—the repeal of the union between England and Ireland. It was not altogether auspicious for Melville to be followed by the man who had referred to Gansevoort's Democratic rhetoric as being of the "gas and glory" style and who had felt the need to warn the public against the luring, hard-to-define immoral tendencies in Herman's early writings. Gansevoort's brother, unfortunately for himself, whatever the extravagance of some of his earlier prose, was proving no Gansevoort on the stage.

After Melville read his lecture at the Tremont Temple for the Mercantile Library Association (fee, forty dollars), several Boston papers, the *Courier*, the *Bee*, the *Journal*, the *Post*, the *Daily Evening Traveller*, and the *Daily Evening Transcript*, all reviewed it politely enough the next day, 3 December. The *Traveller* said Melville's proposition about science being below art had "caused some little discussion in several groups of homeward-bound listeners," as well it might have. Melville's intended distinction was far too complicated for an audience to comprehend, since it had to catch his words on the fly. The *Journal* allowed that the "lecture was quite interesting to those of artistic tastes," but fancied that "the larger part of the audience would have preferred something more modern and personal." Residence at Harvard College now gave Henry Sanford Gansevoort the confidence to express his opinions to his father as well as his friends. From Cambridge on 23 November, before hearing his cousin's lecture, he wrote to his father on Herman's topic, which he reported as "Roman Statuary": "He is able to treat this finely if he will follow 'crassa Minerva,' but if he aims at metaphysical disquisitions he will surely fail. His forte is narration or description in other words a wild, bold word painting—When he essays philosophy he seeks to ascend by waxen wings from his proper sphere only to find his mind dazzled his wings melted and his fall mortifying." Henry had been contemptuous of his poorly educated cousin since about the time young Lem Shaw began putting his own contempt on record. Henry hadn't seen the " 'pint' " of "The Town-Ho's Story" when it appeared in *Harper's*, he had impudently written to his stepmother's nephew Abe Lansing. Now he was prepared to seem very much the professional critic. On 9 December Henry wrote to his father that the lecture "was well conceived and executed but it lacked the force and beauty that characterise his early writings." The audience, he said, was "large and respectable," and Cousin Herman had spoken "with animation and effect" in a hall "badly planned for acoustics," so that his "voice imperfectly reached its remoter parts." Henry thought that Herman would have done better with "a subject with which his name is connected" and in which he would have been "more at home" — such as " 'The South Seas,' 'Oceanica' or a thousand different subjects." Henry then showed the techniques he had learned at Harvard by cribbing long passages from newspaper reports, especially the *Courier* and the *Traveller*, which he coolly offered to his father as the fruits of his own capacious and retentive memory.

On the Sunday after the Boston lecture the Melvilles went out to Longwood for dinner with Helen and George Griggs. Young Henry was there taking notes about Cousin Herman, mixing analysis of Herman's behavior at his sister's with memories of the Wednesday lecture: "He was in a fine flow of humor which I enjoyed exceedingly. There is doubtless positive originality in him. Brilliancy but misanthropy, Genius but less judgement. He evidently mistakes his sphere. He has dropped the pen of candid narration for that of captious criticism. He does the latter well but he can do the former much better." Two days later, on Tuesday, Henry saw his cousin again at the Shaw house: "Yesterday I visited Judge Shaw. I there saw Herman Melville. Both desired me to remember them particularly to you. The Judge is the same droll but earnest man as ever. He is indefatigable in business and at the age of eighty [seventy-seven] still presides on the bench and at his table with the same lynx eye and compressed lip as characterised him of yore. . . . Herman Melville seems considerably improved in health and spirits by his interspersing the spice of variety with the reality of life." All this was in Henry's long letter of 9 December to Peter Gansevoort. On 17 December Peter Gansevoort concurred with his son's educated opinion that Herman "would be more 'at home' in Narrative than in criticism": "It would be a luxury to hear from him a Narrative of his recent tour on the borders of the Mediterranean & Constantinople &c &c I am surprised that he has not made his travels the subject of a Lecture, to be hereafter woven into a Book; which would be not only instructive to others, but very profitable to him." In the draft of this letter, at this point Peter continued: "Such a work would not make a requisition on his imagination." Discretion led to his omitting that passage in the recopied letter, where he contented himself with telling Henry to suggest weaving the lectures into a book when he saw Herman next.

On 9 December Melville left for Montreal, where he stayed with G. H. Frothingham and for fifty dollars delivered his lecture on 11 December. The Montreal *Herald and Daily Commercial Advertiser* on 9 December announced the lecture, claiming that Melville's Boston audience had consisted of two thousand persons, and announcing also that the organizers had made special arrangements with an "enterprising proprietor of the Panorama of Italy" for him to exhibit on Thursday, the night of Melville's talk, "that portion which will illustrate the subject, 'Sight-Seeing in Rome.'" The proprietor displayed his "panoramic view of Rome" on Thursday without Melville, who had been delayed by a railroad accident, then politely let Melville have the hall on Friday, with the splendid visual aids still up behind him.

On his way home Melville stayed overnight in Rutland, Vermont, where he could catch a train to Gansevoort. He arrived carrying a substantial present for Uncle Herman, a pipe and tobacco that cost him $3.25. From there he arranged an impromptu reading of his lecture on 21 December at Saratoga Springs, and faced a small audience since the public was given only "a single day's notice." One of Melville's notes (preserved with the "Lecture Engagements" notebook) lists "6 Fares to & from Saratoga Spgs (Lecture) 2.40" — possibly meaning that three people went both ways, he and his sisters Augusta and Fanny, or Maria and Augusta. The previous entry is for his and Augusta's fares, at an earlier time, presumably, for $2.20, perhaps when he arranged the lecture. On this occasion he lectured before an audience a sizable portion of which was related to him. The ten cents worth of candy he bought at this time may have been his contribution to the Christmas desserts, for he apparently stayed over for his only Christmas at Gansevoort.

In Albany on 28 December Melville called on his Uncle Peter at his office in Stanwix Hall and together they went to the studio of Erastus Dow Palmer, the sculptor, who was at work during 1857 and 1858 on what became one of his most famous pieces (now at the Metropolitan Museum of Art), *The White Captive*, in marble, a young female nude, sixty-five inches high, perfunctorily tied to a chopped-off sapling with no knob at the top to keep any enterprising lass from simply lifting the thongs an inch or two and walking off with a loop still around her wrist. The rumor flaming around town was that Palmer had actually used a nude model, a local girl who had posed for him totally naked. Peter Gansevoort recorded in his diary that his nephew "had just returned from 'Gansevoort' & is on his way to Springfield" — a construction that implies Melville might have been going as directly to Springfield as possible without going home. (He would have had to change depots and trains at

Pittsfield, even if he did not stop there.) In any case, Melville went to Springfield, the railroad junction, and may have stayed overnight there before going on to New Haven, where he lectured before the Young Men's Institute on 30 December for a fee of fifty dollars.

An editorial in the New Haven *Journal and Courier* reassured Melville's prospective auditors that his subject was "purely artistic — and of course can arouse no jealous solicitude in regard to any possible connection between it and questions of current politics, or the vexed questions of theological dispute." Theology was a topic to be avoided in many lecture associations, and by 1857 and 1858 the controversy over slavery was so intense as to threaten the continuance of the associations. The writer also did his best to reassure his readers that Melville might be worth hearing even though he had grown up in an uncultured family and locale and, whatever his subsequent achievements in whaleboats and the literary line, was definitely not a Yale man. A "native of Pittsfield," (not true), Melville was "a farmer of staid and sober demeanor, and a gentleman of scholarly tastes, and connected by birth and marriage with some of the first families of the country"; without "the best advantages of culture in his early youth, he has advanced over difficulties of considerable magnitude, to a position of peculiar elevation as an American literary man." By talking and getting out of town fast, in this case going from New Haven to New York City, Melville may have missed this egregious snobbery. No autodidact needs to be reminded how much he missed out on in early youth or thereafter.

If Melville hoped to lecture in New York City, he was disappointed. He went to Albany then on to Auburn, where he lectured on 5 January. To get to Ithaca, where he lectured on 7 January, required zigzagging to Syracuse, Binghamton (where he stayed the night), and Owego. He may have recorded entries a little out of order, but it looks as if he stayed over in Buffalo, running up a large (lodgings?) bill of $4.37, which included "Ale," while he renewed his tobacco supply for $.06. Travel from Ithaca to Cleveland, where he lectured on 11 January, required getting back to Owego, from there through tiny Hornersville to Buffalo and on to Cleveland. From there he went to Detroit, where he lectured on 12 January. His next known lecture was in Clarksville, Tennessee. Melville got to Clarksville from Detroit by going to Toledo, then crossing the stretch of 450 miles (his estimate) to Evansville, Indiana, where he lodged the night before the lecture. From Toledo he took some sort of "Buss" to Greencastle "(Mud to the hub)" where he lodged, before taking another "Buss" to Vincennes, where he lodged again, then by "buss" to Evansville, and from there across the Ohio River at Smithland, and on to Clarksville, where he lectured on 22 January. Melville lectured at Cincinnati on 2 February, at Chillicothe, Ohio, on 3 February, at Charlestown, Massachusetts, 10 February, then at Rochester on 18 February, and New Bedford two days later.

Ladies had sewn a silken banner for Gansevoort to carry home, and partisans had called out to Gansevoort, "Speak on, speak forever!" As early as 3 December 1857, the Boston *Evening Traveller* was complaining that Melville had talked "too long by one-fifth, covering an hour and a quarter." Other auditors held a watch on him. In Cincinnati the irritated reporter from the *Enquirer* (3 February 1858) claimed that Melville went on for "nearly two hours," so interminable did his lecture seem. After Melville spoke at Cambridge, Massachusetts, the Charlestown and Boston paper, the *Bunker-Hill Aurora and Boston Mirror,* on 13 February itemized the ways that the audience had registered boredom: some people "left the hall; some read books and newspapers; some sought refuge in sleep, and some, to their praise be it spoken, seemed determined to use it as an appropriate occasion for self-discipline in the blessed virtue of patience."

The Auburn *Advertiser* (6 January), having read in the Auburn *American* about Melville's youthful association with a short-lived debating society, lamented that he had "most signally failed to improve his elocution":

> The lecture was completely, absolutely spoiled by his inexcusable blundering, sing song, monotonous delivery. It was the most complete case of infanticide we ever heard of; he literally strangled his own child. The words came through his moustache about as loud and with as much force as the creaking of a field mouse through a thick hedge. Finely formed and well rounded sentences were articulated so feebly that they died long before they reached a twelfth part of his audience, and beautiful poetical quotations fell still-born from his lips. It is inexcusable to come before an audience with an elocution that fails to make his subject, if not interesting, at least understood. The same lecture in the hands of a[n] [Edwin Hubbell] Chapin, a [George W.] Bethune, or [Henry Ward] Beecher, would have been considered brilliant and fascinating.

The Cleveland *Evening Herald* (12 January) kindly said that Melville had "a musical voice, and a very correct delivery," but that his "subdued tone and general want of animation" prevented his being a popular lecturer: "good writers do not make good lecturers." The Clarksville *Chronicle* (29 January) was also wryly ironical, in a gentle fashion: "Some objected to Mr. Melville's subdued delivery; but if we rightly reflect, we will observe a striking congeniality between this quiet manner and those mute forms that stand still and silent amid the venerable ruins of 'ancient Rome.' " (The *Chronicle* perceived a truth about Melville's character, that a "noble nature" lay beneath "the natural reserve of his character.")

The Cincinnati *Daily Commercial* (3 February) gave Melville what praise it could: "His style of delivery is earnest, though not sufficiently animated for a Western audience, and he enunciates with only tolerable distinctness." Another auditor, writing in the Cincinnati *Enquirer* (3 February), likewise managed to put a kindly cast on an inevitable judgment: "His delivery was, in some respects, agreeable, but not in others — it was monotonous and often indistinct, but not devoid of impressiveness, which sometimes approached the ministerially solemn." By the time he got to Chillicothe, Melville "was afflicted with quite a severe cold," the *Advertiser* said on 5 February, and "was aware that he could not command his voice and therefore afraid to trust it." The *Scioto Gazette*, reviewing the same lecture on 9 February, said that although "laboring under a severe cold," Melville's "voice was still rich and mellow, and he had the most complete control of it." This was the highest praise Melville received for his delivery: "He speaks with earnestness and enunciates distinctly; even when he descended, as he sometimes did, almost to a whisper, his words were audible in the remotest parts of the room."

It was not just the delivery that dismayed his audiences: Melville had chosen a topic both too rarified and too unchallenging for the lecture circuit under any circumstances and one almost defiantly unpopular, given his special reputation throughout the country. Once, audiences would have been avid to hear about his adventures in the South Seas. Even after his reputation was lost, there was still residual interest in those adventures but not in much else that he might talk about. A few reviewers tried to justify Melville's choice of subject, but the Ithaca *Journal and Advertiser* (13 January) spoke for most: "His subject, 'Ancient Statuary,' must, from the necessity of the case, be an unattractive one to the masses, who claim, with the lecturer himself, not to be students of art and connoisseurs of beauty in its difficult departments." If Melville didn't know any more than his audience, why should they strain to hear what he had to say? In Clarksville the *Jeffersonian* (27 January) said the subject "was not one calculated to excite general interest or elicit much enthusiasm in any manner in which it could possibly be treated" — yet a more coherent and challenging treatment of the subject and a spirited delivery just might have awakened some interest and enthusiasm.

The best things about the reviews are, first, that they preserved all we have of the lecture, and second, that they contain the most detailed physical descriptions of Melville yet discovered. To have his voice described as "musical" (the Cleveland *Evening Herald* of 12 January 1858) is to learn something new. Even better is to have the *Morning Leader* of the same city, same day, offer a word portrait:

Herman Melville is quite a young man, with a handsome face, innocent of the razor; slightly above medium hight, and well formed; forehead full, and well developed, though neither high nor broad; features prominent and regular; head well-borne like one who is his own master; hair and eyes dark; on the whole a fine *physique*. He stands gracefully and steady, uses little gesture, and speaks well, were it not for a slight indistinctness in articulation, owing, we thought, to the mustache, spoiling the outline of the words as it does a pen-and-ink sketch to draw a camel's-hair brush over it while wet.

(This confirmation of the Auburn *Advertiser* as to Melville's mustache interfering with his speech is curious. The fashion of wearing mustaches was not so new that reporters should have objected out of a dislike of mustaches; more likely, Melville left his unusually thick mustache untrimmed during his travels, so that it actually drooped over his upper lip in a way that bothered some people who had paid to hear him and could hardly do so.) The Cincinnati *Daily Commercial* (3 February) offered another portrait:

Mr. Melville is rather an attractive person, though not what anybody would describe [as] good looking. He is a well built, muscular gentleman, with a frame capable of great physical exertion and endurance. His manner is gentle and persuasive, while a certain indefinable sharpness of features, with small twinkling blue eyes under arched brows, and a rather contracted and rugged forehead, indicates the spirit of adventure which sent him roving a sailor's sturdy life. His face, three parts obscured by a heavy brown beard and moustache, still glistens duskily with the Polynesian polish it received under the tawny influences of a Southern sun, and his voice is as soft and almost as sweet, barring a slight huskiness proceeding from a cold, as the warbling of the winds in cocoa groves.

The Cincinnati *Enquirer* (3 February) called Melville "an unremarkable, quiet, self-possessed-looking man, seemingly about thirty-five or six years of age, with brown hair, whiskers and mustache, bronze complexion, above the medium stature, appearing not unlike the captain of an American merchantman."

For a man so constitutionally restless, so anxious to be on the "go-off," lecturing might have been an ideal escape. But the lecture season was in the dead of winter; the transportation systems still at times primitive and ill connected; innkeepers could still seem like highway robbers gone indoors; and in every town Melville had to present himself before the local arrangement committee, make small talk, deal with the occasional autograph seeker or the inveterate button-holers of visiting celebrities, locate and eat food bad by Maria's standards if not by the standards of South Sea whalers or Mediterranean steamers, pack, present himself to be transported, and do it all over again in the next town on his itinerary (which was not well planned enough to be called a circuit). Almost every report that he was going to lecture and almost every report of his lectures contained sentences to perturb or distress him. Rather than always skipping out of town leaving his bad reviews behind him, Melville sometimes stayed long enough in one place to see them, and indeed he carried reviews home, some of which are still preserved, at Harvard. Lecturing was a form of running the gauntlet where he had the unusual privilege of freezing everyone in their seats for an hour before he made his next exit. Melville probably saw right away some of the complaints about his delivery but he either could not or would not make a great effort to change his basic style, which was ministerial only in the sense of being solemn, not in the more florid style of pulpit thumping. Later, while he was afflicted with the bad cold, Melville may have been trying to speak with exceptional distinctness, but the reviews give no sense that he tried to speak with progressively greater animation every time he had a new audience in a new town. Strangely, men must have come up to him at times (as men had done in London) to tell him quietly that they remembered his magnificent brother, but at least none of the reporters for the local papers mentioned his dismal contrast with "the orator of the human race."

Melville kept meticulous records of his expenditures on his tour, so that we have his expenses for laundry and tobacco and the occasional comforting cigar, as well as a cough medication (Anderson's) either called "Solace" or meant to induce solace—a workaday nostrum, not the Omni-Balsamic salve dispensed by the herb-doctor in *The Confidence-Man*. The mundane record was several times infused with dramatic autobiographical details, as when the "buss" at Greencastle went through that deep mud; or when the bill (for lodging?) at Smithland evoked a comment on the proprietor: "damned rascal"; or when the landlord at Clarksville impressed him by contrast as "fat & honest"; or when he listed "Porter" then before putting down the amount for the item, twenty-five cents, he glossed porter as not the beverage "Brown Stout" but a "stout black" man who carried his bag for him. He had a thirty-seven-cent bath in Buffalo, none too soon, and at Cincinnati he paid fifty cents at the National Theatre to see a travesty of Byron, *Mazeppa; or, The Wild Horses of Tartary* and *Karmel, the Scout; or, The Rebel of the Jerseys*. The income from the lectures amounted to $645.00, according to Melville's records, which after subtracting $221.30 in "Travelling Expenses" left him with a profit of $423.70—enough to pay the taxes and continue the payments to Brewster, but not much else. He gave his last lecture of the tour at New Bedford on 23 February at Liberty Hall, where the New Bedford Lyceum had its meetings. Very soon after that, while at Gansevoort, he collapsed.

[17]

"The South Seas"
March 1858–Spring 1859

>Altho' bound down, from necessity, to a farm, and almost a Hermit in a Wilderness, still I take a no less deep interest in our political affairs, than if I were in a more elevated, & pleasant situation.
>
>>Thomas Melvill Jr., in Pittsfield, to George N. Briggs, December 1834

AFTER HER HUSBAND'S DEATH Elizabeth Shaw Melville recalled that a "severe attack of what he called crick in the back laid him up at his Mothers in Gansevoort in March 1858—and he never regained his former vigor & strength." Melville spent at least several days "laid up"—a poignant reminder for Maria of the times her favorite, Gansevoort, had taken to bed at Lansingburgh in the late 1830s. At least Herman had not collapsed in Cincinnati or Chillicothe. Melville made good use of his time, and pleased his mother in the process, by writing his second lecture. Early in July, the Lansingburgh *Democrat* printed the news, perhaps from Augustus Peebles, that Melville had already prepared "a lecture descriptive of his adventures in the South Seas, which he intends to deliver this winter." Having written the lecture, Melville could lay it aside through the summer as his literary equivalent of a full woodshed against the next winter's cold. The lecture, whether all written on the fringes of the Adirondacks or completed in the Berkshires, was indeed on "The South Seas." Some passages of the lecture as reconstructed from newspaper reports are faulty, but more than half of it was captured by the expert phonologist of the Baltimore *American and Commercial Advertiser* (9 February 1859), in prose convincingly Melvillean.

After "Statues in Rome," Melville was going far toward giving the public what it had said it wanted, but he stopped short of retelling parts of *Typee* or *Omoo:* "I hope you do not expect me to repeat what has long been in print touching my own casual adventures in Polynesia." He launched into a freewheeling justification of why he preferred "The South Seas" to "The Pacific Ocean," in the course of which he paid an evocative tribute to Charles Lamb's depiction of the "Balclutha-like desolation of those haunted old offices of the once famous South Sea Company—the old oaken wainscots hung with dusty maps of Mexico and soundings of the Bay of Panama—the vast cellarages under the whole pile where Mexican dollars and doubloons once lay heaped in huge bins for Mammon to solace his solitary heart withal." Melville was always master of evoking moody connotations, and Lamb's sketch summoned up "the memory of brave old books," and reminded him of the great South Sea Bubble and old books treating not of the Pacific but of the "South Seas"—as in the adventures of Captain Dampier (that eminent and excellent buccaneer), or in "Harris' old voyages."

Having posed a problem—why call it the "South" sea?—Melville explained that the "Isthmus of Darien runs not very far from east and west; if you stand upon its further shore the ocean will appear to the *south* of you." With alluring expansiveness Melville told the story of that "large-minded gentleman, of great latitude of sentiment," Vasco Nuñez de Balboa, "commander of that petty post of Darien," who had laid claim to the ocean that seemed to stretch only to the south of his vantage point on the "western" shore of the Isthmus of Panama. Melville recalled the sufferings of Balboa's men and of a "party of buccaneers" who crossed the Isthmus at the same time, and reminded his listeners of the ghastly suffering undergone in 1854 by the U.S. Navy Lieutenant Isaac Strain and his party of two dozen men. Strain had tried to find a better route across the Isthmus but had followed a river that ran toward the land mass of South America rather than to either ocean; several men died from exposure and disease, and Strain himself was a living skeleton, seventy-five pounds, it was estimated, when he was found. Joel T. Headley, the military writer whom Maria did not approve of because he stayed too long on his first call in 1850, had written a three-part March–May 1855 article in *Harper's* on Lieutenant Strain's disastrous expedition. Melville had read it, for his own "The Paradise of Bachelors and the Tartarus of Maids" had appeared with the middle installment of Headley's "Darien Exploring Expedition."

Melville put credit for the recent exploration where it belonged: "It was California that first brought the Pacific home to the great body of Anglo-Saxons. The discovery of gold in 1848, that memorable year, first opened the Pacific as a thoroughfare for American ships." That discovery, everyone knew, had led to work on the Panama Railroad in 1850. John Lloyd Stephens, the great explorer of Melville's youth and young manhood, had been one of the three partners on the railroad, and had died in 1851 from a disease he contracted in Panama, but the other two, Henry Chauncey and William Henry Aspinwall, carried the railroad through to its completion in January 1855, making them masters of the short route to California and owners of the contract for delivery of U.S. mail to and from the Golden State. Melville's old friend Robert Tomes had chronicled the achievement while it was progressing so that Harper's could publish, in 1855, his *Panama in 1855*, a copy of which Melville had bought that year; meanwhile Tomes had sailed as recording author on the great expedition led by Matthew Perry that opened Japan to Western commerce. In 1855 Melville had also bought Ephraim George Squier's *Waikna*, and he probably knew of Squier's earlier two-volume work, *Nicaragua: Its People, Scenery, Monuments, and the Proposed Interoceanic Canal* (New York: D. Appleton: 1852), published with evocative fold-out maps. Before he wrote his second lecture, Melville knew well enough that many hundreds of human lives had been sacrificed to complete the railroad, but the lecture was no place for commentary on that topic, and in fact he avoided almost every dangerous topic.

Having had lost none of his zest for the Pacific, Melville strewed choice personal anecdotes (true or imaginary) through the lecture, but, at the risk of teasing and not satisfying, he organized much of his talk by citing topics on which he might have expatiated, if there were time. Melville declared that he might have told tales about "tribes of sharks that populate some parts of the Pacific as thickly as the celestials do the Chinese Empire," or about "the devil-fish, over which a mystery hangs like that over the sea-serpent of North Atlantic waters," or about "the birds of those seas." He might have filled "night after night with that fertile theme, the whaling voyage," but he contented himself with a personal anecdote (however doctored) about "the peculiar phosphoric aspect of the water sometimes." He told of spending a long night in a whaleboat, separated from the ship, and watching helplessly while Leviathan came "wallowing along, dashing the pale sea into sparkling cascades of fire, showering it all over him till the monster would look like Milton's Satan, riding the flame billows of the infernal world." Whaling adventures aside, the islands of the South Seas might have made an "endless theme" for lecturers. Melville sacrificed some good will from the audiences by this strategy of naming topics and not elaborating them: some listeners would inevitably become uneasy and resentful, feeling cheated. He must have calculated that he was offering enough substance on each topic that he might charm men and women who, when he spoke the words, would be rigid captives, like him, to winter in the northern latitudes.

Altogether shrewder now than in his first lecture, Melville gave an intimate directive to the auditors, straight word on what his hearers ought to do:

> But, would you get the best water view of a Polynesian island, select one with a natural breakwater of surf-beaten coral all around it, leaving within a smooth, circular canal, broad and deep, entrance to which is had through natural sea-gates. Lounging in a canoe, there is nothing more pleasant than to float along,

especially where Boraborra and Tahaa, the glorious twins of the Society group, rear their lofty masses to the ever vernal heights, belted about by the same zone of reef—the reef itself being dotted with small islets perpetually thick and green with grass.

This stretch of water would become "the last provocative to those jaded tourists to whom even Europe has become hackneyed, and who look upon the Parthenon and the Pyramids with a yawn."

At this point, in hoping that the English yachters who might sail from the "prosy Mediterranean" to the South Seas would not mistreat the natives, Melville indulged himself (for less than a minute of his hour) in obvious and bitter irony:

> They [the natives] esteem us, with rare exceptions, such as *some* of the missionaries, the most barbarous, treacherous, irreligious, and devilish creatures on the earth. This may of course be a mere prejudice of these unlettered savages, for have not our traders always treated them with brotherly affection? Who has ever heard of a vessel sustaining the honor of a Christian flag and the spirit of the Christian Gospel by opening its batteries in indiscriminate massacre upon some poor little village on the seaside—splattering the torn bamboo huts with blood and brains of women and children, defenseless and innocent?

This massacre the Yonkers *Examiner* on 9 December identified as the destruction of Malolo by the U.S. Squadron in 1840: what Melville considered an "atrocity," the *Examiner* considered a well-merited "punishment" for the killing of "two officers of the Squadron."

Toward his conclusion Melville offered some reflections on recent threats to forbid the Hawaiian language in schools attended by Hawaiian children. Still in his mind was Emerson, the author of "Compensation," as a philosophical confidence man: "So the result of civilization, at the Sandwich Islands and elsewhere, is found productive to the civilizers, destructive to the civilizees. It is said to be compensation—a very philosophical word; but it appears to be very much on the principle of the old game, 'You lose, I win'; good philosophy for the winner." Melville would, still, tell truth and shame the devil. Hoping that white adventurers would not "turn an earthly paradise into a pandemonium," he ended in the tone of an earnest philanthropist, a particular friend to the Polynesians, speaking out at a time when European powers were still seizing colonies in the Pacific, as elsewhere: "And as for annexation, I beg to offer up an earnest prayer—and I entreat all present and all Christians to join me in it—that the banns of that union should be forbidden until *we* have found for ourselves a civilization morally, mentally, and physically higher than one which has culminated in almshouses, prisons, and hospitals." This lecture was much better organized, much more evocative, expansive, and liberating than his first year's effort. It should by all rights have sent his audiences away into the cold nights sobered but entranced by this man who had once been incomparable in dramatic storytelling (as the younger Dana had said in 1849) and who could still be alluring and even enthralling.

His conscience assuaged by having written the new lecture so early, and on the subject that everyone wanted him to talk about, Melville in the summer of 1858, despite his impaired health, vacationed with a freer spirit than he had shown since 1851. Evert and George Duyckinck vacationed in Pittsfield at Mr. Butler's on South Street, the road out to Broadhall (George feeling safer from Sarah Morewood with his older brother to watch over him). When the Morewoods took them to Arrowhead, Melville behaved as genially toward the former proprietors of the *Literary World* as he had in 1851. The brothers passed the afternoon of the Fourth of July with Melville, "'bathing' as he called it in these divine breezes." This word (which Evert quoted from Melville in his 5 July letter to his wife) testifies eloquently to Melville's recovered zest and his self-satisfaction at having laid in his literary harvest early. That day, the Morewoods drove over to Arrowhead, where the Duyckincks "remained to tea and walked home at dusk," Evert wrote to his wife (forever tantalized by descriptions but never given a glimpse of the Berkshires). George in a letter on 7 July to Rosalie Baker (who also probably never got her chance to see the Berkshires) revealed greater sweetness toward Melville than ever before: "We have some good friends resident here. One, Herman Melville you know well by his books. I wish you knew, perhaps you do, the man, with his offhand hearty sailor grace. He has a pleasant farm house looking directly at the 'Monarch of Mountains'—of Berkshire—Saddle back or Greylock." George was still seeing the man, as Evert had always done, as sailor first and writer second, but at least he acknowledged a special quality, "his offhand hearty sailor grace." Melville had earned his wind baths.

At some point in the summer of 1858, Greylock thoughts in abeyance or not, Sarah invited George to join her and Mrs. Buckley and the journalist Caroline Whitmarsh ("whom you like") in a drive to Lenox to hear the "Rev Mr Parker Lecture upon 'Beauty and its uses.'" Her appeal was overt: "I have not been out of doors all the day and have battled against the influence of a moaning wind sighing out the doom of August days and the bloom of Summer flowers." George Duyckinck remained in Pittsfield, and on 26 July wrote Evert that after "an early tea" Mrs. Morewood had hustled them "all" into her wagon for a jouncing ride to Arrowhead, "across the fields," not on the public roads, only to be disappointed: "Herman & wife were out but we met them on our way home, and interchanged a few words." On the same day George wrote Rosalie Baker that he had recently passed "a very pleasant afternoon" with her "friend Typee Melville" (that damning sobriquet), and added: "He is busy on a new book." This comment is, most likely, a reference — the earliest known — to the book of poetry Melville finished in the next two years. Sarah was, as usual, surrounding herself with friends, and so were the Melvilles. Sam Shaw arrived at Arrowhead from Boston on 14 August, and at the same time Hoadley was around, presumably with Kate. Tom had been absent for more than three years now, and everyone's longing for him was compounded by the realization that on his last visit no one had been able to give him the usual full quota of loving attention. While Hoadley was visiting at Broadhall on 18 August Sarah prevailed upon him to copy out his seven-page poem "The Sounds I Love," a subject the more poignant because he was already aware of some loss of hearing: "I used to love those gentle sounds / That seemed but silence more intense, / That stole within the spirit's bounds / Almost without the aids of sense." Now his ear was so dull that he delighted, he said, in "all noises, loud and shrill," the "cracking thunder-peal," the "echoing cannon's boom," the "ringing forge, the jarring wheel." Beyond that, there were remembered sounds, the voices "of the loved and lost." George Duyckinck, no substitute for Tom, stayed on in Pittsfield, and when he wrote Evert on 24 August the season had changed: "This morning the thermometer stood at 50° I warmed myself by a walk to Herman Melville's over the railroad and enjoyed it greatly but missed my chief object as both Melville and Shaw were out on a tramp in the woods." "Shaw" was Sam Shaw, who returned to Boston the next day, but George stayed on.

George was still there on 12 September, ready to leave to join Evert on an expedition to Greenport, "when Herman Melville came along with a proposal for a two days trip in the mountains." Later that day George reported to Evert at length:

> It was too tempting an offer to be declined and I was a few minutes after seated along side of him in a buggy and "off" — . . .
>
> Melville was very genial during our ride and we both enjoyed it greatly — The chief features of the trip were the Greenfield river valley, in the adjoining county of Franklin (almost a rival to Berkshire in verdure and picturesqueness) and the Hoosic tunnel. We walked through the mud to the end of the excavation, a little over a thousand feet. It was like a scene in the Mammoth Cave, with German [?] for actors. The tallow dips stuck beside the workmen gave a dull yellow light and the ring of the heavy sledge hammers on the drills

was nerve-jarring and unearthly. As we stood at the entrance we heard the blasts within, like the distant report of cannon.

The tunnel, cutting through the Hoosac mountain range, which separates the beds of the Deerfield and Hoosic rivers, was at the time of construction the longest in the world, excepting only the seven-and-a-half-mile tunnel through Mount Cenis, in the Alps. Work had started under Herman Haupt in 1855; he failed, and the state in the 1860s made a contract with W. & F. Shanly, a Canadian firm, which completed it. Melville and Duyckinck showed up about the time the engineers began using nitroglycerine and dynamite as well as old-fashioned gunpowder for their blasting.

George continued: "We crossed the mountain passing the night at a little inn near the summit, for the sake of the picturesque and to avoid those knaves, the North Adams publicans. The views on either side were magnificent." Any publican, any driver, and any sheriff of North Adams was sure to be a notorious villain, a pack of menaces to all honest tourists, everyone remembered from August 1851. The next day, 13 September, Melville and Duyckinck visited William Henry Aspinwall's manor to see with their own eyes what an ambitious man could do with the endless wealth he was deriving from his interest in the Panama Railroad. The frail editor and the robust-looking author were politely allowed "within Mr Aspinwall's iron gates" and enjoyed "an exquisite drive of miles in his grounds." Then they were granted even greater privileges: "We ascended his tower and paced his piazza." Melville was still the man who hated asking favors of anyone, but the pair were welcomed. George declared that the pleasure of viewing the estate from the tower and the piazza was almost like that of receiving "an extra dividend" from stock in Aspinwall's Pacific Mail: "A capital idea would it not be, for him to throw open his doors and entertain the stockholders." As far as Melville was concerned, he knew that new money never could buy what old money could sometimes cherish and preserve, and he had his memories of the Van Rensselaer Manor House to set against the palace of a plutocrat. More than George Duyckinck, he saw the great estate as a symbol of the opening of the Pacific to commerce, in which he and Gansevoort had played their parts. Indeed, there was solid food for reflection in the Berkshires: the open sore from the construction of the Hoosic Tunnel near at hand, the jungles and swamps of the Isthmus far away, and in both enterprises laborers sacrificed for a worthy cause—thousands of laborers, in the Isthmus.

On 17 September George wrote Mrs. Baker of the "delightful three days ride" he had enjoyed with what he called "your sailor friend Herman Melville," probably meaning only that she was one of his admiring readers: "He was in good spirits; we passed through delightful scenery with constantly beautiful skies; and, as you may imagine, with good talk. He is as robust and fine looking as ever, but somewhat impaired in health by an affection of the spine brought on by too many hours of brain work day after day, following a life of great bodily activity." George at this time was specific about Melville's health being impaired, as Lizzie later confirmed, although once again looking strong and plainly in a mood approaching exuberance. George did not escape to New York unscathed, for on 12 October Sarah Morewood followed his polite note to her with a cross-written lament, "I shrink from the winter this year it will be so desolate here after the sad past and the bitter knowledge false friends have brought me. Now I fear that I shall have to turn to loyal spirits before the spring comes & passes." (Maria had forbidden her children to cross-write to her — that is, to write *across* an earlier-written page in order to save paper and, sometimes, postage; in January 1841 she told Augusta sternly: "write as close as you please but never cross a letter to me.")

Judge and Mrs. Shaw arrived at Arrowhead on 19 September after it had been raining so violently that Herman and Lizzie were sure the bad weather was statewide and would prevent the Shaws from traveling. In fact, the journey was comfortable, and Shaw recruited, as he said, at Arrowhead before starting the court session at Lenox — ruing the absence of his friend Charles Sedgwick. He reported to Lem on life at Arrowhead: "The family here are on the whole very well. Herman is as well as I have seen him for years, & Elizabeth seems quite well, & meets all her household cares with great care and satisfaction. The four children are, as it appears to me, greatly improved, in appearance and conduct." Herman probably seemed better than at any time since Shaw took him to Nantucket and other islands in 1852, and Lizzie had at last become the mistress of her house. That summer Allan and Sophia and their daughters did not visit Arrowhead, for Sophia was dying. At some point that spring or summer Maria went down to New York, as Milie remembered: "Once, it must have been when mama was first sick, grandma Melville came to New York and took Kitty, who I suppose was too noisey, back to Gansevoort with her, and I sat down and cried on the stairs after they were gone." As long as possible Sophia tried to keep her oldest child near her, Milie remembered: "My mother had been sick ever since I could remember, and she could not go about the house. She used to read to me after I was in bed. I remember one book very well. It was the 'Wide, Wide World.' I used to cry, when mother was not looking at me, about it." Then Sophia was unable to read aloud, and through the summer and early fall she was kept alive "by an egg and a small glass of whiskey, her only nourishment, a day. — speaking but a few words and those in a whisper."

Weakening gradually, the strong-willed Sophia had lost all control of the household. Milie recalled guiltily: "As mama was not well, and could not see to us, as she otherwise would have done, we were a dreadful set of children and must have troubled her a great deal." She tormented herself, a few years later, with remorse, recalling a day when she read after breakfast and did not go to her mother's room until about noon: "I well remember the look when she asked why I had not been there before. But I did love her. I used to call her, 'my mamkin.'" "Dear darling mother," Milie sighed, in this recollection written in the 1860s; dear father, she might have sighed, for Allan seems already to have caught the tuberculosis that was killing Sophia. Allan went to Wall Street as usual until the end, coming home for tea and dinner, perhaps absenting himself from Evert Duyckinck's Saturday evenings. On 3 October 1858 Sophia died, thirty-one years old. George Duyckinck saw the news in the paper the next day and wrote to Mrs. Baker that Sophia "was a very gentle, sweet woman." Of Allan he said: "He is as fine, though not as talented a man, as his brother Herman." He failed to elaborate on the word "fine." Allan buried her at the new cemetery—Trinity Cemetery in Carmansville, far up the Hudson side of Manhattan. In Rensselaer County there was current a superstition that unless the person dead of consumption decayed fully, the undecayed part would derive its substance from a living person who loved the dead one, so that the living body decayed. Whatever the case with Sophia's body, Allan began a long wasting away. Almost nothing is known of how the family responded to Allan's new situation as a widower with four small daughters. Members of the family probably came for the funeral from eastern and western Massachusetts and from Gansevoort, and Fanny or Augusta may have stayed on for months. Milie had stayed with Helen and George in the Longwood section of Brookline some summers, but apparently she did not now go there for any prolonged period. Allan probably did not want to separate her from the younger girls. The Thurston family stayed in close contact with Allan and the girls—a large family still, including not only the New Rochelle family, Aunt Abby and Uncle Richard Lathers, but also Grandmother Thurston and Aunt Rachel Barrington (both in Irving Place, near each other), Uncle Charlie and Aunt Carrie Thurston, and young Uncle Henry Thurston's young wife, the girls' second Aunt Elizabeth.

Before Sophia's death, Allan had been representing a local woman, Louisa Jane Dempsey Randolph, in a case involving Vesey Street real estate. Born in 1824 or 1825, a year or so after Allan, Jane (as she was usually called, or Louise or Jennie) was the divorced wife of Henry Randolph, whom she had married early in 1847, and who was still alive and living in Washington, D.C., as late as 1891. A son, John, who died on 9 March 1851 at two years and eleven months, was buried in Fort Lee. The New York *Times* on 10 May 1891 gave this account of the mother of Allan's client, also a Jane Dempsey:

The old lady lived in a classic homestead of the Revolutionary pattern, just beyond Fort Lee; and, besides large possessions in New-York, acquired by the investment of her small change, she was the owner of most of the land in the beautiful little town on the brow of the Palisades. Some say that she was worth half a million when she died at the Waverly Hotel, in Broadway, New-York, nearly forty years ago [1853]; others, that she may have not been worth more than $300,000. But either figure made her for those times an enviously wealthy old lady. Dr. John Dempsey and Miss Louisa were her only children.

John Dempsey, with or without the connivance of his sister, Jane, had hidden the will, and it had remained suppressed for decades. As the *Times* said in 1891, "An atmosphere of romance surrounds the paper which has been produced in the Orphans' Court at Hackensack, in Bergen County, as the last will and testament of Mrs. Jane Dempsey." If Allan's client, Louisa Jane Dempsey Randolph, inherited half of merely $300,000, she was a very wealthy woman in the late 1850s. Multiplying by ten gives nothing like the purchasing power of $150,000—$10,000,000 might be near the modern equivalent. The friendly loan that had kept Herman Melville afloat while he finished *Moby-Dick*, and then proved a five-year curse, involved only $2050. Thus, Mrs. Randolph's money was at her disposal throughout her lifetime only because her brother had suppressed their mother's will, which "did not do all for him that he hoped she would do" (as the *Times* explained in the 1891 article). The moment the will was offered for probate after the death of Allan's client, nearly four decades after her brother had hidden it, his motive in suppressing it became apparent. Under it he and his sister could have claimed only a life estate in the property. The title was to go at their death to their children, if they had direct issue, and they were forbidden to leave the money outside the family. Allan's client disobeyed her mother's intention in the will she left in 1890, and John Dempsey's children were successfully challenging it, with the long-hidden will at last in the open.

After Maggie Van Rensselaer's tumultuous romantic history, everyone in the family had considered afresh the morality of divorce and had been lessoned in its legalities. Allan had been asked to explore the possibility that Maggie could be divorced and remarried in New York State—something not even a Van Rensselaer could accomplish. Whatever her motivations, Mrs. Randolph decided that she would marry Allan Melville; Allan's motivations are less obscure, given his attitude toward money. However soon Allan found himself emotionally available for an engagement to Mrs. Randolph, the family thought it was much too soon, and, however well or ill Allan thought of her, every indication is that for Allan and Sophia's daughters and most of the rest of the Melvilles the immensely wealthy and socially ambitious Mrs. Randolph was a monstrous social climber (however high in society she had started). That the Thurstons managed to keep in peaceful relations with Allan is a tribute to their generosity and their devotion to Sophia's daughters. To the day Allan died, Lathers treated him as a brother, and even after Allan's death Winyah Park remained open to the other Melvilles (which included the Hoadleys and Griggses).

Like Sophia Melville, Priscilla Melvill died of consumption, and soon after Sophia, on 20 October, in Pittsfield. Herman most likely took charge of funeral arrangements in the absence of any of Priscilla's brothers or sisters or her mother, unless indeed someone had come east to care for her. Just over eight years had passed since the opening of the cemetery, reclaimed from eroded and betrashed land to the west of the village, and it had become beautiful, as Joe Smith wrote: "Man had restored to nature something of the symmetry of which his rude and hasty greed had robbed her. The waters of Onota flow in a bold and rapid stream across the entrance of the Cemetery; but some of them had been trained in a winding brook to a beautiful lawn where they spread into a pretty lakelet." Smith was writing in 1890, in *Pontoosuc Lake*, about the cemetery as it was in 1850. In the late 1850s, trees planted in 1850 along the western border of the cemetery already had created some sense of a vista. Priscilla's stone was simple. In November James D. Colt, Shaw's agent in Pittsfield in the early 1840s, was made the administrator of her estate. Charlotte Hoadley was born at Lawrence on 17 December; at New Rochelle Joseph Lathers was born on 20 December, but died the next year on Herman and Lizzie's wedding anniversary.

Others in the circle of friends suffered. Sarah Morewood was dying from consumption, slowly, as Sophia had died, and was both resisting and hastening the end by throwing herself into sporadic physical adventuring. In a year-end letter to her sister-in-law Susannah, Sarah described herself as "able to keep up," and claimed not to cough excessively, but confessed that she was very thin and got very weary if she attempted to do much at all. Around the time Sophia died, George Duyckinck sent Melville an indoor bread-and-butter gift instead of another outdoor gift like Evert's thermometer: a five-volume set of George Chapman's translations of Homer (London, 1857). Melville thanked him on 6 November, explaining that "Indisposition" had prevented him from writing earlier—an unspecified illness, surely aggravated by grief for his sister-in-law and his widowed brother as well as for the woeful cousin whose pride equaled his own. The illness had prevented him from reading, so thus far he had "been mostly engaged in cutting the leaves by way of pastime"—the sort of task Melville found soothing, like cutting tobacco to the precise degree of fineness, or like squeezing sperm before it was boiled in the tryworks, monotonous mindless work, pleasingly engaging the hands. For "Chapman's Homer" he had an explosive plan: "As for Pope's version (of which I have a copy) I expect it, — when I shall put Chapman beside it — to go off shrieking, like the bankrupt deities in Milton's hymn." *Moby-Dick* in 1851 had not driven the bestsellers of the day screaming off the parlor tables of America, but Melville had not lost faith in the power of a great book to assert its own superiority. Always a lover of poetry, and a careful reader of poetry for a decade or more, Melville was in the process of remaking himself as a poet, reading now not only for delight but for models in technical matters such as stanzaic form, rhyme, and diction, as some notes in his books show.

Judge Shaw sent Melville a check on 8 November 1858, the first time, as far as we know, that he sent Melville cash for living expenses: "Believing that in providing your family supplies for the approaching winter, some pecuniary assistance will be convenient to you I enclose you above my check, on the New England Bank above for $100 one hundred dollars, for which I have no doubt, the Bank in your town will give you the money. To avoid danger of loss or miscarriage, I have made it payable to your order. I will thank you to hand half of it, to Elizabeth for her use, though it will all come to the same use in the end." Shaw continued: "We shall sadly miss your visit with that of Elizabeth & your children as Thanksgiving approaches. Our family circle will show a large vacancy. We expect a visit from you however, whether Elizabeth can accompany you or not, as I perceive you have an engagement to deliver a lecture here." Shaw was as loving and respectful toward Herman as ever, despite the fear he must have been feeling for Lizzie's immediate future and for what might happen to her after his death.

The previous year, most of the season's lecturers had been signed and sealed before the Panic of 1857; this year, lecture organizers knew in advance to be more cautious than usual about whom they booked and what they paid, so Melville's bookings must have suffered, after the bad reviews the previous season. Still, his topic encouraged some committees. As early as September 1858 the Boston *Transcript* announced that readers of *Typee* would "be glad to meet the author on his own peculiar ground," in a lecture "descriptive of his personal adventures in the South Seas." The 24 September *Berkshire County Eagle* picked up this notice and used it to urge that arrangements "be made at once for a course of *popular* lectures in Pittsfield, and that, if possible, lectures will be secured by Mr. Melville, George William Curtis, George Sumner, and other gentlemen of similar reputation." The *Eagle* suspected "that *such* a course would *pay* in Pittsfield." By 11 November the Pittsfield *Sun* had seen enough of its "exchanges in various parts of the country" to have a good idea who the season's lecturers would be — and to know that among them would be two locals, the Reverend Dr. John Todd (the inventor of the *Index Rerum*) and "Herman Melvill."

No lecture association where Melville had delivered "Statues in Rome" ever asked him back; he spoke again at the Tremont Temple in Boston but for a different association. Even with the help of his relatives and friends, he was not able to book as many engagements as the first season. He delivered his lecture on "The South Seas" on 6 December 1858 before the Yonkers Library Association, at the Getty House (fee, thirty dollars). The Yonkers *Examiner* in an ambivalent account on 9 December first praised his humor:

> Before last Monday evening . . . we doubt whether he was recognized as a humorist. His success in this field, if it be newly tried, is such as should encourage him, for his audience was not only large, but very sympathetic. It has been related of [Henry] Clay, that at the close of one of his speeches, the effect produced by his eloquence was so intense, that the vast assemblage was unable to manifest any outward applause. Thus was it with Mr. Melville's auditors, though in continuous merriment, their hilarity was too great to allow of other exertion. The facetious tone of Mr. Melville is beyond description.

However, the review concluded in a mood so different as almost to suggest some other reporter had finished it: "Mr. Melville's delivery is anything but pleasant. To use a common simile, the close of his sentences have a descending and rising cadence, which can be likened to nothing on earth but the graceful twist in a porcine after part." Yet, his voice was "susceptible of a modulation, which cannot be acquired without much care." Sentences ending like a pig's tail, down and then up: the victim may shrug off this sort of journalistic wit but can never forget it. Perhaps a speech analyst could make something of the description, knowing Melville's New England–New York family background. At the time this brutal verdict was made Melville had only one other lecture lined up, the one the Pittsfield *Sun* had announced for 14 December "in this town."

On Sunday, 5 December, the day before Herman went out to Yonkers, Cousin Henry Sanford Gansevoort called to see the brothers at Allan's house on Twenty-sixth Street and informed them that his parents and sister had tried to call upon "them" (Allan and his daughters?) but that their good intentions had always been "frustrated by some providential interference" (as he wrote Kitty on 8 December). After his Yonkers talk Melville stayed on with Allan a few days trying to set up other lecture dates. At Clinton Place he talked to George Duyckinck about a lecture at the New-York Historical Society and left two tentative dates in the hope of coordinating one in Jersey City about the same time through the agency of David Davidson, who had befriended him in London. He called on Davidson but missed him and gave up after waiting awhile; he must not have had a card he could leave, so he asked George to tell Davidson he had called. He was in New York when he accepted on 8 December an invitation from James Wilson to lecture in Chicago for the Young Men's Association at fifty dollars, and he eagerly accepted Wilson's offer to try to "make additional appointments" in his "quarter" of the world. Allan was already planning to spend the winter in Savannah, leaving New York a little later in December and staying away until March of 1859. The wealthy divorcée Jane Dempsey Randolph was a woman who did what she wanted to do. Did the usually cautious Allan go alone?

Back at home on 13 December Melville tried negotiating two mid-January dates with George Duyckinck instead of February, either of which now looked to be more convenient for him. That was not possible, and Melville wrote on the twentieth, ready to go to Jersey City if the chance came: "I should be glad to lecture there — or anywhere. If they will pay expences, & give a reasonable fee, I am ready to lecture in Labrador or on the Isle of Desolation off Patagonia." He added, "Bear with mine infirmity of jocularity (which, I am aware, should hardly intrude into a semi-business letter like this)." His infirmity of jocularity was one of his most enduring and endearing qualities. One of his qualities hardest for members of his family to bear was his willingness to go to great lengths to make himself available for their projects after he had waited too long — in this case years too long — to make the projects feasible. For his part, George kept trying, and as late as 31 January 1859 was urging Rosalie Baker to arrange a lecture for Melville at Sag Harbor for fifty dollars and traveling expenses.

Melville was still away when the Unitarian minister Thomas Starr King of Boston, who later showed him around San Francisco, lectured in Pittsfield. On 10 December the *Berkshire County Eagle* touted the next Tuesday's talk: "Mr. Melville is a familiar speaker, abounding in quaint and original thoughts, which adorn and enliven a story told with extraordinary powers of narrative and description." The Tuesday Melville talked, 14 December, was the most stormy and uncomfortable night of the winter, so far, and the place was the notorious Burbank's Hall, "a low, long room" hung around with such atrocious pictures that Dr. Holmes had written a verse tribute to the buying power of a dollar: "It will buy a picture in Burbank's Hall, / That would frighten a spider off from the wall." These were works of art to overpower any speaker, as Joe Smith made clear in his biography of Dr. Holmes (1895), a hundred or more daubs so vile that no one would buy them, even for their frames, until Burbank took the lot of them in 1855 for his rent. Their fate, Smith thought, was to perish "when the hall crashed down under a weight of snow in 1861." Ugly as the room was, Dr. Holmes had spoken from the platform there, and, before the daubs were hung, Fanny Kemble had read Shakespeare there "to a thousand people," Smith calculated wildly. Melville did not address a thousand, and the hall was dark enough that he would not be made as nervous by the daubs as Lizzie could be by patterns on the wallpaper. Melville knew that in the hall were villagers viler than the paintings, some of those who had spread the gossip that *Moby-Dick* had been worse than blasphemous and now wanted to be present to witness for themselves any new flings he might make at religion. He had friends still, and the *Berkshire County Eagle* on 17 December praised the lecture as "written in the style of Mr. Melville's best books, quaint, simple and polished; redolent of the spicy odors of the South Seas, and sparkling with original thoughts." (The day of that report, 17 December, was the day Melville's sister Kate gave birth to her daughter Charlotte Hoadley in Lawrence.)

Melville's third lecture of the series, the first in the new year, was given on 31 January 1859, for the Boston Mechanic Apprentices' Library Association (fee, fifty dollars) at Tremont Temple. On 24 January 1859, fresh from Manila, Thomas Melville (first mate when he sailed, captain when he returned) brought the *Meteor* into Boston Harbor — bringing tea among other cargo into the waters where his grandfather Thomas Melvill had taken part in the Tea Party. He had been away three years and eight months; in 1841– 44, Herman had been away only a few weeks longer than that. Herman may have been in town already, or a telegraphic dispatch about Tom's arrival may have brought Herman east as early as 25 January, when Boston led the country in celebrating the centennial of the birth of the still remarkably popular Robert Burns. The Boston *Evening Transcript* on Wednesday the twenty-sixth reported on "THE BURNS FESTIVAL" at the Parker House, "under the auspices of the Boston Burns Club." If Melville had contributed to the Boston-based *Atlantic Monthly*, as he had been invited to do in August 1857, he might have been asked to attend, and deservedly so, on the grounds of his Scottish heritage as well as his literary achievement. What went on there without him, as was widely reported in the press, entered into Melville's thinking about the destruction of his career, but it also entered into his consideration of what sort of poet he was to make himself into. The organizers had decorated the room "with paintings representing Scottish scenes and places made memorable by Burns." For authenticity's sake they tasted the haggis prepared in Burns's cottage for the Boston admirers and brought across the Atlantic, the substance proving undamageable and perhaps even improved by the ocean voyage. Ralph Waldo Emerson responded to the first toast, decrying himself as "the worst Scotsman of all," before identifying Burns's importance as "the poet of the middle classes," who "represents in the mind of men today that great uprising of the middle class against the armies and privileged minorities — that uprising which worked politically in the American and French Revolutions, and which, not in governments so much as in education and social order, has changed the face of the world." Furthermore, neither Hugh Latimer nor Martin Luther had "struck more telling blows against False Theology" than "this brave singer." Emerson declared that the greatest reformers included the man being honored: "Rabelais, Shakspeare in comedy, Cervantes, Butler and Burns"; he hinted that one other name could be added, but he refrained from specifying Thomas Carlyle. He continued with praise of Burns as having "given voice to all the experiences of common life; he has endeared the farm-house and cottage, patches and poverty, beans and barley; ale, the poor man's wine; hardship, the fear of debt, the dear society of weans and wife, of brothers and sisters, proud of each other, knowing so few, and finding amends for want and obscurity in books and thought." Revisiting his "meal in the firkin" mood from "American Scholar," Emerson spoke powerfully on the sort of lover of nature Burns was, the lover not of Goethe's or Byron's or Moore's majestic scenery but of "the lonely landscape which the poor see around them, — bleak leagues of pasture and stubble, ice and sleet, and rain, and snow-choked brooks; birds, hares, field mice, thistles and heather," a poet of "poor, anxious, cheerful, working humanity," using the "language of low life." After that, the now well oiled celebration rapidly descended into self-praise, for the fourth toast was: "*Pathos and Humor* — Twin sisters of true poetic genius, strikingly illustrated by 'Tam O'Shanter,' 'Hosea Biglow,' and the 'Autocrat of the Breakfast Table.'" The Parker House witnessed, all in all, an orgy of self-congratulation in the name of the people's poet. Only Emerson had risen to the occasion, as Melville saw in one paper or another, and his conviction that "Mark Winsome" was still at large, a national Confidence Man, was tempered by grudging or simply involuntary admiration. In 1862 he put it into words: for all his faults Emerson kept going "nobly on."

Fresh from the Pacific, Tom was in Herman's audience on 31 January to learn still more about that ocean from the lecture on "The South Seas." In their reports the next day, the *Traveller* said the hall was not more than half full, and the *Post* also said the attendance was not large, but the *Advertiser* said the lecture, "a fine production," received "the close attention" of a large audience. The *Journal* (1 February) said Melville was "frequently applauded" — frequently and enthusiastically by Captain Melville, in all likelihood. Luck had it that Melville had not been able to book lecture dates earlier in January and then had three lectures scheduled close together in New York and Baltimore, then Chicago. Once Tom was with him, Melville tried to shuffle his New-York Historical Society date, but George Duyckinck could not manage it. Melville did shift his schedule, as Elizabeth, opening and answering his mail by his instructions, explained to George Duyckinck on 30 January: "It was Herman's intention to pass a few days in New York before the lecture appointment, but the arrival of his brother, Capt. Melville, in Boston, from a long voyage has decided him to pass the intervening time in his company at their mother's in Gansevoort, where they will probably go after the Boston lecture of tomorrow evening." Tom had business aboard his ship, but he had always been able to get ashore at night even during the first days of dealing with crew, cargo, owners, and port officials. In Boston, before sailing the *Meteor* on to New York, Tom saw Helen, whose pregnancy (her secret at the time he left) had ended tragically, and in Lawrence or Boston he got to see the two new nieces, Kate and John's daughters. Tom would have known before landing that the tartest-tongued woman in his mother's generation, Aunt Catherine, had died and that Maria, Augusta, and Fanny had settled into the Mansion House with Uncle Herman. Tom would have learned from family letters of the birth of Lucy, but he may not have known before landing that Sophia was dead — she who had always treated him with casual affection, although being his own age she had infused some irony into her amusement at the family's abject adoration of him. With Herman perhaps talking with unwonted fluency, at times, to fill Tom in, and giving his brother minimal information about the changes in his status as an American author, the brothers could always lapse into companionable silence on their way to Gansevoort on 1 February.

The brothers seem to have taken the Rutland route to tiny Gansevoort and the big house Tom had never seen (like his sister Kate, he may never had laid eyes on his Aunt Catherine). Tom remembered his uncle from the times when he would come down alone to visit Maria's family in Albany and Lansingburgh. They found Uncle Herman feeble, but Maria flourishing. Augusta or Fanny must have been away for long periods the year before, taking turns staying with Allan so there would be a woman to run the household and care for the girls. It is hard to imagine that Augusta, who always had mothered Ally more than Helen had done, would not have lived at Twenty-sixth Street for many months before and just after Sophia's death. Over the next years Tom came to occupy the position in the family formerly occupied by his Uncle Herman, becoming the uncle of whom any of the nieces or nephews might have said what Gansevoort had said of Uncle Herman (when Tom was four), that he was "a very pleasant man in a family, more so than any man I am acquainted with." The difference was that Tom was never constrained by a wife like Catherine Quackenboss Gansevoort.

The brothers separated, Tom to return to his ship in Boston. Herman was in New York for his lecture (fee, fifty-five dollars) on 7 February 1859 in the Hall of the Library of the New-York Historical Society, on Second Avenue at the corner of Eleventh Street. The next day Henry Gansevoort wrote his sister, Kitty, of their cousin's triumph:

> I assure you it was a treat long to be remembered. The rooms were about half filled owing to the want of proper advertising but those who were present evinced their gratification by applause and attention. He treated the subject in so unpretentious a manner, so originally and so carelessly if I may say so that I assure you it was really refreshing. Its very simplicity was its success. He spoke ably for one hour of the phenomena of those unfrequented regions.... He presented the habits of the islanders, their religion their tatto-ing—their dispositions and their institutions in such glowing and gentle colors that every mind seemed to quit its local habitation the while for a short journey through the countries he described.

Having complained about the topic of the first lecture, Henry now pronounced this one to be in "Cousin Hermans true vein": "He was emphatically himself, and the lecture was to me like a quantity tied together — of his vivid and colloquial sketches (always too short) told under the inspiration of Madeira after dinner or drawn forth by some, proper association elsewhere. He should be invited to deliver it at Albany." The *Evening Express* of 8 February declared that the lecture was "full of rich, valuable information, and delivered with ease and grace." The *Century* on 12 February (echoing an unidentified paper of the eighth?) pronounced it "a very interesting lecture, none the less so for its modest and unpretending composition and delivery."

On his arrival in Baltimore on 8 February Melville found that the *American and Commercial Advertiser* was praising him "as the author of some capital books on South Sea subjects, full of the enchantment of shore life in that romantic region, and of perilous adventure in the whale fisheries of the adjacent seas" (the only known reference to *Moby-Dick* in the newspaper accounts of Melville's lectures this season). Encouraged by such praise after the congratulations he had received from Henry and others in New York, Melville acquitted himself well at the Universalist Church that night. The Baltimore *Sun* on the ninth declared that the "lecture abounded in interesting personal narratives, and held the interest of the audience to the close." In New York City on the way back from Baltimore, "while on the wing for Pittsfield," Melville received a note from G. W. Curtis, by then an editor for *Harper's New Monthly Magazine.* Curtis had tried to pique Melville's curiosity by hinting at a Polynesian story in his drawer which he hoped Melville would "do something with," but Melville on 12 February put him off with his usual stubborn vagueness: "I am sorry that some other matters on which I am at present engaged, will prevent me from this. Otherwise, I know no reason why I should not willingly embrace your proposition." He was in the middle of his lecture tour, as Curtis knew, but what he was engaged on was poetry.

While "on the wing" (as he wrote G. W. Curtis on 12 February) Herman probably swept Tom up for his visit to Arrowhead, or what was left of Arrowhead, the farm reduced by half its acreage since his last visit, the population of the farmhouse by more than half the adults. Over the hill to the west, where at the age of two Tom had been the delight of the enormous household, the Broadhall children were growing. Rowland had suffered spells of sickness, and Sarah was weakening, despite her astonishing will not only to live but to flourish. This year, and the next year, especially, Tom became one of Sarah's favorites. Tom found the cousins born in February 1849, Malcolm (Mackey) and Milie, big enough to correspond with each other. On 13 February, for instance, Malcolm wrote Milie that the school he went to had "a firstrate coasting place," on which his "clipper sled" beat all the other boys' sleds—the way Uncle Tom's clipper ship outdid the old-style ships. Malcolm and his friends in one noon hour had built a snowhouse big enough for fifteen boys to go into, and during the week Bessie and Fanny went out to play with their sleds every day, then on Saturday he and Stanny and the girls all had "a nice time together." Malcolm had a "Skating place at school," and another one at home, near the house. He and Milie were fully conscious of their seniority, and he knew to distinguish among his cousins when he said he wished Milie and "the little girls were here too." He and even Stanny were big enough to read the popular Rollo books, and Uncle Oakes had sent the boys the "Aimwell Stories" (first-rate, in Mackey's favorite term of praise) for Christmas, and Augusta had subscribed for him to receive "the Childs Paper every month." Mackey and Milie, and even the younger children, were personalities to be reckoned with by their strange uncle—for Tom had never seen three of his nieces. Florence (Folly) and Stanwix may have remembered him, but perhaps only Mackey and Milie did. From this time, with four young motherless nieces in Manhattan and four young children at Arrowhead needing to be around an easy-going but decisive man who looked just like their father (but younger and happier), as well as two nieces gaining their own personalities under the shadow of the nervously obsessive Kate, Tom took his duties as uncle with great seriousness. These visits to his brothers and sisters marked for Tom a generational change: no one, not even his mother, quite treated him as the baby of the family any more.

Around 14 February Tom gave Henry a tour of the *Meteor*, by then in New York, as Henry wrote his sister on the twenty-fourth, pointing out "the curiosities of the cabin, the mysterious lockers, the Eastern utensils, the cramped state rooms," and other oddities aboard. Cousin of many sailors, he indulged in the fantasy that if he had gone to sea he would not "now be gasping in a heavy atmosphere of law," trying to cast himself in a mold all together too narrow for him. Alas, he was "in the merciless hands of fate." Henry from his Andover days had been profligate, kept from being a publicly condemned ne'er-do-well only by timely infusions of cash from his father. The way things were going, he was set to become the Uncle Wessel of his generation, another alcoholic remittance-man venerealee. Meanwhile, he could dramatize himself in the face of Tom's quiet manhood.

After a few days at home Melville started west, stopping over on 18 February to visit his Uncle Peter, who described the day as "Damp & unpleasant"; he noted in his diary that his nephew "passed the evening with us," perhaps meaning that he stayed the night. (Maria on Saturday the twenty-sixth arrived at Peter's in the afternoon with "her son Thomas, Captain of the Ship Meteor in the East Indies Trade & recently from Manilla after 5 years absence" — almost four years, but Peter was close enough; the time had come to reassert family solidarity.) In Chicago Melville lectured on 24 February at Metropolitan Hall for the Young Men's Association (fee, fifty dollars), having the bad luck to follow the matchless lecturer Bayard Taylor. Melville may have picked up some stage tricks along the circuit, to judge from the *Daily Press and Tribune* the next day: "He said he would direct the gas to be turned down, and repeat to his audience in a whisper the mysterious rites of the 'Taboo,' but the relation would so far transcend any of Mrs. Ratcliffe's stories in the element of the horrible, that he would not willingly afflict any one with its needless recital." The reporter for the Chicago *Journal* on 25 February vaunted himself in exercising his charity toward Melville, then spoke his mind, in syntax that the printer may have mangled: "Whether it was due partially to the lecturer's limited vocal powers, and partially to an involuntary comparison between him and his immediate predecessor, the matchless word-painting and clear-ringing cadences of the handsome Bayard, still lingering in our ears, or wholly to the intrinsic defects of the lecture, we shall not undertake to say." Impervious to anything disrespectful in what he was saying, he informed his readers just how cavalierly Melville had been treated. After Melville finished his lecture, Professor Charles Whitney had taken the podium and announced his own entertainment which was to take place later that evening. Worse, the professor proceeded to awaken Melville's audience with "an admirable impersonation of the eccentric John Randolph, closing with a rendition of Boker's fine ballad of Sir John Franklin," the explorer whose expedition to the Arctic had ended tragically. Melville was most likely trapped on the stage for this quintessentially academic self-promotion. The reporter for the *Press and Tribune* was kinder about Melville's discourse (invested with "warm coloring" and "voluptuous odors and romantic drapery"), but pointed out that "whether owing to defects in the construction of the hall, which the speaker was not aware of, or to a lack of vocal powers on his own part," a large portion of the audience could not hear what Melville said.

William Cramer, the editor of the *Daily Wisconsin*, and his family welcomed Melville to Milwaukee and Albany Hall, where Melville lectured on 25 February for $50 plus $29.50 for expenses. While Edwin Croswell's assistant editor on the Albany *Argus*, Cramer had promoted Gansevoort's political career, and from London Gansevoort had sent him early reviews of Herman's first book, knowing that Cramer would make the most of them. Hard upon his publicizing *Typee*, Cramer had accepted the duty of writing a memorial for Gansevoort, and he had somberly called on Maria at Lansingburgh and had entrusted to the desolate Augusta twenty-four letters he had received from Gansevoort. Removed to the West, Cramer had reviewed *Omoo* generously in the *Daily Wisconsin*, adding to the review some personal comments on the family's love of young Tom. Hospitable before the lecture, Cramer was able to reassure Melville that the audience was larger than usual.

The Milwaukee *Sentinel* (26 February), in an article Melville clipped and carried home, peculiarly headed its report "An Antarctic Hour"; the reviewer tantalizingly said that he possessed "a full report of the lecture" which he could not use "owing to political matters," and instead was contenting himself with "a brief sketch"—a friendly one, which ended: "As a lecturer Mr. MELVILLE sustains the idea we have formed of him in 'Typee,' a soft, voluptuous ease is the predominant characteristic. Romance is breathed into the sterile topography of his subject, and the same drowsy enchantment that makes his writings so fascinating radiates from the speaker, and while we listen, it is to the murmur of the musical waves in coral grottoes, and to the sighing of tropical airs laden with the richness of dream land." The *Daily Free Democrat* (26 February) sketched Melville's plan: "He commenced by saying that he should not detail any of his own personal adventures, which, to our notion, was a great mistake, for had he stated some of the scenes which he passed through himself, and thereby invested his lecture with some life, instead of telling us what the primary geographies told us in our school-days, he would have created a better impression in Milwaukee."

Cramer in the *Daily Wisconsin* (26 February) gave a lengthy report preceded by an extended complimentary passage: "There was no labored effort to set before the audience profound logical syllogisms, nor soaring rhetorical flights; but it was such a feast as one would like to sit down to in a club room, and with the blue smoke of meerschaum gracefully curling and floating away, to listen attentively, though dreamily to, for hours, even till the night wore away." Gansevoort's old friend relished the account of beachcombers and recapitulated the fates many of them suffered, then mentioned also that

Melville had spoken "of a manuscript tradition he had [s]een that was told by a King of one of those Islands. It had much of the grace, strangeness and audacity of the Grecian Fables." The evening had been spent "in delicious literary languor"—so went the account of Gansevoort's old friend. Once again, Melville did not get away unscathed. The *Free Democrat* was sure that many if not most in the large audience "were disappointed in the lecturer and his discourse." The paper called Melville's lecture "a literary effort below mediocrity, and too bookish to please, unless he intended it as a reading." That was the problem: Melville gave a reading, and a dull one, instead of a performance: "it seemed to us as though he had one of his romances before him, and had selected the most uninteresting passages to read for our edification." The reviewer ranted on: Melville treated his general subject too generally; he made the mistake of not detailing "any of his own personal adventures"; the too "few illustrations" were "colored more by his own attempts at word-painting, than by any inherent or thrilling interest appertaining to them." Having endured and survived Melville, Milwaukee was to be rewarded the next Thursday by seeing "BAYARD TAYLOR."

On 28 February Melville spoke, disastrously, at Rockford, Illinois, in Warner's Hall before the Young Men's Association (fee, fifty dollars). To be sure, the *News* the next day began by saying the audience "listened with great pleasure to the discussion of a subject invested with all the gorgeous coloring, and glowing romance of Mr. Melville's peculiar genius," but this was mere faking, for the summary that followed was coolly lifted from the report in the Chicago *Press and Tribune*. The reviewer in the *Republican* (3 March) actually attended the lecture and was outraged: "It has rarely been our lot to witness a more painful infliction upon an audience." Melville had cheated the audience by withholding a personal narrative and giving "a simple presentation of historical facts" already available in books. The reviewer "failed to recognize one really good point throughout the entire lecture," but in the middle paragraph he gave a now-welcome description of the speaker: "Mr. Melville is a youngish man, of good physique, apparently enduring constitution, slightly bilious temperament, and a very good external make up in general. He lacks depth, earnestness, consecutiveness and finish, without which qualities no man need hope of being a permanently successful lecturer. Lecturing is evidently not his forte, his style as well as the subject matter being intensely 'Polynesian' and calculated to 'Taboo' him from the lecture field in the future." The Rockford *Register* on 5 March echoed much of the little that the *Republican* had said, but started with the only known mention of the puffery a lecture association had engaged in for Melville: a "display of his various productions, with euphonious titles" had preceded Melville "on the posters." (One of those posters, brought forth now in mint condition, might sell for enough to buy a substantial house in Rockford.) No man, the *Register* pronounced, "has a right to set himself up as a lecturer at $50 per night, who cannot for one minute take his eyes from his manuscript." In conclusion he swiped at the *News:* that reporter must "have got an advance report of the gentleman's lecture," and not actually heard it delivered. Melville talked on 2 March in the City Hall at Quincy, Illinois, for the Lyceum Series. He was paid $23.50. A local diarist, Orville H. Browning, called the lecture "Erratic but interesting"; no newspaper report is known. As Melville must have realized, whenever he stayed around long enough to read the papers instead of skipping town immediately, he would not be invited west again. In 1859 no less than 1840, it was folly for Melville to seek his fortune in the West— particularly in Chicago (which he remembered as a village huddled against the enormous lake), where he followed Bayard Taylor, the glamorous star of the lecture circuit, far beyond the period in his career when he would dutifully write a valentine for the man he was imitating, Melville. The posters for Herman Melville looked like false advertising, especially to Cramer in Milwaukee, and probably others along the route, who remembered Gansevoort's glory days. As in 1840, Melville would have to seek his fortune elsewhere, and he was too old and infirm to go a-whaling.

Back east in Massachusetts, at Sagamore Hall in Lynn on 16 March, Melville delivered "The South Seas and the Cannibal Islands" (as the Lynn *Weekly Reporter* announced it on the twelfth). He apparently gave his "Statues in Rome" lecture there later on, judging from the *Weekly Reporter* wording on 19 March: "Herman Melville's first lecture was tolerably well attended, but didn't touch the innermost," as those of Emerson and Lowell had done. Melville's was "more 'of the earth, earthy,' or rather of the water, aqueous. It was good, though, of its kind, and went off very well." To get to Lynn, on the coast north of Boston, meant that Melville stayed at least briefly with the Shaws, and probably saw Helen, if not Kate as well. Melville was back in New York before Tom sailed for San Francisco on 26 March, in time to give him an eight-volume set of "Works" — apparently not his own books? — "From *me* to Tom," he annotated the $5.85 charge on the Harper statement. (The Harpers had published only seven of his own books, and they would likely have charged him more than $5.85 for the seven plus another.)

Having heard Shaw's concerns when he was in Boston preparing to lecture at Lynn, Melville did his part in furthering the judge's attempts to leave Lizzie financially secure. On 1 April 1859 George Willis paid Melville $2000, the last installment on the eighty acres he had purchased in 1856. On 7 April, Melville paid off the remainder of his ten-year note for $1500 to John M. Brewster, gaining a $20 discount on the interest for paying it before 14 September 1860. Cleaning up the complex arrangements, on 15 April

Brewster and Willis both granted Melville deeds of discharge on the Arrowhead property, and on 23 April Melville in turn granted Willis a deed of discharge on the portion of the Arrowhead property he had bought from Melville in 1856. Melville waited until Shaw's regular September visit before handing him the deeds to the estate. Shaw then at his own leisure could reflect on just the best course to take.

On 19 April 1859, the anniversary of the battles of Lexington and Concord, two Williams College students, Titus Munson Coan (Munson Coan, he signed himself in his letter to his parents, in Hawaii, on 4 May 1859) and John Thomas Gulick, boarded a stage for Pittsfield on a "literary pilgrimage" (according to the version of his adventure that Coan gave to Arthur Stedman for "'Marquesan' Melville," in the New York *World* of 11 October 1891). They arrived at six, so they had time to look around before retiring to their lodgings. In Pittsfield Coan (then a lad whose skinniness made his face V-shaped, his Websterean forehead angling straight down from either side to meet at his pointed chin) visited "the Dunhams and Deacon Taylor" and "Mr Young," thereby picking up village opinion of Herman Melville. The next day Gulick and Coan took "a weary walk through the dust" to Melville's house on his "comfortable farm" (Gulick's journal) — a trudge that resulted in their feeling "well paid" for their efforts. Coan, who omitted mention of Gulick in his letter to his parents, wrote that he found Melville "dwelling in rustic style in a large and somewhat loosely-ordered farm-house"; when he copied the letter for quotation in 1891, he changed the phrasing to "spacious farm-house" to spare the feelings of Melville's widow. Obligingly, Melville had showed them the fine view of Greylock from "his north piazza," and to the south "the Berkshire hills with Washington peak in the centre" (Gulick). Gulick decided that Melville had "a form of good proportions, is about 5 ft. 9,in. in height, stands erect and moves with firm and manly grace." He was good to look at, all in all: "His head is of moderate size with black hair, dark eyes, a smooth pleasant forehead and rough heavy beard and mustache. His countenance is slightly flushed with whiskey drinking, but not without expression. When in conversation his keen eyes glance from over his aquiline nose." (However dark they seemed that day, his eyes were in fact blue.) Melville invited them inside, for Gulick was able to observe that his "conversation and manner, as well as the engravings on his walls, betray little of the sailor."

Some of Melville's parents' engravings may well have been hanging at Arrowhead, since Maria would not have denuded the walls on the public rooms when she went to Gansevoort, where her brother already had family regalia and paraphernalia to spare, on the walls and in chests and cupboards. Some of the furnishings that the students saw on this occasion were fine old pieces—splendid French chairs with dolphin heads carved on the arms, for example, which Allan Melvill had imported. In the Melville and Gansevoort families, furniture was something to be inherited, not purchased, and by the vagaries of taste and distribution what was there for the Williams students to see was subdued, old-fashioned, and irreplaceable.

Melville's habit of reserve came out strongly, to the point that the young men could not get what they wanted out of him. Coan thought his introducing himself as a Sandwich Islander would evoke reminiscences from Melville. It did not. Coan soon found Melville "in full tide of talk—or rather of monologue," but his host "would not repeat the experiences" (1891) which Coan had been rapturous about when reading his books. Coan wrote his parents:

> Of his own works, however, he seemed unwilling to say anything; preferring to pour forth his thoughts and theories of life rather than to speak of the past. . . . By judicious conduct toward the philosophic cynic, I managed nevertheless to draw him out very freely, and when I left him he was in full tide of discussion upon all things sacred and profane. He seems to have laid away the *objective* part of his life, and now delights to display himself as a thinker[,] talks about Aristotle and Plato very fluently, but not a word of Fayaway "Omoo" or of "White-Jacket."—He is a valuable acquaintance; and an independent enough, if somewhat perverse character.

This is from the 1891 rewriting: "In vain I sought to hear of Typee and those Paradise islands, but he preferred to pour forth his philosophy and his theories of life. The shade of Aristotle arose like a cold mist between myself and Fayaway. We have quite enough of Greek philosophy at Williams College, and I confess I was disappointed in this trend of the talk. But what a talk it was!" This is yet another version, rewritten by Coan long afterward, for the Boston *Literary World* of 19 December 1919: "In vain I sought to hear of 'Typee' and those paradise islands; he preferred to pour forth instead his philosophy and his theories of life. The shade of Aristotle arose like a cold mist between myself and Fayaway. . . . He seem[ed] to put away the objective side of life, and to shut himself up as a cloistered thinker and poet." Gulick also testified to the talk:

> Though it was apparent that he possessed a mind of an aspiring, ambitious order, full of elastic energy and illumined with the rich colors of a poetic fancy, he was evidently a disappointed man, soured by criticism and disgusted with the civilized world and with our Christendom in general and in particular. The ancient dignity of Homeric times afforded the only state of humanity, individual or social, to which he could turn with any complacency. What little

there was of meaning in the religions of present day had come down from Plato. All our philosophy and all our art and poetry was either derived or imitated from the ancient Greeks.

Coan saw his host as "transformed from a Marquesan to a gypsy student, the gypsy element still remaining strong in him" (1891), a comment that tells nothing for certain about his (or Melville's) knowledge of Matthew Arnold's "Scholar Gypsy" in 1859, since this passage was not in his letter to his parents. Coan, especially, testifies to the extraordinary power of Melville's talk—this from a young man just making his escape from learned lectures at Williams College. Gulick gives a better sense of the scope of Melville's talk; indeed, his account has the reliability of a student trained to take good notes during lectures. On the content of the talk the pilgrims agreed—Melville had celebrated classical civilization as the epitome of human dignity and freedom and denounced the present condition of "Christendom" as derivative and superficial.

To his parents in 1859 Coan gave a frank depiction of Melville as a man embittered against his criticism—not so much his literary critics as his neighbors who had never bothered to disguise their hostility: "His air is that of one who has been soured by opposition and criticism; with his freethinking way and his infidel tenets, he is evidently considered worse than a heathen by the good folks of Pittsfield; and his attitude seemed to me that of a man whose hand is against every man's and every man's against him—but perhaps I judged too hastily." The phrasing "worse than a heathen" gains force from its similarity to Maria's saying the neighbors were gossiping that *Moby-Dick* was "more than Blasphemous": the Pittsfieldites did not merely criticize Melville, they uttered anathemas against him. Here is Coan's modified 1891 version:

> And this contradiction gives him the air of one who has suffered from opposition, both literary and social. With his liberal views he is apparently considered by the good people of Pittsfield as little better than a cannibal or a "beach-comber." His attitude seemed to me something like that of an Ishmael; but perhaps I judged hastily. I managed to draw him out very freely on everything but the Marquesan Islands, and when I left him he was in full tide of discourse on all things sacred and profane. But he seems to put away the objective side of life and to shut himself up in this cold North as a cloistered thinker.

By contrast, Gulick, perhaps having been spared some of Deacon Taylor's gossip, had ascribed Melville's disappointment and souring to his disgust "with the civilized world and with our Christendom in general and in particular." Together, the students gave the shrewdest known analysis of Melville's mood in the late 1850s.

In 1859 for Melville to become absorbed in older English poetry, and to steep himself in Greek and, especially, Roman history and philosophy, required a willed turning away from the crisis in what he then and always (taking the long view) regarded as the American political experiment. Slavery was an atheistical iniquity, he had always thought, but others would have to play their parts trying to hasten or retard its inevitable abolition as an institution. For a time in 1848 Melville had thought he might be an effective national political commentator, and for a time in the mid-1850s he had yielded to the urge to publish his reflections on what had become of the American national character. Now, estranged from the values of his own time — the celebration of the achievements of science and technology, the exaltation of the insubstantial Crystal Palace over the long-enduring Parthenon and the indestructible Pyramids — he retreated into the classical past. The best time in all human history, he decided, was the Greece of Homer's time or the age of the Antonine emperors of Rome. Melville had tried, year after year, to sell his wares to a public ever less interested in buying them, and when he tried, belatedly, to placate the public and ingratiate himself with it by going on the public stage, he found himself unable to please in person. He had no way of making a living, in short — torture for a supposedly independent American citizen with four children and a wife on whom, in an un-American reversal of roles, he was dependent, through her father's repeated magnanimous acts.

Despite the miserable spiritual and cultural state of the country, despite the effects of the recent national Panic and his own poverty, Melville gave the young men lunch (probably there was a cook-housecleaner on the premises) then loaded them (and probably the three children) into his wagon to go to the village "where he was expecting to meet his lady on the arrival of the next train" (Gulick). In view of the alcoholism that recurred in the Melville and Gansevoort families in Melville's generation, Gulick's observation about Melville's face cannot be passed over. Melville had drunk in acceptable quantity with Hawthorne at the Fox & Geese in Southport and at a pub in Chester, and his 1856–57 journal reveals nothing like his intense 1849 quest for the perfect snuggery. Henry Gansevoort's comment on the lecture in New York as like a bundle of "his vivid and colloquial sketches (always too short) told under the inspiration of Madeira after dinner" testifies to Melville's normal tendency to loosen under the influence of wine. Indeed, the implication of a newspaper item on Dr. Francis's guests in a New Orleans paper in 1850 suggests that alcohol had long been known to thaw Melville out: "taciturn, but genial, and, when warmed-up, capitally racy and pungent." Yet Priscilla thought Judge Shaw was an alcoholic, and her concern was not that Herman might drink too much himself but that he might undermine his father-in-law's resolves by offering him just a little wine.

Melville may have drunk too much at times: "bilious," a western critic had just called his face. Morning drinking was an American custom widely remarked on, and Melville may have taken the opportunity of the young men's visit to bring a bottle out, early though it was, and he may have showed the liquor's effects because he wasn't used to drinking—just what had happened to poor Poe again and again. A verse epistle Melville dated 6 July 1859 and addressed to Daniel Shepherd (Allan's partner), inviting him to come to visit him in Pittsfield, deals with the realistic problem of what drink to offer a guest in the farmhouse when "Not a pint of ruby claret / Cooleth in our cellar-bin; / And, ripening in our sultry garret, / Otard glows no flask within." A guest might go to bed "*unwined*" but not without alcohol: "Of Bourbon that is rather new / I brag a fat black bottle or two, — / Shepherd, is this such Mountain-Dew / As one might fitly offer you?" And if cold water would content him, Shepherd should have plenty: "Thanks to late floods, our spring, it brims." The Morewoods could have sent a servant down to their wine cellar under the great joists of Broadhall, but if Melville were to give a visitor anything alcoholic, it had to be locally produced and probably still raw whiskey.

[18]

The Poet and the Last Lecture, "Travel"
Summer 1859–Early 1860

> Ours is a poetical age; but has it produced one Great Poem? Not one.
>
> "An Hour's Talk about Poetry," in the Christopher North
> (John Wilson) volume of *Modern British Essayists*, which Melville
> bought in 1849

EVERT DUYCKINCK REPORTED to his brother on 30 July 1859 that Melville was "doing nothing in particular." Melville in fact had lectured in the East and West, had cared for the three older children while Lizzie was away in Boston with Frances, and had done some farm work. Besides that, he had been making himself into a poet. The epistle to Daniel Shepherd on 6 July 1859 is in verse too competent to be the first Melville had attempted (not counting the primitive effusions in *Mardi* and elsewhere). Before he wrote this epistle, Melville had been writing poetry long enough to have formulated and have begun to struggle with what he called there "poet-problems, fancy-fed." Thinking of publishing some of his poems, Melville went to New York City, perhaps as early as 18 May 1859. Henry Gansevoort wrote his father from there on 23 May saying that Herman was "in town looking well and hearty." Melville put "Pittsfield" as his address in a note to a publisher that day, but he seems to have written it in New York City. The note says: "Here are two Pieces, which, if you find them suited to your Magazine I should be happy to see them appear there. — In case of publication, you may, if you please, send me what you think they are worth." He may have left the note off at the publisher's, since it was endorsed as received the day it was dated. The provenance of the note links it, shakily, to the Harper brothers, and in any case *Putnam's*, his alternative outlet for short pieces, had been defunct for more than a year. Presumably the Methodist brothers rejected the pieces, for nothing appeared in *Harper's*, and this latest insult may well lie behind Melville's flat directive the next year that Allan not submit his book of poems to the Harpers.

When, saturated with Byron and brine, young Melville took up his pen in Manhattan late in 1844, he learned, fast enough, that most critics who hoped for the emergence of great American literature were looking for it to come in the form of poetry. That was no surprise, for all his life he had heard the poets and critics say that the surest way to achieve ultimate immortality in literature was to write great poetry. The idea persisted through Melville's early career that the great American literary work would be a poem. The Washington *National Intelligencer* (23 November 1855) opened the review of *Hiawatha* this way: "We have in this newest Poem of Mr. Longfellow perhaps the only American Epic. . . . What the greatest Poets have done for their lands Longfellow has done for his." Even throughout the decade after Melville published his last work of prose, the theory still prevailed that for a lover of literature the highest and richest rewards were to be found in poetry and that the greatest writers were poets. "Why write poetry?" was not a question Melville would have thought to ask.

In his youth and young manhood Melville knew many poems by Edmund Spenser, John Milton, Samuel Butler, John Dryden, Alexander Pope, John Gay, James Thomson, Edward Young, Mark Akenside, William Shenstone, William Collins, Thomas Gray, Samuel Johnson, James Macpherson, Charles Churchill, Oliver Goldsmith, William Cowper, Robert Burns, Samuel Rogers, Walter Scott, Thomas Campbell, George Byron, Alfred Tennyson, and many other poets, particularly eighteenth-century poets, those famous when his grandparents were young, and also those of his parents' generation. He knew poems by hearing them read aloud, by reading them aloud, by memorizing portions of them. At seven, he had heard his brother Gansevoort recite Collins's "Ode on the Passions" many times while memorizing it. The same year he heard Gansevoort memorizing Fitz-Greene Halleck's "Marco Bozzaris." Melville was familiar with much of the glorious British poetry published in the first decades of the century, and he knew these poems soon after they were published. He had declaimed poetry as a whaleman and heard poetry declaimed, notably parts of Luis de Camoëns's *Lusiads*, Jack Chase's favorite. He even knew many early ambitious attempts to write great poetry in America. His Uncle Thomas had been acquainted in Paris with Joel Barlow, the author of the *Columbiad*. He knew Richard Emmons's *Fredoniad*, which he may have read in the Pacific where some of the stirring action was set. In the *Tribune*, on 27 September 1848, G. G. Foster declared that Melville's acquaintance the cranky Rufus Griswold was "as familiar with the pedigree of every tyro and blue-stocking, from the Fredoniad down, as a Virginia turfman with that of his stable." Melville knew something of John Quincy Adams's *Dermot MacMorrogh, or, The Conquest of Ireland*, possibly some lines of it that have been lost, for Duyckinck in the *Literary World* of 18 March 1848 had announced that among the unpublished works of the late president were poems, "including two new cantos of Dermot MacMorrogh." By the time Melville was writing his best prose, in the years beginning in 1850, he had been reading and rereading great poets, not just Shakespeare, his obsession early in 1849, but also Spenser, Milton, Wordsworth, and many others (such as Robert Herrick, whose poems he acquired late in the summer of 1859). He was also reading, as later became clear, a pair of living English poets who set a standard for his efforts, Alfred Tennyson and Robert Browning.

At the time he was becoming a poet, Melville read one contemporary American poet carefully, and skeptically. Sam Shaw visited Arrowhead in the summer of 1859, bringing Melville a copy of a recent (1858) printing of Emerson's *Poems*. Perhaps reading these poems for the first time, Melville paid close attention to poetic techniques. In "Merlin" he scored the injunction that a poet should not try to write poetry in "weak, unhappy times" but should wait "his returning strength" (after which his rhymes might again be "efficacious"). He scored the injunction not to force poetry into existence through the use of mere "meddling wit" but, again, to wait until the mind is "propitious," for the mind of the poet will publish, produce, only when it is inclined to do so. It might have been better for Melville to read advice less in accord with his own early vaunting of the certain something unmanageable in a writer, but he got from Emerson's poem confirmation that elsewhere in the United States, and in fact in his own Massachusetts, someone had been grappling with some of his own "poet-problems."

To prepare himself to become a poet Melville reread the great English poets. He had absorbed Shakespeare early in 1849 and went back and back to some of the plays, particularly *Macbeth*. Melville had long treasured his father's copy of Spenser, and may have drawn on his own experience in adolescence when he portrayed Pierre as awakening to sexuality and aesthetic sensuality, simultaneously, while reading *his* father's copy of *The Faerie Queene*. He had reread much of Spenser before he plundered him for epigraphs to some of the sketches in "The Encantadas." In his thirties and forties Melville knew so much poetry that he could not reread *The Faerie Queene* and Spenser's shorter poems without tracking Shakespeare, Milton, Pope, Wordsworth, Keats, and even Poe through their own plunderings of Spenser. He found in Spenser a special point of personal contact, marking lines 204–7 of "Colin Clout's Come Home Again" — the passage on the meaning of going to sea: "Who life doth loath, and longs death to behold / Before he die, already dead with fear, / And yet would live with heart half stony cold, / Let him to sea, and he shall see it there." Melville annotated this: "Absolute coincidence here between Spenser's conceit and another person's, in connection with a very singular thought." Perhaps the most poignant record in his Spenser has to do with the lines about Scudamour after

Blandamour has denounced him (*Faerie Queene*, 4.1.45): "He little answer'd, but in manly heart / His mightie indignation did forbeare." Melville turned the little volume around so the spine was facing him and wrote across the back flyleaf: "He little answered, but in manly heart / His mighty indignation did forbear."

Always alert to literary echoes, Melville could not reread Milton without thinking of lines in Lucan, Dante, Spenser, Shakespeare, Sir Thomas Browne, Campbell, and Byron. Melville always thought of Milton as the author of the conversations of the fallen angels on the topics recurrent in his own thinking: "providence, foreknowledge, will, and fate, / Fix'd fate, free will, foreknowledge absolute" (2.559–60), topics he recurred to with George Adler, Nathaniel Hawthorne, and others. When he identified with Milton, it was as rebellious thinker. John Mitford in the introductory "Life of Milton" mentioned the poet's "wanderings in religious belief," spurring Melville to comment: "He who thinks for himself never can rema[i]n of the same mind. I doubt not that darker doubts crossed Milton's soul, than ever disturbed Voltaire. And he was more of what is called an Infidel." Knowing the grandeur of his own literary achievements, whatever the opinion of the world, Melville did not scruple to acknowledge the "singular coincidence" that both he and Milton avoided churches, especially those in any way connected to the state, and both rejected "any settled articles of belief." In book 9 of *Paradise Lost*, at the passage where Satan tells Eve that God forbade her to eat from the tree of knowledge in order to keep her and Adam "low and ignorant," Melville wrote: "This is one of the many profound atheistical hits of Milton. A greater than Lucretius, since he always teaches under a masque, and makes the Devel himself a Teacher & Messiah." Melville had no doubt what was the "grandest of all grand thoughts" — God's challenge to Adam in book 8: "Seem I to thee sufficiently possest / Of happiness, or not, who am alone / From all eternity? for nonc I know / Sccond to me or like, equal much less." Yet Melville could never be at ease with Milton. When the Chorus in *Samson Agonistes* declares that God "made our laws to bind us, not himself," Melville protested: "Noble rhetoric but vile reasoning." There was, Melville decided, "a twist to Milton," revealed obliquely in Delilah's comparison of herself to Jael. In the decade before the War between the States, Melville looked hostilely upon the "two-handed engine" passage in "Lycidas": "Mark the deforming effect of the intrusion of partizan topics & feelings of the day, however serious in import, into a poem otherwise of the first order of merit."

Melville read Wordsworth with distaste for the man but with admiration for the poetry, including some works now seldom read, such as *The Excursion*. Chances are *The Prelude* was published too late to be important to him, except for portions that had appeared earlier, particularly "Vaudracour and

Julia" (included in his edition of Wordsworth's poems), which may have influenced the depiction of Isabel in *Pierre*. Edgy as he was about Wordsworth's character, he was able to recapture, with Wordsworth, the delight of encountering a particular passage in "Colin Clout's Come Home Again." In his Spenser, Melville marked the line "Now in the valleys wandring at their wills" and glossed at the bottom of the page: " 'The river wanders at its own secret will' / Wordsworth." Then he wrote: "How W. W. must have delighted in this stanza." By the 1850s Melville's head was a hive of thousands of lines of poetry, and he construed the borrowings he recognized as loving tributes that poets paid to their great predecessors.

Melville may have recognized as a poet-problem the difficulty of connecting his admiration of the classical past with genres he might imitate in his own poetry, but he had little guidance. In Akenside's "The Pleasures of Imagination" (his father's courtship gift to his mother) Melville had read the vague address to the "Genius of Ancient Greece!" which ends with the poet's suggesting that his "compatriot youth" imitate the high example of the Greek poets and urging that the British lyre be turned to Attic themes: from this, could Melville derive anything suggestive for tuning his American lyre to Attic themes? Poetry about aesthetic and political issues was always worth pondering, and all through his early career as a prose writer, Melville had access to the best new critical essays *about* poetry. The American press routinely pirated British weeklies, monthlies, and quarterlies, and publishers, even in smaller towns such as Albany, reprinted whole issues of the more salable periodicals, many containing reviews of poetry.

Earnest about studying criticism rather than contenting himself with what he found in periodicals, Melville bought some handy collections of British poetry criticism of the first quarter of his century, most notably (in 1849) the seven-volume set of *Modern British Essayists*. In one volume Melville read the curmudgeonly John Wilson (Christopher North) on the question of whether there was a great English poem (answer: only *Paradise Lost*). There he read several challenging comments on Wordsworth, and read, with hostility, Wilson's praise of doctrinally correct sacred poetry. Another volume in the set contained the essays on the great Romantic poems that Francis Jeffrey (who had been so hospitable to Allan Melvill) had published in the *Edinburgh Review* as the poems were appearing. *Lyrical Ballads* pre-dated the establishment of the magazine, but the poetry section of the Jeffrey volume contained his reviews of Campbell's *Specimens of the British Poets*; Byron's *Sardanapalus* and *Manfred*; R. H. Cromek's *Reliques of Robert Burns*; Campbell's *Gertrude of Wyoming* and *Theodoric*; Scott's *The Lay of the Last Minstrel* and *The Lady of the Lake*; George Crabbe's *Poems, The Borough, Tales*, and *Tales of the Hall*; Keats's *Endymion* and *Lamia, Isabella, The Eve of St. Agnes*; Samuel

Rogers's *Human Life;* Robert Southey's *Roderick: The Last of the Goths;* Byron's *Childe Harold's Pilgrimage* and *The Prisoner of Chillon;* Thomas Moore's *Lalla Rookh;* Wordsworth's *The Excursion* and *The White Doe of Rylstone;* Felicia Hemans's *Records of Women* and *The Forest Sanctuary.* This was an extraordinary cache of classic criticism, all the more notable because Jeffrey's reviews constituted not only excellent examples of practical criticism but explicit attempts to write criticism from aesthetic principles, to explore what we would call theoretical issues, precisely what Melville needed, as his first lecture woefully showed.

When Melville decided to be a poet, he began testing literary criticism against actual poems. He wrote out facing the opening of book 1 of *Paradise Lost:* "The music of the P. L. / Like a fine organ — fullest & deepest tones of magesty, with the softness & elegance of the Dorian flute. Variety without end, scarcely equalled by Virgil." This passage he identified as coming from a letter of William Cowper defending Milton against Dr. Johnson. On blank pages in his books of poetry Melville noted archaisms and other unusual words which he might want to use. He made little lists of rhyme words. Humbly wanting to learn, he tried out ridiculous suggestions by pedantic scholars: when he put bow lines linking rhyme words in "Lycidas" he was applying a critic's theory involving the mathematics of musicality. Melville developed a scholarly habit of reading one translation of an epic poem with another at hand, so he could make comparisons between the English versions, not knowing Greek, Latin, or Italian. He was serious the way only a passionate autodidact with time on his hands is serious. All along, he agreed with Hazlitt's "On Poetry in General," the introduction to *Lectures on the English Poets* (New York: Derby & Jackson, 1859), where in 1862 he marked the pugnacious opening proposition: "It [poetry] is not a mere frivolous accomplishment (as some persons have been led to imagine,) the trifling amusement of a few idle readers or leisure hours — it has been the study and delight of mankind in all ages." He checked Hazlitt's tough comment on the relevance of poetry: "If poetry is a dream, the business of life is much the same."

Melville knew that if Apollo and the Muses inspired anything, it was poetry, not prose. "Tasso's invocation," Melville noted, when he read Milton's appeal to Urania at the start of book 7 of *Paradise Lost.* (He also marked heavily Wordsworth's obviously Miltonic "Preface" to *The Excursion,* where Wordsworth also invokes Urania.) Melville came to see, after 1857, that his own most prolonged mature wrestling with the Angel, Art (a struggle memorialized in his short poem "Art" in *Timoleon*), would always be in poetry, whether short poem or poetic epic. Without believing that Apollo or Urania had descended upon New York or Pittsfield and swept him to the top of

Trinity Church or Greylock, Melville knew that he had the true "godlike gift" depicted by Collins in the "Ode on the Poetical Character." There Collins's God as Creator imagines the universe into existence, just as, in Collins's daring analogy, the poet imagines a new literary world into existence. Aside from his late work on the prose of *Billy Budd* (which began as poetry, the ballad that now concludes the work), Melville devoted almost all of his creative energies for three decades to poetry.

Very little is known about the summer of 1859, when Melville was making himself into a poet. In late June, Evert Duyckinck visited Winyah, where he cast a professional eye about Lathers's library, by anyone besides Evert's standards a magnificent collection — and one which has disappeared with hardly a trace. One book known to survive, curiously enough, is one that caught Evert's attention, "a copy of Hazlitt's Abridgement of Tucker's Light of Nature with a presentation inscription from Herman Melville." That summer, on Helen's birthday and Herman and Lizzie's wedding anniversary, Joseph Thurston Lathers died, not yet eight months old. That summer, also, William Morris Hunt painted what some consider an American masterpiece of portraiture, a full-length oil portrait of Judge Shaw.

Despite his lack of income, Melville continued to run up his account with Harper's, buying on 18 June 1859 *Poets of the Nineteenth Century* (to be picked up by Allan?) and on 20 June subscribing for two years to *Harper's Weekly* for his mother, then on 16 August subscribing for two more years to *Harper's Magazine* for himself (four dollars), and ordering two books (again to be picked up by Allan?): *The Land and the Book* by William McClure Thomson and *Clouded Happiness* by the Countess d'Orsay. On 8 September the Harper account showed that Melville owed them $287.53. Allan had taken a trip, perhaps alone, perhaps a therapeutic one, for on 30 July Evert Duyckinck wrote George that Allan had been to see him "with an entertaining account of his Virginia travels." He did not yet know that the "new book" George had reported Melville as "busy on" in his letter of 26 July 1858, a year earlier, was a book of poems.

In early September 1859 George was again in Pittsfield. About this time Melville acquired Francis James Child's *English and Scottish Ballads* (Boston: Little, Brown, 1854–57) and read through much of it. His cousin Helen Jean Melvill was in the village, perhaps at Arrowhead, later in the month, visiting acquaintances and visiting her half-sister Priscilla's raw grave. By September or October 1859 Melville had probably finished his third lecture, on "Travel: Its Pleasures, Pains, and Profits." He delivered it only in Flushing, New York, and Danvers and Cambridgeport, Massachusetts. Judging by the length of his previous two lectures, only about a quarter of this last lecture is known, from the single report yet located, that in the Cambridge *Chronicle* of

25 February 1860. Since Melville did not give the lecture in any metropolis, he was never reported in major newspapers, and the known account is so brief that it is impossible to tell whether it represents a condensation of different parts of the lecture or whether it reflects only the opening of the essay (if so, Melville gave an initial survey of pleasures, pains, and profits — presumably before going back to discuss each separately, in more detail).

If the first sentence in the *Chronicle* was the beginning of the lecture, Melville had started close to home:

> In the isolated cluster of mountains called Greylock, there lies a deep valley named The Hopper, which is a huge sort of verdant dungeon among the hills. Suppose a person should be born there, and know nothing of what lay beyond, and should after a time ascend the mountain, with what delight would he view the landscape from the summit! The novel objects spread out before him would bewilder and enchant him. Now it is in this very kind of experience that the prime pleasure of travel consists. Every man's home is in a certain sense a "Hopper," which however fair and sheltered, shuts him in from the outer world.

The requisites of a traveler were those Melville had possessed in 1840 and 1841, not 1856: "One must be young, care-free, and gifted with geniality and imagination, for if without these last he may as well stay at home." The man sour of nature would derive no pleasure in traveling, "for joy is for the joyous nature."

Authentic bits of Melville come through all parts of the fragmentary report. He praised being "a good lounger," in order to "derive pleasure and instruction from the long galleries of pictures, the magnificent Squares, the Cathedrals, and other places that require leisurely survey." He passed over fleas and other insects lightly ("though they by no means pass lightly over the traveller"). In the vein of his letter to N. P. Willis in 1849, he expatiated over grievances involving the passport, the inspection of which always required money: "Open passport, open purse." The remedy for customs officials and for extortionate guides was the same: "full pockets." The profits of travel included (in a Melvillean understatement) the chance to "get rid of a *few* prejudices." Enough of the text survives to show that Melville vigorously went about shaking up cultural prejudices in his usual relativistic way:

> The native of Norway who goes to Naples, finds the climate so delicious as almost to counterbalance the miseries of government. The Spanish Matador, who devoutly believes in the proverb, "Cruel as [a] Turk," goes to Turkey, sees that people kind to all animals; sees docile horses, never balky, gentle, obedient, exceedingly intelligent, yet *never beaten*, and comes home to his

bull-fights with a very different impression of his own humanity. The stockbroker goes to Thessalonica and finds Infidels more honest than Christians; the teetotaller finds a country in France where all drink and no one gets drunk; the prejudiced against color finds several hundred millions of people of all shades of color, and all degrees of intellect, rank and social worth, generals, judges, priests and kings, and learns to give up his foolish prejudice.

Among the minor liberalizing effects of travel was the new emphasis on comfort in clothing and the acceptance of men who wore beards. Melville was stretching to make his cultural relativism as broad as possible, attributing to a Norwegian his own ambivalence about beauty as a counterweight to tyranny in Naples. (Submerged in this passage was Melville's lifelong horror at the way cartmen in Manhattan beat their horses and literally worked them to death.)

Toward the end of the text that survives, Melville praised travel even in a narrower range: "A trip to Florida will open a large field of pleasant and instructive enjoyment. Go even to Nahant, if you can go no farther — *that* is travel. To an invalid it is travel, that is change, to go to other rooms in the house. The sight of novel objects, the acquirement of novel ideas, the breaking up of old prejudices, the enlargement of heart and mind, — are the proper fruit of rightly undertaken travel." (The reference to Nahant in this passage sounds like a variant for the Danvers and Cambridgeport audience; he may have recommended something nearer to the Flushing crowd — Rockaway, for instance.) What survives is only a good approximation of a tantalizing fragment of the lecture.

Melville delivered "Travel" at Flushing, Long Island, before the Young Men's Association on 7 November, for thirty dollars, apparently when Augusta was in New York City with Allan and the girls. On 4 January 1860, Augusta wrote Kate Gansevoort, Uncle Peter's daughter, that she had not heard it but had "read it in M S. & thought it highly interesting." One of the Sanford in-laws of Peter Gansevoort (through his first marriage) may have arranged the Flushing engagement. William R. Prince, a botanist and nursery owner, and his nineteen-year-old son Lebarron, the precocious chairman of the lecture committee, entertained Melville hospitably there for "over night and part of a day" (according to Augusta), and presented him with "a bouquet of lovely flowers" — probably the first time a man had given him flowers since the memorable Henry at the Doney in Florence. The audience may well have felt that they were hearing from a man strangely out of touch with the realities of American life, a man who could generalize about traveling only three weeks after John Brown's raid on Harper's Ferry. No record is known of the reception of Melville's talk at Flushing.

Melville went down to New York again in mid-November, while Augusta was still with Allan. This time he took Bessie with him so she could play with Kitty (eleven months her elder) and her other cousins. Augusta told Kate in the 4 January letter that Melville was then "feeling much stronger," which implies that through the preceding months he had not been well. From Evert Duyckinck's library Melville borrowed for reading through the winter Giorgio Vasari's *Lives of the Most Eminent Painters, Sculptors, and Architects* (London: Bohn, 1850–52) and Luigi Lanzi's *History of Painting in Italy* (London: Bohn, 1847). He probably was still contemptuous of aesthetical grimgribbing, as he had been in his first lecture, but now he wanted to refresh his memory of what he had seen and to become familiar with basic concepts and principles which he could use in refining his thinking about aesthetic achievement. Evert and George may have thought Melville particularly perturbed during this visit, for after he had gone home Sarah Morewood on 21 November was correcting George when she wrote: "Herman Melville is not well — do not call him moody, he is ill."

Small wonder Melville was moody seeming and unwell. However much he turned his back on the trial of John Brown, he could not shut out the recognition that he had nothing to be thankful for as the great New England holiday approached: his career as a lecturer had dried up like his career as a fiction writer. Once again not a single organization had invited him back for a repeat performance, and his friends and relations were twisting arms, often futilely, to get him bookings. On 30 November Hoadley pressured a friend in Charleston, South Carolina, for Herman: "Can't you manage him an invitation? — an engagement? — You can't do a better action, for a better fellow; nor oblige me more deeply." Judge Shaw called in favors, evoking a painfully long letter from A. M. Livingston in Salem on 29 December ("the list of lecturers for the 'Young Mens Union', so called, is already filled; if any vacancy should occur, I think Mr. Melville will be invited to fill it.... The old Salem Lyceum ... has one or two vacancies, and I have reason to believe that Mr. Melville will be invited to fill one of them"). Neither materialized, but Livingston got Melville an invitation from the "Peabody Institute, in S° Danvers" and promised to use his power as a trustee to help get Melville on the "Young Mens Union" list for the next season.

On 28 November, the Monday after Thanksgiving, Washington Irving died at Sunnyside. In the next days all newspapers printed memorial articles and described the funeral. Even in Pittsfield, Melville would have seen at least the *Herald* and the *Tribune*. He may have persuaded himself that John Brown's raid was one more isolated insurrectionary outbreak which he had to ignore, if he were to continue his efforts to lead a quiet emotional life. Certainly he was not letting the events in Virginia obsess him as, at the same time, Thoreau was doing — to the degree that Thoreau said that if Irving had died at any other time his passing would have absorbed all attention, but as it was any mourning for him had to be postponed. Melville, now or in stages, experienced a tangle of emotions over Irving's death. First, perhaps, was spontaneous grief for the writer who at the time of his own birth in 1819 had been in the process of breaking down the resistance of British reviewers to writings by Americans. The Albany *Evening Journal* said on 9 December that the promised biography by Pierre M. Irving might be expected to explain the magic of that power which subdued the ferocious criticism of London and Edinburgh. And as the New York *Times* had said earlier, on 30 November, Irving had been "the patriarch of American letters, and the last link that remained to us between the age of Scott and Campbell and Southey and Byron, and our own."

This link Melville had been amply aware of, and touched by. Melville had absorbed Irving's *Sketch Book*, especially, early in life and still deeply cherished it; he had imitated it in his early works, as Evert Duyckinck had long ago observed, and had relished a chance to rework Irving's subjects and his prose cadences in so recent a piece as his "Paradise of Bachelors." Many literary men and historians stepped forward as mourners. Melville's friend Dr. Francis was among those suggesting that New York City erect a statue of Irving. Theodore Tilton by great good luck had just published in the *Independent* an account of his recent visit to Sunnyside, so it was reprinted avidly. Willis had visited Irving at the end of October and written about it in the *Home Journal*, paragraphs that now were also reprinted in many papers. For the funeral the express train was ordered to stop at Tarrytown, so Manhattanites could leave at eleven in the morning and be back at four. The *Herald* on 2 December listed many people Melville knew among those attending — Evert and George Duyckinck, N. P. Willis, George P. Putnam, and Henry T. Tuckerman. Melville was so generally forgotten that no one seems to have sought him out for tributes to the great dead master. The Cambridge *Chronicle* reported that Melville said in his lecture the following February: "As Washington Irving has remarked, the sea-voyage, with its excitements, its discomforts, and its enforced self-discipline, is a good preparation for foreign travel." Melville probably wrote the reference into the lecture in the fall, while Irving was alive, since he seems not to have interpolated many remarks, except a few local allusions, into his lectures and since in the report that survives no point is made of Irving's having died. Years later, after Joseph Jefferson had routed all the other enactors of dramas based on "Rip Van Winkle," Melville at last came fully to terms with "happiest Irving," whom he eulogized as "A Happy Shade" in his "Rip Van Winkle's Lilac."

At the end of January Melville was in New York, with a lecture scheduled for Danvers in two weeks and Cambridgeport in three. If he was trying to get new invitations to lecture, he failed, and before going home he laid in his intellectual provisions, as Evert Duyckinck noted in his diary: "Herman Melville called for some volumes of the Essayists to take with him to his winter reading at Pittsfield. Says that the mealy mouthed habit of writing of human nature of the present day would not tolerate the plain speaking of Johnson, for instance, in the Rambler—who does not hesitate to use the word *malignity!*" Melville borrowed *The Tatler; A Daily Journal of Literature and the Stage* (4 vols., 1830–32); *The British Essayists*, edited by Alexander Chalmers; three volumes of *The Observer*; and three volumes of *The Looker-On*—an apposite title for a man who had decided his role was as nonparticipant. In Boston, ready to lecture at South Danvers, Melville bought *The Poetical Works of Andrew Marvell* (Boston, 1857), in which he scored this passage in "Upon the Hill and Grove at Billborow": "Learn here those humble steps to tread, / Which to securer glory lead." It had been a long time since he had heard of Krakens.

Melville understood before going to South Danvers that the Peabody Institute had been endowed in 1853 by a native of the town now long resident in London, George Peabody, the "very fine old fellow of fifty or thereabouts" who had found occasion to speak to him of Gansevoort "with much feeling" late in November 1849. In 1853, Peabody had practiced benevolence on a smaller and personal scale by hospitably entertaining Peter Gansevoort and Judge Lemuel Shaw in London. Nevertheless, even if Judge Shaw had just referred to his own happy memories of Peabody, Melville could hardly have been prepared to lecture in the Lyceum Hall with his back to a twelve-foot-high canvas centered in which was a full-length portrait of this biblical anomaly, a very wealthy and a very good man. Melville's fate was to experience momentous collisions of life roughly a decade apart. In 1839 he had sailed out the Narrows on his first voyage, jumping to obey unfamiliar orders while recalling his visit to Fort Tompkins with his father and his Uncle John, around 1828 or 1829, and contrasting his present condition with what might have been, if his father had not died so early and so deeply in debt. The most consequential collision of past and present he had yet experienced dated from 1849, when the New York wharf scene of 1839, Gansevoort seeing him off on his first voyage, was reenacted, Herman playing Gansevoort and Tom being Herman. Another such scene, perhaps as powerful, would occur in 1869, in Lenox. Melville was constitutionally vague about dates, recalling his Nantucket visit as sometime about 1850–53, looking at the Nelson statue in Liverpool in 1856 mindful of twenty years earlier (instead of seventeen and a few months), yet he experienced momentous collisions of times, places, and people in years he turned twenty, thirty, forty, fifty. He may have been aware of such an emerging pattern. Vague as he could be about dates, he was, after all, a sailor who on a ship packed with men had found private ways of asserting individuality and continuity, the way a child in a big family learns to do. In 1849 he had made a narrator confide a very private practice: "there is a particular day of a particular month of the year, which, from my earliest recollections, I have always kept the run of, so that I can even now tell just where I was on that identical day of every year past since I was twelve years old" (*White-Jacket*, ch. 42). Now, his reputation gone, defeated at every attempt to earn a living, Melville lectured under the kindly gaze of the man he had met in London when he was an internationally famous young author. (Melville was not done with the collisions of times involving this Massachusetts man: when the *Harper's Weekly* of 3 November 1866 appeared, he gazed at the depiction of the Lyceum Hall, the portrait dominating the great room.) Besides the South Danvers lecture on 14 February 1860 (fee, twenty-five dollars), Livingston's efforts led to Melville's lecturing at Cambridgeport a week later at the Dowse Institute (fee, fifty-five dollars), as an eleventh-hour substitute for Emerson, whose cancellation was announced in the Cambridge *Chronicle* of 11 February. That was the end of Melville's career as a lecturer, which Maria in 1854 had been sure would bring them "fame & fortune."

In New York Melville had learned perturbing news of an old acquaintance: Dr. Francis was at last being driven out of his beloved No. 1 Bond Street by the "encroachments of trade upon the upper part of the city," for a stove factory rose where the house of the Reverend Dr. Spring had stood, and "theatres disgorged nightly their crowds in the adjacent thoroughfare," Broadway, while "barbers, milliners, dentists, and boarding-house keepers, asserted squatter sovereignty upon this once select domain." (The widowed Mrs. Thurston had fled in 1854.) There was more perturbing news close at hand, for Allan must have informed Herman about his courtship of Jane Louisa Dempsey Randolph, that very wealthy woman with a concentration of property in lower Manhattan. The Real Estate Evaluation Records for Vesey Street, North Side, between Greenwich and Washington, shows her ("Jane Dempsey") as owning Numbers 74, 76, 78, 80, 82, and 84, valued at $53,000. The same records for 1860 identify J. Odell as lessee of all those properties. It is puzzling and suggestive that in 1858 Allan Melville and David E. Oak sued Elias Ponvert and his wife and Jane Louisa Dempsey's brother and his wife, John and Lavinia C. Dempsey, over a plot of land on Vesey Street between Greenwich and Washington, and that on 8 November 1859 Allan won the suit, gaining title to the property at the corner of Vesey and Greenwich, since in the meantime Oak's claims had been transferred to Allan. How this facilitated or complicated Allan's relationship with Jane Dempsey is not clear, but in 1890 John and Lavinia, children of the current John and Lavinia, sued to break her will, and succeeded, at least in part, in 1891.

Aghast when she heard of the engagement (whether or not knowing any details of the bride's marital history), Sarah Morewood wrote to George Duyckinck on 9 April 1860: "I am so sad to hear of Allan Melville's engagement to be married so soon—God help his dear little family. I am disappointed in Allan Melville—he is now only an acquaintance of the past." This was probably before she had a chance to see how disastrous a choice Allan had in fact made, at least for his daughters. The wedding took place in Philadelphia, on 18 April, at the Tenth Presbyterian Church, conducted by the Reverend H. A. Boardman, author of *The Bible in the Family: or, Hints on Domestic Happiness* (Philadelphia, 1859), a book that he may have presented to the bride. The minister may not have known that she had been married before and was divorced; certainly she would not have been permitted to marry Allan in New York City. The bride moved into the household at Twenty-sixth Street, counted afresh the number of stepdaughters still alive and underfoot, and promptly surveyed boarding schools in the city with the aim of disposing of the surplus, starting, of course, with the willful Milie, the eldest and most disposable. Come September, Milie and perhaps one or more of her sisters went into the care of Mrs. Hoffman on Thirty-ninth Street. Allan acquiesced in anything Jane wanted; having married a woman at least a little like his Uncle Herman's wife the first time, now he had married someone quite unlike anyone else in the family—pretentious, cold, selfish, domineering, ruthless, hedonistic, a woman who raised insensitivity to exponential heights, as a woman could do if she were, like Jane, almost fabulously wealthy, a multi-millionairess in modern monetary equivalents. All the Thurstons (including the Latherses) behaved magnanimously, keeping the interests of Allan and the girls in view, although Allan's former mother-in-law must have winced now and then at Jane's contempt for the modest property on which she (Mrs. Thurston) still held the mortgage. It took her three years, but Jane drove even Lizzie to the point of having to break out with a denunciation or suffer a bodily explosion. There was nothing good to say about Allan's second wife, and no one ever said it, except, much later, Uncle Peter's poor deceived daughter.

Tom sailed the *Meteor* into Boston on 28 April 1860. He went to Arrowhead as soon as he could, and apparently his mother came there rather than waiting for him to visit her in Gansevoort. Tom made himself universally welcome. At Pittsfield a local girl, Fanny Wright, sized him up, and during the next year, she would sometimes ask whether they ever heard "from *the big brother of Mr Melville's, the C-a-p-t-a-i-n,*" as Sarah told Tom on 23 June 1861. Perceived as the "big brother" because of his abounding health and vitality, Tom late in April or early in May extended an invitation to an invalid to accompany him as a passenger when the *Meteor* next sailed. The Massachusetts family was facing up to new circumstances too, and decisions were being made. After February there was no use pretending Melville could contribute to the support of his family by lecturing, and everyone remembered that his last book, *The Confidence-Man*, had earned him nothing. *The Isle of the Cross*, if Melville still had it, was not regarded as an asset (as it may have been as late as 1856), nor was any fragment that might have remained unpublished from the tortoise book. Unable to earn money by writing or lecturing, and too weak physically to run the farm, Melville in early May decided to sail with Tom on the next voyage of the *Meteor*—a voyage expected to be a circumnavigation of the globe. This time there was not even a pretense that he was going with the purpose of renewing his literary resources. He was going on a voyage to regain his health, and was quite prepared to take no thought for who would provide for Lizzie on the morrow: he did not have to, because his father-in-law would. On 11 June, after Melville sailed, the Pittsfield Valuation Book listed the Morewood acreage of 250 (value $9000) and $1000 in "Money" with taxes of $60; the Melville 80 acres (value $4000) and $1000 in "Money" with taxes of $60 also. George S. Willis was listed as owning 307 acres worth $40,000. The State Valuation Book for 1860 listed Herman Melville as tilling no more than one acre of land (excluding orchards); as having 25 acres of "upland mowing"; as harvesting 18 tons of hay from those acres; as having 42 acres of pasture land; as having 12 acres of woodland from which 75 cords of wood was harvested per acre; as having one horse; under the category "Amount of personal estates doomed" (a legal survival from the time of the Domesday Book) the amount set down was $1000, a pretty fiction.

 Melville's decision to go with Tom on his next voyage was a clear renunciation of the role of breadwinner: he would be leaving his wife and four children with no income except what she received from the trust fund her father had set up for her (enough to pay the taxes, but not much beyond that) and what her father would advance to her. Shaw could hardly have been more understanding and forgiving than he was in his long letter on 15 May, in which he declared himself "very glad" that Herman intended "to accept Thomas' invitation to go on his next voyage": "I think it affords a fair prospect of being of permanent benefit to your health, and it will afford me the greatest pleasure to do anything in my power to aid your preparation, and make the voyage most agreeable and beneficial to you." In summing up the motivations behind his earlier suggestions that Herman get legal documents together, Shaw now specified that for "a considerable time" the father-in-law and son-in-law (and now probably Lizzie as well) had had "under consideration, a settlement of the matter of the Pittsfield estate." It was with that settlement in view that Herman had paid Dr. Brewster's mortgage off early and acquired a grant deed from Brewster and proffered one to George Willis, then (not rushing matters, not using the mails) he had "handed" Shaw his deeds when the judge was in Pittsfield the previous September for his usual session in Lenox. Now the prospect of Melville's "early departure" rendered it proper and necessary to bring the subject to a definite conclusion. Shaw thereupon recapitulated the conspicuous instances in which he had advanced Melville money. First was the money for Herman's part of the payment for the house on Fourth Avenue in 1847: "You will recollect that when you proposed to purchase a house in N. York I advanced to you $2000." Second, without receiving any of that $2000 back, and indeed before the New York house was sold, Shaw advanced Melville another $3000 so he could purchase "the Brewster place" in 1850. Later, presumably in 1856 or later, perhaps as recently as 1858 or 1859, Shaw had made him a third loan of $500. For all three of these loans, for the total of $5500, Shaw had taken Melville's notes.

Before 1 March 1860, Melville had sold yet another portion of Arrowhead, apparently only a small portion (ten acres?), and had loaned the city of Pittsfield $600, which represented part or all of the proceeds. Shaw proposed to purchase the note from Herman "and then apply it to Elizabeth's use"; in case Herman might think this unfair, Shaw reminded him that the loans he had made could have earned by this time hundreds of dollars in interest. But in addition to the $5500, Shaw had advanced through Allan $1400 or $1500 in the fall of 1856, for Herman's "outfit" and the expenses of his tour, and Herman could think of "that sum as a set off against the note of $600," the proceeds of which, in any case, Shaw intended to appropriate "to its original use" — the purpose for which Herman had sold the small plot of land, namely "to build a barn," in which case it would "go to increase the value of the estate already Elizabeth's." Now Shaw offered to Nancy Wroe Melvill's nephew an even exchange: Shaw would cancel Herman's indebtedness to him in return for what was left of "the Brewster purchase"; once the estate was vested in Shaw, he would "execute a deed conveying the same in fee to Elizabeth," subject to Herman's "rights as her husband." Shaw would protect Herman's pride by trying to not to give "the business any more notoriety" beyond what might "arise from putting the deeds on record," a legal necessity.

Melville would then, for the first time since 1847, be out of debt (except for what he owed the Harpers, thanks to their charging him for their costs in the fire of 1853): "The effect of this arrangement will be to cancel and discharge all debt and pecuniary obligations of every description from you to myself. You will then leave home with the conscious satisfaction of knowing that you are free from debt; that if by a Providential dispensation you should be prevented from ever returning to your beloved family some provision will have been made at least for a home, for your wife and children." This document is known in the form of a transcript made at some later time by Samuel Shaw: sooner or later, within the family, Shaw's generosity had to be known, if not to become notorious. In accordance with Shaw's letter, Melville signed a document conveying to the judge "a certain tract of land," the remaining Arrowhead property. Elizabeth became party to the actions by paying her father one dollar. James Colt, who was winding up his administering of Priscilla's estate, would once again act as Shaw's lawyer in Pittsfield, and would willingly explain to Herman anything he was uncertain about. Everything would be expedited, everything would be legal, and Herman would never again be in a position to jeopardize Lizzie's safety even if some winsome fellow from Lansingburgh offered him a friendly loan. Having provided for his daughter's house if not for her support, Shaw was free to do what he had been unwilling to face under all the circumstances—to resign as chief justice of the Supreme Court of the commonwealth of Massachusetts, effective 21 August 1860. On 16 August the *Berkshire County Eagle* reported: "*Chief Justice Shaw* is on a visit to his daughter, Mrs. Herman Melvill of this town"—the first time he had been free to visit her in August rather than September, the time of his regular session in Lenox. He did not exercise such freedom again.

Melville's decision to sail on the *Meteor* with Tom precipitated a literary decision as well as the legal machinations, for he had a book of poetry ready for publication. A clue to the contents is that in *Timoleon* (1891) Melville included eighteen poems under the subheading "Fruit of Travel Long Ago," all poems set in the Mediterranean regions he had visited on his 1856–57 trip. One of these is "Venice," in which Melville played upon the "worm," the "little craftsman of the Coral Sea" who upbuilds his "marvellous gallery / And long arcade"; a prouder agent, man, proved the power of Pan when "Venice rose in reefs of palaces." Robert Browning's lurid poem of adulterous passion, "In a Gondola," had been widely available in the United States since Ticknor & Fields published their edition of his poetry late in 1849 (dated 1850). An offhand companion piece to Browning's poem, Melville's "In a Bye-Canal" is an account of temptation and resistance, an analogue to the story of Joseph and Potiphar's wife or more specifically Ulysses' and Aeneas's flights from the sirens. Here, as in "The Town-Ho's Story,"

Melville associated Lima and Venice as sexually corrupt cities. The speaker has faced dangers before:

> Fronted I have, part taken the span
> Of portents in nature and peril in man.
> I have swum — I have been
> 'Twixt the whale's black flukes and the white shark's fin;
> The enemy's desert have wandered in,
> And there have turned, have turned and scanned,
> Following me how noiselessly,
> Envy and Slander, lepers hand in hand.

"All this" high adventure, physical and psychological, is nothing to the danger of the woman's glance from the window down at him in a gondola in the bye-canal. Rather than sexual danger, most of the poems in "Fruit of Travel Long Ago" deal with artistic achievements or concepts. "The Parthenon" ends with the declaration that when the last marble tile was laid Aspasia said "Hist! — Art's meridian, Pericles!" This is the whole of "Greek Architecture": "Not magnitude, not lavishness, / But Form — the Site; / Not innovating wilfulness, / But reverence for the Archetype." Chances are, these poems were in the 1860 volume, more or less as they survive in manuscript, but one cannot know.

"Pausilippo (In the time of Bomba)" — sixth of the "Fruit of Travel" group — at some time was part of the long poem called "A Morning in Naples" or "An Afternoon in Naples" (later still, "Naples in the Time of Bomba"). "Pausilippo" was the episode concerning Silvio Pellico (1789–1854), the man who had been long kept a political prisoner for having written a patriotic ode construed as treasonous. The whole of the "Naples" poem as it then stood, including this section on Silvio but lacking a reference to Garibaldi, might well have been part of the 1860 *Poems*. The surviving manuscript shows that the ascription of the poem to the character Jack Gentian was an addition of the late 1870s, and nothing prevents one's taking the speaker as "Melville" or an invented character reenacting Melville's own adventures and elaborating his own thought processes as he went about Naples, looking from superb palaces to smoking Vesuvius, visible from the main square.

"A Morning in Naples" (sometimes titled "Afternoon in Naples") is a vignette of Melville's own travel, closely based on his journal and his memories. On 19 February 1857 he had pushed into the vast crowded Neapolitan streets that reminded him of Broadway until there was a show of armed force: "Palace — soldiers — music — clang of arms all over city. Burst of troops from archway. Cannon posted inwards." Two days later he visited the museum, and on leaving it had the adventure he put into the poem:

> Went in voiture to Cathedral of St. Januarius. Very fine. Thence a promiscuous drive through the older & less elegant part of town. Long narrow lanes. Arches, crowds. —
> *Tumblers in narrow street.* Blocked way. Balconies with women. Cloth on ground. They gave way, after natural reluctance. Merriment. Turned round & gave the most grateful & graceful bow I could. Handkerchiefs waved from balconies, goodhumored cries &c — Felt prouder than an Emperor. Shabby old hack, but good fellow, driver. —
> Wonderful number of shops &c. Crowds of idlers. Lazzaroni troublesome. Stopped in at curious little old chapel. Statue in net. — Dismissed hack at hotel. — Walked on mole. Military continually about streets.

What Melville made of this was in part a continuation of and variation on the thought processes he had ascribed to Amasa Delano in "Benito Cereno." The speaker as tourist seeking guilt-free charm of the picturesque is pulled in two directions — toward a denunciation of the displays of military power and an amelioristic acceptance that vineyards glow even if bayonets flash, that Nature's beauty makes living in Naples possible and even agreeable, even under an oppressive dictatorship. He cannot exclude doubts: perhaps the capering mountebanks are not displaying "mirth's true elation" but some "patched despair." Then Melville put the "burst of troops" from the journal into the poem as "Bomba's sortie," the palace-guard enacting an intimidating drill, replete with "martial din." His recurrent temptation is to surrender to the beauty, embodied in a red rose which a girl pins to his lapel, and dwell "no more on things amiss" such as the clanging of muskets on the pavement. He broods over Virgil, "here inurned / On Pausilippo, legend tells — / Here on the slope that pledges ease to pain" (Pausilippo meaning freedom from pain). This leads into a passage, so far imperfectly transcribed, on the world as two laureates knew it, Virgil and now Tennyson, a "Melancholy sphere" set in motion by some Deistic force ("Ruled by the primary impulse given — / Forever revolving on"). In this sphere "Opinion and vogue" are "recurring still," although some things wait long before recurring: "life's too brief to note some long returns." In this melancholy sphere wise unconsciousness is lord, and "reason, that gladdens not the wise, / Alarms the fool"; in this world there is more to fear from life than there is from death; and in this world "truth takes falsehood graft, and hence / Equivocal friend — ." Here the speaker checks his brooding. No wonder Virgil and Tennyson turn melancholy.

"A Morning in Naples" ("Naples in the Time of Bomba") is structured on the speaker's vacillation of moods, just as "Benito Cereno" is structured on Amasa Delano's. The speaker wants to surrender to the Picturesque without the tinge of present poverty and military oppression. Here the sirens, one named Parthenope, had lured Ulysses; now poets had made Parthenope a name for Naples, the alluring city. The "Siren's seat for pleasurists lies / Betwixt two threatening bombardiers, / Their mortars loaded, linstocks lit— / Vesuvius yonder—Bomba here." In any political uprising Bomba's batteries might be spiked, but who could seal up Vesuvius's vent reaching down toward hell? The narrator is unable to suppress his historical memory any more than he can suppress awareness of present military displays. A "flash of thought" carries him back to the Queen Joanna, the cool murderer of her husband, then that scene is replaced by an older one, Agrippina, the granddaughter of Augustus, who starved herself to death when "In cruel craft exiled from Rome / To gaze on Naples' sunny bay." Pulled as he is by the rose, the symbol of present beauty of life, the speaker is haunted by fearful images from history: "Spectres of Naples under Spain"; an "incensed Revolt" in the seventeenth century, led by Tomaso Aniello (Masaniello); and the Terror imported from France, so that beautiful and bountiful Naples became "Hell's cornucopia crammed with crime!" As Melville wrote this part, he included the lines published in *Timoleon* on Silvio, seized from his house, at night, never tried, imprisoned for many years and kept at hard labor, all because he wrote a "patriot ode / Construed as treason." How the complete poem ended is uncertain, since later Melville added a few lines on the conquest of Bomba's son by Garibaldi's Red Shirts, but what's clear is that the rose has dropped its petals even as the speaker carries it on his ride. When Melville saw Naples, it was not a siren: he saw Naples as St. Anthony, gyved, stung by pain, hung between two tittering hussies—political tyranny and physical beauty.

Poems (1860) may have included some of Melville's better poems. One may have been "The Age of the Antonines," printed in *Timoleon* (1891), for it looks back to a golden age such as the pilgrim lads from Williams College, Coan and Gulick, said Melville talked of in 1859: "While hope awaits Millenial years, / Though dim of late the signs, / Back to the past a glance be cast— / The Age of the Antonines!" On 31 March 1877 Melville asserted to Hoadley (perhaps facetiously, but perhaps seriously) that he had found the poem "the other day—came across it—in a lot of papers." The 1860 volume may have included "After the Pleasure Party" (the second poem in *Timoleon*), in which the principal character is a female astronomer like Maria Mitchell, who had made a strong impression on Melville in 1852 during the evening he and Shaw spent "with Mr. Mitchell the astronomer, & his celebrated daughter, the discoverer of comets." If the topic of the title of the poem is a clue to the composition, then one would look for a date in the late 1850s also, when some of Sarah Morewood's entertainments were magnificent, for example the one on 7 September 1855. Joe Smith revelled in describing how the costumes made "the shores of Melville Lake look quaint and gay," less like a somber American gathering than "those scenes of Italy, France and Spain, which charm us in painting and poetry," and when, in fact, the fete was cosmopolitan: "not only were the picturesque nations of Europe represented in their costumes, but natives of France, Spain, Italy and Germany, were among the party, and joined in its praises, as like the scenes of home." If anything, the 3 September 1856 picnic was grander, with the patriotic tent made by Moakly of Albany. These were not commonplace rustic gatherings — these were splendid affairs, evoking ducal or even regal comparisons.

The essential elements of the situation in "After the Pleasure Party" were available by 1858 or so. Melville had met Miss Mitchell in 1852, he had attended great pleasure parties half a mile away in 1855 and 1856, in 1857 he had seen superb vistas of the Mediterranean Sea, and he had encountered striking recent British examples of dramatic monologues or soliloquies such as those in Browning's *Poems* (Ticknor, Reed, & Fields, 1850) and *Men and Women* (Ticknor & Fields, 1856). Perhaps more important, Tennyson's *The Princess* was available in the Ticknor & Fields 1848 edition and the 1855 one (lacking some lines criticized by the first reviewers). Here the new poet laureate explored the topic of female education, specifically the challenge that "with equal husbandry / The woman were an equal to the man" (1.129–30), and the proposition that men hate "learned women" (1.442). Some of the names and images in *The Princess* and "After the Pleasure Party" are suggestively but not conclusively similar. There is a collision of Cupid and Uranian Venus: "The seal was Cupid bent above a scroll, / And o'er his head Uranian Venus hung" (1.238–39). Melville's poem begins with "Lines Traced Under an Image of Amor Threatening," Cupid warning virgins not to slight him. In Melville the name of the female astronomer is "Urania," but she is not Milton's or Wordsworth's muse. Melville's Urania prays to an "arm'd Virgin," the "Helmeted woman" Athena, and there is a bust of Pallas (Athena) in Tennyson's poem (1.219). (In *The Princess*, 1.131, is a woman "that arm'd / Her own fair head.") This is *The Princess* (3.283–85): "either sex alone / Is half itself, and in true marriage lies / Nor equal, nor unequal"; this is Melville: "For, Nature, in no shallow surge / Against thee either sex may urge, / Why hast thou made us but in halves— / Co-relatives?" Melville was thinking of Plato's *Symposium*, but also of *The Princess*, which dealt with the topic of "After the Pleasure Party"—educated women's repressed sexuality, the idea that "One's sex asserts itself." (Melville may have wondered if one line in *The Princess* was an allusion to him: "Cramp'd under worse than South-sea-isle taboo" [3.261].)

None of this speculation about "Naples" or "After the Pleasure Party" is conclusive. There is no particular reason to think the title of the section of

Timoleon has to mean old fruit of long-past travel as opposed to new fruit of old travels, except the unlikelihood that Melville, while writing *Billy Budd* and after working on *John Marr* and on much of what became *Timoleon*, would suddenly take it into his head to plunder the journal that everyone had assumed he would plunder profitably in 1857 and 1858. Nor is there any particular reason to think that only a young man like the author of *Typee* or (at the extreme limit) a man in his late thirties or early forties would be driven to write poems about sexual temptations and sexual anguish. In fact, Melville in the early 1870s wrote into *Clarel* some of his most complex sexual depictions. Yet when a large number of poems associated with long-ago travel are published late in life, some of them in a section called "Fruit of Travel Long Ago," as part of a grand erratic campaign aimed at cleaning accumulations out of a writing desk, the sensible thing to assume is that some of the longer and more complex pieces may have languished in the desk for a long time, especially when some of them demonstrably were taken out of the desk and worked on over a period of many years, especially when the author was engaged, in those last years, in a difficult, burgeoning, time-and-energy-consuming new project about a sailor named Billy Budd, perhaps fruit of fatherhood long ago.

The first known reference to the poems as a collection to be published is Melville's letter to Duyckinck, 21 May—starting with a casual reference to his brother, who had taken his second wife only the month before: "If you have met Allan lately he has perhaps informed you that in a few days I go with my brother Tom a voyage round Cape Horn. It was only determined upon a short time since; and I am at present busy, as you may imagine in getting ready for a somewhat long absence, and likewise in prepareing for type certain M.S.S." This led to a request for Duyckinck's editorial services in Melville's absence:

> Now may I with propriety ask of you, conditionally, a favor? Will you, upon the arrival of the M.S.S. in New York—that is, in the course of two weeks, or less—look over them and if they seem of a sort that you care to be any way concerned with, advice [advise] with Allan as to a publisher, and form of volume, &c.... In short, may I, without seeming too confident, ask you, as a veteran & expert in these matters, and as an old acquaintance, to lend something of an overseeing eye to the launching of this craft—the committing of it to the elements?

Evert's response, "a very welcome one—quite a wind from the feilds of old times" (as Melville called it in his next letter, 28 May), included an agreement to help see the poems into print.

The next day after he wrote Duyckinck, 22 May (Bessie's seventh birthday and perhaps the seventh anniversary of his completing *The Isle of the Cross*), Melville hastily jotted down what he labeled "Memoranda for Allan concerning the publication of my verses." This "Memoranda for Allan" constitutes the fullest instructions he had ever given for the publication of one of his works, as far as we know, and with the possible exception of *Clarel* or his last two volumes, *John Marr* and *Timoleon*, it is by far the most detailed set of instructions he was ever to give.

> 1 — Don't stand on terms much with the publisher — half-profits after expenses are paid will content me — — not that I expect much "profits" — but that will be a fair nominal arrangement....
>
> 2 — Don't have the Harpers. — I should like Appletons or Scribner — But Duyckinck's advice will be good here.
>
> 3 — The sooner the thing is printed and published, the better — The "season" will make little or no difference, I fancy, in this case.
>
> 4 — After printing, dont let the book hang back — but publish & have done.
>
> 5 — For God's sake don't have *By the author of "Typee" "Piddledee" &c* on the title-page.
>
> 6 — Let the title-page be simply,
>
> Poems
by
Herman Melville.
>
> 7 — Dont have any clap-trap announcements and "sensation" puffs — nor any extracts published previous to publication of book — Have a decent publisher, in short.
>
> 8 — Don't take any measures, or make inquiries as to expediency of an English edition simultaneous with the American — as in case of "Confidence-Man".
>
> 9 — In the M.S.S. each piece is on a page by itself, however small the piece.... Of course in printing two or more pieces will sometimes appear on the same page — according to length of pieces &c....
>
> 10 — The poems are divided into books as you will see; but the divisions are not *called* books — they are only numbered ...
>
> 11 — Anything not perfectly plain in the M.S.S. can be referred to Lizzie....
>
> 12 — Lizzie should by all means see the printed sheets *before* being bound, in order to detect any gross errors consequent upon misconstruing the M.S.S.

These twelve points reveal the seriousness with which Melville took the poetry he had been writing during the past two years or more. Most of the points are self-explanatory, but the reason he did not want the Harpers may have been that they had turned down poems he had submitted early in 1858, and in any case he held old resentments against the brothers, even aside from the high probability that because of his debt to them they would not agree to publish the poems. Numbers 11 and 12 take for granted that Lizzie could be trusted to read his handwriting accurately, and they constitute the earliest evidence that she was so intimately familiar with the poems that she could explain anything that was confusing and would have to be the one to exercise final judgment over the proofs.

Keenly aware of the insignificance of a volume of American poetry in a glutted market ("Of all human events, perhaps, the publication of a first volume of verses is the most insignificant"), Herman nevertheless admitted that it was "still of some concern to the author, —as these *Mem.* show," and left Lizzie, Allan, and Evert Duyckinck all aware of their responsibilities toward him and his poems. No one preserved a table of contents, however, so we are left to what deductions we can make about such matters as the numbered sections (not "called" books, the way the sections of, say, *Paradise Lost* are called books, but nevertheless *constituting* books in the sense of separate, unrelated sections). In the letter Melville wrote to Duyckinck on board the *Meteor* in Boston Harbor on 28 May, he explained that his wife would send "the parcel" of poems "in the course of a week or so—there remaining something to be finished in copying the M.S.S." His wife, he explained, had "interested herself a good deal in this matter," to the point that she seemed "to know more about it" than he did, "at least about the *merits* of the performance." George, he hoped, would also look over his "scribblings"—this he added before breaking off his "egotistic" requests. Constitutionally Melville loathed asking favors of anyone, as Maria had observed long before, so his "egotistic" placing of his poetry in the capable editorial hands of the Duyckincks reveals how momentous to him the publication of his *Poems* was.

Evert's acquiescence took the burden off Herman's mind: Lizzie could answer any questions of reading or design, Allan could handle all legal matters (more expeditiously than he had handled *The Confidence-Man*, since no English publication would have to be arranged), and the most professional literary man in New York would see *Poems* by Herman Melville into print. It was a done deal, and Melville would not have to suffer any of the annoyances of negotiating with publishers and correcting proofs. When he had reached London in 1857 *The Confidence-Man* was waiting for him, brought into print by the efforts of Allan and Nathaniel Hawthorne; now when he reached San Francisco his *Poems* would be waiting for him, brought into print by the efforts of Lizzie, Allan, and the Duyckincks. Melville would open his package from Lizzie, take out a decorous little volume (not in the hackneyed blue and gold binding); it would be a doubly precious little volume, since it would have traveled down the Caribbean to the Isthmus of Panama, across it and up the Pacific to San Francisco. On the shores where Sir Francis Drake was thought to have anchored his *Golden Hind* Melville could read his *Poems*, seeing them in print for the first time. This odyssey would be a fit initiation for some of the poems, if, as seems likely, the volume included poems based on his experiences in the Mediterranean. Nothing would go wrong: Poet would leave early and take the long way, *Poems* would leave late but take the shorter way, and Poet and *Poems* would reunite in San Francisco.

In the last days before sailing Melville probably had enough forethought to obtain from Orville Dewey a letter of introduction to Thomas Starr King (if not, Lizzie had one waiting for him in San Francisco). He had a confidential chat with Malcolm about the behavior that was expected of him during the year when he would be the man of the family, obedient to his mother, helping her all he could, and saving her trouble. Melville apparently laid fewer responsibilities on Stanwix's shoulders. He packed "a good lot of books," he wrote to Evert, and "plenty of old periodicals — lazy reading for lazy latitudes." Writing in a confidential tone, and feeling in a confidential mood, Melville nevertheless gave no indication that there was anything systematic in his choice of books for the voyage. Before departing, the brothers had an ambrotype taken at Davis & Co. in Boston, both in long dusters, Herman sitting half-sideways and Tom standing, face forward, alike in their dark hair and luxuriant beards, Tom a younger Herman. They were handsome men; Allan looked much like them; how had Gansevoort looked?

Melville left behind Pittsfield at its best, as Sarah Morewood wrote to George Duyckinck on 27 May: "The country is looking a very Eden of beauty just now — the fruit trees white & rosy with their promises for an Autumn harvest and the early sown grain, vegetables, grass, above the sod and thrifty as life and health can make them. I do not think I ever saw the green of the trees darker or fuller in leaf than they are just now." She asked why he had not come up with her husband last week, adding: "A trip here would do you good I am very sure and you know that you are as welcome as a brother at any time you choose to visit us" — as a very close brother. She told him about Melville's trip, giving the expected duration, "a year's voyage." She also relayed the news that Dr. Holmes's "nice house" had been bought by a heartless Mrs. Hart ("tis a hard case for we are worse off than if we had no neighbours in that direction"). Further news involved an improvement in the over-the-hill route to the Melvilles: "We have a road through our own grounds to Arrowhead & shall not therefore often pass the Doctor's old home" — that is, by going north and then east through the village before turning south past the Holmes place to get to Arrowhead. She lamented losses: "Alas for the changes of time they drag our feelings up to the stake and make us own the change."

One of Melville's remarks to Duyckinck on 28 May reveals how he thought about himself just then: "I anticipate as much pleasure as, at the age of fourty, one temperately can, in the voyage I am going." The auspices at least were "very happy auspices so far as ship & Captain is concerned." Wind caught in his sails as he expatiated: "A noble ship and a nobler Captain — & he my brother. We have the breadth of tropics before us, to sail over twice; & shall round the world. Our first port is San Francisco, which we shall probably make in 110 days from Boston. Thence we go to Manilla — & thence, I hardly know where." He "devoutly" wished Evert were "going along" — a reminder of the time in 1849 when he had stirred Evert into momentary thoughts of joining him in a voyage to England. He continued with some echoes of his last lecture: "The prime requisite for enjoyment in sea voyages, for passengers, is 1st health — 2^{d} good-nature. Both first-rate things, but not universally to be found. — At sea a fellow comes out. Salt water is like wine, in that respect." When the *Meteor* weighed anchor on 30 May, George Griggs and Fanny came out into the harbor with Tom and Herman, then Herman assisted her into the tugboat before it went ahead to tow the *Meteor*, so she and George watched them to the end. Then Herman entrusted himself to his baby brother, "Commander" of the ship. He promptly began a shipboard journal, in which he recorded that S. Endicott Peabody (the co-owner of the *Meteor*) stayed on board and lunched with them in the cabin. It was after one when the pilot and tug left, and the brothers waved their handkerchiefs to Fanny. That night the merchant sailor, whaler, ordinary seaman, and author of *Moby-Dick* was "Quite sea-sick," and for more than a week suffered from "seasick qualmishness."

[19]

An Epic Poet on the *Meteor*
May–October 1860

> Rely upon it, subjects for genius are not wanting; genius itself, steadily and perseveringly directed, is the thing required. But genius and energy alone are not sufficient; courage and disinterestedness are needed more than all. Courage to withstand the assaults of envy, to despise the ridicule of mediocrity . . . . An heroic mind is more wanted in the library or the studio, than in the field.
>
> "Homer, Dante, and Michael Angelo," in Archibald Alison's volume of *Modern British Essayists*, which Melville bought in 1849

MELVILLE MADE A FEW entries in his journal on the *Meteor*, beginning with the 30 May description of sailing down Boston Harbor at half past ten in the morning. He made no mention in the journal of his thoughts on the ship's figurehead of Atalanta picking up the golden apples, fit subject for moralizing though it was, the swift princess delaying to take on cargo. On 8 June he summarized: "During the past days cloudy, foggy rainy weather, with good breeze generally, and sailing Eastward, or little south of East"; then the sky had turned clear and bright. The crew sent up the skysail yard, to his delight, and were "busy in rigging &c" but this time he did not at once show off his skills. At thirty-seven he had brooded about what sort of joy was possible at his age, and he had been extremely cautious in what he said to Duyckinck about anticipating pleasure at the age of forty. Now he was nearly forty-one, and had been intermittently sick for almost a decade. Nevertheless, by 9 June, in the fine weather, "growing warmer each day," he felt "very sensibly improving in appetite &c," and paid more attention to what he could see over the rail ("flying-fish, weed, Portuguese-men-of-war, and several sail lately").

On 9 June an English brig from Pernambuco bound for Liverpool blundered down across their bow, and for a time was locked with the *Meteor*, "ripping & tearing her sails" and damaging her "fore-yard & main" in a scene reminiscent of *Israel Potter*. The dangerous moments were followed by bathetic explanations for dereliction of duty involving alcohol:

At the moment of collision the Steward of the brig being in jeopardy, leaped aboard of us, and, the vessels separating, remained aboard, till taken off by boat sent from the brig. He told me that the Captain was asleep in his berth when we came together, and added the Mate was half-blind &c. It was altogether an instance of the grossest heedlessness possible on the part of the brig—quite unaccountable.—When it was plain that she purposed crossing our bow, and that it was out of the question for her to do so, Tom at once put his helm up, and by so doing, we came off with less damage than could have been anticipated.

Such drunkenness on duty was a failing of the brothers' nautical cousins, Thomas Wilson Melvill most spectacularly in 1832 and Guert Gansevoort (most recently on 18 September 1856, in Mare Island, California, when Captain David Glasgow Farragut suspended him for being drunk at eleven in the morning). Melville as passenger had experienced, within two weeks of sailing, his first and last collision at sea.

The next day, 10 June, Melville went on deck in light clothes, always a delight for him, and a reminder of the other times he had sailed into warmth, most recently how he had exultantly thrown open his coat after the *Egyptian* reached the Mediterranean and was in sight of the Spanish coast. Four days "in the Doleful Doldrums" united the whole ship's crew in misery ("given up to melancholly, and meditating darkly on the mysteries of Providence") and gave Melville a chance to identify with them. A wind came and made everyone feel better. Taking the trades, they crossed the northern tropic, and on the night of 17 June he saw "the Southern Cross—the North Star sensibly sinking." Cheered by the unvarying fine weather he went "out to flying-jib-boom end" for a "Glorious view of the ship"—the first time we know of his using the term "glorious view" since the Mediterranean trip, although he may have used it in some of his Berkshire outings. Down from the flying-jib-boom end, he spent "the day dipping into the 'Quarterlies,'" finding "methodical reading out of the question." He took stock of his bodily condition: "Not yet completely settled in my stomach. Head all right, tho'."

At the end of June "the Carpenter made a set of chessmen" (Melville recorded this with no indication that his resourceful Carpenter in *Moby-Dick* was vibrating in his memory), then he and Tom began playing a game or two regularly every evening. On 21 July they were so far south that they put a stove up for Herman, and when he started a fire in it the next morning he felt "Quite comfortable & domestic in the cabin now," and was keeping up the routine of daily chess games—a curious business, playing opposite Tom, like facing a rejuvenating mirror. His forty-first birthday was marked by a sudden gale from the east-south-east, "with snow and hail; continuing three days," according to the San Francisco *Daily Evening Bulletin* (13 October). In early August they experienced "several gales, with snow, rain, hail, sleet, mist, fog, squalls, head-winds, refractory stove, smoky cabin, drunken ship &c &c &c"—not great weather for reading. Days became "short—but not sweet": it was winter. Despite the brevity of the day as they passed through the Straits of Le Maire, Melville had "a fine view of the land on both sides": "Horrible snowy mountains—black, thunder-cloud woods—gorges—hell-landscape. Signaled ship 'Black Prince' from New York. — There are three on the Sick List. The man hurt by the sea—one with a fever—the third, a boy with general debility." The next day, 8 August, he thought he might not be able to see anything at all of the coasts, but just before sunset, "in a squall, the mist lifted & showed, within 12 or fifteen miles the horrid sight of Cape Horn— (the Cape proper)—a black, bare steep cliff, the face of it facing the South Pole;—within some miles were other awful islands & rocks—an infernal group." Tom tried "to weather Cape Horn, as sloops weather Castle Garden Point N.Y. —but were headed off," and tacked to the southward.

In the terrible gale of the next day there was a catastrophe, blamed on a sailor's having gone aloft wearing constricting clothing in an attempt to keep warm:

> Ray, a Nantucketer, about 25 years old, a good honest fellow (to judge from his face & demeanor during the passage) fell this morning about day-break from the main topsail yard to the deck, & striking head-foremost upon one of the spars was instantly killed. His chum, Macey (Fisher) of Nantucket, I found alone in the upper cabin sitting over the body—a harrowing spectacle. "I have lost my best friend", said he; and then "His mother will go crazy—she did not want to let him go, she feared something might happen." —It was in vain to wash the blood from the head—the body bled incessantly & up to the moment of burying; which was about one o'clock, and from the poop, in the interval between blinding squalls of sharp sleet.

Tom conducted the ceremony before burial at sea, reading "some lines from the prayer-book" before "the plank was sloped, and—God help his mother." During the ceremony Herman and the rest stood "covered with Sou-Westers or Russia caps & comforters," miserable "under the lee of the reefed spanker where the wind eddies so"—all except Macey, Ray's chum, "who stood bareheaded" in his grief. On 1 September Melville retold this whole episode in a letter to young Malcolm, personalizing it ("Well, all at once, Uncle Tom saw something falling through the air, and then heard a thump, and then,—looking before him, saw a poor sailor lying dead on the deck.... Then Uncle Tom, as Captain, read a prayer out of the prayer-book, and at a given word, the sailors who held the plank tipped it up, and immediately the body slipped into the stormy ocean, and we saw it no more.") Melville continued in a moralizing vein: "This sailor's name was Ray. He had a friend among the crew; and they were both going to California, and thought of living there; but you see what happened."

Melville's private response the day after the death of Ray was recorded in an extended meditation on the indifference of nature and the indifference of human beings who must go on as usual after such calamities:

> — Calm: blue sky, sun out, dry deck. Calm lasting all day — almost pleasant enough to atone for the gales, but not for Ray's fate, which belongs to that order of human events, which staggers those whom the Primal Philosophy hath not confirmed. — But little sorrow to the crew — all goes on as usual — I, too, read & think, & walk & eat & talk, as if nothing had happened — as if I did not know that death is indeed the King of Terrors — when thus happening; when thus heart-breaking to a fond mother — the King of Terrors, not to the dying or the dead, but to the mourner — the mother. — Not so easily will his fate be washed out of her heart, as his blood from the deck.

The passage echoes the conversation between Amasa Delano and Benito near the end of "Benito Cereno," with the difference that the human beings who go about their ordinary affairs "as if nothing had happened" are not exposed as somewhat less than human: they are simply human, and it is simply human of the fond mother, when she learns the news, to be less philosophical than Melville and the crew (excepting Macey), less able to forget that death is indeed the King of Terrors.

The description of washing Ray's blood from the deck is the last journal passage that survives, and probably the last Melville wrote. During the long sail into warm weather up the west coast of the Americas to San Francisco, from mid-August to mid-September, Melville took time to write some letters home, probably expecting to send at least one to Lizzie by Pony Express (new that year, an almost two-thousand-mile route between San Francisco and St. Joseph, Missouri). He expected to send the others by the less expensive Overland Mail and still others by the much cheaper Panama-route steamers rather than to entrust them to any homeward-bound ship, as he had needed to do nineteen years before in these waters. There survives the long letter he wrote to Malcolm by installments and a letter to Bessie, sent by Overland Mail. These provide a disproportionate bulk of the evidence about the trip as well as the sort of tone he took as a father. To Bessie he gave a description of the seabirds that followed the ship from the Cape to the warmer latitudes, where they left off — birds as big as chickens, fluttering, cackling, chasing after scraps thrown overboard, never lighting on the ship, and homeless, unless they lived on "some wild rocks in the middle of the ocean." Supposing that Malcolm had been following his route on the map, he offered a special privilege: "my *globe* were better—so you get Mama to clean it off for you." The route from Boston to San Francisco, he assured Malcolm, who was big enough to appreciate humorous understatement, was "further than from the apple-tree to the big rock."

By sailing at the end of May, Melville had missed the fruit season, and now visualized Bessie having had "a good many walks on the hill," and having picked the wild strawberries. He drew a picture of the way Bessie should go up the hill with Fanny, hand in hand, so Fanny would not fall. He continued to put more serious information into the letter to Malcolm, on 16 September adding a description of a gam:"The other day we saw a whale-ship; and I got into a boat and sailed over the ocean in it to the whale-ship, and stayed there about an hour. They had eight or ten of the 'wild people' aboard. The Captain of the whaleship had hired them at one of the islands called Roratonga. He wanted them to help pull in the whale-boat when they hunt the whale." This was the last time he was ever aboard a whaler (unless an anomalous one washed up at the docks of Manhattan years later and came under his inspection).

On the Line, that day, Melville reminded Malcolm of his parting injunctions and exhorted him: "Now is the time to show what you are—whether you are a good, honorable boy, or a good-for-nothing one. Any boy, of your age, who disobeys his mother, or worries her, or is disrespectful to her—such a boy is a poor shabby fellow; and if you know any such boys, you ought to cut their acquaintance." This was very much in the manner Gansevoort had exhorted him and Allan, as evidenced by the letters the more dutiful Allan preserved, such as this one of 11 April 1840, when Gansevoort was in New York and Allan in Albany: "I am confident that during Mammas visit you will exert yourself to render the time agreable, & to perform all those little services & pay those attentions which should in themselves be a source of great pleasure to an affectionate son, & right feeling gentleman." How Mackey received his father's equally formal but sterner moralizing wholly depends upon the relationship Melville had maintained with him over the past years. Mackey may well have been morally certain that his father knew he was no such shabby fellow and was only whimsically and quite unnecessarily reminding him of the duties of the young fellow who was temporarily the man of the house. Melville was open about his fatherly love: "Now, my Dear Malcolm, I must finish my letter to you. I think of you, and Stanwix & Bessie and Fanny very often; and often long to be with you. But it can not be, at present. The picture which I have of you & the rest, I look at sometimes, till the faces almost seem real." At some point on the voyage Melville drew a picture of Arrowhead from a vantage point across the road, south of the

Holmes house, and annotated it: "Drew this at sea one afternoon on deck — & then in the calm. — Made me feel as if I was there, almost — such is the magic power of a fine Artist. — Be it known I pride myself particularly upon 'Charlie' & the driver. — It is to be supposed that I am in the carriage; & the figures are welcoming me."

During the early weeks of the voyage Melville's reading was desultory, as he noted in his journal. On the day they crossed the Line, 29 June, he inscribed to Tom *Sketches of Life and Character*, by Alexander Campbell (Edinburgh, 1842), a fair indication that he had just finished reading it, just as the almost total absence of marks indicates that he found little of value in it. In July he read some or all of *The Marble Faun*, which Sarah Morewood had given him as a going-away present (the time being long past when Hawthorne had Ticknor & Fields include Melville among those to receive a presentation copy). He ignored most of his friend's inept art criticism but took issue with the assertion in chapter 12 that "Perugino was evidently a devout man": "On the contrary, if I remember right, he is said, in 'Lives of the Painters,' to have been a jeerer at all religion." (He had made good use of Duyckinck's loan-volumes.) In his youth Melville apparently had conducted piratical forays into books, boarding them and plundering them, reading and absorbing so fast that he seldom was witnessed, as Gansevoort often was, with book in one hand and pen in the other for notetaking. As far as we know, he never possessed anything like a physical *Index Rerum*, but instead relied on a retentive memory and repeated forays to keep phrases in mind. He had become capable of the sort of systematic reading the family had associated with Gansevoort, and he had time to accomplish it.

Once his qualmishness subsided, and once Cape Horn had been rounded and left to the south, Melville could not only indulge in lazy reading in lazy latitudes, but could read methodically, purposefully. Besides many old quarterlies, he took with him, as he had told Evert Duyckinck, a good lot of books, being free to carry all he wanted, since once they were installed in his cabin they could stay there as the *Meteor* sailed around the world, or to Calcutta and back to Boston or New York. There must have been odd items among them, carried aboard for incidental reasons, as the timely Hawthorne volume was, but he had exercised a rigorous selection policy. This time rather than stuffing a shirt or two into his old carpetbag and heading to Cape Horn and the Pacific he had taken a small library of great poetry, classical epic poetry in English translation, modern European poetry in translation, and English poetry with an emphasis on the epic or very long poem. Some of these works he had already read with great care over a period of a decade or more, some he had owned for at least two years and may or may not yet have worked through. Enough of these books survive, with notations made during the voyage, so that we can be sure he was not, for instance, steeping himself in contemporary fiction, and also know something of the sequence and intensity of his reading.

Acutely conscious of the grandeur of this episode in his life, which he thought would be a circumnavigation of the globe, Melville relocated himself even in books already inscribed with his name and town (such as the Milton *Poetical Works*, already inscribed "H. Melville / N. Y. 1849"). He displayed his epic mood by repeatedly locating himself grandly in the world: "Cape Horn" — "Pacific Ocean" — "Gulf of Mexico." In his father's eight-volumes-in-four set of Spenser he marked in the upper left front flyleaf of at least two volumes "C. H. 2." (The convention was to designate this voyage "Cape Horn 2" although he had just made his third rounding of the Cape.) Mindful of the fact that he was headed for Indian waters, if not specifically to the port of Calcutta, he took Thomas Duer Broughton's *Selections from the Popular Poetry of the Hindoos* (London, 1814), writing on the recto of the front flyleaf in pencil: "C. H. 2." In his copy of Pierre Béranger's *Songs* (Philadelphia: Carey & Hart, 1844) he wrote: "Pacific Ocean / Sep 4th 1860 / 19 S.L." In his copy of Wordsworth's poems he wrote: "Pacific Ocean, Sep. 14th 1860 / 5° 60″ N.L." In the set of Milton he wrote on the flyleaf of the first volume "C. Horn 1860" and in the second volume "Pacific Ocean / N. L. 15° / Sep. 21th 1860." In a copy of Dante he wrote "Pacific Ocean / Sunday Afternoon / Sep 22 1860." In a copy of Schiller's *Poems and Ballads* (Leipzig: Tauchnitz, 1844) by the last stanza of "To Emma" he wrote: "Sept 25th 1860 / North Pacific." On the front flyleaf of the first volume of Chapman's translation of excerpts from Homer, Hesiod, Musaeus, and Juvenal (the set of Chapman that George Duyckinck had given him in 1858), Melville wrote "C. H. 2." On the front flyleaf of the first volume of the *Iliad* in the same set he inscribed "C. H. 2."; in the front flyleaf of the second volume he wrote "'Meteor & Derby'" and "Cape Horn 2." On the front flyleaf of the first volume of Chapman's *Odysseys* he wrote "Pacific Ocean / Oct 3d 1860 / 700 miles from San Francisco / C H 2." On 15 October while he was in San Francisco he wrote the date in his copy of *Songs of England. The Book of English Songs*, edited by Charles Mackay (London, 1857), which he may have brought with him or may have acquired there. Returning to his copy of Wordsworth's poems, he annotated it "Gulf of Mexico Nov 6th 1860 / Steamer 'North Star.'" These particular books which he marked during the voyage cannot be the only volumes he took with him: others must have been destroyed, some may survive with no record that they went round the Horn, and some may survive unrecognized, as the Wordsworth was until the 1970s, the Milton until the 1980s, and the Spenser until the 1990s.

One clue to what else Melville carried comes from his repeatedly making cross-references between writers he had with him, such as Milton and Spenser, Wordsworth and Spenser. This practice suggests that his frequent citations of lines from Pope's Homer in his annotations in books he had with him (for instance, putting in the pages of Chapman's Homer some of Pope's renderings of particular lines) means that he had that volume of the Harper's Classical Library with him too. In the Dante he noted a variant rendering of a line by John Carlyle, although in this case there is no other evidence that he had further knowledge of the Carlyle translation. Melville was in the habit of reading a translation of an epic poem with a second translation at hand. He may have had with him his Classical Library copy of Dryden's translation of Virgil's *Aeneid*. On the basis of his marginalia that seems to date from the voyage, it is likely that he had translations of Tasso and Ariosto. He may have had with him Chaucer (perhaps in the 1835 expurgated, modernized edition he picked up at some time). He refers to all six of these authors in his annotations in some of the volumes he demonstrably took.

In marginalia possibly dating from this voyage Melville refers to Byron, Keats, and Poe, and it is possible he had some of their poetry with him. It is hard to imagine that he traveled with no Shakespeare, although the good set he bought in 1849 does not bear any indication that he had it along. (Tom might have had his own Shakespeare on board.) Melville knew Joel Barlow's *The Columbiad*, if only from Francis Jeffrey's *Edinburgh Review* article (October 1809), included in Melville's set of *Modern British Essayists*. Jeffrey had not been impressed by the idea that the United States ought to be celebrated in epic poetry since epic poetry had often been the earliest "production of national genius." As he coolly pointed out, "though the American *government* be new, the *people* is in all respects as old as the people of England." Allan Melvill had picked a rose from Jeffrey's garden for Maria, and Barlow had felt the Scotsman's thorns: "Mr Barlow, we are afraid, will not be the Homer of his country; and will never take his place among the enduring poets either of the old or of the new world." Jeffrey had offered a personal opinion which Melville (like Tennyson and Browning) was prepared to ignore: "If it will be any comfort to Mr Barlow, we will add, that we doubt very much whether *any* long poem of the Epic character will ever again be very popular in Europe." This is the place where Jeffrey added that men certainly endured long poems "with more patience of old, than they do now."

Melville may have carried with him or recently have looked at the epic by John Quincy Adams, *Dermot MacMorrogh, or, The Conquest of Ireland: An Historical Tale of the 12th Century: in Four Cantos* (Boston: Carter & Hendee, 1832), for he referred to it in an annotation in the Milton, quoted below. Melville may have looked over a number of such American epics, not excluding the *Fredoniad*, which he mentioned in his essay on Hawthorne, as he thought about the shape a long serious American poem might take. His only known copy of Camoëns (London: Carpenter, 1824) he dated 1867, but he had heard parts of the *Lusiads* from the lips of Jack Chase. On a great clipper ship commanded by his brother Thomas, a veteran of several mercantile voyages to the Orient, Melville would have been in the mood to appreciate more than ever Camoëns's epic poem about Vasco da Gama's 1497–98 voyage around Africa to India, a celebration of the birth of modern commerce particularly significant in the light of the new California commerce. He might have had his copy of Ossian, James Macpherson's *Fingal, An Ancient Epic Poem* (London, 1762), which he had bought in 1848 and still remembered well in March 1862, as he showed in markings in Hazlitt's *Lectures on the English Comic Writers* and *Lectures on the English Poets* (2 vols. in 1; New York: Derby & Jackson, 1859). There he underlined Hazlitt's remark that Ossian "is even without God in the world" and wrote in the top margin: "True: no gods, I think, are mentioned in Ossian," and applauded a passage in which Hazlitt praised Ossian: "I am rejoiced to see Hazlitt speak for Ossian. There is nothing more contemptable in that contemptable man (tho' good poet, in his department) Wordsworth, than his contempt for Ossian. And nothing that more raises my idea of Napoleon than his great admiration for him. — The loneliness of the spirit of Ossian harmonized with the loneliness of the greatness of Napoleon."

This biography may well flush more of Melville's books out of hiding, perhaps even books he carried on this voyage. In the present state of knowledge, it is safe to generalize that aside from the "old periodicals" he carried in abundance, the books Melville brought along were mainly volumes of poetry, and often epic poems or else very long poems (such as *The Excursion*, contained in his one-volume Wordsworth). And now we can be fairly sure what he meant by referring to "methodical reading." He was giving himself an intense course in the interconnections between earlier and later Western poetry, and especially English poetry.

Melville had read so much poetry, and read it so attentively, that familiar lines set off alarm signals when he came across sources for them or echoes of them. He could by now have lectured, lovingly, on a kind of indebtedness for which no one went to debtors' prison (as his Uncle Thomas had done). In his Spenser he copied the tribute from "The Passionate Pilgrim," assuming it was by Shakespeare, was elsewhere reminded of Spenser's tribute to "Dan Chaucer" the *"well of English undefyled,"* and noted passages that had influenced several later poets. (This set of Spenser is the only known extant place where Melville wrote Poe's name; he gave his wife his edition of Poe on New Year's Day 1861; it was accidentally destroyed in the twentieth century.) In reading Wordsworth's *The Excursion* he noticed a debt and copied lines from

Spenser for comparison: "Sleepe after toyle, port after stormie seas, / Ease after warre, death after life does greatly please"—exactly the reading in his father's copy, except for his omission of a comma after "life." Elsewhere he saw a similarity between something in Wordsworth's "Character of the Happy Warrior" and a line from Schiller's *Don Carlos*, "'Keep true to the dream of thy youth'." In reading "Laodamia" Melville turned a criticism of Wordsworth against Dr. Johnson for tautology back on Wordsworth, remembering something he had read in Hazlitt's *The Spirit of the Age*. In the Milton volumes Melville marked comparisons to Virgil, Tasso, Ariosto, Dante, Johnson, Shakespeare, Campbell, Lucan, Sir Thomas Browne, Byron, Spenser, Plutarch. Into his Dante he inscribed a quotation from Walter Savage Landor, was reminded of Blake (and Botticelli), and on a free leaf in the back he jotted down several lines and the initials "J. Q. A."—apparently not from *Poems of Religion and Society* (1848). Adams as a poet was on his mind.

As scholar-like as comparing two translations was, Melville was not reading in order to acquire knowledge for its own sake: his evident purpose in reading epics of Western civilization was to learn how to write great poetry in his own time, perhaps even to write epic poems of his own, despite Jeffrey's warning. Any study of the demand that Americans produce epic poems would have to deal with the magazine and newspaper reception of American poems such as *Evangeline* (1847), *The Golden Legend* (1851), and *Hiawatha* (1855). Such a study would treat seriously, not with contempt, American aesthetic treatises and manifestos, American long poems, and American reviews of those poems published in the 1840s and 1850s and later decades in American newspapers and magazines. Influential American literary people gradually stopped looking for the great work of American literature to come in the form of a long poem and began looking for the great American novel, but no literary historian has yet pinpointed the year, or even the decade, when that shift occurred. The date may be a good deal later than the time when critics began self-consciously watching for the great American novel (as J. W. DeForest did in the *Nation* in January 1868). Somewhere there is a turning point, after which more of the best authorities looked for the great American masterpiece to come in the form of a novel rather than in an epic poem—but it wasn't in the 1840s or the 1850s, and it may not have been in the 1860s. At the time Melville sailed on the *Meteor*, fewer ordinary British and American readers were reading the long poems by Spenser, Milton, once-popular eighteenth-century writers like Thomson, even Scott's beloved *The Lady of the Lake* (stretches of which Gansevoort had memorized) and Byron's long poems, but critics and the most devoted common readers of literature were still willing and even eager to read long poems. People were still willing, in short, to come to poetry for their highest literary experiences. Melville began, as far as we know, writing short poems as a way of learning his craft, but the nature of the books he carried on the *Meteor* suggests that by then his ambition was to write at least one epic poem.

Melville may have adopted some ideas from editors of the poetry he was reading, as he often did, paying close attention to what they said in their biographical and critical material and testing everything against the poets themselves. Melville read carefully Milton's justification "Of that Sort of Dramatic Poem which is Called Tragedy," his preface to *Samson Agonistes*, absorbing the idea that "Heretofore men in highest dignity have laboured not a little to be thought able to compose a tragedy": "Of that honour Dionysius the elder was no less ambitious, than before of his attaining to the tyranny. Augustus Caesar also had begun his Ajax, but unable to please his own judgment with what he had begun, left it unfinished. Seneca, the philosopher, is by some thought the author of those tragedies, (at least the best of them,) that go under that name." Melville put an X in the margin by the passage about Augustus's leaving his tragedy about Ajax unfinished and at the bottom of the page adduced a contrary example from the history of the young American Republic: "J. Q. A. might have followed his example." Melville knew Adams's *Dermot MacMorrogh* well enough to have brooded both over the high intention of the man from Quincy and his failure. Melville read Michael Drayton's praise of Chapman's translation of the *Georgics* of Hesiod:

> CHAPMAN, we find, by the past-prized fraught,
> What wealth thou dost upon this land confer,
> Th' old Grecian prophets hither that hast brought,
> Of their full words the true interpreter;
> And by thy travall strongly hast exprest
> The large dimensions of the English tongue.

Melville put a check mark by this last line, identifying a hope for himself as a poet. He checked and underlined "To build with level of my lofty stile" in Spenser's "The Ruins of Rome" and wrote at the foot of the page, "Build the lofty rhyme / Milton."

In Richard Hooper's introduction to the *Iliad* he drew a box around the word "passion," underlined "the all in all in poetry" and put brackets around this entire sentence: "But passion, the all in all in poetry, is everywhere present [in Chapman's translation], raising the low, dignifying the mean, and putting sense into the absurd." He boxed a reference to Chapman's "primitive power." He was strongly interested in this sentence:

When we consider the subtle influence of poetry upon the rising spirits of the age, it tempts me to hazard the speculation that, if Chapman's noble paraphrase had been read instead of Pope's enervating monotony, and as extensively, the present class of general readers would not only have been a more poetical class — as the fountain-head from the rock is above the artificial cascade in a pleasure-ground — but a finer order of human beings in respect of energy, love of nature at first-hand, and faith in their own impulses and aspirations.

Melville drew three vertical lines along "subtle influence of poetry upon the rising spirits of the age" and underlined those words, and he underlined from "but a finer order" on through the rest of the sentence. Far from remaining in his state of alienation from the contemporary world, Melville was now thinking of how through poetry he might arouse "a finer order of human beings," at least among the English-reading world.

In going to the best authorities to find out how to write a great poem, Melville was using not only editors but essayists. His old periodicals (which he specified were the "Quarterlies") were his main source for literary criticism and what we would call literary theory. Most likely he was referring not only to individual volumes of the *Edinburgh Review* and other periodicals but also a set of compilations *from* the quarterlies which he had owned since 1849, his *Modern British Essayists*, a distillation of the best criticism of the best critics of his age: Thomas Babington Macaulay, Archibald Alison, Sydney Smith, John Wilson (Christopher North), Thomas Carlyle, Francis Jeffrey, James Stephen, Thomas Noon Talfourd, and James Mackintosh; possibly his set also included a volume of Sir Walter Scott's essays. The type in his set was painfully small, but somehow he managed to read widely in the volumes, over a period of many years.

The Archibald Alison volume in *Modern British Essayists* contained "The Copyright Question," originally published in the January 1842 *Blackwood's Magazine*, and of obvious paramount interest to any American author. Melville had probably read the essay repeatedly, judging by the way he echoed a section of it in the essay he wrote on Hawthorne's *Mosses from an Old Manse* in August 1850. He found in Alison an imperative that England not content itself with the works of Milton, Shakespeare, Johnson, and Scott but must "prolong the race of these great men, or her intellectual career will speedily come to a close." Alison saw himself stranded in a modern England where "the whole talent of the nation is directed to periodical literature, or works of evanescent interest," with the consequent degradation of the national character. The present danger was not merely the "gradual extinction of the higher and nobler branches of our literature" but the "termination of the more elevated class of works in history, philosophy, and theology, which are calculated and are fitted to guide and direct the national thought." Standing against the tide of mediocrity are the "master-spirits" who for good or for evil "communicated their own impress to the generation which succeeded them." (The term "master-spirits," which Melville used in his essay on Hawthorne, derived from *Julius Caesar*, but his use of it may have been suggested by Alison's application of it to great geniuses who are too profound to be appreciated by their own times.) Alison enunciated a distinction between popular writing and "profound" writing. ("it is no longer necessary for an author to make himself profound before he writes"): "if we look abroad in France, where the reading public is much less numerous than in England, a more subtle and refined tone is prevalent in literature; while in America, where it is infinitely larger, the literature is incomparably more superficial."

The last essay in the Alison volume, "Homer, Dante, and Michael Angelo," from the January 1845 *Blackwood's*, concluded that great subjects remain for treatment:

> Nature is inexhaustible; the events of men are unceasing, their variety is endless.... Rely upon it, subjects for genius are not wanting; genius itself, steadily and perseveringly directed, is the thing required. But genius and energy alone are not sufficient; courage and disinterestedness are needed more than all. Courage to withstand the assaults of envy, to despise the ridicule of mediocrity — disinterestedness to trample under foot the seductions of ease, and disregard the attractions of opulence. An heroic mind is more wanted in the library or the studio, than in the field. It is wealth and cowardice which extinguish the light of genius, and dig the grave of literature as of nations.

All this was heartening. In a copy of the New Testament he had with him, Melville underscored in Romans 14: "Hast thou faith? have it to thyself before God" and commented: "The only kind of Faith — one's own." He had that kind of faith now, as a published poet, his apprentice work behind him and a major work ahead. All the way to San Francisco he expected to find waiting for him a precious volume, *Poems*, by Herman Melville; after a brief stay he and Tom would be off across the Pacific, his library of poetry augmented by his own volume.

As they sailed up the coast of South America Melville was writing poetry already, or else luxuriating in remembering some pieces that would be in the book waiting for him in San Francisco. One moonlight night he overflowed with his own poetry, from *Poems* or newly composed:

I cant help thinking what a luckless chap you were that voyage you had a poetaster with you. You remember the romantic moonlight night, when the conceited donkey repeated to you about three cables' length of his verses. But you bore it like a hero. I cant in fact recall so much as a single *wince*. To be sure, you went to bed immediately upon the conclusion of the entertainment; but this much I am sure of, whatever were your sufferings, you never gave them utterance. Tom, my boy, I admire you. I say again, you are a hero.

This was in a letter to Tom on 25 May 1862, in which he facetiously assured Tom that he had disposed of his doggerel to a trunk-maker for linings. Tom was a lucky captain who had on board the *Meteor* in the late summer of 1860 a brother who was a poet (they thought), not a mere unpublished poetaster.

It may be folly to try to imagine Melville planning an epic poem he never wrote, since we have so much trouble imagining two books he did write, *The Isle of the Cross* (1853) and *Poems* (1860). Because his first book of poetry was never published, and because we cannot with absolute certainty identify the parts of it that may survive, we treat the 1860 "*Poems*, by Herman Melville" not as if it were lost but as if it never existed. It existed. Melville wrote it, Lizzie copied it, Evert and George Duyckinck read it, publishers looked at it. Melville himself, by the time the *Meteor* reached the Pacific, assumed that it had already been published, and was being reviewed. A powerful consequence of its existence, in his mind, was that when he read poets in the Pacific, even more than in the first weeks of the voyage, he thought of himself as a poet reading *other* poets, Spenser, Milton, Wordsworth. He was (he had every reason to think) already a published poet, and he was not merely deluded in thinking that his next step, the way of achieving the greatest prestige as a poet, lay in writing a long, ambitious poem. He had, by now, thought long and hard about how to do it.

On the voyage Melville may have been experimenting with a Pacific epic. A Boston businessman and politician, Gorham D. Gilman, who had been in Hawaii when Melville was, at some time entrusted Melville with some of his manuscripts of Hawaiian tales in the hope that he might write them up. On 29 November 1862 Melville returned the documents, including "Umi: A Tale of Hawaii as Narrated by King Kamehameha III." Melville said that he had been charmed by the traditional Hawaiian tale of Umi, in which an illegitimate son of the king ultimately inherits the throne, and had found it "graceful & Greekish." This indicates that Melville had kept the manuscripts for years, for in his 1858–59 lecture he had alluded to a "traditional Polynesian legend" which might particularly appeal to the ladies in his audience, since it was a "love legend of Kamekamehaha, Tahiti, and Otaheite, that was told by a king of one of these islands, and which has much of the grace, strangeness, and audacity of the Grecian fables." "Grecian" or "Greekish" is significant, since, as the Williams College pilgrims testified, Melville had saturated himself in Greek epic, myth, and philosophy in the late 1850s, and in the second lecture obviously delighted in making cross-cultural parallels. His friend William Cramer in the Milwaukee *Daily Wisconsin* said that in the lecture Melville spoke "of a manuscript tradition he had [s]een that was told by a King of one of those Islands. It had much of the grace, strangeness and audacity of the Grecian Fables." Cramer's saying "manuscript tradition" helps rule out the possibility that Melville was taking his information from a book.

In his letter to Gilman, Melville declared that he had actually taken Gilman's suggestion seriously: "Some time ago I tried my hand at elaborating it, but found I bungled, and gave it up." Now, late in 1862, Gilman was the one who "ought to do something with it — Show it to people." For all we know, when Melville tried his hand at elaborating the Hawaiian legend he may have done so in prose, and it is faintly possible that Gilman gave him the documents after the voyage on the *Meteor*, although the letter and the seeming allusion in the second lecture make it seem that Melville had kept them for a matter of years, not months. Since Melville said he had tried to elaborate the legend, he may have done so on the *Meteor*. That is, he may have tried his hand at writing a Greekish poetic epic of the Pacific, based on a traditional Hawaiian legend, as he sailed up the coast of South America, bound for San Francisco, and, as he expected, then south of the Hawaiian Islands on his way to Calcutta. The tale of Umi must have appealed ironically to the man who had put some of his earliest poetry into the mouth of "Yoomy, or the Warbler," the "youthful, long-haired, blue-eyed minstrel" introduced in chapter 65 of *Mardi* (the title of which may have come from "Mar di Sur" on some old map of the Pacific). Did he laugh at the coincidence, in the late 1850s, when he tried to pronounce "Umi"? Or had he encountered the tale of Umi long before, in William Ellis's 1826 or 1827 *Narrative*, even before he introduced Yoomy into *Mardi?*

As the *Meteor* approached the California coast it came in sight of another clipper ship, the *Derby*, under Captain Hutchinson. Melville noted in the front flyleaf of the second volume of the *Iliad* " 'Meteor & Derby' " — good indication that he was steadfastly progressing in his reading of Chapman's Homer, an indication confirmed by his noting in the *Odysseys* on 3 October that he was in the Pacific Ocean "700 miles from San Francisco." The *Meteor* was becalmed four days 160 miles west-south-west of Point Reyes, perhaps the calm in which, one afternoon, Melville drew his picture of his return to

Arrowhead. He was homesick, and as always the more restless when becalmed, wherever that was — whether on a visit to Lansingburgh with his mother or far off Point Reyes, California. The *Meteor* anchored temporarily on the bar off San Francisco at 8:30 P.M. on 11 October, and the next day made its way into the bay in hazy weather, with a light wind from the west, 134 days from Boston. They must have passed by the recently wrecked steamer *Grenada*, "imbedded in the sand a few hundred yards away from the southern pillar of the Golden Gate" (the 20 October report of "Glaucus," printed in the New York *Times* of 15 November 1860).

Tom anchored the *Meteor* at the Vallejo Street wharf and prepared to deliver his cargo of merchandise to C. T. Meader & Co. He and Herman went eagerly to the harbormaster for their mail, Tom already well experienced in the fastest way to get the letters from home which always awaited him. While the *Meteor* had been rounding the Horn, the letters had beaten them there, coming by steamer to Aspinwall (once and later Colón), across the Isthmus to the town of Panama, then onto another steamer to San Francisco. Herman saw at once that there was no package for him, no little package the right size to convey his *Poems* across the Isthmus. He knew what he would read even before he opened the first (probably not the only) letter from Lizzie.

She must have laid out what had happened, and anything she failed to write to him she would have told him later. In the weeks after he sailed, she had done her best by his poems. On 1 June she had written Duyckinck to add a thirteenth item to Melville's memoranda, one which he had "omitted in his haste — and that is, that the book should be plainly bound, that is, not overgilt." Furthermore, Melville had "a decided aversion" to the currently fashionable "blue and gold" bindings. On 4 June she accompanied the manuscript with a letter in which she begged Duyckinck to tell her his honest opinion of the poems, an opinion she was especially anxious to hear since no one had seen the sheets, "excepting two of Herman's sisters, who are now with me — and I want to know how they would strike an unprejudiced person." Evert promptly sent the manuscript to Charles Scribner, who had made an enormous amount of money by publishing the Duyckinck brothers' *Cyclopædia of American Literature*. Feeling no excess of loyalty to Evert, Scribner returned the poems on 19 June with a perfunctory comment ("I have no doubt they are excellent, they seem so to me, and I have confidence in your judgement") and the cool decision that he had issued enough poetry for the season, E. C. Stedman and G. P. Morris's volumes, neither of which he expected to pay.

Melville probably never learned all the ironies operative in this situation. It was Richard Henry Stoddard who persuaded Charles Scribner to publish the first book of poems by Stedman, whom Stoddard had just met; it was Stedman who a quarter of a century later took great interest in Melville. The first part of the story is revealed in *Poets' Homes. Pen and Pencil Sketches of American Poets and Their Homes* by "R. H. Stoddard and Others" (Boston: D. Lothrop & Company, 1877), in Stoddard's chapter on Stedman:

> My good friend Bayard Taylor and I were living together in the same house when these poems [by E. C. Stedman] appeared [in the *Tribune*], and I remember his coming home one afternoon and telling me that he had that day, or the day before, met their author in the editorial rooms of the *Tribune*, and had had a talk with him, and that he liked him very much. A few evenings afterwards this likable young poet came to see me, and I was charmed with him. . . . I read them ["his poems printed and unprinted"] with great care; I corrected them where I thought they needed it, and I tried to get a publisher for him. I think that my opinion was not without weight with the gentleman who became his publisher — the late Mr. Charles Scribner.

It was a small world. If Stoddard had not intervened on Stedman's behalf, Scribner might have published Melville's *Poems*.

After receiving the news, Elizabeth on 23 June expressed her gratitude to the Duyckinck brothers for their help as well as their praise of the poetry. She had absorbed from Herman the idea that rejection by the publishers was no indication of literary merit: "I suppose that if John Milton were to offer 'Paradise Lost' to the Harpers tomorrow, it would be promptly rejected as 'unsuitable' not to say, denounced as dull." Evert and George had confirmed her "own prejudice in its favor," and had prepared her to think well of Herman's poetry, whatever the fate of this volume. She saw that Herman's being away might even work in the book's favor: "he might be disheartened at the outset, by its rejection, and perhaps withhold it altogether, which would be a great disappointment to me." She was, nevertheless, disappointed, despite the best efforts of the Duyckincks and Allan. Evert Duyckinck tried again, sending the manuscript to Rudd & Carleton, who soon rejected it in turn. (Rudd & Carleton were intent on pushing forward their translations from the French classics, according to "Blox," the correspondent of the Washington *National Intelligencer*, 1 November 1860.) Then Duyckinck probably gave up, and returned the manuscript to Allan or sent it to Elizabeth.

There were probably other letters from Lizzie, written later, certainly one describing Allan's attempt to bring his new wife into intimate contact with the family, for on 30 July Allan had signed three lines of the register of the Red Lion Inn in Stockbridge: "Mr & Mrs Allan Melville — New York / Mrs Herman Melville — Pittsfield / Mrs George Griggs — Boston." Presumably this was a treat for Lizzie and Helen, possibly a chance to show the new Mrs. Allan Melville some of the natural wonders of the region. Other members of the family wrote Herman. There must have been at least one letter from the family at Gansevoort, and at least one from Allan (well taught by his oldest brother). There was one from Sam Shaw, a substantial one from the way Melville described it in his reply, which he enclosed in a letter to Judge Shaw. But the news was all in the package that was not there. Melville's behavior compellingly suggests he took the news as a violent psychological blow and decided at once to turn around and go home as soon as he could and by the fastest way. Very likely he was making that decision even while Tom (opening his own mail) learned that he would not sail immediately for Manila, as he had planned, but instead would soon begin taking on a cargo of a hundred tons of wheat to transport not to the Far East but back around the Horn to Falmouth, England. (The loading had begun by 31 October, according to the New York *Times* on 12 November.) Tom probably read his news about his ship while Herman was reading his about his book. Herman's decision may have been made, at once, on the double grounds that he would be stuck for many days in San Francisco, if not weeks, if he continued with Tom (on a comparatively mundane voyage). There were versifiers everywhere, but anyone who did not publish his poems was only a poetaster, not a true poet. It was wholly improper for a mere poetaster rather than a genuine poet to indulge himself in more months of reading epic poetry and contemplating the great poetic work which would follow up his "minor" (to use the conventional term) *Poems*, especially if that meant retracing the path of the *Meteor* back around the Horn. He abhorred "a right-about retrograde movement" still, as in *Typee* (ch. 8).

Melville knew as well as anyone that there was never one motivation for any human action, but he settled at once on the reason to be given the public: the voyage had not benefited him. Perhaps it hadn't. Perhaps it had, until he got his news in San Francisco. Melville soon wrote Lizzie by Pony Express, spending at least five dollars on the letter, and on 8 November the *Berkshire County Eagle* had the public version of events, from Lizzie or indirectly from another source: "Mr. Melville's health is better in some particulars than when he left home, but we regret to learn that he has not experienced the full benefit hoped from the trip, and as the voyage will be prolonged beyond what was first anticipated, Mr. Melville will return via the Isthmus, and reach home early in the winter." The voyage was not being prolonged, but shortened; only Tom's stay by the Golden Gate was being prolonged. There was no being precise in anything involving human psychology.

On the day of Melville's arrival the San Francisco *Daily Evening Bulletin* — on the basis of private letters from Boston — announced his presence on the *Meteor*, "A Noted Author Coming to San Francisco." The item explained: "Mr. Melville is traveling in pursuit of health, and new experiences to turn to account in a literary way. He will remain in San Francisco some time; and our Mercantile Library Association, or some other society, might possibly secure his services for a series of lectures. We like to taste the quality of all the celebrities who fall upon our shores." Word got out at once in San Francisco that Melville had arrived, and that he planned to turn around and go back home on the next steamer, so on 18 October the *Daily Alta* (the newspaper of northern as distinguished from Baja California) suggested that "some of the literary Institutions might prevail on him to favor us with a lecture or two before his departure." Melville gave no lectures in San Francisco. If *Poems* had been waiting for him, elegantly printed by Scribner's, would he willingly have talked about monumental poems in the English language and their power to energize a sluggish populace?

On 15 October, Monday, Melville signed and wrote the date (automatically writing "N. Y.") in Mackay's *Book of English Songs*. This curiously anomalous inscription suggests that Melville had been living in the present in the vast spaces of the Pacific, where he wrote down the latitudes and longitudes where he was reading poetry, but that when he was in San Francisco he did not really feel he was there. If he bought Mackay in San Francisco, it could have been the subject of talk there with Thomas Starr King, for King soon went around saying that Mackay's "verses seem as though they were composed on an even, hard-trotting horse upon a macadamized road" (in his "Books and Reading" lecture). When Melville wrote Lizzie by Pony Express "saying he was not at all benefitted by the Voyage," he asked her to convey to his mother and the others at Gansevoort that he had written them a letter "to come by Steamer," much more economically. A surviving envelope addressed to Lizzie is postmarked 19 October. Even before that he must have written to her, because he wrote to her father on 16 October, enclosing a note to Sam Shaw:

> My Dear Sam: In a few days I shall be at sea again, and as I want to see what I can while here, you may imagine I have not much idle time. I have just written to your father, and slip this little note in, just to say that your letter received here was really interesting to me, and merits a longer & more communicative reply than I shall be able to make. Indeed, as I write by night (rather unusual for me) and my eyes feel tired, all I can add here is, that I hope you are a good enough Christian in this matter of correspondence to be willing cheerfully to give much and receive little.

What Melville did besides write letters in the days between Friday the twelfth and Friday the nineteenth is not known (he seems belatedly, on the nineteenth, to have sent to Lizzie the letters he had written to the children on shipboard).

Knowing Melville's sightseeing habits as detailed in his journals, chances are he saw all he could see, keeping a lookout for superb views. For several days just preceding 20 October, the "surf had been rolling quite heavily," making the *Grenada* seem afloat, though at low water she could be boarded dry-shod ("Glaucus" in the New York *Times* of 15 November 1860). The Melvilles must have gone near to inspect her. According to "Podgers" in the New York *Times* of 10 November, the clipper ship *Storm King* had sailed on 13 October with "a lot of horses and live Chinamen on deck, ditto in the cabin, ditto in the steerage, and a hundred or so defunct Celestials in the hold, besides grain and other vegetables." (The dead so blithely referred to were Coolies worked to death, being returned to China to be buried.) The New York *Herald* on 3 November printed a letter from its San Francisco correspondent dated 11 October, which said that the *Storm King* had already sailed with two hundred living Chinese and nine baskets full of dead Chinamen deep in the hold, so Melville may have missed the cautious loading of horses and less delicate loading of Celestials, living and dead, but gossip would have been rife around the port, and he would have recalled the thousand Celestials sacrificed by Aspinwall's company in the cause of safe, rapid transportation across the Isthmus.

On the streets Melville may have seen a vision reminding him of his past, for as luck had it, Prince Kamehameha, a son of the present Kamehameha IV (a nephew of the Kamehameha III of 1843), had arrived from Honolulu in his yacht a week or so before the *Meteor*, and was conspicuous about town, "Podgers" said in the 10 November New York *Times:* "The Prince is a splendid specimen of humanity, a little off color, it is true, but nevertheless a very handsome man, being over six feet high, and finely formed.... I saw him the other day flattening his nose against a window, looking at some painting in a picture frame shop, and stop at a fruit stand and invest a dime in a big red apple.... He wandered about town, ate, drank and slept just like an ordinary mortal, in plain clothes, and at the hotel never once called for roast baby or missionary steak." The prince was to sail on 15 October, ample time for Melville to observe him as they both made their ways around town.

On Thursday, 18 October, Melville was bombarded: from "sunrise to sunset half-hour guns were fired from the Fort, Alcatraz Island, and the *Seranac*, then from three until five minute guns were fired, in honor of Brigadier-General Newman S. Clarke, the Commander of the California Division of the United States Army," whose funeral was held that afternoon. (This is from a report in the New York *Times* on 15 November.) The cannonading was augmented by uproarious Republicans after the Oregon senator-elect Edward D. Baker arrived on the *Brother Jonathan* late in the morning. Republicans set guns blazing away from Rincon Point and Telegraph Hill, "so that the echoes from the 200 guns of joy over Baker got mixed and confused with the minute guns resounding the general grief over the deceased Commander." Baker, British-born, a friend of Abraham Lincoln's since the Black Hawk War, was a hero of the Mexican War who had run for office in California as a Whig in 1855 then took himself north early in 1860, where he had won the election as senator because the Democrats were so divided over slavery. Later it seemed to many that he had held the Pacific Coast for the Union. If Melville was baffled by the political intricacies (was Baker the third senator from California?), he knew a "Grand Contested Election for the Presidency" when he saw and heard one.

With his letter of introduction from Orville Dewey, Melville called on the Reverend Mr. Thomas Starr King, the Unitarian minister and a successful lecturer, who had in fact lectured in Pittsfield without Melville's meeting him, and who had been in San Francisco only a few months. Melville may have particularly wanted to meet him because he knew King's *The White Hills: Their Legends, Landscape, and Poetry* (Boston: Crosby & Nichols, 1859), a rhapsodic, poetry-stuffed tribute to a terrain sacred to Herman and Lizzie. Probably he presented his letter promptly, for what he and King did together on 19 October seems planned in advance. Melville may have felt for himself what Edwin P. Whipple in a memorial tribute in 1864 (printed in the 1866 *Character and Characteristic Men*) said was King's secret — "the rare felicity, in everything he said and did, of communicating himself, — the most precious thing he could bestow." That felicity had once been one of Melville's own special powers. Melville had ample occasion to take his measure of this unprepossessing man (lacking "a grand stature or striking physiognomy," Henry W. Bellows, minister of All Souls Unitarian Church in Manhattan, said in his 1 May 1864 memorial sermon, delivered in San Francisco) who was nevertheless formidable. Bellows asked, "Oh, how can I forget the evenings passed in the society of his most familiar friends in Boston, with HEDGE, and BARTOL, and FIELDS, and WHIPPLE, and ALGER," offering this superlative praise:

> I need not say that in this medley of sense and nonsense, earnest and fun, Mr. KING bore his part with equal vigor and success in either branch, and in the department of anecdote and humor, excelled all by a distance too great to be measured. He was, in short, the best story-teller of his time; and while you seldom got anything from him that you could have recognized in the original, had you been then present, the change was only that legitimate one by which

genius transmutes into precious stuffs, the fabrics that continue mean and coarse in common hands.

Melville was not in a state to be preternaturally alert to other men's or women's qualities, but he must have acknowledged that he was spending some hours with a momentous man. For his part, King soon wrote a lecture on "Books and Reading," which "had an extraordinary popularity in every city and town in California where it was delivered"; in it he mentioned many writers, American as well as British, but not Herman Melville.

Leaving Tom to his duties, on that Friday Melville and King went to Black Point, the "cottage" of Colonel Charles Frémont, the 1856 Republican presidential candidate. The house was at the bluff, on a point projecting out into the bay across from Alcatraz. King called it "The Porter's Lodge," because it commanded the Golden Gate (so named, it was said, by Frémont). There Jessie Benton Frémont, the daughter of the Missouri senator Thomas Hart Benton, reigned over the city's most celebrated political-literary salon, where her favorite was the still-juvenile Albanian Bret Harte, and where she often entertained Carleton E. Watkins, who was photographing the American West. The Frémonts were connoisseurs, and may already have had hanging there Albert Bierstadt's *The Golden Gate*, which Tuckerman cited in 1867 as in their possession. Soon after his arrival King had made the acquaintance of the Frémonts, and on 10 September had written to his friend Bellows: "I rode to Mrs. Frémonts, two miles off, and sat in her lovely cottage, hearing her talk and enjoying it." To a friend in Boston, Randolph Ryer, King described his and Melville's activities:

> I have just returned from Mrs Fremont's where I have made a visit with Herman Melville, who is visiting San Francisco. He brought a letter of introduction to me from Dr. Dewey. We had a fine time with Mrs. F. The Col. was at home. It is the 19th Anniversary of her wedding, when all Washington was horror struck as she said, because she had made "*such* a foolish match." Now that Fremont's mills turn out $16,000 a week in solid gold, I suppose Washington would pass a different judgment. She *is* a superb woman.

She was a superb woman indeed. No other record is known of Melville's conversations on this day; Mrs. Frémont's papers went up in flames in New York City in the early 1890s.

In San Francisco national politics took first place in the newspapers, since some Southern politicians had gone far beyond the old familiar talk of nullification and were threatening secession if Lincoln won. But Melville also caught up on world news, particularly the recent events in Italy, having sailed with Tom just after Garibaldi sailed from Genoa with his thousand Red Shirts. He would have learned now, if not earlier, of Garibaldi's taking Palermo and in early September entering Naples and claiming Sicily and Naples for Victor Emmanuel II of Sardinia. Italy was united now, except what the Austrians held in the north and, most rankling, except for Rome (which Garibaldi tried to take in 1862 and again in 1867). Newspapers which the Melville brothers read in San Francisco gave full coverage to the news from Italy, for Italian immigrants had thronged to the region on the Pacific which everyone said possessed a Mediterranean climate, and were growing Italian plants already, even grapes. The newspapers of 19 October had the news of the voyage of the *Meteor* and other ships that had arrived between the tenth and the seventeenth. One of them, the *Tropic*, from Liverpool, had endured a hard-luck voyage rivaling Melville's *Perseverance* in *Typee*—"Was 60 days to Cape Horn; was off the Cape 30 days, with strong westerly gales; was 126 days to the equator in the Pacific"; it had been "within three days' sail of this port for the last 30 days." The only good news from the *Tropic*, printed two or three inches below the item on the *Meteor* in the *Mercantile Gazette and Prices Current*, leapt off the page at Melville: "off Monterey, saw schr Fayaway, which ran alongside and threw some papers on board, for which Capt Nowell returns his sincere thanks." Once again the author of *Moby-Dick* had to acknowledge that his most popular character was still Fayaway.

On 20 October, the first nasty day of the season (it "rained in the morning enough to convert the dust into mud," wrote "Glaucus" in the New York *Times* of 15 November), Melville boarded the Panama steamer *Cortes*. Tom had hands available to stow his brother's books onto the steamship for him, but without porters Herman would not easily get them off ship and onto the train across the Isthmus then onto another ship and off ship in New York. He kept at least the Wordsworth and the Schiller with him, but it is possible that he left some of the bulkier and heavier volumes aboard, for Tom to carry back around the Horn and up and across the Atlantic. The urgency of Melville's need to have Homer and Milton and other epic volumes at hand may have evaporated when *Poems* was not awaiting him in San Francisco.

If what he had written had been printed, we would know Melville as the man who published these volumes between 1846 and 1860: *Typee*, *Omoo*, *Mardi*, *Redburn*, *White-Jacket*, *Moby-Dick*, *Pierre*, *The Isle of the Cross* (1853), *Israel Potter*, *The Piazza Tales*, *The Confidence-Man*, *Poems* (1860). (Incidentally, we might now think of "Morning in Naples"—or "Afternoon in Naples"—in relation to "Benito Cereno" and to Melville's then-recent 1857 observations rather than as a waif from Melville's last decade and a half.) The loss of *Poems*, like the loss of *The Isle of the Cross* (not to mention slighter losses like some of the tortoise pages and the bungled attempt at a Hawaiian legend), has meant that we cannot see Melville's working life as a whole and cannot see the interrelationships of his works, *The Isle of the Cross* and "Bartleby," for instance, or *Poems* and any poems in *Battle-Pieces* (1866).

His books taken care of, one way or another, Melville "left for Panama between 9 and 10 o'clock" on the morning of 20 October amid the hoopla for that night's Republican mass meeting glorifying the senator from the Pacific Coast. (A soldier-senator, Baker was killed almost exactly a year later, in command of some young Massachusetts and New York men whom Melville memorialized in "Ball's Bluff. A Reverie.") In April 1853 Davis-Brooks (26 Broadway, New York) published an advertising poster for their New-York & San Francisco Steamship Line ballyhooing the *Cortes* as "the new and magnificent side-wheel, double engine steamship," their Panama connection to California. After a few years of hard service, earlier in 1860 the Pacific Mail Steamship Company had bought the ship from Cornelius Vanderbilt. On this trip the ship carried "the mails, 250 passengers, and $1,022,566 in specie," according to the *Daily Evening Bulletin* (the New York *Times* of 5 November added that it "also took silver ore to the value of $60,000"). The *Bulletin* got the news in time to say that their readers would note among the cabin passengers "Herman Melville, the author of 'Omoo' and 'Typee,' who arrived here but a few days since from around Cape Horn." The departure of the *Cortes* was enlivened by the discovery of an "unusual number of stowaways," who were sent ashore after the steamer got into the stream.

Nothing is known of Melville's companions or his states of mind on his return voyage, other than that he read in Wordsworth and Schiller after he crossed the Isthmus. The San Francisco *Daily Evening Bulletin* on 26 November relayed word on the *Cortes*: "6½ A.M., arrived at Manzanillo, took on board $315,000 in silver and left at 10 o'clock the same morning; October 28th, 5 P.M., arrived at Acapulco, took in coal, water and provision, and sailed same evening at 9 o'clock, arriving at Panama, November 4th, at 2.15 P.M." As he showed in his lecture on the South Seas, Melville had long known histories and sailor-stories about Panama, and was unusually well informed about the recent history of the Isthmus, from Robert Tomes's *Panama in 1855* and well as Ephraim Squier's book on the exploration of the Mosquito Coast (Honduras). He also knew John Lloyd Stephens's *Incidents of Travel in Central America* (1841) and read letters and personal accounts from Guatemala by Sam Savage, a favorite of both Herman and Lizzie.

No one wanted to linger on the Caribbean side ("that side of the Continent where the *Vanderbilt* shadow falls," as "Glaucus" put it in his letter printed in the New York *Times* of 15 November), but ordinarily Melville might have wanted to linger on the Pacific side, even if he was at the mercy of "the glib-tongued Isthmus Arabs." He might have wanted, as a fellow lover of Chapman's Homer with Keats, to scale that poetic peak in Darien. What happened, most likely, is that he and the other members of the throng were hustled aboard the railroad cars (as Howard Horsford says in his edition of Melville's journals, "forty-seven miles, four hours, $25 plus ten cents a pound for baggage"). At Aspinwall the railroad extended out to an island so that passengers could board the steamer without being expelled into the city. Melville had lost touch with the Danas, it seems, but the author of *Two Years before the Mast* the year before (in the summer, the worst season) had loathed Aspinwall: "Dismal place. Swamp, torrid marsh, hot, damp, a mist of vapors, like smoke, at sun-rise, all full of miasmas" — emphatically "not intended to be lived in by white[s]," the worst place he ever saw. That "plague-spot," Tomes had said, an oozy marsh "seething in a constant summer heat" and engendering "intermittent, bilious, congestive, and yellow fevers, and the other malignant results of impure miasmatic exhalation." Melville may have seen some signs of the current dispute between the United States and Great Britain, a "misunderstanding between the American and British Naval Commanders at Panama." British sentries on shore at Panama had arrested American officers, and a detachment of troops had been dispatched from New York and had arrived in Aspinwall safely, ready to defend the national honor. The ship Melville returned on carried news of the arrival of those troops (as reported in the New York *Times* on 14 November). If he went directly on board the Vanderbilt steamship *North Star* (A. G. Jones, master), he may have not stepped foot in Aspinwall. No longer taking the cheapest modes of transportation, as he had done in 1856 and 1857, he registered as a passenger in the first cabin, which then cost an exorbitant $200 ($225 in the package-deal including the railroad leg) — more money than he had earned since 1858. The voyage may have provided graphic illustrations of the "Pains," if not the pleasures and profits of travel, for John H. Kemble in *The Panama Route* quotes a passenger in 1860 when eight stewards had to wait on 350 passengers, serving them in eleven sittings in a far from capacious cabin, as well as caring for the staterooms. There were only a few privies, and those filthy. Vanderbilt, a hard driver like the worst of the whaling captains, worked his stokers and firemen brutally, twelve hours a day; two of them died from overwork on one voyage in 1860. Melville was far from fastidious, but Vanderbilt ships could be hellholes. He managed to read a little in his father's Spenser and in his volume of Schiller's poems, but his reading could not have been anything like methodical.

In New York the family had been needlessly confused, though not actively alarmed, by a garbled item from San Francisco in the *Tribune* of 31 October, reporting a wreck and concluding, in elongated brackets: "{This vessel is probably the Meteore, from Bordeaux.}" On 4 November the *Herald* under "NEWS FROM THE PACIFIC" identified the vessel lost off the Heads as the steamer *Grenada* "instead of the ship *Meteor,*" and the next day the *Times* made the same correction. Maria had not been worrying about the *Meteor*, for on 5 November she wrote to Peter about a different concern, that Herman "was not at all benefitted by the Voyage": "I feel so much disappointed, I had fondly hoped that a Voyage to India under kind Tom's care would have quite brought Herman back to health." In Pittsfield on 8 November the *Berkshire County Eagle* expressed its good wishes, ignorant of any report about the loss of the *Meteor*: "We trust and think that the trip home will be of more benefit than out, and that Mr. M. will reach us in the full vigor of health that used to distinguish him." There had been clear good news on 12 November in the *Times*, dated from San Francisco on 31 October: "The clippership *Meteor* has commenced loading a cargo of one hundred tons of wheat for the English market." The confusion had been cleared up well before the *North Star* docked in New York at 10 P.M. on 13 November. The ship had at least been fast. No one willingly would have stayed aboard overnight unless he had to, so chances are that Melville disembarked as soon as he was allowed. Unless the ship had touched a port, likely in Florida, or learned the news from another ship, no one on board knew until the *North Star* reached Manhattan that Abraham Lincoln had won the election on 6 November. It may have been with that stunning news fresh in his head that Herman knocked up the peaceable inhabitants of East Twenty-sixth Street toward midnight on the thirteenth. Although he probably startled the family, for his part, Herman must have been shocked, despite himself, to see Jane (instead of Sophia) with Allan, by this time (so many months had elapsed) completely settled in, the unquestioned queen of Sophia's household. And the Herman Melville who presented himself at Twenty-sixth Street was a failed poetaster, not the triumphant author of *Poems*.

[20]

The Dream of Florence, a State Funeral, and War

November 1860–December 1861

❧

The gloomy lull of the early part of the winter of 1860–1, seeming big with final disaster to our institutions, affected some minds that believed them to constitute one of the great hopes of mankind, much as the eclipse which came over the promise of the first French Revolution affected kindred natures, throwing them for the time into doubts and misgivings universal.

Melville's first note in *Battle-Pieces*, to
"The Conflict of Convictions"

IN NOVEMBER 1860 after arriving in New York from California, Melville went directly to Boston. Augusta saw him there, and on her return home to Gansevoort she stopped over at Albany, where she told Uncle Peter the news about Herman and that John Hoadley had "purchased a fine house with extensive grounds in the suburbs of 'Lawrence' " (as Kitty wrote Henry on 23 November). At Gansevoort, Augusta, Fanny, Maria, and Uncle Herman welcomed Lizzie and Herman for a pre-Thanksgiving visit. Then Herman and Lizzie returned to Boston for the great New England holiday on the twenty-ninth. Sarah had the news at Broadhall by 23 November, when she wrote George Duyckinck: "Were you not surprised at Mr Herman's return. I am glad that we shall have them for Neighbors again this winter." Rather than hurrying home, the Melvilles enjoyed Boston, Herman more sociable than usual, for George W. Wales on 3 December wrote Henry S. Gansevoort that he had seen him "several times" and had learned from him that Uncle Peter and Susan (as well as Henry and Kitty) had returned at the end of August 1860 from well over a year in Europe. In her illness Sarah Morewood was avoiding urban distractions, but she invited the whole Melville troupe to stay at Broadhall until Melville and Lizzie could open Arrowhead. On 2 December, from Mt. Vernon Street, Melville informed her of a change in plans: "Lizzie and the children will remain here till Thursday; and I—in advance,—will go to Pittsfield, on *Tuesday*, to get matters in readiness for them—putting up the stoves, airing the bedding—warming the house, and getting up a grand domestic banquet. I shall leave here in *the morning train on*

Tuesday; and will be very happy to accept, for myself, your kind & neighborly invitation for a day or two." Remembering the circumstances of 1857, Lizzie added a note to Sarah: "You see the order of things is completely reversed, since Herman is going on to Pittsfield to get the house ready for *me* — that is, to get Mr. Clark to put the stoves up, and get it *warm* for me to go to work in — A new proverb should be added 'Wives propose — husband dispose' — don't you think so?" Sarah had always thought so. None of them attached any special solemnity to the occasion, but Lizzie's good-bye to her father in Boston was the last time she saw him alive.

Back at Arrowhead, Melville placed a running advertisement in the *Berkshire County Eagle*, starting 13 December, for a woman "to do cooking and general Housework in a small family three miles from Pittsfield Village." Horace Greeley lectured in Pittsfield on 14 December ("America West of the Mississippi"). Melville had no reason to drive to the village for the lecture, given the long, mixed history of Greeley's personal ambivalent animosity toward the older Melville brothers, even in the light of George Ripley's fairness as a reviewer for Greeley. Did Melville need to hear the man who had proclaimed there was something undefinably and insidiously unwholesome about the tone of his first two books? Even before Christmas, winter was brutal. The Springfield *Republican* on Christmas Day reported that the weather had been "very cold and the sleighing superb in Berkshire"; on Saturday the twenty-second and Sunday the twenty-third in Pittsfield "the thermometer at sunrise indicated 10° below zero." So presumably did Evert Duyckinck's gift, the thermometer on the piazza at Arrowhead.

Promptly enough Melville caught up on the mail that had arrived in his absence. On 18 December he wrote to Oliver Russ, a shipmate on the *United States*, informing him of his recent voyage, and trying to convey how simply he was living. From Richville, far north of Utica, near the Canadian border, Russ replied on Christmas Eve: "I live like yourself in rather primative stile only a little more so." The world was small: "I live but a short distance from Mr Green the father of Toby I often see the old gentleman but have never seen Richard (Toby) but learn that he is now in Mishagan, and that he is not a very desirable patern for a husband and father but perfection is not to be found in man." Herman was hardly a desirable "patern for a husband and father" either, and he found himself depriving his own family in order to make the magnanimous gesture Russ expected. Oliver Russ was first to hint at a memorial gift, second to receive. Melville apparently sent a gift to him early in January 1861. Russ promised to treasure it as a reminder of "all those circumstances which made us acquainted and all the incedents which happened while we were togather." Reading that Melville would be lecturing in Ohio, Toby Greene had written him in January 1858, wishing they could meet. Subsequently he had hinted that gifts might be in order, and before the end of 1860 Melville had responded by sending engraved spoons to Greene's son (Herman Melville Greene) and Greene's nephew (Richard Melville Hair), and inviting Toby to visit him at Arrowhead. In his 4 January 1861 reply, Toby said he hoped that Herman could yet stow away his " 'five shares of duff'!" — a revealing reference to young Herman's appetite — and wished that they could drink while Herman talked ("I would be delighted to see you and 'freshen the nip' while you would be spinning a yarn as long as the Main top bowline"). He had known Herman as a phenomenal eater and an enthusiastic drinker; Toby's alcoholism was subsequently blazoned in dozens of government documents related to his applications for a military pension. No one from the past could comprehend how impoverished Melville was, how severe a drain engraved silver spoons were to the budget, even if he started with plain silver spoons that had been resting in drawers at Arrowhead.

The bitter cold of Christmas 1860 in the Berkshires continued into 1861. Marooned there now, out of Space, out of Time, no longer purposefully aloof from the petty battles of the literati in New York, Melville kept up the Dutch tradition of giving New Year's gifts by signing over to Lizzie something he had bought in 1860, probably in May or earlier, *The Works of the Late Edgar Allan Poe* (New York, 1859); most likely he had carried the volumes around the Horn and home with him. Looking back from the warmth of late June, Sarah Morewood lamented to Captain Melville what the Broadhallers had suffered, what "depth of ice and snow" they had "travelled through! Ugh!" In that intense cold, life had been "a mean sort of thing." Sarah told Tom not to return in "the Winter time," needless advice, since he always cowered by stoves and fireplaces when he arrived home in January or February, as he seemed fated to do. The Melvilles had come to regard the winters as Sarah did. Chances are Melville was reading but not writing. Having learned in San Francisco that his *Poems* did not exist, he hardly could have been in the mood for writing little verses on his way home or during the family visiting that followed, unless he had roused himself for a little poetical toast to Tom that dates from around this time.

Melville had returned to a country in crisis, when several members of the family were deeply involved in last-minute efforts to prevent secession, and, failing that, to prevent war between the states. Hoadley, the most partisan, had been passionately pro-Union in 1850 at the cost of justifying the return of fugitive slaves to the South, but he was now in the Republican camp of his good friend Charles Sumner. There was no satisfactory moral standpoint for any of the rest of them, and it had become harder and harder to satirize even the most accommodating man in their midst, Shaw's great friend and Melville's Berkshire neighbor, Orville Dewey. In an 1852 lecture before the

Mercantile Library Association in New York Dewey had decried being misunderstood in his 27 December 1850 speech at the great Union meeting in Pittsfield: "I did not discuss the present fugitive slave law, though I was immediately represented as a violent advocate for it, but rather addressed myself to the question whether we at the North could, in conscience, yield our assent to *any* such bill — to *any* bill that should give the Southern master the power to reclaim one of his slaves that had fled to us for refuge." He was not the sort of man, he insisted, "to join the malcontents in decrying the law"; and being that sort of man he could have pleased neither abolitionist, unionist, Southerner, nor slave. He made a friendly visit to Charleston in 1856–57 and the next August in a speech under the "Old Elm Tree in Sheffield" he "made some observations upon the threatened extension of the slave-system," that dashed nearly all his "agreeable relations with Charleston." In all cautious mildness, Dewey had said in the Sheffield speech that slavery involved "such a wrong to humanity, such evil to the South, and such peril to the Union of the States, that it was a proper occasion for speaking earnestly and decidedly." Dewey had been "altogether unprepared for the treatment" he received from Southerners. Seeing so many sides to any issue, Dewey could not convey in words the infinite complexity of his thoughts on any controversial issue, so he was fated to be misunderstood by all sides. "Human Destiny" was so much happier and simpler a topic than black slavery.

By late 1860 Lemuel Shaw was as profoundly perplexed as his friend Dewey. The month after his retirement, while his son-in-law was on the *Meteor*, Shaw had been approached to become an elector at large ("a revered mediator between the Northern and Southern extremes of party") on the ticket of the Constitutional Union party, which had nominated John Bell of Tennessee for president and Edward Everett of Massachusetts for vice president. The party was a motley mix of old-fashioned unionists left over from 1850, stray Know-Nothings or Americanists, and many Whigs like Shaw who had outlived their party; some of them, like Shaw, had outlived both the Federalists and the Whigs. Banded together, they hoped to prevent secession, and, failing that, to prevent war. On the back of the letter Shaw wrote: "nomination declined / Sept 4." After Thanksgiving of 1860, while Melville was at Mt. Vernon Street, Shaw put his dwindling energies to the service of a last-ditch attempt to save the Union by appeasing the South. A group of Massachusetts unionists (including remnants of the old Webster coalition majority of 1850) in December 1860 published an "Address To the Citizens of Massachusetts" urging conciliation toward the South. The unionists went so far as to declare that Massachusetts itself had violated the great national contract as flagrantly as Southern states were proposing to do by seceding. This violation was the passage of the "Personal Liberty" laws following the remanding of Anthony Burns, the intended effect of which was to nullify the Fugitive Slave Law within the borders of the state. Forty-two men signed this humble apology from Massachusetts to the South, among them Melville's late second cousin's husband, Benjamin R. Curtis, a principled man who had resigned as a justice of the U.S. Supreme Court in protest against the Dred Scott decision; Jared Sparks, the historian (who had witnessed war, the British plundering of Baltimore); Levi Lincoln of Worcester (governor 1825–34); and Emory Washburn (governor 1854–55). The first signature on the list was Lemuel Shaw's. It was too late for appeasement: within the week of Lemuel Shaw's signing the document, South Carolina seceded.

Richard Lathers, generous and self-deluded, thought that because of his Southern rearing and his Northern business career he could personally help hold the Union together. On 28 November 1860 he wrote to five citizens of Charleston urging them to realize that many Northerners were working against "the fell spirit of fanaticism" and "the fanatical prejudices and sectional demagogism" of the "powerful and aggressive" Republicans who had just been victorious in the election. He urged them to hope that he and likeminded men were "overcoming the fanatical sectionalism and corrupt demagogism" of the North, and reminded the Charlestonians that in New York the Republicans had received only a little more than half the vote. Lathers gave not only his own opinion but that of others he had consulted, including John A. Dix and Charles O'Conor, that many Northerners would be conciliatory toward the South, and that if the South felt it had to secede in the face of Republican fanaticism Lathers and others like him would understand that secession was "the only remedy left for the South," and that the North should be "powerless to resist it." Lathers held a meeting of prominent men (among them Dix, Edwin Croswell, William B. Astor, Augustus Schell, and James W. Beekman) on 15 December, at which O'Conor spoke passionately for national unity, to be achieved by "colonization" of blacks to Africa — an idea held by many abolitionists: "Now, gentlemen, there is no inhumanity, there is no selfishness, there is nothing that men can find fault with in laying down the rule that America was made for a free white Caucasian race and its development. We but follow the judgment of Almighty God when we say, 'America for the white Caucasian, Africa for the negro who was born in it, who is adapted to its climate, and there, in a physical sense, at least, can best flourish.'" Free blacks sent back to Africa might even in a century or two create a "mighty empire," both "civilized and Christianized." (American Indians, being doomed to sufficiently swift extirpation, did not have to be taken into consideration.) The men voted to send Millard Fillmore, Bronson C. Greene, and Lathers himself south on a mission to head off secession and war.

The other two excused themselves, the former president on the grounds of ill health, but in February 1861, when the Confederacy was already in existence, Lathers set off with his wife, Abby Thurston Lathers, at first to the Peace Convention, then in session in Washington, and presided over by Robert Melvill's one-time boarder, former president Tyler, who gave Lathers letters of introduction to the president of the Confederacy, Jefferson Davis, and other prominent men. Abby kept with her husband through this quixotic mission. In Montgomery, then the seat of the Confederacy, Lathers met with President Davis and read him the "Appeal to the South," the product of the December meeting Lathers had convened. By that time seven states had seceded, South Carolina on 20 December 1860, five more in January 1861 (Mississippi, Florida, Alabama, Georgia, and Louisiana), and Texas on 1 February. Sure of his own right-mindedness and reposing total confidence in his friends in the South, Lathers was addressing a large meeting in Mobile on 12 April when (according to his *Reminiscences*) his remarks were interrupted by news that "Fort Sumter had been fired upon and the War of Secession thereby opened." The Southerners paused to give him a vote of thanks for what he had said so far, then quickly adjourned. Undeterred, Lathers went on to New Orleans with Abby, thinking he could talk to the chamber of commerce "on the issues of the day and their effect on trade." They were at breakfast when the mayor called to tell him to leave at once, "as an *alien enemy*," continuing bluntly: "After the capture of Fort Sumter, the first victory of the Confederate States, it ought to occur to such an intelligent gentleman as yourself that the discussions you refer to are clearly out of place. You would be mobbed should you remain." The mayor put them on a train (Arkansas did not secede until May, and Missouri, despite its Southern leanings, did not secede), by which they managed to get north, "traveling night and day through a most disturbed region crazy with enthusiasm."

Toby Greene's letter to Melville from Chicago on 4 January had included fresh personal word of the president-to-be: "I often have the pleasure of seeing our future President. 'Old Abe' looks all right, and its my opinion, he will take the oath of office on the Capitol Steps in spite of all fire eating braggadocios." The fourth of March had begun to loom in Allan's mind, and then in Herman's, as a possible turning point—a new president, new appointments. Sometime in the early winter, perhaps soon after the election when Herman arrived in New York, Allan began a campaign to gain for his brother the consulship in the Sandwich Islands or to get Herman some other appointment that would remove him from Pittsfield. Characteristically, Herman did not immediately bestir himself in his own behalf. On 2 February 1861 Peter Gansevoort recorded a visit from Melville in his diary. On the third, a Sunday, he went to church with his wife and daughter Kitty, accompanied by his sister Maria and his nephew Herman. After the service they walked over to inspect "the New Cathedral St Josephs." The comings and goings were unusual, but they may have involved Uncle Herman's health or some other family matter, not a consultation about how to obtain a political appointment. On Tuesday, 5 February, Kitty recorded that "Aunt Melville & Cousin Herman left for Gansevoort in the 4:30 Train" — on the Saratoga & Whitehall Rail Road. Herman lingered on with his mother an exceptionally long time before returning to Albany on Monday the eleventh and dining with the Gansevoorts, then taking the 4:30 train to Pittsfield. He was home for Malcolm's twelfth birthday, 16 February, the day Elizabeth received her semiannual interest on her trust fund, ninety dollars. Melville had accepted his position as one of Shaw's pensioners, his place of residence and even his food dependent on the fact that he was married to Shaw's daughter, the lady owner of Arrowhead. In 1853, during the last concerted effort to gain him a consulship, Melville had been completing *The Isle of the Cross*, which he assumed would revive his literary fortunes after the disaster of *Pierre*. Now Melville was ready to participate in the drive to gain a political office, even one which would not pay all his living expenses.

Hawthorne had sewn up his plum consulship before the election of 1852. "The Rush for the Spoils" of the current election had been under way for months, the Philadelphia *Ledger* had declared in an article which the Washington *National Intelligencer* reprinted on 12 November 1860. Allan started his campaign on Herman's behalf in January or early February 1861, and without Herman's full acquiescence, as is shown by a blunt letter Lemuel Shaw, now a private citizen, wrote later in February, appalled at Allan's effrontery in initiating inquiries without Herman's "own consent and desire." Shaw was outraged at Allan's proposing to send Lizzie and the children to islands in the middle of the Pacific Ocean at a time when the South might seize or hinder access to the islands and when his own life was nearing its end. Since Allan had now "given up this proposal," Shaw did not feel obliged to spell out to Lizzie's insensitive brother-in-law the grounds on which he "should have disapproved of Herman's removal with his family to so great a distance."

In mid-February, Allan decided to work on behalf of the consulate in Florence. As Melville had prepared to sail with Tom on the *Meteor*, Garibaldi had sailed from Genoa with his thousand Red Shirts; now in early 1861 he had united Italy, except what the Austrians held in the north and, most ranklingly, Rome. In Lawrence early in 1861 Hoadley was chairman of a committee to congratulate Italy upon its unification; he wrote the resolutions out "most beautifully" in the French language and the secretary of state forwarded them to their destination. Newspapers and magazines in January 1861 declared that Garibaldi was bringing peace to a largely unified Italy, and

Melville's friend Tuckerman published the definitive article on Garibaldi in the January 1861 *North American Review*, an essay readily available to reassure any fearful member of the family. Herman and Lizzie would not be entering a dangerous war zone: indeed, what could be more dangerous than the no longer United States?

Melville himself harbored wild hopes that his office-seeking might, this time, succeed. Nourished by breakfasts at the Caffè Doney, he had walked Florence in rain and sun, absorbing and marveling, and seeing what the great Hiram Powers, his countryman, had made of his residence in that city. Italy was the Holy Land of Art, and Florence, perhaps more than Rome, was the ideal city for an artist. Melville knew Vasari's lives of the artists from his reading of Duyckinck's set—a reading so careful that he was able to correct an assertion in *The Marble Faun* from memory, while he was on the *Meteor*. He did not have his own copy until the next year, but he knew the section on Pietro Perugino, who was brought up in poverty and had been put out as a "shop-drudge," as young Herman had been. The young Pietro would ask his instructor and other well-traveled people in what city the best artists were formed, and was always told Florence, Florence, "the place, above all others, wherein men attain to perfection in all the arts, but more especially in painting." In that ideal city, everyone was an aesthetician, quick and free with sharp independent criticism that judged a new work of art on its own merits, regardless of the reputation of the artist. When he had his own copy of Vasari, Melville approvingly scored this passage: for years he had wished that works of art could be anonymous and that his own identity could be as sheltered as that of Junius.

Vasari gave two more reasons that Florence was the ideal city for an artist to live in. Florence did not then draw substantial foodstuffs and manufactured products from the immediate area, so its citizens needed to gain money for trade, which meant that artists had to hone their skills constantly. Florence was not (Melville perceived) the Marquesas, where means of life might be supplied "at light cost," the country being one where produce abounded. Vasari concluded with the third cause, "the desire for glory and honour, which is powerfully generated by the air of that place," so that the talented drove themselves to become masters. Melville may have felt that way about New York City for a time in the mid-1840s and even as late as 1848 and early 1849. By the time he went to Pittsfield for a vacation that turned into a thirteen-year residence, he could no longer feel, even in Dr. Francis's house on Bond Street, that he was part of a literary and artistic society in which fiction writers, poets, painters, and sculptors were all working together toward the creation of high aesthetic culture in the young United States. He would go to Florence, if he could. Who wouldn't?

On 18 February, two weeks before Abraham Lincoln was to be inaugurated, Allan Melville wrote to Lemuel Shaw and to George Griggs urging their help in obtaining the consulship at Florence for Herman. George promptly made inquiries and learned that it was "worth only about $500 per year," not enough to support Herman and his family, so on the twentieth he answered discreetly: "Perhaps if that is the fact it will not be desirous to make any great effort to secure it for Herman. What think you[?]" He had resisted Allan's suggestion that he confer with Shaw ("He is now unwell and I feel disinclined to call on him to make exertions for what may not be worth the trouble it would occasion him"). There was another obvious objection to the scheme: "Would not a knowledge of the French and Italian languages be essential to our consul?" Finally, George was unwilling to perturb the judge "until the efforts of younger persons have been exhausted."

For his part, Shaw was still angry at Allan's effrontery in thinking, earlier, of the Sandwich Islands, but in his response on 20 February he agreed on "the necessity" of Herman's getting away from Pittsfield, where he was "solitary, without society, without exercise or occupation except that which is very likely to be injurious to him in over-straining his mind." The ideal would be "easy employment and moderate exercise of mind & body" as well as "an opportunity to associate habitually with others." Shaw, who knew that Herman would not have to live on the proceeds of the appointment, thought the consulship at Florence "would be extremely beneficial," and assumed that Herman's ignorance of Italian would not matter, since he could cheaply hire a clerk to assist him occasionally. Shaw had ruminated over the implications, devoting much effort to the problem despite his severe illness: "All the circumstances of his residence at Florence would have a tendency to promote his comfort and improvement in health of body & mind. I presume english schools are to be found there for the children. I will do any thing in my power to promote this appointment. Herman's literary reputation would be in his favor, as a candidate for such a place as Florence." With a realistic goal in view, Shaw had practical advice: "Could at once means be found, to apply to Mr. [Secretary of State William] Seward on the subject? The appointment must depend much on him." Florence failing, Shaw hoped that Allan would manage to get Herman an office in the New York Custom House: "I should hope that he could do the moderate daily labor required there, & thus be enabled to live in N.Y. & remove him from Pittsfield."

With this encouragement from Shaw, Allan began mobilizing forces. A week after Lincoln's inauguration, Hoadley wrote to Charles Sumner, requesting his influence in support of Melville's appointment; Hoadley suggested that since Melville was a literary man his appointment "would be thought a graceful act by men of all classes and parties, and would add to the popularity and support of the Administration." Three days later, on 14 March, several citizens of Pittsfield, including Julius Rockwell and James D. Colt, signed a recommendation to President Lincoln for Melville. The next day Herman wrote his Uncle Peter, allowing that in "many respects such an appointment would be desirable" for him, even though the "emoluments" were "not very considerable." Herman stayed with Peter and Susan the night of the eighteenth (Peter wrote in his diary) and left the next morning "at 10.30 A.M. for New York by Hudson R. Road." Hoadley on 19 March organized some prominent Lawrence citizens to urge President Lincoln to give Melville the consulship at Florence, and Alexander W. Bradford, who had put Herman up before he shipped on the *St. Lawrence* in 1839, wrote to Lincoln: "I have known him from his youth, and believe him competent to occupy any post." Bradford signed a letter to Lincoln along with prominent New Yorkers (E. P. Hurlbut, Samuel Blatchford, R. M. Blatchford, George F. M. Davis, David Dudley Field, and John A. Dix): "We believe that Mr. Melville is not only highly competent to fill the Station referred to, but that he is a patriot, & a gentleman of fine attainments, & would do honor to his country abroad."

From New York on 20 March Melville wrote to Richard Henry Dana Jr. to ask him to write Senator Sumner a strong letter himself and to procure for him "other strong letters from suitable persons in Boston." This for Melville was putting himself forward in an unwonted and distasteful fashion, and Dana reacted with persnicketiness, influenced by the earlier coldness between him and Shaw over the fugitive slave issue. Dana's public reputation concealed a core of priggishness, and now he wrote stiffly to the infirm former chief justice that he had made it his policy not to write personal recommendations and that if he were to write on Melville's behalf it would have to be after Sumner asked his opinion. Shaw, despite his weakness, on 21 March wrote a formal letter to Sumner and a personal letter. The letter contained this analysis of Melville's case: "He has suffered somewhat in his health, as his friends believe, by devotion to study, and a life of extreme solitude, and they fully believe, that with the improvement to be derived from a mild climate, a more free social intercourse with artists and men of letters and refinement, he would be able to perform the duties of American Consul at Florence, with great credit to his country." In the personal letter Shaw expended energies that would have been wholly saved if Dana had behaved more generously. He acknowledged that Dana had refused "to volunteer a recommendation to office in favor of any body." If asked by Sumner, Dana would give "all the information in his power." Shaw therefore had to ask if Sumner would "take the trouble to drop him a line of inquiry." What Dana grudgingly wrote to Sumner on 21 March, not as a letter of recommendation but as a mention in private correspondence, was a general blessing and a particular warning: "I like the notion of such consulships going to men of letters,—of note in the Republic of letters; & Melville is a capital good fellow, good manners & feelings. Duty requires me to suggest a doubt whether his health is sufficient. Of that I know nothing, & you can judge, on seeing him." Melville's sea-brother had let him down—not as damagingly as Duyckinck had done when he did his Christian duty in reviewing *Moby-Dick*, but roughly enough. Better an outright enemy like G. W. Peck than stiff-necked friends doing their moral duty.

In Manhattan Herman was reduced to chasing a man he had known by sight since his boyhood, Thurlow Weed, a founder of the Whig party, still owner of the Albany *Evening Journal*, but now a Republican who had supported former New York governor Seward the year before instead of Lincoln. Writing Weed that he had already taken "steps to secure strong letters to Senator Sumner" ("strong" was his operative word), Melville now tried to cover his old New York base by obtaining "earnest" letters from Weed and Seward, the latter to be requested by Weed, not by Melville directly. He went to the Astor House to deliver the letter to Weed, but the "bird" had "flown back to its perch—Albany." Melville sent the letter to Uncle Peter, asking him to forward it to Weed along with a note of his own. Herman was for once serious about his efforts: *"it ought to be done immediately."*

Those efforts behind him, Melville on 22 March went to Washington, expecting to press his cause there "for the next eight or ten days," which would bring him up to April Fools' Day. George Griggs armed Melville with a letter introducing him to Sumner. Melville chased Sumner about the capital, calling at his house on Friday the twenty-second and finding that he was out to dinner somewhere. That night, in company with Dr. Nourse (Herman never called him Uncle Amos—he was a second husband, a latecomer to the family), he went to Lincoln's second levee at the White House, as he wrote Lizzie:

> There was a great crowd, & a brilliant scene. Ladies in full dress by the hundred. A steady stream of two-&-two's wound thro' the apartments shaking hands with "Old Abe" and immediately passing on. This continued without cessation for an hour & a half. Of course I was one of the shakers. Old Abe is much better looking than I expected & younger looking. He shook hands like a good fellow—working hard at it like a man sawing wood at so much per cord. Mrs Lincoln is rather good-looking I thought. The scene was very fine altogether. Supurb furniture—flood of light—magnificent flowers—full band of music &c.

Melville's description of Lincoln as sawing metaphorical wood at so much per cord indicates a high degree of fellow-feeling, since it was the image he used of himself in 1849 about the way he had composed *Redburn* and *White-Jacket*.

When he wrote Lizzie on Sunday, 24 March, Melville had not "in fact been able as yet so much as even to *see* any one on the subject" of the consulship, and he was waiting for letters from New York and Massachusetts. He was boarding "in a plain home — plain fare plain people," and could not resist the punning elaboration: "in fact all plain but the road to Florence." He was still linked up with Dr. Nourse, a fellow office-seeker, on Saturday evening: "After leaving Sumner's I went with Dr. Nourse to a little sort of a party given by the wife of a man connected with one of the Departments. Had quite a pleasant evening. Several Senators were there with wives, daughters &c. The Vice President [Hannibal Hamlin] also & wife. Mrs. Hamlin is in appearance something like you — so she struck me at least. I need not add that she was very pleasing in her manner." Sunday morning he relaxed in Lafayette Park, luxuriating briefly in the early spring some four hundred miles south of Pittsfield: "This morning I spent in the park opposite the White House, sunning myself on a seat. The grass is bright & beautiful, & the shrubbery beginning to bud. It is just cool enough to make an overcoat comfortable sitting out of doors. The wind is high however, & except in the parks, all is dust." At least, he wrote Lizzie, he would "derive good from the trip at this season," although he already felt "home-sick at times, strange as it may seem." That afternoon he visited the Washington Monument, incomplete, work on it suspended. He wanted to get inside, but could not, and contented himself with externals: "Huge tower some 160 feet high of white marble." By dark he had "overwalked" himself — Melville, who had thought nothing of walking a dozen miles as late as the time of Stanwix's birth.

In an addendum the next morning Melville told Lizzie he still felt "rather overdone" from walking, but that the trip would do him good. He sent "Kisses to the children," signing himself: "Thine, My Dearest Lizzie / Herman." This is the only letter from Melville to his wife that is known to survive. In 1861, after almost fourteen years of marriage and four children, Herman complimented his wife by comparing her to the vice president's wife, whom he had just praised, and he addressed her not by some formal salutation such as "Dear Wife," but as "My Dearest Lizzie," and signed himself not merely "Yours," or "Your Husband," but "Thine, My Dearest Lizzie." Lacking the evidence of the dozens of letters Melville wrote to his wife, some commentators have been skeptical that there was any depth of conjugal love between the two. The confession of homesickness in this letter, the obvious affection for the children (even big Mackey, twelve, gets kisses), the compliment, the affectionate close — all these seem unforced, normal, as they probably were. Lizzie kept until she died a great many letters containing just such signs of deep affection as she deserved as a devoted wife. After her death they remained in the apartment in the Florence (the early apartment building with an ironic name), in the possession of Bessie, until her own death. Thereafter, the Melvilles' younger daughter, Frances, destroyed them after thoughtfully laying up stores for autograph seekers: she cut "Mrs" off the envelopes and left "Herman Melville" — salvaging what anyone would take as Melville signatures, indubitably his own name in his own handwriting. If Lizzie had not lived until two of the grandchildren were grown women, interested in Melville's works, Frances might well have destroyed the pile of manuscript pages about Billy Budd too.

On 25 March Melville's neighbor Julius Rockwell wrote a generous letter to Charles Sumner; on hearing of it, Melville wrote gratefully to Rockwell on the twenty-seventh, apologizing for being a "hurried and flurried" novice at office-seeking. When Melville at last got to see him on Thursday morning, Sumner told him that the consulship at Florence had just been filled, and suggested that Melville apply for another post. A letter from Lizzie or someone in Boston telling him of Shaw's worsening condition forced him to leave town early the next day, writing Sumner: "I desire to be considered as an applicant for the consulship at Glasgow." (Florence went to Dr. John S. Prettyman, editor of a Republican newspaper in Wilmington, Delaware. After Prettyman assumed his duties in Florence one of the senators from Kentucky had him replaced by his own favorite. Dr. Prettyman survived the costly humiliation better than Herman and Lizzie would have done.) Leaving his "affair" as it had been ("pretty much entirely" in Sumner's hands), Melville went home. Sumner faithfully bundled the recommendations together and transferred them to the Glasgow file.

Even if he left Washington near dawn, Melville could not have reached Arrowhead before Friday night, 29 March 1861. Lizzie was packed and ready when he arrived, having received a telegram that her father was very ill indeed. Shaw had ridden out through the city at noon that day and on returning home had taken "some refreshments such as wine and water." In his last illness Shaw had moved into the bedroom that his mother had occupied for many years. Over the fireplace were twelve engravings of classical scenes (ruined temples, Roman pines). The bed was hers — a narrow old four-poster, the posts massive and elaborately carved, full skirted, the canopy hanging almost two feet down on the sides, curtains at the head and side arranged so they could hold back any drafts. There were furnishings from the Savage family house (a small rocker — its legs decorously skirted — and a fire screen Hope's mother had embroidered in raised work). Hope wrote in her diary that Shaw lay down but was very restless, talking out loud: "His mind was continually talking about bondages, corporations, and business of all kinds," in a voice she could hardly understand. She led him to his mother's white-covered armchair, where he "appeared to breathe better," but did not speak a word before expiring "Saturday morning about thirty minutes before eight o'clock." In his wallet were two letters from Herman's Aunt Nancy, which he had carried with him for forty-eight years, since 1813, and which for a decade and a half had been linked in his mind with his love for his son-in-law.

Lizzie and Herman, probably with the children, must have taken the first train on Saturday, 30 March. In the noble house on the street that crossed the topmost height of Beacon Hill, Lizzie found her father dead. There was no uniting in simple grief. The three Shaw sons may have begun some work on legal matters, with or without their sister's advice and consent, but otherwise they had little to busy themselves with, for the legal community in Boston took the funeral out of the hands of the family. This was to be a state funeral, not a private service. The arrangements were made by a committee of the bar while the sheriff, John M. Clark, as chief marshal, was charged with carrying out their orders. Scheduling the funeral for 2 April gave ample time for more of the Melville family to call at Mt. Vernon Street, surely the Griggses and Hoadleys, and perhaps some of Herman and Lizzie's other relatives such as the D'Wolfs, the Nourses, Haywards, Dows, or Savages, however forbidding the weather remained. Shaw's old friend Jacob Bigelow and his wife (a cousin of Herman's) must have called. The day of the funeral, a Tuesday, the family awoke to a continuation of the "driving snow storm" *(Transcript)* that had begun the day before. After breakfast, the family and a few intimate friends gathered downstairs, most likely in the parlor where Lizzie and Herman had been married almost fourteen years earlier. The body, clothed in white, rested in a casket "covered with black velvet, richly studded with silver nails and handles" (the *Post*). A plate on the lid, said the *Courier,* "was inscribed with the name and age of the deceased." There by the casket the family's private services were conducted, led by Orville Dewey, Shaw's old friend from Sheffield, who had made Boston his temporary residence.

Some of the railroads were blocked by the storm, and even street traffic was disrupted to the point that some old friends of Shaw were unable to be at Summer Street when the doors of the New South Church opened at 11:30. Mourners filled all the pews on either side of the broad aisle, and there was what the *Post* called "a goodly assemblage in other portions," including the galleries. The *Courier* said the church was "densely thronged," and the *Post* emphasized that "a large number of ladies appeared to have braved the storm for the purpose of joining in the tribute of respect which the sad and solemn occasion constituted." Only the *Advertiser* emphasized that the church was not filled to capacity, the ferocity of the storm having kept away some mourners. Meanwhile, beginning at eleven o'clock, the assistant marshals, among them Charles F. Adams Jr., assembled in the Supreme Court room at the courthouse, where they were joined by other public officials and President Felton and the Fellows of Harvard University. A few minutes before noon the judges of the state and U.S. courts left from the courthouse in carriages for the meeting-house, while some two hundred members of the bar followed on foot, among them "many of the oldest and most eminent members of the legal profession" *(Advertiser).*

Most of the Boston newspapers described the scene in detail, so the public gained a better overview than was available to the members of the family. The *Advertiser* of 3 April described the scene at the point when everyone was seated, front pews on the right of the broad aisle "occupied by the relatives of the deceased, and back of them the friends and members of the New South Church, and others." On the left of the broad aisle the pews were occupied "by the President [Felton] and Fellows of Harvard College, Ex-Presidents Everett and Sparks, past and present Professors of the College, Governor Andrew, the Judges of the Supreme Court" and several other courts, including Benjamin R. Curtis, former justice on the U.S. Supreme Court, and many other officials and representative members of the Suffolk County bar. The mayor and members of the city government were assigned the "wall pews on the left of the altar"; the members of the state government the seats on the right. Some of these details are inaccurate (the teller of the story of the sailor and Agatha Hatch, John H. Clifford, was listed in the papers but had been prevented from attending by his "miserable" condition, suffering "with great depression & debility," as he noted in his diary the next day). In addition, the *Post* recorded the presence of groups who had assembled there as witness to particular aspects of Shaw's life, among them "members of the Cape Cod Association," members of the Massachusetts Historical Society and of the New England Historical and Genealogical Society, as well as many "members of the reverend clergy." As the *Post* said on the third, "the assemblage which gathered to pay the last public tribute of respect to the honored dead was large, and composed to a great extent of the most distinguished representatives of literature, law, and the sciences, in the Commonwealth." It was around 12:30 before the last of the procession was seated.

Then the family arrived outside the church in carriages from Mt. Vernon Street, accompanying the casket, and at 12:40 the organist began the requiem. The coffin was "followed up the aisle by those to whom the deceased was more particularly a great bereavement" — Hope Shaw, Oakes and Caroline, Elizabeth and Herman, Lem and Sam, perhaps some of Shaw's grandchildren, perhaps other relatives. As the casket and the family passed, the entire congregation arose, and remained standing until the casket (now with a white wreath on top of the black velvet) was deposited in front of the altar. The *Post* added that one of the pallbearers placed "an elegant cross of evergreen and white flowers" on the coffin. The services began with the choir chanting the Twenty-third Psalm. According to the *Post*, Dr. Dewey "then read selections from the Scriptures appropriate to the burial of the dead, making the last clause of the quotations the text for felicitous comment— 'And their works do follow them'" (Revelation 14:13). Dewey went out of his way to acknowledge Shaw's son-in-law the writer as well as the writers whom he expected to be in the church (Holmes, Longfellow, Lowell, among others, by virtue of their connection to Harvard): he first applied the text generally to all good men, then observed that it was especially true "of those distinguished in art and science, law or literature—their thoughts still live, and are a guidance to those who come after" (the *Atlas and Bee*).

The *Transcript* printed a revised report which may be closest to Dewey's actual words. Before eulogizing Shaw as "a just man, and one that feared God" (like Cornelius the centurion in Acts 10:22), Dewey gave a penetrating analysis of the qualities of the judge's mind, according to the *Transcript*, guessing shrewdly what the judges and lawyers present would say if they were allowed to speak at the bier:

> they would say that in him who for a long time was their head, they had as safe a wisdom as they ever knew in any man. Learned he was, but he was far more than learned. There is a rectitude of judgment, which sometimes is said to come from the head, and sometimes from the heart; his came from both. He clearly saw the right, and felt no temptation to swerve from it. There was no sophistication of any matter, possible with him. "This austere intellectual conscientiousness," it has been well said, "which would as soon tell a lie as hazard a sophism [palpable sophism, said the *Courier*], gave a grandeur to his mind and impressiveness to its decisions."

Dewey then conscientiously extended the implications of his observation: "It was this which caused his counsel to be so widely sought, not only in his profession, but out of it—in our University, of whose corporation he was many years a member, in a number of charitable associations, of which he was among the directors, and in the private walks of life."

Dewey faced up to Shaw's reluctance to talk about religion, a diffidence which had coexisted with his all but invariable attendance of services at the New South Church. Then a transitional sentence (given in the *Atlas and Bee* as "His venerable form would be seen no more in the holy place") led Dewey into comments on the judge's remarkable personal appearance, which had so often been described as awesomely ugly. About to be lost to them forever was that "face, in which not only grave and masculine wisdom was expressed, and each separate, prominent feature seemed the post for keenest observation, — that face which could brighten into humor or soften into tenderness." The reporter may have misheard, for the *Courier* referred to the face in which "grave and massive wisdom was depicted, but which could brighten into humor or sink into tenderness." The revised account in the *Transcript* was fullest:

> We shall see his venerable form no more in the holy place. Let me mark and signalise his *person — because* we shall see it no more. A form in whose ample dimensions, neither intellect nor feeling was buried, but which was but the larger and more sensitive vehicle for both; — a face, such as we rarely see — in which not only grave and massive wisdom seems to have seated itself, but in which each separate, prominent, protuberant feature appeared to have been a post of keen attention and observation; — and over which, if something like somnolence seemed at times to gather — as is often the case, where deep thought broods — yet could it brighten into humor, or soften into tenderness.

Dewey may have said that Shaw's wisdom had been massive, not masculine. Whichever words he spoke, whatever words Herman Melville and the others heard, still echoed in the heads of the mourners when they once more gazed at the large head of the judge.

The *Post* confirmed Dewey's words on Shaw's face brightening into humor or softening into tenderness, then added that the minister had "made an eloquent application of this remark to the present occasion." Dewey recited powerfully the conclusion to his Unitarian friend Bryant's "Thanatopsis" (here quoted as printed in the *Post*):

> So live, that when thy summons comes to join
> The innumerable caravan that moves
> To that mysterious realm where each shall take
> His chamber in the silent halls of death,
> Thou go not like the quarry slave at night,
> Scourged to his dungeon; but sustain'd and sooth'd
> By an unfaltering trust, approach thy grave,
> Like one who draws the drapery of his couch
> About him, and lies down to pleasant dreams.

Afterward, Dewey read appropriate prayers from the funeral service, and then the choir (said the *Post*) "performed in a style peculiarly suited to the occasion, the Funeral Anthem composed by Dr Calcott." ("I heard a voice from Heaven saying Arise," the *Courier* recorded; the heathenish reporter from the Democratic *Post* misheard the voice from Heaven to say something more appropriate for a deceased author: "I heard a voice from Heaven saying unto me, write, Blessed are the dead who die in the Lord: even so saith the Spirit, for they rest from their labors.")

The lid of the coffin was then opened and the cross of evergreen and white flowers was laid on the chest of the white-shrouded body. Hope, Elizabeth and Herman, all the Shaws, and other intimates of the judge were then allowed to look upon the hardly altered face. ("He was cut down so suddenly that his features had as yet undergone very little change," the *Post* said.) After the family had moved aside, others filed past the coffin, "in succession, the officials present, the members of the Suffolk bar, and the public generally." Then the members of the bar re-formed in procession and escorted the remains to King's Chapel on Tremont and School streets, where, as the *Atlas and Bee* said, the body was "temporarily deposited on account of the severity of the storm." Melville with his way of juxtaposing disparate places, times, and persons must have recalled his and Shaw's encountering the minister of King's Chapel, Ephraim Peabody, in Naushon, and driving about the island with him. Now, in King's Chapel, Hope Shaw, the three Shaw sons, Elizabeth, Herman, and Caroline, along with other intimates, had their last chance to look upon the face of the great Lemuel Shaw. They made their way to Mt. Vernon Street through the storm, feeling oddly inconclusive, since some of them would have to go through another journey and a briefer ceremony, once the weather allowed them to transport the casket to a tomb at Mount Auburn, by Shaw's beloved Harvard College.

The funeral had been for Herman Melville one of the great public scenes in his life, as full of historical significance as the "ovation" for Lafayette which he may vaguely have remembered from 1825. It was awe-striking, like a scene he had heard of from the Boston family, the dedication of the Bunker Hill Monument in the presence of Lafayette, or like the Torchlight Parade through downtown Manhattan before the election of 1844. Now, in the outward storm, Melville's memory was thronged with scenes from the 1820s with his Grandfather Melvill and his father, Shaw's intimate friend, and with wildly contrasting memories of his exuberant steps up to the door of 49 Mt. Vernon in 1844 and the next years before his marriage there in 1847, memories of Malcolm's birth there in 1849, memories of Thanksgivings more and more strained in the last decade during the slow aftermath of his career.

There were the odd gaffes and discrepancies in the Boston news reports, which must have caught the eyes of some of the inmates of the house, and for Melville there were strange distractions. The *Daily Evening Traveller* on 2 April reported from the Sydney *Herald* of 21 January an "Awful Massacre of the Crew of the American Whaling Ship Superior," and the Boston *Herald* on 3 April reported "The Massacre of the crew of the Whale Ship Superior" (the massacre of twenty-six New Bedford whalemen by natives of Treasury Island, in the Solomon Group). Herman's cousin Nilly Van Rensselaer Thayer, still a Mt. Vernon Street neighbor, may have tried to relieve Hope Shaw of some of her responsibilities by inviting the mourners over for a quiet dinner with family and old acquaintances. Governor Clifford, at least, before or after Shaw's death, had been invited to the Thayer house for the third, but had to decline because of the same severe indisposition that had kept him from the funeral the day before.

Herman and Lizzie, probably with the children, stayed on in Boston for some days after the funeral. Shaw's will was probated on 8 April and less than two months later, on 3 June, Herman and Lizzie were back in Boston to accept Benjamin R. Curtis's condolences and his resignation of Lizzie's trust fund in favor of her half-brothers. Even before the funeral her half-brothers may have let Lizzie know that she would inherit some money right away and more later, to a total of some $15,000, a substantial sum, since she already owned Arrowhead free and clear. Lizzie apparently left at least $5000 worth of the money in Boston properties, from which for some years she received about $500 annually, once the accountings had been made. With her inheritance, however little of it was cash in hand, Lizzie and Herman could more easily give up the wild idea of exiling themselves to Europe and consider how to keep their capital (the first they had possessed) from dwindling away before Herman was able to find some way of making money. Even without a job, Herman felt he could afford to begin buying books again, for he put the date 9 April in *The Poetical Works of Shelley* in two volumes (Boston, 1857) and in a recent set of *The Poetical Works of Edmund Spenser* in five volumes (Boston, 1855). Presumably he bought them in Boston, where there were real bookstores, although he wrote "Pittsfield" after the date each time. Odd memories of the dead were at work in the purchase of each of these books, the Shelley reminding him of the aged artist William Edward West, who had told stories of Shelley and Byron at Dr. Francis's house in Bond Street, the Spenser inevitably reminding him of his poring over his father's set, which he may already have promised to give to Augusta when he found a replacement set.

Going to a bookstore on 9 April 1861 was one of those odd persistences of the quotidian amid extraordinary circumstances. The state funeral for Judge Shaw on 2 April was followed four days later by news that Lincoln was sending a relief expedition to Fort Sumter, in the harbor of Charleston, now declared by its residents to be in the Confederate state of South Carolina. On 12 April the War between the States began when Confederate shore batteries at Fort Moultrie opened fire on Fort Sumter. In *Clarel* Melville looked back upon the "dolorous winter ere the war" as a "sad arch between contrasted eras" (pt. 4, canto 5). Melville's United States had burgeoned geographically and the flag had been altered again and again to accommodate new stars, but the government had seemed fixed, the Constitution never altered by an amendment in his lifetime. Early April 1861 was phantasmagorical: just as Shaw had been stowed temporarily in a vault awaiting proper burial, the United States had been placed in suspension, awaiting its own burial — or resurrection.

At Arrowhead on 12 April the Melvilles must have focused simultaneously on the impersonal significance of the assault and their personal connection with the locality, for Charleston was Richard Lathers's home, and Abby had lived with him there early in their marriage, and they all must have known that the Latherses were at that moment somewhere in the Confederate states, in a country at war with their own. From the start, like most Americans, the Melvilles were touched by the war both as bystanders and as participants. Three days later the president who had shaken hands with Melville so sturdily called for 75,000 volunteers to suppress the insurrection. On 20 April sailors loyal to the Union destroyed the frigate *United States* at Gosport Navy Yard, Norfolk, Virginia, to keep it from falling into Confederate hands — news Melville must have received as if he were an Englishman of Dr. Johnson's time hearing of the destruction of Lisbon, or, more precisely, as if he had heard of the destruction of a populous city where he passed many months in his early manhood.

By June, Melville's name was on the Militia Roll, as it had been earlier, although every local knew that he had been ill for years. On 23 June Sarah Morewood outlined to Captain Tom, at sea, the way the war was affecting Pittsfield: "I suppose you hear something of the state of these, no longer *United* States, some 'rumors of War.' Indeed this is the truth. War is in our Midst, as yet the people who have gone off to fight have not met Army to Army, but small companies have met and human blood has been spilled, so that we are looking at the heading of every newspaper for tidings of A Battle, a fight upon the Soil of Free America." She reported the local war efforts from her personal knowledge: "We have had rather an exciting time of it in the village this spring getting our Volunteer troops off to the War, two full Companies have gone from our little Town. Such fine fellows many of them were. I have given Capt. Chipp's Company the Guide Colours, they are made from Chinese Silks and are very bright and pretty. God Guide the Men and march them to victory." Sarah threw herself into encouraging the morale of the soldiers, many of whom wrote to her after they went south. Like everyone in Pittsfield, Melville witnessed the equipping of the companies and the martial drilling that preceded the departure of the men by railroad.

For Melville the next months in 1861 may have dragged out their lengths as wearily as any months on the *Acushnet* or the *United States*, but evidence is fragmentary. Lizzie may have remained in Boston after the funeral. Stanwix apparently had been taken to Gansevoort, for on Bessie's eighth birthday, 22 May, he returned (but only for a visit?) to Pittsfield, in company with his Aunt Fanny and his Cousin Lucy, then almost five years old. As he wrote his Grandmother Shaw weeks later, his father had been in sight on the platform when the train pulled in, and had carried them home in "the great waggon," the old brown lumber wagon. The girls were there at Arrowhead, but "Mamma" and Mackey were not, and the "next day papa went to Boston," so the implication is that Lizzie and Malcolm stayed on at Mt. Vernon Street for mutual consolation with the Shaws, and Melville had to return to Boston to sign legal documents, his signature now being supplementary to his wife's.

Melville put himself out to witness some of the military activities, for Stanwix's letter relates an event of 10 June: "Papa took me to the cattle Show grounds to see the soldiers drill, but we did not see them, because one [of] the factories was on fire, it was too bad." While smoke rose above the Pittsfield Woolen Company, Melville took Stanwix to the west of town for "a ride all through the Cemetery," a special treat, for every year the once-raw terrain was becoming a more and more beautiful place for meditative driving. Melville's sister Fanny may have stayed on at Arrowhead to help, or Augusta may have replaced her, since sometime in June Melville gave Augusta *The Bijou; or Annual of Literature and the Arts* (London, 1828), which someone noted had been "Originally Priscilla's" — probably Cousin Priscilla, whose grave Melville would have driven by with Stanwix. Tom was corresponding with both Ellen Brittain and Sarah, and he preserved Sarah's letter of 23 (she dated it 22) June. By then Lizzie was home, and she had probably brought Helen back with her, for Sarah wrote her "Dear Friend Capt. Tom": "Your brother Herman and his wife and your Sister Helen have just gone from our house, they have been over to take a Sunday dinner with us which we all enjoyed." Despite the war and personal cataclysmic events, Tom was in their minds: "We thought of you and spoke of you, and wished you were here," and since he was away she set herself to "have a little talk" with him on paper, partly to guy him with news of "how the 'gall in the pink dress gets on,'" but also to tell him "how we are trotting our road in life, how the Farm, Country, things in general, get on, that is the things about us here in our World of a mile south of the Town." She was "growing old, growing thin," weighing only "ninety two pounds." Still, she hoped to meet him again, so urged him to "keep out of the Pirates way, for the South have sent out a number of ships and rascals to seize upon our Merchant ships and property." No, she decided, "the Meteor will shoot by the Pirates like a true Meteor I trust."

On 28 June (in preparation for Herman's arrival in New York) Allan invited Evert and George Duyckinck out to spend a day in New Rochelle on the estate of Richard Lathers. By 1 July Herman was in town and the two crossed to the Brooklyn Navy Yard, as Evert recorded in his diary, so Melville could see his cousin. Guert had been charged with refitting ships to be used in warfare, immediately, and was overworked to the point that his commander reported to Washington on 6 May that "Commdr. Gansevoort has perhaps more than he and his assistants can perform, in attending to his many arduous and legitimate duties in the Yard." Those words may have conveyed a covert warning that Guert was best left where he was. Devastated by guilt, pride, and the exhausting power of self-justification after his complicity in the hangings on the *Somers* in 1842, Guert had performed gallantly at Vera Cruz during the war with Mexico, and as recently as 1856 as commander of the U.S. sloop-of-war *Decatur*, had defended Seattle, Washington, from a force of Indians estimated at some two thousand, providing what the secretary of war (in a letter to the secretary of the navy, 6 March 1856) called "very efficient aid" to the military forces "in their efforts to protect the inhabitants of the Territory of Washington from the incursions of the Indians." Yet on 18 September 1856, from Panama, Commodore William Mervine wrote to the secretary of the navy that Captain Farragut, commandant of the Navy Yard at Mare Island, had suspended Guert Gansevoort for being intoxicated at eleven in the morning. Mervine knew Guert: "I was not surprised to hear of the circumstances having long known indirectly that his habits in this respect are bad; but there is such a strong disposition generally prevailing among the younger officers to screen such acts, that it is seldom that any officer so offending can be brought to proper accountability." Removed from command, Guert had hung on in the service. In November 1857 he begged the secretary of the navy to give him "the Command of any sea going ship" that he might think proper, or at least to put him in line for the soon-to-be-vacated post of "U.S. Naval Rendezvous" at the Brooklyn Navy Yard, and on 9 April 1858 wrote his Uncle Peter to help in winning that post for him.

Guert won his Brooklyn position, but continued to drink. He and his brother the bulbous-nosed Stanwix were often in the Glens Falls area. In the Adirondacks, just when the region was beginning to be recognized as a great resource for wealthy sportsmen, they improved their acquaintance with the old navy man and dime novelist Col. Edward Z. C. Judson, better known as Ned Buntline, who was living at Eagle's Nest, his cabin at Blue Mountain

Lake, where his literary subject William Cody later visited several times. On his trips into Glens Falls, Buntline had the reputation of sitting next to a barrel of whiskey until he had drunk it dry, according to one tall tale told by Harold Hochschild, a mining executive, who wrote *Township 34* about Ned and other characters. Buntline was the kind of drinker to inspire such stories. One anecdote, by Frederick Eugene Pond, in a 1919 book, *Life and Adventures of "Ned Buntline,"* has Ned entertaining Guert and Stanwix at dinner and forming "a striking trio" as they stood together, being "about the same size" and " 'bearded like the pard.' " Commented an old bystander: "There's three of the handiest men with weapons that ever struck Northern New York." This story is the likelier to be true since the author shows no awareness that the Gansevoort brothers were cousins to an American novelist named Melville. Just before the war Guert and Stanwix Gansevoort had been doing some hard drinking around hard customers. Guert now hoped to make a contribution to the war effort worthy of his Gansevoort grandfather, the Hero of Fort Stanwix, and despite his spotted record, the whole family now looked to Guert for military glory.

On this trip to Brooklyn, Melville and Duyckinck were not only going to visit Guert, they were there to see for themselves a tragic sight which was blazoned in the newspapers and mournfully signaled by flags flying at half-mast. First, they eased their way into their mission (as Duyckinck recorded in his diary): "Visited the Savannah, the Iroquois, fresh from the Mediterranean and Garibaldi. Lt Buckner of deck of the former delivered a brief lecture on his Dahlgren gun." Then they boarded the receiving ship *North Carolina* and went on the quarterdeck to see the solemn spectacle: "the body of Capt [James H.] Ward was lying, with lighted candles at the feet and head, brought from his vessel the Freeborn in the Potomac where he was slain at his gun by a *secessionist* shot from Mathias Point. Who shall fathom the iniquity of this rebellion?" The body of Captain Ward that Melville and Duyckinck saw was that of the first Union naval officer to be slain in the war. Melville in his journal, only eleven months earlier, had brooded about death as the "King of Terrors" to a mourning mother: "Not so easily will his fate be washed out of her heart, as his blood from the deck." Now he had a realizing sense that everyone in the North, and the South, was face to face with the King of Terrors.

Yet Melville's life did not change immediately. He was still buying poetry, on 3 July *The Poetical Works of James Thomson* (Boston, 1854), containing poems familiar to him from his youth. Perhaps he picked up the volume on his rendezvous for the promised excursion to New Rochelle, which took place that same day, the day before the strangely altered "Glorious Fourth." Evert recorded in his diary: "With Herman & Allan Melville and George to

Mr Lathers at New Rochelle. Siddons in the cars—joined us for the day at Mr L's. A hospitable open handed entertainment—the beauty of nature, the tranquillity of the landscape stretching to the blue waters of the sound reflecting the azure of the skies a happy relief to the war agitations of the times." The man who joined them was Joachim Hayward Stocqueler, who under the pseudonym J. H. Siddons had lectured in February 1860, one assumes coincidentally, on a topic familiar to Melville: "Travel, Its Pleasures, Advantages, and Requirements," delivered at Clinton Hall, New York.

Already, after only a few weeks of war, Winyah Park was a refuge, all the more precious because the master of the house had astonishing stories to tell of his and Abby's adventures in the Confederacy in early springtime. George Duyckinck left an account of the day in a letter to Rosalie Baker on 5 July: "We had a stroll through the woods . . . a rest on the rocks, a glass of blackberry wine . . . a long talk on the pi[a]zza looking out on the Sound—a fine dinner. It was an effort to resist the hospitable invitation to stay all night and tear ourselves away a little after six . . . for the last train to the city." During the session on the piazza, most likely, Lathers had in his hands the copy of Abraham Tucker's *The Light of Nature* which Melville had given him in 1853, and which Evert Duyckinck had paid particular attention to during a visit to Winyah in 1859. Perhaps Evert pulled the volume down to show George. In any event, Lathers in the book sketched a frail George Duyckinck, the peculiarly curved lips, the wispy chin beard, the long straight nose, the mass of long hair. Melville's escape to otherworldly Winyah was magical, but tormenting, given the story of Richard and Abby's escape from New Orleans. That evening they saw a comet, described in Evert's diary as "a brilliant apparition in the north near the head of the Great Bear which first made its appearance in the heavens a few nights since." Signs and portents or not, Herman was back in Pittsfield in a few days, and poor George was still being pursued by the failing Sarah Morewood. From Troy on 8 July, that far on her way with Dr. John Todd toward "the great woods of the wild Adirondack range," Sarah urged George Duyckinck to join them, alone, or perhaps to come up with her husband, if he were to decide to join the party. Dr. Todd was minister of the First Congregational Church in Pittsfield, long ago the inventor of the *Index Rerum*, the autodidact's bible so cherished by Gansevoort, and the author of the *Student's Manual* from which Allan had learned to refrain from onanism: he could chaperon even a woman with Adirondack Thoughts.

Once Aunt Catherine had died and Maria had settled at Gansevoort with Augusta and Fanny, the center of the family began to shift from Arrowhead to the Mansion House. Around 1860, Uncle Leonard and Aunt Mary Chandonette Gansevoort's surviving family moved from Brooklyn to Glens Falls, up on the curve of the Hudson, a sleigh ride away in winter. Cousin Len had been there in 1841. Now railroad extensions put the hamlet of Gansevoort in immediate proximity to Lake George to the northeast as well as Saratoga Springs and Albany to the south, so visits to Uncle Herman's did not mean days of imprisonment in a village with two general stores and two competing Sunday schools, one controlled by Augusta, and a total population (counting inhabitants of farms roundabout) of 162, in 1860. It took a while, but others in the family gradually realized that if they were to see Maria, Fanny, and Augusta very often, or see more than one of them at a time, they would have to travel to Gansevoort. Helen went there in August 1862 and September 1863, but now, in July 1861, she stayed at Arrowhead with Bessie and Frances and perhaps Malcolm as well while Herman and Lizzie, improbably, got into the buggy and drove off on their first cross-country excursion together in many years.

This is what Stanwix wrote his Grandmother Shaw, from Gansevoort, on 11 July: "Aunt Augusta had a letter from papa, and he sent me a stamp with Benjamin Franklin head on it. . . . I was very glad to hear th[at] Papa, and Mama are coming in the buggy to Gansevoort, I hope they will find some way to bring Mackey along." In a postscript to Stanwix's letter Augusta confirmed: "We are expecting a visit from Herman & Lizzie very soon. Helen has promised to stay with the children." It might be thought that Stanwix had misunderstood some joke of his father's about modes of transportation and Augusta had let stand what he wrote, especially since Melville was thought to have been in Albany on 12 July, when Cousin Kitty received a message which she relayed to her brother, Henry, on the thirteenth: "Herman M. wishes to be most kindly remembered & hopes you are sound on Affairs of the country." The message probably came by mail, for in early August Herman and Lizzie went directly to Gansevoort without stopping in Albany. Their purpose may have been to deliver the buggy and Charlie to his mother and Uncle Herman. After all, Maria and Augusta had proved ten years before that they could manage Charlie, and Maria could not be without local transportation. Charlie in any case was getting too old for Herman's preferred style of driving. Lizzie and Herman had their long slow drive together, with three children safe at Arrowhead and one safe at Gansevoort. They could stop over to recruit themselves and Charlie at the Van Schaick house in Troy or at the house of Aunt Maria Peebles and the Lord of the Isle in Lansingburgh, if they were so inclined, and they could luxuriate in knowing the children were well cared for and that no horror-striking telegraphic dispatch was apt to await them along their route. On 10 August, during their visit, Melville reported to Uncle Peter: "I am glad to say, that Uncle Herman, although feeble, and almost entirely confined to his sofa during the day, is yet, for the most part, free from pain, has a pretty good appetite, and sleeps well." Herman and Lizzie wanted to visit Uncle Peter on their way home, between trains, but failed because Peter had just left with Aunt Susan and Kitty for a vacation at the Pavilion at Rockaway, Long Island, and Melville used a few free minutes of the layover to buy at the shop of B. E. Gray *The Poetical Works of Alfred Tennyson* (Boston, 1861), in two volumes.

To make up for being away, Uncle Peter on 12 August invited Herman and Lizzie to come and stay with him for several days, later, realizing they had never paid him such a visit. Everyone was punctilious during this time, Uncle Peter relieved to have Maria caring for their brother Herman, close at hand yet not financially dependent on him, and the older cousins tiptoeing around old resentments in Kitty's presence, since she knew absolutely nothing of the estrangements and conducted herself as if the world had begun afresh with her maturity. If there were a few loosenesses in family connections, then a sensible girl like her should go about tightening them without worrying too much about past history. As the remaining children of the Revolutionary General Gansevoort grew old (the three acceptable ones and the remittance man Wessel), affection suffusingly covered over the resentments. Uncle Peter, partly because he had ignored Malcolm so long already there was no point noticing him now, partly because the name Stanwix could only be received as a compliment to himself, however incidentally, put himself out to be kind toward Stanny, scaring him a little in the process. From Gansevoort Stanny wrote Uncle Peter on 5 September: "I think the reason that Aunt Susan did not answer my letter was that I wrote it so badly. I could have written a better letter, and now I write this one to you to show you that I can." Stanwix witnessed Augusta's efforts just then to assemble a collection of family photographs, and his papa cooperated to the momentous extent of sitting for a new portrait at Rodney Dewey's studio on North Street. Melville's looks were not delicate enough to seem handsome to his contemporaries who saw him in the flesh, and he denied the public chances to have his mug engraved in the magazines, but the man in this portrait is prepossessing, self-possessed, stalwart, and (say it) handsome.

On 11 September in Pittsfield former governor George Nixon Briggs, leader of the Temperance movement, president of the American Tract Society, died of a wound inflicted when he reached for something on a shelf where a loaded gun had been placed for safety. Pittsfield mourned: "flags were displayed at half mast, the places of business were closed, and all the bells tolled as the procession moved along the street." The funeral procession was long, as befitted what was in effect a second state funeral in the same year. The pallbearers and the eight coffin-bearers were men known to the Melvilles, and (according to William C. Richards in his 1866 *Great in Good-*

ness) among "the strangers from abroad" were ex-governors Washburn and Clifford, close associates of Judge Shaw, and many other prominent politicians and officials of the American Tract Society, the Baptist Missionary Union, and the American Temperance Union. Briggs's death marked an end of a political era at the western end of the commonwealth almost as powerfully as Shaw's had done in the east. Even as far as Arrowhead, the tolling of the bells could be heard, and Herman and Lizzie, there or at the funeral, recollected their past associations with the dead man and the mourners. Knowing what eminent men were in town, Melville would have recalled a night with Judge Shaw in Nantucket when John Clifford told them the story of Agatha Hatch.

In late October Melville was in New York, for on the twenty-seventh he bought there Henry Taylor's *Notes from Life in Seven Essays* (Boston, 1853) and Leigh Hunt's *Rimini and Other Poems* (Boston, 1844). Sometime that fall Peter Gansevoort visited his nephew Guert at the Navy Yard, where Guert showed him the new sloop-of-war *Adirondack*, then "on the stocks," and told his uncle that "he desired & hoped to command" her. Peter's daughter, Kitty, may have been with him, for she wrote her brother, Henry, on 4 November, from Albany: "Guert is well — & very busily engaged — exceedingly anxious to be ordered off — but the Sec-of-the-Navy tells him he is doing his country greater service by his presence at the Navy Yard than if he was on ship board." On 15 November the New York *Tribune* carried news strange and moving to Melville — the fate of the "terrible stone fleet, on a mission as pitiless as the granite that freights it." The Union navy had loaded fifteen old whaleships with stones at New Bedford and sent them off to be sunk in the channels of the harbors of Charleston and Savannah so as to prevent blockade runners from getting through (with mundane supplies, but also with medicine, it became clear to the public). Charleston became "an inland city," and the already dwindling American whaling fleet further reduced.

Instead of wintering in Italy, the Melvilles faced the prospect of wintering in the Berkshires again, and, fearful that the previous year's Arctic torture would be part of a continuing pattern, decided to rent a place in Manhattan for a few months. Probably they went first to Boston so Lizzie could be at Mt. Vernon Street, where the family was celebrating Thanksgiving for the first time without the chief justice. An item on 12 December in the *Berkshire County Eagle* announced that Melville had "left town for the winter, which he is to spend in New York and Boston." Sarah Morewood had wanted to visit New York before Christmas but delayed, partly because she wanted to stay there until the Melvilles had left for New York; then on 12 December, after they had gone, she herself was "ill in bed," as she wrote George Duyckinck. She described taking a barrel of fine eating apples on a sleigh to the "regiment of soldiers in Camp on our Fair grounds." The "Boys" were more playful than hungry: "we had a regular scene, a mimic battle, the apples serving for balls," and at the end "the regiment drew up and closed us in their lines and cheered us till our own horses were frightened at the din." This complicated woman revelled in earning the adulation of soldiers and exciting herself by that adulation: "I never saw or heard such a row, and was quite innocent of creating it, going quietly to give an apple apiece to the troops." She was not quite innocent.

Melville rented a house at 150 East Eighteenth Street, his address in January 1862, but there is another unaccounted-for address, 103 East Tenth Street, inscribed without a date in a set of Byron, which may be the place he rented for part of December when he was in New York City alone. Melville wrote "learn by heart" beside section 3 of the third canto of *The Island: or Christian and His Comrades*, beginning "A little stream came tumbling from the height," and by a passage in the eleventh canto he noted: "this is excellent—the practical abandonment of good-humored devil-may-care. Byron is a better man in Don Juan than in his serious poems." While he was so close, Melville called on Henry T. Tuckerman at 15 West Tenth Street, the Tenth Street Studio Building where many artists had studios. Melville missed him, and Tuckerman could not return his call because, as he told Evert Duyckinck on 17 January, he was laid up "with a severe neuralgic attack."

Herman took Bessie for a pre-Christmas 1861 visit to Gansevoort to see Stanwix, his mother, and his sisters Augusta and Fanny, and on the twenty-third, heading for Boston with his sister Fanny and his daughter Bessie, he stopped in Albany. According to Uncle Peter's diary, they dined at his home and visited until 8 P.M., "when they went to Stanwix Hall, to lodge & proceed to Boston at an early hour tomorrow morning." The Hoadleys and Mary Curtis, the daughter of George and Catherine Curtis, came down to see them in Boston and took Fanny back to spend the winter in Lawrence. By Christmas the family was rejoicing in the news that Tom would return home soon. In Boston or Dorchester, John D'Wolf gave Melville his *A Voyage to the North Pacific and a Journey through Siberia More Than Half a Century Ago*, (Cambridge, 1861) (and a copy to his sister-in-law Priscilla Melvill, who subsequently gave it to Kate Hoadley). Perhaps it was at Christmas that Elizabeth inscribed a copy of *The Holy Bible* (London: G. E. Eyre & W. Spottiswoode, 1859): "Malcolm Melville from his Mother — 1861."

[21]

A Humble Quest for an Aesthetic Credo
January–April 1862

> Never will that artist advance to perfection who cannot perceive his own defects, and who has no fear of finding himself surpassed by the works of others; much more safely does the hope of the modest and timid student conduct him towards his object, while, earnestly pursuing an upright walk in life, he does due honour to the works of good masters and labours with all diligence to imitate their productions.
>
> Melville marks this passage in Vasari's *Lives* (3.324),
> at the start of the section on Bartolommeo da Bagnacavallo

MELVILLE WAS IN BOSTON with Lizzie and the children, except for Stanwix, on New Year's Day of 1862, when Tom arrived—by train from Portland, of all places. Tom stayed with Herman and Lizzie at the Shaw house or with Helen a night or two, then the two brothers and the sister went to Lawrence, leaving Lizzie at Mt. Vernon Street with the girls and Malcolm, unless he was at school in nearby Newton already. At Lawrence the visitors could delight in Kate's daughters and husband, and see Fanny. The sisters promptly extracted a promise from Herman to be photographed in New York City, and badgered him through the next months to fulfill his promise, but by April they still had not received the carte de visite they expected. Tom had admired John extravagantly from early 1854, and Herman by this time may have lived past some of his apparently entrenched hostility, or perhaps only edginess, toward their brother-in-law. Herman may not have realized even yet just how brilliantly John infused aesthetic values into the machines which Herman distrusted on principle, but John was, at close range, irresistible, a slow, low talker who formed his sentences elegantly and forcefully and whose views were, like Herman's, apt to be expressed philosophically. As his hearing deteriorated he spoke more softly. Those who leaned closer to him in order to hear him and to make him hear them found that the enforced proximity led to genuine intimacy, since the man himself was so sensitive, open, and decent. Besides, he loved Kate and was making her as happy as she was capable of being, given her panicky way of enacting the maternal injunctions to achieve what Augusta more benignly called "beautiful order." More obviously damaged by the disruption of her childhood than the others, Kate still imposed system rigidly, warring against chaos albeit by proxy: she managed to have her sisters and servants do more for her than any of her sisters would have let anyone else do for them. Her brothers could not be around her without being reminded afresh just how hard it was to live with someone compulsive about the alignment of the vinegar cruet with the North Star.

In the first days of January the travelers and the Hoadleys, with Fanny, all went down to Boston to visit Lizzie and Mrs. Shaw, as Maria in Gansevoort wrote to her niece Kitty Gansevoort on 6 January. Then Fanny returned to Lawrence to help with what was expected to be a temporary move of the Hoadley family to New Bedford in February, when John took control of the Copper Works there. The stay would be brief, lasting only the duration of the Rebellion, but in that interval the navy needed copper sheathing in bulk, and immediately. John was the man for the job.

Herman and Tom left Boston for New York to see Allan and his daughters, and Jane. On the way Tom had ample opportunity to tell something of his amazing adventures. We know his travel route, at least, from Kitty Gansevoort's report to Henry on 16 January: "He sold I suppose you know his 'Ship Meteor' to the Bengal government & then his Ship owners — Peabody & co gave him permission to journey home by the *over land route*, which he wisely did — Left *Calcutta* for *Madras* then to *Point Galle* thence to *Aden* up the *Red Sea* to *Suez* thence to *Cairo*." From Alexandria, then Malta, he went by steamer to France, "by rail to Paris — twenty one hours then to London & then Liverpool where he sailed by the *'Norwegian'*" — to Portland, Maine, then to Boston on New Year's Day, "almost the 1st New Years he has spent in the U.S. in sixteen years." While he was in New York seeing Allan and Jane and the four nieces, Tom made his will, with Allan's help and surely at Allan's suggestion. In it he left his entire estate to Allan's four daughters, nothing to Herman's children, or Kate's. Then the shipless captain departed for Gansevoort on 6 January, leaving behind a happy lawyer no longer burdened with fraternal dread that Tom might die intestate. Herman stayed on in New York in the house at 150 East Eighteenth Street. Lizzie stayed in Boston until 18 January, when, leaving Malcolm at school in Newton, she took the girls to New York.

At Gansevoort the women were busy. Maria looked over Kitty Gansevoort's "Diagrams for army socks & army mittens" and pronounced (in a 6 January letter): "However much disposed to knit for our good Soldiers, I cannot promise to do so this winter." Her responsibilities lay at home, especially while Tom was there. Having visited the family in Gansevoort, Tom paid his respects to his Albany relatives. In her 16 January report to Henry,

Cousin Kitty said she found Tom "very much improved both in mind & personal appearance," so much improved that she elaborated: "He is looking remarkably well—has developed very much & in my opinion is the most agreable of Aunt Melville's sons." The most tactful of Maria's living sons, Tom asked "all about" Henry and showed himself gratified by being granted "a *grafic* account." Tom went back to Boston with the intention of sailing again, in a few days, "as Captain of the 'Bengal,' " bound, he thought, for Calcutta—a Bulkington, whose feet seemed scorched by the earth, even in a New England or New York January.

Herman Melville spent the last week or so of January in the newly rented house at 150 East Eighteenth Street lying in bed, "rheumatism-bound," having been stricken before he had a chance to give Evert Duyckinck his new address; the last address Duyckinck had was from December. It was before the rheumatism flared up that Melville called on Henry Tuckerman. On 17 January 1862 (miswriting 1861) Tuckerman asked Duyckinck: "Do you ever see Herman Melville? If so, will you be so kind as to explain to him that the reason I have not returned his call, is that I have been laid up for several weeks with a severe neuralgic attack." He added: "Had I known his address I should have sent him a line," a fair indication that he had the December address and knew that it had been only temporary. Duyckinck did not yet know Melville's new address, and Tuckerman was probably not the only one who turned to Duyckinck for help in tracking Melville down at this period: this may be when S. Lorimer Graham Sr. sent a messenger to Evert asking for Melville's address. Soon Melville was in touch with Duyckinck, who then relayed Tuckerman's message promptly. Once they had both recuperated, Tuckerman and Melville met, presumably in February, and very likely met more than once in the next months as Melville sallied out on book-buying expeditions, down Fourth Avenue, below Fourteenth Street, in the Broadway-Bowery area of Astor Place, near where he had lived from 1847 to 1850.

Genuinely fond of Melville, Tuckerman was working a compliment to him into his long memoir for his new edition of the 1858 *Old New York: or, Reminiscences of the Past Sixty Years* by Dr. John W. Francis, their gracious host at Bond Street, who had died on 8 February 1861. Tuckerman was a loyal man. By now it was a relief to Melville to find someone of the old days, another liberal spirit who might appear old fogyish to the younger generation. A writer on Tuckerman in the New York *Tribune* on 18 December 1871 gave some hint of qualities the men shared: "Conservative in his tendencies, he had little tolerance for innovations in style, or for audacious theories in speculation. He . . . could never disguise his aversion to the eccentricities of reform, which, however consecrated by genius or eloquence, defied the proprieties of social life, and ventured on the borders of chaos in pursuit of the millennium." The house the Melvilles had rented was suitable for modest entertaining, but the natural thing would have been for Melville to call on Tuckerman at his study (built as a painter's studio) in the Artists' Building in Tenth Street. Like Hoadley, Tuckerman suffered from "a partial deafness," Duyckinck put on record, so he preferred his own rooms, where he could seat himself to best auditory advantage. For his part, Melville's sensibilities were offended by any rented house whether with bare walls or walls hung with other people's notions of art, a rented house with, most likely, minimal and modern furnishings. Tuckerman's place was just the sort of cozy quarters he could have furnished if he had been wealthy and a bachelor. Duyckinck described the "order and neatness" of his studio as indicating the qualities of Tuckerman's mind: "Here, as Mr. Tuckerman sat in the subdued light at his small neat desk, the walls clothed with books and pictures and various memorials of art about him, he might be fancied one of those devoted students of the olden time symbolized to us in the paintings of the age of Dürer, when learning was the devotion of a lifetime, when men grew old in writing folios, and the length of their labors was an anticipation of the duration of their fame." We know many of the books and paintings and memorials of art, for the Tuckerman family auctioned possessions after his death. If they took the choicest items for themselves, they left enough to indicate the range of the collection, and it was Tuckerman's collection, as much as Richard Lathers's, which inspired Melville to make the best art collection he could make, for the rest of his life, beginning with the money Lizzie had inherited, and continuing after he was earning some himself. He could not think seriously of collecting paintings, although he acquired a few in the next decades. As a collector of engravings he would always work with far less money than Tuckerman could lay out, but with a comparably educable and eventually a highly educated eye.

Tuckerman shared his art works with Melville, not as a proud possessor, a role even good-hearted Lathers could fall into, but as a fellow lover of beauty and fellow appreciator of skilled craftsmanship. In Tuckerman's rooms Melville saw the works later auctioned, among them portraits of American writers and scenes illustrating American literature. These were among the many paintings and engravings: *Head of an Old Man* (by Daniel Huntington, who painted Lathers); *Portrait of Washington Allston* (by James Jackson Jarves, whom Melville had hoped to meet in Italy); a portrait of Franklin; *Tomb of Caius Cest[iu]s* and *Grave of Keats* (sites Melville had visited, by "R. S."); and *Washington Irving at Sunny-Side*. There were reproductions of works by one of the Van Eycks (Hubert or Jan) and one by Andrea del Sarto, already familiar to Melville from Vasari and Browning; a Flemish *Boors Drinking;* and a sketch by Melville's friend Felix Darley, unframed. Seventy-two lots of

Tuckerman's engravings were auctioned, including these: a full set of four engravings of Thomas Cole's *Voyage of Life* (the originals of which Melville had seen in 1847); Correggio's *Madonna;* Edwin Henry Landseer's *Combat of Stags;* a colored *Ishmael;* and *St. Michael* (Raphael). These were among the framed engravings: *Dr. Johnson and Goldsmith;* Frederic Church's *Heart of the Andes; Humboldt; Washington* (a proof copy of the William E. Marshall engraving); *Daniel Webster; Tennyson; Burns; Bryant; Garibaldi; Madonna* (Thomas Crawford); *Washington; Everett; Irving; Dr. Francis;* and *Judge Kent* (who had honored young Gansevoort in 1826). Others included a *Tropical Scene* by Church; *Noon on the Sea-Shore* by John F. Kensett; and a *Scriptural Sketch* by Crawford.

Among the engravings in several portfolios were views of Berlin and Newport; a portrait of Charles Loring Elliot by Asher B. Durand; a combat of horses by Landseer; and a colored *Venice by Moonlight.* Tuckerman owned many framed photographs of works of art, including one of the Tribuno in Florence and San Marco in Venice, both of which Melville had visited. He had sculptures, among them a bust of Bryant; he had a bust of Daniel Webster on a pedestal; he had busts or statuettes of Tasso and Dante; he owned five John Rogers groups *(Country Post-Office, The Foundling, Coming to the Prison, Picket Guard,* and *The Town Pump).* He had at least one bas-relief, a mask of Shakespeare.

Tuckerman did not have long runs of important early newspapers and magazines (such as another Duyckinck acquaintance, Oakey Hall, still possessed at this time), but he had a set of *Blackwood's Magazine* in half-sheep, volumes 1–84 (78 missing at the time of the sale, perhaps borrowed and not returned). He had Elizabeth Barrett Browning in quantity, as well as her husband (in 1869 adding the Boston *The Ring and the Book*). Among his American contemporaries he had works by William Allen Butler and George Duyckinck (the *Life of George Herbert*). He had two copies of Darley's illustrations of Sylvester Judd's *Margaret.* He had ten Hawthorne volumes, including a first edition of *The Scarlet Letter,* and four Thoreaus, including a first of *Walden.* No Whitman was listed in the auction catalog.

Unmarried, yet moored in his life's work on American artists, psychologically secure as Charles Fenno Hoffman had not been, Tuckerman was a man Melville could respect and envy—envy for his receiving a cosmopolitan education in which "mental cultivation" was given its own good time rather than being forced into bloom, with all the awkwardness that had marked his own *Mardi;* envy for the formal grand tour and the prolonged stay that allowed Tuckerman to write *Isabel; or, Sicily. A Pilgrimage* (Philadelphia: Lea & Blanchard, 1839) while still a young man (and then have Putnam publish a new edition in 1852, *Sicily: A Pilgrimage*); envy for the respectable, apology-free, semi-monastic life that Melville might himself, after all, have been best fitted for. Their friendship by this time was almost a decade and a half old, nourished by Tuckerman's respect for *Moby-Dick* during years when almost no one mentioned it (who could resent a reference to its having the rare fault of redundant power?), and nourished by their mutual saturation in art history and in aesthetic questions. In 1862 Tuckerman was hard at work on his masterpiece, *The Book of the Artists* (1867). At this time, already, Tuckerman may have had on his wall "a cabinet likeness" of Dr. Francis "in pastel by Julius Gollmann," later engraved by Charles Burt for the frontispiece of the new edition of *Old New York*, delayed by the war. With Dr. Francis dead, with his deafness proving progressive, Tuckerman did not seek out new society. Melville was accustomed to leaning forward to hear the confidential voice of John Hoadley, and when he sat with Tuckerman he had to lean toward him, companionably, and try to speak distinctly through the hedge of a moustache that journalists in the West had complained about. Focused thus confidentially, Melville was acutely aware of the decency and simple charm of the man, who in spite of his brilliance "lived in the affections rather than in the intellect" (as a writer in the *Tribune* wrote on 18 December 1871).

A Bostonian, Tuckerman knew to express the most earnest condolences on the death of Judge Shaw the previous year. Melville's failure to get the consulship in Florence did not have to be lamented afresh, but it was common knowledge through Allan's association with the Duyckincks. Melville and Tuckerman could recur to old topics, such as Tuckerman's imitation of Irving, the *Italian Sketch Book* (1837), or his book on Sicily, or even Tuckerman's venture into naval biography with *Life of Silas Talbot, a Commodore in the Navy* (1850). This time, the old friends had a fresh topic, the partial unification of Italy by Garibaldi (the "sailor-boy," Tuckerman had called him in the *North American Review* of January 1861). Perhaps as early as when Melville was finishing *Mardi*, Tuckerman had drawn Melville into awareness of Garibaldi's presence in New York, where the Italian was plotting with Tuckerman and other supporters to return to Italy at the head of an expedition meant to liberate the fragmented land, if not in 1848 then later. Given the likelihood that Melville had already written his "Naples" poem in 1858 and 1859 and was soon to write new lines about Garibaldi for the end of it, the friends must have talked about the modern hero.

Melville would have known already that in 1851–53 Garibaldi had lived in New Brighton, on Staten Island, and worked at times as a candlemaker while he stayed with Antonio Meucci, on Forest Street. For the New York *Times* (2 June 1878), Charles H. Farnham interviewed Meucci, by then a "portly old gentleman," and found him willing to reminisce about the tenor Lorenzo Salvi, who was his partner in the candle factory across the street, and about Garibaldi's working there, when he liked, for no wages, in 1851–53. The Bull of the Pampas had gotten by as best he could: "Our compatriots helped him; but he gave away as fast as he received. He was generous and democratic in every way. He used to fish off the dock at Clifton, or in a boat I owned. And we used to go hunting. Sometimes we went to the city, but he lived very quietly. Then, in 1853, he resumed his profession of seaman." Upstairs in a bedroom Meucci kept mementos, the scarlet shirt Garibaldi "wore in the streets of Rome in the Revolution of 1848," a "bronze medal that the Italians struck in his honor," a "dagger, with a carved Mazeppa for the handle," brought from Montevideo, a cane, the whole room a shrine. By 1878 Meucci had many letters from Garibaldi, as well as other mementos the hero had sent him from Italy. From the Red Year 1848, Tuckerman had witnessed the progress of this strange episode, so like ancient stories of banishments and triumphal returns of heroes.

The Crimean War had astonished Americans with the magnitude of the arrayed forces, Russia poised to conquer Turkey, Great Britain and France sending forth a great combined fleet, but it had not involved them much beyond thrilling to the laureate's poem about the light brigade, a piece which found its niche as something schoolchildren could learn irony from. Turkey was still the villain of the Byronic struggles, and Americans had, after all, a national political crisis of their own, one which killed the Whig party and established the Republican party. A few years later, in the late 1850s, many Americans became eager for a distracting international crisis like the one in 1851, when Kossuth made his empty triumphal tour of the states. In 1860 what Tuckerman called "the sacred cause of Italian nationality" had come home to the educated classes in the United States as a good-enough equivalent of their parents' cause of Greek independence, a liberal topic easier to talk about at the dinner table than, say, John Brown's raid on Harper's Ferry. During Melville's voyage on the *Meteor* the quiet Tuckerman had roused himself in a meeting at Newport (the Boston *Daily Transcript* reported on 1 August 1860) "to express sympathy for Garibaldi and devise measures to aid the cause of Italy." There Tuckerman "spoke graceful and weighty words from personal observation of the state of Sicily and the providential fitness of Garibaldi for the present crisis, and closed with a series of admirable resolutions," the fourth of which was most practical, "to contribute promptly and generously to the fund now collecting to furnish arms and ammunition to Garibaldi in his holy crusade to free the oppressed and establish Italian independence."

Tuckerman's 1861 article constituted a remarkably full biography, based on more knowledge of both Garibaldi and of Italy than any other American possessed. He recalled his first sight of Garibaldi during his exile, in Manhattan, at a meeting called to deal with the funds raised in the Italian cause in 1848, before its "unfortunate termination"—the cause familiar to New Yorkers from Margaret Fuller's on-the-scene letters to Greeley's *Tribune*. There was undisguised hero-worship in Tuckerman's description of Garibaldi as "one of Nature's noblemen," his complexion "bronzed by exposure to the elements; his gait rather that of a sailor than of a soldier; but through, within, and above all these traits was distinctly visible the hero." Tuckerman then, in 1848, at the time of his early acquaintance with Melville, another sailor, had been reminded "of some masterly portraits of mediaeval celebrities which haunted our memory, almost alive with courage, adventure, and loyalty,—whose effigies hint a stern romance and a chivalric history." In 1862 Melville could have seen many old articles printed during his absence at sea, but Tuckerman's in the *North American Review* provided him most of the details he used when he added the lines about Garibaldi to the end of "A Morning in Naples" (perhaps already changed to "An Afternoon in Naples"). The action of the body of the poem occurs, as a later title makes plain, in the time of Bomba, before Garibaldi liberated Naples, so the completed "An Afternoon in Naples" needed to be finished off differently, given Garibaldi's sudden emergence in Italian history. Melville wrote a new hundred lines or so devoted to Garibaldi's liberation of Sicily and his crossing the strait to free Naples from "King Fanny, Bomba's heir," perhaps intending it as a new ending to the "Naples" poem. Later, he placed it before what he wrote as, or altered into, a companion poem, "A Symposium of Old Masters at Delmonico's," later called "At the Hostelry." These new passages dealing with Garibaldi are poetically confident, as in the plosives in his calling Garibaldi "The banished Bullock from the Pampas":

> Ye halls of history, arched by time,
> Founded in fate, enlarged by crime,
> Now shines like phosphorus scratched in dark
> 'Gainst your grimed walls the luminous mark
> Of one who in no paladin age
> Was knightly-him who lends a page
> Now signal in time's recent story
> Where scarce in vogue are "Plutarch's men,"
> And jobbers deal in popular glory. —

Yet Melville glorifies Garibaldi less than Camillo Benso Cavour, whose wise statecraft might transcend even the hero's glory in redeeming "Art's Holy Land." On the main point Melville was in total accord with Tuckerman: Garibaldi's actions were to be cherished as knightly behavior in an unknightly age.

"A Symposium of Old Masters at Delmonico's" could possibly have been in *Poems* (1860); Melville later associated and intertwined it with the "Naples" poem, placing them in the reverse order of composition, the "Symposium" first. Some of the characters are Italian artists (the "Old Masters" of the title); others are Dutch and German old masters, treated together with the Italians. Already in 1857 Melville had carried in Italy a book by Antoine Claude Pasquin (known as Valery), *Historical, Literary, and Artistical Travels in Italy, a Complete and Methodical Guide for Travellers and Artists* (1852). He may have had access to a history of Dutch painting with biographical sketches of the painters rather early. He borrowed a four-volume set of Vasari's *Lives of the Most Eminent Painters, Sculptors, and Architects* from Evert Duyckinck in November 1859 along with the three volumes of Lanzi's *The History of Painting in Italy*, then he bought his own five-volume Vasari in 1862. His surviving *The Works of Eminent Masters*, two volumes in one, was acquired in 1871, but it consisted of reprintings of magazine articles. Hoadley gave Melville Jarves's *The Art Idea* on 12 March 1871, "with kind and fraternal regards." Access to information about Italian and Northern artists came early and came late, in short, and offers no firm evidence for dating "At the Hostelry." As it survives, the poem contains many lines on Garibaldi which could not have been in any version ready for *Poems* in 1860 but could have been written in the next year or two, when Melville was seeing Tuckerman.

"A Symposium," to which the new Garibaldi lines were ultimately attached, is a poetic interchange of old masters on the topic of the Picturesque. After the preliminary passages on the current political events in Italy, the "Symposium" (or "At the Hostelry"), in its surviving form, continues with some 475 lines in which two dozen old masters converse together on the theme of the Picturesque, some attempting to define it, some evading definition, several trying to identify it by example rather than analysis. These painters are promiscuously Italian, Spanish, Dutch, and German (Jan Steen, Fra Lippo Lippi, Jusepe de Ribera [called Lo Spagnoletto, the Little Spaniard], Herman van Swanevelt, Claude Lorrain, Frans Hals, Anthony Vandyke, Adriaen Brouwer, Carlo Dolce [or Dolci], Jan van Huysums, David Teniers, Rembrandt, Willem van de Velde [father or son], Gerard Douw, Rubens, Paolo Veronese, Antoine Watteau, Turburg [Gerard Ter Borch], Diego Velázquez, Salvator Rosa, Nicolas Poussin, Albert Dürer, Fra Angelico, Leonardo, Michelangelo). In his two trips to Europe Melville had seen works by many of these artists, and had commented on works by half of them, a dozen or so, in his journals: Claude, Hals, Vandyke, Dolci, Teniers, Rembrandt, Rubens, Veronese, Velázquez, Rosa, Poussin, Dürer, Leonardo, and Michelangelo. He may have seen works by Steen, Lippo Lippi, Lo Spagnoletto, Swanevelt, Brouwer, Huysums, Van de Velde, Douw, Watteau, and Fra Angelico (probably, in Venice), without noting down their names.

He could have seen images by some of these artists in New York, for his friend Tuckerman had engravings of *Head of Laughing Boy* (Lo Spagnoletto); *Knife Grinders* and *Bagpipe Player* (Teniers); *St. Thomas* (Rubens); and *The Assumption* (Poussin). He also had access to many art books containing reproductions of their works. Aesthetically, the arguments Melville attributes to the masters are not complex, and the interest of the reader is less in what the masters say about the Picturesque than in the way Melville characterizes their interaction and in his sometimes vivid allusions to their lives and works.

Melville introduced his theme in the light of current events: "Ay, but the *Picturesque*, I wonder— / The *Picturesque* and *Old Romance!* / May these conform and share advance / With Italy and the world's career?" This is a theme pondered at "little suppers," where the narrator is present, by his "artist-friends," who turn out not to be Darley or grander masters such as Church and Bierstadt but an assemblage of old masters. Melville had known many American artists since the late 1840s, and continued to have chances to see them. (Three years later, for example, on 24 February 1865, Bayard Taylor invited Melville to meet "The Travellers": "Many of the members are no doubt old friends of yours—Darley, Church, Bierstadt, Gottschalk, Cyrus Field, Hunt, Bellows and Townsend Harris. We simply meet to talk, winding up our evenings with a cigar and frugal refreshments.") To some extent "At the Hostelry" reflected the vogue of "composition portraits," those painting or engravings of groups of friends such as *A Party at Sir Joshua Reynolds's*, or *Sir Walter Scott and His Friends*, or *Washington Irving and His Friends*—a genre of which Dr Francis had been fond, Tuckerman recalled. Melville was bringing such a gathering into his life. Melville (or the "speaker" of "At the Hostelry") first met these old masters, he says, "with other illustrious ones in row" (as if they were an elongated Last Supper in Leonardo's arrangement), "at that brave tavern / Founded by the first Delmonico, / Forefather of a flourishing line!"

In Melville's lifetime the social history of New York City could be read in the expansions and removals of the restaurants owned by members of the Delmonico family, from the earliest he could remember, the one the two Swiss brothers ran at 23 William, to the splendid new building he knew from 1839 through 1840 (at South William and Beaver), to the one on Broadway that flourished in his first years as a writer in New York, to the spectacularly renovated Moses Grinnell mansion at Fifth Avenue and Fourteenth Street, which opened in 1861. Later, in 1876, perhaps triggering Melville's renewed fiddling with these poetical pieces, a new branch opened just to the west of the Melville house, on Twenty-sixth Street between Fifth Avenue and Broadway. That Twenty-sixth Street Delmonico's was too expensive for the Melvilles. Nor did this end the great American saga of the Delmonicos during Melville's lifetime. Yet the saga is to some extent irrelevant, for Melville may have been envisioning not the early building near Wall Street, the one at Beaver and South William, but an imaginary "brave tavern" (in Italy rather than Switzerland?) presided over by the archetypal ancestral Delmonico, a tavern where artists could gather in a vaguely biblical "upper chamber" never seen or even suspected by the "dolts" who ate in the rooms below.

Melville as aesthetician had started from an impulse toward things beautiful and powerful. His vocabulary for appreciation ranged between "Nothing could be finer than this" and (in his satirical vein while Joe Smith read his own poem aloud) "great glorious" — "By Jove that's tremendous." When he first skimmed "The Artist of the Beautiful" Melville took it seriously as aesthetic commentary rather than seeing that it weakly glorified art for the artist's sake. This was a very bad influence on Melville, who at some point destroyed the manuscript of *The Isle of the Cross*. In "The Piazza" Melville began his skeptical challenging of Hawthorne's aesthetic pronouncements and was astounded to find them not very intelligent, but his own ruminations about the real and the imaginary were still fluid and suggestive—all to the good, given the purpose of that story-essay written to preface some of his evocative and elusive stories. The naïveté of his lecture on "Statues in Rome" was not what drew denunciations from the reviewers, since what he said was on a critical or theoretical level with the sort of vague solemn pronouncements on art for which Orville Dewey and many other lecturers were routinely applauded. Out of his depths, he had chosen to talk on a topic on which he could not, as yet, say anything original.

As Melville made himself into a poet he began to gain a sense of what the best doers and thinkers had said of the nature of the creative process and the nature of the created product. He *heard* better aesthetics than he read: to spend an hour or two with Hiram Powers in Florence was to have a tutorial in aesthetics. He had seen great art and architecture, and had for much of his life a strong visual memory of those that struck him. Never mind that he had written *Moby-Dick*; he was a self-taught American who could articulate, still, only rudimentary aesthetic concepts. For a long time he was more a man who wanted to move among creators of the beautiful and to imagine their pronouncements on the beautiful rather than to learn about aesthetics by watching what happened when he himself confronted art created by others and by watching what happened when he himself was deep into a creative state. He had tried watching his own mind in *Mardi*, *Moby-Dick*, and *Pierre* with disastrous results. In 1861 or 1862, around then, he was able to put good descriptions of artists and their preoccupations into "At the Hostelry" and tie those passages back neatly to Garibaldi at the end, but he was not able to say anything significant about the Picturesque, however he had mastered it in some of the pieces in *The Piazza Tales* or in "Jimmy Rose" and other stories. What is best datable to 1861 and 1862 are the lines in both poems dealing with Garibaldi, the chivalric hero of Melville and his friend Tuckerman. In late 1861 or early 1862, Melville was writing poetry again, after the disastrous failure to get his *Poems* published, and was thinking energetically, although a little at loose ends, intellectually speaking, as he began to feel stronger physically.

By the first of February 1862 Melville and Lizzie were settled into the Eighteenth Street house and had put the girls in the Quaker school by what is now Stuyvesant Park. Melville invited Evert and George Duyckinck to call any evening, and he was focused enough on his intellectual needs to make specific requests (probably by way of a hired lad): "I want you to loan me some of those volumes of the Elizabethan dramatists. Is Deckar among the set? And Webster? If so, please wrap them up and let the bearer have them. — Send me any except Marlowe, whom I have read." Melville made the invitation specific, for 2 February: "If you have nothing better to do, come round tomorrow (Sunday) evening, and we will brew some whiskey punch and settle the affairs of the universe over it—which affairs sadly need it, some say." The oddity is that whatever his purpose in wanting to read more of the Elizabethan dramatists, and whatever the number of plays he was able to lay hand on, his attention was quickly deflected from them, and indeed he may have put off reading some of them until the last months of his life, when he occupied himself with "readings in the 'Mermaid Series' of old plays, in which, he took much pleasure," according to Arthur Stedman in his introduction to *Typee* (1892). After all, Melville may not have read whatever dramas he borrowed, and he seems not to have bought copies of his own, for, enabled by whatever portion of her inheritance Lizzie had received, he embarked on what became sharply focused book-buying. Over the next weeks he made increasingly systematic purchases of volumes of recent and contemporary poetry, including works by second-rank or not-yet-established poets, along with some works which discussed aesthetic ideas and one classic multivolume art history. He was reading what he was buying, and reading purposefully. The man who had invented Ahab's search for the White Whale had embarked on what soon became a quiet but obsessive search for an aesthetic credo.

As far as the surviving evidence shows, Melville's first purchase in this series was on 14 February 1862, *The Poetical Works of Thomas Hood* in two volumes (Boston, 1860). There in Richard Monckton Milnes's "Memoir of the Author" his eye caught an allusion to "the full extent of that poetical vigour which seemed to advance just in proportion as his physical health declined." Among other passages, Melville marked the one where Milnes said that Hood "used to write out his poems in printed characters, believing that the process best enabled him to understand his own peculiarities and faults, and probably unconscious that Coleridge had recommended some such method of criticism when he said he thought 'print settles it.'" Melville also marked a curt realistic poem on "The Poet's Fate." The next day he bought *Ancient Spanish Ballads; Historical and Romantic* (New York, 1856), translated by John Gibson Lockhart, the frigid son-in-law and biographer of the warm-hearted Scott; it contained poems from *The Cid* linked by extensive plot summaries. He or someone else pasted in a review and a caricature portrait of Lockhart which (remembering Lockhart's superciliousness at dinner in London) Melville praised ironically as not being ugly enough: "Some friend hath done this"; in the review he marked a passage on the "sad want of real poetic feeling" revealed in Lockhart's translations. He also bought on 15 February *Poems of James Clarence Mangan* (New York, 1859), whom he knew as a translator of his edition of Schiller, and marked many of Mangan's translations of German poems, as well as a passage in the introduction which specified the predictable results of Mangan's rebelling "against the whole British spirit of the age": "Hardly anybody in England knew the name of such a person." In the back, he noted a few archaisms and rhyming words for his own use. On the same day he carried home *The Poetical Works of Thomas Moore* in six volumes (Boston, [1856?]), where he marked in the preface to "Lalla Rookh" Moore's admonition: "I have been, at all times, a far more slow and pains-taking workman than would ever be guessed, I fear, from the result." On 17 February he acquired *The Works of Robert Fergusson*, edited by A. B. G[rosart] (London, 1857), in which he scored, in Grosart's "Memoir" of this predecessor of Burns, some advice on polishing before publishing, along with some human interest or local color details such as a storm at sea, the price of eggs, and Scottish names.

On Wednesday, 26 February, Melville laid out five dollars of Lizzie's inheritance for *The Works of Isaac Disraeli* in seven volumes (London, 1860), where he marked a sketchy history of English literature. Melville may have associated this volume with some of his friends, for Tuckerman in 1865 asserted that the late Dr. Francis had been thoroughly versed in the anecdotal history of literature "and knew by heart the materials from which D'Israeli the elder constructed his voluminous record of the fortunes of authorship." In the chapter "Poets" Melville marked a passage on someone who risked his life to save his beloved manuscripts from flames then ten years later "condemned to the flames those very poems he had ventured his life to preserve"—an ominous analogue to something that (very likely) Melville had already done or was soon to do to many pages of his writings, including *The Isle of the Cross*. (Probably earlier, perhaps in the 1850s, he had marked in

Wordsworth's "Essay Supplementary to the Preface on Collins" this passage: "The notice which his poems attained during his life-time was so small, and of course the sale so insignificant, that not long before his death he deemed it right to repay to the Bookseller the sum which he had advanced for them, and threw the Edition into the fire.") In chapter 17 Melville marked a passage applicable to the celebration of the something unmanageable in creative geniuses: "This abandonment of their life to their genius has, indeed, often cost them too dear, from the days of Sophocles, who, ardent in his old age, neglected his family affairs, and was brought before his judges by his relations, as one fallen into a second childhood." In *Calumnies and Quarrels*, another volume in the set, Melville underlined and scored with three parallel marks in the margin this sentence: "No man is wiser for his learning: it may administer matter to work in, or objects to work upon; but wit and wisdom are born with a man." One thread in his obsessive analysis was snarled in the mystery of his own creative powers—so tumultuous, yet all but a secret for his first quarter century.

On 1 March Melville purchased a work he had already read in Duyckinck's copy, and had recalled while he was reading *The Marble Faun* in the Atlantic: his own five-volume set of Vasari's *Lives of the Most Eminent Painters, Sculptors, and Architects* (London: George Bell & Sons, 1850–52). He read it again with some care, marking all the volumes, especially 2 and 5, revelling in this vast library about the working lives of artists. In March Melville bought Hazlitt's *Lectures on the English Comic Writers* and *Lectures on the English Poets*, two volumes in one, inscribing "1862 March N. Y." opposite the title page. He read the zestful Hazlitt with renewed gusto of his own, happily expatiating on the virtues of Ossian, on which he agreed with Hazlitt, or taking issue, as he did on page 177 in "On the Living Poets," when Hazlitt ridiculed Samuel Rogers's *Pleasures of Memory* as unintelligible. Hazlitt had pronounced: "The whole is refined, and frittered away into an appearance of the most evanescent brilliancy and tremulous imbecility.—There is no other fault to be found with the Pleasures of Memory than a want of taste and genius." Melville objected, on the basis of his personal acquaintance as well as his reading: "This is pretty much all spleen. Rogers, tho' no genius, was a painstaking man of talent who has written some good things. 'Italy' is an interesting book to any person of taste. In Hazlitt you have at times to allow for indigestion." ("Painstaking" Melville may already have picked up from Moore; the idea was lodged in his mind.) Reading this book reminded Melville of people he had met in London, paintings he had been impressed by in the National Gallery, and even the thespian powers of Mr. Farren, whose acting, despite his advanced age, had been wonderful ("I had never seen anything like it").

The likable, erratic, and opinionated Hazlitt was just the sort of fellow Melville could engage with in his marginalia in good-fellow fashion, especially on so exciting a topic as Wordsworth's poetry, which Melville knew thoroughly, except possibly for the posthumous *The Prelude*. On page 199 Melville marked Hazlitt's quotation from Wordsworth's "Immortality" ode:

> I do not grieve, but rather find
> Strength in what remains behind;
> In the primal sympathy,
> Which having been, must ever be;
> In the soothing thoughts that spring
> Out of human suffering;
> In years that bring the philosophic mind!

Melville put a bow enclosing "In the primal sympathy, / Which having been, must ever be;" and he drew a check mark by the last line, but by the third and second line from the end he made an elaborate symbol, a large X-shape with a firm dot in each of the four more or less right angles. At the foot of the page he repeated the symbol and commented: "A rigid analysis would make this sentiment appear in a different light from the one in which it is, probably, generally received. Its vagueness makes it susceptible of many interpretations; but Truth is susceptible of but one." "Its vagueness" made it easy for the superficial to use in sentimental and pious reassurances, made it especially useful to some of the Unitarians of his acquaintance who did not take other people's suffering very seriously. Having probed deeper into the nature of human suffering than such acquaintances, Melville felt he had attained to a genuinely Wordsworthian sense of the deeply soothing thoughts that can, in momentous men and women, spring out of the most profound human suffering.

Soon after buying Hazlitt's lectures Melville may have had another conversation with Tuckerman on Italy in which the talk turned to Victor Alfieri, the great Italian dramatist, whose grave Melville had visited in Florence. Tuckerman had devoted a chapter to Alfieri in *Thoughts on the Poets* (New York: C. S. Francis, 1846), a volume with a striking title-page motto from the "Defence of Poetry," then only recently published, long after Shelley's death: " 'Poets and Philosophers are the unacknowledged legislators of the world.' Shelley." Tuckerman may have retained, left over from his research years before, the January 1810 *Edinburgh Review* which contained Francis Jeffrey's long article on the *Memoirs of the Life and Writings of Victor Alfieri, Written by Himself* (2 vols.; London, 1810). Tuckerman might well have owned the Jeffrey volume in a set of *Modern British Essayists*, where this essay on Alfieri was reprinted. Melville himself owned this Jeffrey volume, and may well have glanced at the Alfieri article in 1851 or earlier, interested in parallels between his career and the Italian's.

One way or another, Francis Jeffrey's article on Alfieri came to Melville's attention, probably not for the first time, and very likely through conversation with Tuckerman. The article was apt to appeal to Melville both for the subject, the Italian dramatist who had led an unintellectual early life like himself, and for the Scottish reviewer, whom Allan Melvill had called upon in Edinburgh. Now in New York Melville read the essay with great care for what Jeffrey said of Alfieri's aesthetic principles and practices. His problem was that he decided to make some elaborate notes on the essay but was not able to mark up whatever text he was reading. His own Jeffrey volume was printed double-column with little space between and almost no gutters or margins for notetaking, but if Melville had brought his copy to New York he could have made his notes in the endpapers. Chances are that he had borrowed the essay, in one printing or another, from Tuckerman, who hoarded books and papers, and was the American authority on Alfieri.

Under other circumstances, Melville might have marked up other passages in Jeffrey's essay, particularly the ones on Alfieri's achieving success by a "confident and fortunate audacity," a life history that somewhat paralleled his own. That particular passage in Jeffrey's essay must have frozen his attention, at least momentarily, but he had thought through that topic in January 1852, when he was writing book 18 of *Pierre*. Now, in 1862, reading purposefully for present information and for future reflection on new aesthetic, not autobiographical, problems, Melville was powerfully struck by this passage in Jeffrey:

> These pieces [Alfieri's Italian tragedies] approach much nearer to the antient Grecian model, than any other modern production. . . . As they have not adopted the choral songs of the Greek stage, however, they are, on the whole, less poetical than those ancient compositions; although they are worked throughout with a fine and careful hand, and diligently purified from every thing ignoble or feeble in the expression. The author's anxiety to keep clear of figures of mere ostentation, and to exclude all showpieces of fine writing in a dialogue of deep interest or impetuous passion, has betrayed him, on some occasions, into too sententious and strained a diction, and given an air of labour and heaviness to many parts of his composition. . . . There are no excursions or digressions, — no episodical conversations, — and none but the most brief moralizings. This gives a certain air of solidity to the whole structure of the piece, that is apt to prove oppressive to an ordinary reader, and reduces the entire drama to too great uniformity. . . .

> With regard to the diction of these pieces, it is not for *tramontane* critics to presume to offer any opinion. They are considered, in Italy, we believe, as the purest specimens of the *favella Toscana* that late ages have produced. To us they certainly seem to want something of that flow and sweetness to which we have been accustomed in Italian poetry, and to be formed rather upon the model of Dante than of Petrarca. At all events, it is obvious that the style is highly elaborate and artificial; and that the author is constantly striving to give it a sort of factitious force and energy, by the use of condensed and emphatic expressions, interrogatories, antitheses, and short and inverted sentences. In all these respects, as well as in the chastized gravity of the sentiments, and the temperance and propriety of all the delineations of passion, these pieces are exactly the reverse of what we should have expected from the fiery, fickle and impatient character of the author.

Melville opened his copy of Hazlitt's *Lectures* and on the blank page opposite the introductory piece ("On Wit and Humour") he started some elaborate notes where he summarized, within quotation marks, some of Jeffrey's comments about literary style which were directly relevant to his late winter's search for a satisfying aesthetic credo:

> "Worked throughout with a fine and careful hand. — Figures of mere ostentation. — Show-pieces of fine writing. — Nature is not confined to conciseness, but at times amplifies. — Too sententious & strained a diction. — The solidity of the structure is apt to prove oppressive to the *ordinary* reader. Too great uniformity."   *Jeffrey on Alfieri.*
> "Wanting flow & sweetness. — Strives to give a factitious force & energy by condensation & emphasis & inversion. — Chastized gravity. — Temperance and propriety of delineation of the passions."

At the top of the next page, above the start of "On Wit and Humour," he wrote "Discerning with *a mind that has refined from the subject* the best thoughts & rejecting the dross. (Alfieri himself)."

In making his notes, Melville jotted down some negative versions of what Jeffrey had said. That is, he wrote "Figures of mere ostentation" to remind him that Jeffrey had exonerated Alfieri of using such figures. The ideas in Jeffrey's passage involved careful craftsmanship, the avoidance of ostentation, the avoidance of purple passages, the desirability of avoiding minuteness when amplification is required, the need to avoid overly sententious and strained diction, the need for flexibility in structure, the need for graceful "flow & sweetness," the desirability of avoiding forced, overmannered style, the ideal of "Chastized gravity. — Temperance and propriety of delineation of the passions." For a man who had created the mannered style of *Pierre*, the warnings were salutary, and for the man who had exulted in the amplification and variety of styles in *Moby-Dick*, here was confirmation that his instincts had been true. By now Melville may have reflected on just how unsophisticated, aesthetically speaking, his friend Hawthorne had been in "The Artist of the Beautiful," which had so impressed him at first reading. The true ideal was not Owen Warland but an artist who could carry poor Owen's painstaking labors to his muscular friend Robert Danforth's transforming forge: in a Melvillean version of "The Artist of the Beautiful," Danforth would be the true creator. The ideal was a chastised (Jeffrey wrote "chastened") gravity, controlled flexibility. Melville here may have consciously confronted the likelihood that his once-vaunted "unmanageability" was a delusory aesthetic concept. He was going to school to a true master critic and being a good pupil.

And Melville continued to search out textbooks for his course of study. On 4 March he bought the two volumes (fifty cents per volume) of *Germany*, by Madame the Baroness de Staël-Holstein (New York, 1859), and read here and there in the first volume. In its front cover he wrote:

> "*It is not French*" said Napoleon's Minister of Police, and suppressed this book. — There it is. The Minister said but the truth, &, from his point of view, the suppression was just. —
>
> "You are modernising the laws and are dangerous to the young" said the judges to Socrates. They said the truth, & from their point of view, were just in condemning him. —
>
> What then?
>
> Why, as a self-constituted agent for the conservation of useful persuasions, —
>
> I suppress the inference.

Melville suppressed the inference, ironically, rather than the book. The comments are significant for showing something of his sense of himself at this time, left behind by the literary world, and utterly out of the war effort. He had become a self-constituted agent for the conservation of useful unpopular persuasions, and was stocking up his magazine of those unpopular ideas. "Malignity" was one idea too unpopular for mealy-mouthed moderns, and if the idea of malignity in the universe or human beings had to be suppressed, why bother with the idea of Original Sin, one of the notions popularly discarded, he held — long before he wrote *Billy Budd*. Later in *Germany* the statement "A man, regarded in a religious light, is as much as the entire human race" provoked Melville to his autobiographical comment: "This was an early and innate conviction of mine, suggested by my revulsion from the counting-room philosophy of Paley." Instinctively, innately, he recoiled from the ideas of the British Utilitarian-Unitarians who provided whatever intellectual framework American Unitarians could claim.

Melville's longest notation in *Germany* dealt with the suppression of unpopular ideas, but what he was reading to find were ideas about aesthetic problems. By now he had opinions, if not reasoned convictions, on such matters. When he read the statement that "the effects of poetry depend still more on the melody of words than on the ideas which they serve to express," he agreed: "This is measurably true of all but dramatic poetry, and, perhaps, narrative verse." He marked a passage on the terror that can be caused by repetition of the same words, something he was familiar with from Poe, among others. He marked a passage on the "morbid sensibility of Tasso" and "the polished rudeness of his protector Alphonso, who, professing the highest admiration for his writings, shut him up in a mad-house, as if that genius which springs from the soul were to be treated like the production of a mechanical talent, by valuing the work while we despise the workman." At some level this may have associated Alphonso with Duyckinck, who had been his own polished protector in his early years in New York, where, long before, at the time of *Mardi*, Duyckinck had valued the work while remaining a little superior to the workman, and who two years later could not generously estimate the new work, *Moby-Dick*, and had become deeply uneasy about the workman. About this time in his winter reading, Melville began marking passages he encountered on the way genius may be treated as madness. He knew something about that, already.

While Melville sat out the winter, reading, but making forays into the bookstores, his mother and Augusta were nursing Uncle Herman. Early on 18 March, Maria telegraphed to New York (probably to Allan, easily found) that Uncle Herman had died and that the funeral would take place the next day, a Wednesday. She expected both Herman and Allan to come, but (as Kitty Gansevoort reported to Henry) "Cousin Herman" was "sick in New York & was unable to come up"—even for the funeral of the man whose name he bore. Maria must have been pained both by the cause of her son's absence and the fact of it, and for his part Melville must have felt shamed at being too weak to take the train up and console his mother. If he was concerned at the effects of Uncle Herman's illness and death on Stanwix, who was about two years younger than he himself had been when his father died in 1832, he was not concerned enough to summon the lad to New York City, interrupting whatever schooling (starting with religious indoctrination) Augusta was providing for him. Getting Stanwix to New York City would have been easy, since Allan and Jane both went up (leaving the girls with Herman and Lizzie), and stayed over at Gansevoort, Allan giving his mother legal advice on how to probate Uncle Herman's will and assure an orderly course for inheriting the much-contested estate. Herman and Lizzie took the girls to Twenty-sixth Street on Sunday, 23 March, and found that Allan and Jane had returned at midnight the night before. From them Herman and Lizzie received an account of how the family had borne up, and from New Rochelle came the good news of the birth of a daughter, Ida, to Abby and Richard Lathers. It was shocking to recall that at this time the previous year Richard and Abby had been in the Confederacy.

On 22 March, three days after the funeral of Herman Gansevoort, Melville ventured out and bought two volumes by Emerson: *Essays: First Series* (Boston, 1847) and *Essays: Second Series* (Boston, 1844). There were never enough ideas in Hawthorne to argue with, but Emerson was a challenge to Melville, who could write "True" at one point and "False" at another on the same page of Emerson. What he marked most vigorously and argued with most vociferously was his old complaint: to Melville, Emerson was still a national Confidence Man who went about denying the existence of evil. At one point Melville raged against the implication that evil was subjective, not real: "Perfectly good being, therefore, would see no evil. — But what did Christ see? — He saw what made him weep. — However, too, the 'Philanthropist' must have been a very bad man — he saw, in jails, so much evil." (John Howard, he meant.) Still fuming, Melville added: "To annihilate all this nonsense read the Sermon on the Mount, and consider what it implies." Emerson wrote, "Trust men, and they will be true to you," and Melville, who had trusted, among others, Tertullus D. Stewart, ranted incredulously: "God help the poor fellow who squares his life according to this." Emerson benignly observed that although the storm buffets the drover or the sailor all day, "his health renews itself as vigorous a pulse under the sleet, as under the sun of June"; Melville commented: "To one who has weathered Cape Horn as a common sailor what stuff all this is." Part of his anger came from the fact that Emerson, the former Unitarian minister, was employing standard Unitarian thought, very much like what Elizabeth Melville heard from Orville Dewey and other ministers. Lizzie seized her opportunity to attend her old church, All Souls, and Melville could rage in his marginalia as he could not safely rage against anything Lizzie reported from Henry W. Bellows's latest sermon.

At one point, what Emerson said was so asinine that Melville was reduced to noting, "Alas! the fool again!" He worked and raged his way through "The Poet": "What does the man mean? If Mr Emerson travelling in Egypt should find the plague-spot come out on him — would he consider that an evil sight or not? And if evil, would his eye be evil because it seemed evil to his eye, or rather to his sense using the eye for instrument?" Acknowledging an admirable thought, he defined Emerson's failures: "His gross and astonishing errors & illusions spring from a self-conceit so intensely intellectual and calm that at first one hesitates to call it by its right name. Another species of Mr Emerson's errors, or rather, blindness, proceeds from a defect in the region of the heart." He read skeptically Emerson's comments on the deterioration of artists who lead a life of pleasure and indulgence: "No, no, no. — Titian — did he deteriorate? — Byron? — Did he. — Mr E. is horribly narrow here. He has his Dardenelles for his every Marmora. — But he keeps nobly on, for all that!" That last comment is Melville at his most magnanimous, for over and over again Emerson appalled him, to the point that he could never take Emerson's essays as companions the way he had taken Montaigne's, Carlyle's, and Hazlitt's, could never take him as a companion in arms, a fellow writer attempting to contribute a great American stream to the course of literature in the English language. Once, in the late 1820s and 1830s, a challenge to the literary and philosophical establishment, Emerson for many years had been giving philosophical countenance to the fast-spreading superficiality in American life, and was yearly earning his increasing popularity by flattering the public. His example gave Melville no encouragement, and, when taken up a few days after Uncle Herman's death, Emerson's lightness seemed more than ever a profanation from a national Confidence Man.

Remarkably, Melville kept on buying books as they stayed on in the city into early spring. On 3 April he bought *The Poetical Works and Remains of Henry Kirke White* (New York, 1857), and marked a passage on the absence of sublimity and fire in fashionable modern poetry, where harmonious modulations and "unvarying exactness of measure" are the qualities most valued. By now he had in mind what Jeffrey would have said about that sort of uniformity. In April Melville also bought *The Poetical Works of William Collins* (Boston, 1854) and *The Poetical Works of Charles Churchill* (Boston, 1854). (Months later, during a trip back to New York City in late September, he bought *The Works of M. de la Bruyère*, in two volumes [London, 1776]; his marginalia there at times are unwontedly cynical, as when he marked "There are few men so accomplished, or so necessary, but have some failings or other which will make their friends bear the loss of them with the greater patience" and footnoted his opinion from *Timon of Athens*: "True, Shakespeare goes further: None die but somebody spurns them into the grave." Late the next month, October, on still another trip, he annotated the second volume of *The Poetical Works of Thomas Moore*, probably a volume from the set he had bought in February.)

The sixth of April was a Sunday, probably not a day bookstores were open, but that was the date Melville put in what turned out to be the most important of his 1862 purchases, in the short term: Matthew Arnold's *Poems*

(Boston, 1856). The preface, which had first appeared in the 1853 edition, was an aesthetic document being taken seriously by Arnold's and Melville's contemporaries, and within a generation it was treated as on a theoretical level with some of Dryden's and Wordsworth's aesthetic arguments. Among Victorian aesthetic documents, it was almost on a par with the third volume of John Ruskin's *Modern Painters*. Whatever Melville thought of Arnold's poems, he recognized the Arnold of the "Preface" as a thinker worth grappling with. Fresh from Emerson, he encountered this from Arnold: "it is not enough that the Poet should add to the knowledge of men, it is required of him also that he should add to their happiness. 'All Art,' says Schiller, 'is dedicated to Joy, and there is no higher and no more serious problem, than how to make men happy. The right Art is that alone, which creates the highest enjoyment.'" Melville exploded: "The 'Laocoon' is not dedicated to Joy, neither is 'Hamlet.' Yet there is a degree of truth in this, only it dont imply that the subjects of true art must be joyful subjects.—Schiller was at once helped & hurt by Goethe. This saying is a Schillerized Goethecism." Although at moments Melville found in Arnold an ameliorative spirit too near to Emerson's, he found some of the ideas provocatively expressed. Melville underlined "the all-importance of the choice of a subject," scored what Arnold said about "one moral impression left by a great action treated as a whole," marked the qualities Arnold praised in classical works ("their intense significance, their noble simplicity, and their calm pathos"), marked the warning against "the jargon of modern criticism," and heavily marked this sentence: "If they are endeavoring to practise any art, they remember the plain and simple proceedings of the old artists, who attained their grand results by penetrating themselves with some noble and significant action, not by inflating themselves with a belief in the preëminent importance and greatness of their own times." He also marked a passage quoting Goethe on two kinds of *dilettanti* in poetry: "he who neglects the indispensable mechanical part, and thinks he has done enough if he show spirituality and feeling; and he who seeks to arrive at poetry merely by mechanism . . . without soul and matter."

Melville took Arnold as a friendly interpreter of Greek theories of tragedy, paying attention to what Arnold said about greater actions and nobler personages, as in this passage: "For what reason was the Greek tragic poet confined to so limited a range of subjects? Because there are so few actions which unite in themselves, in the highest degree, the conditions of excellence. . . . A few actions, therefore, eminently adapted for tragedy, maintained almost exclusive possession of the Greek tragic stage." From Aristotle, Arnold quoted: "All depends upon the subject." Throughout the essay Melville also focused upon Arnold's allusions to "expression": "a certain baldness of expression in Greek tragedy"; Shakespeare's "wonderful gift of expression"; particularly a summation of three things for a modern writer to learn from the ancients: "the all-importance of the choice of a subject; the necessity of accurate construction; and the subordinate character of expression." Melville responded profoundly to the peroration, in which Arnold discounted modern chauvinism and argued that serious poets, steeped in the past, will not "talk of their mission, nor of interpreting their age, nor of the coming Poet." At last Melville had found a contemporary whom he could respect (on the whole) as a soul mate, or at least, in the political idiom of his youth, a good-enough Morgan of a soul mate. Reading Arnold's "Preface" concluded Melville's prolonged phase of gathering and testing ideas on aesthetics. Now, however odd it was to have Arnold as his liberator, Melville began to distill what he had been learning for months and to integrate it with his own long-held convictions about his own experience as a reader and writer. If he had been working on a manuscript, he could have written his new ideas into it. Instead, he put aside the all-important copy of Arnold and took up his Vasari, perhaps wanting to record his aesthetic ideas in a convenient place, a set he intended to be consulting over and over again, now that he possessed his own volumes. He began his notes on the recto of the front flyleaf of the first volume of the Vasari. "Attain the highest result. —" he wrote, echoing what Arnold had said about the old artists in his peroration. Next Melville wrote: "A quality of Grasp. —" He was thinking of Browning's Andrea del Sarto, the artist who knew that the great artist's reach should exceed his grasp. For decades Melville scholars often minimized Wordsworth's significance to him because no one had seen his copy of Wordsworth; we now wrongly minimize Browning's significance to him simply because no one has seen his copy or copies of Browning, whom he had read at least since 1849, when Thomas Powell introduced "My Last Duchess" (under another title) to readers of the *Literary World*. Here in the Vasari (which Melville knew was Browning's source for "Andrea del Sarto") Melville alternated between Arnold and Browning, reverting next to Arnold for the ideas that clustered about the single word "Expression." What Melville jotted down was "The habitual choice of noble subjects. — / The Expression. —"

The idea that aesthetic finish was fullness and not polish had been one of Melville's own for many years (witness in *Moby-Dick* his tribute to the crane left on the tower of the Cathedral of Cologne — an image derived from an essay on Wordsworth as well as his own visit to Cologne). After "The Expression. —" he continued: "Get in as much as you can. — / Finish is completeness, fullness, / not polish. —" Then he continued with lines on greatness: "Greatness is a matter of scale, — / Clearness & firmness. — / The greatest number of the greatest ideas. —" At that point he stopped listing and began to elaborate: "Greatness is determined for a man at his birth. There is no *making* oneself great, in any act or art. But there is such a thing as the development of greatness—prolonged, painful, and painstaking." He had marked in Disraeli's *Calumnies and Quarrels* the comment that learning made no man wiser: "wit and wisdom are born with a man." Greatness was determined at birth—despite Allan and Maria's focus upon the undeniable greatness of Gansevoort and their blindness to the genius of their second son. But Melville had also, for months, been marking and using the term "painstaking" as he tried to weigh the significance of hard application in the production of art. He had marked what Moore said about being "a far more slow and pains-taking workman than ever would be guessed" from the result, and he had himself defended Rogers as "a painstaking man of talent." Now, at last, Melville was summing up the disparate injunctions and admonitions he had been absorbing (and had been testing against his own experience), and was able to jot down, in a place where he could keep it, an integrated aesthetic credo. With his notes from Jeffrey in his Hazlitt and his notes from Arnold and others in his Vasari, Melville's aesthetic investigations of the previous months came to a satisfying conclusion. He had done his winter's research and reflection, and was ready to go home to Arrowhead. In "At the Hostelry" he said that Claude Lorrain found no gain "Wavering in theory's wildering maze." This winter Melville was not wavering in theory's wildering maze: he had distilled practical advice from people who had thought seriously about aesthetic issues, and at the end of his quest he had "refined" or distilled his own aesthetic credo.

[22]

Farewell to Arrowhead and the Overthrow of Jehu
April–December 1862

> All country people hate each other. They have so little comfort that they envy their neighbours the smallest pleasure or advantage, and nearly grudge themselves the necessaries of life.
>
> Melville marks this passage in William Hazlitt's appendix, "On Wordsworth's 'Excursion,'" in his *Lectures on the English Poets*, and annotates the first sentence: "That's a great truth."
> (William S. Reese Collection)

FOR THE NEXT MONTHS the extant family letters are mainly from Herman's and Allan's children. On 24 March 1862 Kitty Melville wrote her Cousin Stanwix, the only child at Gansevoort, that she had seen his "father and mother and sisters very often," at their rented house in New York City, and she asked the practical sort of question her dead mother might have asked: what did he do all day alone by himself? Thirteen-year-old Milie wrote him also: "Papa does not like me to read the newspapers much, so only now and then I read them; but papa often reads the part about the war aloud to us, so I learn just as much." Improvements in telegraphy and photography brought the war home in the papers, and in 1861 many Northerners stored up newspapers, recognizing that they would be valuable as a historical record and knowing that storage would not be a problem because the conflict would be over so soon. Southerners were far less able to accumulate and preserve newspapers. In the course of the next years many Southern presses were destroyed and newspaper archives burned—historical evidence gone forever. Allan was subscribing simultaneously (for much of the war) to at least these New York papers and probably others: the *Herald* (1861–65), the *World* (probably 1861–65); the *Tribune* and the *Evening Post* (at least 1861 and probably the whole time), the *Times* (at least 1862–64), and the *Commercial Advertiser* (at least 1861). This by no means exhausts the list of papers Allan and Jane received (in 1865, for instance, he was receiving the Troy *Daily Whig*).

About the middle of April 1862 Herman and Lizzie left New York with the girls to visit Gansevoort, where they were reunited with the much-changed Stanwix and saw Maria and Augusta for the first time since Uncle Herman's death. They stayed on for a week or so—a long visit for them—before going home to Arrowhead. The Unitarian mother encountered a Stanwix who had been indoctrinated at Augusta's Sunday school. The author of *Typee* and *Omoo*, once portrayed as the traducer of the missionaries, confronted a son who now propounded a question fit for a reviewer in the *Evangelist:* "How much money have you sent away to buy Bibles for the heathen?" Stannie's piety probably went uncommented upon: after all, what Augusta was teaching was what Maria had taught, a familiar fanaticism, and Melville had every reason to have known what he had been exposing Stanwix to. Home at Arrowhead on 24 April, Stanwix wrote a letter which Augusta marked, "on leaving me": "I am very sorry that I am to leave you as I have been so long with you." He was looking forward to seeing Mackie, who was not yet back from school in Newton. Augusta had extracted promises, writing them herself "on that sheet of paper" (which Stanwix inadvertently left with her) and having him copy them before he left: "There are three particular things that I will try to do . . . to speak the *truth*, to *obey* Mamma, and Papa, and to say my *prayers*."

From letters written in 1863 (the only year after 1855 in the "Augusta Papers"), and from letters in the original Gansevoort-Lansing Collection, we can construct the normal life at the Mansion House at Gansevoort for the previous several years and the rest of the 1860s. It is worth doing because the Gansevoort house became for some years the family hearthstone, inconvenient as it seemed until the family became accustomed to the idea that it was not the end of the world, as Aunt Catherine had treated it, but now an easy ride on the train from Albany and Saratoga Springs, and also approachable from the north, by the Rutland route. Much of Uncle Herman's income had come from the mill, the only mill on the Snook Kil anywhere in the area, so in effect a monopoly. Spring, mid- or late May, was his profitable season, because farmers let their grain dry over the winter before having it ground. Uncle Herman took cash for grinding, but he could routinely have taken a portion of the grinding when his own supplies of buckwheat, for instance, were low; he rented much of his land. For decades Uncle Herman had ruled as something between a lord of the manor and an old English squire.

After Herman Gansevoort's death through the rest of 1862 Maria, Augusta, and Fanny, managing with only one servant, "the factotum Georgia," ran "that great house" (as Helen called it, thinking of how much there was to clean). Maria retained her brother Herman's men or hired other men herself for outdoor work. Uncle Herman had not milked his own cows, and Maria continued his arrangements. By 1863 the closest neighbor, "Mr Landon," had "the charge of them" and was sending to the Mansion House "three lbs of butter a week & two quarts of milk a day," while keeping enough himself to make the deal worthwhile. By the next spring, early May of 1863, Maria's hired man "Lewis" had come every day it did not rain and had "cleaned the cellars, looked over the potatoes & worked all round cleaning up, finishing the wood &c." No one could keep Maria from supervising the garden and seeing that work was done to her specifications, which meant doing some of it herself. Much of this routine life at Gansevoort, such as Maria's supervising the garden, was typical of American village life in the North during the Civil War era.

But much went on that was not typical of village life, as is clear from a letter Fanny wrote in mid-March 1863, when she had replaced Uncle Herman as the one who dealt with the local people. She had already endured, despite the cold weather, "a great deal of company of a certain kind!" She itemized that day's calls, business mixed with the impertinently social. She had rented the pasture lot to Billy Anderson for the season at twenty-eight dollars; she had listened to Mrs. Hurd for "a long time" as she paid her month's rent; "Chalk" had talked about next year's rent, the upshot being "that he should put the house in good order &c & pay less rent." Willie Mott came with "a roll of the 'Home Journals'" (N. P. Willis's gossipy paper) he had borrowed. Mrs. Harriman came on poultry business and seated herself in the parlor where she "remained for two long hours," saying such "comical things" about the war and her "daughter-in-law Maggie, who she informed us belongs to the old aristocracy of Ireland!" Ironically, Fanny exclaimed, "Now have we not been very gay?" Aside from mention of the war, everything Fanny described in this letter was recurrent, part of the pattern of life at Gansevoort, where humbler folk came to the Mansion House to report and negotiate, and where free American citizens, equals to the Melville women in their own eyes if not the eyes of the Melvilles, intruded on them. The Melvilles were educated and worldly women who had in their time had "a great deal of company of a certain kind!" quite unlike their present kind, and they knew what being "gay" at a tea table or dinner in Boston or Manhattan could be. In dealing with their tenants and in controlling the mill Maria and her daughters were living out their lives in a survival from feudalism.

Maria owned 139 acres, according to the 1871 Hamilton Child *Gazetteer*, most of it farmland. While visiting the Mansion House Maria's older grandchildren could fish in the Snook Kil and get to know each other as the goldfinches darted around them. The sisters could have their reunions under the maternal eye, and the sons could visit when they were able to. Tom, at least, would string up the hammock and make himself at home in it, inhaling the Adirondack air and absorbing undisguised adoration from all the rest.

The women thought in the first years that Allan should take charge of bigger problems such as repairs to the mill, but he found it hard to leave Manhattan and Jane. Augusta had charge of one of the two rival Sunday schools, and she and Maria both took a great deal of specific interest in the condition and behavior of their minister and in raising money for his salary, usually from Peter Gansevoort, who owned much property in and outside Gansevoort still (including one of the "groves"), and whose brother-in-law George Lansing was there with his family, in hard-scrabble conditions.

Once Herman and Lizzie returned to Arrowhead at the end of April 1862 they started reorganizing for the summer. Melville got a horse to replace Charlie, and placed a notice in the *Berkshire County Eagle*, to run on 1 and 8 May, for a "woman to do the cooking and house-work in a small family, two miles and a half from Pittsfield village. No dairy-work required. To a competent person the HIGHEST wages will be given." One servant was not enough, and since he was not doing any farming Herman could at least milk the cow. Stanny helped, as he reported to Augusta on 30 April: "I have a good deal to do, to bring in wood, and water, and help papa, and Mamma, and a host of other things so, I could not write to you before." He explained that "Papa" had purchased the new horse from Mr. Nash, on trial, for the high price of $145. That was the big news, but Stanny added the information that Malcolm was coming home that day (Sam Shaw's diary says 1 May) and that Papa was well but that Mamma had been "sick in bed since Monday morning," 28 April. Stanny was feeling the dismay of a lad who had been living in the Gansevoort household run in "beautiful order": "My time is so taking up that I have not had my lessons. My things are in my trunk. Everything in the house is upside down, topsy turvy." Mrs. Chapman, he added, "came and stayed all day and night with us"—a neighbor woman helping them while Lizzie was sick, "a very gentle pleasant woman."

The Arrowhead remnant was in more than usual flutter even aside from Lizzie's illness. Neither Herman nor Lizzie had done the preliminary chore of putting up stoves which Lizzie had heroically performed in 1857 and which Herman had done in 1860. Herman was trying to be systematic when he picked out a horse to replace Charlie and advertised for a woman to cook and clean. While Stanwix was still chafing at not being able to unpack his trunk, Mackie arrived from Boston with *his* trunk. Stanwix wrote touchingly to his Aunt Augusta: "I knew Macky the very half a second I saw him." The Melville daughters had been uprooted since December themselves, though always with their mother or else both parents, and needed to unpack and reestablish some sense of belonging in a place. Household and personal affairs were confused still on 2 May, when Melville added a note to Augusta on Stannie's letter: "Stannie wrote this note two days since. It is my fault it has not gone ere now. We have been in a state of great commotion since arriving here. No help. Lizzie has overexerted herself & been confined to her bed. But is now better. We have managed to procure assistance from the neighbors & in a day or two hope to get permanent 'help.'" Melville marked through "No help," by which he had meant that they had had no help during the days of "great commotion," although they had made do later with the kindness of neighbors. He added at the top of the page: "P.S. Dont write to Helen or Fanny or Kate about our affairs here." This was a reasonable request that Augusta not disturb the sisters, since chaos was a temporary state at Arrowhead, and the news would alarm them and make Helen or Fanny feel obliged to rush to Pittsfield, when Herman and Lizzie were reasonably confident that they could get "help" on a less transitory basis, even if "permanent" was a wistful concept.

As Stannie's letter to Augusta on 8 May shows, his mother had been seriously ill: "Mamma is getting a good deal better, but she can[n]ot walk around the house all over." Mackie had returned in scholastic triumph, having "passed the examination better than any boy in the school except one and he was 18 years old." The boys diverted themselves by playing marbles before they went to school on 9 May, Mackie to "the *Hight School*, and I to the *Grammar School*," Stannie said. In this letter Stannie repeated the information that "Papa has got a nother horse on trial" (not yet another but the one from Mr. Nash). The horse was much on Stannie's mind, understandably, since they depended on him for transportation. In their first days back, Melville had made a comment that went over Stannie's head, indoctrinated in the Bible though he was. Stannie reported that the "horse will go as fast as Jehu." What his Papa had said was that he was driving the horse like Jehu (in 2 Kings 9:20). With the young horse and buggy rather than the old lumber wagon, Melville saw himself as driving furiously, like the punisher of Jezebel. Humorously or not, that is, Melville figured himself as a biblical king noted as a great charioteer and figured his buggy as a war chariot.

Despite Melville's expressed wishes, word got out and Helen and Fanny both came to help. A grateful Herman presented Helen with his newer set of Spenser on 15 May 1862. Even earlier, with little money to buy gifts, Herman had begun giving his old books, marked up or not, to members of his family on important days, and it is hard to know how he felt without those books around; he must have looked around for them at times, forgetting they were gone. Often, he retained a different copy or set: he had given Tom a work by Seneca and kept another copy; when he gave Helen one set of Spenser he retained the one that he later gave Augusta, his heavily marked and annotated set that had been their father's. It is hard to imagine his being without a Spenser, having saturated himself so deeply in his father's set, but for the last third of his life he may not have had all of Spenser's poetry in the house. He may have felt he knew Spenser so well that he would never again commit himself to a prolonged spell under that particular enchanter. At this time, in 1862, Helen compared her Spenser with their father's set, while she had easy access to both, and made a start at transferring Herman's marginalia into her copy—the only proof we have that any of his brothers or sisters ever valued his annotations. (After his death, in 1895, Lizzie read a passage in one of his books about a widow's communing with her husband through his marginalia, but by that time she had sold off cartloads of his books, and probably it was she who erased or snipped out some of his more irreverent annotations.) The next week, on Monday, 19 May 1862, Melville gave Fanny his set of Cooke editions: *The Poetical Works of Shakspeare* (bound with *The Poetical Works of William Collins*), *The Poetical Works of Will. Shenstone*, and *The Poetical Works of James Thomson*.

After helping Herman and Lizzie at Arrowhead, Helen went on to Gansevoort. She and Augusta this summer tried hard to persuade Maria that she could simplify her entertaining during "war-times" by dispensing with "desserts & second courses," but they met implacable resistance from their mother, who was not about to let a national crisis interfere with proper New York Dutch hospitality now that she was at last situated so as to extend largesse to her descendants unto the next and subsequent generations. Helen had the fantastic idea the next year that they might persuade their mother to the simplification if they let her know that it was *"the fashion"* ("perhaps her mind may change with modern manners"). Helen of all the children should have known better.

By 21 May Melville had given up on Arrowhead, and for nearly three months ran a "FARM FOR SALE" advertisement in the *Berkshire County Eagle*: "The farm (With large dwelling-house) now occupied by subscriber, two and a half miles from Pittsfield village, on East road to Lenox, embracing about eighty acres, wood, pasture and meadow. H. Melville." For a time Mackie kept up a correspondence with his schoolmates at Newton, and Stannie played a variety of games with marbles (as he wrote to Augusta on 24 May): "big-ring, little-ring, pea hole, three hole, and others." He and Mackie went fishing in Melville Lake ("Mackey did not catch anything, but I caught a sunfish. I had good luck!") Aunt Kate had sent him "a slate rubber, and a picture of Gen. [Ambrose] Burnside," and he was homesick for Augusta and Gansevoort. As late as 25 May Lizzie was only getting better, not yet well, but the children were all well. Mackie was studying Latin, going manfully at it every night. On 26 May Bessie wrote new details to her Aunt Augusta at Gansevoort (where Minnie Hoadley was visiting), itemizing the presents she had received on the twenty-second, her ninth birthday (and the ninth year since the completion of *The Isle of the Cross*): "I thank you and Aunt Fanny for the cards that you sent me for my birthday.... Mama gave me a little stamp with a dog on it, and Papa gave me a napkin-ring and a picture and some envelopes, six of them. Mama goes out to ride most every day, she is better than she was." Stannie gave Augusta more information about Papa's new horse. Just as each new cook became a Mary, the second horse was again called Charlie. He was much younger than the previous Charlie, only five years old, and Mackie, almost thirteen and a half, was allowed to ride him "most every day." On 8 June Stannie wrote to his Grandmamma Melville: "Mackie and I get home at five. We saw a wild rabbit coming from School one day. Last Saturday Papa went on an excursion, and Macky, Bessie, and Frannie, and myself. We found some young winter-greens. I went down to the Depot to see the Allen Guards go off." That last is to say that on 27 May the Allen Guard (the local militia company, reorganized and sponsored by Thomas Allen) of 122 men had marched to the depot where a crowd, including Melville and Stanwix, watched them board a train for Boston; the guard was allowed to return home just after the Fourth of July rather than being sent to the front. These eyewitness descriptions make Arrowhead sound like a much-changed home — one where the needs of four children were often paramount.

On 25 May Melville wrote to his brother Thomas, grandly addressing him in the ship *Bengal*, care of Augustine Heard & Co., Hong Kong, China. Maria and Augusta had forwarded Tom's "long and very entertaining letter" written from Pernambuco, and Herman responded in kind. Tom had dubbed someone a jackass for good and specific reasons, notably sleepiness and general laziness, but Herman launched into a mock defense of the fellow:

> For my part I love sleepy fellows, and the more ignorant the better. Damn your wide-awake and knowing chaps. As for sleepiness, it is one of the noblest qualities of humanity. There is something sociable about it, too. Think of those sensible & sociable millions of good fellows all taking a good long friendly snooze together, under the sod — no quarrels, no imaginary troubles, no envies, heart-burnings, & thinking how much better that other chap is off — none of this: but all equally free-&-easy, they sleep away & reel off their nine knots an hour, in perfect amity. If you see your sleepy ignorant jackass-friend again give him my compliments, and say that however others may think of him, I honor and esteem him. —

This wasn't up to Herman's old best intense, verbally inventive badinage, but it was charming and happy-spirited. The tone of the letter in places and the distanced attitude toward wartime activities is oddly reminiscent of the last letter he wrote to Gansevoort (after Gansevoort was dead) sixteen years earlier.

Having quoted *Don Juan* in some further badinage about corporal punishment, Melville was, he said, reminded of his own doggerel:

> You will be pleased to learn that I have disposed of a lot of it at a great bargain. In fact, a trunk-maker took the whole stock off my hands at ten cents the pound. So, when you buy a new trunk again, just peep at the lining & perhaps you may be rewarded by some glorious stanza stareing you in the face & claiming admiration. If you were not such a devel of a ways off, I would send you a trunk, by way of presentation-copy. I can't help thinking what a luckless chap you were that voyage you had a poetaster with you. You remember the romantic moonlight night, when the conceited donkey repeated to you about three cables' length of his verses. But you bore it like a hero.

Three cables' length is comical, but the moonlit night recital seems a real event on the *Meteor*, so Tom was one of the few people who had any sense of what had been ready for publication in 1860 and what Melville had composed on the voyage. Herman had marked in Isaac Disraeli's *Amenities of Literature* an extended passage on the vicissitudes of the manuscripts of Ralph Cudworth and he had just read in Disraeli's *Curiosities of Literature* the unsettling story of Baron Haller, who rescued his poems from his flaming house, then ten years later "condemned to the flames those very poems he had ventured his life to preserve." Chances are that the trunk-maker and even the disposal of the poetry were mere fantasy, but there seems a clear message here: for some months Melville had not been writing poetry.

Melville's course of reading earlier in 1862 shows that he was gathering momentum to begin again, but for a man who was to write a book of poetry on the Civil War, he sounded curiously distant: "Do you want to hear about the war? — The war goes bravely on. McClellan is now within fifteen miles of the rebel capital, Richmond. New Orleans is taken &c &c &c. . . . But when the *end* — the wind-up — the grand pacification is coming, who knows. We beat the rascals in almost every feild, & take all their ports &c, but they dont cry 'Enough!' — It looks like a long lane, with the turning quite out of sight." Melville added: "Guert has recently been appointed to the command of a fine new sloop of war." He saw the appointment as therapeutic for Guert ("It will do him good in more ways than one") almost as much as beneficial to the country, and his elaboration may be tinged with both irony and wistfulness: "He is brave as a lion, a good seaman, a natural-born officer, & I hope he will yet turn out the hero of a brilliant victory."

Lieutenant Guert Gansevoort had been a gay, bantering favorite of

Helen's in 1841, a cousin who looked strikingly like Herman, whose going to sea distressed him more than it seemed to distress Herman's own brothers and sisters. Then during the *Somers* mutiny at the end of 1842 Guert had helped to hang three young men, one of them the son of President Tyler's secretary of war. The experience wrecked Guert's health and drove him to alcoholism (perhaps only further into alcoholism) a century before there was effective treatment for that disease. While in the Boston Navy Yard at the end of 1843 he had been gallant to Helen and Lizzie, but without the old lightness. Like Gansevoort Melville and to some extent like Herman Melville, in childhood Guert had been destined for a secure high station in life, only to be deprived in adolescence of the father who might have guided and guarded him into such a station. From Uncle Herman he had inherited the badge of the Cincinnati that had belonged to the Hero of Fort Stanwix—an ironic trophy of lost family pride and security. Uncle Peter's son, Henry, was still too young and untried, and the truth was that Guert was almost too old and, sad to say, already tried and proved lacking in the highest qualities of leadership.

In the fall of 1861, Guert had hoped to command the new sloop-of-war *Adirondack* (it was his by right, since he was the navy man with a marauding Eagle's Lake author-friend, the great Astor Place rowdy Ned Buntline, and with family in Glens Falls, at the edge of the Adirondacks). He had other pressing assignments, such as the one that came on 19 February 1862, when the U.S.S. *Monitor* arrived in the yard and he began arming her with two nine-inch Dahlgren guns taken from the gunboat *Dacotah*. There was intense competition for the command of the *Adirondack* from John I. Almy, who, writing to Henry A. Wise on 21 March, remembered Guert's record: "he has had his Commander's command—that is the Sloop-of-War 'Decatur' in the Pacific until he had the command of her taken away from him on account of habitual Drunkenness, and his habits are not over and above steady and correct now." The urgency of the situation led to hasty decisions, and Guert got his wish. On 20 March 1862 Kitty Gansevoort reported to her brother: "Cousin Guert Gansevoort has been appointed commander of the 'Adirondack'—a vessel that has been fitted & built under his eye it is now in the stream & being *iron bound*—or *clad*—I am so glad he will belong to the Dupont Squadron—just where he wants to be." Uncle Peter wrote his congratulations at becoming "Commander Guert Gansevoort of the U.S. Navy," and in a letter on 31 March told Henry he had been very anxious that Guert "should have an opportunity of exhibiting his patriotism in this unholy war against the integrity of the Union, in sustaining the great principles for which his grandfather so nobly and manfully struggled in the War for our Independence." This was all very pious, but unrealistic: the time for Peter to have taken a protective avuncular interest in Guert had passed four decades earlier. For his part, Melville would take Stanwix, and perhaps the other children, to see the Allen Guards march onto the train, uncertain when they would return, but when he looked at the family's role in the war he focused on Guert Gansevoort as the potential hero, not on himself as poet of the war. It was as if the disruptions involved in reuniting the family and reconstituting life at Arrowhead had made him put in abeyance all the fine purposeful reading of the first months of the year, in Manhattan, until he knew where he would be living.

On 23 August Samuel Shaw arrived from Boston and two days later, on a Monday, set out with Herman "on an Excursion to the mountains," perhaps taking a train part way, perhaps driving, for at Arrowhead, according to this year's valuation book, there were three carriages, perhaps including the lumber wagon. They passed the night in an old (abandoned?) house near Saddle Back (Greylock) in Cheshire. For the ascent of the mountain they had a horse, perhaps rented, and their "Driving & walking" was "interspersed with much news of the war," a suspenseful time, since late on 26 August Stonewall Jackson struck the Orange & Alexandria Railroad at Bristow Station and before dawn the next day had destroyed the Union supply depot at Manassas Station, the start of the Second Battle of Bull Run. This came home to Melville, since Jackson's Union opponent was General John Pope, and young Henry Gansevoort was serving under Pope in that battle, at first retreating, then engaging Jackson's troops at Gaines's Mountain, Henry wrote his father on 8 September, after weeks of battle in which he sometimes ate, in a twenty-four-hour period, only a single "small army cracker." On the way back down from Greylock Herman and Sam left "the" horse, lame, at Chester and caught a train to Pittsfield on an unusually "Hot Day." If this was the new Charlie, and not a rented horse, Melville had to arrange to get it home when it healed. Sam returned the next Monday to Boston by the evening train, with nothing remarkable noted in his diary.

That first week of September 1862 Melville made a trip. He arrived at Uncle Peter's in Albany at five in the evening, took tea with them, then took the night boat for New York, cheaper transportation than rail, and curiously nostalgic. What his purpose was in going is not known. The decision made or being discussed at Arrowhead was whether, or when, to move into the village for the winter, but what connection that had to New York is not clear, unless Herman wanted to talk to Allan about a topic that had been raised before, Allan's purchase of the farm. The Melvilles would have known that soon (22 September, it turned out) Elizabeth would receive her share of Boston real estate, the value of which was calculated at $15,064.75. (The Mt. Vernon Street house was now Hope's.) "The other day Papa went to New

York and brought home a basket full of peaches," Stannie wrote on 30 September to Augusta — perhaps meaning three weeks or so by the phrase the "other day," perhaps meaning that Melville had gone down twice. All these records of Herman in motion need to be read in the light of Lizzie's explicit statement the next February that in the summer of 1862 he was so infirm that he could not have walked from Arrowhead to the village and back without injury — before or after his excursion to Greylock with Sam Shaw?

Allan was to be found in Wall Street any working day, but he and Jane were established in New Rochelle near Winyah for the summer. From the letter Kitty Melville wrote to her Aunt Augusta on 2 September we get a strong sense of what life was like there, near the Latherses. The Melvilles had rented a very handsome house with a very nice garden, and had everything they wanted in it, even given the requirements of Allan and Jane. There were three parlors and one sitting room with velvet carpets and a dining room on one floor, and "six bedrooms on the next and two bedrooms two closets and two large rooms on the third floor." Jane had been making lint from clothing to stuff into the wounds of soldiers, something Lizzie also did at Pittsfield — and something Allan should have been kept as far away from as possible, given the state of his lungs. As for Aunt Augusta, although in the winters she was isolated with Maria and Fanny, the Mansion House at Gansevoort was becoming the hearthstone of the family in the summer, for Kitty sent her love to "Grandmamma aunt Kate Minnie and Lottie and Hellen aunt Fanny" besides Augusta herself.

The children at Arrowhead were living what seemed like normal lives. During the last years the name Melville Lake was going out of the family's speech, and Stannie now referred to having "a picnic at Mrs Morewoods pond." There Gansevoort had rowed the Melvill and Melville children thirty years before, the summer after Allan Melvill died, and now Stannie wrote, in all ignorance of family history, that "Mackey rowed us children out in the middle of the pond, and we began to fish, we did not catch any thing." Another day the boys "went a fishing down to the river, Mackey caught a little bit of a fish down to the river called a shiner, then he snared a good sized pickeral we used the fish we caught for bait, but we did not catch anything else." At some point in 1862 (or 1861?) when Lizzie went to Boston, either taking the boys with her or placing them at Gansevoort or elsewhere, Herman had proved unable to care properly for Bessie and Fanny, according to what Lizzie wrote Augusta on 4 March 1863, after they had moved out of Arrowhead and into the village. Then, in 1863, Lizzie wanted Augusta to come "and overlook matters" while she went home to Boston: "I cannot leave them and Herman alone — there were such 'goings-on' the last time I left them, but then the boys were *not* at home — and in the village it would be still worse." When the "goings-on" occurred is not clear, for there is no documentation of her leaving Herman with the girls in either 1861 or 1862, and what the term "goings-on" covered is anybody's guess, but the very use of the slang term suggests that it was on the order of rowdyism by the girls rather than any dubious behavior by their Papa. When she wrote this Lizzie had a new reason for not leaving Herman with the children: the lingering effects of an accident he had suffered. Whatever the goings-on were, the girls had gotten at least a little out of hand. Helen on 6 March 1863 thought Lizzie was making too much of the problem of leaving Herman with any of the children:

> Just bring the little girls, with their clothes & their school books, and let them stay with us. You shall have no more care of them, (& not half so much anxiety) than if they were in Pittsfield, & I will engage they shall not lose any of their lately acquired erudition. I consider myself competent, with suitable elementary books as aids, to infuse into two youthful minds the very first principles of science, & George can exercise their mathematical faculties.
>
> As to the boys, if with Herman for authority, & restraint, & wholesome correction, if needed — and your household treasure [the latest "Mary"], for the care of their bodies and stomachs, their outer & inner man, or *boy* — cannot keep said souls & bodies together for a few weeks, without any startling outbreak of boyish outlawry, you had better send said boys to the House of Correction.

There would be no point worrying the issue if it had not been rumored, much later, that Melville had somehow neglected or deprived the girls, or if the boys' fates did not suggest the possibility that unwholesome correction might have been administered, or (most particularly) if, a century and a half later, Melville had not been recklessly charged with physically abusing his wife.

Most likely, in 1862, the apparent time of the goings-on, Herman had merely let the girls go wild, barefoot, and unkempt, wearing what clothes they wanted or did not want, sleeping when they felt like it and eating whatever they wanted — letting them behave as he had always wanted to behave, to the dismay of his more proper brother Gansevoort. Given the chance, also, Herman had a way of wearing fewer and looser clothing than most respectable men, a carry-over of his South Sea days which caused his youngest child, at least, some embarrassment when she was a young woman. The "intolerable infliction of 'dressing' " to go into society (Melville's words in his 1850 comments on the binding of Cooper's *The Red Rover*) was not an infliction he had imposed upon himself at Arrowhead in its reduced status. Melville was probably guilty of nothing more, at this time, than laxness in supervision.

Across the hill Sarah Morewood was still pushing herself beyond all reasonable limits. In his 30 September letter, Stannie wrote: "That evening Mrs Morewood invited us to go to camp [the soldiers' encampment] with them, Mackey went, but I staid home with Allie" (Alfred Morewood, conceived about the time of the great Greylock excursion of 1851). Sarah's grand masked picnics for hundreds of guests were now part of Berkshire history, but she continued to entertain small groups of the local elite and visitors, as Caroline S. Whitmarsh described a year after this, and she still had time and strength to take Mackie down to camp with her to see the brave soldiers.

Allan was regularly commuting from New Rochelle to Wall Street still, but on 15 June 1862, a Sunday, he went down to Brooklyn and Guert took him on a tour, all "over his vessel of which he is justly quite proud." Guert was awaiting orders, expecting to sail toward Charleston. In a letter to Henry on 27 June, Allan reported that Guert was "anxious to do something." Allan believed he would if he had a chance. Meantime, he drew up Guert's will, and Allan being Allan the signed will repudiated the rules of primogeniture and left old Peter Gansevoort's insignia of the Order of the Cincinnati and certificate of membership to Henry Sanford Gansevoort rather than to Leonard Gansevoort, Guert's next older brother. Eventually, aged Uncle Peter inherited the medal. On the Fourth of July, Allan took the whole family to see Guert's ship, as Jane wrote to Henry months later: "Did Allan ever write you of our visit to Cousin Guert, on board the Adirondack? We went down on the morning of the 4th of July—and passed the whole day & evening there. Allan, *all* the children & your humble servant, It was a delightful day." On 17 July they went to see Guert carrying two cans of ice cream, and "Allan went down the Bay with him, and the kind wishes of many hearts went with him and his ship." At sea Guert opened the sealed orders to sail the *Adirondack* to Nassau and determine the status of the Confederate cruiser *Oreto*. En route, it captured a Confederate schooner, and as it approached Nassau the *Adirondack* shelled the steamer *Herald* when it refused to stop. On entering Nassau, Guert Gansevoort received a protest from British authorities.

Then, five weeks after he took command, Guert Gansevoort was courtmartialed for his dereliction in the Caribbean: "on or about the twenty-third day of August . . . the said Captain Guert Gansevoort, being then in command of the United States steamer, Adirondack, did, through negligence, suffer the said vessel to be run upon a rock and wrecked near Man of War Key, Little Bahamas." As early as 7 September, his old ally, Flag Officer Samuel F. Du Pont, assured Guert: "you did all that I fully looked for from the energy and manliness of your character and skill as a seaman." At the naval shipyard in New York on 22 September a court of inquiry was opened in the loss of the *Adirondack*. Herman Melville went down to New York about that time (a few days before 30 September, according to Stannie), possibly to let Guert sense his cousinly presence, if Guert could bear to see him at all. (Guert had a history of holing up after disaster, be it the *Somers* or the *Adirondack*.) The court of inquiry exonerated him on 30 September. Uncle Peter still knew no details on 7 October, when he wrote his son: "I unite with you in sympathy for the loss of his ship & the effect upon his future."

The secretary of the navy rejected the court of inquiry's opinion on 8 October and ordered a court-martial of Guert Gansevoort for "Suffering a Vessel of the Navy to be run upon a rock through negligence." The court-martial convened on 15 October. From a hotel in New York on 6 November Kitty Gansevoort wrote Henry: "Have you heard any further about Guert G's court martialing. I hope it may turn out for the best—as you say our name & family credit are at stake." Allan called on her the next day with miserable news: "he told us that Guert was in Brooklyn at the 'Pierpoint House'—that he felt very miserably, & had in every way avoided the subject of the loss of his pet the Adirondack—It was a mortification to his pride for full forty long years he had waited for the command of a vessel & when he had rec'd it, everything so complete—he was happy, but its loss has completely broken him down." Jane Melville wrote to Henry on 11 November: "And now only think the beautiful ship is lost and Guert is here and has been tried by *Court-Marshal!* his friends think he will not suffer from the decision, but only think of his *pride!* He had waited *40-years* in the navy for the command of a gun-boat, poor fellow—he does not wish to see any of his '*tribe*'." The next day in Washington the Secretary of the Navy Gideon Welles issued an order declaring that in the case of Captain Guert Gansevoort "the specification is not proved *& Capt. Gansevoort is* not guilty *of the charge.*" Once again his old navy associations had buffered Guert. The New York newspapers had the story on 15 November. Still in New York, Kitty Gansevoort wrote Henry on the sixteenth: "By yesterdays Herald I saw that Cousin Guert Gansevoort who[se] case came off at the 'General Court Martial' had been acquitted. I am glad to hear of it.... I do not blame Guert, it was probably misreckoning—I hope he will be able to get another vessel & serve his Country—he is indeed anxious." Everyone in the family had ignored Guert's decades of alcoholic behavior and looked to him to uphold the family tradition in the war. Within a few months or a year it was possible for some members of the family to hope that Henry Sanford Gansevoort might prove the grandson of the Hero of Fort Stanwix to glorify the family name again, after almost a century, but Herman must have known that to place confidence in Henry was like placing confidence in Guert, a triumph of wishful thinking over experience.

Melville's attitude toward Guert was always complicated, and now he must have wished that this scandal had been like the *Somers* tragedy of 1842, one he did not have to hear of for many months, until word reached ports and ships at sea in the Pacific. There was no thought of his staying to console Guert. Melville knew about holing up in bad times, and he had his own problems in leaving Arrowhead. Stannie in the 30 September letter to his Aunt Augusta gives the best picture of the move from Arrowhead to a "square old-fashioned house on South street in the rear of Backus block" (as Joe Smith recalled). Stannie is not entirely clear whether the move was to start on 1 or 8 October: "This week Wednesday Papa is going to have the first load of things taken up to the new house and I will have vacation when Mamma is up to the new house getting it ready to move into. I am going to ask Mamma if I can't go up to the village with her to help her. . . . This week Wednesday, Thursday, and Friday, will be Cattle Show and Papa says perhaps he will take us up two days." Stannie was not anticipating that the move to the village would result in his world being turned topsy-turvy again: "I am going to get some colored leaves, and press them, and then paste them in a book." Contemporary descriptions show that the Melvilles were moving into a dreary, dark, undistinguished village in a spectacular setting. There were no public buildings of any pretense to architectural interest. The Reverend John Todd's Congregational church was a "handsome but low and inconspicuous structure of stone." The medical college, "conspicuous and ugly," was "like a big brick with a blister on the top." There was "no good hotel, nor public hall." A "low, long room there used to be for lectures," Burbank Hall. The streets were "not lighted, except here and there by private enterprise; and if you would know what is the blackness of darkness, spoken of by the prophet, 'when the light itself is as darkness,' grope your way home on a cloudy night, beneath the double rows of maples that shade these sidewalks. The darkness seems to separate you from the body, and you have the queerest feeling of having got home before yourself, and being seated at ease by the fire while out in the pitchy night." So Caroline Whitmarsh wrote in "The Town in Gross" ("No Public Buildings in Pittsfield" and "Darkness Visible"), in the Springfield *Republican* a year later, 30 September 1863, when conditions were much the same, and the Melvilles were still in the village.

A year after the Melvilles moved into the village, the Springfield *Republican* of 24 September 1863 printed another visitor's description of an overnight ordeal, there being no night train to connect out of Pittsfield with his 9:00 P.M. train. That piece evoked the ambivalent response from Caroline

Whitmarsh dated 28 September 1863: "The first drive through the village reveals all, — broken off spires, low ware-houses, station in a cellar, and the bald old elm holding out one green bough as a warning to all that dare meet the mountain wind; mills at every bend of the wild little Housatonic, and ambitious private residences — these go together; vehicles tied up and down the principal street, like a fair, — these show how the hamlet is scattered up and down the hillsides." There was nothing in the village to delight the spirit. The worst of it was that Melville was moving into a house with no views comparable to the view of Greylock from his study. What was the point of living in the Berkshires if he could not look out of his study window toward Greylock or sit on his piazza and look toward the mountain? Yet Stannie reported to Augusta on 28 October that they liked it very much and that it was "very convenient" — probably to school; and the first week they were there they all "went to Church" except Stanwix ("I did not have my new coat I shall go next Sunday"). Did Melville go? "All except me," Stanwix said.

In the weeks that followed the move, Melville stayed outdoors when he could, and took the children along. A few days after Stannie's eleventh birthday Melville took all four on an outing, then gave Stannie a special treat, a drive alone with his father:

> Papa took Mackey, Bessie, Fannie and I a chesnutting at Lulu Falls, we all took some bags for chesnuts, when we got there we looked along under the trees, to see if we could find any nuts, we did not find many, there were great long logs put up on the trees for people to climb up, we took the horse out of the wagon and gave him his oats, when we started to go home there was a small bridge over a little brook and the horse would not go over it, he was afraid, so Papa got out and tried to lead him over, but he would not go so Mackey took the whip and struck 3 or 4 times but he would not go over, then we took him out of the wagon and tried to lead him Mackey had to hit him pretty hard to make him go over at last we got him over.
>
> One night Papa said that he wanted to take a ride the next day, so the hostler at the Livery Stable where Papa keeps him harnessed the horse and we put him in buggy, and then we started off, Papa and I, we went up Lebanon mountain I had to walk all the way up the mountain and down the very steep hill, we passed through Lebanon Springs, Hand Cock shakers, and Stearnsville, we had a nice ride.

This seventeen-mile route was one of the recognized drives in and around Berkshire, No. 43 in the list of drives in Clark W. Bryan's 1887 edition of *The Book of Berkshire*. Melville was in good spirits and fair health and was enjoying his children more than ever as they became old enough to be his companions in his outings: according to Stanwix, who would know if anyone would, when

Melville decided he wanted to take a ride the next day he had no thought of going alone.

After 7 November Melville never again drove like Jehu, and probably never again took the children on outings alone. The *Berkshire County Eagle* gave the story on the thirteenth:

> On Friday forenoon last, as Mr. Herman Melvill, accompanied by Mr. J. E. A. Smith, was riding, in his box wagon, from his house in the village to his farm house, from which he had recently removed, a portion of the iron work of the wagon gave way, letting down the thills about the heels of the horse. The animal, which is a young one, naturally took fright and ran, throwing Mr. Melvill violently to the ground, where he fell into the angle made by the rise of the bank from the road. Mr. M., we regret to say, was very seriously injured, having his shoulder blade broken and several ribs injured, and his whole system badly jarred.
>
> Mr. Smith was also thrown to the ground and, falling on his head, was stunned and considerably bruised, but not seriously injured.
>
> Fortunately Col. Geo. S. Willis, near whose farm [on Williams Street] the accident occurred, happened to be at hand, and procuring assistance lifted Mr. M., who was in great pain, into his own carriage and conveyed him with the utmost kindness and care to his home, where he was attended by Drs. [O. S.] Root and [Frank A.] Cady.

This Willis who lifted Melville from the ground had done it before, metaphorically, by buying eighty acres from him in 1856 just when Melville needed a stroke of good luck. In Joe Smith's later account, Melville "fell with his back in a hollow of the frozen road." Ironically, instead of driving in his usual hell-for-leather Jehu style, Melville had been, as Smith remembered, "driving at a moderate pace over a perfectly smooth and level road, when a sudden start of the horse threw both occupants from the wagon; probably on account of an imperfectly secured seat." What happened was a freak accident, partly due to the condition of the wagon, partly the fault of the skittishness of the young replacement Charlie, who had been put into a position of responsibility without a sufficient trial period.

In 1891, after Melville's death, Joe Smith shared his guess that the accident "had something to do" with Melville's decision to leave Pittsfield, "and also with other changes in his life, which accompanied it." Lizzie properly notified family members, explaining that she could not get home for Thanksgiving. By the holiday Melville was writing almost normally, if the 29 November letter to Gorham D. Gilman is correctly dated to 1862. With this letter Melville returned the manuscripts of Hawaiian tales which Gilman had sent him — probably a few years earlier. Sam Shaw wrote a sympathetic letter, which Melville answered on 10 December, when he was still carrying the left arm in a sling and suffering neuralgic love-pinches (as he said) in the cheek. He claimed to have rethought his attitude toward death and life:

> I once, like other spoonies, cherished a loose sort of notion that I did not care to live very long. But I will frankly own that I have now no serious, no insuperable objections to a respectable longevity. I dont like the idea of being left out night after night in a cold church-yard. — In warm and genial countries, death is much less of a bugbear than in our frozen latitudes. A native of Hindostan takes easily and kindly to his latter end. It is but a stepping round the corner to him. He knows he will sleep warm. —

Then Melville drew a comical picture of a skull, one tipping the wink, as he said. He added that Lizzie was "quite well, though a little jaded by her manifold cares, we not yet being quite in order yet," and the children were "flourishing as usual." Maria was expected on 11 December for a long visit, there being no longer anyone at Gansevoort for her to nurse.

When Melville began to recover he went about a changed man, according to Smith's recollections — written down much later, but detailed and plausible:

> He suffered painfully for many weeks. This prolonged agony and the confinement and interruption of work which it entailed, affected him strangely. He had before been on mountain excursions a driver daring to the point of recklessness; but he always brought his ride to a safe conclusion, and his sometimes terrorized, passengers to a safe landing place. After this accident he not only abandoned the rides of which he had been so fond, but for a time shrank from entering a carriage. It was long before the shock which his system had received was overcome; and it is doubtful whether it ever was completely.

It was the sort of injury from which one is never made "whole" again, in the delusory term of insurance adjusters. Melville the timid wraith haunting bookstores in the Manhattan of the 1880s is prefigured in his behavior immediately after the accident.

In New York Allan and Jane had a beautiful Christmas tree and a party attended by "a good many Ladies and gentlemen besides children," Kitty Melville wrote to Augusta on 29 December ("But first I will tell you about my presents"). In the rented house on South Street at Pittsfield the celebration was more modest. Stannie hung up his stocking and "got a pocket comb, a chain, two cents, and a paper of candy," and Mackie and he shared a joint gift from Aunt Fanny and Aunt Augusta, a book called *Learning to Think*. Mrs. Brittain dined with the Melvilles in the village on Christmas Day, bringing

Allie and Annie (Sarah, very ill, being in town with her husband). Mrs. Brittain, holding down Broadhall with the two younger children, returned the hospitality the day after Christmas, inviting them all to a Christmas tree that Annie and Allie got up. ("Allie brought the tree home on his shoulder it was a very large one.") A little gray and white puppy had taken to coming to the South Street house every day to be fed, and before the year's end Stannie had made a collar for him and his mother had supplied a buckle for it. Melville was weak and subdued (for another month or more he could not dress himself without assistance), and did not figure at all in Stannie's letter to his Aunt Augusta on 30 December.

By year's end Melville's brush with the King of Terrors had left Lizzie subdued as well as her husband. What with their immediate concerns about him, and with her grief for her father (which naturally overshadowed his own mourning for his Uncle Herman), they were probably not touched much by other family births and deaths that year. Milie and her sisters had a new cousin on 6 May, Helen Barrington Thurston, born (in Nashville?) to Eliza Blunt Thurston and Dr. A. Henry Thurston. Eliza, Milie's second "Aunt Lizzie," died in Nashville on 8 September, leaving two children. Young Dr. Thurston, a Surgeon of Volunteers with the rank of major, had charge of the University Hospital in Nashville, now transformed into a military hospital. On 1 November Melville's Aunt Priscilla stopped talking at last and died at the age of seventy-eight, having survived her first executor, Lemuel Shaw. She left the muddy copy of the Copley portrait of her father's friend Samuel Adams to Harvard College, perhaps thinking it was an original, and she left nine hundred dollars to Herman. In Chicago on 23 December Uncle Thomas's son John Melvill died, and on Christmas Day his brother George brought the body home to Galena, accompanied by John's widow, Catherine, and his three children. Robert Melvill's son Robby "walked up from Davenport to spend Christmas with us, a sad Christmas for us all" (so Aunt Mary wrote to Maria). Guert was exonerated by the old boys of the navy but still without a command. It had not been anyone's very best year.

[23]

Displacements
January–June 1863

Master Allan . . . is however the cock of the walk among them [the children], he is one of those sturdy champions, who bear down all opposition by the mere force of dogmatical will, arguments are straws with him & he scorns to reason on any subject, — have his way he must.

Allan Melvill to Peter Gansevoort,
26 September 1826

HAVING HER OWN HOUSE at last and able to reciprocate all courtesies extended to her, Maria happily made a visit to the Curtises in Glens Falls, as Helen's special friend Kate Curtis wrote on 13 February 1863: "We are enjoying at present, a visit from our dear Aunt Melville — What a wonderful woman she is — I think she is one of the most remarkable persons I ever knew — I look at her with wonder, and astonishment and can not realise, she is over *seventy* — How active she is; and youthful in her feelings — I must say; she is a splendid old lady." While Maria was settled, with surprisingly easy access to the Curtises, many members of the family were uprooted. Herman and Lizzie were making do in the rented house in Pittsfield. Allan and Jane moved from Twenty-sixth Street to Thirty-fifth Street, a new venture far uptown for Allan. In Brookline, but not desirable Longwood, George and Helen were still living in a rented house, as Helen wrote to Augusta (26? January): "George took it until the first of June; but I am in hopes that the family [who owns it] may be detained longer in France. We have never been so pleasantly situated a *winter* before, even at Longwood, this house is so sunny and warm." As late as May (past the usual moving time) the Griggses were still hoping to extend their lease.

The Panic of 1857 had been disastrous for his Machine Shop, but Hoadley had rebounded with a small, highly adaptable product with a sure-fire name, "portable steam-engine." The Lawrence *Sentinel* reported (9 May 1863) that about forty men were employed making his "portable-steam-engines" there, and that he was "pressed with orders constantly, not only from Pike's Peak and California and remote parts of our own land, but from

Egypt, from Peru, from Eastern Siberia, far up the Amoer River." Early in 1862 Hoadley had also taken charge of the New Bedford Copper Works in the modern manufacturing area in the northern part of town, on the east side of North Front Street, territory familiar to Herman from the end of 1840; Hoadley's office was at Front and Rodman. Begun in 1860 to manufacture copper sheathing for the hulls of whalers, along with bolts, nails, and other essential equipment, the company suddenly was a major military asset. Millions of pounds of copper and other metals, the copper from the Great Lakes in the form of ingots, arrived by the Erie Canal to New York then through Long Island Sound to New Bedford — so there was no danger from Southern "pirates." The main product was "bronze sheathing" for ships, but the company also did "an immense business" in the manufacture of printing rollers of copper used to engrave patterns upon cloth. Hoadley commuted while waiting for Kate to join him, then rented a handsome Italianate house at the southeast corner of Madison and Orchard, about a dozen blocks west of his office. The house was new, built in 1855, and too large for the owner, a woman newly widowed. It had high ceilings, fine double parlors, a bow window in the dining room, fireplaces in all the main rooms, and a wide sweeping staircase to the second floor.

After visiting the Curtis-Gansevoort family in Glens Falls, Maria visited Uncle Peter, Aunt Susan, and Kitty (the Melvilles were all getting to know Kitty again, and had begun calling her Kate Gansevoort, in more or less clear distinction from Kate Gansevoort Curtis and Allan's daughter Kitty and Maria's daughter Kate Hoadley.) In the spring Rowland Morewood, one time, and Sarah and her sister Ellen another time, stayed with the Melvilles in the village before Broadhall was ready for habitation. Augusta sacrificed her own comfort in the spring in order to help Herman in Pittsfield and then Kate in New Bedford. She had not been to Boston or Lawrence to visit Helen or Kate for five years, not since the late spring of 1858. Lizzie and Herman were barely settled in their rented house themselves, since his injury had taken precedence over household affairs, and since from the first they regarded the arrangement as only temporary.

The most momentous shift was yet to come. In late January 1863, as soon as he "found that he could dress himself without assistance," Melville decided that, recent damage aside, his general health was "better this winter" (Lizzie's words to Augusta on 11 February), enough so that he could think about going to New York. He tested himself by walking out to Arrowhead and back without injury ("which he could not have done last summer"), then left for New York around the first of February. In her letter Lizzie said Herman was enjoying New York "very much" and had performed the pedestrian feat of walking from Trinity Church to Thirty-fifth Street — a trifle to the great Melville walks of the old days. Thirty-fifth Street meant Allan and Jane's new house, Allan always trading up and Jane wanting a newer, bigger house and one on which Sophia had not placed her stamp, however infirmly. The lot (between Fourth Avenue and Lexington Avenue) was 22' by 98' 9" and the house, a row house, took up the full width and went back 50'; an advantage over the Twenty-sixth Street house was the extra 2' of width and 5' in length: more important, this house had an extra floor, for it was four stories, five if you counted the basement, where the kitchen was. A great advantage was that it faced south. From New York Herman wrote his mother a letter she found "quite amusing," as she described it in her 13 February letter to Augusta and Fanny; she cheerfully hoped that New York would "continue to amuse him," and she particularly hoped to hear "that he went to Grace Church to witness the queer couple that were so splendidly attended, & so peculiar in all respects." That is, she hoped to receive from the author of *Typee* a graphic ethnological report about the 10 February 1863 wedding of Tom Thumb, Barnum's featured dwarf (Charles Sherwood Stratton, born early in 1838), to Lavinia Warren, a woman of stature suited to him. Helen in writing Augusta on 25 February was less amused at this example of thinly veiled post-*Typee* Victorian obsession with the combination of exoticism and eroticism, comparable only to the general fascination with the marriages and the accumulating progeny of the "Siamese Twins," Chang and Eng: "I saw a great crowd about a photographic saloon, the other day in Boston, & seeing an opening, thought I would take a look, and there was a framed picture of the two little goslings, looking silly at each other—the bride & groom forsooth in their bridal array." This year in particular the family relished Herman's amusing letters so much that they exchanged them.

Despite the Barnum-managed media sensation of the wedding of the year, the war was inescapable for anyone of the family in New York City. Colonel Henry Gansevoort, now stationed at Fort Hamilton, out at the Brooklyn side of the Narrows, was much underfoot at Allan's office and home. Allan was not only the will-maker for the family but a lawyer with a thriving practice, and for Henry the incomprehensibly wealthy and divorced Jane was exciting company. Henry had always been close to money he could not quite touch enough of; he and Allan were blood cousins who shared some crucial experiences and attitudes. Henry had been at ease with very fast women from his school years. On 12 February 1853 he had boasted to his friend Abraham Lansing, Aunt Susan's nephew, of being under the care of "Dr C⎯⎯ for all the time I left you for the disease I mentioned," and on 1 May 1853 he boasted that he could introduce Abe to the prettiest girl in New York City on the basis of having "visited every house of *any reputation* there." The Melville brothers never talked that way. Henry and Jane took each other's measure and liked what they saw. On 8 February Henry had Sunday dinner at Allan and Jane's, with Herman present. There Herman heard (not for the first time) of Henry's war service. Melville saw his Cousin Henry at least three times during this trip, once on a formal visit with Allan and Jane to Fort Hamilton, where Henry acted as guide, as Melville wrote to Kate Gansevoort on the seventeenth, after he had returned home: "He politely led us to the ramparts, pointing out all objects of interest. He looked well and war-like, cheerfully embarked in the career of immortality."

Yet Henry wanted a softer way to Glory than he had experienced the previous summer in the Second Battle of Manassas, and the way to get it, any Albany boy knew, was through influence. As he explained to Allan on 25 February, he was willing to accept a leave of absence from his regiment "to take a Command less than that of a Colonel in the Volunteers" or "Position on Staff of Major Gen¹" that would give him "at least the rank of Major." Uncle Peter had been at work behind the scenes and had a promise from Governor Horatio Seymour that Henry would get the first vacancy in the line of the volunteers, provided he got leave from the War Department. Lathers, Henry and Allan were sure, could ask his friend Edwin Stanton, the secretary, "to make such appointment with rank of Major as a personal favor." Lathers was going to Washington, and Allan and Henry gave him information that Lathers presented to Stanton before leaving for Europe. The military lineage on her mind, Henry's sister, Kate, prepared pictures of her Gansevoort grandparents to send to Herman and other cousins. Herman's were waiting when he arrived back at Pittsfield, and he assured Kate Gansevoort that the one of their grandmother was "clear and admirable" (he remembered her well and Kate had never seen her): "But alas for the Hero of Fort Stanwix!" (whom he had never seen), Melville exclaimed; in the photograph he seemed "under a sort of eclipse, emblematic perhaps of the gloom which his spirit may feel in looking down upon this dishonorable epoch." He then backed off: "But don't let us become too earnest. A very bad habit." A little later Melville heard that Henry Gansevoort had received "his leave from Washington (through Mr Lather's influence with his friend Mr Stanton in a great measure) to take position on *Lieut Col. in state volunteers*." (This was Fanny's report on 28 March, from Allan.)

Herman could retain his jocular tone toward Henry's chances of achieving immortality, but he would have seen that Allan's anxieties about the war were by now self-damaging. Following the war on all fronts, at sea and on land, kept him agitated, and the normal press of work exhausted him. No wonder that his weakened body yielded to the tuberculosis he had contracted from Sophia. Toward the end of March, Fanny reported to Augusta: "Letter from Allan to-day — all well, that is Jenny & the children, he does not feel very strong himself, he writes that a part of every day 'he seems to give up, but comes out bright in the morning.'" The daily cycle involved brightness and alertness in the morning, a feverish, frenetic period in the afternoon, lassitude at night, followed by brightness and alertness the next morning. There was no point telling him that worrying about the war was bad for his failing health; his extreme anxiety about the war was itself to some extent a manifestation of his disease. Yet Maria expected services from Allan just as she had when "Ally" had been expected to bring her a demijohn of Schuyler's best brandy from Albany the next time he went up to Lansingburgh. Even from the coast of China came instructions: Tom wrote to his mother and sisters at Gansevoort that he was sending a package home on the clipper ship *Samuel Russell*, and that Allan would see that the precious cargo got to Gansevoort. Maria and the girls became impatient with Allan when he wrote them without saying "a word about the Mill repairs." In a letter of 25 January, Helen tried to tell the Gansevoort women not to accuse Allan of neglect: "He says he is so tired at night, what with his business, and the excitement of politics & the war, he is too exhausted to do anything."

In Allan's mind the repairs on Maria's mill (important as it was to her as a source of income) ranked low against the alcoholism and venereal infections that he saw destroying the two military Gansevoort cousins. Allan was also keeping track of the other Gansevoort cousins at Glens Falls, and they were no better: by March Leonard was sick and confined to his room "& Stan was staying at the house to take care of him." (Stan was "the same odd fellow," as Fanny said on 20 March; peculiar, Stan was, and with that bulbous drunkard's nose everyone still hoped would not sprout on Stanwix Melville's pinched face.) Young Ned Curtis had been commissioned a third assistant engineer in October 1861 and assigned to the *Sciota*. Because of ill health he resigned from the navy, on condition that a replacement for him could be found, and he wrote home that he would be returning to Glens Falls ("Mary said Cousin Kate looked ten years younger since the news came," Fanny heard). Ned finally returned in the middle of June 1863. Now Allan had no chance of containing quite everything within red bands on legal documents filed neatly in their cubbyholes. He could perform significant rituals, as when (on 26 November 1863) he labeled an envelope: "Enclosed piece of cloth given to me by my cousin Annie Downer DeMarcini. It came from my grandmother Melville and lint was taken from it during some of the Revolution Battles. See the name *Melville* on it." He could attempt to alter the disposition of the badge of the Cincinnati, against all honorable laws of primogeniture. He could arrange the astonishing terms of his baby brother's will. Perhaps he could recuperate if he had his own country house, preferably a historic property in the Berkshires, ill kept or not.

Allan still had the power to arrange Herman's affairs and to assure a second safe haven for himself. Herman at last understood that he could never hope to run Arrowhead as a farm. His days of running up the rigging and climbing trees were over, and now even his wood-chopping days were finished. The Pittsfield locals were gossiping contemptuously that he had let Arrowhead run down, even the plot of ground immediately north of the house, between the imprudently commissioned but now-famous piazza and Greylock, and they knew that no one would buy it when he advertised it for three months in 1862, in the summer, the best selling-season. During Herman's visit to New York the brothers again conferred on real estate matters. Allan was prepared to take Arrowhead off Herman's (that is, Lizzie's) hands, and he had just the right property in Manhattan, the house on Twenty-sixth Street that had been good enough for him and Sophia for a while but was not good enough for him and Jane. Then numbered 60 East Twenty-sixth Street, it was the second house on the block, starting from the Fourth Avenue (later Park Avenue) side, and the mirror-twin of the first house. The lot was 98' 9" long, like Allan's new lot, and the house took up the entire 20' of width, and was 45' long. Even allowing for sidewalk and stoop, there was a narrow back yard stretching 40'. It was three stories high—four, counting the basement, which contained the kitchen and dining room. It was dark— no windows on either side, and fronting the north. Herman had sold half the acreage of Arrowhead for $5500 and now Allan would buy the other half (minus a few more acres already sold off), including with the house and outbuildings, for $3000, not paying over the cash but taking it in part payment for the house on East Twenty-sixth Street. "War-prices!" was what the brusque clerk snapped at Helen when she fingered silks; had real estate values in the Berkshires plummeted in wartime, while those in Manhattan had soared?

Herman and Allan seem to have made the decision themselves. There was talk of Lizzie's having to go to New York in March, as Helen wrote Augusta on 25 February (Hope Shaw had "said something about Lizzie having some thought of going to New York, instead of coming to Boston, next month. What does that mean? Sam Shaw is in New York now, and is to return via Pittsfield, & then we shall hear about it"). As it turned out, Sam Shaw (representing Lizzie) had been able to handle matters without Lizzie's going down to New York. Sam made no recorded protest against the arrangement, and seems not to have blamed Allan for his hand in it, so it may have seemed reasonable to him at the time. Sam visited the Melvilles in the village from 25 to 27 February 1863, and on 2 March Herman Melville and Elizabeth S. Melville signed a warranty deed conveying Arrowhead ("a certain tract of land together with the buildings thereon standing") to Allan Melville in consideration of three thousand dollars. This is Lizzie's much later memorandum: "Lived there [in Pittsfield] till Oct. 1863 when he moved into a house in New York 104 East 26th st bought from his brother Allan giving 7,750 and the Arrowhead estate valued at 3000 and assuming a mortgage of 2000 to Mrs. Thurston which was afterwards paid off [by] Dr Hayward's legacy to me of $3000 in May 1864 — about $1000 Aunt Priscilla's legacy was spent in repairs." Unable to pay the full price of $10,750, Lizzie had been forced to take over Allan's mortgage to his first mother-in-law, his various moves having been made possible by advances from Mrs. Thurston. This means that Lizzie paid over to Allan approximately $5750 of her inheritance — a third? or half? of the cash she had received, unless she sold some of the stocks that had been put to her portion. It is hard to know what to make of the value placed on real estate by the city of New York in the house-by-house descriptions, but in 1855 the Twenty-sixth Street house was valued at $4000, and in 1867 at $5500; the Thirty-fifth Street house was valued at $8500 in 1861, before Allan bought it, and at $10,000 in 1866 and at $11,500 in 1867. It looks as if Allan, now dubiously the husband of a fabulously rich woman, took advantage of Lizzie both on the low price of Arrowhead and the high price of the Twenty-sixth Street house, which needed a thousand dollars or so of fixing up before it could be habitable to the new set of Melvilles. Whether or not she overpaid, Herman and Allan's deal deprived Lizzie of an enormous percentage of her inheritance and left her anxious about how the rest of it would dwindle away month by month unless Herman found some way of contributing to the family income, something he had not done at all since the beginning of 1860.

Why Jane was willing to take Arrowhead as a summer house is hard to say: the house Allan had rented at New Rochelle in 1862 was more her style, and struck the family so in 1863. Allan himself had never liked the country. If a boy or a man was not careful, the sun tanned him, and even on a dry summer day the road between the Melvill place (now Broadhall) and the village was dusty, as Allan remembered from the mid-1830s, and Arrowhead was much farther from the village than Broadhall. No one ever said that Uncle Thomas's farm was *Allan's* "first love" (as Cousin Priscilla said it was Herman's) — no one ever said that Allan even *liked* the Berkshires. Take him to the top of Mount Greylock and he snored all the memorable night while the rats ran over Augusta's blanket and Sarah made *sotto voce* sexual innuendoes and indited her illicit "Greylock Thoughts" about George Duyckinck. But Allan was a man who wanted every interesting property or fine house he ever visited, and Herman had made Arrowhead famous. Its grand location was described in newspapers or magazines (or both) every year. No enterprising Yankee had yet portrayed it on a picture postcard, but every respectable library owned the Duyckincks' *Cyclopædia*, which contained W. Roberts's engraving of Arrowhead (looking from Holmes Road toward South Mountain, so as to show the piazza, instead of looking toward Greylock). Allan had prudently provided this picture of Arrowhead along with a draft of the biographical section, in lieu of an engraving of Herman's "mug." To his credit, Allan was the first person to understand that Herman's occupancy had made Arrowhead a historic house. Arrowhead was good enough for him, as a summer house, never mind its lack of grandeur; money and attention would work wonders. All this had been prefigured in Allan Melvill's depiction of his namesake as the bully boy who every night, fast asleep, did his best to kick his bedfellow out of the nest.

What Herman got in exchange for Arrowhead is hard to say. If he ever wanted to obtain some sort of non-literary work, his chances were better in New York, and the grandson of the old Major Melvill could never put the possibility of a Custom House job out of his mind. The bookstores and art stores were there, as well as Evert Duyckinck, Henry Tuckerman, and perhaps a few other literary friends. Herman had always loved walking along the wharves and the Battery, and if he were ill he could take short walks until he was ready for longer ones. New York was a Babylonish brick-kiln in summer, and it had doubled in distance up the island, almost, since he had left, and was formidably bigger in population — not a Constantinople, quite yet, but thronged in many streets. Pure water had come into the city for two decades, now, but privies stank up the air on hot days, and the cholera raged through the tenements at Five Points and environs. Still, a man living on his wife's money in a house the mirror image of the next house could disappear into the city the way the London husband had done in Hawthorne's story "Wakefield," and no neighbors would complain that he was letting the narrow brick front of the property run down. He might even get well enough and lucky enough to be offered some sort of job he could bear to accept.

What Lizzie got and what she gave up is unpleasant to contemplate. Her home was Boston, always, where her stepmother and half-brothers, and her brother nearby, all loved her, and where 49 Mt. Vernon Street was a fine house on the best block in the hub of the universe, and where nearby were cousins and even aged aunts. The move depleted her new capital and, agonizingly, put her in a mortgaged house again, and it turned out that she even had to pay movers twice, once to leave the furniture at Thirty-fifth Street, and again (about the same amount) to take it from Thirty-fifth to Twenty-sixth Street. She would no longer be just a few hours' ride from Boston, and her children would lose the chance to be real Shaws, just when Malcolm was old enough to be put on the train by himself and soon could take the grown-up duty of escorting his mother or an aunt on the cars and just when Stannie could be turned loose on the crooked-streeted town with his Cousin Oakey Jr., free to try to get entrance to the dome of the State House together. A smaller loss was the friends she had made in Pittsfield (on a visit to Boston she asked Augusta, who was staying with Herman in the house in the village, to write on her slate the names of callers, the locals not having adopted the custom of having cards printed bearing their names). Lizzie's annual allergies would strike in Manhattan as hard as in Pittsfield. She had never liked making the calls that Maria had relished in the old days in the Fourth Avenue house, and there was nothing likable about Jane (particularly since the Allan Melvilles were coming out so disturbingly far ahead in the real estate transaction), and Jane had her own fast set of friends, so no one expected much socializing. Lizzie would at least be near Milie and the other nieces, even though her access to them might be limited (huddled away as they were at Mrs. Hoffman's boarding school). The eight children could be together on some urban outings and family gatherings.

Perhaps the best inducement for Lizzie was the prospect of having better schools for the children. When Herman and Lizzie came to terms with Allan on the exchange of houses, there was no talk of leaving Malcolm in Newton or leaving Stanwix at Gansevoort. Herman's sense of personal chronology was defective and his arithmetic was downright shaky. Former schoolteacher or not, there was no thought of his tutoring Mackey. Malcolm had gotten so far in his arithmetic that Lizzie was "sometimes posed," and could not "do the sums without studying up the rules—not being familiar with Banking business." Neither of them could teach Mackey any foreign languages, ancient or modern, and Mackey's needs in 1863 would be Stannie's needs in 1865. Joe Smith was probably right as far as Lizzie was concerned, when, long afterward, he said the time had come that they had to find better schools for the children: "If Mr. Melville left Pittsfield on that account, his is not the only instance in which it lost or missed getting valuable citizens by its delay in providing the best possible schools and libraries." Lizzie could comfort herself in doing what her father had thought best, for shortly before he died her father had advised Allan to take some measures to get Herman "an office in the N. Y. Custom House." Lizzie got from the move the possibility, however remote, that someday in Manhattan her husband might contribute something to the family income for the first time in years. All in all, Lizzie was the loser in this, and it remained to be seen whether or not Herman would be a loser too.

George Duyckinck died on 30 March in New York City—a devastating blow to Evert and the family, but also brutal news for Sarah Morewood, who had continued to pursue the Saint, although more discreetly than in 1851.

The best tribute to George came from Oakey Hall, one of Herman's most perceptive admirers, now the district attorney of New York County. On 31 March, from Hoosick, near Troy, Oakey wrote to Evert:

> In a little town to which business called me: in the midst of a driving snowstorm: just toward dusk: and with everything cheerless about me I learn of the death of George. It is a great shock: for I did not even know he was ill: & I shall not, I fear, reach town to attend the funeral, but shall try.
>
> You know Evert I have knocked around the edges of society of all sorts & have for a man of my years seen a great deal of the bad side of life without being in it or of it. I can therefore well admire & esteem such a meek and unaffectedly just man as was George. To *me* he stands out in very bold relief as such a man. He was guileless, charitable to the failings of others, detesting wrong & deceit. You see I dwell on the things which to me seem *great* virtues. Others will speak of his talents, & literary labors & of his mind & its acumen. But to me a *good* man & that *my* friend is praise above all praise.

Manly Oakey Hall grieved, whether or not he made it back for the funeral. In Manhattan, Hall dealt every day with Tammany men, but he had bound his *Pierre* and his *Shirley* in half-sheep, making his own loving library classification where Herman Melville's despised book (which he, against the tide of opprobrium, had praised to readers in the Crescent City) huddled snugly with a work by one of the once-scorned and indistinguishable Bell brothers or Brontë sisters. Momentous New Yorkers like Oakey Hall moved just outside whatever little circle Melville might draw around himself there, and in their libraries copies of books by Herman Melville were still cherished. Allan must have gone to George's funeral. Herman had his set of Chapman's Homer to remind him of George, but this was no season to die and be properly mourned.

On 30 April Allan arrived at Pittsfield to inspect his property, and "seeing that it was such fine weather and dry roads here, he telegraphed to Jane to come up next day, and bring all the children, which she did," so Lizzie "had a house full—children enough as Mary said to 'shingle a house.'" (This was the current generic Mary, whatever her name had been in Ireland.) Luckily the weather continued splendid, and Lizzie got everyone out of the rented house, as she wrote Fanny on 7 May: "Saturday we started off in two vehicles—12 Melvilles of us and had a grand picnic, on our old 'trailing arbutus' ground where Tom had such 'a good time' on one occasion. We staid the whole day, made fine, boiled tea & eggs—fried ham &c. The children enjoyed it highly, and we all came home loaded with flowers, a box full of which the children took to N. Y." The next day, 3 May, Lizzie said, they "'simmered down'" as much as possible—Lizzie marshaling "the 6 Misses

Melville & the 2 masters Melville into church" while Allan and Jane took their time but appeared at Dr. Todd's low stone church (Lizzie bit her lip as she wrote) "in time to hear the benediction"; Herman rested in his room. The family knew what a strain Jane had been on the household. On 11 May Maria sent Lizzie's letter to Augusta, at Lizzie's request, commenting: "She must have had a fatiguing time with the 6 Miss Melvills two Master Melvills & the four old Fathers & Mothers."

Having surveyed her new property, Jane made her mind up to take possession fast, although Lizzie told Maria she hardly believed it could happen: "possibly Allan & Jenny may come up and occupy the farm house this summer—Jenny is very desirous to do so, but seeing that they will have to transport all their furniture from N. Y. and that it would hardly 'pay' for so short a time, I think that Allan will dissuade her—at least, I hope so." Helen could scarcely believe it either; in a 14 June letter she asked Augusta, "How long do you predict that Madam will be satisfied & contented in such a quiet corner of the earth?" Nilly Van Rensselaer Thayer, ensconced from birth higher than Jane could ever buy or bully her way, was coolly skeptical in writing to Augusta on 24 June: "I hope Mrs Allan will enjoy her quiet country life, but I fancy she will soon tire of it, unless she finds gay society in Pittsfield." In a letter to Fanny on 7 May Lizzie set her own new moving month: "we move in October. Yes. *'Move'*—We shall only wash paint & windows"— so she thought then, not thinking she would have to renovate the whole house. On 22 May, Maria, anxious about Kate's removal to New Bedford and Helen's shift as well, wrote to Augusta, then at New Bedford after her stint at Pittsfield. She had received a letter from Herman with the real estate news: "Herman seems to be much pleased with the prospect. He has always liked New York, & is not the first man who has been beguiled into the country, & found out by experience that it was not the place for him." It was odd how passively Herman and his mother saw some of his most momentous behavior.

An era in Melville's life was ending, but (as no one quite realized) his departure was not going to remove his association with the farm. Already the article on celebrities who had lived or still lived in the Berkshires had become an established journalistic genre, and the hasty authors of this annually recycled prose took a long time realizing that Herman was not at Arrowhead any more, just as later the public was told he was working at the Custom House long after he had retired. Allan and Jane and his daughters and the Lathers and others thought otherwise, but Allan had the deed to Arrowhead and that was all: Arrowhead would always be Herman Melville's. There was no stopping Jane. Stannie on 30 May wrote to Augusta, still with the Hoadleys in New Bedford: "Did you know that Uncle Allan was going to live out at the farm, this summer? they are coming out some time this week. All their furniture has come. Uncle Allan has got a horse her name is Kate" (therefore obviously a high-strung, skittish beast). From New York on 2 June, Jane wrote imperiously to her sister-in-law Lizzie, a letter breathtakingly arrogant, selfish, snobbish:

> I cannot sufficiently thank you for all your kindness and attention in arranging *all the little things* which are always *most* troublesome. Allan & I feel deeply obliged to both Herman & yourself—The "Man" you speak of may do—I trust he will, but when there are so many growing *girls*, & so many girls as help in a family we cannot be too careful but I trust may still. It would relieve Papa of a great deal of labour-besides we should be at once *settled*. I think to put Matting on my Parlor, or as Mrs Thurston said last evening that *carpet* was better, perhaps I may put down a pretty little carpet, will you be so kind as to make a drawing of the room (parlor) & measure the recesses, the width of Mantle, the window recesses (if any,) &c let me know—as I can have it cut & made here at half the price upholsterers would ask.—Allan had not told me about the painting, how glad I am that he has thought of it. Poor Allan! . . . About the stove we think it would be better to wait & select it after we arrive. You are very kind to offer to get one & to send the coal out. . . . I do wish we could find a match of size, speed &c—to Katy our horse—as much of our pleasure will depend upon our drives &c &c—I trust the painters have been out to Arrowhead and that the ceiling are *all* whitewashed by to-day. We shall use the open fireplace until we buy a *stove*—can we get eggs, milk &c—about the neighborhood. I am much obliged for your kind offer about the Ham but I think we can boil one *here* and get eggs &c *there*, and we can dine thus for a day or so. . . . Will you oblige me by getting 3 dozen or 4 tomattoe plants, & 3 dozen egg-plants, & some vegetable oyster-plant, say 1 dozen also—some fine *dahlia plants* for the garden—& some *Petunia Plants* to be placed in the front of the house & around the trees, they are *hardy*, & bloom until *November in Boston.* 1 doz Dahlia plants or roots of different colors—in front of house & by the *piazza, Madeira* blue is pretty please get two & plant in sunny place—
> . . . . Do get me some *dahlias*—& any other plant *you* think pretty. . . . Arrowhead would not be so attractive if I could have no garden—I shall have some visits from New York friends who go to visit Mrs *Lanman* alas what will they think of poor simple *Arrowhead*—?

Lizzie read every word she could decipher in this royal edict, and obeyed many of the commands. On 12 June Allan and Jane were back at Herman and Lizzie's (so Lizzie told Fanny on the fourteenth) for "the purchases of furniture, kitchen utensils, cook-stove &c—" then discourteously "went out in the evening," improving their social contacts.

At the end of April Lizzie had taken Jane to Lebanon to see the Shakers and, after prevailing upon Sister Sary Ann to give them dinner, they had spent "some time in the 'shop' there," Lizzie watching as Jane ostentatiously "made large purchases" of the Shaker products. Being repeatedly subjected to such doses of Jane sharpened Lizzie's irony, as in this report to Fanny in her 14 June letter: "The great event of the season has transpired. Allan and the whole family (3 servants) came up last Thursday, the furniture, in part, having been sent up previously—Jane, Kity & Lucy staid with me that night & Allan and the rest went out" (out to Arrowhead). Lizzie restrained her responses as she witnessed for the second time in her life the original shop-till-she-dropped woman in action: "the children staid with me till last eveg. when *Jennie* drove in with Milie & Florence and staid so late making purchases that she was afraid to drive home alone, & Malcolm had to go with her (in his Saturday wardrobe).... Among other purchases she bought 3 *doz* Tomato plants,—*lots* of material for *pickle* she will have." Mackey walked back to the village the next morning before Jane was up.

By mid-June Lizzie was sure that the "lady" was somewhat homesick already ("homesick" meant "bored") and declared that she would "not be surprised if she left the place in a month." She continued: "Selfishly speaking, I hope she *will*—I enclose a specimen of the sort of letters I have been having, which will amuse you, especially the part about Mrs *Lanman's visitors*—This came when I was in the midst of 'cooking my own dinner' do you wonder I was cross on *trying* to read it?" (The latest Mary had left about two weeks before, finding Lizzie's work too hard, the New York infusion being more than she had bargained for.) When Lizzie said "*trying* to read it" she was referring to the wretchedness of the handwriting. Lizzie was hurt, naturally enough, by Jane's haughty view that Lizzie for a decade and more had lived in something slightly above a hovel, although a hovel good enough to do as a summer house for Jane, at least for the time being, if only it could be spruced up inside and out. Lizzie was justifiably furious at the relentless demands Jane had made upon her—treating her like a servant, in fact. She was absolutely confident of her own social status. She was, after all, the only daughter of the great chief justice of the Supreme Court of the commonwealth of Massachusetts, and had been all her life part of the best society of Boston, whatever her sufferings as the wife of an unemployed former writer. She was also secure enough in the Melville family to trust her sisters-in-law to understand just how appalled she was and to be sure they would be equally appalled as they read Jane's letter—which survives only because Lizzie sent it to Augusta as a "specimen" of what she had been receiving.

All plans were complicated by Bessie's becoming so sick late in June 1863 that Lizzie took her out of school for the summer, regretting it because she had been the best scholar of her age at the school. On the twenty-ninth Lizzie reported to Augusta that a doctor had advised her to take Bessie out of school at once in the hope that she would have "a mild run of low fever" then throw it off and be well again. Fanny, Lizzie added, "has twice the vigor of constitution that Bessie has — she walked out to the farm with Macky the other day, and did not 'feel tired a bit' she said." Bessie's health suffered after this, horribly if not immediately and continually, but rather than growing up "a perfect dunce," which Lizzie would have preferred to making her go to school when sick, she never lost her intellectual bent. She needed, and Frances would need, proper schooling.

Whatever Lizzie's problems with Bessie and the loss of her cook, Jane continued relentlessly. In mid-June she dispatched a typically haughty note to Lizzie, while Augusta was in Pittsfield, the day being so warm that Jane did not dare ride into the village in the carriage but instead sent "two of the children so that one may hold an *umbrella*." She said, "You might let two of the little girls, or one of the boys come out with Milie. But come in a carriage yourself by all means, & oblige." Jane knew Milie's name but had trouble with the other girls' names, sometimes resorting to their first initial; the Melvilles somehow all learned the names of children and used loving nicknames for them. Before the end of June Lizzie sent word to Augusta, home in Gansevoort, that "that Jenny got very much disgusted with a 'cold spell' of weather, and took Milie and went down to New York." She left the three younger girls " 'out in the cold' " with four servants to care for them, including the Irish "Man" whom Jane had envisioned as a marauding sexual predator (not the only time Jane too eagerly shared her lurid or outright pornographic fears with previously innocent souls). The weather became warm again. Lizzie was also, as they said then, "warm." She exploded, for the only time on record, alluding to a current anecdote about Horace Greeley and the "nigger," the point of which was that even the most self-suppressed of people would burst under extreme provocation, like a steam boiler: "I *must* relieve my feelings — *Great fool!* — say it — or 'bust.' " Lizzie had been like a sister to Helen, Augusta, Kate, and Fanny for more than two decades now, and they all grieved for the loss of Sophia, whose touch of Aunt Catherineness had been, after all, endearing. Unspoken was their anxiety about Allan's health and the possibility that Madame might become the sole parent of Sophia and Allan's daughters.

Uncle Peter had entertained his sister Maria in the spring, sending a coach and coachman to meet her at the depot. Encouraging this new spirit of benignity, Herman responded in a wholly uncharacteristic way to Peter's invitation to him to attend the celebration of the semicentennial anniversary of the founding of the Albany Academy: he not only accepted but attended. Leaving Lizzie with the children (all of whom were still in school, except poor Bessie), Melville went to Albany for the celebration on 26 June. For a wonder, he actually marched through the streets in the procession led by the music of Screiber's band, then at three in the afternoon he attended the meeting at Tweddle Hall, which was presided over "by the Honorable PETER GANSEVOORT, the President of the Board of Trustees," according to the memorial volume. Seated near Peter and "warmly welcomed" was "HERMAN MELVILLE, whose reputation as an author" had "honored the Academy, worldwide." The "Honorable ALEXANDER W. BRADFORD, LL.D., of New York, a former student of the Academy," gave the principal oration, a piece of nostalgic patriotism delivered as best he could, though he was still no Gansevoort Melville. Melville stayed to the end, although he did not partake of the "collation which the thoughtful liberality of the Committee of Arrangements had provided"—a committee of which he was a nominal member. He kept Bachelor's Hall with Uncle Peter that night, Aunt Susan and Kate being at Saratoga, and the next day accompanied his uncle to Saratoga and went on to Gansevoort by himself. To Augusta, still in New Bedford and now unwell, Fanny reported on 29 June that Herman looked well "& enjoyed his visit in Albany." He and his mother talked of going to Glens Falls or to "the springs for a day also." The weather was fine and Herman was "enjoying his visit."

Despite Guert's wreck of the *Adirondack*, the family still hoped for military distinction from him as well as from Henry Sanford Gansevoort. On 15 July Captain Guert Gansevoort was detached from duty at the New York naval shipyard and ordered to command the *Roanoke*, then at Hampton Roads. Maria wrote to Augusta on 24 July: "I was rejoiced to hear of Guerts appointment to the command of the Roanoke, I saw that she was at some place in complete order." Maria had not lost her sense of reality ("may he be more fortunate"). Across the Potomac at the headquarters of the Thirteenth New York Cavalry Henry Sanford Gansevoort had moaned to his father on 6 July that his regiment was "yet as undrilled as can well be," no drilling but much "detached duty,—patrolling, scouting, and skirmishing." It was such "an outrage to expect cavalry to be made in a day" that he moaned, "Oh, how I wish I could return home, and let this war be ended!" On the same day Guert was given his new command, 15 July, Henry wrote his father from Washington rejoicing that his regiment had been ordered back from the front, it being at last recognized that it needed "drill and instruction." On 23 July he expressed his delight that Cousin Guert had "again a vessel under his command." Guert's new chance with the *Roanoke* should have been cause for perturbation. Guert was Guert, and Henry seemed to be campaigning for favoritism as much as campaigning against the secessionists. No wonder that Herman Melville began to think that he might be the cousin to take a national role in the war, after all.

There were fewer moments when the war seemed quite secondary to more pressing problems. At Gansevoort, Maria and her two daughters for news of the day were still subscribing to the *Home Journal*, Herman's friend N. P. Willis's paper, and to the semiweekly edition of the New York *World*. When the war news became too much to absorb in two sittings they shifted to the daily edition of the *World*. Like many Northern families, the Melvilles went through the war without deaths in the immediate family. Nevertheless, before it was over the war marked everyone, evoking a wide range of attitudes and experiences, and shortened lives. The family worried about George and Kate Curtis's son Ned, Herman's first cousin once removed, even after he had resigned and they expected him home. Fanny wrote Augusta on 4 May 1863: "From Ned, they have not heard one word & of course are anxiously expecting him every day." Ned's sister Mary Curtis saw a notice "in one of the N. Y. papers of the funeral of Herman Gansevoort Radclift, he died of wounds in one of the hospitals," Fanny wrote to Augusta, at New Bedford. "What a blow to his parents!" Lizzie later on (spelling the name "Ratcliff") said she had not seen any death notice at Pittsfield but would watch for one. On 3 May 1863 at Salem Chapel, in Virginia, Captain John De Peyster Douw, son of Valcourt P. and Helen L. Douw, and nephew of the eponymous husband of Margaret Van Rensselaer, led his own company of the 121st Regiment of New York State Volunteers in that day's terrible battle. In that family where a third cousin like Hun (or Hunn) Gansevoort was simply "Cousin Hun," connections unknown to us died and were grieved for.

The family was more than normally fearful for Tom Melville. He was captaining the *Bengal* when Kate Gansevoort wrote Henry from Saratoga Springs on 30 June 1863 that one of the owner's of Tom's ship was vacationing there, and had informed her of Tom's attempts to evade capture: "He is at present at San Francisco & from thence will sail for South America — so as to keep free from the Rebel privateers." On 29 June Lizzie wrote to Augusta that Dr. Nourse's dynamic daughter Clara was to be in Pittsfield for much of the summer while recuperating from overwork in Cincinnati, where she had started a school in a large house which she had rented "to Gen. Burnside & staff, till September when her school opens again." By 5 November Julia Blatchford Potter protested to Augusta that dressing for a gay "Russian ball" that night was money misspent: "it seems wrong to me that when so many brave soldiers are suffering, so much money should have been spent upon this unnecessary testimonial I would rather have had it given to the Sanitary Commission" — the organization women had founded (with Henry W. Bellows as front man) to see to the welfare of the Union volunteers before they all died off in camps.

The family expressed all degrees of opinion on the war, from Hoadley's espousal of the views of his friend Charles Sumner to the Van Rensselaers' overt admiration of the fine Southern aristocrats they had been friends with all their lives. Kate Berry, the mother of little Walter (much later Edith Wharton's great friend in Paris), raged to Augusta on 7 May 1863 about the black regiment, the Massachusetts Fifty-fourth, then recruiting: "What splendid soldiers those Southerners are and they have had all the victory since the war has commenced." She was horrified that "these abominable Massachusetts abolishionists," seeking glory, did not care "if this war continues ten years to come." Sumner, one of "the greatest cowards & hypocrites that we have at the North," would "clap his hands and sing March again and try to be defeated but he will take good care that he will never die fighting for the restoration of the Union." That was one extreme. Lizzie did volunteer work in Pittsfield during that summer. Young Frances remembered almost nothing of it, as she wrote to her own daughter Eleanor Thomas Metcalf on 30 April 1925: "My only remembrance of the Civil War, is, that your grandmother took beef tea to the sick soldiers (Pittsfield) and we all scraped old linen to make 'lint'—to be used in dressing wounds." Yet Lizzie did enough to warrant being named, with other women, in *Life with the Forty-Ninth Massachusetts Volunteers*, by Henry T. Johns (Pittsfield, 1864), as one who had nursed the wounded, giving "all the attentions that patriotism allied to Christianity, working through women's hearts and hands, could inspire," disregarding "questions of rank or residence" and thinking only of "the measure of illness and necessity." Many "a stricken soldier" would "ever think with gratitude, and many a soldier's widow will, in her loneliness, invoke Heaven's blessings on them" (Lizzie being one) "who so tenderly handed *their* loved ones to God and His mercy."

In Gansevoort a little into 1863 Maria had a new factotum, Frances (not Frances Priscilla Melville). In early April the resident daughters timed their Dutch housecleaning efforts around Maria's visit to Peter, causing Helen to worry to Augusta on 4 April: "For pity's sake, dont go to Kate's, with a long pale care-worn physiognomy, all ready to take cold, and get sick, on the first provocation.... Now mind Gus, *dont, please dont*, pull the whole house to pieces at once, & you on the eve of making a visit." On 18 May, Fanny wrote to Augusta (then at the Hoadleys' in New Bedford) not to hire a woman because "Mamma says we 'may be away part of next winter'!!" Temporarily, the local Frances would be "better than any one from a city." On 10 April Mary Curtis wrote from Glens Falls to her "dear Cousin Gus": "We are at present and have been for three weeks, without any cook or servant of any kind excepting a little contraband in the kitchen to wash up pots and kettle." "Contraband" was a wry application of the new slang term from the decree that in some circumstances blacks might be liberated as contraband of war. Lizzie found it so hard to keep help in Pittsfield that she resorted to doping one woman, a generic Mary who threatened to quit then decided to stay on " 'a spell longer' "; at that point Lizzie began giving her "a daily dose of 'Bourbon & Bitters' " which "so propped her up," that she felt " 'quite smart again.' " Mary's daughter "S'liny," after substituting for her mother while Lizzie was away in Boston, impudently told Lizzie that " 'Miss Gusty' " had found no fault, when she was in charge, years earlier (Lizzie to Augusta, 16 April). On 14 June Lizzie wrote Fanny that Mary had left: "I was nearly a week without 'help'! for though I had numerous applications, I would not take a woman without a good recommendation." On 29 June she reported success in her letter to Augusta: "I have got a new 'help' as you know, and am more than satisfied with the exchange. The new Mary is a treasure, so far." At the Mansion House Frances had to be dismissed in the summer, and Lizzie wrote sympathetically to Augusta on 16 August, wishing she could send her latest Mary to Gansevoort but knowing it would not work: "as she is a devout Catholic she would not be willing to go anywhere, where she could not worship at her own Church, and of course would not consent to have Willie put under other than Catholic influences." Lizzie thought servants might be available "at the break up of the Saratoga season." In New Bedford Kate imposed her ways as best she could, as Helen wrote to her sisters at Gansevoort (29 September); the new cook could "do, probably, if she condescends to stay when the lady requires her sheets to be folded the lengthwise of the article, a thing 'never heard of in New Bedford' " and "the children's stockings to be stretched in the width before ironing, 'which no other lady in New Bedford would ask a girl to do!' "

The war had exacerbated the servant problem. Immigration had fallen off as Irishmen and other newcomers found themselves liable to being drafted to fight a war about black slaves while they themselves were in economic competition with free blacks. The New York City draft riots of July 1863, in which Irishmen hung black men from lampposts and Irishwomen cut off their penises, burned themselves into the consciousness of Northerners like Melville, who was in Pittsfield but who could now see realistic pictures in newspapers and magazines. Augusta had to take extreme measures to reassure and console servants, as when she paid Allan to put a notice in "Personal" columns of the New York *Herald* of 12 October 1863: "INFORMATION WANTED — OF JOHN WALSH, who left his home in Tipperary May 17 and landed in New York June 19, from the ship Chancellor. It is thought that he may possibly have enlisted." Any men who had crossed the ocean with Walsh were asked to "please communicate" their information "by letter to Ellen Walsh, Gansevoort, Saratoga county, N. Y., who will relieve the anxiety of his family in Ireland." It was one thing for Herman to think about the theological and philosophical implications of such mob violence in the draft riots and the subsequent Draconian law enforcement and for him to make the events the subject of a poem, "The House-top," but women needing to run households had to act, not merely to meditate, and they needed the help of servants.

John Hoadley as a partner in the McKay Sewing Machine Association had given each of the sisters a sewing machine for Christmas 1862 and a few shares of stock in the company; apparently he had given a sewing machine to Lizzie also. On 25 January 1863 Helen wrote to Augusta and Fanny: "What a treasure your little sewing machine must be. I expect to find the sheets tucked, and the pillow-cases puffed, and the table cloths, & napkins, & counterpanes ruffled, or otherwise ornamented by the aid of this magic machine." Magic or not, the women still needed a seamstress semiannually. When Fanny wrote Augusta from New Bedford on 8 December 1863, the seamstress had been there several days and was not nearly finished, even with Fanny's help. Fanny was then wearing, for the first time, a brown dress of Mary Curtis's that had been made over and looked "'bran new.'" Everything salvageable was reused, one way or another, as always—and more carefully now, in wartime. The women who ran the households were more concerned, day by day, about the problem of hiring and retaining good help than about the problem of Negro slavery or the stalemate beyond the Potomac, although everyone read the war news.

More than a decade and a half away from the impetuosity of his wartime satire of Zachary Taylor, Melville was now by settled temperament unwilling to respond to any present national crisis directly. For months into the war, he was able to follow his bent of mind, as long as it seemed that Guert Gansevoort at last would have the chance to redeem himself and with it the Gansevoort name and as long as it seemed possible that Henry might embody the family honor instead of Guert. It was Allan who was obsessed with war news, and Herman who remained more outwardly aloof, stoical, more philosophical. By the time Hoadley began distributing elegantly printed copies of his "The Sounds I Love" that summer, however, Melville was becoming ready to start his own poetic record of the war. It may have been the battles and riots of July that at last drew him out of the refuge he had found in the age of Homer, which was, after all, itself a time of warfare.

[24]

Wartime Second Honeymoon and Manhattan

Summer–Fall 1863

※

all proudly concur in the opinion, that New York, the Empress Queen of this vast Continent, either as a Port of Trade or as a personal residence, is without contradiction the very best of all cis-atlantic Cities — & will most unquestionably before the close of the present century, equal London in arms, Commerce, & population, if not in arts, wealth & splendors —

Allan Melvill to Lemuel Shaw, 16 January 1819

IN PITTSFIELD THERE WAS no official civic observance of the Fourth of July 1863 — no parades, no fiery young orator allowed to read the Declaration of Independence as Gansevoort Melville had done in 1836 in Albany. Like the rest of the North, Pittsfield was awaiting news of the outcome of battles on two fronts, the Mississippi and, terrifyingly, south-central Pennsylvania, and unwilling to celebrate a glorious past in an ominous present. This was the sober report of the day in the *Berkshire County Eagle* of 9 July 1863: "Not a bell was rung or a cannon fired. There was neither orator, toast, or jubilant music, procession, or public fireworks; consequently the rain was not a public misfortune, but rather the contrary. — However, the sovereign people thronged the streets and a very liberal display of fireworks contributed by private citizens enlivened the evening." Word got around the village that some of the higher ranking citizens were displaying flags "of historic interest," General Henry Briggs "the old flag of the 10th regiment at Camp Brightwood"; Colonel Thomas W. Clapp a flag that had "passed through the fires of Bull Run"; and "over the entrance to Lieut. Col. Whelden's store, hung the tattered remains of the original flag which was hauled down at Fort Pike when Louisiana seceded." Historic flags and other military trophies had ennobled the old Gansevoort house in Albany in Melville's childhood, and his Uncle Peter still possessed the great banner of the Third New York Regiment, which Catherine Quackenboss Gansevoort had helped to stitch — a flag that had witnessed Cornwallis's surrender. Melville was alive to the symbolism and stunned that the present day had become historic, that a battle at Gettysburg, which no one in the family had ever seen, might prove as decisive as the Battle at Fort Stanwix.

The "glorious news of the surrender of Vicksburg, following close upon the victories in Pennsylvania," reaching Pittsfield on 7 July, had "thoroughly roused the patriotism" of the citizens by that evening: "the bells were set ringing merrily, the cannon boomed, fireworks streamed through the air. Bonfires blazed in North street, to which merchants cheerfully turned out their old boxes and other combustible material. The streets were thronged, and every man, woman and child was full of patriotic joy" (the *Eagle* on 9 July). As great good fortune had it, a family historian arrived to witness and make his own record of the scene; otherwise we would not know that Melville took part in the celebrations. The luck was John Hoadley's arrival at the depot with Kate at 8:10, just before late summer nightfall on the seventh. From Rochester on 10 July he wrote a vivid description to Augusta, who was keeping house for him and Kate in New Bedford. Herman and Malcolm had been waiting at the depot, and drove John and Kate to the rented house on South Street through streets gone mad with joy at the news of the victories: "The village was all ablaze with bonfires, rockets were whizzing, streaming, flashing, exploding, and expiring in the air; roman candles popping, flashing and dying away in infinity; — Bengal lights lending the unreal effect of their spectral light to trees and houses and the surging throng; bells were peeling from every steeple, groups of people on balconies were singing the Star Spangled banner, — and through all these outbursts of joy for deliverance and victory, we drove to the house." Lizzie and the girls and Stannie were waiting at the gate on South Street. Herman (and John?) somehow got the horse back to the livery stable.

After tea Kate, always careful of herself, went to bed, but the other grown-ups, John, Herman, Lizzie, and Fanny (Melville's sister, who was already there), "with Mackie attendant," traversed the short distance north to the common, John called it from his Boston experience, meaning the square, where the old Pittsfield elm still held up one great arm. They felt like "skirmishers" on a battlefield as they "sallied out to the Common, to see the spectacle, which was kept up with great spirit to a late hour." Pittsfield's could not rival the celebrations on the Boston Common or at City Hall Park in New York City, but the wild rejoicing in the square brought the war home to Herman and Lizzie as nothing yet had managed to do, since the victories on two fronts allowed both of them to think that the war would not drag on until young Malcolm was of an age to be sacrificed to it. On Wednesday, 8 July, the *Eagle* exulted on the topic of "Victory": "One word, one thought, one feeling, has filled all hearts, has been first upon all tongues, has thrilled every hearer. Victory continued, glorious, almost unqualified has been ours—has been our country's." The seventh of July 1863 may have been a private as well as a public turning point: henceforth, Hoadley was recognized as a friend who stuck closer than a brother, especially a brother like Allan. The new owner had been at Arrowhead during the wild celebrations, and must have seen some of the fireworks above the trees. Allan, Jane, and the four girls were all at Arrowhead when Herman and John (and others?) took a hack out there on Wednesday the eighth before driving to Broadhall, where John saw Sarah: "Poor lady! she looks very feeble."

Maria wanted the greatest number of delightful grown children, grandchildren, and cousins of all sizes at the Mansion House while the food was most bountiful and varied and the weather was invigorating. On 16 July 1863—July being jam-making month—Fanny wrote to Augusta: "Helen & I made *18 quarts* of raspberry & currant jam, it is fine. To-morrow we are going to make *shrub*. There never was such a season for the small fruits." On 24 July Maria reported to Augusta: "The garden is full of the best vegetables & small fruits, raspberries are superabundant . . . plenty of gooseberries & currents the peace [pease] never looked better." No one could live on fruits and vegetables, but the butcher made his semiweekly visits, and they had their chickens. At Gansevoort, the third week of July, while Helen was there, Maria wrote to Herman "urging the coming on of the children, Malcolm Bessie, & *Milie* alone," since Augusta's "coming on had been put off so long," but a week later there had been "no reply of any kind." On 31 July Lizzie scrawled a note to Augusta, still in New Bedford:

> Mother and Sam are here, and we have been riding about early & late, so that I could not get around to write—so many household duties when I am at home. They leave tomorrow for Red Hook & Gansevoort—Come on the 4th Aug, by all means, and stay as long as you can—(I think we shall let Macky & Bessie go on before that to Gansevoort as Macky's vacation is nearly over). Herman will meet you on that day, eveg train. I *always* have a place for you somewhere, but do not anticipate having any other visitor but yourself at that time.

Maria and Lizzie were both anxious that Mackey and Bessie might not get to Gansevoort at all before his vacation ended, since they had been waiting for Augusta to be home before he made his visit. As Lizzie said, Samuel Shaw had taken his mother visiting, leaving for Pittsfield on 27 July. The next day, Hope wrote in her diary, "Mr Melville took a carriage and carried us to the top of Mount Washington the road was bad but the scenery was magnificent" —a long hard drive for a man recently injured. Early in August Herman and Lizzie sent Malcolm up to Gansevoort, escorting Bessie, for a short visit before his school began. In mid-August Lizzie was hoping that Herman would be able to take Stanwix and Fanny "to see Grandma before cold weather"—a fourteen-year-old lad being fit to escort a ten-year-old girl, but a twelve-year-old boy not being quite old enough to take an eight-year-old girl in the "Cars."

Herman had made plans that involved only him and Lizzie. On the morning of 10 August, a Monday, having sent Malcolm to Gansevoort with Bessie and having "seen Stanny and Fanny off on their way to Arrowhead where Jane was kind enough to receive them," Herman and Lizzie started off in a buggy. They "dined at Great Barrington and reached 'Smiths'" (Milo Smith's) "near the Dome of Taconic by night fall & passed the night there." (So Lizzie wrote to Augusta, 16 August.) To what the Melvilles (in 1853 as now in 1863) designated as the "Dome of the Taconic," to the south or southwest of Great Barrington, was a formidable drive. The next morning, Tuesday, Herman signed the register, putting the date as 12 August instead of 11, and it was after they had stayed Monday night, for he made a notation on it: *"Good Time"*—not as fancy an inscription as he had made in Nashua in 1852, but the place was not as fancy either. What he wrote down is less interesting than the fact that he was still the sort of man who politely recorded his impressions of a place in the space allotted for clients' comments. Tuesday they drove from the Dome to Bash Bish Falls, at the New York border, where a Melville family party had gone in the summer of 1854. Having traveled along a precarious road, they reached the twin falls which had been painted by almost every American landscape painter of any reputation and which repaid any attempt to see them from various angles.

Herman and Lizzie stayed overnight at Bash Bish, in the single primitive hostelry, open only in the summer. A rough board seat on the piazza commanded a majestic view of the falls, for seated there you saw "the waterfall spring whitely over the sheer perpendicular front of the mountain, bounding and rebounding till it twirled like a spiral plover and lost itself in the dense shade underneath." (This was Caroline S. Whitmarsh's description a few months later.) Wednesday Herman and Lizzie drove the few rods further into New York state (she had written to Malcolm from Bash Bish and mailed it at Copake) then circled around to Barrington by a new route. Having dined there, as Lizzie wrote to Augusta on 16 August, they "took an easterly turn into Hampshire Co. and northward to Monterey (in Berkshire Co.)," where they spent the third night, having made a formidable loop. On Thursday they drove north from Monterey through North Becket and slept the night at Peru Hill, east of Ashmere Lake, and far east of Pittsfield. On Friday, taking a northeasterly course, they "drove through East & West Cummington a most charming drive along the Westfield river and finely wooded," then veered to the northwest "and passed the fifth night at Savoy Hollow." They reached home about noon Saturday, both having enjoyed it very much, and both relieved that Herman's left shoulder had not given out on him. Lizzie had been to Bash Bish, perhaps only once, but she had been left out of many of the excursions in the Berkshires, and now saw many vistas for the first time: "We passed through some of the wildest and most enchanting scenery, both mountain and valley and I cannot sufficiently congratulate myself that I have seen it before leaving Berkshire. . . . It has been a very hot week, but we were so high on the mountains most of the time that we always had a fresh breeze." Lizzie could leave satisfied, able to talk to New Yorkers and Bostonians about some of the less accessible areas of the region where she had been living for thirteen years, stretches farther away than the trailing arbutus ground where they had picnicked with Tom or even Greylock, the frequent destination for visiting family and friends.

Augusta returned home to Gansevoort, just missing Hope and Sam, but finding Helen still there with their mother and Fanny, and Malcolm and Bessie there for a little time more. Allan had finally bestirred himself, as John wrote to Augusta on 13 August: "I am truly happy to learn that Allan has arranged satisfactorily about the Mill, so that our dear Mother's mind may be at rest." Nilly on 14 August tracked Augusta down from her home in Lancaster, near Boston, amused both at her father's anxiety lest a *"whaler"* catch Augusta in New Bedford and her own imaginings about the new mistress of Arrowhead: "Has Mrs Allan honored you yet, how does she flourish in the seclusion of Pittsfield? though at this season I suppose she finds Society enough there." Cornelia Van Rensselaer Thayer had never needed to find Society anywhere. On 11 September Maria wrote to Kate Gansevoort after inviting her to come with Anna and Abe Lansing, niece and nephew of Kate's stepmother, Susan Lansing Gansevoort: "I wish your Father Mother & Aunt Sarah would also come the weather is beautiful we have plenty of chickens to boil, & sweet corn to boil & a profusion of garden vegetables to cook in the most approve'd manner." Furthermore, there was a man's shoulder for Peter to lean on if he left his valet in Albany: "*George* shall be ready equipt to wait upon you."

On Saturday, 22 August, a week after Herman and Lizzie got home, the Forty-ninth Massachusetts Volunteers returned to Pittsfield, by ship from New Orleans, then by railroad. Lizzie was glad that Malcolm and Bessie were home so all the children could see the decorations—"triumphal arches" put up over some streets of the village, houses decked out, their own rented house dressed with "Flags and festoons." Melville later wrote about Colonel William Francis Bartlett's entry in "The College Colonel": "He rides at their head; / A crutch by his saddle just slants in view, / One slung arm is in splints, you see, / Yet he guides his strong steed—how coldly too." Sarah was having a respite, feeling "pretty well just now." She had gone with Mrs. Brittain to take the waters at Saratoga Springs; now she helped see that Broadhall "was handsomely illuminated" for the return of the Volunteers. She and Rowland arranged "a fine display of fireworks" the evening of the return of the Forty-ninth, with Colonel Bartlett as an honored guest, the Pittsfield Liederkranz group serenading him, and Sarah putting on a very handsome entertainment, according to the *Sun* of 27 August.

Herman and Lizzie seem to have been waiting for the Twenty-sixth Street house to become free (was it rented to someone else until 1 November?), or waiting for a break in the children's schools, for they lingered on. In September Orville Dewey, whom they may have seen last at Judge Shaw's funeral, baptized the three youngest children in "Pittsfield Village," in the house on South Street. Why they had not been baptized earlier is not clear, but if Dewey was going to do it, better now than later, since his years of going regularly from Sheffield to New York City were long past. As so often before, with the Harpers, with the Duyckincks, and others, Melville behaved cordially to a man whose behavior or ideas had outraged him. At least there had never been an open break with the authority on Human Destiny that would have cast Melville in the wrong: Dewey probably never read *Pierre*.

Sarah's friend Caroline Whitmarsh, one of Samuel Bowles's stable of correspondents for the Springfield *Republican*, sent in an effusion printed on 17 September, based in part on visits to Broadhall: "These Berkshire woods are flashing with such brilliant tints as promise a glorious autumn." Just as the Berkshires in 1850 had put on one of their most vivid and long-sustained displays of foliage during the Indian summer, as if in honor of Melville's return to the place he loved, this year the Berkshires were again glorious, as if for his going. On 25 September Jane in a dutiful letter to her mother-in-law at Gansevoort mentioned that she presumed Herman would be going down to New York in a few days, adding: "Lizzie I trust will make my house [on Thirty-fifth Street] her home for as long as she finds it convenient." By delaying her own trip to Gansevoort, Jane was going to miss Helen's visit. "I have never seen her but once," she said, the time when Allan Melville took her, Helen, and Lizzie to Stockbridge and all stayed at the Red Lion Inn, in 1860—while Herman was on the *Meteor*. She added a religious note: "Dr [Henry] Thurston is in N. Y.—he has taken Rachie on a visit to Washington for a few days. They are both Roman Catholic I believe." Not high Episcopalian, as Allan had become?

From the village, or staying at Broadhall, the roving correspondent Caroline Whitmarsh on 28 September wrote to the Springfield *Republican* about some of the artists working in the Berkshires. One was John O'Brien Inman, the son of Henry Inman (whom Gansevoort and Helen had met in September 1841 while he was on "a professional visit" to Lenox). He painted "flowers so that a bee would mistake them for real; and landscapes so that a child would recognize and praise." Whitmarsh had seen him "in twenty minutes, on a wager, begin, finish and frame a landscape more elaborate than half of those in the stores:—snow on the Alps, sunshine on the woods, reflections in the lake, lichens on the pine, haze in the hollow, and shadow under the cottage eaves!" He was, as it happened, Sarah's last protegé. Her oldest son, Willie, was not around to watch his mother try to brave out another season: he was in England, at school, worrying, his uncle James McConnel wrote him on 1 October, about boyish things: "I notice your solicitude about the length of the coat tails of your new coat and the possession of a watch, both which you deem emblems of respectability in the big school."

In the press of planning to move, Lizzie made a decision about a valuable item she had inherited. On 1 October the Springfield *Republican* reported that she had "presented to the Berkshire bar a statue of her father, made some 15 years since" (1839) "by an eminent Boston artist." The statue was to "occupy a prominent position in the court house at Lenox," and "keep in mind the memory of a man pre-eminent for judicial learning." Salem had the magnificent portrait by William M. Hunt, which Lizzie knew about, although she may not have seen it, and Lenox would have the bust. Lizzie was not the sort of woman who discarded heavy items when moving and then regretted the loss: she was sacrificing the bust because she felt it belonged at Lenox where her father had held court so many times. On 8 October the North Adams *News and Transcript* elaborated. The bust was "similar to those in marble in the Boston Court House and Athenaeum," it "was executed about twenty years ago by Clevinger, a young Vermont artist, then very popular in Boston," and the chief justice had been "so well satisfied with it that he declined to sit for another." Another item in the *Eagle* of 1 October involved family news: "J. C. HOADLEY, formerly of Pittsfield and Lawrence, and now agent of the New Bedford copper company, has gone to England for two months to inspect the cannon and other munitions of war, manufacturing there for the state of Massachusetts."

Peter's daughter, Kate, having now become an arc in the circle of the Melvilles' correspondence, Helen gave her the news of Hoadley on 5 October: "I suppose you know that John has gone to England, by request of the Gove[r]nor, to inspect cannon now in progress, and which may ultimately be bought for Massachusetts 'coast defense.' Our grand old State has voted one million for that purpose, and I suppose our own arsenals and work-shops are too busy to supply any extra demand. He is to be gone two months, and I came here to await Fanny's arrival, who is to be here this week. John begged us not to leave her alone." (Helen was in New Bedford to care for her sister Kate; the secret of Kate's outliving her sisters by two decades was she arranged to be so fragile that they had to care for her.) Hoadley was now intimate with Charles Sumner, and for months he had been following the fate of the Fifty-fourth Massachusetts (there had been a recruiting office in New Bedford), the black regiment headed by Robert Gould Shaw, who was killed in early July, in the early stages of the prolonged assault on Fort Wagner, at Charleston. In his quiet way Hoadley may have contributed more to the war effort than the cousins in the military.

On 6 October Sarah Morewood rose from her sickbed and attended the Cattle Show at (according to Caroline Whitmarsh) "the society's park on a commanding eminence a mile and a half north of the village," at the height "of nature's gorgeous adorning in crimson and gold and red.... No wonder the people of Berkshire flock to their annual cattle show in crowds." Herman may have been in Pittsfield for the Cattle Show, but by 12 October he was in New York City. Lizzie wrote on the sixteenth, of Sarah: "only last week, on Tuesday she was up on the Cattle Show grounds all day about as well as usual apparently." At the fair J. O. Inman was showing two little paintings of flowers which Caroline thought were "real gems." Just before or after the Cattle Show, Sarah gave a party at Morewood Lake. In the 21 October *Republican* Whitmarsh wrote of driving with Sarah through some woods at Broadhall a few days earlier. Sarah had called horses to her and patted them, then they had driven on to the lake, "where her guests were assembled for a picnic,—poets, artists, scholars, saints,—the highest society on earth." Whitmarsh wrote: "Her house was the resort of men and women of genius; her library, pictures, grounds, vehicles, material, for every conceivable art, were placed at their service with a hospitality which made them feel the givers and not receivers of bounty; and the poor and the wicked claimed from her, as tender a pity as if she were one of themselves." Such a tribute challenges our imagination in several ways, reminding us how very little we know about just which men and women of genius or merely high talent were brought together at Broadhall under her aegis. Sarah entertained more people of more diverse and extraordinary talents than we can document. Besides the writers Melville, Catharine Sedgwick, and Dr. Holmes (now removed from the Berkshires), Sarah had met the writer-artist John James Audubon. She surely knew many of the artists who painted Bash Bish and Greylock and other Berkshire scenes (Asher B. Durand, Albert Bierstadt, George Inness, Frederic Church, besides her current favorite, John O'Brien Inman). She knew the great Orville Dewey and other philosophical churchmen who lived or summered there. Few gatherings of the Boston and New York elite in their respective cities could compare with the finest groups Sarah could assemble at Broadhall, where she could entertain local celebrities along with the best of both Boston and New York.

Most likely it was on or after 8 October that Sarah set out with young Inman and Caroline Whitmarsh, along with servants and possibly other guests, on a trip to Bash Bish, eighty-five miles round trip, "over the steep, hard roads of Berkshire." Whitmarsh wrote: "Arrived at Bash-bish intending to linger for the night, we found the hotel closed; and for rest, only a rough board seat around the piazza. There she lay, hardly willing that we should fold shawls together for a pillow, for it was her choice not to be ministered unto but to minister; lay in the sweet October afternoon, too tired to brush away the curls that fell over her face, but looking unspeakably happy." On "the long hill between Stockbridge and Lenox," on the way home, Sarah remembered the soldiers and asked her friends to pick bright leaves and mosses so she could "make a great fernery for the sanitary fair" and to pick "milkweed down" ("'I should like to fill a pillow or two for those poor fellows in the hospital; I can do so little for them now'"). So went a small portion of Whitmarsh's tribute, "A Representative Woman," which appeared in the Springfield *Republican* for 21 October and was reprinted in the 29 October *Berkshire County Eagle*. The title, readers would have recognized, was a play on Emerson's 1850 *Representative Men*, and therefore the signal of a feminist statement, a labeling of Sarah Morewood as an extraordinary woman, if not quite the equal of Emerson's six men, Plato, Swedenborg, Montaigne, Shakespeare, Napoleon, and Goethe.

Herman lingered in New York City, "busy with his house," and expecting to go to Pittsfield on Thursday, 15 October, and then bring Lizzie and the children down the week of the nineteenth. About 13 October Sarah began to sink rapidly. She died on 16 October, and Lizzie wrote a full report to Augusta later the same day. That morning, Friday, Lizzie had walked out South Street to Broadhall directly after rising from the breakfast table, and at nine found Sarah unconscious and suffering no pain. Dr. Frank Cady expected her to live only a few minutes, and told Lizzie that both Rowland Morewood and Ellen Brittain desired her to come upstairs to her bedside. The three watched together until half past two. So placid was Sarah's death, Lizzie said, "that no one knew exactly *when* she ceased to breathe — Dr Cady came in for the third time, felt her pulse, & listened for a heart-beat & pronounced it over!" Since Sarah had repeatedly expressed her wish that "no professional person should come about her," someone sent for a neighbor, Mrs. Lee, and with her help and the help of Sarah's favorite servant, Margaret, Lizzie prepared the body for the coffin. It was, she wrote to Augusta, the first death she had witnessed, and altogether "a very solemn and eventful day":

I feel that I have lost a very dear and much attached friend — for thirteen years we have been on the most intimate terms without the least shadow of a break in our friendship — Poor Mrs Brittain feels the blow most keenly, it came to her as to us all, most suddenly, for Mrs Morewood had been ill and up again so many times, that it was impossible to realize that this was the last — . . . . She was much surprised herself when she knew that her hours were numbered — said she did not want to die, but was calm in view of it, and left messages for Willie & gave instructions to Mr Morewood on various matters.

Herman had delayed beyond the time Allan thought he would leave, and was due the next day, Saturday. Lizzie took comfort where she could: "I feel that my delay here has been providential, for I feel that my presence there today has been a comfort to Mrs Brittain, and I should not have felt right to be absent." Practical comfort came from Mrs. Lee, who stayed on at Broadhall with Ellen Brittain till after the funeral. Not knowing of the death, on 19 October, Caroline Whitmarsh stayed up "till the small hours" writing a letter to Sarah, then saw the death notice in the morning *Republican* and began her essay on her friend. The world was very small, and talent was concentrated visibly: Caroline Whitmarsh worked for Samuel Bowles, the "Master" (many think) to whom had been addressed in the previous years some of the greatest poems ever written in the United States; another "Representative Woman," Emily Dickinson, had every chance to read of Sarah Morewood in the *Republican*.

Sarah's funeral was held on the morning of Wednesday, 21 October. She had declined so fast that no one thought of sending to England for Willie in time, but Annie and Alfred were home. Rowland and Ellen had wanted Herman as a pallbearer, but he was still in New York. Elizabeth attended (as she wrote Augusta on 28 October), carrying a wreath selected for her by Sam and delivered to Pittsfield the day before: "it was very beautiful, and I know the attention pleased them. I felt that it was the last thing I could ever do for the friend who has been so kind to me, and that were I in her place & she living, it would be the very first thing she would think of for *me*, and I could not *help* doing it." Herman sent up from New York "another wreath, smaller, all white, and Allan and Jane sent a cross." Herman's selecting a wreath must have evoked strange emotions, for one of Sarah's boldest actions involving him had been her premeditated crowning of him with a wreath, almost a dozen years before, and (despite his refusal to be crowned) her running into the cold to bestow it on him as he prepared to drive away from Broadhall. No woman would ever again attempt to crown him with a laurel wreath.

The coffin, rosewood studded with silver and covered with flowers, was borne into church on the shoulders of six pallbearers. The services were stark, Lizzie thought. Mr. Stearns and Mr. Parker of Stockbridge read the Episcopal burial service at St. Stephen's, Uncle Thomas's church, where Kate and Helen had been married: "& that was all—no address, & nothing to mark it from any funeral of any indifferent person in the parish . . . as the church regulations admit of no extemporaneous prayer (a great deficiency it seems to me) no mention was made of the absent son or any of the relatives." Sarah was not buried after the services but placed in a temporary vault, despite the wording of Annie's letter to her big brother in England: "mama was buryed this morning at Eleven oclock she looked so sweet that I did not want to have her buryed but I had to see her buryed some time or other she was put in the coffin this morning she was buryed from the church and we went up to the cemetery and saw the box shut up and put in the vault for a few days untill Papa can get a plot to put Mama." By the time Lizzie wrote her 28 October letter to Augusta the pieces of the Morewoods' lives were being sorted out. Rowland had gone back to New York for a few days (he probably saw Herman and Allan there), and Alfred (eleven years old) had been put (back?) into a boarding school in Stockbridge and Annie kept on at "the Institute as a day scholar": "Mr M. wished every thing to go on as before, as far as possible, & Mrs Brittain is to stay there this winter & to ask any one she pleases to be with her," Lizzie reported.

A week after the funeral Lizzie was downcast, all the more from the strain of her suspended life: "I expect Herman home tonight, and if he comes, I know I shall have no further time for letter writing for some time. . . . I am out of all patience living in this forlorn uncomfortable condition, carpets up window shades down, & every thing in boxes, but it could not be helped and I hope we shall get settled before long." She had, at least, a new "carte" of Herman that she had already sent Augusta, and she asked Augusta to send back the one she had previously given her for Tom, so she could send a new one. Herman had become spoiled by buckwheat from the family mill, and now Augusta was offering to send potatoes and buckwheat both, to stock their New York larder, when they would have a larder. Herman did return that evening, and the word was that they would leave Pittsfield on Tuesday or Wednesday, 3 or 4 November.

Before that, on 1 November, the Melvilles saw Sarah Morewood buried. Rowland wrote to Willie:

> I went up to Pittsfield on Friday last, the 30th Oct., and on the following day I had the remains of your dear Mamma removed from the vault where they had been temporarily placed, to their final resting place in Earth, in a plot of ground which I have bought in the Pittsfield Cemetery. Mr Stearns, our

clergyman, read a short service at the grave, as on previous occasion, the whole service had been in the Church, and M^r and Mrs Herman Melville, and a few others of her intimate friends were present, besides ourselves. Thus the last office that we can perform for her on earth has now been done, and we must for the future think of her only as a dweller in another and happier home, where we may hope to meet her hereafter, if we too faithfully strive to do our duty in this life, till GOD in his Providence shall ordain that we, like her, shall "rest from our labours."

Rowland exhorted his "dear Willie" to keep his "mind & heart fixed upon that future meeting," and prayed for Sarah's influence to be over him still, "now that she is separated from you, so far as flesh or sense are concerned, though not, as I trust & believe, in spirit."

Henry T. Tuckerman had been in Lenox in October and from there had sent "Authors in Berkshire" to the Philadelphia *American Literary Gazette and Publisher's Circular*, which printed it with what looked like ironic timing on 16 November: "'Moby Dick,' indeed, has the rare fault of redundant power; the story is wild and wonderful enough, without being interwoven with such a thorough, scientific, and economical treatise on the whale; it is a fine contribution to natural history and to political economy, united to an original and powerful romance of the sea. Impaired health induced him [Melville] to retire to this beautiful region, and in the care of his fruits and flowers, and the repose of a domestic life, he seems to have forsworn the ambition of authorship, but we trust only for a time." The wording indicates knowledge of Melville's life at Arrowhead rather than the village, where he would have been less apt to be found caring for his fruits and flowers. Perhaps Tuckerman had visited Melville in an earlier year, not 1863, and wrote now from that experience. In any case, Melville was neither at Arrowhead nor in Pittsfield.

The Melvilles moved to New York on 3 or 4 November, not directly into the house on Twenty-sixth Street but to Thirty-fifth Street. On 9 November Hope Shaw told Helen that Lizzie was "staying at Allan's, & they are deep in furniture getting, and fixing generally." They had made the disheartening discovery that it cost "as much to carry their goods through the city to the house, as it did to bring them from Pittsfield to the city." Helen would have sympathized, for in May she had written to her sisters Kate and Augusta in New Bedford: "There is something truly pitiable, to my mind, in the condition of any one, on the eve of moving from one house to another. No matter whether the move is up or down the ladder of social position, or housekeeping convenience, for the time being their household gods are dishonored, and the outraged Lares & Penates fly shrieking and homeless through the air." There had been discussion about Fanny's going to New York, and she had decided against it, as she wrote Augusta on 16 November: "I have determined *not to go* this time. I do not want to go & why should I make a martyr of myself. After I have made Helen a short visit I am coming straight home and that is a fact." The emphasis recalled Gan's phrase "that is a positive fact"; in what way going to New York would have been making a martyr of herself is not clear: which would have been worse, living in the same house with the intolerable Jane or living in an unsettled house with Herman and Lizzie? Living in John and Kate's rented house in New Bedford was not, apparently, making a martyr of herself.

Lizzie worked in New York City with no help from the family. Late in November, having renounced any hope of going to Boston for Thanksgiving, she wrote to Augusta: "If I were not so tired this evening, I would write you more than this pencilled line or two — I have been 'up to my eyes' in work lately fitting window-shades, which of course will none of them fit the new fixtures. I am getting along steadily but dear me what a world of things are to be done! 'It is a great move to move' as one of our country neighbors said the other day! — We are all well, & hope for a visit from one or all of you before long." At Broadhall on 30 November Ellen Brittain wrote to Willie of Sarah's often saying, " *'Willie is a good boy,'* and 'if *I live* he will be a great comfort to me.' " Ellen assured Willie: "No stranger hands were around her, but those she loved (Mrs Melville & Mrs Lee) prepared her for her last sleep & she rests in a lovely spot in our Villiage Cemetary." (Three decades later Lizzie and Ellen made their pilgrimages there together.) Rowland called on Herman and Lizzie and received from her one of her new cartes de visite of Herman. In his letter, written around 4 December, on his new black-bordered stationery, Rowland explained that he was sending the photograph because Willie would "value it for its associations." Willie needed any such associations he could find.

Even as late as 10 December the Melvilles were "involved in a thousand and one botherations incident to a removal of one's household a hundred & sixty miles, the fitting up & furnishing of a house &c &c." In explaining this to an autograph seeker in Cincinnati (a friend of Sarah Morewood's?), Melville made the most direct statement we have from this period about what he did with personal letters: "I should be very happy indeed to comply with your request to furnish you with autographs from old letters, were it not that it is a vile habit of mine to destroy nearly all my letters. Such as I have by me would hardly be to your purpose." Had he already destroyed his letters from Hawthorne, including the one about *Moby-Dick?*

John Hoadley turned up from his trip to England unexpectedly, and sick, on 20 December, a Sunday, probably finding his way to the house he knew was occupied, 109 East Thirty-fifth Street, instead of 60 East Twenty-sixth Street. He seems not to have reached home until the twenty-fourth, so he was too sick to leave New York at once. An 18 January 1864 letter from George Curtis in Glens Falls to Maria (preserved because it was misdated 1863 and stored with that year's letters in Augusta's papers) alludes to his need to confer with her about some indiscreetly disclosed news of her having become proprietor of some valuable commodity—perhaps something as innocent as having two or three good hens. George had heard from Mary, his daughter, about John Hoadley: "she speaks of Mr Hoadley's return, and noting naught, of his illness, I infer, he quite recovered, after the *Crossing*—Singular too, he *should* have grown worse." Late in December Evert Duyckinck sent Melville a book for review—presumably to be done gratis, like his early reviews, rather than a way of earning a few dollars. On 31 December Melville returned the book, which he had read with great interest: "As for scribbling anything about it, tho' I would like to please you, I have not spirit enough." Not having spirit enough to spend on the review did not mean that Melville was ill. He and Lizzie were having what passed as a New Year's Eve party in that saddened year. Allan and his family were coming, Ellen Brittain, in town for Christmas, "& one or two other friends, who will come early, stay sociably & go early." Melville said to Evert, "If convenient, pray, join us." Evert would be among people who had respected George, and people who had loved Sarah, who had sustained such an unlikely alliance with "the Saint," as Evert now knew in excruciating detail from his redaction of George's diaries and letters. It was a subdued party of mourners who said good-bye to 1863 in the new Melville residence.

[25]

The War Poet's Scout toward Aldie
1864

&c.

> We yet shall rise, correct our errours past,
> And virtuous Freedom will return at last.
> Discord will die, and, lock'd in Union's chain,
> Sublim'd, eternal will the States remain!
>
> Words attributed to President James Madison
> in Richard Emmons, *The Fredoniad* (Boston, 1827),
> book 4, canto 5, "Washington City"

A PERMANENT RESIDENT of Manhattan, Herman Melville again haunted the newspaper reading rooms, finding fewer daily papers than in 1850, but thicker ones. Allan still subscribed to several New York City dailies; on 29 January 1864 he wrote a hasty note to Jane in the top margin of the first page of the *Herald:* "I take the 'Times' with me — Don't fail to go out early. Splendid day." As a Massachusetts landowner, Allan subscribed to the *Berkshire County Eagle*, from which Pittsfield news could be passed on to Herman and Lizzie. Oddly, one of the items that most shook Melville had nothing to do with the present crisis but was in the fourth volume of Pierre M. Irving's *The Life and Letters of Washington Irving.* There was a long review in Greeley's *Tribune* on New Year's Day. When he held the book, in a bookstore or at Duyckinck's or Tuckerman's, Melville found pages about an unnamed villain, the "Virginian" who wrote "Hawthorne and His Mosses," the part printed in the *Literary World* on 24 August 1850. Working from Thomas Powell's arguments about imitation versus originality, Melville, in the arrogant impudence of youthful ambition (and doubly shielded by a pseudonym and the paper's policy of anonymity), had declared his independence from one of his literary fathers, that writer who perhaps owed "his chief reputation to the self-acknowledged imitation of a foreign model, and to the studied avoidance of all topics but smooth ones." Melville's words had caused the old man acute distress, and Irving's nephew Pierre long remained outraged at the "Virginian" for maliciously twisting Irving's own words against him. In the biography Pierre Irving described his uncle as having responded benignly to the essay. Any twinges of regret Melville felt for grieving the elderly Irving must have become inextricably fused with his complex feelings about Hawthorne, whom he had boldly exalted over Irving. When Melville saw this fourth volume of the Irving biography, the excesses of his early ambitions came back to haunt him—not merely remorse for his harshness to the old man but the irony of his sweeping pronouncement on failure: "He who has never failed somewhere, that man can not be great. Failure is the true test of greatness." Melville had passed that test within a year or two of writing the *Literary World* essay that had so pained the Irvings. Reckless ambition and spectacular failure equally distant from him now, on 9 February Melville found a good use for some of Lizzie's dwindling fund of cash and paid the Harpers two hundred dollars (they had been charging him interest), thereby reducing his debt to less than fifty dollars. Before long he would have the Harpers paid back for the advances that had helped support his early career and for the thousand dollars or so they had extorted from him in covering their losses in the fire of 1853.

Both Melville brothers in New York City became anxious in February at word from Gansevoort that their mother had been ill since December. For her part, Fanny came home from Boston as soon as she could, on 23 February, having been detained a week by bad weather. The next day, Herman arrived at Gansevoort alone (business having kept Allan in the city), but bringing with him his own bounties for his mother, "many delicacies to tempt her appetite." On the twenty-ninth Augusta reported to Kate Gansevoort that Maria had been "improving ever since his arrival, the effect of seeing him she said." Herman left with the indefinite plan of stopping by Albany (Augusta said) to see Uncle Peter and Aunt Susan and "have a peep at the great Bazaar," the Albany Army Relief Bazaar held under a vast tent over the trees of the park, as the Albany correspondent, "Sentinel," explained in a report to the New York *World*. Herman did manage to stop in Albany. Relieved that his mother was "much better," in his opinion, he arrived at Uncle Peter's house on Washington Avenue at nine at night on 29 February. Besides his family, the attraction that lured him was indeed the Albany Army Relief Bazaar held at Tweddle Hall to raise money for the U.S. Sanitary Commission. A precursor of the Red Cross, the Sanitary Commission was the quasi-private women's organization that with the blessings of Secretary of War Stanton and President Lincoln was supplementing the Quartermaster Corps and the Army Medical Corps in providing for the comfort of the ordinary volunteer soldier in the Union army, nursing the sick and wounded, giving food, and guiding men and their families through paperwork involving benefits and pensions as well as helping men write letters home. Men were used to front the Sanitary Commission, most prominently Lizzie's minister, Henry W.

Bellows, and some men performed real work. In this case the organizers of
the exhibition were the sculptor Erastus Dow Palmer and the portrait painter
Charles Loring Elliot, a student of John Trumbull, who had worked with the
strange early illustrator of Irving, John Quidor, and recently had painted
Fletcher Harper and Erastus Corning, and a little later painted Frederic E.
Church. Tuckerman, who greatly admired Elliot, thought a "certain manly
vigor" distinguished all his portraits.

Melville particularly wanted to see the "Arts Exhibition" housed at Palmer's studio, which he had visited in 1857, when Palmer had been working on *The White Captive*. Peter and Susan Gansevoort arrived early, that first of March, braving the steady snow to look at 148 works of art, most of them by American artists and almost all of them either loaned by Palmer himself or by the elite families of Albany, Uncle Peter's friends, and even by Peter himself. Melville met the Gansevoorts and the sculptor, then looked more or less intently at the paintings. More works exhibited were owned by Palmer than anyone else, and his own *White Captive* was on display along with a few of his other sculptures. Many of the paintings were long-separated canvas brothers and sisters, some never in the studio or an owner's room together, now for the duration of the show able to talk familiarly to each other, almost, Church to Church, Cropsey to Cropsey. Peter and Susan saw the paintings with different eyes than Melville did, having examined some of them many times in a Corning or a Pruyn or a Rathbone parlor, or at home, although never before all under one roof. Looking at the names of the donors, Melville recognized the Albanians as brilliant collectors, the habitual purchasers of just the sort of new paintings he himself would like to have owned. Richard Lathers, Melville would have realized ruefully, was buying what he thought was safer European art and therefore had amassed few true masterpieces. There were paintings to dazzle Melville and to tantalize him, since he had to hurry through the exhibition — among them many that caught his eye because he knew the painter, the subject, or the owner. These are a few: *Boston Harbor* (F. H. Lane, owner David I. Boyd); *Landscape, with Cattle* (John Constable, owner J. F. Rathbone); *Bareford Mountains* (J. F. Cropsey, owner J. V. L. Pruyn — John Van Schaick Lansing Pruyn); *Piety and Folly* (Daniel Huntington, who painted the portrait of Richard Lathers that went to the New York Chamber of Commerce and painted a fine portrait of Tuckerman, owner R. H. Pruyn); *Lake Como* (J. W. Casilear, owner Palmer); *Catrina Van Tassel* (D. Huntington, owner G. M. Vanderlip); *Ruth and Naomi* (L. Terry, owner R. H. Pruyn); *Twilight* (George Inness, owner E. L. Magoon); *Beatrice Cenci* (no artist named, owner E. C. Delavan); *Home of the Pioneer* (Church, owner Palmer); *The Italian "Nooning"* (J. E. Freeman, owner Peter Gansevoort);

White Mountains (H. Ferguson, owner E. L. Magoon); *The Evening Star* (Church, owner Palmer); *Scene in South America* (Church, owner Palmer); *The Coming Storm* (R. S. Gifford, owner Palmer); *Katskill Falls* (Thomas Cole, owner J. V. L. Pruyn); statue, *White Captive* (Palmer); *Indian Maiden* (Palmer). The bazaar earned a net profit of $81,908.50, according to a letter Kate Gansevoort wrote to Henry on 3 May—a great deal of money.

Melville tore himself away to pack his gear. Alone with the servants at Washington Street, he had a little time to stroll around the east room quizzing "several family portraits by Gilbert Stuart" and reflecting on the vagaries which had left in this room what a later observer referred to as so "much fine old furniture" and "cases of books and china and on the walls and mantel a general air pervading of inheritance from the past." Then Peter and Susan returned and gave Herman lunch, a cozy meal in the little eastern breakfast room with the Dutch black-and-white-tiled floor, not a meal in the grand octagonal dining room, which was hung with more paintings (including portraits by the man long called the "Gansevoort Limner") and treasures of Dutch, colonial, and Revolutionary silver. A nephew did not have to be as covetous as Allan to be struck with a basic inequity in life. As he walked out into the snow to take the streetcar to the depot for the 4:10 train Melville may have devoted a moment to reflections on the comparative financial status of his mother and her brother Peter and his own permanent status of poor relation.

Melville was by this time not only a poor relation but a poor poet, writing poems again, perhaps a good many poems, all of them short and most if not all of them about the war. He may have written some poems through the previous year, 1863, disrupted as he was, ousted from his study in Arrowhead and making do with provisional conditions in the house on South Street, then in the chaotic conditions of Twenty-sixth Street. The length of the poems would have allowed him to do some composing at odd moments, perhaps even outdoors, memorizing or carrying notepaper and pencil with him. The title he ultimately used for his Civil War collection, *Battle-Pieces*, derived from his interest in the visual arts, since it was the standard term for battle scenes, especially nautical, as depicted in paintings and engravings, and just may indicate that some of the earliest poems he wrote included nautical ones such as "Dupont's Round Fight (November, 1861)," "The Stone Fleet: An Old Sailor's Lament (December, 1861)," "The Cumberland (March, 1862)," "In the Turret (March, 1862)," "The Temeraire," and "A Utilitarian View of the Monitor's Fight." Once reestablished in Manhattan, Melville had begun accumulating poems, for in March when Lieutenant Colonel Alexander Bliss wrote from Baltimore to request a manuscript to be reproduced in facsimile in a volume entitled *Autograph Leaves of Our Country's Authors*, he responded willingly, indeed, over-hastily, with the poem "Inscription For the Slain at Fredericksburgh":

> A glory lights an earnest end;
> In jubilee the patriot ghosts ascend.
> Transfigured at the rapturous height
> Of their passionate feat of arms,
> Death to the brave's a starry night, —
> Strown their vale of death with palms.
>
> HERMAN MELVILLE

Subsequently Melville realized that in the hurry of dispatching his contribution he had sent an uncorrected draft, and on 22 March he mailed a corrected copy. He felt so strongly that he wanted to "suppress" the one he had sent by mistake that he asked Bliss to drop him from the volume unless the corrected poem could be substituted—the kind of request a hard-pressed editor hates to receive. As it turned out, Bliss managed only to put a variant of the correct title into the table of contents ("Inscription to the dead at Fredericksburg") but printed the draft Melville had first sent him. At the Metropolitan Fair in Aid of the U.S. Sanitary Commission on 19 April, Patriots' Day, copies of *Autograph Leaves*, containing facsimiles of the contributions, went on sale at the high price of six dollars. The sequence of the composition of Melville's Civil War poems is unknown, in most instances. Melville may have started with nautical poems, he may have started not just with the "Inscription For the Slain at Fredericksburgh" but with the group of poems he separated in the published volume as "Verses Inscriptive and Memorial"—a timely continuation of an established Romantic genre.

By the time he submitted the poem to Bliss, Melville was far enough committed to the idea of writing about the war to feel he needed to witness it first hand. Early in April he decided to join Allan in an excursion in which they would try to see Guert Gansevoort, stationed in the North Atlantic Blockading Squadron off Fortress Monroe at Hampton Roads, the entrance to Chesapeake Bay, and Henry Gansevoort (Thirteenth New York Cavalry) in the Union camp at Vienna, Virginia. Lizzie took Bessie and Fanny home to Boston for a visit, and the brothers left on Thursday evening, 7 April, on the all-night journey to Washington, accompanied by Henry's former law-partner George Brewster, recently become Allan's partner, who was joining Henry's regiment. There Herman and Allan made their way to the Ebbitt House on F and Fourteenth Streets, across from Willard's Hotel. Richard Lathers still had connections despite the opprobrium heaped upon him in 1861, from both North and South, and Allan appealed to him: "My brother

Herman & I arrived here this morning. He is very anxious to go to the front, but it appears that it is difficult to get a pass—It has occurred to me that perhaps you might address a line to Secretary Stanton introducing Herman & stating his wish, as a literary man he might be favored. As such men should have opportunities to see that they may describe." This was explicit: writers should be allowed to witness what they would write about. What Melville was writing was poetry. Herman took the practical measure of going to the Capitol to find Senator Charles Sumner, who, remembering his old ties to Shaw and his newer ties to Hoadley, readily requested that the Provost Marshal issue a pass to the front for Melville, "a loyal citizen & my friend." From the War Department Edwin M. Stanton issued the pass: "Herman Melville Esq & his brother Allen Melville Esq have permission to visit the Army of the Potomac & return." (It survives because Allan kept it.) Jane, with fifteen-year-old Milie in tow, arrived at the Ebbitt House only to find that the men had left "for the *front*" on Sunday, 10 April.

No evidence has been found to show that Melville saw Guert Gansevoort, although his visit to Henry Gansevoort's camp is well documented. Anyone knowing the family would agree with Stanton Garner in *The Civil War World of Herman Melville* that the Melvilles must have tried to see both their Gansevoort cousins, and, as Garner says, a visit to Guert is the only plausible explanation for what the brothers did in the days beginning 10 April:

> Virtually the only place worth seeing that they could have visited without difficulty, and that would have required a trip of that duration, was the anchorage of the North Atlantic Blockading Squadron off Fortress Monroe. They had good reason for going there. Guert Gansevoort would welcome them, and a visit to his ship would be the naval equivalent of a visit to Henry's camp and even more congenial to the sailor in Herman. . . . Their pass would by implication have entitled them to visit any forward area, and there was a steady traffic of government vessels plying the route to Fortress Monroe from Baltimore, Annapolis, and the Washington Navy Yard. From the fort, a visual signal to the *Roanoke* would have brought one of Guert's boats to the landing to pick them up.

This is, as Garner says, speculative. One cannot safely argue from poems Melville later wrote that, for instance, he must have seen the sunken masts of the *Cumberland* near the fortress for him to write the poem on its ramming, but the brothers would have tried to see both their military Gansevoort cousins, not just one, and several undocumented days need to be accounted for. As in 1844, when Herman stayed an extra day or two in Boston before going to New York City and then Lansingburgh, to see his mother, the obvious explanation is the best.

On 13 April Jane picked up Allan's letter for her at the Ebbitt House before checking in at the Willard, from whence she wrote blithely to her stepdaughter Florence (Folly): "we arrived here safely, but did not find *Papa*. We learned he had gone with Uncle Herman to the *front* of the Army of the Potomac on Sunday last.... We hope to see Papa tomorrow—unless the Guerrillas have got Papa & Uncle Herman." This was quintessential Jane, the woman who had inveighed to Lizzie against male servants who might turn into sexual predators, then promptly had abandoned the three youngest and most vulnerable girls in an isolated, rundown country house with foreign-born servants, a man or two among them. Now Folly could have nightmares that John Singleton Mosby's guerrillas would capture Papa and Uncle Herman and hang them from any tree left standing in a battleground. Jane was, as always, egregiously selfish and irresponsible, and abusive toward children in ways she could pass off as airy jesting. On Wednesday, exasperated at waiting in the capital without an escort, she wrote Henry a letter that remained unclaimed for several days. Whatever Herman and Allan did, it involved them until late in the week, when they joined Jane and Milie at the Willard. In a comedy of errors, Henry checked into the Ebbitt House and stayed there three days, Garner shows, without encountering his cousins.

Herman and Allan left for Henry's camp on Saturday, 16 April. Garner worked out the logistics by which the brothers were transported to the battlefield:

> The conventional route was via the Orange and Alexandria Railroad. One crossed the Potomac River to Alexandria on a ferry from the 7th Street pier. Once in Alexandria, any question of ways and means could be answered by Brigadier General Henry Briggs, the former captain of Pittsfield's Allen Guard, who was now in command there. The journey to Fairfax Station was brief and relatively safe from Mosby's guerrillas, although a little farther down the track Grant had narrowly escaped capture the previous day. Fairfax station was guarded by the Corcoran Legion.... From the station, there were four bumpy miles of corduroy road (road made passable and uncomfortable by logs laid across it) to Fairfax Court House, which Herman and Allan may have traversed on one of the many government wagons that lumbered to and fro along it. A short distance beyond that was the cavalry camp, which the brothers must have reached about midday.

Having in 1849 renounced his wild longing to go to the Vienna on the Danube, Melville now irrefutably arrived at Vienna, in Virginia, about fifteen miles from Washington. The joke, he may have been told, was that the camp was part of "Sharon," the biblically named farm of Commodore

Thomas ap Catesby Jones, formerly of the frigate *United States*, Melville's ship, and the man who had, metaphorically at least, "seized" California for twenty-four hours in October 1842.

The regimental chaplain, Charles A. Humphreys, in his *Field, Camp, Hospital and Prison in the Civil War, 1863-1865* (Boston: George H. Ellis, 1918), described the camp as "surrounded with a heavy abatis of felled trees branching outwards to guard against sudden attacks of guerrillas." The troopers had left some trees standing, but the photograph Humphreys published in 1918 shows just how few survived after the abatis was constructed. As Humphreys knew, Melville in "The Scout toward Aldie" had described the same scene, great trees felled by the troopers and leaned around the circle of tents in "antlered walls" — that is, with the tree trunks toward the tents and the limbs and branches fanning out to keep Mosby's men from galloping into the camp. Once at camp, Melville took stock of his position, especially in relation to the terrain he had just covered. In his note to "The Scout toward Aldie" Melville described the irony that the "chase of Mosby" ("chase" meaning private hunting grounds, as in Sir Walter Scott's usage) was so near to Washington:

> South of the Potomac in Virginia, and within a gallop of the Long Bridge at Washington, is the confine of a country, in some places wild, which throughout the war it was unsafe for a Union man to traverse except with an armed escort. This was the chase of Mosby, the scene of many of his exploits or those of his men. In the heart of this region at least one fortified camp was maintained by our cavalry, and from time to time expeditions were made therefrom. Owing to the nature of the country and the embittered feeling of its inhabitants, many of these expeditions ended disastrously. Such results were helped by the exceeding cunning of the enemy, born of his wood-craft, and, in some instances, by undue confidence on the part of our men.

There was no Dumbarton Castle here frowning down on the confluence of rivers, no Stirling Castle with its back to the mountains and its face to the Firth of Forth, yet from pine-tops or from little hilltops anyone could catch sight, on a clear day, of the "Capitol Dome — hazy — sublime — / A vision breaking on a dream." In this border warfare the overwhelming strangeness was that "Mosby's men / Should dare to prowl where the Dome was seen" — the Dome completed only a few months earlier.

On their way to camp the Melvilles may not have quite realized how dangerous the country was they were traversing, but once there they heard firsthand accounts of the guerrilla leader and began to understand just how "shrewd, able, and enterprising" the wary Mosby had proved himself in "partisan warfare," and to know that wild tales were investing Mosby with heroic associations. Melville knew already that Mosby was legendary for his phantomlike harassment of the Union troops, and he learned more now about this young Virginia lawyer who as a prized scout for Jeb Stuart had helped prepare for Stuart's already legendary ride around George Brinton McClellan's army in the Peninsula Campaign. Stuart afterward had allowed Mosby to raise his own battalion of partisans. A brilliant, dashing tactician and strategist both, Mosby snapped Union supply lines, disrupted field communications, and threatened the forces guarding Washington. Inventively disguising himself on some of his missions, he was a tough, daring, fast Confidence Man of a soldier whose men accompanied him at night, then rode on with him or melted back into the civilian population until summoned again. He was a master of psychological gamesmanship: Who else under cover of night would remove planks from heavily guarded Union bridges? Who else would ride into a Union camp and roust a general from bed by slapping him smartly on the rear?

Talking to men "personally familiar with the irregular fighting in Virginia" (as he wrote in his note to "The Scout toward Aldie"), Melville learned of the high repute Mosby held among his superior officers and his reputation for kindness to the wounded he captured as well as his civility to officers and civilians captured by forces under his immediate command. Mosby was a momentous man — the man who forced the North to commit great numbers of its troops against a piddling number of guerrillas. As far as Melville was concerned, Mosby did not maunder like the present generation of Gansevoorts. And he had a literary bent, having loved Byron's poetry from childhood, as Melville had done; the difference was that Melville was a child of his times and Mosby in his allegiance to Byron was looking a little backward, or perhaps he was only a Virginian rather than a New Yorker. Mosby was still a great spouter of Byron, as Melville had once been, and a brilliant talker. Melville in an annotation to "Lycidas" declared that he had never been a partisan in religion or politics, and always regarded political partisanship in poetry as a blemish, but this was his kind of partisan, just the sort of border warrior Sir Walter Scott had immortalized. Newspapers were already calling Mosby the Modern Rob Roy. As the bearer of a noble Scottish name and a pilgrim to Scottish strongholds, Melville knew about border warfare, and relished the experiences he might have. He also knew about imaginary conversations in literature. One man of his own time that he ought to have sat down with, knee to knee in convivial confabulation with cigars and brandy, was young John Mosby — the Modern Crusoe face to face with the Modern Rob Roy.

Over the winter the officers of the Second Massachusetts Volunteer Cavalry Regiment had settled into camp near Vienna. According to Humphreys, they had board floors in their "wall-tents," brick fireplaces, and chimneys made of mud and sticks; the chaplain's had a barrel on top to improve the draft. Colonel Charles Russell Lowell had his headquarters in a farmhouse, although he and his wife slept in a tent. The chaplain's tent had a little platform, an unroofed piazza, on which rested a small box for firewood. The tent had a wooden front door, framed in, and a hitching rail on either side. A photograph of lank, bearded Humphreys on horseback by his tent shows three other tents, with no chimney, no wooden door, no piazza, and no evidence of wooden floors. Henry was absent from the camp when the brothers arrived, but Aunt Susan's nephew Edwin Yates Lansing (son of Christopher Yates Lansing) was there: Melville later gave him a copy of his Civil War poems as "a souvenir of his soldier hospitality at the cavalry camp in the Virginia woods, April 1864." They met Lowell (whose uncle, Melville had been told, had wept over the ending of one of the sketches in "The Encantadas") and his wife, Josephine (the daughter of Francis G. Shaw and sister of Robert Gould Shaw, the already glorified leader of a black regiment). Her brother had been, less interestingly, the chaplain's classmate, and she was a sister-in-law of George W. Curtis. She was not the only wife to accompany her husband to that war. The Hawthornes had once been Melville's ideal of a married couple, but the Lowells were a glamorous, intellectual, and chivalric pair the like of which he had never encountered before, and he idealized them as far as his pervasive irony would allow ("Ah, love in a tent is a queenly thing"). They knew who Herman Melville was from their Boston-Cambridge circle. Lowell was Harvard-educated, and Lemuel Shaw had long been one of the Harvard overseers. Melville also met the brigade surgeon, Dr. Oscar C. DeWolf, who had studied then taught at the Berkshire Medical Institute. His name must have provoked a few trial runs up the family tree, and Melville may have known him from Pittsfield, at least by sight.

 The brothers stayed overnight, awaiting Henry, then the next morning, Sunday, 17 April, young Lowell invited Herman to go with him the next day, when, under orders from Brigadier General Robert O. Tyler, he was leading an expedition against Mosby. Allan's health may already have been too precarious for the ride (aside from the fact that he had never been good with animals). Jane and Milie were expecting Allan back in Washington, but Herman, since Lizzie did not know his whereabouts, was free to go somewhere else—always an appealing state of affairs. Allan was the kind of man who left forwarding addresses before he walked out a door, but Herman still had in him the restless irresponsibility that had sent him to the ends of the oceans. The eighteenth of April was honored by Massachusetts men like Lowell, Humphreys, and Melville as the anniversary of Paul Revere's ride, and all of them, as well as the men, must have been aware of the irony that they might be fighting a battle in another war on American soil on Patriots' Day, the nineteenth. This expedition, Humphreys recorded, was "made only a few days before the grand movement of the Army of the Potomac across the Rapidan. It was doubtless a preparatory reconnaissance to make it certain that there was no especial danger to Washington in Grant's uncovering its front as he was about to do." Humphreys chose this particular scout to record in detail in part because the famous writer went along.

At the bugle call "Boots and Saddles" a large detachment of the brigade assembled, every man carrying "two days' rations and three days' forage." Garner envisions the departure: "There were perhaps three hundred troopers in smart blue uniforms with field caps and waist-length jackets decorated with gold, each wearing a saber and carrying a carbine, though because of the grim business at hand the guidons of the troopers were not flying and bugles ceased their nasal blare as soon as the camp was left behind." Humphreys had been writing in his tent when he heard "Boots and Saddles," but he got permission fast and had someone put up his rations and forage, and then galloped after the column on his horse, "Jaques" (which later passed into Mosby's possession). According to his record of the scout, Humphreys caught up with Colonel Lowell ("Elate he rides at the head of his men; / He is young, and command is a boyish thing," Melville later wrote). Lowell had an odd companion, an older civilian in a flannel shirt (hastily borrowed from George Brewster, now a captain, and in the camp), a writer:

> With him [Lowell] was the noted traveller Herman Melville, who had charmed all lovers of the wild and picturesque by his accounts of his adventures among the savage islanders in the Pacific Seas in the books "Omoo" and "Typee," which I had in my camp library, and who shared with Richard H. Dana the honorable distinction of a pioneer in the work of lifting into popular literature the life of the merchant seaman. He was out now to learn something of the *soldier's* life and to see a little campaigning with his own eyes, preparatory to the writing of the book which appeared two years later, entitled "Battle Pieces and Aspects of War."

For his part, Melville was marveling at the youthful strength and vitality of the riders ("Tingles the tendoned thigh with life"), as well as the colorful display ("Their cavalry-jackets make boys of all — / With golden breasts like the oriole"). A few days later Humphreys gave his Melville books along with the rest of the camp library to Anna Lowell at Amory Square Hospital in Ward K, Washington, since he knew he could not lug them around during the spring campaign. Some anonymous soldiers — too young to have been readers in 1846 and 1847 — thus were able to devour *Typee* and *Omoo* along with the other books, for Miss Lowell wrote to Humphreys: "I wish you could have seen the eagerness with which my men took them out when the box was opened."

They rode, Humphreys recorded, "till four o'clock, stopping every hour and a half to rest the horses a few minutes, and adjust the saddles to prevent galling." Garner traces the route as "west along the abandoned railroad track as far as Guilford Station," then up Church Road "toward a mill along Goose Creek between Aldie and Leesburg" — a route littered from previous military engagements ("ravaged land," Melville called it). The raiders rested at Ball's Mill on Goose Creek for an hour, attending to their horses, then eating something themselves; the chaplain had dry bread with some ham he cooked on the end of a stick over a cornstalk fire. They were passing through tobacco country, and Melville was far from alone in resorting to the calming influence of his own supply of that sacred weed ("Halting, and slackening girths, they feed, / Their pipes they light, they loiter there"). At five they crossed the swollen creek, the current too fast for a man to stand in it and "just fordable for cavalry," Humphreys said. At dusk they approached Leesburg, "the hotbed of secessionism in those parts" (Humphreys), about twenty-five miles from the camp at Vienna. Leesburg was full of Confederates, who fired upon the advanced guard. Hoping to capture Mosby's troops, Lowell at once ordered the charge in which Melville perforce took part, for "the whole column immediately broke into a trot and then into a gallop." The first squadron dashed on with sabers drawn, the chaplain wrote, while the rest rode "holding their carbines in their hands ready to fire." Melville and the chaplain experienced simultaneously what Humphreys called the "first taste of the intoxication of battle," as opposed to the mere "charm of *adventure*": "It was very exciting to hear the commands — 'Steady! Wait for orders! By platoons left, gallop, march! By fours, march!' — all shouted at the top of the voice, above the noise of the column, itself almost deafening with the clattering of the sabres and the thumping of the horses's hoofs upon the stony pike. At such times one is borne along in the rush and tumult of the onset, and can hardly think of fear." The Confederates fired a few shots before scattering "through the woods like leaves before the wind," and the troops dashed into a Leesburg seemingly emptied of graycoats. After confiscating Mosby's leavings from Leesburg's corn supply, Lowell decided to bivouac overnight, just outside the village.

His shoulder severely injured only a year and a half earlier, Melville suffered that night, perhaps with his feet in wet shoes, almost certainly with inadequate clothing, despite the flannel shirt he had borrowed. He could not unsaddle his horse, and could not light a fire, for they were in enemy country, and "the frequent signal-rockets from the hilltops" in front of them "showed that the Confederates were gathering their clans," Humphreys recalled:

The night was very cold, too cold to sleep; and besides there were several attacks upon our pickets that brought us to our feet and made us stand to horse till the danger was past. It was about as easy to stand as to lie down that night. If we lay down, it was at our horses' feet with the bridle rein in our hands; and — not to speak of their uneasy stamping with their iron shoes upon the ground which was our bed, — if they got lonesome they would poke us with their noses, or if they got tired standing they would lie down at our side — either of which movements was, to say the least, not conducive to sleep. It seems a wonder that — crowded together as we were, the horses standing in column four-abreast in a narrow road — none of us were trampled under their feet.

The horses somehow avoided stepping on those masters who dared to sleep. Melville may have stood or leaned all night, but his poem confirms that men attempted to stretch out on the ground: "down they lie, / Their steeds still saddled, in wooded ground: / Rein in hand they slumber then" — while the young colonel and a grizzled major (Melville's self-portrait?) stayed awake, talking, the major smoking ("A contrast here like sire and son, / Hope and Experience sage did meet"). It was, as such nights are, endless — and unforgettable, but some of the men had only a short time for remembering.

Lowell sent scouting parties out early in the morning of 19 April, and some returned with prisoners, an officer and ten men, all mounted — "quite a catch, considering the wooded nature of the country and the open chances of escape," Humphreys thought. Melville got to see the captured Mosby's rangers and to hear them talk, and he probably got to witness an escape attempt which ended in a tackled ranger's crashing his head into a tree. At ten Lowell led his men over Goose Creek again, and camped for "rest and refreshment." They were quietly dining at four when word came that Mosby and one other man were nearby — a vague report which nevertheless caused Lowell to order "Boots and Saddles" sounded and to break camp, "with abbreviated dinners." A lieutenant and ten men were sent on Mosby's trail, while the main column, Melville included, "took a direct line across the country," to head Mosby off if they could, aided by flankers who were "thrown out a distance of half a mile on either side of the advancing column."

The party with Melville struck for the pike between Middleburg and Mosby's headquarters near Rectortown, but reached it forty-five minutes too late to encounter Mosby. In the twilight they turned back to Ball's Mill and camped for the second night — time for the well-deserved respite which Humphreys described: "Now, for the first time since we started out, we had an opportunity to boil coffee and make ourselves comfortable with fires, and to unsaddle our horses and give them a refreshing rest." At odd moments, and surely in the early parts of this evening, Humphreys enjoyed his "discussions with Colonel Lowell on metaphysics and mental philosophy — subjects in which he delighted and which now were the more fascinating as they were the farthest removed from the work which most employed our thoughts." It is impossible to imagine Melville letting himself be excluded from any such discussions, and hard to imagine any better luck than his finding "good-enough Morgans" to replace his old philosophical companions, Dr. Franklin Taylor and Professor George Adler on the *Southampton* or George Campbell Rankin on the *Glasgow*. Talked out, Humphreys prepared for rest: "I made a luxurious bed of boards and dried leaves for Colonel Lowell and myself, and we lay down for the night, after the Colonel had sent a dismounted party towards Leesburg to take the city by surprise." Melville observed and diagnosed the "pale young Chaplain," who, he later wrote, "went to the wars for cure of souls, / And his own student-ailments." Melville may have fared almost as well as the colonel and the chaplain, since Lowell would not likely have let the American author, an almost exact contemporary of his literary uncle, sleep less snugly than he did, and since he plainly had decided at the outset that he wanted Melville nearby, where he could protect him even while profiting from his company.

The Leesburg raid was a result of word that Mosby would be attending a late-night wedding at which "the beauty and chivalry of the country round might be expected." There is an air of "Young Lochinvar" about Humphreys's description, but the Union troop was after the rangers, not the bride, and they came in time to see the wedding place, a hotel, brilliantly illuminated, half an hour too late for the chance to bag "a good number of Pickett's and Mosby's men." They were too late to do anything but suffer a few losses when they were fired upon. The troop abandoned the wounded and dead where the marriage had been celebrated, and returned to the night camp at two in the morning to report the sad news. Before full day on 20 April Lowell crossed the ford again and took his men into Leesburg, where they found that the landlord of the hotel had cared for the wounded. Melville got his impressions of what the war was really like as the wounded were bandaged up and put onto the ambulance (the encumbrance they had thoughtfully brought with them), along with the dead. At ten they turned toward Vienna, stopping once they had crossed Goose Creek so they could feed their horses and eat in safety. After dinner they rode twenty miles to camp, where they "were welcomed with patriotic music by the band, and were glad enough to get a good supper and rest." Humphreys summed up the scout: "We had been out three days and two nights, and I had slept only two hours, and was so stiff from a cold caught the first night that it seemed as if I could count by its special ache each muscle in my body." Melville likewise probably had slept only two hours or so, and suffered more than most of the healthy young soldiers.

Henry was there to welcome his cousin amid the playing of patriotic airs, and on 25 April he reported to his father that he had "spent a day" with Cousin Herman: "He was well and seemed to enjoy it." Melville was going on nervous energy, and no one could have forced him to bed right away. After cleaning up a little, he went to Henry's tent, and was there when Henry introduced Dr. Benjamin Rush Taylor, the regimental surgeon. Henry then took Melville for a long ride to the Fairfax courthouse—a long ride that Melville did not need, just then, but at the end of the ride they met General Tyler, "charming, curly-headed, cherub-faced, and slightly overweight," as Garner says, the curly hair parted right down the middle of his head. This Tyler was a man worth meeting (Garner again): "He was the sort of man who appealed to Herman, an affable, whiskey-drinking, cigar-smoking lover of books. But he was more than that, one of the most experienced of all the Union officers in the East. Conversing with him was like thumbing through an encyclopedia of the war, Fort Sumter, rebellious Baltimore, Yorktown, the Seven Days, Fredericksburg, Chancellorsville, and Gettysburg." Tyler rose splendidly to the occasion, bestowing at least two gifts on the sailor-author—Jean Paul Richter's *Titan* and a translation of Terence. After this Herman and Henry had to ride back, all boozily, to the camp at Vienna, where Herman at last had a chance to get as much sleep as he could in such circumstances.

Garner examines the possibility that Melville went from Vienna directly back to Washington, "since he attempted unsuccessfully to contact a doctor there, probably Doctor Taylor, and he appears to have claimed a letter that awaited him at the post office" (a letter advertised in the 22 April *Evening Star* but not on the twenty-fourth). Melville's "further travels," Garner acknowledges, "are almost completely undocumented," traceable "only through his poem 'The Armies of the Wilderness (1863–4).'" Garner sketches what Melville would have seen at Rappahannock Station, then Brandy Station, the headquarters of the Army of the Potomac, and after that Grant's headquarters at Culpepper Station. Garner assumes that Melville's prestige as an author and his connections to the Galena Melvills may have induced Grant to receive him graciously and welcome him into the house he occupied inside the circle of tents. Melville's note to "Chattanooga (November, 1863)" contains a shadowy character, a "visitor" who converses with Grant about that victory. In that note Melville describes the November day ("in character an October one—cool, clear, bright, intoxicatingly invigorating; one of those days peculiar to the ripest hours of our American autumn") in which the Union soldiers at Chattanooga had amazingly disobeyed orders to pause and dashed on to victory ("the army took the bit between its teeth, and ran away with the generals"). One of the topics of conversation between the "visitor" and Grant was this extraordinary day of the previous fall: "General Grant, at Culpepper, a few weeks prior to crossing the Rapidan for the Wilderness, expressed to a visitor his impression of the impulse and the spectacle: Said he, 'I never saw any thing like it:' language which seems curiously undertoned, considering its application; but from the taciturn Commander it was equivalent to a superlative or hyperbole from the talkative." Like Garner, I take the visitor to be Melville himself and the anecdote to be a truthful personal account of his visit to the general. This modesty and obliqueness, so unlike Gansevoort's or Allan's or Lathers's way, so unlike Henry Gansevoort's way, recalls how Melville avoided naming the eminent John Clifford to Hawthorne as the man who gave him the Agatha story.

Elizabeth Shaw Melville's statement in her little memoir of her husband provides the corroborative evidence: "Herman went to Virginia with Allan in April 1864 Visited various battlefields & called on Gen. Grant." She had some normal lapses of memory, but her record for veracity is unimpeachable on any matter so important as whether or not Melville visited Grant. In this war private citizens did indeed venture onto the battlefields, and generals did indeed take time to socialize with private citizens, especially those with a famous name and connections in remote Galena, where Grant had spent years on about as low a social scale as the declassed Melvill family, whom he knew by sight and reputation, if not more intimately. The daughter of Chief Justice Shaw would never have claimed her husband had met a famous general if he had not done so. They met, and smoked together, and talked sparingly.

During the late winter Peter had agreed to pay for a suitable banner for Henry's regiment and with unwonted lack of caution he authorized Henry (he said on 4 April) "to order it without regard to cost." In early May the regimental flag was finished, the finest Tiffany had ever made, the bill from Tiffany asking Peter to remit $295 for "Cavalry Guidon silver mountings." Peter suggested that there might be "some mistake," this being three times what he had expected. Peter paid up, even though Henry denied him the pleasure of having his cousin, Representative John Van Schaick Lansing Pruyn, or Senator Ira Harris make the presentation, and in early June Kate Gansevoort was sending out Albany papers describing (as Robert Sanford wrote to Henry on 25 June) "the handsome & appropriate present of the Flag that your Father gave to your regiment." The Gansevoorts once again would serve under a magnificent banner. What would Catherine Van Schaick Gansevoort have thought, after putting her own stitches into her husband's flag in the Revolution? Like her father, Kate Gansevoort found warfare hard to envision, and wished *she* could attend the ceremony and see "something of a military life" (she wrote Henry on 21 April) rather than remaining "a simple civilian."

In her letter of 3 May Kate told Henry that Allan had given "quite a graphic account of his visit to your camp" — an account she did not commit to paper; the other news was that "Herman M. is suffering from a terrible attack of Neuralgia after his exposure in visiting the front of Our Army of the Potomac." On 10 May, long back in New York, the neuralgic attack having delayed his thanking Henry for his hospitality, Melville wrote his military cousin. By that time Melville knew that Tiffany was to make Henry a flag, not that it was ready, and astonishingly expensive. In the letter Melville naturally enough, but perhaps slyly, mentioned a flag, and then worked in a double-edged allusion to another Henry: "I enjoyed my visit very much, & would not have missed it on any account, and can only regret that you happened to be away when we arrived. But as when the sun reappears after being hidden; so — &c &c &c. Your imagination and modesty will supply the rest." He plainly did not expect his cousin to have at hand a pocket edition of *Henry IV, Part 1*, where at the end of act 1, scene 2, Prince Henry imitates the sun, temporarily permitting the base contagious clouds to smother up his beauty from the world. Herman must have known more about Cousin Henry's venery and his venereal infections, and more about his alcoholic sprees, than he wanted to know. No Falstaff was needed to entice his young cousin to sin, and Henry's past efforts at reformation showed no high likelihood that he would ever reign over the Washington Avenue house, moving among the ancestral portraits as King Henry Gansevoort. Henry's reservoir of "imagination," Herman knew, was even lower than his supplies of "modesty."

Melville now sent his respects to General Tyler and asked Henry to deliver his book reports: "say that I agree with him about 'Titan.' The worst thing I can say about it is, that it is a little better than 'Mardi' The Terence I highly value; indeed both works, as memorials of the hospitalities of an accomplished General & jolly Christian." Melville inquired in jocular fashion about George Brewster: "How is Captain Brewster? Coke on Lyttleton, and Strap on the Shoulder. My friendly regards & best wishes to the Captain & say to him that I hear the neigh of his war-horse in my dreams, Likewise that I have a flannel shirt of his in my keeping; which I hope one day to exhibit as the identical shirt worn by that renowned soldier shortly after his entrance into the army." He also sent word to Aunt Susan's nephew Edwin Lansing: "remember me to him. Tell him I frequently think of him & his tent & there is pleasure in the thought. Tell him to tell Dr Wolf (savage name, but sweet man) that my prayers ascend for him." At last Melville was ready to address his cousin directly:

And now, Col. Gansevoort of the 13th N.Y. Cavalry, conceive me to be standing some paces from you, in an erect attitude and with manly bearing, giving you the military salute. Farewell. May two small but choice constellations of stars alight on your shoulders. May your sword be a terror to the despicable foe, & your name in after ages be used by Southern matrons to frighten their children by. And after death (which God long avert, & bring about after great battles, quietly, in a comfortable bed, with wife & children around) may that same name be transferred to heaven — bestowed upon some new planet or cluster of stars of the first magnitude. Farewell, my hero & God bless you.

This was Melville in an ironic highfalutin mode which must have left Henry a little off balance — Henry being conspicuous for his inability to get what he called (in reference to "The Town-Ho's Story") the "'pint'" of his cousin's prose. What the tone of all this praise of Henry shows is that Herman had quietly decided that he himself would be the grandson of Peter Gansevoort who would glorify the martial honor of the family in his generation — an ambition that would have struck both the naval and the army cousin as grotesque.

In the middle of April, better but not at her best, Maria arrived for a visit at Peter's in Albany; on the twenty-first Kate reported to Henry that Maria had responded to their "good care & cheer," and was feeling "very much improved — but still not as strong as usual." On 24 May Augusta packed for the Manor House amid consultations with her mother and Fanny about the summer schedule. As Fanny explained to Kate Gansevoort that day, they were hoping that the Albany Kate could meet Kate Hoadley or at least the Hoadley daughters, since Kate and John would be going on to Rochester: "If you are fond of little girls, you will be delighted with Lottie, she is such a bright, comical child, has such a roguish look out of her dark eyes, and enjoys what she calls a 'hard play' with her whole heart." In her letter of 3 May to Henry, Kate gave news of the peripatetic Jane and Allan, who had stopped by after "making arrangements for the summer at their place — 'Arrowhead.'" Mrs. M. (Kate was still formal with Jane) had been "full of her visit to Washington of having seen Genl Grant" (something Herman did not boast of) and had professed herself as *"so sorry"* that Henry "should have been so long — three days next door to them & not have seen them." (This is when Allan gave "quite a graphic account" of his [not "their"] visit to Henry's camp, and relayed the news that Herman was "suffering with a terrible attack of Neuralgia" as a result of exposure.) Melville's letter to his mother about his adventures traveled about (directed to Albany, where Peter forwarded it to Maria at Gansevoort, from whence she sent it back to him to read) and is apparently no longer extant.

On 29 March, shortly before Melville left for Washington, the New York papers had carried the news that the publisher William Ticknor and Nathaniel Hawthorne had arrived at the Astor House, both ill. Even if Melville learned of their presence in the city, diffidence at his altered circumstances would have kept him from calling, but the news exacerbated the odd emotions he had begun to feel when he encountered praise of Hawthorne in the papers and in books. Less than two weeks later the family all saw the notices of Ticknor's death in Philadelphia ("Mr Hawthorne was the friend that was with him. They had been intimate for years"—so Fanny wrote to Kate Gansevoort on 24 May). Then worse news came during a bad time in New York City, when (in Lizzie's complaint that Maria quoted to Peter on 24 May) that the " 'smell of the Streets is very disagreeable, that a short time ago there was a strike among the men who carry away the garbage, & for a week the barrels before the door were untouched, sending forth most villanous odors." During this hourly reminder of decay and stench came the news of Hawthorne's own death on 19 May in Plymouth, New Hampshire, while on a therapeutic trip with another dear friend, Franklin Pierce. Melville was "much shocked," Lizzie wrote to the family at Gansevoort, "at hearing of Mr Hawthornes sudden death." On 24 May Maria wrote to Peter, apparently drawing her details from a news account (such as Peter would have seen) rather than from Lizzie's letter:

> I was quite shocked to see the sudden death of Nathaniel Hawthorne, in New Hampshire where he was on a visit, & was found dead in his bed, he had left home for the benefit of his health. A few weeks, since he visited Philadelphia with his friend W. D. Ticknor, the Boston publisher, who was taken sick & died, Mr Hawthorne never leaving him from the time he was taken sick, & was holding his hand at the moment he was breathing his last. Mr Hawthorne was deeply affected at his death, & not being well; then travelling for his health. It is very probable the sudden shock was too much for him, Herman was much attached to him & will mourn his loss. He staid with him a few days in Liverpool, & I beleive has not seen him since.

The letter from Lizzie had just arrived, and Maria was showing concern in her coupling of the "sudden shock" that killed Hawthorne and the report of Herman's being "much shocked."

On 20 May many of the major newspapers carried stories, not just items about Hawthorne's death at the age of sixty, but full obituaries and retrospective articles such as they had printed for Irving. The Boston *Post* declared that Hawthorne (well known as a Democrat) now held a place in American literature by the side of Irving. No one has scoured the surviving Southern newspapers (Sherman and other incendiaries saw to it that few files survived the war intact), but a recurrent minor strain in the obituaries in New York and New England was the regret that Hawthorne had been so closely allied with Democrats, who had long tried to appease the South, and that he had, as the Springfield *Republican* said on 20 May, never "expressed a word of sympathy for the cause in which we are fighting, or manifested any interest in the preservation of our national integrity." The *Tribune* mentioned his having written *The House of the Seven Gables* at Lenox, but said nothing more about those months. The *Tribune* concluded: "Thus, one by one, the writers who have created for us an American literature, original and self-sustaining, are departing. It is not enough to say that they will be remembered through their own productions; but we may fondly hope that they will always stand as the foremost pioneers of a literature yet to achieve more signal and important triumphs." The line of pioneering American writers hardly stretched out to the crack of doom: "one by one," Cooper, Irving, Hawthorne? It is hard to know what others Greeley's staff-writer could have had in mind. Hardly Thoreau, despite Greeley's affinity for him. Melville would have seen this article, and brooded about the death, one by one, of the writers who had created "an American literature, original and self-sustaining." Hawthorne's death did not immediately propel him into the literary empyrean; Melville witnessed that transformation as it took place over the next few years. Melville was never mentioned in any known obituary or memorial article on Hawthorne in 1864. It was as if he were not a mourner.

The year 1864 saw the first grand Melville family gathering at Gansevoort — really, the first such gathering anywhere, since Arrowhead was smaller and Herman had been so deeply in debt during the years the family tried to gather there, and since Jane had evinced no unconquerable urge to gather all the Gansevoorts and Melvilles there. About 15 July Herman came up to Gansevoort with his sons, and then or soon afterward John and Kate Hoadley came with Lottie and Minnie. This crew was in residence on 19 July, when Samuel, one of Uncle Peter's servants, returned from Gansevoort ("where his Cousin lives in Aunt Melville's Family," Kate Gansevoort wrote Henry on 20 July) reporting "all well & the place he says looks 'Splendid Elegant.'" They could not put the war out of mind, but they could revel in being with loving, intelligent people where books and magazines were ready for idle or serious reading. One day (this year, it seems) Lottie had an adventure — "rescued from a watery grave by the Farmers son, who pulled me out of the spring — just back of the house — into which head first I had fallen" (so she wrote to Victor Hugo Paltsits on 21 March 1936). In any case, this was the summer she became dangerously ill at Gansevoort with what they called "billious" fever. The illness complicated things. To Kate Gansevoort on 4 August, Maria reported that John had rushed there from New

Bedford, after "travelling all night coming the Rutland route." He had stayed a week, leaving on 4 August, the anniversary of his first marriage (according to Lizzie's information), and of Herman and Lizzie's, and Helen's birthday. Helen and George left together from Boston but went separate ways, Helen to Gansevoort and George to Canada before visiting them to escort Helen and Kate Hoadley and the girls home ("if Lottie should then be able to travel"). Later, on 8 September, Kate Gansevoort gave Henry her tart view of Helen's decision: "Kate & Helen have spent most of the Summer with their mother, but have now returned to their respective domiciles—Mr Griggs has been out West—making a tour, through Canada to Detroit, thence by Steamer to Superior City, & then 160 miles through the Woods to St Pauls Minnesota—Helen would not accompany him." Kate added: "How I should like to visit our Western Country." Maria had all her living children there for part of the time, except her baby, and a letter came from him, written in Shanghai, dated 5 May 1864, and giving November as the month of his return.

While he was at Gansevoort, Herman received the news that the literary and hospitable General Tyler had been grievously wounded in the ankle during General Grant's attack on the Confederate army at the crossroads of Cold Harbor, ten miles from Richmond, on 3 June 1864, when the Union army suffered four or five times as many casualties as Lee. On 21 July Melville wrote Tyler one of his bantering, flattering letters:

> Though I hope I *am* patriotic—enthusiastically so—yet I will not congratulate you, General, upon your wound, but will reserve that for the scar, which will be equally glorious and not quite so irksome.—I am glad it is no worse with you, and rejoice to learn that you are in a promising way. I trust that you are in a condition to enjoy your book and your cigar, also (but this should have gone before) the sweet eyes of the sympathetic ladies, who, you know, have a natural weakness for heroes.

As best he could, he disengaged himself from this heavy whimsy: "But methinks I hear somebody say, Dont bore him with too long a yarn." Brooding on his recent adventures as he was, Melville may well have worked on his "Scout toward Aldie" there at Gansevoort, where he could be outdoors much of the time at the edge of the Adirondacks, such contrast to the devastated terrain of a Virginia literally torn apart by war.

Herman celebrated his forty-fifth birthday with his mother. On 3 August, on the page facing the frontispiece of the third volume of his father's set of Bell's edition of *The Poetical Works of Edmund Spenser* (London, 1788), he wrote: "Gansevoort / Aug 3^d 1864." At this time he inscribed the first volume

"Augusta Melville, from Herman" and left the set with her. This was the family Spenser, given to Allan Melvill by his friend Obadiah Rich Jr., on New Year's Day, 1803, the volumes which very likely had simultaneously aroused Herman's aesthetic and sexual excitement in the early 1830s. On his seventeenth wedding anniversary Melville and Augusta boarded the cars with the boys to go to Glens Falls for the day — perhaps the first time the boys had visited their Gansevoort relatives there, although Stanny had been so much at Gansevoort that he at least knew the cousins in Glens Falls well, including the odd older Stanwix. Herman and Augusta had their chance to see Leonard, now seriously ill with dropsy of the heart, as the diagnosis went, liable to die any time, and they heard news about Ned Curtis, who had been serving in the navy. After Herman and Augusta left for New York on 8 August, Maria wrote Kate Gansevoort on 19 August, there was a "severe storm of wind rain & hail" that felled several trees in Peter's lot, and on Maria's property uprooted "one large apple tree, apparently sound, full of fruit," forty feet high, which exposed "Mr Landons out houses to view." There was still other damage. That was a Saturday. Then on Monday the fifteenth, a week after Herman and Augusta left, there was a religious spectacle which fascinated Malcolm, as Maria told Kate Gansevoort:

> We have a large Camp meeting here held in your Fathers Lot, my daughters walked over to see them & met M^rs [George] Lansing & her little boy Albert.... We all went again in the Eveg to see the place lighted up, I staid but a very short time & returned home with Malcolm. Helen staid to hear the Sermon which she said was an excellent one. The short time I was there a woman it was said had "got religion" she lay on her back in front of the Pulpit with hands upraised & screaming with all her might. I did not see because of the crowd but Malcolm struggled through & saw her.

Malcolm, fifteen years old, had been transfixed at this quite un-Bostonian form of worship, Stanwix apparently less so, given his Calvinistic Dutch church training there at Gansevoort. At least the theology was not shocking to Stanwix. Class distinctions had crumbled. The Unitarian Sedgwicks earlier in the century could drive to the outskirts of a camp meeting in the Berkshires and survey the scene in patrician amazement, the way they might have watched a pagan orgy in an unchristianized land. Here, fashionably dressed women (from Saratoga Springs, even) intermixed with the lower classes, and Maria and her families did not shun the meeting, although neither she nor Helen could ever take anything but an ironic view of such goings-on. Cousin Kate relayed the news to Henry on 29 August, tartly doctoring Maria's account the way she always did: "She gave me quite an account of the 'Camp Meeting' at that Place, held in Fathers Lot. There were more then [than] 1000 persons there and all of them seem to have 'got religion.'" Malcolm's response is the most curious, and the least sharply defined: was he riveted in horror or disgust? He had things to tell his Unitarian mother when she arrived in Gansevoort on 20 August.

Perhaps Lizzie had taken the girls to Boston, perhaps she was still at Twenty-sixth Street, but she soon came to Gansevoort. The exorbitantly priced Twenty-sixth Street house was now hers, free and clear, thanks to a three-thousand-dollar legacy from Dr. Hayward, enough to pay off the mortgage held by Mrs. Thurston. Three days after Augusta and Herman arrived in New York, Julia was born at New Rochelle to Abby and Richard Lathers, a new cousin for Allan's daughters. Augusta stayed in New York with Herman while Lizzie and the girls spent three weeks in Gansevoort (and perhaps visited Boston as well). The family visits to Gansevoort did not cease until very late in the summer. On 9 September Lizzie left for New York with her four children ("they all look better than when they came, & profess to have passed their time very pleasantly," Maria wrote Kate Gansevoort that day). For a few days, until Augusta returned, Maria and Fanny expected to be "quite alone"; and "for a novelty" they were prepared to enjoy it. Word was received from Tom in Manila confirming that he would be home in mid-November and announcing his intention to stay with his mother a whole year—heartwarming news for the women at Gansevoort.

A few weeks after his return to New York City Melville read the 3 September *Harper's Weekly Journal of Civilization*, which featured Thomas Nast's semicircular full-page cartoon on the recent convention of the Democratic party in Chicago, entitled, at the top, "Compromise with the South." On the upper left the Union flag flies upside down, while the North (represented by a young woman on her knees and a bedraggled Northern soldier) grieves at a tombstone engraved "In Memory of the Union Heroes who died in a Useless War"; in the upper right the Confederate flag flies, emblazoned with reminders of the starvation of Yankee prisoners, while the South is represented by a triumphant, well-clad Confederate soldier who pulls the Northern man by the hand toward the gravestone. At the foot of the picture are the words: "Dedicated to the Chicago Convention." Elsewhere in the issue "Compromise with the South," a commentary on this picture, accused the Democrats of forgetting "the massacres of Lawrence and Fort Pillow, and the burning of Chambersburg, and the long, long story of the hanging and torture of Southern Union men at home and of Union prisoners in rebel hands." Melville mailed this issue to his mother at Gansevoort, and she in turn commented (5 September) to Kate Gansevoort on the "most melancholy picture, headed Compromise with the South, Dedicated to the Chicago Convention," and declared herself against the president: "I rejoice at McClellan's nomination, hope he will be elected."

Maria was less than pleased when her fiftieth wedding anniversary was celebrated by McClellan's opponents, "hundreds of waggons & carriages" filling tiny Gansevoort. She wrote Kate Gansevoort on 4 October that a "full band of music, playing very finely & hundreds of 'ladies & gentlemen' dressed in their best are riding & driving about," all bound to "a great Lincoln Mass meeting in the Grove" — Buckley's Grove, not Peter's. Alert to fashion still, Maria reported that the young ladies were wearing "Red Garabaldi's & dark brown or blue skirts," topped "by the pet head dress of the day, a jockey as the hats are called here." Just as all of Kossuth's triumphal processioning over the United States resulted in nothing more than a fad in headgear, the slouch hat with an ostrich feather plume, the distinctive garb of Garibaldi's thousand had inspired fashionable headgear for young ladies. At that time, Americans were known for a capacity to simplify, trivialize, and even pervert a potent symbol.

That fall the military Gansevoorts, Guert and Henry, each faced crises. On 14 September 1864 Captain Guert Gansevoort was detached from command of the *Roanoke* and ordered to duty as inspector of ordnance at the New York Navy Yard, but that order was modified. As Maria wrote to Kate Gansevoort on 4 October: "Guert has been at Glen's falls for a week or more on a visit, he while there had a letter giving him the choice either to return to his old place on board the 'Roanoke' at, or near Fortress Monroe, or take his old position at the Navy Yard in Brooklyn. Guert went to New York yesterday, to take up his old, or new quarters." Leonard died on 8 October, so Guert must have turned round and gone back to Glens Falls. Young Kate Gansevoort wrote to Henry after Leonard was buried: "I wish we had known him during his life time — but the Gansevoorts are a strange family — Guert certainly behaves *strangely*." Maria Gansevoort Melville and Mary Chandonette Gansevoort had raised their children to be discreet, and no one explained to young Kate that it was her father's selfishness which had split the family for a quarter century and more, after Catherine Van Schaick Gansevoort's death at the end of 1830.

On 19 September at Fairfax, Colonel Henry Gansevoort reported to another officer that "in the skirmish with the Thirteenth New York Cavalry, on the last scout of that regiment, Colonel Mosby was seriously wounded, a pistol bullet striking the handle of the pistol in his belt and glancing off in his groin." Mosby was able to ride away but collapsed a little later, Henry claimed in a report to his father on 31 October. Henry boasted of surprising "the artillery camp of Mosby on the summit of the Little Cobbler mountain, one of the Blue ridge peaks about a mile high," and capturing four "peices of his Artillery, a full complement of ammunition," one of the "peices" being "a 12 pounder presented by Genl. Early to Mosby, a fine brasspiece." The capture of this artillery, Henry exulted, had deprived Mosby "of his sting and admitted & secured the opening of the Manassas Gap Road (R R) which had been delayed by him." According to Henry, Mosby had "even threatened Washington" with the now-captured artillery, so Peter Gansevoort could, if he wanted to, exult that his son had saved the capital even as Peter's father had saved New York from the British. Mosby, in fact, regained his sting swiftly.

On 19 October, the day of the Battle of Cedar Creek, Henry was across the Blue Ridge Mountains, keeping a lookout on the rebuilding of the Manassas Gap Railroad. The Confederates under General Jubal A. Early launched a surprise attack while most of the men of General George Crook were still sleeping, and had routed them, it seemed. General Philip Sheridan heard the cannon from Winchester, and his sudden appearance on the battlefield around noon, after a fourteen-mile horseback ride, animated the troops into a counterattack of such unexpected ferocity that the Confederate troops panicked, utterly ignoring Early's exhortations. In the terrible cost of victory, Melville's gallant companion young Lowell was killed. Reporting to his father, on 31 October, Henry compared himself to Harry of the North: "During my absence the battle of Cedar Creek was fought in which 'the flower safety was so valiantly plucked from the nettle danger' by the noble Sheridan." Henry had "champed the necessity" which held him near the fight but out of it. He was "wearied of this thankless task of fighting guerrillas—a task that no matter how zealously performed is but service ignored." "Party spirit" was running high that election year: "I have studiously kept aloof from all interferance but I regret to say that my enemies are savage & numerous. Every endeavor that evil genius can make is against me. I have criticised the military but never the political measures of the administration." As Garner explains, on 24 October, while Henry was sick in bed, two of his officers had handed out absentee ballots and urged the men to vote for McClellan against Lincoln. To the War Department this was a sign of unreliability if not disloyalty.

Just after this, the humorless young zealot George Armstrong Custer captured six of Mosby's men and, rather than granting them the status of prisoners of war, executed them. Mosby executed seven Union men and attached to one of the bodies an eloquent note to General Sheridan, dated 11 November 1864, offering a way out: "Hereafter any prisoners falling into my hands will be treated with the kindness due to their condition, unless some new act of barbarity shall compel me, reluctantly, to adopt a line of policy repugnant to humanity." Throughout the fall and winter Mosby devoted himself to incessant harassing of Sheridan, interrupting his transportation and communication lines. Melville followed all these events very closely. Soon after 19 October he probably wrote what became one of his most famous poems, "Philip," also called "Sheridan at Cedar Creek." In it "Philip" is "king of riders," but the poem is structured on a series of imperatives in which Melville orders honors for the horse, not the rider, beginning "Shoe the steed with silver / That bore him to the fray." Sheridan had been riding the Michigan-born horse since 1862, and named him "Winchester" after the ride and the victory at Cedar Creek.

The vicissitudes of her Gansevoort nephews and the poetic struggles of her oldest living son were nothing to Maria in comparison to the news that on 18 November 1864 Captain Thomas Melville had returned to New York on the *Bengal*. By 21 November Maria was en route to see him, stopping at Peter's while equipping herself. Augusta and Kate on the morning of the twenty-second "saw her safely seated in the Harlem Cars, & happy in the anticipation of a very charming visit at New York, not having been in the Metropolis in five years." Maria was expecting to be "met at the cars in 26th St." (Kate wrote Henry on 23 November) "by her four Sons, Tom, Herman, Allan & Mr. John Hoadley." Hoadley was in New York "on his way to the Petroleum Regions in Va.," looking ahead: "He is very much interested in these wells & hopes to make a fortune out of a tract of Land which he has lately purchased." Two Melville brothers had killed whales for lamp oil, and Hoadley was to exploit a cheaper, safer source of illumination. Aunt Melville, Kate said, "is to dine with her four sons, two daughters in Law — & eight grandchildren Thanksgiving Day — & expects to enjoy the family party." Cousin Kate was not necessarily invidious in not mentioning the absent son-in-law, George Griggs, but he had been less gentle to Helen and the rest of the family since shortly after the stillbirth of their son. Critical, Fanny called him; "gruff" was his reputation among the descendants down through the next century. Tom was as always resplendent and charming.

Lizzie apparently did not go to Boston for Thanksgiving in 1864, as she always needed to do, but did not do for a dozen years, according to an 1871 letter. She gave Malcolm a Bible that year, and he wrote into it in his youthful hand eight lines of poetry:

> Little travellers Zionward,
> Each one entering into rest
> In the kingdom of your Lord,
> In the mansions of the blest,

> There to welcome Jesus waits
> Gives the crowns his followers win
> Lift your heads ye golden gates!
> Let the little travellers in!

It should have been unthinkable that little travelers were headed Zionward, but that terrible year many thousands of young men, among them the poet Lowell's nephew, who had treated Herman Melville so kindly in camp, had headed Zionward long before their time.

[26]

Two Years—of War and Dubious Peace
1865–1866

> If there be one conclusion more forcibly pressed upon us than another by the review which has been given of the fortunes and fate of Poetical Works, it is this,—that every Author, as far as he is great and at the same time *original*, has had the task of *creating* the taste by which he is to be enjoyed: so has it been, so will it continue to be.
>
> Wordsworth, echoing Coleridge,
in "Essay Supplementary to the Preface," marked by Melville
with two parallel vertical lines in the margin

THE MELVILLE AND GANSEVOORT family dynamics shifted momentously but almost imperceptibly in the two years 1865 and 1866. Maria's living in the Mansion House at Gansevoort drew her children and grandchildren to her in the summers, and, through proximity to Albany, gradually brought her and her brother Peter back into easy, loving familiarity. The healing was hastened by Peter's daughter, Kate, who now took a mature interest in her aunt and her seldom seen Melville cousins, and who encountered for the first time, through Maria, some of her Gansevoort cousins. Since no one wanted to explain to young Kate why the estrangements had occurred, everyone began to behave as if nothing was wrong, and before long they all realized that they still loved each other. Tom, a figure of great interest to Allan's young daughters and to Kate Gansevoort (eight years his junior), was home from the sea and casting about for a role on land. Malcolm was put to work and Henry Gansevoort cast about for some easy way of supporting himself until his already aged father died and left him wealthy. Around this time, presumably after the move to Twenty-sixth Street, the domestic situation had become such that Lizzie had at last begun to accept the possibility that the accusations long leveled against her husband in the press, and surely at 49 Mount Vernon Street, after her father's death, might be true—that Herman might really be insane. She had never been a woman who trusted her own judgment. Once she accepted the idea that her husband was insane, she sought the sympathy of her Boston family more and more.

Melville, not at all insane and perhaps ignorant of his wife's desperation, wrote a book of poems and published it, and at the end of 1866 he took a job, nothing to depend on and therefore nothing for the family to become excited about.

On 22 December 1864 Kate Gansevoort wrote Henry that Maria was "still in New York staying at Hermans—she returns to Gansevoort Farm after the Holydays." That did not happen. Maria found it so good to be around her three sons, eight grandchildren, and several old friends that she prolonged her visit to New York until mid-April 1865. Augusta stayed at the Mansion House, all alone, for several weeks after Fanny went to New Bedford in March 1865 to help care for the two girls, Kate being newly pregnant and anxious. Staying with Allan and Jane, Maria was easy enough for Herman and Lizzie to visit. Tom saw the Albany Gansevoorts on 18 and 19 December 1864, prompting this judgment from Kate to Henry: "He is looking finely. We enjoyed his visit very much. I never knew any one more informed than he is—Tom has improved the advantage offered by travel & is well read & quite an elegant young man." When he was in New York at Allan's, Tom could escort Maria to Herman's and Lizzie's house, where she could see four grandchildren more often than Allan's daughters, who were in boarding school. Since he was only writing poems, Herman had nothing to do but escort her when requested to do so. Maria was near enough to witness any undue tensions in Herman's household, and made no comment of any in her known letters if she observed any. She had not been, up to this point, a woman who missed much.

On 28 January 1865 "Mrs. E. S. Melville" paid two hundred dollars for rental of pew 209 in the gallery of All Souls Church, the third least expensive available. She attended, with at least some of the children. Herman was writing, and the composition of "The Frenzy in the Wake" can be dated to mid-February 1865:

> With burning woods our skies are brass,
>   The pillars of dust are seen;
> The live-long day their cavalry pass—
>   No crossing the road between.
>   We were sore deceived—an awful host!
>   They move like a roaring wind,
>   Have we gamed and lost? but even despair
>   Shall never our hate rescind.

In his note in *Battle-Pieces* Melville says this poem "was written while yet the reports were coming North of Sherman's homeward advance from Savannah." Melville continued to lead something of a literary life. Bayard Taylor extended an invitation on 24 February 1865: "On Monday evening next, the 27th, 'The Travellers' meet ... and it would give me great pleasure to see you among the guests of the Club. Many of the members are no doubt old friends of yours—Darley, Church, Bierstadt, Gottschalk, Cyrus Field, Hunt, Bellows and Townsend Harris. We simply meet to talk, winding up our evenings with a cigar and frugal refreshments." This was company fit for Melville: the illustrator Felix Darley, who had made his way to Arrowhead; the painters Frederic Church and Albert Bierstadt; the New Orleans composer Louis Moreau Gottschalk; Dudley Field's brother, the Atlantic Cable entrepreneur; one of the Hunt brothers, either the architect Richard Morris Hunt or William Morris Hunt (the painter of Judge Shaw); Henry W. Bellows, the minister of All Souls, or possibly the painter Albert F. Bellows; and Townsend Harris, the country's first consul general to Japan. Melville may not have gone to the meeting, and there is no evidence that he was invited again. There was a death and a birth. Maria Van Schaick Peebles, Maria's first cousin, died in Lansingburgh and was buried on 7 March. On 18 March a daughter, Mary Bankhead Thurston, first cousin to Allan Melville's children, was born to Mary S. and Dr. A. Henry Thurston.

In March a Philadelphia firm, T. B. Peterson & Brothers, reprinted *Israel Potter* from the old plates under the title *The Refugee*, after touting it for a month. The advertisements in the New York *Times*, the *Daily News*, and the *Tribune* on 11 March added insult to injury in describing the book as "by Herman Melville, Author of 'Typee,' 'Omoo,' 'The Two Captains,' 'The Man of the World,' etc. etc." Lizzie clipped the *Tribune* notice and labeled it "Fraud." On the title page Peterson printed notices not known to modern Melville scholars, but possibly genuine, either recycled reviews of *Israel Potter* or new reviews of *The Refugee*, reading in part: "We advise no one to take up 'The Refugee' until he has leisure to finish it; for when he has once dipped into its fascinating and adventurous pages, he will not be disposed to leave them until he has reached the very last"; "This is a really delightful book, in which one may find food for laughter and sterling information into the bargain." The Boston *Commercial Bulletin* on 18 March derived a few remarks from these dubious but handy notices, and, oddly enough, *The Refugee* brought a brief spate of generally good attention to Melville at a time when he was all but neglected. Polite comments appeared in New York, Boston, Albany, Philadelphia, Cincinnati, and surely elsewhere, doing Melville's reputation no harm. The re-publication in 1865 even had a certain timeliness for the country and for Melville, since it dealt with stirring adventures on land and sea and portrayed the humble hero's adventurous early years, in which he encountered momentous men of the time, followed by a miserable afterlife.

Melville's anger at Peterson was compounded by his helplessness, since Peterson had bought the plates fair and square. Years later, on 28 January 1876, Melville protested that he had conveyed "a remonstrance" to Peterson's long ago, presumably in 1865, for foisting two unknown books on him and for publishing *The Refugee* as if that were his own title, and the title of a new book. The attribution to him of books he had never written, *The Two Captains* and *The Man of the World*, profoundly troubled Melville. It was if he were long dead and liable to have works ascribed to him the way new pieces got put into the Joe Miller joke books or new rhymes into printings of Mother Goose. He had thought he would have wanted to write behind a mask, like Junius, but not to have books foisted on him. He had been "prevented" from publishing *The Isle of the Cross* and *Poems* and at least one story, "The Two Temples," and now Peterson in a real book with a spurious title was attributing to him imaginary books with imaginary titles.

Sometime this year, Melville accepted an invitation to one of the Sunday night literary receptions at the nearby Twentieth Street residence of Alice and Phoebe Cary, the poets from Ohio whom Horace Greeley had persuaded to better their fortunes in Manhattan. Charles Hemstreet in *Literary New York* (New York, 1903) said that he not only went, but once again proved himself incomparable in dramatic storytelling: "Melville told the company, and told it far better than he had ever written anything (at least so one of his hearers has recorded), the story of that life of trial and adventure" — his boyhood, his "shipping as a common sailor," his "youthful wanderings in London and Liverpool" (London, as in *Redburn* if not in life?). Then he retold *Typee*, "with picturesque detail," as he had stubbornly refused to do in his lecture on the South Seas. Although the great fame of the late 1840s was long past, there continued to be printed the odd public reference to Melville, as when G. W. Curtis in his "Editor's Easy Chair" column in *Harper's* for April 1865 mentioned his "wonderful chapter upon whiteness in 'The Whale.'" With modestly renewed public attention, and an infusion of Lizzie's money into the coffers of the Harpers, came solvency: On 13 November 1865 the seventeenth Harper & Bros. account contained astonishing figures: "Balance due Herman Melville, Esq. $43.17."

Melville was in New York City during the fall of Richmond on 3 April, then Lee's surrender to Grant at Appomattox Court House on the ninth, then the horror of Lincoln's assassination in his box at Ford's Theatre by John Wilkes Booth on the fourteenth. Day by day, he witnessed the joyous flags and parades, the thunderous cannoning, then the flags at half-staff, the black bunting, the great confused noises of a city exhausted and aghast. That month, sometime, Melville made his way to the National Academy Exhibition, where two paintings suggested poems to him, *The Coming Storm*, by Sanford Robinson Gifford (which he had seen in Albany), and *Jane Jackson, Formerly a Slave*, by Elihu Vedder. Like many New Yorkers in the weeks after the end of the war, Melville on walks downtown observed a strange phenomenon, Confederate soldiers released from Northern prisons, wandering "penniless about the streets" (he later wrote), or lying "in their worn and patched gray uniforms under the trees of the Battery, near the barracks where they were lodged and fed," awaiting transportation south. For him they were living specters, strange as the specter of the damaged, impoverished Israel Potter which had risen in March. Henceforth the Battery was more haunted for Melville than ever.

Melville was reading very little not connected with the war, but he made an exception in May for some of Hawthorne's *Mosses from an Old Manse*, making private judgments based on his acquaintance with the author. In "Monsieur du Miroir" he underscored seven words ("Will he linger where I have lived, to remind the neglectful world of one who staked much to win a name") and, taking the words as spoken in Hawthorne's own voice, he commented, "What a revelation." He marked the sentence "He will pass to the dark realm of Nothingness, but will not find me there" and commented on it: "This trenches upon the uncertain and the terrible." He marked and underlined the passage in the Vanity Fair episode of "The Celestial Railroad" on the way people vanish like soap-bubbles and others, accustomed to "such little accidents," hardly realize they are gone. When the narrator says, "But it was otherwise with me," Melville commented: "Nothing can be finer than this. May 1865." But the surviving books from his library show pretty clearly that this was a year for writing, not for reading.

On 3 May 1865 Kate Gansevoort wrote from Albany to Henry: "Tom spent a day with us on his way to Boston — He & Mr Hoadley are deep in the Petroleum Speculation — have purchased quantities of Land in Western Virginia and are making money very rapidly." Tom had come back from the latest voyage of the *Bengal* with capital to invest, and was ready now to cash in on the postwar economy. The women could not keep him at the Mansion House, where they were still seriously inconvenienced by the war, which had swallowed up laborers and had slowed immigration to the point that servants were almost impossible to find. Augusta became so desperate that she took a train to New York City without an escort, as Maria wrote Kate Gansevoort on 5 July: "Augusta driven by dire necessity took on Thursday morning the 29 June the early train of cars, to New York. She arrived there at three ½ O clock & quite astonished Herman & Lizzie at her unexpected appearance." Augusta brought back Wilhelm and Anna Muller, a German couple with almost no English, although Wilhelm proved a fast learner, and both could milk a cow competently. Besides the Mullers, Maria had the Landons, "my farmer & wife."

In mid-August 1865 Herman visited at Gansevoort along with Allan's three younger daughters, as Maria wrote to Kate Gansevoort on 17 August. Melville was entertained on Sunday the sixteenth by "a band of music the Cornet band of Fort Edward, thought here to be wonderful performers, they were dressed in long red coats & made a fine appearance, fifteen in number, large fine looking men." Augusta shepherded Herman, Florence, Kitty, and Lucy "to the Picnic," where they "had a grand supply of iced cakes, sugar-plums, peaches nuts, biscuit &c, quantities left were given to the poor." Some of the younger girls, Maria said, perhaps meaning her granddaughters, "wore white dresses wreaths on the head bare arms & pink cotton bows behind crossing the bust." Fifteen hundred persons were there when "about three O clock a tremendous wind came up filling the air with sand, the sky became black, & all the picnickers, rushed to the Church or tumbled into their waggons, galloping home, Augusta & her party returned blew home for the wind was fair." Then the rain "fell in torrents." After such a long season of watching for and of witnessing prodigies conjointly meeting, as in *Julius Caesar*, it was hard now for people like Maria and her son Herman to take the simple view again, and say, " 'These are their reasons: they are natural.' "

Lizzie was expected at Gansevoort in a few days with Bessie and Fanny. Malcolm and Stanwix spent their vacation with their Aunt Fanny at the Hoadleys in New Bedford, Fanny having gone there in March, when Kate found she was pregnant, and remained. It was probably this year that Malcolm (and Stanwix) went with the Hoadleys to Horseneck Beach, between New Bedford and Newport, across the horse's neck of land that protects Westport Point from the Sound, perhaps taking a ferry rather than making a complicated land and water trip by Westport and then down to the Sound. Herman, Lizzie, and their girls returned to New York early in September, and Allan's daughters went to Pittsfield, leaving Maria and Augusta alone after early September. It may have been this year that the Melvilles stopped by Albany and gave Uncle Peter a chance to traumatize their younger daughter when he noticed her silence at the dinner table in the grand octagonal room: "Fanny, lay down your knife and fork, and make a remark!" On 26 September Colonel Henry Gansevoort wrote Kate that Allan had brought his children down from Pittsfield so they could go to school, and that Allan had plans for himself and Jane: "He thinks of going abroad." In early October 1865 the Melvilles assured the family at Gansevoort that Herman had been "unusually well" ever since his visit there. Both Herman and Tom began urging Maria and Augusta to come down to New York, but the mother and daughter delayed, Maria going to Pittsfield. Maria wrote to Kate Gansevoort on 12 October from a scarcely recognizable Arrowhead: "The country looks splendid gorgeous, some of the woods look like a garden of gigantic tulips. Allan has made great improvements here, both within & out of doors —Arrowhead looks like a different place, it is now a beautiful place. Allan has put out a great many Norway pines, & dwarf fruit trees, built a new barn & out houses—laid out new paths &c." All Herman had needed was money.

On 24 October 1865 Kate Hoadley gave birth to her third child and first son, Francis (Frankie). Fanny had been with her, and Helen probably came down to New Bedford also. The second week of November, Allan and Jane sailed for Europe, having sold the Thirty-fifth Street house and left the girls at Mrs. Hoffman's boarding school. Maria and Helen went to Albany about the time Allan and Jane sailed, staying with the Gansevoorts while they attended a wedding, easier now, month by month, about taking advantage of Peter and Susan's hospitality. Allan's daughters, Maria wrote to Kate Gansevoort on 12 October, were "well & full of happiness in the prospect of passing Thanksgiving at Winyah." The Latherses, with their eldest daughter, Carrie, had just returned from England and France, and had "brought a great many pretty things with them, which the dear little girls are so anxious to see." Far better a Thanksgiving with their own Aunt Abby and Uncle Richard than their stepmother.

Henry Gansevoort was stationed at Fortress Monroe, having evaded an assignment to the Dry Tortugas. Kate wrote him on 28 November that "Aunt Melville" had given "a very bad account of Cousin Guert Gansevoort —that he is failing gradually. The Doctors say he has dropsy of the heart— the same disease Leonard died of last Spring." Resisting the urgings of Herman and Tom, Maria and Augusta stayed on at Gansevoort, Augusta wanting to "close the Sabbath School with the year" and Maria wanting to wait until the tax bill came and she could pay it. Helen stayed on with them at Gansevoort for Christmas, as Maria reported to Kate Gansevoort on 21 December: "We have been reading aloud, 'Faith Gartneys Girlhood,' 'The Gayworthys,' by the same author [Mrs. Adeline Whitney]—Helen brought us 'The clever woman of the Family' [by Charlotte Mary Yonge]—which we are now reading in the eve^g aloud." They were expecting "the Capt on Saturday Eveng," 23 December, and hoping he would stay till after New Year's, to escort them to Boston. In New York, wanting *Harper's Weekly* around the house, Melville providently bought bound volumes as Christmas presents: 1861 for Malcolm, 1862 for Stanwix, 1863 for Bessie, 1864 for Fanny, and 1865 for Dolly (Lizzie). Malcolm gave little Fanny an appropriate book: *Ethel's Story: Illustrating the Advantages of Cheerfulness*, by the Child's Friend (Philadelphia). The most painful family loss that year may have been the old one, most keenly felt on 6 December, when Maria Melville and her surviving children consoled each other while remembering that Gansevoort would have been fifty years old. All their lives would have been unimaginably different and better if he had lived.

Two documents that survive from these years are fantasies celebrating perfect family relationships. One is John C. Hoadley's January 1866 letter to Robert Pomeroy, a friend from Pittsfield, declining the invitation to him and Kate to attend the Pomeroys' silver wedding celebration, "that Harvest Home of a quarter of a century of happy wedded life." The Pomeroys shone forth amid the "sordid, low, cold, earthly matches and mis-matches, which almost banish trust in the divine origin of the marriage tie." The other is Milie's essay on "Thanksgiving-Day," written anomalously on 3 April 1865: "Grandma and grandpa are at the head and foot of the table and look down on both sides on a long vista of happy faces. There is Tom, the sailor just promoted to be a capt. happening to arrive in port just in time to rush home for Than[k]sgiving." Allan, "a successful merchant in a large city," brings his wife and children to see Grandma. After dinner, the children play games, and Uncle Tom, "almost buried among the children," recounts "wonderful stories of what he has seen in far off countries." Tom Melville, home from the sea, was a fantasy father, not just to Milie but to her sisters and to her Melville cousins.

In his new status as an author who owed his publisher nothing, Melville seems to have negotiated the publication of *Battle-Pieces* by the Harpers before the end of 1865. Why he would choose the Harpers is hard to understand in the light of his vehement command to Allan in 1860 *not* to have them publish his *Poems*. Perhaps his paying off his debt to them made it easier for him to deal with them, perhaps he had some good personal dealings with Alfred Hudson Guernsey, editor of *Harper's New Monthly Magazine*, or William H. Demarest, the long-time cashier of the company, whom the New York *Tribune* in July 1876 referred to as "a veritable Tim Linkinwater" (the clerk in *Nicholas Nickleby* who glories in the perfection of his ledgers), a goodhearted and popular man. Perhaps he simply lacked the spirit to approach unfamiliar publishers once he saw that for whatever reason the Harpers would be favorably disposed. Their motives are as elusive as his, but perhaps they saw it as enhancing the value of Guernsey's massive compilation of pieces from *Harper's Weekly*, which was finished with the help of Henry Mills Alden in 1868, *Harper's Pictorial History of the Great Rebellion*. No contract has been found, but the Harper accounts of costs and half-profits shows that, without giving Melville an advance, the Harpers took the book at half-profits. The size of the edition is specified in a letter from Demarest to Melville on 7 December 1866 as 1260 copies. Part of the agreement, apparently, was that poems would be featured in *Harper's New Monthly Magazine* before book publication — as it turned out, "The March to the Sea" (February 1866 — copies available by the third week of January); "The Cumberland" (March); "Philip" (April); "Chattanooga" (June); and an anniversary poem for the July 1866 issue, "Gettysburg: — July, 1863."

Far from having to be ashamed of what Herman was now publishing, the Melvilles and Hoadleys and Gansevoorts admired the impeccably patriotic poems. In Albany on 20 January 1866 Kate Gansevoort read "The March to the Sea," in eight stanzas, the last beginning:

> For behind they left a wailing,
>   A terror, and a ban,
> And blazing cinders sailing,
>   And houseless households wan,
> Wide zones of counties paling,
>   And towns where maniacs ran.

She wrote to Henry: "I have been over looking the Harper for Feb^y & find there a piece of Poetry entitled 'The March to the Sea' — I think it is written by Herman Melville as Aunt Melville when here told us a piece of Poetry by Herman would appear in that magazine — I never have read any of his poetry before — *This piece* is very inspiring & describes Sherman's Grand March." From New York on 29 January Tom confirmed her belief: "You were right in your idea that Herman was the author of the 'March to the Sea' in Harpers of Feb. 1866, do you not think it is good. John read it aloud in New Bedford the other evening, he thinks it is splendid." Reliable John Hoadley, whose poetic judgment everyone else in the family deferred to! From New Bedford on 8 February Fanny Melville wrote to Kate Gansevoort: "Did you read 'The March to the Sea' in the last Harpers? It is thought grand by all."

Dr. John Wakefield Francis in the 1858 enlarged and revised edition of *Old New York; or, Reminiscences of the Past Sixty Years* had named Melville in close association with Hawthorne, Tuckerman, and the Duyckincks. Early in February 1866, when Henry T. Tuckerman published his new edition of that book, in his introduction he quoted from an unidentified 1850 New Orleans newspaper a remarkable tribute to Dr. Francis himself; to Rufus Griswold (who had died 27 August 1857), Tuckerman's collaborator on an edition of the poems of Felicia Hemans; to the artist William Edward West ("the friend of Shelley and Byron," who had died on 2 November 1857); and two living friends, Duyckinck and Melville. At Dr. Francis's evening gatherings in the old days Duyckinck could be relied upon to be "critical" (in the sense of judicious?), Melville "taciturn, but genial, and, when warmed-up, capitally racy and pungent." Tuckerman may have written the article; in any case, he had saved it, and printed it as reaffirmation of his affection for Duyckinck and Melville.

Tom decided to extend his stay at East Twenty-sixth Street well into February. Maria visited the Hoadleys and the new baby, and on 6 March was in Brookline, expecting John to escort her when he went to New York the next month, so she could make her own "visit to Herman & Lizzie." She had news for Kate Gansevoort: Malcolm's schooling was over and he had been put to work at Lathers's Great Western Marine Insurance Co.: "He is but 17 years old gets a salary of $200 a year. They all have a fine lunch at the office equal to a dinner, & if kept in after six in the Evening have a regular supper Mr Lathers who is President, is an active industrious man—Prompt, energetic, & just the Man for Malcolm or any other boy." Malcolm's uncles Lem and Sam Shaw made no offer to help prepare him for their own Harvard College or for any other college or to pay any of his educational expenses. Soon after her arrival in New York Maria became ill. On the twenty-third Augusta wrote Kate Gansevoort: "On Tuesday afternoon I received a few lines from Herman saying that Mamma had been quite sick for three days, & although she was then able to sit up, he thought I had better come down as soon as possible." Accordingly, Augusta had packed up at once and took the morning train down on 21 March, arriving to good news: "Found Lizzie & Stannie waiting for me at the dépôt who told me that my dear Mother had improved much since Herman had written me. I found her sitting up but looking very pale & feeling very weak. The doctor however says she will be quite well in a few days." That week, 24 or 26 March, a son, Edmund Griffin Lathers, was born to Abby and Richard Lathers—news that Malcolm would have brought home, even if Lathers had not called at Twenty-sixth Street to share it. On 30 March Melville's aunt Jean Melvill Wright died in Boston at the age of seventy-eight, but probably only Helen attended the funeral: Maria's health absorbed the interest of the others.

Meanwhile, Allan Melville was being dragged through Egypt by the redoubtable Jane. On 23 March 1866 Augusta reported to Kate Gansevoort on letters from the two dated "from Nubian Assuan Feb. 11th when they had begun their voyage up the Nile & closing on their return to Cairo Feb. 26th." Augusta had just received a clipping from the Boston *Daily Advertiser* (21 March) or the Boston *Evening Transcript* (22 March) about how a group of patriotic Americans, including ladies, had celebrated Washington's birthday in Cairo at the "Hotel des Ambassadeurs." Brief speeches had been made "by Messrs. Hale ["the United States Consul-General"], Melville, Atterbury, Tiffany and Appleton, and a number of patriotic songs were sung." That account was just the sort of publicity Jane may have arranged, from Egypt.

The right phrase for her was coined a century later: Jane was ego-tripping, in two senses.

Allan's lungs were affected, Leonard was dead of dropsy, Guert was suffering from the same disease, and Henry Gansevoort was affected by venereal and other infections, perhaps already what was named as his cause of death, gastric fever ending in tubercular consumption. Outwardly healthy enough, still, Henry was behaving badly. The United States, he had decided, owed him a great sum for capturing what Peter Gansevoort referred to as "Mosebys Artillery." He might resign from the army, he might pursue those claims, he might continue to play at being a lawyer and sponge on his father. On 9 March 1866 Peter wrote impatiently, "you now are old enough, to judge for yourself." He queried, "are not your prospects of promotion in the Artillery, much better, than to be a Major of Cavalry?" Malcolm had been placed with Lathers—could no one place the restless, irresponsible Henry? Peter continued: "As you did not like your legal profession—what will you engage in?—This is for you to determine, after careful deliberation—What business, have you thought of? When you let me know, I can give you my opinion."

On 3 April Kate wrote Henry less challengingly, having in her possession a letter Augusta had sent her, from Jane at "Assuan," dated 15 February 1866. The Melvilles and a dozen other Americans had "chartered a steamer which belonged to the Viceroy or Pascha of Egypt & had a very charming time." Jane had laid in her stores in advance:

> Before leaving Cairo they purchased an American Pennant & the materials for a Flag which Mrs M. made on the Steamer & it was used on the Steamer with great ceremonies—a speech was made, "Rally round the Flag Boys" was sung, *Mrs Melville* was complimented, cheers for the flag was given, *cheers* for Mrs Melville & a *"tiger"* & salutes were fired from an American pistol—This flag Mrs M says was the *first* American *flag* that ever floated on a *steamer* up the Nile. So there was some glory in their trip up the Nile.

Not knowing her Cousin Herman's *Pierre*, Kate innocently continued: "You know Henry the Ancients believed that one of the Statues on Memnon uttered Sounds of music as the first rays of the rising sun touched its lips & also as the last rays of the setting sun departed." Having quoting so many of Jane's further observations that she thought she might weary Henry, Kate was pleased that he found the account was "particularly interesting." Captivated by Jane, Henry on 7 April told Kate he was sure he would have "great pleasure in listening to her adventures with Allan in the East and West." Henry the child of privilege added sententiously: "Happy are they who can enjoy such a luxury as the gratification of curiosity in these days of depreciated currency." Maria had never had the luxury of gratifying her curiosity, but she was less worried about money than she had been for perhaps a full half-century. Leaving Augusta "at the 'Manor House' in Gansevoort Cleaning house," all alone, "a jewel in *good works*" (so Kate wrote Henry on 19 April 1866), Maria visited Peter and Susan in Albany. "Aunt Melville is here & looking very well — so subdued & much more congenial & agreeable than ever," Kate wrote. Finding the Gansevoorts barely functioning without a waiter, the resourceful Maria had written to "an *Intelligence Office*" in New York "for a man — after *Father's precise* & perfect order!"

By late April 1866 Maria had received a letter from Jane written from "Jaffa the Ancient Joppa," as Kate explained to Henry, adding serious news (in her letter of 8 May): "Allan was very ill with . . . Fever — a German Physician resident at Jaffa had taken him to his home just out of the city wall's where he was recieving every kindness — Mrs M. has proved herself a kind generous woman. She was alone for two days in the Convent with Allan delirious — & was so faithful to him." Jane never lacked for a heroine in her stories. On 24 May Kate reported belatedly that Maria had heard from Allan three weeks earlier, a letter written himself, from the harbor of Messina, when he had reported himself as "quite recovered from his illness." By early June Allan and Jane had arrived in London, where he made a nuisance of himself at the legation. On 4 June the secretary of the legation, Benjamin Moran, wrote in his diary: "Mr. Allan Melville, a brother of Herman Melville and of Gansevoort Melville, who died when secretary of Legation here . . . brought me a letter from Capt. Hoadley. This is rather a pleasant good looking man, but rather exacting and inconsiderate. He has been in Egypt all winter & altho I was busy wanted to tell me all his adventures." The tourist was a bad penny: "Mr. Allan Melville has been here again. He is considerable of a bore." Moran already knew that a big river ran through Egypt to the Mediterranean and that near the sea there were big old pyramids and a sphynx, and he had a job to do.

In 1866 Tom and John were still speculating in petroleum, and Tom was on the move. On 30 May he was ready to leave Gansevoort for some weeks in East Twenty-sixth Street. When she wrote to her Aunt Fanny (in Brookline) on 17 June, Milie explained that Alice the cook would not go up to open Arrowhead, despite Jane's instructions from London. In this letter she portrayed Tom at family play with Herman's and Allan's children: "We saw Uncle Tom after he had come down from Gansevoort, and he took us eight children around to get some soda water. The man asked if we were all his children. Uncle Tom laughed and said that we were his nieces and nephews, 'because,' said the man, 'my sister has twelve.' 'I pity her,' replied Uncle

Tom." Milie was anxious for the return of the travelers, and perplexed about the possibility that she would have to leave Mrs. Hoffman's: "sometimes I feel so sad, to think it may be my last at boarding school. I love it so, it is a second home to me, this my sixth year here, and I expect to come for two more. I love Mrs Hoffman so much, and I feel so much interest in all concerning it." Milie had been unable to have "much merrymaking" on Lucy's birthday because 14 June came on Thursday, a school day, but on Saturday someone (Tom? Lizzie?) took Allan's and Herman's daughters to "an ice-cream saloon," and "being a warm day it was very nice." They didn't have ice cream at school as often as they had had it at home, when Sophia was alive. Milie sent much love to Uncle George and Aunt Helen, who had cared for her during some summers of her woebegone and what she self-reproachfully called her willful childhood.

The Melville and Gansevoort women knew politicians were fighting about Reconstruction, but on a day-to-day basis the women were struggling with the now-intractable servant problem. On 8 June 1866 Kate set Henry straight about his suggestion that he select "a black waiter for Father." As children in Albany, Peter and Maria had lived in a household with slaves, and there were black Gansevoorts in the area still, so their attitudes toward black servants tended to be matter of fact. The Great Famine had filled the Northeast with young Irish girls willing to work for their keep and a pittance more, but the supply had dwindled in the war, and now servants could pick and choose their employers. Kate wrote Henry: "The female portion of our domestics would not live here with a black waiter so that is out of the question." The Gansevoorts were making do with "a young Irish lad about 17 years old," slow, "rather inclined to be lazy," not possessed of "a very attentive memory," but acceptable to the female servants. Maria hired blacks without thinking much about it. On New Year's Day, 1867, "surrounded by heaps of snow & a daz[z]ling whiteness covering every thing," Maria wrote Kate Gansevoort: "We have a darkey at work sawing & splitting wood in the wood house another darkie in the kitchen which gives an occasional dark shade to surrounding whiteness." (Attitudes were unpredictable: Melville's John Paul Jones might hotbunk it with a black at sea, but Melville's daughter Frances in her old age would not eat food she knew had been prepared by or served by a black person.)

Allan and Jane returned from their tour abroad on 29 June 1866. Jane had brought gifts, some of too personal a nature (two white muslin neck ties for Henry); Lizzie could not have approved, nor Maria. Allan found himself overwhelmed with documents to deal with. By 20 July he had caught up enough with some old news to write Cousin Henry about Herman: "Did you see his poem 'The March to the Sea' in Harpers monthly for February. It is published in advance of a volume of Poems he has in press shortly to appear." Allan had not yet gone up to Gansevoort to see his mother, but Herman, he reported, was going up the next morning. Tom returned to Gansevoort from Parkersburg in the second week of July, and went down to Albany to escort Kate Gansevoort up to Gansevoort on the seventeenth. Kate Curtis had been there for some days. On 18 July Kate Gansevoort reported to her stepmother, Aunt Susan, that "Gus & Fanny" were at home, that "Kate Hoadley & her three children" were there (baby Frank's first visit), and that they expected "Mr Hoadley, Herman, & Allan" on Saturday. Further news was that an unpredictable member of the family, Stanwix Gansevoort, had shown up: "By invitation not to our surprise Cousin Stanny Gansevoort arrived here from Glens Falls this morning." Kate thought him (as she wrote her stepmother) "a small man" and "out of 'his sphere'" even around his sister, aunt, and cousins. He avoided "the 'refining sex'" and devoted his attentions to the vegetable garden instead, longing, she may have guessed, for the company of hard-drinking fellows like Ned Buntline and his brother Guert. And he brought bad news: "Cousin Guert is a miserable sufferer — the neuralgia is gradually killing him." She asked Henry if he had ever seen their cousin Stanwix Gansevoort, adding: "he is a very *peculiar* man, one I should judge had thrown away his advantages — He seemed so out of his sphere here, among his cousins & with his sister too!" She continued: "Never throw away refinements & the restraints of society Henry — they assist in the civilization of man." She knew nothing of Stanwix's mother's appeals to Peter Gansevoort, about the time of Kate's birth, to settle the estate while she most needed the money, while Stanwix was in hourly need of education.

On 19 July Tom and Kate Gansevoort and little Lottie Hoadley went walking to the mill, the dam, and in the woods. Tom was helping at Gansevoort again. On 21 July Kate Gansevoort wrote her stepmother that Tom was "out showing their man 'Henry' how to work," and emphasized the hopes the women at the Mansion House had for Tom: "He seems quite to like Gansevoort & when his oil duties in Parkersburg East [West] Va. allow he spends his time here. This place needs a man & they all hope Tom will eventually settle here." Kate was so impressed with her Cousin Tom that she deputed Susan to spend an enormous sum, anywhere from ten to eighteen dollars, at Wendells & Roberts for "a gentlemans *travelling bag, large* enough to hold something & not be too heavy," and marked with the name "Thomas Melville." The schedule at Gansevoort was set: "We Breakfast at 7 A.M. Dine at 12. M[eridian]. Tea at 5.30." Their fare was "delicious, fresh fruit (berries) cream & butter & vegetables." One took turns swinging in the hammock, and one took a nap (a rule of the house). Herman and John arrived at Gansevoort on Saturday night, 21 July, having traveled together all the way or rendezvoused in Albany. Kate Gansevoort wrote Henry on 23 July that she thought Herman looked "thin & miserable"—a telling description.

That summer, on 23 July 1866, Augusta got a rare treat, for once, joining an excursion to Lake George with Kate Gansevoort, John and Kate Hoadley, and Tom. Kate Gansevoort wrote Henry on 2 August a description interesting in itself, not least of the various modes of transportation required on land and water. Tom's nautical skills were put to good use: "In the Evening when the moon was up we took a row on the Lake—The Loch Katrine of America—I never shall forget that hour. Nature was so calm & serene & the pale moon shone on us in all her beauty—Mr Hoadley & Capt. Tom. Melville were our oarsmen & Augusta Melville & I the fair dreamers on that moonlight ride... quite congenial spirits." They took a steamer and coaches to "the Fort & *Hotel* just *on the* banks of Lake Champlain," where they watched passengers landing from Whitehall. Kate Hoadley rested while the others walked to the ruins of the old fort. In 1866 all that was left were the walls of the officers' quarters, but the visitors "could trace the *fortifications*—built on the form of *a star.*" They had "a jolly loquacious driver who amused the passengers by telling, in his 'peculiar manner', about the Hero's—& history of the Early days of our glorious Republic!" This was just the sort of guide to make historically minded pilgrims recite Ethan Allen's thunderous command to the British in 1775 to surrender the fort at once "in the name of the Great Jehovah and the Continental Congress!" Kate Gansevoort could still visualize one particular spectacle, near the highest of the mountain peaks, when "the sun was shining brightly & it rained in torrents, each drop seemed a diamond & on the other hand was a rainbow & we were steaming just in the arc of the bow." That being late July 1866, she saw both the green foliage of what seemed early spring and also "deep autumnal hues." As an Albany aristocrat from a family which patronized contemporary artists, Kate thought in practical terms: "I wish some artist could have sketched it as it appeared to us. It would scarcely seem a natural view—perhaps Bierstadts pencil might portray it correctly."

Herman missed this excursion in 1866, although he was still at Gansevoort. Lizzie was in Boston, and Malcolm (separately?) had "gone East during his vacation" from his job, perhaps again to New Bedford. During at least part of her visit to Boston, Lizzie left her daughters in Brookline with Helen, for she was in profound distress and needed to speak freely with her family. At this time, as at earlier times, Lizzie and the other Shaws conferred about her marital woes; this is clear from the letter Samuel Shaw wrote to Dr. Henry W. Bellows on 6 May 1867. On this occasion, and not for the first time, Sam urged Lizzie to acknowledge that Melville's treatment of her warranted her leaving him. The reasons are not named, other than that

Elizabeth seemed convinced her husband was insane. At some time between 1861 and 1866, Sam and Lem, at least, had resolved that Lizzie should "come to Boston as if on a visit . . . and that when here her friends" (meaning relatives) "should inform her husband that a separation, for the present at least, has been decided on," and that they would rely upon the testimony of Herman's long-time acquaintance Dr. Augustus K. Gardner as to her soundness of judgment. This 1867 statement makes it explicit that Lizzie had consulted Dr. Gardner in New York well before that year. Malcolm can hardly have escaped some of the conferences, even if they were merely whispered. Malcolm, on the scene, and half a Shaw (but not the worst, not a Savage), was just the age to see himself as obligated to be his mother's knight. If not quite yet the slayer of the tyrant Macbeth, he had, long before, proclaimed himself the gallant Cornishman who slew the giant Cormogan. Poor Malcolm was caught in the middle, unable, at seventeen, to interpose himself between his father and his mother, however sad she was, however deeply she was suffering.

On his forty-seventh birthday, 1 August, Herman and Tom spent a day at Saratoga Lake. On 24 July the Harpers had sent Melville their eighteenth account with him, showing a balance due him of $64.31, and they or someone had sent early copies of *Battle-Pieces* up to Gansevoort, for on his birthday Herman inscribed a copy to his mother and another to "Mrs H M Griggs from her affectionate brother H. M." Melville inscribed copies to his wife and his stepmother-in-law as well, though where he was when he inscribed them is not known. Augusta mentioned to Kate Gansevoort on 2 August that the hammock was still "in high favor." Augusta herself "enjoyed a quiet swing last evening" (the birthday) while the others played croquet, Herman showing himself "quite a hand at it." On 4 August, Kate Gansevoort, back in Albany, wrote in her diary: "Tom Melville came down and spent two hours with us." Herman had been uncertain about whether he could make "a flying visit" to Albany, since he had to be in New York on Thursday, 9 August, when Malcolm would arrive from Boston. Herman did manage to pay the Albany Gansevoorts the visit he had talked of the day after Tom went down, stopping in the morning in Lansingburgh and arriving "before 2 Oclk to Dinner," then leaving on the sixth after an early breakfast.

On 8 August Allan was at last at Gansevoort, doing what he liked best. Maria signed an indenture conveying to Allan Melville and Thomas Melville (for one dollar) a large lot in the village, lot No. 17 roughly between the Snook Kil on the west at the Saw Mill Lot, along the water course used as a tail race of Uncle Herman's Grist Mill, then southeasterly along the center of the road leading to Glens Falls to a point where the center line of Catherine Street intersected then went northeasterly to the center line of Birkby Street then west to the first point on the Snook Kil, "excepting therefrom the Dutch Reformed church Lot & also the Cemetery Lot." She covenanted and agreed to leave Allan, Tom, and their heirs and assigns in "Quiet and Peaceable Possession" and she swore to "forever Warrant and Defend" the conveyance "against any person whomsoever lawfully claiming the same or any part thereof." Maria may have thought that the lot was in danger of being claimed by another person, as the whole of the property had been for many years, and that Allan and Tom would be in a better position to defend it than she would. But the transaction could not have been pleasant for her, especially since on 9 August she had to appear before Harlow Laurence, justice of the peace, and sign the indenture drafted the previous day.

On 8 August Tom reported to Kate Gansevoort that Allan would take Maria with him to Arrowhead if she would go, and that he, Tom, would pick her up on his return from a trip to Boston. Meanwhile, Tom, not Allan, was supervising repairs on the dam and the mill in hope of having them "in running order" soon: "As I have four different sets of men employed it keeps me very busy looking out for them, as they all need watching." Maria and Allan surprised the Albany family on the eleventh, on their way to Arrowhead, where Maria intended to pass ten days or more with "M^{rs} M & the grand children." In writing Henry that day, Kate said Allan looked well, but had told her he had "not yet recovered his strength." Tom wrote Kate Gansevoort on 21 August, rejoicing that Henry was home for a visit and wanting to show him the improvements at Gansevoort: "The 'Dam,' & 'Mill,' I am happy to say are now finished, and the Mill is running better then it ever did before, having a[n] abundant supply of water, and superior cleaning works. I was unable to leave here last Thursday, on account of a[n] alteration that I wanted to make in the Dam." John Hoadley was there, unexpectedly, and having been "cultivating his side whiskers according to Kate's directions" ("is he not a[n] obedient husband"). Kate and the children were staying until 10 September, but John and Tom were going east together on 22 August. Peter and Susan vacationed in Nantucket.

Back at Fort Monroe on 1 September, Henry wrote his father: "Have you seen Herman Melvilles new work 'Battle-Pieces.' There are some beautiful things in it. Unfortunately he has so much of Emerson & transcendentalism in his writing that it never will really touch the common heart. Still I must say that this work shows him to be a poet of high order & certainly of originality." Henry, the arrogant wastrel who had not seen the " 'pint' " of "The Town-Ho's Story" when he looked it over in *Harper's* a decade and a half earlier, was the first in the family to cavil. He had spent too much time in the classrooms and around Lemuel Shaw Jr. in Boston. By that time, reviews of *Battle-Pieces* had been appearing for a week. (The book and the reviews are the subject of the next chapter.) Tom wrote Kate Gansevoort on 2 September from Brookline, having bought his own copy of *Battle-Pieces* the previous week in Boston: "Mamma has got tired of waiting for me & has returned to Gansevoort. I am staying at Helens & having a very pleasant visit, what a lovely place Brookline is & what delightful drives there are around it. John is staying here & has his horses at the village, which makes it very pleasant. George went to New Bedford & drove them up for him, they are a very fine pair & we have had some splendid drives with them. Helen is very well, Hermans two girls are staying with her, so she has quite a houseful." Tom had been to 49 Mt. Vernon Street and had found nothing amiss: "I have called on Mrs Shaw what a lovely old lady she is and what a pleasant interesting person to talk to. She lookes as young as she did when I stayed at her house fourteen years ago." Andrew Johnson had been in Albany, so Tom wanted to know if Kate had seen him and what she thought. Eastern Massachusetts was Radical Republican territory: "The Bostonians, run him & his speeches down fearfully, and think that he is trying to destroy all the good effects of the war."

In Albany Kate Gansevoort also got a copy of *Battle-Pieces*, but wrote her brother on 17 September: "I must say I cannot get interested in his style of Poetry. It is too deep for my comprehension." Tom wrote Kate Gansevoort from New York on 23 September with news that John Hoadley had resigned his position in New Bedford and was either going to Europe or moving to Boston in 1867. More important was his sister's servant problem: "Kate is all alone, not a servant in the house & no prospects of getting any. Helen & George are well, Helen is looking splendidly she is a *dear good sister*, a *noble woman*, George is a lucky man to have such a wife." Allan and Jane were expected back from Arrowhead, and planned to "go to housekeeping again in 35th Street, near where they lived before." By then Kate Gansevoort had expressed herself on the Boston Radicals: "Like yourself Kate I hope, & trust, that the Conservatives will gain the election this fall, although from present appearances I am afraid that the Radicals will carry the day by a large majority, & if they do I expect their [there] will be troublesome times in Washington this winter." They had seen Major Edwin Lansing in town, and Herman had inscribed a copy of *Battle-Pieces* to him as "a souvenir of his soldier hospitality."

From Fort Monroe on 26 September Henry asked his father for an allowance of sixty dollars a month, since military pay had been reduced. Peter at once agreed. In the middle of October Peter and Susan spent a night in Saratoga and took the train the next day to stay with Maria for three days, a visit Maria had long hoped for. Kate wrote Henry on 22 October: "They found Mr Greenleaf an old friend of Father's at Gansevoort saw Uncle

George Lansing, Mr Markle the Clergyman of the Dutch Church at Gansevoort & all the old residents at Gansevoort—and had a very delightful time, were really sorry to come home again—Aunt Melville, Augusta, & Fannie are alone at Gansevoort[.] Tom. is at Parkersburg Va. & will probably remain there this winter perhaps make it his home, Farming does not seem his Specialty." Augusta soon went to the Manor House to help the Van Rensselaers.

In Boston on 2 November Elizabeth Shaw Melville's aunt Lucretia Knapp died. Four days later her will was probated, showing the four principal heirs to be nephews and nieces, Charles Dillaway, Mary E. Dillaway, John Oakes Shaw, and Elizabeth S. Melville. She had left Lizzie thirty dollars to buy a memorial gift, also her fur coat, all her books, and the furniture in her bedroom. Politics continued to be fiery everywhere, as if the war had not been won. Maria wrote to Kate Gansevoort on 4 December about "a union meeting" at their church, to which Methodists had come. She and Fanny stayed home, but Augusta had gone and heard a sermon from Professor King of Fort Edward Seminary: "It seems Dr King is a red hot Radical, it was a fiery discourse. He said he would like to tear up our Constitution & write another, for our Constitution might have been written by infidels. He would impeach our President Andrew Johnson &c, &c, and thumped our Bible at a great rate, so that its friends feared for its safety. Many persons looked uneasy, uncomfortable as if they could not agree with the noisy demonstrations, & wild words of the speaker." Milie had written her grandmother about being allowed to attend a reception at the Century Club for the layer of the Atlantic cable, Cyrus Field. Maria sent the letter to Kate Gansevoort: "She is so young & artless that her first appearance in public in its full impression upon her mind is very interesting to me, & thought you would perhaps be pleased to read her description of the great event & I begged Fanny to let me enclose it to you for perusal—Please return it to me."

Then something happened that may have seemed insignificant to many in the family, something that would not amount to much; on the other hand, it may have seemed momentous, at least to Melville himself. On 28 November, the day before Thanksgiving, Henry A. Smythe, the collector of customs for the port of New York, wrote to the secretary of the treasury, nominating Melville as inspector at four dollars per diem. This was the "Mr Smyth merchant of N.Y." who had traveled with Melville in Switzerland and Germany in April 1857. On 30 November, Melville's appointment was approved in Washington by William E. Chandler, assistant secretary of the treasury. On 5 December, Melville swore the usual (and much-violated) oath that he would use the best of his endeavors "to prevent and detect frauds in relation to the duties imposed by the Laws of the United States," and that he had not bribed anyone to obtain the office, and that he would support the Constitution. He also took the new oath prescribed in an act of 2 July 1862 (the loyalty oath he had discussed in his "Supplement" to *Battle-Pieces*, published more than three months earlier):

> I, Herman Melville, do solemnly swear, that I have never voluntarily borne arms against the United States since I have been a citizen thereof; that I have voluntarily given no aid, countenance, counsel, or encouragement to persons engaged in armed hostility thereto, that I have neither sought, nor accepted, nor attempted to exercise the functions of any office whatever, under any authority, or pretended authority; in hostility to the United States; . . . and that I will well and faithfully discharge the duties of the office on which I am about to enter, saying nothing, doing nothing, and encouraging nothing which tends to weaken loyalty and strengthening treason and rebellion within the United States of America. so help me god.

Afterward, Melville called on Richard Lathers, but he was "too early" and missed him.

It was Lathers, perhaps calling in some chit from Smythe, who had assured Melville his position, for Melville wrote to him, apparently on 6 December: "Accept my sincere thanks for your friendly and successful effort on my behalf." He had received his warrant "yesterday" and was ready to "go at it to day." He went at it for nineteen years. That first day, when Melville reported to work James S. Benedict gave him a note to carry to Richard Henry Stoddard, whom Hawthorne had helped to this job, in another room: "He seems a good fellow, Dick, and says he knows you, though perhaps he doesn't, but anyhow be kind to him if this infernal weather will let you be to anybody." Stoddard was the American Keats, author of an ode to Autumn immortalized in the Duyckincks' *Cyclopædia* ("Divinest Autumn! . . . / Sometimes we see thee stretched upon the ground, / In fading woods where acorns patter fast. . . . / Sometimes at work where ancient granary-floors [doors?] / Are open wide . . . / And sometimes fast asleep at noontide hours, / Pillowed on sheaves, and shaded from the heat, / With Plenty at thy feet, / Braiding a coronet of oaten straw and flowers!") He was the husband of the magnificent Elizabeth (a cousin of Hawthorne's, and like Emily Dickinson an American Brontë), and the intimate friend of Bayard Taylor. Stoddard recalled that looked up when Melville handed him the note, and "recognized a famous writer" he had met some years before: "no American writer was more widely known in the late forties and early fifties in his own country and England than Melville." Stoddard had read some of Melville's war poems already, and perhaps had reviewed *Battle-Pieces* in the *World*. Soon he asked for and received from Melville a handwritten copy of "Sheridan at Cedar Creek," which Melville made for him, under the title "Philip," as in the April *Harper's*. This was flattering attention that eased Melville's entrance into his work at his first post, District Office No. 4, North River, at 207 West Street. ("North River" was still being used for the Hudson.) It was a while before the courtesies ceased: on the nineteenth Melville gave a copy of *Battle-Pieces* to another employee of the Custom House, Colonel Henry L. Potter, and even a whole year later he gave a copy of *Typee* to Smythe. This year, 1866, in the Christmas Day issue the Springfield *Republican* reported that Smythe had been "completely worn out by the pressure upon him by office seekers and their friends, and announces that he is going to take a vacation."

On Christmas Day, 1866, Maria wrote again to Kate Gansevoort, explaining that Milie was determined to take refuge in school, the unexpressed alternative being to stay in the same house with Jane and her friends: "She is yet at School & does not dream of leaving it, indeed she told me she would rather continue going to school for several years longer than go into company." The girls had stayed on at Arrowhead, "waiting for their house in 35th Street to be repaired &c." — a different house near the old one on Thirty-fifth Street. They were to return to Mrs. Hoffman's school after the holidays. Tom had returned from New Bedford on the twentieth, bearing gifts from the Hoadleys, but suffering: "The first three days he was nearly petrified by the excessive cold weather." She did not mention Herman's new occupation in that letter. Perhaps she did in another; but perhaps she did not think that Herman would be able to keep it for very long. By the time Melville started work in the Custom House, all the significant known reviews of *Battle-Pieces* had appeared except the ones in the *Independent* and the *Atlantic Monthly*. By the time those two appeared, in January and February 1867, Melville had become habituated to his six-day-a-week, four-dollar-a-day job.

[27]

Battle-Pieces
Poet, Poems, Reviewers, 1866

※

> In this ["his spirit of partisanship"] Milton resembles Dante (the only one of the moderns with whom he has anything in common,) and it is remarkable that Dante, as well as Milton, was a political partisan.
>
> Melville marks this passage in William Hazlitt's
> "On Shakspeare and Milton," Lecture 3 of *Lectures on the English Poets*
> (William S. Reese Collection)

ABOUT THE TIME he moved to New York, Melville had come to see himself as the Gansevoort grandson who would take on the role for the nation in the Civil War that the Hero of Fort Stanwix had taken in the Revolutionary War. By early 1864 he had taken up his patriotic and poetic duty to record the war. In a note prefixed to *Battle-Pieces*, his book of Civil War poems, Melville said that "with few exceptions" the poems "originated in an impulse imparted by the fall of Richmond" — which is to imply that most of the poems were composed after 3 April 1865. More precisely, the end of the war may have determined him to make a book of poems he had been composing "without reference to collective arrangement" and others he had not yet composed. He had been writing his war poems long before the fall of Richmond. He probably wrote "The Scout toward Aldie" in 1864, soon after his adventures in the desecrated terrain of Virginia, near the Blue Ridge Mountains, perhaps during his stay at the contrastingly bucolic, placid Gansevoort, at the edge of the Adirondacks.

A dozen years earlier Melville had striven with what he later called the Angel, Art, in dubious battle on the slope of Arrowhead, in the most intense aesthetic struggle in the English language yet engaged in on the continent. The writing of *Battle-Pieces* involved no such Miltonic contest, but required instead shifting strategies to master the flood of war news so as to evoke a specific, personal mood in every poem. At no time did Melville set out to give an unvarnished picture of what war really was like. On the contrary, he had marked and taken to heart this passage in Wordsworth's "Essay Supplementary to the Preface":

> The appropriate business of poetry, (which, nevertheless, if genuine, is as permanent as pure science,) her appropriate employment, her privilege and her *duty*, is to treat of things not as they *are*, but as they *appear*; not as they exist in themselves, but as they *seem* to exist to the *senses* and to the *passions*. What a world of delusion does this acknowledged principle prepare for the inexperienced! what temptations to go astray are here held forth for them whose thoughts have been little disciplined by the understanding, and whose feelings revolt from the sway of reason!

Melville had at least made it his business to witness war at first hand, but he emphasized that he was capturing in the poems the aspects which episodes of the strife took on in his memory, his variable moods coloring the way he recalled the battles. Like Wordsworth, he was attempting to do the proper business of poetry by treating of things as they appeared to him, as they *seemed* to exist to his senses and passions. Melville's decision not to aim for Dutch realism or what was then being called Pre-Raphaelite realism was not designed to win him the widest audience, but it was a conscious literary choice made under the influence of the former poet laureate, dead only a decade and a half.

Melville also decided very consciously that a spare diction would befit a poet determined to repudiate gaudy idealizing of military glory, especially since (a confirmed Utilitarian might say) this war exalted impersonal mechanical power over personal heroism:

> Plain be the phrase, yet apt the verse,
>   More ponderous than nimble;
> For since grimed War here laid aside
>   His Orient pomp, 'twould ill befit
>   Overmuch to ply
> The rhyme's barbaric cymbal.

These lines from "A Utilitarian View of the Monitor's Fight" are fitted to the speaker, one very like the "Englishman of the old order" in the previous poem, "The Temeraire." Not just for this poem but others, Melville was following "The Verse" section preceding *Paradise Lost*, where Milton declared that "Rime" was "no necessary Adjunct or true Ornament of Poem or good Verse, in longer Works especially, but the Invention of a barbarous Age, to set off wretched matter and lame Meeter." (The underlining is Melville's in his copy of Milton.) True "musical delight," Milton declared, "consists only in apt Numbers, fit quantity of Syllables, and the sense variously drawn out from one verse into another, not in the jingling sound of like endings" (again, the underlining is Melville's). Apt the verse! In *The Poetical*

Works and Remains of Henry Kirke White, which Melville had bought during his quest for an aesthetic credo in 1862, he had read (and underlined four words in) the comment that "Harmonious modulations, and <u>unvarying exactness of measure</u>, totally precluding sublimity and fire, have reduced our fashionable poetry to mere sing-song"—a good modern affirmation of Milton's principles.

In the whole of what became *Battle-Pieces* Melville eschewed insistent rhyming and ostentatious diction, specifically under the influence of Milton, but also very much under the influence of Jeffrey's essay on Alfieri, which he had read so carefully early in 1862. Melville would do what Jeffrey said Alfieri had done: he would work with "a fine and careful hand," avoiding "Figures of mere ostentation. — Show-pieces of fine writing." Alfieri had sacrificed "flow & sweetness" in striving to give "force & energy by condensation & emphasis & inversion." Alfieri had achieved, Jeffrey said, a chastened gravity and had displayed "Temperance and propriety of delineation of the passions." The aesthetic tenets he had written down in his Vasari were in his mind as he wrote his war poems; he would value "completeness, fullness," even in a short poem, over "fine writing" and high polish.

Battle-Pieces was a more literary book than the reviewers realized, and not only in Melville's choice of Wordsworth for authority on poetic distance from subject and his choice of Milton (and of Alfieri as interpreted by Jeffrey) as authorities for a spareness in rhyme and diction. The poems Melville relegated to the back of *Battle-Pieces* under the subtitle "Verses Inscriptive and Memorial" (such as "Inscription for Graves at Pea Ridge, Arkansas") demonstrate how closely he was working in another British literary tradition. Just as he had borrowed the idea of "Extracts" for *Moby-Dick* from Southey's *The Doctor*, now he borrowed the genre of "Inscriptions" from Southey, the poet laureate from 1813 throughout his youth in Albany and Lansingburgh, and indeed until 1843, when he was in the Pacific, as well as from Southey's successor, Wordsworth, who wrote a group of "Inscriptions" (pp. 331–34 in Melville's edition) as well as an appendix called "Essay Upon Epitaphs." At least one "Inscription," "A Requiem for Soldiers lost in Ocean Transports," reflected Melville's painstaking analysis of "Lycidas," but the inspiration for "Inscriptions" was Romantic. Being brief by their nature and taking only a matter of hours to compose after reading a particular account of valorous deaths, they would naturally have been among those written before Melville had a fuller sense of what kinds of war poems he might write. When Lieutenant Colonel Alexander Bliss had asked him in March or so of 1864 to contribute a manuscript to be reproduced in facsimile, what Melville very promptly sent was "Inscription For the Slain At Fredericksburgh." Long before the fall of Richmond, Melville had written this particular "Inscription," which he did not collect in *Battle-Pieces*. Just as the "Inscriptions" were conventional, however odd-looking to twenty-first-century readers, so was the "Supplement" part of a literary convention as honorable, almost, as an "envoy." In particular, Melville had pored over Wordsworth's "Essay Supplementary to the Preface" in the 1815 *Lyrical Ballads*.

In contrast to his frequent practice (in *Mardi*, in *Moby-Dick*, especially, and later in *Clarel*), Melville did minimal book-buying for use in *Battle-Pieces*. After the winter and early spring of 1862 he had paused in his book-buying, and toward the end of the year he moved all his books from Arrowhead into the rented house on South Street. He may have bought almost no books in 1863, the year he moved his library and everything else he owned twice, first to Allan's house on Thirty-fifth Street in New York, then to Twenty-sixth Street. He bought *Poems* by Elizabeth Barrett Browning (2 vols.; New York, 1860) in June 1864, and marked it casually. (No one has ever reported seeing his copy of any of Robert Browning's poems, which he must have owned in one or more editions.) After the war, on 18 August 1865, late in his work on the poems, he charged on his Harper's account a copy of *The Story of the Great March* (Sherman's march from Atlanta to the sea) by Brevet Major George Ward Nichols, and may have made some use of it.

Melville's notes to some of the poems in *Battle-Pieces* ("The Stone Fleet," "The Frenzy in the Wake: Sherman's advance through the Carolinas") suggest that through the war he may have been clipping from newspapers items that caught his eye. Much of the time, Allan was in a position to supply him with papers when he needed to look up a second or third article on a particular battle or to locate a piece he realized he would need. Melville's old friend Robert Tomes, who had written *Panama in 1855*, later had gone to Japan with the Matthew Perry expedition and written *The Americans in Japan* (New York: Appleton, 1857). Just before the war, Tomes had made himself into an American military historian, and then had issued three volumes on *The War with the South: A History of the Great American Rebellion*, the last ready in 1865; some of the many engravings were from drawings that Melville's illustrator friend Felix Darley had made for the volume. In 1864 and 1865 Melville saw much of Evert A. Duyckinck, who had been collecting documents for what turned out to be another three-volume *National History of the War for the Union, Civil, Military and Naval, Founded on Official and Other Authentic Documents* (copyrighted in 1861 by Johnson, Fry & Company of 27 Beekman Street, but not published until after the war was over). As Duyckinck's title pages explained, the volumes were illustrated with highly finished steel engravings, including battle scenes by sea and land, and full-length portraits of naval and military heroes, engraved from original paintings by Alonzo Chappel (a phenomenally speedy brushman) and by the young Thomas Nast, not yet known as a political satirist. Melville may never have owned a set, although John C. Hoadley bought the three volumes and had them bound in half-calf, gilt. Still, Melville had access at need to documents that went into the *National History of the War* as well as the rest of the massive array of documents which Duyckinck gathered before ultimately rejecting many of them from the compilation. Nothing has been adduced to show that anything in Duyckinck's volumes was irrefutably the *specific* source for anything in *Battle-Pieces*, but supplementary information was available to Melville, in abundance, in Duyckinck's working files. Whether Melville knew the volumes or not is not known, but he would naturally have consulted his friend's trove of documents.

Melville had access all through the war to *Harper's Weekly*, a lavish source of news and engravings made from on-the-scene photographs and sketches. Melville also had access to some of the eleven volumes of the *Rebellion Record*, the first volume published in 1861, three more in 1862, two in 1863, two (including the supplemental volume) in 1864, one in 1865, and one in 1866; another followed in 1867 and the last in 1868. The volumes consisted of, as the subtitle said, *A Diary of American Events, with Documents, Narratives, Illustrative Incidents, Poetry, Etc.*, and became Melville's source for many newspaper reports of battles (as he specifies in his note to "Rebel Color-bearers at Shiloh: A plea against the vindictive cry raised by civilians shortly after the surrender at Appomattox"). The note to one of the "Inscriptions," "On a natural Monument in a field of Georgia," states that the poem was written before the founding of the National Cemetery at Andersonville, the death-camp for Northern prisoners of war, where some fifteen thousand were "reinterred." In the note Melville described a postwar pamphlet: "A glance at the published pamphlet containing the list of the buried at Andersonville conveys a feeling mournfully impressive. Seventy-four large double-columned pages in fine print. Looking through them is like getting lost among the old turbaned head-stones and cypresses in the interminable Black Forest of Scutari, over against Constantinople." Melville must have read many war poems which appeared in newspapers and magazines, but no one has demonstrated that he read and was influenced by any of the volumes of poems on the war that appeared before *Battle-Pieces*, such as Henry Howard Brownell's *Lyrics of a Day; or, Newspaper-Poetry* (New York: Carleton, 1864). (Brownell saw war service as secretary to Admiral David Farragut.) Apparently the only books which were Melville's major sources were the collections of documents, mainly newspaper stories.

Melville was well aware that the "events and incidents of the conflict" could be seen as making up, in retrospect, a unified "whole, in varied amplitude, corresponding with the geographical area covered by the war." From the information that was generally available, someone else could have attempted to write the poetic history of all the campaigns of the war on sea and land. As Melville knew, Richard Emmons had attempted to cover all the major nautical battles of the War of 1812 in his *Fredoniad*, as well as some land battles. Melville made no such attempt. Whatever his early impulses, Melville specified in the preface to *Battle-Pieces* that, out of the enormous number of events and incidents of the conflict, he had chosen to treat only a few themes, and those not by any rigorous scheme but merely "such as for any cause chanced to imprint themselves upon the mind." Disavowing any single point of view in the poems, he acknowledged that the "aspects which the strife as a memory assumes are as manifold as are the moods of involuntary meditation — moods variable, and at times widely at variance": "Yielding instinctively, one after another, to feelings not inspired from any one source exclusively, and unmindful, without purporting to be, of consistency, I seem, in most of these verses, to have but placed a harp in a window, and noted the contrasted airs which wayward winds have played upon the strings." Melville probably already delighted in an Aeolian harp on his little back porch off the second floor of the Twenty-sixth Street house, and now he was not being disingenuous. He wanted to be understood as not imposing his aesthetic or political designs on the shape of his volume. The diffidence could be taken as irresoluteness, but it was a choice made.

   The book begins with a dedication to the memory of the three hundred thousand "who in the war for the maintenance of the Union fell devotedly under the flag of their fathers." Then comes the untitled and elusive note that starts with the assertion that with "few exceptions, the Pieces in this volume originated in an impulse imparted by the fall of Richmond." The contents page lists everything that follows, except, oddly, "The Portent (1859)" which immediately follows it, the poem about the hanged John Brown as the "meteor of the war." Fifty-two poems follow, beginning with "Misgivings" and "The Conflict of Convictions" and ending with "On the Slain Collegians" and "America," arranged roughly in the chronology of events depicted. (The longest of these, "Donelson," was the ninth.) Then there is a section of sixteen "Verses Inscriptive and Memorial." Following that section is the longest poem in the book, "The Scout toward Aldie," distinguished in the contents by being printed in capitals and small capitals. The book closes with the poems "Lee in the Capitol" and "A Meditation," nine pages of prose notes to some of the poems, and a prose "Supplement" running to fourteen pages.

   Although *Harper's New Monthly Magazine* began making a feature of his poems in January 1866, Melville had not then provided the brothers with final copy for the entire manuscript; "Lee in the Capitol" was one late addition. On 17 February 1866 Robert E. Lee testified before the Reconstruction

Committee of Congress. Apparently the publication of the testimony was long delayed because of what the Washington *National Intelligencer* attributed to the absence of Michigan Senator Jacob Merritt Howard, "before whom all of it was taken." On 28 March the *Intelligencer* printed the testimony of General Lee in full, and it was rapidly picked up by New York papers. Lee's assurances to the committee were reported in third person:

> He represents that nothing like a sentiment of hostility to the United States Government exists in Virginia; that there are no combinations or conspiracies having that end in view; that the people, though disappointed and saddened by the result of the war, accept that result submissively, and are only looking now to their material interests, and that the surest and speediest means of reconciling the people to the Government, and making them its cardinal supporters, is to extend to them equal political rights with the people of other States.

Later Senator Howard said to Lee: "If there be any other matters about which you wish to speak on this occasion, do so freely." In answering, Lee merely clarified what he had said about the politicians of the country being responsible for dividing the great masses of the people: he had not meant to imply that he himself "had been individually wheedled by the politicians."

This dramatic moment caught Melville's imagination so that he violated the historical fact and put an appropriately eloquent response into Lee's voice in "Lee in the Capitol (April, 1866.)"—the date identifying, most likely, the month Melville completed the poem. Melville gave Lee a richly historical argument against punishing the South ("Shall the great North go Sylla's way? / Proscribe? prolong the evil day? / Confirm the curse? infix the hate? / In Union's name forever alienate?"), ending with a plea against copying "Europe in her worst estate." The committee dismisses him (and Melville dismisses him):

> Forth he went
> Through vaulted walks in lengthened line
> Like porches erst upon the Palantine:
>   Historic reveries their lesson lent,
>   The Past her shadow through the Future sent.
>
> But no. Brave though the Soldier, grave his plea—
>   Catching the light in the future's skies,
> Instinct disowns each darkening prophecy:
>   Faith in America never dies;
> Heaven shall the end ordained fulfill,
> We march with Providence cheery still.

Thus far could Melville bring himself to override the lessons of history in the hope of promoting reconciliation at the end of a book which had begun with contemptuous misgivings about the "optimist-cheer" of many of his fellow citizens. He mythologies the man who had endured a public renunciation of military glory—something parallel to the grandeur of his own renunciation, for years now, of literary glory: informing the poem is Melville's profound though covert identification with Robert E. Lee. Even Melville's depiction of Lee's choosing not "coldly to endure his doom" and speak out is infused with his own decisions to write and publish *Battle-Pieces*. And once again he followed rhetorical precedent, classical and Shakespearean, as well as American classroom exercises, in inventing an imaginary oration for a real historical figure.

In the next weeks of 1866 the fury of Radical Republicans intent on punishing the South led Melville to add the "Supplement," introduced this way: "Were I fastidiously anxious for the symmetry of this book, it would close with the notes. But the times are such that patriotism—not free from solicitude—urges a claim overriding all literary scruples." He dated his writing as "more than a year since the memorable surrender," and further dated it by alluding to recent histories and biographies written by Southerners and already "freely published at the North by loyal houses," and widely read. He also alluded to the "mourners who this summer bear flowers to the mounds of the Virginian and Georgian dead"—a strong indication, although not proof, that he wrote the "Supplement" some weeks after the actual anniversary of the surrender. On 11 July he bought from Harper's a copy of J. W. Draper's *Thoughts on the Future Civil Policy of America* (1865), probably wondering if he should have used it for the "Supplement"; in fact, although it made much use of Machiavelli, as Melville did in the "Supplement," it had almost nothing to say about Reconstruction, despite the title. (Duyckinck may have piqued Melville's interest by commenting on Draper's lectures at the Historical Society, lectures which had gone into the book.) As he looked over the postwar histories and biographies, Melville had recognized his own battle-pieces as constituting a parallel "poetic record" of the war, however unsystematic and uncomprehensive his approach.

Melville knew Shakespeare's passages on brother against brother and father against son in warfare, but the "Supplement" shows he had been brooding not over the War of the Roses but over the Stuart-Hanoverian parallels, especially George IV's rearing a monument "over the remains of the enemy of his dynasty, Charles Edward, the invader of England and victor in the rout at Preston Pans"—a gesture that mitigated against the ugly possibility that Grant's descendants might "pursue with rancor, or slur by sour neglect, the memory of Stonewall Jackson." The course of events was controlled by Northern politicians who had not yet learned to act like statesmen, but Melville dared to hope that the South could be defeated without being shamed:

> Supposing a happy issue out of present perplexities, then, in the generation next to come, Southerners there will be yielding allegiance to the Union, feeling all their interests bound up in it, and yet cherishing unrebuked that kind of feeling for the memory of the soldiers of the fallen Confederacy that Burns, Scott, and the Ettrick Shepherd felt for the memory of the gallant clansmen ruined through their fidelity to the Stuarts—a feeling whose passion was tempered by the poetry imbuing it, and which in no wise affected their loyalty to the Georges, and which, it may be added, indirectly contributed excellent things to literature.

Melville saw himself like Robert Burns, like Sir Walter Scott (whose *The Lady of the Lake* Gansevoort had drummed into his ears), and like James Hogg, the Ettrick Shepherd (a profound influence on Wordsworth), a poet daring to be fair to defeated rebels while contributing to the poetic record of the victors.

In the "Supplement" Melville urged Radicals to apply in their legislation "prudence, not unallied with entire magnanimity":

> Benevolence and policy—Christianity and Machiavelli—dissuade from penal severities toward the subdued....
>
> The blacks, in their infant pupilage to freedom, appeal to the sympathies of every humane mind. The paternal guardianship which for the interval government exercises over them was prompted equally by duty and benevolence. Yet such kindliness should not be allowed to exclude kindliness to communities who stand nearer to us in nature. For the future of the freed slaves we may well be concerned; but the future of the whole country, involving the future of the blacks, urges a paramount claim upon our anxiety. Effective benignity, like the Nile, is not narrow in its bounty, and true policy is always broad.

"Something may well be left," he urged, "to the graduated care of future legislation, and to heaven." Melville found it hard to check his "crowding thoughts," but forced himself to cease: "Let us pray that the terrible historic tragedy of our time may not have been enacted without instructing our whole beloved country through terror and pity; and may fulfillment verify in the end those expectations which kindle the bards of Progress and Humanity." Among those bards, of course, Melville could not include himself, so his rhetorical struggle, at the end, was not to alienate his readers by his truth-telling. His book did not lend itself to sloganeering quotations.

Hoadley was now in an intensely Radical phase, identified with Charles Sumner's determination to punish white Southerners. Melville was much closer to the complicated, ambivalent feelings of Lemuel Shaw, Richard Lathers, John A. Dix, and their 1860 associates. Melville inscribed a copy of his war poems to "Major General Dix with the respects of the author" (now in the William S. Reese Collection), a tribute to a national hero, who as a fifteen-year-old boy had fought at Lundy's Lane, in the Niagara campaign, the bloodiest recorded battle on Canadian soil. Major general of volunteers, he was first on the list, outranking all other volunteer officers through the Civil War. As such, he worked out the Dix-Hill Cartel, the prisoner-exchange program (later repudiated by Secretary of War Stanton), and he was in charge of suppressing the New York City draft riots in 1863. (He crowned his career as governor in 1872–74; in World War I Fort Dix in central New Jersey was named for him.) Melville knew momentous men who found no such simple answers as Hoadley could take refuge in. Some "three hundred thousand" Union soldiers had died, to use Melville's number. The South was devastated. The political, economic, and social fate of the freed blacks was uncertain. It was one thing to believe, all along, that slavery was an atheistical iniquity, as Melville had done, according to his "Supplement," and another to feel that the war had solved all racial problems.

Orville Dewey, looking before and after, seeing from the point of view of his Southern friends in Charleston and feeling in his core that slavery was wrong, a little after the war wrote in his autobiography that the freedmen were, "at present, upon their good behavior," and "acting under the influence of a previous condition." What might happen to the freed slaves later on concerned him:

> when I look to the future, and see them rising to wealth, culture, and refinement, and, as human beings, entitled to consideration as much as any other, and yet forbidden intermarriage with the whites, as they should be for physiological reasons, — when, in fine, they see that they have *not* any fair and just position in American society and government, — they may be sorry that they were not gradually emancipated, and colonized to their own native country; and for ourselves — for our own country — the seeds may be sowing, in the dark bosom of the future, which may spring up in civil wars more terrible than ever were seen before.

As Dewey was aware, such "speculations and opinions" would "meet with no favor" in the postwar North. Dewey's words were not published while he lived; Melville's similar forebodings in the "Supplement" met some favor and much antagonism.

On 12 August 1866 a note in the New York *Herald* added a comment about one of the new books from Harper's, *Battle-Pieces:* "for ten years the public has wondered what has become of Melville." The public was to learn from a good number of reviews what Melville had recently done, if not what had become of him. Much of the commentary in the still highly politicized months of the reviewing dealt with the "Supplement." The Boston *Daily Advertiser* (24 August) did not recall a literary precedent, despite Wordsworth's famous essay: "Rather a novel feature, for a volume of poems appears in a political essay inserted at the close under the head of 'Supplement.'" Henry Raymond, the editor of the New York *Times* (no longer merely a juvenile intruder in the newspaper world), had been campaigning for a policy of non-punitive reconciliation toward white Southerners, so on 27 August it may have been Raymond himself who seized on the "Supplement" as showing that Melville did not have "the fear of the Radicals before his eyes" in advocating a position like Raymond's own. Barely mentioning the "poems themselves" (a "succession of lyrics, many of them vivid battle pictures, which were dashed off from time to time during the war"), the *Times* managed to praise them particularly for their political stance: "They make all the more pleasant a contribution to the literature of the war, because they are not marked by those extravagances in which nearly all our bellicose poets have so freely indulged."

In his summary of the "Supplement" the reviewer in the *Times* played ironically with Melville's authority as an anthropological political philosopher:

> Mr. Melville ventures to advise that we should "be Christians toward our fellow whites, as well as philanthropists toward the blacks, our fellow men;" that "something may well be left to the graduated care of future legislation, and to heaven;" and, he adds, that "in all things, and toward all, we are enjoined to do as we would be done by." The use of such treasonable language as this shows a singular hardihood on the part of one who has studied and written about the ferocious inhabitants of the South Sea Islands, who were accustomed, as we all know, to keep cold missionary on their sideboards, and it is perhaps unkind to Mr. Melville to draw down upon his devoted head Radical wrath by calling attention thus publicly to his views.

In warning the Radicals about the "Supplement" the *Times* claimed to be acting with "the most benevolent intentions," to keep the followers of Thaddeus Stevens and Charles Sumner from "pitching the book out the window." The warning, however, was ambidexter, as Melville would have said, and may have kept such Radicals from picking up the book at all.

On 31 August the Augusta (Maine) *Kennebec Journal* decided that Melville "did not help his reputation any by his prosy supplement, which is a sort of apology for some of the sentiments in his poetry which, less than some others required any apology and a rather discursive and uncalled-for essay on the present situation." The reviewer added that one "hardly knows after reading it what opinions the author holds." On 3 September the New York *Herald* directed "special attention" to the "Supplement," insisting that "far from spoiling the symmetry of the book, this supplement completes it, and converts it into what is better than a good book—into a good and patriotic action." Writing under the threat of Radical triumph, the *Herald* welcomed Melville's " 'words in season,' not only as the deliberate, impartial testimony of a highly cultivated individual mind, but as hopeful signs of a change in public opinion and sentiment." (On 14 September the Baltimore *Sun* coolly plagiarized this excellent passage to deck out a brief notice.) The extract in the *Herald* was from the prose "Supplement," not the poetry. On 5 September the New York *Commercial Advertiser* also excerpted the "Supplement," "in which the author ventilates his political philosophy." For the Radical taste of the Boston *Traveller* (8 September) there was "too much said about generosity to the vanquished" in the "Supplement." On 6 October the Portland (Maine) *Transcript: An Independent Family Journal of Literature, Science, News &c.* was harsh on Melville: "he so far violates literary taste as to add a 'Supplement' in which, in somewhat stilted prose, he urges the duty of moderation and magnanimity to a fallen foe on the part of the victor. All will agree that a generous forbearance should be exercised towards the South, but the nation will not forget that it is bound to be just as well as generous."

The "Supplement" outraged the Radical New York *Independent* (10 January 1867), which called Melville "this happy optimist" for saying Northern whites were "bound to be Christians toward our fellow-whites as well as philanthropist toward the blacks" and declaring that something "may well be left to the graduated care of future legislation and of Heaven." A portion of the denunciation shows just how dangerous the ground was on which Melville had so cautiously trodden:

> Does Mr. Melville really believe that, if William Lloyd Garrison had not called the Constitution "a Covenant with Death and Agreement with Hell," or if Robert Toombs had never hoped to call the roll of his slaves on Bunker Hill, red Wrong would not one day have arraigned Right for being Right, and been compelled to hear her terrible justification! Almost a century the North labored with the dull mechanic oar, to find at last, through a fearful awakening, that "the strong wind is blowing, and the strong current flowing, right onward to the Eternal Shore." We speak at this length because gentlemen of

Mr. Melville's class are mischievous men in these troublous times. Only absolute justice is safe. Peaceable, by all means peaceable, in God's name; but *first pure*, in God's name, also.

(Robert Augustus Toombs was the fiery Georgian, first Confederate secretary of state, notorious for defiling the hallowed monument at Bunker Hill by exercising his constitutional rights to enumerate his slaves.) This was hard reading for the family from the paper that had warned Melville and the Harpers of hell-fire, hard reading for Melville as he went about his daily rounds in the district office and the docks.

One small decision about rhyme made Melville a laughingstock among the reviewers. The Philadelphia *American Literary Gazette and Publishers' Circular* (1 September) decried the rhymes as "fearful": "The first one [poem] in his book makes 'law' and 'Shenandoah' rhyme," then Melville went from bad to worse, making " 'war' and 'Shenandoah' rhyme." On 8 September the Cincinnati *Enquirer* condemned some of the rhymes as "hardly canonical" and some of the lines "would be prose but for the typography." Still, some of the pieces had "more than mere spasmodic force; and some have hardly as much" — a two-sided reference to the British Spasmodic poets of the previous decade. On 15 September the New York *Round Table* called some of the rhymes "positively barbarous": "In his first poem, *The Portent*, 'Shenandoah' rhymes with 'law,' and 'John Brown' with 'shown.' " The reviewer in the New York *World* (19 October), possibly Richard Henry Stoddard, declined to enumerate "such technical blemishes as the rhyming of 'law' and 'Shenandoah,' 'more' and 'Keneshaw,' " lest he should seem to be "carping at a book which, without having one poem of entire artistic *ensemble* in it, possesses numerous passages of beauty and power." The *Independent* had no such scruples, and enumerated the various words Melville had rhymed with "Shenandoah," "regardless of incompatibility," then added that "Shenandoah" made "another Mormon marriage with half-a-dozen unfit terminations, of which 'star' is the least unlike." Only a handful of reviewers got far past their contempt for the rhymes to "Shenandoah." Melville was renouncing rhyme's barbaric cymbal — but was he also carrying into his middle years some pronunciation derived from his Boston-born father and wife, just as he wrote "Happar" to identify the Marquesan tribe others called "Happa"?

The Springfield *Republican* (29 August) decided that none of the poems was "absolutely bad, but many of them cannot be called good." The Boston *Post* (30 August) decided that the verse was "pregnant, but not artistic," and that the volume was "likely to fall into its place among the subordinate depositories of war verse, which the time has been so prolific in." He wrote verse much as Bulwer did, "understandingly, scholarly, but not imaginatively in the fine poetic sense of that word." One of the briefer and terser comments was in the 31 August Boston *Christian Witness and Church Advocate:* "This is a series of descriptive and lyrical poems, on subjects and incidents fresh in the memory of us all. It is full of a certain offhand heartiness but will not bear severe criticism." The *Kennebec Journal* said Melville's poems were "inspired by particular events" which followed "each other so rapidly as to demand of the writer a fresh poem every few days," so they could not be meritorious; however, some were "musical in their rhythm" and showed "some poetical talent," particularly "the descriptive pieces, such as 'Donelson' and 'The Scout towards Aldie.' " The New York *National Quarterly Review* (September 1866) was blunt: "Had this really been a book of poetry, as it purports to be, it would have had a different imprint; it would have reached us, not from New York, but from Boston." The reviewer in the New York *Nation* (6 September) read the book "with a certain melancholy," finding proof that Nature did not make Melville a poet. In Taunton, Massachusetts, the *Daily Gazette* (8 September) thought that probably not one poem in the collection would be remembered, since it lacked "that free and musical flow of fine words and fervid fancies which give verses a place in all newspapers." The Boston *Traveller* asserted that the war had given birth to "little poetry that is worth preserving, but Mr. Melville's poems are an exception to the rule, for they have both vigor and sweetness, and often rise to the element of grandeur."

The New York *Albion* (15 September) elaborated with a good memory the "few short 'swallow-flights' " in *Mardi* which were "not so poetical as the prose" in which they were set. The writer had thought about the subject: "Mr. Melville's prose, indeed, was less prose than poetry in the rough, resembling, we take it, the spirited but careless memoranda which poets throw together in their moments of inspiration as the skeleton of future poems. It was rich in diction, full of colour, and, after its fashion, imaginative." The "interval of silence" on Melville's part was now broken, and not agreeably, for the volume showed that his mind, "while lying fallow," had "changed in many respects, and not to his advantage in a poetical point of view." The merit in the poems was intermixed with much that was "worthless," for Melville was "less an artist now than ever": "His conceptions are frequently obscure, and his style uncouth and harsh. Of verse as verse — meaning thereby the falling together of words in rhythmical order — he knows but little, seldom writing a stanza that is melodious throughout. Some of his discords are fine, but music has other and higher qualities than mere discords." On 29 September the San Francisco *Evening Bulletin* thought some of the pieces were "spirited and full of poetic fire; but taken as a collection" they were "rather mediocre": "They are cast in unfamiliar metre, and the versification is at times harsh and limping." The reviewer in the New York *Evening Post* (10 October) mentioned

Pierre twice — highly unusual — and offered a cautious praise: "These war-lyrics are full of martial fire, and sometimes are really artistic in form, but often the thought of the author is too vaguely expressed." Melville's "style in verse" was "as unfettered by ordinary precedents as in such of his prose works as 'Pierre.'" The long review in the New York *World* cautiously observed that "the poetic nature and the technical faculty of poetry writing are not identical": "Whole pages of Mr. Melville's prose are, in the highest sense, poetic, and nearly all the battle-pieces would be much more poetic if they were thrown into the external prose form."

Reviewers often singled out for comment the longest poem of the first section, "Donelson." The New York *Evening Express* (25 August) said the book's "principal 'piece' appears to be a versification and attempted idealization of the bulletin board of some daily newspaper office during the Fort Donelson excitement." The September *National Quarterly Review* resisted taking many of the pieces, including this one, as poetry: "Mr. Melville has great faith in difference of type; sometimes he prints whole pages in *Italics*, as if he thought he could render them more poetical by the process. Thus, for example, the poem entitled Donelson is chiefly in that type; but the amount of poetry it contains may be pretty safely inferred from the first stanza" — which it then quoted in full. On 3 September the Philadelphia *Inquirer* complained that "Donelson" exemplified the "fault of needless and commonplace detail," a fault Melville had "generally" avoided. The New York *Round Table* enumerated defects, and found counterbalancing virtues, "nervous phrases and energetic passages, and fine bits of description, now of landscapes and now of battle movements," such as in "Donelson, in some respects the most original poem of the collection." The *Albion* called it one of the most "sustained" poems, "the execution of which is fantastic enough, the effect depending upon the reading on a city bulletin of the daily telegraphic reports of the battle." The New York *Evening Post* offered an example of Melville's style as unconventional: "His account of the impressions produced by the various reports from Fort Donelson — about the time of its surrender — is a specimen of this, yet it presents a faithful picture of the times, and recalls them vividly to the mind of the reader."

Several reviewers praised one of the most conventional poems, one comfortingly in the genre of Browning's "How they Brought the Good News" — "Sheridan at Cedar Creek" ("Shoe the steed with silver / That bore him to the fray"). The *Albion* described it as best of all the poems and advised "Mr. Melville's readers to turn to it first, since it ought to cover the multitude of his poetic sins." The *Round Table* called it "the best thing in the volume" and pronounced that it far surpassed "Mr. Buchanan Read's poem on the same theme," being imaginative and having "the true lyrical ring." It was often

30 Richard Lathers, from *Reminiscences of Richard Lathers,* edited by Alvan F. Sanborn (New York, 1907).

31 "George Long Duyckinck," 1861. Original pencil sketch by Richard Lathers in the copy of *An Abridgment of the Light of Nature Pursued,* by Abraham Tucker, presented to Lathers by Herman Melville, August 1853. Courtesy of Between the Covers— Rare Books, Inc., Merchantville, New Jersey.

32 "The Finest Home in the World for Needy Sailors. The Famous Sailors' Snug Harbor at Staten Island," from *Leslie's Weekly*, 12 August 1899. Courtesy of The Boston Public Library.

33 *(left)* Catherine (Katie) Bogart Melville, ca. 1868. Carte de visite by J. Loeffler. Berkshire Athenaeum, Pittsfield, Massachusetts. 34 *(right) Portrait of Thomas Melville, Governor of Sailors' Snug Harbor*, artist unknown. Oil on canvas, 1884. Collection of The Sailors' Snug Harbor, Sea Level, North Carolina.

35 "Admission of an Old Sailor to the Harbor," from *Harper's New Monthly Magazine*, January 1873. Courtesy of Mark Twain Papers, The Bancroft Library, University of California, Berkeley.

36 "Governor's Residence, Sailors' Snug Harbor, S. I.," New York, ca. 1905. Collection of Doris Lane.

37 Dr. John W. Francis, from *Cyclopædia of American Literature*,
by Evert A. Duyckinck and George L. Duyckinck
(New York, 1855).

38 Henry T. Tuckerman, engraving by Capewell & Kimmel, in
A Memorial of Henry Theodore Tuckerman, by Evert A. Duyckinck (New York, 1872).
By permission of the Houghton Library, Harvard University.

39 *(left)* Orville Dewey, from *Autobiography and Letters of Orville Dewey, D. D.*, edited by his daughter, Mary E. Dewey (Boston, 1883). 40 *(right)* Henry W. Bellows, ca. 1870. Photomechanical print, photographer unidentified. Courtesy of the Massachusetts Historical Society. MHS image no. 1217.

41 All Souls Unitarian Church, ca. 1855. Photograph by Victor Prevost. Collection of The New-York Historical Society. Negative no. 26114.

42 Elizabeth Shaw Melville, 1872. Carte de visite by Warren's.
Berkshire Athenaeum, Pittsfield, Massachusetts.

43 *Portrait of Herman Melville*, by Joseph Eaton. Oil on canvas, 1870. By permission
of the Houghton Library, Harvard University. Shelf mark *61z-4, Melville Family,
Portrait of Herman Melville, 1870.

44 Maria Gansevoort Melville, ca. 1870. Photograph.
Berkshire Athenaeum, Pittsfield, Massachusetts.

45 Gansevoort Mansion, Gansevoort, New York, 1880. Helen Melville Griggs
and Frances Melville on the porch. Photograph. Berkshire Athenaeum, Pittsfield,
Massachusetts.

46 *(left)* Helen Melville Griggs, 1879. Carte de visite. Berkshire Athenaeum, Pittsfield, Massachusetts. 47 *(right)* Augusta Melville, ca. 1855. Carte de visite by R. H. Dewey. Berkshire Athenaeum, Pittsfield, Massachusetts.

48 *(left)* Catherine (Kate) Melville Hoadley, after 1880. Cabinet card. Berkshire Athenaeum, Pittsfield, Massachusetts. 49 *(right)* Frances (Fanny) Priscilla Melville, 1879. Carte de visite. Berkshire Athenaeum, Pittsfield, Massachusetts.

50 "Along the Docks, New York City—View from West Street," from *Harper's Weekly*, 4 September 1869. Museum of the City of New York.

51 *(left)* Malcolm Melville, ca. 1866. Tintype by Thwaites & Co. Berkshire Athenaeum, Pittsfield, Massachusetts. 52 *(right)* Stanwix Melville, ca. 1880. Cabinet card by Cramer. Berkshire Athenaeum, Pittsfield, Massachusetts.

53 *(left)* Elizabeth (Bessie) Melville, 1884. Cabinet card by Rockwood. Berkshire Athenaeum, Pittsfield, Massachusetts. 54 *(right)* Frances Melville, 1870. Tintype. Berkshire Athenaeum, Pittsfield, Massachusetts.

55 *The Library of Colonel Richard Lathers, Winyah Park, New Rochelle*, by George Henry Story. Oil on canvas, 1880. Gibbes Museum of Art/CAA, 18.01.01.

56 Catherine Gansevoort Lansing seated in front of a portrait of her husband, Abraham Lansing, 1916. Photograph. Berkshire Athenaeum, Pittsfield, Massachusetts.

57 Hand and Torch of the Statue of Liberty, displayed in Madison Square Park, 1876. Collection of The New-York Historical Society. Negative no. 58889.

58 "A Brisk Gale," 1763. Engraving by P. C. Canot after the painting by Willem (or William) Van de Velde the Younger. Private Collection.

59 "Beatrix Cenci," ca. 1838. Engraving by Vincent Biondi after the painting by Guido Reni. Courtesy of William S. Reese.

60 "House of the Tragic Poet at Pompeii," ca. 1888. Lithograph. Printed and published by Eduard Hölzel. Private Collection.

61 Elizabeth Shaw Melville, 1885. Cabinet card by Rockwood. Berkshire Athenaeum, Pittsfield, Massachusetts.

62 Herman Melville, 1885. Cabinet card by Rockwood. Berkshire Athenaeum, Pittsfield, Massachusetts.

63 Elizabeth Shaw Melville, 1905. Photograph. Berkshire Athenaeum, Pittsfield, Massachusetts.

reprinted, in the Boston *Commonwealth* for 6 October, for example, and in the New York *Leader* for 8 December. This is the poem Melville copied for Stoddard, by request.

Other poets of the war had done better. The reviewer in the New York *Nation* had thought the matter through and decided that Melville did not compare with the true war poet, James Russell Lowell, whose "Commemoration Ode" "takes its place securely, not only among the finest works of our generation, but among the noblest poems of all time." Granted, even lesser poets are inspired by great events, but not to worthy achievement: "the same storm that piles up the waves of the sea sets all the duck-ponds in ineffectual commotion." Melville's duck-pond had been ruffled, as *Battle-Pieces* bore witness, and the reviewer, having responded to Lowell's mastery, confessed to feeling "a little impatience and weariness with the common handiwork of the journeymen and apprentices, however much he may approve their industry or sympathize with the emotion which, in their degree, they experienced and attempt to express." Melville, to be blunt, "must take his place with the herd of recent versifiers." Furthermore, it "was Melville's bad luck that his 'Shiloh: A Requiem' would almost inevitably suggest, by contrast, the very striking poem of Mr. Forceythe Willson's, of which a great part of the scene is laid on the battle-field of Shiloh, called 'The Old Sergeant.'" The reviewer could hardly stop praising this great poem, which, if his memory served, had first appeared in mid-war in the Louisville *Journal*. The Philadelphia *Inquirer* concluded that as "a singer of soldierly deeds" Melville was "preferable even to Brownell; possessing all the vivid powers of that warrior poet, without his fault of detailing minutely all the accessories of an action." This was Henry Howard Brownell, whose *Lyrics of a Day* (1864) had been followed by *War-Lyrics and Other Poems* (1866). On 8 September the Boston *Commercial Bulletin* elaborated a contrast: "Some of the battle-pieces remind one of Brownell, but the resemblance goes not beyond the quality of brusqueness. With more polish and less freedom than Brownell, Mr. Melville writes what he thinks rather than what he feels."

The New York *National Quarterly Review* looked abroad for cruelly limited comparisons: "Lee in the Capitol" was "nearly, if not quite, as long as Campbell's 'Hohenlinden,' or Goldsmith's 'Traveller;' but we cannot point out any further resemblance." The *Albion* also made comparisons: "We read his [Melville's] songs, if we may call them such, and wonder while we read, first, that the events should have presented themselves to his mind in the shape that they did; and, second, that, with his genius, he has not succeeded in placing us more *en rapport* with them. Mr. Brownell has this last power in many of his patriotic pieces, while Mr. Walter Whitman, the most shapeless of all our versifiers, possesses it in a remarkable degree. We fail, however, to sympathize with the mass of Mr. Melville's poems, which are scarcely intelligible, as he has handled them." The "Yea and Nay" of the end of "The Conflict of Convictions" was "Emerson at second-hand." The San Francisco *Evening Bulletin* knew Melville's place: "The author delights in grotesque metaphors and strained similes, and uses strange phrases to express the most simple ideas. We can pardon barbarism of style in men like Carlyle or Emerson, who are original thinkers; but when Herman Melville affects the obscurely-profound and dislocates the parts of speech from sheer contempt of good English, we confess it makes our gorge rise." Greeley's *Tribune* ignored *Battle-Pieces* (except for a Harper publication notice ["this day," 24 August] and a later advertisement), but on 4 October it lavished more than two columns on James A. Dorgan's *Studies* under the heading "A New Poet": "Of all the so-called young poets of America, we are much mistaken if he is not quite the best that has appeared since the death of Poe." The Portland *Transcript* made a comparison to the writer who may most have warranted Melville in some of his stylistic experiments: "Though the lines have not a very melodious flow, they are not lacking in spirit and vigor, and some of the descriptive pieces remind one of Browning in his more intelligible mood."

Not unexpectedly, the New York *Independent* was vicious, not least in seeming to praise the early works it had condemned when they were published: "The odorous South winds which blew through Mr. Herman Melville's earlier books might have filled the sails of his graceful bark, and wafted him to Cathay, for all the world has known of him of late. It seems, however, that he has been coquetting with the Muse—and we say advisedly, coquetting—for the majestic presence has not possessed and enthralled him. It is rather as if he were the humble 'meejum' alternately influenced by the overmastering personalities of Walt. Whitman, Dante, Emerson, Brownell, and Mother Goose." (The odd "meejum" means "medium," the conduit of greater spirits, from the current excitement over "spiritualism.") The *Independent* continued scathingly: "He coins words and phrases with the prodigality of Elizabeth Browning, and without her fine fitness." Even "Sheridan at Cedar Creek," which had received some praise when printed in *Harper's*, seemed "founded on the two familiar poems of an earlier writer: one beginning 'Ride a black horse to Banbury Cross, to see an old woman,' etc., etc.; the other 'Shoe the old horse, and shoe the old mare, but let the little colt go bare.'" Melville may have ruined the subject of "Sheridan's Ride" for any real poet, and it was certain that he had *"not* written" the poem the subject deserved. "'A Canticle significant of the national exaltation of enthusiasm at the close of the war' out-Whitmans Whitman," the *Independent* continued, before offering strange mitigation, recognizing "the real power which underlies his vagaries, and carelessnesses, and crudities." There were "poetic hints enough" "to set up half a dozen popular poets in life-long business," and there were even "lines strong as Robert Browning, pictures vivid as life, phrases clear-cut as Emerson." The conclusion was downright charitable: "when a man needs to eliminate, rather than to strengthen, there is hope for him."

The privilege of driving the last nail into the coffin devolved upon young William Dean Howells, in the February 1867 *Atlantic Monthly* (as the most respected American monthly, the worst possible place for a grudging review). Howells had kept well informed of the actualities of the war from his charming villa in Venice, suffering there only from the occasional severe affront to his aesthetic sensibilities, as when he surveyed disdainfully the green drapery marble in the Jesuit church which Melville had so admired. Now, home in a peacetime United States, he pronounced the events and characters in Melville's poems ghostlike rather than realistic:

> Mr. Melville's work possesses the negative virtues of originality in such degree that it not only reminds you of no poetry you have read, but of no life you have known. Is it possible—you ask yourself, after running over all these celebrative, inscriptive, and memorial verses—that there has really been a great war, with battles fought by men and bewailed by women? Or is it only that Mr. Melville's inner consciousness has been perturbed, and filled with the phantasms of enlistments, marches, fights in the air, parenthetic bulletin-boards, and tortured humanity shedding, not words and blood, but words alone?

With "certain moods or abstractions of the common mind during the war," Melville's faculty was "well fitted to deal," but even when he treated events "realistically" the events "seem to have presented themselves as dreams," and "at last they remain vagaries, and are none the more substantial because they have a modern speech and motion." Melville's "quality of remoteness" was heroic but it separated "our weak human feelings" from his subjects "by trackless distances"; the description of the death of General Nathaniel Lyon's horse was undeniably noble but the passage was "as far off from us" as any of the poetry of Ossian's. The curious aspect to this specific criticism is that Howells identified quite precisely what Melville, following Wordsworth's dictum, had attempted to do, but never thought that he might have intended doing it. One passage he praised without reservation: "We have never seen anywhere so true and beautiful a picture as the following of that sublime and thrilling sight,—a great body of soldiers marching:—'The bladed guns are gleaming— / Drift in lengthened trim, / Files on files for hazy miles / Nebulously dim.'" By late January 1867, when these words were read everywhere, Melville had other things to think about besides his stature as the poet of the war. His new job was only one of these.

As it happened, *Battle-Pieces* brought Melville new grievances against the Harpers, involving the poems which appeared in *Harper's New Monthly Magazine*. The editor of *Harper's Monthly*, Albert H. Guernsey, wrote the Harper brothers a memo, probably in late June 1866: "I think you ought to agree with Mr Melville what should be paid for these poems for this use in the Magazine, apart from their use in the volume." Melville was given this memo, and noted on it: "I never got." Melville grimly had to acknowledge the almost universal opinion that he was no poet, and as the months passed he had to face the book's failure to sell more than a few hundred copies. On 7 December 1866 William H. Demarest of Harper & Brothers wrote to Melville: "According to promise I beg to report that there were printed of the 'Battle Pieces,' 1260 copies: there have been given to Editors, say in round numbers, 300: There were on hand yesterday 409. So there were sold, or in hands of booksellers on sale, up to yesterday, say 551 copies." More than half as many copies had been given away as had been sold. It was just as well Melville did not know precisely which booksellers were stocking *Battle-Pieces*, for in Philadelphia (according to the *Inquirer* on 3 September) one could buy it at T. B. Peterson & Brothers. Peterson had ignored Melville's letter of remonstrance about *The Refugee*. In Hannah Mary Bouvier Peterson's *The National Cook Book* he had included a page of advertisements for Peterson books, all $1.75 in cloth or $1.50 in paper. Between Annette Marie Maillard's *The Jealous Husband* and *The Life, Writings, and Lectures of the Late "Fanny Fern"* was *The Refugee*, by Herman Melville. How did the egregious Peterson display *Battle-Pieces*? Cheek by jowl with *The Refugee*? Squashed between *The Two Captains* and *The Man of the World*?

The reviews almost all made hard reading for the Melville household. This was the first time that Malcolm was old enough to notice reviews in newspapers and magazines outside as well as inside the house, and old enough to compare notes, however furtively and diffidently, with Stanwix. What they learned, and what Melville's daughters soon learned, was that their father, still famous as the author of two good books, *Typee* and *Omoo* (unless you asked the opinion of an evangelical Protestant) was no poet. It looked as if the praise John Hoadley had heaped upon the poems in *Harper's Monthly* was well meaning but ill founded, even Uncle John's opinion not being fit to weigh against the judgment of professional critics. Now, very likely, long before *Clarel* was reviewed in 1876, Melville's daughter, "little" Fanny, tainted already by what she had absorbed at 49 Mt. Vernon Street, internalized the world's opinion of her father's poetry, so that many decades later she could "deride" (her daughter Eleanor recalled) Melville's declaiming his own verse around the house. For the first time, as reviews were published the children saw them, one by one—not all the ones mentioned here, but many of them, and others that have been destroyed or remain undiscovered. If their mother could not defend her husband, how could the children defend their father against such an onslaught?

How could they defend him against daily behavior? Melville's daughter Frances told her daughter Eleanor that once when she made a comment about property, having overheard adults use the word, Melville had shamed her as "Little Miss Property." Lizzie, the story went, had calmed her, saying "Papa doesn't mean anything. Run along to school." Did this happen after 1864, when Tennyson's *Enoch Arden* was available in the United States and Melville could read, somewhere, "Northern Farmer. New Style," where the horse canters to the refrain "Proputty, proputty, proputty"? Did he say in an attempt at a strange accent, "Little Miss Proputty"—giving the words a cruelly hurtful sound? Then did he give her *The Holy Grail* in 1870 remembering that the "Northern Farmer. New Style" was cantering through it again? (Once printed in London, or Boston, a new poem by Tennyson could appear anywhere: in October 1864 *Harper's* printed the "Northern Farmer. Old Style"—the one without the "proputty" cantering.) Chances are Frances told a true story, but skewed, only the part of the story she knew, not the part about the sensitive genius living in a private world of literary voices and about the failed father jealous of his daughter because she was a granddaughter of the propertied Shaws. Melville in these years did not make it easy to love him. One of his younger granddaughters, who had not known him, told her children, long after the Melville revival, that the price of genius was too high for a family to pay.

[28]

The Deputy Inspector amid Domestic Maelstroms
1867

They err, who deem Love's brightest hour in blooming youth is known.
Its purest, tenderest, holiest power, in after life is shown.
When passions chastened and subdued to riper years are given,
And earth, and earthly things, are viewed, in light that breaks from Heaven.

An entry in Augusta Melville's commonplace book that she "Copied from Lizzie's book. April 2nd 1849 / New York"

ON 7 JANUARY 1867, for the only time in their lives, as far as we know, Herman and Thomas Melville went to the theater together, a performance of *Elizabeth of England* by Paolo Giacometti, seeing the actress Adelaide Ristori in her "Last Night . . . before her departure for the West." That was a Monday night affair, an anomaly for a working man. Melville's new job was bringing him into contact with whalemen occasionally as well as men from merchant ships and passenger steamers, and he took home a keepsake now and then, a memento from some foreign place. One such item may be a whale tooth Captain Francis S. Worth of the New Bedford ship *Swift* had taken from an eighty-barrel sperm whale "On the Line" in 1860, and given to Melville, who gave it to "E S Doolittle" in January 1867. Following Irving and Cooper, Melville used "Doolittle" as the New Yorker's slur for a busy-looking but inefficient Yankee, as when he referred to Robert Melvill in December 1850 as "Cousin Doolittle." Could the recipient of the tooth have been E. S. Melville, the Cypherina Donothing of the 7 September 1855 costume party? Allan had coped with Sophia's independence by comparing her to Aunt Catherine; it is not pleasant to think that Herman, the gainfully employed husband, might have dubbed his wife "Doolittle" in what passed, according to the rules of marital engagement, as affectionate badinage.

Tom visited his mother late in January 1867, and early in February (he wrote Kate Gansevoort) on his return to New York had "reached Herman's ten minutes to eleven P M, just as Lizzy was shutting up the house, Herman having gone to bed with a bad cold." On 28 February the entire Gansevoort contingent, Maria, Augusta, and Fanny, arrived on the Harlem train to stay out the rest of the winter at Twenty-sixth Street. (The number 60 East Twenty-sixth Street was still being used; later in the year it was consistently 104 East Twenty-sixth Street.) Kate Gansevoort reported to Henry on 2 March that "Herman & his family met them" at the train. Tom was living somewhere else—probably in Allan and Jane's new Thirty-fifth Street house, where there was plenty of room, no children around. On 11 March Maria wrote to Kate Gansevoort: "Tom has a bad cold & does not seem to feel well he dined with us yesterday, nobody went to church but Augusta—for it rained all day. . . . Herman's health is much better since he has been compelled to go out daily to attend to his business. He is one of the District Officers in the Custom House. He has been in Office about three months." Maria was slightly exalting Herman's position in the Custom House, and she was saying what she wanted to believe about his employment's benefiting his health. She gave Kate the impression that she was "delighted with the change from the quiet of Gansevoort." Kate extracted from her Aunt Melville's letter the formula that Gus was "devoted to church going" and elaborated to Henry on 19 March on the news of "Cousin Herman": he had been "quite well this winter" (presumably barring that cold in early February) and his "intercourse with his fellow creatures seems to have had a beneficial effect he is less of a misanthrope." When Kate relayed information, as she often did, she invariably imposed her wry slant on the news.

The second week of April, the Albany Gansevoorts were expecting Tom to stay with them "a few days en route to Gansevoort before sailing for Brazil," as Kate wrote to Henry on the ninth. Uncle Peter had suffered a paralytic stroke in January, but Susan and Kate both welcomed Tom. His intention was to "command the 'Equator' if she sails & the money is deposited in the Bank at New Orleans." Augusta was at Justine Van Rensselaer Townsend's (in New York) and Maria was still in New York City and planning to be there until May. In caring for Peter Gansevoort, Kate and Susan had much to do, starting at seven, as Kate wrote Henry on 30 April. He had to be washed and dressed, and a servant helped him eat. He could smoke his pipe, and tried to read the Albany *Argus*, understanding more and more. Then he was able to walk before napping. Peter's sister was also infirm. Tom wrote to Kate of an accident to Maria in late April, and Kate relayed the news to Henry: "It seems that Gus & she were in 5th Avenue & in coming down the steps of a friends house Aunt Melville slipped & sprained her ankle badly. She had to be taken home in a carriage & has not walked a step since. Dr. [Augustus K.] Gardner her physician say she will not be able to walk in sometime." Fanny had returned to Gansevoort, but now planned to go back to New York to take care of her mother so Augusta and Tom could "go on to Gansevoort & prepare the house" before bringing her up. All during Maria's visit with Herman and Lizzie, Malcolm, her eldest grandchild, was "devoted to her, & so kind in his little attentions," as she wrote Kate Gansevoort (who repeated what she said to Henry on 16 September). The only concern being expressed in the extant correspondence is for the frailties of the older members of the family.

In May, John Hoadley completed the preparation of a gift to the city of New Bedford. The City Library possessed two enormous and historic shells, weighing 420 pounds each, presented on 6 April 1865 by a New Bedford native then stationed at the U.S. Arsenal, Captain James W. Grace of the Fifty-fourth Massachusetts Regiment. As a lieutenant, early in 1863 Grace had opened a recruiting office in town to enlist black men for the Fifty-fourth Volunteer Infantry, an effort aided by visits to New Bedford by Frederick Douglass, Wendell Phillips, William Lloyd Garrison, and other prominent abolitionists. In making the gift, Grace explained that the shells had been thrown from Union monitors (low-sided, heavily armored war vessels, slow, but steady as gun platforms) during the bombardment of Fort Wagner on Morris Island in July 1863, the distance from the monitors to the fort being three thousand yards. Owing to some "disarrangements of the Fuze," these two had not exploded, and subsequently all explosive matter had been removed: "no danger need be apprehended from handling them, they are simply globes of Iron." No Bannadonna as in Melville's "The Bell-Tower," Hoadley had unleashed his metals at the copper mill triumphantly, and had contrived the means for displaying the sacred relics. At the city council meeting on 23 May someone read aloud his letter presenting to the city (as the *Republican Standard* said on 30 May) a memorial gift to go with Grace's gift: "a pair of cast iron brackets, in the form of human hands, with plates to fasten them to a wall, for the purpose of supporting the two 15-inch shells in the possession of the city, which were thrown into Fort Wagner during the siege of that fort." These were literally colossal hands, such as Melville had seen at the Capitoline Museum, and the wall to which the brackets were affixed must have been massive. This magnificent gift has disappeared. Melville must have been interested in this news, since he had been entertained in camp by Josephine "Effy" Lowell, the sister of the commander of the Fifty-fourth Massachusetts, Robert Gould Shaw, who had died in the first assault on Fort Wagner.

Melville's getting out of the house during the day and earning a little money did not remove the tensions which had been building in his home life for many years and which early in 1867 had grown turbulent, at least for Lizzie. What happened between Melville and his wife and between him and his children must be inferred from the few facts and some family legends now known. The house which Maria had been visiting with such aplomb had been to some of its occupants a place of sadness or even acute misery. By this time, early in 1867, some of the Melvilles knew that the Shaws were saying Lizzie believed that Herman was insane, and by this time, at last, some of the Melvilles were willing to say nothing against her if she left him. Lizzie had gone in confidence to her minister at All Souls, the renowned Henry W. Bellows. The pulpit had been an aphrodisiac to Bellows, as to other churchmen of that particular period, but was it also a hotbed of dime-novel fantasies? The minister proposed a harebrained scheme by which Samuel and Lemuel would stage a kidnapping—that is, carry Lizzie off apparently against her will.

Sam, a lawyer and a cautious man, rejected that plan out of hand in the letter he wrote to Bellows on 6 May 1867, some parts of which are quoted in a preceding chapter. Lizzie's "case" had been "a cause of anxiety" to all of them "for years past." Melville had so "ill treated" his wife that she was at last forced to consider very seriously a separation from him. Repeatedly, Sam and Lem had assured her that they would assist her to the best of their ability. At last, "quite recently," possibly early in 1867, "the Melvilles" (whoever that means) had "expressed a willingness to lend their assistance." Samuel emphasized to the minister a newly united front against Melville. The Shaws may well have involved the Griggses and Hoadleys, and even Augusta and Fanny; a later note by Hope Shaw in her diary is quite explicit about a session in which she told Helen Griggs what she expected her to do in regard to Lizzie's sufferings. Sam laid out an alternative to Bellows's scheme:

> The whole family understands the case and the thing has resolved itself into the mere question of my sisters willingness to say the word.... we must base our claim to act on what *she* knows and *not* on what *we* know.... But I think that [your plan] would only obscure the real merits of the case in the eyes of the world, of which she has a most exaggerated dread.... The simplest way and the best way seems to me to be the one often talked about and once resolved upon viz that she should come to Boston as if on a visit... and that when here her friends [that is, Lem and Sam, or perhaps Oakes as well] should inform her husband that a separation, for the present at least, has been decided on. That it should *not* appear to be the work of persons who urge her against her inclination but the deliberate decision of her judgement, which everybody believes to be good, assisted by the counsel of friends, and the professional advice of Dr. [Augustus K.] Gardner.
>
> But if *we* are to seem to be the real putters asunder of man and wife and she is merely to acquiesce I do not think it could be managed better than by

having her at our house and by keeping her there and carefully preventing her husband from seeing her, and telling him and everybody that we had made up our minds not to let her return....

It may well be said Here is a case of mischief making where the wifes relations have created all the trouble. "She says *now* that her husband ill treated her so that she could not live with him but why did she not say so before..." &c &c &c

And her very patience and fortitude will be turned into arguments against her belief in the insanity of her husband.

I think that the safest course is to let her real position become apparent from the first, namely that of a wife, who, being convinced that her husband is insane *acts* as if she were so convinced and applies for aid and assistance to her friends and acts *with* them.

If this letter to Bellows were from Lem, it would be easy to discount, for the older of Hope's sons, like Lizzie's full brother, Oakes, had been contemptuous of Herman since reading the reviews of *Mardi*. Oakes had deflected toward Herman his own perverse and unutterable resentment toward Herman's older brother: would he have gotten free of his foolish liaison if Gansevoort had not persuaded a minister to unite him and Caroline Cobb in holy matrimony? Would he then have stolen from his employer in Chicago if he had not had a wife to support? Lemuel Jr. had been given everything and took it as his by right; his father's name and money carried him safely through Boston society. Sam, gentle, companionable, unselfish, had no such obvious causes of resentment and no such obvious defects of character, and in recent years, even after the great confession of Melville's indebtedness of 1856, as late as 1862, had presented himself at Arrowhead as a companion for Herman in Berkshire excursions. As a witness he must be taken for about as fair-minded as one could expect under the circumstances.

What had Melville done? One of Melville's great-grandsons reported a rumor passed on to him by the poet Charles Olson, supposedly derived from Eleanor Metcalf, Melville's oldest granddaughter, that Melville had pushed his wife down the stairs. Olson is not a source a responsible biographer can put much faith in, and in any case the stories that came down in the family were often skewed. Eleanor was the source for most of the domestic anecdotes that scholars have heard, and, although she gained some information from Sam Shaw and others, her own main source was her mother, Frances. Eleanor recounted an instance from the early Arrowhead years when Melville regularly referred to a neighbor as Mrs. Pecksniff, with the embarrassing consequence that his mother politely greeted the woman by that name when she came to call. This story Frances used to tell Eleanor with "a slightly malicious pleasure." The problem with it, first, is that Frances would not have been old enough to witness the scene. More importantly, it distorts Maria's sophistication. Maria knew her Dickens as well as anyone in the house. She was present at all novel-reading sessions, and indeed she established the family habit of reading novels aloud in the evenings. She read newspapers always, and given the controversial nature of *Martin Chuzzlewit* in the United States in 1843 and 1844, it is impossible that she did not know the name Pecksniff. As so often, family stories distort real events: perhaps Maria, the inveterate coiner of nicknames, was so used to referring to the woman as Mrs. Pecksniff that she simply spoke the insulting name before she caught herself. Frances did not like her Grandmother Melville, and did not judge her fairly.

Elizabeth Shaw Melville thought her husband had ill treated her, and she may even have thought he was insane. Melville ill treated her by borrowing a great sum of money in secret and not being able to pay it back. When she finally inherited a competence he ran through an enormous portion of it in the exchange of Arrowhead for the New York house, it appears: yet Sam had been involved in that transaction and had not protested, and seems not to have blamed Allan afterward. Melville spent his wife's money on books, in 1862, especially, when he was not earning a penny. If he had really paid Harpers to publish *Battle-Pieces*, with his wife's money, that would have been abusive if not clear proof of insanity, but that assertion by Eugene Exman in *The House of Harper* (New York: Harper & Row, 1967) cannot be true, the Harper accounts show. If Melville gave a whale tooth to his wife inscribed to her as "E. S. Doolittle," then that was psychological abuse, even if the rules of the marriage dictated that she take it as sportively affectionate. If Herman taunted her with her intellectual inadequacies, or if he merely made literary allusions designed to go over her head and leave her *knowing* that something had gone over her head, then that would have been psychological abuse.

How badly could he have mistreated his family? The English confidence man Thomas Powell in his revised article in 1856 in the New York *Daily News* had accused Melville of setting out to make himself "a Psychological Cerberus," presumably by growing, above his shoulders, heads of three dead prose writers, Sir Thomas Browne, Swift, and Rabelais, *Mardi* being the result. Melville in 1849, when Powell knew him, a dog with three heads, a serpent's tail, and a snaky mane, admitting the shades of dead writers into his private Hades and never letting them out again? Was Melville now carrying three heads, yet remaining cur enough to bark, snap, and lash out at his living wife and four children, snarling words which struck them as brusque, gruff, ironic, or sarcastic missiles? Whatever he was doing, his wife may never have wanted to leave him. She wanted the Shaws to understand her sorrows, and they may have been the ones to think of ways she could leave him without scandal.

A complication is that it is impossible to draw the line between what the Shaws concluded from Lizzie's reports and what they had concluded over the previous eighteen years from the public prints and what they led Lizzie to believe. The Shaws all believed the worst of what they read in the papers about Herman, always excepting the judge, who during the Harvard murder case had experienced foul personal abuse in anonymous letters, some of them vilely scatological and containing violent threats. He had taken by far the longest view of Herman Melville as a human being. Which living Shaw could forget the way the January 1852 *Southern Quarterly Review* used Ahab's speeches to attack Melville himself: "His ravings, and the ravings of some of the tributary characters, and the ravings of Mr. Melville himself, meant for eloquent declamation, are such as would justify a writ *de lunatico* against all the parties." Or the Boston *Post* on *Pierre*: "'Pierre; or the Ambiguities' is, perhaps, the craziest fiction extant"; and it might have emanated "from a lunatic hospital rather than from the quiet retreats of Berkshire." Or the *American Whig Review* on *Pierre:* Melville "might have been mad to the very pinnacle of insanity" without deserving utter condemnation, but he had been worse—he had been immoral. In July 1853 "Sir Nathaniel" in the London *New Monthly Magazine* (reprinted in Boston in *Littell's*) had been extravagant about *The Whale:* "The style is maniacal—mad as a March hare—mowing, gibbering, screaming, like an incurable Bedlamite, reckless of keeper or strait-waistcoat." No one could forget that little news item in the New York *Day Book* headed "HERMAN MELVILLE CRAZY." These words were read and remembered, even if Lem and Oakes did not keep a file of them handy.

Perhaps even harder to deal with than the public accusations that Elizabeth's husband was insane were the long public analyses of his defective character, as when the *United States Magazine and Democratic Review* (January 1852) declared: "his vanity has destroyed all his chances of immortality, or even of a good name with his own generation." Melville's vanity was "immeasurable," he would "centre all attention upon himself, or he will abandon the field of literature at once." In Boston, in the review of *Pierre* in the *Daily Times*, the family had read not only commonplace criticism ("No man has more foolishly abused great original powers") but a detailed attack on Melville's lack of qualifications to try to reform any part of the world: "Ambitious of the character of a reformer, he has been playing away at social evils, with about as much skill, and with results as useful, as Mr. Winkle [Nathaniel

Winkle in Dickens's *Pickwick Papers*] made war on the pheasants." This reviewer could sound reasonable enough to Hope, Oakes, Lem, and Sam. What Charles Creighton Hazewell had said in the Boston *Daily Times* in 1852 was especially appealing to such good Unitarians as the Shaws were, taught that those who declare themselves to be impoverished have little legitimate cause for their grumblings. The Shaw family had evidence of Herman's defects of character in his willingness to take and misuse money from the ever-indulgent Judge Shaw, beginning with his letting his father-in-law subsidize the disastrous self-indulgence of *Mardi*.

One of the worst things Melville could have done, as far as the Shaws were concerned, was to make any offhand ranking of himself as a writer along with indisputably great writers. If any member of the Shaw family, after 1852, or especially after 1856, or in 1866, after Lowell's great "Commemoration Ode" had been published, heard Herman make a casual comment about his being a prose writer who ranked with Washington Irving, or as good a poet as Professor Longfellow, that person (not just Hope, Lem, or Oakes, but even Sam and Lizzie) would necessarily have thought him insane, at least temporarily, for making such an absurd claim. In 1859, and probably as early as 1858, Melville's writing poetry had been a secret shared, for a long time, only with Lizzie, and they had been like conspirators, allies in an exciting campaign. In 1860 Lizzie had learned that publishers did not share her husband's confidence that he had made himself into a true poet, and her own trust in her husband's judgment of himself was broken. What Lizzie says of him indicates that he did not defend himself against reviewers, but if he ever burst out, in the early 1860s, with some comment implying that he was a great poet, then that was clear sign of madness. In 1849 Lizzie had written to her stepmother: "When you hear any individual express an opinion with regard to it *[Mardi]*, I wish you would tell me—whatever it is—good or bad—without fear of offence merely by way of curiosity." In 1860, in all the intervening years until 1867, Lizzie still wholly lacked the capacity for making a personal judgment that her husband was a great writer, and if she retained much lingering faith in his greatness, particularly as a poet (she had showed some such faith in her letter to Duyckinck about how John Milton's *Paradise Lost* would be received in New York in 1860), she lacked the strength to interpose her opinion against the well-educated authorities in the Boston newspapers. Not many wives would have been able to believe in Melville's genius after he had been denounced by all the best authorities (many of whom were personally known to the Shaws) year after year. It is hopeless to try to separate whatever Melville did to Lizzie to make her feel ill treated from everything she and the other Shaws had read about him in the papers and magazines. Even subjecting her to such shame in the public press was a form of mistreatment. Yet in May 1867 once again she was not willing "to say the word" and attempt to separate from him.

More than that, Lizzie was already schooling herself in patience and, indeed, in fortitude. On 8 May 1867 she wrote down these lines:

> II Timothy 4th Chap 7th verse
> "Hold on," my soul, with courage for the "fight"
> "Hold out," my feet, the weary "course" to run
> "Hold fast" my faith, bring patience to the "rack"—
> Oh, God, thou knowest each hour of need! look down,
> Give thine own help for courage, strength and faith,
> Or never may we win the victor's waiting crown.
> All Souls church May 8th 1867 E. S. M.

(First she wrote "hope to win" the crown, then marked through the words "hope to.") Below, perhaps years later, she made a note: "A sermon of Dr Bellows suggested these lines to me." She had made her decision while the Shaws and Dr. Bellows were still plotting to rescue her.

After receiving Sam's letter Dr. Bellows paid a long pastoral call on Elizabeth Melville at East Twenty-sixth Street while her husband was at work, and then on 18 May, in the midst of his last-minute preparations for a voyage to Europe and the Levant, he stopped by at Twenty-sixth Street, only to miss his parishioner. He may even then have been on his way to the *Ville de France*, which he boarded in the early afternoon of that day. Elizabeth wrote to him on 20 May, perhaps hoping he was still in the city:

> My dear Sir, I cannot refrain from writing to say how troubled I was at having missed seeing you on Saturday, and how much I appreciate your kind attention in calling in the busy moments of your departure. . . . I also wanted to thank you for the active interest you took in my behalf. I do so now—most sincerely—and whatever further trial may be before me, I shall feel that your counsel is a strong help to sustain, more perhaps than any other earthly counsel could. I think you will be glad to know that your long talk with me has been a very great comfort.

The next family document that survives demonstrates the strength of Melville's legal position: on 23 May Elizabeth S. Melville and Herman Melville signed an authorization for proceeds of a mortgage held by Judge Shaw to be paid to Samuel S. Shaw; their signatures are followed by those of the Boston family, Hope S. Shaw, Lemuel Shaw, and Samuel S. Shaw.

Soon after her marriage Elizabeth had copied some lines on "The Love of Later Years" into her commonplace book (from which Augusta copied it into her own on 2 April 1849): "They err, who deem Love's brightest hour in blooming youth is known. / Its purest, tenderest, holiest power, in after life is shown. / When passions chastened and subdued to riper years are given, / And earth, and earthly things, are viewed, in light that breaks from Heaven." Lizzie had written Sam Savage in September 1847, "with Herman with me always, I can be happy and contented anywhere." Now she could test that resolve. Neither her situation nor her character would change at once. She would still unburden herself to Hope about her unhappiness, but she would not again be party to plotting about how she could leave her husband. Years would pass before she believed in his genius, but when she did at last believe, on the basis of praise from England, where critics were even more infallible than Boston newspapermen, she kept that faith passionately until she died. During all of this period of Bellows's involvement in the Melvilles' marital crisis, Herman Melville himself may or may not have suspected that his wife had thought that he was insane and may or may not have known that she had thought of leaving him. For all the elaborate scheming and plotting revealed by Samuel Shaw's letter to Henry Bellows, the possibility remains that Herman Melville may have lived through that spring of 1867 absorbed by his attempts to master and retain his job, then may have lived through the summer and the fall and the rest of his life wholly ignorant that his wife had ever been badgered to separate from him and had ever for a moment considered doing so. Who would have mentioned it to him? Not his wife.

Maria in her long visit to Twenty-sixth Street had seemed oblivious to any abnormal strains in the household. She had reason to be happier than she had been in many years, now that Tom was home from the sea, and she was happy to be home in the old Mansion House at Gansevoort after so long an absence. After the war, in 1865, 1866, and especially in 1867, the Mansion House had become the summer gathering place for all the family. The house was large but absolutely unpretentious; the nearest thing to an architectural flourish was a Greek key design in the double-block of wood ornamenting the middle of the lintel over the front double door (whereas the corner blocks and the blocks at the outside corners of the window lintels were ornamented merely with diamond-angled centers). The main floor was divided so that there was no such hall running the depth of the house as distinguished Uncle Thomas's real mansion, now Broadhall, but instead a front and a back hall. One of these, presumably the south one, was big enough that it could be designated "the hall sitting room"; there in the mid-1860s Maria and Tom could play chess while others sewed and chatted. There was (on the east side of the house?) a south parlor and north parlor (the one facing the road, and containing the most furniture), a bedroom off the south parlor, with an attached closet, a room at the (west) end of the back hall, a closet under the stairs. The "*canopied* bed" that Maria in the mid-1860s offered to let Peter and Susan sleep in was probably in one of the first floor bedrooms.

On one "Glorious Fourth" (4 July 1870) Augusta wrote Aunt Susan about the layout of the house:

> And now I want to ask you which room you think Uncle would prefer. The room off of the parlor or the large room up stairs? I am afraid the stair case would be too fatiguing for him. The three rooms there are at your service, for Albert [Peter's valet] can have the one we have always given to the nurses when here. You will have all that part of the house to yourselves, quite like Saratoga and Congress Hall, a suite of apartments. But I am fearful that the stairs would be too much for Uncle. Would he not like the lower room better, & then he can go out on the piazza whenever he wants to. It is perfectly charming there.... Ah how you would all enjoy the piazza this morning. I have the hammock up & will soon be swinging in it with my book. I told Mamma she might have her turn, hour about.

There was a north rear bedroom. Off or in one of the bedrooms, now or later, was an "earth closet," a dry toilet with dirt, lime, and charcoal, that did not have to be emptied every day. On the second floor the southeast room was sunny in the mornings (from two of the three east windows on that floor as well as a south window). A room adjoining it was used as a study. There was a servant's room, a storeroom, the small upper hall, the main upper hall (big enough to store at least one chest with ancestral military clothing), a big middle back bedroom, a northeast bedroom (with one eastern window and one or two north windows of the five on the north side), and a room adjoining it.

The attic sloped sharply to the south and north, but a wide center section was available for the usual garret storage, and there was light from two windows on either end, east and west. The kitchen, dining room, and a closet were in the basement, which on the east was at ground level, so that it could be entered from the outside and would be well lighted for breakfast, especially. By the mid-1860s one little room was designated as the "tea room," where they "tea'd" in a hearty way in the early evening, and after a late chat on the north piazza the family would meet in the front room (the front parlor) until nine, then have prayers together and retire. There was something on the first floor called "the *Slate* Apartment" presumably because of the floor. (Cousin Kate Gansevoort's hand is hard: perhaps, being ironic, they were calling it the "State" apartment.) There was a back piazza also, to the south, mentioned in 1880, when Fanny had both front and back piazzas painted.

Maria's family gradually became familiar with the house now that rooms were no longer explicitly or tacitly reserved as Uncle Herman's domain, but none of them ever explored anything like all of the treasures of Revolutionary costumes and documents stashed away there. All the chests, drawers, and shelves were full, as Helen ruefully wrote Kate (Peter's daughter) much later, 28 October 1885: "the furniture is nothing—in comparison—it is the contents of the pantries, and closets, the chests, the trunks, & the drawers." There were many books about the house—as Kate Gansevoort said in 1867, "the most interesting of books, good books, & novels, Travels & Poetry, Biographies & History"—rows and rows of books. Some had been purchased by Allan Melvill, Maria's husband, some by Gansevoort Melville. Long before Helen complained in 1885, the library had gotten wholly out of hand, to the point that Augusta or Fanny had some local artisan take the paperback books, probably hundreds of them, and amateurishly bind several together, higgledy-piggledy, under cheap thin leather, and then crudely stamp and gild "NOVELS" on the spine—anything to control the sprawl and to help preserve the books, some of them more important for their inscriptions than their bibliographical value. Maria and Tom played chess, as Herman and Tom would also do. There was a piano and even a local piano tuner, although this was not Maria's girlhood piano, which she had left behind at Arrowhead and which Allan and Jane had junked; the more respectful Lizzie spotted it and managed to save some of its wood for use in memorial picture frames. The hammock was put up on or beside the piazza every summer, at least in the 1860s, under one of the locust trees, and there was a swing put up under an old butternut tree. On dry afternoons women as well as men played croquet.

The village changed a little every year. By 16 August 1867 Kate Gansevoort reported to her father that the "square in front has been enclosed & several new stores built & they say Gansevoort has grown very much." The Hamilton Child directory for 1871 reported "two churches, a hotel, two stores, a woolen factory, a grist mill" (Maria's) and "several mechanic shops." Peter Gansevoort still owned lots opposite the hotel and he owned one of the groves. Someone built "a large store on the street & rail-road line," the second or third store in the village. Kate, by then a regular visitor, approved the enclosing of the square—enclosed and sown with buckwheat because it had been used for some years "as a base ball ground & made disagre[e]able by a collection of men & boys using profane language & making noises," within hearing of anyone (even a woman) on the piazza, some of them, evidently, direct descendants of the louts who had tried to intimidate Uncle Herman a third of a century earlier.

An orchard with very large apple trees near the house blocked the view of the Landon outbuildings. At the edge of the circular drive in front of the house had been a good-sized beech tree, until it was broken in two in a storm in 1864 and had to be removed. There were beautiful balsam firs, even after one was blown down toward the end of 1869. Gansevoort offered pleasant walks which were especially appreciated in the mid-1860s, when Tom and Herman were more on the scene. Maria wrote Kate Gansevoort on 5 September 1864, wishing she could have been there while Helen was, since Helen "is always so cheerful & happy & being fond of walking she would have taken many pleasant walks with you." Even Lizzie and her daughters some summers took time from their more essential visit to the aging Hope Shaw and the other Shaws in Boston. As the years passed, traditions grew up. Captain Tom had a sailor's expertise with a knife, and showed his skill on a tree, so that on 20 August 1867 Kate Gansevoort wrote in her diary about walking with Tom "over to *the Dam*—the old mill & Forest to the tree where *our names* are cut had a lovely walk—Played croquet too"—all this besides enjoying the great new dessert: "Had Ice Cream for Dinner—Deacon Lem's furnished the Ice, Cousin Helen made the custard & Tom & I froze it." There were errands that were pleasant enough in the brilliant summers, as when Kate Gansevoort recorded on 21 August 1867: "Walked over to Delia's the washerwoman about Kates clothes Cousin Helen made Ice Cream alone today as a surprise—Florence Melville is a devoted knitter & crochets very nicely under my tuition." Maria could return favors to the Albanians, as when she reported on 5 September 1864 that *"Those shirts"* were "being made by a sister in Law of 'Stella Martin' the celebrated colored Preacher, who preached to large crowded houses in London, and in America."

By the mid-1860s Kate Gansevoort was coming regularly, and the fare was better all the time. On 9 September 1864 Maria thanked Kate Gansevoort for sending up on the train fruit baskets, plums, delicious grapes, and pears that needed some time to ripen. In winter, after regular trade was reestablished, postwar, fruit from the Caribbean islands or Florida was always a good gift for the Albany Gansevoorts to send. On 15 March 1865 Augusta thanked Kate: "The oranges are most excellent; please tell Uncle & Aunt Susan, with my love; very sweet & thin skinned." Augusta being Augusta, she enjoyed only a few of the oranges herself and devoted others to a higher purpose: "I have some poor sick persons to whom I have sent them." It became a tradition for Susan to send up a substantial supply of old-fashioned New Year's Cakes, the enormous round ones that Dutch children (that is, the Albany Dutch) used to make last for hours, nibbling around the edges. Something Maria said on New Year's Day, 1867, was especially poignant: "The Basket with New Years cake arrived last Eveg. Mr Lawrence kindly sent it in, immediately. I was sorry Tom was not here to see them. He has not seen so many of the festive cakes since he was a lad of fourteen." (Maria may have meant sixteen, but with her record for accuracy Tom may have been away from home earlier than we know, perhaps making a voyage before 1846.)

Flowers in winter were welcome, as Tom made clear in a letter to Kate Gansevoort on 1 February 1867: "Mamma was very, very, much pleased with your beautiful present of flowers, & when she saw them exclaimed 'Kate is a dear good girl' to which I mentally rejoined, she is indeed, a dear [double underlined], good, kind, *sweet*, *lovely* & *loviable* girl." Tom had run errands for Aunt Susan all over the Orient, even when he knew her only slightly. In 1864 he had been unable to bring cashmere shawls for Kate, "not having been to India this Voyage," but that November he had for Aunt Susan "a box of Chinese Tea — The finest English Breakfast *Congon*" and for Kate "a sett of Chinese cups & Tea pot. The Tea is delicious — aromatic & delicate & the cups & tea pot curious. Tea made in China always is better (to my tastes) & *my China* is very useful." Tom's services continued, his way of repaying Kate's and her parent's gifts to his mother. On 12 February 1867 from New York Tom sent Susan by express mail a "15 lbs box of Japan Tea" ("I have tasted the same kind of tea on board the ship & think it very fine") and "a case of Canton Ginger." On 30 July 1868 Augusta sent thanks to Uncle Peter and Aunt Susan for "a splendid piece of sturgeon," from which Maria had already "enjoyed three meals . . . , broiled, boiled & pickled," with "enough for an appetizing little meal yet for her." On 21 December 1869 Augusta wrote Peter and Susan to tell them that they were sending "a roll of sausage by the evening train" the next day and that if she could "manage to get it in a basket" she was "going to add a piece of head cheese," entirely of her own making, and, she thought, "remarkably fine." On 16 April 1870 Fanny thanked Aunt Susan for the pigeons they had sent home with her; she and Augusta had eaten them for breakfast and found them delicious ("Ellen understands cooking them").

Later, on 3 June 1870, luring Peter and Susan back to Gansevoort, Maria recommended the air, walks about the grounds and the garden instead of "the hot pavement in the Avenue, & the pure fresh air as improvement on the dust & noise of the Street," and itemized foods: "We have fresh butter, fresh eggs, fine cheese, & remarkably fine pork." They could send to Saratoga Springs for anything Peter might desire: everything was within reach if not in hand: "The whole house is at your service to select such rooms as you may prefer, & I do think that you would enjoy your stay here & have more comfort than a Hotel can furnish. The warmest welcome awaits you. Water from the Springs can be brought here, as often as you wish. We get a box of high Rock Spring water of two Dozen send it back & have it refilled whenever it is empty. Our house with its new paint & paper is much improved & freshend, & I think if you try it you will be as comfortable as possible." She had already invited Albert (Peter's valet) to come with him: "He is indispensible to your comfort, & I shall be glad to see him."

The Mansion House was in its glory when Melville arrived at Gansevoort late in the day on 29 July 1867 for the start of his vacation. Soon Malcolm, and then Stanwix, joined him. Kate Gansevoort reported to Henry on 30 or 31 July: "I had a letter from Gus Melville this morning—They must have a full house at Gansevoort just now. Mr. Hoadley, Cousin Kate—three children & nurse—Malcome & Maria from Pittsfield—Cousin Helen, & Cousin Herman are there—*only ten*, besides their own family—& what a delightful time they have." "Maria" (Milie) was Kate's mistake—Malcolm had escorted his Cousin Florence from Pittsfield to Gansevoort. Malcolm did write Milie, on 30 July:

> Flory and myself arrived here safely, last evening at about seven o'clock and found all the good people well and expecting us. We had rather a comfortable ride from Pittsfield, than otherwise; had to change cars twice, once at Greenbush, and once at Troy. Grandmama and all your Aunts, Uncles and cousens were real disapointed that you did not come on with us; but I consoled them by saying that you hoped to make a long visit, later in the summer, which they thought would be much better than to make such a short visit now. We found Papa here, he came up Monday evening; Stan is expected this afternoon; and I can tell you that we shall have a housefull. I had a real plesant visit at Pittsfield, and enjoyed myself very much, and now thank you for your hospitality to me when there. It is a magnificent day to day just such another one as yesterday was.

Malcolm added that he had "just come in from carrying Frank around the walks" near the house; sweetly Malcolm said of his cousin, not yet two years old, "he and I have become great friends." Hoadley watched this new friendship and put it in a larger context of Malcolm's behavior—"his purity, his gentleness, his truthfulness," "his playful fondness of children, his hearty enjoyment of nature on Horseneck beach and among the Berkshire hills," and in the foothills of the Adirondacks.

Cousin Kate Gansevoort went up shortly after Melville left to return to work, and on a rainy Friday, 16 August, re-inventoried the inhabitants to her father: "Cousin Kate Hoadley, her three children, Cousin Helen, & Stanwix Melville (Cousin Herman's youngest son—) Fanny, Gus, Aunt Melville, & K. G. form the household here." Kate Gansevoort's letters describe happy family life. Here is her description to her stepmother on 17 August, after Herman had gone back to work:

> Dinner is over. Aunt Melville has retired for her afternoon nap. Cousin Helen and Kate are in their rooms, Cousin Gus putting her work basket in order and entertaining at the same time the three children, Minnie, Lottie, and Frank. Florence Melville is writing home, and Tom Melville lying in the hammock reading Harpers Magazine, and Fanny busy with the domestic affairs. Gus is the upper housekeeper and Fan has care of the Culinary Dept.
>
> Aunt Melville looks quite well, but feels the want of regular exercise. She walks about the house, but has taken only one meal downstairs since October. She finds the noise of the family so fatiguing. The other morning I saw her breakfast served on a *salver* in the parlour-onions, cheek [beef cheek? cheese?], bread rolls and tea—so you see Papa and Aunt Melville's tastes are alike.

Two days later she wrote Henry that "Stanwix Melville went fishing this morning & caught *three* small fish for his Grandmother. . . . He is a pupil of Cousin Gus, who is the strictest of teachers & truly a good woman." On the same day, Kate Gansevoort elaborated on the division of responsibilities at the Mansion House in a letter to Henry: "Fanny attends to the culinary dept. & Gus has the entire care of her Mother & the upper part of the house—I never saw such a devoted, & lovely household—all stirring to do good & benefit each other." By then Tom had been pressed into service: "They have one servant girl—Their man servant left the day I came & Tom supplies his place early & late in waiting upon the females of the family & Henry you know the Gansevoorts are helpfull, but give a great deal of advice & Fanny & Gus—are descendants of that family." That summer of 1867 the Mansion House was a "full house" where the family had "a delightful time."

After Malcolm returned home from Gansevoort tensions increased on Twenty-sixth Street. The calm young man who had made such good friends with his baby Cousin Frank at eighteen and a half was of an age to see himself as his mother's best protector, after his Shaw uncles had failed. No surviving evidence, only observed patterns in family psychology, links the marital crisis of the spring with the events of the late summer. Although the war was a year or more over, Malcolm "joined a volunteer regiment," finding he had "a boy's newly awakened enthusiasm for whatever related in any way to weapons, arms and military equipments," Hoadley later wrote. After his vacation, apparently in early September, he received his new uniform and "tried [it] on in the evening, to gratify his desire to see himself in the habiliments of a soldier, and to amuse his sisters younger than himself, who teased him with harmless banter on his martial vanity." A pistol was part of his accoutrements, and he "carried it in his pocket and slept with it under his pillow for weeks, as he had told his fellow clerks and his brother Stanwix." This "fondness for arms, for military discipline, and for athletic sports," Hoadley saw as "exactly proportionate in strength and intensity to the purity of their character, and their freedom from degrading vices, ignoble aims and debasing pleasures." In early September Malcolm was "a member of a base ball club, and was looking forward with a lively interest to a 'match game' to be played" in a few days, a chance to win back the laurels his team had recently lost.

By early September, or some weeks before, Malcolm had pushed against his parents' ideas of proper hours (Hoadley said), staying "out sometimes pretty late in the evening after joining the military organization." Sam Shaw reported to his mother on 12 September that Malcolm had formed a habit of staying "out late at night recently so much so that his father took away his night key from him," and both Herman and Lizzie talked "very seriously about it but they both say that they believe that there was nothing in his dissipation more than a fondness for social frolicking with his young friends, and acquaintances that he made down town." Sam continued: "They know he had *no* vices." Malcolm was sexually innocent, and not debauched by alcohol, his Uncle John was also sure:

> Eighteen years of age, tall, manly, engaging, full of frank and generous confidence, yet possessing a noble reserve and power of self-control; pure, free from low tastes, or bad companionships; fond of the society of his gentle and amiable mother; the delight of his little sisters, in whom he also delighted, pleased with the society of well-bred ladies in company with his mother; with bright business prospects, good social position, the love of all who knew him, not one of whom even suspected him of a wrong action or an evil thought.

On the night of 10 September Lizzie sat up for him, and Malcolm at last came home at three o'clock Wednesday morning, the eleventh, claiming to have "been at an entertainment at Yorkville given by some friends." Lizzie thought he "showed no signs of having had any liquor," and "remonstrated with him kindly" but "did not scold him in the least." Hoadley heard that he kissed his mother when he found her waiting up, "sat down by her side, put his arm round her neck, begged her pardon for keeping her up so long," and "promised not to do so again." Then he kissed her good night and went to bed, according to what Sam wrote to his mother on 12 September.

In the morning when Malcolm did not rise to prepare for work in Lathers's office, Fanny or Bessie went up to call him:

> He answered "yes" but did not come down — Time went on and Herman advised Lizzie to let him sleep, be late at the office & take the consequences as

a sort of punishment — and then went himself down to his business. The day went on and though Lizzie tried to wake him by knocking & calling, she did not succeed — a not un[u]sual thing she says — and it was not till Herman got home in the evening unusually late that the door was broken down and Macky found in his night clothes in bed with a pistol shot in his head and apparently several hours dead.

Hoadley described the scene:

There is no doubt indeed that he died by a shot from a pistol held in his own right hand; for when he was found dead, he lay as if asleep in his night clothes, and in his natural attitude on his left side, with his left hand under his knee, as had been his life-long habit, his right hand fallen across the body holding the fatal pistol; calm, smiling, the eyes closed, the lips just parted, as they always were when he slept, a wound in his temple, his door locked, his watch, his money, his clothes, all disposed as he left them on retiring.

The Melvilles summoned Dr. Augustus K. Gardner somehow (Stanwix was not there to be sent on that horrible mission), once the young author of *Old Wine in New Bottles: or, Spare Hours of a Student in Paris* (1848) and soon to be the eminent author of the 1870 *Conjugal Sins*, dedicated to the "Native American People" — whites before the Irish invasion, that is. A few months earlier Gardner had been willing to support Lizzie in her decision to leave her husband. Now he at once advised that the coroner should be called.

At the cost (paid by the city?) of $11.31 and a quarter cent, the coroner's jury held an inquest and came to this verdict: "That the said Child came to his death by Suicide by shooting himself in the head with a pistol at said place while laboring under temporary insanity of Mind." This verdict, printed in the city papers, horrified the parents, and not the parents only: many others also acted as if suicide were as grievous a sin as the new Irish immigrants thought it. In the midst of their grief, the family mobilized forces to alter this verdict, and on 16 September the city papers (the New York *Evening Post* was one) began printing corrections:

The jurors on the inquest held in regard to the death of the son of Mr. Herman Melville have made the following explanation of their verdict:

"We, the undersigned jurors in the inquest of the death of Malcolm Melville, on the 11th inst., desire to correct any erroneous impressions drawn from our verdict of 'suicide.' We believe that his death was caused by his own hand, but not that the act was by premeditation or consciously done, no motive for it having appeared during the inquest or after it. It has since been learned that out of a boyish whim he had been in the habit (unknown to his parents) of sleeping with his pistol under his pillow, and whether the act was committed in a state of aberration incident to disturbed or somnambulistic sleep, or whether the death arose from an accident in carelessly pulling out the weapon from under his head, it is impossible now to determine. Justice to the deceased, whom some of us knew personally for an upright and amiable young man, impels this added statement."

In that paper William Cullen Bryant, a member of Dr. Bellows's church, printed, after the names of the jurors (neighbors of the Melvilles), a letter from Dr. Samuel Osgood, the minister of the Church of the Messiah on Broadway, who was in charge at All Souls in Dr. Bellows's absence abroad. As the Melvilles' spokesman, Osgood corrected the "wrong impression of the cause of the death of young Malcolm Melville." Hoadley in the Boston *Weekly Advertiser* likewise repudiated the thought that Malcolm's memory "should lie under the imputation either of such a crime as suicide or of such a fearful scourge as insanity." In the twenty-first century one of Melville's great-grandchildren remembers being told fiercely by Melville's granddaughter Frances Thomas Osborne *never* to allow anyone to refer to Malcolm's death as suicide: it was an accident.

Stanny had still been in Pittsfield, and he and his Uncle Allan were on the train when Sam boarded it from the connecting train he had caught in Boston, so the three went down together, "straight to Elizabeth's house," Sam wrote to his mother. He explained: "The circumstances of Macky's death are very mysterious . . . today they have been subjected to the distressing ordeal of having an inquest . . . . Poor Lizzie is much exhausted but has not had time to realize the situation." The *Times* on the thirteenth, calling Malcolm the "son of a well-known literary gentleman," announced the time of the funeral: "Saturday, the 14th inst., at 8½ o'clock A.M." — early, so that no gawkers would be on the street. On Friday, 13 September, the *Tribune* began its "HOME NEWS" column with an item which would have been of interest to the family, under other circumstances: "Col. Richard Lathers of this city has purchased about 300 acres on Middle-st., at Pittsfield, Mass., and will erect a handsome Summer residence there." It went on, in the same column, with two more items:

> The Sanitary Inspectors, searching for filth and other predisposing causes of cholera, had occasion to make complaint last week against . . . 16 waste pipes and drains, 47 full and offensive privies, 9 gutters, &c., 1 hide and fat house.
>
> At No. 104 East Twenty-sixth-st., yesterday, Coroner Wildey held an inquest over the body of Malcolm Melville, a native of Boston, aged 18 years. . . .

This *Tribune* column was schematic in the trajectories of the fame and prosperity of Lathers and Melville — one ascending, crossing the other in descent; and the last juxtaposition of piggery, cesspools, and privies against the little that would be in print about Malcolm Melville — this last juxtaposition was unbearable to the parents.

Samuel Osgood, Orville Dewey's successor as minister of the Church of the Messiah, on Broadway, the rival Unitarian church, had bulldog jaws and what the Duyckincks had called a clear, "well toned" voice. He had been a writer of theological articles for the Unitarian weekly *Christian Inquirer,* and as such may have been the man of the world who took the time to review *Omoo* so approvingly or the manly admirer of *Moby-Dick* who observed only perfunctorily that there might have been "a little more reverence in the spirit of the book" (22 November 1851). Fond of German literature, and a translator of works from German, Osgood "never yielded to the rationalism characteristic of German theology," the Duyckincks had been happy to record. He was not the sort of man to intrude into the private grief of the family as he conducted his duties, but he may have comforted simply because, in an un-Unitarian way, almost, he believed that Jesus had a divine nature and was the mediator between God and mankind. He was also about as high church as a Unitarian dared to be, wearing the silk gown in the pulpit but regretfully eschewing the bands.

The fullest description of the funeral and burial is Kate Gansevoort's, in a letter to Henry on 19 September; despite the thick detail Kate may not have been present but merely paraphrasing closely from what Helen and others had written or told her, including an indirect report from Augusta through Kate's Aunt Melville:

> Well the funeral took place last Saturday morning Dr. Osgood (their Clergyman) read a chapter from the Bible — the 15th Chap. Corinthians the one used in the Episcopal Burial Service, made a short address & a prayer — Then after a pause — the young Volunteer Company to which Malcom belonged & who had asked the privilege of being present & carrying the coffin from the house to the cars — filed in at one door from the hall & out at the other — each pausing for an instant to look at the face of their lost comrade. Cousin Helen says they were all *so young* & it was really a sadly beautiful sight — for the cold limbs of the dead wore the same garments as the strong active ones of the living — Cousin Lizzie — his almost heart broken Mother having dressed her eldest son in the new suit he had taken such pride & pleasure in wearing — Four superb wreaths & crosses of the choicest white flowers were placed on the coffin & it was lifted to the shoulders of six of the company & born[e] down the steps, through the street to the car (on the Harlem R.R. I think) which Allan had secured for special use.
>
> The family, & mourners followed — They left the car at the entrance of the

> *Woodlawn Cemetery,* & the young bearers carried the coffin to the hearse — others bearing the flower, — What a sad sight — "The stone was rolled from the mouth of the cave —" as the scripture saith — & the remains placed in the receiving vault. Cousin Herman Lizzie the children, Gus & Allan selected a location & the others wandered through this new cemetery which she says will one day rival Greenwood.

The lower Manhattan cemeteries were filling up fast, as Allan had discovered in 1858. Why Herman and Lizzie selected the new Woodlawn, far away in the Bronx, rather than the more accessible Greenwood is not known, but probably it was much cheaper, and Herman and Lizzie wanted to buy lots for all of them. If Malcolm had not died so early, Melville himself may well have been buried much closer to where he lived, for by that time Lizzie could have afforded a more expensive plot.

Lizzie and Herman dealt with their pain in their own ways, and oddly, as such ways always seem to outsiders. To John Hoadley, Melville wrote about 13 September: "I wish you could have seen him as he lay in his last attitude, the ease of a gentle nature. Mackie never gave me a disrespectful word in his life, nor in any way ever failed in filialness." To end his life by intolerable carelessness, if not by willfulness, Melville apparently did not see at that moment as a lapse in filialness. And Melville was defending Malcolm, not defending himself and not reproaching himself. According to Augusta, Herman remained "quite composed," and Lizzie "had not shed a tear" that she had witnessed, "but poor little Stanwix seems heartbroken." At the house were Tom, Allan and Jane, Milie (Malcolm's twin in birth), and — perhaps because he had escorted Augusta — Gus Peebles. To Henry on 15 September Kate wrote: "I pity the poor parents — both Cousin Herman & Lizzie are of such nervous temperaments I should fear for *their peace* of *mind*," and the next day she added an analysis and some philosophical musings:

> Cousin Herman is I think a very strict parent & Cousin Lizzie thoroughly good but inefficient. She feels so thankful she did not scold him or remonstrate as she intended So she cannot blame herself for having induced him from despair at her fault-finding, to put an end to his life.
>
> I sometimes wish we mortals had the power of seeing the heart & feelings of our friends — I believe there would be greater happiness were such the case — We so often distrust & blame where we should not, because we judge wrongly — & mistake the motives of the actions of others.

During these days of stress, Herman and Lizzie gave away something precious. Lizzie may never have regretted giving the bust of her father to the Lenox Bar, but she soon regretted their giving a tinted photograph of Malcolm to his volunteer company. Later, with some inconvenience, they retrieved it.

After the funeral Melville gained permission to take off work for a week, and he and Lizzie fled to Arrowhead, apparently without the three surviving children. Less than two months earlier, Malcolm had made a visit to a much altered Arrowhead. During the last four years Allan had become the Lord of Arrowhead as Herman never had been, and his daughter Florence is the source of a detailed contemporary description, a composition she wrote at boarding school in March 1868 on "My Country Home." She mentions that the parlor, on the southern side, is shaded "by an arbor overgrown with a clustering grapevine," and she names the color of the house. Some of her Uncle Herman's phrases seem already to have passed into family usage as common property, as if Herman's words went with the deed to Arrowhead:

> It is a spacious farmhouse, of a dark red color originally but which many storms of wind and rain have gradually converted into a dingy nondescript hue. The rooms are large but with low ceilings, the windows narrow and the panes small. The chief attraction of the house is its great chimney, which, twelve feet square at the cellar, rises majestically through the centre of the mansion and terminates its diminished proportions about four feet above the roof. . . . There is an engraving in this room [the dining-room, once the kitchen] which I regard with considerable awe, a dark sketch whose subject seems to be taken from the Paradise Lost, and represents Satan enthroned upon the world and surrounded by crowned heads who are bowing before him. A strange picture which has a certain fascination for me. [The teacher accurately commented: *"Martin's probably."* It hangs now in the Berkshire Athenaeum.] The mantel which is of oak is decorated with a huge pair of antlers, swords which were wielded in the Revolution, a pair of pistols, a tomahawk, fencing foils, two old fashioned brass lamps and a Chinese joss.

(Some of this paraphernalia had been left by Herman and Lizzie: the joss is the household deity their daughter Frances reclaimed when Milie sold Arrowhead in 1927; maybe they left the mantel ornaments intact, as inappropriate for New York parlors.) Florence's account continues:

> Two weddings have been celebrated in this room and the walls have often resounded with merriment. In the front of the house and opening into the dining room are two rooms used respectively as library and parlor. The former is on the southern side and is shaded from the burning rays of the midday summer sun, by an arbor overgrown with a clustering grapevine. In the autumn when the leaves begin to fall, you can see from the side window, a carriage drive with a bright border of flowers succeeded by a vegetable gar-

den, and then a long piece of meadow, dotted with crooked old apple trees, which is dignified with the name of orchard. The parlor commands a more extensive view, and one of which I never tire. Thirty miles away to the north lies our sublime mountain Greylock in profound repose; on either side rise hills of lesser magnitude, noble indeed but far below this monarch of the valley, who, in his royal robes of purple, his peaks crowned with the golden mist of the setting sun, seems in truth what he has once been called, "Charlemagne among his Peers."

Nowhere can he be seen to such advantage as from our parlor, where the distant mountain and all the lovely expanse which lies between of velvet lawn sloping to the river's edge, dark woods rustling in the autumn winds and little villages nesting in the valley, are set around by the old window-frame, forming an everpresent, exquisite picture.

(The "Charlemagne" allusion is from "The Piazza": Melville's nieces knew his words about Arrowhead and the Berkshires.) Allan had the money to keep the property up, and watching him make his improvement was Richard Lathers, no less his brother-in-law for Sophia's death and his remarriage. From the time of Herman's occupancy, Lathers had been a visitor at Arrowhead, and now, on 16 August 1867, he sketched out a floor plan for the drawing room and for "Arrow Head Parlor." That summer Lathers's highest domestic vision was not of window treatments for Allan's summer home. On 19 August Kate Gansevoort reported to Henry the news from Pittsfield: "Mr Richard Lathers has been there visiting, & became so fascinated with Berkshire, that he has purchased three farms near Allans & will probably occupy *one* of the country seats. Aunt Melville thinks it a mere speculation, but Florence think's he will only spend a month or two there each summer." This was only the start of Lathers's purchases of farms across Holmes Road. He began with the property across from Arrowhead and over the next two years bought several more farms, until he commanded a spectacular view much of which consisted of property he owned.

Herman and Lizzie must have hoped to cherish better memories of Mackey at Arrowhead than in the city. When they arrived, with Milie the chatelaine, the autumn foliage was near the height of its glory, and they were poignantly aware that almost exactly seventeen years had passed since they moved into Arrowhead during Herman's exultant work on *Moby-Dick*—and they may have remembered their concern over Malcolm's temporary lameness during the bustle of getting settled. Herman and Lizzie were greeted by words from "I and My Chimney" painted on the chimney boards, Allan's way of enforcing the historical associations of the house. Lathers was probably there at Arrowhead when Herman and Lizzie arrived, for he snapped up another farm on 26 September. Herman always seems to have liked being around Lathers, despite his open pleasure in his ostentatious spending and his compulsive name-dropping, but there was no escaping the moral in the *Tribune*'s "HOME NEWS" column. Lathers (and Allan) were borne upward still farther, just as the cruelest blow yet had descended on the household at Twenty-sixth Street. In these years other shifts in Herman's relationship with Allan must have become obvious. One was the question of who inherited the Pittsfield friends. Sarah Morewood had regarded Jane Melville with disdain, but in the years after her death the pious widower Rowland Morewood saw more of the pious Allan and Jane than of Herman and Lizzie. He and Allan were now responsible owners of adjoining rural estates in the Berkshires (young Willie now lived at Broadhall and managed it year-round, under his father's close supervision). Rowland was a prosperous business man in Manhattan where Allan was a busy lawyer, and both were conscientious church-goers (who sometimes went to Episcopalian services together) and parents of promising children who were coming into maturity together.

While they were at Arrowhead Herman and Lizzie took some comfort not only from the air and scenery of the Berkshires and the familiar rooms of Arrowhead but from some of their old friends and acquaintances. Ellen Brittain, now the mistress of Broadhall, during this visit gave Lizzie a copy of Frederick W. Faber's *Hymns*, newly published in Northampton, and into it Lizzie seems later to have placed the inscription used for Malcolm's grave: "So good, so young, / So gentle, so sincere, / So loved, so early lost, / May claim a tear." Herman took the occasion to present a copy of *Battle-Pieces* to "The College Colonel" — Major General William F. Bartlett, pale, sharp-featured, now one-legged. Nothing else of their activities is on record, though in all likelihood they got out for drives on dry autumn days.

After about a week Herman and Lizzie were home, benefited by the visit, as Tom reported to Cousin Kate. In the weeks that followed the Melvilles did what had to be done. Melville worked, they bought lots in Woodlawn, they had Flossy (Florence) and Kitty to dinner late in October while Milie stayed out the season at Arrowhead. From Arrowhead Milie wrote a note saying Mackie had been "always obliging and affectionate" to her and her sisters. Touched, Melville on 22 October wrote her that what she said "was but of a piece" with Malcolm's "whole nature and conduct." Melville told her he and Lizzie had been doing sad duties, getting new photographs of Malcolm made from two tin-types, "one representing him in his ordinary dress, and the other in the regimental one." Sam Shaw took his mother on her first visit to Washington, and the two stopped back by Twenty-sixth Street. Herman may have seen Evert Duyckinck, as usual, now easier to be around than most other men, since his own first son, Evert, had died, at sixteen. For once

Duyckinck really did know something of how Melville felt. By early November Herman and Lizzie could talk to Cousin Kate about Malcolm with outward calm, Kate wrote her stepmother, and even what she perceived as "pleasure." On his return to New York from Europe in mid-August 1868 Henry Bellows repeatedly quoted to Lizzie the precept in Revelation 3:2: "Be watchful, and strengthen the things that remain." (So she said to Kate Gansevoort Lansing, on 30 November 1902.)

There were reminders through these months that Melville had once had a literary career. He continued to make belated presentation copies of *Battle-Pieces*. From San Francisco late in 1866 Charles Warren Stoddard sent him his newly published *Poems* along with news that in Hawaii he had found no traces of Melville. A homosexual who had written even more fervently to Whitman, Stoddard had been excited by *Typee*, finding Kory-Kory so stimulating that he wrote a story celebrating the sort of male friendships to which Melville had more than once alluded. From the poems Stoddard sent, Melville may have sensed no homosexual undercurrent, and the extant draft of his reply in January 1867 is noncommittal. Late in the year, November 1867, someone asked him to contribute to the revived *Putnam's*. Melville responded politely, and the invitation from *Putnam's* might have proved momentous, for in January 1868, in the first issue, Charles F. Briggs posed this problem: "where, let us ask, is Herman Melville? Has that copious and imaginative author, who contributed so many brilliant articles to the MONTHLY, let fall his pen just where its use might have been so remunerative to himself, and so satisfactory to the public?" Elsewhere in the issue was the news that Melville was one of the "eminent writers" who had agreed to be listed among "probable contributors" and had expressed himself as "much complimented" at the invitation. He did not in fact contribute.

[29]

A Snug Harbor for the Melvilles
Late 1867–1868

> And through the hall there walked to and fro
> A jolly yeoman, marshall of the same,
> Whose name was Appetite; he did bestow
> Both guestes and meate, whenever in they came,
> And knew them how to order without blame,
> As him the steward badd.

In Spenser's *The Faerie Queene* (2.9.28), where Alma escorts her guests through the House of Temperance, Melville marks the first four lines on the left and underlines the first two and a half lines (Priscilla Ambrose Collection)

AFTER 1866 MELVILLE'S brother Tom had found himself less and less willing to captain another ship. He prepared one ship for another captain, he even thought of making a short voyage, to Brazil, but he was no longer eager to go back to China or India. He thought he and Hoadley could make fortunes in petroleum speculation in the new state of West Virginia. He needed to be around his family after so many years and was even happy to act as escort for any traveling female in a family where a woman almost never took a train trip alone, whatever women of a slightly lower class might have to do. As Kate Gansevoort had said in July 1866, the Gansevoort "place" needed a man, and the women in the Mansion House hoped Tom would "eventually" settle with them. Their hopes went counter to Tom's needs, but Maria through her connections helped him to become something better, the governor of the Sailors' Snug Harbor.

The Sailors' Snug Harbor, the American equivalent of Greenwich Hospital for aged and decrepit sailors (which Melville had made a point of visiting in 1849), was an almost fabulous institution, easy to rhapsodize about, as Louis Bagger did in the January 1873 *Harper's New Monthly Magazine:* "There is nowhere another institution conceived in the same spirit of liberal and unlimited benevolence, the famous Greenwich Hospital not excepted; nowhere else does the old sailor, after having braved many a storm and frequently faced death, find so safe and snug a harbor." The 1801 will of Robert Richard Randall had directed that the income from the leases of his Manhattan farmland, out in the country north of town, should be devoted to a home for aged, disabled, and destitute sailors. The trustees of the Sailors' Snug Harbor, fighting off decades of legal challenges to Randall's will, had created the richest and haughtiest charitable institution in the world, for by midcentury the farmland, now owned by the Harbor, had become Washington Square and its environs — the richest farm in America, wags said.

Young Herman had been taken by his father and John D'Wolf on an excursion as far as the Narrows, sailing past northern Staten Island when it was farmland. In the early 1830s, gambling that Manhattanites would like their own resort nearby, especially if it bore the name of the Prince Regent's seaside wonderland, developers built a row of mansions along the north side of Staten Island so that, on a bright day, they gleamed from the Battery, five or six miles away. Having purchased some of the best land, the trustees moved Sailors' Snug Harbor from Manhattan to New Brighton, Staten Island, in the early 1830s, after the Melvills left for Albany and Allan Melvill died. First the trustees constructed the main building with its two wings. True Greek temples might have been more splendid, but New Brighton was undeniably picturesque from the Battery by the time the Melvilles were all there in the 1840s. In 1846, the year of *Typee*, the trustees built the Governor's House on the west and the Physician's House on the east, both designed by William Ranlett. The three-story Governor's House had thirty rooms, including two parlors and a library; at some point in the century it had a designated billiard room as well. A staff of eight, give or take one or two, was required to keep it maintained. The Governor's House and the Physician's House were roughly paired in size and comforts, and the custom was to match renovation in one house with improvements in the other — new wallpaper in one, new wallpaper soon in the other, and so with new bays or piazzas or marble mantels, as requested by governor or physician and approved by the trustees.

In 1855 a large dining hall was built behind the main building and a chapel constructed to the east of it, not far behind the Physician's House. Flagged walks connected all the main buildings, including the houses. In front of the main entrance of the center building, surrounded by an iron railing, was "the plain marble monument that covers the remains of the founder of this noble charity," Captain Randall, as Louis Bagger said, having visited the Harbor and interviewed Governor Melville for his article. The hospital, begun in 1850, was southwest of the main buildings, set well behind the Governor's House. Between the hospital and the chapel were the service buildings such as the engine house, the blacksmith shop, and the morgue,

A Snug Harbor for the Melvilles: Late 1867–1868 653

and on the west were cottages for the senior employees such as the engineer, gardener, baker, and farmer, and the actual farm buildings were on the extreme southwest. This was a formidable institution, a town in itself. There was excellent cheap ferry service, two Manhattan–Staten Island steamboats arriving and leaving the dock once every hour from six in the morning until nine in the evening, a delightful twenty-minute voyage of roughly seven miles, ten cents one way, twenty cents round trip.

Joseph Greenleaf, the friend and intermediary between Peter Gansevoort and Allan Melvill in the 1820s, was a connection of Catherine Gansevoort, Uncle Herman's wife, and visited them at Gansevoort every fall, continuing to do so during Maria's occupancy. As treasurer of the Harbor for three decades, he was in a position to influence the other members of the board of trustees. The aging governor in 1867, Augustus De Peyster, bore Gansevoort family names, and was a close enough connection that Peter had taken Kate to see him at the Harbor when she was young. In the first weeks of mourning for Malcolm, Tom was busy escorting his sisters home from New York and in general smoothing the lives of the family, but in November, when Governor De Peyster had become obviously incompetent to perform his duties, Greenleaf began maneuvering to replace him with Captain Thomas Melville. Uncle Peter was too ill to help, but at Allan's instigation Kate Gansevoort procured letters in Tom's favor from Albany friends, as she explained to her brother on 21 November: "I applied to Hon. Robert H. Pruyn who wrote a strong recommendatory letter, to Mayor Hoffman which he signed as also did Father & Judge Parker—I forwarded it as was desired, but could get no one to write to Senator Morgan or Rev. Morgan Dix Rector of Trinity Church"—Morgan Dix's father being the Major General John A. Dix of Bond Street, Peter's old friend, the boy-hero of the War of 1812 and now a Civil War hero. John T. Hoffman was especially important, since as mayor of New York City he was *ex officio* a member of the board of trustees of the Harbor. As Allan had written Kate on 13 November, "Such aids are often necessary to present ones claims, or to secure such places, and unless offered are seldom obtained without the asking." Hoffman presented her letter in person to the board of trustees. Greenleaf had to argue strenuously for Tom against other candidates, for the office was extremely desirable, paying two thousand dollars a year (a munificent sum that was expected to be doubled soon), not to mention extraordinary housing.

Tom was named governor on 19 November 1867. The election came just in time, as far as the Harbor was concerned. Too ill to vacate the Governor's House promptly, Governor De Peyster wandered outside in January 1868 in what his sons called an aberration of mind, and, it was thought, fell off the pier. No one wanted to say the word suicide. Tom had been the least well educated of the children, but, as he wrote in a diary when he was nineteen, he was eager to have the mate of his ship "learn" him something. In 1867, having learned a great deal the hard way, he took over an institution with some four hundred decrepit men. The numbers changed all the time, but according to his report to the board of trustees two years later, on 1 January 1870, the breakdown of the inmates of the Harbor by nationality was United States 197; England 44; Ireland 33; Sweden 26; Germany 16; Scotland 14; Norway 10; Denmark 10; France 5; Prussia 8; Finland 4; and a scattering of men from other countries. There was no policy preferring one nationality or race over another, only proof of service in an American ship. A black inmate had been among the population when the Harbor opened its doors (on Herman's birthday in 1833), and Tom on 20 January 1877 drafted a response to a query about subsequent black inmates (spelling his): "The next collored Inmate was admitted in Sept 1842, the next in Aug 1843 since then there has been over one hundred colored men admitted as Inmates." On ships, berths had not been assigned on the basis of race (as Melville made John Paul Jones vividly recall in *Israel Potter*), and it had never occurred to anyone to go to the expense of trying to make separate wards for whites and blacks at the Harbor. (By 14 August 1880 the total number of inmates had grown to 725, according to Governor Melville's letter to Lieutenant Commander Edward Hooker, U.S.N.)

The new governor paid a visit to Gansevoort and called at Albany on his way back to New York, receiving plaudits of ecstatic family members in his regal progress. On 25 November with well-justified pride Kate Gansevoort wrote Henry: "He is delighted with this appointment, & will make a home for himself, Mother, & sisters at Staten Island. . . . Quite an unexpected change for him he says, & he owes it to his kind friends & Allan's indefaticable exertions on his behalf." ("Governor" proved as hard to spell as "indefatigable.") The immediate thinking was that the Mansion House might be closed up, at least for the winters, since the Governor's House would need serious direction by at least two competent women. Tom must have gone over to the Island with Herman and Allan on scouting expeditions, despite the long hours both the older brothers were working. What they saw from New Brighton itself, over the narrow Kill von Kull and a sliver of low New Jersey pastureland, was a vista of the whole harbor as well as Manhattan and Brooklyn. In 1867, all the commercial shipping bound for docks around both sides of lower Manhattan, all the pleasure boats, and all the vessels bound for the Navy Yard (then commanded by Charles H. Bell, the man who could say he had met Lord Byron in 1822 and Herman Melville in 1857), came into sight of the Sailors' Snug Harbor in clear weather.

From the bay there was not a Persian pleasure dome to be seen, despite the developers' fantasy name of New Brighton, but the site and the existing buildings were extraordinary, as Charles Farnham confirmed in the New York *Times* a decade later (1878):

> The terrace or road along the shore each side of New-Brighton is a delightful walk. The road is covered with elms and maples; on one hand are large houses surrounded by lawns, flowers, shrubs, and trees; on the other is a green sod sloping down to the wall or the rocks, where the surge breaks in soothing murmurs. The bay stretches far away, bearing its multitude of ships. The horizon of twenty miles of cities bounds the scene with masts, piers, and stores, with steeples and domes, that rise like hills above the distant haze. It is the great circle of human life.

Louis Bagger described the view an inmate had from within the Harbor buildings on a winter's day: "There, seated in a warm and comfortable room, he can through the window look out upon the scenes of his former life as a mariner; there is the deep blue sea, covered with numerous craft, reminding him of the time when he himself braved its dangers, and recalling adventures in foreign climes, that, sitting there by the window in his easy-chair, he is fond of relating." An inmate described the location in the 1879 *History of the Sailors' Snug Harbor* as "very pleasant, having from its front a view of the 'Kil[l] von Kull,' upon which are constantly plying numerous crafts of both steam and sailing power." Later, industrial buildings desecrated that thin strip of New Jersey and totally blocked the Sailors' Snug Harbor and much of New Brighton from panoramic views of the bay and the skylines of Manhattan and Brooklyn.

Some of Herman Melville's friends and acquaintances already knew the bay side of Staten Island well. Tuckerman had visited often when Garibaldi lived there, a decade and a half earlier, and G. W. Curtis had been living there for the last decade. The village of New Brighton was especially attractive, "one of the most charming places on the island, with its shady street, good walks, orchards, and pleasant houses," Farnham wrote in his celebrity tour. Up Davis Avenue, off the main road, was the large frame house of Curtis's father-in-law, Francis G. Shaw (the father of the commander of the Massachusetts Fifty-fourth, Robert Gould Shaw, and of Mrs. Charles Lowell, whom Melville had met in camp), and General Antonio López de Santa Anna (or Ana) and his staff had lived in the blue granite house near by. The house of Sidney Howard Gay, the abolitionist and Greeley's managing editor on the *Tribune* since 1862, was "further up with columns and architraves like Greek temples, and visible on the avenue, on the left, among large pines and firs along the fence." Before Francis Parkman married Melville's second cousin, the historian had lived in New Brighton "to have the medical aid of the oculist, Dr. Elliot," and had worked on a farm where streets had since been run. Farnham gave particular attention to Melville's *Putnam's* editor, G. W. Curtis, who lived "on the west side of Bard-avenue." Near the Curtis house, Theodore Winthrop had lived with his sister. Though he was killed at the Battle of Great Bethel at the start of the war (10 June 1861), Winthrop's posthumous books (*John Brent*, 1862; *The Canoe and the Saddle*, 1863; and *Life in the Open Air*, 1863) had had a posthumous vogue outlasting any vogue "Guy Winthrop" had — that name Melville thought Bentley might attach to *Pierre*. The most celebrated former resident without question was Garibaldi, who had spent "three years at Signor Antonio Meucci's house, on Forest-street, standing just east of the Clifton Brewery," Farnham wrote. Melville knew of Meucci, from Tuckerman, and after 1867 had ample occasion to walk as far as Forest Street and savor the oddity of Garibaldi's residence here, odder than William E. West's telling stories of Byron and Shelley at Dr. Francis's house on Bond Street, as odd, perhaps, as the juxtaposition of the Taghconics and the Tuileries in his memories of his Uncle Thomas. This was just the kind of juxtaposition and superimposition of images and times that appealed to Melville powerfully, and Garibaldi's image haunted him all his last decades, when he turned back, over and over again, to his verses about the sailor-boy turned liberator.

Because the bereft (and presumably widowed) Mrs. De Peyster was not immediately ejected from the Governor's House after her husband disappeared, Tom accepted Dr. Stephen V. R. Bogart's kind invitation to spend the winter in the Physician's House. The name suggests that Dr. Bogart may have been related to the Gansevoorts and Melvilles through the Van Rensselaers; in any case, some of the Albany Gansevoorts were already acquainted with Bogart's son John. On 23 December 1867 Maria Melville wrote to her niece Kate Gansevoort that a room in the main building had been furnished "very handsomely" as an office for Tom, and that he had a "fine room" and was "very well pleased" to be boarding with Dr. Bogart and his wife, "a lovely old lady." Maria added: "We must make him a visit next fall, he told me he would not be ready to see company until Sept — . *a long time*." Kate Gansevoort understood the implication and as usual translated Tom's intention pointedly when she wrote her brother: "That means I take it . . . he does not want the family on his hands just yet!" Having Tom's great fortune to talk about, everyone except Hoadley managed better at ignoring politics during the impeachment trial of Andrew Johnson from 5 March to 26 May 1868. (They all knew the president's chief defense lawyer, Benjamin R. Curtis.)

Before Tom could welcome his family, he had acquired a wife, Kate Bogart, one of the doctor's unmarried daughters. Since sometimes there were four or maybe even five Kates in a room, the family on occasion referred to Kate Bogart as "Katie" to help identify her, and Katie she is in this biography except in a few quotations. Born in 1842, Katie was in her midtwenties when she met Tom, very pleasant looking, and, the family was happy to learn, she had great teeth. She was, like Maria Gansevoort Melville and her daughter Augusta, an earnest member of the Dutch Reformed church. Furthermore, she knew and respected social forms. Upon becoming engaged, in April 1868, Katie Bogart wrote a "sweet" note to Maria Gansevoort Melville at Gansevoort, and Tom sent his mother "the ladys Photograph." Augusta was at Herman and Lizzie's on Twenty-sixth Street, so the "Capt with Miss Kate called to see Augusta & invited her to Staten island," where she stayed overnight with the Bogarts. Augusta was given the full effect of the doctor's water view ("with a constant passing of vessels of all kinds & sizes," as Cousin Kate later described it). On 23 April Maria relayed to Kate Gansevoort that Augusta had reported herself "much pleased with the family & the surroundings, particularly with Miss Kate." She went back "with Lizzy" (Herman's Lizzie) "& passed a day with the Bogarts," and Lizzie was delighted with *her* visit. Maria wrote Kate Gansevoort on 23 April 1868: "Tom will have possession of his house next month the place will be put in fair order, some alterations Tom wishes to make inside, & then it will have to be furnished, as neither party are rich. I presume they will make themselves happy in enjoying the comforts of life, without disturbing themselves about the empty show & glitter of the world. Tom writes 'he is a happy happy man.'" He was a happy happy man who was having the governor's mansion retrofitted with gas and modern plumbing, neither of which had graced any house he had lived in and few he had visited in, although Uncle Peter had done *his* retrofitting in Albany in 1851.

Rather ridiculously, Kate Gansevoort had finally announced her engagement to her stepmother's nephew Abraham Lansing, after much soul-searching about marrying so close within the family, they being raised almost like brother and sister. They were not related by blood, except in the complicated and more or less remote ways that made all members of the old Dutch Albany families double or triple cousins. In her 23 April letter Maria could not resist a reproving comment along with her congratulations: "I must say that I was rather puzzled at the tardiness of the communication!" Long-homeless Tom revelled in the plans for his own wedding, inviting groomsmen joyously, letting his fiancée and especially his sisters deal with the knotty diplomacy of choosing bridesmaids, one of whom had to be Cousin Kate, to whom Tom wrote this description on 25 April:

> The Wedding will take place on the 6th of June next A.M. at the D. R. Church New Brighton. The Rev Dr Paxton of N. Y. one of the S. S. H.

Trustees will perform on the occasion & the reception will be at Dr. Bogarts afterwards. I enclose a note from MY KATE who by the way I will not describe but will send her photograph & let you judge for yourself. Hoping Kate that you will like a good girl gratifye your Cousin's & write at once accepting, I remain as ever your Afft. Cousin Tom.

Katie, excellent young woman, explained that they *both* wanted Kate to act as her bridesmaid. Melville's granddaughter Eleanor Metcalf was rather contemptuous of Katie, many decades later, as stocky and stolid, but no one in Melville's lifetime thought Katie ever did one thing wrong: we would know it if she had.

The Snug Harbor wedding was as good for the family as the birth of a baby, after the tragedy of the previous September. For Maria and Augusta the death of Stephen Van Rensselaer in the Manor House on 25 May was a new grief; Augusta must have gone to Van Rensselaer's funeral at the old North Dutch Church, the Reverend Rufus W. Clark officiating, assisted by the Reverend Dr. Kennedy, of Troy. The sermon was preached by the Reverend Dr. Thomas Vermilye (who had united Oakes Shaw and Caroline Sarah Cobb in marriage); and the Reverend Dr. William Buell Sprague (who had asked for young Herman's autograph) delivered the benediction — a mustering of familiar faces and voices. There was no feudal procession as there had been for the Last Patroon in 1839. Maria was lame from a fall, but on 6 May she reported to Kate Gansevoort that her sons were determined that she recover speedily for the wedding: "Tom writes me that I must get strong, & Herman & Tom have sent me strengthening cordials. Allan sent me a bottle of rare French Brandy brought out with him from France, & fresh fruit & every thing to make me strong & active." The Bogarts invited her and Augusta and Fanny to stay with them, as was only proper, but Herman insisted upon their coming to his house. Everyone behaved well. Even Jane, seeing advantages in access to the Governor's House in New Brighton, deigned to invite Miss Bogart to her house and herself risked the perilous passage of the bay to take lunch at the Physician's House. Tom made it all easy for his mother, she told Kate Gansevoort on 15 May: "About going to the Island on the 4th Tom wrote me that I should have no fatigue on that day, for a carriage would be at Hermans door, which would take me to the Church door at New Brighton, & after the Ceremony would take me to Dr Bogarts." On 29 May Maria and Fanny took the Hudson River Railroad down to New York. Herman met them and conducted them to Twenty-sixth Street, where Kate Hoadley and her children were already on the scene. At Maria's instigation, Melville then invited Kate Gansevoort to stay there also. In his 29 May letter to Kate, his tone was hearty: "We shall be a little crowded, but, on these occasions, the more the merrier, you know." She arrived on 4 June, two days before the wedding.

Tom and Katie were married at the Brighton Heights Dutch Reformed Church very early on 6 June 1868. The subsequent festivities are described by Kate Gansevoort in her diary and letters to her stepmother and to Abe Lansing. The Herman Melville group was back at Twenty-sixth Street at eleven and most of them promptly took a train to the New Rochelle station. Richard Lathers was an inveterate party-giver, and no one else in the immediate family had anything like his resources (since Allan's second wife did not put her wealth at his disposal). Lathers had several carriages at the station waiting for "the whole bridal Party & friends numbering over thirty." Kate had never before been out to Winyah, which she called "a lovely English home," one that quite met her idea of "an old English Country Seat," despite her having made a prolonged European tour with her parents just before the war. Italian, A. J. Davis had thought when he designed it, a Tuscan villa, but Kate understood the restrained splendor and marveled at a house "so complete & elegant without the modern newness of the present city mansions." Richard and Abby Thurston Lathers met them on the double piazza. Being Southern-bred, Lathers knew what travelers needed most when they arrived, so everyone was sent upstairs to refresh themselves "by a delicious wash" before coming down to feast on ice water, claret punch, and cake. Later Kate itemized: "Our Party consisted of Dr. S. V. R. Bogart—Madame Melville Mr. & Mrs. Allan—Milly [Milie] & Florence—Cousin Herman & [daughter] Fanny—Mr John C. Hoadley & Minnie & Lottie & Kate Hoadley—Cousin Helen Griggs—Fanny Melville Mr Greenleaf, & daughter Tilly[,] Mrs. Barrington [Abby Lathers's and Sophia Melville's sister Rachel], Miss Effie Bogart & the Brides maids & grooms men C[hristopher]. Y[ates]. L[ansing Jr., one of Abe's brothers] & Belle Bogart—Mr Whittemore [husband of one of Katie's sister's] & Milly [Milie, listed twice] Melville Miss Minnie [Bogart—a second Minnie] & Mr Osgood [presumably Dr. Samuel Osgood], Mary Curtis [Kate Gansevoort Curtis's daughter, a bridesmaid because Fanny had declined in her favor] & Kate G" herself.

Abe Lansing declined the honor of being a groomsman (he was always "miserable as a visitor in a private house") and made one of his regular escapes north or west into the wilds with anglers and hunters as dedicated as he, sportsmen who always happened to be, almost to a man, well-established or rising politicians. Abe's brother "C. Y." feasted at Winyah and kept up satirical badinage directed against the young women. Her "party" included "the Melville family," Kate said in a letter to her stepmother the next day—a group not including Lizzie and Bessie? Bessie may have been too tired to go, and Lizzie may have stayed with her. Kate was shown some of Lathers's treasures: "heard & saw the famous 'Orchestrian' which includes some 22 different musical instruments, & plays over a dozen Overtures. The music is soft & like a full band & it is one of the two instruments of the kind in America altho' there is one for sale at the 5th ave. Musical Store." She "wandered over the house — & looked at the pretty Articles of Vertu picked up in Europe," and marveled at "*one* of the first Editions of Shakespeares works only seven of which are in existence" — not a first but a 1685 Folio. She was used to seeing superb old Dutch paintings and she had seen dozens of magnificent contemporary paintings of the Hudson River School in Albany homes, including her own, but a few small Swiss scenes caught her eye. Lathers's paintings were mostly European and for that reason, possibly, more impressive to her than what she was used to at home or in her friends' homes. What she was used to, day in and day out, were some of the greatest paintings ever executed in America. Anytime he was at Winyah, Herman's eye was caught by a Piranesi, one of the great prison scenes, categorized by Lathers as one of many "Rare Engravings in frames," such as Melville alluded to in *Clarel* as "Piranesi's rarer prints" (pt. 2, canto 35).

The Latherses gave their guests a "splendid" entertainment, "bride's cake and all, in honor of Capt. Melville — Madame Melville the Mother was toasted as well & the others of the party — toasts given & we had a merry time." Maria had "looked like a Queen Dowager Surrounded by her children & grand children." The Staten Island party left at five and others remained to take the evening train down. From the Tuscan Tower they had a splendid view, all across Manhattan Island: "The Hudson Palisades were visible & the Country looked lovely." They walked off the feast on the grounds, plucking wildflowers, circling the trout pond, until after seven. Rain came the next day, but Tom and Katie's wedding and Richard and Abby's party had beautiful late spring weather, and the party had all of Lathers's warm-hearted hospitality. A man who had "but once dined his friends," Melville had said in *Moby-Dick* (ch. 34), "has tasted what it is to be Cæsar." Richard Lathers relished his power to give pleasure to his family, which always included all the Melvilles, and even a stray Melvill.

After this there was no packing up the next day for a trip back to Albany. Very late on the sixth, Kate wrote hastily to Susan Gansevoort that she was "having a very lovely time all are so kind." Stanwix was one of the kind ones, apparently, and Bessie and Fanny were "lovely girls," and "Cousin Herman Allan & Aunt Melville" all desired her to send "their best love." Soon Maria and her daughter Fanny were planning to visit Peter and Susan on their way home. The bride and groom went to Lake George by way of Hartford before going down to Gansevoort, where Augusta received them, and then to Albany to see the Gansevoorts before returning to Staten Island. Susan had sent Tom a beautiful box which he said he would use for matches, and Peter's gift of spoons was the richest present of all. Sensible Kate Gansevoort could not help wishing that she had suggested to John Hoadley that the silver gifts be made in Albany, where the best silversmiths were found, so the quality and markings could have been identical. Later, she became a redoubtable authority on historical Albany silversmiths, but already she knew where to find the best current workmanship. She passed on to her stepmother the most reassuring judgment she could have made: "Tom is to have a lovely home & a large roomy house & has chosen a systematic amiable woman as his companion. I know you will be pleased with her."

Looking back on the events of the wedding day Kate had nothing but praise for the Melville family:

> The Melvilles have all been so very kind to me. I never fully appreciated them & am willing now to acknowledge they are a very lovely family. Aunt Melville —Madame M. as she is called is the center of all, & a dignified old lady she is. At the Lunch yesterday Mr Lathers paid the Matron Mme M. a compliment & charmed the Bridal Party. Mr Hoadley paid his wife Katerine a sweet compliment. He bears the same chivalrous love my Father does to you my dear Mother. Oh that all husbands were so truly & heartfully *in love* with their wives. Cousin Lizzie & Herman are well & *all* of us desire lots of love to you & Papa. I do so wish you & Papa could have been with us these two festive occasions—I never saw such happiness & unostentation & we had a congenial party too.

Susan Gansevoort's nephew Edwin (or C. Y.?) Lansing, one of the groomsmen, would escort her home the next day, she concluded.

Kate's letter to Abe Lansing on 7 June contained new details. The "happy groom & willing Bride" had seemed self-possessed even though "the gallant Capt. never before had attended a wedding." The new in-laws were already known enough to the family to require mitigating comment: "Dr Bogart has a charming family & really the excentricities of the Bogart family are to be overlooked when we meet so much kindness & hospitality—they are a loving united family & Tom I consider a very fortunate man to have won the heart of *his Kate*, who is such an amiable & gifted young woman. Dr Bogart is an old fashioned gentleman & Mrs B. a lady." (Luck had determined that there were no "excentricities" among the Gansevoorts.) Kate had received an invitation to visit Tom in the "Autumn" in the Governor's House, greatly improved, she noted, by his "modern improvements water, gas, &c." The Island was very beautiful, she thought, but Westchester County, "dotted with beautiful country seats," surpassed anything she had seen, especially Winyah, where Lathers entertained "with true Southern hospitality." Lathers's own

Reminiscences, published decades later, do not quite convey the sense of the Lathers family that Kate caught at once — the "elegant comfort" of the country seat; the grace of the hostess and "her lovely daughter Carrie," Milie's cousin, a young woman, just turned twenty, and already "so lovely gentle & accomplished"; the generosity of the host, a man "well fitted for his life, pleasures do not spoil him & he is a lover of the beautiful in art & nature & a true lover of music." Thanks in large part to the Bogarts and the Latherses, this was the best wedding any Melville ever had.

From the first, the family (all except Allan's wife) delighted in everything about the Sailors' Snug Harbor and the neighboring parts of Staten Island. Maria Gansevoort Melville on 4 January 1869 wrote to her brother Peter: "This seems to be a very social place little family whist parties, private Billiard tables, or I should say perhaps Billiard tables in private houses — are very general." There was even a relative on the island, a granddaughter of Maria's brother-in-law Captain John D'Wolf. Uncle John, nearing ninety, visited and gave Tom the honor of showing him proudly around the Sailors' Snug Harbor to the awe of the old salts, many of whom were formidable naval historians and knew all about "Norwest John" and the great traveler Langsdorff. Maria decided that "a residence here would be delightful in Summer." Staten Islanders were unfazed by the weather: "they go every day, wet or dry to New York." The walking was fine, despite Maria's lameness, because of the flagstone walks between the Harbor buildings, and the air was tonic. When Maria left after her first visit (which lasted two and a half months), she went with Tom and Herman as her escorts to Twenty-sixth Street: "The day was lovely & we enjoyed the water & its views, the ride to Hermans &c."

Visitors — even female visitors — regularly declared "that the sea air had given them uncommon appetites for their lunch," and no one ever wearied of seeing the light on water in the New York bay. On 30 November 1870 Fanny Melville wrote to Kate Gansevoort: "Katie & I were out driving this afternoon, oh how beautiful the water did look as the sun went down." On 18 June 1869 Kate Gansevoort wrote to her stepmother from the Harbor:

> Kate Melville & I came over safely in the 4.PM. boat yesterday afternoon. We dined at Dr Bogart's, & I enjoyed myself exceedingly in that pleasant [home].
>
> Tom has a lovely home here, & a charming Mistress. Kate is a splendid woman frank, & able, & cultivated. The Island is radiant. Strawberries, & cherries are in abundance — the country looks fresh & beautiful & a rare treat after the dust & ever lasting turmoil of New York City....
>
> New York is very warm & this Island a Paradise I only wish we had a home here. The views are beautiful & the air so refreshing.

While she was staying at the Harbor, on 13 June 1872, Elizabeth Melville wrote Cousin Kate of being "obliged" to pass the day before in the "Babel of New York," and of being grateful to return "in the evening to this peaceful retreat." Only Allan's wife complained of the difficulty of getting to the Island, as in her 11 December 1870 letter to Kate Gansevoort: "Allan was down at the Island today—he found his mother looking remarkably well—The journey to Staten Island in winter, is to me rather formidable." Jane also complained of the discomforts of rail traffic when the rest of the family rejoiced at the good class of people they happened to travel with, counting themselves "fortunate enough to have a clean and well ventilated car, scarcely half filled," and being "entirely exempted from the usual discomfort of railway travel." One of Jane's strictest principles was to do whatever she wanted to do; corollaries were to do nothing because she was expected to do it or because doing it would have made Allan's family happier.

From the time Tom occupied the mansion until he died, the Sailors' Snug Harbor was the family hearthstone, the most convenient and comfortable gathering place for the family for Thanksgiving, Christmas, and New Year's Day (still a big Dutch holiday) and, indeed, for wintering. As far as that goes, everyone thought it was a cool and bracing resort in the summer. There had been no place the Melvilles could gather in the winter, and only Gansevoort where they could gather in the summer, everyone pretending it was not a little remote, despite the improvements in transportation. The baby of the family, who had gone to sea as a whaler at sixteen and spent the next two decades at sea, at last gave the family a snug harbor—often imperiled, but lasting until his death. His sister Fanny defined his role in 1884, writing specifically of Christmas Day: "Ever since Tom's marriage he has been the centre, the warm hearted centre, of all the family joys and pleasures at that time." Once he was at the Sailors' Snug Harbor, Tom was the man of the family, superseding his two surviving older brothers, Herman and Allan.

Tom's position meant that the socially ambitious Allan could mingle with the trustees and also could invite particular friends to join the trustees at the annual dinner, for instance, Herman's old friend the editor Evert Duyckinck on 25 June 1869: "It will be a pleasant occasion & you will meet some friends Drs *Dix* & *Paxton* are among the Trustees as well as Mr Dodge. Herman Mr Lathers Mr Wilson G. Hunt will be present only a few invited." He added: "12 oclock is the best hour to go as all are going by that Boat." At the 26 September 1870 quarterly meeting, for another example, there were trustees Captain Ferrier, Dr. Morgan Dix, Captain Ambrose Snow, and also "Col Lathers, W. G. Hunt & several Gentlemen present." Tom's trustees' dinners also gave the increasingly reclusive Herman Melville a rare opportunity to mingle socially with leading businessmen, ministers, and politicians. (One politician, Mayor Oakey Hall, a trustee by virtue of his office, had hero-worshiped Melville two decades before.) Melville's sister Fanny on 4 March 1879 wrote to Cousin Kate: "Tuesday evening, *Tom* gives a party, has invited about fifty of his gentlemen friends to be with him from '8 to 11.' Herman is coming, & no doubt, . . . will enjoy the affair." These meetings were, as far as we know, almost unique examples of Herman Melville socializing in the 1870s.

During all his years at the Island Tom was always pushing forward at least one construction or renovation project. In his first report to the trustees, Tom was blunt about the Harbor's farm: "I should advise hiring a practical farmer, one who thoroughly understands farming and whose wife would take charge of the milking, also a Vegetable Gardener, one who has experience and a thorough knowledge of the business. . . . The S. S. Harbor farm is as good land and ought to be in as good Condition as any farm on Staten Island, and I hope that in a fue [few] years it will be the best" (report in clerk's hand, Maritime College). On 5 April 1870 Tom's sister Augusta wrote to Kate Gansevoort: "All at Staten Island is going on famously, the season is so forward, that the farmer & gardener are both busy putting in their seeds." Peter, she was sure, would be interested to hear that the "Institution used about $10000 worth of what was raised, while the expenses of the farm amounted to only $3500," and at the recent annual meeting of the trustees Tom had "received many high compliments for the manner in which he conducted affairs at the Harbor." Here is a typical entry in Tom's work diary for 6 June 1872 (now in the Maritime College): "6 masons & 4 laborers in M[ain] Building / Miles & one carpenter— / Moors men at Bake House / 2 carpenters at Old Parsonage / 3 painters & one paper hanger at Old Parsonage / 3 men putting foundation under Bath room . . . / 3 painters on church & woman cleaning Hospital." The next day's entry mentioned farmhands, stonemasons, and a driver of an ox team that was hauling stone. Routinely, Tom noted in his diary that he had consulted city officials, especially the mayor, on Snug Harbor business, as on 26 January 1870: "Went to town gave my Requisition to Mr [Joseph] Greenleaf[.] Saw A Oaky Hall the mayor." Poor beleaguered Oakey Hall looked at the governor, but what he saw was the slightly battered image of the young Herman he had idolized two decades earlier; Hall did his business as trustee and thought his private thoughts.

For Tom, the running of the Harbor was hazardous to his peace of mind and his health. Any institution where men are housed has problems involving gambling, sex, food, and alcohol. Tobacco was not a problem but a weapon: it was assumed that men smoked, chewed, sniffed, and dipped tobacco, and the governor could maintain order by threatening to deprive them of it temporarily. Gambling was more a problem for inmates than the governor, but being sailors (see ch. 73 of *White-Jacket*) the men must have gambled on anything, whether a yacht would pass the Quarantine Station before a ferry did, whether fog would block the Battery before three o'clock, whether they would have turnips for supper, whether three or four men would die before the month was out, whether, a little later in Tom's administration, the Frenchman's Statue of Liberty would ever be erected. Sexual assaults at sea are a matter of recurrent record, but not, as far as is known, at the Sailors' Snug Harbor. The men thought of sex much of the time but they were experienced enough to take care of their own and each other's needs and to police themselves. Men living in the twenty-first century have assured me that while playing on the grounds of the Harbor they received a sexual instruction from the inmates. The more restricted any group of men are by lameness or other illness, the more they fixate on the quantity and the quality of food being served to them, resenting it when others get more food than they do, even food that they had earlier not desired, and becoming quick to charge the management with stealing foodstuffs that ought to have been served up to them.

If many of the men thought about sex and food most of the time, most of the men thought about alcohol almost all the time. During their years at sea the pensioners had been given a daily ration of rum and whiskey, however watered down as "grog," and many of them had two purposes in life which were in direct conflict: to keep enough alcohol in their systems and to keep their berths in the Harbor. From the way they had lived before breaking down physically, it was inevitable that many of the old salts (not necessarily old in years) were alcoholics, and outright drunkenness at the Harbor led to their being "tabooed." That meant they were confined within the grounds rather than being allowed to roam the Island or take the ferry to Manhattan — tabooed and therefore irrationally resentful because they needed alcohol. When there are so many men confined together with time on their hands, when there is so much money to be spent and the men have so little control over the spending, when discipline is to be enforced on men addicted to gambling, alcohol, and tobacco, and obsessed with food and sex, the possibilities for complaints multiply, especially since some of the men were of that captious, argumentative breed disdainfully called sea-lawyers.

The pensioners did not want to work, even if they were able to. Tom laid out stern new regulations about the labor expected of the younger and more agile pensioners, and he seems to have been the one who introduced into the Harbor the term "taboo," which his brother (as much as anyone) had put into the English language. Any able-bodied inmate had to work at least five hours per day for at least three days a week, unless given a certificate of unfitness by

Dr. Bogart: "Any inmate without such certificate, refusing to work when required, shall be 'tabooed' for two months, his tobacco shall be stopped, and he shall not be allowed to make baskets or mats, or to do any work by which he can earn money. Any inmate breaking this 'taboo' shall be forthwith expelled from the Institution." These rules were an invitation to abuse, and once Tom became the son-in-law of the staff physician in 1868 the possibilities for collusion multiplied. Tom's position and his behavior in it subjected him to strong criticism during his tenure at the Harbor, so the fact that he and Dr. Bogart were never quite accused outright of running a work farm for their own profits is fair indication that they did not fully exploit the more malign possibilities open to them.

The Harbor was regularly in the news, as on 6 March 1870, in an article in the New York *Times* on "The Worn-Out Sailor. Closing Days of the Men Who Toil Upon the Sea," describing two Staten Island institutions, first the financially precarious Seaman's Retreat Hospital, then the more secure Sailors' Snug Harbor: "There are three men in each room, the floors of which are cleanliness itself. Spotless sheeting, blankets and coverlets cover the beds, and neat little bureaus hold the inmates' knicknacks and clothes." All this was good, for the moment, but much of the attention was unwelcome, since Tom served at the will of the trustees in the face of repeated accusations of mismanagement and outright thievery and monstrous brutality. In his 28 September 1868 report to the trustees, Tom wrote: "Several of them [the inmates] have been very active in Spreading false & Scandulous reports about the management of the Institution and its funds, and have collected money from the Inmates to give Mr Nash a Lawyer to prosecute the Trustees." Worse, they had gone "to New York and given testimony under Oath in which testimony they have Stated & Sworn to the foulest lies against the S. S. Harbor and its management & food, they have Accused the Officers of Swindling & the Trustees of Squandering the S. S. H. money, and of being defaulters to a larg[e] Amount." The week after Maria left the Island in 1869, the New York City newspapers were full of attacks on the Harbor and on Dr Bogart and on Tom himself — attacks impossible for the family to ignore.

The *Herald* put "Snug" in ironic quotes in its headline, and subheaded its 12 March 1869 report "A Full Disclosure of the Inner Workings of the Institution — Inhuman Treatment of the Inmates — The sick in the Hospital Beaten and Otherwise Maltreated — Insufficient Food and Clothing — High Life Among the Officials — The Way the Money Goes." The *Herald* was still one of the most sensationalistic papers in the city, and it quoted the worst charges with delight: "Another testifies that he has seen the men most shamefully beaten in the hospital, and neglected and lying in their filth; that afterwards he saw them die; that he saw men who were paralyzed and in the last stages of existence maltreated by blows and human excrements mopped up and dashed into the faces of the sick." Even the respectable *Evening Post* repeated some of the allegations under the heading "Abuses at Sailors' Snug Harbor." The New York *Dispatch* on 14 March 1869 printed a long article entitled "Poor Jack! Poor Jack!" — lamenting that "one of our most esteemed New York charities is charged with loose management and positive inhumanity in its domestic matters." It repeated the charge that the doctor gave about thirty minutes a day to hospital visits and the allegation that one of the inmates "heard the governor say that he 'had got into a situation now where he could make money.'" The local weekly *Richmond County Gazette* joined in (17 March 1869), lamenting that the "poor, aged, decrepid and worn out seamen" had been made "the victims of somebody's avarice and rascality." It took a week for the trustees to undertake serious damage control in the *Times* with a "Reply to Recent Attacks upon the Institution." Tom denied everything: the allegations under oath had been "simply an effort to place before the public certain damaging mis-statements, under the color of a judicial proceeding." Having already repeated the allegations in the *Herald*, the weekly *Richmond County Gazette* backed off publicly. Tom was vulnerable. The lad who had spent his childhood with his mother and sisters in a rented house in Lansingburgh and had gone to sea in his early adolescence now was the master of a magnificent house, with incomparable views of the harbor from several rooms and with incomparable grounds, but the job was always under siege. Tom was vulnerable, but he met the recurrent threats by proving himself adept at backscratching and arm-twisting — wholly unlike Herman, more like Gansevoort and Allan.

At the same time, in the Custom House, Herman was simply vulnerable, and he was reenacting the early 1830s in a strange, sad way — stuck in a menial job, while around him other members of the family were rich — Lathers, Hoadley, young Abe Lansing, and now Tom. Allan was prosperous but unwell, and only Henry could envy a man married to Jane. Melville was in debt again. The February 1868 account from Harper's showed that despite a sale of 486 more copies of *Battle-Pieces* Melville still owed the firm $338.93. When Charles Dickens came to town to give his readings in March 1868 Melville and Lizzie seem to have gone to hear him, for Maria reported to Kate Gansevoort on the twenty-third that all the family in New York and Boston had heard him, and had varying opinions on his performance. By this time no one would have thought of inviting Melville to meet Dickens privately, as would very likely have happened if Dickens had braved these insulted shores in 1849 or early 1850. Meanwhile Lathers's interest was steadily growing in the Berkshires as country seat and agricultural base (and perhaps as political base if he decided to make it his voting residence).

Through the spring of 1868 Lathers had bought one farm after another, piecing together a fabulous stretch of land, and deciding not to demolish the farmhouse across from Arrowhead but to envelop it "in a great rambling new edifice" named for his wife, "Abby Lodge." Lathers (with Allan the silent listener by his side) was making a reality of a mansion in the Berkshires instead of the sort of towered house Melville had once imagined, just as Allan had transformed Arrowhead so that it was almost a showplace.

Strangely, Nathaniel Hawthorne was now lodged in a structure very like his early "Hall of Fantasy," a palatial edifice of posthumous literary fame which every year acquired metaphorical new wings, towers, and battlements, "balconies and balconies"—square, demi-lune, circular—a Celestial Abby Lodge. The words Melville had used of Bayard Taylor in 1856 applied now to Hawthorne, who was borne up as if by the gods, however untimely a death he had suffered. In early January 1868 Melville bought the 1863 Boston edition of *Our Old Home: A Series of English Sketches* (and on the fifteenth he accepted with pleasure an invitation—to dinner?—from his old publisher, Sophia Hawthorne's cousin G. P. Putnam). By purchasing Hawthorne's book on his British experiences Melville was filling in the years between 1857 and 1864, when he seems to have had no more personal contact with his friend, except, in one report, the receipt of a kind of card there was a new fad for, a Christmas card. Now at least he could follow some of Hawthorne's experiences and reflections beyond what he had learned in 1856, then glimpsed momentarily in 1857. Almost incidentally, he would see his own name. When *Passages from the American Note-Books* reached the bookstores in early November 1868, Melville did not buy a copy right away, but he must have seen the long review of it in the *Tribune*, perhaps written by George Ripley, the reviewer of *Moby-Dick*. In one bookstore or another he would have scanned Hawthorne's apparently laconic note on 5 August 1850: "Drove with Fields and his wife to Stockbridge, being thereto invited by Mr. Field of Stockbridge, in order to ascend Monument Mountain. Found at Mr. Field's Dr. Holmes and Mr Duyckinck of New York; also Mr. Cornelius Matthews [Mathews] and Herman Melville. Ascended the mountain . . . and were caught in a shower." He would have read also the entry for 7 August 1850: "Messrs. Duyckinck, Matthews, Melville, and Melville, junior, called in the forenoon. Gave them a couple of bottles of Mr. Mansfield's champagne, and walked down to the lake with them." There was *nothing* else about him— nothing to indicate that he had been of any significance to Nathaniel Hawthorne. By this time he had probably destroyed Hawthorne's joy-giving letter about *Moby-Dick* along with other tangible mementos. Had he imagined that they had been friends? If Hawthorne was in his own Hall of Fantasy, was Melville in one of Piranesi's Carceri?

Guert died in Schenectady on 15 July 1868, a blow to Helen more than Herman, since she had known him better than other members of the family when he was a cheerful, teasing lieutenant, before the catastrophe of 1842. For Melville, Cousin Guert was another example of the cheapness of life among his first cousins — Gansevoort dead at thirty in London of a grotesque concatenation of diseases, Thomas Melvill dead before he was forty of alcoholism and venereal disease in Hawaii. Guert and Herman had borne enough family resemblance that people remarked on it, and had felt for each other the special ambivalent affection people have for others of their blood who remind them uneasily of their own more or less desirable features of body, manner, or character. Melville did not attend Guert's funeral in Schenectady but he went to Gansevoort at the start of his two weeks of vacation. After several days there he went to Albany on 15 August, where Aunt Susan and Cousin Kate and a friend drove with him out to the Rural Cemetery to visit what Kate in her diary called "this home for our dead." They made a long tour, stopping at the Dudley monument (that for English-born Charles Edward Dudley, who had been mayor and senator in their early years in Albany, and an astronomer in the years before his death in 1841) and that of Prince John Van Buren ("a cross — entwined with Ivy"), the once-dazzling son of the president, the kind of success Gansevoort Melville might have become if Allan Melvill had survived and prospered. The sight of the family graves and the memorial statuary of their townspeople loosened Herman's reserve, and Kate declared they had had "a lovely time — Herman is so interesting in conversation." The next morning Herman went with her to St. Peter's Church, and walked the familiar streets, up to St. Joseph's Church, then up Second Street to Swan and down Clinton Avenue. They dined at 103 N. Pearl, at the Lansing family house. In the afternoon Abraham Lansing and Major Edwin Yates Lansing "escorted 'Typee' as Papa calls him to Kenwood Convent, for a view of the City — the Hudson & surrounding country." (Melville still loved superb views.) The next day Kate went with him to General Rathbone's great garden (and perhaps inside the house, so Herman could see again some of the great paintings he had glimpsed at the Bazaar in 1864). After a two o'clock meal he caught the 3:50 train for Pittsfield. Uncle Peter was not able to drive out while Herman was there, but Herman had some quiet conversation with him at the house. All in all, it was the kind of visit Melville could best tolerate, one involving much change of place by various means of conveyance and a shifting cast of supporting players, but the late lunch flustered him, and what with his "bundles" and his "luggage" and "the catching of the car," he forgot to tell Kate good-bye, and had to write his apology (18 August). There he expressed his pleasant memories of his "most agreeable visit to Albany, full of diversified pleasure."

The ride to Pittsfield was "very pleasant." In his 18 August letter Herman told Kate that at Arrowhead he had found Lizzie and the children (only three children). They had arrived from Boston a few hours before, and were "well and frisky." Allan's family was all absent, "leaving only Kate to preside." This was Kate Hoadley, who could function when she wanted to, for Melville went on: "But Kate, like all the Kates, inherits the good old Dutch talent for housekeeping, and takes good care of us." The "country hereabouts," he decided, was looking as fresh as a rose — or as fresh as Cousin Kate Gansevoort. He had displayed much of his old charm in Albany, perhaps because he felt less guilt away from Lizzie and the surviving children than with them, and, leaving his family at Arrowhead, he returned to New York City, still in better spirits. There, as he told Cousin Kate on 9 September, he was discomfited at Lizzie's having thoughtlessly subjected his room to "a horrible cleaning & setting-to-rights" before she left on her separate vacation, so that now he could not find a particular obituary notice of Guert's to send Kate.

On 25 August Melville was excused from work for the funeral of George Adler, whose body was buried at the rapidly filling Trinity Cemetery, after a funeral at St. Michael's Church. Melville was one of only a handful of mourners at the funeral. When he was earning no money, in late 1859 or early 1860, and before Lizzie inherited money, Melville had subscribed for a copy of Adler's translation of a book on Provençal poetry — the test of friendship. Most of the intervening years Adler had remained confined at Bloomingdale's Asylum. Duyckinck was there at the funeral, riding from St. Michael's with the Dr. Houghton who was conducting part of the service. It was a sorry affair, a man of genius living in confinement and dying almost unmourned, Duyckinck recorded in a letter to his son George: "Herman Melville, [F. W.] Downer with me & two others were at the funeral and Dr. [D. Tilden] Brown of the Asylum in whose face and mien you may read the secret of Adler's regard for him." At least the staff physician had been one of the mourners. Now a year bereaved of his eighteen-year-old son, Melville stood with Duyckinck, both aware that *his* oldest son had died at sixteen, while Melville was in Athens.

In early September Cousin Kate Gansevoort sent Herman a photograph of a mausoleum. It was all in all too much of funerary associations for Melville: "What an imposing mass of masonry. But a critic must needs be fastidious. There appears on the central pediment a sort of dilated sentry-box, which seems to be without due foundation. Look for yourself, and if you agree with me, drop a polite note to the architect, and quote Vitruvius the great classic authority, — though old as our Era, — in architecture, you know." This response to Kate was written on 9 September, two days before the first anniversary of Malcolm's death. Lizzie marked the anniversary of Malcolm's death in Boston. Not mentioning that date, in this surviving page of her diary Hope Shaw on 14 September wrote tartly about what had happened while Lizzie was out with the three children: "Not well at house all day—Mrs Helen Griggs called here and I had a full and plain discourse with her about not writing to Mrs Melville, & giving her a sympathy for her distress relating to her husband when all Mrs M asks [is] a little sympathy from her friends." Hope could be blunt with Helen, who had spent winters at Mt. Vernon Street a quarter century before. Helen's brother was still distressing his wife, by unspecified behavior. Melville was, just about this time, exercising tact in soothing Uncle Peter's feelings over Stanwix's not coming over from Pittsfield ahead of his mother and sisters (he had a "violent cold," Melville told his uncle). He could not assure Kate that the remaining members of the family would be more courteous: "As for Lizzy-Ann and the young ladies, I enjoined upon them not to omit that visit. But Lizzy-Ann is wilful, and I can't make her mind. However, she may obey in this present instance." ("Lizzy-Ann," like "Dolly," was Elizabeth Shaw Melville.)

On 23 October 1868 Kate Gansevoort called on the Melvilles at Twenty-sixth Street but did not stay with them. Her father seems to have come down later, and twice called at his nephew Herman's house without finding him at home. Uncle Peter, the son of the Hero of Fort Stanwix, was taking unwonted interest in Stanny, now a shy lad of seventeen who was the only assistant in Allan's law office, a temporary post, Lizzie assured Cousin Kate in a 10 November letter, until his health improved. Apparently some of Stanwix's problems were inherited from Judge Shaw: "his hearing we think is improving under the treatment for catarrhal weakness—and as it is, perhaps he had better give it a fair trial before doing anything else—& he seems to feel much encouraged about it himself." Kate may have been unaware of the worst of the tensions in the Melville household, but Lizzie went to some pains to soothe any ruffled feelings in Washington Street: "Be assured we most fully value and appreciate your father's & mothers kindness & interest —Stanny would take much pleasure in visiting Albany, & I hope he may at some future time—as I much desire that all the children should be acquainted with their father's relatives as far as possible." Stanwix dutifully thanked his granduncle for an invitation to come up to see him, but explained that he was needed "in Uncle Allan's Office." He continued: "My deafness has been a great trouble to me lately, but I am glad to say that it is getting better." Stanwix may, like Kate, have been ignorant of these undercurrents, but to plead the necessity of working in Uncle Allan's office was to remind Peter Gansevoort of the frustrations that had attended his employing Maria's impudent third son in his own law office. The only evidence we have shows

Herman and Lizzie both trying to smooth feelings and Hope ruffling feelings in her determination that Herman's sisters would continue to recognize that her stepdaughter was suffering from the behavior of their brother the Custom House inspector.

In Manhattan Herman and Tom were both at the depot on the evening of 22 December 1868 to meet the party from Gansevoort, Maria with Augusta and Fanny, and escort them to Staten Island, where they settled in for a long visit. Maria described Christmas to her brother Peter: "On Christmas day the whole family dined here, Dr Bogart, wife & three daughters, Dr Edward Bogart wife & child, Herman Lizzie, Stanwix Bessie & Fanny, those five came in the morning & remained until the next day at Noon." She had, as she wrote, seen her "thirteen children & Grandchildren they are all well & seemed to enjoy the Christmas & New Years holidays." Three days after Christmas Jane wrote to Kate Gansevoort a blithe revelation of her disdain for the Melville family and for the welfare of her stepdaughters:

> Allan was at Staten Island on the 26th — There was quite a gathering of the Melvilles — I did not go — nor did the girls as I had visitors in the house — and a dinner party in the evening, which went off charmingly. I have a young friend from Irvington staying with me — she sings divinely. I wish you could hear her. I believe they are all well at Lizzies — Stanwix escorted us to Church on Christmas night, and heard some most delightful music. Was the day pleasant in Albany — Mrs Trotter was at Tom's on the 26th. Helen came on from Boston with Allan. Should you hear soon from Cousin Henry, do let me know how he is —

One way of putting it is that there was "quite a gathering of the Melvilles" — Herman, Lizzie, Stanwix, little Fanny, Bessie, Helen, Allan, Tom, and Katie — but not Milie or her three younger sisters, since the incomparable Jane had arranged to have visitors in the house, and a formal meal for them at night. Malcolm was on the mind of all the Melvilles (and it must have seemed strange that he had been dead before they knew the Bogarts). Maria reported to Peter that in the evening of the twenty-sixth, after their return to Twenty-sixth Street, Lizzie made "a little party for her nephew, Oakes Shaw, who is said to resemble Malcolm so much." At least all of the closer relatives among the Gansevoorts and Melvilles got through the year of 1868 except Guert, who had been said to resemble Herman so much.

[30]

The Man Who Had Known Hawthorne
1869

Though it is a good many years now since the present reviewer first read in Hawthorne's "Note Books" of Herman Melville, he even then looked upon that brilliant author and singular man as one who had long ago passed over to the majority.

The anonymous author of "A New Edition of Herman Melville,"
in the Philadelphia *Evening Bulletin* (21 September 1892)

HAVING CLOSED THE Mansion House for the winter, Maria and her two unmarried daughters stayed on at Sailors' Snug Harbor, where she found its ample spaces and ready servants (more servants than had been at her command since her childhood in a slaveholding family) altogether more preferable than the cramped and tense situation at Twenty-sixth Street. In January 1869 Lathers was still buying up land east of Holmes Road and (perhaps through the winter, even) was continuing the construction of Abby Lodge. In early February Augusta left Herman and Lizzie to join Maria at Tom's. About the same time, Fanny left Staten Island escorted by John Hoadley to make her visits to Lawrence and Brookline, John having booked her one of the new sleeping compartments on the train. In mid-February 1869 the Twenty-sixth Street household took the ferry to the Island in order to talk openly about Stanwix's new obsession, for, as Augusta wrote Kate Gansevoort on 23 February, seventeen-and-a-half-year-old Stanwix was determined "to go to sea, & see something of this great world." He used to talk to her about it, Augusta said, but she "always tried to talk him out of it." In this wanderlust Stanwix's model was not his father but his Uncle Tom, the great captain of a great clipper ship who knew all about San Francisco, Calcutta, Falmouth, Canton, and Shanghai. Stanwix was so "bent upon it," Augusta said, "that Herman & Lizzie have given their consent, thinking that *one* voyage to China will cure him of the fancy." The helpless parents tried to make the best of it by arranging for him to sail with "Captain Paul," a friend of Tom's. Augusta's palliative in her letter to Kate sounded like Gansevoort's letter to Shaw decades before about Herman's luck in his crewmates on his

673

first whaler: "there are three other boys, gentlemen's sons, who are also going, & they have a room to themselves" — whatever "a room" meant. Even when the topic for consultation was distressing, the family delighted in confirming that the ferry ride to and from Staten Island was a pleasure when the weather was good. With Tom's help, Herman brought his mother and Augusta to Twenty-sixth Street on 5 March, and the next week the weather was fit enough for Lizzie to get Maria out for a walk in the morning and for Herman to tempt his mother to nearby Madison Park in the afternoon, where (Maria wrote Kate Gansevoort on the thirteenth) they "stopt to look at the fat little Sparrows hopping about who seem to have feet, but no legs." Life seemed to be returning to something like normal.

On 4 April 1869 the *Yokohama* sailed for Canton, with Stanwix aboard. The family put the best face on his departure, making up "quite a party" to go down to make Captain Paul's acquaintance. Augusta reported to Cousin Kate on 1 April: "I like him much, & so does Lizzie who had a long talk with him. Herman has known him for years I believe," a fair indication that one way or another, through Tom or through his work, Herman had been in contact with a good many nautical men. In mid-April Maria arrived at her brother Peter's on the way to Gansevoort, and Augusta returned for more weeks on Staten Island. What Maria said in Albany made it clear just how hospitable Tom and Katie had been. Cousin Kate wrote Henry on the sixteenth: "Aunt Melville is quite rejuvenated by her stay on the Island & prefers it to Herman's home in 26th St. N. Y. City." She preferred it also to Allan's house, where the master was absent all day and the daughters were absent at boarding school, and where Jane displayed neither a maternal feeling for Sophia's daughters nor a strong familial feeling for any of the Melvilles. On 30 April Augusta reported to Uncle Peter and Aunt Susan from the Governor's House that she had seen everyone at Herman's and Allan's and that they were all well. "Well" was relative, for in these years the Melvilles knew that Allan had one "bad" lung and, they told each other, a spare good one.

In his evenings and Sundays Herman was pursuing his study of art. For some years now, and from this time forward, whenever he could, Melville studied engravings (separate and bound in books) and scrutinized paintings and other works of art in galleries, studios, and, on rare occasions, other people's houses. Over the years he made himself a serious aesthetician through his study of the best historians and critics of art from Vasari to Hazlitt and Ruskin. His study of aesthetics by looking at art and reading about art was not only to enhance his appreciation of sculpture, painting, and other arts but also to apply what he learned to the art of poetry. From mid-May 1869 a somewhat pathetic little document survives, a note to Elias Dexter, a framer with a shop on Broadway: "That mezzotint, The Healing of the Blind [by Nicolas Poussin], which I left at your place—pray, be good enough to cause the Lettering at bottom, when cut off, to be glued upon the back of the frame.—I am glad, by the way, that my chance opinion of that picture receives the confirmation of such a judge as yourself.—Let me thank you for the little print after Murillo." Melville was taking his aesthetic companionship where he could get it, from a framer if not from an artist friend like Darley, and willing to minimize his own judgment as a "chance opinion."

On 10 May railroad tracks from east and west linked at Promontory Point in the Utah Territory—a feat staggering to the imagination of people as old as Maria and even Herman, both of whom grew up in the age of stagecoaches. The emerging family pattern was not of linkage but division: Lizzie had begun to go her separate way in the summers. By early June 1869 she had made plans to go to Boston with Bessie and Fanny, leaving Herman in town until time for his August vacation. Before the family divided, Kate Gansevoort came to visit, and on 13 June, Lizzie's forty-seventh birthday, accompanied her to hear the Reverend Mr. Bellows speak, writing his name in her diary phonetically, probably from Lizzie's Bostonian pronunciation, as "Belors." By coincidence, Bellows that week published in *Appletons' Journal* a letter from Florence dated 1 May 1868 but not included in his *The Old World in Its New Face* (Harper & Bros., 1868). This was an interview with Hiram Powers in which he quoted the sculptor's theory of the primacy of form over expression, which Melville already shared. The four Melvilles took Kate out to Staten Island to see Tom, whom Herman was calling "His Excellency the Governor" of Sailors' Snug Harbor (as in his 9 June letter to Uncle Peter). On her return to Albany on 26 June Kate reported to her brother: "I made a delightful visit at Staten Island & in New York. Cousin Lizzie & Herman Bessie, & Fanny—Kate & Tom M so kind." Lizzie and Herman were at least keeping up appearances, and Tom seems never to have been anything but happy around his family. On 28 June the trustees of Sailors' Snug Harbor held their annual dinner, Allan inviting Evert Duyckinck. This was one of the few occasions when all three surviving brothers could get together.

Left alone in Manhattan, Herman on 10 July 1869 bought Matthew Arnold's *Essays in Criticism* (Boston: Ticknor & Fields, 1865) and read with a pencil in hand. He underscored the words "Genius is mainly an affair of energy, and poetry is mainly an affair of genius." He noted "G. W. C." (George William Curtis, his editor at *Putnam's* and *Harper's*, and a neighbor of Tom's) alongside Arnold's observation that "It is comparatively a small matter to express one's self well, if one will be content with not expressing much, with expressing only trite ideas." As he progressed through *Essays in Criticism* Melville boxed a passage where Arnold was quoting Maurice de

Guérin: "The literary career seems to me unreal, both in its essence and in the rewards which one seeks from it, and therefore fatally marred by a secret absurdity." Melville commented: "This is the finest verbal statement of a truth which every one who thinks in these days must have felt." Alone with his thoughts, Melville brooded, other annotations show, about the evanescence of fame and the sheer drudgery of being forced to produce writing on demand, but he also was thinking, as he had done so strenuously in 1862, about the essential components of great poetry. Now as then, his most provocative contemporary was Arnold.

Allan had been free to attend the trustees' dinner because on 26 June his wife had gone up to Arrowhead with the two younger stepdaughters, who had not gone ahead. At Arrowhead entertaining required serious planning. A list of expected visitors was made out early and the time allotted for each visit. Because her father was weakening and her stepmother was irresponsible, young Milie had been declared competent to supervise the opening and closing of Arrowhead. Rather than making a simple diary, Milie composed "The Story of the Summer of 1869" as if it were "Told by the Old Chimney" and she the scrivener. This shows literary ambition, however humble, in a niece of the once-famous author, and shows that "I and My Chimney" (like "The Piazza") was something like a private possession for the new inhabitants of Arrowhead, something that came with the deed. The account shows the young Maria Gansevoort Melville carrying on the extraordinary rigor of her paternal grandmother's annual Dutch housecleaning. It shows the effects the occupancy of Abby Lodge had on the inhabitants of Arrowhead and Broadhall while describing the amusements of the household and providing a list of visitors. A few days in late August were reserved for Uncle Herman.

At the start of the second week of June 1869, after the housecleaning at Arrowhead was completed, Milie brought down and cleaned "the time-honored mantel ornaments" and put them up in their accustomed places, everything orderly at Arrowhead under Allan's rule. Allan supervised the putting out of a fine garden, and they were harvesting early green peas and new potatoes in mid-July, when Richard and Abby arrived to oversee the furnishing of the newly completed Abby Lodge. Much later, Allan's granddaughter Margaret Morewood described the double-sidedness of Abby Lodge: "The view of the house from the road had a monastic stiffness about it, it was even dull and cold, and very simple. But view it from the other side, and it resembled an Italian Villa." The furnishing was complete by late summer, and Abby Lodge occupied and enjoyed: "Those who came into the house from the road, when they stepped through the center door, found themselves still outside upon the very wide spreading piazza, which was like an open room. From this piazza one looked upon a panoramic view, up and down the Housatonic valley." *That* was a piazza, and decorated so as to delight from near as well as for the views, for there were terraces "rolling off into the fields, and fountains played about a sweeping drive-way." Lathers "placed statues of Greek and Roman Women in niches about the piazzas, and urn-shaped jardinier[e]s filled with bright flowers, and at their base were cannon balls from Fort Sumpter." No matter what Herman had heard of the changes across the road, he was astounded when he arrived for his vacation. Alexander J. Davis had restrained Lathers's more eccentric impulses at Winyah, but Abby Lodge was gaudy, not a chastened old Hotel de Cluny of a place that Melville would like to have lived in. Still, the basic decency and warmth of the hospitable Richard Lathers was, as always, irresistible.

Visitors to Arrowhead before Melville arrived that summer included a Miss Curtis, probably Kate Curtis's daughter Mary, and the attractive young George W. Dillaway, a New York lawyer, the son of a first cousin of Lizzie, Charles Knapp Dillaway, former master of the Boston Latin School and a writer of Latin textbooks. The young people of Broadhall, Arrowhead, and Abby Lodge kept up a series of entertainments. On Melville's birthday Willie Morewood joined the Melville and Lathers cousins in an excursion to a rugged part of Monument Mountain, the awe-inspiring rock formation called Devil's Pulpit. The next day they spent on the Morewood Lake, the new name for Melville Lake, picnicking, rowing, and racing (perhaps in canoes); their table talk afterward included the topics of Dickens and Thackeray. A group went to see the Shakers, a never-failing entertainment, although the number of members in the sect was already dwindling from the success of their policy of celibacy. A party at Arrowhead brought the young people together for croquet, and after the chilly afternoon drove them in, they took tea and danced. Also before Melville arrived, Mrs. Brittain gave a party, after which some of the young people, including Miss Curtis and Mr. Dillaway, sat about the table in the dining room talking and laughing until one in the morning. Next there was a visit from the Thibaults, not otherwise identified, who "enjoyed the beautiful drives around Pittsfield & Lenox, but two days out of their visit were rainy." Herman Melville arrived the evening of the day the Thibaults left, 16 August, having concluded to go to Arrowhead before going (or instead of going) to see his mother and the others at Gansevoort.

On 19 August, Melville probably was present at a picnic on Morewood Lake along with most of the best people of Pittsfield, the presence of the Lathers and Melville families having inspired Mrs. Brittain and Willie to pattern themselves after the inimitable Sarah. On the twentieth the new Mr. Pond and Mrs. Pond (the former Rachel Turner) came for a little visit; Melville was to write a poem in her memory. He may have displayed his skill at a croquet party on the twenty-sixth which surpassed the earlier one, according to the "Old Chimney"; on that occasion the "rooms were dressed with flowers & there were a great many young people present & a great deal of dancing." Another guest arrived on the twenty-fourth, and about this time Herman retreated to the Curtis Hotel in Lenox—the Little Red Inn, it had been called in his time there.

There was no hiding from local news. Allan, most likely, had left at the office of the Pittsfield *Sun* a fine specimen of oats grown at Arrowhead, a tall specimen of farming by a "City Farmer," declared the paper, on the day of the second croquet party. The item created some ambivalence and even chagrin, for it pointedly contrasted the present owner of Arrowhead with his less competent brother, Herman Melville:

> By the way, we passed on Thursday afternoon the "Arrowhead Farm" and also the Farm opposite of RICHARD LATHERS, Esq., and were surprised and delighted to witness the great improvements which Mr. [Allan] MELVILLE and Mr. LATHERS have made and have in progress in this locality. The Dwelling-Houses, Barns, &c., have been enlarged and modernized, and present an elegant and attractive appearance.
>
> We commend to the notice of our Farmers and others the process by which Mr. [Allan] MELVILLE has made the former unsightly lot north of his mansion one of the most beautiful plats in the Berkshire Valley.

Nothing was new here in this casual slurring. All of his books had been botches, Melville had lamented to Hawthorne; *Moby-Dick* had been no botch, but undeniably he had made an unsightly botch of the first rods of the beautiful vista that stretched to Greylock. A mote this was to trouble the mind's eye, for the raw grave in the Bronx bore mute witness that Melville had made an unsightly botch of beautiful things besides literary works and a bit of the local terrain.

The next day, 27 August, a merry contingent from Arrowhead went back to see the Shakers. Probably Melville missed the festivities on the twenty-ninth, "such a merry dinner table the merriest I think of the many merry out of the summer." There were, Milie recorded for the Chimney, "Mr Lathers, Mr & Mrs Pond & Miss St. John Mrs Bradford besides the usual family & the conversation on the 'Women of India' will not readily be forgotten by those who heard it." Being expelled from Arrowhead to the Little Red Inn meant that Melville would be sleeping in Lenox for the first time since his visit to the Hawthornes in the summer of 1850, before he bought Arrowhead. This was a situation ready-made to trigger disturbing memories, some of them dating back long before he knew Hawthorne. Melville knew the proprietor of the hotel casually, the now calmer if not sedate William Curtis who as a lad had so thrilled Fanny Kemble by his daredevil driving on the roads in and around Lenox and the road west to the port of Hudson, a truer Jehu than Melville because he had fine horses to drive so furiously.

One of the most extraordinary events in Melville's life had occurred there in the Little Red Inn in mid-November 1851, when he had reserved the dining room after the hotel guests had eaten so he might hold his publication party for *Moby-Dick* with Hawthorne, all alone together, although spied on, to the subsequent titillation of the Lenox "belles and beaux." In 1869 Melville was still a man for whom momentous events marked—most often, scarred—the places where they occurred, so that to revisit them was to have past superimposed upon present, contrasting eras in his life colliding, as when he had scrutinized the Nelson statue in Liverpool in 1856, again, after seventeen years of adventure, literary achievement, and failure. Five years after Hawthorne's death, during the early posthumous apotheosis of his friend's reputation, Melville, now a humble employee of the Custom House in New York City, found himself again, and day after day, in the dining room, still much the same as it had been, for the Curtis Hotel had not yet been expanded into its grandiosity as a Berkshire Behemoth. Now instead of being alone with Hawthorne he was surrounded in the dining room by wealthy patrons of the glamorous summering place. The Springfield *Republican* of 20 September 1869 listed more than a dozen of "the notabilities" who had been summering there, among them "Herman Melville of New York" and "Gen John A. Dix and family of New York." At the hotel Melville renewed his acquaintance with Uncle Peter's old friends Dix and his wife, who twenty-two and a half years earlier had failed to win him a job in the Custom House. Dix may have made proper comments on some parts of *Battle-Pieces*, which Melville had presented to him, most likely soon after its publication, and they would naturally have chatted about Morgan Dix, the Dix son who was so much a part of Tom's life at the Harbor. Melville may have been sociable enough with other guests of the hotel, who were of his social class, although wealthier. The clientele Melville met and observed in 1869 was not greatly unlike the guests written about in the New York *Herald* fifteen years later, 15 July 1883: "It is estimated that on chilly evenings Mr. Curtis, the keeper of the hotel, gathers around his wood fire, without any of the liquid attractions deemed necessary in most taverns, fully $60,000,000 of capital represented in those who go there for an evening's chat." Even in 1869, Melville was harboring for the nonce with people of wealth, but seeing, as he looked about the dining room, only his dead friend, and remembering his own high exaltation, his absolute certainty that *Moby-Dick* was a great book and would be hailed as such. The experience was hallucinatory for Melville, "the occasional victim of optical delusion" (as he had said in "The Encantadas"). Instead of seeing the ghost of a gigantic tortoise crawling heavily across the floor of the Curtis Hotel, "with 'Memento ****' burning in live letters upon his back," Melville now saw Hawthorne paging through the fresh presentation copy of *Moby-Dick* and fixing his gaze on the humbling and exalting dedication. During the past few years he had begun to brood over Hawthorne's inexplicable posthumous fame. Now, in Lenox, and later, back in Manhattan, Melville paid the price of his hallucinatory visions of Hawthorne's superb living face superimposed over the faces of "notabilities" such as the Danish minister, or Captain H. Stockton of Newport, R.I., or Judge Skinner of Chicago, or Colonel Schuyler Crosby, or R. Rangabe, the chargé d'affaires for Greece. He paid the price during the last four months of 1869 even as he began to collect the prize.

Melville gave no sign that anything had happened. He was back at work on 30 August while the family vacationing continued. Cementing the new relationship, Dr. Bogart paid a call at Gansevoort, probably with Allan, then helped Allan escort Augusta to Arrowhead on 7 September, where she probably just missed Henry Gansevoort, who was morose and hard to entertain, despite his bringing along a companion named Andrews, the law-partner of George Dillaway at 54 William Street in lower Manhattan. Dillaway left the day Augusta arrived at Arrowhead and the day Rachel Thurston Barrington arrived at Abby Lodge. (Andrews, like Dillaway, was to play a part in Jane Melville's later history.) Seriously ailing, Lizzie soon sent the girls home to go to school, tainted with Hope Shaw's innuendoes about their father, and stayed on at Mt. Vernon Street through September. Bearing fresh news of Cousin Henry and other visitors at Arrowhead and Abby Lodge, Augusta came down from Arrowhead to Twenty-sixth Street, as she wrote to her Uncle Peter on 29 September, "to be with Herman & the children until Lizzie was able to leave Boston." On 8 September, just after Augusta left, Jane gave "quite a tea party, all her own large household & all at Abby Lodge. A merry dance took place in the evening in which all joined."

The early autumn passed with Herman and Lizzie divided, while at Arrowhead wealth and leisure conspired with youth and propinquity to lead, in due course, to the mingling of Melville and Morewood blood and to linking a Lathers and a Morewood in a childless marriage. Richie Lathers flirted with a charming visitor at Arrowhead, Florence St. John (once he "brought her water lilies which gave rise to a great deal of fun," according to the Chimney), but his attentions later settled on little Annie Morewood, born in November 1853. Willie Morewood and Milie Melville had known each other since earliest childhood, and now saw each other as possible marriage partners. As for prospective visitors, it was hard to tell who would naturally find a room at Arrowhead and who would go to Abby Lodge, for the Thurston blood linked Allan Melville's and Richard Lathers's children, and whatever her undisguisable faults, Jane Melville knew just how desirable it was that her stepdaughters keep up their intimacy with Uncle Richard and Aunt Abby.

The guests soon left, and "Arrowhead seemed a little lonely," but the loneliness did not last long, according to the Chimney and Milie, for one evening "the Lathers family would come over to Arrowhead & have a dance and the next evening Mr Melvilles' [family] would go to Abby Lodge in the same manner & twice some very accreditable characters were got up." The then-unborn Margaret Morewood heard these stories from her mother, the ghostwriter: "The young people of the Colonels family must have had many merry times. One can imagine them dancing impromptu over the moon-flooded piazza and through the round dancing room, which opened on to the piazza, to the accompaniment of some darky servant fiddle, or perchance a sister[']s piano accompaniment. And often again with guests and people from the villages of Pittsfield and Lenox when it was worth while to hire an orchestra." The young people of Broadhall, Arrowhead, and Abby Lodge had been marked by tragedy, but for all their emotional griefs they were golden children when set against the surviving children of Herman and Lizzie: Malcolm dead; the shattered Stanwix already at some watery part of the earth; Bessie, whose arthritis mirrored the constriction of her life; Fanny, determined to marry a rich man and escape a harsh impoverished household. Herman and Lizzie each in his or her way knew the gulf between the lives of their children and the lives of the children's cousins by blood and cousins by courtesy. For Herman it was an old story, his late childhood years repeated in the lives of his surviving but maimed children.

Back at Winyah at last, on 30 September Richard and Abby Lathers gave a fete to celebrate their silver anniversary, and, although it was a Thursday, Herman managed to be there. He went with a lighter heart for having received, two days earlier, Stanwix's first letters home, written from Shanghai, saying (as Maria wrote Kate Gansevoort on 8 October) that his deafness had nearly left him, that "he had been well, and that he liked the sea even better than he had thought he would." At the end of the first week of October Lizzie was well enough to return from Boston, though still suffering from neuralgia and general weakness, and Augusta, thinking it was "high time" (as she put it in her 29 September letter to Peter), turned her face homeward. The family's peregrinations between New York and Pittsfield continued despite unseasonable weather that temporarily stopped railroad traffic. In late October Peter and Susan Gansevoort came to New York and sought their comfort in a hotel rather than imposing on Herman and Lizzie. On the twenty-third bad weather prevented the Melville daughters from accepting some invitation from their granduncle. Lizzie's neuralgia kept her at Twenty-sixth Street, and she was worried about what the visitors might say to her husband, asking Aunt Susan on 28 October: "If you see Herman, please do not tell him that I said he was *not well* but if you think he looks well, I hope you will tell him so." Herman made plans to take his daughters to call on the Gansevoorts, without Lizzie.

In early November Maria wrote to Cousin Kate an account of Lizzie's medical history and present symptoms, apparently on the basis of a report from the older Gansevoorts:

> I am sorry to hear our dear Lizzie looks so ill, she has not been well since last summer. Her visit to Boston did not seem to restore her strength as she has fondly hoped it would, & always had done before. Every Spring she seems to lose her strength & appetite & with the fresh breath of spring Flowers every spring she suffers from "Rose cold," which is in its effects a severe influenza lasting from six to eight weeks. Judge Shaw had during his lifetime what is called "The Hay Fever," attacking him in the month of September & continuing its uncomfortable visit for six weeks or more.

In these circumstances, there were no grand family reunions at Thanksgiving. As Augusta put it to Kate Gansevoort on 27 November, the residents of the Mansion House "had letters from all the scattered members of our family giving an account of their Thanksgiving." Lizzie wrote about a splendid turkey sent all the way from Boston, to be enjoyed only by the grim four in the house where Sophia had died and Malcolm had shot himself and from which another son had fled to China. Christmas was no such gathering as the year before, either. Fanny was back in Gansevoort with Augusta and her mother after visiting Helen, and Justine Van Rensselaer Townsend spent Christmas with them, Augusta wrote Kate Gansevoort on 3 January 1870. The week before Christmas Henry Gansevoort dined with Allan and Jane, and on Christmas Henry's friend Andrews "dined at Allan's, making one of a very pleasant party," Augusta gallantly said, knowing enough to be concerned. Helen herself had come from Boston, escorted by Allan, to spend Christmas at Tom and Katie's, not with Allan. Poor Allan, and poor daughters of Allan and Sophia. Peter and Susan's basket of New Year's cakes arrived, as usual, on New Year's morning; some delicacies were not worth eating if they were not made in Albany.

All this autumn, after returning from Pittsfield and Lenox at the end of August, Melville had been intensely roiled up from his memories of Hawthorne, from new questions about his relationship with Hawthorne, and, as the weeks passed, from a resurgence of his profound epic aspirations. Julian Hawthorne in the *Literary Digest International Book Review* (August 1926), on the basis of a visit in 1883, observed that Melville seemed "to have pondered much over his brief intercourse with Hawthorne, conjecturing some baffling problem in his life." Melville had in fact "pondered much" over both the Hawthorne he knew and the Hawthorne of literary history, more and more in the years after 1864, during which his friend had been exalted beyond even Washington Irving as America's greatest fiction writer. In only two minor aspects of that new fame was Melville publicly involved. First, the articles that appeared from year to year on literary people in the Berkshires gave pride of place to Hawthorne and almost always recalled Melville, and now would often mention their acquaintanceship. Second, articles specifically on Hawthorne that dealt incidentally with the year and a half at Lenox when he wrote and published *The House of the Seven Gables* sometimes mentioned Melville as the sea-writer who had enlivened the romancer's brief stay in the Berkshires. Herman Melville was beginning to be remembered, if remembered at all, as a man who had known Hawthorne, *the* literary man who had known Hawthorne during the Lenox months, and already some younger readers were first encountering Melville's name in one of Hawthorne's books or a book about Hawthorne. With his own reputation besmirched then all but obliterated, Melville, after his spectral encounter with Hawthorne in the Curtis Hotel in 1869, began to reflect (jealously, skeptically, judiciously, and still lovingly) on the mental, aesthetic, and physical characteristics of the man who had so bewitched him and now so outshone him.

A dozen years after his visit to the Holy Land, Melville had not put it to literary use, but his experiences at the Curtis Hotel at last let him see his way clear to begin writing his epic poem about a pilgrimage in the Holy Land. What happened in the dining room at Lenox, that collision of times and people at a single evocative place where some momentous life-event had occurred, was precisely the hallucinatory state that in May 1849 had hurtled him into the composition of *Redburn*. Now after very much the same sort of collision of two scenes at the Little Red Inn he was hurtled into beginning the actual work on *Clarel*. Melville may have been thinking about a plot for the poem, off and on, for several years, may have had in mind already the challenge of putting a young divinity student in contact with representatives of the Americas and of Europe and the Near East. The chaplain Humphreys, in particular, may have lingered in his memory as a type character who might be individualized in his imagination. Melville may have had a good many of the characters in mind, yet have been stymied for many months by the lack of one immediate powerful personal motif that he could weave in and out of a very long poem. If that was the case, now he had such a motif. In the summer of 1851 he had longed for a little vagabondizing with Hawthorne, once his whaling book was off his hands. Now in the barrenness of his life, a failure as a writer, a failure as a husband, a tragic failure as a father, he would not have to go on the pilgrimage alone: he could take Hawthorne with him and reevaluate their friendship at leisure, dramatizing his memories and later perceptions in the form of a "tournament of merits" (Walter E. Bezanson's perfect phrase) between him and his friend, Hawthorne as the character Vine, himself as Rolfe.

In the late 1930s Walter E. Bezanson discovered that Vine was in some ways a portrait of Hawthorne. The identification depended on traits shared by Hawthorne and Vine (an "almost fierce shyness"; a fascination with blackness; a habit of watching rather than participating; strong personal attractiveness; and a strength "compromised by anti-intellectualism"). Bezanson pointed to Vine's pelting his own shadow with stones as "not only Hawthornesque; it is Hawthorne's" — that is, it is from a scene in *Passages from the American Note-Books* (1868). By deciding to work a partial portrait of Hawthorne into his characterization of the fictional Vine, Melville had guaranteed that his most profound personal emotions would suffuse the poem, however long it became, and however little Vine might play a part in some of the action. Ahead of Melville in September 1869, after his return from the Berkshires, was a long autumn's contemplation of possible characters and plot lines, and perhaps a good deal of experimentation with poetic forms. Melville did not have to work all the complications out, for in the poem he would not announce what he thought about his friendship with Hawthorne: in the course of writing the poem he would *discover* what Hawthorne had meant to him.

The time had been propitious for one overwhelming emotional experience to let Melville know what he had to do next, just as he knew what book he would write to follow *Mardi* when he saw Tom off on the *Navigator*. Witnessing the dazzling shift in his friend's fame, Melville had already begun to fill out his shelf of Hawthorne books with the January 1868 purchase of the 1863 Boston edition of *Our Old Home*. That book belatedly supplemented the many volumes the Hawthornes had given him or his family, as well as Sarah Morewood's gift of *The Marble Faun*. Melville would have seen in the *Atlantic Monthly* the mawkish sections from one of the inchoate and truly "abortive" romances Hawthorne had become entangled in and strangled by during his last years, *The Dolliver Romance* (1864, 1871). Melville must have handled *Passages from the American Note-Books* when it was published in 1868, after being serialized, but his surviving copy is signed 8 June 1870 in New York, a few days after *Passages from the English Note-Books* reached bookstores: Melville bought the English and American *Note-Books* at the same time and happened to inscribe the date in only one of them, the one published two years earlier. In New York in July 1870 he signed what may have been a replacement copy of *The Scarlet Letter*, a book that never meant much to him in comparison to Hawthorne's stories, especially the earlier ones. He put the date 6 January 1871 in *The Snow-Image* (the 1865 printing); *Passages from the French and Italian Note-Books* (1872) he signed 23 March 1872 in New York; and he received the 1872 *Septimius Felton* that year as a birthday gift from his wife.

Melville would not have considered putting the pilgrimage in prose. In his mind he had been a poet for a decade, almost the length of his career as a writer of books in prose. Nor was he being obdurate and self-defeating, despite the unpopularity of *Battle-Pieces*. The evidence from contemporary reviewing is overwhelmingly clear that in the 1860s most Americans still considered poetry the highest literary form, not the novel, however many writers and critics had begun to look about them for the arrival of the great American novel. Intensely absorbed in British poetry of several centuries, Melville had kept up with the reception of new long poems from modern English poets, whether he read all of them all the way through or not. He knew about the reception of Tennyson's *In Memoriam* (1850), Tennyson's *Maud* (1855), Elizabeth Barrett Browning's *Aurora Leigh* (1857), Tennyson's first four *Idylls of the King* (1859) and *Enoch Arden* (1864), George Eliot's *The Spanish Gypsy* (1868), William Morris's *The Earthly Paradise* (1868), and Robert Browning's *The Ring and the Book* (1868–69). Melville bought Tennyson's *The Holy Grail* as a Christmas present for his daughter Frances in 1870. As late as 1868, any American could read praise for Morris's *The Earthly Paradise* as "an achievement of which the author may be proud, and for which the lovers of English poetry can hardly be ungrateful" (the *Athenæum* as reprinted in the 11 July *Littell's Living Age*). *Harper's* (September 1868) said *The Earthly Paradise* was "much the most notable poem recently published."

Most important for Melville's sense of how intellectually complex a modern long poem might be was Browning's *The Ring and the Book*, which Fields, Osgood & Company had published in two volumes in March and May of 1869. No one professed to believe the poem needed to be so long, especially when the second volume brought the whole poem to 21,000 lines. In March 1869 *Putnam's Magazine* paid Browning dubious compliments: "He possesses an equally strong and nervous organization, which can sustain the most intricate mental processes far beyond the point to which our lagging attention desires to follow him." In May the *Harper's* Editor's Book Table advised that it would "tax the patience of ordinary readers." Also in May the New York *Eclectic Magazine* complained: "the poem is too long, not simply in the number of lines, but it is longer than the story renders necessary, we had almost said justifies." Melville could have taken warning from any number of such typical reviews. In planning and pursuing the composition of *Clarel* he was aiming for poetic greatness with a Browning-like ambitiousness and with a self-consciously stoical disregard for the public's view of his poem, if it were ever published. Especially after the reviews of *Battle-Pieces*, Melville knew what he was getting himself into, but he decided that a long narrative poem would give him better opportunity to display his powers than the separate short poems in the Civil War volume had done.

In his decision to cast his book about the Holy Land as a long narrative poem, Melville was looking far back to the poetic form of Sir Walter Scott's *The Lay of the Last Minstrel* and *The Lady of the Lake*, of Lord Byron's *The Giaour, The Siege of Corinth*, and *Mazeppa*. John Greenleaf Whittier's *Snow-Bound* had been the literary sensation of 1866 (the year *Battle-Pieces* had *not* been a literary sensation) despite being written in the by-then-unpopular iambic tetrameter, most often couplets but also irregularly rhymed. In the March 1866 issue the *Atlantic Monthly* said: "What Goldsmith's 'Deserted Village' has long been to Old England, Whittier's 'Snow-Bound' will always be to New England. . . . After a perusal of this new American idyl, no competent critic will contend that we lack proper themes for poetry in our own land." The "American Muse," it declared, "need not travel far away for poetic situations." *Snow-Bound* dealt with a situation Melville was sensitive to: family chores and amusements during a New England snowstorm that isolates a farmhouse from the outside world. Incidental details would have intrigued him — a passage adapted from the sea-going Quaker Thomas Chalkley's *Journal* (1747) on cannibalism providentially averted; a passage on the Isles of Shoals, associated in his mind with Hawthorne and *The Isle of the Cross*; the character of an idealistic young country-school teacher, better educated than he himself had been as a schoolteacher in 1837–40; a portrait of the "crazy Queen of Lebanon," Lady Hester (or Esther) Lucy Stanhope, who "under Eastern skies" awaited the second coming of Jesus; the war for Greek independence against the Turks; and an intensely felt passage on the direction Reconstruction should take. Infused, even saturated with well-earned emotion, the poem avoided mere sentimentality, and the variety of tone Whittier achieved was a sufficient reminder of the capaciousness of the form that had been good enough for Scott and Byron. *Snow-Bound* was crucial in Melville's decision that the comfortable, old-fashioned iambic tetrameter would be ideal for *Clarel*, since Byron, especially, had demonstrated how flexibly it could be rhymed, in couplets, in quatrains rhymed *abab* or *abba*, occasionally in triplets or other variations.

Around January 1870 Melville began buying books on the Holy Land and other parts of the Middle East. As Leon Howard said, "normally, book collecting on a single subject by Melville meant either that he was getting his mind worked up to the point of beginning a book of his own or else that he was nearly through one and needed additional material in order to finish it."

He was beginning *Clarel*. His major source was at hand, his 1857 journal of his visit to the Holy Land. He had known one minor source, John Lloyd Stephens's *Incidents of Travel in Egypt, Arabia Petræa, and the Holy Land*, from the time of its publication in the late 1830s, and had alluded to it in *Redburn*. He seems to have had access to Bartholomew Elliott George Warburton's *Travels in Egypt and the Holy Land; or, The Crescent and the Cross* (Philadelphia, 1859). Allan would likely have turned over to Herman some materials gathered for his own trip to the Near East in 1866. Lizzie may have bought Bellows's work, *The Old World in Its New Face*, which would have enraged Melville with its casual racism (the best thing to do with American Indians was to finish extirpating them), but it would have reminded him of what he had seen and given him something provocative to dissent from. Needing other sources, on 31 January 1870 Melville bought two books (editions unidentified) by W. H. Bartlett, *The Nile Boat* and *Forty Days in the Desert, on the Track of the Israelites; or a Journey from Cairo, by Wady Feiran, to Mount Sinai and Petra*. On 4 April he acquired Arthur Penrhyn Stanley's *Sinai and Palestine in Connection with Their History* (New York: Widdleton, 1863). On 1 November he ordered from Harper's *The Rob Roy on the Jordan, Nile, Red Sea, and Gennesareth, &c. A Canoe Cruise in Palestine and Egypt, and the Waters of Damascus* (1870) by John Macgregor. For Christmas 1870 he thoughtfully gave Lizzie *Walks about the City and Environs of Jerusalem* (London: Virtue, [1860?]) by W. H. Bartlett. The Harper's account of 12 June 1872 shows his purchase of E. H. Palmer's *The Desert of Exodus* (1872).

Melville marked in his Milton the passage on the poet's starting *Paradise Lost* in his forty-eighth year and finishing it in his fifty-seventh, and he marked also the contradictory reports on the seasons of the year when Milton was most prolific, so speculation about the composition of *Clarel* he would have recognized as legitimate. He wanted to know about *Paradise Lost* just as we want to know about *Clarel*. In all likelihood Melville wrote pretty much sequentially, in the order in which his epic was published. How fast or how steadily he wrote we can guess by dividing a total of nearly 18,000 lines (lines that he retained — for he must have drafted many more) by the number of days that might have passed between the day he started and the day he finished. He began around the start of 1870, the time he began buying books on the Holy Land. We know that the poem was complete (except for subsequent tinkering) in August 1875, and the implication is that it had been complete then for some time — months? a year? If it took Melville five years, that amounts to some 1800 days. That would work out to 10 lines a day for five years, or some 300 lines a month for sixty months in succession. Looked at another way, it would mean 30 cantos a year, two and a half cantos a month. Melville never before or after wrote a long work while holding a steady job. Like it or not, he had a routine at the Custom House, six days a week, and that may have encouraged him to hold to a routine with the poem. There were severe disruptions during the years that Melville was working on *Clarel*, so it must have progressed at varying speeds, with pauses and bursts, but he must have applied himself to the poem day by day for very long stretches, weary and disturbed or not. He was fatigable, and often desperately fatigued, but he persisted; "indefatigable" is offered as perfunctory praise only by superficial critics who have no idea what real work is. Melville toiled on *Clarel*, as he had toiled on *Moby-Dick*, in hours when he was exuberantly energized and other hours when he was crushed by fatigue and strain. Chances are that the opening "Part" ("Jerusalem," forty-four cantos) went rather slowly until Melville had achieved a manageable working schedule, and that the end, Part 4 ("Bethlehem," thirty-five cantos), went a good deal faster than the earlier ones not only because he had become more competent but because he surrendered himself to what in *Moby-Dick* he had called the final dash. This is speculative, but we need to take the composition of *Clarel* out of the realm of the magically appearing artifact and see what writing it must have meant if Melville spent four or five years on it. At a guess, the composition of "Jerusalem" was carried forward in 1870 in the strength of the original impulse. By sometime in 1871 Melville might have gotten well into or through Part 2 ("The Wilderness," thirty-nine cantos). Progress may have been slow in 1872, but by 1873 Melville may have been writing Part 3 ("Mar Saba," thirty-two cantos), and in 1874 he may have been working on Part 4. By the end of 1874, or early 1875, at the latest, he was bringing the poem to a close. In the absence of other external evidence and in the absence of any conclusive relationship between historical events (the Commune in France, for instance) and topics in *Clarel*, or between the daily events in Melville's life and the events in *Clarel*, we can only speculate. So many new documents have come to light in recent years that one may hope for the discovery of oblique if not overt references to the progress of the poem. As it is, we must keep in mind dual sequences of Melville's life—the imperfectly known episodes of his life, season by season, over several shadowy years, and the imperfectly dated sequence of his concurrent labors on the poem. Whatever else he was doing in the years 1870–74, and perhaps into early 1875, Melville was making his rounds as deputy inspector of customs and he was writing epic poetry.

From the start, an obvious publication date loomed before Melville. As soon as the Civil War ended, patriotic and provident Northerners turned their minds to the value of civic and commercial celebrations of the centennial of the Declaration of Independence. Planning committees sprang up all over the North and West, and eventually in the South. And at the outset, in

1870, Melville was consciously preparing to write a Centennial Poem — an epic for America's centennial year. His would not be a mindless celebration, given his sense that the dreams of the founders in Philadelphia had been betrayed repeatedly and progressively in the years since his return from the Pacific in the *United States*. In a late passage the English cleric, Derwent, fails to comprehend what lies behind cryptic writing on a wall at Mar Saba: "What's here / Half faded: '. . . teen . . six, / *The hundred summers run, / Except it be in cicatrix / The aloe — flowers — none*'" (pt. 3, canto 27). The American century-plant was flowering only in scars, not magnificent blossoms. Melville had tried to be a political prophet in prose, in *Mardi*, and had resorted to prose as a would-be national voice of moderation in the "Supplement" to *Battle-Pieces*. Now prose for the Centennial was out of the question. Melville had come to see, after 1857, that his own most mature wrestling with the Angel, Art, would always be in poetry, and that his most prolonged wrestling would be in the poetic epic. Taking an inventory of himself, after the loss of Malcolm and so much else, he found that he still possessed reserves of emotional commitment, intellectual rigor, aesthetic complexity, psychological insight, and the requisite physical strength. If he started now and worked steadily he could have something befitting the Glorious Fourth in 1876. He would write his own *Paradise Lost*.

[31]
West Street, and "Jerusalem"
1870

>He knew
>Himself to sing, and build the lofty rhime
>
>In Milton's "Lycidas"
>Melville twice checks this phrase and underlines the last five words.
>His footnote: "Spencer"

IN 1870, as he had since December 1866, Melville walked the docks six days a week, checking cargo on newly arrived ships against the ships' manifests, and he walked to the Battery and elsewhere for brisker exercise. In "A Day on the Docks" (*Scribner's Magazine*, May 1879) Charles H. Farnham described scenes such as Melville witnessed in the course of any few weeks during his early years as a customs inspector, before he worked farther uptown. Farnham opened with a run past the area where Melville was first assigned. Starting at the Battery, Farnham "jumped on a car (a Horse car) to ride up town to begin the regular tour of the water-front." Going up along the Hudson, the car seemed to sail "through a canal of filth, fetlock deep with black mud," through "rat-holes and rotten cribs, gin-mills and junk-shops." The great seaport city did not boast a modern waterfront "occupied by warehouses, large docks, industries connected with ship-building and other conveniences for maritime trade." Instead, the docks were home to miserable structures "given up to every kind of trumpery retail trade." Inclement though the weather was during Farnham's tour, most of the piers were uncovered: "Only here and there a shed covers a wharf and shelters the traffic of a ferry or an ocean steamer." The piers themselves, "too narrow even for the circulation of a junk-cart," were "disgraceful," a few piles driven into the mud, timbers laid over them, and planks nailed to them with spikes.

Having reached the Hudson River at West Thirty-fourth, Farnham described his passage back down the docks (at times specifically on West Street, near where, at No. 470, stood the little office Melville shared), on to the Battery, and then up the east side to the Dry Docks north of Market Street. The waterfront along the Hudson was busy and befouled. The Thirty-fourth

Street pier on Farnham's visit had five brigs unloading forty thousand bushels of potatoes, and there was a grain elevator and a mill ("dimly lighted, and obscured by mists of flour"). There was a coalyard where men were shoveling two hundred tons of coal a day from a canal boat into the elevating buckets on the pier. A little down the river was a lumberyard, beyond that an icehouse, then a great shadowy cavern of an ironworks, then a cotton press and a woodyard. A full mile of the shore below Thirty-fourth Street was given over to lumberyards. Massive as the machinery was, these docks "devoted to the bulky commodities of grain, lumber, iron, and ice" were comparatively quiet. Vagabonds occupying the stretch of shore from below Thirty-fourth Street down to around West Eleventh Street knew it as Timber Town Hotel. At dawn they spruced themselves up at hydrants and blended into the city, at night returning "to the hospitality of misery."

At West Eleventh Street began "the beach of humanity" which extended "for miles, all around the lower half of the city." Here lines of men and teams of horses surged up and down, "farther than the eye can see or the ear can hear their busy march," and along the piers lay "fleets of ships from every quarter of the globe." The oyster market, Eleventh Street to Tenth, was a "long block of two-storied sheds built on boats," and enormous, some 2.5 million barrels a year being sold in the city; the place was "a net-work of masts and rigging, with here and there a basket hoisted by a tackle, and a sail hanging in shaded folds." Below Tenth Street ocean steamers occupied "several consecutive piers"; one ship was bringing mahogany, one taking on grain from a canal boat. Below Christopher, some of West Street was built over the water on piles, Farnham said. At Spring Street and West he encountered a crowd of a hundred or more longshoremen standing in two parallel lines waiting for a stevedore to come along and offer work, selecting men by walking up and down, inspecting them, before hiring a few to help unload one of the freight steamers. South of Spring was a pier "where the Southern steamers" landed their cotton, hundreds of bales covering the quay.

Below Spring, Canal Street hit West Street, and there West contracted "to its original meanness," tough and ugly, a narrow street crowded with trucks and horse-cars moving slowly past No. 470, the little office where Melville did some of his paperwork. The docks there and farther south were busy day and night in the early summer, when "large quantities of fruit, and other perishable articles" arrived every day and had to be "delivered to the commission merchants and market men before daylight, to be ready for sale in the early morning." The railroad freight depots on the docks were "also busy centers for man and beast." Garbage was dumped onto a lighter for transport out into the bay: "The pier is built quite high, that the carts may rise above the heap of refuse on the deck of the lighter even at high tide."

Still farther south on West Street, toward Castle Garden, was Washington Market. Past it, on the way to the Battery, were "more freight depots, more ferries, more shipping." The Battery was "the only oasis of the docks" —clean, "after miles of dirty bustling wharves." Farnham contrasted the "granite sea-wall and the clean walks" with "the rickety and disgraceful piers!" From the Battery, one could forget the ugliness of the docks in looking out at New Brighton (where the Greek columns and architraves at the Sailors' Snug Harbor gleamed on any clear day, if you knew what the shiny dots were): "The bay stretches away in front, showing cities on every shore, islands, busy ferries and steamers puffing about, and fleets of great ships from the sea. It is the meeting-point of two worlds, — the commerce of the continent and the trade of the ocean; yet it is a quiet nook, where your dreams are quickened, not broken, by the distant whistle of the locomotive, the strokes of the ship's bell, the roar of the city, and the murmur of the ocean." The "rush of commercial life" took up again at South Ferry, after the Battery was rounded. First, the flour trade extended along South Street and up the side streets. Coenties Slip, which Melville had named in "Loomings," the first chapter of *Moby-Dick*, was now "one of the oldest parts of the docks." Farnham found the "view up the wedge-shape street" to be "quite picturesque, with the converging rows of old houses, and here and there a dormer-window above the pinched and faded fronts." By the late 1870s this picture of the past was marred by the new elevated railroad.

Just east (north, up island) from Coenties Slip was the "finest view of ships in the port of New York"; indeed, the ships impended over the street: "For several blocks one side of the street is a row of high bows at the edge of the docks. Bowsprits run in over the wagons and the traffic of the street, and beyond these masts and rigging make a forest. The vessels are all noble clippers, pressing close to the city. You can put your hand on their anchors, their figure-heads, and their shapely bows. They seem almost human in their confident intimacy." These piers were "uncovered" and "quite animated with the loading and unloading of ships." Farnham described the unloading of a smack at Fulton Fish Market (across South Street from the more inclusive Fulton Market, which Melville had long known as the place sailors bought cheap pornography). Vessels "from the tropics" were "unloading oranges, bananas and lemons," with the "eager figures" of the enterprising poor on the dock "diving into the barrels of damaged fruit for now and then a half-sound orange." There were "busy freight depots along the South street" with steamers from as far as the Mediterranean and others from as close as New England. Some canal boats were always "stowed away here and there in a slip for the winter," while the captain and his family lived in the cabin and enjoyed "a season of metropolitan life."

Farnham rejoiced at "a welcome sign of civilization among all this roughness of the docks — the Bethel ship with its cross and its church bell" — a daily sight that aroused Hawaiian memories in Melville. South Street had strong maritime characteristics, with "a large fleet of ocean clippers along the dock" and "the sailors themselves," near their vessels, not jolly tars rigged out in neat sailors' shirts but "a lot of dull-looking men, unshaven, dressed in patched coats and caps, and devoted to their black pipes." The area Farnham described next was evocative for Melville to walk past, the nautical-supply area north of Market Street (about halfway between the Battery and Corlears Hook, just below Pike Street): "The houses are full of ship-chandlery, — great cables, blocks, anchors and wheels; the signs of sail-lofts flap from upper stories; boats run their bows out-of-doors; spar-yards are full of men hewing great timbers; and shipsmith shops glow with forges and echo with blows on the anvil." Shop windows were enticingly "full of quadrants, compasses, chronometers and other navigating instruments." On the waterside were "the dry-docks where some large ocean steamers were being repaired by gangs of men," the "great hulls" imposing, "their high masses contrasted with such mites as men." There Farnham found a figurehead carver "making a woman for a new vessel," a four-to-six-day job. (In the late 1870s, after the celebrated death of George A. Custer and his regiment, the most fashionable image for a ship was an American Indian woman.)

What Melville saw in his daily work was grimy and smelly, but gaudy. Farnham said South Street from "curb to curb, and as far as you can see," was "full of wagons as closely packed as the pieces of a puzzle," a "long line of piles of merchandise; a driver is perched on every pile, and a team is before it." He itemized: "There are loads of oranges, boxes of tea, four-bushel bags of pea-nuts, cases of silk and Indian shawls, a steam-boiler, and coops of geese that stick up their heads and look concerned." The wagons, he said, were "emblazoned with the modern heraldry of commerce — signs and trademarks." All this was familiar to Melville. Except for the Pittsfield years and his time in the open sea he had lived his life surrounded by commerce and its florid heraldry. He was a New Yorker, where almost everything worth having came to you by water, even if the water was only that in the Erie Canal and not one of the world's oceans. The one good thing that did not come into Manhattan by water was the pure Croton water.

What Melville did during his work day must be gathered from Custom House regulations, supplemented by a few comments in the family papers. The surveyor was "the outdoor executive officer of the Port," charged with "superintending, directing and assigning to duty" all the inspectors, weighers, measurers, gaugers, and laborers. He supervised the discharge of cargoes and the landing of merchandise. There were two classes of inspectors. Boarding inspectors met ships released from the Quarantine Station (off Staten Island), then literally boarded them, by climbing up rope ladders, and demanded of the master "the manifests of his cargo and passenger list" and (if American) the crew lists, and mustered the crew and checked the men against the list. The boarding inspector then certified the manifest and crew list and turned the vessel over to the discharging inspectors on the dock. Nothing indicates that Melville ever acted as a boarding inspector, even temporarily. Instead, he worked on the docks under the deputy surveyor. He may have worked at times as one of the inspectors who examined the baggage of arriving passengers and consulted with an appraiser who was always at hand to decide on the value of undeclared dutiable items. Surviving comments suggest that he most often dealt with cargo rather than passengers, as a discharging inspector "assigned to vessels for the purpose of examining the cargoes and superintending the unloading, and in the case of goods entered for warehouse, sending the same to store, so as to prevent the loss to the revenue of the United States through failure to secure any lawful duties." (For a note to Duyckinck in early 1877, Melville used paper that was at hand, the blank verso of a customs form for the Discharging of Vessels.) As a discharging inspector, Melville went on board ships in order to secure all mail and send it to "the nearest post-office." He obtained from the masters of vessels "lists of the articles reported at the Custom House as ship stores" and took possession of specie and valuables entrusted to the care of pursers. As a discharging inspector he reported to the collector any perishable and explosive articles in the cargo, seized all illegal goods, and used his judgment in attempting to save owners of goods any charges for carting and storage if he thought the owners would be able to take possession and transport the goods immediately. Inspectors kept such goods on the vessel or the wharf until the owners appeared with a permit allowing the goods to be delivered to them. As inspector, Melville sent runners (lads? or grown men?) to notify owners that goods had arrived and needed to be claimed. Meanwhile, the goods had to be guarded. He was required to submit to the surveyor a filled-out discharging record for each ship, "supported by the permits and orders of discharge and the acknowledgements of delivery as vouchers." Somewhere in storage (a warehouse in Bayonne?) may be a great many such documents filled out and signed by Melville.

In his job Melville inspected cargoes almost every working day, and as he worked memories were triggered by sights and sounds and smells, and by reminders of foreign ports he had known or heard of. Every day, also, Melville saw the brutalizing effects of unrestrained commerce on both human beings and their work animals. He saw men maimed and diseased, figures from the City of Dis such as he had portrayed in *Redburn* and *Israel Potter*. Horses were mistreated in his sight every day. Carting, Farnham explained, was "one of the most important divisions of wharf life," for horses every day moved "thousands of tons of freight and thousands of people." Two horses might haul "fourteen bales of cotton, four hogsheads of tobacco, or twenty-five barrels of flour or sugar." Melville concluded much as Farnham did, that even "with the best of feed and care the average service of a horse in this overwork is but four years." Melville had worked his old outrage at this abuse into "Travel," and in *Clarel* (pt. 4, canto 9) he has Ungar say, "Let the horse answer," pointing out that it is the cruel Anglo-Saxons who made a proverb of *"As cruel as a Turk."* This offhand unelaborated remark (typically Melvillean in its rejection of cultural stereotyping) may strike a modern reader of *Clarel* as baffling ("let the *horse* answer"?), but the context was Melville's daily life.

For four or five years, starting in early 1870, Melville walked two sets of passageways at once, the squalid, jammed streets of Manhattan Island and the narrow streets of Jerusalem and its environs, and then Manhattan streets and the trails through the desert to the Dead Sea, on to the monastery of Mar Saba and its stairways up and down the precipice, and across the desert to Bethlehem. In 1870, and perhaps into the next year, in "Jerusalem," the opening "Part" of *Clarel*, he sent his title character up and down the lanes and outside the city walls, drawing on his own memories, his journal, and sourcebooks. After work he reminded himself of the terrain of the Holy Land by poring over maps and printed accounts. Inevitably, he tried out lines of poetry to himself at intervals as he walked along the docks of Manhattan.

As early as *Mardi* Melville had taken a pair of adventurers through an erratic island-hopping topic-hopping symposium, and in *Clarel* he created a much more tightly controlled version of the traveling literary symposium, around a simple, flexible plot. The title character (whose name rhymes with "barrel") would be a still-inchoate young theological student, something like the youths of genteel capacity Melville had once held in contempt. During Clarel's visit to Jerusalem and other parts of the Holy Land, Melville explores the young man's emotional life through his ambiguous psychological and sexual responses to a series of young men and older men. Guided by an old American Protestant millennialist, Nehemiah, Clarel enters upon a perfunctory romance with Ruth (the daughter of Agar, a Jewess from Chicago, and Nathan, a fanatical American farmer who had converted to Judaism), more colorless than even he. When Ruth's vividly portrayed father is killed by Arabs, she is withdrawn from Clarel into ritual seclusion. At loose ends, Clarel joins a group of men come together for a brief journey from Jerusalem through the wilderness to the monastery of Mar Saba, around to Bethlehem, and back to Jerusalem. The men, representing different ways of responding to modern religious, political, and cultural forces, accrue other companions along the way and lose some of their number to desertion or death. Diffident around men of worldly experience, Clarel keeps silent through most of the scenes, but many of the other travelers talk, and their talk constitutes the substance of the poem.

Through the pilgrims' conversations, Melville explores the bitter legacy of Christianity, which he sees as separating man from nature. In the view of Rolfe, the character nearest Melville himself, Christianity "Made earth inhuman; yes, a den / Worse for Christ's coming, since his love / (Perverted) did but venom prove" (2.21). Melville scrutinizes the appeal of Catholicism, and the possibility (raised by the Dominican priest) that if "Rome could fall / 'Twould not be Rome alone, but all / Religion" (2.25). In long discussions of Catholicism and Protestantism; Revolution, Democracy, and Demagoguery; Science and Faith, Clarel is swayed one way then another, always listening conscientiously, if in dismay. Before the poem is finished, Clarel has been challenged by a range of controversial topics: Deism's liberating power in the post-Revolutionary generation, the meanness of spirit in rural America, the warring attitudes of Greek cheer and Hebraic grief, and the Romantic conflict of science and poetry under "Doubt's heavy hand." Recurrent is the theme of social, intellectual, and aesthetic leveling, where the rule of "King Common-Place" is seen as yearly extending, "in vulgar sway," until it absorbs "Atlantis and Cathay" and reaches "toward Diana's moon, / Affirming it a clinkered blot, / Deriding pale Endymion" (1.34).

Vine is not the main character in *Clarel*, but he is unavoidable in Melville biography because he is based (however loosely) on Hawthorne. My strategy is to haul myself along the twisted cord of Melville's treatment of Vine at the pace of a "Part" of *Clarel* a year, the likely rate of composition, citing works by and about Hawthorne published in the early 1870s when they may have influenced Melville's evolving depiction of Vine. By the end, the depiction of Vine contains the best evidence for the dynamics of Melville's lonely struggle to anatomize some still perturbing and some newly perturbing aspects of his long-past relationship with Hawthorne, the most intense personal involvement he ever had with a living writer. Aside from all that, anyone who has not yet read *Clarel* will find that having followed Vine through the poem has removed most real or imaginary obstacles to enjoying it.

Before setting out for Mar Saba, Clarel has met the two men who represent choices of ways of behavior, Vine and Rolfe. Vine cultivates a stance of detachment from current issues. He is the object of some of the most intense spiritual and sexual urges of Clarel, and the reader gauges Clarel's growth in intellectual and psychological insight largely through his altering responses to Vine. The earnest, questioning Rolfe engages, tests, challenges every issue that is raised. Strongly drawn to Vine at the outset, Clarel is repelled at first by Rolfe's intellectual energy and fearlessness. Rolfe displays throughout the poem a quick and thronged historical memory, as in this leap ("Rolfe," 1.31) from Matthew to Cicero and to the present:

> "To Cicero,"
> Rolfe sudden said, "is a long way
> From Matthew; yet somehow he comes
> To mind here — he and his fine tomes,
> Which (change the gods) would serve to read
> For modern essays. And indeed
> His age was much like ours: doubt ran,
> Faith flagged; negations which sufficed
> Lawyer, priest, statesman, gentleman,
> Not yet being popularly prized,
> The augurs hence retained some state —
> Which served for the illiterate.
> Still, the decline so swiftly ran
> From stage to stage, that *To Believe*,
> Except for slave or artisan,
> Seemed heresy."

The gods, Rolfe concludes, are gone. In a century when Melville had been denounced as worthy of hell-fire, the best citizens had moved so far from Calvinism that they scarcely believed in hell even as metaphorical. From Maria Gansevoort Melville's Dutch Calvinism to Henry Whitney Bellows's Unitarianism was a precipitous decline in religious faith. From Andrew Jackson to Andrew Johnson was a precipitous decline in the presidency. Even from Irving and Cooper to G. W. Curtis and Thomas B. Aldrich was a precipitous literary descent into inanity.

Melville introduces Vine at the Sepulcher of Kings ("Tomb and Fountain," 1.28), "a waste where beauty clings":

> But who is he uncovered seen,
> Profound in shadow of the tomb
> Reclined, with meditative mien
> Intent upon the tracery?
> A low wind waves his Lydian hair:
> A funeral man, yet richly fair —
> Fair as the sabled violets be.
> The frieze and this secluded one,
> Retaining each a separate tone,
> Beauty yet harmonized in grace
> And contrast to the barren place.

The tracery proves to be an image of Vine himself, his personal beauty not merely contrasted with the waste but harmonized with it. Habitually, we see, Vine meditates upon things he sees as images of himself, a refined form of the destructive egotism which Hawthorne anatomized in such a story as "The Bosom Serpent." In "The Recluse" (1.29) Melville strongly implies that Vine has "gifts unique." We are told that he has an inexplicable "charm" and a suggestive power, "suggestive more / Of choicer treasure, rarer store / Reserved, like Kidd's doubloons long sought" (1.31). In canto 29 Melville analyzes Vine while Clarel, Nehemiah, and Vine are approaching Kedron (the "verge and line") on their way to Gethsemane:

> Ere yet they win that verge and line,
> Reveal the stranger. Name him — Vine.
> His home to tell — kin, tribe, estate —
> Would naught avail. Alighting grow,
> As on the tree the mistletoe,
> All gifts unique.

Family is irrelevant. Vine's unique gifts are like wind-borne "seeds of fate" which graft to the stock on which they alight. In his own life, Vine curbs the flesh. But Melville says Vine mortifies desire less "by moral sway / Than doubt if happiness thro' clay / Be reachable." Vine's skepticism is philosophical; it does not arise from the moral sway of his conscience. Vine compulsively *moralizes*, draws morals from what he reads or hears or sees, but moralizing is not necessarily proof of a keen moral sense. Compulsive moralizing can be a means of shielding oneself from the ambiguities inherent in any complex ethical situation. Moralizing is that sort of shield for Vine. He never concerns himself with right or wrong, never weighs the conflicting ethics of a problematical situation any more than he grapples with an aesthetic problem. If he does little strenuous thinking or acting in the aesthetic world, he does even less in the moral world.

Melville then weighs the contradictory qualities of Vine's manner. His shyness might imply a "lack of parlor-wont," a lack of acquaintance with polite society, but he has grace of manner even if he lacks the "polish of veneer." Furthermore, he has remained unstained by struggles which scar or mar most men who have reached his age — presumably thirty-five or more, the age when life is "half ferried o'er." The question in Melville's mind is how one manages to preserve a smooth exterior unblemished by the trials of ambition or time. One possibility is that Vine has not struggled but has simply waited for a time when his labors would be justifiably spent: he might not have served any use but have been merely waiting, forbearing, delaying. If so, such indolence might be excused or understood as a decision to bide one's time in "dearth of rich incentive high." The new question is whether Apollo should slave in Mammon's mine, and the answer is that it is better to lie unknown as Admetus's shepherd, an unrecognized, unaccomplishing Apollo. The passage leaves open the possibility that some rich, high incentive might yet come, one strong enough to rouse Vine from his indolence to great achievement.

Melville next considers another aspect of Vine's strange attraction, his unattributable "charm of subtle virtue" (power), a personal influence others might covet—an inexplicable, untraceable charm. The question arises: is Vine saintlike? And the answer is that Vine has "no nature saintly fine, / But blood like swart Vesuvian wine," whose current is nevertheless cooled. Under "cheer" (appearance) of "opulent softness, reigned austere / Control of self." Vine is curbing flesh, mortifying desire. But he is not controlling pride, and he is imposing these restrictions on himself less out of morality than a philosophical conviction—a "doubt if happiness thro' clay / Be reachable." He is contradictory, "in sort Carthusian / Tho' born a Sybarite"; he may not forget the beauty and charm of the world, though he may keep it from warming him. Melville characterizes Vine's isolation not as hermit-like but nun-like: "His virgin soul communed with men / But thro' the wicket." Vine's aloofness is not caused by mere reclusiveness: "Was it clear / This coyness bordered not on fear— / Fear or an apprehensive sense?" And winding strangely behind all these qualities is an ambiguous elfishness, as if Vine were "an Ariel unknown," an unseen trickster. Melville evokes the imagery of the monastery, only to reject it:

> Thronged streets astir
> To Vine but ampler cloisters were.
> Cloisters? No monk he was, allow;
> But gleamed the richer for the shade
> About him, as in sombre glade
> Of Virgil's wood the Sibyl's Golden Bough.

The shade about him—his dark clothing but also his funereal air—enriches his glow. Other pilgrims perceive Vine as richly gleaming. Only later does the reader have grounds for speculating about what Vine himself sees and cannot see.

When Clarel, Nehemiah, and Vine reach "The Site of the Passion" (1.30) Clarel wants to speak to Vine about the gnarled olive trees, the "survivors" of the Agony: "but as well / Hail Dathan swallowed in the mine— / Tradition, legend, lent such spell / And rapt him in remoteness so." Vine knows his Bible, knows tradition and legend, too, and responds powerfully to the past, however it is recorded. Clarel himself relives the "night-scene," while Nehemiah turns in his Bible to the Gospel of John but forgets what he was going to read and goes to sleep. Vine avoids the talkative monk, then returns to Clarel with "The shadow of his previous air / Merged in a settled neutral frame — / Assumed, may be." Ready to go, they see Nehemiah sleeping:

> Then died the shadow off from Vine:
> A spirit seemed he not unblest
> As here he made a quiet sign
> Unto the monk: Spare to molest;
> Let this poor dreamer take his rest,
> His fill of rest.

The validity of this quiet sign, one of the few sympathetic gestures Vine makes in the poem, is cast in doubt by the role he is playing: we have just been reminded that it was Jesus who said at that place, "Sleep on now, and take your rest" (Matthew 26:45).

A more disturbing episode follows. A "brisk dapper man," a tourist, "alertly glances up / By grotto of the Bitter Cup — / Spruce, and with volume light in hand / Bound smartly, late in reference scanned." He is an "Inquisitive Philistine," the tourist violating the sanctity of the place which our pilgrims had respected. What follows is complex, involving Vine's facial reaction to the tourist and Clarel's own reaction to Vine's reaction. Clarel sees on Vine's face a "ripple" of "freakish mockery," and this ripple allows him to see something else: "O angels, rescue from the sight! / Paul Pry? and in Gethsemane?" The syntax is cryptic, but the two possibilities are that Clarel saw in Vine's face the tourist revealed as a Paul Pry or that Clarel saw in Vine's face Vine revealed as a Paul Pry. If the former, it is hard to see why Clarel is so upset: realizing that a tourist is violating the Garden should cause dismay but not such pain. For Clarel to be as distressed as he is, he must have felt something unexpected about Vine's own character; Vine must have been revealed not merely as (in a much later scene) "shy prying into men" (3.14). He must be seen as more overtly prying, in the manner of many of Hawthorne's characters, such as the young Reverend Mr. Clark of Westbury or Miles Coverdale. We are reminded of Hawthorne's explorations of the morality of prying into other people's minds and we are reminded that Vine, having just indulged himself in playing Jesus, is in no position to mock anyone else for profaning the Garden.

In "Rolfe" (1.31) Melville presents ironically Clarel's sense that Rolfe and Vine are peers who "needs . . . must pair": "Clarel was young." Melville wastes no time on this illusion: "Crude wonderment, and proved but vain." Just afterward he describes Vine's behavior in medieval imagery:

> The informal salutation done,
> Vine into his dumb castle went—
> Not as all parley he would shun,
> But looking down from battlement,
> Ready, if need were, to accord
> Reception to the other's word—
> Nay, far from wishing to decline,
> And neutral not without design,
> May be.—

Vine's withdrawal is so obvious that Rolfe bursts out with speech meant "to fill trying pause alone." Vine mocks Rolfe: "Hard for a fountain to refrain." Vine himself is later described as a fountain sealed. (Melville could not have read Sophia Hawthorne's descriptions of the way his own words had washed up against her husband the way waves wash against a bluff, but he remembered how he had behaved and remembered what she had said to him on those occasions when they had talked confidentially about their mutual admiration of her husband.) In "They Tarry" (1.34) Vine "twitched from ground a weed, / Apart then picked it, seed by seed." As Walter Bezanson says, this is an expression of ennui: Vine is bored by Rolfe's long discussion of the fate of religion. Much of what we learn of Vine is from mere gesture. Vine's speeches are most often short—even one-line outbursts. Sometimes they seem involuntary, as when he responds to a biblical setting ("How solitary on the hill / Sitteth the city; and how still— / How still!") before relapsing into silence like a "motionless lone fisherman / By mountain brook" (1.34).

In 1870 Melville put pages of manuscript poetry with other pages, week after week, month after month, perhaps writing now and then in sustained bursts, but more likely for the first time in his life writing, for the most part, steadily, a few lines most days, or many lines most Sundays, accruing pages, every canto written (three or four, ten or twelve manuscript pages) making another small stack placed in a drawer. There is in the surviving family letters of 1870 no hint that Melville had begun writing poetry again. During the early mild weeks of the winter, Melville started buying his sourcebooks. On 27 January 1870 Augusta wrote to Kate Gansevoort with news from New York. Allan had been "very seriously ill with bronchitis," but, Milie had written, was "now able to drive out." Mary Curtis had taken Allan's daughter Florence out to "the Island," as they had begun to refer to Sailors' Snug Harbor. Herman and Lizzie wrote that they were all well and wanted the women of the Mansion House to come down in February, but, lulled by the

January thaw, Maria demurred. Tom was in the news again on 6 March 1870, in a descriptive article in the New York *Times* on "The Worn-Out Sailor. Closing Days of the Men Who Toil Upon the Sea." Here the reporter took for granted that old salts notoriously growl and grumble, so this was no exposé. He wrote about men Herman may have talked to, the last of several centenarians at the Harbor. One was "Captain Webster, who is 104 years old, and, it is said, was intimately acquainted with the naval heroes of Revolutionary renown" (and with Lafayette and General Washington). Another was "a colored man named 'Morris,'" 105 and near death; a cook at sea, he still told "many stories of his voyages as marvelous as the travels of Gulliver." For the men in Tom's family, notably his sailor-brother, such an article was a pleasant reminder of old salts they had chatted with on visits to the Island. As the years passed, Herman Melville paid more and more attention to the inmates at the Harbor, some of whom worked their way into poems he wrote.

On 11 April 1870, Augusta reported to Peter and Susan Gansevoort that all was well with the "respective households" of "Tom, & Helen & Lizzie & Kate." Escaping house painters, Maria visited her brother and Susan in Albany and prolonged her stay until late May, grateful to Peter and Susan for making her welcome in their "hospitable mansion" and giving her the chance to attend the "loved old Church." Seeing her "very few old friends," a dwindling number, left her "truly sad to think of the changes so silently going on around us" (as she wrote to the Albany Gansevoorts on 23 May). John Hoadley had come up in her absence and found that the painters expected to put up some inferior wallpaper, not up to the quality of the paint, and took action: "So without saying a word about it he sent on some handsome paper for three rooms, & the girls had two rooms papered, leaving my room for another time. The graining certainly is perfect I never saw any so well done."

News had come that Stanwix had jumped ship, apparently in England, abandoning the kindly Captain Paul. "Poor Cousin Lizzie," Kate Gansevoort fretted to her brother on 1 February, "She will be almost broken hearted." Kate analyzed Stanwix's psychological state, sure Stanny was manifesting some delayed consequences of being repressed during his adolescence: "if boys are not boys in their childhood they will run away & explore for themselves when they should be preparing themselves for the duties of life." Stanny wrote from London in late January, a letter that reached New York in February, then he fell silent, keeping both his parents concerned, even through Frances's fifteenth birthday party on 2 March, at which Melville presented her with a good book to have in the house, *The Buried Cities of Campania: or, Pompeii and Herculaneum* by W. H. Davenport Adams. Stanny showed up at his step-grandmother's house on 18 July, "taller & stouter," and was there when his unsuspecting mother arrived from New York with her daughters the next day (news Augusta relayed to Peter Gansevoort on 30 July).

That spring John Hoadley thought of the perfect gift for Maria, better even than that fine wallpaper for the Mansion House—a portrait of Herman by an excellent painter, Joseph Oriel Eaton. By 5 May Herman had already had two sittings, presumably at Eaton's studio in Manhattan. About that time Herman wrote the daughter of the Hero of Fort Stanwix about a recent experience. Hoadley recognized the value of the letter and copied it out:

> The other day I visited out of curiosity the GANSEVOORT HOTEL, corner of "Little twelfth Street" and West Street. I bought a paper of tobacco by way of introducing myself: Then I said to the person who served me: "Can you tell me what this word 'Gansevoort' means? is it the name of a man? and if so, who was this Gansevoort?" Thereupon a solemn gentleman at a remote table spoke up: "Sir," said he, putting down his newspaper, "this hotel and the street of the same name are called after a rich family who in old times owned a great deal of property hereabouts." The dense ignorance of this solemn gentleman,—his knowing nothing of the hero of Fort Stanwix, aroused such an indignation in my breast, that disdaining to enlighten his benighted soul, I left the place without further colloquy. Repairing to the philosophic privacy of the District Office I then moralized upon the instability of human glory and the evanescence of —— many other things.

Among things evanescent were Herman's letters to his mother: only this one survives, and only because his brother-in-law made a copy of it.

The time was ripe for reflections. The failed author was sitting for a fine portrait, after rejecting opportunities in his young manhood to have engravings of his face look out of hundreds of copies of magazines opened all over the country. Now the scion of a great family was reduced to humble toil in an alien age, working on the docks at the foot of Gansevoort Street where the local inhabitants were ignorant of the historical significance of the Gansevoort name. There was no escaping reminders of the "instability of human glory" such as that which had befallen his Gansevoort grandfather, for on a visit to Tom's "Paradise" on Staten Island in early June Tom handed him "a handsomely framed engraving of the Hero of Fort Stanwix," explaining that Herman "was to regard it as a gift from Uncle Peter." Herman thanked his uncle, adding that when Fanny made her expected visit to the Island with Peter's daughter he hoped that Tom would "not wholly imprison them in his Paradise," but would "permit the people of 26th St to have a share of their company." He was behaving correctly, as Maria had taught him, and even genially, toward the man they all regarded ambivalently. And he was thinking about how in his Centennial Poem he might develop the theme of the brevity of historical memory in what his soldier of fortune in *The Confidence-Man* had sarcastically called "free Ameriky."

By late May, Eaton was finished, and Hoadley had arrived in New York to supervise the framing. Even Jane was impressed, as she wrote Henry Gansevoort on 26 June: "I had a small party on the 4th of June, and had determined, if possible to have Hermans portrait to grace my parlor. So, with Lizzies permission, I took a carriage and brought it home and stood it on the Piano. It was much admired." The portrait stayed at Twenty-sixth Street, apparently, for many months. On 7 November Melville's sister Fanny wrote Cousin Kate from Tom's that it was "a splendid likeness," and that she (and Maria) were going to carry it to Gansevoort with them when they went home. The Eaton portrait was recognized at once as a worthy addition to the family portraits, which would have made a striking gallery if they had been united together, Maria's family portraits along with Uncle Peter's portraits by the "Gansevoort Limner" and his Gilbert Stuart portraits of his parents.

A few days after Jane's party, Melville acquired the new *Passages from the English Note-Books* and at the same time bought the 1868 *Passages from the American Note-Books*, giving a day's pay, four dollars, for each of them. In 1870 he had in hand what he must have scanned in a bookstore earlier, Hawthorne's two notes from August 1850 made both laconic and tantalizing by Sophia's ellipsis dots, an invitation to Melville to fill in the blanks with his own memories as well as to speculate on what else Hawthorne might have recorded about their meeting. The quotations in chapter 14 above are uncensored; in what Melville saw in *Passages from the English Note-Books* Sophia had strewn the first two pages of the 30 November 1856 entry with ellipsis dots:

> A week ago last Monday, Herman Melville came to see me at the Consulate, looking much as he used to do, and with his characteristic gravity and reserve of manner. . . . . We soon found ourselves on pretty much our former terms of sociability and confidence. . . . . He is thus far on his way to Constantinople. I do not wonder that he found it necessary to take an airing through the world, after so many years of toilsome pen-labor, following upon so wild and adventurous a youth as his was. I invited him to come and stay with us at Southport, as long as he might remain in this vicinity, and accordingly he did come the next day. . . . . On Wednesday we took a pretty long walk together, and sat down in a hollow among the sand-hills, sheltering ourselves from the high cool wind. Melville, as he always does, began to reason of Providence and futurity, and of everything else that lies beyond human ken. . . . . He has a very high and noble nature, and is better worth immortality than the most of us. . . . . On Saturday we went to Chester together.

The account of the visit to Chester stretched over four pleasant pages, uncensored by Sophia because less dangerous. Here Melville saw the description of his opening a cupboard in the cathedral and discovering "a dozen or two of wine-bottles" which the guide told them "were now empty, and never were meant for jollity, having held only sacramental wine." Sophia also printed some of Hawthorne's account of their visit to the Yacht Inn, where they saw what was said to be Swift's satirical commentary on the clergy of Chester, written on a windowpane with the diamond in his ring, and the encounter with a printer who showed them about his office affably without having an inkling that the two Americans had "given a good deal of employment to the brethren of his craft." This made a good story, American writers companionably keeping their identities to themselves as they saw the sights of a Roman city near the Irish Sea, but it was strange for Melville to read, especially while engaged in his own evaluation of what Hawthorne had meant to him.

Melvilles and Gansevoorts made their usual peregrinations. By early June 1870 Fanny and Cousin Kate Gansevoort were planning a trip to Tom's Paradise. Herman started his vacation in late July, a little earlier than usual, and with Lizzie. He stopped at Boston to leave the girls with Hope Shaw then accompanied Lizzie to North Conway, New Hampshire, where she hoped to escape the worst of her rose cold. This was two years before the Eastern Railroad extension opened for travel as far as North Conway, so that Boston tourists could "reach that place now in five hours, getting to the White Mountains the same day." In July 1870, the Melvilles experienced what the Boston *Post* on 15 July 1872 reported as the bad old way of getting to North Conway, when the train set visitors down at Conway Centre, where they had to change to a coach. There were never "enough coaches to hold the greedy crowd of pleasure-seekers," and "there was always a downright Thermopylae fight to get the inside places." If you were accompanying women you had "to make a separate fight for every one of the dear creatures and hold the coach down if you happened by good luck or good muscle to secure one, against all comers till your ladies should see fit to make their way to your side; and then there was the baggage." Melville with his bad back fighting for Lizzie is not pleasant to imagine, but he had a quiet assertiveness that made him noticed, and he got them safely to the hotel, and stayed on for a time.

According to the Boston *Post* in 1872, a vacationer could board in North Conway "for from six dollars a week in a mile-away farm-house," and ten dollars a week would rent a room in "the upper stories of the Kearsarge and the Sunset," the summer hotels. For the hale, there was the challenge of Mount Kearsarge: "The view from there is, in some respects, superior to that from the Tip Top House, for this view includes Mount Washington in the landscape." In 1870 the social mix was much what the *Post* described in 1872: "pulpit orators of national fame, several of our distinguished Congressional legislators in Scotch tweeds, and at least one English lord." North Conway was "a sort of compromise between the extremes of summer pleasuring," lacking "in the feverish excitements of Saratoga, or Newport," featuring no races, possessing no gambling houses. Women did not have to worship Fashion: "neither is dress the sole thought of the ladies, nor are toilettes thrice a day a *sine qua non* to recognition at the hotels." There was, on the other hand, "a good deal of social merriment," and "the goddess Flirtation" reigned paramount among the young. Lizzie may not have thought of Bessie as marriageable — she may already have developed debilitating arthritis — but here was a place for Frances, if not Bessie, in a later year, to meet eligible bachelors. Young people, even city sophisticates, who might have revelled in the "whirl of Mammon at the specifically great summer resorts," genuinely enjoyed themselves here in North Conway, "hedged in among these glorious hills, with the vista of Washington and Jefferson in the hazy distance, and by the banks of the Saco," at this point "scarcely less romantic than the Thames from Richmond Terrace." (Saco *was* romantic, made so forever by Herman Melville in "Loomings.") Young "men and maidens" still favored croquet, in which Melville could take part, if oldsters were allowed. Conway was unparalleled as "a loafing place," with big verandas, no flies, "just people enough to make the siesta merry without being boisterous, variety of view without weariness, cooling draughts at hand and a soft stillness all around — these the Conway mansions of hospitality offer to all who prefer the *otium cum dignitate* to mountain climbing, river fishing, or excursion making." For those with a chair in the right corner, there might be a glimpse of a natural phenomenon as interesting as Hawthorne's great stone face: they might see "the 'white horse' on the ledge with silvery distinctness."

The reporter for the *Post* had a good idea of men like Herman Melville the customs inspector, the "Paterfamilias, who is usually miserable and totally uncomfortable at Saratoga and Newport, and spends his time there sitting disconsolately on the hotel piazzas the livelong day, with a tattered Herald five days old spread across his lap." Here, he "is braced to good spirits by the mountain air, he is refreshed by the rides to Echo Lake and Artists Falls and the Cathedral, and what not, and he has always floating in his head the tranquillizing reflection that he is paying ten dollars a week instead of thirty." To beguile himself on the piazza Melville might well have carried along the famous book by his guide around San Francisco, dead now, Thomas Starr King, *The White Hills; Their Legends, Landscape, and Poetry.*

King made an unabashed comparison and contrast of the air of Italy and the air of North Conway: "for pomp of bright, clear, contrasted flames on a deep and transparent sky, the visitors of North Conway, on the sunset bank that overlooks the meadows, enjoy the frequent privilege of a spectacle which the sun sinking behind the Notch conjures for them, such as he rarely displays to the dwellers by the Arno or the inhabitants of Naples." There were times when King longed for "the miracle of Joshua—for some artist-priest, like Turner, to bid the sun stand still, that such gorgeousness might be a garniture of more than a few rapid moments upon the cloud-flecked pavilion of the air." Melville was a kindred spirit, not to be disappointed in Nature, however much he might avoid his fellow-boarders.

In July Tom and Katie went to Boston (Maria wrote the Albany Gansevoorts on the seventh) "to visit Helen in her new pleasant home, & then go to Lawrence & visit Kate Hoadley. After which Tom & Katie will come to see us," Katie remaining after Tom returned to duty. Maria (Milie) was already in Brookline with Helen, and planning to be with her grandmother in August. Allan and his family went as always to Arrowhead. About this time *Appletons'* printed a pleasant mention of Arrowhead (the author under the impression that it was Herman's still), and, conscious of the value of the association, Allan chose a way to glorify his property for its literary associations. In early August he hired C. Seaver, the local photographer, to capture the chimney place at Arrowhead (in the room converted from kitchen to dining room); by this time Allan had ornamented the chimney place with a quotation from "I and My Chimney." Lizzie took one of the carte-de-visite-sized copies of the photograph which Allan gave her and Herman and had an enlargement "especially made for Herman at considerable cost"—at a time (she wrote to Cousin Kate decades later, in 1902) when she "could only afford to have the one example" enlarged.

Herman swung by Gansevoort, perhaps for days, leaving on 13 August, when he paid a "short visit" in the evening to Peter, Susan, and Kate, who reported to Henry (about 14 August) that he was looking "remarkably well—& was very cheerful." Hope Shaw's diary entry on 20 August says that Mr. Melville stopped on his way to see his sister Helen—Allan, since Herman could not have taken a month's vacation. By 22 August Stanny was with his Grandmother Melville at Gansevoort, and Lizzie was "off to the sea side" with Lem. Stanny managed to overcome what Augusta in a letter to Aunt Susan on 27 August called "his diffidence, & the little difficulty about his hearing," and stopped by to see Uncle Peter, who was always happy to see the Hero of Fort Stanwix memorialized in any fashion. There was talk of Stanny's going into his Uncle John's machine shop in Lawrence, Cousin Kate Gansevoort reported to Henry on 29 August, "as he has a decided taste for Machinery," but this reflected the hopes of some of the family, not Stanny's desires. Lizzie prolonged her own stay in New England. By early September she was with Sam (not Lem) at the Glen House, one of the better hotels, returning to Boston on the seventh. Lizzie was there when Allan and Jane stayed overnight on the ninth, but on 12 September she left with her daughters for New York, Hope Shaw recorded in her diary. Katie Melville wrote to Kate Gansevoort on 3 October: "Poor old Gansevoort will soon be deserted, is it not a good thing that Mamma will be away from there, this winter, I am sure it will do her good, Jane Millie & Lucy have returned to the city, also Herman's family. Tom is as *splendid* as ever & sends with me much love."

The family continued its visiting in the fall. Hoadley stopped by Twenty-sixth Street unexpectedly in early November, between trains, while Melville's sister Fanny was there, and in Boston picked up Maria and Augusta at the Shaws' and escorted them for a few days' stay at Lawrence. Fanny went to the Governor's House at the Harbor for Thanksgiving, apparently, before returning to Herman's. She had been "at Herman's yesterday" (29 November), she wrote Kate Gansevoort, and also "saw Jenny when in town." (None of them stayed at Allan and Jane's with any regularity.) Tom and Katie argued hard for everyone to come to the Harbor. On 17 November, Fanny reported to Kate Gansevoort: "Helen has partly promised to come on with Mamma & Gus & Mr Hoadley & Kate will accept, if they can leave home at that time." Through the holidays Cousin Kate was wild with concern about the health of her brother, who in early November was confined to his room on Washington Avenue. Jane wrote her on 11 December, pained that Henry was "in such delicate health—that it is considered necessary for him to pass the winter in a warmer climate." The sooner the better, she thought, and added with her usual insensitivity: "the trouble in most cases is—that people so often delay going south until it is too late." Allan also was ailing, having had "a slight attack of the same thing he had last winter," and had been warned to "exercise great care of himself this winter," and "go away somewhere" warm. Allan had been down at the Island that day and had "found his mother looking remarkably well." Jane as usual had let him go out alone: "The journey to Staten Island in winter, is to me rather formidable." Augusta had been at Allan's on the tenth, preparing "for the great festive Christmas," Jane said.

In mid-December Kate accompanied Henry down on the boat to New York, where he took passage to sail to Nassau on the fifteenth, alone, Kate feeling she must be with her father and stepmother, but torn. "I only wish I was going with him," she wrote Susan on the fourteenth: "It seems so cheerless & lonely for him to go so without any one who particularly cares for him." The day before Henry sailed, the Melvilles rallied around him and Kate at the St. James Hotel, corner of Broadway and Twenty-sixth Street:

> Cousin Lizzie Melville & Augusta called here this afternoon & this eveg. we had a meeting of the Lansing & Melville clan's in the parlour — all very kind in their messages & wishes for our dear boy — I will write & let you know as often as I can — Coz. Lizzie wants me to stay with her to-morrow night & Tom & Kate want me for a few days at Staten Island & I have concluded to accept & will let you know when I will be home. A. L. has attended to all Henry wanted.

Herman gave Henry a note of introduction to Lizzie's cousin Ellen Gifford, who was already in Nassau for her health. The day Henry sailed, the fifteenth, was his thirty-sixth birthday. Augusta wrote to Susan and Peter, then Kate wrote that she had seen "the steamer out of sight" and they "waved 'bon voyage,' & blessings to the vessel bearing one we all love so tenderly." She wished "Robert Sanford, or Abe. could have gone to Nassau & remained only a week." The Melvilles had behaved lovingly, and Kate readily left the hotel "& went to Cousin Hermans for the night," she wrote Henry, then on the seventeenth "the gallant Capt." (Tom) escorted her to the Island. The forces were divided: "Aunt Melville, & Fanny, are staying with Tom & Kate, & Cousin Gus at Hermans." Cousin Lizzie had been "very nice"; Aunt Melville, Gus, and Fanny were well. They all weighed the possibilities. Henry's cousin Robert Sanford was talking of going to Nassau to see him, and Allan thought he might go too, in January, and escort Kate. Tom and Katie held the family Christmas for at least Herman's family, Maria, Augusta, and Fanny. Melville gave Bessie *Characteristics of Women*, by Mrs. Anna Jameson (London, 1870). To his daughter Frances he gave Tennyson's *The Holy Grail* (Boston, 1870), a volume that reprinted the "proputty" poem.

Not content with the construction of Abby Lodge in 1869, Richard Lathers had made another bold move in early 1870, one which pretty much removed him from contact with the Melville family for most if not all of the year. On 21 February 1870, he bought in Charleston the antebellum mansion at 20 South Battery, which afforded "a fine view of the harbor entrance, neighboring islands and rivers that sweep by them." Lathers was ready to pursue his mission to heal the wounds of the recent conflict by bringing together political and military leaders of the North and South at his and Abby's large and elegant receptions. This meant that he was away from Winyah and even from Abby Lodge during months when Allan Melville's health was noticeably deteriorating, with one lung pronounced definitely bad.

In November 1870 Melville had acquired Emerson's *The Conduct of Life* (2d ed.; London: Smith, Elder, 1860) and, adopting the role of "Western

Critic," he read it aggressively, measuring the progress and fixity of his contemporary. In the essay "Considerations by the Way" he marked a passage on "the first lesson of history," the good of evil, and made this comment: "He still bethinks himself of his Optimism—he must make that good somehow against the eternal hell itself." When in "Culture" Emerson proclaimed: "You do not think you will find anything there [in Europe] which you have not seen at home?" Melville demurs: "Yet possibly, Rome or Athens has something to show or suggest that Chicago has not." Nevertheless, he could exclaim "True & admirable! Bravo!" when Emerson declared that the reality of simple virtues "is the foundation of friendship, religion, poetry, and art." He was reading Emerson with such zest because he too was still engaged in thinking his way through some of the great issues of the century. Through many months, probably beginning in 1870, Melville read and marked the more than a thousand pages of Thomas Warton's *History of English Poetry from the Twelfth to the Close of the Sixteenth Century* (London: Ward, Lock, and Tyler, n.d.), taking it as necessary accompaniment for his epic task, much as he had taken the reading of epics in 1860. Dennis Marnon, who, with Steven Olsen-Smith, rediscovered this book, has pointed out that Melville marked Warton's comments on religious and social history about as often as he marked literary commentary; marked virtually every mention of Shakespeare; marked mentions of hallowed names like Dante and Petrarch, but also marked names of obscure writers, many of whom he had some familiarity with. Month by month, Melville was putting himself through an intensive course in the early history of English poetry. He had his aesthetic credo, but he still needed to put on all the pieces that constituted the armor of an epic poet.

    Melville was living a hidden life, what journalists a decade or so later would begin calling a buried life, away from his old literary associates, almost lost to fame. Nevertheless, there are reports of his going into public. Henry Holt, in *Garrulities of an Octogenarian Editor*, recalled: "late one night about 1870 he [Melville] was one of a cheerful group of four who walked up Fourth Avenue from the Century Club, which was then in Fifteenth Street. . . . I often recall him as one of the very most agreeable men I have ever met." His international fame survived, in private. On 21 October 1870, visiting Portslade, near Brighton, Shirley Brooks, the editor of *Punch*, made a note in his diary: "Pretty churchyard. Among monuments, one to a gentleman killed by a coach accident at Carlisle, 10 days after marriage, & to another, I think his brother, who sailed from Singapore, & of whom, or of his Ship, nothing was ever heard again. Reminded me of the capital description of a seaport church in my favourite book, 'The Whale.'" That Christmas, a few hours before the Melvilles were celebrating Christmas in Tom's Paradise, Dante Gabriel Rossetti wrote to F. S. Ellis: "I am going to add two to my list of high-class orders which you have already been favoured with: viz: a *Lemprière* and a book called *Pierre, or the Ambiguities*, by Herman Melville, which I believe is not easily met with like others of his, as it has not been republished in England."

[32]

The Last Mustering of the Clan, and "The Wilderness"

1871

❧

> The great mistake with us seems to be, that we feel that we cannot do any great thing, unless we have all our time to devote to that particular thing.
>
> Marked (in 1839?) by Allan Melville in John Todd's
> *The Student's Manual* (Northampton, Mass.: Butler, 1837)

O<small>N</small> 6 J<small>ANUARY</small> 1871 Jane wrote to Kate Gansevoort, offering to "chaperone" her to Nassau; a male escort is what she needed. Ready to vacation in the warmth of Nassau while Kate watched her brother die, Jane was equally cavalier about Allan's health: "Allan thinks he cannot come [to Nassau] unless on business, he is quite over whelmed with business now, but I really think he will have to take great care of himself this winter" (without her, she meant), and she added that Allan might "be obliged by his health to go south" (as a doctor had recommended) even before March, when the Latherses would have their Charleston mansion ready for a proper housewarming. She consulted her own pleasures always, Jane did, and could do with a winter vacation in Nassau, shaken as she was from contemplating a ferry ride to Staten Island in December. On the same day, Melville's sister Fanny wrote her Aunt Susan from Staten Island, back from her post-Christmas visit to Winyah. Tom had arrived home from Manhattan when they received Kate Gansevoort's telegram asking him "to engage a state-room for the twelfth 'conditionally'" for her voyage, but he arranged her passage the next day. Fanny had planned to go home with Helen in mid-month and make her Brookline and Lawrence visits then, rather than later in the year, but she offered to go to Washington Avenue to take Kate's place, as far as she could, knowing that Susan and Peter could not run the house in proper Dutch fashion without the help of a strong attentive younger chatelaine.

On 7 January Augusta wrote to Kate Gansevoort from 104 East Twenty-sixth Street, having taken the 9:00 A.M. boat over from the Island. Herman had been thinking of Henry and Kate at breakfast, and had directed Lizzie to see "that a letter goes to Kate Gansevoort inviting her to come right here," while she was arranging to sail to Nassau. Lizzie herself, "very busy in making up Swiss muslin" for the girls' party dresses, had asked Augusta to reply to Kate's letter of 3 January, saying, typically, "I am so busy, would you write Kate for me, & say that we would be very happy to see her here when she comes to New York." Stanwix was there, ready to meet Kate at whatever train she took. "Command my services," Augusta told Kate. In the middle of this distress, on 10 January, Tom had to spend all day with a reporter from *Harper's Magazine* who was "getting Information about the Harbor & Inmates for publication"; two years passed before the article appeared. Kate sailed on the *Missouri* and reached Nassau on 16 January. When Abe Lansing decided to follow Kate, Tom introduced him to the captain and officials of another boat to Nassau so that, as Abe wrote his Aunt Susan on the fourteenth, he would "sail as our Kate did under good auspices." He did, but left her there sooner than he should have. Lizzie received an independent, encouraging report about Henry from her cousin Ellen Gifford, also in Nassau. Kate was "an angel of mercy," Henry wrote to his stepmother on 22 January 1871 (dictating the letter to the angel). The doctor had told Henry that "three months ago this could have been stopped," but now it was too late "to be radically cured," Henry wrote, adding, "however I hope for the best — but I suffer considerably," the opium having begun to numb his right arm. On 7 April Kate and Henry arrived in New York on the *Moro Castle*, unannounced, and made their way to the Wadsworth House at Fifth Avenue and Thirteenth Street. Herman and Lizzie saw Henry there the next day, then on 12 April Kate got Henry aboard the *Drew*, where, as they were passing Rhinebeck, on the way home to Albany, he died.

Riding to Rhinebeck in an open one-horse wagon, the Hudson blocked by ice, had brought on the last illness of Allan Melvill, Maria and Peter remembered at once; now Allan Jr., who could barely remember his father, wrote Henry's cousin Robert Sanford at Uncle Peter's house, saying that he and Augusta would go up with Tom and Katie for the funeral. Kate arranged the west parlor to accommodate Henry in his coffin, so the funeral service could be read over his body there at three o'clock on 15 April — six years after the national tragedy. Lizzie took the trouble to acquire multiple copies of some verses meant for consolation (perhaps asking her church to have them "re-published"), so she said Aunt Susan could keep the copy she sent her on 24 April. The verses are lost, but Lizzie's own comments survive: "The enclosed lines are so filled with the spirit which I feel that we ought to cherish on the pain of parting with our loved and lost dear ones, and they have been of so much comfort to *me*, that I enclose them, hoping that you may find in their breathings some soothing influence in this sore time of trial when the Father's hand has fallen so heavily on your household." Lizzie tried to make herself believe that Kate would accept the loss: "May she be able to say from her heart: It is for the dear one's sake and shall I rebel when he is safe and *at rest?* Tell her so for me, please, and do I not know! — it is the only way to bear it *at all*. And then, we shall meet our loved ones again, we *must* believe, or despair would be ours indeed." This is the voice of a woman talking from her own deepest experience: *"and do I not know!"* On this topic Lizzie offered commonplaces, but commonplaces that had kept her alive and sane, and she feared for Kate with good reason.

Maria stayed on and on at the Harbor, hoping, in late April 1871, that Helen could come to meet her and go to Gansevoort with her, and in the last week of April she visited both Herman's and Allan's houses, where she found "all well." At last on 4 May Augusta left for the Mansion House "with the Servantman" ("Old John" from the Sailors' Snug Harbor), "preferring herself to open the Sunday school on the next Sabbath which has sadly fallen off since her absence," as Maria wrote to Kate Gansevoort. Milie was "taking Augusta's place" as her grandmother's companion, so Maria asked permission to bring her oldest granddaughter with her to Albany: "would you or your dear father or mother object to seeing her at your house," she asked, adding: "She is a dear good girl quiet & sensible, & *a pious Episcopalian.*" Neither Peter nor Susan knew Milie as a young woman, and they had to be forewarned, for she might shock the Dutch church Gansevoorts by making the sign of the cross in prayer. "My especial favorite," Lizzie called her in a letter to Kate on 17 May. They were eager to have Milie make new friends in the family as a way of sheltering her from Jane; Jane deftly manipulated Kate Gansevoort to keep that from happening.

In early May 1871 from Kansas City, Missouri, Edwin Lansing sent word to Melville about Stanwix, and then Stanwix himself wrote. Lizzie relayed the news to Maria through Kate Gansevoort in her 17 May letter: "Please tell Mama (and I know that you will be interested to hear) that we had another letter from Stanny today, from the interior of Kansas, on the line of the Santa Fe R.R. whither he had gone by advice of Mr Lansing (or Brewster, or both) both of whom he found on his first arrival in Kansas City. They have been exceedingly kind to him, and it is a great relief to me that he has found such good friends." Kate Gansevoort was kind, also. In the aftermath of Henry's death Kate began sending clothing which Lizzie could remake to fit her and the girls. The women of Uncle Peter's family, like their Van Rensselaer cousins, always bought for quality, not for fashion, so any used garments were well worth making over. Lizzie the rich man's daughter took the charity with perfect self-possession, glad (as she wrote on 17 May) that she had "no absurd pride" and considering "the stitches already set" as an immense gain, having "just been over ears in spring sewing." In late May Lizzie had problems with servants again, while she was house-bound with a sprained foot. On the twenty-eighth she wrote Kate Gansevoort that "Mary" (probably her correct name, but also still the family's generic name for an Irish cook) "must needs get married on four days notice to me"—four days' notice after living at the Melville house over three years. The lame Lizzie had to find a "new dispensation" (a maid or cook) and try to overcome the novice's "*very* inefficient endeavors."

Lizzie continued in her letter of 28 May with a passage that reveals much about her attitude toward money. In her memorandum book she found a record that she owed "K.G. 25 cts.," which she now paid by enclosing a twenty-five-cent stamp: "I think I can hear you say 'What did our Lizzie do *that* for,' I have never forgotten what I have heard my father tell us so often—'Always be *precise* about money matters to the *smallest sum*' and 'never forget the smallest debt—not so much for your creditors sake as your own.'" Herman was Allan Melvill's son, and Lizzie, forced to take over the finances of the family, drew now on her early Franklinesque indoctrination. Other news was that Ellen Gifford had been in the city for a week at the New York Hotel, and Lizzie had not seen her yet because of her lame foot, but she and Herman were going to try to see her that evening. The family had personal interest in her being able to go about, for the spring exhibit at the new white-marble-walled National Academy of Design at Fourth Avenue and Twenty-third Street included the Joseph Oriel Eaton portrait of Herman Melville, loaned by "Mrs. Melville"—presumably Maria Gansevoort Melville, the owner of the painting.

Late in June 1871 John Hoadley escorted his Kate and the children and Fanny (and a "Maid" named, ludicrously, Catherine), the children "delighted at the idea of spending their vacation at Grandma's" and Kate and Fanny "happy at the thought of going home" to their mother (as Fanny wrote her Aunt Susan on 20 June). They would see Helen on their way. Hoadley's being in the party was good news for Cousin Kate, who would be able to consult him at the Mansion House. She had already begun talking of a memorial volume for Henry, and Allan Melville had made an inquiry of Edwin Lansing about Henry's war service. Stanwix came home on a visit in late August, and this time willingly called at 115 Washington Avenue in Albany on his way north to see his grandmother and aunts. At Gansevoort Augusta thought he had "grown a great deal" in stature and had "improved," apparently in health; she wrote Kate Gansevoort on 25 August that he would "improve still more before he is a man"—not the sort of thing anyone said about Herman, who had been a man at that age. After Henry's death Peter wanted more than ever to see Herman and Stanwix when they were anywhere near Albany, but that summer, 1871, Melville did not go to Gansevoort. Instead, he went to North Conway with Lizzie and the girls.

Kate's grief for Henry had turned morbid, as Lizzie had dreaded. On 3 July Kate wrote to Henry's doctor with a useless question: "May I presume to ask if *You* really thought my poor Brother had not such a short time to live when he left Nassau?" She moaned to him: "It is past the sorrow of my life, my only Brother, my pride my nearest tie on Earth, to die so young." She blamed doctors; she blamed herself; she blamed her father; she did not blame her profligate brother. Katie Melville wrote her on 21 July, while visiting Gansevoort: "I do pray my dear Kate that though you have lost a dear and only brother, you may be able to lean on Jesus, the Elder Brother, and receive His strength and consolation." Kate's grief affected everyone she knew. On 11 September George Wales, a cousin of Lizzie's who shared an interest in porcelains with Kate, reproached her for mourning excessively, reminding her that she had a duty "to the living" as well as the dead. Everyone knew Kate was behaving abnormally and self-destructively but no one could stop her. As months passed her grief manifested itself in psychological states oddly like some of Herman's.

Herman's brothers and sisters vacationed strenuously, but he, Lizzie, and their daughters did not join them. By mid-August, as Augusta wrote Kate Gansevoort, the Mansion House was diminished: "Our household of twelve is now reduced to six. Helen, & Lucy, Lottie & Frank are still with us. For some weeks our long table presented quite a hotel-appearance." Stanwix Melville was the only one in the immediate family to visit Gansevoort that year, needing to see his grandmother and Augusta. On 2 September Fanny wrote Kate Gansevoort that she and Augusta and their mother would probably not leave home until after New Year's, having been away from Gansevoort so long the previous winter. Melville was probably home when a charming tongue-in-cheek article appeared in the New York *World* on 3 September: "Staten Island Savages." One of the few articles known to link Herman Melville to the governor of Sailors' Snug Harbor, this is a Swiftian, and in places specifically a Melvillean, account: "within a short distance of the City of New York there exists an island whereon the primitive simplicity of savage life is still maintained, almost untrammelled by any of the restraints of artificial civilization. . . . and when the history of Staten Island comes to be written by Captain Melville (who was some time ago cast upon its shore), its customs will be found to rival in their happy innocence those of Omoo and Typee." The Staten Islanders were "savages" because in the summer they go about nearly as naked as the Polynesians in *Typee*, "lining the shore of the Kill von Kull and disporting themselves in the flood in happy carelessness of observation." Among the naked savages were Irishwomen ("robust naiads of

Hibernian mould") disrobing on the bank; "brawny youths clustered on a public wharf in a costume slightly modified from the classical fig-leaf"; scullers wearing no top garment, only "a pair of thin drawers, with both legs amputated high up" (primordial cut-offs), and paddling or sunning themselves in "full view of the ferries." Any of several commuters to New York City, G. W. Curtis, for one, or Sidney Howard Gay, would have been capable of writing this very clever piece.

In 1868 Augusta had written Aunt Mary in Galena for details of the life of Uncle Thomas, perhaps at the instigation of Allan, who had been prodded by J. E. A. Smith to help him gather material for his *History of Pittsfield*. Smith's triumph, perhaps with Allan's help, was that Herman agreed to write for the history a brief memoir of his uncle for the second volume. The first volume was published early in 1869, and reviewed in the New York *Tribune* on 5 March, with respect for the antiquity of the town but uneasiness about Smith's style ("prolix," often "cumbersome," and failing to achieve effects "through its lack of simplicity"). In 1871, while Kate Gansevoort was compiling material for Henry's memorial volume, Smith plodded on with his history of Pittsfield. On 25 October he wrote Allan Melville to thank him for the volumes of Herman's works that Allan had donated to the Berkshire Athenaeum. Smith was grateful for a photograph of a painting of Thomas Melvill Jr., and dared to hope also for "Mr. Herman Melvilles on steel for our history which will go to press about the first of next June."

Kate Gansevoort had intaglio memorial rings made for her male cousins, and sent Herman his in early November. On 13 November Melville responded, though pressed for time: "Be assured that I shall sacredly preserve the ring, esteeming it as if it had been given me by the living hand—*his* who now lies so honorably at rest." He added, "Promptitude must atone for brevity." From Thirty-fifth Street Milie also wrote Kate Gansevoort on 13 November, giving news of the three brothers and their families: "Lucy is spending Sunday on the Island and we expect Uncle Tom & wife this evening to spend the night. I see Aunt Lizzie often. They are all well. Bessie is at home this winter and is a great assistance & comfort to her mother. Aunt Lizzie expects to go to Boston for Thanksgiving, she has not been at home for that day in twelve years. She asked about you & seemed sorry not to have seen you." In Albany, there was a ferocious family outburst on 16 November when Peter Gansevoort wrote checks to Kate totaling ten thousand dollars, with this note: "for my darling child with her fathers sincere Love & best wishes—that she will use it as remembrance from her devotedly attached Father May God bless you Peter Gansevoort." Another daughter might have written him a heartfelt note of thanks, or spoken her thanks directly. Kate replied: "what shall I do with the money? I am not ungrateful, but oh how sincerely *I wish you had given it*, to *our beloved Henry!* If he had only had it" (here she added above the line: "two years ago"), "he might have resigned & gone away from the coast, & I have no doubt, that a new life, would have moderated his disease, & preserved his precious life to us." Having punished her aged father as her duty to Henry required, she then acknowledged that he had always been "so kind" to her and thanked him for this and for his lifelong kindnesses. From Gansevoort on 11 December Helen wrote Kate Gansevoort that her mother and Augusta were going down on the fourteenth to stay a few days on their way to New York (" 'if nothing unforeseen happens to prevent,' as the county people say"). Fanny and Helen would go later, but with so much luggage that they preferred to go straight to New York rather than stop in Albany overnight. Peter was unwontedly querulous, and asked Augusta why Herman had not been to see him, so Herman sweetly explained, the day after Christmas: "About not coming to see you. — I am only allowed two weeks' vacation. This I take in the summer; and last summer I spent it, for a change, at North Conway, with Lizzie. Had I gone to Northumberland as usual" (Northumberland being the township in which Gansevoort was located), "I should not have failed seeing you on the way, going or returning."

On 17 December Herman's old friend Henry Theodore Tuckerman died. In New York City on 18 December the *Tribune* printed a hastily written but elegant obituary: "Although he never possessed a robust physical constitution, he had of late been in the enjoyment of more than his usual health, and his last illness was unexpected and rapid in its fatal action." Bryant's *Evening Post* printed the obituary by Dr. Samuel Osgood, the minister of the Church of the Messiah who had stepped into Henry Bellows's place to deal with the press after Malcolm's death. Despite a snowstorm on the nineteenth, Bellows conducted the funeral services for Tuckerman at All Souls Church, Fourth Avenue and Twentieth Street, on Wednesday morning, the twentieth. Melville may have been granted time off to attend; he would have gone with Duyckinck, who was preparing a memorial tribute for a meeting of the New-York Historical Society the next month.

Melville could have testified with the writer in the *Tribune* that few men "would go so far out of their way to oblige a friend" as Tuckerman, particularly to let a friend know that he was still highly esteemed in some quarters, whatever adversity had befallen him. As late as the year before, 1870, Tuckerman had mentioned Melville in his "Sketch of American Literature" revised for Thomas Budd Shaw's *Outlines of English Literature*. Melville must have continued to visit Tuckerman among his books and pictures in his "large southern rooms of the old Studio Building in West 10th Street, the home of many of his artist friends" (Tuckerman's nephew Bayard's words), and communed with him quietly, for in his last years Tuckerman was quite deaf. The naturally silent man and the deaf man managed to talk about consuming topics—artists, works of art, art theory. For Melville, as for Duyckinck, the loss was hard to bear. His mourning gift to himself was one he might have talked about with Tuckerman: *The Works of Eminent Masters, in Painting, Sculpture, Architecture, and Decorative Art* (London: Cassell, 1854), two volumes in one, which he signed "Dec. '71 N.Y." In it he made the marginal comparison to "'Pictor Ignotus' of Browning," evidence, like the 1862 annotations in his Vasari, that he had long known Browning's poetry.

Maria's trip south for Christmas with her unmarried daughters was disastrous, the train delayed, and ice slowing them all the way, so they reached New York very late on the nineteenth—after Herman, poor Bessie, and Allan had given up. On the twenty-first, Augusta described the trip to Peter Gansevoort:

> The train of cars was very long & the crowd immense, but dear Tom soon found us, & Mamma was so happy to see him. Coming in so late, nearly two hours behind time, Herman had got tired of waiting in the cold, & he & Bessie had gone home, & Allan had an engagement which called him off. So Tom took us at once to the carriage & we drove into Fifth Av, down to "Washington Parade Ground", & through it to the new st. opened *South Fifth Av.* to Canal st, & so on to Dey st, in good time for the 7 O'clock boat. Glad were we to reach Tom's home, refresh ourselves with a good tea, & go to bed. Kate gave us a warm welcome.

In the morning Tom confirmed that the twentieth was "the coldest day of the season:—thermometer 3° below zero."

For Christmas dinner 1871 Thomas Melville planned to serve the inmates of Sailors' Snug Harbor with "Roast Turkey and smoked Ham. (the Hams are cured and smoked at the Harbor)"—this according to his quarterly report to the board of trustees, 18 December 1871. Tom also hosted a great Christmas dinner for his mother and his brothers and sisters—all except Allan and his daughters and his ineffable wife. On the twenty-sixth Augusta wrote to Peter and Susan:

> Mamma has been quite well since recovering from her fatigue, & was able to make a bright appearance at the Christmas-board yesterday. I wish you & Uncle, & our Kate could have looked in at the hour of five upon the circle gathered about it. As John said it was artistic, comprising as it did such a variety of form & feature with types of every style, fair & dark, black eyes & blue, hair ebon & flaxen; & all ages from Grandmamma to the little Frank, who seemed to enter into the very spirit of the festival & gave his toast with

the rest. We wished that you & dear Uncle could have been with us, & your Kate. All were together, except Allan & his family.

Poor Allan had come over on Sunday, Christmas Eve, with Lucy, "to take his Christmas dinner with his Mother." He explained that "Jenny would insist upon his dining at home, she having invited guests to their Christmas dinner!" Driven to extremity, as Lizzie had been eight years earlier, Augusta ventured this comment (how extreme a judgment, only an intimate would know): "There are some funny people in this world." Jane's selfishness had kept the family from being united:

> So there were only seventeen at the table this time. George made his appearance on Monday morning, John, Kate & the three children, much to our surprise, Friday, we not having expected them until the evening. They left Boston Thursday noon, intending to sleep at Springfield, but were detained some hours when thirteen miles from that place, by a collision of freight trains which had strewn the track with smashed-up cars. So they reached us sleepy and famished, having been obliged to exist upon their lunch. Herman & Lizzie with their three children came over in the noon boat yesterday. They were all looking remarkably well, & made many inquiries about yourself, uncle, & Kate. Stanwix has grown & expanded wonderfully. That Western trip was a good thing for him physically.
>
> Now to return to the dinner—It was a beautiful one, so well cooked & handsomely served, & the Christmas greens & flowers were lovely. As to our host & hostess:—they were Tom & Kate, & saying that, I need add nothing more. They both looked their best, & acted out their own warm-hearted selves, & every one seemed happy. Mamma never looked better, & was the Queen of the feast, whose good health formed the toast of our little Frank, her youngest grand child.
>
> After the noble turkey & other Christmas grand dishes had been satisfactorily discussed [meaning "eaten," as used in *Typee*], the huge plum pudding & mince pie, & beautiful dessert received due attention, then came the "flow of soul," & John & George Herman & Tom shone their brightest. You should have heard their bright sallies, & the toasts which so quickly followed each other....
>
> And then Tom rose, and proposed the health of the dear absent ones who had thought of us & our Christmas feast, & sent us such a pleasant remembrance—And all standing we drank to the good health of our dear Uncle & Aunt Gansevoort—Tom & Kate raising to their lips the little magic glasses they had sent, but, tell dear Uncle, that done, the sip of bright sherry followed—& all hearts were in Albany.
>
> When all were again seated a pause followed which Herman broke by

proposing "The souls in Paradise," Tom took the idea at once, & all rose once more, as he gently uttered the words "We will drink to the memory of Mackie, & Henry Gansevoort." And there were tears in the eyes of some who did so. It was beautiful to see the quiet feeling which seemed to steal over all.

There was a "shower of Christmas gifts," especially from the Hoadleys, since Kate and every other Hoadley had "something handsome for every one," so that the "parlor looked like a Fair." But Allan, Milie, Florence, Kitty, and Lucy were at Thirty-fifth Street with Jane's delightful friends.

That was Augusta to Peter and Susan Gansevoort. This is Herman's description to Uncle Peter:

> Yesterday (Christmas) we all dined on Staten Island at Tom's, who gave us a bountiful and luxurious banquet. It was a big table, belted round by big appetites and bigger hearts, but the biggest of all the hearts was at the head of the table — being big with satisfaction at seeing us enjoying ourselves. Mama looked uncommonly well; and Helen, Augusta, Kate (two Kates), Fanny, Minnie, Lottie, Frankie, Bessie, Fanny, Stanny, Mr Hoadley, Mr Griggs, not excluding the present modest writer — we all looked very well indeed.
>
> Among the toasts Uncle Peter was remembered, Aunt Susan & Cousin Kate; nor was Henry forgotten. Tom offered that toast to his memory.
>
> Stanny and I were obliged to leave at an early — or rather early hour, in order to take the last boat for New York. We left them still enjoying themselves in the parlors.

The boxes from Kate Gansevoort for Tom and Katie had "afforded a fund of amusement & merriment at our Christmas dinner," leading Augusta to tell her: "You sly puss you!" On 9 January 1872 Lizzie added her own deepest feelings in a letter to Kate Gansevoort: "It was a pleasant meeting though it comes at last that these anniversaries bring as much of sadness as gladness, and the places left vacant by the dear ones who have 'gone up higher' seem more empty still. And were it not for the sympathy and interest in the young branches who are able to hail these seasons with delight, I for one would almost be glad to let them pass without outward notice."

If Allan and his daughters had been allowed to come, it might have been less painful for Lizzie. On 28 December 1871 at last the family was invited "to a grand lunch at Allan's." Maria and Fanny stayed in the Harbor. Augusta wrote Kate Gansevoort: "We had a perfectly charming time at Allan's the day of the Collation. The Thurston family, Mr Lathers' & Mr Morewoods' & Mr Duyckincks' had been invited to join us." The table was very handsome, "& the little tables scattered round with the attentive waiters." On 29 December one of Allan's best friends, the actor James H. Hackett, died; in June he had written Allan about their respective summer plans. First Herman's loss of Tuckerman, then Allan's loss of Hackett. More souls in Paradise. And at year's end Herman Melville owed Allan fifty dollars: did Lizzie know?

During this year, aside from his brief vacation, Herman Melville had mainly confined himself to his work as deputy inspector of customs and his more and more private life as a poet. On 6 January 1871 he had bought a copy (not his first) of Hawthorne's *The Snow-Image* and marked the passage in "The Devil in Manuscript" where Oberon burns his tales and cries, "May my hand wither when it would write another!" As early as "The Piazza," during his rudimentary attempts to articulate just how his aesthetic views differed from his friend's, he had taken Oberon as a self-portrait by Hawthorne. Later in January 1871 he bought another edition of Shakespeare's sonnets and read some of them, triple-checking a line in Sonnet 65: "Tired with all these, for restful death I cry." He bought *In Memoriam* (again not the first copy he had held).

Sometime in 1871 Melville bought Thomas Arnold's *Travelling Journals, with Extracts from the Life and Letters* (London, 1851). He was caught by a passage "On the Lake of Como," in which Dr. Arnold reflected on what it would be "to bring one's family and life" to a place of "such voluptuous enjoyment" instead of continuing his life of "usefulness and activity" in England. Some countries were for pleasure, but England had "other destinies." Melville marked what followed on the duty of the English "to do good to themselves and to the world," underlining "to do good to themselves" and at the bottom writing "This is very curious." Melville had proclaimed in *White-Jacket* (ch. 36) that American national selfishness was "unbounded philanthropy" because "we can not do a good to America but we give alms to the world." Now he was bemused by Dr. Arnold's solemnity about England's high destiny. In a section on "Theology" in the "Extracts from the Life and Journals," Melville marked a passage where Dr. Arnold argued that the king is a better representative of God than the clergy. Better trust the king's supremacy, "which is, in fact, no other than an assertion of the supremacy of the Church or Christian society over the clergy." At the bottom of that page Melville marked this passage: "And my fondness for Greek and German literature has made me very keenly alive to the mental defects of the Dissenters as a body; the characteristic faults of the English mind, — narrowness of view, and a want of learning and a sound critical spirit, — being exhibited to my mind in the Dissenters almost in caricature. It is nothing but painful to me." Melville commented: "How this is developed & applied by his son, M. Arnold." Dr. Arnold helped Melville comprehend how a certain kind of man could defend the divine right of kings and project all the unpleasant national characteristics onto a modern set of Malvolios — helped him with his portrait of Derwent, the overly sophisticated literary Anglican cleric in *Clarel*.

On 13 February 1871 Melville bought *New Poems* (Boston, 1867) by the son, Matthew Arnold, and marked this passage in "Empedocles on Etna" on mankind's having "no *right* to bliss, / No title from the Gods to welfare and repose." Here Melville wrote: "A Western critic here exclaims—'What in thunder did the Gods create us for then? If not for bliss, for bale? If so, the devel take the Gods.'" Then he read on: "The mass swells more and more / Of volumes yet to read, / Of secrets yet to explore," bursting out again: "'Damn the volumes,' exclaims the Western critic.—'What could a sage of the nineteenth century teach Socrates? Why, nothing more than something about Cyrus Feilds and the ocean telegraph, and the Sewing Machine &c.'" Contempt for the sewing machine as one symbol of modernity is perturbing because it shows so little awareness of how much labor it was saving the Melville women, and especially because it shows that Melville was still associating Hoadley, the sewing machine maker, with contemptible modernity, as he had done in 1857. Melville may have felt that the sewing machine had brought a tremendous racket into the house, which he needed to be a quiet haven after his hours on the tumultuous streets and docks of New York City. The racket the machines made is undeniable, for Augusta in 1872 wrote Kate Gansevoort: "Fanny is making such a tremendous noise with the sewing machine right in my ear that I fear this letter will not be as good as I could desire in acknowledgment of yours." Lizzie put her sewing machine in her little south room, as far away from Herman's study as she could get it, on that floor.

From London on 25 October 1871 Lemuel Shaw Jr. wrote to Sam Shaw: "We are to bring home the Rev. Mr Alger who is hopelessly insane, in a hospital in Paris." Perhaps news of this prodded Melville to buy a book by this close friend of Tuckerman's, William Rounseville Alger, *The Solitudes of Nature and of Man; or, The Loneliness of Human Life* (Boston, 1867). He marked a passage on "the kindly Emerson" as illustrating "the temptation of the great to scorn the commonality," where Alger cited these phrases from Emerson: "enormous populations, like moving cheese,—the more, the worse"; "the guano-races of mankind"; "the worst of charity is, that the lives you are asked to preserve are not worth preserving"; "masses! the calamity is the masses." Melville commented: "These expressions attributed to the 'kindly Emerson' are somewhat different from the words of Christ to the multitude on the Mount," and signed the note "H. M." An annotation on a later page is partly recovered: "It is not aspiration but ambition that is the mother of misery in man. Aspiration is a . . . . H. M."

The marginalia tells something, but Melville's inner life in 1871 is best revealed in *Clarel*, presumably in Part 2, "The Wilderness." There, influenced by Dr. Arnold, a prominent character is Derwent, the highly secularized Anglican cleric who embodies, as Walter Bezanson says, a "meliorist view of man and society" and a "benign view of God and nature." A Dominican joins the pilgrims at the Jordan long enough to advance the argument that the Catholic Church "is the Protestant to-day" (pt. 2, canto 25), in a reversal of historic roles. The developing portrait of Vine is likely affected by what Melville read about Hawthorne in the periodicals and by what Melville read by Hawthorne, since excerpts from his Italian notebooks were available during 1871 in newspapers and magazines. On 14 March the *Tribune* mentioned that Lippincott was reprinting the London *Good Words*, with new Hawthorne material entitled "First Impressions of France and Italy." The *Tribune* also passed on the news that Hawthorne's experience in Rome had been unhappy: "He arrived in Rome in the month of February, which is generally considered the finest season in the fickle climate of Italy, but it struck a chill to his heart from which he scarcely recovered during his residence in that world of enchantment."

In "The Cavalcade" (2.1), as the pilgrims leave Jerusalem by the Via Dolorosa, Vine rides "in rear of all the train / As hardly he pertained thereto / Or his right place therein scarce knew," and he "frequent turned again / To pore behind." Even though he holds the reins with "lurking will," he is looking backward, living in the past. Once again Melville raises two possibilities in attempting to account for Vine's behavior: that he lags as if he hardly pertains to the train, or that he lags as if he scarcely knew his "right place" in the train. Then once again Melville is unable to content himself with a single possibility: either Vine is "In reminiscence folded ever" or else he is always wrapped in "some deep moral fantasy." The latter possibility gains credence for the reader because it is given fuller elaboration:

> At whiles in face a dusk and shiver,
> As if in heart he heard amazed
> The sighing of Ravenna's wood
> Of pine, and saw the phantom knight
> (Boccaccio's) with the dagger raised
> Still hunt the lady in her flight
> From solitude to solitude.

Such a "deep moral fantasy" is associated with revery, musings, and daydreaming — in this instance about a particularly ghoulish story, which Bezanson succinctly describes: "A violent, expiatory tale of a knight who committed suicide for love, and of his contemptuous lady who joyed in his death. Daily they reenact their punishment: he pursues her through the Ravenna wood, disembowels her, and feeds her heart to pursuing dogs." This literary episode may recall some analogous horror in Vine's earlier life or may merely establish his fascination (outwardly manifested by a facial "dusk and shiver") with a terrifying and a notably misogynistic old story about sin, guilt, and revenge. The passage also emphasizes Vine's habit of living in the past, whether his own experience or recollections of something he has read about the past.

In "Through Adommin" (2.9), after Nehemiah has retold the story of the Good Samaritan, Vine whispers "to the saint aside: / 'There was a Levite and a priest.'" Nehemiah is not disturbed: "'Whom God forgive,' he mild replied, / 'As I forget.'" What baffles the reader is why Vine would have the impulse to remind the dotty saint of something that could not possibly make him feel better and might well cause him pain. In "A Halt" (2.10), the Scottish Presbyterian Elder (embodying what Dr. Arnold called "the mental defects of the Dissenters" — "narrowness of view," a "want of learning and a sound critical spirit") provokes from Vine "a vivid spark — / Derisive comment, part restrained." (Unable to unbend to the free-and-easy manners of the others, the Elder turns back.) When the Druze, Djalea, the chief guard and guide and himself the son of an emir, employs a "courtesy peculiar" toward Vine, Rolfe explains the deference to Clarel: "few, believe, have nicer eye / For the cast of aristocracy / Than Orientals," and goes on to describe Vine as being "in mold / Of a romanced nobility," his "chary speech, his rich still air" confirming the desert people in such conjectures.

In "The Banker" (2.12), disconcerted by the way the wasteland along Kedron affects many of the travelers, Clarel turns "to meet the grace / Of one who not infected dwelt — / Yes, Vine, who shared his horse's pace / In level sameness, as both felt / At home in dearth." Melville was recalling "Tomb and Fountain" (1.28), where he had introduced Vine as reclining in the Sepulcher of Kings, intent upon sculptured leaves and fruits which bloom while "Involved in dearth." He was also recalling "The Recluse" (1.29), where he speculated about Vine's non-productivity as possibly resulting from his pining "In dearth of rich incentive high." Now Vine's "level sameness" is "thoughtful" but we are not told what those thoughts concern. In "By Achor" (2.14) Melville briefly describes Vine's behavior near Achor's gorge, a site that sparks in Nehemiah an unwonted and rather eerie vehemence and leads to an exchange between Derwent and Rolfe in which Rolfe supports Nehemiah: "roundabout" Achor Nature is "Calvinist" insofar as her aspect may be construed as at all devout. While this conversation is taking place, "Vine, o'ercast, / Estranged rode in thought's hid repast." Nothing suggests that Vine is actively, vigorously thinking about old thoughts so as to create new thoughts. By now, we begin to know what unproductive order of "thought" we are dealing with, and we may begin to pay special attention to what it means to feed upon thought's hid repast: self-cannibalism. There is a law of diminishing provender: every time you feed upon your unrenewed thoughts there is less left. Tellingly, the character in "The Wilderness" who fascinates Vine is the Swede, Mortmain, a disillusioned veteran of European revolutionary fervor who bleeds into his own armor, Vine thinks, and feeds on himself as Vine does, even (later, in 3.15) gnawing his own hand in his sleep. In his father's copy Melville had marked 4.6.1 of *The Faerie Queene*: "What equall torment to the griefe of mind, / And pyning anguish hid in gentle hart, / That inly feeds itself with thoughts unkind, / And nourisheth her owne consuming smart? / What medicine can any leaches art / Yeeld such a sore." Then Melville wrote: "Macbeth to the doctor." Mortmain and Vine are Spenserian sufferers, and of all Melville's friends in his mature life the one he most associated with *The Faerie Queene* was Hawthorne, the father of Una.

In "The Fountain" (2.15) Rolfe's good fellowship has struck on "a chord long slack" in Vine. Then Melville focuses on Vine's reactions to the place and the situation: "But how may spirit quick and deep / A constancy unfreakish keep? / A reed there shaken fitfully / He marks: 'Was't this we came to see / In wilderness?' and rueful smiled." Vine apparently sees a real reed there, although he is playing on Luke 7:24, where Jesus speaks to the people about John the Baptist: "What went ye out into the wilderness for to see? A reed shaken with the wind?" Jesus is being ironical — he goes on to explain that they had come to see a prophet: "Among those that are born of women there is not a greater prophet than John the Baptist." Vine is here characterized vividly as being easily distracted (even when one might expect him to be brooding upon the fact that someone had just struck on a chord long slack), and he is indulging his old habit of playing Jesus or at least echoing Jesus' words. Struck chord of friendship or not, Vine is apparently making some analogy to Rolfe as a reed shaken in the wind rather than the great prophet they might have expected to encounter in the wilderness. Later in "The Fountain" Vine, further distracted, suddenly rises and, excessively humble, helps Nehemiah feed the ass: "Nay, / Me too, me too let wait, I pray, / On our snubbed kin here." He has gone from quoting Jesus to imitating Jesus' model of humility — more play-acting (like Hawthorne on Monument Mountain, looking "wildly" about for the Great Carbuncle?).

In "Night in Jericho" (2.16), after Rolfe recalls from history some prior pilgrims to the place, Vine says, "why disown / The Knight of the Leopard," referring to the fictional character in *The Talisman*. Delighted, Rolfe acknowledges that "Scott's dreamed knight seems all but true / As men which history vouches," and then expatiates on the theme. At times Vine breathes a word because he wants to evoke personal speculation (psychological gossip) about another character, as when in this canto he says, "You spake of Mortmain." Then in "The Syrian Monk" (2.18) and "An Apostate" (2.19) Vine takes up thorn-weeds "by the peasants named Christ's Thorn" and plaits them into a "thorn-wreath" — a Crown of Thorns — in mockery of the Syrian monk's self-imposed suffering. Sometimes Vine breathes a few words just to get a conversation going, as in "Rolfe" (1.31), where he spurs Rolfe on by asking him if he is hinting that "In Christ Osiris met decline / Anew?" In "Concerning Hebrews" (2.22), Vine provokes Derwent to talk about the significance of the atheist geologist Margoth's being a Jew. After the discussion turns to various roles Jews have played in modern society (a discussion taken over by Rolfe), Vine tries to turn it back to the level of personal speculation about Margoth. Unable to proclaim Spinoza's superiority to Margoth, Rolfe falls silent, and Derwent speaks in confidential, empty encouragement to Clarel, who rejects him in his thoughts: "Pray, and what wouldst prove? / Thy faith an over-easy glove." "Meanwhile" — perhaps even before the end of the discussion — "Vine had relapsed":

> They saw
> In silence the heart's shadow draw —
> Rich shadow, such as gardens keep
> In bower aside, where glow-worms peep
> In evening over the virgin bed
> Where dark-green periwinkles sleep —
> Their bud the Violet of the Dead.

What the pilgrims see when they watch Vine in his relapse is an image of elegant morbidity and moribundity, an exotically and perhaps erotically beautiful place of living death.

Rarely does Melville give Vine long speeches or thoughts such as he gives Rolfe. The first of Vine's longer speeches occurs in "Vine and Clarel" (2.27), a wryly comic canto in which Vine and Clarel proceed on parallel tracks with few inklings as to each other's states of mind. The scene is the Jordan, where John baptized Jesus, and Clarel is wrought up with emotions over the site as well as over his extraordinary good fortune in finding himself all alone with Vine in such an evocative place. Vine is indulging himself in one of the few things which give him pleasure, play-acting — and in a setting he finds worthy of him. His standards are high: Gethsemane will do, the Jordan will do. During the course of the canto Clarel passes through an agonizing sequence of sexually tinged longings for brotherhood with Vine, then abases himself over what he thinks Vine may be thinking of him. Vine may have barely noticed that anything was happening, for by the end of the canto he is not thinking of poor Clarel and his psychological contortions at all. Self-involved Clarel and play-acting Vine are thinking and talking past each other.

At the beginning of the scene, baffled by the Dominican and Rolfe, Clarel discovers Vine lounging on the bank above the Jordan, hidden by leaves as if by Venetian blinds (another reminder of a swart, sensual—if not supersensual—Venetian quality in Vine): "As were Venetian slats between, / He espied him through a leafy screen, / Luxurious there in umbrage thrown, / Light sprays above his temples blown." Vine looks "an overture" but says nothing until Clarel has "leaned—half laid— / Beside him." Vine reveals that he has been indulging a bad habit—he has been "moralizing" there like "any imbecile," and he actually offers Clarel a specimen of his moralizing. Long before this point we have heard wonderful talk and have witnessed tough thinking. Melville does not turn the word "imbecile" against Vine, but here is what Vine says he has been fancying that the willows say to the waves which they over-weep:

> "Fleet so from us?
> And wherefore? whitherward away?
> Your best is here where wildings sway
> And the light shadow's blown about;
> Ah, tarry, for at hand's a sea
> Whence ye shall never issue out
> Once in." They sing back: "So let be!
> We mad-caps hymn it as we flow—
> Short life and merry! be it so!"

"Surprised at such a fluent turn," Clarel "did but listen—learn." There's not much to learn from this folderol, but Clarel is not concerned with the precise purport of what Vine says about avoiding danger rather than rushing merrily into danger. What counts is that Vine is there with him alone and is talking freely to him.

Then Vine's attention shifts. Putting aside the twigs, he directs Clarel's attention elsewhere, toward the route the sheik had taken, and he continues talking in something like free association:

> Look; in yon vault so leafy dark,
> At deep end lit by gemmy spark
> Of mellowed sunbeam in a snare;
> Over the stream—ay, just through there—
> The sheik on that celestial mare
> Shot, fading.—Clan of outcast Hagar,
> Well do ye come by spear and dagger!

> Yet in your bearing ye outvie
> Our western Red Men, chiefs that stalk
> In mud paint — whirl the tomahawk. —
> But in these Nimrods noted you
> The natural language of the eye,
> Burning or liquid, flame or dew,
> As still the changeable quick mood
> Made transit in the wayward blood?
> Methought therein one might espy,
> For all the wildness, thoughts refined
> By the old Asia's dreamful mind;
> But hark — a bird?

The topic of deep-thoughted aboriginals is an interesting one, as is the comparison between the splendid barbarians of East and of West, and one should not object when a character interrupts himself at the song of a bird. Or should one? This is not the only time Vine will break off his talk at a sound: he is easily distracted, unlike Rolfe, who would be so involved in the complexity of a thought that he would plunge on, birdsong or organ music or windstorm — or, for that matter, ready dinner or no ready dinner, as when Melville and Holmes cost Maunsell Field his repast by their intense discourse on East Indian religions.

Clarel has not paid a whit of attention to what Vine is saying: he is in a trance over Vine's proximity and his gorgeousness:

> Pure as the rain
> Which diamondeth with lucid grain,
> The white swan in the April hours
> Floating between two sunny showers
> Upon the lake, while buds unroll;
> So pure, so virginal in shrine
> Of true unworldliness looked Vine.
> Ah, clear sweet ether of the soul
> (Mused Clarel), holding him in view.
> Prior advances unreturned
> Not here he recked of, while he yearned —
> Oh, now but for communion true
> And close; let go each alien theme;
> Give me thyself!

Vine to all indications is oblivious of this intensity of yearning. Perhaps Melville means that Vine is making a point of dwelling "upon his wayward dream," but it looks as if Vine has no inkling of "Clarel's thrill / Of personal longing" and wants merely to ramble still, to hear himself talk. Clarel is ecstatic that Vine continues to talk to him, or at least to talk in his presence, but in the previous canto the discussion about the leveling and desavoring of American life had been pithy, and what Vine says about loss of aristocratic forms and virtues is comparatively thin:

> Methinks they show a lingering trace
> Of some quite unrecorded race
> Such as the Book of Job implies.
> What ages of refinings wise
> Must have forerun what there is writ —
> More ages than have followed it.
> At Lydda late, as chance would have,
> Some tribesmen from the south I saw,
> Their tents pitched in the Gothic nave,
> The ruined one. Disowning law,
> Not lawless lived they; no, indeed;
> Their chief — why, one of Sydney's clan,
> A slayer, but chivalric man;
> And chivalry, with all that breed
> Was Arabic or Saracen
> In source, they tell. But, as men stray
> Further from Ararat away
> Pity it were did they recede
> In carriage, manners, and the rest;
> But no, for ours the palm indeed
> In bland amenities far West!

Vine continues with an extraordinary proposal. Just as he had been moralizing there "Like any imbecile" (his moralizing is always unstrenuous), he now invites Clarel to share his game: "Come now, for pastime let's complain." Vine is playing Richard II now, not Jesus, studying how he may "complain," if not "compare" — something a would-be poet might do when he does not have any real work to do.

Then Vine continues with his improvised poem: "Grudged thanks, Columbus, for thy main! / Put back, as 'twere — assigned by fate / To fight crude Nature o'er again, / By slow degrees we re-create. / But then, alas, in Arab camps / No lack, they say, no lack of scamps." By this time Clarel is working himself up into a frenzied state. He has enough judgment to label these little extravagances of Vine's as "sallies," but his "heart's desire" is keeping him from giving undivided attention to them:

> How pleasant in another
> Such sallies, or in thee, if said
> After confidings that should wed
> Our souls in one:—Ah, call me *brother!*—
> So feminine his passionate mood
> Which, long as hungering unfed,
> All else rejected or withstood.

Here Clarel lets fall some "inklings" of his feelings, although Melville spares us his actual words. Writing this passage, Melville was remembering the substance if not the exact words he had written to Hawthorne on 17 November 1851—"Whence come you, Hawthorne? By what right do you drink from my flagon of life? And when I put it to my lips—lo, they are yours and not mine. I feel that the Godhead is broken up like the bread at the Supper, and that we are the pieces. Hence this infinite fraternity of feeling." And he had written of what he had felt the night before, when he first read Hawthorne's letter about *Moby-Dick:* "I felt pantheistic then—your heart beat in my ribs and mine in yours, and both in God's." It may never have entered Melville's mind when he wrote this canto of *Clarel* that Hawthorne had preserved his letter and that Sophia or one of the children might publish it.

Melville also specifies that Vine reacted to the inklings by a change, a shadow which "slid" over his face. What Vine's look meant is left very much in doubt. Instead of telling us, Melville offers possibilities: "Does Vine's rebukeful dusking" ask why bring pain to someone already acquainted with pain? Does Vine go on to say that Clarel must live out his doubt? Does Vine then comment on Clarel's longing for fellowship? "But for thy fonder dream of love / In man toward man—the soul's caress— / The negatives of flesh should prove / Analogies of non-cordiality / In spirit." At the end of this set of possible meanings for Vine's look, offered as if it were in Vine's words, we find that "such conceits" existed only in Clarel's head—that they are even "such conceits" as "could cling / To Clarel's dream of vain surmise / And imputation full of sting." At this stage, Clarel is unreliable as a gauge of what Vine is looking like, much less what he is thinking, so when Clarel looks up and finds "serious softness in those eyes / Bent on him," we have to reserve judgment. Clarel, however, reacts accusingly: "Enslaver, wouldst thou but fool me / With bitter-sweet, sly sorcery, / Pride's pastime? or wouldst thou indeed, / Since things unspoken may impede, / Let flow thy nature but for bar?" Then he returns to self-accusations: "Nay, dizzard, sick these feelings are; / How findest place within thy heart / For such solicitudes apart / From Ruth?—Self-taxings." Self-taxings indeed! At this pitch of Clarel's turmoil

Vine, wittingly or not, distracts him by pointing to Nehemiah, who is kneeling in prayer, in a "golden shaft of mellow light."

The scene between Vine and Clarel, or the scene in which Vine and Clarel are at least together, fades out with the description of Nehemiah in prayer, and the narrative resumes when they see the saint later, as the train is mustering in line. Nehemiah is trying to dress the ass with a wreath of river-palm, but she flaps it off and stomps on it. We are given Vine's thought: "Meek hands (mused Vine), vainly ye twist / Fair garland for the realist." That is, Melville tells us what Vine was thinking while the ass was tromping the wreath. Vine was *not* thinking, for example, that he had narrowly escaped from an embarrassing scene with Clarel and was *not* worrying about whether he had handled the situation well. Vine is *not* thinking about any confusion of his own and not thinking about any awkwardness Clarel might be feeling. There is some possibility that he distracted Clarel, once, out of kindness, but we can by now conclude that Vine is, to put the case mildly, easily distracted, if not quite a scatterbrain. (Or, a man with a scattered brain, Melville might have thought of his friend, as he read the posthumous *Dolliver* in the *Atlantic Monthly*.) Vine may be able to concentrate on a fellow-sufferer like Mortmain, but he concentrates better on his memories and on himself than on anyone else.

In "Lot's Sea" (2.33) two passages confirm aspects of the portrait of Vine adumbrated as early as "Tomb and Fountain" (1.28). The first is a description of Vine as Clarel catches sight of him by the Dead Sea: "Upon a rock / Low couchant there, and dumb as that, / Bent on the wave Vine moveless sat." Clarel joins him, without speaking, then Rolfe also comes and lingers with them. Rather than describing what they think, Melville describes an object by the water, thereby implying that Vine has been brooding upon it and that Clarel and Rolfe's attention is also focused on it:

> At Vine's feet
> A branchless tree lay lodged ashore,
> One end immersed. Of form complete —
> Half fossilized — could this have been,
> In ages back, a palm-shaft green?
> Yes, long detained in depths which store
> A bitter virtue, there it lay,
> Washed up to sight — free from decay
> But dead.

The reason Vine is moveless is that he is contemplating, as at the Sepulcher of the Kings, an image of his own fate: an image of what he was, a palm-shaft green, and what he has become, half-fossilized, "free from decay / But dead."

Nothing is said about Clarel's and Rolfe's comprehension of why Vine is moveless there. After Margoth has intruded upon their company, Vine takes impish pleasure in implying that the hideous hee-haw of the ass is a comment upon Margoth's geological harangue, but he remains behind by the wave while they move off to the accompaniment of the ass's renewed brays: "Vine tarried; and with fitful hand / Took bits of dead drift from the sand / And flung them to the wave, as one / Whose race of thought long since was run — / For whom the spots enlarge that blot the golden sun." Vine was earlier seen as having a glow about him like the golden bough in shade. Now we learn that his own perception of the golden sun is darkening, darkening progressively. This passage not only specifies that Vine's aesthetic capacities are progressively declining ("the spots enlarge" — in the present tense), but also locates the period of Vine's intellectual striving as having occurred long in the past. Thought and aesthetics are linked: Melville makes no attempt to show that Vine possesses high artistic sensibilities while his rational faculties deteriorate; he has not thought for a long time, and his ability to respond to beauty is waning — maybe waning fast, judging by the successive scenes in the poem. For in the action of the poem (again, not so much over the literal span of the journey as over the years Melville lived with the poem) Vine is not stable: he deteriorates as we watch. The spots that blot the golden sun *enlarge*, so that the result must sooner or later be that the sun will be entirely blotted. The passage may be complicated by a faint Miltonic echo which would tend to further ennoble the earlier Vine, for in his text of *Samson Agonistes* Melville marked the lines where the hero refers to his "race of glory" as having been "run."

Insofar as Vine is a portrait of Hawthorne, Melville is generous and protective still: what would he have said if something like the *Dolliver Romance* had been published under Irving's name, or G. W. Curtis's? What must Melville have thought as he read the serialized sections of the Italian notebooks, seeing his friend as smug Philistine, unable to enjoy Rome because of the dog and human ordure in the streets, not writing anything down about the paintings by Domenichino, Rubens, and others in the Casino because he "cared really little or nothing" for them, declaring the faded ceiling of the Sistine Chapel "forlorn and depressing," revealing himself as so miserable a tourist that Sophia interpolated a justification for his complaining "of grimy pictures and tarnished frames and faded frescoes." Hawthorne had been distressed beyond measure at the lack of perfection in what he saw: he was too sensitive for Italy. He was also imperceptive, unseeing, not too perceptive for his own good, as Sophia argued. In his thoughts of his friend and in his poem, these months, Melville was leading a steady, poised life.

[33]

Death, Death, and Flight to a Snug Harbor
1872

> ... and talking of Titian's work, Buonarroto, declared that the manner and colouring of that artist pleased him greatly, but that it was a pity the Venetians did not study drawing more, "for if this artist," said he, "had been aided by Art and knowledge of design, as he is by nature, he would have produced works which none could surpass, more especially in imitating life, seeing that he has a fine genius, and a graceful annimated manner."
>
> From a paragraph Melville marked in Vasari's *Lives*, vol. 5

AT NIGHT ON 2 JANUARY 1872, a Tuesday, Melville may have gone sadly down to the New-York Historical Society at Second Avenue and Eleventh Street to hear Evert A. Duyckinck read his memorial to Tuckerman. The only good days any of the Melvilles had in 1872 were the first days. In the afterglow of Christmas, John Hoadley hired Joseph Eaton to go over to New Brighton to paint the matriarch Maria while she was "looking so well" (Augusta's description to Peter on New Year's Day), and the sittings began auspiciously enough. On 3 January Augusta left the Island in a "party of 6" (including all the Hoadleys). They lunched "at Herman's" on the way to an overnight rest at Springfield, then on to Lawrence. On 9 January Lizzie urged Cousin Kate Gansevoort to come down "while so many of the family are here," meaning Maria, Helen, and Fanny: "If you would come and stay with us, we should be most happy to have you, and I would do all in my power to make you comfortable — You know you could not come to a quieter house than this, where you might be at liberty to do just as you liked." She sent all their love to Uncle Peter, with gratitude that he was "so well at this trying season for the strongest," meaning the pain of the holidays, with Henry dead, as well as the bitterness of the winter. Helen spent several days with Herman and Lizzie and they all went to Allan's on the twelfth. On the thirteenth, just after Helen returned to the Island from Herman's, leaving all well, Fanny explained to Kate Gansevoort that she could not make a visit to Albany because she was afraid to leave her mother at Tom's, even with Helen and Katie to care for her. Maria had been ill, but came downstairs on Sunday the fourteenth for tea, in order to see Allan, who came and stayed overnight, looking miserable but telling them that he and Jane were planning an entertainment for family members, on the evening of the sixteenth. After that, he was "thinking of a trip to St Paul on business." Milie was at the Island a week, intending to stay for Tom's birthday, the twenty-fourth. Helen went to see Allan on the twentieth and returned with bad news about his health, so that Tom went over on the twenty-first, perhaps escorting Milie. On the thirty-first Fanny described Allan to Aunt Susan as "now very ill indeed," so bad that Hoadley had come down from Lawrence, alone, and had been at the Governor's House since the day before, and that Helen was staying at Herman's "so as to be near Allan." The doctor had instructed Jane to send for Tom once, the night of the thirtieth.

Augusta, in Lawrence, with Kate Hoadley needing much attention, was slower than she should have been to understand the seriousness of Allan's condition. She was sorrowing for Kate Gansevoort on the anniversary of Kate's sailing for Nassau. On the strength of that sympathy, Kate dared to write Augusta, not directly to Hoadley, to ask a very great favor, that John would edit a memorial volume for her brother. Augusta talked to John, and assured Kate on 25 January: "When my beloved brother Gansevoort died, the same intense longing possessed my soul that something might be written to preserve the memory of one so gifted, so good, so noble, so dearly loved & deeply mourned. Had I known a John Hoadley then, it would have been done." Having done her part, she asked Kate to write directly to John: "He is very busy now, but he will do I know any thing he can for you in carrying out your wishes." It proved a severe sacrifice on Hoadley's part, damaging to his health, and a prolonged test of his innate courtesy and devotion to his own Kate and her family.

On 2 February Fanny wrote Kate Gansevoort that Allan was very sick, and that her mother had not been able to go downstairs for several days. The sittings with Eaton had been interrupted. Hoadley returned to Lawrence on the third, and Augusta quickly passed on encouraging news to Kate Gansevoort: "Mamma was feeling better yesterday, & able to go down stairs to her meals. And dear Allan was more comfortable." On 3 February Augusta wrote Kate Gansevoort that they were "all sorry that Mamma's indisposition should have put a stop to the sittings for her portrait," which Fanny reported as "excellent so far." On 8 February Augusta wrote Kate Gansevoort that she and John had been looking over memorial volumes in his library and had "selected those of *The Harvard Memorial Biographies*' as most nearly approaching" what they thought Kate desired. Allan on Tuesday (6 February) "'was better upon the whole' but still forbidden to see any one, or even to sit up for a few moments as the attempt to do so the day before had been followed by a more than usual restless night." Maria was better but still very weak, "& had only been up since Friday (the day John left New York) long enough to have her bed made."

On 9 February Allan died. The next day Abraham Lansing escorted Cousin Kate to New York, where she wrote to her father and stepmother: "We arrived safely a few moments after 7 P.M. came directly here—(Cousin Herman Melville's—104 E. 26 St.) found Bessie & Fanny" (the Melville daughters) "waiting for me & Cousins Lizzie & Herman up at Cousin Allan's house—Abe very kindly took me up to 109 E 35th St.—& left me—I saw them all—Jennie & the girls—& they are so heart broken at the sudden Death of their Father & of *her loved husband*—the rudder of the household." She got an imperfect account: "*The change* was very sudden & Allan died in great agony his *well lung* having *collapsed* as far as I can judge from what I have heard." The body was of course in the Thirty-fifth Street house, and she declared that "Allan looks *so young & so fair.*" She imagined Allan's "first Sabbath in the unknown world of spirits: "Sophia & he have met, & he has seen (I hope) our darling Henry!" She thought of her own generation, but Gansevoort Melville, brimming with admonitions and advice, eager to compare symptoms, was the first spirit Allan met. The funeral was at Zion Church on 12 February, and the family went up the Hudson to Carmansville for the burial in Trinity Cemetery.

The day after Allan died, a scandal broke into the open in New York City politics. Indicted for corrupt neglect of official duty, Mayor Oakey Hall addressed the court: "I am not here to move to quash the indictment, nor to demur to it, but simply to demand the earliest practicable day for an investigation . . . I wish an immediate trial. . . . I have a great many remarks to make, but I shall reserve them until I confront a Judge and jury" (the *Times* of 11 February). Under other circumstances, Hall might have written Thomas or Herman the kind of noble letter he wrote Evert Duyckinck when George died. On 16 February the *Times* reported cases of "WHOLESALE SMUGGLING: An Extraordinary Series of Operations in Linen and Jute Goods" involving the steamship *Wisconsin* and the steamship *Baltic*, and built on fraudulent invoices and faulty examinations: "What with undervaluation at such a rate, and large importations, a pretty profitable business must have been realized." This came home to Melville and his fellows in the Custom House, since any scandal might hurt the innocent and might not necessarily punish the guilty.

Augustus Peebles wrote at once to console Herman on Allan's death, a letter which Herman forwarded to his mother. In answering Augustus on 12 February, Helen quoted the letter the Episcopal Bishop Southgate had written to Jane and the girls: "If the conviction may sink into your hearts that your bereavement is the act of a Father who doeth all things well, Who cannot err, Who is Himself love surely you will not grieve without an all sufficient consolation." (This was the apostate Congregationalist Horatio Southgate, denounced along with Herman Melville in the New Haven *New Englander* for July 1846, when denominational differences still mattered to Protestants.) The grieving Kate Gansevoort was getting just such advice on all sides. Abe tried on 17 February: "While we do not forget those who have gone before us, and love to reflect upon their excellence and worth and to recall the incidents of their lives, let us never my dearest Kate forget that we owe much to ourselves and to the living." Katie tried, not for the first time, on 19 March: "I cannot wonder that you feel alone in this world, and that your heart is weighed down with sorrow, but with God's help rise above that, do His will, by faithfully & quietly walking through the paths *He chooses for you.*" Everyone except Jane was concerned enough about Kate Gansevoort to attempt to help her get past her obsessive grief.

Maria was broken by Allan's death. Cousin Kate wrote her parents on 11 February: "Aunt Melville is very feeble — & confined to her bed & wants me to come over & see her." Kate stayed a night or two on the Island to be with her aunt, and went back to Herman's on the fourteenth, "leaving Aunt Melville very miserable." That day Susan wrote her, pained for Milie: "she seemed so dependant on her Father & so loving to him — tell her I do grieve with her." Fanny gave her own report to Aunt Susan on the eleventh: "Mamma has hardly spoken since we told her [of Allan's death], is perfectly quiet, but you & Uncle would hardly recognize her, she is so changed. She has been confined to her bed now ten days. She has been slowly but surely, losing strength all winter." Herman went to the Harbor on Saturday morning, 17 February. That day Lizzie went to Jane's, and went back again all the next afternoon and evening. Augusta and Helen relieved Fanny at Tom's, and Maria had days when she seemed more comfortable, for on 20 February, Augusta wrote Kate Gansevoort the next day, she was "able to see Herman & the children."

Augusta again wrote Kate Gansevoort on 22 February: "She has been able to see Herman, Florence, & Milie, & also Mrs Bogert, & Lizzie too before she left us this morning, She came over with Fanny yesterday, & passed the night here." Augusta described the concern the family was showing: "Every day since you left us the morning boats have brought over some kind friends to inquire about dear Mamma — Mrs Charles Thurston, Rachel Barrington, Mr William Morewood, Cousin Hetty, & Fannie Trotter, Mr. Curtis, Mrs Brittain, Miss Annie Morewood, Allan's children, Herman & Lizzie & Stannie, Bessie & Fanny. Thus we have had company at lunch every day." (The deeply grieving widow Jane Louisa Westervelt Dempsey Randolph Melville had not showed herself.) Nowhere else than the Governor's

House could such callers have been accommodated. Nowhere else could suitable rooms be found for the day-and-night watchers, Augusta and Fanny, and overnight guests such as Lizzie and her daughter Fanny. Any member of the family could stay over at the Governor's House, sure that Tom and Katie would make them welcome.

Maria rallied, not enough to determine to live but enough to manage the manner of her death, as is clear from Augusta's letter of 26 February to Peter and Susan:

> Mamma just called me to her bedside, & said "Augusta, I want you to write to your Uncle & Aunt Susan, & tell them how comfortable I have been to-day, & was yesterday; that dreadful oppression has left me, & I have no pain nor uneasiness now. That I am in God's hands to restore me to my usual health, or take me to himself. His will be done."
>
> "And tell them that Dr. Irving was here this afternoon & administered to me the Communion[,] That all my children were with me, my four daughters, & Herman & Tom, & John & Katie, & that Mrs Bogart & Evie joined us; & that they sang sweetly that beautiful hymn
>
>> 'Abide with me
>> Fast flows the even-tide
>> The darkness thickens,
>> Lord with me abide'"
>
> I wish you both, & dear Kate, could have heard that lovely chant. Never shall I forget those sweet notes, nor the impressive scene of this afternoon. The western sun shining in so brightly, & that group around the bed, Mamma's perfect composure, & Dr. Irving's solemnity.

Everyone (except Jane) was devotedly attentive to Maria, Dr. Bogart in particular, and a minister from the Island came and read Scripture to her and prayed at her bedside. John and Kate Hoadley came to the Harbor, and went home on the last day of February. Helen went back to Boston the next day, 1 March, and found that George had taken a room at the Parker House, where they were "very pleasantly situated," although still considering taking a cottage on Longwood Avenue on the first of April. Early in March Jane decided she was the one who needed special consolation, so, almost unbelievably, she summoned Augusta from her mother's deathbed.

Not needing to wait around, Stanwix wrote to Kate Gansevoort on 3 March. He thanked her for the "very handsome pair of sleeve buttons, a last token of remembrance" of his Cousin Henry, of whom he had seen very little, "but entertained a high regard for, and long desired to know him better." He had told her in New York that he was taking a steamer on the "briny deep" but his plans had changed, so he was "deliberating," and had "almost come to the conclusion to stay ashore and pursue the profession" he had been studying for the past few months. He asked her, all ingenuously, "What do you think?" He had to remind her of his status as a world traveler: "Spring, entered with quite a heavy snow storm this year, but I hope we have a hot and early summer with the thermometer at a 100° in the shade to remind me of the East Indies." On 8 March Maria's brother-in-law Captain John D'Wolf died at the age of ninety-two. There would have been a time for proper grieving at such news, but this was not it. Helen, who knew him better than the others from her visits to Boston in the early 1840s and from her residence in Brookline, attended her uncle's funeral on the eleventh, "from the residence of Samuel Downer, Pleasant street, Dorchester." The 9 March *Evening Transcript* in "DEATH OF A VENERABLE SHIP MASTER" remembered D'Wolf as "the first American that travelled overland from the East, across China and Siberia to St. Petersburg." Jarred now into generosity to his daughter, to Augusta and Fanny at Christmas, and to other nieces and nephews, Peter Gansevoort sent his sister a "fifty-year-old bottle of wine." Acknowledging the gift on the sixteenth, Augusta assured him: "my dear Uncle, she knows how to appreciate, & I have no doubt will derive strength from each glass she takes." Susan sent Maria warm bed-caps. John was back down, Helen having gone to stay with Kate. Hoadley was being especially attentive to Maria partly because he feared he would have to be away when she died, for he and Kate were planning a railroad trip to San Francisco, the first time one of the family had gone across the continent on the recently constructed lines. He wrote Kate Gansevoort on 24 March of their plans to leave Lottie and Frank with his sister in Louisville and take Minnie with them to San Francisco. He refused " 'to make a Hotel' " of the Gansevoort house for fear of disrupting Uncle Peter's schedule in a harmful way.

Melville may have mourned for Allan and suffered with his mother by absorbing himself in some cantos of his poem; at least, while working in the Custom House and doing his family duties he somehow managed to buy a few books and perhaps even to read in them. Before Allan was known to be seriously ill, on 5 January, Herman bought Horace Walpole's *Anecdotes of Painting in England* (London: A. Murray, 1871), and on 23 March he bought Hawthorne's *Passages from the French and Italian Note-Books* (Boston: Osgood, 1872), scoring a confession: "My receptive faculty is very limited, and when the utmost of its small capacity is full, I become perfectly miserable, and the more so the better worth seeing are the things I am forced to reject." This could only have reminded Melville by contrast of his own insatiable gallery-going during his two trips to Europe and the capaciousness of his own receptive faculty through much of his life. He had seen similar passages the year before, in serialized versions of the *Note-Books*, the most likely time he was elaborating in "The Wilderness" his depiction of Vine's waning ability to perceive beauty.

Lizzie responded to the grief in her life by arranging for Dr. Bellows to baptize her at All Souls Unitarian Church on 31 March, a rite oddly omitted until now. Sometime in late February or March, Maria Gansevoort Melville received her first and only installment of her annuity from her son Allan, seventy-five dollars. Insofar as Allan's intention was to make life at the Mansion House easier for Augusta and Fanny as well as his mother, that intention was thwarted, for the fund reverted to the estate rather than being Maria's to pass on to her unmarried daughters. She died on the first of April, at the age of eighty-one. The newspapers that day reported the death-watch on Twenty-second Street for the painter and the inventor of the telegraph, Samuel F. B. Morse, and the next day reported his death. The death of the daughter of the Hero of Fort Stanwix and the widow of a 1820s Manhattan importer was not news.

Kate Gansevoort came down on the second of April to Herman's house, and on the third he took her over to the Island by the noon boat. Kate described the scene at Sailors' Snug Harbor in her diary: "saw Aunt Melville & the girls—all *her children* & sons, & daughters in law were there Aunt Melville looks so naturally—dressed in white Alpaca dress—tulle cap—& just as *she* directed—What a remarkable woman—Dr Thos. E. Vermilyea [Vermilye] officiated at the Funeral services which took place at 3 PM. A large number of relatives & friends filled the house—& afterwards left, *the remains*, with us, for the night." On the fourth the family rendezvoused at the uptown depot in Manhattan: "Tom. Melville & wife, Fanny, Kate, & Mr Hoadley.—Helen, Dr Bogart—Mrs Allan Melville & her four daughters—Cousin Herman & Stanwix[,] A. L[ansing] & K.G. met at the Depot 42 St, to convey, by the 10:30 Train the remains of their dear Mother . . . to Albany to be interred in the Vault at the Cemetery." Herman had accompanied Gansevoort's body by boat from Manhattan to Albany a quarter century before. Now the six surviving children were together, for the last time: Helen, Herman, Augusta, Kate, Fanny, Tom. Uncle Peter was not able to meet them, but Aunt Susan was at the upper depot, and after "a terrible quick drive to the Cemetery" a local minister "made *some* remarks" to the exhausted mourners and they all drove to Uncle Peter's and Aunt Susan's for dinner. Kate asked herself, "How many more of those I love must I see buried?" Herman and Stanny left for home that night, after the burial, so Herman would not have to miss work another day.

The strain on the household at Twenty-sixth Street was such that around mid-April Lizzie took her daughters to Boston, where she collapsed, unable to go out on a drive, and resting for days longer before proposing even to walk out "for the air" (as Lizzie wrote Katie, words Augusta quoted in her letter to Hope Shaw on 22 April). Herman and Stanwix joined Augusta at the Governor's House of Sailors' Snug Harbor, from which Melville commuted to work by ferry. Not able to choose his hours, he had to be part of the morning and afternoon crowds. Charles Farnham described the rush for the ferries as a "funnel for folks," who "converge at the wicket from all directions, and slip in out of sight as if engulfed in oblivion." Whitman's "Crossing Brooklyn Ferry" was idealized; Farnham was realistic: "As the people come in close columns, you see a panorama of hats and chins; as they pass, hats and noses, and as they crowd about the ferry entrance, hats and back hair. They are a crowd devoted to bundles, for every one has a package or a bag." Claustrophobiac since his forecastle days and nights, Melville changed his seat repeatedly, seeking air and a little elbow room, so that accompanying him could be an ordeal, as Stanwix perhaps knew best, since a fellow male was easier to desert than a female he was escorting.

From New Brighton on 22 April Augusta wrote to Hope Shaw her anticipation that Lizzie would soon be able to join Herman there at the Harbor: "He & Stannie left us with Tom for New York after our seven O'clock breakfast. He [Herman?] is quite like his old natural self, & seems to take an interest in every thing; & it is very pleasant having him here. . . . Last evening he [Herman] went with us to hear an eloquent minister at New Brighton. Stannie took care of the house for us. He is full of the idea of going West again. Herman, I believe, has written Lizzie about it." Augusta's hope that Lizzie would soon join Herman at the Island was in part a hope that Lizzie could restrain Stanny, but he departed for Kansas, perhaps after his mother left her daughters in Boston and joined her husband.

By early May the Hoadleys and the untraveled Fanny Priscilla Melville were in San Francisco. On the train had occurred "one of those strange incidents which make us half believe that the world contains after all only a few men and women, — and that even those few which it appears to contain may after all be only projections of our own internal consciousness, — subjective universalities." On 4 May from San Francisco, Hoadley described the incident to the person who would best appreciate it, Peter Gansevoort. Hoadley had offered a young man in the parlor car a drink of wine "in a little silver cup which Kate had in her lunch basket," Gansevoort Melville's baby cup, and the stranger recognized the engraved name because his grandfather, General Willet, had "commanded a regiment in the Revolutionary army, and served with Gen. Gansevoort." In Salt Lake City Hoadley had been granted a private audience with Brigham Young, "a very interesting interview," apparently not recorded in Mormon church daybooks. From the session Hoadley emerged thinking that in the mountainous desert many a portable steam-engine might be put to good use and deciding that Mormonism was no longer a "fearful portent": "Propriety, worldliness, and the inevitable individuality of man, will bunch them up into half a dozen societies of varying manners, some of which will take their place among the various dissenting denominations, and become as harmless and inoffensive as Ana-Baptists, Pseudo Baptist, Campbellites, Moravians, Dunkers, Quakers, Shakers, Sanderainians [?], Swedenborgians, who knows what?" On 1 July Augusta, in Boston, heard from her sister Fanny, now a great traveler, having been "through Calaveras County, Cal. where the 'big trees' are" and seen other wonders. The Hoadley party had taken "the palace car" from Truckee all the way to Denver. Fanny's being along meant that she could take care of Kate and relieve John of some of the strain, but it also gave her the first vacation trip she had been granted since her visit to Black River in 1848.

Tom accompanied Augusta up to Gansevoort to check on the Mansion House and arrange for its care. This year the daughters closed the mill, according to a letter Fanny wrote Kate Gansevoort (by then with a new last name, Lansing) on 15 February 1876: "since the mill was closed, four years ago, we have just managed to get away without getting into debt—*now* we can feel easy. We have always had such a horror of being in debt." Lizzie being sick and Herman deeply grieved, they simply closed up the house in Manhattan and took refuge with Tom and Katie, planning to stay there "for the present." Lizzie wrote to Kate Gansevoort on 6 May, from the Harbor, answering a letter she had received while in Boston, in which Kate had enclosed a photograph of Henry. On the serious matter of an appropriate likeness of Henry for the memorial volume, Lizzie was straightforward about the opinions of her brothers and Hope Shaw: "They *all* think that it is not as natural as some of the earlier ones taken before Henry was ill. The face seems to them too thin, & the expression of the eye not quite natural. I do not myself like it as well as the one I gave you from my book, and when you have that copied, do not forget your promise to send me one. I should think that one might be copied larger, & finished in ink to advantage. Have you no good photographer in Albany to try it?" Now, at the Harbor, Lizzie relaxed: "it is a great relief to me to have a *rest* for a while, & I hope to get stronger & better in this refreshing air—for indeed I have got terribly 'run down'—so that sometimes I think I shall never get 'wound up' again." Dealing honestly with the bad photograph of Henry led Lizzie to enlist Kate's help in recovering a portrait of Malcolm which she and Herman had too hastily given away during their first grief. Soon "after the dear boy's death" Herman had presented it to Malcolm's "comrades in arms" of Company B of the "Second Reg^t of Infantry, First Brigade First Division, N.Y.S.N.G.," after having the frame inscribed to the company. When the company had disbanded, its effects were transferred to Albany. Now Lizzie and Herman wanted Kate to appeal to Adjutant General Edward Davis Townsend to retrieve it. Lizzie was sure Kate would recognize it ("a colored photograph of the full length figure"), and in any case Augusta was visiting Kate and could assist her: "If you could get that picture of Macky for me, dear Kate, I should be so happy — it seems as if we might have it, when it is of so much value to us, and so little to anyone else where it is."

On 8 May Lizzie was able to go to visit Jane Melville, and more and more felt the peace of the Harbor in contrast to what she called "the Babel of New York." in writing Kate Gansevoort on 13 June. After Lizzie's visit, Jane wrote Kate Gansevoort on 8 May: "I must hold my great bereavement — my life sorrow — close to my heart, mentally weeping over it never loosing sight of it waking or sleeping." Resourceful woman, she had made up her mind just how to console her inconsolable self: "Do you know that I am going to Europe in the Autumn, — then, my dear Cousin — wont you come over to Arrowhead and make us a good visit this summer, indeed you must, for I want to show you what a place my husband has made it, have there too, associations recollections of dear Cousin Henry — that noble soul — come — and let us take our work and our books — and you and I — will go up on the hill — sitting in the shade of the trees — we will look down on the valley of the Housatonic, before Pittsfield and 'Arrowhead.'" Jane was planning to go to Arrowhead the next week and wanted Florence to go: "she is very modest — and timid — and dwells upon her great loss, — she is looking *so sad*, but when I urge her to go — she says she does not want to go any where — I have told her, if she will go — I will come back by way of Albany — and run up to Schenectady for a call — but all seems useless, what am I do to with her?" What to do, obviously, was to abandon her and the other girls and go to Europe, after encouraging Kate Gansevoort to welter in her loss of Henry.

Allan's executors on 27 May paid off his bond to Richard Lathers for $2140 and his note to John C. Hoadley for $504.96, and at some point in the next year Herman repaid the estate the $50 he had owed Allan. On 1 June James Gordon Bennett died — in honor of which the office of the *Herald*, no longer the scurrilous paper that had welcomed Thomas Powell's lies about Melville in 1850, was closed all the next day. This sort of event came to Melville as a reminder of a past far removed from the new public humiliation of Oakey Hall and the Custom House scandals. Stanwix went back to Kansas, then left for more exciting places: "I thought I could do better South, so I came down through the Indian Nation, & then into Arkansas, I stopped at a number of towns on the Arkansas river till I came to the Mississippi, then down that river to Vicksburgh I staid there a few days, & then took the train to Jackson, from there by Railroad to New Orleans, I found that a lively city, but no work" (this was his summary, months later, on 23 February 1873). That summer Melville wrote his son a letter of which only a few words survive. He had learned of Stanwix's departure from Kansas and was dealing calmly with his son's traveling on, but apparently unable to restrain himself from expressing a cautionary opinion.

While living in the Governor's House Melville saw, from six in the morning until dusk, almost anywhere on Staten Island, "one or more old sailors either walking along, lying or reposing under a tree, or perched upon some fence, so great has been their habit of roving around," as Louis Bagger would say in the next January's *Harper's*. Around the Harbor the men played dominoes and checkers, "as many of the inmates are too old to indulge in many sports." There was a fiddler, Jerry, who sometimes played. Mainly, they told stories: "Many are the groups and many the yarns spun by one and another of hair-breadth escapes and scenes they have passed through during their lives on the ocean wave. Some seeming intent to beat the others, I fear, tell some things that have never happened, but what matters that? Let the old sailors enjoy themselves in any harmless manner they can." This summer was Melville's best chance to improve his acquaintance with the more notable of the four hundred or so pensioners at the Sailors' Snug Harbor. Only half of them were Americans by birth. Their average age was fifty-five, only slightly more than Melville's own, but several were veterans of the War of 1812. Many of the inmates had led momentous lives and were fit to be consulted by any former ordinary seaman with an interest in naval history. On a lowlier level Melville could hardly have escaped seeing " 'the bone man,' " whose passion for dogs amounted "to a monomania" and who filled his pockets with bones and wandered off "into obscure haunts and by-ways," where he could "be seen surrounded and followed by his not entirely disinterested clients." Years later Melville invented a character, John Marr, whose memory was thronged with the faces of seamen he had known decades before. By that time, in the 1880s, Melville's own memories included not only the seamen he had known in the Atlantic and the Pacific but also the seamen he had known only on land, including the Baltimore Negro he had met in Greenwich and the pensioners of the American Greenwich to which he had such miraculous access because of Tom's job.

Living there at the Harbor made Herman and Lizzie part of the Bogart family entertaining. In 1932 Mabel Abbott recorded what she had been told by Mrs. H. Cleaver Brown, a niece of Belle Bogart, who, as Mrs. Belle Bagley, was still living, in Bronxville, in May 1932, but very old and apt to confuse generations. Mrs. Brown was sure, however, that before she became so confused Mrs. Bagley had told her of being "at a dinner where Herman took her to the table and she was 'thrilled by his charming and gracious manners.'" Belle reported that he "talked about the sea all the time" — even more than Captain Tom, her brother-in-law, did. (It was at that time, in 1932, that the "Melville family bed — 'on which Herman and all the sisters and brothers were born' according to Mrs. Brown," was reported to be still at the Snug Harbor, in the then-standing Governor's House, a bed too large for Mrs. Brown to take home with her.)

Melville would have read about the auction of the library of Henry T. Tuckerman that started on 10 June in Manhattan, at 7:30 P.M. in Clinton Hall. The next three nights the auction continued with his collection of paintings and engravings and statuary, many of which Melville was familiar with. Just possibly, Melville took some last glances at the items in Clinton Hall before crossing to Staten Island after work. Being on the Island meant that Herman and Lizzie were caught up in plans for the trustees' dinner, on 17 June. It may have been smaller than usual, judging from Tom's diary: "Trustees Meeting held at the S. S. Harbor Dr Dix, Dr Paxton & Capt Ferrier present. Dined at my house." Katie was going away with her sister Evie Bogart the next day after the dinner, and Lizzie was "to keep the house from running away" while she was gone — which meant through almost all of July, since Katie was going to Boston and then on to upstate New York.

In early July Melville enjoyed the novel prospect of becoming an anthologized poet. On the fifth he thanked Richard Henry Stoddard for "the generosity" which prompted him to include seven poems from *Battle-Pieces* in his forthcoming revision of *Poets and Poetry of America*, the popular anthology created by Melville's irascible acquaintance Rufus Griswold. One of the poems was "Sheridan's Ride," which in 1903 led Stoddard to call Melville "one of our great unrecognised poets"; the others were "Battle of Stone River, Tennessee," "An Uninscribed Monument on One of the Battle-Fields of the Wilderness," "The Victor of Antietam," "The Mound by the Lake," "The Returned Volunteer to His Rifle," and "Shiloh." Melville concluded his note to Stoddard floridly: "Happiness attend you up to the gate of Paradise."

Very sudden arrivals at that gate of Paradise were much in the news. In his diary Thomas Melville recorded a heat wave lasting from July first until the night of the fourth. During this hot spell the New York *World* for 3 July 1872 printed an article on many dozens of New Yorkers dying of heat: "TORRID, TRUCULENT TUESDAY" (2 July). While Melville continued his commuting into this surreal Manhattan, Lizzie (as she wrote Kate Gansevoort on 17 July) rejoiced in her escape, and Herman's escape for the nights, at least: "The *weather* is the general theme, and we cannot very well ignore it — I am so thankful to be here, rather than in New York — I feel the prostrating effect of the heat so much — Kate [Katie Bogart Melville] is still absent but is coming home tomorrow — Bessie & Fanny are still enjoying themselves diligently in Boston and thereabouts." Boston also sweltered, and in the midst of the heat wave, on the fourth, the travelers returned from the West, brought out to Brookline by George. There Augusta and Fanny were with Helen. "They were quite wilted down with the heat; but after refreshment & rest, we could see how much they had all gained," Augusta wrote Susan on the sixth: "They are as brown as berries, hands as well as faces, & presented quite an unique appearance with their Yosemite dusters & hats. Frank has thriven . . . having grown a couple of inches." Melville's sister Fanny went with the Hoadleys to Lawrence in the hope of bringing Kate and the children with her to Gansevoort in a few days. Bessie and Fanny, the Melville daughters, returned from "their three days visit to Way-land" just too late to see the Hoadleys. Augusta left to open the Mansion House, stopping one night at Pittsfield and another in Albany, where Abe put her safely on the cars with two new servants.

During the heat wave, Herman and Lizzie learned that the picture of Malcolm they were seeking was in the possession of Robert Coster on Fifty-third Street in New York City. Melville called at that address, missed Coster, and located him at his place of work. Young Coster and his wife had been displaying the picture over the mantelpiece "in their pretty little parlor" (Lizzie wrote Kate Gansevoort) "and not wishing to leave the place absolutely vacant," Herman "carried a pretty water-color, handsomely framed, to replace it." Thus Herman and Lizzie rectified their first impulsive gesture, made when looking on Malcolm's image seemed unbearable. On Melville's fifty-third birthday Lizzie gave him *Septimius Felton; or The Elixir of Life*, probably thinking only of the fact that the author was Nathaniel Hawthorne, not that the subject was physical immortality. Lizzie and Herman were expecting to leave for Pittsfield on the afternoon of Saturday, 3 August, after his work for the day was done, to get the jump on his vacation, which would start on Monday the fifth. Jane had invited Bessie and Fanny to reunite with their parents there at Arrowhead. Herman and Elizabeth observed their silver wedding anniversary in the company of their daughters and Allan Melville's widow and daughters, at Arrowhead. Melville probably saw there a new portrait of his Uncle Thomas, a photograph Allan had commissioned from a painting; just after Herman's visit Jane fulfilled Allan's intention by presenting it to the Berkshire Athenaeum. At Pittsfield Herman and Lizzie found Lathers, as successful as usual, but losing his zest for Abby Lodge after Allan's death, and also losing his zest for the new life he had hoped to build in Charleston. Allan's granddaughter Margaret Morewood understood some of the reasons: "after some happy summers spent there, the youngest son of the colonel died" (Edmund Griffin Lathers, born in March 1866), "and his neighbor from over the way died, (He had been a good listener) and soon after the Colonel wearied of his Italian Villa" — that is, Abby Lodge. Allan had been not only a good listener but also one of the colonel's few ties to the 1840s when both young men had married daughters of the Bond Street banker.

Lizzie quizzed Kate Gansevoort about Fire Island as a possible refuge for her, especially if she could board in a private house rather than the expensive Surf Hotel. From the Mansion House, bereft of Maria, Augusta wrote Kate Gansevoort on 31 August 1872: "Since I wrote you last we have had visits from Herman; & Tom; & Lizzie & Samuel Shaw. The latter left us on Wednesday for Canada & the White Mountains, where Lizzie hopes to find relief from her annual cold." Lizzie had found *Autumnal Catarrh*, by Professor Morrill Wyman of Harvard, which cited as notorious sufferers two friends, Judge Shaw and Daniel Webster. The family studied Wyman's colored maps showing "the non-Catarrhal regions," a boon to them and certain resort areas. Lizzie planned to return to the Mansion House, if nothing prevented, "after her trip to the White Mountains," and before that they expected to see Jane, who was "going to New York to place Lucy at school." As it turned out, Sam Shaw took Lizzie to Quebec in a severely debilitated condition. On 2 September he reported to his mother: "Elizabeth's catarrh is somewhat relieved here but I am sorry to see how generally feeble she is, and prematurely old." At the end of September or the first days of October Jane left the girls at Arrowhead and stayed "at Lizzie's in New York" (probably while Herman was living with Tom and Katie); after all, she knew her way around the house, and could fit a servant or two into place.

All summer Tom had been making great aesthetic improvements to the center hall of the main building at the Harbor, having the walls painted (according to his quarterly report submitted on 30 September) with these inscriptions: on the south wall, "Robert Richard Randall, 1801"; west, "Rest after dangerous toil"; north, "The Cross is my Anchor"; and east, "Port after stormy seas." Tom dealt with artists as well as artisans. Herman was probably at the Harbor and Lizzie still in Boston when Tom's Paradise was threatened by yet another marplot. On 2 October George Porter, formerly the clerk of the governor of Sailors' Snug Harbor, appeared before the board of trustees to read a series of charges against Thomas Melville, including mismanagement of the institution and embezzlement of funds — specifically, that Tom had diverted milk, bread, and chickens from the use of the pensioners to the use of the residents of the Governor's House. Tom and Katie went to Pittsfield early in October. Herman and Lizzie seem to have returned to Twenty-sixth Street in late October; in a letter of 11 November

Lizzie refers to the house as having been long closed up and not yet restored to its usual functioning.

In mid-September Kate Gansevoort put herself through yet another punitive journey, to Boston to see where Henry had been stationed. As her Cousin Fanny said cautiously (11 September), "Your visit to Fort Independence will be one fraught with deep feelings, for the spot where Henry spent so many months will possess a tender & ever living interest to you." On the fourteenth Helen wrote to Kate Gansevoort too, about the death of Susan's brother: "as death, year by year, narrows the family circle, each of those who are left should cling closer to the others, and keep bright and clear all the well-springs of true affection." She put in words what everyone felt more and more strongly: "I have had long letters to-day from Fanny, and Milie. What a comfort and blessing these family letters are! We each know all that occupies or interests the others, and are as much bound together as when we were sheltered under one roof-tree." Helen was making a special effort to stay in close touch with Allan's daughters, and she invited Kate Gansevoort to visit her out of her determination to keep hold of all close family ties. Kate arrived, and on 18 September wrote her father and stepmother on mourning paper, reproaching herself for not coming two years earlier, when Henry was alive, but gathering a store of memories. The fort, Harvard, much of Boston, was "hallowed ground" because Henry had been there. On the twenty-first in Lansingburgh Augustus and Mary Peebles's only son, Charles, died at nine years old. Susan and Peter were simply too feeble to go to the funeral.

Expecting to sail for Europe in November, Jane made visits, sending Florence and Kitty to Gansevoort, and for a wonder, coming up with Milie, then taking "F and K" (her brutal abbreviations for Sophia's daughters, so hard to differentiate one from the other) to Helen's while Jane visited Hope Savage Shaw. Jane suffered terribly, she told Kate Gansevoort on 13 October, from "the changing that seems to be done between here and Gansevoort. I don't know how many times we shall change cars." On 14 October, a stormy day, Helen wrote Kate Gansevoort about the forthcoming election: "I hope it will clear before evening, for there is to be an enormous torch-light procession this evening; that is, for our small town, some three thousand torches, including expected visitors. As it is to be a *Grant* demonstration, perhaps you will not care whether it rains or not, and I suppose, the few Greeley-men among our townspeople, would rather that it should." From the Shaw house on 24 October Jane wrote Kate Gansevoort that she would be met in Hamburg by friends from Hanover: "I have good and kind friends in several of Continental Capitals and they all express a desire to have me come at once." This high sophistication impressed Kate. As for mail, Kate was to address her "care Andrews & Dillaway, 54 William st New York," as her movements were uncertain; and even Lizzie might not always know just where she was, "and for how long." George Dillaway was Lizzie's young first cousin once removed who had visited Arrowhead in 1869. On 5 November Jane wrote Kate from New York, having visited not Herman Melville or Herman and Lizzie but, as she put it, Lizzie: "I saw Lizzie yesterday—and shall see her again this evening. She is looking very well indeed." She went on, still not commenting on Herman, "There is considerable excitement here this evening owing to the Election returns." On the fifteenth Lizzie wrote Kate saying that she and Jane "had arranged matters so that you and Milie would come and take Florence and Kitty's place and I hoped you would both come together." Helen's understanding was that the girls "were to be at Herman's." After all that planning, Jane stayed on in New York at the Gramercy rather than sailing for Europe.

On 9 November a new calamity occurred—the great Boston fire, which destroyed some seventy-five million dollars in property, the worst physical disaster Bostonians had ever suffered. Sam Shaw watched its progress: "Saw the great fire make its way up Summer St. and afterwards from other points. Helped move valuable articles from my brother's office. The city alive all night with teams and people." He continued the diary the next day, 10 November: "Dismal Sunday though weather beautiful. Street thronged and bustling, churches deserted. Fire stopped towards afternoon." By Monday Lizzie had heard that the house on Mt. Vernon Street was safe, as she wrote Kate Gansevoort: "Thank Heaven the dear old *home* was spared—the loss of property is easier to be borne than the tearing up of family altars and all the desolation that must follow." She was still greatly agitated, "& still in a state of suspense, as to *our* actual *loss* thereby." Helen, the Melville of her generation who knew Boston longest and best, on 14 November gave a heartbroken eyewitness report to Kate Gansevoort: "The 'Old South' church, which on one corner stayed the progress of the fire," was to be repaired as "a temporary Post Office." She asked, "Can you realize that so many of the pleasant 'corners,' round which we used to circulate in Boston are obliterated from the face of the Earth?" She "could have wept over the ruins," but Boston was "to be re-built, more glorious than before." Lizzie went back to Boston for Thanksgiving, having so judiciously packed her pie that it was only a little flattened during the long ride. At the great New England festival even Lizzie's pie was not wholly at home, as she wrote Cousin Kate (10 December): "you would have been amused to see my brothers look askance at *anything* in the place of one of 'mother's pies' on the table." She saw for herself some of the physical damage to the city and what had been her inherited property, although she remained "in a state of suspense, as to *our* actual loss." In fact, the loss was severe. Her property in Boston, worth five thousand dollars, had regularly been bringing her an annual income of five hundred dollars—an enormous sum when her husband made only four dollars a day. Alert as usual, Kate saw to it that her stepmother suggest to Uncle Peter that a check would be appropriate as a delayed silver wedding present, and around Thanksgiving her father sent Herman a check for five hundred dollars.

December began in New York with a snowstorm that "chilled the beggar's body, frosted his tatters, put white patches in the rents of his clothes, and caused him to hide in convenient areas," said the *Times* the next day, 2 December, the day Kate Gansevoort arrived at Twenty-sixth Street escorted by her cousin Robert Sanford and carrying an elegantly engraved soup ladle as her anniversary gift. Herman was there with the girls. During her visit Kate and Robert Sanford talked business, trying to settle Henry's estate, and dealing with a Tiffany's bill larger than Herman's annual salary by far ($1715.25); in January she wrote Sanford that she was sorry to have overdrawn ("you told me at Cousin Herman Melville's in 26th St. New York that you thought I had some 800 Dollars for my use from the Estate"). On 6 December Bessie had to write the thank-you note to Kate, for her father had suffered "a very bad attack of influenza which keeps him in the house." For some days he could "not use his eyes at all." As soon as he was well enough (9 December), Herman wrote her his own thanks for her remembering the "Silver Wedding": "Lizzie and I will ever think of you at our soup; and I shall always pour out a libation from the tureen to the angelic donor, before helping a mere vulgar broth-bibbing mortal like myself." Augusta was visiting in eastern Massachusetts in mid-December, and came to see Lizzie and Hope along with Helen and Minnie.

Early in December Herman wrote Lizzie about "the beautiful soup ladle" Kate had brought and about Uncle Peter's gift of five hundred dollars. On the tenth Lizzie wrote to Kate, "much relieved" by Peter's "kind and generous gift to Herman." She said it removed "the necessity of renting our house or part of it," which she had feared, and made it easier for her to bear her loss in the Boston fire with equanimity, explaining: "I say *I*, because Herman from his studious habits and tastes being unsuited for practical matters, all the *financial* management falls upon me—and one cannot make bricks without straw—you know—Mother and my brothers feel much relieved on my account." She consoled herself about her losses in the fire as best she could: "friends on every side have met with losses greater or less—I have plenty to keep me company." In alluding to Exodus 5 she meant that she could not make the brick of responsible household management without the essential straw, money. Lizzie's stepmother and half-brothers could have taken more active steps to relieve her mind and their minds about her had they wished, but such measures would have been out of keeping. Lizzie's dreading having to rent all or part of the house at Twenty-sixth Street sounds absurd, but it was not. In a situation dire enough the whole household could have moved in with Tom and Katie at the Governor's House, or, more easily, Lizzie and Herman could have stayed there while Bessie and Fanny moved into Mt. Vernon Street, where they could fulfill Hope Shaw's need to be surrounded by young girls dependent on her favor and where they could best meet marriageable young men, and where Lizzie could spend much of the time with them, sure that Tom and Katie were seeing to Herman. Lizzie was her father's daughter; all the "*financial* management" did indeed fall upon her; and she had seriously taken renting the house as a last resort, knowing that she and Herman could take refuge at the Island—as long as Tom was able to retain his post.

On 20 December George P. Putnam died suddenly, and two days before Christmas his funeral was held near the Melvilles' house at the Madison Avenue church. On such an occasion the natural thing would have been for Evert Duyckinck and Melville to have attended together, as they did Adler's funeral. Herman must have been forcibly reminded of Putnam and Gansevoort in 1846, when the two Americans in London had boldly arranged the American publication of *Typee* under the sponsorship of Washington Irving: all three dead, now, the youngest first. "Christmas time," as Lizzie wrote to Kate Gansevoort on 29 December, was "a very quiet and sad one": "The losses in our family circle come home forcibly to our hearts at these anniversary times—as you well can realize—Jenny and the girls dined together with us—very quietly," the girls having come from the Island "to attend Zion church, where Jenny had a beautiful memorial flower cross hung over their pew." Jane said on New Year's Day that two of the girls had spent Christmas with her, two with Herman and Lizzie, by which she meant that Kitty and Milie had stayed overnight with her in the Gramercy Hotel, while Florence and Lucy were with Herman and Lizzie. Kitty wrote to Kate Gansevoort: "The next day the great snow storm prevented us from returning to the Island, but on Friday we managed with some difficulty to get to the boat." Lucy was still in boarding school, but the other three girls stayed on at Tom's, and were there when their father's estate was settled the next year. For the girls it was miserably far from Sophia and Allan's Christmases with child-sized tables heaped with gifts. They were orphans, "Mamma at the Gramercy" or not.

The year 1872 was one for passing on family heirlooms as mourning gifts and for buying new mourning gifts. After Allan Melville's death Jane gave Herman a silver dessert spoon inscribed on the handle "C. Gansevoort" and on the reverse, "H.G. to A.M. March 18, 1862," the death date of Herman Gansevoort. Jane ordered from Tiffany four identical gold mourning lockets, superb pieces, onto each of which were inscribed the initials of one daughter, and inside each of which she placed a lock of Allan's hair and a carte-de-visite photograph of him in his little round Horace Greeley–Cornelius Mathews glasses. The photograph shows Allan as a white-haired, frail man, and the locks of hair were white. These gifts probably constituted most of the items for which Allan's executors on 13 May paid Tiffany $158 — serious money for serious jewelry. I hefted Florence's, in the possession of Milie's daughter-in-law Anna Morewood, in the late 1980s: heavy, superb Tiffany work. After Maria Gansevoort Melville's death someone took the two spoons in memory of her parents which were received from her mother's estate by her son Gansevoort in 1845 (and subsequently engraved with the date of Gansevoort's death), and had engraved upon them also Maria's name and her birth and death dates. Herman Melville like the rest of his family took a chastened pride in such memorials, and of course wore mourning for their dead. That year, shorter of money than usual, even, Herman gave to "Capt. Thomas Melville" the two-volume work Herman Gansevoort had given him in 1846, Ephraim Chambers's *Cyclopaedia; or, An Universal Dictionary of Arts and Sciences* (London, 1728).

Augusta and Fanny adjusted to their responsibilities as the dowagers of the Mansion House. They worked out a trial inscription for their mother's tombstone and showed it to Tom before sending it to Herman for his approval or criticism, wanting to hurry so the work could be done before winter. As Augusta wrote Kate Gansevoort on 28 October, they wanted "The *name* & *dates* merely, under papa's" so it would continue, "and his wife / Maria Gansevoort Melville. / born April 6th 1791 / died / April 1st 1872." It was good that Augustus Haebig was conveniently located, farther up Washington Avenue. (His business card specified "manufacturer of Marble Monuments, headstones &c., in Italian and American Marble.")

The year ended miserably. On 30 December the trustees of the Sailors' Snug Harbor considered the allegations against Governor Melville and Melville's testimony in his own defense, then in the absence of "conclusive proof" of Melville's having embezzled funds they voted "to notice and express their most emphatic disapproval of certain views of the Governor as stated in his examination in respect to extra compensation being made to him for certain services in a manner different from what is contemplated by and provided for in the existing By-laws," and recommended that in the future the governor "be wholly relieved of the duty which under the original By-laws devolves upon him to purchase all Supplies for the Institution." The upshot was the creation of an office in Manhattan to "transact all business," requisitions going from the governor to a comptroller rather than directly to a supplier. This time word got out all through the family of the danger to

Tom, and on 4 January 1873, from Brookline, Fanny wrote to her Uncle Peter, as she had promised: Katie had written on 31 December that "the meeting took place yesterday and every thing [was] most splendidly settled for Tom," and that he had been told "that he was on a surer footing & would be better sustained by the Trustees than ever before." Fanny then sighed, "You will all rejoice with us, that the affair is settled." The matter was not splendidly settled at all, but the family needed to put the best face on Tom's troubles. At least Maria did not have to suffer through this episode.

On 31 December Kate Hoadley (Kate herself, for a wonder) wrote to Kate Gansevoort about the "very delightful gathering at Helen's on Christmas day" — delightful but painful, "being constantly reminded of the day at Tom's last year, & of the two dear ones who have passed to their eternal rest, casting a sadness that was felt by us all, without making the day a sad one, for the children." Lizzie was not the only one who felt the strain beneath the bright sallies. Some of the strains still involved Herman and Lizzie. Half a century later Tom's widow, by then Katie Melville White, told Melville's daughter Frances, in regard to Herman Melville's state of mind and behavior, that his "sisters felt very badly about it all," whatever it all was, "but did not say *much*."

[34]

A Family in Disarray, and "Mar Saba"
1873

To build with level of my lofty stile

Melville checks and underscores this line
in "The Ruins of Rome," stanza 25, in his father's Spenser; he annotates it:
"Build the lofty rhyme / Milton." (Priscilla Ambrose Collection)

BEFORE THE NEW YEAR BEGAN, the January 1873 *Harper's New Monthly Magazine* was available with the long-promised article by Louis Bagger, "The Sailors' Snug Harbor," in which two engravings depicted the neatly bearded governor, Thomas Melville. Bagger described the library but made no mention that the governor's brother Herman had been an author. At some time, one of Herman's nautical books, John Turnbull's *A Voyage Round the World* (Philadelphia, 1810) got into the library. New Year's Day was sparkling, but Tom's dog, "Boatswain," had run away (as Florence Melville wrote Kate Gansevoort on that day) and was "supposed to be detained by the expressman at Brighton with whom he has been seen." Tom's first New Year's duty was "to compel his restoration," celebrity portraits in *Harper's* or not. The trustees had exonerated him of the worst charges against him, and he would have his dog back. ("Boatswain" was a double literary allusion, from the dog in *Typee*, which had been named for the canine Boatswain of a poet with nautical connections, Lord Byron.) Jane spent a few hours "at Herman's" on New Year's Day then wrote a maudlin letter to Kate: "even if I would I cannot escape the dearest memories that a sorrowing woman can know. I cannot stop living—and yet—I hate myself for living—The world has become so small since Allan *died!*" They all survived the great duplicitous thaw that was followed by heavy sleet and rain, the great sleet storm of Sunday, 5 January. Allan's daughters continued to see much of Herman and Lizzie. Augusta explained to Kate Gansevoort on 14 January that Milie would not visit Albany that winter: "I thought she would become so much interested in the plan she had laid out for improvement this winter, taking music lessons, & French, & readings with the girls, that she would find it difficult to leave Tom's, even for a few weeks." There was much of her serious, dogged father in Milie, who was able to set out a program for study like him, and to pursue it with something of the determination of her Uncle Gansevoort. Lucy went back to school on 7 January, "rather regretfully," Milie wrote Kate Gansevoort on the eighth. Florence spent Sunday the fifth "in town at Aunt Lizzie's," where all were well, and saw her stepmother. Milie also said that "Bessie is spending a few days here, and we all are enjoying her visit." Tom and Katie had put a framed crayon picture of Henry "on the piano at present till they decide on a good place to hang it." Allan's Kitty was staying with Herman and Lizzie, and Jane visited her there on the ninth.

Jane wrote absurdly to Kate Gansevoort on 9 January: "I have delayed writing because I have found communication with Staten Island almost impossible." Rather than escaping to Europe, Jane was amusing herself by systematically seducing the vulnerable Kate to her side, uniting with her in grief rather than trying to help her get over her grief for Henry: "Oh my dear cousin I cant write you and perhaps can never tell you how well I now understand your great grief—once I could not understand it, but now, why it is so like my own poor life—and loss—that it seems to me as I know you better—you become so near and dear to me." On 13 January Bessie Melville wrote to Kate Gansevoort so Kitty could carry it up, since Jane and Kitty were leaving for Albany. Milie had come up for Saturday and Sunday with the Melvilles, then insisted on "going down to the Island this morning to practice," although Bessie wished "she could stay longer." The two sets of uncles and aunts, Herman and Lizzie, Tom and Katie, were making Allan's daughters welcome, although Herman's job was threatened and Tom, still under a cloud, was dealing with the inconvenience and indignity of submitting petty financial decisions to a comptroller.

On 22 January 1873 Melville's sisters Helen and Fanny called at 49 Mt. Vernon Street where (Fanny wrote Kate Gansevoort) they "found Mrs Shaw better, though still confined to the library—oh, how sweet she did look with her bright eyes, & a pretty flush in her cheeks." Hope was anticipating John Oakes Shaw Jr.'s graduation from Harvard in the class of '73 (no one had put up such money for Malcolm's education, nor for Stanwix's). Bessie went back to the Island to visit Kitty on 30 January, apparently by herself—being almost twenty years old. The Hoadleys were planning a trip to Washington for the end of February, which involved spending one night at Herman's on their way. Before the Hoadleys arrived, Stanwix returned, on the steamer *Henry Chauncey*—named for one of the three founders of the Panama Railroad. Stanwix had worked for a time with Dr. Alfred Starr, the neighbor at 58 East Twenty-sixth Street who had been on the coroner's jury after Malcolm's death, and had also done a little work for a Dr. Read. Now he planned to go back to his "old business in dentistry again in a few weeks," as soon as he could get a chance. On 23 February 1873, he regaled his step-grandmother with his adventures after passing through the Indian Nation to New Orleans, which he found to be "a lively city," but with no employment for him:

> so I thought I should like a trip to Central America, I went on a steamer to Havana, Cuba & from there to half a dozen or more ports on the Central America coast till I came to Limon Bay in Costa Rica. I walked from there on the beach with two other young fellows to Greytown in Nicaragua, one of the boys died on the beach, & we dug a grave in the sand by the sea, & buried him, & travelled on again, each of us not knowing who would have to bury the other before we got there, as we were both sick with the fever & ague.

Stanwix's father on hearing this could visualize the experience all too vividly, since he had read Headley's gruesome three-part *Harper's* article on the Strain expedition in 1855, as well as his friend Tomes's *Panama in 1855*.

The Melvilles were lucky to have Stanwix alive, especially in view of his adventures scouting the right spot for a ship canal and his arrival in Aspinwall on a schooner that was "wrecked there in that heavy gale of wind where four or five other vessels got lost, & the Pacific Mail Steamship Co. lost such a large amount." He had himself lost all his clothes "& every thing" else and been taken sick "again" with fever. He announced: "I find the cold weather agrees with me much better, than the sun of the tropics." Now, Stanwix declared, "I say New York forever." From Stanwix any good resolutions had a hollow ring. Augusta went to Nilly Thayer's for a week or so, starting 26 February, but Helen (in writing to Kate Gansevoort) insisted that she could not spare her longer than that. Among other things, they had been reading *Middlemarch* to each other. In Boston the walking had been "unspeakably disagreeable," and Helen, in her mid-fifties, suffered from the biting cold and "icy paths, devious & dangerous." Kate and John Hoadley stayed over in Boston at the Parker House, so they saw both Helen and Augusta before leaving "for New York en route for Washington." Hoadley had his own business, but he probably called on George Boutwell, the secretary of the treasury, about Herman, having on 9 January 1873 written Boutwell a long letter on his behalf. The Hoadleys had further plans, to go on to Charleston to visit the Latherses.

From Hoadley's letter to the secretary of the treasury, we can piece together a portrait of Melville as deputy inspector to supplement that in the rules and regulations. According to Hoadley, Melville was endeavoring to avoid notice (much as White Jacket had done on the *Neversink*): "Proud, shy, sensitively honorable, — he had much to overcome, and has much to endure; but he strives earnestly to so perform his duties as to make the slightest censure, reprimand, or even reminder,—impossible from any superior." Corruption was so pervasive in his daily life that Melville devised strategies for dealing with outright attempts at bribery. Knowing that complaint to his superiors would be self-defeating—that is, would quickly cost him his job— he did not report the "low venality" which surrounded him. Specifically, "corrupting merchants and their clerks and runners" offered him money, often approached him and slyly put money in his pocket, sure that "all men" could be bought. With all these Melville dealt mildly, unreprovingly, so as to avoid offending them and bringing down official disfavor: "he puts it all quietly aside,—quietly declining offers of money for special services,— quietly returning money which has been thrust into his pockets behind his back." Not only did men attempt to bribe him, others attempted to extort payoff from him, "the corrupt swarms who shamelessly seek their price." Hoadley declared that in the midst of all this Melville was "quietly, steadfastly doing his duty, and happy in retaining his own self-respect." In the aftermath of the Boston fire everyone in the family knew the importance of keeping Melville employed in his position, always precarious in a branch of the government notorious for job insecurity. Melville at work was exercising formidable self-control, the sort of fearful caution that affected his hours at home as well as at work.

Timidity, reminiscent of his behavior after his accident in 1862 (when according to Joe Smith for a time he "shrank" from entering a carriage) seems for some years to have tinged much of Melville's life outside his house. In earlier years he had been an eager rummager in bookstores and bookstalls, quick to strike up conversations with dealers. Now, although he still haunted bookstores which were open after his working hours, he was subdued. In the early 1870s, Dr. Samuel Arthur Jones repeatedly observed him in the Luyster Brothers' bookshop on Fulton Street. Then a young man, Jones became a great Melville collector when he snapped up part of Allan Melville's copies of his brother's works dumped by Jane's executors. Looking at Melville's portrait in the 1892 edition of *Typee*, he recognized a man whom he had frequently seen. Melville and Richard Grant White, another veteran of *Yankee Doodle* and his superior at the Custom House, had often enough wandered in Luyster Brothers' at the same time. As Jones later reconstructed their routines, he saw that after finishing their day's work at the Custom House both "would drop in before going to their up-town homes," but there "did not appear to be any intimacy between Melville and White; at least I never saw them conversing." Dr. Jones's impression of Melville was of a self-effacing man: "In the flesh he did not show either strength or determination; on the contrary, he was the quietest, meekest, modestest, retiringest man you can imagine. He moved from shelf to shelf so quietly—I never saw him speak to anyone—and his air was that of shrinking timidity: by no stretch of the imagination would one have thought him an author of any repute." This portrait squares with Hoadley's characterization of Melville as trying at work to escape notice, to avoid offense, to forestall reprimand. Melville did not always act this way, but it was a role that he knew how to take on.

Stanwix did apprentice himself to Dr. Read, a dentist, with the promise that pay would begin in a few months, as his skills improved. On 3 March he wrote Hope Shaw piously: "Patience is indeed a virtue and which, for one, I wish I was the happy possessor of, for as the days roll slowly along, at times I think the year will never draw to a close, so that I will find myself better off than when I started; but I know that if I am steady at the profession I am learning that in a few years I will be independent of any man." On 25 April he wrote Hope Shaw that he had "encountered a serious obsticle"—that he was "too near sighted" to become "a number one dentist." He could not "find anything in New York," he decided, not wanting to be "a clerk in an office." "Fate is against me in most of my undertakings," he lamented, and announced that he would go "to Southern California on a farm or something like that." Still disturbed by the precariousness of his own job, Melville collapsed just when Stanwix began talking about going to California, for on 4 April Jane wrote Kate Gansevoort, "Do you know that Herman is quite ill?" Stanwix sailed on 30 April on the *Henry Chauncey*, again, from Pier No. 42, North River, which became one more haunted spot in Manhattan for Herman to revisit on his rounds. Lizzie was in despair when she wrote Kate Gansevoort on 26 May: "We all thought he was foolish to give up his place, especially as the Dr. was desirous to keep him, but he seems to be possessed with a demon of *restlessness*, and there is nothing to do but let him go." The parents were helpless in the face of that "demon of restlessness" which haunted Stanwix—a hereditary demon Maria could have identified. Melville must have seen himself in Stanwix, but must have contrasted himself and his son. He had been fatherless and poorly educated himself, but Stanwix was more weakened by hereditary flaws and more damaged by life. In her 26 May letter Lizzie informed Kate Gansevoort: "Herman is quite well again now—you heard through Augusta, of his sudden & severe illness—and also of Stanny's going to California." She made no connection between the events; perhaps she should have, given the timing of Melville's illnesses in the mid-1850s.

In the 4 April letter Jane told Kate Gansevoort of her plans to sail "in the steamer 'Abyssinia,' of the Cunard line—on May 10th with a charming party" from Gramercy Park House, a five-story hotel. She would be accompanied by her personal maid, Annie, but none of Allan's daughters. Among the passengers might be young Dillaway's partner, Andrews, she coyly mentioned ("I am sure that you will be surprised to hear that Mr Andrews goes in the same steamer—so he says—but possibly, he may go before"). She informed Kate that she was giving to the Century Club "a beautiful likeness of Allan" in crayon, "much larger than any heretofore made," elaborately framed, perhaps still extant. Allan, she said, "was much interested in the Century," and had taken her there "the Sunday the day before that dreadful Monday—when he came home to lie down and die." The Hoadleys may have timed their Charleston visit so they could be there on 4 April when Lathers entertained Governor Horatio Seymour of New York and the aged poet and editor William Cullen Bryant. That news reached a Boston paper on the seventh, so Helen got to enjoy it all vicariously. There may have been a gathering on the docks on 10 May to see Jane off, for the Hoadleys had been in New York for several days on their way home, leaving on the eleventh. Milie (she wrote Kate Gansevoort on 11 May) and her next two sisters were leaving also, spending a night with Herman and Lizzie before starting for Pittsfield on the thirteenth "at 8 A.M — Uncle Tom, we three girls, three servants, a dozen pieces of luggage, & a liberal allowance of bags, shawls, umbrellas baskets etc." Lucky Tom.

From Albany Kate Gansevoort continued to send clothing to Lizzie and the girls, and sent Herman some of Henry's clothing, particularly a coat, which almost fit him, although it was (Lizzie said on 26 May) "a little snugger than the loose sacks he is accustomed to wear" (that is, it was much too tight). Lizzie agreed that Herman's "figure" and Henry's "were very similar," and specified that the Boston relatives, who saw much of Henry toward the end, "constantly noticed how much they were alike in various ways — but *mainly*, in figure and carriage." As the generation shrank, familial characteristics were more and more valued. Kate came to New York in June of 1873, twenty-six months to the day after they buried Henry in Albany (for she kept less obvious dates than annually occurring ones). She was flooded with memories of times in New York, as she wrote Abe on the fifteenth: "that all came over me — & with the familiar scenes here — the very streets & stones are all full of memories — Cousin Herman is so like Henry in manner & in appearance & in little trifling ways — It does me good to see him." On 23 June Kate wrote Abe: "Cousin Herman & Lizzie are well & anxious to have me remain until the latter part of this week & as I have not been able to get some things I have left my return home until Wednesday — most probably Thursday."

Kate's cousin Helen Sanford spent a day there, and kept her company in her rigorous shopping which she liked to perform with another expert beside her. Kate was clear about her strategy, saying, in a letter to her parents on 23 June: "I always search until I find what I think will suit or answer." Cousin Lizzie had gone out and left her in charge of the house for an hour. It sounds like a normal household — Stanwix away in California or somewhere, the two girls in Boston, and the parents Lizzie and Herman hospitable, Cousin Kate Gansevoort coming and going. On the twenty-second Lizzie took Kate to hear Dr. Bellows preach, as Kate wrote Abe the next day: "he had a pure Unitarian sermon putting forth the idea, that 'works was better than faith' — & that creeds were useless for man or woman, seldom lived up, to them & the living a good, honest pure & true life was better than all else — nor *belief in God was essential.*" Kate knew politely phrased heresy when she heard it: "Such a contradiction to an orthodox belief — but very beautiful & very moving — but oh Abe — how much better in Faith & hope that our Risen Saviour stands ready to recieve & forgive *all* who come to him in humility & trust & able to wipe out all our sins, tho' they be scarlet, if we only have tried to do our duty & believe — for our Creator God — has given us through the inspired writings the news of forgiveness to all who believe on his dear Son Jesus Christ!" Like Herman, she found New York heartless except to those who lived there, and luxuriated in the sadness of places she had been to with Henry: "So many spots here are hallowed with associations, painful & yet sweet." Kate saw Henry everywhere: "Poor Henry how he suffered here, there are streets, & corners, & houses, & windows, where he shadows forth & I almost yearn for his coming — that can never be again." She was getting easier about Herman's resemblance to Henry: "Cousin Herman is so like my darling Brother Henry in voice, manner, & little ways that is really fascinating." In Kate's obsession she was feeling emotions not wholly unlike those which Herman himself felt at times while walking his rounds. It would have been impossible for him not to see his father on the Courtlandt Street dock, or Allan at Wall Street with the bushel of notices of Gansevoort's speeches, or Gansevoort in the torchlight parade in Manhattan, or Tom going aboard the *Navigator* in 1849, or his mother as she boarded a ferry for Staten Island. What was self-destructive obsession in Kate had been, repeatedly, and probably more often than we know, the impetus to creativity in her Cousin Herman, even to the hallucinatory metamorphosis of body into body, Herman seeing himself in Tom in May 1849 even more vividly than Kate saw Henry in Herman in 1873. In his prose headnote to the poem about John Marr, Melville defines the way an aureola sheds light over phantoms of those one has loved, "for reunion with which an imaginative heart passionately yearns." They were true cousins.

In late May the Harbor was in turmoil. Isabella (Belle) Bogart was becoming Belle Bogart Bagley, and much sewing was taking place. In the 1868 renovations gas-lines had not been laid in the Governor's House, after all, or not laid in all the right places, so Tom and Katie were in upheaval. Lizzie wrote Kate Gansevoort on 26 May that they literally had "not a room that is in comfortable order." The occupants at Twenty-sixth Street were also busy, Lizzie said: "the girls are getting ready to go to Boston somewhat earlier this year, to be in Cambridge on Class Day. My brother's son [Oakes Jr.] graduates, and a 'good time' is expected—The pique skirt comes in very opportunely—we are dressmaking with all our might, as usual 'on our own hook,' and are independent of dressmakers and their frightful charges with the exception of an occasional 'cut and baste.'" Lizzie expected to be home until Herman took his vacation, "probably the last of July or August," and until then Kate was welcome any time: "you have only to write us a day or two beforehand, & let us know the day and train." About this time the auditors prepared their account of the estate of Allan Melville for the executor, "Capt Melville." Schedule A showed assets of $34,356.72 (diminished on Schedule B by $208.04). Among the assets in Schedule A, collected since Allan Melville's death, was $50 in cash "from Herman Melville." Schedule D itemized Allan's debts of $19,431.78, including a bond to Richard Lathers, another to Charles Thurston, and a note to John C. Hoadley. Maria G. Melville, Florence Melville, and Catherine G. Melville were listed as "with Capt. Melville Governor Sailors Snug Harbor, New Brighton N.Y." The address of Lucy Melville ("a minor of 17") was given as "Mmes Da Silva & Bradfords school West 38th New York."

Lucy joined Milie and Florence at Arrowhead and let them know that Kate Gansevoort was "at Uncle Herman's." Milie, running Arrowhead by herself, on 16 June invited Kate to visit, still juggling dates, since after Rachie Barrington she was "to have Uncle Herman & Aunt Lizzie and the girls," and after that the aunts Augusta and Fanny and Kate Gansevoort herself. She had a favor: "will you ask Aunt Lizzie if she received a postal card which I sent to her on Saturday it had been put in our box here." Milie added that she supposed Bessie and young Fanny were about to start for Boston (they did, on the eighteenth), and showed a certain quiet wit: "Have you been visiting Tiffany's as much as usual?" Milie had begun a patchwork quilt, "having nothing to do or think of you know"—an ironical allusion to something that was keeping her quite busy enough. Lizzie's letter to Kate on 2 July sounded calm. She and Herman had enjoyed the loaf of bread Kate sent. The weather had been hot, and the trees "'smellier' than ever," so that her rose cold was still very bad. The heat and stench of New York oppressed Lizzie, and she experienced an unaccustomed emotion, especially after Kate had visited and left: "I miss you very much and wish you were here to help me get along with this dreary time without the children—When Herman is gone all day, or the largest part of it, the house seems utterly desolate—it is quite a new sensation for me to have the days seem *long*." As the time for Herman's two-week vacation approached both he and Lizzie were "counting the days for going to

Pittsfield and think with longings of the refreshing breezes from the hilltops." Herman was now seeking refuge in the new Central Park, walking there, Lizzie reported, in the long summer dusk. Strange — a park where farmland had been during their days on Fourth Avenue. Herman tended to walk uptown for pleasure now, partly because his work still was taking him downtown, partly because downtown was more thronged every year, while great open spaces had been preserved to the north.

Lizzie was tempted by the idea of meeting the Gansevoorts at Catskill, but knew that would make Herman's short vacation too complicated. The girls, Bessie and Fanny, had been staying in Brookline, with Helen, not with old Hope Shaw, and they wrote often. Herman sent love, and volunteered to find a book for Cousin Kate Gansevoort if she had not found it. Lizzie wrote Kate again on 16 July, wanting the return of *Autumnal Catarrh* by Morrill Wyman, needing it "for reference" — so she could consult the colored maps of danger zones and safe havens. On 20 July Lizzie reported to Kate that Jane was in Scotland, adding cautiously with an allusion to a Dickens title: "I have not seen or heard of our 'Mutual Friend' since you left though I keep up a great *thinking* about him." The women of the family knew things they did not put down on paper. Which young partner was the friend: Andrews or Dillaway? Jane was taking her consolation abroad, perhaps having carried consolation with her on the *Abyssinia*. Herman and Lizzie were still planning to leave for Pittsfield on the twenty-sixth for Herman's two weeks of vacation. While Augusta was writing to Kate on 21 July Minnie and Lottie called to her, having caught sight of Tom and Katie: "Yes. There they come!!" August was hectic at Gansevoort, much coming and going, with trips to Saratoga Springs for Augusta, even (as she wrote on Herman's birthday to Kate Gansevoort).

On 13 August Richard Lathers sailed with his daughters Carrie and Emma to tour Europe, so he was not at Abby Lodge when Herman and Lizzie visited Arrowhead, but Abby kept her house open and hospitable. There was news in Pittsfield — the best news for the family since Tom was given the governorship of Sailors' Snug Harbor, but deeply poignant, since it involved Milie, the cousin inextricably linked in everyone's mind with Malcolm, her near twin in birth. Milie Melville and Willie Morewood had known each other since early childhood, and they had been thrown together intimately in 1869, when Abby Lodge was opened to such gaiety among the Lathers and Melville and Morewood children. They had been attracted to each other but the log had burnt out (Lizzie's phrase) and it was assumed in the family that they had lost interest in each other. In the interim Willie had formed a Chicago connection, since broken off. Now Willie bided his time, waiting until Lizzie had gone to Boston before seizing an opportunity to talk to Herman about his desire to marry Milie.

Lizzie received the news in Boston. Suffused with memories—most powerfully her hours of watching by the deathbed of Sarah Morewood and helping to prepare the body afterward—Lizzie wrote Willie from Mt. Vernon Street on 12 August: "When I tell you that there is no one to whose keeping I would be more willing to confide the happiness of my beloved Milie than to you, dear Willie, you may well believe that I cannot better express my approval of your engagement, for apart from other considerations, you have always seemed nearer and dearer to me than you can ever know from associations which you can hardly appreciate." She signed herself "your affectionate friend & (prospective) 'Aunt Lizzie.'" On 12 August Melville returned from his vacation, a day late, accompanied by Bessie and a young friend of hers. On the eighteenth Milie reported sweetly to Kate: "We had a very pleasant visit from Uncle Herman and Aunt Lizzie, and I think it did them both good." The logistics were complicated:

> Lucy went on to Boston with Aunt Lizzie on the 8th, to visit Aunt Helen. We were very sorry to have Aunt Lizzie leave us so soon, but she looks forward so much to her Boston visit that it seemed too bad to shorten it even by extending her time here. Uncle Herman stayed till Monday, for which I was very glad. . . . Aunt Lizzie did receive the [Hay Fever] book from Mrs Sanford. Uncle Herman told me after she had left, I had forgotten to ask her. . . . N. B. Have you heard that you are to have a new cousin—initials—W.B.M.?

She wanted the Gansevoorts to visit Arrowhead soon, "while the weather is bright and windows are open to let in 'all out doors.' And in September we are not so sure of pleasant weather."

Lizzie on 15 August, from Boston, wrote Kate Gansevoort at Prospect House, Catskill, New York: "Herman and I had a *delightful* visit in Pittsfield—and—have you heard the news?—it has happened since I left—Maria is engaged to young Mr. Morewood—Willie, as we always call him—we have known him from infancy, and feel sure that his character and standing are such as to make the match a very suitable one—." Lizzie rejoiced in every aspect of the match, Willie's known character and affectionate family behavior, his success in the mercantile business in New York, and a "mutual attachment" with Milie "based upon a long tried *friendship* which is the best ground for married happiness." Practically, it meant that Milie and her sisters would have "a kind protector" (she did not say "in addition to Tom"). She explained: "Herman was there a few days ago *after* I left, (as I wanted to see Bessie *here* [in Boston] before she went home) and Willie took that opportunity to talk with him and have it settled. He approves of it very much" — as well Herman should have done, since it would unite Milie to the son of the memorable if erratic Sarah and the stable Rowland and place her as heiress to Broadhall. She would be as secure financially and emotionally as her family could hope. Lizzie went on:

> So the young people are likely to "have a wedding in the family" as they wished and Kitty will "have a brother-in-law" at last, as *she* longed for. Fanny, (my Fanny) came to Pittsfield before we left, and is there still. Herman and Bessie are in New York, & she has a young friend to keep her company....
>
> Our visit to Arrowhead did us both much good, and I wish you could go there and see how delightful it is. We spent nearly all the time walking, or driving, or sitting out doors — and it seemed as if we could not get enough of the reviving air, after being nearly suffocated in the heat and *smell* of New York. The girls get along admirably and the place looks as neat as a pin. With their aunt's [Abby Thurston] family "over the way" they have both protection and company, and all goes on well.... My brother [Lem?] and nephew [Oakes Jr.] are "doing London["] for a short time, and are well. Please give my kind love to your papa and mama. I hope they are gaining strength in the mountain air. I am not quite sure of your address, but send this at a venture.

From Mt. Vernon Street Lizzie wrote Kate Gansevoort on 31 August more about Milie's engagement, explaining the "'Chicago engagement'" as "one of those inexplicable, sudden affairs, that will happen sometimes under 'aggravating circumstances'"; "Milie was the *first* love, and you know the French proverb 'one always returns &c' Anyway, I am glad it is so settled now for I think there is all the material on both sides for a happy union." She continued in pointed reference to Kate's nebulous plans: "And it is *not* proposed to be a 'five years engagement.' I suppose, though I do not know, that the marriage will take place this fall." There was no reason for delay: "he is well settled in a prosperous business, and their acquaintance dates from infancy. Now, are *you* going to let Maria get ahead of you!! — We will see." Helen was very well, Fanny was in Pittsfield still, and Bessie still keeping house for her father "with a young friend for company." Lizzie was "*resting* mind & body*," suffering only very lightly from "the *cold*."

At the time, the family letters say nothing of the Panic which started in Vienna and hit New York in September of 1873. On 8 September Jay Cooke, the financier of the Northern Pacific Railway, failed, and the New York Stock Exchange was closed for ten days late in the month following "Black Friday" (19 September). Soon it was clear that Hoadley had been devastated. Apparently unperturbed, Kate Gansevoort arrived at Pittsfield on 12 September, met (she wrote her parents the next day) by "Kitty M. & Bessie M.," who drove her to Arrowhead, where Milie was waiting. Kate found the "old home" cheerful and bright. Florence and Lucy were coming from New York and their aunt Fanny Melville from Gansevoort, after stopping to see the Gansevoorts in Albany. It was perfect: "The trees sound beautifully in the breeze & Berkshire looks so fresh & green." Old Greylock loomed in the north, and the old home had "many associations," as everything had for Kate, even Rouser, the horse Henry had bestridden. Willie she pronounced "a very sensible fellow, not handsome but agreeable." Lizzie wrote from New York on 25 September: "The household machinery has begun to revolve, and we are getting into our usual routine again. And whenever you feel like coming to make us a visit we shall be delighted to welcome you. You know, as I have said before, you have only to write and say so, and I hope you will before the pleasant fall weather is all gone." Herman sent "his special thanks for the pears, with his kind remembrances." Now the Albany Gansevoorts were sending food south as well as north.

Kate kept reminding Hoadley to keep her advised of his work on the memorial volume for her brother. On 3 October she sent him "extracts of letters written home by Henry & some letters to his Father I have taken out of the book file — They are all numbered so that they follow in date — & you can read them with interest. Some I think you might use with your judgement." The last week of October Herman and Lizzie, both looking well, stayed overnight with Tom and Katie on the Island. On the thirty-first Lizzie invited Kate Gansevoort, any day after Tuesday, when they would have concluded "some housecleaning operations." To the delight of all the Melvilles, Kate Gansevoort announced that her engagement, mysteriously suspended for several years, would proceed promptly to marriage. On 11 November Augusta could not refrain from reproaching Kate for her tardiness in giving them "our long, longed-for Cousin, Abraham Lansing." Acerbic Kate wrote Abe on the fourteenth that "even Cousin Herman says if you are not happy it will be *my fault*." Yet Kate was behaving very strangely still. On 11 November she wrote to Peter and Susan reproaching Peter for not having given even greater sums to Henry: "Oh if I could only share all you are so good & kind as to give me with our beloved Henry. *If he had only been spared to us.* — all here is so associated with him, that I live over our loss & have scarcely the heart to select & buy the things which you want me to get." She was keeping weird memorial days: "You may think me foolish but I cannot keep this, pardon all, for it comes from a full & very sad heart for to night the day of the week, & month 2 years & 8 months ago I was on my way home with my darling Henry." Abe would always be "a devoted & kind Son in Law," she told Peter, but she added: "I want you *never* to let him fill *Henrys Place*. We let *him die*, & *God* means us always to feel and bear in mind how he *afflicted us.*" Everyone congratulated her, and on 19 November Lizzie declined an invitation for her and Herman to come several days early and stay for the wedding, adding carefully: "I hope the excitement and bustle necessarily attending such 'doings in the family' will not be too much for your father." Jane arrived at the Fifth Avenue Hotel on 21 November, and sent her own congratulations.

Lizzie's letter of 23 November accepted the invitation for Bessie: "Tom & Kate will take her with them, and leave her at your house." As Kate should have known, Herman could not "leave his post at this very pressing time of business," but sent his "very best wishes," as Lizzie did. She was afraid to miss a Thanksgiving in Boston now that Hope Shaw was so old: "I have had such very earnest desires expressed that I should be with the family at Thanksgiving, at Boston, that I have decided to go *there*. You know it is the grand high hearthstone festival of us New Englanders, and in these times of change, we feel that every meeting *may* be the last one, and I think I ought to join them, mother desires it so much." Bessie would represent the Melvilles, while Frances remained (as Lizzie wrote Aunt Susan on 29 November) "to keep the household machine in running order." Jane, Lizzie said pointedly to Kate Gansevoort, was well, and would go to the wedding, "she says, if 'invited.' "

On 26 November Kate Gansevoort became Mrs. Abraham Lansing in the seldom-used west parlor of the house on Washington Avenue. On the honeymoon poor Abe wrote the Gansevoorts (30 November) to tell them he was awash in associations of places with Henry, as she was. In order to keep peace, Abe had to forget the sexual profligate drinking and brawling in lower Manhattan and boasting to Abe of having a venereal disease and of having been to all the brothels of any reputation in New York City, so he could introduce Abe to the prettiest girls. The price Abe paid for peace with Kate was lying about Henry's character as long as he lived, and he started his life of lies right, for Kate's idea of a honeymoon was a pilgrimage of pain—next stop, Fort Monroe, where Henry had served so nobly. In Boston Helen and George represented the family at Faneuil Hall's "Boston Centennial Tea-Party" on 3 December, where "Mr Quincy, Mr Winthrop, and other celebrities held forth" (according to Helen in a letter to Peter Gansevoort that month). There were times when it was good to be old Thomas Melvill's granddaughter. Lizzie stayed on in Boston past the middle of December, two weeks after the centennial, so she may have attended also, as bearing the Melville name. She was home before 20 December, when she reported to Aunt Susan that they had "heard from Stanny after a long interval during which he was off on a cruise 'taking deep sea soundings' in the naval service — and is now at the Navy Yard at Mare Island near San Francisco and doing well."

On 30 December Hoadley wrote from Boston to explain to Kate Gansevoort Lansing that he was not getting on as hoped with his "labor of love on the biography, or Memorial." In the Panic, western railroad construction had all but come to a halt, and the demand for engines, locomotive and otherwise, all but ceased. Hoadley's debtors were not paying him, so he had to carry them; dividends had fallen off; his low prices had to be lowered still further. "Nobody pays me"—a mournful statement. In New York, for Christmas Melville gave his daughter Frances *Pearls of Shakespeare*, illustrated by Kenny Meadows (London, 1873), a new book that was for her, not his research. It was a grim Christmas. Four days afterward Elizabeth wrote to the All Souls treasurer to explain her giving up pew 209 because she could not afford the rent. She would still attend, sitting in the gallery until she could "become a legitimate pew holder again."

While Kate was dragging Abe along on her pilgrimage of pain, Herman in *Clarel* had long since worked his way out of the Via Dolorosa and into the desert (Part 3, "Mar Saba"). The meekest, modestest man you could imagine was writing thousands of lines of poetry a year, and becoming a great poet. Good evidence is the nocturnal conversation of "The High Desert" (pt. 3, canto 5), Melville's somber meditation on the likelihood that the American experiment had descended into debased culture and corrupt politics, culminating in the triumphal march of "Mammon and Democracy." All this he conveyed indirectly, not by quoted speeches from the well-individualized characters. Instead, Rolfe, Mortmain, and Derwent, at least, converse, but no specific speech is assigned to any one of them. The thoughts sweep naturalistically from topic to topic, a slow whirl and wash of opinions, the way the best talk can rush, pause, circle, push forward—the way the men had talked in the Ocean House at Nantucket in July 1852, John Clifford, Judge Shaw, Herman Melville, perhaps Thomas Macy. To the talk in the high desert Clarel listens "ungladdened" and Vine listens impatiently, ill brooking what he takes as the "weary length of arguing." Dead a decade, Hawthorne was still saying things new to Melville, in 1873 (in the serial publication of the 9 June 1858 notebook entry) grumbling that Robert Browning's poetry could "seldom proceed far without running into the high grass of latent meanings and obscure allusions"—ill brooking complications, like Vine. Hawthorne was unavoidable throughout 1873, conspicuous in the magazine and newspaper reprints of sections from the Italian notebooks. The successors of Ticknor & Fields, "Fields, Osgood & Company," then "James R. Osgood" (not yet Houghton Mifflin), were proving themselves masterful repackagers. This year they reissued *Our Old Home* in a volume along with *Septimius Felton*, sending out old stuff in different formats. In an article on "Mr. DeForest's Novels" in the November 1873 *Atlantic Monthly*, *Typee* was listed as one of "a dozen American tales" just below the preeminent works of Hawthorne. Foremost in Melville's depiction of the Hawthorne-like character at this time was Vine's lack of intellectual daring or even intellectual curiosity — something Melville remembered well enough but that was freshly made manifest to him by passages from the notebooks.

During "The High Desert," when the other characters ponder the fate of the American experiment, Vine is so bored that he tosses bits of stone down into the valley "Or pelted his own shadow there" — a gesture of self-contempt (since Melville in the poem "Shelley's Vision" defines it as revealing the emotion opposed to "self-reverence"). On the same occasion, apparently, Vine finds time to rear a pile of stones, a cairn, as a monument to the barrenness of the discussion. This symbolic cairn is hardly a high product of artistic creativity; like the thorn-wreath earlier, it is a fairly simple satirical artifact. Several of Vine's hand actions are explicitly disintegrative, acts of taking things apart and throwing them away rather than amassing things and building intricate new artistic edifices with them. Vine's gestures appear neither normal nor innocent but vaguely unpleasant, even spooky, fitful, erratic, distracted, and distracting; they are analogues, oddly enough, to his gibing short speeches.

A late example of Melville's comments on Vine comes in "Bell and Cairn" (3.7). Seeking solitude at the memory of Jesus' moan on the cross, "ELOI LAMA SABACHTHANI!" Clarel goes among the crags, where he sees Vine, alone and quivering:

> He wore that nameless look
> About the mouth — so hard to brook —
> Which in the Cenci portrait shows,
> Lost in each copy, oil or print;
> Lost, or else slurred, as 'twere a hint
> Which if received, few might sustain:
> A trembling over of small throes
> In weak swoll'n lips, which to restrain
> Desire is none, nor any rein.
>   Clarel recalled the garden's shade,
> And Vine therein, with all that made
> The estrangement in Gethsemane.

The source of the century's fascination with Beatrice Cenci was Shelley, but in 1873 Melville had probably seen one or another serial publication of Hawthorne's 19 February 1858 notebook entry: "I might as well not try to say anything, for its spell is indefinable, and the painter has wrought it in a way more like magic than anything else." In "Bell and Cairn" the man who had held his reins with lurking will now gives himself over to sobs with no rein. Melville uses a strangely minimizing word: "small." What Clarel witnesses is not a gushing over of great throes, as in a Niagara, or even a Bash Bish, but a trembling over of small throes. While an image used just below implies that the woe is of size and significance (Vine's heart is compared to a heated anchor under the forge's mound of ash: "Raked open, lo, the anchor's found / In white-heat's alb"), here the skeptical memory of Vine's behavior in Gethsemane reminds us that small throes are not to be compared, for instance, to Jesus' agony either in the Garden or on the Cross. Instead, Melville offers a perturbing but aesthetically conventional image of suffering, suggestive of the not-unpleasing woe Guido Reni depicted in his portrait of a historical sufferer, Beatrice Cenci. Her story through its association with Shelley and other poets had become for Hawthorne, if not for Melville, almost as safely legendary (and perhaps as appealingly misogynistic) as the story of Boccaccio's lady and pursuer. Understanding what the image meant is complicated: in 1863 Kate Hoadley sent, as a welcome Christmas present, "'Beatrice Cenci' to hang in Gus's room." At this point Clarel slips aside "quite noiseless," renouncing any hope of "winning Vine / Or coming at his mystery." Instead, Vine will remain, perhaps all unwittingly, a puzzle with uncanny powers to tease. When Vine speaks at all it is usually in freakish, impish gibes at the expense of one or more of his companions; once in a while (as in "Tents of Kedar," 3.8) he may even include himself in a gibe.

In "The Beaker" (3.11) Vine, himself partaking of wine, "humorously" (according to his humor, characteristically) moralizes about the imparadising effects of liquor and wishes he could "joy in it" himself: "But no!" It is old news that Vine can take no joy in sensualizing, but at this late stage we may be newly realizing that our powerful initial impression of the darkly dressed man with "meditative mien" is gradually being eroded by what we see of his erratic, abruptly veering, self-checking mental processes. Finally, in "The Revel Closed" (3.14) Melville not only has Vine sing but also gives his comments on the song, one he has borrowed from an artist in Florence. In the "sweet impudence of wine" Derwent has begged from Vine a contribution to the mirth, either tale or song, and Vine's response is described in terms from Scottish legend: "Vine's brow shot up with crimson lights / As may the North on frosty nights / Over Dilston Hall and his low state — / The fair young Earl whose bloody end / Those red rays do commemorate, / And take his name." Beset by all the "Bacchic throng," Vine agrees to hum the song he heard an artist trill "one morning fine" in his loft in Florence, provided only that he is allowed to "recline / At ease the while." The song has two stanzas:

> What is beauty? 'tis a dream
>   Dispensing still with gladness:
> The dolphin haunteth not the shoal,
>   And deeps there be in sadness.
>
> The rose-leaves, see, disbanded be—
>   Blowing, about me blowing;
> But on the death-bed of the rose
>   My amaranths are growing.

Vine continues with this comment on the song: "*His amaranths:* a fond conceit, / Yes, last illusion of retreat!" This is something of a gibe—a gibe at the painter whose song he has taken. In Vine's opinion the last illusion of retreat is that even if beauty dies, something more important replaces it: immortality (to judge from the qualities associated with the amaranth in *Pierre*), presumably immortality from his artistic achievement. Earlier, in "The Cypriote" (3.4), Vine had indulged himself in unstrenuous mocking revery over the young Cypriote whose songs are scarce "self-derived." Now, after borrowing a song himself, he mocks the artist's fond conceit of immortality. Vine's earlier perception of beauty is not about to be replaced by any sort of immortality, whether through art, religion, or anything else. Pronouncing the song "hopeful" or "if part sad, not less adorning," Derwent insists that Vine come to the table: "So Vine sat down among them then— / Adept—shy prying into men." Next, in "Vine and the Palm" (3.26) Melville presents a long passage of musing followed by a self-conscious apostrophe. The darkly clad Vine is "Reclined aloof upon a stone / High up," where a shadow creeps over him. He "muses" about his solitariness, remembering the fabled "gushing amity" of "Achmed with his hundred brothers" and acknowledging the divineness of philanthropy (in the root sense). Such sociability is not for him: "For my part, I but love the past— / The further back the better; yes, / In the past is the true blessedness; / The future's ever overcast— / The present aye plebeian." Vine's love for the monastery of Mar Saba is a response to its age, yet he will leave the next day "With right good will."

When Vine sees the famous Mar Saba Palm he does something "to pass the time"—something creative people do not do. Young sailors may "kill time" locked on shipboard in view of Rio de Janeiro (ch. 42 of *White-Jacket*), but after Melville's twenty-fifth year, whatever year that was, he was never bored: creative people are never bored. No thought impels Vine, no work roils inside him, he literally has nothing to do except pass time, and likes to think only about time already past. So he announces his subject and his style: the Palm, and "an invocation free" in "a style sublime, / Yet sad as sad sincerity." This is a substantial invocation—thirty-four lines long. Vine first asks the Palm why it stands there — to make the desert dream of Eden? Then he asks if the Palm claims kinship with Apollo's Palm on Delos — a Palm which ended with the death of the Greek gods, none of whom saved it. He sees it as a pledge of heaven, but precarious, since it hangs "suspended / Over Kedron and the night!" so that it suggests the question: "Shall come the fall? shall time disarm / The grace, the glory of the Palm?" If the Palm falls, "Who then shall take thy office on — / Redeem the waste, and high appear?" Without answering the question, Vine changes direction and takes comfort that the Palm is still fair: "Every age for itself must care." Vine ends with a Poesque injunction to the Palm:

> Braid thy green tresses; let the grim
> Awaiter find thee never dim!
> Serenely still thy glance be sent
> Plumb down from horror's battlement:
> Though the deep Fates be concerting
> A reversion, a subverting,
> Still bear thee like the Seraphim.

After the measured optimism of this injunction, Vine loiters, "lounging on the stair," apparently with the Palm quite off his mind.

Melville was steadily coming to terms with Hawthorne, both the improbably beautiful and mysterious writer who had so fascinated him in the summer of 1850, and for a long time thereafter, and the literary immortal Hawthorne had since become. Vine's character is very gradually clarified in the course of the eighteen thousand lines — not so much a sign of Melville's planning before he began the poem as remarkable evidence of his arriving at his own conclusions in 1870 and through the next years. Melville may have found backing for his iconoclastic view of Hawthorne from a review of *Passages from the French and Italian Note-Books* in the *Nation* (14 March 1872), anonymous, but by the younger Henry James. Under the cloak of anonymity, James ventured a cautiously phrased warning that the "posthumous productivity" (that is, relentless scraping of the bottom of barrels by the family and indefatigable repackaging by the publisher) might ultimately be to the detriment of Hawthorne's fame. The documents in this latest *Passages* James found frankly "superficial":

> His journals throw but little light on his personal feelings, and even less on his genius *per se*. Their general effect is difficult to express. They deepen our sense of that genius, while they singularly diminish our impression of his general intellectual power. There can be no better proof of his genius than that these common daily scribblings should unite so irresistible a charm with

so little distinctive force. They represent him, judged with any real critical rigor, as superficial, uninformed, incurious, inappreciative; but from beginning to end that cast no faintest shadow upon the purity of his peculiar gift.

Hawthorne was indeed an odd case, having "genius" but not "general intellectual power." Nothing like this had been said about Hawthorne's inexplicable allure except what Melville was writing in *Clarel*. James delicately ventured the opinion that "simplicity" was the word that came to mind for Hawthorne's observations abroad: "He looks at things as little as possible in that composite historic light which forms the atmosphere of many imaginations." Hawthorne, for all his antiquarian streak, his love of annals, had no historical sense to compare to Melville's thickly thronged historical memory. Melville was not alone in his revisionist analysis of Hawthorne.

At some time in 1873, despite the reduced income, Melville bought Shelley's *Essays, Letters from Abroad, Translations and Fragments* (London, 1852). He also bought *Songs from the Dramatists*, edited by Robert Bell (London, 1854), in which he checked a stanza on enduring what cannot be avoided, choosing "wise contentment" instead of complaining. Melville was not forgotten. He was mentioned in reviews of books of travel or adventure, especially books about the South Seas. In Honolulu someone found among the papers of the merchant Isaac Montgomery the contract Melville had signed with him on 1 June 1843. The editor of the *Friend* printed it in August 1873 as "A CURIOSITY RELATING TO A LITERARY AUTHOR"—an author who now resided in New York and whose brother was superintendent of the Sailors' Snug Harbor on Staten Island.

[35]

The New Generation, and "Bethlehem"
1874–1875

... Florence finished her quilting before she left. They all came over and staid with me the last week leaving on Wednesday for Boston, we miss them very much. Fortunately we had some young ladies arrive from Charleston to visit us. Maria & Willie opened the house on Monday for a tea party prepared by themselves[,] the last sewing party (of Patchwork) for the season. Hoping we shall have the pleasure of seeing you again in Berkshire.

Abby Lathers to Kate Gansevoort, written from Abby Lodge,
across from Arrowhead, 23 October 1873

WHEN AUNT SUSAN sent a basket of New Year's cakes down to Twenty-sixth Street for the start of 1874, Herman asked Lizzie in her letter of 2 January "to say particularly for him that he was much gratified and that they reminded him of the 'days of his youth' when the chief occupation for himself and the other youngsters on the first day of the year used to be to 'nibble round' their new year's cakes from morning till night." On 14 March, when Lizzie thanked her stepmother for two dollars, she told her that Orville Dewey had preached at All Souls the previous week. Lizzie had spoken to both Dr. Dewey and his wife after the service, and they had seemed very glad to see her. She called at W. C. Bryant's house where the Deweys were staying (Dewey and the poet-editor being Berkshire men and Unitarians), and saw Dewey, who looked "very well" for a man turning eighty. Thirteen years after his funeral oration for the late chief justice, he inquired about Hope Shaw "with much interest" and asked about "all the family." Lizzie had read much about Charles Sumner's death on 11 March and had a pertinent judgmental question for Hope: "Do you know who Mrs. S. is going to marry next?" They had at least "better news from Stanny." He was on a sheep ranch in Merced under the promise of twenty-five dollars a month. George Nourse, Dr. Nourse's son, on the scene in California, was encouraging Stanny with the hope that eventually he would be able to care for sheep on halves then get a flock of his own. Sheep-raising, according to Nourse, was "*now* the most profitable business in California — and if Stanny will only *persevere* he will come out all right." Stanny had never persevered in anything, and after hoping that Sam would write to him or send him a paper, now and then, Lizzie concluded, "I suppose it is very hard work, for Stanny, but *every* thing is hard work."

Milie chose to be given away by her Uncle Thomas at her wedding on 10 June. The wedding was at St. Paul's Memorial Church (completed in 1870) in Edgewater, near the Tompkinsville landing, and the Governor's House was more than adequate for the reception. Lizzie had forewarned Kate Gansevoort Lansing on 22 May that it would be "about such a wedding as Tom's was," and so it proved, except that things were handled badly. Enclosed with each wedding invitation was a card that conveyed other essential information: "Boats leave South Ferry for Tompkinsville at 12 M. Returning every hour. Carriages in waiting." Abby Thurston Lathers gave a benign account the next day to her daughter Julia, saying that on the ferry the Lathers group had encountered "Mrs Brittain & Mrs Fisher, Mrs Melville with Mrs Lansing," but at the landing beer wagons had blocked the carriages, and at the church the wedding party had to wait "for their boquets." Lizzie without Herman: this was a Wednesday, and the deputy inspector had a job. Kate Gansevoort Lansing's letter to her father and stepmother specified that the "Bridal Party" was excessively late, "¾ of an hour." Kitty Melville had walked in with Richie Lathers, Carrie Lathers, and Annie Morewood with their escorts (not family members), Florence with Allie (Alfred) Morewood, Katie Bogart Melville with Willie, then Milie with her Uncle Tom. Afterward the "Bride & Groom — & the four groomsmen & Bridesmaids returned to New Brighton," Kate Gansevoort Lansing wrote to her father and stepmother, but the "rest of the party did not get there until after 2.30 as there was great detention." Things went worse: "a more hungry & tired set of people I never saw, & a good while after our arrival salads & tongue sandwiches Strawberryies & Cream, Champagnes &c — were served to the exhausted guests." The older guests knew that either mother, Sophia Thurston Melville or Sarah Huyler Morewood, would have kept everything moving faster and more smoothly.

According to Kate Lansing, "Every one looked well as they always do. The Melville Clan was strong powerful & very defensive" — defensive against unspecified onslaughts from outsiders. She added that "All are well in 26th St" — meaning the Melvilles but also their guests (Helen, Minnie, and Lottie), while John and Kate Hoadley stayed in the Physician's House and Fanny and Augusta at the Governor's House. For all the fatigue of the guests, the day was pleasant, and there was a formidable regrouping of many of the Thurstons and Melvilles at Twenty-sixth Street, well after Herman's working hours, according to Abby Lathers's letter to Julia and others at Winyah.

Richard Lathers saw to it that the New York *Evening Telegram* ran a vulgar item, "A Recherche Wedding on Staten Island."

From Irving Place on 11 June 1874 Kate reported to Abe on the chat she and Jane had engaged in the previous evening, "about *the Wedding* & affairs in general." For all Kate's shrewdness, Jane had taken her in, and now Kate wrote Abe that "Mrs Allan Melville felt her position yesterday & it was hard not to be noticed as Maria's fathers widow." She judged wrongly, seeing Allan as embarrassed for his daughters rather than by his wife: "I think it must have grieved Allan for he was proud & had for twelve years taught his four daughters to respect & look up to his wife." Jane's story was that the four sisters had liked it better at the Harbor than in New York and that Jane "could not bear the surroundings" at Thirty-fifth Street, so, Kate said, "in breaking that up she unwound the chain—which strands are getting looser & looser & will at length I fear break & unwind entirely." The girls, Lizzie could have told Kate, had never been allowed to live at Thirty-fifth Street: they merely perched there (or, often, with the Lathers family, or some of the Thurstons, or Helen, or the Melville women at Gansevoort) between sessions of boarding school. Kate understood nothing of Jane's deliberate sabotaging of Allan's last Christmases, the selfishness that had pushed even Augusta too far. Kate's excessive grief over Henry kept her vulnerable to Jane's dramatic role as grieving widow, and her feelings toward her own generous stepmother further distorted her perceptions. This new alliance between Kate Lansing and Jane Melville was Milie's loss, and her sisters' loss, and Kate's own loss, for it created an awkwardness between Kate and Lizzie, who knew more than she could say to Kate. A week after the wedding, when the bride and groom had been seen off for England, the older generation of Melville sisters were still around New York. Augusta came in from Staten Island for the fourteenth and fifteenth, as she wrote the Gansevoorts. On Monday, the fifteenth, Kate Hoadley came in, so all the sisters lunched together with Lizzie, and perhaps Herman, with Florence and Kitty there, as well as Herman and Lizzie's daughters. Helen returned to the Harbor with Augusta to prepare for the journey up to Gansevoort, where they would be joined by Allan's three younger daughters. In the aftermath of the wedding Herman punned on Abe's new post as state treasurer, sending word by Cousin Kate (as she wrote Abe on 20 June) that he was surprised Abe would go off on a fishing trip leaving all his *"treasures,"* the most valuable of which was Kate.

At the end of June 1874 Lizzie wrote Kate Lansing her thanks for a suggested medicine: "I have heard of the remedy before, and have tried a quinine preparation by snuffing it up, but never with a 'nasal douche'—I have my medical recipe for the quinine, and think I will get a douche, and try it, as I am suffering much now from the 'June cold.'" The extreme heat was making her feel "so 'used up'" she could only write Kate very briefly. This year Melville went with Lizzie for two weeks in the White Mountains. He could "not tear himself away" from there, he wrote the sisters in Gansevoort, and went directly from the White Mountains to Manhattan, and was back at work by 10 August. New Hampshire was honeymoon territory, and Herman and Lizzie were husband and wife still. Augusta and Fanny heard from Bessie that she (and her sister?) had endured a "hot ride" on the train to New York from somewhere, but had found Melville there before them, and "looking very well after his fortnight among the mountains," so Augusta at Gansevoort assured Kate Lansing on 21 August that "Herman is quite well & enjoyed the White Mountains." At the end of the month Sam Shaw took Lizzie on a trip—probably to the seashore.

Kate and Abe Lansing had moved into 166 Washington Avenue in the last week or ten days of August 1874, down the street from Peter and Susan's Washington Avenue house; then on 28 October Susan Lansing Gansevoort died. The next day Herman wrote a note to Uncle Peter to assure him of his and Lizzie's "true sympathies," adding: "how we share in feelings which on such an occasion it is hardly for words to express.—May God keep you, and console you." He also wrote the next day to Abe, Aunt Susan's nephew by blood: "All of us here—Lizzie and I particularly—sympathise and mourn with you. My recollections of Aunt Susan are of a kind to make me keenly alive to the loss which has befallen Uncle Peter as well as all others united by blood or socially to so true a woman." After the funeral a new routine was established, and Kate as usual did her duty, carrying out her late stepmother's wishes to provide black silk dresses for the Melville girls, and being thoughtful enough to ask Abe to make the checks out in the girls' names, "as it will save Cousin Herman the trouble of either endorsing the drafts or going to the Bank." (Early in 1877 Lizzie wrote Kate that they were making new black silk dresses for the girls, the first they had possessed in two or more years; this would mean that in 1876, when the publication of *Clarel* cost $1300 or so, the Melville daughters did not get new silk dresses, an injustice Bessie may have marked with resignation but young Fanny with asperity.) Kate had no doubt that her grief for Susan was shared. Augusta wrote her on 7 November that Aunt Susan was "still ever present" in her thoughts, "& Fanny's too"; she assured Kate, "Your and our great loss, I cannot forget one moment, it is ever present with me, & my heart mourns with a never ceasing mourning for one who was so tenderly loved by us all." Confident that they would all "meet again on the other shore," Augusta resolved: "let us then follow her in her devoted, unselfish life, & try hourly to live out the faith, hope, & charity which she so truly impersonated."

The Gansevoorts being adept at inventing trouble, Peter would not accept that his wife had died under the best possible conditions, and Kate was not allowed to mourn normally for the only mother she had ever known. Peter reproached Kate for not being with Susan when she died, then would not listen to her reply, so on 13 December she wrote him a letter designed to make both of them feel even more miserable than they did already. Their cousin Edward Hun "had no right to give *Hartshorn* & *Morphine* to any one who had tendency to *disease of the heart*, of which Dr. Hun says Mother died." Dr. Hun wrote her almost fiercely on 21 January 1875, about Susan and also Henry, for Kate had rejected his and other medical opinion on Henry's illness: "you have on account of some notion of mistaken or bad management, persistently treated me with rudeness and disrespect and have indulged in improper remarks which have pained me on your account more than on my own, and have been the cause of much mortification to your friends." Another grievance was that one of Abe's sisters, Aunt Susan's niece Anna, had in the last hours inveigled Kate into absenting herself from the death chamber so *she*, not Kate, would be with Susan at the last moment. Kate protested: "I *did not desert* my dear Mother, *either*, that *Tuesday* or the night she died or the morning she was found dead—I came as you know a number of times that day to see Mother[—]every time Anna Lansing sat there & gave me no chance to talk to Mother or find out about her." Kate's moans, justifications, and reproaches were extreme; she suffered more than Cordelia, and more noisily. This episode colors our understanding of a later occasion when Kate took offense at something Herman did or said: he may not have behaved very badly at all.

At Thanksgiving 1874 Lizzie and the girls were in Boston, for Sam Shaw noted in his diary on 26 November: "Family Dinner. All my father's descendants present except Stanwix—Party in the evening—Mother unexpectedly well and bright." Herman Melville was there. On this visit, if not earlier, Lizzie went against her husband's explicit wishes and confided that he was writing poetry. She managed to alert everyone to the fact that her husband was in a precarious state of mind because of his literary activity and that the family might sooner or later have to endure the shame of another onslaught of reviews, a serious problem all along: it had been two decades since Lem wrote to Sam that Herman had written more than enough books for his reputation. Everyone missed Stanwix, and some weeks later Hope wrote him so: "Last Thanksgiving day you were wished with us. You little know how much we think of you." Before Christmas he wrote her from San Francisco, typically confessing his follies and his having been "deaf to the counsel of older heads": "Eighteen months in California! and though I have had more experience seen more of the ways of the world, and learned more about this State since I came here, I am still stationary, and sailing in about the same boat as when I left home; but I hope to retrieve the past, & for better times in the future." Hope wrote him by the end of the year, confident, like him: "the worst is over — You are beginning a new life — Perseverance is my *motto* & never be *discouraged*." Having decided she was a pondering woman, she offered her own Unitarian thought to cheer him after his intensely Calvinistic training at Gansevoort: "I am delighted that you attend Church — I think the essence of Religion consists in being intimate with our *Heavenly Father*." For Christmas 1874 Herman gave Elizabeth *The Handbook of Engraved Gems*, by C. W. King, M.A. (London, 1866), and to his daughter Frances he gave Jakob L. K. Grimm's *German Popular Stories* (London, 1868). Peter continued the tradition of sending out baskets of New Year's cake, what Hoadley on 27 December 1874 called this "thoughtful continuance of dear Aunt Susan's bounty." There may have been a Christmas gathering at the Harbor.

Over the holidays Lizzie remained uneasy about having broken Herman's secret at Thanksgiving 1874, and recurred to the topic in her 9 March 1875 letter to her stepmother: "Herman is pretty well and very busy — pray do not mention to any one that he is writing poetry — you know how such things spread and he would be very angry if he knew I had spoken of it — and of course I have not, except in confidence to you and the family." She went on with still worse news: "We have been in much fear lest his pay should be reduced, as so many others have, but it has not been, so far — it is hard enough to get along at all." Lizzie was simultaneously reminding Hope of her having confided to the family that Herman was writing poetry again and reminding her that the news was to be kept secret for fear of greatly angering him. Herman writing poetry was to be dreaded and Herman angry was to be dreaded, but Lizzie always needed sympathy, and she was an inveterate confider. In 1874, this year of Stanwix's wandering, Milie's wedding, Kate's wedding, Aunt Susan's death, Herman was indeed writing poetry. He was writing what might be called great poetry. Part 4 of *Clarel*, "Bethlehem," is notable for the introduction of two scarred New World characters, the part-Indian Ungar, a Confederate veteran who has hired himself to Egyptians and Turks, and a Mexican, Don Hannibal, who has lost an arm and a leg in fighting for Mexican freedom. The New World has maimed them both, and exiled them to the Old World. Ungar is quick to identify another source of maiming in industrialization, whether in the young United States or the old England: "How many Hughs of Lincoln, say, / Does Mammon in his mills, to-day, / Crook, if he do not crucify?" ("The Shepherds' Dale," pt. 4, canto 9). Taking up a theme already pushed by Rolfe and others, Ungar fervently denounces the leveling down of American culture (where what we have is "the mean intelligence / That knows to read, and but to read — / Not think," 4.10). Ungar rails against American national crimes (4.9):

> *As cruel as a Turk:* Whence came
> That proverb old as the crusades?
> From Anglo-Saxons. What are they?
> Let the horse answer, and blockades
> Of medicine in civil fray!
> The Anglo-Saxons — lacking grace
> To win the love of any race;
> Hated by myriads dispossessed
> Of rights — the Indians East and West.
> These pirates of the sphere! grave looters —
> Grave, canting, Mammonite freebooters,
> Who in the name of Christ and Trade
> (Oh, bucklered forehead of the brass!)
> Deflower the world's last sylvan glade!

Ungar speaks for the others in condemning the "impieties of 'Progress' " ("Ungar and Rolfe," 4.21) and identifying an America which, having lost the lofty republican ideals of Washington and Jefferson, would soon give "New confirmation of the fall / Of Adam," and where one could view

> Myriads playing pygmy parts —
> Debased into equality:
> In glut of all material arts
> A civic barbarism may be;
> Man disennobled — brutalized
> By popular science — Atheized
> Into a smatterer —
> . . . .
>   Yet knowing all self need to know
> In self's base little fallacy;
> Dead level of rank common-place:
> An Anglo-Saxon China, see,
> May on your vast plains shame the race
> In the Dark Ages of Democracy.

The other American pilgrims (including Vine) do not rebuke Ungar, but rather agree that in the United States mankind has squandered the last inheritance, so that they might well cry: "To Terminus build fanes! / Columbus ended earth's romance: / No New World to mankind remains!"

The last long passage about Vine is in canto 15, "Symphonies." Clarel and Vine are together "in friendly neighborhood" after the young Franciscan Salvaterra has memorably confronted Ungar: "True sign you bear: your sword's a cross" ("Soldier and Monk," 4.14). For once Vine speaks words without an "equivocal tone / Freakish" and without leaving much for his listener to infer. In "unconstraint," his "chord" moved again, as his "long slack" chord had tightened in response to Rolfe, Vine says: " 'Tis very much / The cold fastidious heart to touch / This way; nor is it mere address / That so could move one's silver chord. / How he transfigured Ungar's sword!" Vine wonders if Salvaterra is deluding himself into serving in "melancholy's dale / Of mirage" — literally in Bethlehem, figuratively in the service of the Catholic Church. Then Vine offers to interpret Salvaterra by "a swallow-skim / Over distant time," to Mexico, where a Franciscan "Saw in a bud of happy dower / Whose stalk entwined the tropic tree, / Emblems of Christ's last agony," and named it "the passion-flower." Struck anew by the "beauty in that sad conceit," Vine suggests of Salvaterra that "where'er he turns / For him this passion-flower burns; / And all the world is elegy." Vine makes over Salvaterra into something like his own image (earlier, Vine has been willing to mix Bible with folklore just as he has been willing to mix history with fiction). This long period of "unconstraint" continues a few more moments before it breaks off: "A green knoll is to you and me / But pastoral, and little more: / To him 'tis even Calvary / Where feeds the Lamb. This passion-flower— / But list!" The reader is irresistibly reminded of Vine's distractedness at the River Jordan—"But hark—a bird?" Here the interruption is formidable enough, the rising of organ music, but the fact remains that Vine's single attempt at open speech has ended in his interrupting himself because of an external distraction: he can't keep his focus on anything.

What Melville shows about Vine is that while he may once have possessed genius, he does not possess much of it when we meet him. Melville by this time had put himself through prolonged academic sessions in aesthetics, most intensely in early 1862. And during the course of the poem Melville shows Vine's aesthetic sensibility as deteriorating. He shows Vine changing, for the worse, reflecting Melville's altering comprehension of Hawthorne. Reading some of the *Twice-Told Tales* early in 1851, Melville had recognized an earlier vintage superior to *Mosses from an Old Manse:* the early Hawthorne was the greater Hawthorne. Despite the ecstatic essay on the *House of the Seven Gables* that Melville wrote for the *Pittsfield Secret Review*, he had not changed his mind. While the posthumous works Sophia and the Hawthorne children put into print in the mid-1860s and 1870s were patently more laxly written than the great early tales, none of Hawthorne's frustrated laments about the death of his inspiration got into print, none of those baffled, despairing admissions of mental collapse that infiltrate the manuscripts of his late romances. Hawthorne had moaned in the "Etherege" draft of the "Ancestral Footsteps" manuscripts: "All this amounts to just nothing. I don't advance a step." "I can't possibly make this out, though it keeps glimmering before me." "'Twont do. Oh, heavens!" "What unimaginable nonsense!" "Try back again." Even without knowing such secret evidence of intellectual and physical decline, Melville, having known the man, had proof enough of decline in the infantile passages of the *Dolliver Romance*, so cruelly exposed in the *Atlantic Monthly*.

After this point Vine fades out of the poem; there is little more about him until the rapidly glossed over departure of Rolfe, Vine, and Derwent from Jerusalem, each of them loath to leave Clarel in his grief at the news of Ruth's death. In "Passion Week" (4.32) Melville says that Clarel from Vine had "caught new sense / Developed through fate's pertinence"; apparently, Clarel in his own pain guesses better at Vine's own secret pain. Vine's elusively powerful presence, whatever its mysterious source, still makes itself felt to Clarel at the end. Fascinating though Vine is as a psychological portrait of a non-practicing artist-figure (one of the "non-producers," a phrase Melville employed around 1876 or 1877 of men who sit in Madison Square), his greatest interest, after all, is biographical. Walter Bezanson finely says that Melville's depiction of Vine shows that he had decided that "beneath his shy and opulent serenity Hawthorne was scared." Melville also came to understand—during the years he worked on *Clarel*—that Hawthorne, simply by writing well, looking as gorgeous as any Romantic poet could, and keeping silent—had been granted unearned credit. The implications of Vine's longer speeches and thoughts are that Melville had decided that Hawthorne had not merely burnt out as an artist at an early age; in later life Hawthorne had coasted on an unmerited reputation for moral force, not to say deep intelligence. Given the complexity of Melville's need to include in the poem the autobiographical "tournament of merits" between Vine and Rolfe, given the anguish of his loss of reputation and career just when Hawthorne's own renown was becoming enormously inflated, it is immensely pleasing that Melville could play as fairly as he did. Play fair he did, portraying the glamour and mysterious power of Vine's person, then letting Vine's actions and words speak for themselves, allowing the reader at last to perceive the discrepancy between the way Vine is introduced and his ultimate status in the poem, between, on the one hand, the admiring response Vine evokes from several characters, and, on the other hand, his deeds and words. For Vine's deeds often reveal an erratic staginess and contempt for himself and others, and his words, however prettily melancholy they are, reflect the shallowness and discontinuity of his mind—the mind of a man "Whose race of thought long since was run— / For whom the spots enlarge that blot the golden sun" (2.33). In reality, Melville had concluded, Hawthorne had none of Melville's own "strange power to reach the sinuosities of a thought" (young William Butler's phrasing in his review of *Moby-Dick* in the Washington *National Intelligencer*), let alone the ability to move cogently from one gnarled thought to another.

Sometime in 1875, more likely than early 1876, George Parsons Lathrop, the husband of Rose Hawthorne, the baby born at Lenox in May 1851, wrote Melville (according to his statement in 1890) asking "for permission to use two or three letters" in his forthcoming *A Study of Hawthorne*. He claimed to have "received his consent given with a sort of gloomy reluctance," and in fact quoted from one letter only, the 16 April 1851 letter in which Melville took on the role of the critic reviewing *The House of the Seven Gables* for the *Pittsfield Secret Review*. The irony of having his letters used in a study of Hawthorne, the irony of being now so belatedly associated with Hawthorne in print, could not have been lost upon the man who had lavished some of the most elusive passages of his poem upon a Hawthorne-like character during the past years. Melville was being moved from the audience to a walk-on role in Hawthorne's life and his posthumous fame. When Lathrop's letter came, probably early in 1875, Melville had no prospect of publishing his own retrospective analysis of Hawthorne: he might as well have been writing *Clarel* for the *Twenty-sixth Street Secret Review*.

Augusta and Fanny opened the Gansevoort house in the summer of 1875, after it had been boarded up for half a year. At the end of April and early May Helen visited the Harbor then went to Twenty-sixth Street, where on 1 May she reported to Kate Lansing on Herman's daughters: "Bessie & Fannie are very busy preparing spring garments, to put on, when the sudden change all are anticipating in the temperature, arrives." On 19 June, before the summer influx of visitors to the Mansion House started, Harriet Elizabeth Bayard Van Rensselaer, widow of Stephen Van Rensselaer, died in the Manor House. Lizzie's 7 June 1875 letter to Kate says she was late replying because of her current servant crisis: "I have been so upturned in my kitchen department by Maggy's leaving and so hard worked to get on at all that I hardly know 'whether I stand on my head or my heels'. I have the second candidate for the vacancy now on trial (the first one's snuff-taking habit being a positive objection) and I don't know when I shall ever feel settled again." A smoking husband was one thing, but a snuff-dipping cook was another. Lizzie reported to Kate that Stanny was due home. She was, as always, ready to believe that this time things would be different for her son, and she had long since perfected her story about Stanny. Favorable opportunity always arose (a "very favorable opening for his going back to his old business, *mechanical* dentistry offered itself"). Stanny always was about to learn from experience and display a new character. Now he "had undergone a very marked change in his ideas and purposes, born of his own experience (which is the best teacher)." Stanny was always diffident and shy, fearful of what his relatives would say, but he was given an excuse for returning ("He naturally feels some compunctions about coming back no better off in fortunes than when he left, & fears his friends may look coldly on him—but I told him I should say, and I want it to be distinctly understood that *we sent for him*"). He would need clothing, something like Henry's coat, which was a little too tight in the shoulders for Herman but which Lizzie would not give to Stanny if Kate had any scruples at all about his wearing it instead of Herman. On 24 June 1875 Stanwix Melville returned home in the steamer *Acapulco*. As Lizzie wrote to her stepmother (20 July), he soon was very well ("with the exception of a little bowel trouble") and had a good appetite. He went off to work at "his old place at the Dentists," and reported the first bad news, that "this is the dull season when every one (that can get away)" is out of town, so there was not much to do.

In her 20 July letter to Hope Lizzie said that when the heat allowed it she and Bessie were working as hard as they could to get their "things ready to make a decent appearance among strangers"; the Melvilles' daughter Fanny was in Pittsfield, "taking her vacation." Lizzie, perhaps alone, went over to Elizabeth, New Jersey, where the young Morewoods were living until they opened Arrowhead, and visited Milie for "a day or two," Fanny Priscilla wrote Kate Lansing on 30 July. Lizzie and Fanny were going to Boston on 13 August, a Friday, passing Sunday with Hope and then Monday going to Jefferson, not North Conway—to coincide with the predicted arrival of her rose cold. Lizzie and Bessie were "quite worn out" and longing to get away from New York, Lizzie wrote her stepmother on 8 August. This is the first year when concern for Bessie's health is explicit: "she looks very pale & thin, but please do not tell her so—I hope she will recruit soon—We have all had a very hard summer." That presumably means Lizzie and Bessie, and perhaps Herman. Fanny was not there, having been in Pittsfield with Milie from the middle of July, and planning to return to New York on 10 August, to keep house for Stanwix, whom Lizzie called "quite well." Herman had left on 7 August for Gansevoort, for his two weeks of vacation.

With Stanwix home for the moment, and the poem done at last, Melville began planning his vacation with more than usual zest. He stopped at Albany on the way to Gansevoort. Abe had offered to come to the wharf to meet him, but Melville had refused grandiloquently on 5 August: "When the Shah of Persia or the Great Khan of Tartary comes to Albany by the night-boat— *him* meet on the wharf and with salvoes of artillery—but not a Custom House Inspector." Besides, he was disembarking so early on a Sunday morning, 8 August, that he would find his breakfast before arriving at Uncle Peter's, since his appetite would be "clamorous at an hour too early for any rational household to satisfy." He was brimming with secret triumph, having outdone Milton's *Paradise Lost* twice over in length, having outdone Wordsworth's *Excursion* twice over in sheer interest, having rivaled Browning's *The Ring and the Book* in gnarled, toughly intellectual poetry. As usual, he was traveling light: "As for my plunder or impedimenta, I shall carry nothing but what I take in my hand." But once again he knew he was one of the Divine Inert, and in denying that he was the Great Khan of Tartary he was recalling the night he read Hawthorne's letter giving him the crown of India. At some time in the last months or years he had come to terms with both his ambition and his involvement with Hawthorne. He was at an equilibrium for the first time in many years. In his Milton he had marked Capel Lofft's claim that the poet had begun *Paradise Lost* "in his forty-eighth year, and finished it in his fifty-seventh," and marked also reports and speculations about when the lines flowed most readily, "from the autumnal equinox to the vernal," or "in the spring and autumn." Whatever his own seasonal variations in productivity, Melville had begun his great epic at fifty and finished it at fifty-six, close enough that he could feel a kinship with Milton.

Melville had been unable to prevent his wife from telling secrets, but now with the completion of *Clarel* he was ready to talk about it, discreetly, with his Uncle Peter in Albany. Uncle Peter had hoped for almost two decades that his nephew's visit to the Holy Land would result in some popular travel account. On 8 or 9 August 1875, inspired by the spirit of Aunt Susan, Melville said later, Peter "made known" his intention to subsidize the publication of the poem, and Melville then spontaneously expressed his sentiments of gratitude and affection. Helping Herman now, as he had more or less tried to do in 1837 with a bland letter to the governor, deprived Peter of nothing he needed for the rest of his life, and pleased Kate. Despite the little transaction between Peter Gansevoort and his nephew, the family book in 1875 was not a poem that lay complete in manuscript. The book that obsessed Kate Lansing and that damaged the health of Hoadley, bedeviled just then with huge financial losses, was Kate's memorial volume for Henry. She repaid Hoadley the money he laid out for supplies for the book, when he billed her, but it was a time when waiting for a check from her, even for five hundred dollars, put a strain on him. Still suffering from the Panic which had begun the previous fall, in the spring he "passed through a very severe financial trial," which almost broke his heart, he said, and left his property "so locked up in unavailable assets, largely real estate," that he welcomed any income, however small. He had much money in Treadwell & Company, which failed, as he told Kate Lansing on 11 June 1874: "The failure of Treadwell & Co. has inflicted on me a heavy loss, — just how much I don't know, — $15,000. to $22,000, (depending on whether certain machinery have been sold or not,) — with probably some salvage." Sorry for his plight or not, Kate drove Hoadley ferociously on the memorial volume, so that he made an infinite number of suggestions and decisions, most of which were qualified or countermanded several times. There were questions of the type, whether the page would be bordered with rule in either black or red, questions of photographs and engraving and heliotypes—matters on which Herman Melville had never had control in any of his books. Kate acknowledged on 19 May 1875: "I know you have had great care & trouble with this book & only wish I could help you—The heavy part is done—& now the finishing I fear will monopolize more time than you can spare before you go away for the summer—rather leave part unfinished than neglect your own business & personal duties—it ought to be a secondary thing in your labors—Thanks sincere & true for your precious time & strength given in my behalf." But she continued to hound him.

Melville arrived at Gansevoort by the evening train on 9 August 1875, carrying macaroons from Kate Lansing and carrying (if not sharing) the news that his poem would be published. He was understandably content, for he could tell himself that he would never have to work so hard again, however long he lived. Augusta later (9 October) wrote to Hope Shaw that his visit had been "charming," and added: "I dont know when I have seen him better." Three sisters were at the Mansion House, Helen having timed her visit to correspond with Herman's, and staying on until late in the month, when she left for a week at Arrowhead before returning to Brookline. With his sisters around him, Herman relaxed, "lounging on the sofa" (a phrase he always associated with the poet Gray) in the room they all still called Mama's parlor. While lounging there he wrote Kate Lansing to persuade her to discard an engraving of Henry from her memorial volume. The letter is interesting not only for its evidence of his mixture of tact with forthrightness in a delicate matter but also for its hint at the tastefulness of the Mansion House under his mother's and his sisters' rule. "Michael, the angel of truth," he said, had inspired this note to Kate:

> my eye chanced to fall on a photograph of Henry in a gilt frame hanging under my mother's portrait. I took it down & brought it to the window, & looked at it.—
>
> Now let me say, that the engraving you showed me of Henry, meant for the book, is detestable. Also, I have seen other pictures, claiming to be he, which do not look like him, and are a caricature of him. The picture for the book is the one that I referred to at the outset. It is he, and is not bad-looking, and it has character.—

Fanny had told him "that Mr Hoadley much dislikes the engraving. There's confirmation," so Melville told Kate, "Stop tinkering, and do the right thing,

I pray you, and impute to the right motive my outspokenness." Tinker Kate did, going to the engraver (as she wrote Hoadley on 10 August) and having him work on the image: "It has been well studied an Artist here has made changes in the nose — eye-brows — & moustache, & all of us — Papa, Fanny, A.L, & I think them all imprvts" (improvements). On the twenty-fourth she enclosed to Hoadley the "characteristic note from Cousin Herman," telling its own story. She enclosed a photograph from which a new engraving might be cut, from an artist in Boston or in New York, offering infinite possibilities, and commenting at last on the photograph: "This Photo — was taken in 1864 while in command near Washington and is a military picture." Poor Hoadley. He could always (her letter of 23 September) have the photograph engraved and they could "see which of the two suits best."

The East River bore a different look than on any other return to New York: the Brooklyn tower of the Brooklyn Bridge had been completed in May, the New York tower in July. After Herman had returned to New York and Helen had left for Pittsfield, Augusta wrote Abe Lansing on 26 August about their having been importuned all summer by "dear Allan's girls" to come to Arrowhead themselves, but that they had both felt they could not "leave home again so soon." Whatever her inadequacies, Jane was plainly not depriving her stepdaughters of chances to see their aunts: anything to get them off her hands. The family feelings ran deep. As Augusta said, she and Fanny both were missing Helen "terribly every hour in the day," although they were glad she was with the girls at Arrowhead. This seems to have been a vacation at the Mansion House for lounging, not for riding or driving or playing croquet — a quiet, nurturing double-handful of days in the house filled with memories of Uncle Herman and Maria. When Herman was home, Tom and Katie took the ferry over and found him "looking very well," a condition he shared with his daughter Fanny after her visit to Arrowhead (as Augusta reported to Kate Lansing on 26 August).

Melville not only went out of his way to see that his blood cousin was memorialized suitably, he emphatically expressed his admiration of Kate's new husband, who had just endeared himself further to the Melville sisters by sending two baskets of peaches. In her 26 August letter, Augusta told Kate: "Oh, I wish you could have heard all that Herman said about him. I must tell you of one remark he made in speaking of what constituted a *true* gentleman. 'There is Abraham Lansing — He is a gentleman, *instinctively* he is the gentleman.'" On the basis of Herman's renewed praise, Augusta said to Abe (in her 26 August letter to him): "I do not know any one he thinks more highly of than he does of you. It is quite refreshing to ones soul to hear one gentleman speak of another as he does of you, Abe." For years Hoadley had been the relative by marriage whom Melville had most reason to respect, and now, with Malcolm dead and Stanwix seldom around long enough for anyone to expect him to be there the next month, Melville found comfort in the generosity and courtesy of his cousin's husband, of that next half-generation he had little familiarity with. What it came down to was that Abe Lansing was as unlike the arrogant, contemptuous, and malicious young Lem Shaw as an in-law could be. And Kate needed all the comfort she could receive. As late as 28 October 1875 Augusta wrote Kate, consoling her on the anniversary of her stepmother's death: "We were so glad to hear that your dear father was able to enjoy Mr Hoadley's little visit, & hear the Appendix read, & look at the Index. We were much interested in them. How I long to see that book out. What a beautiful volume it is going to make, and that touching tender appendix seems the fitting Crown."

On 25 August 1875, while Lizzie and Bessie were still "enjoying the mountain air at Jefferson," Melville received from Abe a check for $1200, which he had written for Uncle Peter. The next day Melville wrote: "And now, My Dear Uncle, in receiving this generous gift from you, so much enhanced by the circumstances, I feel the same sentiments which I expressed to you in person at Albany when you so kindly made known your intention. I will not repeat them here; but only pray God to bless you, and have you in His keeping." In early October Kate Hoadley came to the Mansion House, and during her visit went down to Albany with her sister Fanny to visit Cousin Kate. On 8 October Herman asked Cousin Kate to pass on an invitation to his sisters: "both must come down & see us before leaving for the East"—pretty clear indication that he was not already deeply involved in preparing his poem for publication.

Lizzie may have gone home for Thanksgiving, for on 28 December George Wales wrote to Kate Lansing that Lizzie and her daughter Fanny had dined with him ("It was only a few days before I received your letter that Mrs Herman Melville and Fanny were dining here and she told us how feeble your venerable father had been"). Tom and Katie arrived at Gansevoort the day after Thanksgiving, judging from Augusta's letter to Kate Lansing of 27 November. There was little to be thankful for at Twenty-sixth Street. On 3 December a memorandum went out from the Treasury Department in Washington to the New York Custom House, ordering cuts in salaries, all 282 inspectors to be given only $3.60 a day instead of $4.00. This cut in pay, after the loss of income from Lizzie's property in Boston, pointed up the irony of Melville's position—or his sheer selfishness, as it seemed to his daughter Frances. Melville had money in the bank! For he had at once deposited the check Abe had written for Uncle Peter "in a Savings Bank, there to remain till needed for the purpose designed." He had money in the bank while his children wore Kate's old clothes. (In 1875 Tom requested a raise of a thousand dollars, and received it, making his salary four thousand dollars, a thousand more than his father-in-law received as the Harbor's physician.)

Two days before Christmas Katie wrote to Kate Lansing that she had "been constantly occupied with Christmas work, now that is about over and the gladsome Day is very near." She resolutely called it "such a bright and happy season to me, 'the merriest of the year,' and full of sweet recollections," and hoped that Kate despite her mourning might "experience the love and peace the dear Saviour can impart." The year's most festive Christmas was the one Augusta gave at the Mansion House for the Sunday school children, and which she described to Kate and Abe on the twenty-ninth in a letter containing sidelights on the characters of the sisters. She wished "for the inspiration of a *poet*" so she might do justice to the description of their "*first S. S. Xmas Tree!* Transport yourselves to *Gansevoort* now! — It is Xmas Day! Snow has fallen during the night. Two ladies [Augusta and Fanny] are seated at breakfast in the south parlor." She described the way she and Fanny entertained eighty guests, the first floor of the house "hung with wreathes, & garlands, & waving vines & holly (pepper pods) for the mistletoe":

> The lights burn brightly, the chandelier throws down a glow upon the "Colored Paris Views" on the opera porte folio, with its huge stereoscope, round which is gathered a group of the older ones.... A bell sounds! & the *three* hall doors open as if with one hand. The glories of the Gansevoort S. S. Xmas Tree burst upon the dazzled eyes of the little ones! (The little candles twinkled like stars) with its golden balls, & bright reflectors; its waving flags & gorgeous cornucopias; its beautiful bon-bon boxes & its lovely chromos; its colored picture books & its loaded boughs! The children stand spell bound!

But the tract-delivering girl of Lansingburgh was not one to let childish awe and lust at aesthetic splendor stay in the way of revealed truth. The eyes of the children were "directed to the 'star of Bethlehem'" high on the eastern wall, and they were told "the story of the Babe of Bethlehem" and asked if they had no gifts for the baby Jesus. "Yes, *hearts* of gold, give Him *those*. He gives *Himself* to you." They were allowed to gather fruits under the tree, but the lesson was not over: "Then high over their heads 'the rod' is held! 'Children what is this?' 'A whip.'" After indoctrination in theology and warnings that a whipping might await the villains of "*sad* stories of broken glass in church, & S. School; of books torn, & walls & benches disfigured, & many other sad things," Augusta, "'Shepherdess of the Lambs,'" took her position at the tree "to distribute the cornucopias & boxes of candy." Afterward the sisters distributed New Year's cakes for 1876 along with their good wishes before the sleighs drove up to carry off the guests. "So ends the

Gansevoort S. S. First Xmas tree!" The local children were thus treated and taught, but in the long run what should have mattered to everyone in the family was the quiet little Stanwix who had been exiled to the Mansion House for many months when it was not so glorious a place and he was a part-Unitarian little vessel into which Augusta had poured the Calvinism of her Dutch ancestors and her cousin Stephen Van Rensselaer, the son of the "last" Patroon. Before the end of December 1875 Stanwix, twenty-four years old, deprived of his older brother, restless, hopelessly confused, incapable of purposeful behavior, left for San Francisco, bearing his "heart of gold" to the Golden State.

[36]

Clarel

Melville's Centennial Epic, 1876

A "cynic," perhaps, you might call him, a rover at heart, he knew people only too well, used to say I was told, there was no such thing as gratitude, the word even was not mentioned in the bible.

Charlotte Hoadley to Victor Hugo Paltsits, 7 January 1947

BEFORE THE END OF 1875, amid the immense effort to get *Clarel* into shape for a typesetter to follow, Melville had begun negotiations with G. P. Putnam's Sons to print, bind, and distribute his poem. He would be spending the money as Uncle Peter had wanted, but his daughter Fanny, for one, saw it as spending money on himself, and even Lizzie was acutely aware that he was laying out such an enormous amount of money just as he was earning less every day. Melville had not been acting with any special haste in these arrangements, but on the morning of 4 January 1876 he received a letter from Augusta warning him that Uncle Peter was dying, and that day, by previous appointment, he completed arrangements for the publication of *Clarel*. His intention was to publish the poem anonymously, but word spread among the New York press and on 12 January among the "Literary Notes" in the *Tribune* was the news, surely unwelcome at Twenty-sixth Street, that a "narrative and descriptive poem on the Holy Land, by Herman Melville, is in press by G. P. Putnam's Sons." Peter died the day Melville was at Putnam's, and on the same evening Melville received the news in a telegram from Abe. Melville wrote him: "Uncle is released from his suffering. — *In pace*. — The event happens at a time which brings it home to me most sensibly, since, as it happens, only to-day I made arrangements for that publication which he (inspired by the spirit of Aunt Susan) enabled me to effect." The parenthetical comment on Aunt Susan was delicate, since she had been Abe's aunt by blood.

For the funeral on Saturday, 8 January, Melville went up for the day and returned the same evening. He found Albany in mourning, Kate and Abe having decreed that "the flag upon the mast surmounting the hotel," Stanwix Hall, would float at half-mast. At the funeral were the "officers and staff of the Burgesses Corps, in full uniform; the members of the 'Old Guard,' in citizens' dress, of which the deceased was a member." Prominent mourners included Robert H. Pruyn and Howard Townsend, the husband of Justine Van Rensselaer Townsend. The body was "enclosed in a rosewood casket bearing a solid silver plate, and floral decorations were tastily placed about it." The pallbearers, among them a nephew of James Fenimore Cooper and a Van Rensselaer cousin, "all wore large plaited white sashes of ancient style, which were especially provided for the occasion." Kate did things right, Peter being notorious for favoring an old-fashioned white cravat despite polite ridicule. The funeral services were conducted at the North Dutch Church, then the body was conveyed to the Albany Rural Cemetery. "P" wrote a long article which the *Argus* printed on Friday and the *Evening Journal* reprinted on the day of the funeral, too late for Melville to pick up a copy before he caught the train home. Tom and Katie were there, and stayed on until the tenth, in Kate and Abe's house, across the street from Uncle Peter's. Kate as usual saw to the dissemination of newspapers, sending Herman a copy of the *Evening Journal* with the article by "P." Word got back to Kate through Lizzie and Augusta in their mid-January letters that Herman had said gratefully that "it told him many things he did not know" concerning family history.

About this time, Melville saw a new advertisement for "*The Refugee*; by Herman Melville," and on 28 January 1876 he wrote to the editor of the New York *World*: "I have never written any work by that title. In connection with that title Peterson Brothers employ my name without authority, and notwithstanding a remonstrance conveyed to them long ago." Grieving for Peter, annoyed by Peterson, annoyed by the *Tribune*, Melville began the formidable task of seeing his poem into print. The process disrupted the household at Twenty-sixth Street more than anything since Malcolm's suicide, and required not only Melville's but also his wife's obsessive attention, and even required some help from Bessie and Frances as well. Soon after the funeral Augusta decided to come to see Herman, but Lizzie wrote her that Herman could not have her at Twenty-sixth Street under the present circumstances, and she went to Tom's instead. Tom met her at the depot and escorted her to the Harbor through intense cold, fierce wind, and "immense" dust—altogether the worst journey she had made to the Island. Augusta was sick. She had just finished unpacking her trunks when Lizzie came, miserable at not inviting her to Twenty-sixth Street. Once Lizzie saw Augusta, she decided to stay overnight. Augusta wrote Kate Lansing: "Lizzie is seated at my side reading one of Edward Barrett's books." (The 1863 *Dead Reckoning, or Day's Work?*) Lizzie sent her love, as did Tom and Katie.

Lizzie was so diplomatic that Augusta did not take offense at not being asked to stay with her and Herman, and Herman's sister Fanny did not sense that much was amiss on Twenty-sixth Street, for she soon suggested that Kate Lansing might visit there. Having been too discreet in her letter to Augusta, Lizzie now corrected any misapprehension she had created. She warned Kate off with a public letter and a private letter on 2 February. The first, which she let Herman see, was frank enough about their preoccupation:

> I have just received Fanny's letter [suggesting Kate's visit] and hasten to reply that I am sorry it so happens just now that we cannot receive any visitor, not even Augusta and Fanny. The book is going through the press, and every minute of Herman's time and mine is devoted to it—the mere mechanical work of reading proof &c is so great and absorbing. You know dear Kate, how happy Herman and I always are to have you come here freely, and make yourself perfectly at home, and will I am sure understand the exigency of seeming want of hospitality at this time. Just as soon as the stress is over, I will let you know & then hope you will come down and make us a good visit. We are so sorry to hear that Augusta is ill, & hope that Fanny's good nursing will soon set her right again—
>
> Herman sends love and so do we all—Ever your affectionate Cousin Lizzie.

She added across the first page: "Excuse this plebeian paper!" Then she wrote a second, secret letter indicating that the household was not merely disrupted but was in a near-frenzied state:

> I have written you a note that Herman could see, as he wished, but want you to know how painful it is for me to write it, and also to have to give the real cause. The fact is, that Herman, poor fellow, is in such a frightfully nervous state, & particularly now with such an added strain on his mind, that I am actually *afraid* to have any one here for fear that he will be upset entirely, & not be able to go on with the printing. He was not willing to have even his own sisters here, and I had to write Augusta before she left Albany to that effect—that was the reason she changed her plan, and went to Tom's. If ever this dreadful *incubus* of a *book* (I call it so because it has undermined all our happiness) gets off Herman's shoulders I do hope he may be in better mental health—but at present I have reason to feel the gravest concern & anxiety about it—to put it in mild phrase—please do not speak of it—you know how such things are exaggerated—& I will tell you more when I see you—which I hope will be before long. You know how I enjoy your visits— And I count on your affection for us, not to say your good sense, to take this as you should & in no wise feel hurt at it—Rather pity & pray for yr ever affectionate Cousin Lizzie.

What Kate knew of earlier phases of the Melvilles' marriage was limited, but she would have taken "all our happiness" to mean any happiness they had managed to put together for themselves after Malcolm's death. Lizzie's language is too extreme to be accounted for as a state induced by Melville's grief for Uncle Peter and the other losses summoned up by the latest death. Herman had been, according to Lizzie, in "a frightfully nervous state" even before that month (for she specifies that matters were "now" worse because of the "added strain on his mind"). She feared he would be so upset as to be unable "to go on with the printing." He was in a bad mental state (for she hoped he might soon "be in better mental health"). At present she had reason (and this was using "mild" phrasing) "to feel the gravest concern & anxiety about it" ("it" being his mental health). She wanted Kate not to repeat what she had said ("you know how such things are exaggerated") and promised to tell more in person the next time they met.

How long and for what reasons had Herman been so upset? Since Uncle Peter's death, surely, and perhaps well before that time, perhaps during much of the fall and early winter, a period we know little about, except that Melville had spent his free hours in the fall of 1875 preparing his manuscript for publication. Perhaps all along, for years, he had been making clean copies in his best hand as he finished the cantos of the poem. If he did that, he also may have discarded all rough drafts as soon as he had cleaner ones—for not a scrap of manuscript has been found. More likely, he had drawers or little boxes stuffed with hundreds of pages of his poem in copy which was final (or nearly so) in wording but which was not in a state that could be handed to a printer to set from. Chances are, judging from the first of the two letters of 2 February 1876, Lizzie took on her old role and copied out much or all of the poem, with her husband's help in interpreting the manuscript pages. In the meticulously honest if not grudging inscription Melville made in Lizzie's copy of the poem on 6 June 1876, three days after publication, he wrote that he hardly knew how he "could have got the book (under the circumstances) into shape, and finally through the press" without her help. Copying over some parts or even all of an enormous manuscript in shape clean enough for the printer was an immense task, but it should not have been so disturbing in itself. Part of the problem may have been that once Melville looked hard at the manuscript he saw dozens or hundreds of passages which he felt compelled to improve, so that the chore of copying (a merely arduous chore) was complicated by his revisions.

Melville's compulsive revising, or that uglier thing, rewriting, would have been enough to drive tensions high in the household, but another possibility needs to be set down. Melville must have known how good *Clarel* was during the lonely years he was working on it, and he was too fine a reader not to recognize its greatness as he read parts of it again and again with an eye to publishing it. Small wonder if Melville's mental state grew agitated. Small wonder if the poor fellow! — the patronizing phrase used of him — small wonder if he dared to hope, in the face of the bitter lessons of *Battle-Pieces*, that he might after all gain respectful attention or even admiring recognition during the high solemnities of the American Centennial. If once again, as had happened in 1850 and 1851, Melville dared to hope for praise commensurate with his achievement, he could easily have worked himself into a state such as Lizzie described.

Lizzie's words of deep woe contain factual evidence about the preparation of the poem and the first phases of its printing history. "If ever this dreadful *incubus* of a *book*" was of course less than tactful, since Kate's late father was paying for the publication of *Clarel*. Aside from that, the use of "ever" implies a considerable previous duration of suffering. Just possibly, Lizzie had been copying behind Herman for years; more likely, she may just have put in many weeks of intense copying, under the specter of Peter's approaching death. She and Herman were "reading proof" by the start of February (and possibly by mid-January, when Augusta came down), not (not primarily, at any rate) preparing printer's copy. If the printer was setting from Melville's own manuscript, then correcting proof was harder than correcting proofs on books which Lizzie or his sisters had copied, aside from the fact that there are many more possibilities for error in printing a poem than in printing prose, since lineation and indentation can easily go awry and so many words were unfamiliar and so many word forms were poetically elided or otherwise altered. Decades later the Melvilles' daughter Frances remembered outrageous mistreatment, her father's rousing her (and surely her older sister?) out of bed at two in the morning to read proof with him. As with any such anecdote, we ask questions: did Melville roust Fanny out of bed at two o'clock one night only, or two or more nights? Did he regularly keep both his daughters as well as his wife occupied evenings on the poem? Did he struggle alone as long as his strength held out, then, one time, collapsing from fatigue, implore the help of one or both of his daughters, who could, after all, nap during the day when he was out of the house? Fanny never forgave Melville for dragging her out of sleep to proofread what she and every reviewer knew was not really poetry. A reporter, Minna Littmann, put Frances's view bluntly in the New Bedford *Sunday Standard* of 11 August 1929: "She does not reminisce of her distinguished father. He had the failings of genius, and her memories of him are not wholly happy ones." During the Melville revival of the 1920s, Frances did not recognize "H.M." in "the new light." To acknowledge that he had been an important writer (let alone a great writer) would have forced her to admit that she (and her Shaw relatives) had cruelly misjudged. In her old age, when she managed to be a loving, patient grandmother, her image of her whole earlier abused life depended upon her having been right in 1867, in 1876, in all those years, and having been right about her father ever since.

Lizzie was part of the problem. As Maria had long believed, Lizzie had not been taught sufficient self-discipline. She could not *will* herself into more healthy attitudes, as Maria's daughters had been taught to do. She was, in comparison to Maria's daughters, even Kate, inefficient. She was the only member of the family who regularly started a letter by explaining why she had not gotten around to writing it before, although she had been wanting to write. Neither Susannah Shaw nor Hope Savage Shaw ever taught her to "Do it now." Using time inefficiently, she seemed never to have time. Herman had shown himself incapable of managing money, beyond doubt, so all the burden of managing it fell on Lizzie, who was habitually overwhelmed by the responsibility, habitually overwhelmed, dragged down, complaining, and dragging down others. Lizzie had a set of clichés—she was up to her eyes in housecleaning; she was someone's friend through joy and sorrows; she did not know whether she stood on her head or on her heels; she grieved for the "dear ones" who had "gone up higher"; she wished things were different "but 'Such is life' "; she was so "terribly 'run down' " that she thought she should never "get 'wound up' again." If you lived with her, you could anticipate phrases coming out of her mouth—as you could *not* anticipate what would come out of Maria's or Helen's mouths. Herman derived his high standards from his mother and his older sister. For many years Lizzie talked herself into thinking that she took care of Herman, but she neglected him badly. At a time when he was working fifty or fifty-one weeks a year, six days a week, she disappeared on him for weeks at a time, longer and longer as she got older and had more money to escape with. She left him alone in the house, or she left him to the care of an untried housekeeper, or she left him to take his meals at a nearby boardinghouse. She was suffering, so she had to get out of New York City; she was in terrible physical condition for several months a year, and made everyone feel her suffering, never even trying to be stoical. It was hard on others to witness her suffering, and after a few years and decades hard on them to put up with her complaining about her suffering, especially in view of her customary inefficiency. In a post-1900 letter to Cousin Kate she says Kate is lucky not to have to abandon her home for four months of every year, the way she does. Lizzie simply would not admit that Herman had anything to feel bad about. Her own physical and emotional sufferings were real, but his were not. All of his sufferings were "needless"; his sufferings were all in his mind. She was a Unitarian.

Meanwhile, Augusta's sufferings were not in the mind. She had been in

Albany for Uncle Peter's funeral, then had arrived at the Harbor in the middle of January, unwell, so that Tom and Katie at once placed her under the care of Dr. Bogart. Augusta herself soon after she arrived at the Harbor apologized to Kate Lansing for being incapacitated, in her 15 January letter making a humorous allusion to a "crick" in her back ("they are fashionable here"), a pain which in fact interfered with the free use of her pen. Crick in the back was a family diagnosis if not a family disease — it is what Herman called his problem at Gansevoort in 1858. Kate had sent down a "big Sanford apple" which Katie, identifying it as a " *'Northern Spy'* & a very fine variety & specimen," displayed "on the mantel-piece to the admiration of all beholders." In writing Kate on 25 January, Katie put the situation in plausible terms, though the disease was organic, not a result of fatigue: "I am afraid the Christmas Tree, was too much for her." Augusta was ashamed of herself when she wrote Kate Lansing on 27 January: "I was real sorry, dear Kate, that I could not go to N.Y. myself & execute your commission as I had hoped to do." Katie had gone in "twice about them, the cards not being ready the first time," but Augusta was able to report: "The box was sent from Tiffany's yesterday, & I hope has reached you safely."

Soon after her arrival in New Brighton with Augusta, as Fanny wrote to Kate Lansing on 18 February, "at Dr. Bogert's particular request, 'a consultation' was held . . . to ascertain *the cause* of the intense pain & weakness Gus suffers — Dr. Bogert & the physician from New York decided after a careful study of all the symptoms, & seeing just how Gus was, that it was an *internal hemorrhage.*" Realizing the seriousness of matters, Kate and Abe decided to tell Fanny at once that Uncle Peter had left her and Augusta fifteen hundred dollars each and that the money would be forthcoming, before the will could be proved. On 25 February, Fanny gratefully replied: "How like Abe — ever thoughtful for others — to have you write of dear Uncle's generous legacy to Gus & me — would that Uncle could know, the help it will be to us, for since the mill was closed, four years ago, we have just managed to get away without getting into debt — *now* we can feel easy. We have always had such a horror of being in debt." She promised to watch for Augusta to show a moment of strength, so she might tell her. Fanny could not imagine life at Gansevoort without Augusta: "oh Kate, what will I do, if I lose Gus? What will become of our *home then?*" Everyone showed the strain, even Tom, for two months later, in mid-March, C. Henry King, physician-in-chief, Seamen's Retreat, Stapleton, Long Island, said bluntly, "you looked badly the last time I saw you." The two brothers and the three sisters mobilized as best they could, Kate Hoadley deputing her husband to do the first visiting, Lizzie being able to leave Herman and go out and stay overnight more than once. Lizzie was distressed about Augusta, but also about Herman. By 21 February, Fanny reported to Kate Lansing that Augusta "sees no one, cannot bear the excitement of a new face, & her room is kept perfectly still." Hoadley came down in February, and Herman came over on his day off, but being in the Harbor did not mean that visitors got to see Augusta. Helen and Kate Hoadley came down, and stayed on. On 26 February Herman "saw Gus for the first time, he was deeply moved, could hardly control his feelings while with her," Fanny wrote to Kate Lansing. Three of Herman's and Allan's daughters came out, "Florence, Lucy & Bessie" together, one day. In early March Kate Lansing came down, but Augusta was not aware that she had been there. Helen wrote to Kate Lansing on 13 March: "Fanny *will not* allow anyone to take her place at night, so that one cannot feel as if one were of any use to her, except sparing her a few steps by day."

Once again, only the advantages of the Governor's House could have allowed Fanny and the others to feel that they at least were doing everything possible for Augusta, and only the Governor's House could have allowed those nursing her to be spared any distracting household duties. Here one could take refuge, and here one could die properly, with any number of the family well accommodated, assisted by a staff of servants. You wouldn't, of course, let anyone but family members do the actual nursing. Years later, on 7 July 1885, Lizzie wrote Kate Lansing frankly about Augusta's illness: "In Augusta's case of 'fibrous tumor' I think we all regretfully feel that an operation at a suitable stage would have saved her life, and restored her health, but that a fatal false delicacy & pride prevented her taking the best medical advice at the outset. You know she suffered for not only months, but *years*, without letting even her sisters know that aught was wrong with her, and when it *had* to come out, it was too late, and *her* valuable life was sacrificed." If Maria had been alive, she would have accompanied Augusta to a doctor and stayed during the examination; as it was, Augusta's female modesty about letting a man examine her body had doomed her unnecessarily, Lizzie was certain. On 4 April, four years to the week after Maria's death at Tom's house, Augusta died there. Tom's house at times seemed less like "Paradise" (as Herman had called it) than a port for launching voyages thither. Funeral services were at the Governor's House on Friday the seventh at two o'clock. A death notice advised friends how to get to New Brighton: "Boat leaves Pier 1, East River, at 1:15 P.M." (The day of the funeral services the Melvilles' family physician, Dr. Augustus Kinsley Gardner, died.) Abe went down to New Brighton alone, and from there on the sixth wrote his eulogy to Kate: "She sought to know her duty and she did what seemed to her, *wholly* cheerfully and without one thought of variance or compromise. She took counsel of her conscience and her God and nothing swerved her from her sense of right and duty, which she pursued with buoyant and cheerful enthusiasm."

Herman once again went up the Hudson with a body, as he had done in 1846 by ship, as he had done by train in 1872. Interment was in the Albany Rural Cemetery.

Things had been confused in Albany for months, what with Kate and Abe moving out and Peter dying; then Kate and Abe moved back across the street to her old home, leading Fanny to ask on 29 February who had "taken" 166 Washington. This meant that Kate and Abe were able to make Uncle Peter's house available for those who went up with Augusta's body, including Herman but not Lizzie. After the return to New Brighton, Helen and Fanny wrote Kate and Abe on 11 April that they had gone to Herman's and lunched ("found Lizzie better, as the tonic she has been taking, has begun to build her up again"). Then they had taken an omnibus for the ferry, and got to the Harbor in time to rest before dinner. They thanked Kate for all she had done, and added: "Under the reign of Abram & yourself, 'Uncle's,' will keep up its old traditions, of genuine, Dutch, open-hearted, and open-handed hospitality. Long may you both reign!"

When Tom took the time to go up to check on the Mansion House at Gansevoort and to leave orders for its care until Fanny could return, he found that some callous neighbor (perhaps alerted by a death notice) had taken the chance to pry out some nails and vandalize the vacant house. There was a broken bottle of wine, some wine left in it. Tom did not think to open the pantry door to see what state it was in, something that gave Fanny and Helen pause. Helen insisted on going up with Fanny when the time came. They arrived at the house sacred from its associations with their mother and sister (as well as Uncle Herman) and cleaned up the evidences of the desecration. Lizzie was disconsolate at the news, writing Kate Gansevoort on 22 April: "How could any one be so *mean* and *heartless*, as to disturb that house at Gansevoort—the very silence and repose of which, just as poor Augusta left it, would seem to make it almost sacred—Most of all, my heart aches for poor Fanny—how will she ever bear the desolation & *change* that is now brought to her—Thank Heaven for *Divine Help*—surely it cannot fail us— and how could we endure life without that strong assurance within us." Helen stayed on for a time. The family had begun to realize that some of the old furnishings were superb. Two years later, an artist inveigled his way inside to sketch the furnishings, prompting Helen to laugh that the "Turkey carpet" was sitting for its portrait. In 1877, Fanny dug through the older papers when pestered by historical societies for documents dealing with the battles of 1777. No one in the rest of their lives thought there was any value in Augusta's vast, methodical archive, bundled up by year from the 1830s on, now left undisturbed, in her room.

Augusta had wanted to come to Twenty-sixth Street three months too soon. On 22 April Lizzie and Herman had lived through most of the crisis over *Clarel*, for Lizzie invited Kate to come visit any time after the first of May:

> Congratulate us that the book is *at last*, in type, to the last page of Ms. and a few days more will finish up the *plate-printing* and the various little odds and ends of the work—Herman has consented on the *very strong* representations of the publishers, to put his name on the title-page, for which I am very glad—and *therefore* he has changed his mind about having a dedication— Now, he wants me to tell you he is going to inscribe that book in your father's name, as seems most natural and fit—I have been all along in strong hopes that he would, but he seemed averse to having *any* dedication whatever or any name on the title page—I shall be so thankful when it is all finished and off of his mind, and cannot help hoping that his health will improve when he is released from this long continued mental strain.

She specified that she herself was "better a good deal, & gaining strength, as I always do, slowly"; she meant she was regaining strength slowly, as she always did after a period of illness (not that she always regained strength). Before Kate's arrival she wanted to cap her recovered health with an escape to Tom's: "I am going to try to spend a day or two at the Island before long and want to time my visit accordingly—A little change of air, scene &c often helps me wonderfully, to recruit." Herman went with her. After Maria's death in 1872 the Melvilles had fled to the Island for months; now a briefer visit might suffice.

For all the evidence, Melville was seeing almost no one socially outside his family except Evert Duyckinck, who was by this time immersed in his own labors on an edition of Shakespeare that William Cullen Bryant was going to attach his name to. Duyckinck's record on his ink blotter shows that Melville visited him in the evening of 30 April. Kate Lansing on 12 May wrote to Abe that "Cousin Herman is well." She was there for a dental appointment and for memorial business: "This morning I went to Bierstadts to see about my mothers Heliotype, and to-morrow go to Hall & Sons to see about Papas engraving." Kate also paid for all of Augusta's funeral expenses, judging from Fanny's depth of gratitude in her letter of 11 May: "when I took up your note, I read it—what you had done in Uncle's name flashed upon my mind—and I was speechless, and am so yet. What can I say to you Kate?" Kate did not know about her father's old mistakes, but she had learned from his recent ones involving Henry. All the rest of her long life, Kate Gansevoort Lansing laid out money when it was needed, not when it was too late to do any good. Having lived in debt so long, Lizzie never learned to let money go even when she became wealthy: after Herman's death she badgered the

Galena relatives to repair Priscilla's grave at Pittsfield rather than paying ten dollars herself and getting the job done.

On 14 May, Kate relayed an invitation to Abe to come down to the city on Friday the nineteenth and stay over Sunday. The strain at Twenty-sixth Street had lessened, for she reported that Cousin Herman "seems very well & is very entertaining — *The Book* will be out by June 1st." (By then she may have known that the "Book" would consist of two small volumes.) Abe began looking forward to passing "many a Sunday afternoon this summer" in the company of the poem, he said in his 16 May reply to Kate, about the most endearing thing Kate could have reported to the author. Abe was going to take the book slowly, in a way commensurate with its composition and its significance. The family began mobilizing for the publication. At Lizzie's request Kate sent John Hoadley the address of G. P. Putnam's Sons. Kate had not been shown the page proofs, for in her unspoken wish (in a letter of 25 May) that Hoadley might do something for the book's reception in his area she said, "I hope the Boston Papers will notice the Book it is called I believe 'Clara or the New Jerusalem.'" Cousin Kate learned more about the financial facts than the title; Lizzie had admitted that there had been unforeseen expenses for the book, and during her visit Kate decided that her father would have wanted her to pay for them, but knowing her cousin she waited to tell him so until they were at the depot for her return to Albany. After Kate left, Melville saw Duyckinck again, on the twenty-sixth, and again on the thirtieth, the new holiday, Decoration Day. After so many years of producing a book Melville needed companionship during the countdown of days before publication, when there occurred what Lizzie called (in a 4 June letter to Kate Lansing) "a series of the most vexatious delays." It appeared on 3 June. And about that time someone came from downtown with a kitten in his pocket for "Fanny the little"; it was welcomed despite the jealousy of the Maltese cat that already owned 104 East Twenty-sixth Street.

Melville had wavered as to putting his name on the title page. The fact that the *Tribune* had announced the book in January may have weighed in his decision not to have the book published anonymously, but also as the time for publication approached it became more and more obvious that he owed something to the memory of Peter Gansevoort. The final decision was to sign the book, to include a proper dedication to his uncle, and to assuage his irrational impulses by putting this truculent note across from the first page of the text: "If during the period in which this work has remained unpublished, though not undivulged, any of its properties have by a natural process exhaled; it yet retains, I trust, enough of original life to redeem it at least from vapidity. Be that as it may, I here dismiss the book — content beforehand with whatever future awaits it." On the level of information the note is far from satisfying. We do not know who had divulged its existence during composition except Lizzie or who had divulged its existence after it was completed except the *Tribune*. What governed Melville's sense that the poem remained long unpublished may simply have been the literal fact that any parts written, say, in 1870 or 1871 had indeed remained long unpublished. He was not asserting that the entire poem had remained completed and unpublished for years. In his early career, Melville had experienced little delay between writing a book and seeing it in print. He had worked his thoughts about the European revolutions of 1848 into his supposedly completed manuscript of *Mardi*, and less than a year later he was in print as a commentator on still-current history.

Melville gave out no presentation copies at all at the time, except the one to Lizzie in which gratitude was rather too finely calculated: "This copy is specially presented to my wife, without whose assistance in manifold ways I hardly know how I could have got the book (under the circumstances) into shape, and finally through the press." Lizzie made it clear in her 4 June letter that she hoped Herman would send Kate a copy "by-and-by if he does not now" — evidence that his strange behavior was not at an end. His mourning ring for Peter Gansevoort, a gift of Kate, "came from Tiffany's — all nicely marked," and Lizzie was able to report that "he wears it frequently." Sometime in June George Parsons Lathrop's *A Study of Hawthorne* came to Melville's attention. Lathrop here revealed Hawthorne had been "much interested in Herman Melville, at this time living in Pittsfield" and that there "was even talk of their writing something together." Surely without permission, he quoted part of Melville's private review of *The House of the Seven Gables*, commenting, "This really profound analysis, Mr Melville professes to extract from the 'Pittsfield Secret Review,' of which I wish further numbers could be found." Public quoting of Melville's private correspondence was new (aside from Willis's use of a letter from London in 1850), and it did not go unremarked. The Brooklyn *Daily Union* on 9 June mentioned that Lathrop's *A Study of Hawthorne* was "enriched by letters from Hawthorne, J. L. Motley, H. W. Longfellow, J. R. Lowell, Dr. Holmes, Miss Mitford, Charles Sumner, and Herman Melville." There was no stopping the reverberations. In October a reviewer of the Lathrop book in *Scribner's Monthly* took Melville's words (beginning "There is a certain tragic phase of humanity") from his "review" of *The House of the Seven Gables* out of context and worked them into a paragraph on the evidence for and against Hawthorne's being "a gloomy, morbid or morose man."

If Herman was still unpredictable, the rest of the family behaved splendidly. Tom and Katie came to dinner to celebrate the publication of *Clarel*. Kate Lansing bought up several sets of *Clarel*, apparently, and gave them as gifts, one set to Amasa J. Parker (who had done his best for Herman on more than one occasion) and his wife. She gave her husband a copy. She gave a copy to Paul Fenimore Cooper, one of her father's pallbearers, who wrote her on 2 August: "I expect to derive much pleasure from reading it; for I was always a great admirer of Mr M.'s writings." She lent a copy to Asa W. Twitchell, who had painted Melville in the early days of his fame. Visiting her sister Kate in Lawrence, Fanny wrote to Kate Lansing on 18 June that she had not seen *Clarel*, Mr. Hoadley having not returned with his copy, but that she had heard from Helen "of the beautiful inscription to Uncle." Hoadley had acquired his volumes as he was hurrying to catch a train (away, not home to Lawrence), and in the next weeks read and reread it with great attention. On 30 June Tom wrote to Kate Lansing: "Have you seen Hermans Book yet & what do you think of it"? Kate's uncle Edward Sanford, a respected poet himself, was reading it carefully in March 1877, when he wrote her about it.

Willie and Milie were living in Elizabeth, New Jersey, most of the year, but Florence, with Lucy, opened Arrowhead. In her 18 June letter to Kate Lansing, Melville's sister Fanny summarized goings and comings: "Tom & Kate, were to pass this Sunday at Winyah — Mr Lather[s]'s place — Kitty was at Staten Island, but is soon going to Arrowhead with Bessie. Florence & Lucy have been there since the first." The girls — the young women — had invited Bessie to come to Arrowhead for the Berkshire air and for drives with Rouser, the horse that Henry had ridden, still able to pull a carriage. Lizzie on 21 June wrote Kate Lansing that she often saw Charles Brewster, the brother of Henry's law-partner, George Brewster. Charles had been in George Armstrong Custer's postwar regiment and had led a troop in the Black Kettle Massacre, then afterward had resigned. Now he lived just "over the way" and could be heard calling out for his little boy, who was named "Henry Gansevoort": "Where are you Ganny" — "What you doing Gan?" Lizzie and both Bessie and Fanny were going to the mountains around Herman's birthday, through her "good brother Lem's kind provision." A little belatedly, Lizzie was "trying to arrange for comfortable quarters for Herman" during their absence, "so as to shut up the house." She offered a self-consoling opinion: "I think the change will benefit him also — take him out of himself." Most likely, Melville stayed in the house alone.

Irritation must have been mixed with jealousy, for, after having worked out his feelings about Hawthorne in *Clarel*, Melville had to stand by and read reviews of books by his friend, *Fanshawe* and *The Dolliver Romance*, as well as the Lathrop book. Even worse, a controversy between Lathrop and Julian Hawthorne was taking whole columns of newspaper space. On 8 July a "Letter from Julian Hawthorne" in the *Tribune* (dated London, 20 June) protested against Lathrop's "Study" of his father's life, making an issue of papers including some or all of Melville's letters to Hawthorne. Julian claimed to speak "as the chosen mouthpiece of all surviving members of the late Nathaniel Hawthorne's family who yet bear his name," and to speak "in behalf of those whom death has deprived of the power to defend themselves." The papers Mrs. Hawthorne left, "among them many letters of a peculiarly private and delicate nature," were Julian's by right; Lathrop in Julian's absence had taken possession of "most of the personal effects, including the legacy of papers and letters." On 15 July the controversy continued in the *Tribune* with Lathrop's reply, dated Boston, 13 July: "I used only such parts of the family papers as I supposed myself entitled to control under my wife's right, and with her consent. . . . They consist of letters from other persons to Nathaniel Hawthorne; and the consent of the writers was obtained in all cases, except where the writers were dead." Melville knew this last was not true. The exchange was widely reprinted, and while his name was not mentioned in it, Melville was one of those most closely touched by Lathrop's intrusiveness and indelicacy, and most concerned that his extravagant, intimate letters were in the hands of warring mercenary heirs.

At the very least, the controversy, along with the flurry of reviews of Hawthorne's posthumous books, detracted from the resolution of emotions that Melville thought he had achieved, besides taking up space that might have been given to *Clarel*. Melville had made it Hawthorne's turn for attention in August 1850 when he wrote his essay for the *Literary World*, and he had forgone his own turn in November 1851 when he asked Hawthorne not to write a word about *Moby-Dick*. Now it was his turn, by rights, but he did not get that turn. Instead, just at this time, the reviewer in the once-friendly Springfield *Republican* (18 July) in the first of five sentences declared that "Herman Melville's literary reputation will remain, what it has fairly become, a thing of the past." In his concluding sentence the reviewer became the first, as far as we know, to use a phrase like "posthumous life" of Melville or his reputation: "Mr Melville lives in his novels,—a sort of posthumous life, it is true, yet they are worth reading," particularly *Moby-Dick*, "with those preposterous heroes, the White Whale and Capt Ahab." The *Republican*, the best Massachusetts paper west of Worcester, if not Boston, was widely read in Pittsfield by year-round residents and summer people alike. The dead Hawthorne was having a great vogue, posthumously, and the living Melville might as well have been dead, since his fame was already posthumous.

Putnam distributed review copies of *Clarel* mainly in the Northeast, apart from a few sent to London. On 10 June the reviewer for the Boston *Daily Evening Transcript* had looked over the "two handsomely printed and bound volumes" of *Clarel* and commented that so many pages of rhymed verse were "rather apt to create a disgust for poetry if one is obliged to read them conscientiously and crucially." He was spared that disgust, for the "heat of the season" allowed him to "forgo" the pleasure of attacking the volumes. On 16 June the reviewer in the *Tribune* began: "After a long silence, Mr. Herman Melville speaks again to the world. No more a narrator of marvelous stories of tropical life and adventure, no more a weird and half-fascinating, half-provoking writer of romance, but now as a poet with a single work, in four parts, and about 17,000 lines in length." He was respectful of the "distinctly poetical side" of Melville's genius, remembering "still his stirring lines on Sheridan's ride," the first two of which he quoted. *Clarel* he found "something of a puzzle, both in design and execution." He had read carefully enough to list and tersely describe some of the main characters and outline the simple action, which he could not honor with the word "plot." He would have tolerated better "the theological doubts, questions, and disputations indulged in by the characters, and those whom they meet," had all this talk had an obviously "logical" course or led "to any distinct conclusions." Appreciative of Melville's poetic achievement, he was bewildered that anyone capable of writing excellent passages could write such poor ones: "The verse, frequently flowing for a few lines with a smooth, agreeable current, seems to foam and chafe against unmanageable words like a brook in a stony glen: there are fragments of fresh, musical lyrics, suggestive both of Hafiz and of William Blake; there are passages so rough, distorted, and commonplace withal, that the reader impatiently shuts the book." His conclusion was far from contemptuous: "There is a vein of earnestness in Mr. Melville's poem, singularly at variance with the carelessness of the execution; but this only increases the impression of confusion which it makes."

On 26 June the New York *World* printed a shorter review by a shallower reviewer than the one in the *Tribune*. This reviewer had read carelessly (as his account of the characters shows), but he sounded much like the reviewer in the *Tribune* in his irritation at the mixture of worthless and poetic passages, the rare "passage of striking original thought" or "the true lyrical ring" merely tricking the reader onward for "another thousand lines or so" in search of the next fine moment. He concluded that he could not recommend *Clarel* because "a work of art it is not in any sense or measure, and if it is an attempt to grapple with any particular problem of the universe, the indecision as to its object and processes is sufficient to appal or worry the average reader." On the first of July the reviewer in the Chicago *Tribune* professed to be favorably disposed toward "any new literary effort" by the author of what the paper spelled as " 'Amoo' and 'Typee,' " but he was put off first by the length and the subject then by the dedication, which he took as revealing that

Clarel was the typical product of a vanity press and therefore not worthy of being reviewed with real books. After claiming to have examined the poem faithfully "from end to end," he offered this grudging tribute: "The manufacture of the poem must have been a work of love. It bears internal evidence of having been labored over as a blacksmith hammers at his forge, and only a mastering passion for the severest task-work could have sustained the author through it all."

Hoping the best for Herman but wholly incapable of reading his poem, Thomas Melville on Staten Island helped to celebrate the national jubilee. The *Herald* on 5 July wrote that the "morning of the centennial Fourth opened on Staten Island with the booming of cannon, the cracking of small arms and firecrackers and the ringing of bells. . . . All the public institutions, the Sailors' Snug Harbor at New Brighton and the Seamen's Retreat at Stapleton were handsomely decorated." In Manhattan there were fireworks in City Hall Park, again according to the *Herald*; there "all" those who lived in "the lower wards of the metropolis congregated in the part fronting the City Hall last evening to hear the music given by Dodsworth's band and to witness the pyrotechnic display in honor of the national jubilee." The great celebration, very properly, was held in Philadelphia, and a great American poet read his Centennial Poem, which began with an address to the "Sun of the stately day." The poet was not Walt Whitman and not Herman Melville but Bayard Taylor, who read his verse "in a strong, full voice" (the *Herald*, 5 July 1876). With any luck Melville was spared the sight of the Philadelphia *Press* of 5 July, which called Bayard Taylor "more like an inspired singer of old than a modern writer for an occasion" and declared: "If 'Bayard Taylor's National Ode' had been written and spoken by William Shakespeare three centuries ago it would have been enshrined among the choicest memorials of English literature." One place or another, Melville saw accounts of Taylor and his National Ode and weighed it against his own American *Paradise That Need Not Have Been Lost*.

The Glorious Fourth passed without any known comment on Melville's own Centenary Poem, but on 6 July the New York *Independent* gave it three sentences, the third of which read: "It is destitute of interest or metrical skill." In a letter on 8 July to Abe Lansing, Hoadley scoffed at the earlier "criticism" in the *World* ("if such it can be called even by courtesy"):

> It was flippant and foolish in the extreme.
> "Clarel" is not easy reading. It requires determined study, and my attention must be at its freshest, to relish it until after several perusals.
> But it will grow on thoughtful reading, and will give Mr. Melville a firm footing on a higher plane than anything he has before written.

> I wish it might make him at once rich, famous and happy! — Noble Fellow! He deserves to be all three! —

Not since the first years of his career had a member of Melville's family defended him so stoutly, and no family member had ever defended him on the basis of such good literary judgment. Hoadley wrote when for three days eastern newspapers had been filled with news of the massacre of General Custer's regiment at a place the first reports called "Little Horn River" (not the "Little Big Horn"). On 6 July the news had crowded aside delayed reports on the Centenary. While the papers printed confirmations and corrections, accusations and cross-accusations, Herman Melville, John Mosby, the survivors of the six young rangers Custer had murdered for practice, anyone with any historical memory, could ruminate on just how exceeding small the mills of God did grind (as Longfellow put it in "Retribution"). And the Melvilles on Twenty-sixth Street could listen to voices over the way and marvel at the timeliness of Charles Brewster's decision to come home from Custer's regiment to play with Ganny.

Custer, like Hawthorne, may have crowded Melville's poem out of some papers, but on 10 July the New York *Times* reviewed *Clarel*, as the New York *Tribune* had done, respectfully. Melville's talent was recognized as "undoubted," and a two-volume poem from him could not "fail to be a matter of interest to a wide circle of readers." The reviewer would have been happier had Melville included Miltonic arguments before each book, but he worked through most of "Jerusalem," at least, and laid out the story as it concerned Clarel, Nathan, Agar, and Ruth, up to the point where Clarel is excluded from the mourning for Nathan and "starts for a short journey with a company of friends." He understood that Melville was employing the octosyllabic line which Sir Walter Scott had used "in his narrative poems," and remembered also that Byron had declared that a "'fatal facility'" inhered in that verse form, although Melville belied Byron's claim by finding the form difficult to work in. Skipping from "Jerusalem" to the epilogue, the reviewer concluded: "Such merit as Mr. Melville's poem has is in its descriptions and in the Oriental atmosphere which he has given his work. There is no nonsense about the book; it is written in an honest and sincere style, but verse is certainly not the author's forte." This was superficial, but it was not vicious, and would not have been hard to live with, not crushing in the way the reviews of *Pierre* had been.

Melville continued to see Evert Duyckinck occasionally in the evening, and late in July Lizzie and he took the ferry to see Tom, "starting in 5 P.M. boat, & returning in 9 P.M. Quarantine [boat]," as Herman told Cousin Kate on 25 July. Tom and Katie were well, but Herman and Lizzie were taken aback by a grisly spectacle off Stapleton, the wreck of the *Mohawk*, owned by Vice Commodore William T. Garner. Six lives had been lost, through "the carelessness or incompetency of the sailing master." Herman commented to Kate: "How tragical a thing that oversetting of the yacht. We passed the wreck in the boat—the two masts projecting from the water." Bessie may have gone on ahead to Boston, for Herman wrote that "Lizzie & Fanny (Fanny the Little) are busily completing their arrangements for the White mountain campaign." His sister Fanny was with Kate and Abe, obviously less than eager to stay alone at the Mansion House after Augusta's death and the vandalizing. Melville apparently received a letter from Stanwix and forwarded it or news of it to Lizzie in Jefferson, New Hampshire, but Lizzie still felt "very anxious about him," and on 6 September told her stepmother that when she arrived in Boston she wanted to send Stanwix "all the clothing that Sam has to spare for him." In Manhattan Herman suffered, especially on 6 August, what the *Sun* called "One Hot August Sunday," ninety-three degrees in the afternoon, rivaling "the highest temperature of July's hottest days."

Reviews of *Clarel* were still appearing. The New York *Galaxy* (August) dismissed the poem: "It is not given even to the gods to be dull; and Mr. Melville is not one of the gods." The New York *Library Table* (August) was vague but friendly ("we doubt not it will meet with some readers who will not object to linger with the author by the way and who will think it none too long"). Melville was not basking in praise for *Clarel* when he left on 12 August to spend his two-week vacation at Jefferson, New Hampshire, with Lizzie and his daughters. Toward the end he managed to get to Brookline to see Helen and George then took the Fall River route for an overnight ride home, where he took his meals at the Hartnett sisters' boardinghouse on Twenty-fifth Street. He wrote Cousin Kate on 27 August that he had left Lizzie and the girls "jolly," and declared further: "I myself am ever hilarious, & pray sincerely that you & your Abraham may likewise ever be so." He was in good spirits, having picked up on Nassau Street a set of Chaucer: "What with his other volumes Chaucerian, Abraham will now have quite a variorum library of the old poet who did'nt know how to spell, as Artemus Ward said."

After his vacation Melville soldiered on alone in Manhattan, suffering in early September "a jumping tooth-ache." On the eighth he wrote Cousin Kate while holding his left hand to his "'jole.'" Again Abe and Kate decided to send pears down to him, but he advised deferring the gift until Lizzie's return late in the month from the mountains, where she and the girls had all "been greatly benefited by the mountain air—entirely escaping the annual cold, &c." Kate had mentioned "the present whereabouts of Fanny & Helen," news to him, for he wanted to write Fanny and "hardly knew where precisely she was." Helen as big sister was making a point of spending as much time with Fanny as possible. The Lansings decided that their plums (which followed the pears) would not wait until Lizzie had returned, so on 12 September Melville shared his bounty at the boardinghouse. That day Edwin Lansing and George Brewster dined with him "at the Misses Hartnett's" (he wrote Kate on the thirteenth), then spent the remainder of the evening with him in his room at Twenty-sixth Street—one of the few times in these years that we know of his having male companionship in the evenings; they must have joked, a little queasily, about the state of Melville's neighbor Charles Brewster's scalp. One Sunday, rain poured down all along the Hudson, and to Kate's complaint Herman replied on 26 September: "By the way—your rainy Sunday was also experienced by me, alone here as it chanced, to chew the cud of sweet and bitter fancies. I doubt not there was no lack of others—a plentiful sprinkling of them all over the world." He was treating her more and more as her own person, now that she was orphaned and married, a "blood cousin" indeed rather than a mere child of a younger generation. Lizzie and the girls returned on 18 September, and three days later in a letter to Kate Lansing Lizzie referred to the "delightful country sojourn" they (presumably including Herman) had experienced there—but of course she and Bessie were already suffering "from the hay fever which came on as soon as" they "left the safe mountain region." She added, "the first good frost will bring us deliverance so we wait in patience." Kate and Abe had shipped down pears again, "good thing at breakfast," and a pleasant reminder of the Lansings at the start of each day.

Herman invited Kate and Abe to visit on their way to the great Centennial exhibition in Philadelphia—the Big Show, as the Philadelphia *Bulletin* was calling it. Soon after her return Lizzie urged Kate also, "We all 'second that motion' and hope you will." The restoration of his pay to four dollars a day on 1 October may have lessened Melville's guilt at going down to Philadelphia himself on 11 October. The next day he described it to Kate (who had not yet gone down) as "immense—a sort of tremendous Vanity Fair." While at the exhibition, Melville saw the much-ridiculed arm and torch of Frédéric Auguste Bartholdi's proposed gift to the United States, the truly colossal Statue of Liberty. He may also have visited the display of portable steam-engines by the J. C. Hoadley Company of Lawrence, Massachusetts. (In February 1877 Hoadley learned that he had won a medal from the Centennial Commission for excellence of design and construction "without departing from the simplicity of mechanism which is the feature of greatest value in the ordinary slide valve.") Melville bought himself a handsome amber mouthpiece there, later handed down to his son-in-law, who used it with a large meerschaum pipe and at the end of 1931 labeled it for his descendants.

Abe was in the long tradition of fishermen who were also bookish men, and Melville found he could show his appreciation for various kindnesses by doing preliminary book scouting in Manhattan for his cousin's husband. Hoadley, by now intimate with Abe, in a long, news-filled letter on 20 October let his financial woes and his political attitudes bleed into each other. The situation was almost hopeless: "our unique and peculiar danger is in the momentary issue of our pending political contest. Never *before* in the history of the world, did a people seem to invite a bitter, unrelenting, malignant enemy, just removed, with pain, from his clutch at their throat, — almost before drawing one long, free breath, — to come into its naked bosom and do its will!" He felt that all the Union soldiers had died in vain and that he himself was politically alienated as well as financially all but ruined: "I may have to go out into the cold world, — a bundle on my thatch, a stick in my hand, in tattered rags and worn out shoes, to beg my bread, — I *have* gone through that for *ages* in imagination; but then to be without a country!" No wonder Kate Gansevoort a few years before had pronounced him an *"ultra"* in Reconstruction politics. Insensitive to the political views of others, Hoadley talked wildly of fears for the nation and in the next sentence fears for his own impoverishment. There was something to be said for Herman's attempts at stoicism.

By early September copies of the London *Academy* of 19 August had reached the United States. In that issue a reviewer declared *Clarel* "a book of very great interest, and poetry of no mean order," shrewdly accounting for the varying levels in the poetry: "The form is subordinate to the matter, and a rugged inattention to niceties of rhyme and meter here and there seem rather deliberate than careless. In this, in the musical verse where the writer chooses to be musical, in the subtle blending of old and new thought, in the unexpected turns of argument, and in the hidden connexion between things outward separate, Mr. Melville reminds us of A. H. Clough." He concluded with this blunt comment: "We advise our readers to study this interesting poem, which deserves more attention than we fear it is likely to gain in an age which craves for smooth, short, lyric song, and is impatient for the most part of what is philosophic or didactic." The identity of the reviewer is not known, and there is no known record of any of Melville's later admirers having read this comment. If he had given any indication of knowing other works by Melville, there might have been a chance of identifying him or of associating him with a literary group, but as it is this stands as an isolated bit of intelligent and sympathetic criticism in an important reviewing organ a decade ahead of the known strong stirrings of interest in Melville in England. On 8 September the Springfield *Republican* responsibly quoted from the review in the *Academy*, allowing that "Herman Melville's poem, 'Clarel,' receives kindlier countenance in England than it has in his own land." (Curiously, Melville and Clough had been reviewed together, along with Longfellow, in the New Bedford *Mercury* on 8 June 1849.) Hoadley got a copy of the *Academy*, perhaps borrowing it, since Minnie copied out the entire review, neatly, for him to preserve in his set of *Clarel*.

In London the *Saturday Review* (26 August) gave a one-sentence dismissal: "We have to note the unusual phenomenon of a poem in two volumes — *Clarel*, a versified account of a pilgrimage in Palestine, not remarkable either for elevation of sentiment or for poetic excellence." In Philadelphia, *Lippincott's* (September) commented sadly on the problem-world of the poem: "The personages are used, like figures in landscape-painting, to animate the scenes through which we follow the author: their conversation turns chiefly on the religious doubt and disbelief which beset many — Mr. Melville seems to think all — thoughtful men in our times, and the social, political and scientific questions interwoven with them." Like the reviewers in the *World* and the *Times*, the writer in *Lippincott's* expected answers and protested that "no new light is thrown upon these questions." He found "a few striking descriptions, such as that of the monk of Saba feeding the doves, which is like a picture of Mr. Holman Hunt's, and some good images and metaphors, especially those drawn from Mr. Melville's old sea-life." In October the *Westminster Review* declared that "we do not understand a single word," then went on with a bit more sarcasm: "Talleyrand used to say that he always found nonsense singularly refreshing. He would certainly have set a high value on 'Clarel.'"

Throughout the summer and fall Hoadley read in his light green copy of *Clarel*, pondering sets of lines, alertly reading the entire poem. They show him as a man with a practicing poet's notions of what is proper in matters of punctuation, grammar, syntax, and rhyme. He watched for typographical errors and what he saw as nonstandard punctuation. That much was pedantic and puristic. Hoadley also identified actual people and things Melville was referring to, including a literary source, Martin Farquhar Tupper, and noted some scientific errors. Hoadley brought his own religious and political (and specifically Radical Republican) biases to *Clarel*. In "The Priest and Rolfe" (pt. 2, canto 21) he marked the lines on the world's becoming "a den / Worse for Christ's coming, since his love / (Perverted) did but venom prove," and in the margin identified the perverter: "Rome! — even if the author didn't mean it!" Alongside Rolfe's bitter meditation which moves from the suffering of the South from war and Reconstruction to the loss of belief in the Adamic American ("Of the Stranger," 4.5), Hoadley wrote: "Strong: but sympathy ill-bestowed." Putting his mind to *Clarel* during the tense Sunday before the November election, Hoadley interpreted according to his own fears the lyric in which Ungar apparently foresees retribution to the Radical Republicans for their harshness toward the South: "Tilden? No[v]. 5/ '76." Hoadley was fearing that a victory for the Democrat Samuel Tilden (Gansevoort's old friend and later a great benefactor of the New York Public Library) would exalt the South to its pre-war power. At Ungar's denunciation of Anglo-Saxon materialistic imperialism and Northern cruelty in wartime ("The Shepherds' Dale," 4.9), Hoadley burst out in an impassioned protest against Northern kindness to the South after the war: "No grace — So faith-foolish, So stupidly forgiving the unrepentant, was ever accorded under heaven or among men, by men, or gods, as by North to South!" Beside Ungar's diatribe against Democracy as the "Arch strumpet of an impious age" ("A New-Comer," 4.19), Hoadley wrote woefully in the margin: "Truer, in literal sense, than the Author meant: O *Democracy!*" Toward the end of the first volume, in "The Sleep-Walker" (2.38), Hoadley marked lines 4–25 as "very beautiful." In "Before the Gate" (3.10), Hoadley surrendered to the poetry, writing "All this is fine" beside the "Pilgrim and Perizzite" passage, then along the reception at the monastery writing "Fine, very fine description." At Ungar's passionate denunciation of the debasement of values in Democratic America ("Ungar and Rolfe," 4.21), he wrote "Powerful!" Melville's devoted, generous brother-in-law (despite his increasingly rabid political views) was the best nineteenth-century critic of *Clarel*. As he read, Hoadley commented aloud to his wife and children, saying that in order to read it he was forced "to have available all the books of Reference etc — possible." ("This the idea if not his language," Charlotte Hoadley wrote to Victor Hugo Paltsits on 12 September 1930.)

For months during the reception of *Clarel* Cousin Herman and Cousin Kate acted out intermittent episodes of a farce on who should pay the last expenses on the poem, both of them demonstrating the stubbornness that allowed their grandfather to hold Fort Stanwix against the British, but both of them, also, exhibiting genuine affection and admiration for each other and deep solicitude for each other's abnormally sensitive natures. On learning that her father's twelve hundred dollars had not covered all the "supplementary charges," Kate in August sent Melville a check for one hundred dollars. What followed was a long exchange in which Melville and Mrs. Lansing proved themselves to be cousins indeed, each outdoing the other in pride, punctiliousness, and courtesy. Herman's pride turned Uncle Peter's gift into a problem for Kate rather than a matter of sweet charity freely bestowed with comfortable results. Melville accepted the five hundred dollars Peter had left him in his will: no quarreling there.

Fanny pursued her visits away from the Mansion House, for in mid-November Cousin Kate wrote Abe from New York that she and Fanny had "arrived at Cousin Hermans," where "Cousin Lizzie—Herman Bessie & Fanny gave us a warm welcome." "It seems very natural here," she said, and a week later she relayed an invitation to Abe: "Cousin Herman invites you to spend Sunday with him. It is his free day"—implying that he worked six days a week still. Lizzie may have gone to Boston for Thanksgiving, leaving Melville especially eager to welcome Abe down. Around the first of December in San Francisco Stanwix played out his usual pattern. He got a clerkship in a wholesale house, "at a pretty fair salary to start with," and (from what one of the partners said) he at first "expected to get a steady situation & a larger salary after this work of dissolving partnership was over." What followed was predictable, unreliable partner, vulnerable victimized Stanwix, told four days after Christmas that he was being fired so the man's son could have his job. Stanwix wrote his half-uncle Lem on 29 December: "That was the last straw that completely upset me, for I thought to obtain a respectable & steady situation here, but was disappointed." Having "borrowed money here in San Francisco on the strength of a speculation & lost," he asked Lem for sixty dollars, "at the least," and as an outright gift, not as a loan since repayment would have been uncertain. His plans for 1877 were more hazardous-sounding than anything since the Central American ordeal, in view of the battle at the Little Horn River:

> There is a party of five or six of us that are going to start for the Black Hills country about the middle or last of January two of them who were there before & were doing well until driven away by the Indians, & I am going with them if I can get this money, I put it at the smallest amount possible to do me any good, if I do not get it, I shall start now as quick as I receive an answer to this, on my own account and foot it till I get there, if it takes all winter. I have made up my mind, this is a chance, & I may be lucky there, at any rate I can get miners wages which is more than I can make here; and I am going this winter if I die of starvation or get frozen to death on the road.

He asked Lem not to let anyone know of his intention to go to the Black Hills, but by late January Lizzie probably had the distressing news.

Melville sent Abe his own copy of *The Songs of Béranger*, and Abe sent him a Christmas story in which St. Nicholas lamented over "these 'degenerate days' which we account such an 'advance,'" opinions much to the liking of the recipient, and an almanac, probably not a new one for 1877 but a quaint old one Abe had come upon, for Melville in a 2 January 1877 letter called it a "venerable almanac, which bears witness to the old times when some imagination yet lingered in this sort of publication." Melville relished "looking over it mightily," and set about "getting from Boston a similar almanac which still continues to be published there." Melville gave his daughter

Fanny a copy of Goldsmith's *Deserted Village*—not a lesson in social change apt to appeal to a resentful young lady of twenty-one who that year had watched her father spend more than a thousand dollars publishing a poem that the papers and magazines had dismissed; but she kept it all her life. It is not known whether there was a Christmas gathering of any size. At some time this year J. E. A. Smith at last published the second volume of his *The History of Pittsfield (Berkshire County), Mass., from the Year 1800 to the Year 1876*, including an anonymous contribution by Melville, a memoir of his uncle Thomas Melvill Jr., quoted in the first volume of this biography. This Allan's daughters would have learned about promptly enough, since Allan, long before, had helped persuade Herman to write the piece.

The reviews of *Clarel* were almost a closed chapter when the January 1877 issue of the New York *International Review* gave the poem two long paragraphs. This issue may not have appeared in late December, the usual date, for the New York *Times* did not notice it until 5 January 1877. The reviewer was astounded that "the hero of whaling and Polynesian adventures, whose model seemed to be Defoe, should become a theological mystic in his ripened years." He arrived at an opinion not unwarranted by Melville's prefatory note, and drew an explicit comparison between Browning's recent experiment (presumably in *The Ring and the Book*, 1869) and Melville's. In *Clarel* Melville had written "for himself, and not for the reader," following "the bent of his own interests and fancies," as Browning had just done. If Browning had failed, how could Melville succeed, a man "who has not yet achieved a recognized place as a poet"? Moredock in *The Confidence-Man* chews wild news and wild meat at the same time; Melville could more tamely chew this review along with the old-fashioned New Year's cake that Cousin Kate had sent down.

For all his forearming himself against failure, his vaunting himself that he could dismiss the poem content beforehand with whatever fate awaited it, Melville had hoped for recognition that he, all surprisingly, had written the great American Centennial poem. He wanted to be popular again for a while, to be part of the society he was deploring. He deserved, as kind John Hoadley said, to be rich, famous, and happy, and at some irrational core of his being (at least early in January 1876, fresh from reading the entire poem and full of his sense of the power of his achievement) Melville had hoped that one or two of those qualities might again be his. Instead, once the reviews of *Clarel* ceased, Melville found himself declining toward the nadir of his reputation, rarely mentioned in literary histories or encyclopaedias, very rarely mentioned in contemporary magazines and newspapers. Even some articles on nautical fiction failed to mention him. In the years between *Clarel* and 1880 or so, he remained one of the chief authors associated with Pittsfield; indeed, it was only in items on Berkshire authors and new articles or books on Hawthorne's time in Lenox that he was almost invariably mentioned. But with the fate of *Clarel* his ambition and his lust for fame gradually dissipated. The bulk of his writing in the next years may well have consisted of the words he wrote into the blanks of Custom House forms.

[37]

"Old Fogy" and Imaginary Companions
1877–1879

Monday P.M. [about 1877?]
By-the-bye-, you should read, or at least look over D.D. It is well worth any one's reading. It is the last leaf out of the *Omnium Gatherum* of miscellaneous opinion touching the indeterminate Ethics of our time.
With which Johnsonian sentence, I conclude.

Melville's note to Evert Duyckinck
when returning a book he refers to as "D.D."

ON 2 JANUARY 1877 the Melvilles received a letter from Stanwix, and Lizzie promptly wrote to Lem: "he is employed in an 'iron & steel firm' at present, engaged in settling matters previous to dissolving partnership—he has 2.50 a day, and a *prospect* of a steady engagement with the partner who goes on with the business—I earnestly hope he will be able to make it sure." That was old news. Within a week or so Lem had received Stanwix's plea of 29 December, and three weeks later Stanny thanked Lem for the check for seventy-five dollars and announced his latest plans, to go to the mining country to take his chances with hundreds of others: "I am satisfied that something will come of it I start in a few days"; his Uncle Lemuel would hear from him "in a few months." Stanwix was alive, although even Lizzie's hopes for his having a responsible and happy life were dimmer every year.

Lem had given his Melville nieces their usual New Year's "tip," as Lizzie wrote Kate Lansing on 25 February 1877, at the start of the new sewing season. Kate was also donating to the "'black silk fund'"—a good thing, since the girls' dresses were shabby, their "present black silks being nearly on their last legs, or arms rather, having done most faithful duty these two years and more past." Lizzie lamented: "Oh, if we *could* only be clothed like the birds, and renew our coverings as easily and efficiently what hours and days of weary work might be spared us—that woman's work that is *never done*. I get heartily sick of it, and I don't know who dresses as plainly and gets along with so few 'furbelows' as I do." Man's work kept Melville out of the house six days a week, until mid- or late afternoon, but he was still sorting through his poems, if not writing many new ones. On 25 February Hoadley sent Melville his poem "Foundation Stones," based on a legend of Samarcand told by Marco Polo, and "He Wins Who Highest Aims," a condensed paraphrase from Virgil. He may have sent "In Memoriam," which Melville's sister Fanny quoted on 12 January to Kate Lansing: "That expression 'this activity was so great that it seemed like repose,' comes into my mind every now & then—there is so much in it." On 31 March, a Saturday morning when he was not working, Melville acknowledged receiving poems from Hoadley and made two offers of his own. The first involved the brig *Carolus* from Girgenti: "Where's that? Why, in Sicily—The ancient Agrigentum. Ships arrive from there in this port, bringing sulphur; but this is the first one I have happened to have officially to do with. I have not succeeded in seeing the captain yet—have only seen the Mate—but hear that he has in possession some stones from those magnificent Grecian ruins, and I am going to try to get a fragment, however small, if possible, which I will divide with you." He shared something more than a fragment of a Greek ruin: for the first time we know of, he exchanged poems with the engineer-poet, copying out "The Age of the Antonines" and describing it as something he "found the other day—came across it—in a lot of papers." The poem begins "While hope awaits Millenial years, / Though dim of late the signs, / Back to the past a glance be cast— / The Age of the Antonines!" In that golden time, no "demagogue beat the pulpit-drum," no one "stifled the fluent thought," no levelers threatened "Orders and grades and due degree," and men were freer than in post–Civil War America, for the rulers then were the best men and the world reposed under law internalized as individual will. Melville went on: "I remember that the lines were suggested by a passage in Gibbon (Decline & Fall) Have you a copy? Turn to '*Antonine*' &c in index. What the deuce the thing means I dont know; but here it is." Melville must have heard how much Hoadley had admired *Clarel*.

Copying out "The Age of the Antonines" for Hoadley (whether it was from among the old manuscripts or more recent) may have inspired Melville to get it (or another poem) into print. On 17 June his sister Fanny wrote to Kate Lansing: "Ever so much love for Abe. Did he receive the paper containing those lines by Herman? 'Why I am A Churchman' has arrived; many thanks for sending it on, I wanted to read it." The context, members of the family passing on reading material, shows that Fanny or someone else had sent Abe a newspaper containing some poetry ("lines") by Herman in it, but a century and a quarter later the "paper" has not been located and the lines have not been identified. He may well have taken out for a fresh look whatever survived of the manuscript of the 1860 *Poems*, some of it already reworked in the early 1860s, before he began on *Battle-Pieces*. Freed from the long intense concentration of *Clarel* and having endured the pain of seeing it reviewed, he may have drafted now, in 1877, some of the poems he published in *John Marr* (1888) and *Timoleon* (1891) or left unpublished at his death. One of his great poems, "Art," may date from this period, when his artistic and physical powers were still at their height, and after he had moved far away from the simplicities of "The Artist of the Beautiful." He had measured the distance between having "bright conceptions" of works he might write and actually embodying a happy thought in a work of art. To give form to daydreams, to create "pulsed life" out of a "brave unbodied scheme," required the fusion of opposites, the meeting and mating of unlike things:

> A flame to melt—a wind to freeze;
> Sad patience—joyous energies;
> Humility—yet pride and scorn;
> Instinct and study; love and hate;
> Audacity—reverence. These must mate,
> and fuse with Jacob's mystic heart,
> To wrestle with the angel—Art.

A pondering autodidact all along, he had needed to define an aesthetic credo, in 1862, when he was still an unpublished poet. In "Art" he described the creative process in eleven lines. What he left out is what any great artist leaves out of the account—the cost to the artist and people around the artist.

Working as hard as ever at his job, and writing at his own speed, not so assiduously, Melville was freer to share his now more limited bookish pleasures, with young Abe Lansing as well as Hoadley. Having sent Abe his own copy of Béranger for Christmas 1876, over a period of months he helped Abe gather different editions of Chaucer. Melville was also eager to share his interest in civic architecture with Abe. In June 1877 he told Cousin Kate he wanted Abe to come and go with him to see the Lenox Library (well worth seeing, Kate wrote to Abe on 17 June, a little incoherently, "for its superb building & its valuable endowment fund") before it closed temporarily. He was even able to do belated kindness to the Albany poet Alfred Street, Augusta's friend, whom he had so wounded in 1852. From Gansevoort on 14 August 1877, on the piazza in faultless weather, he wrote to Abe and Kate: "I have just been reading in a copy of Frank Leslie's Illustrated paper [of 18 August] 'The Old Garden' by Mr Street. How beautiful, and poetically true to nature it is! It is like a flower-and-fruit piece by some mellow old Fleming.—There, I wont bore you any more.—H.M." Uncle Peter would not know it, but he was making amends, at whatever cost to his high aesthetic principles.

As the months passed it became clear that Melville was not the man he had been when he began *Clarel* in late 1869 or 1870. The death of Malcolm, and other deaths; the loss of his career; the failure of *Clarel;* the relentless pressure of his vulnerable position at the Custom House—these, and age, took their toll on him. In June of 1877 there was again a serious threat that Melville would be fired; he was kept on, but with longer working hours, a hardship for a man almost fifty-eight. (He was now working out of an office at 6 State Street, according to the 1877 directory.) In early August 1877 in a letter to Cousin Kate he referred to her and Abe as "people of leisure," bluntness born of the new physical weakness and exacerbated by the increase in his working hours. It was a descriptive phrase, meaning that they were in command of their own hours. Cousin Kate, who single-handedly made sure the family plot in the Albany Rural Cemetery was maintained, who shopped assiduously (keeping Tiffany's afloat with her requirements for mourning jewelry alone), who entertained, who received callers and paid calls on a grand scale, who was year by year making herself into an authority on silver-making in the colonial period and the early Republic (the way Lizzie's cousin George Wales was making himself one of the foremost experts in ceramics), had all but absolute command of her time. She could do what might seem frivolous things—such as taking her dog Di down to the great "Dog Show" in the Hippodrome in May. She could dragoon Herman into looking in at the show for a few moments in the evening of 9 May, and she could take due satisfaction that Di was commended in her class. ("This is something at such an Exhibition," Abe loyally assured her on the eleventh.) Melville apologized when Kate challenged him on the "people of leisure" remark, but in that 5 September letter he added: "it amused me—your disclaiming the thing, as if there was any merit in *not* being a person of leisure. Whoever is not in the possession of leisure can hardly be said to possess independence. They talk of the *dignity of work*. Bosh. True work is the *necessity* of poor humanity's earthly condition. The dignity is in leisure. Besides, 99 hundreths of all the *work* done in the world is either foolish and unnecessary, or harmful and wicked." Melville would hardly have counted his work at the Custom House as qualifying for that blessed 1 percent. Nothing about it bestowed dignity upon him, as the governorship of the Sailors' Snug Harbor (despite all the complaints against him) indubitably bestowed upon Tom.

Now for the first time Melville talked regularly about the effects of aging. His older sister Helen, who understood this best, wrote him on 31 January 1877, lacing her letter with Scottish phrasing. Her nieces Minnie and Lottie ("blackbirds," Herman called young girls like his own daughters, dressed up for parties in their silk dresses—always mourning dresses) had gone to an assembly and "returned 'among the sma' hours,'" and she wrote to Herman: "ah me! what a thing it is to be young, to be sure!" Melville's sense of weary fatalism came out in a letter to Cousin Kate on 7 March 1877: "How about President [Rutherford B.] Hayes? I chanced to turn over a file of your Albany Argus yesterday, and was all but blown off the stool by the tremendous fulminations of that indignant sheet. — But what's the use? life is short, and Hayes' term is four years, each of 365 days." In August 1843 Gansevoort had campaigned with Samuel Tilden, the man from whom the 1876 election had been stolen, and Allan had written Gansevoort a rueful narrative of a fruitless "chase after Mr Tilden," who had learned somehow that Allan "had been in pursuit of his excellent self" but had rendezvoused with Gansevoort without seeing Allan. Melville's older and next younger brother had flourished among that little world of Democratic lawyers and law students on Pine Street or Nassau Street or Wall Street while Herman was in the Pacific. Melville was not one to reflect on his being one or two dead brothers away from intimacy with the man who had received the most votes for president, but he saw the eclipse of Tilden, after the disgrace of Oakey Hall, as a falling away of the young lawyers who had been part of the milieu in which he started writing *Typee* late in 1844.

In the 31 March 1877 letter to Hoadley Melville had offered an explanation "in palliation" of his "incivility" in delaying a few days before answering Hoadley's own friendly letter: "You are young; but I am verging upon three-score, and at times a certain lassitude steals over one — in fact, a disinclination for doing anything except the indispensable. At such moments the problem of the universe seems a humbug, and epistolary obligations mere moonshine, and the — well, nepenthe seems all-in-all." Later in the day he looked over the letter and feigned an apology for it:

> It is a queer sort of an absurd scribble, but if it evidences good-fellowship and good feeling, it serves the purpose. You are young (as I said before) but I aint; and at my years, and with my disposition, or rather constitution, one gets to care less and less for everything except downright good feeling. Life is so short, and so ridiculous and irrational (from a certain point of view) that one knows not what to make of it, unless — well, finish the sentence for yourself.
>
>   Thine
>   In these inexplicable fleshly bonds
>   H. M.

He added: "N.B. *I aint crazy.*" He wasn't insane, but he was bone tired, and getting old.

In his weariness Melville may have behaved irascibly in the privacy of his house, although when Mary Lanman Douw Ferris, a granddaughter of the abandoned John De Peyster Douw (plainly ignorant of *her* scandalous family story), in 1901 sent proofs of a piece she had written on Melville, Elizabeth

Shaw Melville challenged the word "gruff": "I do not think my husband's manner ever could be called 'gruff' though being approached at times when his mind was absorbed in some phase of his literary work it might have seemed so." He seemed tyrannical with his daughters and with the succession of Irish servants in the kitchen, yet what others saw as tyranny was suppressed panic: susceptible to caffeine jags, he required the cook to serve him just the right amount of coffee which he could then dilute with hot water. After the failure of *Clarel*, Lizzie saw evidences of a heightened susceptibility to states of morbid sensitivity to fancied slights by members of his family. Some of the slights must have been real, for Lem, at least, habitually went out of his way to insult Melville. On 25 February 1877 Lizzie wrote to Cousin Kate a specific plea: "I want you *always* to mention Herman's name in your letters, especially if it is to say anything about coming down — I know your feeling is always right to him, and so does everyone else, but he is *morbidly* sensitive, poor fellow, and I always try (though I can't succeed to my sorrow) to smooth the fancied rough edges to him wherever I can — so I know you will understand why I mention it." Perhaps the morbid sensitivity Lizzie described (if in fact she accurately perceived it) derived specifically from his disappointment with *Clarel*, and had something to do with Melville's prideful determination not to take more from Kate than the original twelve hundred dollars for the subsidy of the poem. It is possible that Lizzie was accurately assessing the response Herman would have if Kate simply wrote a family letter without mentioning his name, but it is also hard to imagine that Kate would ever have written without conveying her love to Herman and the children. A shift was in fact occurring: people were already saying that they had seen Lizzie when almost surely they had seen both Lizzie and Herman, and he may have observed and resented instances of this emerging pattern in which he was treated as if he were not there.

People were still visiting at Twenty-sixth Street, whatever they knew about long past or more recent tensions there. George Wales visited at least Lizzie in May before leaving for a year abroad, as he wrote Kate Lansing on 23 May: "We had a very pleasant visit of a week in New York and was glad to find Mrs Melville so well." On 5 June, just after Abe sent Melville his share of Peter Gansevoort's estate, five hundred dollars, Lizzie assured Kate of her welcome: "Of course, come down this week, any day you like, it is *perfectly* convenient, and we shall all be very happy to have you." Lizzie assured Kate that the legacy gave Melville great pleasure and that she hoped it would "make him really happier to have something to call his own — poor fellow he has so much mental suffering to undergo (and oh how *all* unnecessary)." She declared that she rejoiced when anything came "into his life to give him even a moment's relief." Perhaps the mental suffering was from Melville's failure to make money and keep his fame as an author, but the notion that it was "*all unnecessary*" indicates Lizzie's inability to understand the depth of the injustice Melville had suffered from the literary establishment and the reading public. Underlying everything else was Lizzie's Unitarian conviction that (while her own physical and mental sufferings were real) her husband suffered unnecessarily in his mind. His suffering was all unnecessary only if the cause was unimportant, only if he had been wrong to be so ambitious for literary success long ago, and again in early 1876.

Melville's sister Fanny on 13 February 1877 had reported to Kate Lansing that Tom was "very busy with plans for building in the spring." Tom showed the sculptor Augustus St. Gaudens around the Harbor so he could look over sites for a proposed monument to the founder, Captain Randall. St. Gaudens then presented a design at the 26 March meeting of the trustees of the Sailors' Snug Harbor in their Manhattan office, and the ensuing contract called for St. Gaudens to erect "in the Sailors' Snug Harbor a full length bronze statue not less than nine feet tall and to design a suitable pedestal," for which he was "to be paid $10,000, in installments." He did not design the pedestal, as it turned out, but gave the job to Stanford White, whose base for the statue of Captain Randall was to be eighteen by six feet, according to a telegram White sent Tom on 15 October 1879. Melville and Duyckinck knew young White as the son of Richard Grant White, their literary acquaintance from the 1840s who more recently had been a fellow employee of Melville's at the Custom House. In June 1877 the senior White, then in charge of the Revenue Cutter Bureau, was a member of Collector Chester Arthur's committee for (according to the *Tribune*) "CUSTOM-HOUSE PRUNING/SELECTING THE VICTIMS." The papers referred to the job-pruning as Collector Arthur's "Golgothur," but once again Melville was spared.

The St. Gaudens commission was on Tom's mind when Melville went down on 12 April and "anchored for the night in the 'Snug Harbor.'" Herman and Allan years before had made Evert Duyckinck welcome at Tom's Harbor, and in April 1877 Duyckinck, through Herman, presented four watercolors of the Battle of the Nile. On the thirteenth Herman reported that he and Tom had visited the new wing and "selected a good place for the Prints, where the old Salts can look up at them from off their dominoes—a favorite game with them." With something like his old jocular grandiosity (this is the time he wrote on the back of a customs form for the Discharging of Vessels), Melville elaborated, the style in deliberate contrast to the stationery: "All you have now to do, is to provide for an annual Lecture, to be delivered before the old veterans in the big hall of the Institution, on the Battle of the Nile, the pictures serving to illustrate the matter." The four did not constitute a veritable panorama to be commented upon scene by scene, but it was in fact a splendid gift and gave pleasure for many years before neglect took its toll on them. Nelson's victory over Napoleon's fleet was already part of Melville's historical memory, but now he was reminded afresh of the French ships, including the *Timoleon* (a name which he used as the title of a book) and the *Franklin;* and the British, including the *Bellerophon* and the *Swiftsure* (that accursed name from 1830, when the eleven-year-old Herman made his agonizingly slow escape from Manhattan with his father up the North River).

In the two years after the publication of *Clarel*, Melville had continued to call on Duyckinck with some regularity, and seems to have had some sociable contact with others of Duyckinck's friends who came calling at the same time in the evening that Melville did, picking their way, according to an obituary which Richard Lathers preserved and quoted, to 20 Clinton Place, "which of late had queer surroundings for a man of quiet and retiring habits. But he so disliked changes!" That fall of 1877 Melville continued his visits to Duyckinck, on 13 November being there in company with Henry Thayer Drowne, a balding man with low jaw-whiskers and a goatee, who in 1872 had edited a Revolutionary account by his grandfather Dr. Solomon Drowne, *Journal of the Cruise in the Fall of 1780 in the Private-Sloop of War, Hope.* Drowne, then president of the National Fire Insurance Company, was an amateur historian and genealogist, and a collector of engravings. He was even more passionately interested than Melville in the Society of the Cincinnati, especially its early French members, and inherited the badge of the Cincinnati the next year. (With a name like his, in that company of Hawthorne-readers, Drowne had to expect racy jokes about what wooden image he had been chipping away at.) A fourth man that evening was Alexander Jackson Davis, the architect of Winyah, who like Melville, in anything like a club where Burgundy might flow, was ready to fulminate for hours about the degeneration of American culture and especially of New York City architecture. Like Melville, Davis, the great collaborator with Andrew Jackson Downing, was out of favor. The Civil War broke his career, for much of his work had been in the South, and that was gone. After the war, taste had changed, and Second Empire and high Victorian Gothic were triumphant. Davis was bitter about Richard Morris Hunt's Lenox Library, to name one building, and bitter about the failure of his long struggle to have architecture recognized as an art. Melville was ready to rant in his turn, having witnessed the precipitous decline of American letters.

In 1877 new patterns were emerging for the Melvilles' vacations. In 1877 Lem paid for Lizzie and the girls to go to the Plaisted House in Jefferson for six weeks, the only problem for Lizzie being how Herman would manage in

New York. The first plan was that Herman would spend his full two weeks at Gansevoort, where his itinerant sister Fanny would be in residence with some of the family from eastern Massachusetts. Poor Fanny felt less and less at home at the Mansion House in Gansevoort. On 13 July she opened the house, as she wrote to Kate, and faced her memories, especially her "overpowering thoughts of Augusta," and struggled "to retain composure of manner & voice." Cousin Kate persuaded her to come to Albany frequently, and as the months passed with her visiting her remaining brothers and sisters and the Lansings it became obvious that she was uprooted. Lizzie put it plainly in a letter to Kate Lansing on 25 February 1877: "she will hardly know where she belongs." On 11 August Melville stopped off in Albany and spent the day with the Lansings, who took him for the evening to the showplace home of Judge Elisha P. Hurlbut and his wife, the former Kate Van Vechten.

Melville stopped off also at Saratoga Springs for three hours, and rather than shrinking away he positioned himself conspicuously. Something of the nature of the moving spectacle is suggested by the observations of a correspondent of the Boston *Post* (12 August 1872), for five years had not changed the essentials: "Saratoga, whatever its other qualities, is death on good resolutions. It is astonishing how a man's courage and energy ooze out when he finds himself squarely and comfortably planted on this big Congress Hall piazza," watching people, but, better, watching the "crowd of equipages—a perfect whirlwind of them, of every size, shape and color, drawn by thoroughbreds of every breed and hue." Much like this reporter, Melville self-consciously sought the best vantage point (as he wrote the Lansings on 14 August): "I lunched at a neat little restaurant I found there, and visited the hotels, presenting no doubt a distinguished appearance in my duster, and finally took up a commanding position on the piazza of the Great Union, and surveyed at my leisure the moving spectacle of fashion and—in some instances—folly. A New York paper also of the day helped to occupy the time." Recollections colored his broodings, as far back as stories of his Grandfather Gansevoort, the hero of Saratoga as well as Fort Stanwix, as recent as the latest news from Stanwix. After this unwonted ostentation on the piazza, Melville caught the train. At Gansevoort he found his sisters Fanny and Kate Hoadley and her son Frankie—"all well and warm in welcome." On the fourteenth he rejoiced to the Lansings: "To-day is faultless weather and I shall dedicate it to leisure and the piazza," the long front porch on the Mansion House, a quieter vantage point than the piazza of the Great Union, but still a place apt to provoke ruminations on the evanescence of family glories. In 1877 the Mansion House at Gansevoort had women in it and for masculine company had only young Frankie and, briefly, Herman. Rather than staying on until Helen and a niece arrived at Gansevoort (perhaps one of Allan's daughters, perhaps one of Kate's), Melville joined Lizzie and their daughters at Jefferson.

At Plaisted's in 1877 a new part of the family life began, for there Fanny met her future husband, Henry B. Thomas. In 1929 Harry Thomas recalled that summer when he first saw his future wife, and also when he first saw Melville: he told an interviewer then that he was "engaged in the prosaic act of buying a cigar at the desk at the Plaisted House in Jefferson, but he was such a striking figure and so dignified in the transaction that Mr. Thomas was profoundly impressed." A later variant of the story is given by Melville's granddaughter Eleanor:

> It was in Jefferson that my father first saw Herman Melville, in the summer of 1877, and where he fell in love with my mother at first sight, as she sat on the railing of the Plaisted House piazza. She was very beautiful in feature, coloring, and expression.
>
> Of Herman he once told me, "He came into the lobby to buy a cigar. He did it with a certain air. I did not know who he was, but he bought a cigar and walked out in a way that impressed me"—as much as to say, this simple act showed him to be no ordinary man. Perhaps it was partly the erect bearing and squared shoulders that imparted a dignity that seemed to add to his height. Many who knew him would have said he was six feet tall, whereas he was two to three inches short of that.

Back in New York, Melville wrote his Cousin Kate on 5 September 1877: "You mention having spent a peaceful Sunday at Gansevoort, enjoying it much, with Abraham. I should have liked it well to have been of the company. I was so sorry that, purposing my main visit among the mountains, I was not able to devote more time to Gansevoort. Helen, Kate, Fanny, & Minnie must be having a pleasant time there together." Melville felt "decidedly lonely often in the house," but he saw people at meals at the boardinghouse nearby run by the Hartnett sisters. On 25 September Tom reported on him to Kate Lansing: "Herman is very well & expects Lizzie & the girls home next week."

On 30 September Lizzie herself reported to Kate Lansing, having visited her stepmother in Boston on the way home: "We have had a very pleasant vacation and return much refreshed. Now we have to go at it 'hammer & tongs' to get the house cleaned and in winter order and expect to be upset generally for about two weeks. We are going to make some change on the upper floor so as to have a comfortable guest-chamber for two, and hope when we get to rights that you and Cousin Abe will both come down and occupy it." She and Bessie had been entirely free of hay fever in Jefferson, and now were suffering, but only moderately. Jane Dempsey Melville's behavior with young George Dillaway had reached the point that on 9 October Lizzie alluded to it in a letter to Kate Lansing delicately, and only because Kate had pushed the issue: "About the 'shell necklace' you speak of, if it refers to possibilities of an approaching marriage in the family, I will say that George D. has returned, and has not seen Mrs. M. since she sailed from here. He had business in *London* and did not go out of that place & was there on acct of a firm here in the city who paid his expenses, and a $300. fee besides, so much for that 'mare's nest.'"

Herman and Elizabeth (with their daughters?) were in Boston for Thanksgiving. On 1 December (according to Hope Savage Shaw's diary) Melville and Sam went "to Mr. [James Freeman] Clark[e]s Church" (Clarke being the man who had given communion to Lizzie on her wedding day) and in the evening the two went "to Mrs. Kimball," perhaps the widow of John Hoadley's first father-in-law, the classmate of Chief Justice Shaw. In December Lizzie stayed on, for Helen reported to Kate Lansing on 7 December that on the evening of the fifth Lizzie had attended "a grand 'regardless of Expense' party, given by an old friend of hers, to introduce two pretty young daughters, fresh from a two years abode in Europe." Jane had come to Boston to attend it also, and "was beautifully gotten up, for the occasion." Helen added coolly: "She is at the Tremont House, I hear." Lizzie reported to Kate Lansing on 31 December: "I had a *very, very* delightful visit in Boston the weather was so fine and I went about and saw many old friends. I am glad to be as much as possible with my dear mother, for I cannot help feeling that she is declining in many ways, though she keeps well, and has no special ailment." Lizzie added the clear news of how her stepmother was fading: "She inquired for you most kindly and talked a great deal about Henry, seeming to think he was still living."

At the Governor's House at Sailors' Snug Harbor, indisputably the family seat, Tom and Katie again in 1877 gave Christmas dinner for Herman and Lizzie and the girls and for all four of Allan's daughters (but not his widow). Willie must have accompanied Milie, and their baby, Allan, performed: "on this occasion he sat up at the table for an hour or more as straight and good as any one" (Lizzie wrote to Kate Lansing on 31 December). Memorials of the dead continued to reach Twenty-sixth Street. In June 1877 Kate Lansing had sent Herman her father's sleeve-buttons, which Herman on 12 July promised to preserve always "as a lasting memorial" of one whom he had "more than one reason to remember with love." At the end of the year she sent the Melvilles a copy of Hoadley's *Memorial of Henry Sanford Gansevoort*, the production of which had obsessed her and exhausted Hoadley. Other deaths in the family had continued. Hoadley's mother died in Cincinnati in mid-March, a month short of eighty-three. On 7 April 1877 Dr. Amos Nourse died—the second husband of Melville's Aunt Lucy. Lizzie knew him better than her husband did. Half a year later, on 24 October, Aunt Lucy died. (Captain Thomas Melville received a keepsake, probably after Aunt Lucy's death, a cup and saucer marked "T.M." that had belonged to Aunt Lucy's father, old Major Melvill, the recipient's grandfather.) In 1877 a temporary footbridge was opened between the looming Manhattan and Brooklyn towers of the Brooklyn Bridge: could Herman Melville have resisted walking it?

In February 1878 the Harpers account showed $64.38 due to Melville from the sales of *Omoo* (33 copies), *Redburn* (35), *White-Jacket* (58), and *Moby-Dick* (66) since 1 August 1876. He was an author who received royalties again—much better than a poetaster in search of a publisher. While visiting Herman with his sister Fanny in late March, Kate Lansing gave him "the Oriskany & Schuylerville Centennial Volumes"—memorials of their Grandfather Gansevoort. Kate Lansing continued to stay at Twenty-sixth Street on her visits to town. On 31 March 1878 she wrote her husband: "Cousin Herman wished for you at dinner & drank to you." In late May and June of 1878 Melville's hands pained him severely, so that his sister Fanny was relieved when his right hand was good enough for him to write to her, while his left was not yet entirely recovered. In June 1878, while Herman was recovering from this incapacitating affliction of the hands, Charles Thurston died. Able again to use his right hand, Herman wrote to Fanny, with the Hoadleys, and Fanny was struck enough by what he said to quote a bit in a 14 June letter to Kate Lansing: "Speaking of Mr Charles Thurston's sudden death—he says, 'whose end by the way may hardly be thought unhappy—the manner of it I mean—since he died in summer and suddenly, and in the open air, and in a garden.'"

On 21 April 1878, Easter Sunday, the Melvilles' daughter Fanny became engaged to Harry Thomas, and Lizzie rejoiced that she had a chance for happiness. On 28 April Lizzie wrote to Kate Lansing, having already arranged that Melville's sister Fanny tell her the news. Young Thomas had made "a chance visit" to his vacationing mother and sisters, who had already impressed Lizzie favorably "by their marked refinement and good breeding." They had been assured of Harry's "good principles and unblemished character" and a "small inherited property" not tied up in his business, which was a "comparatively a safe one—commission business in which he is well started in partnership with a reasonable prospect of success." Heretofore Fanny had declared that "the 'coming man' would have to be a *rich* one anyway—having had enough of the other kind of way of getting along," but she had "modified her ideas considerably." This was in Lizzie's eyes a highly suitable match—financial and social responsibility on the side of the Philadelphia Thomases and with admirable ancestry on the bride's part (and the prospect of eventual inheritances). Harry Thomas did not win a happy young woman, but he won the chance to offer her respite and eventual contentment away from her father. In May 1878 young Fanny wrote to Kate Lansing: "Last Saturday evening, Uncle Tom and Aunt Kate, Florence Kitty & Lucy were all here to meet the 'gentleman from Philadelphia' and the girls spent Sunday with us. You can imagine that with all those girls in the house and Bessie, I did not get much peace." She supposed they would get tired of teasing her "after a while." On his fifty-ninth birthday Melville took Harry Thomas over to the Sailors' Snug Harbor to see his brother, Thomas, making him ever more part of the family he was to marry into.

Tom had invited Herman and his family to spend the Fourth of July at the Sailors' Snug Harbor, so Fanny, at Lawrence, wrote Kate Lansing that she supposed they had a merry time. At the Harbor Herman saw some artistic work beyond basket-weaving, for (according to Charles H. Farnham in the New York *Times* of 2 June 1878) one of the inmates furnished Tom with "appropriate designs for decorating the ceiling of the reception room with anchors, compasses, ropes, and knots in a tasteful combination." At least one other inmate was proficient at spinning yarns "in acceptable rhyme" — about the level Herman himself was achieving in some retrospective nautical verses he was writing. That year Arrowhead was still kept open as a summer house and Rowland Morewood probably was still summering at Broadhall, for when the Melvilles divided up at the end of July Bessie left early for Pittsfield, Lizzie went to Boston with her Fanny, then Bessie joined them to "start for the Mountains" on 7 August, where Melville was to show up later, when his vacation started. His sister Fanny was hoping he would go by Lawrence on his way so she and the Hoadleys could see him "as Gansevoort is not open" (as Fanny wrote Kate Lansing on 28 July). The happy summer reunions of Melville brothers and sisters and their children were approaching the end after all the deaths, and there were always new deaths. Katie Melville's sister Belle's husband, the Reverend Dr. Bagley, died suddenly on 12 July — after entertaining Tom and Katie the evening before. This summer of 1878, the Mansion House remained closed far past the usual time, since no one was able to go with Fanny. Instead, Allan's daughters urged her to go to Arrowhead, which had been freshly painted for the first time since well before Allan's death. Fanny and Helen arrived in Gansevoort on 12 September and the next day opened the house and took "a general look at things, in doors & out" and found it as left the previous fall. They made themselves "comfortable in the south parlor & Mamma's bed-room" and urged Kate and Abe to come up: "You ask if you can do anything for us — thanks for the kind thought, but we have all we will need while here, this Garden of Eden life, calls but for little." In 1878 Melville must have visited at Gansevoort at least briefly, and he stayed three days in Albany with the Lansings. Back in New York City he wrote the Lansings on 12 August that his pleasure at being with them enhanced the loneliness on his return to his "solitary house": "I don't know that I shall visit you & Abraham again, if the eventual result is but an augmentation of the blues. — Howsomedever, every one manages to rub along." (Lizzie was away with the girls at Jefferson, New Hampshire, with Fanny's fiancé, Harry Thomas, close at hand.)

On his birthday in 1878 Herman had agreed to act as Kate Lansing's agent "in presenting to the Lenox Library a copy of Henry's Memorial," so on his way to work, far uptown at Seventy-sixth Street and the East River, he picked up the memorial volume at the Adams Express Office at Twenty-third near Fifth Avenue when it arrived a few days later and carried it up. He did not find his acquaintance, "Mr Moore the librarian," but he assured Kate on the sixth that he had left the volume "with the janitor in perfect security," arranging to stop by to see Mr. Moore himself about it. This was the new Lenox Library much inveighed against by Herman's friend Davis as an example of "hideous deformity." In 1878 Melville continued to call on Evert Duyckinck some evenings, usually finding him alone, but on 30 January being joined by A. J. Davis and on 23 February by "Bouton Robinson" (unidentified — one man? or Mr. Bouton and Mr. Robinson?). Shortly after Melville turned fifty-nine, the one remaining link with the publishing world of his young manhood was severed: on 13 August, Evert Duyckinck died. Surely he attended the funeral on 16 August. What the loss meant to Melville is unimaginable. He had long forgiven Duyckinck for doing his Christian duty in regard to *Moby-Dick* and *Pierre*.

Two and a half months after Duyckinck's death — just possibly because of his death, because this private outlet for his fulminations was sealed off — Davis published a vehement public statement in the 28 October 1878 New York *Sun*. The piece, "An Old Architect on Modern Architecture" was addressed "To the Mayor of New York and the Public through the Press." He railed against "the New Court House, as at variance with the harmony of the structure and disgraceful to the honor of every citizen." He denounced the city "committee-men" who let public money be spent on "unmeaning, irrelevant ornament," in "ostentatious waste," and in inculcating "a diseased thirst for novelty and the picturesque" such as had already resulted "in hideous deformity, like the several hospitals, Female College, Lenox Library, Presbyterian Church, corner of Lexington avenue and Seventy-third street, and the Park Observatory." These structures disgraced the city "by their ill-proportioned exteriors, multiplied breaks, discordant colors, string courses and lintels, capricious, fantastic, broken heaps of littleness, and whimsical designs, costly and deformed, puerile, wasteful, and often incendiary." He named more buildings that defied any principles of architecture: "Witness the new Post Office — is it not a broken pile of costly vulgarity? — the *Tribune* building; the new Jefferson Market Court House; . . . hybrid churches, of uncertain doctrine, where meretricious, irrelevant ornamentation is no uncertain symbol of 'ways that are not my ways;' the Lenox Library, and neighboring hospitals; losing all sight in audience halls of fitness, phonics, and sight; in stores and dwellings, security against fire and hostile elements; in churches, simplicity and dignity. These deformities are again and again repeated." This was dated "September, 1877" and signed "Alex. J. Davis," the 1877 an error, for the date of publication was 1878, and the piece was nothing if not timely. After Tuckerman's death Davis was the only man Melville regularly saw who ranked as an original aesthetician, and his roll call of buildings provides a remarkably specific reminder of the changing face of New York that Melville made his way through month after month, year after year. The letter to the *Sun* is the best commentary on parts of some prose sketches Melville may have already been working on as well as the introductory essay, "House of the Tragic Poet," which he wrote a few years later. The structures which so offended Davis did not necessarily offend Melville, who was pleased, as well he might have been, with the Lenox Library, one of the buildings Davis decried. Duyckinck's death cut Melville off from the society of Davis and the chance to take wry pleasure in railing with Davis against most things modern. He still railed in the privacy of his house, as his daughter Frances always said, but that was no fun compared to the joy of railing companionably with another great old fogy.

Melville may have seen Duyckinck many more times than we have record of, and have encountered Drowne, Davis, and other admirable men there. After Duyckinck died, Melville apparently lost touch with these men. If Davis went public with his comments on current architecture partly because he could not express himself adequately in private, Melville may have done something similar. Perhaps before Duyckinck's death, as early as late 1876 or 1877, perhaps after Duyckinck's death, Melville created a society he could enjoy at home. He began sketching, in prose, portraits of invented characters, Major Jack Gentian, the Marquis de Grandvin, and other members of an imaginary Burgundy Club, who carry the values of an older time into the alien era of Reconstruction. In these sketches, which he did not live to publish, are references to the death of Charles Sumner (11 March 1874); to Memorial Day as falling "the last Tuesday of every May" (it fell on Tuesday, 30 May 1876, and Melville later corrected the manuscript to read the "Thirtieth of every May"); to the celebration of the Fourth of July "getting along now in its second century"; to Grant's presidency as being in the past (he left office on 4 March 1877). (He added a few other datable references to these manuscripts while he was working on them in the last half dozen years of his life.)

Melville may have begun with a "Portrait of a Gentleman," Major Jack Gentian, a transplanted Southerner like Richard Lathers, who had been a soldier on the frontier in his early years, a Major in the Union army in the Civil War, and is now embarked upon "the after-mission of his life, namely, the dispensing of those less abbreviated greetings on the avenue and considerate old-school hospitalities of the board." A social being, as Melville decidedly no longer was, Gentian shares with his creator "a certain impulsive straightforwardness at times" at war with the Chesterfieldian definition of the gentleman. Again like his creator, in his advancing age he permits himself "an easy latitude in his dress," and, on hearing "some story of perfidy or brutal behavior," is even capable of "incontinently" rapping out an expletive. He is accused not only of "a tendency to the aristocratic in general" but even "a weakness for certain gewgaws that savor of the monarchical," conspicuously "wearing on his left lapel the eagle-wings in gold of the Cincinnati, a venerable order whereof he who still reigns 'first in the hearts of his countrymen' was the original head." Melville wore his inspector's badge on his left lapel, that being the one most men find easiest to pin a badge to, but in recent years he had been thinking of his Gansevoort grandfather's badge of the Cincinnati, and at Duyckinck's had met Drowne, the authority on the society. Melville has the Major boast (in surviving drafts) that the badge is better than "the insignia of the Knights of the Golden Fleece or the Knights of the Spanish order of the Holy Ghost." Those were the true gimcracks, and the last "in fact as in name, but a ghostly sort of vanity."

Later Melville drafted several prose pieces which survive in somewhat duplicative fragments, three of some length. In "Jack Gentian" Melville depicts men seated in Madison Square, "disreputable nondescripts, nonproducers in deplorable attire, plunged in lugubrious reveries on their doubtless misspent lives"—a mocking self-portrait, since Melville often walked the couple of blocks from his house to sit in the park, especially at tulip time. Melville managed a dig at pieties he lived with: "This is America, Christian America, thank God; where, be it what it may, one's bank account is of no account whatever in an American's estimate of a fellow American." He followed this with having an old fellow declare that at a dinner given by Mrs. Jones "there was twenty three million represented by the guests, twenty three million dollars"—just the sort of comment he might have seen in any of the papers. The question "What are you worth?" in Christian America could be answered only by a number of dollars. Another sketch, "Major Gentian and Colonel J. Bunkum," contains some patriotic rhetoric by the Colonel in denunciation of the Major's badge of the Cincinnati: "'And is such a man, — I put it to your consciences — the sort of man to take place with the law-makers of a people, the chosen people, the advance-guard of progress, a priestly people, the Levite of the nations, to whose custody Jehovah has entrusted the sacred ark of human freedom?' (Cries of no no, and riotous applause.)" This sort of game Melville had pretty much abandoned after the anecdotes about Old Zack in 1847, but he still knew how to play it. Even after Bunkum denounces "McClellan's Fabian tactics," the Major forgives him charitably, leading the speaker to decide that this is "Christian charity with a vengeance," and to make an unflattering judgment on the Major: "But some of us ere now have thought that by such charitable construings (or, are they but indolently stoical ones?) of words or actions not charitable, thy failing to take the trouble to resent them, however absurd they may be, and vindicate thyself, thou hast — and more than once or twice, too — been something of a loser." Melville could identify with a man who had been something of a loser. Another longish fragment, "The Cincinnati," consists mainly of a meditation by the "philosopher" of the Burgundy Club, the possessor of a great library of Americana, on the public's loss of historical memory. The average man on the street no longer can identify the white border on the blue ribbon of the badge of the Cincinnati as an allusion to the Bourbon allies of the colonies in the American Revolution. The philosopher sounds very much like Melville himself in his letter to his mother (1870) about his visit to the Gansevoort Hotel; it may owe a good deal to Henry Thayer Drowne. Here also Melville used the comparison of the badge of the Cincinnati to the insignia of the old Spanish Order of the Knights of the Holy Ghost.

Melville brought another prose sketch to completion and at some point entitled it "To Major John Gentian / Dean of the Burgundy Club." In this depiction of the Major's thoughts on the Fourth of July in the present, the mid- or late 1870s, the Major is declared to be one-armed, having lost one in the Battle of the Wilderness under Grant. Despite his mutilation "no superfluous syllable" fell from his lips condemning the South. He graciously honors the memory of Charles Sumner, though far "from sharing in all his advocated measures" — punitive measures toward the South such as Hoadley championed. The Major enters into a humorous diatribe on the young boy who provides himself with explosives for the Fourth of July, a boy who makes himself "a spluttering blunderbuss" and may hurt himself or members of the crowd or burst his toy-cannon with his discharges. What then, Gentian asks; will he go to Hades for it? If so, "*Dulcit amor patriae!* That's the inscription, Sir, on General Worth's monument you and I pass everyday. Ten to one you never noticed it — the inscription, I mean." General William J. Worth was a hero of the war against Mexico, a man (Grant later recalled in his *Memoirs*) who moved his troops so fast he wore them out in a few days without accomplishing much, although his fighting qualities kept his men and officers loyal to him. The monument to Worth, with his tomb under it, had been constructed by James G. Batterson in 1857 at a traffic island formed by the crossing of Broadway and Fifth Avenue just below Twenty-fourth Street, across from Madison Square. Melville passed the monument regularly, and looked at it, inscription and all. While speaking all this the Major is seated at his customary place at a bay window of the Burgundy Club, very like the University Club, which until 1888 was at 1 West Twenty-fifth, facing the Worth monument. Melville would have loved such a place, cozy, quiet corners in winter, cool nooks in summer. By early disposition he could have been a club-man, as Lemuel Shaw Jr. conspicuously was, but for much of his life he was a failed farmer in a rundown farmhouse eight hours from Manhattan (where neighbors were bigoted gossipmongers, fanatics in religion and politics) and then for many years a man in a dark, north-facing study in a row house whose only regular intellectual companions were imaginary.

Asked if he knew General Worth personally, the Major broods a moment then replies:

> The last time I saw Will Worth was on the night-boat coming down from Albany—by Jove, it seems but a week or two ago—he then being bound for Mexico to pay his military respects to General Santa Anna in the field.—But he came back horizontal who went forth so erect!—Ay, but like the great Gustavus, Sir, from Lutzen field, if dirged yet laurelled. Pray, sir, can you repeat the battle-names on the monumental shaft, *Cherumbosco, Buenna Vista, Rescaca de la Palma, San Antonio, Cerro Gordo.*—There's a volly for you of vowels and victories! Ay, and *Monterey* too, that superb dash of arms, one inspiring my chivalric friend, Charles Fenno Hoffman—remember Charlie, Sir? No, no; you don't go back so far—inspired his fine lyric.

The Major recites some lines about storming home the towers of Monterey, lines Melville had learned from his real friend Charlie's poem three decades earlier—the friend whose fate, to be forgotten in a Pennsylvania lunatic asylum, was even stranger than his own.

Older memories than those from the Mexican War recur to the Major—memories of the doughnut and cider booths that ringed the little triangular City Hall Park every Fourth of July (the park where Gansevoort later had his first chance at political glory). Flooded with memories, and quoting Horace on the speeding of time and the inevitability of death, the Major remembers another stanza from Hoffman's poem, and stirs himself to welcome friends to dinner: "Not good for a man to be alone, especially on the immortal Fourth." The Major glorifies the Fourth, but he shuns the new holiday, Memorial Day, as being too partisan, a self-serving device of the Radical Republicans.

He remembers scenes from the war, "the scouting, the foraging" such as Melville knew from one intense experience. It emerges that, like Melville, the Major has been to Naples—nominated by President Grant as consul at Naples, he had arrived there to take his post only to learn that he was stranded there "unconfirmed by the Senate"—the fate of Mr. Prettyman from Delaware, who received (so he thought) the Florence consulship that Melville had longed for.

Madison Square was becoming Monument Square. The colossal hand holding the torch (waiting to be placed on the Statue of Liberty) had been in Philadelphia at the exhibition when Melville visited there in 1876, and after March 1877 Melville saw the hand holding the torch regularly in Madison Square Park for a time, before the completion of the monument on Bedloe's Island. Augustus St. Gaudens's monument to Admiral David Glasgow Farragut was installed in 1881 at the southeast corner of Fifth Avenue and East Twenty-sixth Street, facing Melville's direction. The Farragut Monument was democratically hospitable. Melville pored over the center of the Farragut base with its sword and waves and admired the fluid lines of the female figures on the wide base above the seat, and, as the passerby was invited to do, sat down on the south or the north side and leaned back against Loyalty or Courage, which the figures were meant to represent. According to Nelson, whose monument in Liverpool was the first important sculpture Melville ever saw, England had expected every man to do his duty, but Farragut had been idiomatically American: "Damn the torpedoes! Full speed ahead!" There were dolphins at home in Twenty-sixth Street on chair arms, and here there were dolphins at either end of the exedra. This was a place Melville the non-producer could visit and revisit.

Apparently after most of the pieces about the Major were written, Melville began a sketch about an ineffable inspirer of the Major, the Marquis de Grandvin—a "countryman of Lafayette and Frédéric Auguste Bartholdi," an "honorary member of most of the Fifth Avenue clubs," but elusive, since he is the spirit of wine. Bartholdi had been in the news in the United States intermittently since his first visit shortly after the war to scout out locations for his proposed gift from the French nation and to arouse interest in the project with the goal of having Liberty ready as a Centennial gift. That proved impossible, but the project proceeded, with enough bursts of anti-French sentiment to make Melville reflect on his own grandfathers' and his Uncle Thomas's acquaintance with Lafayette and the significance of the French support in George Washington's success. In the sketch of the Marquis Melville avowedly takes on the personality of De Grandvin "as the prophets of old, announcing the mind of their deity, in some instances dramatically put on his personality."

Melville may have drafted several of these prose sketches set in the present before he realized that he could employ them in a salvage operation on some old poems which he had "found" while going through some old papers, as he said to Hoadley about "The Age of the Antonines." What turned the trick may have been his giving the Major his own experience in Naples. When the Major entertains the younger men of his club with the story of his "Afternoon in Naples," one of them, the speaker of the sketch, volunteers to put it into verse, and — by a frugal coincidence — the verse he writes turns out to be identical or nearly so to what Melville had written many years earlier. The Marquis de Grandvin, invented subsequently to the Major, was then (quickly?) given the role of introducing "At the Hostelry" (renamed "A Symposium of Old Masters at Delmonico's"). In divine afflatus borrowed (he feigns) from the Marquis de Grandvin, Melville offers these two old but slightly reworked poems, in reverse order of their composition, now with prose comments interspersed through each of them.

At this stage (around 1878 or 1879) Melville drew up this title page:

<u>Parthenope</u>
<u>A Morning in Naples</u>
<u>In the time of Bomba</u>
with
An Introduction
merging into
A Symposium of Old Masters
At Delmonico's.
Liberally rendered from the ideal
of
The Marquis de Grandvin.

Later on this page he changed "A Morning in Naples" to "An Afternoon in Naples" and deleted the line "At Delmonico's." "Parthenope" (four syllables) he knew as a name for one of the Sirens but also as a poetical name for Naples. In his copy of Wordsworth was the poem written on the departure of Sir Walter Scott from Abbotsford to Naples: Melville was working within poetic conventions, as always. He was puttering with unambitious literary endeavors, aware of a very natural physical weakening and aware also that mental decline might soon manifest itself. Melville had ample reason to keep a ready reckoning of the state of his own mental agility, since he had lived already almost to the age Hawthorne had been at his death, Hawthorne whose mental disintegration had occurred in full public view, albeit posthumously, thanks to his widow and his publisher's exploitation of the *Dolliver*

Romance and other unfinished romances and notebook passages not designed for publication. Whether he had heard any jocular comments about his own decline or not, or made any such comments himself, in "Jack Gentian" Melville let the narrator recount "various bits of unflattering gossip concerning the declining faculties of the aging major." For some months, or for two or three years, Melville was deflected from poetry into prose sketches which he ultimately tied back to two unpublished poems. All this was private, written in the seclusion after work which he tried to keep inviolable.

Lizzie left for Boston on 29 July 1878 with her daughter Fanny. Bessie had been at Pittsfield but went to Boston to meet Lizzie and her sister, so after a week they could "start for the Mountains" (as Melville's sister Fanny wrote Kate Lansing on 28 July). By the time they left Boston, Bessie was unwell. They went to Jefferson, apparently, for this seems to be the year that Melville received a letter from "Jeffers Hill" from Mr. Thomas—while his daughter Fanny was there. Presumably Lizzie had both daughters with her. In her 28 July letter Melville's sister Fanny told Kate Lansing that Herman was planning to go to New Hampshire also, and perhaps "take Lawrence on his way," so she and the Hoadleys could see him. In October 1878 Fanny reported to Kate Lansing that she and Helen had received letters from young Fanny, Lizzie, Tom, Katie, Lottie, and Herman, all within a day or two. While they supervised the repair of fences and the building of new ones, Fanny and Helen took stock of the way their primitive life looked to the outside world, all of them slow to acknowledge that the Mansion House contained treasures in furnishing; none of them ever understood the value of the historical clothing and documents. A young artist was sketching "draperies" and "furniture & any thing old & odd that catches his Artistic eye," Fanny wrote Kate Lansing; by the end of October Helen reported that he had progressed upwardly: "The Turkey carpet is sitting for its portrait today, and 'our artist' has just gone up the stairs again, after standing by the fire awhile, to thaw his fingers." She was comical as usual about the calls "all the elite of the town" (yokels, they seemed to Helen) were paying upon her and Fanny, especially one woman and her daughter who had called "both in full war-paint and feathers." They kept the house open later than usual. On 7 November Helen wrote Kate Lansing that they were going to close it on the twelfth.

Lizzie and the girls stayed away until almost the end of September, then Bessie remained in Boston and Fanny stopped at Arrowhead on the way home. Lizzie suffered in New York, unable to go to church until 27 October, by which time Bessie had returned, bearing a gift from Hope to Lizzie, a dollar. Hope had also paid her fare to New York. The household was constricted. Just as he had let Arrowhead deteriorate in the last years of his residence there, Melville was unable to maintain the house on Twenty-sixth Street. The rooms that had been in good shape under Allan and Sophia's early tenancy had deteriorated during her illness, and Jane had regarded the cramped dwelling as not worth maintaining. Lizzie had paid dearly for refurbishing when they moved in, but then had to postpone any new improvements for many years. In the late 1860s and early 1870s, in any case, no one had the spirit to freshen up Mackey's room. Only in the years after *Clarel* was there money and desire even for cosmetic improvements. In 1877 Lizzie tried to make a "change on the upper floor so as to have a comfortable guest-chamber for two" that Kate and Abe could occupy. In 1878 there was astounding news, as Melville's sister Fanny wrote to Kate Lansing on 13 September: "We are all rejoicing over Lizzies great fortune & I write to tell you, knowing well how glad Abe & you will be to hear, that *she* has been left $10,000. Stanwix $4,000. Bessie & Fanny *each* $3000 a piece, by the will of her Aunt Mrs Marett who died this month—your friend Mrs. Gifford's mother—as the children would say, is it not splendid!" On 6 November 1878 Lizzie reported to Kate Lansing that Stanny was working in Quincy, California, and that he was "quite well" after having been sick ("poor fellow") and having to be in a hospital at Sacramento: "he has seen some very hard times, and deserves much credit for his pluck and patience under difficulties and disappointments." Thus she excused and hoped for him.

Kate Gansevoort Lansing worried about Herman's comfort as winter came on, and sent him a carpet in early November 1878. Before leaving for work on the sixth, Herman gave Lizzie "a long message" for Kate:

> He thinks it a very handsome one, and thanks you very much for your kindness in thinking of it for his room, and sending it, and hopes you will not think he does not appreciate it, if he hands it over to Bessie for her room—which it just about fits, and which is sadly in need of some kind of covering—especially as it nearly matches her grey mats—of course she is very anxious to have it, as her old *red* one with her *blue* trimming has been an "eye sore" to her for some time, and I was just contemplating whether we should try to worry through the winter with it, or put down matting.

Herman's spartan tastes had hardened: "As to Herman's room he is so enamored of a *floor* without a 'stuffy carpet' that he does not want to have it covered at all but only have a mat here & there—I fear it will be cold for him in the winter, but as all the cracks have been filled up, he thinks not—The carpet is a lovely one and we are all pleased at your kindness in sending it." Renovations had been proceeding, not with the prospective grand legacy from Mrs. Marett but with Lizzie's "special legacy" from Herman's Aunt Lucy, one hundred dollars already in hand. Thinking she could not do better than to put it in some form that they "might all enjoy together," she was spending it on the back parlor, where she promised Kate would see a great improvement on her next visit, but the pressing reason for sprucing up the house was the expected several days' visit from "the *Sisters Thomas.*" Frances had less reason than before to feel humiliated about its condition. She was able to receive Henry B. Thomas there, in the front parlor, during the many months of their engagement before their marriage in 1880, although (according to Melville's granddaughter Frances Thomas Osborne) Melville once strode "down the hall to the front parlor door" and shouted: "Young man, do you prefer oatmeal or mush for breakfast?" That night, according to the story, Henry Thomas fled, and his fiancée "wondered whether she would ever see him again." Lizzie was now content with the back parlor, and Bessie was happy with a better carpet. Having done her duty, Lizzie left for Boston, and Herman and the girls managed their "little Thanksgiving affair," of which "'the young man'" was "the central figure" (as Melville put it to Kate Lansing on 26 November). Lizzie arrived home from Thanksgiving on 19 December, in time for Christmas. Fanny wrote her sister Helen what Helen called on 4 January 1879 "a long and most interesting account of the Christmas festivities at Staten Island," which Helen had missed because of George's illness. Kate Lansing left the Island to visit the Melvilles at Twenty-sixth Street, where (as she wrote her husband on 27 December) she gave Herman a "Photograph of the Old Revolutionary Flag presented to Genl. Peter Gansevoort Col. of the 3^d N.Y. Regt. at the surrender of Lord Cornwallis"—the flag now at the Albany Institute of History and Art.

In the middle of February 1879, Herman took his sister Fanny up to the Lenox Library, which captivated her so that several hours passed quickly and she was eager to return to it. Such institutions were to be shared with out-of-town members of what was, still, a bookish family. (Abe on 2 June 1879 wrote his wife that *Daisy Miller* had made him reflect on his own Hudson River experience: "Thank God all American girls are not Daisy Miller, but the character of some of them is portrayed very vividly in her you must read it, & I must know more of Henry Jame[s]'s writings.") Kate Lansing, in New York early in February 1879, encountered Herman and Fanny (probably his sister) walking on Fifth Avenue, then took tea with them at Twenty-sixth Street. She met Abe on the tenth at the Japanese store near Seventeenth Street and "went to the Lenox Library 67th St via 4th Ave. cars—stayed there till 3 P.M."—making sure that Mr. Moore was caring properly for the memorial volume. Melville's daughters went up to Albany on the thirteenth for a week's visit; Kate and Abe met them and took them home in a sleigh. Tom suffered not only from the gout but also from bad publicity, for on 16 February the *Times* printed "Sailors' Snug Harbor—Dr. Hebersmith's Charges of Favoritism in Management." As she recorded in her diary, Kate entertained Melville's daughters lavishly, introducing them, in an intimate setting, to Judge Amasa Parker and his wife, among others. Judge Parker read them "the 'Hog Story.'" Abe took them all three to their private tour of "the new Capitol 'Assembly Room' & 'Court of Appeals Room' where the Senate now sit," and on to "the Bazaar." Fanny was receiving every day a letter "from Mr Thomas her accepted lover."

The Melville daughters returned, escorted by Cousin Kate Hurlbut, to find their mother unwell (Fanny reported she was having "one of her 'run down' turns, as she calls them"), and Bessie prepared for a new regimen, as she wrote her Albany hostess on 28 February: "This is the last letter I expect to write in some time; and you may imagine me sitting with my hands folded, for a month to come, as Mamma thinks I had better try the experiment by all means." Through March the doctor had her fingers "bound up in splints," although she managed to sew a little every day, which, her sister wrote to Kate Lansing on 2 April, seemed "to be a great comfort to her; her general health is, I think much better than it has been for some time, other people have noticed a change in her for the better, also. She has not seen the doctor you speak of." Judging from Lizzie's letter to Kate Lansing on 7 March 1879, Kate had taken a great interest in Bessie's physical problems while the two girls were visiting her. She may actually have taken Bessie to a doctor in Albany, for Lizzie reported in a way that indicates long-distance follow-through. The doctor had bound Bessie's fingers "in splints at once with a *very marked* favorable effect towards straightening out," at the cost of such pain that they sometimes had to loosen the tie. She was also taking powders, and Lizzie was willing for her to try "homeopathic treatment if Dr Cox can prescribe for her at such a distance." Lizzie was swayed by Kate's stronger personality, but not quite convinced: "Only one thing he ought to know & that is her *extreme delicacy* of constitution, and want of vital force—how little strain on her strength she can bear & how anxious we feel about her generally, so perhaps he could not do with her as with a *strong* patient, she says she did not tell him anything about her general health—his suggestion of straightening her fingers at once, *by force*, if carried out I believe would kill her." Kate, "so full of life & vigor" (for which she "ought to thank Heaven daily") could "hardly appreciate what it is to be in the weak and prostrated condition" that Lizzie and Bessie suffered "from more or less nearly all the time," and which in Lizzie's case dragged her down to the point that she could not "walk across the room without staggering." Lizzie had exhausted herself in writing "this scribble," the best she could do at such a time (she wrote Kate Lansing on 7 March): "The 'last feather' was change of 'help'!!! But I have Ellen back now for a time at least." Kate Lansing had Herter's (the furniture makers) deliver a green chair to Twenty-sixth Street, where it fit into the parlor, its temporary home, because other furniture there was also upholstered in green. Perhaps without consulting the Melvilles, Kate and Abe loaned money to Stanwix Melville, aware that he was manipulative and unreliable, yet eager to spare Herman and Lizzie as much pain as they could. On 4 March 1879 Tom gave an enormous entertainment for Sailors' Snug Harbor trustees and politicians, and perhaps for architects and others involved in his ongoing improvements. Melville's sister Fanny had reported to Kate Lansing on 2 March that Tom had "invited about fifty of his gentlemen friends to be with him from '8 to 11.'" She added then: "Herman is coming & no doubt, but will enjoy the affair."

Melville's capacity for pain, not joy, was tested later in the month, for his old misery of seeing *Clarel* fail was compounded when Putnam's, run now without the sensitive founder who had accepted *Typee* in London under the friendly joint pressuring hands of Washington Irving and Gansevoort Melville, requested Melville's presence in their offices. On 27 March Putnam's extracted from Melville the following authorization on their letterhead: "Please dispose of cases 2 & 3 ('Clarel') containing two hundred and twenty four copies, on my account, to paper mill." Someone at Putnam's noted on his letter, "Sent to Paper Mill April 18 / 79 . . . 220 Sets 110 Pounds of Covers 305 Pounds of Clarel." If case 1, like 2 and 3, had contained 112 copies, some of which must have been sent out for review, the total number printed would have been 336, or perhaps a run of some 350. In a letter Lizzie wrote to the New York *Times* in 1901 to correct a statement about her husband's books, she said that he withdrew *Clarel* from circulation "on finding that it commanded but a very limited sale." For Melville as for any author, having a book printed is to give it a chance not just for immediate success but (if it fails) for an afterlife. A book does not have a real chance for a life of its own if so few copies are distributed that it seldom turns up in the used-book market. The copies of bound books at Putnam's had been paid for by Uncle Peter's legacy, so Melville might as well have carted them home, if there had been room for them. Another man might have put little volumes in his left and right coat pockets and salted them in bookbins throughout Manhattan, or stashed them behind other books in bookstores, so that they might have a chance of surviving, much as Herman's mad cousin Harry Crosby did in Paris in the 1920s with books from Cousin Walter Van Rensselaer Berry's library. By authorizing Putnam's to pulp the unsold copies that Uncle Peter had subsidized, Melville had "withdrawn" the book from circulation in the most extreme fashion. Putnam's had required Melville to acquiesce in a suicidal act, and not even a fiery immolation but a more sordid pulping of his high aspirations for his American *Paradise Lost*. To destroy *Clarel* must have been bitterer for

Melville than many of the human deaths he had witnessed. Did it help to remember the passage on Collins he had marked in his Wordsworth, "Essay Supplementary to the Preface"? — "The notice which his poems attained during his life-time was so small, and of course the sale so insignificant, that not long before his death he deemed it right to repay to the Bookseller the sum which he had advanced for them, and threw the Edition into the fire." There was in Melville's character a willingness to be annihilated rather than to be hacked to pieces; better to destroy *The Isle of the Cross* than to save it as a reproach to him, better to pulp *Clarel* rather than salvage a few dozen sets.

Travel became harder for the older members of the family, especially George, who was in New Rochelle on business in May 1879 twice but was so busy with his client that (Helen wrote Kate Lansing on "Decoration Day") "he did not have time to go and see Herman, even, and of course not, Tom, who is so much further off." Earlier, none of the family except Jane would have taken much account of the ferry ride to Staten Island. In June the household at Twenty-sixth Street was all "sick & miserable," Kate Lansing wrote in her diary after taking tea there and bringing Fanny (probably Herman and Lizzie's Fanny) back to sleep with her in the hotel. Sick as he was, Herman was better, and before 2 June had been to Elizabeth, New Jersey, to inspect Milie's daughter, Agnes. Hoadley on 1 June had returned to Lawrence from New Bedford, "after an absence of some days on business for the Board of Health" and on 2 June Florence and Lucy were to leave for Arrowhead, "the rest follow in a few weeks." The Morewoods were "at their cottage" (perhaps meaning Broadhall, in the Newport sense of "cottage"), and the Latherses were to open Abby Lodge later in June. As Fanny wrote to her Cousin Kate from Lawrence on 2 June, "This warm weather makes one long to be in the country."

In June Kate had the engaged couple up, preparing her old room for Fanny and Henry's old room for Henry Thomas. At the end of the visit Kate packed cherries for them to eat on the train down, enough so that Fanny's parents and Bessie got to enjoy the remainder. Fanny properly wrote her hostess a bread-and-butter letter, adding particular details about her mother's allergies: "she is able to come down stairs to meals now, and I think when those disagreeable trees cease to be disagreeable, she will be much better." Secretions from "sticky" trees were harmful, and the heat brought out the secretions. Fanny conveyed an invitation to her father, with predictable results: "Papa wants me to thank you for yours and Cousin Abe's invitation to spend next Sunday with you, but says he will not be able to come as he does not like to leave home when mamma is feeling so miserably." When Kate and Abe sailed for England in July, Edwin Lansing saw them off, and Abe gave him a commission involving Melville. Melville's sister Fanny had known the plans well in advance, but no one had told the Melvilles, and Abe was concerned not to make Herman feel slighted. Edwin went downtown from the wharf to the Custom House to find him, but was told he would have to go up to Seventy-sixth Street and the East River, so he asked one of the Brewster brothers to deliver Abe's "message of farewell" to Herman soon. There was some awkwardness involved in the Lansings' not making a proper farewell to Herman, for Melville's sister Fanny on 30 August wrote to Abe, in London: "Herman met your brother Edwin in the street, & heard of Kate & you having gone abroad, from him — Too bad that your note turned up in London & not, at 104 East 26 Street."

In early August 1879 Lizzie and the girls went to the Overlook Mountain House in the Catskills near Woodstock, and enjoyed themselves so much that Herman thought about joining them there. A telegram announced the death of Hope Savage Shaw on 13 August, at the age of eighty-six. Herman most likely stayed at his job, but Lizzie and her daughters made their way to Boston for the funeral on 16 August, James Freeman Clarke officiating. The service was at the house, at noon, on a rainy day. The night of the nineteenth, Lizzie left with the girls for New York, prior to returning to Overlook, leaving the sorting of Hope's possessions for a later visit. Herman joined them, with Harry in tow. Melville returned to work on 15 September, apparently missing Sam at Overlook when he arrived on the twelfth and found only Lizzie and Bessie there. Minnie and Frank Hoadley were vacationing with Tom and Katie on Staten Island.

Fanny and Helen were at the Shaw house on 19 September, before leaving for Gansevoort, where they kept the Mansion House open until at least late September. In October 1879 Melville's sister Fanny divided her time between Twenty-sixth Street, Elizabeth, and Twenty-sixth Street again, before going to the Island. Lizzie had been unwell in the middle of the month, grieving. Hope Savage Shaw left no will, so all of her estate went to her sons, Lemuel and Samuel Shaw, nothing to John Oakes Shaw or Elizabeth Shaw Melville, who were not her blood kin, although Lizzie may have forgotten that fact. Neither of the lawyer sons of the chief justice had arranged that their mother make any other provision, even though her death was anything but unexpected. Lemuel for several years had ceased being an active member of the bar, and was confining himself "to office work and the care of the numerous trusts committed to him," according to a report in 1884: "Mr. Shaw was of a retiring disposition and never took an active part in politics; he occupied many responsible positions, however; he was president of the Boott Company, president of the Rockport Granite Company, trustee of the Public

Library, the Athenaeum and the Provident Institution for Savings, and a director in several financial institutions. He was for several years president of the Union Club." He was making, these years, frequent visits to Europe.

Something unpleasant happened the next time Kate came to stay at Twenty-sixth Street, before Thanksgiving 1879, soon after her return from Europe. She arrived on 18 November in a heavy rain and received a warm welcome, and found everyone well. One day her Cousin Fanny accompanied her far up to Eighty-ninth Street to look at a monument and headstones, then she went back alone, hoping the marble would look as well in the lot at the cemetery and brooding over her plight: "sad work to do *all alone.*" On 23 November she (and presumably Lizzie) went to hear Dr. Bellows in the morning and went to St. Thomas's Church in the afternoon, then took a carriage to the Grand Hotel, where she was to meet Abe the next day, when he returned from duck-hunting in Maryland. He had intended to go to the Grand Hotel if he arrived on Saturday, so it was not as if Kate were stalking out of the house and hailing a carriage in high dudgeon. But Kate concluded her diary entry: "My last visit to 104 I never will be so awkwardly situated—at the mercy—of the politeness of friends." The Melvilles knew she had taken offense. Obsessive, irascible, passionate, Herman and Kate were more alike than either of them cared to admit. They were both quick to feel slighted, although he now tried to appear stoical, as she did not.

Lizzie had left on "a beautiful bright night, to go to Boston by boat, & not cold either," around 25 November, Melville's sister Fanny wrote Kate Lansing the next day. Lizzie wrote to Kate Lansing from Boston on 4 December: "Our Thanksgiving was, as you may suppose, a very sad one, only our own immediate family were assembled. My brothers are just as kind as they can be, but the house seems strange and empty to me and it is hard to believe that mother will never more be seen in the familiar places. Yes, time brings changes faster and faster as we advance in life, and we must accept what comes, painful though it is." In this letter, she apologized to Kate for Herman's behavior:

> It has laid heavily on my mind that the last part of your visit to New York was not as pleasant as it might have been and I have felt so sorry about it—but there is nothing to be said or done except to bow to inexorable fate—I wished you were with me today, for I know you would have enjoyed seeing the collection of Mr [William Morris] Hunts pictures which are now on exhibition at the Art Museum—father's full length portrait from the Salem Court House holding the most conspicuous place.

Bowing to inexorable fate meant bowing to the inevitability and relentlessness of Herman's moods. Others in the family knew of the situation, and did their best to smooth it over. Helen was in Pittsfield in December (late for Milie to have Arrowhead open), and wrote from there to Kate Lansing: "*Dear* Kate, I know you are tried *sorely*—but 'Blessed are the Peace Makers,' and if there is any 'giving up,' to be done, *do it*—Kate dear!.... At whatever the cost of hallowed associations, and bitter heart pangs, let it go!" Helen was cryptic, as the Melville women were when they did not want to put unpleasant matters in writing; still, the reference to "hallowed associations" pretty much nails the offense as something Herman said concerning Henry Sanford Gansevoort or Kate's grief for him. The offense seemed great, whatever it was, but Kate forgave him, and as token of her good feeling sent him a package of tobacco, undoubtedly of a special nature designed to give him pleasure (what she brought back from London for the men in the family, including Melville, was the best George Griggs had ever smoked, he said). Lizzie was home from Boston on the thirteenth.

Tom was too strong a figure not to provoke criticism. In October 1879 *A History of the Sailors' Snug Harbor Together with Incidents of a Life in It for Eighteen Months* slurred Tom: "The Governor of the Institution was once a ship master, (for a short time, however, I think.)"; the author wanted him fired. On 10 January 1880 "A Looker On" at the Harbor gave instructions to the mayor of New York to catch an unsupervised look at the hospital to "see how things are carried on here" and the kitchen ("Dying men cannot eat such coarse food"). Again Tom held his place in his Paradise. In mid-December 1879 Morgan Dix sent Richard Grant White's young son Stanford over with this letter: "I have much pleasure in introducing to you Mr Stanford White, who wishes to examine the grounds at the Harbour with a view to design a base for the statue of Capt. Randall. Any facilities you can give him will be highly appreciated by yours very truly, Morgan Dix." For Christmas Fanny gave her brother Herman a photograph of "General Gansevoort's Phaeton, still to be seen in the carriage house at Gansevoort, N.Y." The centennials (including 1877, during which Fanny had been pestered for Revolutionary documents) had made them more conscious of the historic treasures they lived with. Before Christmas, she received from Kate an article on "The Arms of the State," which she "sent to Herman to read."

In 1879 Kate and Abe determined to have the family Christmas dinner, and sent out invitations early, in mid-November, "to Cousin Herman Lizzie Bessie Fanny & Mr Thomas Capt. Tom & Kate E.M. Mr Hoadley Kate Minnie Lottie & Frank & Mr Griggs & Helen M. Griggs." Melville's sister Fanny determined to go to Abe and Kate's "in good season to help" with the big Christmas preparations. Herman declined the invitation on 17 November by citing Lizzie's health: "The truth is Lizzie is not very robust—and the journey northward at midwinter—why, she rather dreads it." From Boston on 4 December Lizzie put the refusal to go to Albany on Herman: "I should like, ever so much to join you at the Christmas dinner, dear Kate, but fear I shall not be able to — if Herman would go, it would be different, but as it is, I shall have to forego it." The travel with babies was too much for Milie, so she declined on behalf of herself and Willie and her sisters. Melville's sister Fanny explained in November that she would come but Tom could not possibly come: "Oh, Kate, I am sorry to tell you, that Tom as Gove[r]nor, has never been away from his post on a Holiday — any other day he could, so he & Kate will not be able to join the party, it is too bad, for he would enjoy the day so much — delights in these family gatherings." The Lansings ended up with a rival Christmas dinner. In her diary Kate listed those present. Between the host and the hostess, on his right, were: Mr. Hurlbut, Augustus Peebles, Nellie Hurlbut, E. Y. Lansing, Minnie Hoadley, Morris Miller. Then Kate, and beginning at her right: George Griggs, Mary Ann Peebles, Frank Hoadley, Fanny P. Melville, Gansevoort Hurlbut, Mrs. Griggs, then the host at the head. If Herman had been willing to go, Lizzie would have gone — so she said.

[38]

The Shadow at the Feasts
1880–1885

> ... wild boar meat; humps of grampuses; embrowned bread-fruit, roasted in odoriferous fires of sandal wood, but suffered to cool; gold fish, dressed with the fragrant juices of berries; citron sauce; rolls of the baked paste of yams; juicy bananas, steeped in a saccharine oil; marmalade of plantains; jellies of guava; confections of the treacle of palm sap . . . .
>
> Part of the menu at the House of the Afternoon, *Mardi*, ch. 84

> My grandfather was afraid we wouldn't have enough to eat, and he had a very good appetite — really had a very good appetite.
>
> Frances Thomas Osborne, misremembering the Great Blizzard of 1888, in Sealts, *Early Lives*

MOST OF THE RECORD of Fanny Melville's wedding on 5 April 1880 comes from the diary of Kate Gansevoort Lansing, who got together presents, including forks and spoons in memory of Fanny's Granduncle Peter and Grandaunt Susan. Kate said in mid-March that everyone at Twenty-sixth Street was well, and did not specify how Bessie's fingers were. Back at Twenty-sixth Street on 4 April, she "saw all the family The Bride & groom Elect," and judged that "all seemed rather uncomfortable." On the next afternoon, Henry W. Bellows officiated at Fanny's wedding to Henry B. Thomas at All Souls Church, Fourth Avenue and Twentieth Street. Even on that occasion, Herman had to work part of the day, since it was Monday. Abe, Nettie Hurlbut Miller, and Kate went together in a heavy shower, only to find the church dark and a general "want of arrangements," the lack of a fine directing hand such as Kate or her Aunt Maria would have wielded. Afterward members of the family and a few guests congratulated the bride and groom and admired the wedding gifts in a parlor at Twenty-sixth Street. After a week's honeymoon, Fanny completed her escape, across the Hudson to Orange, New Jersey. Lizzie was so terrified of an allergic reaction if she went across the Hudson in June that she did not see Fanny for months. By late May, Jane Dempsey Melville had moved from Irving Place to the Florence, the early apartment building on Eighteenth Street.

Lizzie and Bessie took a summer vacation, in the mountains, Melville's sister Fanny mentioned in November. (Despairing of keeping her own identity after Melville's daughter was a grown woman, she had begun signing herself "Fanny Priscilla" or even "Priscilla," and family members began referring to her as "Fanny P." or "Fanny Priscilla.") Melville may have stayed at home, boarding out. After Lizzie's return in late September, she was "so taken up with getting the house in order" that she did not rush out to Orange. On 10 October Lizzie told Kate Lansing that Herman was "well as usual," and reported on Fanny Thomas: "she is very well and happy—she is coming in this week to make some preserves for me and will stay over Sunday —she and Harry." Lizzie and Herman were both going to Orange soon. That month all three Melvilles took meals at the Hartnetts for a time until Lizzie got new help ("two girls who impress us favorable so far"—meaning after two days). As if to counter the tendency of Gansevoort, New York, to fade out of the lives of most of the family, and to memorialize good old times, in September 1880 Fanny Priscilla had a photograph taken of the Mansion House. Two women (Fanny and Helen?) dressed in long, full skirts, sit on the porch. Fanny sent framed copies as special gifts to the few surviving members of the immediate family, using oak for all except Kate and Abe's, knowing (she said to Kate on 31 December) that Kate would want to frame it herself, being critical "on the subject of frames"—as indeed others in the family were, including Herman and not excluding Lizzie. Fanny and Helen held on at Gansevoort until 21 October, by which time they had learned that Hoadley had taken rooms at Boston Highlands, and he and Kate were leaving Lawrence before the first of November. Changes now were harder for everyone.

Kate Lansing went to church in Manhattan on 7 November 1880 then "went to Cousin Hermans," where she found the family at dinner. While she was there she picked up the picture of the Mansion House that Fanny had left for her. That month Melville may have seen two of Sarah Bernhardt's performances, Eleanor Metcalf was told long afterward. Lizzie and Bessie visited Fanny Priscilla in New Brighton the next week, and Hoadley was there briefly, reporting that he and Kate were settled in nicely, in walking distance of Helen and George. When Lizzie left for Thanksgiving in Boston, Fanny Priscilla transferred to Twenty-sixth Street for two weeks, but in the longer term she was "flying about between Orange, Elizabeth, New York, & the Island" (she wrote to Kate Lansing on 1 December). Lucy stayed with Fanny Priscilla and Herman and Bessie that Thanksgiving, spending the time "very pleasantly," and not cooped up: "The weather being bright, we have been out a good deal with Herman & by ourselves"; probably Fanny felt she was caring for Lucy as well as the other two. As a married woman Fanny Thomas could tolerate her father better than before, and in early December 1880 she was willing to go back with Harry to Twenty-sixth Street to help run the house for Melville and Bessie while Lizzie prolonged her usual Thanksgiving visit to Boston. Then Fanny Priscilla and Allan's daughter Lucy relieved the Thomases, Lucy there more to be cared for than to care for the others. In early December Abraham Lansing invited the Melvilles to a reception for mid-month at the Fort Orange Club, across the street from what was now the Gansevoort-Lansing house. Herman declined. As he said in his reply of 8 December, Lizzie was in Boston and Bessie was keeping house, and, the clincher last: "I am an—old fogy; so none of us can comply, much as we regret it."

Christmas at the Harbor in 1880 included Lizzie, looking well, Fanny P. wrote to her Cousin Kate, and, arriving in shifts, Frank Hoadley, then "John, Kate & the girls," then on morning of the twenty-fifth "Lizzie & Bessie Harry & Fannie, Will & Milie Florence & Kitty"; Lucy was there, and Milie's children "Agnes & Roland, & the nurse" (three-year-old Allan having died the previous January). All the guests "from New York & Elizabeth & Orange" would stay over Sunday. Five of the Bogarts would be at Christmas dinner, but not Helen and George. It was a Saturday: did Herman have to work? how could Fanny P. not have named him, if only to say he was prevented from coming? The disturbing possibility that he was not there is worsened by the count of the guests Fanny P. made in her post-Christmas letter to Kate Lansing, where she made her thanks for gifts and described the day at the Governor's House: "We numbered at the table twenty-one, the dining-room was brilliant with Holly & other Xmas greens—& the family filled it from one end to the other. All was bright with Xmas cheer & warmth." Others are accounted for: "John had to leave for Boston that night, as business called him immediately back—to our great regret—The next morning Harry, Florence & Kitty, & Fanny left, & the next day Bessie. Lizzie went home Sunday early." It had been so bitterly cold since the Hoadleys arrived on the twenty-third that the two sisters had taken the ferry to Manhattan only once: "we lunched at Herman's they were all well—The photos you sent all were glad to have for their Albums just the right size." Was Herman at Christmas dinner, as insignificant as the woman in "Shadow at the Feast," his poem about the widowed bride at other people's Christmas celebrations? An often-verified optical phenomenon is that younger people of either sex are unable to perceive old gray-haired men. Was Herman Melville now so old, gray, and quiet as to be invisible—as insubstantial as his Marquis de Grandvin?

Melville was substantial enough to have known that Oakey Hall's library was auctioned beginning 17 January 1881 at Bangs & Co., New York, "arranged by subjects, which comprehend Dramatic, Legal, Journalistic and Local Literature; Travels; Poetry; Fiction; Biography, etc., etc." There were treasures from the years of Hall's association with the Duyckinck group, including three of Duyckinck's ventures, *Arcturus*, the *Literary World* "in full," and *Yankee Doodle*, and Hall had owned "the 'Figaro' that preceded 'Punch,'" a magazine now known only in partial runs of varying formats and lacking an issue of great interest to a biographer of Melville, the one with Thomas Powell's promised essay on Evert Duyckinck, missing from Duyckinck's own copy (the one at the New York Public Library). Among the books auctioned were *Moby-Dick* and *Pierre*. Do they survive?

Fanny Priscilla wrote Kate Lansing on 29 January 1881 of visiting Milie and having a "merry sleigh ride" from Elizabeth to Orange to see young Fanny Thomas, and then bringing her and Bessie home to Elizabeth (New Jersey) for dinner. On her way back to the Island, Fanny "staid over night at Herman's." In late April Hoadley sold the Lawrence house for eighty-five hundred dollars, possession to be given on 15 May, which meant that the books, china, and glass had to be stored and some of the furniture sold. (The former Lawrence house had sold for eight thousand dollars in May of 1863.) The Hoadleys moved into the Norfolk House at 29 High Street, Boston, Hoadley still reeling from his losses in the Panic of 1873, talking the language, as he had for years now, of homelessness, taking his idiom from the fear evoked in the phrase "Tramp Menace." He wrote Kate Lansing on 19 May 1881: "We have got moved, — our house in Lawrence is vacated, and we are houseless. — Still, we fare very well at the Norfolk House, for tramps!" Visiting New York in mid-May, Kate Lansing made calls on Mrs. Allan Melville then "at Cousin Hermans 104 E. 26th St."

In 1881 there was little to rejoice about. Cousin Robert Melvill died in Davenport, Iowa, on 20 July 1881 at the age of sixty-five, "of paralysis of the heart." That summer fifteen-year-old Edmund Griffin Lathers, the son of Richard and Abby Lathers, died in New Rochelle. For literary people, the death in April of James T. Fields marked the end of an era. The national tragedy of the year was the slow death by assassination of President James Garfield. Herman's brother and sisters and their families vacationed strenuously in 1881. Lizzie and Bessie went to Fire Island, where on 23 June Kate Lansing wrote Lizzie at the Surf Hotel; they stayed on through July, if they kept to their plans, then went to Arrowhead. Afterward they went to the Overlook Hotel in the Catskills, where Lizzie reported so favorably, as Mrs. Pruyn did, that Kate and Abe went there the middle of August. In late July Lizzie and Bessie were at 49 Mt. Vernon Street, where Kate Lansing and

Helen and Fanny P. all visited one day. Gruff George Griggs, phenomenally, sailed at the end of July 1881 for England and Scotland, where he did everything he had heard other people talk of doing, even following Hawthorne and Melville to the old cathedral at Chester. With George gone, Helen was able to go with Fanny Priscilla to their "dear Gansevoort house," as Fanny wrote Kate Lansing at the end of June. Young Fanny and Harry breakfasted with Kate and Abe on their way to Saratoga and what was probably Harry's first visit to the Mansion House. In the known correspondence there is no mention of Herman's vacationing anywhere. Increasingly, as he became older, quieter, easier at last to ignore, Herman Melville ceased to be mentioned in family letters where he should have been mentioned, in a pattern strangely analogous to the way he had dropped out of lists of American authors in the late 1850s and the 1860s.

In midsummer occurred something that Herman and Lizzie may never have known about. Stanwix wrote to Kate and Abe asking a loan, sweetening the plea with the disingenuous suggestion that he had in his possession a nugget from what he was calling the "Gansevoort Mine." This precipitated an exchange of letters, Abe in Albany and Kate on Fire Island. On 27 July 1881, observing that "Stan writes a good letter," Abe wrote to Kate, but a good letter did not require "a well to do cousin, on the other side of the continent" to come to his rescue "at the critical moment." Knowing Abe was right, Kate sent Stanwix a draft for $110. Either he had not yet received his part of Mrs. Marett's legacy or he had wasted it. On 31 October loyal Sam Savage came to Twenty-sixth Street after long years away. "I called on Lizzie," he wrote his wife that day: "She was very kind. Saw Herman & the visit did me good." Kate and Abe dined at Delmonico's on Thanksgiving Day—right by Herman's house—perhaps with politicians. On 27 November after attending church Kate "called at 104 E. 26th St. Saw Cousin Herman Lizzie & the girls." For Christmas 1881 Tom held the "family party," but the Hoadleys and Griggses could not attend.

The year 1882 was marked, early and at the end, by family births, Eleanor Thomas on 24 February, Milie's son Thomas Melville Morewood on 27 December. At year's end Milie had three living children, Agnes, born in 1879; John Rowland (or Roland), born in 1880; and Thomas Melville Morewood—evidence if it was needed of just how much Tom's nieces loved him. The wedding of the year was that of Annie Morewood to Richard Lathers Jr., but a brother of the groom had died in 1881, so festivities were muted. Henry W. Bellows, a man in the prime of life, he thought, with adult children and with tiny children by his new wife, died on 30 January. The Lansings' intimate friend Robert H. Pruyn, Lincoln's minister to Japan, died suddenly in early March. The national death of the year was that of Longfellow. On

12 April Helen in writing Kate Lansing gave a sense of how much he had meant: "Longfellow's death cast a shadow for some days over the city, and its suburbs." The Longfellow family had boarded with Cousin Robert at the Melvill house (Broadhall) in the late 1840s, and Lizzie had her own special association (as she wrote Kate Lansing on 14 April 1897): "I suppose you know that in Longfellows 'Tales of a Wayside Inn' the *Student* who figures as one of the characters was Dr Henry Wales, George's brother. I knew him very well."

In 1882 Herman faded further out of the surviving family correspondence. Still he worked six days a week for the Custom House, and had only two weeks' vacation. His pattern was recalled long afterward by Henry Thomas: "He would devote his mornings to this [Custom House] work, which would keep him busy until 1 or 2 P.M. Then he came home to dinner, after which he would shut himself up in his room, and no one knew or dared inquire as to what busied him there." (There may have been a seasonal pattern, longer hours some of the time, shorter hours other times, for Lizzie's surviving comment stresses that Herman was gone all day or almost all day.) In March he gave an autograph collector his signature with the words "Honor bright"—slightly less perturbing than "Tell Truth and shame the Devel." A few slight mentions of Melville have been found in new books and the newspapers and magazines, but the eight or so years after *Clarel* were the lowest of his career. This October the Authors Club was founded, and he accepted an invitation to attend, but rescinded his acceptance, saying "he had become too much of a hermit," and that "his nerves could no longer stand large gatherings," according to some reminiscences of the Authors Club by Charles De Kay.

Melville behaved normally, although in a more subdued way than before, able to muster less and less energy after the end of his work day. In February 1882 he sent Fanny Priscilla a San Francisco newspaper, perhaps from a ship he had boarded, perhaps from Stanwix. On 24 February, after Fanny Thomas's daughter, Eleanor, was born, Lizzie went to Orange in April to help Fanny "to break in the 'babby' to going without its nurse," as Melville told his sister Kate on the twelfth. He made a trip over to inspect the baby. There was less and less chance for Tom to share his magnificent home, as Helen became incapable of winter travel and as both John Hoadley and George Griggs were often ill, though still pushing themselves to make business trips. Frank Hoadley spent his Easter vacation on the Island, then John and Kate Hoadley visited later in April, only to find a disastrous situation. Dr. Bogart had been summarily demoted to "Consulting Physician" (though with the old salary, for a time), and was being pushed out of the physician's mansion—at first told the house was to be given up at once, then graciously told to take an entire month to move everything out. Tom opened the Governor's House to the Bogarts, until they could make other arrangements, but their presence meant that fewer rooms would be available for visiting Melvilles or Gansevoorts, and that prospective visitors might be inhibited about descending on the Harbor. And as Fanny P. said to Kate Lansing of the Bogarts on 21 April 1882, "You can feel what a trial it must be for them all, this breaking up of the old home with all its associations, particularly for the doctor & his wife at their age."

Fanny Thomas and her husband had not fully settled in when she wrote Kate Lansing on 23 May, sounding like her mother (who had been over to help with the packing): "We have just moved in our house, and are in a state of confusion there is so much to be done, I don't know where to begin." Herman wrote affectionately to his sister Kate on 12 April in regard to a note he had received from his niece Minnie, a note "Wherein, among other interesting matters, she says — what she previously had heard distant rumors of — or did we read it under the head of *'Personal'* in the newspaper? — I say, she says that you and John propose a visit to these parts some time next week." His avuncular whimsy was lax, now. On his way to visit Tom for Easter vacation from his school at Poughkeepsie, Frank Hoadley (now five feet eight inches) had visited at Twenty-sixth Street, and had gone with Bessie to the zoo, where he shook hands with P. T. Barnum himself. "How he has grown!" Herman exclaimed of his nephew; Minnie was hoping he would turn out a "six footer." Herman still saw his Cousin Kate during her trips to New York City, when normally she called first on Jane Dempsey Melville at the Florence then went farther uptown to Twenty-sixth Street. (Kate read Henry James's *Portrait of a Lady* in March, oblivious to any resemblance between Madame Merle and Jane Melville.)

After Fanny P. and Helen opened the Mansion House on 25 July 1882, Helen rejoiced to Kate Lansing: "I am writing on the piazza; the air is just genial, neither hot nor cold, and entirely free from the easterly 'Hub,' quality, which has been almost poisonous to me of late years." Herman wrote Fanny P. and Helen that he hoped to join Lizzie and Bessie at the Overlook House but could not go to Gansevoort. He may have joined Lizzie briefly, but much of his vacation he spent alone in New York City, driven out of the house by the heat, dropping into bookstores, and walking the streets until bedtime, a summer pattern now. In late August or early September Melville sent word (Lizzie's curious phrasing) that he was laid low with his old "crick in the back," and she went back home briefly to see to him before returning, determined to escape the evil effects of staying in the city. For Herman and Lizzie it was hard to know what was worse — not hearing from Stanwix for long periods, as in earlier years, or now hearing ominous news frequently.

From Woodstock on 8 September 1882 Lizzie wrote to Kate Lansing: "We hear constantly from Stanny — I wish I could say he is materially better — but he keeps about the same, & cannot yet get rid of his cough — I feel very anxious about him — that it holds so long." The "demon of restlessness" was the best Lizzie could do to explain his behavior. By contrast, young Harry Thomas came of a good stable family, had a small but significant inheritance, held onto a good job, and managed to keep on cordial terms with his now unsociable father-in-law.

Annie Morewood, the baby born in November 1853, the month the first installment of "Bartleby" was published, married Richard Lathers Jr. on 21 September 1882 in St. Stephen's Church in Pittsfield (still the 1832 church that Uncle Thomas had attended — not demolished until May 1889). That reception at Winyah, later in the fall, was formidable. Colonel Lathers's hand was obvious in all the arrangements, particularly the prenuptial hoopla in the press, although the celebrations were muted because of the death the summer before of one of the Lathers sons in New Rochelle. Melville probably stayed home. There survives a piece of paper, apparently a letter, which Melville inscribed with the location Albany and the date 13 November, but if he was then in Albany, nothing is known about the purpose of his visit or its duration. The thirteenth of November was a Monday, a working day, so he would not have been making a flying Saturday-Sunday visit.

Lizzie went to Boston after Thanksgiving, on 4 December 1882, having arranged that her daughter Fanny and her baby would stay at Twenty-sixth Street the week she was gone (stay with Bessie, said Fanny Priscilla, meaning with Bessie and Herman — an instance of his name dropping out of the roll call). Lem and Sam Shaw had a dinner party on 9 December, so the Griggses and Hoadleys were invited "'to meet Mrs Melville,'" as Fanny Priscilla humorously put it in writing Kate Lansing on the seventh. Christmas 1882 was at the Harbor, where the doctor and his wife found accommodations, and had become settled. Tom was suffering from the gout in both feet, and temporarily confined to the house. Katie reported to Kate Lansing on 26 December that Tom had been a little better: "We enjoyed our Christmas, eighteen sat down to our dinner, and Tom was able to get down which of course brightened all for me, as a few days ago he was suffering too much to enjoy anything, he has not been down stairs to-day, but is better & free of pain. Lizzie, Fanny her husband & baby, Bessie, Florence, Kitty, Lucy, my father, mother & sister, and Mrs Van Vechten and two of her boys comprised our party, we received some very pretty & useful presents." (This is Hannah Van Vechten, who was sick, and remained there for months, sick, and cared for by Katie, who became worn down herself in 1882.) Like the 1880 list, this one does not add up, and does not include Herman, invisible, if there.

Most likely Melville was present when Eleanor was christened in Orange on 25 March 1883, Easter Sunday. For that occasion Herman and Lizzie took his memorial spoon for Herman's Grandfather Gansevoort (received in 1845 after such bitter delay) and had it inscribed on the reverse of the handle: "Eleanor Melville Thomas Christened Easter Sunday 1883": one treasure better out of the house, where it could accrue new and more cheerful memories. When most needed Lizzie went to Orange to help Fanny, although she had never become a genuinely expert and efficient housekeeper herself. Melville went over the Hudson to see Fanny still less often. Milie's stepmother did not rush to Elizabeth to see the new Thomas. She wrote Kate Lansing on 10 January 1883: "I took lunch with Mrs Brittain—the other day, and heard about Maria's new—boy—baby—'very fine child' &c &c I care little or nothing for children, except those of larger growth." She had cared "little or nothing" for Allan's children from the time she met them, however much larger they were then and how much larger they grew. The first in the family to complain of taking a ferry to New Brighton, now on 24 April Jane complained about taking the railway car to Orange: "I was to have gone to see Fanny Thomas with Lizzie—last week but Lizzie said for some reason—we had better wait. I cant say I like suburbia visits much as I may like my friends, I find it a tax to move by steamboat—and thence by rail-ways." Maneuvering up the Nile, riding to Jerusalem on a road of loose stones so thick the horse could not find a place to put his foot down (as she wrote Milie, 23 March 1866), dashing around Europe—all that was easier than getting to New Brighton or Orange or Elizabeth. Jane went abroad again that summer, where transportation was civilized.

Alfred Morewood married on 9 May 1883. Then on 19 June there was "A Fashionable Wedding and Reception" at Trinity Church in New Rochelle—Emma, one of the daughters of Richard and Abby Lathers, to Matthew Verner Simpson, son of Bishop Simpson, of Philadelphia. This was the "society event of the season in this part of the state," a newspaper reported. There was a reception at Winyah for fully a thousand persons, among whom many notables and a few family members were named. A clipping names as guests "Mr. and Mrs. J. C. Hoadley, Miss [Charlotte] Hoadley," "Mr. J. R. Morewood," and "Capt. Thomas Melville." At this last of the great family celebrations in these years there is no record of the presence of Herman and Lizzie or either of their daughters. The pregnant young Orange matron Fanny Thomas and her Philadelphia in-laws would have known the details from the papers: Lathers had presented the young couple "with an elegant house in Philadelphia," which was "to be their future home, and Bishop Simpson added the furniture." Fanny Thomas's own house was minuscule (the best translation of what Fanny Priscilla called "the pretty home," which was "*so* cosey & compact," her description after going out with Tom in November 1883).

Melville knew William E. Dodge, one of the Sailors' Snug Harbor trustees, whose funeral Tom attended on 12 February 1883, and described in his diary as the largest funeral that he ever saw. Lizzie knew Melville's first cousin once removed Lucy Cushing Scollay Whitwell (born in 1788) better than he did; she died in September, an ancient lady. The Melvilles had all met Kate Lansing's friends, and mourned with her when Cora Parker died in December. Fanny Priscilla wrote kindly on the twenty-first: "I know how this sorrow coming at this season will affect you, for though apart we are yet *together*, & always will be — be the years long or few." Kate was still keeping her anniversaries, as when she wrote in her diary on 28 October: "*Nine years ago this morning Oct. 28. 1874*, mother was found dead in her bed — nine years of regret & disappointment with care and anxiety." As state senator Abe Lansing took on serious entertaining, giving a large party for the new governor, Grover Cleveland, and inviting family members. Kate and Abe stood with Cleveland in the west parlor, receiving some three hundred guests; the grand reception ended at three in the morning. On 10 February 1883 Fanny P. asked, "Were you not the first in the city, to entertain Governor Cleveland?" Hoadley had moved his office into the same building with George Griggs and was "busy, busy," Fanny P. reported to Kate Lansing on 14 April 1883. Tom was supervising Augustus St. Gaudens's calculations about the relation of Stanford White's base to his statue of Captain Randall. On 24 May Kate Lansing, as the wife of a state senator, attended the opening of what they had not yet learned to call "the Brooklyn Bridge." She wrote in her diary: "The ceremonies of the *New York & Brooklyn Bridge*, took place today. Went to the 5th Ave. Hotel & saw *President Arthur* & Cabinet & *Gov. Cleveland* & staff — A.L. went down town in a carriage with the Procession — & such a crowd that he was unable to hear the orations & do anything but see the crowd & be uncomfortable." This was a Thursday. Herman was working, but he could see the bridge anytime now. Bessie went to Boston in late January and February 1883 to see the Hoadleys, Griggses, and Shaws, and to visit her friend Miss Wells. Helen was never in good health for long now, yet she managed to help Fanny Priscilla open the house in Gansevoort in late July 1883. The rest of the family, always excepting Herman, took long vacations.

Something of Melville's isolation is clear from what Harry Thomas recalled in 1929. Melville "had an extensive district to cover" in his duties for the customs service and walked miles, in the mornings, on the job. What Melville did in his room after that was read and write — read much more widely than we presently have evidence of, since so much of his library was dispersed soon after his death. On 10 August 1883, while all alone in Twenty-sixth Street, Melville replied to a letter from Julian Hawthorne, who as a boy had declared he loved Melville as much as his parents and his sister Una. Julian had questions to ask, for he was then writing *Hawthorne and His Wife*, and had in his possession letters Melville had written and hoped for his father's side of the correspondence. The idea that Julian possessed his letters, and might quote from them as Rose's husband George Lathrop had done in 1876, was distressing to Melville, who wrote him that the information he had to give ("little enough, I think, it will prove, at least for the purpose you name") could "be more conveniently conveyed personally than by note." He set a time for Julian to call at Twenty-sixth Street: "Wednesday next the 15th about 7½ P.M." Julian told the story of this interview several times, whenever he could make a few dollars more by retelling it, and as time passed he became more and more hostile, baffled by Melville's fame at the end of the first quarter of the twentieth century, after many decades of living in his father's reflected glamour and becoming a confidence man, jailed for swindling.

What follows is conflated from Julian's different versions. Melville opened the door on this "quiet side-street" (1901) and greeted his guest kindly, "with a low voice and restrained manner" (1927), looking, Julian said (1903, while Lizzie was still alive), "pale, sombre, nervous, but little touched by age," or, alternatively, "a melancholy and pale wraith of what he had been in his prime" (1927). By 1927 Julian remembered the visit this way: "During the incoherent talk between us on that occasion he let fall several hints as to his interpretation of the source of Hawthorne's insight into the human soul." When Julian asked about his father's letters to him Melville said, "with agitation, that he had kept nothing; if any such letters had existed, he had scrupulously destroyed them" (1927). Alternately, Melville made "a melancholy gesture" and said "that they had all been destroyed long since, as if implying that the less said or preserved, the better!" (1926). Melville told Julian that the story he had offered to Hawthorne had been tragic, "and that Hawthorne had not seemed to take to it" (1884). In 1927 Julian said that when he mentioned knowing that Melville "had once proposed to Hawthorne to join him in some literary work," Melville had "made no intelligible response": "His words were vague and indeterminate; and again and again he would get up from his chair and open or close a window with a stick having a hook at the end, which he kept by him seemingly for that purpose." This is from 1901: "he seemed nervous, and every few minutes would rise to open and then to shut again the window opening on the courtyard. At first he was disinclined to talk; but finally he said several interesting things, among which the most remarkable was that he was convinced Hawthorne had all his life concealed some great secret, which would, were it known, explain all the mysteries of his career." In particular, this secret would account "for the gloomy passages in his books" (1903). Julian concluded that Melville seemed "to have pondered much over his brief intercourse with Hawthorne, conjecturing some baffling problem in his life" (1926). In 1903 he turned back on Melville the thought that Hawthorne had kept some dark secret: "It was characteristic in him to imagine so; there were many secrets untold in his own career." In 1927 Julian wrote: "It was a sad interview"; Melville had "seemed partly to shrink from the idea that obsessed him, and partly to reach out for companionship in the dark region into which his mind was sinking." In this 1927 account Julian wrote: "When I tried to revive memories in him of the red-cottage days — red-letter days too for him — he merely shook his head."

Perturbed, uneasy already about what Julian would write of him, helpless to control the quotation or misquotation from the letters he had written so recklessly in 1851, Melville stayed on alone in the city for two weeks before leaving on his vacation on 31 August 1883. At first he joined Lizzie and Bessie at Richfield Springs (enjoying "the beauty of the country all about exceedingly," he wrote Fanny P., as she reported to Kate Lansing on 14 September), and he went to Gansevoort just for Sunday, 16 September, on his way home, the plan being that Lizzie and Bessie would also visit Gansevoort, later. By 17 September Melville was back at his job, working out of the office at Seventy-sixth Street and the East River. At the end of October, Helen and Fanny P. stopped over in Albany for a week with Kate and Abe then went to the Sailors' Snug Harbor rather than Boston. Helen had been a stranger to New York for so long that the family gathered around, as Fanny Priscilla wrote to Kate Lansing on 13 November: "While at Tom's we saw all the family, as they came to see Helen, making it quite a Christmas gathering. Kate having invited for every day & night. I was only in the city once, spent the morning at Herman's." Tom met her there and took her to Orange to see Fanny Thomas and Eleanor, "a darling, sweet winning little thing." Fanny the little was Fanny the big, enormously pregnant now. In Boston, Kate Hoadley had looked "blooming, after the sea & mountain breezes," but John had left for New York for a few days.

The Thomas's second daughter, Frances Cuthbert, was born on 3 December 1883, and to help care for her and Eleanor, as well as the new baby, Lizzie and Bessie took turns staying at Orange until Christmas, leaving the other to see to Melville. (Melville at some time, perhaps at her christening, gave the child the memorial spoon he had received in honor of his grandmother Catherine Gansevoort, after having this inscribed on the reverse of the handle: "H.M. to F.C.T.") On 26 December Lizzie wrote to Kate Lansing that she had "scarcely had a thought to give to Christmas till the very day," since she had been "out at Orange for the greater part of the last three weeks," and then to Tom's at Staten Island — for Christmas Day. Fanny was "progressing favorably towards recovery" and "Little Eleanor" was "much delighted with her 'tunnin little baby sister'" and "always begging to 'kiss her.'" Eleanor was, Lizzie reported, "as good as child can be, but is very active and needs constant watching." After the baby was born Jane called at Twenty-sixth Street to offer to take Bessie out to drive, but "she was not well enough, she was under the weather" (Jane to Kate Lansing on 8 December). Christmas 1883 at the Harbor was "a very quiet time" for Lizzie without her daughter Fanny, she wrote Kate Lansing; "Dr Bogart was there, and Belle but none of the others." Katie also wrote to Kate Lansing: "We had a pleasant Christmas, and many kind remembrances. All the Elizabeth family, Lizzie, Hannah V. V. & two young cousins of mine dined with us, the day was wintry, & the deep snow made it much like the traditional Christmas." Fanny Priscilla later wrote Kate: "Tom's party numbered sixteen, Hannah V. V. & Leonard among the guests." (Apparently Hannah's son Leonard Van Vechten.) The names still don't total sixteen. If Herman was there, Katie did not name him. Perhaps it was this Christmas when Herman gave Tom a copy of the three-page manuscript poem, "The Admiral of the White" (not "The Haglets," which was published in 1885 as "The Admiral of the White").

The year 1884 was the worst for the family since 1872. At the start, the sickest family member was Helen, who simply did not complain. Even Kate Hoadley, now living nearby, nursed Helen. Kate Lansing wanted Fanny Priscilla to visit Albany and Tom and Katie wanted her to come to the Harbor, but on 1 January 1884 Helen wrote Kate Lansing that Fanny would not hear of leaving her: "You see, to parody Longfellow — 'When I am well, I am very *very* well!' and, as I wrote Lizzie the other day, I am afraid my friends do not take any stock in there being another side to the matter." On 15 January Fanny Priscilla wrote Kate Lansing that the postman had just brought "Tom's weekly letter," reporting "All well on the Island," Saturday the twelfth having been Mrs. Bogart's eightieth birthday. Tom had been suffering from gout, and later in 1884 Herman was diagnosed as having some sort of rheumatic gout, Lizzie was always sick or about to be sick, Bessie was becoming an invalid, and Lucy was seriously ill. Fanny Priscilla seemed to be the healthiest one of Maria's surviving children. In mid-February, Kate Lansing went to the city and on the thirteenth dined "with Cousin Jenny at the Florence with Mr Merowitz, a very pleasant young gentleman & went to the Theatre." Then on the fifteenth, she noted in her diary, getting the address wrong: "Called at *104. E. 25th St* saw *Cousin Lizzie & Herman*." Tom turned fifty-five on 24 January 1884, after a stretch of terrible "London fogs"; night whistles had been blown everywhere, fog bells rung, and the streets of Manhattan and Brooklyn utterly dark (according to the Boston *Saturday Post*). Everything seemed normal enough, except for Helen's illness.

On 5 March, Tom "reached his residence at the Harbor at 8 o'clock, and was apparently in the best of health. Soon afterwards he complained of a suffocating sensation and died three hours later" (the *Nautical Gazette*). The stronger remnants of the Melville tribe gathered. Abe and Kate had invited Governor Grover Cleveland to dine with them and a few others, but when the telegram came Kate countermanded the invitations, telegraphed Katie ("poor Kate my heart aches for her—her broken home & shattered life"), and prepared to take the train down. At the Sailors' Snug Harbor on 8 March Kate Lansing "met a heart broken sorrowing household Cousin Helen—Mr Hoadley & Kate, & Frank—our dear Fanny & Tom's Kate—Oh how my heart aches for them." Herman collapsed with "a kind of Rheumatic gout" (perhaps an involuntary sympathetic manifestation, the body choosing to mimic Tom's minor ailment, gout, rather than heart failure). Herman may have taken to his bed already, for Kate Lansing did not name either him or Lizzie as being at the Harbor. The casket and the "families" were in the living room, where Kate looked at the body of the cousin nearest her in age: "Dear Old Tom looks so natural I can scarce realize him dead." Rain delayed the burial until 10 March. As Kate recorded, the inmates of the Harbor, inveterate grousers and all, paid tribute to the governor: "Nearly ten o'clock this morning the funeral left this pleasant hospitable home & carried its dear Master Capt. Thomas Melville to the gate . . . lined with the old sailors with bared heads, & tearful eyes saying farewell to their devoted friend & Governor." Tom was buried in "the Moravian Cemetery at *New Dorp* on the other side of the Island," so Katie could visit the grave, alone or with her sister Belle, whose husband, the Reverend Dr. Bagley, had been buried there in a lot Tom had chosen. Herman was not even able to go downstairs when Cousin Kate Gansevoort Lansing came to Twenty-sixth Street on the evening of the eleventh.

John C. Hoadley, functioning better, wrote an obituary notice which survives in another hand in the Berkshire Athenaeum and in a damaged copy of the 12 March 1884 *Staten Island Gazette and Sentinel:* "Like most really strong men, he was one of the tenderest. Although the cadet of the family, he was for many years a great stay and support to his mother and sisters. All who knew him respected him, all who knew him intimately loved him, loved him the more the better they knew him." Hoadley was tactful, thinking of Herman's seniority, but the truth was that Tom from the time he became governor of Sailors' Snug Harbor had been not "a great stay and support" but the *greatest* stay and support to the family, including his brother Allan's daughters. Besides that, he had been the member of the family who gave to all his brothers and sisters untarnished delight. As Kate Lansing wrote in her diary: "Tom's life was full of usefulness & a happy enjoyable life & so soon cut off from us all."

Tom's death left Katie much more bereft than anyone would have thought. She was given notice to vacate the Governor's House as soon as she possibly could, for the new governor, G. D. S. Trask, took charge on 26 March. Lizzie came out for lunch on the eleventh, the day after the burial. On 15 March "Cousin Hetty's daughters Kitty & Sarah" came out, and that night Hoadley and his Kate returned to Boston, leaving Helen and Fanny Priscilla. Mary Curtis was there, "such a stay & support to us all—a perfect treasure," Fanny Priscilla wrote to Kate Lansing on 16 March, adding that "Mr Curtis & cousin Kate" (Cousin Kate Gansevoort Curtis) were "so kind to spare her," in George Curtis's own illness. Fanny Priscilla wrote to Kate Lansing on the fifteenth: "The full extent of what has come to her [Katie], has yet to come home to her poor heart, with crushing force, oh, the loneliness that is before her, is more than I can bear to think of." On 24 March Lizzie, now the strong one, accompanied her old friend Helen back to Boston, leaving Fanny Priscilla, who insisted on staying with Katie, who needed her most. Morgan Dix, whose mother, Catherine, had recently died, wrote Katie a memorable letter, according to Fanny Priscilla. The 29 March 1884 eulogy in the minutes of the trustees of the Sailors' Snug Harbor praised Governor Melville's achievements. He had "built four big dormitories; extended the iron fence; built two gatehouses, added the church tower, redecorated the main hall of the center building," and now was commissioning a statue of Randall from St. Gaudens.

There were formidable legal problems, for it was discovered that the only will Tom left was the one made in 1862, with Hoadley and Allan as witnesses, five years before his marriage, in which, Allan being Allan, everything Tom owned was left to Allan's daughters. Judge Stevens, Fanny Priscilla wrote to Kate Lansing on 26 March 1884, was "kindly attending to business affairs for Kate with the assistance of a friend of Tom's, Mr White on the Island." A good thing she had a friend of Tom's to help her, under the circumstances; I assume this is the Mr. White she later married. Packing as best she and Fanny could, Katie moved in with her previously displaced father (just turned eighty) in his own smaller quarters, abandoning some family furniture in the governor's mansion. As for Allan's daughters, they were at first uncertain who would "take charge for them, probably some lawyer in New York"; Fanny Priscilla added: "They feel as if they had lost their Father again. Mr Hoadley being so far away & so busy, would not have time or be near enough to see often." There was no thought of Herman's somehow taking Tom's place in their lives. On 10 April, Mary Ann Peebles wrote to

Kate Lansing: "We were very much surprised about T.M.'s will. Shall be much interested to hear about it." How the will was resolved, whether Katie was given what she deserved, has not been discovered. Kate Lansing was concerned enough to send Katie a check for fifty dollars on 6 May. Early the next year the trustees "offered to have a copy made of Tom's portrait for her, which she had gladly accepted," Helen told Kate Lansing; the portrait may be hanging on a wall in Staten Island to this day. During the Melville revival of the 1920s no one thought to interview Katie Bogart Melville White.

Tom's death meant the end of the Melvilles as a clan. Milie had made her own successful life (and carried her sisters with her); she was a Morewood now. For several years, the Mansion House at Gansevoort had been a retreat more for Fanny P. and Helen than anyone else. Now the family hearth, the governor's mansion, was lost to the Melvilles, so there was no place to go for refuge when someone needed to spend a day or two away from the busyness and dirt and smell of the city, no place to go for refuge when someone needed to recuperate from an illness, no place to go for a death made as easy as a death could be made. On 30 May was the ceremonial unveiling of the statue of Captain Randall by Augustus St. Gaudens, to which Herman and the others would have been invited if Tom had lived. For Herman the loss of Tom meant the loss of companionship with some of the sailors at the Harbor, surely, as well as an excuse for taking the ferry into New York Harbor and looking back at the island of the Manhattoes and the work progressing on Bedloe's Island.

Even aside from the desolate widow, the survivors were stunned. Fanny Priscilla, in particular, was shattered by the suddenness of the loss. Helen in the aftermath of the death behaved recklessly, as a Brookline neighbor, Mary Whitney, reported to Kate Lansing on 3 April 1884: "She is chronically imprudent, and I imagine always has been. If Miss Fanny had not been with her this winter, she would have gone out in all weathers." For Lizzie the loss of Tom was blurred by another death. In his diary for 6 May 1884 Sam Shaw wrote: "My brother Lemuel died of an attack of apoplexy at 11.45 PM at the Union Club, Park St." He had been of that utterly useless breed, an authentic clubman, so his death could not have been more appropriate, judging from the obituary in the 7 May Boston *Evening Transcript:* "Mr. Lemuel Shaw of Boston died at the Union Club House on Park street at a quarter to twelve o'clock last night. He had been in excellent health for many years, and spent yesterday in attending to his customary duties. In the evening he visited the Union Club, and after smoking a cigar he started to rise from his chair but was unable to do so and fell back and died in a few minutes, an attack of apoplexy causing his death." Kate Lansing saw Lizzie a few weeks later and reported to Fanny Priscilla, still in Brookline with Helen, that she was looking sick. Fanny wrote back on 7 June: "She feels deeply the sorrows of the past months, the loss on both sides, & has little strength to bear the coming [rose] cold, with all its discomforts." Lemuel had made some special provision for Josie, Oakes's crippled daughter, and he had left his share of 49 Mt. Vernon Street to Sam, but he had divided the rest among Oakes, Lizzie, and Sam. The estate was substantial, some $153,250 in real estate and some $170,200 in personal property. From this time forward Lizzie was a very rich woman, although a sorrowful one and often a sick one. Since he never went to Boston any more, Melville did not have to see that Thomas Bailey Aldrich, editor of the *Atlantic Monthly*, was now the proprietor of Herman's cousin Dr. Jacob Bigelow's mansion at 59 Mt. Vernon Street. Melville knew that the purchase was in progress, for on New Year's Day 1883 he gave Lizzie *The Poems of Thomas Bailey Aldrich*, musing on how the exaltation of Aldrich to Mt. Vernon Street was symbolic of the way the country rewarded triviality. For that matter, from glory to mediocrity in American literature was the distance from the last voyage of Captain Ahab to *The Story of a Bad Boy*.

The deaths came so thickly that the family had no time to absorb one before the next came, Kate Lansing grieving for her friend Cora Parker still, when Tom died; Lizzie reeling from Tom's death and Katie's condition when Lem died; Melville, a week after Tom died, having to deal with the death of his traveling companion and employer at the Custom House, Henry A. Smythe; then everyone having to grieve when Cousin Kate Curtis's husband, George, died on 27 May 1884, having sacrificially allowed his daughter, Mary, to leave him to help Katie and Fanny P. close up the Governor's House at Sailors' Snug Harbor after Tom's death. On 28 March Fanny Priscilla wrote to Kate Lansing of her other Cousin Kate: "Dear Cousin Kate & Mary 'the nearness of a great grief,' has come to them. I wanted to go on at once, but Helen would not listen to my even thinking of it, as I have been sick since Thursday, quite shut in." Ned Curtis reached home in time to accompany the body from Schenectady to Brooklyn, where George was buried near his mother-in-law, Mary Chandonette Gansevoort, who (dying while Melville was writing *Moby-Dick*) had wanted nothing but to be buried by her husband —in Albany. Only the older generation grieved when Aunt Mary Melvill, Uncle Thomas's widow, died on 30 July in Illinois (Hoadley and Griggs may never have met her).

Kate Lansing was in New York at the end of May or the first of June 1884, probably for George Curtis's burial. She wrote hastily to Fanny Priscilla, who queried her more closely on 8 June: "Where did you see Katie? Was she to lunch with you at the Hotel? I am sorry that you found Lizzie looking sick.... I will be glad when she gets to Fire Island." The Hoadleys insisted on Helen and Fanny's visiting them at their rented cottage at Nantasket Beach south of Boston (where old Thomas Melvill had done Revolutionary duty), "saying the salt air will do wonders," so they were going for a few days, trying to live normally. Abe went fishing as usual and caught a twenty-nine-pound salmon which he designated for Governor Cleveland, who responded handsomely, saying he had received it in beautiful condition and he and his household had enjoyed it exceedingly. Fanny P. and Helen opened the Mansion House in mid-August, finding it harder and harder, Helen told Kate Lansing on the eighteenth, to manage the physical chores, such as manipulating the "sashes, and shutters, and blinds." They stayed only briefly, two weeks or so, drawing the days out as a "furlough" expiring too soon, so that they did not stop at Albany on their way home to Boston.

On 12 September 1884 Fanny Priscilla needed again to comfort Kate Lansing, who was made sad and wretched by dealing with the contents of some family trunks: "Oh, it does not do to live in the past, for it perfectly unfits us for our daily life. We must look away from self, or our sorrows will make us selfish and unmindful of what we can do for the happiness of others." Mrs. Bogart was slowly dying; even Fanny P. exclaimed ruefully, "oh, this nursing & watching, how sad it is." On 25 November Fanny P. passed on news from New York: "Bessie has had a severe attack of 'muscular rheumatism,' & has suffered greatly, but the doctor assures Lizzie, that the worst is over. The strain of night & day attendance was too much for her mother, & they have a nurse from the training school, which is a great aid & comfort." The plan was for young Fanny and Harry to spend Thanksgiving in Philadelphia, the Hoadleys to be with the Griggses and Fanny Priscilla. On 7 December Kate Lansing noted in her diary: "Went up to see Cousin Lizzie — & hear how Bessie is getting along." After the diagnosis of typhoid fever was made, belatedly, Lizzie and Herman had to count several days until the twelfth, at which time, if all went well, the danger should be over. Bessie's life hung in the balance these days. Kate Lansing went to New York again and on 14 December after church "called on Mrs. Allan Melville & at Cousin Hermans." Later in December, Fanny Priscilla wrote Kate Lansing, Bessie's "long beautiful hair" had to be all cut off: "Is not that a loss?" Kate saw her on 19 January 1885, and noted that she was improving but had "had her hair cut & her head shaved."

When Kate Lansing asked Fanny Priscilla where she would have her 1884 Christmas dinner, she evoked a lament. Fanny (in her 19 December reply) said that she would try to think of the "Holy joys" of the season, but never could be "merry" again. Then Caroline Cobb Shaw died on 13 December 1884. When she wrote on the nineteenth, Fanny Priscilla asked Kate Lansing: "How was Lizzie looking? The death of Mrs Oakes Shaw — Josey's mother — brings home to her another loss & sorrow." Fanny wrote to Kate what everyone felt: "Ever since Tom's marriage he has been the center, the warm-hearted centre, of all the family joys and pleasures at . . . [Christmas] and the day can *never* be again to any of us, what it has been in years past." That first Christmas after Tom's death Katie got away just far enough, to Orange, to spend Christmas with the young Thomas family, which by then included Tom's two grandnieces, Eleanor and Frances. Fanny Thomas wrote Kate Lansing on 28 December from Orange: "Bessie is improving, but very slowly, the fever still continues, but the doctor says all her symptoms are favorable, and we need not feel anxious about her, it seems to be a very long and tedious illness." Sometime in these months after Lem Jr.'s death Elizabeth began putting twenty-five dollars in Melville's pocket every month, Eleanor heard much later, an allowance he could spend on books and prints without reproach or remorse. This year Melville was listed in the book of communicants kept by Dr. Theodore Chickering Williams, the successor to Henry W. Bellows as minister at All Souls, which wags were calling the Church of the Holy Zebra from its alternating courses of limestone and red brick. This long after Malcolm's death, Melville was mellowing toward youths of genteel capacity like his Clarel, especially if they were of a literary bent and possessed the power of recognizing an old fellow like him as a human being, still. Becoming a communicant was little enough to do for Lizzie, the year her brother Lemuel died.

In early October 1884 Melville received a letter from a young Englishman, James Billson, of Leicester. Three years earlier, the poet James (B. V.) Thomson had gone to Leicester for the opening of a new Secularist hall and formed a friendship with J. W. Barrs, who lived nearby. During his visits that year he introduced some of Melville's works to Barrs and (directly or through Barrs) to Billson, a young solicitor who for years regularly taught classes in Latin and Greek at the Working Men's College there. In class Billson gave rein to "his strong and racy sense of humour" as he taught artisans "enough Greek to enjoy Aristophanes." Two years after Thomson's death in 1882 from dipsomania, young Billson, spurred by the enthusiasm he now shared with Barrs and other friends, wrote Melville his first admiring letter (21 August 1884), in which he made clear that in his experience in the provinces (unlike D. G. Rossetti's in London) all of Melville's books were scarce, not just *Pierre*, and "in great request." Billson added: "as soon as one is discovered (for that is what it really is with us) it is eagerly read & passed round a rapidly increasing knot of 'Melville readers.'" Melville responded noncommittally on 10 October 1884, a few days after receiving the long-delayed letter. In it he answered Billson's question as to other works he had published, listing *White-Jacket, Battle-Pieces,* and *Clarel* ("a metrical affair, a pilgrimage or what not, of several thousand lines, eminently adapted for unpopularity. —

The notification to you here is ambidexter, as it were: it may intimidate or allure"). He sent best wishes to Billson and his "circle."

Melville led his obscure life still, unnoticed, or noticed by people who later saw his photograph and realized who he was, but mentioned more in the newspapers and magazines than in several years. In November 1884 Julian Hawthorne violated Melville's privacy by putting into *Nathaniel Hawthorne and His Wife* the most intimate letters Melville had ever written to anyone outside his family, and more intimate than any of the family letters known to survive. The letters revealing his ecstatic hopes for *Moby-Dick* were printed for the amusement of any flippant browser in any bookstore, making him more than ever the man who had known Hawthorne. Worse, he was the man who took up too much space in the book about Hawthorne, for in the February 1885 *Atlantic Monthly* T. W. Higginson, admirer of "The Encantadas," correspondent of Emily Dickinson, friend of George Wales, fulminated: "The letters, published in full, of his few American correspondents betray habitually the tone of secondary minds, not of men meeting him on high ground.... In some cases the letters are given so fully as to give an impression of 'padding,' as where we have nine consecutive pages of not very interesting epistles from Herman Melville." Even as a friend of Hawthorne, Melville was not very interesting. How low could his American reputation sink?

And what was he to make of a "circle" of readers in a Roman town in northern England? In October 1884 James Billson had sent him James Thomson's *Vane's Story . . . and Other Poems* (London, 1881), and in January 1885 he sent him Thomson's *The City of Dreadful Night and Other Poems* (London, 1880). Billson sent him also "The South Sea" from the London *Daily Telegraph* of 16 January 1885, containing this praise (which Melville assumed was by Billson himself): "There have been scores of books written about the South Seas, since 'Typee' and 'Omoo' were given to the world, but nothing has been expressed by pen or pencil that does not send the mind hastening back to the lovely imaginations which the very name of Herman Melville arouses." When the Brooklyn *Eagle* reprinted this article on 14 September, someone named C. F. Kane sent Melville a copy, which he retained. Billson was the author of yet another article he sent Melville, one in the Liverpool *Daily Post* for 10 February, "James Thomson: Poet, Essayist, and Critic." On 22 January 1885, Melville wrote to thank Billson for *The City of Dreadful Night*, contrasting "Sunday up the River" ("a Cuban humming-bird, beautiful in faery tints") with "The City of Dreadful Night" ("the tropic thunder-cloud" against which the humming-bird flew). Since Billson had not "unearthed" *Clarel,* and fearing that he would never get at it by himself, Melville had "disinterred" a copy for him; forgetting the copy of

Clarel he had so cautiously inscribed to his wife, Melville added: "It is the sole presentation-copy of the issue."

Then Fanny Priscilla, who had nursed others tirelessly, became very ill in Brookline, and the family's concern shifted away from Bessie. Helen broke the news to Kate Lansing on 8 February: "She has never recovered from the shock, so totally unlooked-for, and so without the *shadow* of softening preparation, that came upon us last March [with Tom's death]." Now Helen had her "in bed, where she cannot 'make believe well,'" trying "all healing and strengthening means" to restore her. Kate Hoadley and Minnie were "always on hand, to aid and comfort" them. On 14 March Helen reported, again to Kate Lansing, that Kate Hoadley and Minnie were alternating days, and offering to stay at night, but lately Fanny had been sleeping, so Helen got her own "night's rest." She reiterated what everyone knew, no doubt thinking how different Fanny was from their sister Kate Hoadley: "You know Fanny is not one to demand much attention,—not a querulous or exacting invalid, and we get along beautifully with Lizzie's aid, who takes a deep and affectionate interest in the patient." (Lizzie was the servant.) Kate Hoadley now did what needed to be done.

When he first wrote Melville, in 1884, Billson had not seen a piece by the sea-novelist W. Clark Russell, "Sea-Stories," in the September 1884 London *Contemporary Review*. There Russell daringly denied that *Moby-Dick* should be categorized as a sea-story: "it is a medley of noble impassioned thoughts born of the deep, pervaded by a grotesque human interest, owing to the contrast it suggests between the rough realities of the cabin and the forecastle, and the phantasms of men conversing in rich poetry, and strangely moving and acting in that dim weather-worn Nantucket whaler." Some of the sayings in the "Forecastle" chapter "might truly be thought to have come down to us from some giant mind of the Shakespearean era." *Moby-Dick* was "like a drawing by William Blake, if you please; or, better yet, it is of the 'Ancient Mariner' pattern, madly fantastic in places, full of extraordinary thoughts, yet gloriously coherent—the work of a hand which, if the desire for such a thing had ever been, would have given a sailor's distinctness to the portrait of the solemn and strange Miltonic fancy of a ship built in the eclipse and rigged with curses dark."

The Melvilles may not have known about this article for months, but they did learn, amid all the new concern over Fanny Priscilla's illness. Kate Lansing visited New York late in March 1885. On the twenty-sixth Lizzie called at her hotel while she was eating breakfast. Whoever had the news first, the two black-clad women consulted and went out together, purposefully, to the bookstore of August and Simon Brentano on Union Square West, where

Kate ordered an old magazine, the *Contemporary Review* for September 1884 —just that one issue where Russell's article had appeared. Kate's terse diary entry masks a dramatic scene, Lizzie and Kate going in pursuit of a copy of the magazine which contained an article they had heard of somehow, and which Herman may well not have seen, since it was not reprinted in this country until June, as far as is known, and then in the Philadelphia *Times*, not a New York paper. At some time Hoadley obtained a copy of the article (taken out of the issue) and preserved it. Hoadley's pages may be from the issue Kate Lansing ordered, since she knew how highly he had praised *Clarel* to Abe. No comment from any of the Melville family on Russell's article is known, but someone called it to the attention of Harper & Brothers. On 25 December 1885, the weekly Harper's Handy Series published *In the Middle Watch*, a collection of sea-pieces by W. Clark Russell, including an expansion of "Sea-Stories." As the Harper brothers died off (in 1869, 1870, 1875, 1877), the company was beginning to see the value in the author who, the brothers had told their friends confidentially in 1852, was a little crazy.

In 1846 Gansevoort was dying in London as Melville's first book (published by Gansevoort's efforts) was being reviewed there. In 1885, as Fanny Priscilla lay dying, Melville's reputation was slowly coming back to life. On 17 May the New York *Tribune* published thirty stanzas of a version of Melville's "The Haglets," entitled "The Admiral of the White," and beginning:

> By chapel bare, with walls sea-beat,
> The lichened urns in wilds are lost
> About a carved memorial stone
> That shows, decayed and coral-mossed,
> A form recumbent, swords at feet,
> Trophies at head, and kelp for a winding sheet.

Two days later the Boston *Herald* reprinted the lines, and the faithful John Hoadley dated a copy "May 1885" and made two corrections on it; in 1930 his daughter Charlotte gave it to Victor Hugo Paltsits. Kate Lansing's copy of the *Contemporary Review* came promptly enough from London. Not quite believing what he had read in Russell's article, perhaps, Abraham Lansing began reading *Moby-Dick* for himself, or possibly even reading *The Whale*, for Cousin Augustus Peebles's wife, Mary, wrote him on 29 June, asking: "How are you getting on with the Whale?" Like everyone, Mary had been reading Julian Hawthorne's *Nathaniel Hawthorne and His Wife*, and found it "very entertaining, principally because it is so indiscreet": "I wonder if Herman Melville was consulted about the appearance of his name? I should think some of the allusions would be very trying to a person of his sensitive nature." Lizzie in June gave a copy of Julian's two-volume book to Herman, so that, oddly enough, he now owned a book containing those dubious nine consecutive pages of his own intimate letters, published without his permission. He felt the strangeness of reading Julian's room-by-room description of the little red cottage so that he could have re-entered it and again read Emerson's essays in the "boudoir." He dealt with weirdnesses as well as he could, groping to remember that a casual salutation like "Buenos días, Señor," lay behind the claim in Julian's "Index" that Melville had worn a "Spanish disguise" when he called upon Hawthorne. Suddenly, it seemed, Melville was almost newsworthy—a cumulative result of years of simmering, brought perhaps to a boil by the notoriety occasioned by the publication of Russell's praise and by the publication of *Hawthorne and His Wife*. Melville's own knowledge of Russell's praise lies behind his comment to an admirer he wrote on 12 July: "You tell me you like my sea-tales. I am glad to know it. But have you read something yet better—the sea-tales of *W. Clark Russell*, the author of the '*Wreck of the Grosvenor*'?"

In 1885 another national deathwatch proceeded, too soon after that for Garfield. Former president Grant had been taken ill the previous summer at his house in Long Branch, New Jersey, down the coast, where Tom and others had vacationed. From March until his death on 24 July reporters kept a vigil outside Grant's brownstone on West Sixty-sixth Street. Simultaneously, the family kept a deathwatch for Fanny Priscilla, whose great characteristic in her intensely private life had been unselfishness that verged on the self-sacrificial, despite her determination, on one occasion, not to be a "martyr." Her last months seemed harder for everyone than any of the earlier sicknesses, even Maria's and Augusta's, because of the cumulative weight of the deaths and the increasing fragility of the remaining brother and sisters and cousins. In Boston for a visit, Bessie reported that Bright's disease, one of Gansevoort's diagnoses, was being mentioned along with kidney problems and some trouble with a hip, then a massive tumor in the hip. Herman and Lizzie, and others, begged Helen to hire a nurse, and she at last agreed. As Lizzie described it in relaying the news to Kate Lansing on 25 April, the treatment was barbaric, attaching a weight to keep "the bone of the leg" from slipping "up over the hip bone."

On 28 June 1885 John Hoadley visited the Griggs house and was allowed to see Fanny Priscilla. He wrote to Kate Lansing that Fanny's eyes had "a strange, far-away look" which he could hardly endure. Kate came herself to check out the situation, while Kate Hoadley, from her new residence in Brookline, took herself out of her sickbed for the duration and helped Helen; Kate Hoadley and her daughter Minnie were "always on hand, to aid and comfort," Helen said on 14 March. On 26 March Mrs. Bogart "died very quietly," Helen wrote Kate Lansing, reporting also that Cousin Kate Gansevoort Curtis and her daughter Mary were "sadly engaged in packing up their furniture for storage," clearing out before renters took possession on 1 April: "There is a world of sadness in the mere mention of these changes wrought by death!" Ned Curtis, she added, was in Omaha, unable to help. Harry Thomas escorted Bessie to Boston, to visit family and her special friend Miss Wells in Cambridge, leaving Fanny and the babies at Twenty-sixth Street. Bessie felt "braced" by the winds, and was able to visit her aunts, but not to help nurse her Aunt Fanny Priscilla. The first week of May, Katie Melville came up from Staten Island, feeling comfortable enough as Tom's widow to stay at Sam Shaw's house, he being now the sole owner of 49 Mt. Vernon Street. She went to Fanny Priscilla's doctor for the news from him before going out to Helen's. On 5 May Herman sent his sister Fanny a "box of superb flowers," Helen wrote Kate Lansing. Katie stayed on through the month, part of the time with the Hoadleys, so as to be near and to help. The doctors having warned her to make arrangements if she had any arrangements to make, Fanny Priscilla asked Helen to ask Abe to make some alterations in her will, and if possible to make a new will "as it would condense the contents." Helen wrote Kate Lansing on 12 May: "We do not give up hope; but Fanny with calm, quiet, thoughtfulness, has dictated these changes; she would 'set her house in order'—and she wishes to do what seems wisest and best, in view of the changes that have taken place since her will was written." Perhaps young Fanny Melville's wedding to Henry Thomas had changed things, perhaps Tom's death and the problems his old will had caused for Katie, perhaps other deaths.

And there was a new death: Lucy Melville died on 11 May 1885 at Bloomingdale Asylum, before any of her sisters could reach her. Milie could hardly have gone, even with more warning, since her new baby was only a few weeks old—and named Alfred Pierpont Morewood in honor of his uncle, dead earlier in the year. Sophia's sister Rachel Barrington called at Twenty-sixth Street to inform the Melvilles of Lucy's death, and Lizzie and her daughter Fanny went to the funeral, knowing it would have been too much for Bessie, a service in "that little out-of-the-way church" and the interment in hard-to-reach Carmansville, maimed rites for a young woman long, perhaps congenitally, weak in mind and body. According to Lizzie's account to Kate Lansing on 7 July, there were few mourners: "only one sister could be there, the cousins numbered eight"—Florence or Kitty there, Fanny Thomas, three or more of the Lathers cousins, most likely, perhaps Minnie or Lottie or both. It was the first funeral conducted by and for the younger and female generation, with Lizzie perhaps the only representative of what was now the older generation except the uninvited stepmother, Jane Dempsey Randolph Melville, who learned of Lucy's death in a newspaper and came with a friend. Herman, as usual, went to work out of his office by Simonson's lumberyard at the foot of Seventy-ninth Street on East River, the other side of the island from Carmansville, fearful of asking favors that might jeopardize his job.

The Lansings went back to Boston in mid-May, so Fanny Priscilla got her new will, and with it some peace of mind, judging from Helen's cryptic comments on the twenty-second: "You cannot tell, what a relief to her mind, was the result of your intervention. Now, there is an opportunity, or opening, for a return to old relations; and all may be again as it was before." This is probably something mundane, her concern with a renter in Gansevoort, perhaps, not some allusion to a breach in the family: Herman's flowers had not been a gesture of atonement. As usual, the Lansings helped out with cash for doctor bills. On 22 June, Katie, back in New Brighton somewhere, perhaps with her widowed father, wrote Kate Lansing that an operation on Fanny Priscilla was "simply impossible as the growth was so great and involved so much of the body, that it *must* take her life, but she would probably live some time as the natural conditions were unusually good—digestion &c.—that the growth probably began six months or more ago, it began in the hip joint & was rapidly extending, pushing the bladder & other parts much out of place." They had gotten the best consulting physician in Boston, Sam assured the family.

In the summer of 1885 Herman went to his job, but the others who were not nursing Fanny Priscilla separated. In June Lizzie went to the Surf Hotel on Fire Island Beach with Bessie, enjoying the "reviving sea air," she told Kate Lansing on the twentieth. Katie went to Orange to care for "Fanny's babes and household," so the Thomases could attend Harry's brother's wedding in Stockbridge. Florence and Kitty may have seen them there, probably the first time after Lucy's death. On Friday, 3 July 1885, Herman came down to Fire Island "& staid till Monday morning, and seemed to enjoy it very much," Lizzie wrote to Kate Lansing, serenely confident that it would benefit him even after he returned to New York City. Lizzie gave further plans in a letter to Kate Lansing on 7 July:

> You ask about our summer movements. When the hay fever time comes (near the middle of Aug.) Bessie and I expect to go to Jefferson N. H. where we are *sure* to escape the enemy—it is important that she should have no drain upon her system that way this year, but meantime, as Herman does not care to spend his vacation in Jefferson, we have it under consideration to take it early in Aug. and go somewhere, perhaps only on short excursions together, for a couple of weeks—or just whenever [the word could be "wherever"] he wishes.

> I am so fortunate this year as to have an excellent woman to leave in the house which makes Herman much more comfortable in my absence; and relieves me of much anxiety on his account, and though he protested against it vehemently at first, he feels the benefit of it, and is now glad to have her.

In her worry about Fanny Priscilla, Lizzie was haunted by the specter of misdiagnosis and delayed treatment because of her conviction that Augusta could have been saved if she had gone to the right doctor in time—something she laid out for Kate in this letter, so the younger woman would know. Lizzie was hoping, sometime, that she and Kate could "get out to Orange together," after the summer, and after the confusion consequent to the extension being added to the all too "cosy" Thomas house. Summer plans were imposed upon Herman, the only member of the family with a regular job with set hours.

Frances Priscilla Melville died on 9 July 1885. Kate Lansing, who had just comforted the sisters Fanny and Helen by promising to see that their father, Allan Melvill, had a properly repaired and marked tombstone, came to help. In her diary, Kate wrote of Fanny Priscilla: "Her death is to them what mother[']s was to us." A delegation took the cars for Albany, the body in the Undertaker's Wagon, a freight car designated for such cargo. There were John and Kate Hoadley and Kate Lansing, then at Pittsfield Mary Curtis and Florence and Kitty Melville got aboard. Others met them in Albany for the drive to the cemetery. Kate Lansing listed those at the cemetery. Frank had come, from Poughkeepsie or elsewhere; Katie had come up, two days before sailing for Europe; Fanny Thomas had come, probably with Katie; Augustus and Mary Peebles were there; some Lansings, including Will and his wife; and Mrs. Alfred B. Street, wife of the poet. Kate's dear friend (and distant cousin to her and to Fanny), Mrs. John Van Schaick Lansing Pruyn came, bringing her children, one of whom, then twelve, was Huybertie Pruyn (later Hamlin), much later a local historian, and the author of the posthumously published *An Albany Girlhood* (an eyewitness to Fanny's burial in 1885 who survived until 1964). Kate as usual sent out an obituary notice, this time from the Albany *Argus*, to Mr. and Mrs. Herman Melville, to Florence and Kitty Melville in Pittsfield, and to Abe's uncle George Lansing in Gansevoort, among others. Ignorant of Fanny's death, Abe was still on his fishing trip on Restigouche River, in Canada. Helen, who could not make the trip to Albany, on 5 May thanked Kate Lansing for the family: "Kate Hoadley was here yesterday, and told me of all your active goodness about the cemetery arrangements, and of your abounding hospitality, to the friends who were present."

Abe wrote to Herman on 27 July telling him that he would take steps at once to probate Fanny's will, if Herman approved, as he did. Lizzie returned to Manhattan just as a late July heat wave settled in. She wrote Kate Lansing on 29 July: "It does seem the strangest, and most inscrutable thing, that Fanny of all the sisters who seemed to be the strongest and most active and the most useful to all, should have been laid upon such a bed of sickness and death, when so many who would have been *glad* to go, are kept to linger on!" Lizzie was sure Helen would not long survive Fanny, but hoped that for now Helen would go to Milton with the Hoadleys, without George, for a while. Kate had asked something about Herman's job, for some obscure reason, perhaps involving Fanny's will, and Lizzie answered in detail:

> Herman's position in the Custom House is in the Surveyor's Department—a *district inspector*—his work is all on the uptown piers nearly to Harlem, and he has held office since Dec. 1866. Of course there have been removals, and he may be removed any day, for which I should be very sorry as apart from every thing else the *occupation* is a great thing for him, and he could not take any other post that required head work, & sitting at a desk. If Cousin Abe has an opportunity to say anything for him, I should be glad, but *do not let* Herman know that the subject has been mentioned between us. He *did* receive "The Argus" and sent you *a paper* in response.

Now a very rich woman, Lizzie knew so little of her husband that she could assert that his work at the Custom House was still "a great thing for him" when in reality it was wearing him down, more brutally every year. What he needed was a chance to do his own "head work" at his own pace, "sitting at a desk" when he felt like it, walking when he felt like it. Lizzie may well have worried about having him too much underfoot, remembering what it was like in the house before December 1866. Now she and Bessie were leaving for the Plaisted House in Jefferson, New Hampshire, on 5 August, the day after her wedding anniversary. Once again she congratulated herself: "I am fortunate in having a good reliable woman to stay in the house, which makes me feel less anxious about Herman in my absence, and is more comfortable for him." As it turned out, there was what Helen (in a letter to Kate Lansing on 4 September) called "quite a colony of the clan Melville at Jefferson" through August: "Lizzie & Bessie, Milie & her family, even to gran'pa [Rowland Morewood], Florence and Kitty; and Sam Shaw was up for a while. They must have enjoyed being together, all free from family cares."

Helen was not so free. On her birthday, and Herman and Lizzie's wedding day, she wrote to Kate Lansing, unconsoled and inconsolable: "Kate, & the girls often, one or other of them, pass a day with me; but companionship, does not make my loneliness less felt, it rather only emphasizes the 'vacant chair.'" Herman's birthday present from Lizzie was *Balzac*, by Edgar Evertson Saltus (Boston, 1884). According to Joe Smith's much later recollection, Melville spent his vacation at Pittsfield, with almost no one else in the family around, except perhaps some of the Latherses. He stayed "at the Homestead Inn, the Pomeroy homestead on East street, which was for a short time converted into a fashionable hotel," not evincing "the slightest aversion to society," but appearing "to enjoy the hearty welcome which it gave him; time having enhanced instead of diminishing the local pride in and regard for him." Smith thought that perhaps "his manner was a little more quiet than in the old time; but in general society, it had always been quiet." Smith emphasized that in this visit Melville "bore nothing of the appearance of a man disappointed in life, but rather had an air of perfect contentment, and his conversation had much of his jovial, let-the-world-go-as-it-will spirit."

On 17 August 1885 Melville went back to work after his vacation. That week he signed a waiver regarding Fanny's will, at Abe's request. In Milton, Hoadley made a bitter choice. Feeling he could not spare the money it would have required to send Frank to an institute he had helped to found, the Massachusetts Institute of Technology, he saw him off for a job in the engineering corps of a railroad working between Chicago and St. Paul. As Minnie wrote Kate Lansing on 23 August: "He had fully determined not to return to the Institute of Technology in the fall, for various reasons, (all good ones,) the *chief* being, that Papa was quite unable to bear the expense, and was looking about in every direction for an opening of this kind." Herman Melville's surviving son had gone to school longer than he had done but was less well educated; Frank had gone to school longer than Hoadley but would never be as well educated.

At the end of August or the beginning of September, Melville received from Billson the 15 August 1885 issue of the London *Academy*, the magazine which had praised *Clarel*, albeit briefly. Now the *Academy* had published a poem by Robert Buchanan, the notorious author of the attack on the Pre-Raphaelites, "The Fleshly School of Poetry." The poem in the *Academy* was "Socrates in Camden, With a Look Round," an exaltation of Walt Whitman at the expense of the popular writers of the day, the "haberdashers," notably Henry James and William Dean Howells, and containing lines on Melville:

> Meantime my sun-like music-maker [Whitman],
>   Shines solitary and apart;
> Meantime the brave sword-carrying Quaker
>   Broods in the peace of his great heart, —
> While Melville, sea-compelling man,
>   Before whose wand Leviathan
>   Rose hoary white upon the Deep,

> With awful sounds that stirred its sleep,
>   Melville, whose magic drew Typee,
>   Radiant as Venus, from the sea,
>   Sits all forgotten or ignored,
>   While haberdashers are adored!

Melville, "ignorant of the drapers' trade, / Indifferent to the art of dress," had "Pictured the glorious South-sea maid / Almost in mother nakedness." Fayaway "*lives*," Buchanan declared, and would live "Long as the sea rolls deep and blue, / While heaven repeats the thunder of it, / Long as the White Whale ploughs it through, / The shape my sea-magician drew / Shall still endure, or I'm no prophet!" Buchanan felt the need to identify Melville in a footnote: "Herman Melville, author of *Typee*, *The White Whale*, &c. I sought everywhere for this Triton, who is still living somewhere in New York. No one seemed to know anything of the one great imaginative writer fit to stand shoulder to shoulder with Whitman on that continent." The praise of Melville was astounding, but the other comment was puzzling. Melville was in the city directory, and Buchanan had visited E. C. Stedman, who then was already or soon afterward became an adherent of *Moby-Dick*, "its tale often on his lips, and the recommendation by all odds to read it at once to nearly every young writer who sought his counsel."

Not for three and a half decades had Melville read current praise like this. He knew enough of Whitman's poetry to accept the comparison at face value, not, for once, to have to feel uncomfortable at someone's praising him for the wrong thing, or praising him along with his inferiors. This was unexceptionable praise, and it may have created a storm of exaltation in him he had not felt since the first weeks of 1876, when he understood anew just how magnificent *Clarel* was. Yet when he got around to thanking Billson on 5 September 1885 he controlled his feelings: "For more than one reason, this Piece could not but give me pleasure." Buchanan had "intuitively penetrated beneath the surface of certain matters here," but did not specify that he referred to the self-glorification and mutual-glorification of literary mediocrities. The tribute to Whitman had "the ring of strong sincerity." The "incidental allusion" to his "humble self" was "overpraise, to be sure," but he couldn't help that and was "alive to the spirit that dictated it." Humility was not his characteristic state of mind, but Melville was conscious that his words would be read by more than Billson — by the Leicester "Melville readers," at least, and he was a cautious man, concluding quietly: "But a letter on almost any theme, is but an inadequate vehicle, so I will say no more."

Bessie came home alone at the end of September or the beginning of October 1885, Lizzie, ailing, having stayed over with Sam. That September or early October, Melville had his photograph taken at Rockwood's, since Billson and Lizzie's cousin Ellen Gifford, and others, had requested a photo of him. Melville sent one to Mrs. Gifford on 5 October with a whimsical comment: "Well, here it is at last, the veritable face (at least, so says the Sun that never lied in his life) of your now venerable friend—venerable in years. —What the deuse makes him look so serious, I wonder. I thought he was of a gay and frolicsome nature, judgeing from a little rhyme of his about a Kitten, which he once showed you" (the rhyme being Melville's own "Montaigne and His Kitten"). He enclosed some rose-leaves, it being a set thing between them that he presented her with a rose-leaf as a token, no matter the season. Jane was in Europe as well as Katie, so (to Kate Lansing on 20 October) Helen mused about the possibility that "the two 'wandering widows,' the two Madams Melville, should meet," in Paris or elsewhere. Lizzie came home and got sicker at once, with hay fever and asthma, after having escaped illness all the time she was at Fire Island and Jefferson.

Kate Lansing made a trip to Boston to talk to Helen about the Mansion House and lands. Helen was in such great physical pain that she apologized, on 28 October: "I was so miserable the afternoon you were here, that you must have thought me most weak, & unreasonable. But the pain was more than could be quietly borne, & worked upon my mental powers, so that mole-hills were mountains." Abe was right, Helen understood: "That Gansevoort business must be done, and the sooner the better, if Abe thinks best." All the obstacles seemed insurmountable as Helen tried to explain: "As to lodging in the house itself, it would never do to attempt it. And Kate, I think, even you, have no idea of the magnitude of the undertaking. The furniture is nothing—in comparison—it is the contents of the pantries, and closets, the chests, the trunks, & the drawers." She knew the job had to be done, somehow, even if Kate Hoadley had to bestir herself and help her do it with Kate Lansing's help.

Helen forced herself to visit New York and environs for Thanksgiving 1885, taking the actual dinner on the Twenty-sixth with Herman, Frances, Harry, and the babies, while Lizzie and Bessie were in Boston with Sam. Lizzie's widower brother, Oakes, had moved into the Parker House, permanently. On 30 November Lizzie wrote Kate Lansing from Brick Church, Orange, the newly enlarged Thomas house. Kate had been in New York, and Helen had parted from her in a slightly bewildered state, not quite realizing that they would not meet for some time, since she was going to "the Jerseys" and Kate might return to Albany before Helen returned to Manhattan. Herman was the "most polite escort," seeing to a safe passage for himself, Helen, his daughter Fanny, her two babies, and a nurse, four bags, and his own essential cane, triumphantly maneuvering them on all but the last stage of the journey, which involved "two separate lines of horse-cars, a ferry-boat, a steam-car, and a carriage" — enough to have deterred Jane permanently. Herman got them aboard the steam-car before returning to New York, and his job, it having been arranged that Harry would meet the steam-car. Florence and Kitty were coming from Elizabeth to see Helen on the thirtieth, and on 2 December Milie and Ellen Brittain were coming to lunch.

Kate Lansing stayed on for Thanksgiving, on 26 November 1885, at Delmonico's, in the new location a stone's throw from Herman and Lizzie's house: "*Our Wedding Day* Anniversary & *Thanksgiving Day* — . . . . Dined at *Delmonicos we four* [Abe, Kate, and the Peebles] & no more — Cousin Helen went to Dined [i.e., dine] at Cousin Hermans with Fanny & Mr Thomas & the children." Kate Lansing was still there on 3 December, calling on Mrs. John Bogart in East Twenty-third Street and on Cousin Lizzie, during Herman's working hours. Nothing in these documents shows Herman as anything but loving brother to his older sister, and obliging father and grandfather. Helen lingered on with Fanny Thomas, loving it (she wrote Kate Lansing on 8 December) that the babies had adopted her as an aunt, and also that they were "sweet little maidens, being trained up in the way they should go" — both Eleanor and Frances. Helen was naturally full of rue (perhaps thinking of 6 December, when Gansevoort would have been seventy): "at each remove, the chain only lengthens; and the coming on of the holidays, brings back the thought of happier days, passed in company with those who did so much to make them happy." After going to Elizabeth to see Milie and her children, Helen was thinking of returning to Brookline without accepting renewed invitations from "Elizabeth, New York, and Staten Island." She added tellingly, since she never complained: "I have half promised to pass a day at each of the two latter places; but it takes so ridiculously little to tire me out, that I am afraid to venture."

Around Thanksgiving, between work and escorting Helen, Herman had been observed by someone who thought his mere appearance was striking enough to make inquiries: "Dropping into a bookstore the other day, my attention was attracted by an old gentleman with white hair, but whose eyes are still bright and his movements quick." This witness was "Stylus," the New York correspondent of the Boston *Literary World*, which published this item on 28 November, in time for Lizzie to hear about it at Mt. Vernon Street. American newspaper comments on Melville were almost always annoyingly inaccurate as well as patronizing if not outright offensive. From late 1884 on Melville knew there was a "circle" in Leicester reading his books, and learned that he had many admirers in London and elsewhere, but he never knew the ramifications of his literary fame, most of which are in fact still imperfectly documented. He knew almost nothing of the English readers who had remembered him from midcentury and had shared their love of him with their friends during the past three decades and more. While the effects of *The Whale* were still reverberating in London, a few readers (mainly young people) had pondered their way toward a further stage in their sense of what was of value in American literature. In this the very young James Hannay, an intimate of the Rossettis, played a significant role. The rankings of these younger critics did not jibe with the opinions of the British reading public and the British literary establishment, in whose view Henry Wadsworth Longfellow was a poet almost if not quite the equal of Alfred Tennyson and in whose view Nathaniel Hawthorne was the equal of most living British novelists. It took time for an anti-establishment evaluation of American writers to crystalize—it took the publication of *Walden* in 1854 and *Leaves of Grass* in 1855, then more years, for only a few copies of these books reached England in the mid-1850s. *Walden* was first published in London in 1884 and first actually printed there in 1886, while part of *Leaves of Grass* was first printed there, without "Song of Myself" and otherwise sanitized, in W. M. Rossetti's *Poems of Walt Whitman* of 1868. It took time to reassess the American canon, but by the late 1860s and the 1870s some of the brightest, most vigorous young British lovers of literature and art, men (the available evidence is almost exclusively about men) who shared idealistic and iconoclastic social views as well as aesthetic values, were deciding that great literature had come from one or another of three American writers (or perhaps two of the three) who at the time were all practically unknown in Great Britain and were all somewhat marginal figures in their own country: Melville, Whitman, Thoreau.

The younger members of the British literary world who constituted the admirers of Melville, Whitman, and Thoreau belonged for the most part to several overlapping groups. Some were members of the Pre-Raphaelite Brotherhood of artist-writers, or their associates. Some were adherents of the workingmen's movement (datable from 1854, when F. D. Maurice, the Christian socialist, founded the Working Men's College in London). Some were latter-day Shelleyans too young to have seen "Shelley plain" (Browning's awestruck phrase), but, some of them, lucky enough to have talked to Edward Trelawny and Thomas Peacock, who *had*. Some (a little later) were Fabian socialists. Some were themselves sea-writers or writers about remote countries, for *Typee* and *Omoo* in portable sets of Murray's Home and Colonial Library still accompanied young men to the farthest outposts of the Empire. And the man who had been America's first literary sex symbol—heterosexual sex symbol—at the end of his life became one of three cult American authors (Melville, Whitman, and Thoreau) cherished in England by social radicals and by homosexuals (some of whom were pursuing the scientific study of sexuality). Melville was in no position to trace such ramifications. During several weeks before and after Thanksgiving 1885 he looked at his latest gifts from England, Thomson's *Essays and Phantasies* and *Satires and Profanities*, closely enough to refer to specific essays when he thanked Billson for them on 20 December 1885. As to Thomson's "not acheiving 'fame'" Melville was sanguine: "He is not the less, but so much the more." He did not say so to Billson, but he was going to take his own chances with completing his literary projects, whatever sort of "fame" he might achieve with them: after more than nineteen years, he was retiring from the Custom House at the end of the month.

[39]
Fragments in a Writing Desk
1886–1891

Chaucer's character of Griselda.

Melville's note to himself after looking at "On Chaucer and Spenser" in Hazlitt's *Lectures on the English Poets;* the note faces the title page of *Lectures on the English Comic Writers,* bound first in the two-in-one volume (William S. Reese Collection)

ON 1 JANUARY 1886 Herman Melville had a New Year's cake to eat his way around, for Kate Lansing was keeping up Uncle Peter and Aunt Susan's tradition. He had, that Friday, no duties to send him out far uptown to the frigid docks. He was sixty-six, almost sixty-six and a half, and worn out, as Lizzie described him to Kate and Abe that month, despite his vigorous appearance. Despite the tone she had taken the previous year when she insisted that she and Herman both feared his losing his job, now she said: "For a year or so past he has found the duties too onerous for a man of his years, and at times of exhaustion, both mental and physical, he has been on the point of giving it up, but recovering a little, has held on, very naturally anxious to do so, for many reasons." She added: "He has a great deal [of] unfinished work at his desk which will give him occupation, which together with his love of books will prevent time from hanging heavy on his hands — and I hope he will get into a more quiet frame of mind, exempt from the daily irritation of over work." Healthfully distracting occupation was what she had in mind, not another obsessive drive to create a literary masterpiece like *Clarel*.

Melville was weakening, mentally as well as physically, not capable of writing another *Clarel*. The man who had entered into print with an abortive series, two "Fragments from a Writing Desk" in a row, now could sit and look at his fragmentary literary projects which he might or might not bring to completion. In the next years, at sixty-six, at sixty-seven, and thereafter, Melville made pretty much the expected intermittent progress on putting his papers in order and in revising them and in composing small pieces, with only one, the story of Billy Budd, greatly outgrowing its initial confines. He lived to print two books, privately, each in editions of twenty-five copies: *John Marr and Other Sailors, with Some Sea-Pieces* (New York: De Vinne, 1888) and *Timoleon and Other Ventures in Minor Verse* (New York: Caxton, 1891). Only death prevented him from printing other such volumes. Some of the old manuscripts in Melville's writing desk dated as far back as the mid-1850s, for "The Two Temples" survived, in Augusta's hand. Conceivably, Melville could have printed it if he had tried. *The Isle of the Cross* was not in his desk. In one of the bitterest ironies of his life, the time came when he could have answered an inquiry of one of several British admirers by saying that, as a matter of fact, he had a novel in manuscript which he would be pleased to see published in London. If he had kept the manuscript, he could, at any time in the late 1880s or 1890 or 1891, have become the author of a new book that he had finished the week Bessie was born. Immolations, he called his sacrifices to the god of fire in the spirit of Hawthorne, who had fatuously proclaimed that what counted was that the spirit of the artist possess itself in the enjoyment of the Reality, even though the work of art were destroyed.

Of his earlier poetry, Melville retained a good many pieces from the collection he had thought would be published in New York in 1860 while he was on the *Meteor* with Tom. "Fruit of Travel Long Ago" (appended as the last section of *Timoleon*) consisted of eighteen poems derived from his Mediterranean trip. Some of the previous twenty-three poems in *Timoleon* (such as "The Ravaged Villa" and "The Garden of Metrodorus") were also set in Mediterranean locales. Even laxly applied notions of putting like things with like would have dictated that the poems set in the Mediterranean be printed together, so chances are that the last section was indeed long-ago-written fruit of long-ago travel, not more recent fruit of long-ago travel. Indubitably, the sixth of the "Fruit of Travel" group, "Pausilippo (In the time of Bomba)," the episode concerning Silvio, long kept a political prisoner, had been part of the long poem "A Morning in Naples." "Pausilippo" and presumably the other seventeen poems gathered in "Fruit of Travel Long Ago" were already in Melville's desk when he retired, possibly along with others from the 1860 volume that he later discarded, and along with other poems written since 1860, or even shortly before that. Much of the 1891 *Timoleon* may have consisted of older material (however much reworked) than much of the 1888 *John Marr*.

Melville had in hand, in January 1886, two long poems he had been working on, off and on, for many years, the one once entitled "A Morning in Naples" then "An Afternoon in Naples" and later "Naples in the Time of Bomba," and another once entitled "A Symposium of Old Masters at Delmonico's" and later called "At the Hostelry." They were closely related, the beginning of the "Symposium" (about Garibaldi's liberation of Italy) having been written as an appendage to the "Naples" poem. Associated with these two poems, by the time Melville retired, was a good deal of prose involving Jack Gentian and the Marquis de Grandvin, written in the years just after the publication of *Clarel*, some of it already interpolated within the poems to introduce the sections, some of it surviving as drafts partly or wholly superseded but not destroyed. Under various titles, one of which was "Parthenope" (the poetic name for Naples) and another was "The Burgundy Club," Melville had brought this mixture of poetry and prose nearly to completion around 1879, then, under various pressures, had dropped it, perhaps dropped it more than once, finding it hard to yoke together two disparate things, Naples in the late 1850s and a discussion of the picturesque in art, especially when he was trying to foist upon those poems some post-Centennial prose sketches involving, first, a one-armed Civil War Major commenting on a century or more of military and social issues and, second, the Major's literally insubstantial French friend who represents the spirit of wine.

Between January 1886 and his death, Melville worked for weeks on end on certain projects—most surely on *Billy Budd*. Yet the evidence is that during most of his retirement he pushed one project forward, then another, cutting one (*John Marr*) off in order to declare it publishable at the expense of leaving out "Daniel Orme" and the material about Billy Budd, and including a poem, "The Enviable Isles," which he identified as "from '*Rammon*,'" thereby implying that he was cannibalizing his longer "Rammon" material for a lyric. (He may not have cannibalized his Naples poem for the passage about Silvio in *Timoleon*, since that passage may have been removed from its context long before, not in order to be included in *Timoleon*.) Physical evidence indicates the interconnectedness of Melville's projects though not always the priority of his work on them. The back of the first manuscript leaf of the "House of the Tragic Poet" essay has "Timoleon" written on it in big letters—an implication being that the leaf had been discarded from the poem "Timoleon" or the book *Timoleon*. Leaf 13 of "Rammon" has material from a poem published in *John Marr* on the other side, and the date 4 December 1887. Part of the "Daniel Orme" sketch is written on an early version of the prose headnote for *Billy Budd*. "The Lake" in the unfinished collection *Weeds and Wildings* is partly written on the other side of "To M. de Grandvin." The blank verso of a canceled sheet of poetry from *Weeds and Wildings* was reused in the *Billy Budd* manuscript.

Already on Melville's desk at retirement may have been much of what went into *John Marr and Other Sailors*. An odd source for the title character is a passage in the article on George Crabbe's poems in Melville's volume of Francis Jeffrey's essays. There Jeffrey hooted at Wordsworth for asking the reader to imagine "a captain of a small trading vessel . . . who being past the middle age of life, has retired upon an annuity, or small independent income, to some village or country, of which he was not a native, or in which he had not been accustomed to live." No one has known such a person, said Jeffrey. Rising to the challenge, Melville created one. His title poem, "John Marr," begins with a long prose headnote on the adventurous sailor, who, when disabled, ekes out a living as a sailmaker in one seaport or another, then as a "rough bench-carpenter" migrates far inland to an alien frontier-prairie, very like the Illinois Melville saw in 1840. There he marries. His wife and child die, and he stays on, hoping to cultivate "social relations" with his neighbors, but they know only "their own kind" and admonish him when he tries to talk about some episode of his nautical life: "'Friend, we know nothing of that here.'" For solace the isolated and aging John Marr turns to "retrospective musings" upon his shipmates, some of whom must be dead by this time, others of whom might be alive, but all of whom "as subjects of meditation" were "like phantoms of the dead," all lit "by that aureola circling over any object of the affections in the past for reunion with which an imaginative heart passionately yearns."

Other poems that went into *John Marr and Other Sailors* named actual men Melville had met four decades earlier, and he may have drawn on other men he met during his weeks at sea in 1839 and his years at sea in the early 1840s, when yarn-spinning after labor was a cherished art and a social obligation. In *White-Jacket* (ch. 74) he wrote: "I always endeavored to draw out the oldest Tritons into narratives of the war-service they had seen." As a young man, Melville knew many older seamen who had fought in the War of 1812 and who had heard with their own ears, from *their* elders, stories of bloody maritime struggles stretching back into the eighteenth century, beyond the mutinies on British ships in 1797 at Spithead and the Nore. He had heard, as well, many stories of peacetime calamities at sea. Melville had never wholly banished his old shipmates from his consciousness. In the first years of his literary career, and later, some of his shipmates had corresponded with him. In 1853 or afterward Melville wrote down a full list of "What became of the ship's company of the whale-ship 'Acushnet.'" In 1853 he advised his Uncle Peter to visit an American Negro he had met in Greenwich Hospital. As an older man, Herman Melville had dealt with ship captains in his work in Manhattan; and at Sailors' Snug Harbor, until Tom's death in 1884, he had spent time with men who had stories to tell from his own time at sea, and far earlier. After his retirement, free to live if he pleased in memories of the distant past, Melville brooded over "what became of" his shipmates in whalers and in the U.S. Navy, and perhaps even in the *St. Lawrence*, which had carried him on his only merchant voyage.

The *John Marr* poem "Bridegroom Dick" is given the date 1876 in brackets, perhaps as the date of composition, yet 4 December 1887 seems to be the date Melville completed a revision of it. This poem, an old man's rumination delivered aloud to his aging wife, celebrates the dead from different decades, from different wars, all vivid in the speaker's memory. Among the great poems in *John Marr* is "The Maldive Shark," as much about the pilot fish that attend on it as about the shark itself, the pale ravener of horrible meat. Another is "To Ned," an acute look at what nearly half a century had done to the Polynesia explored by the "Typee-truants" Melville and Greene in 1842. Now, Paul Pry had "cruised with Pelf and Trade," and tourists were exploring the isles "smart in pace," like the tourist at Gethsemane in *Clarel*. In the great port of Manhattan in the 1880s, Melville reflected on what sensuous peacefulness he and Toby had won then, in 1842: the "Indian Psyche's languor," in which they could breathe "primeval balm / From Edens ere yet over-run." Then, in 1842, they could marvel "if mortal twice, / Here and hereafter," could "touch a Paradise." In "To Ned" Melville recorded his comprehension of what his own adventure as told in *Typee* had meant to the popular culture of his century and what the experience had meant to him, in 1842, in 1844 and 1845 (when he wrote *Typee*), and in the 1880s. The creator of a great cultural icon (*Typee*—far more important to the century than *Moby-Dick*) here looked back on it after it had become fraught with meaning to thousands of readers, most of them strangers to him.

Two pieces that survived in Melville's papers may have been intended for *John Marr and Other Sailors*. One, a prose piece about a sailor called Daniel Orme, a moody old Great Grizzly of a man-of-war's-man, may have been conceived as set at the Sailors' Snug Harbor, judging by the location described at the end: "Orme was discovered alone and dead on a height overlooking the seaward sweep of the great haven to whose shore, in his retirement from sea, he had moored." It contains a passage, hardly ironical at all, on the sort of animal decay Melville had begun to recognize in himself: "In his retirement the superannuated giant begins to mellow down into a sort of animal decay. In hard, rude natures, especially such as have passed their lives among the elements, farmers or sailors, this animal decay mostly affects the memory by casting a haze over it; not seldom, it softens the heart as well, besides more or less, perhaps, drowsing the conscience, innocent or otherwise." "Daniel Orme" has close affinities to the prose headnote to "John Marr," and may possibly be a headnote that survived its poem. "John Marr," longish headnote and poem, was published; "Daniel Orme," a prose sketch but with no surviving poem, was left unpublished; the ballad "Billy in the Darbies" led to the composition of an ever-growing headnote, both ballad and prose story left unpublished, the prose unfinished.

Whether Melville drafted the poem "Billy in the Darbies" before or after he retired, the prose headnote to it began (Harrison Hayford and Merton M. Sealts Jr. have shown) not as a late literary departure, a deliberate return to longish fiction, but more simply as a poem for the *John Marr* collection, one which, like "John Marr," acquired a headnote that eventually overshadowed the poem. Gradually the story became a full "inside narrative" (Melville's phrase) which told all that had previously been put on human record about Billy and also told more than had ever been put on record. The inside story of *Billy Budd* became a kind of fictional analogy to the lost true histories of shipmates who had died unknown to fame or who had lived out long lives more obscurely even than Melville. Toward the end of his work, Melville blurred fictional record and factual record by dedicating his fictional narrative to his real comrade, "Jack Chase / Englishman / Wherever that great heart may now be / Here on Earth or harbored in Paradise." By late 1887 Melville was also at times working on a short prose and poetic manuscript, variously entitled, in which Rammon, a son of Solomon (an invented figure, not in the Bible), finds his father's Hebraic philosophy, in which there is no afterlife, challenged by the Buddhistic teachings of immortality and transmigration of souls. Melville attached to the end of "Rammon" a poem, "The Enviable Isles" (the one he published in *John Marr* as "from '*Rammon*'"). The "Rammon" material exhibits a narrowing and faltering of mind, and one can see in it Melville's resorting to expediences (such as disclaiming responsibility for thoughts or arguments) so as to mask his weakening grasp of his material.

During his last years Melville vacillated about what, if anything, to do with the Naples poem, the symposium on the picturesque, and the Gentian and Grandvin prose pieces. By 1890, at the latest, Melville was thinking of publishing the poems "At the Hostelry" and "Naples in the Time of Bomba," without the prose sketches (but with the prose interpolations?). At a late stage he wrote in pencil a prose preface called "House of the Tragic Poet" to precede another preface. As Robert A. Sandberg has shown, the speaker in "House of the Tragic Poet," a character Melville invented late in his work on the "Burgundy Club" material, is a gentleman of mature years who takes on the task of editing the material for publication. This editor (who has never before ventured into print) here argues that the famous "House of the Tragic Poet" excavated at Pompeii is misnamed: anything as lavish as that Roman house and at the same time as inhospitable (there was a "Beware of the Dog" mosaic) must have belonged to a publisher, not a poet, and the canine mosaic must have been there to frighten away would-be authors.

Melville portrays the editor as dreading the attempt to publish the sketches. Consulting an old friend who had "risen to an influential position as a member of the metropolitan press," and knows "all about Popular Opinion and the popular taste," the editor is given a number of reasons a publisher should decline the manuscript. Sandberg elaborates:

> He [the friend] gave a catalog of reasons: the manuscript was not in "the current"; nothing new is told; the theme does not relate to America; the meter is "as old as the hills"; the events described in the "main piece" took place twenty years ago, "an aeon to the popular mind"; his [the editor's] method is "painterly," not photographic; and finally, worst of all — "I fail to see that anywhere you have laid an anchor to windward by conciliating the suffrages of the ladies, and in marked preference to those of the men." The tyro editor responds only to the last criticism: "The ladies?"

The critic explains that just as the ladies are social arbiters so are they arbiters in the "literary sphere, as to every book, the design of which is at all to please." The disheartening experiences of the first-time editor whom Melville invented to try to shepherd the "Burgundy Club" material into print pretty obviously reflect Melville's bemusement with his own situation roughly between the time of his retirement and the months before his death.

In "House of the Tragic Poet" Melville achieved a wry, sardonic attitude toward the current literary scene, where W. D. Howells from the "Editor's Study" in the September 1886 *Harper's* proclaimed that there was no Dostoyevskian tragedy in America, "a land where journeymen carpenters and plumbers strike for four dollars a day" (Melville's salary at the Custom House), a land where "the sum of hunger and cold is certainly very small." This roused Melville's contempt, since it recalled all the smugness of Orville Dewey on the question of poverty in America, and Howells made things worse by recommending that the novelist concern himself "with the more smiling aspects of life, which are the more American." Still more dismaying was Howells's admonition from the "Editor's Study" in June 1889 that writers should keep their novels fit for eyes of young people, especially young ladies. The rueful self-satirizing in "House of the Tragic Poet" reflected Melville's decision after his retirement to put some of his poetry and other unfinished work into shape fit to print, and it reflected also his related decision not to subject anything he printed to the judgment of publishing people holding alien values and to the full glare of journalistic publicity; instead, he would pay for printing the works himself and distribute copies to family and friends. His last two books were in fact printed and bound then distributed privately, not "published."

Early in 1890 Melville became absorbed in arranging a volume of verse under the title *As They Fell*, to consist of two parts, "A Rose or Two" and "Weeds & Wildings," each with thirteen poems. The last of the "rose" poems, "L'Envoi," asks why a man finds himself "aging at three-score" when sunrise is forever young; in an associated prose piece, "Under the Rose," the English ambassador to Persia is said to be sixty-three and dreading death, which had come to his father and grandfather when they were about that old. Aside from these hints at the period when Melville might have worked on the "rose" poems and "Under the Rose," internal echoes show that they were written after he had fallen under the sway of that great piece of Victorian orientalism *The Rubáiyát of Omar Khayyám*, which he may first have known from the 1878 Boston edition of Edward Fitzgerald's version, within a few years of its publication. Early in 1886 Melville received from James Billson a "semi-manuscript" edition of Fitzgerald's free translation of the *Rubáiyát*, a gift that only confirmed his prior sense of Omar Khayyám as "that sublime old infidel" (his words to Billson on 2 April). Soon after its publication Melville bought the more elaborate 1886 Boston edition of the *Rubáiyát*, illustrated by Elihu Vedder, the text lettered by Vedder. Melville pored over the text and pictures by the hour, telling Lizzie that he was proud Vedder was his countryman. The "Weeds & Wildings" poems contain few clues as to their dates, though the subject matter of several (seasons, birds, small animals, insects, flowers, clover, weeds) may suggest that they date from the first years Melville was writing poetry or from a late period of nostalgia for Arrowhead. Both sections, "A Rose or Two" and "Weeds & Wildings," portray a man content to acknowledge that he "came to his roses late" but not too late, and content to celebrate spousal love in old age.

About the first of January 1891 Melville was taken sick after he walked too far "in a bitter cold air" (his wife told Kate Lansing a week later). In the night his "dizziness or vertigo" alarmed his doctor, but he improved enough to resume intermittent work at his desk. Finishing *Billy Budd* now may have taken on a higher order of priority than Melville had given it before. On 19 April 1891, he recopied at least part of the poem "Billy in the Darbies" and wrote after it, "End of Book," perhaps confirming that the poem was to end the work rather than the news account which earlier had done so, or perhaps recording a temporary impression that the work was completed. Each attempt to get the story into fair copy required a new concentration of physical and intellectual energies. In Melville's state of declining health some thoughts could not be completed, or if worked out in the mind were not put down fully on paper, and some tasks which he keenly perceived as essential to complete were never carried out. Sometimes Melville made matters worse, as when he belatedly tried to straighten out the number and personnel needed for a court-martial. Although he jotted down some housekeeping notations about the need to eliminate inconsistencies and to plant necessary information at the right place, he did not manage to achieve all that he saw needed to be done. He reminded himself that he needed to "Speak of the fight & death of Captain Vere" before chapter 29 could make sense, and did so, but he did not live to handle other anomalous details. He may well not have noticed some loose ends which patient students of the manuscript can now discern. He needed help, and if his wife had been free or had felt free to follow after him at every stage, copying after him, as she and his sisters Augusta and Helen had once done, then he might have reworked all the parts of the story to something like an equal degree of finish and might have satisfactorily handled all the unprepared for passages or not yet reconciled passages that obtruded on his consciousness but were too awkward or too baffling for him to resolve at a given time, or simply too difficult, physically, for him to write out. Even if presented with ever-fresh copy he may well have lacked the mental force necessary for reconciling what he was adding with what stood in the latest previous stage as well as what had stood at another stage or had been in his mind but never put on paper.

When he died, Melville was still revising the manuscript of *Billy Budd, Sailor*, having left a chapter on Lord Nelson in a separate folder, out of the manuscript, not having settled the direction in which Vere's characterization was to go, and leaving other minor contradictions. Without the Nelson chapter, and without the late pencil revisions that question Vere's character, the story is fully interpretable. *With* the Nelson chapter and without the late pencil revisions the story is adequately interpretable, with Captain Vere being much like Nelson but not quite of his heroic order. However, after Melville made the late pencil revisions the story became difficult if not impossible to interpret as a whole, since he died leaving clues as to how to read Vere's behavior going in at least two directions. With the late pencil revisions in the text and with the Nelson chapter put back into the text from the folder where Melville had kept it during the last stages of his work on the story, then not only is Vere's behavior questioned, but, even more strikingly, the contrast with Nelson's behavior seems to have been set up to make the reader, from early in the story, see Vere as inferior to Nelson, who could brilliantly, bravely, and patriotically (a reader would feel) have done what Vere never thought of doing: could have pardoned Billy on the spot and then publicly told the crew why, and have won them to his command in doing so. We do not honor Melville by pretending that *Billy Budd* is complete and perfect: to close our eyes to the relation between artistic imperfection and failing health is to dehumanize the creative process and the created product.

Later, perhaps around 4 August 1891, the Melvilles' wedding anniversary, Melville worked on "Rose" and "Weeds" material, reversing the sections as *Weeds and Wildings Chiefly: with a Rose or Two*, and he composed a more-or-less autobiographical dedication to "Winnefred." Among the *Weeds and Wildings* which he proffered to Lizzie was a long prose retelling of the

Rip Van Winkle story in which Melville made clear his late understanding of Rip as an artist figure. He was writing or had written other poems not in the collections as we know them, and he made other notations, including one on Shakespeare, whom he called (in this imperfect transcription) "a [undeciphered] intelligence, with wisdom wiser than the Serpent's yet without his guile; genial; child-like in sincerity; and, what is phenomenal in a modern — for in vital matters Shakespeare was so advanced a modern that not yet have we come up to him — utterly without secular [pessimism?] or secular cant." Melville did not push the *Weeds and Wildings* poems to completion: he went to Fire Island instead, most likely. Almost two years earlier, on 5 December 1889, Melville had rebuffed an admirer by saying he needed to husband his declining vigor "for certain matters as yet incomplete, and which indeed may never be completed." *Billy Budd* was the largest of the fragments on his writing desk, then and later, but for many of the remaining months of his life it was not the "matter" most important to him, just then.

In and on Melville's writing desk in the late summer of 1891 were folders and piles of more or less messy manuscripts in various states of completion, among them manuscripts of poems already printed in *John Marr* and *Timoleon*. At least three books were in active progress: the *Billy Budd* material; the "House of the Tragic Poet" version of the "Burgundy Club" material; and the *Weeds and Wildings* material. Though the paper stocks varied, sheets for the late prose and poetry manuscripts had been torn from larger cream or ivory sheets to create leaves of a fairly uniform size, approximately 7 by 5⅝ inches. For the most part, the surviving leaves bear writing on only one side in ink and pencil. Flashes of color from Melville's green, orange, blue, and rust-brown crayons (the colors often indicating distinct phases of revision) helped Melville find his way among many canceled passages and among decisions and indecisions about paragraphs or indentation, and to find his way through multiple refoliations necessitated by his repeated reworking of texts or sequences. Near to hand was a pile of canceled sheets (texts boldly struck through in crayon) whose empty versos were ready to be called to new service. Many extensively revised leaves of text not discarded had been cut down so their usable parts could be pasted or pinned to uniform base sheets to cancel existing writing or to avoid recopying. Even homemade folders for the various late projects were reused: the folder for "Rip Van Winkle" (title in pencil) was first fashioned for "Small Naval Pieces" (title, now upside down on the rear cover, in blue crayon, underlined in red crayon, and canceled in pencil). On the writing desk were drafts of incomplete works in many stages, some with portions rewritten by Lizzie and all with revisions, cancellations, balloon insertions, crabbed marginal scrawls, and editorial reminders by Melville to himself. Even completed works still existed in manuscript in the study: for *John Marr* and *Timoleon* Melville retained his heavily reworked drafts with many cut-and-pasted or cut-and-pinned leaves. The final draft of the eleven-line "Art," one of the poems in *Timoleon*, consisted of a base sheet of text in ink and pencil and three pinned-on revisions in pencil, each of the revisions itself substantially revised. At hand was Lizzie's fair copy of *Timoleon*, but fair only in the technical sense, for it bears her own reworkings following Melville's editorial instructions, along with his annotations (many barely erased), and the compositors' inky fingerprints that document its trip to the printshop and back. Even printed copies of *John Marr* and *Timoleon* were marked with corrections. Once again, as at the outset of their married life, and again in 1859–60, Lizzie was a willing, active partner in helping her husband give form to his yet-unbodied literary schemes.

After 1 January 1886 Melville was no longer the subject of daily irritation from overwork, but intermittently he was the subject of annoying and ignorant comments in American newspapers and magazines, mainly in New York and Boston. In the recurrent imagery, he was a "buried author," often described as still working at the Custom House. Once, in January 1886, when foolish compliments had been offered to him, he started to draft a reply, then threw up his arthritic hands: "For what can one do" with "the Press"? He answered his question: "Retaliate? Should it ever publish the rejoinder, they can. . . ." No, he would not retaliate. More and more, he was corresponding with English admirers who sent him books and articles, conveyed compliments to him, and assured him of his present and future fame. Cherishing his letters from England, Melville could only remark the oddity that the American comments were almost wholly different in content and tone. In the 1840s British praise almost guaranteed subservient echo of that praise in the United States; now, few American critics had any notion of the momentous changes in Melville's reputation that were taking place in England and elsewhere in the Empire, and those who heard praise from abroad tended to respond with a short exclamation followed by baffled silence.

Then, less than two months after Melville's retirement, Stanwix Melville died in San Francisco on 23 February 1886, at German Hospital, "in the 35th year of his age," the death notice said. There is a tombstone for Stanwix in Woodlawn, where Mackey and Bessie are buried near their parents, so presumably Herman and Lizzie had the body shipped back. They had the money to do it. Helen Griggs wrote to Kate Lansing on 16 March: "Ah! me. The sorrows that lie round our paths as we grow older! I miss Fanny more and more every day — the future looks dreary without her — it is hard to be resigned." They took what comfort they could: a friend had been with Stannie. On 5 May Helen wrote to Kate Lansing: "Lizzie is in Mt. Vernon Street, and I saw her yesterday, she spoke of having seen you lately, and that you were looking remarkably well. She is in great trouble; and seems unable to find solace for her grief—it was *so* hard,—the sickness and death so far away!" One thing is sure: when Stanwix met Malcolm in Paradise he knew him "the very half a second" he saw him.

When Melville thanked Billson for the *Rubáiyát* on 2 April 1886, he did not explain the delay, except to say that it was "from any cause but indifference." Almost incidentally, he was being drawn into new knowledge of literary connections such as always pleased him: "It pleases me to learn from you that Thomson was interested in Wm Blake." About the same time, the Danish artist Peter Toft met Melville and saw a good deal of him. On 7 April 1886 Toft gave Melville two watercolors, one or perhaps both illustrations of Melville's works that are now in the Berkshire Athenaeum. Learning of Toft's plans to return to England, Melville entrusted him with a letter to be delivered personally to W. Clark Russell. It was full of praise for Richard Henry Dana Jr., echoing Russell's own praise. Russell wrote to Melville on 21 July 1886 (relying on his son as amanuensis) of the "very great and singular pleasure" he had felt on receiving this letter and gave Melville assurances he could lay alongside Buchanan's: "Your reputation here is very great. It is hard to meet a man whose opinion as a reader is worth having who does not speak of your works in such terms as he might hesitate to employ, with all his patriotism, towards many renowned English writers."

Late in 1886 Melville had to sign receipts for his sister's Fanny's legacies to him, his wife, and the children who had been alive when Fanny made her will, Stanwix included. Another family crisis demanded enormous effort—the attempt to empty the Mansion House at Gansevoort. The family had dreaded closing the house, as Helen recalled on 16 April 1886 when she wrote Kate Lansing of what the Van Rensselaers had endured: "I remember, when the Manor House in Albany was dismantled—of hearing dear Fanny say—'Well, I suppose that will happen *here*, some day'—it was at Gansevoort—'and I don't envy the person, or persons, who will be called upon to do it.'" Helen was left to empty the house, and she did it, with help from an unexpected source, her sister Kate, and with help from Kate and Abe Lansing and from Augustus Peebles, who did an inventory for Abe, Fanny's executor. The objects were overwhelming in number and variety. Helen wanted to go in logical order, she wrote Kate Lansing on 8 July: "We shall get off Herman's first, as he, Lizzie, & Bessie, together, make the largest lot. Then there is some to go to Pittsfield!, some to Orange!, some to Elizabeth,! some to Staten Island, besides Kate's and mine—it will be a work of time." She added: "Herman wrote me, when I asked how *his* furniture should be forwarded, 'that the packers could proportion what each person's charge of material, & time, should be, and the account should be sent to each.' *Which I have done. To Herman; Milie; Florence; & Fannie.*" Kate Hoadley had helped: "Kate has been indefatigable, but with all we do, from morning until night; and all we give away to humble friends, by Fanny's particular request, like the fabled 'dragon's teeth' more & more seems to spring up, to take the place of what has been disposed of."

That first summer of his retirement, Herman came late to the scene of the carnage and, rather than cording a trunk or looking through cupboards or sorting Gansevoort letters, he recreated himself by driving to Glens Falls, probably to visit his surviving Gansevoort cousin, Stanwix, at Saratoga Avenue in South Glens Falls. He also got a haircut and regaled the locals with a salty tall tale of his sexual exploits in the South Seas, as the editor Ferris Greenslet wrote to the Melville scholar Willard Thorp on 22 November 1946, commenting: "I have thought you might be interested in an anecdote from one who once saw Melville plain" (as in Browning's poem on meeting someone who had seen Shelley plain). Young Ferris was in a barber's chair as witness:

> a buggy drove up and made a dashing stop, and after hitching the horse the driver came into the shop to have his whiskers trimmed, announcing that he had driven up from Gans[e]voort, some eight or nine miles, in a flat hour. Clad in a blue double-breasted suit of a seagoing flavor, he was seventy-ish, with a lot of hair and beard well grizzled, a vigorous body, "plump sphericity," a well tanned countenance, a bright and roving eye, all making up a singularly vital and impressive personality. I remember no one that I have met in the fifty odd years since more vividly.

Melville began "a flow of joyous narrative" of which the "climax came when the barber inquired":

> "Weren't there any girls down there?"
>
> "My God!" said the whiskerando, "I'll say there were! I went back to the island a couple of years after I left there on board a man-of-war and the first thing I saw when I went ashore was my own little son about a year and a half old running around naked in the sun on the beach."
>
> "How did you know it was your son?" asked the barber.
>
> "He had to be," said the story teller. "He carried his bowsprit to starboard!"

On the "surface of him," said the much older Greenslet, "there was every indication of a central *joie de vivre*." In the twenty-first century the anecdote needs glossing: the joke turns on the custom of making men's trousers to accommodate the genitals either to the right or the left—here with the twist that the lad was naked. This is all we have to suggest what sort of "racy" stories Melville told his New York literary friends in the late 1840s: exuberant sexual bragging exploded by a delayed revelation that the whole thing was a humorous fantasy.

Helen exhausted herself, and Abe eventually sold the house, but the removal of some of the bigger pieces was not really completed, even late in 1891. Kate Hoadley on her return to "The Warren," the modern apartment building in Boston, found John very weak. He died on 21 October 1886. Obituaries told the story of a remarkable American life. The death notices specified that interment would be "at the Albany Rural cemetery Monday afternoon on the arrival of 2:50 train from Boston" and that carriages would be waiting at the depot. Kate Lansing did her duty: "Went down town saw *Morange & Burns* from the Cemetery—Had obituary *Death* notice inserted in Journal & Albany Argus." She was dazed when she wrote in her diary on the twenty-fourth: "Everything ready & in order for the sad party tomorrow. Mr Hoadleys death seems like a dream for I had really hoped against hope that he might get well." Katie came up on the twenty-fifth by the 1:10 New York train and Augustus Peebles came and they had lunch then did their duty together: "at 2.20 went to the *Depot* to meet *Kate Hoadley Frank Minnie* & *Lottie* bringing *their dear Father* to be interred in the *Albany Cemetery*." Morange had "attended to every thing." At least, Kate could write, "weather pleasant." Abe, who had been on a fishing trip when Fanny died, arrived home from a duck-hunting trip late that evening. He found the house full of people, "& was much shocked to hear of Mr Hoadleys death & Burial." Kate wrote on the twenty-sixth: "A gloomy day—rain—went down town with Kate E. Melville [Katie] & Kate Hoadley & daughters, and Frank, drove to the Cemetery & left the Flowers that were forgotten yesterday." Melville did not go up for the funeral, but a few days later, on 28 October, he may have walked out to witness some local events, for during the celebration of the unveiling of Bartholdi's Statue of Liberty on Bedloe's Island President Grover Cleveland rode in a carriage down Fifth Avenue from Central Park then took his place on the reviewing stand at Madison Square, just west of the Melville house. Later Melville may have witnessed the unveiling of the Statue of Liberty, visible from the Battery through the rain.

Melville's first cousin John Langsdorff D'Wolf died in Dorchester on the last day of 1886. He had lived a circumscribed life for the past decade with "two very old ladies, cousins of his wife, who cared for her during her long invalidism," Helen wrote to Kate Lansing on 6 January 1887. His carriages had been "stored idle in the stable" since his wife's death. He had "carefully cared for green houses" so as to have flowers to place on her grave every week. There was no one to bring flowers to his grave except his sister, Mrs. Downer, and her children. Early in January 1887 a Boston newspaper printed an article on the upcoming sale of Hoadley's "noteworthy" library. The sale took two full days, mornings and afternoons, in the rooms of Charles F. Libbie at 608 Washington Street, opposite Park Theatre. Among the American works were several first editions of Hawthorne, Longfellow, and Whittier. There was a first edition of Walt Whitman's *Leaves of Grass* (signed by Hoadley in 1855, and now at Kent State University) as well as a first edition of *Drum-Taps* (1865, present location unknown). Kate Melville Hoadley had sent for auction the first eight volumes of *Harper's New Monthly Magazine* (1850–54, where "The Town-Ho's Story" and early tales had appeared), and which Hoadley had bound in cloth, as well as the eight volumes of *Putnam's Monthly* (1853–57, containing all of *The Piazza Tales* except "The Piazza," and other tales), which Hoadley had lovingly bound in half-morocco. So much for sisterly loyalty. And so much for publisher's loyalty: in March 1887, just as interest in *Mardi* was growing in England, Harper's got Melville's permission to melt the plates of *Mardi* and *Pierre*.

In May 1887 Maria Gansevoort Hoadley (Minnie) married William H. Mackintosh in Boston. In 1887 Fanny Thomas took Bessie with her to Stockbridge while Lizzie went to Fire Island, where she kept hoping Herman would join her. Harriet L. Parker on 16 July wrote to Kate Lansing: "your cousin, Mrs. Herman Melville has been here three or four weeks—but leaves next Monday. She has been expecting her husband—but fears, he will not come now. She looks sad & lonely & not in good health." Melville apparently went down to join Lizzie. While the Melville daughters were in Stockbridge someone sent a social item which was printed in a Boston paper: "At Edwards Hall . . . are staying for the summer the daughters of Herman Melville, the friend of Hawthorne and the author himself of some very exciting sea stories extensively read about a quarter of a century ago. Mr. Melville, now a man of sixty odd, is staying at Fire Island." The "friend of Hawthorne"—Julian could not have said it better. The date 4 December 1887 on Melville's poem "Bridegroom Dick" is a fair indication that he was at work on what became *John Marr and Other Sailors* (1888).

More praise from W. Clark Russell was published in the Chicago *America* in January 1888: "one must search the pages of the Elizabethan dramatists to parallel" some passages in *Moby-Dick*. Russell himself on 10 February 1888 called Melville's attention to this article while informing him that he had dedicated a novel, *An Ocean Tragedy*, to him. Perhaps this year a newspaper printed some slightly mangled praise in a chat column. In Washington the columnist had met the magazine writer A. A. Hayes, who showed him a letter from Russell suggesting that Hayes write Melville's biography: "Why not let the world know as much as can be gathered of his seafaring experiences and personal story of the greatest genius your country has produced—leagues ahead of Longfellow and Bryant as a poet." Lizzie kept two copies of this item. In January 1888 E. C. Stedman, newly moved to Twenty-sixth Street near Melville, wrote him, asking for one of his best known shorter poems, in his own handwriting, and for an engraved portrait for an extra-illustrated copy of his *Poets of America*. This led to Stedman's becoming an advocate of the merit of Melville's works. Stedman's son Arthur, named during the mid-century Tennyson vogue, acted as messenger part of the time, forming a greater intimacy with Melville than his father attained, although the banker-poet began to act toward Melville the way some British admirers were acting, sending him books he might enjoy looking at, soliciting his opinion on literary matters. At some point the talk with the senior Stedman turned to Whitman, whose poetry Hoadley had known since 1855 but on whom no comments of Melville's survive before he read Buchanan's poem in the *Academy* and wrote to Billson about it. Melville "said so much of Whitman" that Stedman decided on 1 February 1888 to "run the risk" of sending Melville his chapter on Whitman.

Melville escaped the Great Blizzard of 1888 by taking a sea-voyage to Bermuda (although his granddaughter Frances confusedly remembered being marooned with him and Lizzie as policemen pulled horses out of snow-drifts and she ate "funny food" and drank condensed milk for the first time — a lesser storm, another year). Melville, she said, "was afraid we wouldn't have enough to eat, and he had a very good appetite — really had a very good appetite." Melville sailed on the Quebec Steamship Company's steamer *Orinoco*, Captain Garvin, from Pier 17, North River, at 2 P.M., perhaps wearing a distinctive shawlstrap that his granddaughter Frances remembered from his later outings. The *Orinoco* arrived in Bermuda on 11 March, in fine weather, as the Great Blizzard of 1888 was commencing in New York, but passengers were kept on board two days. Melville checked into the Hamilton Hotel on the thirteenth. The weather turned bad, but braving hail, squalls, and rain, Melville sallied out to buy a wooden book-rack for his wife. On 22 March he left Bermuda on the R.M.S. *Trinidad*, recorded as "A Melville" in the Bermuda *Gazette*, and what looks like an age of "37." On the way home near St. Augustine, Florida, the passage was so rough that he had to get around on his hands and knees, his granddaughter Eleanor recorded.

On his return, Melville acknowledged gifts from James Billson and wrote W. Clark Russell asking his permission to dedicate a volume of poems to him. On 10 April Russell responded from Ramsgate with a heartwarming letter, admitting that he really had not known whether Melville was living or dead when he praised him. Badly crippled by rheumatism, Russell nevertheless rejoiced in the thought of how much, in better health, he should have enjoyed a visit to the Bermudas in Melville's company. For *John Marr* Melville wrote a long "Inscription Epistolary to W. C. R.," actually printed as a dedication. In it he elaborated a theory first advanced by "Hilary," his "companionable acquaintance, during an afternoon stroll under the trees along the higher bluffs of our Riverside Park last June" — which if autobiographical would have been June 1887. According to this, "an American born in England, or an Englishman born in America, each in his natural make-up retains through life, and will some way evince, an intangible something imbibed with his mother's milk from the soil of his nativity" — Russell being New York–born, his father a musician, author of popular songs, among them "A Life on the Ocean Wave" and "Woodman Spare That Tree." Melville rejected this theory as "moonshine," the "amiable illusion of a zealous patriot eager to appropriate anything that in any department may tend to reflect lustre upon his beloved country." In late April 1888 Melville inscribed one of his twenty-five copies of the newly printed *John Marr and Other Sailors* for Russell, but was displeased with it, and inscribed yet another one; the rejected one is at the Berkshire Athenaeum, the one he sent is at Harvard. In his response Russell told an astonishing anecdote about "the author of several boys' books, a Mr Charles St Johnstone," who had asked Russell whether he "had ever read the noblest sea book ever written called 'Moby Dick.'" Thereupon Russell smiled and handed him *John Marr*, with this effect: "'Is Herman Melville alive?' he shouted." Melville preserved such letters now, making no more fiery immolations.

George Griggs had been behaving oddly, even for him. On 26 February 1888 Helen's neighbor Mary Whitney had reported to the only healthy and responsible member of the family she knew, Kate Lansing, railing about "obstinate" George Griggs: "He will go to town in all weathers and not in a carriage but in the horse-cars. The doctor told me that Mr Griggs fell down twice in one day, and was 'mad as a hornet' with the men who picked him up." Helen continued to function admirably, despite the pain she suffered. On 8 May 1888 George Griggs died. His obituaries were short in comparison to Hoadley's, but they are the source of almost all that is known of him outside the family letters. The Boston *Evening Transcript* said only this: "Mr. George Griggs, a well-known lawyer, died Tuesday at Brookline, where he was born Sept. 8, 1813. He entered Brown University and was graduated in 1837; he entered Harvard Law School and in 1839 received the degree of LL.B. Mr. Griggs studied law in the office of Judge Peleg Sprague, and has since continued to practice his profession." Kate Lansing summed it up coolly: "A sad ending to rather an unsuccessful life." They buried him in the Boston area on the eleventh, Kate Lansing riding "to the vault with Mr Mackintoch & Minnie." She reflected tolerantly: "A good kind friend with all his peculiarities." He had been miserly with Helen, never buying her a house of their own and not using the seventy thousand dollars he received for a land sale in 1886 to make her more comfortable, according to Mary Whitney, the neighbor of the Griggses who kept Kate Lansing informed.

On 28 June 1888, preparing to move yet again, in October, to some sort of boarding arrangement, Helen roused herself from her sickbed to write Milie that she was lessening "the amount of small movables, that seem so endless in number when a removal is in prospect." Two items were special: "The package you will receive soon, contains first, a 'superfine' blanket shawl which took the prize at the very first World's Fair in London. Mrs Morewood gave it to me for a wedding-gift, and Mr Morewood [Rowland] will remember it perhaps — that is *for you*. The scarlet shawl belonged to your mother. Your father gave it to Aunt Fanny, and that is for *Florence*." This was Helen, perfectly taught by Maria, giving, among other thoughtful gifts, the ultimately appropriate gift, her own wedding gift from Sarah Morewood, brought from England and lovingly bestowed on Helen, then lovingly cared for since 1854 and now bestowed on the daughter-in-law Sarah had known only as a girl the age of her neighbor Malcolm.

The warning of John's death Melville could ignore, but not both John's and George's — not to mention Tom's and Fanny's and Stanwix's. On 11 June 1888 Herman Melville wrote out his will and signed it:

> I, Herman Melville, declare this to be my will. Any property, of whatever kind, I may die possessed of, including money in banks, and my share in the as yet undivided real estate at Gansevoort, I bequeathe to my wife. I do this because I have confidence that through her our children and grand-children will get their proportion of any benefit that may accrue. — I appoint my wife executer of this will. — In witness whereof I have hereunto set my hand and seal this 11th day of June 1888.

One of the three witnesses was Henry B. Thomas, his son-in-law; the others may have met Melville only this once.

In June 1888, probably, and in early July Lizzie was again at Fire Island Beach and there asked Harriet L. Parker for news of Abe and Kate. Melville may have joined her some of the time again. Abe's executor's sale by auction of the Gansevoort property was on 1 September: "a Fine Country Seat! at Gansevoort, Saratoga Co., N.Y." It brought four thousand dollars. Kate Lansing was there, watching the "Old Homestead" go out of the family. That fall, on 1 October, the first payments were made to the heirs of Lemuel Shaw Jr., $243,551.69 divided into three shares, one to Samuel Shaw, one to John Oakes Shaw, one to Elizabeth Shaw Melville. Eighty-some thousand dollars in 1888 was not what it had been a few decades earlier, but it would buy what several millions of dollars would buy today. This great wealth meant that Lizzie would feel more comfortable as she went on spending precisely what she was used to spending.

About this time Melville inscribed a copy of *John Marr* to E. C. Stedman, making some autograph corrections in it. His copy inscribed *"To Lizzie."* was dated 5 November, and the next day he inscribed one to Lizzie's cousin Ellen Marett Gifford, and about that time gave a copy to Richard Henry Stoddard, who may be the one who reviewed it politely on 20 November in the New York *Mail and Express:* " He is the author of the second best cavalry poem in the English language, the first being Browning's 'How They Brought the Good News from Ghent to Aix'. . . . Nothing finer than his unrhymed poems exist outside of the sea lyrics of Campbell." Melville also sent two copies of *John Marr* to Billson, who passed one on to John W. Barrs. Now psychologically rid of *John Marr*, after disposing of a few copies, Melville decided to tidy up another project, for the manuscript of *Billy Budd* bears a note: "Friday Nov. 16. 1888. Began." — not "began to write" but began a significant revision. About this time he consulted a copy of the Bentley *White-Jacket*, marking in one of the back covers: "192/214 Flogging." He marked a passage in chapter 33 beginning "At a sign from the Captain, John, with a shameless leer, advanced, and stood passively upon the grating." He also acquired *Battles of the British Navy*, by Joseph Allen (London: Bohn, 1852), and W. Clark Russell's *Horatio Nelson and the Naval Supremacy of England* (New York: Putnam, 1890).

On 14 December 1888 Helen Melville Griggs died in Roxbury "at the Williams Mansion kept as a boarding house by Mrs Maloy" (Sam Shaw's diary entry). Kate Hoadley, Frank, and Minnie H. Mackintosh accompanied the body from Boston and saw Helen buried beside Fanny, and then stayed at Stanwix Hall. The next day ("Rained & stormed all day") Kate Lansing took breakfast with them there and saw them off. Then she bucked herself up: "It was all so sudden, so hurried — Such is life — sad, sad enough and while life last *all* must *try & keep up*. — Swim or sink in lifes waters." Lizzie wrote her cousin Ellen Marett Gifford on 4 January 1889 that Helen had died "after many long years of suffering from something like internal cancer in the stomach & liver." By then Lizzie was composed: "It is a blessed release for her, but it is a great grief to us all to part with so faithful a friend." In 1888 Herman rented a pew at All Souls in his own name, whatever that meant for a man who had always found Unitarianism repugnant. On the last day of 1888 (two years after Langsdorff's death, if anyone remembered it), Melville made the effort to write to Billson, who had sent him a book by the late James Thomson ("B. V."): *Shelley, A Poem: With Other Writings Relating to Shelley*. Melville had to "rein up," he said, for his eyes had been annoying him for days, and he hardly knew "anything more disconcerting." He approved Billson's gift of *John Marr* to Barrs, who had sent Melville Thomson's *A Voice from the Nile*, which he called "an appreciated gift." He enclosed an American newspaper comment on Thomson, something Lizzie had called his attention to — good evidence of her interest in his correspondence with English admirers. Since that bleak morning in March 1885 when she and Kate Gansevoort Lansing had sallied out to the Brentano bookstore on Union Square in quest of an old copy of the *Contemporary Review*, she had changed her attitude toward her husband's work, and was changing still as she became an archivist in good earnest, clipping, labeling, correcting, and preserving items about him.

In the middle of January 1889 Melville seems to have tried to escape his grief from Helen and the ravages of winter by going on "a fortnights trip" south, to Savannah, judging from a postcard from Lizzie to Kate Lansing, 10 January 1889, preserved in Kate's copy of *John Marr*. Perhaps he saw young Frank Hoadley there, for in 1891 he was working in a Savannah store. Soon Melville was back at work; a note on the manuscript of *Billy Budd* reads: "Revise — began March 2 1889." In the middle of March Melville received $1123.79 from Fanny's estate, mainly his part in the sale of the Mansion House, Abe handling the administrative chores. (Cornelius Mathews died in New York on 25 March 1889; once important to Melville, he had passed out of his life mysteriously, before *Moby-Dick* was published.) On 15 June Melville, Elizabeth, Bessie, Fanny Thomas, and Fanny's two daughters all registered at the Surf Hotel on Fire Island. On 30 June Lizzie wrote to Kate Lansing: "Herman came down with me on the 15th, and staid a few days, since that," so he apparently returned to New York once, then came back to Fire Island. Lizzie was not intimate with Amasa and Harriet Parker, but she knew them, and their daughter Mrs. Pruyn, so she wrote sincere condolences to Kate when she read that Mrs. Parker was dead. Lizzie pondered on the bonds of long marriages: "And her poor husband, what loneliness is left for him! The ties of such a long happy wedded life can hardly be severed without its serious effect on the survivor. Who will live with him now and minister to his declining years?" For twenty-five years the Parkers had occupied the same rooms in "Cottage" three, and Lizzie remarked that it seemed "strangely vacant" with none of the Parker family there.

Lizzie was expecting Herman to be on Fire Island for his birthday and the next week or two; she bought him *The Correspondence of Honoré de Balzac* in a two-volume edition (London, 1878), which he read attentively. On 9 September 1889 the Boston *Post* printed a bemused item on hearing that Melville was still alive, and saw no reason why Melville's life "should not find a place in the American Men of Letters series." In September, deaths came two days apart. On 5 September the husband of Cousin Kate Van Vechten, Elisha P. Hurlbut, died in his mansion, Glenmont, outside Albany, and on the seventh Lizzie's first cousin Ellen Marett Gifford died in New Haven. Ellen Gifford left a fortune to the Melvilles, but at this stage another fortune made no outward difference at all. The legacy from Mrs. Gifford that gave practical benefit was her New York Society Library certificate, transferred to Herman for life, free from all annual payments, as of 20 November. Melville now had a new library to borrow from—something he would not have laid out the few dollars to purchase but something more practically important to him than the sum of money willed to him.

In November of 1889 Melville received a letter from the man who over the next decades did more than any other person to establish his reputation on this continent and in Great Britain, a young professor from Halifax, Archibald MacMechan: "For a number of years I have read and re-read 'Moby-Dick' with increasing pleasure on every perusal: and with this study, the conviction has grown up that the unique merits of that book have never received due recognition." Finding himself able to devote himself to "literature as a life-work," he was anxious to set the merits of Melville's books before the public, and asked the honor of corresponding with Melville. He had been to the Duyckincks' *Cyclopædia*, but he wanted more particulars of Melville's "life and *literary methods*," for he was a committed Melvillean: "I consider, your books, especially the earlier ones, the most thoroughly New World product in all American literature." It was in his 5 December reply to MacMechan that Melville cited his need to husband what remained of his vigor for projects that might never be "never be completed." In reading Balzac's letters he marked this: "every man has only a certain amount of strength, of blood, of courage, of hope, and my store of all these is exhausted." Melville knew he was weakening.

E. C. Stedman had by now taken a fixed interest in Melville. In 1889 he and his co-editor Ellen Mackay Hutchinson included several poems in volume 7 of their *A Library of American Literature from the Earliest Settlement to the Present Time*. On 9 April 1890 Stedman wrote to Charles Henry Phelps on a meeting of the Authors' Club, saying, "I never yet have been able to get the members to take an interest in Melville—one of the strongest geniuses, & most impressive *personalities* that New York has ever harbored." There are unconfirmed rumors that Melville was tempted out, and one report that Brander Matthews did actually interview him. Enough reports survive to make it likely that Melville did venture out, briefly, into the company of young whippersnappers and elderly non-producers. In November 1889 the *Scottish Art Review* published an article by the Fabian socialist H. S. Salt, a pioneering Thoreau scholar, and the man who later pushed *The Whale* on William Morris ("a week or two afterwards I heard him quoting it with huge gusto and delight") and George Bernard Shaw (who read enough of it to satisfy himself that he knew what the fuss was about). Salt was ambivalent about Melville, and not very well acquainted with his works yet, so his attention was anything but pure gain for Melville's reputation, but he was certain that Melville should not have fallen out of notice and should be "enjoying the wide reputation to which his undoubted genius entitles him." Salt's friend John W. Barrs kept his promise to send Melville a copy of this issue soon after it came out. In December, Salt wrote Melville directly, proposing a new edition of *Typee* in the Camelot series. On 12 January 1890, Melville replied to Salt, explaining that illness had prevented an earlier reply. He was embarrassed somewhat, he explained, since he could not authorize a publication of *Typee* without seeking permission from John Murray, the man to whom Gansevoort had delivered the manuscript in 1845. (Murray still kept both *Typee* and *Omoo* in print in the popular Home and Colonial Library, and very sensibly refused to let it be reprinted by another company.)

On 20 December 1889 the *Pall Mall Gazette* published "The Novelist of the Sea, An Interview with Mr. Clark Russell," in which Russell raved to the reporter about *John Marr*. Thereupon the reporter quoted what he called "words never before published," seven lines beginning with "Implacable I, the old Implacable Sea" (from the very short poems Melville called "Pebbles"). Having made this easy convert, yet another British enthusiast for Melville, Russell wrote on 5 January 1890 to tell Melville he was asking his publishers to send him a copy of his new book, *An Ocean Tragedy*, with an exultant dedication: "My books have done more than ever I had dared dream, by winning for me, the friendship and approval of the Author of 'Typee,' 'Omoo,' 'Moby-Dick,' 'Redburn,' and other productions which top the list of sea literature in the English tongue." Russell still dreamed of seeing Melville face to face. Barrs waited until 13 January 1890 to follow up the *Scottish Art Review* with a diffident letter, himself disappointed in what Salt wrote, and personally fond of *Mardi* and even *Pierre*. Slowly but surely, Melville's British admirers were expanding the range of their reading in his works, determined in part by availability. There was no vogue for *Pierre* or *The Piazza Tales* until volumes appeared in the Constable edition in the early 1920s, and then the surviving admirers who had written to Melville and a new generation of readers burst into ecstatic praise. In his 13 January 1890 letter Barrs pointed to the coincidence of Salt's and Russell's so conspicuously praising Melville: "So you see notwithstanding the inadequacy of the recognition of your books, on this side, they are not without warm admirers." Not one of all these British admirers ever asked Melville what it had been like to be a friend of Hawthorne. They never asked him about Hawthorne at all. They understood that Hawthorne, like Longfellow, was immensely popular but not of the same order of literary greatness as Melville and Whitman.

On 5 March 1890 Melville sent to the executors of the will of Ellen Marett Gifford a receipt for their payment to him of eight thousand dollars as well as receipts from his wife, his daughters, and one for his dead son, Stanwix. Later that month he spent some hours working, labeling a folder of poems "Greece" and recording: "Looked over March 23 '90." Jane Louise Melville (as the death certificate identified her) died on 30 March, at her Florence apartment. Allan Melville's surviving daughters went to her funeral, conducted by the Reverend George Hendric Houghton at the Church of the Transfiguration (the "Little Church Around the Corner") at Twenty-ninth Street between Fifth and Madison. Some of the Thurstons and Latherses came, loyal to the memory of Allan and Sophia and courteous to the end; Lizzie and Bessie Melville came, with Frances Melville Thomas but not Herman Melville; and Kate Lansing came down from Albany, and drove to the cemetery with Lizzie and her daughters. Still wholly deceived in Jane's character, Kate railed in her diary about Jane's "ungrateful step children." In April, Melville had his second attack of erysipelas (the date of the first being unrecorded); both of them, Lizzie said in her memoir, "weakened him greatly." He was able to take care of routine business soon enough. Kate Hoadley and her daughter Charlotte were both visiting the Melvilles on 23 May when Lottie told him he owed Kate Lansing $134 for his share of expenses on the lot in Albany Cemetery: Kate did all the work, but at least he could now happily pay his share of actual out-of-pocket expenses.

Pitchers had possessed ears all during the years of family summers at Gansevoort, and Lottie had developed into an observant young woman. At this time she had a chance to confirm her impression of Melville — a durable impression which she conveyed on 7 January 1941 to Victor Hugo Paltsits, just months before his retirement from the New York Public Library, at a time when her pen was sharpened by her irritation, or even rage, at what Paltsits had sent her, a letter by Eleanor Thomas Metcalf which struck her as slurring Melville's parents out of a taste for "notoriety." She recalled that Raymond Weaver in his biography had called Allan and Maria Melvill " 'monsters' and made various slurring remarks concerning them," and assumed that Weaver's impression was conveyed and authorized by either Frances Thomas (now dead) or Eleanor. Her indignation prompted her to give her own version of Melville and marriage:

> As I look upon it, he was absolutely unfited for prosaic marriage life, but was expected to fill that role — A "cynic," perhaps, you might call him, a rover at

heart, he knew people only too well, used to say I was told, there was no such thing as gratitude, the word even was not mentioned in the bible. This is my idea of him. He was a fine looking young man when he married Judge Shaws daughter.... It is difficult to express myself as I wish. It is so outrageous that they cannot let Herman Melville rest in peace. He knew people only too well, evidently, but one hardly looks for this sort of thing from ones own grandchildren.... He was a very proud man. Mrs Melville may have wanted him to do so [write for magazines, such as *Godey's* and the *Atlantic*] when they badly needed money, and that may account for the other letter which is said to exist written by Judge Shaw.

(Melville had been right: neither "grateful" nor "gratitude" appears anywhere in the King James Bible; the "other letter" is unidentified.) In her old age Charlotte was as good a witness as one could want. She had listened to her aunts talk when she was a child, and knew all the brothers and sisters well except Gansevoort.

Through letters from England Melville was gradually piecing together a sense of the interconnectedness of his admirers, for in asking for information on Melville's ancestry Havelock Ellis on 19 July 1890 regretted that Salt's hope to reprint *Typee* in the Camelot series had fallen through: "At present your books are, practically, not before the public at all in this country, and a very large number of people are thus deprived of the delight which they would certainly derive from them, if they were accessible." Melville was late in writing Ellis, 10 August: "I have been away from town, a wanderer hardly reachable for a time"—at Fire Island? In July 1890 young Edward Garnett wrote Melville from the office of the publisher T. Fisher Unwin in London with an unusual proposal. For an adventure series, he hoped Melville would "recast Redburn, or preface it with an introduction, showing that whereas it was given to the world as a fiction remaking it from the class of fictitious to that of personal adventures." This would have been one moment to offer *The Isle of the Cross*, if he had saved it.

Fanny Thomas had been pregnant since late March 1890, and all autumn was "very 'poorly,'" and worried about the new house they were building, and hoping to get into in the spring. On 14 December she bore her third daughter, Katharine Gansevoort Thomas. Lizzie wrote to Kate Lansing on the seventeenth that, though a little early, she was a "well formed and healthy baby, and as 'plump as a partridge.'" Then she took up an unpleasant subject, especially so since she knew there was a gulf between her feelings and Kate's on the subject of Jane Dempsey Randolph Melville. Allan had taken George W. Dillaway into his office because he was the son of Lizzie's first cousin, the classics teacher. Over the years Jane had formed a strong attachment to young George, and had left him more than ninety thousand dollars of her estate, ten thousand first going to her physician, Dr. George V. Foster. The two children of Jane's brother had challenged the will; Milie and her sisters did not challenge it, having expected nothing and gotten nothing. As Lizzie explained to Kate, the " 'will business' " was "at a stand still for the present," the Dempseys claiming to have found "an old will of their grandmothers never probated which gives all the property to the children of *her* two children or the survivor of them." Jane's will, in short, might "be set aside as null & void" and her Dempsey nephew and niece might "have everything," under the terms of their grandmother's will, now providentially discovered. Lizzie knew how Jane would have liked that: "Just imagine how enraged she would be at such a state of things!"

Lizzie explained to Kate Lansing on 8 January 1891 that she had been out to see Fanny's baby only once, the day after it was born. She had been "much absorbed with Herman," who required "a good deal of attention," having come down with a bad cough. He had enjoyed a spell of clear weather around Christmas time and had gone out every day, taking long walks, and walking "¾ of a mile in a bitter cold air" around New Year's Day, a feat that had been "too much for him." Now Lizzie wrote to be sure that Kate did not hear from anyone else, perhaps in an "exaggerated way," how sick Herman had been. He had suffered "a turn of dizziness or vertigo in the night, which the Dr feared might eventuate in a serious way," but he was better: "I am glad to say that his strength which seemed to leave him in one night has gradually returned and he is improving every day—he has not been out yet or even down stairs, but the Dr says there seems to be no reason why he should not entirely recover and be as well as before." Lizzie had heard that the matter of old Mrs. Dempsey's will and Jane Dempsey Randolph Melville's will was to come to court that day, so she advised Kate to keep a lookout especially for the *Herald* (still sensationalistic after all the decades) and the *Sun*, which she cited as having "had the articles before." Of course, the court might meet "only to adjourn again." Lizzie could not look at the papers—Kate would have to do it in Albany. In fact, the *Herald* reported on 8 January that "Mrs. Melville's Will Stands," her nephew and niece John A. and Lavinia Dempsey having asked that the suit be discontinued, presumably because Foster and Dillaway had agreed to settle out of court. Dillaway was impossible for Lizzie to avoid, living as he did at 7 West Twenty-sixth Street, while keeping his office at 18 Wall Street.

Melville was up and around by 24 February 1891, when he gave Eleanor for her ninth birthday *Landseer's Dogs and Their Stories*, by Sarah Tytler [Henrietta Keddie] (London, 1877). He was working on *Billy Budd* on 19 April, he noted. By May he was working on the dedication of *Timoleon*, a new book of poems, some of them very old. In May, probably early May, he turned over *Timoleon* to the Caxton Press, not De Vinne, and dedicated it to "My countryman / Elihu Vedder"; the title was copyrighted in Washington on 15 May. Late in the month Kate Lansing's historian's impulse was high, and she asked questions about Uncle Herman that Herman could not answer satisfactorily. Lizzie's response on 28 May shows how she tried to maneuver Herman: "I . . . have been trying for the few days past to get from Herman what he might chance to know of Uncle Herman by leading the conversation that way." Some of what she gathered is unrecorded elsewhere: "On one of his first visits to New York he met and married Catherine Quackenboss who cheerfully went to this wilderness and lived the rest of her life. She was a very eccentric character as no doubt you have heard. All her property was sunk in the great N.Y. fire of 1835, and Uncle H. never dared to tell her, but paid her usual dividends out of his own means." Lizzie made it clear that Kate Hoadley, of all incurious people, was the one to be consulted about the documents: "you know what quantities of papers &c Helen found there." Presumably many of these went to Kate Lansing eventually, as part of the family letters Kate Hoadley left to her daughter Charlotte and Lottie then turned over to Kate Lansing, according to her letter to Paltsits, 29 September 1943. When Kate Lansing got the documents she had said to Lottie: " 'The Melvilles are much finer born or superior in birth,' (I do not remember her exact words) 'than the Gansevoorts, but I always from childhood knew they came from the nobility.' " Kate Lansing always knew, she said. In 1891 she wrote to Kate Hoadley, and Minnie replied for her mother on 23 June, explaining that her mother had never been at Gansevoort until after Uncle Herman was a widower. Helen, she agreed with Kate Lansing, could "have given a charming sketch of them," but Kate was too late. Kate Hoadley had destroyed many letters, mostly mere "personal & business letters," but had preserved "any letters giving any family history." The woman who disposed of the bound copies of *Putnam's* was an early member of the most loathsome school of archivists, the deaccessionists.

Herman, Lizzie reported on 28 May 1891, was "tolerably well but not strong." Fanny's children had "been having the measles — Eleanor, just in the midst of their moving — Frances was sick here — both mild attacks — and all well now — but Harry has been laid up with them, and is not out yet." Lizzie and Bessie were planning to go to Fire Island in June — "Herman also, as he is not well enough to be left alone." He would not be gracious about being uprooted: "I suppose he will get very impatient but I have to go there for my rose cold." Impatient or not, Melville inscribed a copy of *Timoleon* to her in June, perhaps on 13 June, her sixty-ninth birthday: "To Her — without whose assistance both manual and literary Timoleon &c could not have passed through the press—with her name I gratefully and affectionately inscribe this volume." Melville was ill enough that in July Lizzie called Dr. Everett S. Warner to see him.

Fanny Thomas's move into the new house led to her writing Kate Hoadley that she would like to have what Minnie called "Grandma's wardrobe," and which Kate Hoadley wanted her to have. This and some other furniture was still at the already-sold house in Gansevoort, apparently, or in storage nearby, for Minnie, in relaying the request to Kate Lansing on 23 June 1891, suggested that it could "be sent by *freight* to her at *South Orange, N. Jersey.*" Minnie wrote again in August, apologizing: "I surely would wait for cooler weather before visiting Gansevoort about the furniture, & I feel uncomfortable about putting you to so much trouble." Presumably after 4 August, the Melvilles' wedding anniversary, Melville worked on *Weeds and Wildings Chiefly: with a Rose or Two*, and composed a more-or-less autobiographical dedication to "Winnefred": "I yearly remind you of the coincidence in my chancing on such a specimen by the wayside on the early forenoon of the fourth day of a certain bridal month, now four years more than four times ten years ago." Now he dedicated to her his "'Weeds and Wildings,' thriftless children of quite another and yet later spontaneous aftergrowth, and bearing indications, too apparent it may be, of the terminating season on which the offerer verges." Rather than pushing the collection toward completion, in August (after his obligatory stays in Fire Island?) and in September Melville at last got around to "readings in the 'Mermaid Series' of old plays, in which, he took much pleasure" (according to Arthur Stedman in his introduction to *Typee* the next year). At last Melville was reading the great contemporaries of Shakespeare he had wanted to read early in 1862, before he got deflected into a quest for an aesthetic credo.

[40]

In and Out of the House of the Tragic Poet
1886–1891

> The name of Herman Melville will not suggest any note of interest to many readers, but it none the less recalls the career of a man of brilliant genius, who practically retired from the pursuit of letters a quarter of a century since, in the prime of his powers.
>
> *Harper's Weekly*, 10 October 1891

IT WOULD NEVER HAVE OCCURRED to the Melvilles to move to a better house now that they could afford one. Both of them, by the mid-1880s, were content enough with what they had at 104 East Twenty-sixth Street. Melville spent his last years in a narrow, dark townhouse, but at least it was filled with objects which satisfied his instinct to be surrounded by beautiful things, and he lived there in peace with his wife and older daughter. Bessie's arthritis got steadily worse, despite barbaric medical strappings of her fingers; she remained brave and loving enough to tie her nieces's bonnet-strings deftly. (Frances Thomas left her daughters at Twenty-sixth Street in black mourning hair-ribbons which her mother removed and replaced with colored ribbons, unwilling to see her granddaughters doomed to black through childhood, deaths coming so fast they might never have been out of mourning.) Bessie improved her mind, becoming adept in French. She inherited Melville's set of Balzac in translation, and gave it to her niece Frances only after the girl proved herself able to read Balzac in the original. She took Eleanor to the theater and to a French church and instilled within her also an enduring love for French. Frances Thomas Osborne remembered her aunt with respect as well as affection—she "had a wonderful mind," was "a remarkable woman," was a "very intelligent woman," with something of her father's capacities. Nothing suggests that Bessie ever became anything like an intellectual companion to her father, but his granddaughter Fanny's testimony suggests that she might have, if he had encouraged her at the right time. Eleanor and Frances remembered Bessie reading them stories in their grandmother's room, and Frances, the granddaughter, became a marvelous teller of stories and skillful at reading aloud. The family habit of reading novels aloud persisted in a straight line from Maria's household well into the twentieth century, when the Frances Thomas Osborne read Dickens novel after Dickens novel aloud to her invalid husband.

Thanks mainly to the two older granddaughters, we know a good deal about the Twenty-sixth Street house. The exterior was brick. The literary interviewer Theodore F. Wolfe (who visited Melville there) in the 1899 edition of *Literary Haunts and Homes: American Authors* (Philadelphia: J. B. Lippincott) called it "a pleasant brick house which is now replaced by flats" — razed a few years after Lizzie sold it in 1892 and moved with Bessie to the Florence on Eighteenth Street. An expert on the local urban architecture before he became interested in Melville, Lewis Mumford in his 1929 critical biography *Herman Melville* said that the house was brick, with, he specified, a muddy-yellow exterior and brownstone trim. Melville's granddaughter Frances Thomas Osborne in her copy corrected Mumford's description at other points and could have corrected him here if he had been wrong. Mumford said the house looked like every other one in the row. Mrs. Osborne herself said the same when describing her bewilderment after being abandoned by her absent-minded grandfather in Madison Square Garden, but she corrected Mumford in the margin, "Only one of two," which the city records confirm. (The house was probably the mirror image of the one on the west.) There was nothing the Melvilles could do to lend the house any architectural interest, but they could stamp it with their character, or more precisely Melville could stamp it with his. Long before the 1880s, Elizabeth Shaw Melville had learned to accommodate herself, as cheerfully as she could, to the fact that her husband was the arbiter in conspicuous matters of home decor. Between them, Elizabeth and Herman Melville had made the house not only comfortable but actually elegant, despite the fact that all the rooms were undeniably small and there was nothing to be done about the darkness of a narrow, north-facing row house.

Eleanor, the older of the two granddaughters born in time to know Melville, may have been less familiar with the house than Frances, who recalled that Eleanor was kept at home because she was headstrong, while Frances herself was docile, easier for the aging grandparents and arthritic aunt to care for. Frances's daughter Priscilla Ambrose pointed out to me an obvious rebuttal to late-twentieth-century New Historical fantasies about violence in the household: her grandmother, the Melvilles' daughter, would never have left a child of hers in an unsafe or even unpleasant house. Melville, his wife, and his older daughter were good caretakers, if you overlook the one occasion when Melville forgot Frances in Madison Square. Although some of the furnishings and art works gave the children real and not entirely delicious frissons of fear, Eleanor and Frances remembered the Twenty-sixth Street house happily. Priscilla Ambrose is emphatic that her mother's memories were good ones, and that even from the experience of being abandoned Frances became proud of her own resourcefulness and exulted in the love Bessie demonstrated by overcoming her infirmities in order to launch the search.

The layout of the house was conventional. The house had three floors, not counting the basement where the kitchen and dining room were located (connected by a sliding pass-through), and where there may have been servants' quarters. (When Allan and Jane were there, they must have had more than one live-in servant; Jane had three or more even when keeping a house alone.) The street door opened into a front hall where hung a print of the bay of Naples (Lewis Mumford said, and Frances Thomas Osborne did not correct him). The parlors were on the first floor. The front parlor, where Melville intimidated young Mr. Thomas, was on the north end, looking out at Twenty-sixth Street. Melville's granddaughter Frances remembered:

> in the front parlor standing behind a highbacked sofa — stood a very white pillar surmounted by a more than life sized bust of Antinous, in order to protect his curls from the city dust he was covered with a veil — this, to an imaginative child was very terrifying to contemplate — & I used to scuttle past the doorway with a backward glance to see if I were being followed — At dusk particularly when I came up from my early supper one could almost see the head turn ever so slightly at my footfall.

The sofa and perhaps some of the chairs in the front parlor were covered in a green fabric, judging from what Melville's daughter Fanny wrote to Kate Lansing, 14 March 1879: the new chair for her had arrived and was "in the front parlor" and looking "very pretty with the green furniture." One had to pass the open front parlor door to go down to the basement, so the stairs were at the street end of the house.

By early 1887, most likely, the Eaton portrait of Melville which is now in the Houghton Library was hanging in the back parlor, and in half-light it frightened Eleanor, who thought the eyes followed her. On Maria Gansevoort Melville's death it had gone to Melville's sister Kate, since John had paid for it. Eleanor definitely saw it in the Twenty-sixth Street house when she was young enough to be so frightened by it, so Kate Hoadley gave it to Lizzie, or Herman and Lizzie, about the time she was disposing of her late husband's library in January 1887; less likely, she could have given it to Lizzie in the few months between Herman Melville's death and the time she sold the house and moved into the Florence.

Also on the first floor (again, not counting the basement with the kitchen and dining room), in the back (the south end), a narrow, roofed porch ran the whole width of twenty feet, across both the main hall and the back parlor. The girls remembered a little differently. Eleanor was apparently Mumford's source for saying that the porch was narrow and iron-trimmed, furnished with Windsor and folding canvas chairs. Mumford said Melville might loll on the canvas steamer-chair placed on the narrow iron balcony, smoking his pipe; in her copy of Mumford's book Mrs. Osborne marked out "iron balcony" and replaced it with "wooden piazza." There Melville would sit and smoke, holding his cane (he carried a cane, even within the house, and pointed out objects with it). An Aeolian harp was kept on the porch. On the wall was a red and blue china butterfly matchholder, removed, it seems, from the piazza at Arrowhead. From the porch Melville watched Eleanor or Frances (one at a time) pick stones out of their grandmother's garden; Mumford (on authority of a granddaughter?) specified that geraniums and pansies grew there, and Eleanor told Leon Howard that Melville grew roses in his last years. Frances specified that Melville took his constitutional on stormy winter days on the "dusty, chill back porch enclosed in shutters."

Melville's library or study was on the second floor, above the front parlor, on the street side, looking north. Frances described his desk and his slippery leather chair with a footrest on which she tripped one time. Eleanor thought of her grandfather, she said, in connection with different parts of the house, including his study:

> His own room was a place of mystery and awe to me; there I never ventured unless invited by him. It looked bleakly north. The great mahogany desk, heavily bearing up four shelves of dull gilt and leather books; the high dim book-case, topped by strange plaster heads that peered along the ceiling level, or bent down, searching blindly with sightless balls; the small black iron bed, covered with dark cretonne; the narrow iron grate; the wide table in the alcove, piled with papers I would not dream of touching — these made a room even more to be fled than the back parlour, by whose door I always ran to escape the following eyes of his portrait, which hung there in a half light. Yet lo, the paper-piled table also held a little bag of figs, and one of the pieces of sweet stickiness was for me.

Frances remembered the study as being "such a wonderful place!":

> There was no wall space at all, just books, books, books. His huge desk had interesting things on it including a rolling ruler decorated with different varieties of green ferns, a large velvet pincushion mounted on an iron stand and a little black metal candlestick for sealing wax. I could play with anything

on those days when I was invited into the study. Sometimes I piled books into houses on the floor. A set of Schopenhauer pleased me most—they were not too heavy to handle and of a nice palish blue color.

The "great" or "huge" desk may be the moderately sized desk preserved in the Berkshire Athenaeum (holding up a tall bookcase), but it may have been one which later stood in Frances Thomas Osborne's home in West Orange, a piece one of the great-grandchildren remembers as "a secretary, rather than a desk, because of the bookcase above"; it had "glass doors and reached to the ceiling," so it was high enough for the shelves Eleanor remembered. (A photograph shows Eleanor Thomas as a young woman standing by the desk that is now in the Berkshire Athenaeum, with no bookcase atop the desk, corroboration of her later assertion that in her grandmother's apartment in the Florence the "tall glassed-in shelves had been removed" from the desk.) On Melville's writing desk was an olive-wood blotter holder (the blotter rocked) and an olive-wood cross with Hebrew lettering, both brought back from the Holy Land. For fastening his salvaged pieces of manuscripts onto other sheets of paper (a device to avoid recopying by arthritic fingers), Melville used straight pins from his iron pincushion holder.

The second-floor study was dominated by books. The collection was most notable for handsome old folios (some purchased in London in 1849), but it included some impressive new volumes as well, such as the 1886 *Rubáiyát* illustrated by Elihu Vedder. Placed in among the books and in front of the books were numerous knickknacks, keepsakes, and trophies, such as a brick pressed from the bloody earth of the first Malvern battlefield. For an author once internationally famous, the perfect paperweight was a foot-long piece of the first Atlantic cable, that early information superhighway, copper core wrapped in gutta percha. (Tiffany's had sold the item as early as 1858, but Melville's piece, thicker in diameter than the Tiffany souvenir pieces, may have been a gift from his acquaintance Cyrus Field.) Framed and hung on a wall or leaned against a wall was Melville's large Persian tile (more than a foot high) depicting (some parts in bas relief) a horseman with a stylized bird of prey. In Melville's study, framed, was the steel engraving of Hawthorne by Thomas Phillibrown from the Cephas Thompson oil painting (one of the five presented to Hawthorne) that Sophia Hawthorne had given him on 12 March 1851—Hawthorne as Melville knew him best, without a moustache.

Also on the second floor, there was a hall like the one on the main floor ("the same hall," Frances Thomas Osborne called it), and near Melville's "study-bath room" (Mrs. Osborne again) was a small room where Melville slept in a large black double bed. Mrs. Melville's bedroom, connected by a passageway to Melville's "study-bath room," was very different from his. On the south end of the house, Eleanor Thomas Metcalf remembered, that room was "sunny, comfortable and familiar, with a sewing machine and a *white* bed like other peoples' "; in the corner stood a big armchair, for Melville to sit in when he "left the recesses of his own dark privacy." There, in his wife's room, he would tell one girl or the other stories of his travels, "wild tales of cannibals and tropic isles." There also he displayed to the five- or six-year-old Frances a tattoo on his arm, a star, which he told her was done by cannibals on an island. More likely, he cunningly inked it on his arm in his study a few minutes before telling the story; imitating him once she got home, Frances punctured a finger with a needle and put ink into the wound, thereby creating a tattoo of her own which endured until her death at the age of ninety-seven.

On the stairway leading to the third floor (still not counting the basement) Mrs. Osborne said Melville's collection of whaling scenes were hung —not engravings, but "oil paintings of the Whalers." "I wonder where they are now," she mused long afterward. Her mother, Frances Melville Thomas, gave to the "Seaman's Institute New York" what *her* mother, Mrs. Melville, had listed as " 'Whale Pictures' " by "Ambroise Louis Garnery," but these seem likely to have been engravings, not oil paintings. The "oil paintings of the Whalers" waylaid the young Frances as she went upstairs from her grandmother's room: "at bed-time there was another ordeal — On the stairway hung large pictures of whaling days — & the monsters who were nameless to me then — were fearful to behold — there was one especially which smote terror to my heart — for a boat-full of men was being turned in the air about to fall into huge red jaws — while other men struggled in the water helplessly. I was glad to arrive in my room & tuck myself into bed." The little room where Eleanor or Frances slept was "on the top floor" — the third floor — next to their Aunt Bessie's, and very likely it was the "little room" that their mother, Frances Melville, had taken for her own in 1877. The guest bedroom (probably still containing its cottage furniture) was also on the third floor.

By the early 1880s the house was filled with art. Melville could not have collected many oil paintings (that was for his brother Allan's brother-in-law, the millionaire Richard Lathers, and in a smaller way for Allan). Nevertheless, his granddaughter Frances specifically recalled the now-lost oil paintings of whaling scenes. In the parlors, besides the Eaton oil of Melville (and the oil of him painted about 1846 by Asa Twitchell), there were oils of some of the ancestors, including a copy of the Gilbert Stuart portrait of Melville's grandfather, General Peter Gansevoort, made by Ezra Ames, listed in his sister Frances's will as "Grandpapa's *portrait.*" Melville's sister Frances also left him his choice "of *papa's portraits*" (the two of Allan Melvill), one of which was to go to the other surviving male in the family, young Frank Hoadley. There was a framed engraving of Lord Cornwallis's *Surrender at Yorktown*, perhaps detailed enough to show a recognizable General Gansevoort and the huge and gorgeous flag—a pity the colors did not show. That was the flag of the Third New York Regiment which General Gansevoort had taken to Yorktown, a trophy Cousin Kate cherished. There too, most likely, was a gift from Melville's uncle, Peter Gansevoort, in 1870, "a handsomely framed engraving" of the Hero himself, Melville's Grandfather Gansevoort. After April 1886, Peter Toft's watercolor illustration of Rock Rodondo in "The Encantadas" was somewhere in the house, perhaps side by side with his *Flamboro Head*.

Besides the marble or alabaster statue of Antinous there seems to have been a bust of Minerva—another of "many beautiful things" (Mrs. Osborne said) which her grandfather bought "just because he couldn't resist them":

> the rooms held a varied collection of objects, not always too appropriate for their setting—He was a great collector of fine engravings—many of ships & the sea—I have often wondered what became of Antinous for he had a rather mysterious ending. When the household was broken up after my grandfather's death—my mother presented to the South Orange New Jersey library Antinous & two very fine alabaster Grecian urns, the trustees accepted them—and seemed glad to have them, the urns looked very well on the mantel & Antinous found a niche where he couldn't startle little girls.

Mrs. Osborne explained Melville's ownership of many beautiful things such as the Aeolian harp on the back porch by citing his comment in *White-Jacket* that (in her paraphrase) "if for any reason one finds ones temper souring—one should try & counteract this by surrounding oneself with pleasurable sights & sounds." She concluded: "I think he did just this." He did it, for years, at the expense of the family's needs, his daughter Frances thought.

Despite the purchase of "cottage furniture" in 1877 to convert a nondescript room into a functional guest room and despite Melville's purchases of decorative artifacts, the pattern was that the Melvilles did not buy furniture—they inherited it. There was an old-fashioned claw-footed chair, and the old eight-day clock which Elizabeth and Herman gave to Fanny Thomas. Melville still had some of the set of Empire chairs with dolphin handrests that his father had imported. In an inventory of possessions Elizabeth itemized these pieces: "Old clock from Gansevoort made by Devereux Bowly London"; "Vases from Miss Magee to Bessie. One 'Copenhagen' the other 'Cypriote' from the collection discovered in Cyprus by Gen. Di Cesnola Director of the Art Museum in New York"; "Grandmother Shaw's old worked chair covers bought May 4th—1774"; "Little mahogany bureau belonged to my grandmother Shaw, when she was ten years old. I have given it to Bessie."; "Two ivory miniatures"; "Linen fire bag—marked 'No 1 J. Knapp 1788' "; "The 'Dana snuff-box' "; "The watch set with pearls" from Mrs. Craigie, a cousin of Judge Shaw's; "Statuette" which the artist Washington Allston (a classmate of her father's) gave to her uncle John Knapp; and, apparently, a reproduction of a statue, "Ariadne sleeping." Herman Melville had his desk and table, and Elizabeth Melville had her own cupboards, cabinets, chests, and drawers for displaying or sheltering treasures of odd family silver pieces, tumblers, plates, cups and saucers, many of them storied pieces, the family equivalents of the historic whaling implements in the Spouter Inn in *Moby-Dick*. A sampling of these objects, preserved at the Berkshire Athenaeum, includes blue and white Wedgwood cups and saucers, a large japanned box, and a vase. Melville took the fine old sideboard from the Mansion House, at least until the Thomases were able to use it.

Young Arthur Stedman, who knew the house better than almost anyone besides family members, said that Melville had gradually made a "notable collection of etchings and engravings from the old masters," those "from Claude's paintings being a specialty." Some of the Claudes, and Poussins as well, have recently been identified. The art historian Frank Jewett Mather Jr. saw much of Melville's collection in Bessie's possession at the Florence Apartments around 1907, after her mother's death in 1906; in 1938 he recalled "silvery prints after Poussin and Claude on the walls." In the Twenty-sixth Street house were framed engravings of gypsies, of the barque *Minerva* (colored), of ships at Rio, large framed engravings of Swanevelt's *Morning* and *Evening*, small framed engravings of Turner's *Calais Pier* and *Dutch Boats in a Gale*, the one of the bay of Naples (colored) that hung in the front hall, and another much cherished one in a simple, elegant gold frame, and later hung above the mantel at Henry and Frances Thomas's house in Edgartown, *A Brisk Gale*, after a painting by Van de Velde the Younger. In addition to fine engravings in many of his books, Melville possessed several hundred engravings which he kept in three or more portfolios, presumably stored flat on the writing desk in his study or the wider table in the alcove. These included Old Master prints from the Italian, French, and Dutch schools; antiquarian prints and biblical subjects; nineteenth-century prints by English as well as French painters and engravers; sequences of literary engravings; and a wide variety of marine scenes. Many of these prints may have been picked up out of bargain bins, but the testimony of Stedman, and later of Frank Jewett Mather Jr., is conclusive that the framed engravings were impressive. More to the point, framed and loose in his portfolios, the engravings were important to Melville, providing inspiration for some of his later poetry as well as stimulating recollections of some of his earlier travel.

Every time Melville passed by the colored engraving of the bay of Naples in the front hall, he would say, both his older two granddaughters recalled, "See the little boats going hither and thither" — the phrase hither and thither coming readily enough to the man who had written *Mardi: And a Voyage Thither* but puzzling little girls. From the two girls we learn other bits of his verbal usages and personal habits. Eleanor thought Melville "used funny words," as when he said "cop" instead of policeman when he warned her against running wild in the park: "Look out, or the 'cop' may catch you!" Frances also said he would use quite big words. He was apt to call Eleanor "Tittery-Eye," a private joke. He did not like the girls to leave food on their plates: "He would say in a warning whisper, 'Jack Smoke will come down the chimney and take what you leave!'" He had his regular jokes, always checking the china butterfly matchholder on the porch to see if it had flown away since he and one of the girls had last looked at it. You never knew when it would fly away.

Melville took Eleanor or Frances for walks when they visited, especially in springtime. Eleanor later remembered many "pilgrimages" with her grandfather to Central Park — the longer ones probably two or more years after his retirement, perhaps between 1887 and 1891. Once the horsecars had delivered them at Central Park, she ran about while he walked more slowly. He took Eleanor and Frances to see the animals in the Central Park zoo, and more than once he hired a swan boat to take one girl or the other voyaging on the lake. If you faced the tail of the swan and did not glance back at the man pedaling the contraption, you had the illusion that the beautiful swan was "drawing you along." Frances also recalled her sense of estrangement when Melville put on his odd sunglasses (rectangular with the corners cut off) for a visit to nearby Madison Square during tulip-blossoming time. It was there that he sat on a bench while she ran round and round the tulip beds and after a while he forgot her and went home. She was too young to know house numbers, yet old enough to remember many details of the experience, so the year was probably between 1887 and 1889. Moments after Frances reached their block with its bewilderingly similar stoops, Bessie, moving fast despite her arthritis, was opening the door to send Melville to look for her.

Three decades and more after he had gazed fascinated upon Zummo's realistic wax anatomical figures in Florence, Melville took Frances and Eleanor, separately, down to Fourteenth Street to see the wax representations of everyday people and historical or royal groupings at the Eden Musée. After Frances was duped by the man who had sat down on a green bench only to discover that the wet paint had come off on his trousers, Melville coaxed her downstairs to see how she would react to the chamber of horrors. As he might have known, she was terrified by the "hideous gorilla" which clutched a beautiful white woman, but she had some of his own odd interest in such matters, for a second visit reassured her, since it was clear to her that the gorilla had made no progress with the abduction since her first visit. If he hadn't gotten off with her yet, he probably wouldn't, she concluded. On rare occasions Melville crossed the river by ferry to Hoboken, the "Elysian Fields" of his remote childhood rambles, and took "the suburban train to East Orange," where he would sit on the piazza watching the girls play "until he had enough of such exhibitions," when he "would suddenly rise and take the next train back to Hoboken." His son-in-law recalled that Melville was fascinated by the Hudson River and the harbor. Together they would take ferry rides—"back and forth endlessly, but nervously prolonged," for Melville (pursued still by the "demon of restlessness" and the itch to occupy the most commanding situation), "never sat still in one seat for long, but moved about trying every place of vantage on the ferryboat." He was, his second granddaughter recalled, "restless—he was very restless at times." In colder seasons he worked off excess energy by walking back and forth on the back porch— an "enclosed" porch, Frances Osborne recalled, possibly roofed by Mrs. Melville's room on the next floor. (Despite her bitterness toward her father, Frances Melville Thomas became a smiling, gracious grandmother, even when, in the 1930s, she had to use two canes and had to back down the stairs, so that she made the trek only once a day, like her own grandmother Maria Gansevoort Melville at times in the late 1860s.)

Melville gave the impression of being reasonably strong still, to all appearances, still a stout-looking man. After meeting Melville in the spring of 1886 Peter Toft conveyed the impression to the English sea-novelist W. Clark Russell that Melville was "still hale and hearty." When his granddaughters were not there to be taken on good-weather outings, Melville went out for a long walk almost every day, whatever the weather. Remembering him from a few years later, his granddaughter Eleanor emphasized Melville's erect posture: "he made a brave and striking figure as he walked erect, head thrown back, cane in hand, inconspicuously dressed in a dark blue suit and a soft black felt hat." In his introduction to *Typee: A Real Romance of the South Seas* (1892), Arthur Stedman said: "After he retired from the Custom House, his tall, stalwart figure could be seen almost daily tramping through the Fort George district or Central Park, his roving inclination, leading him to obtain as much out-door life as possible." When Ernest Rhys visited E. C. Stedman in 1888, soon after Stedman moved near Melville, he (perhaps thwarted by his own diffidence) found it "difficult to get more than a passing glimpse of his 'tall, stalwart figure'" (he was quoting Arthur Stedman), though he gained an enduring impression of Melville's "grave, preoccupied face." Late in 1890 Edward Bok told readers of his syndicated newspaper column just where anyone could see the reclusive Melville: "along East Eighteenth Street, New York City, any morning about 9 o'clock." Melville, he added, "is now an old man, but still vigorous." In his walks about Manhattan Herman Melville was improving on old Thomas Melvill, whom the public had commented on as he crept, stooped and cautious, about the crooked streets of Boston with his three-cornered hat on his head and his cane in his hand; the grandson had made himself a conspicuous figure for erectness and vigor.

Old, much alone, and seemingly self-sufficient, Melville could still be thawed, though when a topic set him off he might fall into harangue rather than genial conversation. His son-in-law paid respectful attention to him, observing him and listening to him. In Minna Littmann's 1929 story for the New Bedford *Sunday Standard*, based on her Martha's Vineyard interview with Henry and Frances Thomas (and their daughter Eleanor Metcalf), the hook was the curious discovery that the Thomases were owners of the Valentine Pease house, and possessors of some Pease furniture deemed too heavy to move. Pease, someone had remembered, had been the captain of the *Acushnet*, a man vilified in *Typee*, although not by name. Harry Thomas told Minna Littmann this about Melville: "He never talked about his writing. If anyone brought up the subject, he'd shut up like a clam." The reporter on that occasion wanted Melvillean anecdotes about the Vineyard, but Mr. Thomas had none: "I never heard him mention Captain Pease or Edgartown." If Littmann had thought to ask if Melville had ever visited his sister Kate Hoadley when she lived in New Bedford, Frances could have responded informatively, but she missed that opportunity. Littmann recorded Harry Thomas's memories of Melville at some length:

> He talked freely and most interestingly on many subjects not connected with his books. He was fond of walks in the country and liked to talk about nature. I remember many interesting talks on politics and religion. He was very much down on politicians. He called them "damn fools." In fact, that was the term he applied to nearly everybody. He wasn't sociable, you know. He didn't care for people.
>
> [Minna Littmann:] "How about you?"
>
> "He was always very nice to me," Mr. Thomas recalled, his kind blue eyes a little misty. "That's one thing I never could quite understand."
>
> "I rather think," interposed Mrs. Metcalf, who has the same blue eyes, "that he must have taken a liking to father because of his sea-blue eyes."

Blue eyes are a simplistic explanation, but Harry Thomas's memories seem reliable, if not quite specific. Where in the "country" (as distinguished from parks) could he and Melville have walked? Perhaps the still-wild area of the bluffs up at Riverside Park.

That Melville liked to talk about "nature" also is tantalizing, especially in the light of the tendency of some of his later British admirers to link him with Thoreau. Extended comments on Thoreau and on Whitman run through many of Henry S. Salt's writings, such as his 1894 *Richard Jefferies: His Life and Ideals*, in which Salt quoted from a manuscript on Jefferies by Dr. Samuel Arthur Jones, whom he identified as "a well-known student of Thoreau" — Jones being the collector who bought many of Allan Melville's copies of his brother's works. In the months before and after Melville's death in September 1891, Salt found that the "litterateurs" of the British publishing world, aloof from issues of human nature and society, were threatened by his proposed collection of essays on "the whole *Nature* subject," to be called *The Return to Nature* and to consist of his articles on "Jefferies, Carpenter, Burroughs, Thoreau, Melville, &c, &c." Had Salt found a publisher for *The Return to Nature*, or had he set himself to write a biography of Melville instead of Thoreau, the course of Melville's reputation would have been incalculably but powerfully altered.

Reports of Melville's tramping about Manhattan in these years have him doing so unaccompanied by another adult, but on occasion he made an exception at least with his son-in-law, who remembered Melville's fondness for walking in the country and talking about nature. The "country" may well have meant Riverside Park. Starting in 1879 or 1880, there had been much talk about Riverside Park and Morningside Heights as being the possible site of a World's Fair, which went to Chicago, in the end, but roads were built there, and Melville could take public transportation most of the way out — seven miles from City Hall to the start of the park. Melville's casual reference in the epistolary preface to *John Marr* to the higher bluffs of Riverside Park suggests that he was familiar with it, whether or not he had taken an "afternoon stroll" there in June of 1887 or 1888 with a genial companion like Harry who might have suggested the "Hilary" of the preface. Harry Thomas meant that Melville talked as he walked with him. Melville was not sociable, Harry said. Certainly he did not want to meet new people, and people who might have known his name did not necessarily connect it with the face of the bearded old man in a blue suit and a low, wide-brimmed hat, walking with a cane.

On 14 January 1886 the New York *Commercial Advertiser* had made comments more personal than Melville could have liked: "Still, he is not very old — sixty-five — and his rather heavy, thick-set figure and warm complexion betoken health and vigor. . . . He is a genial, pleasant fellow, who, after all his wanderings, loves to stay at home — his house is in Twenty-sixth street — and indulge in reverie and reminiscence." A few old acquaintances called upon Melville in his last years and if lucky heard such reverie and reminiscence. Melville had received Julian in the south parlor in 1883, not in his study, and the indications are that all his callers were taken to the back parlor, not to his private workroom on the second floor. Titus Munson Coan, that pilgrim to Arrowhead before the war, visited Melville several times and felt he was just achieving intimacy when Melville died. Theodore Wolfe had the privilege of hearing Melville reminisce about Hawthorne's visit to Arrowhead in 1851. The artist Peter Toft "accidentally" discovered him early in 1886 and became "good friends" with him, although not an unskeptical one:

> Though a delightful talker when in the mood, he was abnormal, as most geniuses are, and had to be handled with care. He seemed to hold his work in small esteem, and discouraged my attempts to discuss them. "You know," he would say, "more about them than I do. I have forgotten them." He would give me no information about the old whaling tradition of the fiendish White-Whale ("Moby Dick,") which was said to haunt the sea about the Chiloe Islands, south of Valparaiso, and was almost offended when I inquired so curiously about his falling from the maintopgallant yard of the frigate — ("White Jacket") — a tour de force of writing, in my opinion.

One visitor recalled: "Though a man of moods, he had a peculiarly winning and interesting personality, suggesting Laurence Oliphant in his gentle deference to an opponent's conventional opinion while he expressed the wildest and most emancipated ideas of his own." Oliphant was a writer for the New York *Times* who had traveled more widely than Melville and written books on Russia and China as well as the 1852 *A Journey to Kathmandu*.

The journalist O. G. Hillard on 5 October 1891 wrote a piece that the New York *Times* printed the next day. He insisted that Melville had made his choices:

> One reason for Melville's obscurity as a man and writer must be looked for in the man himself. He had shot his arrow and made his mark and was satisfied. With considerable knowledge of the world, he preferred to see it from a distance, and was in no sense a man of business. His proud and sensitive nature made him a recluse, and led him to bury himself from a world with which he had little in common. . . . So he was content to be forgotten, and among his cherished books he passed his life. With the few who were permitted to know him he was the man of culture, the congenial companion, and the honestest and manliest of all earthly friends. I once asked the loan of some of his books, which early in life had given me such pleasure, and was surprised when he said that he didn't own a single copy of them.

That little incident told a story of Melville's "own indifference to the children of his brain," Hillard said. Though "eloquent in discussing general literature," Melville "was dumb when the subject of his own writings was broached."

Whatever the reason Robert Buchanan had not been able locate Melville, his footnote to "Socrates in Camden" may have roused E. C. Stedman to make his first polite overtures to Melville. Their acquaintance grew to the point that in February 1888 Melville urged Stedman to call on him: "I have not by any means so many external demands upon my evenings as you probably have. I am the one most likely to be at home in the evening. Pray remember this, and give me the pleasure of dropping in again here when you feel like it." Arthur Stedman summed the matter up in his introduction to *Typee*: "His evenings were spent at home with his books, his pictures, and his family, and usually with them alone; for, in spite of the melodramatic declarations of various English gentlemen, Melville's seclusion in his latter years, and in fact throughout his life, was a matter of personal choice. More and more, as he grew older, he avoided every action on his part, and on the part of his family, that might tend to keep his name and writings before the public. A few friends felt at liberty to visit the recluse, and were kindly welcomed, but he himself sought no one."

Melville was still impressing people who met him for the first time. An apprentice boy, Oscar Wegelin, remembered Melville's first visit to the bookshop of John Anderson Jr. (in *The Colophon*, Summer 1935):

> Late one afternoon in the autumn of 1890 an old gentleman preceded by a beard that was impressive even for those hirsute days walked into the bookshop of John Anderson, Jr., at 99 Nassau Street, New York, where the author of these notes was employed as boy of all work. A neighboring bookseller, it appeared, had directed the visitor to Mr. Anderson as likely to have a copy of a certain title which the visitor sought. If I remembered the title of that particular book, you may be sure I should give it here. I recall only that it was concerned with the sea; I do not even recall whether the Anderson shop was able to supply it.
>
> But I do recall that a conversation was opened between Mr. Anderson and the newcomer — a conversation about the sea and sailors that soon included as an audience the browsers in the shop and the boy of all work. For it was very evident that the stranger knew considerably more about those who went down to the sea in ships and the sorts of ships they went down in than anyone we had ever listened to.
>
> At last Mr. Anderson, giving voice to a curiosity that was consuming all of

us, inquired: "By the way, sir, you have not given me your name. To whom do I owe the pleasure of this visit?"

"My name is Herman Melville," said the visitor. Mr Anderson raised his hands in delighted surrender. "That explains it," he said.

It was the beginning of a brief but pleasant friendship between the pair. Until a short time before his death the following September... Melville was a frequent visitor at the Anderson shop. On at least one occasion Mr. Anderson visited the Melville home and met Mrs. Melville. It was my own good fortune several times in those months to be the bearer of bundles of books to the Melville house—some of them were copies of his own sea tales, of which, oddly enough, he seemed to have had virtually no copies until Mr. Anderson supplied him. When the author was at home I was certain to receive a modest but welcome tip—an offering wholeheartedly appreciated by a 'prentice bookseller who was drawing three dollars a week. If I had only had the foresight to take up a few copies of his books on my own account and ask him to inscribe them!....

I do recall enough about those books to be able to report that Melville was hardly a collector in the sense in which the term is employed today. There was a report current in the booktrade at the time that he spent more of his slender income on books than his family liked, but plenty of people before and since who were not of Melville's literary stature have done and are still doing the same....

Melville, as I recall him, was slightly below the average in stature, and walked with a rapid stride and almost a sprightly gait. He could be depended upon to wear a low-crowned hat and, almost invariably, a blue suit. I particularly recall his gentleness of manner and his pleasant smile. I never found him to be the misanthrope that many authorities accuse him of having been; it is difficult for me to believe that he was a disappointed man—if he was he did not permit his disappointment to come out into the open....

Whether he liked people or simply made believe he did, masking his real self in the presence of a bookseller and his youthful assistant, I am certain that he loved New York. He would take long walks in those latter months, voyaging as far afield as Central Park—a promenade which I doubt if many residents of East Twenty-sixth Street indulge in today.

Lizzie, Wegelin implied clearly enough, did not feel called upon to give him a tip if he happened to deliver books when Melville was not at home. Being wealthy did not mean she had to be wasteful.

In London on 27 August Robert Buchanan published a poem, *The Outcast: A Rhyme for the Time*. In it he mixed the *Typee* story with the legend of the

Flying Dutchman, dedicating canto 2 ("The First Haven") to Melville. He had written new lines to lead into lines recycled from "Socrates in Camden":

> My Homer of the southern seas,
> Who, proudly pagan, Yankee-Greek,
>   Flung out his banner to the breeze,
> Then, wandering onward like Ulysses,
>   Heard Syrens sing of Nature's charms
> Leaping on shore to greet with kisses
> The dainty dimpled nutbrown misses,
>   Found the lost Eden in their arms!
>
> To thee, O HERMANN MELVILLE, name
> The surges trumpet into fame,
> Last of the grand Homeric race,
>   Great tale-teller of the marines,
> I give this Song, wherein I chase
>   Thy soul thro' magic tropic scenes!
> Ah, would that I, poor modern singer,
> Spell-bound with Care's mesmeric finger,
> Might to the living world forth-figure
> Thine Odyssean strength and vigour!
> Alas; o'er waves *you* tost on gladly
> *I* sail more timidly and sadly,
> And find no surcease or protection
> From *mal de mer*, or introspection!

Here the old line "Aid me, O sea-compelling man!" led into other lines from the 1885 tribute. In canto 2 the Flying Dutchman (the outcast) visits the South Seas and has some of the same experiences as the hero of Typee. The American edition of *The Outcast* was published in mid-September, just in time for Melville to learn about it, but not much time to revel in it.

As Lizzie recorded, Melville "died Sept. 28th 1891 after two years of failing health, induced partly by severe attacks of erysipelas terminating finally in enlargement of the heart." Dr. Warner signed the death certificate, certifying that he had "attended the deceased" from July 1891 to 28 September 1891. He had last seen Melville alive on the twenty-seventh, and death occurred on the twenty-eighth at 12:30 A.M., the cause being "Cardiac dilatation, Mitral regurgitation.... Contributory Asthenia." Arthur Stedman wrote the note on the funeral that the *Tribune* published on 1 October 1891:

> The funeral of the late Herman Melville was held at the family residence ... yesterday afternoon, the Rev. Theodore C. Williams, of All Souls' Church,

delivering a short address. Among the relatives and friends present, beside the widow and daughter of the deceased, were Mrs. Thomas Melville, widow of the late governor of the Sailors' Snug Harbor; the Misses Melville, daughters of the late Allan Melville; Samuel Shaw, of Boston; W. B. Morewood, George Brewster, Mrs. Griggs, Miss Lathers, Dr. Titus Munson Coan, Arthur Stedman and George Dillaway.

("Mrs. Griggs" was an error for Kate Hoadley, the surviving sister.) Presumably all three of Allan's surviving daughters came, Milie, Florence, and Kitty. Since Harry Thomas is not listed, "daughter" may be correct: if Fanny Melville Thomas was ill, or Harry, or one of their three children, it is possible that neither came to the funeral. Poor Fanny, in any case, had more resentment to nurse than grief to express. Burial was at the remote Woodlawn in the Bronx, with Malcolm and Stanwix.

The obituaries were few and predictable. The New York *Press* on 29 September 1891 concluded that Melville had "fallen into a literary decline," so deep that "if the truth were known, even his own generation has long thought him dead, so quiet have been the later years of his life." The *Tribune* misdated *Typee* as 1847 and called it his best book. The *World* (now owned by Joseph Pulitzer) said Melville was "formerly a well-known author." On 2 October the *Times* printed a longish piece in which the writer made a challenge: "Whoever, arrested for a moment by the tidings of the author's death, turns back now to the books that were so much read, and so much talked about forty years ago has no difficulty in determining why they were then read and talked about. His difficulty will be rather to discover why they are read and talked about no longer." (The Brooklyn *Standard-Union* quoted these words on 3 October.) On 4 October the Springfield *Republican* printed a memorial article in "The Literary Wayside," calling Melville "one of the most original and virile of American literary men" and declaring:

> it is probable that no work of imagination more powerful and often poetic has been written by an American than Melville's romance of "Moby Dick; or the Whale," published just 40 years ago. . . . Certainly it is hard to find a more wonderful book than this Moby Dick, and it ought to be read by this generation, amid whose feeble mental food, furnished by the small realists and fantasts of the day, it would appear as Hercules among the pygmies, or as Moby Dick himself among a school of minnows.

The *Times* on 6 October printed a piece by "O.G.H." ("H" for Hillard) praising the paper as the only one to have printed an adequate editorial in memory of Melville. Hillard did not use Melville's first name, and the compositor, making a good guess, set *"THE LATE HIRAM MELVILLE"* in the heading. Efforts to chisel it out left the first name obliterated in some copies, "Hiram" barely legible in others. "The Late Hiram Melville" entered American literary history as the one thing memorable in Melville's obituaries. The letter itself, subheaded "A tribute to his memory from one who knew him," recalled Melville as one "whose fame at one time was second to none in the annals of our literature," but the highest claim Hillard made for Melville's greatness was that he was the "equal" of the recently dead James Russell Lowell, though "in a narrower sphere."

The Melville family motto was "Denique Coelum" — "Heaven at Last," not "Heaven All Along." Judging from "Rammon," Melville never stopped thinking about the religious concept of immortality, and judging from the *Billy Budd* manuscript, he had never given up on the idea of setting the uncomprehending world aright by writing an "inside narrative." Since late 1884, thanks to Julian Hawthorne, the public knew that he had once fantasized of sitting down in some little shady corner of Paradise with Nathaniel Hawthorne, by themselves, with a basket of champagne. That was 1851, and over the decades Melville had moved beyond Hawthorne. Even in 1851 he was identifying with Shakespeare, and he found singular coincidings between his ideas and Spenser's and then between himself and Milton. Along the way he had measured himself against his contemporaries Matthew Arnold and Robert Browning. He did not die hoping that he and Hawthorne would cross their "celestial legs in the celestial grass that is forever tropical," and strike their glasses and their heads together, "till both musically ring in concert."

Englishmen and Englishwomen from the beginning had been more comfortable with Melville than his fellow citizens were, and long provided his most powerful critics. In England, even after "Socrates at Camden" was published, Robert Buchanan ranted repeatedly about the neglect of three writers of his century. The "critical snobs" had recognized Tennyson's worth only when he "assumed the laurel, 'greener from the brows' of Wordsworth." Herman Melville, that " 'Yankee-Greek,' greatest and best of all writers of the sea," had broken his pen, "sick of the futile struggle against the platitudinous mediocrities bepuffed by the newspaper critic." And George Meredith had turned "grey before our critical *ciceroni* mentioned — or apparently knew — his name." In January 1856 the *Dublin University Magazine* had celebrated "A Trio of American Sailor-Authors" — Cooper, Dana, and Melville; Buchanan's trio of "Tennyson, Melville, Meredith" was better. In Melville's lifetime, others in England privately were naming George Borrow and Melville as a pair of authors too little known. After a few decades English admirers put Melville in a still higher category. In 1922 T. E. Lawrence (Lawrence of Arabia) reminded Melville's erstwhile young correspondent Edward Garnett that he had collected "a shelf of 'Titanic' books (those distinguished by greatness of spirit, 'sublimity' as Longinus would call it): and that they were *The Karamazovs, Zarathustra, Moby Dick*"; his ambition had been to make an English fourth, with his *Seven Pillars of Wisdom*. In 1927 Lawrence wrote Garnett again: "My notion of the world's big books" (excluding poetry) "are *War and Peace, The Brothers Karamazoff, Moby Dick*, Rabelais, *Don Quixote*." Melville's widow never lived to read such praise, but she read this passage in William Livingston Alden's "London Literary Letter" in the New York *Times* for 5 August 1899: "Herman Melville is far and away the most original genius that America has produced, and it is a National reproach that he should be so completely neglected." The winds of March 1885, on that excursion to the Brentano bookstore, had fanned in Elizabeth Shaw Melville a flame that burgeoned into fierce pride that she had been Herman Melville's wife. Marrying him did not seem the worst thing she ever did.

Genealogical Charts

MELVILL[E]

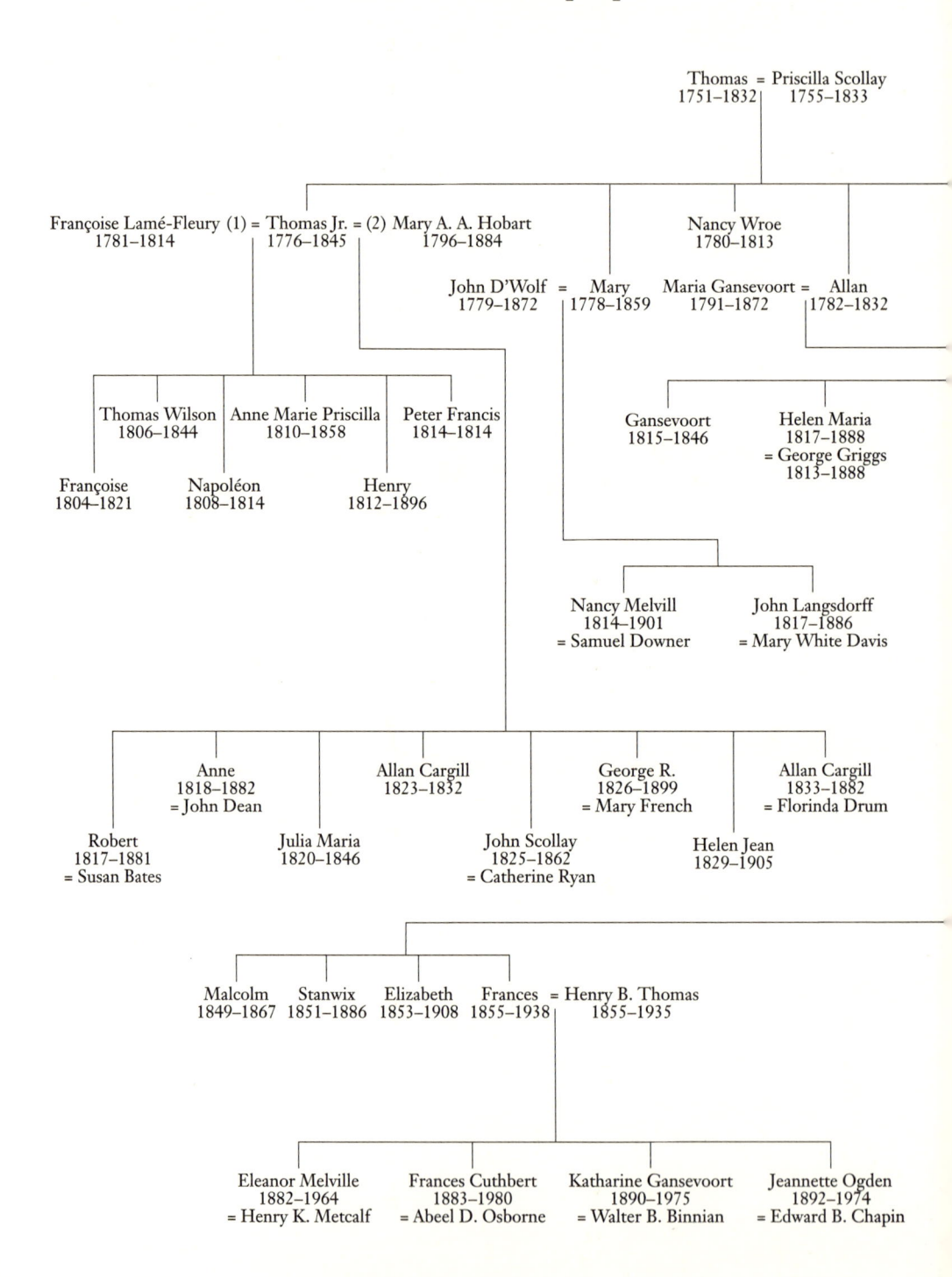

Thomas = Priscilla Scollay
1751–1832   1755–1833

Françoise Lamé-Fleury (1) = Thomas Jr. = (2) Mary A. A. Hobart
1781–1814   1776–1845   1796–1884

Nancy Wroe
1780–1813

John D'Wolf = Mary   Maria Gansevoort = Allan
1779–1872   1778–1859 1791–1872   1782–1832

Thomas Wilson | Anne Marie Priscilla | Peter Francis
1806–1844   1810–1858   1814–1814

Gansevoort   Helen Maria
1815–1846   1817–1888
                = George Griggs
                1813–1888

Françoise   Napoléon   Henry
1804–1821   1808–1814   1812–1896

Nancy Melvill   John Langsdorff
1814–1901   1817–1886
= Samuel Downer   = Mary White Davis

Anne   Allan Cargill   George R.   Allan Cargill
1818–1882   1823–1832   1826–1899   1833–1882
= John Dean   = Mary French   = Florinda Drum

Robert   Julia Maria   John Scollay   Helen Jean
1817–1881   1820–1846   1825–1862   1829–1905
= Susan Bates   = Catherine Ryan

Malcolm   Stanwix   Elizabeth   Frances = Henry B. Thomas
1849–1867 1851–1886 1853–1908   1855–1938 1855–1935

Eleanor Melville   Frances Cuthbert   Katharine Gansevoort   Jeannette Ogden
1882–1964   1883–1980   1890–1975   1892–1974
= Henry K. Metcalf   = Abeel D. Osborne   = Walter B. Binnian   = Edward B. Chapin

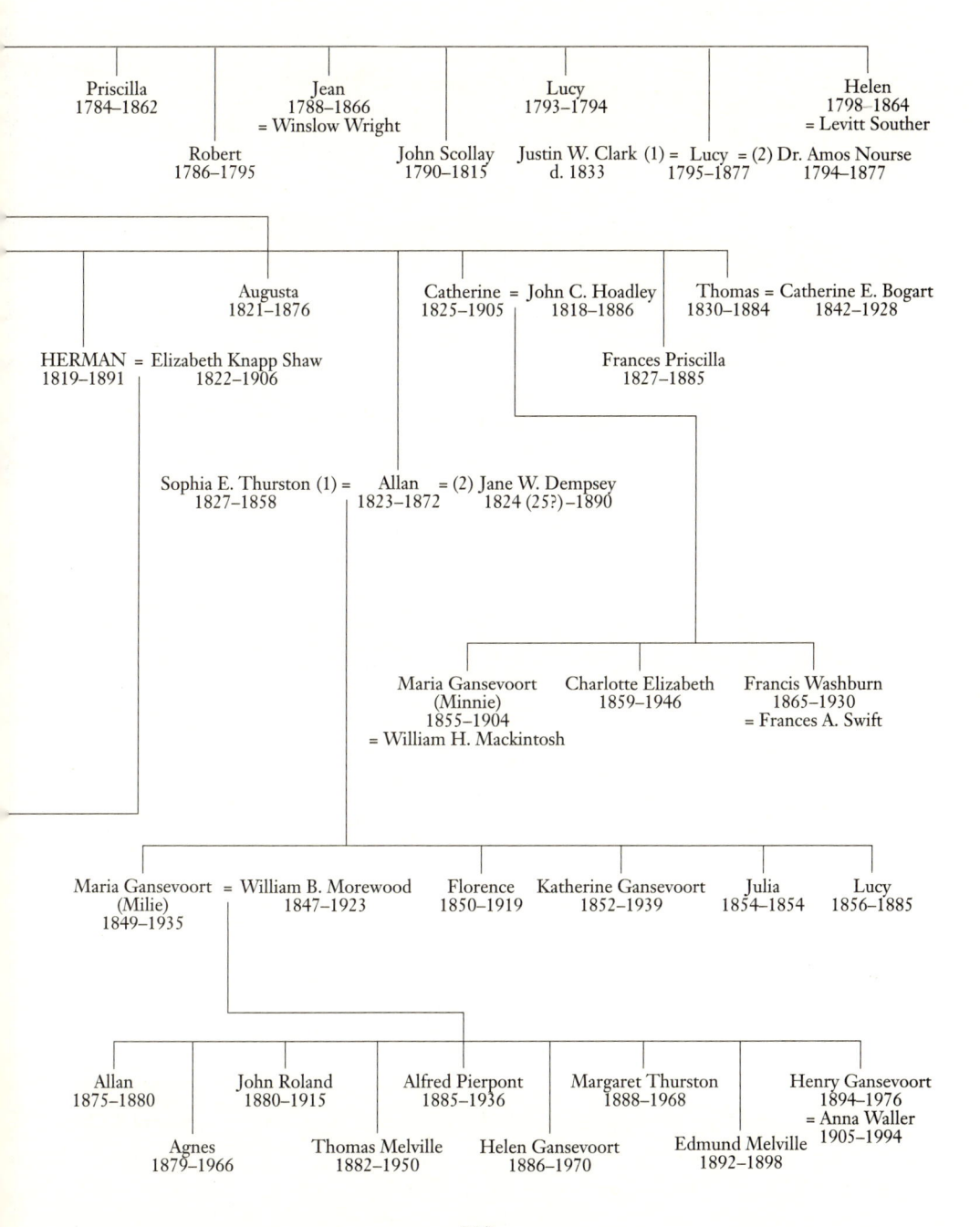

```
Priscilla      Jean              Lucy                                    Helen
1784–1862      1788–1866         1793–1794                               1798–1864
               = Winslow Wright                                          = Levitt Souther
     Robert              John Scollay    Justin W. Clark (1) = Lucy = (2) Dr. Amos Nourse
     1786–1795           1790–1815       d. 1833              1795–1877    1794–1877
```

```
              Augusta              Catherine = John C. Hoadley    Thomas = Catherine E. Bogart
              1821–1876            1825–1905 | 1818–1886          1830–1884  1842–1928
HERMAN = Elizabeth Knapp Shaw                 Frances Priscilla
1819–1891  1822–1906                          1827–1885
```

```
          Sophia E. Thurston (1) =  Allan   = (2) Jane W. Dempsey
          1827–1858                 1823–1872    1824 (25?)–1890

                    Maria Gansevoort    Charlotte Elizabeth    Francis Washburn
                       (Minnie)              1859–1946            1865–1930
                       1855–1904                                = Frances A. Swift
                    = William H. Mackintosh
```

```
Maria Gansevoort = William B. Morewood    Florence    Katherine Gansevoort    Julia       Lucy
   (Milie)         1847–1923              1850–1919        1852–1939         1854–1854   1856–1885
   1849–1935

  Allan        John Roland    Alfred Pierpont    Margaret Thurston    Henry Gansevoort
  1875–1880    1880–1915      1885–1936          1888–1968            1894–1976
                                                                    = Anna Waller
        Agnes         Thomas Melville    Helen Gansevoort    Edmund Melville   1905–1994
        1879–1966     1882–1950          1886–1970           1892–1898
```

927

MELVILL[E]

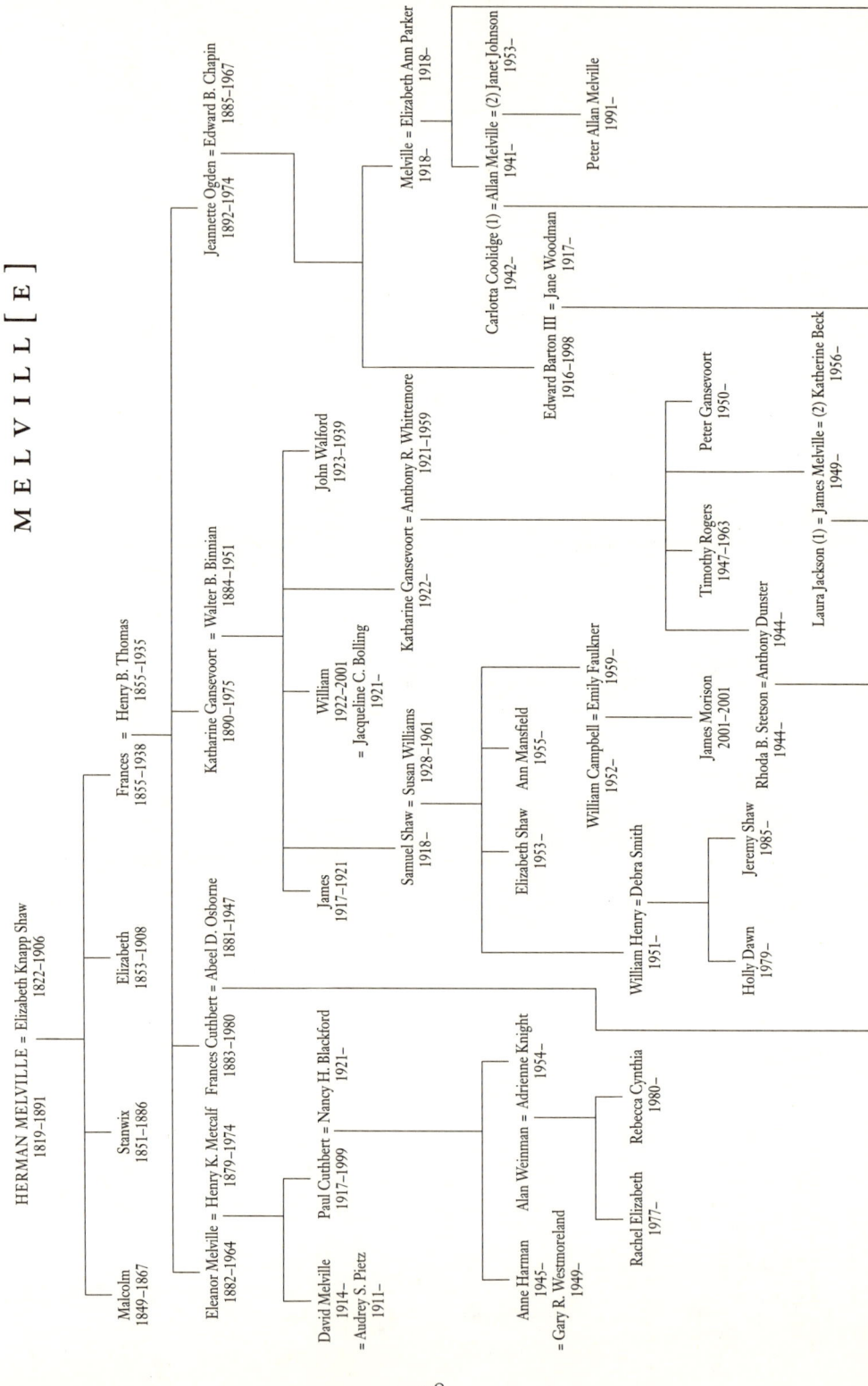

HERMAN MELVILLE = Elizabeth Knapp Shaw
1819–1891   1822–1906

- Malcolm 1849–1867
- Stanwix 1851–1886
- Elizabeth 1853–1908
- Frances = Henry B. Thomas
  1855–1938   1855–1935
- Jeannette Ogden = Edward B. Chapin
  1892–1974   1885–1967

Frances Cuthbert = Abel D. Osborne
1883–1980   1881–1947

Katharine Gansevoort = Walter B. Binnian
1890–1975   1884–1951

Eleanor Melville = Henry K. Metcalf
1882–1964   1879–1974

Paul Cuthbert = Nancy H. Blackford
1917–1999   1921–

James 1917–1921

John Walford 1923–1939

Katharine Gansevoort = Anthony R. Whittemore
1922–   1921–1959

Melville = Elizabeth Ann Parker
1918–   1918–

David Melville 1914–
= Audrey S. Pietz 1911–

Samuel Shaw = Susan Williams
1918–   1928–1961

Elizabeth Shaw 1953–

Ann Mansfield 1955–

William 1922–2001
= Jacqueline C. Bolling 1921–

Edward Barton III = Jane Woodman
1916–1998   1917–

Carlotta Coolidge (1) = Allan Melville = (2) Janet Johnson
1942–   1941–   1953–

Anne Harman 1945–
= Gary R. Westmoreland 1949–

Alan Weinman = Adrienne Knight
1954–

William Campbell = Emily Faulkner
1952–   1959–

William Henry = Debra Smith
1951–

Peter Gansevoort 1950–

Timothy Rogers 1947–1963

Peter Allan Melville 1991–

Rachel Elizabeth 1977–

Rebecca Cynthia 1980–

Holly Dawn 1979–

Jeremy Shaw 1985–

James Morison 2001–2001

Rhoda B. Stetson = Anthony Dunster
1944–   1944–

Laura Jackson (1) = James Melville = (2) Katherine Beck
1949–   1956–

928

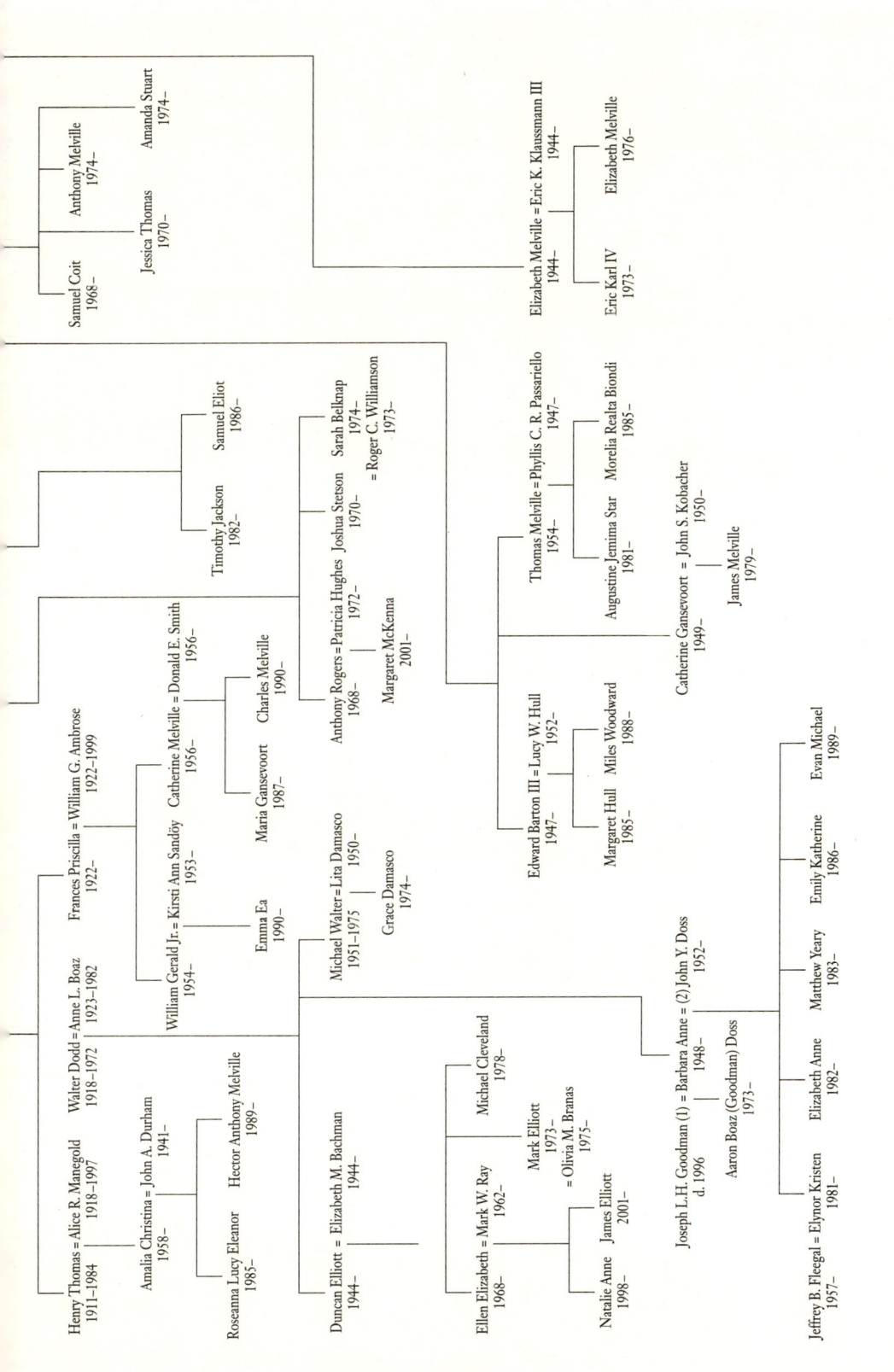

```
                                                                Samuel Coit    Anthony Melville
                                                                1968–          1974–
                                                                      Jessica Thomas    Amanda Stuart
                                                                      1970–            1974–

                                                                                              Elizabeth Melville = Eric K. Klaussmann III
                                                                                              1944–                1944–
                                                                                                    Eric Karl IV      Elizabeth Melville
                                                                                                    1973–             1976–
```

Henry Thomas = Alice R. Manegold   Walter Dodd = Anne L. Boaz   Frances Priscilla = William G. Ambrose
1911–1984   1918–1997   1918–1972   1923–1982   1922–   1922–1999

  Amalia Christina = John A. Durham   William Gerald Jr. = Kirsti Ann Sandiy   Catherine Melville = Donald E. Smith
  1958–   1941–   1954–   1953–   1956–   1956–

      Roseanna Lucy Eleanor   Hector Anthony Melville   Charles Melville
      1985–   1989–   1990–
                                                          Emma Ea   Maria Gansevoort
                                                          1990–   1987–
                                                                                                                  Timothy Jackson   Samuel Eliot
                                                                                                                  1982–   1986–

  Duncan Elliott = Elizabeth M. Bachman   Michael Walter = Lita Damasco   Anthony Rogers = Patricia Hughes   Joshua Stetson   Sarah Belknap
  1944–   1944–   1951–1975   1950–   1968–   1972–   1970–   1974–
                                                                                                                                             = Roger C. Williamson
                                                                        Grace Damasco   Margaret McKenna   1973–
                                                                        1974–   2001–

      Ellen Elizabeth = Mark W. Ray   Michael Cleveland   Edward Barton III = Lucy W. Hull   Thomas Melville = Phyllis C. R. Passariello
      1968–   1962–   1978–   1947–   1952–   1954–   1947–

                Mark Elliott   Margaret Hull   Miles Woodward   Augustine Jemima Star   Morelia Realta Biondi
                1973–   1985–   1988–   1981–   1985–
                = Olivia M. Branas
                  1975–   Catherine Gansevoort = John S. Kobacher
          Natalie Anne   James Elliott   1949–   1950–
          1998–   2001–
                                                                                                                                                        James Melville
                                                                                                                                                        1979–

                                         Joseph L.H. Goodman (1) = Barbara Anne = (2) John Y. Doss
                                         d. 1996   1948–   1952–

                                                       Aaron Boaz (Goodman) Doss
                                                       1973–

  Jeffrey B. Fleegal = Elynor Kristen   Elizabeth Anne   Matthew Yeary   Emily Katherine   Evan Michael
  1957–   1981–   1982–   1983–   1986–   1989–

929

Documentation

EPISODE BY EPISODE, THIS BIOGRAPHY is composed from nineteenth-century Melville family manuscripts and from items in periodicals (especially newspapers), most of them as transcribed into my chronological electronic archive, *The New Melville Log*, now several thousand pages long. (Gordian Press may issue a three-volume selection; I hope that the whole work will eventually be available in an electronic format.) I have also drawn on books Melville knew (some of them never before cited, such as his set of the *Modern British Essayists*). Quotations from manuscript letters are identified in the text by writer, recipient, and date so that the archive holding the document may be determined from the "Chart of Correspondents," below. Newspaper and magazines are dated in the text; full texts of the reviews known as of 1995 are in *Herman Melville: The Contemporary Reviews*, ed. Brian Higgins and Hershel Parker. In his 1951 and 1969 *The Melville Log* Jay Leyda sampled Melville's marginalia; I have added more to *The New Melville Log*, but often I cite Melville's marginalia from my ready-reference transcriptions in duplicates of his sets of Milton, Wordsworth, Hazlitt, Vasari, and other writers. I make every effort to quote from these and other authors from the editions Melville owned. I use the Northwestern-Newberry edition of *The Writings of Herman Melville* for Melville's books, stories, journals (the primary source for much of chs. 14 and 15), lectures (in vol. 9, *The Piazza Tales and Other Prose Pieces, 1839–1860*, a source for parts of chs. 16–18), published poems (in progress), and for his letters and letters to him (except for a few items discovered since 1993, the year vol. 14, *Correspondence*, was published). Melville's works are cited by chapter, not page; any page citation below for a Melville work is to an editorial section of the Northwestern-Newberry (NN) volume. I depart from the NN text only rarely, as when "Travel" has been newly established (by Steven Olsen-Smith) as the correct title of Melville's last lecture. Books and articles by writers other than Melville are cited in "Printed Sources" unless fully identified in the text or the chapter-by-chapter documentation, below. For volume 2 a major resource was the research (including my own) reported in NN volumes, edited by Harrison Hayford, Hershel Parker, and G. Thomas Tanselle (and, certain volumes, by Howard C. Horsford, Lynn Horth, Alma MacDougall, Robert C. Ryan, Merton M. Sealts Jr.). (Work by Merrell R. Davis and William H. Gilman went, posthumously, into the NN *Correspondence*.) I profited especially from two Historical Notes by Walter E. Bezanson, those in *Israel Potter* and in *Clarel*.

Special Sources, Benefactors, and Notes on Evidence

This volume is indebted to many people named in the acknowledgments and sometimes specially identified in these notes. William S. Reese was, as always, magnanimous. Two librarians were unfailingly generous and resourceful: Ruth Degenhardt at the Berkshire Athenaeum (during much of what seemed an interminable cruise) and Dennis Marnon at the Houghton Library (during the final, but drawn-out, Nantucket sleigh-ride). It was a blessing to have the Melville scholar Alma MacDougall Reising as copyeditor. Readers seeking rapid immersion in Melville's American literary and political contexts will value two old books by Frank Luther Mott, his *American Journalism* and his 1850–1865 volume of *American Magazines*. Readers of my later chapters will treasure *New York 1880: Architecture and Urbanism in the Gilded Age*, by Robert A. M. Stern, Thomas Mellins, and David Fishman. Melville was able to lecture in Montreal with a panorama of Rome behind him; I finished the first volume longing for ready access to illustrations, but now a reader with good Internet access can create a magnificent extra-illustrated edition of any historical study like this one.

Working as I did from the archives, I have had few occasions to quote twentieth- or twenty-first-century biographical and critical books on Melville. (I cite the 1951 *Log* and use the 1969 "Supplement" when I can, even if I have fuller transcriptions of the documents in *The New Melville Log*.) All the documents I used in the archives had been open to all comers, but few of the new readers in the late 1980s and 1990s, it turned out, had much prior acquaintance with Melville's domestic and literary milieux or much experience in transcribing nineteenth-century handwriting. In the recent stampede to display golden nuggets, especially from the Augusta Melville papers (acquired, mainly by the New York Public Library, in 1983), pytites flooded the market, flawed, false, and outright fantastic episodes of family history. Places, events, and people were scrambled (any four Aunt Marys were three too many to disentangle); motivations and behavior were misconstrued; imaginary characters and relationships were depicted. ("Reliable," pronounced reviewers who had never dirtied their own hands in the archives.) Of the writers of recent books on Melville, I quote an analysis of evidence only from Stanton Garner, who is "reliable" on facts, although, alas, a poor judge of women's character; from an article by Robert Sandberg I quote a terse summary of a document; and from Clare Spark I quote some transcriptions of 1920s documents.

In the 1980s and 1990s more than one ingenuous aspirant to Boswellhood, having found it inconvenient or downright onerous to visit a library, suggested strenuously that I should hand over my years of work on *The New Melville Log* to serve as his or her ready-made bio-kit. Before Leyda's death in 1988 I knew that for a dedicated biographer the "Silver Platter" theory of research is a delusion: even Leon Howard, wise as he was, could not write a reliable narrative biography from Leyda's working files, although he let Hayford and Leyda "browbeat" him into trying. As I said in the preface to the first volume, I had to become my own Leyda & Company. Doing so, I saw that there is no substitute for seeking documents, transcribing documents, dating them, and identifying people, places, and events referred to in them. Establish chronology first, and, if you are alert enough, you have a chance of recognizing causality and significance; listen hard enough, and you may hope to catch elusive tones of voice. More than half a century ago, I learned that if you want to understand a family there is no substitute for listening quietly to women talking to each other for as long as they go on talking. Never setting myself to prove one point or another, I simply listened for many months as I transcribed Melville family letters, comparatively few of which are quoted from in this biography but all of which resonate in my mind. I emphasize this because Melville's niece Charlotte Hoadley also listened, many hours, to her mother and her aunts talking, while Melville's daughter Frances, who spent far less time around her Melville aunts and her Melville grandmother, later became the source of almost all family anecdotes.

A look backward to the first volume. At 1.179 my guess that Melville might have returned from Illinois in time to take a teaching job near Lansingburgh has been verified by Gansevoort Melville's letter to Allan Melville, 6 October 1840, deposited in the Berkshire Athenaeum by Paul and Nancy Metcalf in 1998. The date 1849 at 1.625 is corrected to 1850 at 2.66, as Walter D. Kring corrected it in Yannella and Parker (1981). The number of servants listed as 1.563 is corrected on 2.197; see Gretchko (1985). While reading Henry T. Tuckerman's *Book of the Artists* for this volume I realized that the friend of Shelley and Byron who visited Dr. John W. Francis (1.572) was the painter William Edward West (1788–1857). Hershel Parker and Harrison Hayford in the Revised Sesquicentennial Norton Critical Edition of *Moby-Dick* (2001) first published Geoffrey Sanborn's discovery that Melville based Queequeg on Tupai Cupa, a Maori described in George Lillie Craik's *The New Zealanders* (London: Charles Knight, 1830). Now any comments on the sequence of Melville's work on *Moby-Dick* (such as that at 1.723–24) must confront the likelihood that Melville had progressed some distance into his manuscript with Bulkington as Ishmael's special comrade before he picked up *The New Zealanders* and saw that he could construct strong scenes based on Tupai Cupa. In 1998 I saw that a word in Evert Duyckinck's 6 August 1850 letter to his wife was wrong in all printed texts (including 1.745): Hawthorne had not looked "mildly" about for his "Great Carbuncle" on Monument Mountain; the excited romancer had hammed it up for his new acquaintance Melville and the others, looking "wildly" about. For other corrections of Jay Leyda's 1951 *The Melville Log* see the notes at 292, 381, and 634, below.

Chapter-by-Chapter Documentation

[Ch. 1] Page 1: The "publication party" is based on an account by "Maherbal" in the Windsor (Vermont) *Journal*. See 1.898 for my several-year hunt which ended in Richard E. Winslow's discovery of a file of that newspaper. A moral for researchers: if I had not been looking in Lawrence papers for something I did not find, I would not have come upon the unknown "Maherbal" description of the Hawthorne cottage near Lenox and would not have started the search for the *Journal*. 5: For Melville's sketch of his uncle, see Sealts, "Thomas Melvill, Jr." (1987).

[Ch. 2] 31: The title: *Moby-Dick*, ch. 81. 33: See Dewey (1864); lectures were an asset, unpublished. 38: The definition of blasphemy is from Levy (1957), 44–45. 40: The contradiction is essentially Melvillean: emotionally an absolutist, in practice a relativist. 40: "great novelist": Maria to Augusta, 5 November 1850. 43: I was wrongly skeptical, in public, when Donald Yannella claimed Sarah Morewood had been obsessed with George Duyckinck; see "Biographers on Biography: A Panel Discussion" (237) in *Melville's Evermoving Dawn*, ed. John Bryant and Robert Milder (Kent: Kent State Univ. Press, 1997), 225–59.

[Ch. 3] 59: Two women: See 1.63–65. 63: "Preparatives" is the word in the 1852 table of contents, echoing "Misgivings"; the word in the title of the "book" is "Preparations." 66: Complaint: Dewey (1852).

[Ch. 4] 74: Charlotte Hoadley to V. H. Paltsits, 14 February 1944. 79: Lathers's *Reminiscences* (52) is the source for Duyckinck's speech mannerism.

[Ch. 5] 94: McKay & Hoadley: *Transactions of the American Society of Mechanical Engineers* 8 (1887). 100: In *Moby-Dick* (1039) is a facsimile of Allan Melville's transcription from the *Leader*.

[Ch. 6] 111: The "Report of the Committee" is printed in the NN *Piazza Tales* volume, 449–51. 111: Saplings: Sealts, "Sheaf" (1987), 285. 117: For Melville's memorandum of his meeting with Pollard, see *Moby-Dick*, 987–88. 118: Naushon register: *Log*, 453. 123: Powell as "English egotist": 1.647. 128: Sea air and ocean bathing did not work a cure: Josie's lameness turned into severe disability, to judge from Clare Spark's transcription (in *Hunting Captain Ahab*, 212) of Raymond Weaver's notes at Columbia on an interview with "Josephine MacK. Shaw" around 1920: "Cousin Josie: Deaf—coarse bobbed hair—walks with a hideous rocking—with strange straps and paraphanalia *[sic]* rattling under her skirt. Loathsome in appearance and as keen as an old Devil." Like her father, Josie hated Herman Melville (no word but "hated" will do); Frances Melville Thomas and Eleanor Thomas Metcalf, according to the latter's book on her grandfather, believed that Elizabeth Shaw Melville had made young Josie her confidante, but they did not specify the period in which they thought this special intimacy occurred.

[Ch. 7] 137: Tom later inscribed his *Life of Franklin Pierce* to a man named Thomas Bishop (Collection of Kent Bicknell). 142: Ferris: See McNeilly (1976). 142–43: Dana, *Journal*, 2.533. 145: Melville ran an errand for Sophia, delivering a gift to the Hawthornes' cook in Lenox, Mrs. Peters, accompanied by a letter from Una Hawthorne (3 December 1852) which explained that "Mr Melville will give it to Mr Steele to take to the Lenox Post office"; she added, "We do not know when Mr Melville will go home"—that is, from Boston. (Hayford's photocopy of the letter was from Samuel Sukel; Thomas E. Steele, of Lee, Massachusetts, was the "Express man," according to Ruth Degenhardt.) 150: In *Moby-Dick* see "Melville's *Acushnet* Crew Memorandum," 997–1004, and "The Hubbard Copy of *The Whale*," 1005–20. 153: As in chs. 15 and 20, most office-seeking letters are from Hayford's National Archives file assembled for the two-part Hayford and Davis study (1949). In this part of Lemuel Shaw to Caleb Cushing, 3 May 1853, Library of Congress-Cushing (Box 64), transcribed by Alma MacDougall Reising (and not in Hayford-Davis or the *Log*), the use of the past tense is striking: "Mr. Herman Melville is probably known to you through his literary productions, some of which were very popular, especially those which related to scenes & incidents in the Pacific. He resided some time in the Sandwich Islands. I think he would be quite competent to the duties of such an office, & would be especially useful at that great port for American Whalers." 154: Stoddard (1903). 157: "London": See *Journals*, 620–23. 159: George Peabody's hospitality to Lemuel Shaw and Peter Gansevoort is a discovery by Dennis Marnon from George Peabody Papers, Phillips Library, Peabody-Essex Museum, Salem, Mass., and Lemuel Shaw Papers, MHS, Boston, Mass.

[Ch. 8] 164: Rockwell: *Log*, 476. 173: Praise of locomotive: Undated clipping in the Berkshire Athenaeum, probably from the Lawrence *Courier* or *American*.

[Ch. 9] 190: Longwood, in suburban Brookline, was an early planned community; even when he became wealthy, Griggs rented, so that Helen never could become settled in her own house. 190: Gifts: In ch. 39 the "Victoria shawl" given to Helen by Sarah Morewood (according to Augusta's inventory) reappears as the " 'superfine' blanket shawl," an especially appropriate gift from Helen to her eldest niece, Milie, by then Mrs. William

Morewood—the wife of Sarah's older son. The Melvilles all lived out their lives amid objects precious because of associations—slept on them, looked at them, ate from them, wore them, carried them around. Objects treasured for associations with the dead acquired new associations in new generations. Beginning in 1846, Herman Melville carried the seal of his much-traveled father, the same seal which Gansevoort had inherited and carried to Jackson's Hermitage, Parliament in London, and Cambridge University. Before Melville was fifty that seal had been worn in the presence of Francis, Lord Jeffrey; the Earl of Leven and Melvill; Henry Clay; Andrew Jackson; James K. Polk; Washington Irving; Samuel Rogers; Nathaniel Hawthorne; Hiram Powers; Abraham Lincoln; and Ulysses S. Grant, as well as assorted forgers, publishers, and reviewers.

[Ch. 10] 218: Brown: Matthew Hale Smith (1868), 39. 219: "Tartarus": See 1.810 and in this volume, illus. 8. 228: hard use of the book: The judgment of Dennis Marnon. 232: In November 1854 Augusta copied Henry Ware's "Testimony of Conscience" into her *Orient Pearls*.

[Ch. 11] 243: Greene's lectures: Hayes (1994). 246: Tuckerman (1866), xlii. 246: Frederick Law Olmsted may have bought into *Putnam's Monthly* with Joshua A. Dix in March 1855, according to Witold Rybczynski in *A Clearing in the Distance* (New York: Scribner, 1999), 134.

[Ch. 12] 261: In the mid–twentieth century Mabel C. Weaks saw this album, and later told Dr. Henry A. Murray that Melville had written in it "Tell Truth and shame the dead"—a formulation that Murray, not recognizing the allusion to Shakespeare (as he acknowledged to me), took as supporting his view of Melville's attitude toward his father. Merton M. Sealts Jr. and Harrison Hayford later agreed with me that Miss Weaks must have misread Melville's handwriting, for he habitually spelled "devil" with no "i" ("devel") and habitually formed the letters "vel" in such a way that they could be read as "ed." 261: Thoroughly magazinish, Curtis said of "I and My Chimney," probably written during this sciatic attack. The Yale scholars who did dissertations under Professor Stanley T. Williams starting in the late 1930s came to regard some of the stories Melville wrote between *Pierre* and *The Confidence-Man* as almost pathological in their secrecy, innocuous enough to be palmed on Melville's genteel publishers and their readers but concealing outrageous religious, sexual, and mock-autobiographical allegories. In *Pursuing Melville* (1982) Merton M. Sealts Jr. looked back on his early reading of "I and My Chimney" as a disguised account of the medical examination of Melville by Dr. Holmes. (The unnamed "individual" who triggered Sealts's study by responding so sensitively to the story in 1940 [174] was Walter E. Bezanson.) Also see *Pursuing Melville* (172) for Elizabeth Shaw Melville's marginal comments in the magazine printing: "All this about his wife, applied to his mother—who was very vigorous and energetic about the farm, etc. The proposed removal of the chimney is purely mythical." 261: "taciturn man": See Parker and Hayford (1970), 141–42, from *Holmes-Pollock Letters*, ed. Mark DeWolfe Howe (Cambridge: Harvard Univ. Press, 1941), 2.68. 265: Marian Chitty's notes: Typescript in Leyda files in my possession. 265: Kurt Bell, through James Alexander Jr. and Alex Liddie, explains that the railroad from 1855 until March 1865 was called the Saratoga & Whitehall; then it became part of the Rensselaer & Saratoga Rail Road, so that its name, like the name of the village, was a standing source of family pride to the descendants of the Van Rensselaers, that old established family in the land. In 1871 the road became part of the Delaware & Hudson.

[Ch. 13] 277: I found Powell's "Ambrotype" on Robert Browning and others in the series while hunting for, and finding, a review of *Piazza Tales;* I stopped looking too soon, and later Steven Olsen-Smith found the essay on Melville which Powell had revised from its appearance in *Figaro!* 284: Carol Borchert found advertisements in the New York *Tribune* quoting the New York *Criterion*, a periodical previously unknown to Melville scholars. In it the Duyckincks seem to have been pursuing their old obsession to create "an able and independent Literary and Critical Journal." 285: Pittsfield Valuation Books: My 1962 notes, when these records were in the basement of Pittsfield City Hall. 285: Lion G. Miles found these mortgages in the Berkshire County Middle Registry at the County Records Office in Pittsfield. 288: See 599 for a family excursion a decade later, at the same season. 292: In the *Log* Leyda misread "sensation" as "vacation." 292: Passport and accompanying letters: Olsen-Smith and Parker (1995).

[Ch. 14] 295: This chapter is built primarily on passages in *Journals*, vol. 15 of the NN Edition, edited by Howard C. Horsford with Lynn Horth.

[Ch. 15] 321: Like the previous one, this chapter is constructed largely from passages in the NN *Journals.* 329: The miniature scenes in cases were by the Sicilian Zummo; Melville may not have realized that some of the larger figures were by Clemente Susini and others. 338: In addition to Gaskell's biography, competing for space in London papers were Charlotte Brontë's *The Professor,* George Borrow's *Romany Rye,* and Anthony Trollope's *Barchester Towers.* 343: Josie: Spark (2001), 299, quoting a "lurid" entry in a notebook kept by Charles Olson, shakily based on notes from Raymond Weaver.

[Ch. 16] 351: Stephen Higginson Tyng Jr. (1800–1885), the Episcopalian minister, was a socially correct choice: "From Philadelphia to the old Beekman Street Church of St. George came Dr. Tyng. A large salary has enabled him to live in good style. He rides in his carriage, owns valuable real estate, and is wealthy" (Matthew Hale Smith [1868], 33). When the former literary pilgrim Dr. Titus Munson Coan asked "Does Life-Insurance Insure?" in the January 1881 *Harper's New Monthly Magazine*, Dr. Tyng, ignoring Jesus' words in Matthew 6:34, reassured the insurance companies in the April issue that "Life-Assurance Does Assure." The "heart" (*Journals*, 29) revealed by Coan in this debate may have been one reason that Melville was willing, late in life, to receive visits from him. 353: Details about the lawsuits over the Gansevoort, N.Y., property are from Kenney (1969), 206–10. 354: The contract is in the Massachusetts Historical Society, Lemuel Shaw Collection; see Barber (1973). 354: Details about Stewart were provided by the Lansingburgh historian Frances D. Broderick. 356: Melville's name was not in the partial list of lecturers (the *Tribune*, 18 September) but was in the full list on 25 September (Colin Dewey, correcting the "October" cited in *The Piazza Tales*, 517). Dewey also found that the *Tribune* ran Phillips, Sampson ads for the new *Atlantic Monthly*, with Melville listed as a prospective contributor, on various dates, such as 19 and 26 September and 3 and 10 October 1857. 357: Under a picture of the Gurrnsey Power Printing Press "traced and engraved from a Daguerreotype," the Lawrence *Courier* (13 April 1855) printed an enthusiastic article on the "Lawrence Machine Shop—.its Products, &c." 363: Photocopies from this scrapbook, now at the Lawrence Public Library, were provided by Frederick J. and Joyce Deveau Kennedy. The keeper of the scrapbook made a number of corrections on the clipping about Melville's lecture, some if not all from Hoadley himself. 365: The Irvington lithograph is reproduced as illus. 10 in this volume. 366: Thanksgiving: On 20 November 1857, from Dorchester, grieving over the death of his wife, Maria, Captain John ("Mad Jack") Percival declined an invitation from Shaw for Thanksgiving Day: "My mind is broken and intellects shattered, yet there is I trust sufficient glimmering of light left to appreciate you and express my gratitude for your innumerable acts of kindness conferred by you and Mrs Shaw, to whom with the rest of your family give my warmest wishes for their happiness." Percival, a favorite of Helen's, may have seen Melville on unrecorded occasions in this decade. 368: Melville in Montreal: Frederick J. Kennedy (1977). 373: Mark Wojnar identified Liberty Hall as the site of the meetings of the New Bedford Lyceum.

[Ch. 17] 380: In "The Panama Railroad" in *Harper's New Monthly Magazine* (January 1859) Melville may have seen the account of deaths of many hundreds of workers—Irishmen, "Coolies from Hindostan; Chinamen from China," English, French, Germans, and Austrians; dead Irishmen and Frenchmen were said to have been "replenished" by "freshly imported" countrymen of the dead. A living contemporary of the Erie Canal, Melville understood that the Hoosic Tunnel, like the Panama Railroad, was making a straight path between Massachusetts and the Erie Canal and the railroad tracks paralleling it to the west, to become part of the "interoceanic" railroad that a decade after the Civil War moved freight speedily to California and made that state an almost convenient vacation spot for wealthy and sufficiently enterprising Easterners and Europeans. 381: In "fine looking as ever" the last word begins with the then-common initial "e" that looks much like "E." For the 1951 *Log* Jay Leyda transcribed the word as "Evert"—not thinking of how slight were the frames of the Duyckinck brothers. 382: This belief about tuberculosis is recorded in *Their Own Voices: Oral Accounts of Early Settlers in Washington County, New York* (Interlaken, N.Y.: Heart of the Lakes Publishing, 1983), 141, collected by Dr. Asa Fitch, ed. Winston Adler (a gift to me from Virginia Barden). 382: I tracked Jane Dempsey Melville in family letters in the Gansevoort-Lansing Collection of the New York Public Library and in 1890 and 1891 newspapers, and Mort Engstrom helped with the related history of George Dillaway; otherwise the details about her (including her marriage, motherhood, inheritance, and divorce) and about Dillaway are from the ongoing researches of John M. J. Gretchko. 384: Sarah Morewood continued: "Rowland's health has greatly improved and he very seldom complains even of a head ache, but I cannot get him to leave off the vile weed tobacco—he is a moderate smoker only using segars three times a day" ("tobacco" underlined twice). Of the characters in this biography, only Sophia Hawthorne objected strenuously to smoking inside her house. Men smoked. The Melvilles and the Gansevoorts smoked, Hoadley and Griggs smoked, the Shaws smoked. The women made no complaints; indeed, her father's inveterate smoking predisposed Lizzie to think she should encourage Herman's smoking. No one associated tobacco with Shaw's and Lizzie's allergies. After Melville smoked himself to death before his time (as any good twenty-first-century doctor would say), his son-in-law inherited, treasured, and smoked his pipes. Tobacco was the herba santa. See Metcalf (1953), 216. 392: This 12 February 1859 letter to G. W. Curtis was auctioned at Sotheby's New York sale 7332 on 22 June 1999. 396: *The Diary of Orville Hickman Browning*, 1 (1850–1864), ed. Theodore Calvin Pease and James G. Randall (Springfield: Illinois State Historical Library, 1925).

[Ch. 18] 413: *British Essayists:* Duyckinck's notation means that Melville borrowed selected items from Alexander Chalmers's 45-volume *The British Essayists with Prefaces Historical and Biographical* (London: J. Johnson, J. Nichols & Son, R. Baldwin, 1803), a reprinting of many eighteenth-century periodicals, among them the *Tatler, Idler, Rambler, Spectator,* and *Observer.* 413: Peabody: This episode was worked out by Dennis Marnon, who first saw the significance for Melville of Peabody's paying for the Peabody Institute, South Danvers, where Melville lectured. At the end of February the chairman of the lecture committee, Thomas M. Stimpson, complained that people had stayed away because the furnace had not kept "the Hall comfortable in cold weather"; Chris Coughlin, from the Peabody Institute Library, "Eighth Annual Report of the Trustees of the Peabody Institute Library of Danvers." 414: The decline of Bond Street is from Tuckerman (1866); confirming details are in Lathers's *Reminiscences*, 40. 414: John Gretchko discovered the records of Jane Dempsey Randolph's property. For the Pittsfield Valuation Book, see note at 285 above. 417: Sale of several acres: Discovered by Mandy Victor. 420: Dennis Marnon provided strategically varied photocopies of the difficult "two laureates" passage from HCL MS Am 188 (386.A.3).

[Ch. 19] 432: Drawing of Arrowhead: Melville's "magic power" had always been verbal; this specimen of his skill in the visual arts is known only by Raymond Weaver's reproduction (itself reproduced in this volume, illus. 13): Eleanor Metcalf never received it back after loaning it to him to be reproduced in his 1921 biography of Melville. 434: Before Melville's father's copy of Spenser was located, Thomas Heffernan (1977), on the basis of an exact quotation from Spenser which Melville wrote into his Wordsworth, correctly guessed that Melville had a copy of Spenser with him. 442: Umi is also named as "a rival king" by James Jackson Jarves in his *History of the Hawaiian or Sandwich Islands* (Boston: Tappan & Dennet, 1843) in an ugly passage about king "Huakau," one of the "Caligulas" being described. 443: Melville did not want to be included in a "blue and gold" series like D. Appleton's (which published Bryant's poems in 1854) or especially the Ticknor & Fields series (blue cloth, die stamped in blind on boards, gilt stamped on spines, all edges gilt, stocky at 5⅝ by 3¾ inches), which included Longfellow in 1857 and Whittier in 1858. 444: Mandy Victor saw the significance of the Register of the Red Lion Inn in Stockbridge and supplied a photocopy of this entry. 446: Either Melville bought Mackay in San Francisco or turned to reading it belatedly, after carrying it around the Horn; King's lecture is in his posthumous *Substance and Show*, 385. "Books and Reading," according to the editor, Edwin P. Whipple, "had an extraordinary popularity in every city and town in California where it was delivered" (354); it contains no mention of Melville. 450: While tracking the *Derby*, Colin Dewey found the name of the Monterey sloop *Fayaway*; throughout Melville's lifetime, Fayaway was his most famous character. 451: See Haskell (1943) for reproductions of the poster and a lithograph of the *Cortes*.

[Ch. 20] 456: Thomas Heffernan loaned me his NA pension records of the First Illinois Light Infantry—miserable reading. 457: Shaw's declining the Bell-Everett nomination is in Levy (1957), 107. 458: O'Conor's speech is in Lathers's *Reminiscences*, 92–101. 464: Dana had been enthusiastic about Melville in his 10 May 1853 letter to Allan Melville. As in ch. 7, I use Hayford's set of National Archives documents and Hayford and Davis (1949). 470: Calcott: John Wall Collcott, the English composer. 475: 6 May 1861 report of Commodore S. L. Breese: Garner (1993), 101, 471 (quoted from "Letters Received from Navy Yards, Navy Yard New York," National Archives). 475: Buntline: Robert Pepper supplied these printed comments on the hard-drinking Gansevoort brothers and Judson. 478: Information about the inhabitants of Gansevoort, N.Y., is from J. H. French's *Historical and Statistical Gazetteer of New York State* (Syracuse: R. P. Smith, 1860 [for 1861]).

[Ch. 21] 485: Tuckerman's deafness and studio: Duyckinck (1872). 485: The Leavitt catalog of the 10–14 June 1873 auction in Clinton Hall of Tuckerman books and art works survives in the American Antiquarian Society. 495: The Hazlitt *Lectures* are in the collection of William S. Reese. 504: Melville used "Good-Enough-Morgan" in *The Confidence-Man* (ch. 9). Masons were accused of murdering William Morgan (1774?–1826?) after he disappeared from Canandaigua, N.Y.; when a body was found in the Niagara River, the anti-Masonic Thurlow Weed, a recurrent figure in this biography, called the body "a good-enough Morgan" until the Masons produced the real one, and the press improved the formula to "good-enough Morgan until after the election." (Weed's *Autobiography* [Boston: Houghton Mifflin, 1883], 1.319.)

[Ch. 22] 506: Southern papers: Such losses weaken all historical scholarship. I have searched every known extant Savannah newspaper for Oakey Hall's 1850 letters, variants (not duplicates) of the letters to the New Orleans *Commercial Bulletin* in which he gave unique information about Melville. 506: Allan Melville's subscriptions: When a mass of newspapers Allan Melville had subscribed to and saved turned up for sale near Albany in 1986, the State Librarian James Corsaro examined them and sent me some photocopies; I later examined some of the papers at the *Sword and Saber*, the Civil War shop at Gettysburg, and bought the few I could afford. The known surviving papers are not mutilated (as they might have been if Herman Melville had clipped items that he later wrote poems about); but any mutilated papers would have been discarded as of no value to collectors of Civil War newspapers, a puristic lot. 507: The Mansion House at Gansevoort: In this generalizing I use letters Augusta Melville received in 1863 from her sisters Frances and Helen, from Lizzie, from Stanwix Melville, and from others, now in the Gansevoort-Lansing Collection of the New York Public Library, as well as the great trove of letters written by the Melvilles, including Maria, to Uncle Peter's daughter, Catherine Gansevoort, who preserved them. Many of these letters are specifically quoted in this chapter and the following ones. 514: Almy to Wise: Garner (1993), 146, 477 n. 50. 518:

Guert Gansevoort's will: Garner (1993), 166. 518: For the Order of the Cincinnati, see Sealts, "Cincinnati Badge" (1987). 518: DuPont on Guert's alcoholism; Guert's court-martial: Garner (1993), 170–71.

[Ch. 23] 525: Lawrence *Sentinel:* Chris Coughlin discovered this article. 526: The "immense business" is described by Everett S. Allen in *Children of the Light* (Boston: Little, Brown, 1973), 110. Allen quotes from Edward King's 1871 letters to the Boston *Journal* and from *New Bedford, Massachusetts: Its History, Industries, Institutions, and Attractions* (New Bedford Board of Trade, 1889). 529: Envelope with piece of cloth: Berkshire Athenaeum. 530: "War-prices": Helen to Augusta, 25 February 1863. The more or less reliable Pittsfield Valuation Book (nominally dated 5 August 1863) showed a shift in taxable assets for the Melvilles. In 1862 they had been taxed on a dwelling worth $600, a barn worth $200, and eighty acres worth $3200, an aggregate value of real estate valued at $4000; now that had been sold to Allan Melville for $3000. In 1862 they were shown as possessing a horse (valued at $50 for tax purposes, not the exorbitant sum Stannie had named), and three carriages (including the old lumber wagon?); in 1863 they were shown with one carriage and no horse. The 1862 valuation showed $1500 cash; the 1863 valuation no cash. 530: Warranty deed: Berkshire Athenaeum. 532: Allan Melvill on his son Allan as a bedmate: 1.36, from Melvill to Peter Gansevoort, 26 September 1826. 533: Arithmetic: Lizzie to Augusta, 11 February 1863. 538–39: See the memorial volume: *Celebration of the Semi-Centennial Anniversary of the Albany Academy* (Albany: J. Munsell, 1863). 542: The chief regional paper, the Springfield *Republican,* as well as New York City papers, provided extensive coverage of the Draft Riots, the subject of Melville's poem "The House-top." It was Uncle Peter's old friend John A. Dix whom President Lincoln assigned to restore order.

[Ch. 24] 544: epigraph: Dennis Marnon provided this passage in advance of his publication of this newly discovered letter. 545: Jay Leyda, Stanton Garner, and I consulted on Hoadley's handwriting in this letter until we agreed on all essentials. 547: The patient, persistent Johannes D. Bergmann was allowed to see the mutilated Milo Smith register in 2000; "autograph fiends" had attacked it more than a century earlier (see Bryan [1993], 145). 548: The "arches" (erected early): Lizzie to Augusta (16 August).

[Ch. 25] 560: Tuckerman (1867), 301. Mary Alice Mackay provided a photocopy of the *Catalogue of Painting and Sculpture, Exhibited at Palmer's Studio, in aid of the United States Sanitary Commission, February 22, 1864* (Albany: van Benthuysen's Steam Printing House, 1864.) (This company had produced the engraving of Hoadley's Irvington.) 560: Robert Hewson Pruyn's wife was a Lansing whose mother had been a Ten Eyck, a family akin to the Gansevoorts in various ways. 561: East room: Clipping at the Berkshire Athenaeum from an unidentified Albany paper, "Last Gansevoort Descendant Dies/Mrs. Catherine Lansing Lived in One House Nearly All Her Life—tribute by Mrs. William Gorham Rice." 562: The originals of the "Autograph Leaves" are at the Humanities Research Center in Austin, Texas. 563: Pass: Berkshire Athenaeum. 564: Jones's ownership of Sharon: Dennis Marnon. 571: Morgan: See note to 504 above. 580: The *Harper's Weekly* commentary on "Compromise with the South" (supplied by Mort Engstrom) continues: "The powerful picture of Mr. Nast's, which we print this week, shows at a glance the condition which compromise presupposes. Those who urge it represent the friends of the Union as in this condition of the Northern soldier in the picture, utterly defeated, crippled, and crushed; while by letters in their papers and by the mouths of their orators they depict the Rebellion as rather more stalwart, vigorous, and victorious than ever. And again, when compromise shall come, the consequence to the North will be the total prostration represented in the picture. For compromise with armed rebellion is abject submission." 581: Henry Sanford Gansevoort's capturing of Mosby equipment: Hoadley (1875), 182–83. 582: note to Sheridan: Mosby (1917), 302–3. 583: Richard E. Winslow found in the 28 December 1900 Portsmouth (N.H.) *Herald* a quotation from *Our Animal Friends:* "Herman Melville, Buchanan Read and many other writers have made this horse the subject of poems, and several sculptors and painters have delineated him in marble and on canvas. On every returning Memorial day many aged survivors of Sheridan's Shenandoah troopers who remember the services of this 'Steed as black as the steeds of night' cross over to Governors island museum and place floral memorials on the glass case that contains all that remains of Winchester." Since Winchester died in October 1878, Melville may well have visited him, stuffed, on Governor's Island; this was his idea of a good exhibit.

[Ch. 26] 586: Pew rent: Walter D. Kring, in Yannella and Parker (1981), 12. 587: Richard E. Winslow was the first to realize that the Peterson issue of *The Refugee* was widely reviewed and to hunt for notices of it; after Higgins and Parker (1995), he also discovered many notices of Melville's others works, especially in provincial New England papers. 587: Lizzie's clipping labeled "Fraud": Harvard College Library–Melville Collection (provided by Dennis Marnon). 588: 1876: The dating of Melville's letter to the *World* (see *Correspondence*, 538), is a new discovery by Steven Olsen-Smith and Todd Richardson (2002). 588: A record by the witness mentioned by Hemstreet, or another of the "hearers," may languish in an extant newspaper (most likely the *Tribune*, given Greeley's love of the Cary sisters' bright drawing room). 590: "fork": Metcalf (1953), 211. 593: Mort Engstrom established from reviews that Henry T. Tuckerman's long-planned new edition of Dr. John

Wakefield Francis's *Old New York* was published early in 1866. 596: Moran's diary: *Log*, 680. 599: Marital woes: See Kring and Carey (1975) and Yannella and Parker (1981). 600: Indenture: Berkshire Athenaeum. 603–4: Oaths: National Archives. 604: In his *Recollections* Stoddard continued: "Whether any of Melville's readers understood the real drift of his mind, or whether he understood it himself, has often puzzled me. Next to Emerson he was the American mystic. He was one of our great unrecognized poets."

[Ch. 27] 606: Because the dating of Melville's Civil War poems is not precisely established, Stanton Garner in *The Civil War World of Herman Melville* (1993) sensibly discussed the poems in the chronology of the battles they deal with. 607: Bertrand Mathieu (1976) identified these verbal echoes of Milton before Melville's copy of Milton was known; likewise on the basis of internal evidence, Henry F. Pommer had written his fine *Milton and Melville* (Pittsburgh: Univ. of Pittsburgh Press, 1950). 619: Melville's early books, especially *Mardi*, were often said to be written in poetic prose, as in the joint review of *Mardi* ("a prose poem in style"), Longfellow's prose *Kavanagh*, and Arthur Hugh Clough's poetic *The Bothie of Topper na Fuosich* in the New Bedford *Mercury* (8 June 1849), discovered by Mark Wojnar.

[Ch. 28] 626: Ristori: *Log*, 685. 626: After I saw the tooth in a display case at the New-York Historical Society, Leyda had it photographed for the 1969 *Log*, 949. 628: The hunt for these colossal hands has been led by librarian Paul Cyr and independent scholar Mark Wojnar, allied with Robert Lovering of the New Bedford *Standard-Times:* ideally, a picture of it would have balanced the picture in volume 1 of the flag made for Gansevoort Melville by the ladies of Nashville. 631: Melville's behavior toward his wife: Spark (2001, 216–17) quotes Eleanor Metcalf to Henry A. Murray (26 May 1926): "In the abusive periods he never used low language to her, nor did his exclamations express disappointment. She had an unpleasant habit of dropping her soiled handkerchief about the house. He would pick it up & give it back to her, calling it by some disgusting name which Mother absolutely refused to repeat." Since she suffered for months each year from her "rose cold" (at times wrapping her head in a towel), Elizabeth Shaw Melville had occasion to drop many a handkerchief. Handing one to her, Melville did not always say something as sweet as, for example, "Could this snowflake be yours, my dear?" Spark's quotations suggest that Eleanor Metcalf played up to Murray's questionings, as if titillated by seeing her grandfather emerge from Raymond Weaver's biography as an international figure of Freudian gothicism. 634: 8 May 1867: Leyda printed this in the *Log* in 1869, misled by Lizzie's tiny loop at the end of the left side of the top of the 7. Another moral for the researcher: dated correctly, the letter becomes dramatic evidence. 635: See 507–9. This depiction of the Mansion House draws on letters from different years in the Gansevoort-Lansing Collection of the New York Public Library as well as the inventory (in the Berkshire Athenaeum) prepared by Augustus Peebles two decades later. 644: Osgood: Evert and George Duyckinck's *Cyclopædia*, 2.572; Matthew Hale Smith (1868), 578. 648: Lathers's drawing: Located at Arrowhead; reproduced in Cohen (1994), 28. 649: Dennis Marnon pointed out to me that the words are not from one of Faber's hymns, as sometimes stated. 649: See Humphreys (1918, facing 306) for a photograph of Bartlett.

[Ch. 29] 651: On the Harbor the basic book is Barnett Shepherd's (1995). 654: 1877 and 1880 letters: Here and later, I quote Thomas Melville's draft letters, diaries, Quarterly Reports, and letters to him from records moved from the Sailors' Snug Harbor to the Maritime College. 660: Piranesi: Lathers, *This Discursive Biographical Sketch*, 82. 667: Rich Mauro discovered this item in the *Dispatch*. 667: Melville was back in debt to the Harpers because, avaricious and disdainful as always, they had charged half the expenses of printing *Battle-Pieces* against his account rather than paying expenses up front and waiting to recoup their investment; this circumstance may account for the claim in Exman (1967, 98) that Melville subsidized the edition.

[Ch. 30] 676: Margaret Morewood's description: Arrowhead. 677: Melville wrote a poem, "Iris," about Rachel Pond after her early death. 681: Margaret Morewood's brother Henry Gansevoort Morewood made these notes (now at Arrowhead) in 1972: "'Abby Lodge' was built in the form of a small European Castle. I recall that it held a music room with a sky-blue ceiling. The slope was terraced with stone and covered with flowers. It had a beautiful view, unobstructed, of the western [eastern] mountains, as the site has today, right down to the railroad track." 681: Bessie's bad health surfaces in the surviving letters in 1875; her hands are severely crippled by 1879. 686: Melville had praised Whittier in the manuscript form of his essay on "Hawthorne and His Mosses." 686: Leon Howard: *Herman Melville*, 290. 689: This allusion to mythical flowering of the aloe every hundred years is, like so much in Melville, a curious mixture of family history and American history. On 13 July 1846, the summer of *Typee* and the resurrection of Toby, the Albany *Evening Journal*, three columns away from "Toby's Own Story," reprinted an article on the century plant from the Boston *Journal* and added that one of these rare plants "was seen, in all its glory, a few years" before, in Stephen Van Rensselaer's garden, exciting interest and attracting thousands of visitors. Even on the Island of St. Croix, where they were abundant, few "were as tall as that in the Patroon's."

[Ch. 31] 690: I thank John B. Putnam and Norman Brouwer for reading a draft of this chapter and Putnam for a photocopy of the *Custom House Sou-*

venir of the Port of New York (1893–1894), quoted (beginning on 693) on duties of inspectors. For a contemporary map of New York City, see vol. 1 (illus. 48 and 49). 701: Bezanson: *Clarel*, 598. 709: The 1870 *Bird's Eye View of Charleston* showed the mansion with the mansard roof complete; the view from the house: Charleston *News and Courier* (5 August 1870). At year's end, on 7 December 1870, Richard Lathers purchased a small portion of the remaining Arrowhead property from Allan Melville (he had some need of a plot on the other side of the road from Abby Lodge and a little south of it). Mandy Victor provided this information. 710: See Sealts (1982), 100, for Charles Olson's examining the Warton in the Brooklyn Public Library in the 1930s; Melville's markings in the Warton (now at Harvard): e-mail to me from Dennis Marnon. 710: Brooks's note is from the foreword to *The American Writer in England: An Exhibition* (Charlottesville: Univ. Press of Virginia, 1969). Louis Becke in his "Introduction" to *Moby-Dick* (London: G. P. Putnam's Sons, 1901), ix–xii (obtained for me by Richard Colles Johnson from the only known surviving copy, in the British Museum), recalled from around 1870 the occasion when a "sweet, dainty, little English lady" came aboard a trading schooner at Apia in the Samoan Islands: "I have brought you some books," she said to our grizzled old captain; "and among them are three volumes by an American writer—Herman Melville. It is called 'The Whale,' and it is the strangest, wildest, and saddest story I have ever read." The Scottish captain read the volumes aloud to the crew, Becke recalled: "And although he would stop now and again, and enter into metaphysical matters, we forgave him, for we knew that he too, like us, was fascinated with mad Captain Ahab and brave mate Starbuck and the rest of the ill-fated crew of the 'Pequod.'" (Reprinted in Parker and Higgins, 1992.) 711: *The Letters of Dante Gabriel Rossetti*, ed. Oswald Doughty and John Robert Wahl (Oxford: Oxford Univ. Press, 1965), 2.917.

[Ch. 32] 715: Dennis Berthold called my attention to this exhibition of the painting of Melville. 716: "Savages": Richardson (1998). 718: Bayard Tuckerman, *The Tuckerman Family* (Boston: Privately Printed, 1914), 170. 719: Quarterly Report to the Board of Trustees (18 December 1871): Maritime College. 722: Melville's $50 debt to Allan is from Thomas Melville's 26 May 1873 account, as executor, of the "Estate of Allan Melville" (Berkshire Athenaeum); by then Herman Melville had repaid the estate. 722: Thomas Arnold: photocopies from Dennis Marnon. 724: Bezanson: *Clarel*, 619.

[Ch. 33] 736: Melvin G. Holli (1999) calls Hall "a front man for the infamous Tweed Ring that fleeced the city of millions of dollars in ill-gotten booty and ran one of the most scandal-ridden and corrupt administrations in the nation's history." Melville would have seen many of Thomas Nast's savage depictions of Hall in *Harper's Weekly*. Hall's significance as a cultural critic awaits the republication of his essays, especially the letters he wrote over a several-year period to the New Orleans *Commercial Bulletin* during Melville's early career. 736: Merton M. Sealts Jr., who justifiably prided himself on his prudence and method, swore that while reading the bound copies of the Boston *Post* at the Boston Athenæum, for the period after Allan Melville's death early in 1872, he encountered an article about some crooked financial dealings of Allan's; he failed to write the date down, went to lunch, and never could find the article again. Harrison Hayford agreed with me that if Sealts said the Boston *Post* he meant the *Post*. I devoted days to pursuing this scholarly will-o'-the-wisp, at first trying to read badly washed-out microfilm; then I dispatched Hayford, Steven Olsen-Smith, Dan Lane, and Chris Coughlin to the Boston Athenæum, and went myself. I gained useful information from the quest (such as the Boston *Post* description of North Conway, N.H.) but what Sealts saw remains unlocated. 741: "funnel": Charles H. Farnham, "A Day on the Docks," *Scribner's* (May 1879), 46. 744: Mabel Abbott's 1932 notes are in the Staten Island Institute of Arts and Sciences. 746: Margaret Morewood: Notes on Abby Lodge, Arrowhead. 752: Jane being Jane, she charged the girls for the lockets: after all, Allan was their father, and they got to keep the lockets. 753: Katie Melville White: Metcalf (1953), 215.

[Ch. 34] 757: Melville's timidity: See "The Jones Copy of *Moby-Dick* and the Harper *Whale* Title Page," *Moby-Dick*, 1021–43. 761: Executor's report on the "Estate of Allan Melville" (Berkshire Athenaeum). 769: Cenci for Augusta's room: Fragment of a letter from Frances Priscilla Melville to Augusta, before Christmas, 1873.

[Ch. 35] 774: Commanding "a grand vista of the harbor from Sandy Hook past the Narrows to Fort Hamilton in Brooklyn," according to *New York 1880* (1004), St. Paul's Memorial Church was "trimmed in Connecticut brownstone, with dark gray traprock walls and polished granite dwarf columns capped by naturalistically carved foliated capitals." Stern, Mellins, and Fishman (1999) accompany their description with a photograph (1003). 775: Mrs. Allan Melville: Anna Morewood, the daughter-in-law of the bride (yes, Milie, born in 1849), told me that Milie and her sisters referred to their stepmother as "Mrs. Dempsey," denying her the proper title of Mrs. Allan Melville. Anna Morewood got the story second or third hand: what the high Episcopalian Milie and her sisters called their wicked stepmother must have been "Mrs. Randolph." To keep this narrative taut I have perforce ignored some of Jane's more appalling behavior. 780: Laments: See in Hawthorne's *The American Claimant Manuscripts*, 58, 200, 230, 269, 286, 323, 327. 781: "scared": *Clarel*, 600; "tournament": *Clarel*, 601. 782: Lathrop, 1890: *Log*,

745. 787: This "Appendix" was a two-part tribute to the late Susan Gansevoort, by K[ate] and by A[nna] P[arker] P[ruyn].

[Ch. 36] 791: The *World:* See note to 588 above. 794: Melville in the "new light": Frances Melville Thomas to Eleanor Metcalf, 17 May 1926; quoted in Spark (2001, 215). 798: Turkey carpet: Helen to Kate Gansevoort Lansing, 25 October 1878; see 835. 799: Lizzie's badgering: Sealts, "Sheaf" (1987), 285–86. 802: Hoadley's copy is now in the William S. Reese Collection. 802: For the Black Kettle Massacre see Stan Hoig, *The Battle of the Washita* (Lincoln: Univ. of Nebraska Press, 1979), 124. 802: "Ganny": Elizabeth Shaw Melville to Kate Gansevoort Lansing, 21 June 1876. 806: Custer crowding out the Centenary: The Boston *Daily Advertiser* of 6 July 1876 gives visual proof, with "THE CENTENARY. Observance of the Day in Boston and Its Vicinity" off to the left of the page, news of Custer conspicuously in the middle. (Provided by Chris Coughlin.) 808: In 1876 and later, Melville understood the Statue of Liberty as Bartholdi intended, a reminder of France's aid to the colonies during the Revolutionary War. In 1883, with a single short poem, "The New Colossus," an outgrowth of her recent work with immigrants from Russia, the New York and Newport poet Emma Lazarus appropriated the statue, before it was completed, as a symbol of America's hospitality to the world's refugees. 808: Hoadley's medal: Clipping from a Lawrence paper (Berkshire Athenaeum). 809: *"ultra":* Kate Gansevoort to Henry Sanford Gansevoort, 14 July 1865.

[Ch. 37] 819: Mary L. D. Ferris: McNeilly (1976). 821: On 3 June 1964 J. J. Boies with his friend Larry Naustrop (an old Danish "Snug"—Snug Harborite) found Duyckinck's four watercolors, each approximately four feet wide by three feet high, in gilded frames, hanging in the "B" House at the Harbor: *The Attack at Sunset,* numbered paper tag 56; *10 O'clock at Night,* #57; *Near Midnight,* #58; *The Ensuing Morning,* #55 (numbered out of chronological sequence). Boies noted the present state of the watercolors as very bad. They were all still covered with glass, but they were stained, darkened, torn, and cracked. (Photocopy of Boies's notes, in Leyda papers in my possession.) 822: Clinton Place: Lathers's *Reminiscences,* 53 . 824: Interviewer: Minna Littmann, "Edgartown Finds New Link with Melville," New Bedford *Sunday Standard* (11 August 1929); Eleanor Metcalf's memory: Metcalf (1953), 251. 825: Dillaway: Titus Munson Coan's papers in the New-York Historical Society indicate some knowledge of Dillaway's entanglement with Jane. Coan knew much but got some details wildly wrong, as in the fantasy that "Grandpa went up the Hudson, got a schooner and went sailing with a British flag waving," in support of England's pro-Southern stance (Spark [2001], 214, quoting Eleanor Metcalf to Frances Melville Thomas, 28 September 1919). 828: "Bouton Robinson": *Log,* 767. 828: The revised edition of

Frank Luther Mott's *American Journalism*, 374–78, makes clear that the editor of the *Sun*, Charles Dana, saw Davis's rant as just the thing he wanted to print. *New York 1880* depicts many of the structures which so offended Davis; they did not necessarily offend Melville. 829: Burgundy Club: These pieces, all in the Harvard College Library Melville Collection, are described here from Sandberg's 1989 dissertation. 830: Personal worth: See in the New York *Herald* (15 July 1883) the speculation about the non-alcoholic gatherings around William Curtis's wood fire in his hotel in Lenox: "$60,000,000 of capital" was "represented in those who go there for an evening's chat." 831: Madison Square was becoming Monument Square. As depicted in an illustration (57) in this volume, the hand holding the torch was displayed in Madison Square Park, which Melville frequented. See the photograph in Stern, Mellins, and Fishman (1999), 377. 834: "Parthenope": facsimile in *Log*, 741. 835: These papers are all at Harvard College Library; the summary of the unpleasant comments on Gentian's decline is quoted from Sandberg (1989), 435. 836: Mrs. Marett: See 1.79. Melville would have remembered that Mr. Marett's men had come to his widowed mother's door, demanding money. 837: Oatmeal: Taped recollections; Metcalf (1953), 216, says "oatmeal or hominy." 839: Loan to Stanwix: Kate Gansevoort Lansing to Abraham Lansing, 7 April 1879. 839: Cousin Harry Crosby: Wolff (1976). 840: "cottage": Milie, as Mrs. Morewood, now summered at Broadhall.

[Ch. 38] 845: Title: In Melville's unfinished "Weeds and Wildings" is a poem, "Shadow at the Feast," about the afterlife, at others' feasts, of a woman widowed soon after marriage. Warren F. Broderick (1997) showed that the Melville family knew of a Lansingburgh woman who was widowed as a bride. An annotation on the manuscript of Melville's poem (at HCL-M) shows that Elizabeth Shaw Melville thought it was about Ellen Brittain; the Melvilles had occasion over the years to see how Ellen Brittain behaved as a widow in situations festive for others. Here, I apply the title to Melville himself. See *Clarel*, 887 n. 5. 846: "two girls": Elizabeth Shaw Melville to Kate Gansevoort Lansing, 10 October 1880. 846: Mansion House: See illus. 45. 848: The New York Public Library has a copy of the catalog of the auction of Oakey Hall's library. 854: See Hamlin (1990), endpapers: Cora Parker was the daughter-in-law of Judge Parker. 854: Henry Thomas: New Bedford *Sunday Standard* (11 August 1929). 861: Special provision for Josie: $50,000, serious money. Lemuel Jr. left his wine to Sam alone. 863: Communicant: See Spark (2001, 214) for Melville's daughter Frances's comment: "*I* never knew him to go to church but twice that I can remember—All Soul's Unitarian"; when Melville went, it was to please his wife, not because he could suddenly tolerate Unitarian ideas. 866: Perhaps influenced by knowing one of Theodore F. Wolfe's accounts of visiting Melville, Moncure Conway in his introduction to *The Blithedale Romance* (London: Service & Paton, 1898) wrote: "Mrs. Melville informs me that when at her house [in March 1851] the two men passed most of their time discussing the profoundest problems of human life, philosophy, and even of theology." 873: Stedman's praise: Laura Stedman Gould in Sealts (1974), 49. 874: I emend here: what Melville miswrote to Ellen Gifford was "his about a Kitten, which you once showed me." 875: No one at 104 East Twenty-sixth Street needed to read what Stylus said of Melville, the "old gentleman": "Had he possessed as much literary skill as wild imagination his works might have secured for him a permanent place in American literature." The ugliest comments did not reach print. See *Log*, 826, for Horace Scudder's wish (22 October 1890) to George Lathrop that "Melville would only let go of life," so they could write freely about him. 876: Continuity of British reputation: See *Moby-Dick*, 735–36. George Worth let me have his microfilm of Hannay's diaries on extended loan.

[Ch. 39] 878: The title: All of Melville's poetic and prose manuscripts surveyed here, including the MS of *Billy Budd*, are in the Harvard College Library Melville Collection; I draw details from scholars cited in the next two notes and from Dennis Marnon. 880: Interconnectedness: Harrison Hayford, Merton M. Sealts Jr., Eleanor Tilton, Robert C. Ryan, Barbara Glenn (letter to me, 1977), Robert Sandberg, and Gordon Poole have identified manuscript leaves which relate to two of Melville's projects. 884: Sandberg, (1989), 442–43. 885: "semi-manuscript": Hand-copied; see *Correspondence*, 497. 886: Nelson chapter: See Parker, *Reading "Billy Budd"* (1990), 110–13, 173–74. 887: Shakespeare: Harvard College Library, Melville Collection (MS Am 188, 369.2). 887: "In and on": I challenge anyone to prove that Dennis Marnon wrote this paragraph. 888: Spark (2001, 217) quotes Eleanor Metcalf to Henry A. Murray (26 May 1926): "About Stanwix, he died of tuberculosis in a public ward of hospital in San Francisco, to which he was removed from a semi-private ward, after his father refused to let any more money be sent to him. Mother believes his illness was brought on by insufficient nourishment and clothing." Did Frances Melville Thomas make this story up out of whole cloth? She complained all her life about "insufficient nourishment" as a child, having only bread and tea for supper (Metcalf [1953], 133). Theorists in the brief heyday of the New Historicism claimed self-exoneratingly that all biography was fiction; a corollary being that all biography is autobiography. I put on record, on the basis of prolonged experiences in semi-private rooms and wards in tuberculosis sanatoria in more than one state, that chances are Stanwix was just as well off in the ward, however he came to be there. 889: Spark (2001, 219) prints Eleanor's and her mother's accusation that Kate Hoadley (and her heir Charlotte) seized more than their share at the dispersal of the Gansevoort, N.Y. possessions. The story I tell beginning on this page, like the whole of this biography, is stringently condensed; a fuller version would show Helen, with Kate Hoadley's help, struggling to empty a house stuffed with treasures, without help from any man in the family. Surviving documents show that the two sisters exercised the most exemplary fairness in distributing goods: their problem was to find takers for the treasures. Frances had absolutely no just grounds for being aggrieved at the behavior of her aunts. 890: Greenslet: Letter to Willard Thorp, deposited by Thorp in the Newberry Library. 891: The obituaries of Hoadley in the Boston *Daily Evening Globe*, the *Evening Transcript*, and the *Traveller* on 22 October were varyingly truncated from a longer form presumably made available at this time and preserved in *The Hoadley Genealogy*. 892: A copy of the Charles F. Libbie catalog of Hoadley's library is in the New York Public Library. 893: Blizzard: Sealts (1974); appetite: taped recollections (August 1968); copy in Parker's files. 893: The ship may have passed off mail or stopped at St. Augustine, judging from part of an envelope, cut up for Melville's autograph, which survives in the Howe Collection, Gainesville, Florida. 898: Frederick J. and Joyce Deveau Kennedy (1999) correct earlier impressions that MacMechan was of marginal importance to Melville's reputation; this long article is basic for study of the Melville revival. 898: Stedman's letter: *Log*, 823. 898: Naming names may flush out a fragile and elusive document: at a Grolier Club meeting in Chicago Philip Krapp read what he identified as Brander Matthews's handwritten notes on his interview with Melville. Krapp subsequently rebuffed Richard Colles Johnson, Donald Yannella, Harrison Hayford, and me whenever one of us asked to see them and to help preserve them. I have a letter from Johnson to Hayford and me on 20 August 1996 recounting his several attempts to copy the manuscript for the Newberry Library files. Hayford heard Krapp's talk and assumed the notes were genuine; I did not hear the talk but remain skeptical because on Christmas Day 1921, reviewing Raymond Weaver's *Herman Melville: Mariner and Mystic* in the New York *Times*, Matthews, plainly still in his right mind, passed up the God-given opportunity to mention any such interview. 898–99: Morris: Henry S. Salt, "Herman Melville," London *Literary Guide* n.s. 311 (May 1922), 70; Shaw: *Bernard Shaw: The Diaries, 1885–1897*, ed. Stanley Weintraub (University Park: Pennsylvania State Univ. Press, 1986), 2.848 (28 August 1892). 901: Garnett: Letter in the Berg Collection of the New York Public Library, reported by John Bryant on Ishmail, the online Melville chat-group.

[Ch. 40] 905: See Parker (1997) for a version of part of this chapter, and see the series of articles by Robert K. Wallace on Melville's art works. I draw on "To a White-Haired Lady, Melville Means Grandpa," the interview with

Frances Cuthbert Thomas Osborne by Gledhill Cameron in the Trenton *Evening Times*, 27 April 1971; this is a variant of the interview reprinted in Sealts's *Early Lives*. Mrs. Osborne's taped recollections (August 1968, 23 minutes) contain unique material. 906: Mrs. Osborne's copy of Mumford's book is in the Priscilla Ambrose Collection. 908: Long ago Leon told me that "Did Melville grow roses?" was the only question he asked Eleanor Metcalf. 911: Mrs. Melville's inventory is in Sealts (1974). 912: *Brisk Gale:* See illus. 58. 912: Portfolios: See Wallace (1986). 913: If Eleanor was brought over from New Jersey for a few hours on a Saturday when Frances was already there, making a longer visit, Melville would sometimes take both girls on an outing, according to Frances's 1968 taped recollections. 913–14: These pages draw on Sealts, *Early Lives*, 177–79 (Eleanor's recollections), and 179–85 (Frances's). 914: Rhys's introduction to the Everyman's Library *Typee* (London: Dent, 1907). 915: Son-in-law recalled: New Bedford *Sunday Standard* (11 August 1929). 917: Coan (1891) wrote of Melville: "He took the attitude of absolute independence toward the world. He said, 'My books will speak for themselves, and all the better if I avoid the rattling egotism by which so many win a certain vogue for a certain time.'" 917: Toft's letter appeared in the New York *Times* (17 March 1900). 917: Oliphant comparison: *Library of the World's Best Literature Ancient and Modern*, ed. Charles Dudley Warner, 30 vols. (New York, n.d.), 17.9868. 919: Wegelin recalls a Melville ready to converse with bookmen, in contrast to the recollections of Dr. Jones (see note to 757 above). 922: Some of the fulminations reached print in *Robert Buchanan: A Critical Appreciation and Other Essays* (London, 1901), by the English Henry Murray (not the Harvard psychologist Henry A. Murray). 923: *The Letters of T. E. Lawrence*, ed. David Garnett (New York: Doubleday; London: Jonathan Cape, 1938).

Quotations from Manuscripts

Rather than footnoting each of the hundreds of quotations from nineteenth-century manuscripts, I have cited them in a chart of correspondents (and a few diaries and other documents), below. Letters to and from Melville are included here only when they are not in the NN *Correspondence* (1993). (See the opening paragraph of this section, "Documentation.") Any author-and-date reference (such as "Olsen-Smith and Parker") indicates that an item is quoted from one of the "Printed Sources," below.

Abbreviations

Arrowhead Berkshire County Historical Society, Pittsfield, Massachusetts
BA The Berkshire Athenaeum, Pittsfield, Massachusetts

HCL-M The Houghton Library, Manuscript Department, Harvard University (Melville family material is shelfmarked bMS Am 188–bMS Am 188.7)
MHS-D The Massachusetts Historical Society, Dana Collection
MHS-S The Massachusetts Historical Society, Lemuel Shaw Collection
NA-S The National Archives, State Department
NYPL-Berg Henry W. and Albert A. Berg Collection, The New York Public Library, Astor, Lenox and Tilden Foundations
NYPL-D Duyckinck Collection, Rare Books and Manuscripts Division, The New York Public Library, Astor, Lenox, and Tilden Foundations
NYPL-GL Gansevoort-Lansing Collection, Rare Books and Manuscripts Division, The New York Public Library, Astor, Lenox, and Tilden Foundations

Chart of Correspondents (and Related Documents)

Catherine Van Rensselaer Berry to Augusta Melville NYPL-GL
Julia Blatchford (see Julia Blatchford Potter)
Charles F. Briggs to Harper & Brothers *Log*
Ellen Brittain to William Morewood Arrowhead
John H. Clifford's diary MHS–John H. Clifford Papers
Titus Munson Coan to his parents *Log*
Robert Cooke to Peter Gansevoort *Log*
Paul Fenimore Cooper to Catherine (Kate) Gansevoort (Lansing) NYPL-GL
Coquette ship's log, 1821 Nantucket Historical Association
Catherine (Kate) Gansevoort Curtis to Catherine Gansevoort (later Lansing) NYPL-GL
G. W. Curtis (the editor and writer) to Joshua A. Dix MacDougall (1983)
G. W. Curtis to Allan Melville BA
G. W. Curtis to Herman Melville William S. Reese Collection
Mary Curtis to Augusta Melville NYPL-GL
George Curtis (husband of Catherine Gansevoort Curtis) to Maria Gansevoort Melville NYPL-GL
Richard Henry Dana Jr. to Charles Sumner Hayford-Davis (1949), 384
Richard Henry Dana Sr. to Evert A. Duyckinck NYPL-D
Charles De Kay manuscript recollections *Log*, 781
Morgan Dix to Thomas Melville State University of New York–Maritime College
Evert A. Duyckinck's diary NYPL-D
Evert A. Duyckinck's record of books lent NYPL-D
Evert A. Duyckinck to George Duyckinck (his son) NYPL-D
Evert A. Duyckinck to George Long Duyckinck NYPL-D
Evert A. Duyckinck to Margaret Panton Duyckinck NYPL-D
George Duyckinck to Rosalie Baker NYPL-D

George Duyckinck to Joann Miller NYPL-D
Catherine Gansevoort (see Catherine [Kate] Gansevoort Lansing)
Guert Gansevoort to Peter Gansevoort NYPL-GL
Henry Sanford Gansevoort's diary NYPL-GL
Henry Sanford Gansevoort to Peter Gansevoort NYPL-GL
Henry Sanford Gansevoort to Abraham Lansing NYPL-GL
Henry Sanford Gansevoort to Catherine (Kate) Gansevoort (Lansing) NYPL-GL
Henry Sanford Gansevoort to Allan Melville BA
Herman Gansevoort's "Checkbook and Remembrancer, 1823–1832" NYPL-GL
Herman Gansevoort's will BA
Peter Gansevoort's diary NYPL-GL
Peter Gansevoort to Guert Gansevoort NYPL-GL
Peter Gansevoort to Henry Sanford Gansevoort NYPL-GL
Peter Gansevoort to Susan Gansevoort NYPL-GL
Peter Gansevoort to Allan Melville NYPL-GL (draft)
Peter Gansevoort to Augusta Melville NYPL-GL
Peter Gansevoort to Maria Gansevoort Melville NYPL-GL
Stanwix Gansevoort to Peter Gansevoort NYPL-GL
Alexander Gardiner to [David Gardiner?] Yale Gardiner-Tyler Papers
Edward Garnett to Herman Melville NYPL-Berg
Captain James W. Grace to the Trustees of the New Bedford City Library New Bedford Public Library
George Griggs to Peter Gansevoort NYPL-GL
George Griggs to Allan Melville BA
George Griggs to Augusta Melville NYPL-GL
Helen Melville Griggs to Catherine (Kate) Gansevoort (Lansing) NYPL-GL
Helen Melville Griggs to Augusta Melville NYPL-GL
Helen Melville Griggs to Augusta Melville and Frances Priscilla Melville NYPL-GL
Helen Melville Griggs to Elizabeth Shaw Melville NYPL-GL
Helen Melville Griggs to Frances Priscilla Melville NYPL-GL
Helen Melville Griggs to Maria (Milie) Gansevoort Melville Morewood Arrowhead
Helen Melville Griggs to Augustus Peebles NYPL-GL
John Thomas Gulick's journal *Log*
James H. Hackett to Allan Melville BA
A. Oakey Hall to Evert Duyckinck NYPL-D
Harper-Melville business records HCL-M (*Log*; see Tanselle, 1969)
Sophia Hawthorne to Elizabeth Peabody (her mother) Courtesy of Department of Special Collections, Stanford University Libraries
Una Hawthorne to Elizabeth Peabody (her aunt) Sukel Collection
G. S. Hillard to Lemuel Shaw MHS-S
Catherine (Kate) Melville Hoadley to Augusta Melville NYPL-GL

Catherine (Kate) Melville Hoadley to Catherine (Kate) Gansevoort (Lansing) NYPL-GL
Charlotte Hoadley to Victor Hugo Paltsits New-York Historical Society (7 January 1941: BA)
John C. Hoadley, manuscript copy of "The Sounds I Love" BA
John C. Hoadley to George A. Gordon (30 November 1859) HCL-M
John C. Hoadley to George Boutwell *Log*
John C. Hoadley to Peter Gansevoort NYPL-GL
John C. Hoadley to Susan Lansing Gansevoort NYPL-GL
John C. Hoadley to Abraham Lansing NYPL-GL
John C. Hoadley to Catherine (Kate) Gansevoort (Lansing) NYPL-GL
John C. Hoadley to Augusta Melville NYPL-GL
John C. Hoadley to Robert Pomeroy BA
John C. Hoadley to Alfred B. Street New-York Historical Society
John C. Hoadley to Charles Sumner NA (quoted from *Log*)
Maria (Minnie) Gansevoort Hoadley to Catherine (Kate) Gansevoort (Lansing) NYPL-GL
Edward Hun to Catherine (Kate) Gansevoort (Lansing) NYPL-GL
Pierre Irving's outline for his biography of Washington Irving NYPL-Berg
C. Henry King to Thomas Melville Maritime College
Thomas Starr King to Henry W. Bellows MHS-Bellows
Thomas Starr King to Randolph Ryer Bancroft–King Papers
Abraham Lansing to Catherine (Kate) Gansevoort (Lansing) NYPL-GL
Abraham Lansing to Susan Lansing Gansevoort NYPL-GL
Catherine (Kate) Gansevoort (Lansing), diary NYPL-GL
Any letter to Catherine Gansevoort (Melville's cousin Kitty or Kate; later called Kate Gansevoort Lansing) NYPL-GL
Catherine (Kate) Gansevoort (Lansing) to Henry Sanford Gansevoort NYPL-GL
Catherine (Kate) Gansevoort (Lansing) to Peter Gansevoort NYPL-GL
Catherine (Kate) Gansevoort (Lansing) to Peter and Susan Gansevoort NYPL-GL
Catherine (Kate) Gansevoort (Lansing) to Susan Lansing Gansevoort NYPL-GL
Catherine (Kate) Gansevoort (Lansing) to John Hoadley NYPL-GL
Catherine (Kate) Gansevoort (Lansing) to Abraham Lansing NYPL-GL
Catherine (Kate) Gansevoort (Lansing) to Augusta Melville NYPL-GL
Catherine (Kate) Gansevoort (Lansing) to Frances Priscilla Melville NYPL-GL
Catherine (Kate) Gansevoort (Lansing) to Robert Sanford NYPL-GL
Catherine (Kate) Gansevoort (Lansing) to Frances Melville (Thomas) NYPL-GL
Abigail Thurston Lathers to Catherine (Kate) Gansevoort (Lansing) NYPL-GL
Abigail Thurston Lathers to Julia Lathers Arrowhead
A. M. Livingston to Lemuel Shaw MHS-S
Longman archives NN *Confidence-Man*

John A. Lowell to Orville Dewey Htn *54M-206: Lowell Institute, Boston, Mass., Papers and Records, 1837–1943
James McConnel to William Morewood Arrowhead
Allan Melvill's draft passages of *Pierre* contract HCL-M (reproduced in Parker, Allan Melvill to Harper & Brothers HCL-M (reproduced in Parker, 1977)
Allan Melvill's penmanship exercise book William S. Reese Collection
Allan Melvill to Peter Gansevoort NYPL-GL
Allan Melvill to Lemuel Shaw (16 January 1819) HCL-Murray Papers Htn *93M-70
Mary Ann Augusta Hobart Melvill (Mrs. Thomas Melvill Jr.) to Maria G. Melville NYPL-GL
Mary Ann Augusta Hobart Melvill (Mrs. Thomas Melvill Jr.) to Lemuel Shaw MHS-S
Priscilla Melvill (later, sometimes, Melville) to her cousin Augusta Melville NYPL-GL
Priscilla Melvill (Melville) to Lemuel Shaw (31 March 1853) MHS-S (27 March 1854: Metcalf, 1953, 150–51)
Thomas Melvill Jr. to George N. Briggs BA
Thomas Melvill Jr. to Thomas Melvill Sr. (27 November 1822) HCL-M *bMS Am 1233
Thomas Melvill Jr. to Lemuel Shaw (14 January 1842) MHS-S
Allan Melville's draft passages of *Pierre* contract HCL-M (reproduced in Parker, 1977)
Allan Melville to Evert A. Duyckinck NYPL-D
Allan Melville to Henry Sanford Gansevoort NYPL-GL
Allan Melville to Harper & Brothers HCL-M (reproduced in Parker, 1977)
Allan Melville to Nathaniel Hawthorne Hayford-Davis (1949)
Allan Melville to Catherine (Kate) Gansevoort (Lansing) NYPL-GL
Allan Melville to Richard Lathers *Log*
Allan Melville to Augusta Melville NYPL-GL
Allan Melville to Helen Maria Melville NYPL-GL
Allan Melville to Robert Sanford NYPL-GL
Allan Melville to Samuel H. Savage (19 April 1850) MHS-Savage (Kennedys, 1977)
Allan Melville to Lemuel Shaw (11 June 1853) MHS-S
Augusta Melville's commonplace book, *Orient Pearls at Random Strung* BA
Augusta Melville's correspondence record, 1849–54 NYPL-GL
Augusta Melville's "Excursions" (1852) William S. Reese Collection
Augusta Melville's inventory of wedding gifts NYPL-GL
Augusta Melville to Herman and Catherine Quackenboss Gansevoort NYPL-GL
Augusta Melville to Peter Gansevoort NYPL-GL
Augusta Melville to Susan Lansing Gansevoort NYPL-GL

Documentation

Augusta Melville to Abraham Lansing NYPL-GL
Augusta Melville to Catherine (Kate) Gansevoort (Lansing) NYPL-GL
Augusta Melville to Allan Melville BA (Arrowhead: 16 May 1851)
Augusta Melville to Frances Priscilla Melville NYPL-GL
Augusta Melville to Sarah Morewood NYPL-GL (draft)
Augusta Melville to Hope Shaw (22 April 1872) HCL-M (Metcalf, 1953)
Augusta Melville to Cornelia (Nilly) Van Rensselaer Thayer NYPL-GL
Catherine (Kate) Melville (Melville's sister; see Catherine Melville Hoadley)
Catherine (Kitty) Melville (Melville's niece) to Augusta Melville NYPL-GL
Catherine (Kitty) Melville to Stanwix Melville NYPL-GL
Catherine (Katie) Bogart Melville to Catherine (Kate) Gansevoort (Lansing) NYPL-GL
Elizabeth (Bessie) Melville to Catherine (Kate) Gansevoort (Lansing) NYPL-GL
Elizabeth (Bessie) Melville to Augusta Melville NYPL-GL
Elizabeth Shaw Melville's memoir of her husband HCL-M (Sealts, 1974)
Elizabeth Shaw Melville to Henry S. Bellows MHS-Bellows (Yannella-Parker, 1981)
Elizabeth Shaw Melville to Evert Duyckinck NYPL-D
Elizabeth Shaw Melville to George Duyckinck NYPL-D
Elizabeth Shaw Melville to Mary Lanman Douw Ferris McNeilly (1976)
Elizabeth Shaw Melville to Ellen Marett Gifford *Log*
Elizabeth Shaw Melville to Catherine (Kate) Gansevoort (Lansing) NYPL-GL
Elizabeth Shaw Melville to Augusta Melville NYPL-GL
Elizabeth Shaw Melville to Frances Priscilla Melville NYPL-GL
Elizabeth Shaw Melville to Maria Gansevoort Melville NYPL-GL
Elizabeth Shaw Melville to Sarah Morewood BA
Elizabeth Shaw Melville to William Morewood Arrowhead
Elizabeth Shaw Melville to William M. Prichard, All Souls Treasurer All Souls Archives (Yannella-Parker, 1981)
Elizabeth Shaw Melville to Samuel H. Savage Kennedys (1979)
Elizabeth Shaw Melville to Hope Savage Shaw HCL-M (Metcalf, 1953)
Elizabeth Shaw Melville to Lemuel Shaw MHS-S
Florence Melville's school composition, "My Country Home" Arrowhead
Florence Melville to Catherine (Kate) Gansevoort (Lansing) NYPL-GL
Frances (Fanny) Melville (Melville's daughter; see Frances Melville Thomas)
Frances (Fanny) Priscilla Melville to Peter Gansevoort NYPL-GL
Frances (Fanny) Priscilla Melville to Susan Gansevoort NYPL-GL
Frances (Fanny) Priscilla Melville to Abraham Lansing NYPL-GL
Frances (Fanny) Priscilla Melville to Catherine (Kate) Gansevoort (Lansing) NYPL-GL
Frances (Fanny) Priscilla Melville to Augusta Melville NYPL-GL (19 February 1854: William S. Reese Collection)

Gansevoort Melville's *Index Rerum* BA
Gansevoort Melville's lost 1834 diary; see Leyda (1950).
Gansevoort Melville to Allan Melville BA
Gansevoort Melville to Lemuel Shaw MHS-S
Helen Maria Melville (see Helen Melville Griggs)
Herman Melville's memorandum book HCL-M (Sealts, 1957)
Herman Melville's notebook of lecture engagements HCL-M (Sealts, 1957)
Herman Melville's 1857 passport BA
Herman Melville's will *Log*
Herman Melville to John M. Clayton NA-S (see Olsen-Smith and Parker, 1995)
Herman Melville to G. W. Curtis William S. Reese Collection
Herman Melville to William L. Marcy NA
Jane Dempsey Melville to Henry S. Gansevoort NYPL-GL
Jane Dempsey Melville to Catherine (Kate) Gansevoort (Lansing) NYPL-GL
Jane Dempsey Melville to Elizabeth Shaw Melville NYPL-GL
Jane Dempsey Melville to Florence Melville BA
Jane Dempsey Melville to Maria Gansevoort Melville NYPL-GL
Jane Dempsey Melville to Maria (Milie) Gansevoort Melville Morewood BA
Malcolm Melville to Maria (Milie) Gansevoort Melville BA
Maria Gansevoort Melville to her niece Catherine Gansevoort (Lansing) NYPL-GL
Maria Gansevoort Melville to Peter Gansevoort NYPL-GL
Maria Gansevoort Melville to Susan Lansing Gansevoort NYPL-GL
Maria Gansevoort Melville to Augusta Melville NYPL-GL
Maria (Milie) Gansevoort Melville (later Morewood), school compositions Arrowhead
Maria (Milie) Gansevoort Melville's "The Story of the Summer of 1869" as "Told by the Old Chimney" BA
Maria (Milie) Gansevoort Melville Morewood to Catherine (Kate) Gansevoort (Lansing) NYPL-GL
Maria (Milie) Gansevoort Melville to Frances Priscilla Melville NYPL-GL
Maria (Milie) Gansevoort Melville to Stanwix Melville 1862 NYPL-GL
Sophia Thurston Melville to Rachel Barrington Arrowhead
Sophia Thurston Melville to Augusta Melville NYPL-GL
Stanwix Melville to Peter Gansevoort NYPL-GL
Stanwix Melville to Abraham and Kate Lansing NYPL-GL
Stanwix Melville to Catherine (Kate) Gansevoort (Lansing) NYPL-GL
Stanwix Melville to Augusta Melville NYPL-GL
Stanwix Melville to Maria Gansevoort Melville NYPL-GL
Stanwix Melville to Hope Shaw HCL-M (Metcalf, 1953)
Thomas Melville's diary on the *Navigator* NYPL-GL

Thomas Melville's work diary and Quarterly Reports State University of New York–Maritime College
Thomas Melville to Catherine (Kate) Gansevoort (Lansing) NYPL-GL
Thomas Melville to Augusta Melville NYPL-GL
Annie Morewood (later Lathers), scrapbook BA
Annie Morewood to William Morewood Arrowhead
Ellen Pierpont Morewood to Rowland Morewood Arrowhead
Henry Gansevoort Morewood's description of Abby Lodge Arrowhead
J. Rowland Morewood to William Morewood BA
Margaret Morewood's description of Abby Lodge Arrowhead
Sarah Huyler Morewood's "Greylock Thoughts" NYPL-D
Sarah Huyler Morewood to George Long Duyckinck NYPL-D
Sarah Huyler Morewood to Augusta and Kate Melville NYPL-GL
Sarah Huyler Morewood to Thomas Melville Arrowhead
Sarah Huyler Morewood to Susannah Morewood Arrowhead
Amos Nourse to Lemuel Shaw *Log* (MHS-S: 8 November 1853; 6 October 1855)
Lucy Melvill Nourse to Augusta Melville NYPL-GL
Amasa J. Parker to Franklin Pierce NA
Amasa J. Parker to Lemuel Shaw NYPL-GL
Harriet L. Parker to Catherine (Kate) Gansevoort (Lansing) NYPL-GL
Augustus Peebles's inventory of Mansion House, Gansevoort BA
Mary Peebles to Abraham Lansing NYPL-GL
Mary Peebles to Catherine (Kate) Gansevoort (Lansing) NYPL-GL
Captain John Percival to Lemuel Shaw MHS-S
Julia Blatchford Potter to Augusta Melville NYPL-GL
Robert Sanford to Henry Sanford Gansevoort NYPL-GL
Samuel H. Savage to his wife MHS-Savage
Samuel H. Savage to Hope Savage Shaw Kennedys (1977)
Samuel Savage to Lemuel and Hope Shaw MHS-S
Samuel H. Savage to Lemuel Shaw Jr. Kennedys (1977)
Charles Scribner to Evert A. Duyckinck NYPL-D
J. C. Sharp to Samuel H. Savage Kennedys (1977)
Caroline Cobb Shaw's diary MHS-S
Elizabeth Shaw (see Elizabeth Shaw Melville)
Hope Savage Shaw's Diaries MHS-S (1 December 1877, *Log*); HCL-M (excerpt, 1868; Metcalf, 1953)
Hope Savage Shaw to Samuel H. Savage Kennedys (1977)
Hope Savage Shaw to Lemuel Shaw MHS-S
Hope Savage Shaw to Lemuel Shaw Jr. *Log* (MHS-S: 4 October 1852; 23 January 1853; ? May 1853; 12 June 1853)

Hope Savage Shaw to Samuel Shaw *Log* (MHS-S: 15 January 1857)
John Oakes Shaw to Lemuel Shaw Jr. MHS-S
Lemuel Shaw's passport NA
Lemuel Shaw's prayer at sea on the *Arabia* on 20 June 1853 MHS-S
Lemuel Shaw's will MHS-S
Lemuel Shaw to Benjamin R. Curtis (draft) MHS-S
Lemuel Shaw to Allan Melville BA
Lemuel Shaw to Maria Gansevoort Melville NYPL-GL
Lemuel Shaw to Hope Savage Shaw *Log* (MHS-S: 1 July 1853)
Lemuel Shaw to Lemuel Shaw Jr. *Log* (MHS-S: 5 March 1853)
Lemuel Shaw to Samuel Shaw MHS-S
Lemuel Shaw Jr. (Lem) to Hope Shaw MHS-S (23 May 1853; 16 June 1853)
Lemuel Shaw Jr. to Lemuel Shaw and Hope Savage Shaw *Log* (MHS-S: 9 May 1853)
Lemuel Shaw Jr. to Samuel Shaw *Log* (MHS-S: 18? July 1856; September 1856?; 29 December 1856; 21 April 1857; 2 June 1857)
Samuel Shaw's diary MHS-S
Samuel Shaw to Henry W. Bellows MHS-Bellows (quoted by Kring, in Yannella-Parker, 1981)
Samuel Shaw to Elizabeth Shaw Melville *Log*
Samuel Shaw to Hope Savage Shaw (1 August 1855) MHS-S
Samuel Shaw to Lemuel Shaw Jr. *Log* (MHS-S: 1 August 1855; 2 November 1856; 23 November 1856)
J. E. A. Smith to Allan Melville BA
Jared Sparks to Lemuel Shaw MHS-S
Elizabeth Stoddard to Margaret Jane Muzzey Sweat Rare Books and Manuscripts, The Allison-Shelley Collection, The Pennsylvania State University Libraries
Charles Sumner to the Provost Marshal BA
Cornelia (Nilly) Van Rensselaer Thayer to Augusta Melville NYPL-GL
Frances Melville Thomas to Catherine (Kate) Gansevoort (Lansing) NYPL-GL
Frances Melville Thomas to Eleanor Thomas Metcalf HCL-M (Spark, 2001)
Howard Townsend to Augusta Melville NYPL-GL
Henry T. Tuckerman to Evert A. Duyckinck NYPL-D
George Wales to Henry Sanford Gansevoort NYPL-GL
George Wales to Catherine (Kate) Gansevoort (Lansing) NYPL-GL
Mary Whitney to Catherine (Kate) Gansevoort (Lansing) NYPL-GL

Printed Sources

Unless otherwise specified, quotations from Melville are from *The Writings of Herman Melville* (Evanston and Chicago: Northwestern University Press and The Newberry Library), General Editor Harrison Hayford, Associate General Editor Hershel Parker, Bibliographical Editor G. Thomas Tanselle.

Thirteen volumes of the Northwestern-Newberry (NN) Edition appeared between 1968 and 1993. For the location of books owned by Melville I have relied on the 1988 edition of Merton M. Sealts Jr.'s *Melville's Reading* and his and Steven Olsen-Smith's supplements. I have made use of the "Historical Notes" in the NN volumes as well as other editorial sections in *Moby-Dick*, *Correspondence*, and *Journals* (from which I have quoted extensively in chs. 14 and 15).

Barber, Patricia. "Herman Melville's House in Brooklyn," *American Literature* 45 (November 1973), 433–34.
Bellows, Henry W. "In Memory of Thomas Starr King: A Discourse Given to his Flock in San Francisco, Sunday Morning and Evening, May 1, 1864." San Francisco: Frank Eastman, 1864.
———. *The Old World in Its New Face*. 2 vols. New York: Harper & Brothers, 1868.
Bercaw, Mary K. *Melville's Sources*. Evanston: Northwestern Univ. Press, 1987. (Bercaw provides "a checklist, keyed to Melville's works, of all the sources scholars have suggested Melville used.")
Bezanson, Walter E. "Historical and Critical Note." *Clarel*. Evanston and Chicago: Northwestern Univ. Press and the Newberry Library, 1991. 505–637.
———. "Melville's Reading of Arnold's Poetry." *PMLA* 69 (1954), 365–91.
Bowen, Croswell. *The Elegant Oakey*. New York: Oxford, 1956.
Broderick, Warren F. "Unmasking the 'Shadow at the Feast.'" *Melville Society Extracts* 109 (June 1997), 19–24.
Bryan, Clark W. *The Book of Berkshire*. North Egremont: Past Perfect Books, 1993. (A facsimile of the 1887 issue.)
Budd, Thomas Shaw. *Outlines of English Literature*. Philadelphia: Blanchard & Lea, 1870.
Butler, William Allen. Letter signed "Jacques du Monde." Washington *Weekly National Intelligencer* (31 August 1850).
Coan, Titus Munson. "Herman Melville." Boston *Literary World* (19 December 1891).
Cohen, Hennig. "Melville and the Art Collection of Richard Lathers." *Melville Society Extracts* 99 (December 1994), 3–25.
Collum, Eric, and Hershel Parker. "The Lost Lathers Collections." *Melville Society Extracts* 99 (December 1994), 26–28.
Cowen, Walker. *Melville's Marginalia*. New York: Garland, 1987.
Curtis, G. W. *Little Journeys to the Homes of American Authors*. New York: Putnam's 1896.
Dana, Richard Henry. *The Journal of Richard Henry Dana, Jr.* 3 vols. Ed. Robert F. Lucid. Cambridge: Harvard Univ. Press, 1968.
Davis, Merrell. See Hayford.

Degenhardt, Ruth T. "The Melville-Morewood Collection, Gift of Paul and Nancy Metcalf: A Detailed Inventory." *Melville Society Extracts* 116 (February 1999), 1–14.

Dewey, Orville. "An Address Delivered Under the Old Elm Tree in Sheffield, with some Remarks on the Great Political Question of the Day." New York: C. S. Francis, 1856.

———. *Autobiography and Letters*. Ed. Mary E. Dewey. Boston: Roberts Brothers, 1883.

———. *Discourses on Human Nature, Human Life, and the Nature of Religion*. New York: C. S. Francis, 1846.

———. "The Identity of All Art. A Lecture before the Apollo Association of New-York" [1840]. *Discourses on the Nature of Religion; and on Commerce and Business; with some Occasional Discourses*. 3 vols. New York: C. S. Francis, 1847. 2.311–35.

———. "The Laws of Human Progress and Modern Reforms. A Lecture Delivered before the Mercantile Library Association of the City of New-York." New York: C. S. Francis, 1852.

———. *The Problem of Human Destiny; or, The End of Providence in the World and Man*. New York: James Miller, 1864.

Duyckinck, Evert A. "A Memorial of Henry Theodore Tuckerman." New York: New York Historical Society, 1872.

Duyckinck, Evert A., and George Long Duyckinck. *Cyclopædia of American Literature*. 2 vols. New York: Charles Scribner, 1855.

D'Wolf, John. *A Voyage to the North Pacific and a Journey through Siberia, More Than Half a Century Ago*. Cambridge: Welch, Bigelow, 1861.

Emmers, Amy Puett. "Melville's Wife: A Study of Elizabeth Shaw Melville." Ph.D. dissertation, Northwestern Univ. 1969.

———. "New Crosslights on the Illegitimate Daughter in *Pierre*." *Critical Essays on Herman Melville's "Pierre; or, The Ambiguities."* Ed. Brian Higgins and Hershel Parker. Boston: G. K. Hall, 1983. 237–40.

Exman, Eugene. *The House of Harper: One Hundred and Fifty Years of Publishing*. New York: Harper & Row, 1967.

Field, Maunsell B. *Memories of Many Men and Some Women*. New York: Harper & Brothers, 1874.

Fields, James T. *Yesterdays with Authors*. Boston: J. R. Osgood, 1872.

Garner, Stanton. *The Civil War World of Herman Melville*. Lawrence: Univ. Press of Kansas, 1993.

Gretchko, John M. J. "Melville at the New-York Gallery of the Fine Arts." *Melville Society Extracts* 82 (September 1990), 7–8.

———. "Remnants of the U. S. Census, 1850–1880," *Melville Society Extracts* 62 (May 1985), 15–16.

Hamlin, Huybertie Pruyn. *An Albany Girlhood.* Ed. Alice P. Kenney. Albany: Washington Park Press, 1990.

Harper, J. Henry. *The House of Harper: A Century of Publishing in Franklin Square.* New York: Harper & Brothers, 1912.

Hawthorne, Julian. *Hawthorne and His Circle.* New York: Harper & Brothers, 1903.

———. "Hawthorne at Lenox." Philadelphia *Booklover's Weekly* 10 (30 December 1901), 225–31.

———. "Herman Melville and His Dog." Dearborn *Independent* 27 (24 September 1927), 3, 26.

———. *Nathaniel Hawthorne and His Wife.* 2 vols. Boston: James R. Osgood & Co., 1884.

———. "When Herman Melville was 'Mr. Omoo.'" New York *Literary Digest International Book Review* 4 (August 1926), 561–62, 564.

Hawthorne, Nathaniel. *The American Claimant Manuscripts.* Ed. Edward H. Davidson, Claude M. Simpson, and L. Neal Smith. Columbus: Ohio State Univ. Press, 1977.

———. *The American Notebooks.* Ed. Claude M. Simpson. Columbus: Ohio State Univ. Press, 1972. (Cited for Hawthorne's full texts; see *Passages*, below, for shorter texts available in Melville's lifetime.)

———. *The Letters, 1843–1853.* Ed. Thomas Woodson, L. Neal Smith, and Norman Holmes Pearson. Columbus: Ohio State Univ. Press, 1985.

———. *Passages from the American Note-Books of Nathaniel Hawthorne.* Boston: Ticknor & Fields, 1868.

———. *Passages from the English Note-Books of Nathaniel Hawthorne.* Boston: Fields, Osgood, & Co., 1870.

———. *Passages from the French and Italian Note-Books of Nathaniel Hawthorne.* Boston: James R. Osgood & Co., 1872.

Hayes, Kevin. "Toby's *Typee* Lecture." *Melville Society Extracts* 96 (1994), 1–4.

Hayes, Kevin, and Hershel Parker. *Checklist of Melville Reviews.* Evanston: Northwestern Univ. Press, 1991.

Hayford, Harrison. See also Melville; Parker.

Hayford, Harrison, and Merrell Davis. "Melville as Office-Seeker." *Modern Language Quarterly* 10 (June 1949), 168–83; (September 1949), 377–88.

Heffernan, Thomas F. "Melville and Wordsworth." *American Literature* 49 (1977), 338–51.

Heidmann, Mark. "The Markings in Herman Melville's Bibles." *Studies in the American Renaissance* (1990), 341–98.

Higgins, Brian, and Hershel Parker. "The Flawed Grandeur of Melville's *Pierre*." *New Perspectives on Melville.* Ed. Faith Pullin. Edinburgh: Univ. of Edinburgh Press, 1978. 162–96.

―――. *Herman Melville: The Contemporary Reviews.* New York: Cambridge Univ. Press, 1995.

Hoadley, John C. *Memorial of Henry Sanford Gansevoort.* Boston: Franklin Press, 1875.

Holli, Melvin G. *The American Mayor: The Best and the Worst Big-City Leaders.* University Park: Pennsylvania State Univ. Press, 1999.

Holt, Henry. *Garrulities of an Octogenarian Editor.* Boston: Houghton Mifflin, 1923.

Howard, Leon. *Melville: A Biography.* Berkeley: Univ. of California Press, 1951.

Humphreys, Charles A. *Field, Camp, Hospital and Prison in the Civil War, 1863–1865.* Boston: George H. Ellis, 1918.

Irving, Pierre. *The Life and Letters of Washington Irving.* 4 vols. New York: G. P. Putnam, 1862–64.

Kemble, John Haskell. *The Panama Route, 1848–1869.* Berkeley: Univ. of California Press, 1943.

Kennedy, Frederick. "Herman Melville's Lecture in Montreal." *New England Quarterly* 50 (March 1977), 125–37.

Kennedy, Frederick, and Joyce Deveau Kennedy. "Additions to the *Melville Log.*" *Extracts* 31 (September 1977), 4–8.

―――. "Archibald MacMechan and the Melville Revival." *Leviathan* 1 (October 1999), 5–37.

―――. "Elizabeth and Herman (Part 1)." *Extracts* 33 (February 1978), 4–12.

―――. "Elizabeth and Herman (Part 2)." *Melville Society Extracts* 34 (May 1978), 3–8.

―――. "Elizabeth Shaw Melville and Samuel Hay Savage, 1847–1853." *Melville Society Extracts* 39 (1979), 1–7.

―――. "Herman Melville and Samuel Hay Savage." *Melville Society Extracts* 35 (September 1978), 1–10.

Kenney, Alice P. See also Hamlin.

―――. *The Gansevoorts of Albany: Dutch Patricians in the Upper Hudson Valley.* Syracuse: Syracuse Univ. Press, 1969.

King, Thomas Starr. *Substance and Show, and Other Lectures.* Boston: Houghton, Osgood, 1879.

―――. *The White Hills; Their Legends, Landscape, and Poetry.* Boston: Crosby, Nichols, 1860.

Kring, Walter Donald. *Henry Whitney Bellows.* Boston: Skinner House, 1979.

Kring, Walter D., and Jonathan S. Carey. "Two Discoveries Concerning Herman Melville." *Proceedings of the Massachusetts Historical Society* 87 (1975), 137–41. (See also Yannella and Parker.)

Lathers, Richard. *This Discursive Biographical Sketch 1841–1902 of Colonel Richard Lathers was Compiled as Required for Honorary Membership in Post 509, Grand Army of the Republic . . . .* Philadelphia: J. B. Lippincott, 1902.

―――. *Reminiscences of Richard Lathers: Sixty Years of a Busy Life in South Carolina,*

Massachusetts and New York. Ed. Alvan F. Sanborn. New York: Grafton Press, 1907.

Levy, Leonard W. *The Law of the Commonwealth and Chief Justice Shaw.* Cambridge: Harvard Univ. Press, 1957.

Leyda, Jay. "An Albany Journal by Gansevoort Melville." *Boston Public Library Quarterly* 2 (October 1950), 327–47.

———. *The Melville Log: A Documentary Life of Herman Melville, 1819–1891.* New York: Harcourt Brace, 1951; 2d ed., with a supplement, New York: Gordian Press, 1969.

Littmann, Minna. "Edgartown Finds New Link with Melville: Author's Daughter Learns She Is Living in Former Home of Captain in Moby Dick." New Bedford *Sunday Standard* (11 August 1929).

MacDougall, Alma. "The Chronology of *The Confidence-Man* and 'Benito Cereno': Redating Two 1855 Curtis and Melville Letters." *Melville Society Extracts* 53 (February 1983), 3–6.

McNeilly, Dorothy V. B. D. R. "The Melvilles and Mrs. Ferris." *Extracts* 28 (November 1976), 1–9.

Mather, Frank Jewett, Jr. "Reminiscences of a Melvillian." *Princeton Alumni Weekly* 38 (25 March 1938), 555–56.

Mathieu, Bertrand. " 'Plain Mechanic Power': Melville's Earliest Poems, *Battle-Pieces and Aspects of the War.*" *Essays in Arts and Sciences* 5 (July 1976), 113–28.

Melville, Herman. See headnote to this list.

Melville, Herman. *Billy Budd, Sailor.* Ed. Harrison Hayford and Merton M. Sealts Jr. Chicago: Univ. of Chicago Press, 1962.

———. *Moby-Dick.* The Norton Critical Edition, rev. ed. Ed. Hershel Parker and Harrison Hayford. New York: W. W. Norton, 2001.

Metcalf, Eleanor Melville. *Herman Melville: Cycle and Epicycle.* Cambridge: Harvard Univ. Press, 1953.

Mosby, John S. *Memoirs.* Boston: Little, Brown, 1917.

Mott, Frank Luther. *American Journalism.* New York: Macmillan, 1941. Rev. ed. New York: Macmillan, 1950.

———. *A History of American Magazines (1850–1865).* Cambridge: Harvard Univ. Press, 1938.

Olsen-Smith, Steven. "A Fourth Supplementary Note to *Melville's Reading* (1988)." *Leviathan* 2 (March 2000), 105–11.

———. "Herman Melville's Planned Work on Remorse." *Nineteenth-Century Literature* 50 (March 1996), 489–500.

———. " 'Travel': New Evidence on Melville's Third Lecture." *Leviathan* 1 (March 1999), 45–55.

Olsen-Smith, Steven, and Hershel Parker. "Three New Melville Letters: Procrastination and Passports." *Melville Society Extracts* 102 (September 1995), 8–12.

Olsen-Smith, Steven, and Todd Richardson. "Melville's Protest to the *World*," to be published in 2002.

Parker, Hershel. See also Collum; Hayes; Higgins; Melville; Olsen-Smith; Yannella.

———. "Biography and Responsible Uses of the Imagination." *Resources for American Literary Study* 21 (June 1995), 16–42.

———. "Contract: *Pierre*, by Herman Melville." *Proof* 5 (1977), 27–44. (Includes photo-reproductions.)

———. "Herman Melville." *American National Biography* 15 (1999), 277–83.

———. *Herman Melville and the Powell Papers*. Under contract (described in the NN *Moby-Dick* "Historical Note").

———. "Herman Melville's *The Isle of the Cross*." *American Literature* 62 (March 1990), 1–16.

———. "Melville and Politics." Ph.D. dissertation, Northwestern Univ., 1963.

———. "The Melville House at 104 East 26th Street." *Harvard Library Bulletin* n.s. 8 (Winter 1997), 37–45.

———. "*The New Melville Log*: A Progress Report and an Appeal." *Modern Language Studies* 20 (Winter 1990), 53–66.

———. *Reading "Billy Budd."* Evanston: Northwestern Univ. Press, 1990.

Parker, Hershel, with Edward Daunais. "Sarah Morewood's Last Drive, as Told in Caroline S. Whitmarsh's 'A Representative Woman.'" *Melville Society Extracts* 93 (June 1993), 1–4.

Parker, Hershel, and Harrison Hayford. *"Moby-Dick" as Doubloon*. New York: W. W. Norton, 1970.

Poole, Gordon, ed. *"At the Hostelry" and "Naples in the Time of Bomba."* Naples: Instituto Universitario Orientale, 1989.

Reynolds, Cuyler. *Hudson-Mohawk Genealogical and Family Memoirs*. 4 vols. New York: Lewis Historical Publishing Co., 1911.

Richardson, Todd. "The Melville Voyagers and the 'Staten Island Savages.'" *Melville Society Extracts* 115 (December 1998), 8–10.

Rothenberg, Albert. *The Emerging Goddess: The Creative Process in Art, Science, and Other Fields*. Chicago: Univ. of Chicago Press, 1979.

Sandberg, Robert. "'The Adjustment of Screens': Putative Narrators, Authors, and Editors in Melville's Unfinished Burgundy Club Book." *Texas Studies in Literature and Language* 31 (Fall 1989), 426–50.

———. "Melville's Unfinished 'Burgundy Club' Book: A Reading Edition Edited from the Manuscripts with Introduction and Notes." Ph.D. dissertation, Northwestern Univ., 1989.

Sanborn, Geoffrey. "The Name of the Devil: Melville's Other 'Extracts' for *Moby-Dick*." *Nineteenth-Century Literature* 47 (September 1992), 212–35.

Sealts, Merton M., Jr. See also Melville.

———. *The Early Lives of Melville: Nineteenth-Century Biographical Sketches and Their Authors.* Madison: Univ. of Wisconsin Press, 1974.

———. "Innocence and Infamy: *Billy Budd, Sailor.*" *A Companion to Melville Studies.* Ed. John Bryant. Westport, Conn.: Greenwood, 1986. 407–30.

———. *Melville's Reading.* Columbia: Univ. of South Carolina Press, 1988. Also "A Supplementary Note to *Melville's Reading* (1988)." *Melville Society Extracts* 80 (February 1990), 5–10. (*Melville's Reading* lists books known to have been owned by Melville or otherwise to have been available to him.)

———. "The Melvilles, the Gansevoorts, and the Cincinnati Badge." *Extracts* 70 (September 1987), 1, 4.

———. *Pursuing Melville 1940–1980: Chapters and Essays.* Madison: Univ. of Wisconsin Press, 1982.

———. "A Sheaf of Melville-Melvill Letters." *Harvard Library Bulletin* 35 (1987), 280–93.

———. "Thomas Melvill, Jr., in *The History of Pittsfield.*" *Harvard Library Bulletin* 35 (1987), 201–17.

Shaw, Samuel. "Lemuel Shaw." *Memorial Biographies.* Vol. 4. Boston: The New England Historic Genealogical Society, 1885.

Shaw, Thomas Budd. *Outlines of English Literature.* Philadelphia: Blanchard & Lea, 1870.

Shepherd, Barnett. *Sailors' Snug Harbor: 1801–1976.* 2d ed. Staten Island: Snug Harbor Cultural Center, 1995.

Smith, Joseph E. A. "Herman Melville." Pittsfield *Evening Journal* (October 1891–January 1892), as reprinted in Sealts's *Early Lives.*

———. *The History of Pittsfield, (Berkshire County,) Massachusetts, from the Year 1800 to the Year 1876.* Springfield, Mass.: C. W. Bryan & Co., 1876.

———. "Pontoosuc Lake and Rolling Rock." *Taghconic* (1852, below), ch. 4.

———. *The Poet Among the Hills: Oliver Wendell Holmes in Berkshire.* Pittsfield: George Blatchford, 1895.

——— [Godfrey Greylock, pseud.]. *Taghconic; or, Letters and Legends about Our Summer Home.* Boston: Redding, 1852.

———. *Taghconic: The Romance and Beauty of the Hills.* Boston: Lee & Shepard, 1879.

Smith, Matthew Hale. *Sunshine and Shadow in New York.* Hartford: J. B. Burr, 1868.

Spark, Clare. *Hunting Captain Ahab: Psychological Warfare and the Melville Revival.* Kent, Ohio: Kent State Univ. Press, 2001.

Stedman, Arthur. Introduction. *Typee.* New York: United States Book Co., 1892. xv–xxxvi.

———. "'Marquesan' Melville." New York *World* (11 October 1891), 26.

Stern, Robert A. M., Thomas Mellins, and David Fishman. *New York 1880: Architecture and Urbanism in the Gilded Age.* New York: Monacelli, 1999.

Stoddard, Richard H. *Recollections Personal and Literary.* New York: A. S. Barnes, 1903.

Tanselle, G. Thomas. "Melville and the World of Books." *A Companion to Melville Studies.* Ed. John Bryant. Westport, Conn.: Greenwood, 1986. 781–835.

———. "The Sales of Melville's Books." *Harvard Library Bulletin* 17 (April 1969), 195–215.

Thurston, Brown. *Thurston Genealogies.* Portland, Maine: Brown Thurston, 1880.

Tilton, Eleanor. "Melville's 'Rammon': A Text and Commentary." *Harvard Library Bulletin* 13 (Winter 1959), 50–91.

Tuckerman, Henry T. "Biographical Essay." *Old New York.* By Dr. John W. Francis. New York: W. J. Widdleton, 1866.

———. *Book of the Artists: American Artist Life.* New York: G. P. Putnam, 1867.

———. "Reminiscences of Fitz-Greene Halleck." *Lippincott's Magazine* 1 (January 1868).

Wallace, Robert K. "Melville's Copy of Turner's *Whalers—the 'Erebus'*." *Melville Society Extracts* 90 (September 1992), 12–13.

———. "Melville's Prints and Engravings at the Berkshire Athenaeum." *Essays in Arts and Sciences* 15 (June 1986), 59–90.

———. "Melville's Prints: David Metcalf's Prints and Tile." *Harvard Library Bulletin* n.s. 8 (Winter 1997), 3–33.

———. "Melville's Prints: The Ambrose Group." *Harvard Library Bulletin* n.s. 6 (Spring 1995), 13–50.

———. "Melville's Prints: The E. Barton Chapin, Jr., Family Collection." *Leviathan* 2 (March 2000), 5–65.

———. "Melville's Prints: *The Gypsies*." *Harvard Library Bulletin* n.s. 8 (Winter 1997), 34–36.

———. "Melville's Prints: The Melville Chapin Collection." *Harvard Library Bulletin* n.s. 11 (2002).

———. "Melville's Prints: The Reese Collection." *Harvard Library Bulletin* n.s. 4 (October 1993), 6–42.

Whipple, Edwin P. *Character and Characteristic Men.* Boston: Ticknor & Fields, 1866.

Wolfe, Theodore. *Literary Shrines: The Haunts of Some Famous American Authors.* Philadelphia: J. B. Lippincott, 1895. Rev. as *Literary Haunts and Homes.* Philadelphia: J. B. Lippincott, 1899.

Wolff, Geoffrey. *Black Sun: The Brief Transit and Violent Eclipse of Harry Crosby.* New York: Random House, 1876.

Yannella, Donald, and Hershel Parker. *The Endless, Winding Way in Melville: New Charts by Kring and Carey.* Glassboro: The Melville Society, 1981. (A reprinting of a 1975 Walter D. Kring–Jonathan S. Carey article along with commentary and supplementary material by Kring and several Melvilleans, in a pamphlet distributed to all members of the Melville Society and many libraries.)

Index

Abbot, John Djékis, 305
Abbotsford, 296–97
Abbott, Dr. Henry (1812–1859), 336
Abbott, Mabel, 744
Abby Lodge, 668, 673, 676–77, 746
Acushnet (whaleship): crew of, 150–51, 881, 915; wrecked, 150
Adams, John Quincy (1767–1848), *Dermot MacMorrogh*, 403–4, 435, 437, 438
Adams, W. H. Davenport, *The Buried Cities of Campania*, 702
Adirondack (U.S. sloop), 514, 518–19
Adler, George J. (1821–1868), 670
"The Admiral of the White," 857. *See also* "The Haglets"
Aeolian harp, 611, 908, 911
Aesthetics, 326–27, 330, 334, 411, 487, 674–75; architectonics, 173; fiction, 270, 287, 734; Hawthorne and, 273, 492, 739; M's aesthetic credo, 504–5; M's study of, 492–505; the picturesque, 491; terminology, 313, 357; theory, 160–61. *See also* Poetics
"Afternoon in Naples." *See* "Morning in Naples"
"After the Pleasure Party," 116–17, 421–22
"Agatha" story. *See The Isle of the Cross* (lost). *See also* Hatch, Agatha; Robertson (sailor)
"The Age of the Antonines," 421, 816, 834
Akenside, Mark, 403; *The Pleasures of Imagination*, 406
Albany Academy (Albany, N.Y.), 539
Albany Army Relief Bazaar, 559–61
Albany Institute of History and Art (Albany, N.Y.), 837
Albany, N.Y., periodicals: *Argus*, 30, 82, 791, 870, 891; *Atlas & Argus*, 345; *Daily State Register*, 138, 179; *Evening Journal*, 255, 412, 791, 891; *Microscope*, 356
Alcohol and alcoholism, 194–95, 217, 400–401, 428–29, 456, 475–76, 514
Alcott, Bronson (1799–1888), 145
Alden, Henry Mills (1836–1919), 592
Alden, William Livingston, "London Literary Letter," 923

Aldrich, Thomas Bailey, 861; *Poems*, 861; *The Story of a Bad Boy*, 861
Alexandria, Egypt, M visits, 310, 313
Alfieri, Victor, 83, 328, 496–98
Alger, William Rounseville, 723; *The Solitudes of Nature*, 723
Alison, Archibald (1757–1839), 428, 439–40
Allen, Ethan, *A Narrative of Col. Ethan Allen's Captivity*, 226
Allen, Joseph, *Battles of the British Navy*, 896
Allen, Phineas (bookstore, Pittsfield, Mass.), 38
All Souls Unitarian Church (N.Y.C.), 66, 232, 501, 586, 718, 740, 767, 845, 863, 896, 920
Ambrose, Priscilla Osborne, 906
American national character, 227, 237–38, 241, 256, 581
American national literature. *See* Literary life (American); Literature, American national; Poetry: American
American Society of Mechanical Engineers, *Transactions*, 94, 180
Ancient Spanish Ballads, 494
Anderson, John, 918–19
Andrews (lawyer), 680
Animals, cruelty toward, 409–10, 694–95
Ann Alexander (whaleship), 23
Anonymity of magazine contributors, 163
Antonio (guide, Venice), 332
Appledore Island, Maine, 137
"The Apple-Tree Table," 271, 276
The Arabian Nights, 308
Arcadia (steamer), 309
Architecture, 817, 828–29
Ariosto, Ludovico (1474–1533), 435
"The Armies of the Wilderness," 572
Armories, 296
Arnold, James, 113
Arnold, Matthew (1822–1888), 366; *Essays in Criticism*, 675–76; *New Poems*, 723; preface to *Poems*, 503–4
Arnold, Thomas (1795–1842), *Travelling Journals*, 722

Arrowhead (Pittsfield, Mass.): Allan and Jane Melville take possession, 535–37; Allan Melville farms, 676, 678; amusements, 677–78; depiction, 271, 432–33, 707; description, 397, 647–48; historic import, 271, 531–32, 535, 648, 707; improvements, 111, 281, 536, 591, 647, 678; M farms, 138, 344; M moves from, 520; offered for sale, 278, 280, 353, 511; sale of portion, 285–86, 396–97, 417; sale of remainder, 515, 530–31; servants, 198–99; visitors, 112, 121, 137, 150, 169–71, 189, 229–30, 253, 261–62, 286, 379, 677–78, 761
"Art," 407, 817, 888
Aspinwall, Panama (Colón), 452
Aspinwall, William Henry, 375, 380
Athens, Greece, M visits, 320
Atlantic cable, 366, 603, 909
"At the Hostelry," 489, 490, 491, 492, 834, 879–80
Auburn, N.Y., M lectures at, 369
Auburn, N.Y., periodicals: *Advertiser*, 370, 372; *American*, 370
Augusta, Maine, *Kennebec Journal*, 616–17, 619
"Authentic Anecdotes of 'Old Zack,'" 292, 831
Auto da Fe, 16, 287
Aventine (steamer), 328

Backus, John (model for Pip), 151
Bagger, Louis, 651–52, 655, 744, 754
Bagley, Isabella Bogart, 744–45, 760, 827
Baker, Edward D., 448, 451
Balance Rock (Lanesboro, Mass.), 46, 58, 229
Balboa, Vasco Núñez de (1475–1517), 375
"Ball's Bluff. A Reverie," 451
Baltimore, Md., M lectures at, 391
Baltimore, Md., periodicals: *American and Commercial Advertiser*, 374, 391; *Sun*, 391, 617
Balzac, Honoré de (1799–1850), 905; *Correspondence*, 897
Banvard, John, 308; *Description of Banvard's Panorama of the Mississippi River*, 257
Barlow, Joel (1754–1812), *The Columbiad*, 403, 435
Barnum, P. T. (1810–1891), 270, 527, 851
Barrett, Edward, *Dead Reckoning*, 791
Barrs, J. W., 863, 896, 897

Bartholdi, Frédéric Auguste (1834–1904), 808, 833
Bartholomew, Edward (1822–1858), 326
"Bartleby, the Scrivener," 164, 176–79; payment, 185; reception, 179, 183, 188; sources, 138, 150, 176, 178–79
Bartlett, W. H., *Forty Days in the Desert*, 687; *The Nile Boat*, 687; *Walks about the City . . . of Jerusalem*, 687
Bartlett, William Francis, 548–49, 649
Bash Bish Falls (Mass.), 174, 229, 547–48, 552
Batterson, James G., 832
The Battery (N.Y.C.), 589, 692
Battle-Pieces, 454, 561; composition, 562, 586, 606; contents, 611; dedication, 611; family response, 601–2, 624–25; genre, 608–9; poems anthologized, 745; poetics, 606–8; presentation copies, 567, 600, 602, 605, 615, 649; publication, 592–93, 600; reviews, 605; reception, 615–24; sales, 624, 667; sources, 562–573, 582–83, 588–89, 609–13; Supplement, 604, 609, 613
Beirut, Lebanon, 319
Bell, Acton. *See* Brontë, Anne
Bell, Capt. Charles H. (1798–1875), 321, 342, 654
Bell, Currer. *See* Brontë, Charlotte
Bella Vascongoda (whaleship), 23
Bellows, Henry Whitney (1814–1882), 448–49, 501, 540–41, 559–60, 599, 675, 718, 740, 760, 842, 845, 849; counsels Elizabeth Melville, 629, 634–35, 650; *The Old World in Its New Face*, 675, 687
"The Bell-Tower," 259, 628
Benedict, James S., 604
Bengal (merchant ship), 484
"Benito Cereno," 14, 269; autobiographical elements, 241; characterization, 238; composition, 235, 240, 242; offered to *Putnam's*, 250; reception, 270, 272; sources, 235–38, 272; style, 239; theme, 237, 241–42
Bennett, James Gordon (1795–1872), 123, 743
Bentley, Richard (1794–1871), 38, 138, 242; losses on M's works, 98–99, 106; offered *Pierre*, 71, 94, 99, 106–7, 108
Béranger, Pierre, *Songs*, 434, 812, 817
Berkshire Athenaeum (Pittsfield, Mass.), 717, 746

Berkshire County, Mass., 64, 111, 165; authors in, 555, 683, 813–14; *Eagle*, 215, 262, 290, 353, 385, 387, 418, 445, 455, 480, 509, 511, 522, 544, 545, 550, 552, 558; eminent citizens, 183, 544; excursions, 111–12, 173–74, 229, 379–80, 515, 521, 547–48; in *Pierre*, 45–46, 58, 62

Bermuda, M visits, 893

Bernhardt, Sarah (1844–1923), 846

Beta (pseud.), 230

Betty, William Henry, 167–68

Bezanson, Walter E., 684, 724, 781

Bible, 39, 256, 481. *See also* Corinthians; Exodus; Kings II; Proverbs; Romans

The Bijou, 474

Billson, James, 863–65, 872, 877, 885, 889, 893, 896; "James Thomson: Poet," 864; "The South Sea," 864

Billy Budd, Sailor, 16, 408, 878, 882–83, 885–86; composition, 880, 896, 902

Binnian, Katharine G. (1890–1968; Mrs. Walter; M's granddaughter), 228

Bird, Francis W., 221

Black Point (Frémont home in San Francisco), 449

Blake, William (1757–1827), 804, 865, 889

Blatchford, Mary (d. 1851), 95

Bliss, Alexander, *Autograph Leaves of Our Country's Authors*, 561–62, 608

Boardman, Rev. H. A., 415

Boatswain (dog), 754

Boccaccio, Giovanni (1313–1375), 724, 769

Bogart, Catherine E. *See* Melville, Catherine E. (Katie)

Bogart, Stephen Van Rensselaer, 656, 666, 850–51

Bond Street (N.Y.C.), 414

Bok, Edward, 915

Bologna, Italy, M visits, 331

Bon Homme Richard (warship), 226

Boston Athenæum, 144

Boston, Mass.: fire of 1872, 749; M lectures at, 366, 386, 388

Boston, Mass., periodicals: *Advertiser*, 54, 389, 468, 644; *Atlantic Monthly*, 355, 605, 623, 686, 732, 861, 864; *Atlas & Bee*, 469, 471; *Bee*, 366; *Christian Examiner*, 248; *Christian Register*, 91; *Christian Witness*, 619; *Commercial Bulletin*, 587, 621; *Commonwealth*, 621; *Courier*, 221, 366–67, 467, 470, 471; *Daily Advertiser*, 594, 616; *Daily Evening Transcript*, 221, 350, 366, 385, 388, 467, 469, 470, 488, 594, 739, 803–4, 860, 894; *Daily Evening Traveller*, 30, 82, 183, 284, 361, 366–67, 370, 389, 471, 617, 619; *Daily Times*, 124, 632–33; *Evening Gazette*, 110, 247–49; *Herald*, 472, 866; *Investigator*, 221; *Journal*, 366, 389; *Liberator*, 65; *Literary World*, 398, 875; *Littell's Living Age*, 163, 276, 632, 685; *North American Review*, 461, 487, 489; *Post*, 18–20, 53–54, 119, 123, 221, 247, 248, 366, 389, 467–71, 576, 618–19, 632, 705–6, 823, 897; *Puritan Recorder*, 349; *Saturday Post*, 168, 858; *Statesman*, 20; *Weekly Advertiser*, 644

Boston Tea Party, 766

Bourne, William O. (b. 1819), 16

Boutwell, George, 756

Bowles, Samuel, 553

Bradford, Alexander W. (1815–1867), 463, 539

Brentano, A. and S. (bookstore, N.Y.C.), 865–66

Brewster, Charles, 802, 808

Brewster, George (1834–1903), 562, 568, 574, 808

Brewster, Dr. John M., 6, 137, 396–97

Briggs, Charles F. (1804–1877), 179, 218, 650

Briggs, George Nixon, 479–80

Bright, Henry A. (1830–1884), 301, 342

Brittain, Ellen Huyler (1814–1897), 41, 553, 649, 677

Broadhall (Pittsfield, Mass.), 4–5, 262–64, 290. *See also* Melvill farm

Brontë, Anne (1820–1849), *The Tenant of Wildfell Hall*, 56

Brontë, Charlotte (1816–1855), 338; *Jane Eyre*, 55; *Shirley*, 166; *Villette*, 201

Brontë, Emily (1818–1848), *Wuthering Heights*, 55

Brook Farm, 119

Brooklyn Bridge, 786, 826, 854

Brooklyn Navy Yard, 354, 475–76, 581

Brooklyn, N.Y., periodicals: *Daily Union*, 801; *Eagle*, 864; *Standard-Union*, 921

Brooks, Shirley, 710

Broughton, Thomas Duer, *Selections from the Popular Poetry of the Hindoos*, 434

Brown (sexton, Grace Church, N.Y.), 218

Brown, Charles Brockden, 284

Brown, Mrs. H. Cleaver, 744

Brown, John, 410, 611
Browne, Sir Thomas (1605–1682), 105
Brownell, Henry Howard (1820–1872), 622; *Lyrics of a Day*, 610; *War-Lyrics and Other Poems*, 621
Browning, Elizabeth Barrett (1806–1861), *Aurora Leigh*, 685; *Poems*, 609, 622
Browning, Orville H., 396
Browning, Robert (1812–1889), 404, 504, 622, 623, 767, 813, 922. Works: "In a Gondola," 418; *Men and Women*, 422; *Poems*, 422; *The Ring and the Book*, 685, 784
Bruyère, Jean de la (1645–1696), *The Works*, 502
Bryan, Clark W., *The Book of Berkshire*, 521
Bryant, William Cullen (1794–1878), 211, 759, 773; "Thanatopsis," 470
Buchanan, Robert (1841–1901), 922; "The Outcast," 919–20; "Socrates in Camden," 872–73
Bulwer-Lytton, Edward George (1803–1873), 618–19; *Ernest Maltravers*, 55; *Zanoni*, 55
Buntline, Ned. *See* Judson, Edward Z. C.
Buonarroti, Michelangelo. *See* Michelangelo Buonarroti
Burbank's Hall (Pittsfield, Mass.), 387–88
"Burgundy Club Sketches," 829–34, 880
Burns, Anthony, 220–21, 458
Burns, Robert (1759–1796), 296, 614; centennial celebration, 388–89
Butler, William Allen (1825–1902), 25–26, 28–29, 82, 134–35, 782
Byron, George Gordon, sixth baron (1788–1824), 306, 332, 333, 342, 435, 481, 654, 754; travesty of, 373. Works: *Childe Harold's Pilgrimage*, 360, 362; *Don Juan*, 481, 513; *The Giaour*, 686; *The Island: or Christian and His Comrades*, 481; *Mazeppa*, 686; *The Siege of Corinth*, 686

Cairo, Egypt, M visits, 310–13
California, 6, 375, 436. *See also* San Francisco, Calif.
Callcott (or Calcott), John Wall (1766–1821), 470
Carolus (brig), 816
Cambridge, Mass.: *Chronicle*, 408–10, 412, 414; M lectures at, 370
Cambridgeport, Mass., M lectures at, 408, 414

Camoëns, Luis Vaz de (1524–1580), *The Lusiads*, 403, 436
Campbell, Alexander, *Sketches of Life*, 433
Camp meeting, 579–80
Cannibalism, 11, 240, 686, 726; by *Essex* survivors, 117; by Marquesan islanders, 117
Cape Cod Folks. See Greene, Sarah P. M.
Carlyle, John, 435
Carlyle, Thomas (1795–1881), 104–5, 132
Cary, Alice (1820–1871), 588
Cary, Phoebe (1824–1871), 588
Cavour, Camillo Benso (1810–1861), 489
Cemeteries: Albany Rural Cemetery, 669, 740, 791, 798, 870, 891; Moravian Cemetery (Staten Island), 858; Mt. Auburn (Cambridge, Mass.), 471; Pittsfield, Mass., 384, 474, 554–55; Trinity Cemetery (Carmansville, N.Y.), 382, 736, 868, 900; Woodlawn Cemetery (The Bronx, N.Y.C.), 646, 649, 921
Cenci, Beatrice (1577–1599), 325, 768–69
Centennial celebration (U.S.), 805
Centennial Exhibition (Philadelphia), 808
Central Park (N.Y.C.), 762, 913
Cervantes Saavedra, Miguel de (1547–1616), *Don Quixote*, 303
Chalkley, Thomas, *Journals*, 686
Chalmers, Alexander (1759–1834), ed., *The British Essayists*, 413
Chambers, Ephraim, *Cyclopaedia*, 752
Chandler, William E., 603
Channing, William Ellery (1818–1901), reviews *The Piazza Tales*, 284
Chapman, George (1559?–1634). *See* Homer
Chapman, Rev. George T., 96
Chappel, Alonzo, 609
Charles Edward (Stuart prince; 1720–1788), 613–14
Charleston, S.C., periodicals: *Courier*, 188; *Southern Quarterly Review*, 73, 124–25, 130, 140, 632
Charlestown, Mass.: *Bunker-Hill Aurora and Boston Mirror*, 370; M lectures at, 369–70
Chase, John, 883
Chase, Owen (1796–1869), *Narrative of the . . . Shipwreck of the Whale-Ship Essex*, 11
"Chattanooga," 572–73, 593
Chatterton, Thomas (1752–1770), 191
Chaucer, Geoffrey (1340?–1400), 435, 807, 817, 878

Chauncey, Henry, 375
Cheever, Henry T. (1814–1897), 25, 82
Chess, 429, 635, 637
Chester, Eng., 301–2, 849
Chicago, Ill., M lectures at, 393
Chicago, Ill., periodicals: *America*, 892; *Daily Press and Tribune*, 393; *Journal*, 393
Child, Francis James (1825–1896), *English and Scottish Ballads*, 408
Child, Hamilton, *Gazetteer... of Saratoga County*, 508, 637
Chillicothe, Ohio, M lectures at, 369
Chillicothe, Ohio, periodicals: *Advertiser*, 371; *Scioto Gazette*, 371
Chitty, Marian, 265
Christmas celebrations, 41, 47–50, 188–89, 345, 368, 523–34, 672, 719–21, 788–89, 843–44, 863
Churches and church-going, 25, 66, 67, 94, 96, 118, 405, 459, 521, 535, 825, 863, 896. *See also* All Souls Unitarian Church (N.Y.C.); Church of the Ascension (N.Y.C.); Church of the Holy Sepulchre (Jerusalem); Church of the Messiah (N.Y.C.); Dutch Reformed Church (New Brighton, N.Y.); Grace Church (Lawrence, Mass.); Grace Church (N.Y.C.); King's Chapel (Boston); New South Church (Boston); North Dutch Church (Albany, N.Y.); San Marco, cathedral of (Venice); St. Joseph's Cathedral (Albany); St. Peter's Cathedral (Rome); St. Sophia, mosque of (Constantinople); St. Stephen's Protestant Episcopal Church (Pittsfield); Zion Church (N.Y.C.)
Churchill, Charles (1731–1764), *Poetical Works*, 502
Church of the Ascension (N.Y.C.), 25
Church of the Holy Sepulchre (Jerusalem), 316
Church of the Holy Zebra. *See* All Souls Unitarian Church
Church of the Messiah (N.Y.C.), 644, 645
Cincinnati, Ohio, M lectures at, 369
Cincinnati, Ohio, periodicals: *Daily Commercial*, 370–71, 372; *Enquirer*, 370, 371, 372, 618
Cincinnati, Order of the, 514, 518, 822, 830–31
City of Manchester (steamer), 342, 351
Civil War (U.S.): Secession crisis, 449, 456–59; *1861*: 472, 473, 476, 480; *1862*: 513, 515; *1863*: 540–41, 544–46; *1864*: 562–73, 581–83; —, M witnesses, 562–73; *1865*: 588; Reconstruction, 602, 603, 613, 615, 616, 656
Clarel, 173, 660; ambitions for, 688–89, 794, 813; "Bethlehem," 778–82; Centennial Poem, 688–89; composition, 315, 687–88, 701; dedication, 799, 800; form, 685–86; genesis, 678–80, 683–84; "Jerusalem," 695–701; M describes, 863–64; "Mar Saba," 767, 768–72; plot, 695–96; prefatory note, 800–801; preparation for publication, 784, 790, 791–94, 799; presentation copies, 801, 864–65; publication, 800; pulped, 839–40; reception, 803–6, 809–10; sources, 683–87, 722–23; themes, 695–96, 697, 703–4, 767, 778–79; Vine's role, 696–701, 724–33, 767, 768–71, 780–81; "The Wilderness," 724–33. *See also* Hawthorne, Nathaniel
Clark, Rufus W., 658
Clarke, Rev. James Freeman (1810–1888), 825, 841
Clarke, Newman S., 447
Clarksville, Tenn., M lectures at, 369
Clarksville, Tenn., periodicals: *Chronicle*, 370; *Jeffersonian*, 371
Cleopatra's Needles, 310
Cleveland, Grover (1837–1908), 854, 858, 862
Cleveland, Ohio, M lectures at, 369
Cleveland, Ohio, periodicals: *Evening Herald*, 370, 371; *Morning Leader*, 371; *Ohio Farmer*, 359
Clevinger, Shobal Vail (1812–1843), 550
Clifford, John H., 113, 114–16, 120, 130–31, 202, 468
Clough, A. H., 809
Coan, Titus Munson, 397–400, 917
Cobb, Edward W., 116
"Cock-A-Doodle-Doo!" 164, 168, 175, 188
Coleridge, Samuel Taylor (1772–1834): *The Friend*, 217; *Lectures upon Shakespeare*, 144
"The College Colonel," 548–49, 649
Collins, William, 403; "Ode on the Poetical Character," 408; *Poetical Works*, 502, 511
Collision at sea, 428–29
Cologne, Germany, 57
Colonial and Home Library. *See* Murray's Home and Colonial Library

Colt, James D., 384, 418, 463
Columbus, Christopher (1446?–1506), 240, 779
Columbus, Ohio, *Ohio State Journal*, 350
Combe, George, *Essays on Phrenology*, 217
Come-Outers (religious sect), 260
Como, Lake (Italy), 288, 334
Composition portraits, 491
Composure of mind, 70
Concord, N.H.: M lectures at, 366; *New Hampshire Patriot and State Gazette*, 363
The Confidence-Man, 10, 16; autobiographical elements, 280; composition, 256, 257–58, 260–61, 270, 279–80, 286–87; contract, 293; family comment, 350–51; prospective profits, 282; publication, 291, 337–38, 349; reception, 338–40, 349–51; sales, 340; sources, 255–57, 263; style, 287, 339–40; stereotype plates, 354–55; themes, 260, 291
"The Conflict of Convictions," 622
Constantinople, Turkey, M visits, 306–8
Constellation (U.S. frigate), 310, 321, 336
Conway, N.H. *See* North Conway, N.H.
Cooke, Robert Francis, 157, 158
Coolies, 447
Cooper, James Fenimore (1789–1851), 350; M's attitude toward, 36–37. Works: *History of the Navy of the United States*, 226; *The Red Rover*, M's review of, 22, 517
Cooper, Paul Fenimore, 802
Copper works. *See* New Bedford Copper Works
Copyright, 71, 222
Coquette (whaleship), 238
Corinthians, First Epistle to the, 258
Corning, Erastus, 346–47
Cortes (steamer), 450, 451
Coster, Robert, 746
Courts-martial, 519
Cowper, William, 407
Craik, George Lillie, *The New Zealanders*, 40, 113, 143
Cramer, William E. (1817–1905), 394–95, 442
Crawford, Thomas (1813–1857), 327
Crimean War, 488
Crook, George (1828–1890), 582
Croswell, Edwin L. (1797–1871), 153
Crystal Palace (London), 340–41
Cultural relativity, 39–40, 323, 409–10
"The Cumberland," 561, 563, 593

Cunningham, Frederick, 314
Cupa, Tupai. *See* Tupai Cupa
Curtis, Benjamin R., 157, 472, 656
Curtis, Catherine (Kate) Gansevoort (1814–1887; Mrs. George; M's cousin), 353, 481, 525, 598, 859
Curtis, George (1789?–1884), 861
Curtis, George W., 354, 391, 588, 655–56, 675, 717; assists M's lecture career, 355–56, 363; edits *Putnam's*, 246–47, 250, 258–59; *Homes of American Authors*, 145
Curtis, Joseph, 177, 220
Curtis, Mary (M's first cousin, once removed), 481, 659, 859
Curtis, Ned (M's first cousin, once removed), 529
Curtis, William, 678
Curtis Hotel (Lenox, Mass.), 678–80, 683. *See also* Little Red Inn
Cushing, Caleb, 154
Custer, George Armstrong, 582, 802, 806
Custom House. *See* New York Custom House
Cyclopædia of American Literature, 270–71; compilation, 246
Cydnus (steamer), 321

Dana, Richard Henry, Jr. (1815–1882), 281, 463–64, 889; M writes to, about *Moby-Dick*, 17; *Two Years before the Mast*, 76
Dana, Richard Henry, Sr. (1787–1879), 179
Dante Alighieri (1265–1321), 13, 328, 434, 435, 622
Danvers, Mass., M lectures at, 408, 414
Darley, Felix (1822–1888), 173–74, 230–31, 587
da Vinci, Leonardo. *See* Leonardo da Vinci
Davis, Alexander Jackson (1803–1892), 74, 659, 822, 829; "An Old Architect on Modern Architecture," 828–29
D. D., 815
Dead letter office, 138
Dearborn, Mich., *Independent*, 343, 855–56
Death and burial at sea, 430–31
Defoe, Daniel (1660–1731), M compared to, 233, 566
Delano, Capt. Amasa, 114; *A Narrative of Voyages and Travels*, 235–37, 239, 272
De Leon, Edwin, 310
Delmonico's restaurant (New York), 491–92, 875

Delos, Greece, 309
Demarest, William H., 592, 624
De Peyster, Augustus, 653
De Quincey, Thomas (1785–1859), 105
Dewey, Rodney, 479
Dewey, Orville (1794–1882), 33, 35, 65–67, 358, 426, 773; baptizes Melville children, 549; conducts Shaw's funeral, 467, 469–71; and the poor, 66, 220; and race, 615; and slavery, 66–67, 456–57. Works: *Autobiography*, 177; *Discourses on Human Nature*, 220; "The Problem of Human Destiny," 33, 35, 67, 80
DeWolf, Oscar C., 567, 574
Dexter, Elias, 674–75
Dickens, Charles (1812–1870), 55, 667; M compared to, 183, 284. Works: *American Notes*, 260; *Bleak House*, 207–8; *David Copperfield*, 49, 55; *Martin Chuzzlewit*, 631; *Master Humphrey's Clock*, 228
Dickinson, Emily, 553
Dickson, Walter, 318, 319
Dillaway, Charles Knapp (1804–1889), 603, 677
Dillaway, George W., 677, 680, 748–49, 825, 901–2, 921
Dillaway, Mary E., 603
Disraeli, Benjamin, 55
Disraeli, Isaac, *Works*, 494
Dix, John Adams (1798–1879), 154, 458, 615, 679
Dix, Joshua A., 250, 259; M offers story collection, 271
Dix, Morgan, 653, 679, 843
Dix & Edwards (publishers), 246, 354; publish *The Confidence-Man*, 257, 258, 349; publish *Piazza Tales*, 271–72, 275, 276, 283
Dockyards (N.Y.C.), 690–93
Dodge, William E., 854
Dog show, 818
"Donelson," 620
Doney, Caffè (Florence, Italy), 328, 329, 331
"Doolittle, Cousin." *See* Melvill, Robert (1817–1881)
Doolittle, E. S. *See* Melville, Elizabeth Shaw
Dorgan, James A., *Studies*, 622
Douw, John De Peyster (1812–1901), 203–4
Douw, Margaret Van Rensselaer (1819–1897), 203–4, 383
Dow, Elizabeth, 145, 169
Draft riots (N.Y.C., 1863), 542, 615

Draper, J. W., *Thoughts on the Future Civil Policy*, 613
Drayton, Michael, 438
Drowne, Henry Thayer (1822–1897?), 822, 831
Dryden, John (1631–1700). *See* Virgil, *The Aeneid*
Dublin, Ireland, *University Magazine*, 103–4, 276, 922
Duckworth (English resident of Salonica, Greece), 305
Dumbarton Castle (Scotland), 296
Du Pont, Samuel Francis (1803–1865), 514, 518–19
"Dupont's Round Fight," 561
Dutch Reformed Church (New Brighton, N.Y.), 657, 659
Duyckinck, Evert A. (1816–1878), 593, 734; and Allan Melville, 246, 345; and "Bartleby, the Scrivener," 188; compiles *National History of the War*, 609–10; death, 828; edits *Cyclopædia of American Literature*, 246, 898; gift to Sailors' Snug harbor, 821–22; lends books to M, 411, 413, 493; literary salon, 345; and M, 79, 93, 107, 291, 799, 822; and *Pierre*, 78–79, 80–81, 121; and *Poems* (1860) (lost), 423, 425, 443–44; reviews *Moby-Dick*, 22–25, 38; reviews *Pierre*, 128–29; reviews *White-Jacket*, 15, 24; sponsors *Criterion*, 284; visits Arrowhead, 378; visits Winyah, 476–77. *See also* New York, N.Y., periodicals: *Criterion*, *Literary World*, *Yankee Doodle*
Duyckinck, George L. (1823–1863), 93, 299; death, 533–34; edits *Cyclopædia of American Literature*, 246; on M, 379–81; on *Moby-Dick*, 23–24; portrait, 477; pursued by S. Morewood, 45–52; sponsors *Criterion*, 284; visits Arrowhead, 378; visits Winyah, 476–77
D'Wolf, John (1779–1872; M's uncle) 662, 739; *Voyage to the North Pacific*, 481
D'Wolf, John Langsdorff (1817–1886; M's cousin), 199, 891
D'Wolf, Mary Melvill (1778–1859; Mrs. John; M's aunt), 200–201

Early, Jubal A. (1816–1894), 582
Eaton, Joseph Oriel, 703, 704, 715, 734, 907, 910
Eden Musée, 913–14

Edinburgh, Scotland, M visits, 296–97
Edinburgh, Scotland, periodicals: *Edinburgh Review*, 406–7, 496; *Evening Courant*, 104
Egbert (fictional character), 279
Egypt, M visits, 310–13
Egyptian (screw-steamer), 302–4
Eliot, George (pseud., 1819–1880): *Middlemarch*, 756; *The Spanish Gypsy*, 685
Elizabethan drama, 493, 904
Elliot, Charles Loring (1812–1868), 560
Ellis, F. S., 711
Ellis, Havelock (1859–1939), 901
Emerson, Ralph Waldo (1803–1882), 99, 256, 388–89, 414, 622, 723; M on, 389. Works: "Compensation," 377; *The Conduct of Life*, 709–10; *Essays*, 501–2, "Friendship," 69, 279; "Merlin," 404; *Representative Men*, 552
Emmons, Richard (1788–1834), *Fredoniad*, 403, 435, 558, 611
"The Encantadas," 165, 210–13; censorship of, 218; epigraphs, 404; reception, 215–16, 218; style, 210–11, 215–16
England, M visits (1856–57), 297–303, 337–42
Erechtheum Club (London), 158
Erie Canal, 180–81
Essex (whaleship), 117. *See also* Chase, Owen, *Narrative*
The Ettrick Shepherd, 614
Evans, Mary Ann. *See* Eliot, George
Exman, Eugene, *The House of Harper*, 631
Exodus, Book of, 750

Faber, Frederick W., *Hymns*, 649
Farnham, Charles H., 655–56, 741, 827; "A Day on the Docks," 690–93
Farragut, David Glasgow (1801–1870), 429, 475, 833
Fauntleroy, Lt. Charles M., 336
Fay, Theodore Sedgwick (1807–1898), 336
Fayaway (schooner), 450
Felton, Mrs., *American Life*, 241–42
Fergusson, Robert, *The Works*, 494
Ferris, Mary Lanman Douw, 142, 204, 819–20
"The Fiddler," 164, 166–68, 175, 213
Fidèle (fictional riverboat), 258
Field, Cyrus (1819–1892), 603, 723, 909
Field, David Dudley, Sr., *A History of the County of Berkshire*, 15, 40–41, 255

Field, Maunsell B., *Memories of Many Men and Some Women*, 230–31
Fielding, Henry (1707–1754): *Amelia*, 257; *Tom Jones*, 257
Fields, James T. (1817–1881), 848
Flint, Timothy (1780–1840), *The History and Geography of the Mississippi Valley*, 256–57
Florence (apartment building, N.Y.C.), 846, 906
Florence, Italy: M seeks consulship, 460–66; M visits, 328–31
Florian's cafe (Venice), 332
Flushing, N.Y., M lectures at, 408, 410
Fly, Eli James Murdock (1817–1854), 93, 206
Forrest, Catherine (1817–1891; Mrs. Edwin), 85
Forrest, Edwin (1806–1872), 36, 74
Fort Stanwix, N.Y., 514, 703
Foster, George V., 902
Fox and Geese (Southport, Eng., tavern), 301
"Fragments from a Writing Desk," 878
Francis, Dr. John W. (1789–1861), 143–44, 246, 414; *Old New York* (1866 ed.), 484, 593–94
Franconi's Hippodrome, 156
Franklin, Benjamin, 225–26
Frederick II (1818–1859; king of the Two Sicilies, 1830–1859), 323
Frémont, Col. Charles, 449
Frémont, Jessie Benton (Mrs. Charles), 449
"The Frenzy in the Wake," 586
"Fruit of Travel Long Ago." *See Timoleon*; see also individual poems under *Poems* (1860) (lost or dispersed)
Fugitive Slave Law, 221
Fuller, Margaret (1810–1850), 119, 489
Fulton Market (N.Y.C.), 692
Furnishings (household), 397–98, 466–67, 485, 798, 835, 889–90, 907–12
Furniss, William, *Landvoieglee*, 307

Gam, 432
Gama, Vasco da (1469–1524), 436
Gansevoort, Catherine (Kitty) (1838–1918; M's cousin): engagement, 657, 764, 765; grief, 713–14, 716, 737, 760, 765; helps T. Melville, 653; marriage, 766; memorial volume for Henry, 715, 717, 742, 765; rapprochement with Melville family, 253, 526,

Index

598; and silver, 661. *See also* Lansing, Catherine (Kate) Gansevoort
Gansevoort, Catherine Quackenboss (1774–1855; Mrs. Herman; M's aunt), 97, 262, 268, 653, 903
Gansevoort, Catherine Van Schaick (1752–1830; Mrs. Peter; M's grandmother), 528
Gansevoort, Guert (1812–1868; M's cousin), 429; alcoholism, 475–76, 529; death, 669; illnesses, 591, 598; M tries to visit, 562–63; naval career, 354, 475–76, 513–15, 518–19, 539, 581; *Somers* mutiny, 475, 514
Gansevoort, Henry Sanford (1834–1871; M's cousin), 585, 595; character, 393, 527; death, 713; estate, 750; health and illnesses, 527, 529, 708–9, 712; on M, 351–52, 366–67, 391, 574; memorial volume, 715, 784–86, 825, 828; orders regimental banner, 573; war service, 515, 528, 539, 572, 581–82
Gansevoort, Herman (1779–1862; M's uncle), 262; death, 500; health, 478–79; leaves estate to Maria, 269; M visits, 265, 266–67, 268; remembered by M, 903; will, 501
Gansevoort, Leonard (1816–1864; M's cousin), 204, 529, 579, 581
Gansevoort, Peter (1749–1812; M's grandfather), 703, 826, 843; memorabilia, 58, 544, 837; Order of the Cincinnati, 514; photograph, 528; portrait, 910
Gansevoort, Peter (1788–1876; M's uncle): attempts political appointment for M, 153–54; death and funeral, 790–91; describes M, 139; estate, 796, 811; health and illnesses, 627; and M, 367–68, 750; pays for regimental banner, 573; relations with family, 201, 581, 585, 718; and Stanwix Melville, 479, 715; subsidizes *Clarel*, 784, 787; travels to England, 157, 158–59; visits Arrowhead, 253; visits Gansevoort Mansion House, 602–3
Gansevoort, Stanwix (1822–1901; M's cousin), 475–76, 529, 598, 890
Gansevoort, Susan Lansing (1804–1874; Mrs. Peter; M's aunt), 253, 463, 526, 559, 776, 784, 790
Gansevoort, Wessel (1781–1862; M's uncle), 393, 479
Gansevoort family, 703, 903
Gansevoort Hotel (N.Y.C.), 703, 831
Gansevoort Limner, 704

Gansevoort Mansion House (Gansevoort, N.Y.), 265, 269; amusements, 637; becomes family center, 477–78, 546–47, 577–80, 585; Christmas, 788–89; contents, 637, 704, 798, 835, 874; description, 635–38; emptied and sold, 889–91, 895; gradual disuse, 823, 827–28, 862, 874; Maria and Fanny move to, 269; M visits, 287–88, 368, 481, 507; photographed, 846; routine life, 507–9, 638–41; upkeep, 601, 702, 742; visitors, 288, 546, 548, 590, 598–99, 602–3, 638, 640, 747, 762
Gardiner, Alexander, 42–43
Gardner, Augustus K. (?–1876), 600, 627, 629, 643, 797
Garfield, James, 848
Garibaldi, Giuseppe (1807–1882), 450, 460–61, 487–89, 581, 655, 656
Garner, Stanton, *The Civil War World of Herman Melville*, 563, 564, 568, 572–73
Garner, William T., 807
Garnett, Edward (1868–1937), 901, 922
Garrison, William Lloyd (1805–1879), 617; "Spasmodic Philanthropy," 65
Gaskell, Elizabeth, *Life of Charlotte Brontë*, 338
Gay, Sidney Howard, 655, 717
Gayhead, Mass., 118
"The 'Gees," 223, 276
Genoa, Italy, M visits, 335–36
George, Lake (N.Y.), 287–88, 599, 660
George IV (1762–1830; king of Great Britain), 613
Germany, M visits, 337
"Gettysburg:—July, 1863," 593
Giacometti, Paolo (1816–1882), *Elizabeth of England*, 626
Gibbon, Edward (1737–1794), *Decline and Fall of the Roman Empire*, 326, 816
Gibson, John (1790–1866), 326
Gifford, Ellen, 709, 713, 715, 874, 896; death and legacy, 898, 900
Gifford, Sanford Robinson, *The Coming Storm*, 589
Gilman, Gorham D. (1822–1909), 441–42, 522
Glasgow (steamship), 294, 295
Glasgow, Scotland, M visits, 296
Godwin, John A., 364–65
Goethe, Johann Wolfgang von (1749–1832), 292, 324

Goldsmith, Oliver (1728–1774): *Citizen of the World*, 257; *The Deserted Village*, 813
Governor's House (Sailors' Snug Harbor), 652, 661, 760–61; Christmas celebrations, 672, 719–21, 825, 837, 847, 849, 852, 856, 857; Katie vacates, 859
G. P. Putnam & Co. *See* Putnam, G. P., & Co.
Grace, James W., 628
Grace Church (Lawrence, Mass.), 193
Grace Church (N.Y.C.), 67, 218
Graham, S. Lorimer, Sr., 484
Grant, Ulysses S. (1822–1885), 572–73, 748, 829, 867
Graylock, Mt. *See* Greylock, Mt.
Great Barrington, Mass., *Courier*, 183
Great Eastern (steamship), 337, 340
Greece, M visits, 304, 309–10, 320
"Greek Architecture," 419
Greeley, Horace (1811–1872), 177, 366, 455, 538
Greene, Herman Melville, 456
Greene, Richard Tobias (Toby) (1819–1892), 23, 151, 243, 455–56, 459, 882
Greene, Sarah P. M. (1856–1935), *Cape Cod Folks*, 160
Greenock, Scotland, 295–96
Greenleaf, Joseph, 653
Greenslet, Ferris, 890
Greenwich Hospital (Greenwich, Eng.), 651
Grenada (steamer), 443, 447, 453
Greylock, Mt. (Mass.): excursion to (1851), 45; excursion to (1852), 112; excursion to (1853), 173; excursion to (1862), 515
Griggs, George (1814 or 1815–1888; M's brother-in-law), 170–71, 182, 185–86, 196, 228, 354, 583, 849; attempts political appointment for M, 462; character, 894–95; death, 894
Griggs, Helen Maria Melville (1817–1888; Mrs. George; M's sister), 201; character, 252; death and funeral, 896; gifts to nieces, 895; health, 854, 857; home, 194–95; intimacy with Shaw family, 202–3; and M, 242; M visits, 228, 242; pregnancy, 243, 251–52, 267. *See also* Melville, Helen Maria
Grimm, Jakob L. K. (1785–1863), *German Popular Stories*, 778
Griswold, Rufus W. (1815–1857), 593; *Poets and Poetry of America*, 745

Grosart, A. B., "Memoir" of Robert Fergusson, 494
Guérin, Maurice de, 675–76
Guernsey, Alfred Hudson (1824–1902), 592, 624; *Harper's Pictorial History of the Great Rebellion*, 592
Gulick, John Thomas, 397–400

Hackett, James H., 721
Hafiz (Persian poet, 14th c.), 804
"The Haglets," 866
Hair, Richard Melville, 456
Hall, A. Oakey (1826–1898), 36, 534; library auctioned, 848; mayor of N.Y.C., 664, 736, 819; on *Pierre*, 133; on *White-Jacket*, 11
Hall, Judge James: *Sketches of History, Life, and Manners in the West*, 257; *The Wilderness and the War-Path*, 257
Hall, John (model for Stubb), 151
Halleck, Fitz-Greene (1790–1867), "Marco Bozzaris," 403
Hamlin, Hannibal, Vice President, 465
Hamlin, Huybertie Pruyn, *An Albany Girlhood*, 870
Hannay, James, 876
"The Happy Failure," 164, 166, 175, 213
Harper, Joseph Wesley (1801–1870), 76
Harper & Bros. (publishers): and *The Isle of the Cross*, 88, 155–56, 159; M's accounts with, 163, 187–88, 232, 276, 282, 408, 559, 588, 600, 624, 667, 826; M's relations with, 74, 88, 125, 209–10, 624; melt plates, 892; nonpayment for poems, 624; not offered *Poems*, 402, 424–25; offices burn, 187–88, 282; and "The Paradise of Bachelors and the Tartarus of Maids," 219; publish *Battle-Pieces*, 592–93; publish M's short stories in magazine, 163, 175, 212–13, 220, 268, 276; publish *Pierre*, 76–77, 84–85, 93–94; recognize M's value, 866; reject *Typee*, 72–73; reprint *Typee*, 74; sales of M's books, 30, 150, 624; and "The Tortoise-Hunters," 186–87, 209, 212
Harper's Classical Library, 435
Harper's Handy Series, 866
Hartnett sisters (boardinghouse owners, N.Y.C.), 807, 808, 824
Harvard Memorial Biographies, 735
Hatch, Agatha, 114–15, 120. See also *The Isle of the Cross*; Robertson (sailor)
Hawaiian legends, 441–42, 522

Hawthorne, Julian (1846–1934), 91, 300, 343, 802–3; *Hawthorne and His Wife*, 855, 864, 866–67; interviews M, 855–56, 917; *Literary Digest International Book Review*, 682–83; uses M's letters, 864

Hawthorne, Nathaniel (1804–1864), 99, 733, 834–35; attempts political appointment for M, 154, 298; death, 576–77; eclipses M, 119, 683, 782, 814; engraving, 909; Lenox, Mass., moves from, 1–2, 17; and M, 3, 31–32, 298–303, 668, 704–5, 801; M remembers, 678–80, 682–83; M visits in Concord, 145; M visits in Liverpool, 297–301, 342; and *Moby-Dick*, 2–3, 15, 25, 679; *Moby-Dick* dedicated to, 1; negotiates sale of *The Confidence-Man*, 297, 299; obituaries, 576–77; political appointment, 137; posthumous literary fame, 668, 680, 767, 876; as subject of *Clarel*, 684, 696, 724, 771, 780–81; vacations at the Isles of Shoals, 136–37, 686. Works: "The Artist of the Beautiful," 141, 160–61, 273; *Blithedale Romance*, 118, 119, 120, 137; *The Dolliver Romance*, 684, 732, 733, 781, 802; *Fanshawe*, 802; "First Impressions of France and Italy," 724, 740; *The House of the Seven Gables*, 683, 780; *Life of Franklin Pierce*, 128, 136; *The Marble Faun*, 433, 684; *Mosses from an Old Manse*, 589, 780; *Our Old Home*, 668, 684; *Passages from the American Note-Books*, 668, 684, 704; *Passages from the English Note-Books*, 684, 704; *Passages from the French and Italian Note-Books*, 117, 685, 739, 771–72; reissues, 767; *The Scarlet Letter*, 684; *Septimius Felton*, 685, 746; *The Snow-Image*, 91, 685, 722; *Tanglewood Tales*, 189; *Twice-Told Tales*, 77, 780

Hawthorne, Rose (1851–1926), 782

Hawthorne, Sophia Peabody (1809–1871; Mrs. Nathaniel), 2–3, 75, 300; describes M, 136, 140–41

Hawthorne, Una (1844–1877), 300

"Hawthorne and His Mosses" (M's essay on *Mosses from an Old Manse*), 358, 439, 558–59

Haydon, Benjamin, 217

Hayes, A. A., 892

Hayes, Rutherford B., 819

Hayford, Harrison (1916–2001), 76

Hayward, Dr. George, 32

Hazewell, Charles Creighton, 123–24

Hazlitt, William (1778–1830), 68; *Lectures on the English Comic Writers*, 436, 495; *Lectures on the English Poets*, 407, 436, 495; *Spirit of the Age*, 437

Headley, Joel Tyler (1813–1897), 375, 756

Hemstreet, Charles, *Literary New York*, 588

Henry (the "young Polyglot"), 329, 330–31

Henry Chauncey (steamer), 755, 758

Hero of Fort Stanwix. *See* Gansevoort, Peter (1749–1812)

Hero of the Tea Party. *See* Melvill, Thomas (1751–1832)

Herrick, Robert, 404

Higgins, Brian, and Hershel Parker, "The Flawed Grandeur of Melville's *Pierre*," 62–63

Higginson, T. W., 864

Hillard, O. G., 917–18, 921–22

Hippodrome, 307, 818. *See also* Franconi's Hippodrome

History of the Sailors' Snug Harbor, 655, 843

Hoadley, Catherine (Kate) Melville (1825–1905; M's sister): character, 251, 483, 545; family papers, 903; home, 194, 232; pregnancies and children, 245, 252–53. *See also* Melville, Catherine (Kate)

Hoadley, Charlotte (Lottie) Elizabeth (1858–1946; M's niece), 74, 321, 384, 388, 575, 577–78, 790, 811, 891; on Melville, 900–901, 903

Hoadley, Francis (Frank) W. (1865–1930, M's nephew), 640, 851, 872, 897

Hoadley, J. C., Co., 808

Hoadley, John C. (1818–1886; M's brother-in-law), 5, 94, 723; assembles M's books, 364; character, 172–73, 196, 197, 363, 482; and *Clarel*, 802, 805–6, 810–11, 816; courts Catherine Melville, 52, 94–95, 171; death and funeral, 891; engineering career, 180, 196, 366, 483, 525–26, 583, 589, 602; family trip to California, 739, 741–42, 746; finances, 356–57, 764, 767, 784–85, 848; gift to New Bedford, 628; gifts to family, 543, 702, 703; helps M, 462–63; houses, 184, 454, 526, 848; library sold, 892; and M, 173, 175, 181, 191–92, 365–66, 546; on M's work, 259; obituary for T. Melville, 858; politics, 456, 615, 809, 810–11; war work, 526, 550–51. Literary works: 184; "Berry Pond," 95; "Destiny," 172; "Foun-

Hoadley, John C. *(Cont.)*
dation Stones," 816; "In Memoriam," 816; *Memorial of Henry Sanford Gansevoort*, 735, 765, 784–86, 825, 828; "A Sermon in Rhyme," 363; "The Sounds I Love," 379, 543
Hochschild, Harold, *Township 34*, 476
Hogg, James, 614
Hoffman, Charles Fenno (1806–1884), 153, 832
Hoffman, John T. (1828–1888), 653
Holmes, John, 354
Holmes, Oliver Wendell (1809–1894), 230–31, 261, 426; *A Mortal Antipathy*, 36
Holmes, Oliver Wendell, Jr. (1841–1935), 261
Holt, Henry, *Garrulities of an Octogenarian Editor*, 710
Holy Land: M buys books about, 686–87; M visits, 314–18
Homer: trans. Alexander Pope, 385, 435; trans. George Chapman, 384–85, 434, 438–39
Honolulu, Oahu, periodicals: *Friend*, 772; *Polynesia*, 324
Hood, Thomas (1799–1845), *Poetical Works*, 493
Hooper, Richard, 438
Hoosac (or Hoosic) Tunnel, Mass., 379–80
Hope, Thomas (1770?–1831), *Anastasius*, 308
Horn, Cape, 430
Hotspur (fictional character), 261
Housekeeping, 197–99, 207, 214, 227, 670, 676
"House of the Tragic Poet," 829, 880, 883–84
Houses, individual: *Albany*: 115 Washington Ave., 561; *Boston*: 49 Mt. Vernon St., 202–3, 466–67; *Lawrence, Mass.*: Hoadley home, 184, 848; *New Bedford, Mass.*: 526; *New York City*: 150 E. Eighteenth St., 481; 103 Fourth Ave., 197; 103 E. Tenth St., 481; 60 or 104 E. Twenty-sixth St. (*see* Twenty-sixth St. home, M's); Thirty-fifth St., 525, 527. *See also* Abbotsford; Abby Lodge; Arrowhead; Black Point; Broadhall; Gansevoort Mansion House; Governor's House (Sailors' Snug Harbor); Melvill farm; Van Rensselaer Manor House; Wayside; Winyah; Woodbourne
"The House-top," 542–43

Howard, Jacob Merritt (1805–1871), 612
Howard, John (1726–1790), 501
Howard, Leon (1903–1982), 686
Howells, William Dean (1837–1920), 35, 864, 872, 884; reviews *Battle-Pieces*, 623–24
Hubbard, Henry F. (1820–1887), 150–51, 235
Humphreys, Charles A., 683; *Field, Camp, Hospital and Prison in the Civil War*, 565, 566–71
Hunt, Leigh (1784–1859), *Rimini and Other Poems*, 480
Hunt, Richard Morris (1827–1895), 822
Hunt, William Morris (1824–1879), 408, 550, 842
Hurlbut, Catherine (Kate) Cuyler Van Vechten (b. 1826; Mrs. Elisha P.; M's second cousin), 823, 838
Hurlbut, Elisha P. (1807–1889), 823, 897
Hurton, William, 276
Hutchinson, Ellen Mackay, 898
Hyer, Tom, 226–27

"I and My Chimney," 223, 259, 271, 276, 648, 676, 707
Imperialism, 5–6
"In a Bye-Canal," 418–19
Independence Day (holiday), 159, 164, 228, 378, 544, 805, 827
Index Rerum: or Index of Subjects, 36, 54, 349
Inman, John O'Brien, 549–50, 551
"Inscription for the Slain at Fredericksburgh," 562, 608–9
International Copyright Act. *See* Copyright
"In the Turret," 561
Irish immigration, 198, 542–43
Irving, Pierre (1802–1876), *Life and Letters of Washington Irving*, 412, 558–59
Irving, Washington (1783–1859), 342, 411–12, 558–59; M's literary model, 37, 412; "Rip Van Winkle," 412, 887; *The Sketch Book*, 219, 412
Irvington (locomotive), 365
The Isle of the Cross (lost), 686; actionable nature of, 120, 159–60; composition, 146–47, 154–55; genesis, 130–31, 141, 145; offered to Harper's, 156; rejected by Harper's, 88, 159; sources, 114–16, 120, 130. *See also* Hatch, Agatha; Robertson (sailor)
Isles of Shoals, Maine, 136–37, 686
Israel Potter: advertised as *The Refugee*, 624,

791; book publication, 232, 243, 247; composition, 223–27, 231; dedication, 243; hallucinatory experience, 225; magazine publication, 232–33, 247; offered to *Putnam's*, 222; pirated edition, 249; reception, 233, 247–50, 587; reprinted as *The Refugee*, 587–88; sources, 223–27; stereotype plates, 355; theme, 166, 227
Italia (paddle-steamer), 320
Ithaca, N.Y.: *Journal and Advertiser*, 371; M lectures at, 369

Jackson, Thomas Jonathan (1824–1863; "Stonewall"), 613
Jacox, Francis (pseud. "Sir Nathaniel"), 162, 341
Jaffa, Holy Land, M visits, 313
James, G. P. R. (1799–1860), 31, 122–23
James, Henry (1843–1916), 771–72, 872; *Daisy Miller*, 837; *Portrait of a Lady*, 851
Jameson, Anna (1794–1860), *Characteristics of Women*, 709
Jarves, James Jackson (1818–1888), 324; *The Art Idea*, 490
Jean-Paul. *See* Richter, Johann Paul F.
Jeffrey, Francis, Lord (1773–1850), "Memoirs . . . of Victor Alfieri," 496–98, 608; *Modern British Essayists*, 83, 406, 496, 880–81; reviews Barlow's *The Columbiad*, 435
Jehu, 510, 679
Jerusalem, Holy Land, M visits, 314–17
"Jimmy Rose," 223, 268, 269
"John Marr," 880–81, 882, 883
John Marr, 817, 879, 880–82, 916; dedication, 893–94; excerpt published, 899; presentation copies, 894, 896; review, 896
Johns, Henry T., *Life with the Forty-Ninth Massachusetts Volunteers*, 541
Johnson, Andrew (1808–1875), 602, 656
Johnson, Samuel (1709–1784), 413
Jones, John Paul (1747–1792), 226
Jones, Samuel Arthur, 757, 916
Jones, Com. Thomas ap Catesby (1790–1858), 565
Journal, 1856–57, 295–342
Journal, 1860, 427–31, 433
Judson, Edward Z. C. (pseud. Ned Buntline), 475–76

Kamehameha, Prince, 447
Kane, C. F., 864

Keats, John (1795–1821), 325, 435
Keddie, Henrietta (pseud. Sarah Tytler), *Landseer's Dogs*, 902
Kemble, John H., *The Panama Route*, 452
King, C. Henry, 796
King, C. W., *The Handbook of Engraved Gems*, 778
King, Prof., 603
King, Thomas Starr (1824–1864), 387, 426, 446, 448–49; *The White Hills*, 448, 706–7
Kinglake, Alexander, *Eöthen, or Traces of Travel*, 321
Kings, Second Book of, 510
King's Chapel (Boston), 118, 471
Kingsley, Charles, *Westward Ho!* 247
Knapp, Lucretia, 603
Kossuth, Lajos (1802–1894), 35, 40, 48–49, 51
Kraken (short form of *Pierre*). *See Pierre*
Kring, Walter, 66

Lafayette, Marquis de (1757–1834), 833
Lamb, Charles (1775–1834), 104, 374
Lansing, Abraham (1835–1899), 657, 659, 669, 713, 766, 775, 802; and M, 786–87, 817, 841, 866
Lansing, Catherine (Kate) Gansevoort (1838–1918, M's cousin; Mrs. Abraham), 766; arranges F. Melville's funeral, 870; character, 777, 799; Christmas celebration, 843–44; dog, 818; gifts to Melville family, 776, 799, 800, 801, 807–8, 815, 825, 826, 836, 838–39, 843; and Jane Melville, 775; memorial volume for Henry, 784–86, 825, 828; silver, authority on, 818. *See also* Gansevoort, Catherine (Kitty)
Lansing, Christopher Yates, Jr., 659
Lansing, Edwin Yates (1841–1937), 567, 574, 602, 669, 714
Lansing, Garret Yates (1783–1862), 153
Lanzi, Luigi, *History of Painting in Italy*, 411, 490
Larnaca, Cyprus, 319
Lathers, Abby Pitman Thurston (1821–1904; Mrs. Richard), 74, 157, 170, 459, 477, 773
Lathers, Richard (1819 or 1820–1903), 74–75, 156, 217, 644; and M, 170, 604; and Allan Melville, 384; entertains, 659–60, 853; political activities, 458–59, 473, 709; purchases land near Pittsfield, Mass., 644, 648–49, 667–68, 673; purchases property

Lathers, Richard *(Cont.)* in Charleston, S.C., 709; receives visitors, 476–77; *Reminiscences*, 170, 459; sketches G. Duyckinck, 477. *See also* Abby Lodge; Winyah

Lathrop, George Parsons, 802–3; *A Study of Hawthorne*, 782, 801

Lawrence, T. E. (1888–1935), 922–23

Lawrence, Mass., M lectures at, 363–65

Lawrence, Mass., periodicals: *Courier*, 228, 364–65; *Semi-Weekly Courier*, 193, 196, 365; *Sentinel*, 525–26

Lebanon, 319

Lectures, M's. *See* "The South Seas"; "Statues in Rome"; "Travel"

Lee, Mass., *Valley Gleaner*, 352

Lee, Robert E. (1807–1870), 611–13

"Lee in the Capitol," 611–13, 621

Leonardo da Vinci (1452–1519), 333–34

Lenox Library (N.Y.C.), 817, 822, 828, 837

Lewis, Matthew Gregory (1775–1818), *The Monk*, 54

Leyda, Jay (1910–1988). *See* Documentation

Life and Remarkable Adventures of Israel R. Potter (1824). *See* Trumbull, Henry

"The Lightning-Rod Man," 216, 222

Lincoln, Abraham (1809–1865), 453, 459; M meets, 464

Literary criticism, 439–40

Literary life (American), 80–81, 586–87, 588, 710

Literature, American national, 99–100, 403, 437, 577

Little Red Inn (Lenox, Mass.), 1, 138. *See also* Curtis Hotel

Littmann, Minna, 794, 915

Liverpool, Eng.: *Daily Post*, 864; M visits, 297–301, 342

Loch Lomond. *See* Lomond, Loch

Lockhart, John Gibson (1794–1854), 54, 297, 494

Lockwood, John Alexander (1811–1900), 310, 321–22, 336

Log (ed. Leyda). *See The Melville Log*, in Documentation

Lomond, Loch (Scotland), 296

London, Eng., M visits, 337, 340–41

London, Eng., periodicals: *Academy*, 809, 810; *Athenæum*, 18, 21–22, 105, 249, 339–40, 685; *Atlas*, 73, 102, 103, 134; *Bell's New Weekly Messenger*, 105; *Bentley's Miscellany*, 104, 138; *Britannia*, 103; *Contemporary Review*, 865–66; *Critic*, 339; *Daily News*, 338; *Daily Telegraph*, 864; *Economist*, 249; *Examiner*, 57; *Globe*, 338; *Good Words*, 724; *Illustrated London News*, 134; *Illustrated Times*, 338, 339; *John Bull*, 102, 103, 104, 134; *Leader*, 99–100, 102, 105, 339; *Literary Gazette*, 1, 90–91, 104, 338, 339; *Lloyd's Weekly*, 249; *Looker-On*, 413; *Morning Advertiser*, 104–5, 134; *Morning Chronicle*, 102; *Morning Post*, 101, 102, 104, 105; *New Monthly Magazine*, 162, 632; *New Quarterly Review*, 102; *News of the World*, 105, 211, 338; *Observer*, 413; *Pall Mall Gazette*, 899; *Punch*, 710; *Reynolds's Newspaper*, 105, 340; *Saturday Review*, 339, 340, 810; *Scottish Art Review*, 898; *Spectator*, 21–22, 103, 339; *Sun*, 337, 338; *Tatler*, 413; *Weekly Chronicle*, 249; *Weekly Times*, 105; *Westminster Review*, 339, 810

Longfellow, Henry Wadsworth (1807–1882), 849–50, 876; "Endymion," 182; *Evangeline*, 131; "Golden Legend," 208; *Hiawatha*, 403; "Tales of a Wayside Inn," 850

Longmans (London publishers), publish *The Confidence-Man*, 337

Lord of the Isle (or Isles). *See* Peebles, Anthony Augustus

Loring, Judge Edward G., 221

Louisville, Ky., *Journal*, 621

Low Countries, M visits, 337

Lowell, Charles Russell, 567, 568–71, 582

Lowell, James Russell (1819–1891), 218–19, 621; *A Fable for Critics*, 219

Lowell, Josephine (Mrs. Charles), 567, 628, 655

Lowell Institute (Boston, Mass.), 33

Luyster Brothers' Bookstore (N.Y.C.), 757

Lynn, Mass.: M lectures at, 396; *Weekly Reporter*, 396

Macgregor, John, *The Rob Roy on the Jordan*, 687

Machiavelli, Niccolò (1469–1527), 328, 335, 613; *The Florentine Histories*, 34–35

Mackay, Charles, ed., *Songs of England*, 434, 446

MacMechan, Archibald, 898

Macpherson, James (1736–1796; pseud. Ossian), *Fingal*, 436

Index

Macy, Obed, *A History of Nantucket*, 114
Macy, Thomas, 114
Madame Tussaud's (Wax Museum, London), 340
Madison Square Park (N.Y.C.), 833, 906
"Maherbal" (pseud.), 1 (the ("new resident"), 44, 122
Maitland, James A., *The Lawyer's Story*, 150, 176
Mangan, James Clarence, *Poems*, 494
The Man of the World, 587–88
Manor House. *See* Van Rensselaer Manor House
Mansfield, Lewis William (b. 1816), *Up Country Letters*, 208
Manuscripts, destruction of, 494–95
"The March to the Sea," 593, 597–98
Marcy, William L. (1786–1857), 292
Mardi, 14, 238–39, 442, 801, 845, 892, 899, 913; M compares to *Titan*, 574
Marett, Martha Bird Knapp (d. 1878), 205, 245, 836
Marett, Philip, 205, 245
Marginalia, M's (including notes): in Alger, 723; in *Ancient Spanish Ballads*, 494; in Matthew Arnold, 366, 503–4, 675–76, 723; in Thomas Arnold, 722; in Balzac, 898; in the Bible, 39, 440; in Bruyère, 502; in Byron, 481; in Dante, 437; in Staël's *Germany*, 68, 499, 500; in I. Disraeli, 494–95, 505, 513; in Emerson, 404, 501–2, 710; in Field's *Berkshire County*, 15, 255; in Grosart's "Memoir," 494; in Hawthorne, 433, 589, 722, 739; in Hazlitt's *Lectures on the English Poets*, 407, 436, 495–496, 506, 606, 878; in Homer, 438–39; in Hood, 494; in Mangan, 494; in Marvell, 413; in Milnes's "Memoir of" [Thomas Hood], 493–94; in Milton, 53, 162, 301, 359, 405, 407, 437, 438, 607, 687, 690, 733; in Moore, 494, 502; in Shakespeare, 722; in Spenser, 111, 231, 295, 404–5, 436, 438, 511, 651, 726, 754; in Vasari, 461, 482, 495, 504–5, 734; in Warton, 710; in White, 502, 608; in Wordsworth, 57, 136, 165, 334, 407, 436, 585, 840; in *Works of Eminent Masters*, 719; on Arnold, 504; on Browning, 504, 719; on Emerson, 723; on Jeffrey's "Memoirs of Alfieri," 498–99; on Milton, 606, 754; on Spenser, 690; on Wordsworth, 496
Marnon, Dennis, 710

Marr, John (fictional character), 744
Mar Saba, Holy Land, 770; M visits, 315
Martha's Vineyard, Mass., 118
Marvell, Andrew, *The Poetical Works*, 413
Masquerade parties, 262–64, 290, 421–22
Massachusetts (steamship), 113–14
Massachusetts Fifty-fourth Volunteer Infantry Regiment, 541, 551, 628
Massachusetts Institute of Technology (Cambridge, Mass.), 872
Massachusetts Second Volunteer Cavalry Regiment camp, 564–67, 571–72
Mathews, Cornelius (1817–1889), 81, 897
Matthews, Brander, 898
Maturin, Charles Robert (1782–1824), 105
Mausoleum, 670
McKay Sewing Machine Association, 366, 543
Meadows, Kenny, 767
Meister, Wilhelm (fictional character), 324
Melvill, Allan (1782–1832; M's father), 713; as cannibal, 11, 117; claim against estate, 59; penmanship exercise book, 90, 275
Melvill, Allan Cargill (1823–1832; M's cousin), 10
Melvill, Anne Marie Priscilla. *See* Melvill, Priscilla (1810–1858)
Melvill, Françoise Lamé-Fleury (1781–1814; M's aunt), 148
Melvill, Mary Ann Augusta Hobart (1796–1884; Mrs. Thomas, Jr.; M's aunt), 861
Melvill, Nancy Wroe (1780–1813; M's aunt), 200, 467
Melvill, Priscilla (1784–1862; M's aunt), 126, 199–200, 201, 524
Melvill, Priscilla (1810–1858; M's cousin), 121, 140, 185, 213, 217, 244, 384; as model for Isabel in *Pierre*, 59–61
Melvill, Robert (1817–1881; M's cousin), 43, 848; called by M "Cousin Doolittle," 626
Melvill, Susan Bates (1814–1885; Mrs. Robert), 43
Melvill, Thomas (1751–1832; M's grandfather), 766; estate, 185, 199
Melvill, Thomas, Jr. (1776–1845; M's uncle), 5, 166, 235, 746; M's memoir of, 5, 717
Melvill, Thomas Wilson (1806–1844; M's cousin), 11, 429, 669
Melvill family, 199–201
Melvill farm (Pittsfield, Mass.), 4–5

Melville, Allan (1823–1872; M's brother), 288; accompanies M to Washington, D.C., 562–63; as archivist, 71–72, 351, 506, 558; and Arrowhead, 121, 530–32, 647, 707; assists T. Melville, 653, 654; attempts political appointment for M, 152, 459, 460, 462–63; character, 205, 483, 525, 529, 531; and Civil War, 506, 528, 543, 562–67; contributes sketch of M for Duyckincks' *Cyclopædia*, 246, 271; courtship and remarriage, 382–84, 414–15; death, 736; depicted, 759; donates M's works, 717; draws family wills, 483, 518; estate, 740, 743, 751, 761; illnesses and health, 204, 229, 382, 516, 528–29, 596, 701, 708, 712, 735; as literary representative, 71, 84–85, 211, 291, 402, 423–25; marginalia, 712; and real estate, 204–5, 216, 271, 414–15, 527, 530–31, 600–601; travels to the Mediterranean and England, 590, 591, 594–96, 597; visits Stockbridge, 444–45; visits Winyah, 476–77

Melville, Augusta (Gus) (1821–1876; M's sister), 263; attempts Custom House appointment for M, 346–47; character, 797; as copyist, 70, 152, 178, 207–8, 243, 261, 286; commonplace book, 626; correspondence archive, 798; death and funeral, 797–98; engagements, 182; housekeeping, 207, 214, 641; intimacy with Van Rensselaer family, 203–4, 603; illnesses, 791, 796–97; religious practice and views, 41, 232, 509, 627

Melville, Catherine (Kate) (1825–1905; M's sister), 52, 94–95, 100, 149; copyist, 152; wedding, 175, 180. *See also* Hoadley, Catherine (Kate) Melville

Melville, Catherine (Katie) E. (1842–1928; Mrs. Thomas), 656–57, 859–60; character, 658, 661; honeymoon, 660; wedding, 657–60, 661

Melville, Elizabeth (Bessie) (1853–1908; M's daughter), 681; birth, 155; childhood, 290, 345–46, 516–17; education, 537–38, 905; illnesses and health, 537–38, 783, 835, 838, 857, 862, 905; infancy, 181; inheritance, 836, 900; intellectual capacity, 905

Melville, Elizabeth (Lizzie) Knapp Shaw (1822–1906; M's wife; also "Dolly," "Lizzy-Ann"): accepts death, 713–14; baptized, 740; character, 31, 347–48, 777, 778; as Cypherina Donothing, 263, 626; daily routines, 174, 344, 761; donates bust of her father, 550; finances, 531, 715, 749–51, 767, 861, 895–96; as "the Genius of Greylock," 290; gifts from M, 228, 456, 626, 778, 893; gives M pocket-money, 863; housekeeping, 214, 381, 555–56, 714–15, 782; helps M, 362–63, 424–25, 793, 888, 903–4; illnesses, 31, 32, 33–34, 91–92, 509–10, 680, 681–82, 715, 740–41; income, 460; inheritance, 157, 396–97, 472, 515, 531, 580, 603, 836, 861, 895, 898, 900; and Jane Melville, 537–38; literary judgment, 110, 444, 633; marriage settlement, 157; marital problems, 585–86, 599–600, 626, 628–35; on marriage, 897; and M's work, 897; move to New York, 530–33, 555–56; as parent, 646, 681; pregnancies and childbirth, 31, 143, 144, 155, 223; and Sarah Morewood, 552–54; tours Berkshire County, 547–48; vacations, 675, 776, 822, 871; visits father's home, 343; war work, 541; as wife, 795, 821

Melville, Florence (1850–1919; M's niece), "My Country Home," 647–48

Melville, Frances (1855–1938; M's daughter), 681; baptized, 549; birth, 243; childhood, 516–17, 590; destroys M's letters, 466; engagement, 826–27; inheritance, 836, 900; relations with M, 624–25, 794–95; relations with Melville family, 630–31; wedding, 845. *See also* Thomas, Frances Melville

Melville, Frances Priscilla (Fanny) (1827–1885; M's sister), 641, 742, 823; character, 95, 865, 867; death and funeral, 870; estate, 889, 897; illnesses, 865, 867, 869; moves to Mansion House, 269; uses name Priscilla, 846; will, 868, 869

Melville, Gansevoort (1815–1846; M's brother), 63, 146, 252, 736, 866; childhood achievements, 49; compared to M, 152–53, 244; helps M, 9; influence on M, 36, 54, 176, 301, 432; remembered by family and friends, 96, 413, 669, 735, 751, 832

Melville, Helen Maria (1817–1888; M's sister): as copyist, 64, 85, 95, 152; courtship, 95, 182; wedding, 190–91. *See also* Griggs, Helen Maria Melville

MELVILLE, HERMAN (1819–1891)
LIFE: accidents, 295–96, 522–23; aging,

effects of, 818–19, 835, 850, 878, 882, 883; ambrotyped with T. Melville, 426; appetite, 845; biography, suggested, 892, 897; books, given, 1, 151, 170, 191–92, 193, 228, 474, 510–11, 578–79, 591, 702, 709, 752, 767, 778, 812–13, 861, 902; books, purchases, 143, 406, 408, 413, 472, 476, 479, 480, 493–96, 499, 501–3, 609, 613, 675, 684–85, 686–87, 704, 709, 722–23, 772, 807, 896, 919; cats, 800, 874; character, 139, 151, 163, 370, 387, 632–33, 739; Civil War, witnesses, 562–73; collects art, 485, 910–12; conversation, 5, 37, 231, 291, 300, 343, 398, 399, 669, 915, 917–18; daguerreotyped, refuses to be, 81, 139, 219; daily routine, 850; death, 920; death, attitude toward, 431, 523; debts, 6, 37, 122, 137, 241, 255, 282, 286, 667; defaults on loans, 142, 155, 180, 185, 225, 232, 245, 251, 264, 269–70; demeanor, 757–58; destroys letters, 556; dogs, 126, 524; employment as customs inspector, 603–4, 756–57, 871, 877; enrolled in Militia, 473; family relations and responsibilities, 34, 37–38, 92–93, 216, 416, 624–25, 628–35, 874–75, 906; as father, 91, 426, 430–32, 474, 512, 516–18, 521, 646, 681, 744, 875; finances, 37, 92, 192, 280–82, 285–86, 289, 396–97, 416–18, 750, 787, 900; friends, 170, 173–74, 175, 828, 832; gossip, subject of, 25, 38, 41, 51, 397, 399, 530; as grandfather, 906, 910, 913; and Hawthorne, 1–3, 6–8, 37, 62, 75, 298–302, 342–43, 559, 576–77, 678–80, 682–83, 771–72, 781, 784, 803; horse, 126, 509–10, 512; illnesses and health, 152–53, 161, 209, 244, 261, 286, 288–89, 314, 320, 326–27, 371, 373, 374, 411, 427, 484, 500, 516, 574, 758, 792–93, 826, 857–58, 871, 900, 902; inheritance, 524, 811, 820, 897, 898, 900; invisibility, 820, 847, 849, 850, 852, 857; as lecturer, 196, 242, 344, 355–56, 357–76, 408–10, 413–14; literary pilgrimage, subject of, 397–400; marriage, 142, 213–14, 215, 465–66, 517, 585, 626, 628–35, 671, 885; obituaries, 905, 921–22; offends C. G. Lansing, 842–43; photographed, 479, 482, 554, 874; physical descriptions, 277, 292–93, 371–72, 395, 397–400, 479, 875, 890, 914, 919; pipe, 808; political appointment, seeks, 143, 146, 152–54, 155–56, 346–47, 460–66; portraits, 703, 704, 715, 907, 910; poverty, attitude toward, 220, 304; psychological development, 9–12; reading, 144, 217, 262, 402–8, 411, 413, 429, 433–40, 490, 493–505, 558, 589, 815, 854–55, 864, 885, 897, 904; reclusiveness, 142, 663–64, 710, 799, 850, 915–18; Reconstruction, views on, 613–15; religious and philosophical views, 5, 31, 38, 39–40, 48, 68–69, 74, 231, 300, 358–59, 405, 499–500, 571, 922; resemblance to cousins, 10, 759, 760, 811, 842; residence in N.Y.C., 480–81, 535; retreats to Sailors' Snug Harbor, 741, 742, 799; returns to N.Y.C., 493, 532, 552, 555–56; sanity questioned, 73, 88, 123, 125, 132, 140, 585–86, 600, 630, 631, 632; as sex symbol, 44–45; silver wedding anniversary, 746, 750; slavery, attitude toward, 220–21, 241–42; social responsibilities, 139, 263; as storyteller, 588, 890–91; teaches school, 44; tours Berkshire County, 111–13, 379–80, 515, 521, 547–48; tours Italy, 321–36; tours the eastern Mediterranean region, 303–20; vacations, 287–88, 378–81, 478, 669–70, 705–7, 718, 746, 776, 783, 785–86, 807, 822–24, 851, 856, 872; values, 400; visits Albany, 669; visits Bermuda, 893; visits Glens Falls, 890–91; visits Savannah, 897; visits Scotland, Liverpool, and Chester, 295–303; visits Washington, D.C., 464–66, 562–63; visual arts, appreciation of, 325–27, 330, 334, 485–86, 490, 560–61, 588–89, 660, 670, 674–75; voyage of 1860, 416, 426, 427–53; walks, 914–16, 919; will, 895; work, attitude toward, 818

LITERARY WORK: accounts with publishers, 6, 93, 98–99, 163, 187–88, 232, 559, 588, 667, 826; aesthetic theories, 160–61, 270, 273, 313, 334, 358, 492–93, 503–5, 710; agrees to stop writing, 343, 351; ambition, 6, 88–89, 438, 439, 559, 575, 682, 685, 723, 784, 813–14; as reviewer, 557; autographs requested, 261, 850; bio-critical surveys, 271, 277–78, 555; career, M's analysis of, 16, 83–85, 142, 633, 922; career, retrospective surveys, 150, 162, 183, 211, 271, 276, 349; Civil War, 543, 545–46, 548–49, 561–75; compositional methods, 164, 880, 887–88; Dante's influence on, 13; eclipsed by Hawthorne, 119,

MELVILLE, HERMAN
LITERARY WORK *(Cont.)*: 673, 682–83, 782, 864, 892; fragments, 880, 882–87; growth as a writer, 9, 179, 215–16, 239, 270, 922; Hawthorne as subject, 684, 696, 780–81; imagery, 12–14, 57, 164–65; lectures *(see* "Statues in Rome"; "The South Seas"; "Travel"); magazine contributions, 138, 163; marginalia *(see* Marginalia, M's); offers topic to Hawthorne, 130–31, 141; payment for, 185, 209, 211, 212, 216, 218, 219, 222, 232, 234, 247; poetry, 379, 385, 392, 402–8, 440–41, 493, 513, 561, 710, 777, 778, 784, 816–17; possible subjects, 114–15, 120, 563; profits or losses, 98–99, 588; pseudonyms, 107 ("Guy Winthrop"), 211 ("Salvator R. Tarnmoor"); psychological phenomena in, 9–10, 12–15, 61–64, 134–35, 225, 656; publishers, 73–74; recognition, 710–11, 850, 863–67, 872–73, 875–77, 888, 889, 899, 901, 922–23; reputation, 16, 650, 673, 772, 803, 813–14; responses to reviews, 81; reviews by *(see* "Hawthorne and His Mosses"; "Mr. Parkman's Tour"; "A Thought on Book-Binding"); Shakespeare's influence on, 12–13; short stories, 163–68, 174–75; theory of creativity, 10, 679–80, 682–85; unfinished projects, 878, 882–87; Wordsworth's influence on, 164–66, 606–7, 609. *See also individual titles:* "The Admiral of the White"; "After the Pleasure Party"; "The Age of the Antonines"; "The Armies of the Wilderness"; "Art"; "At the Hostelry"; "Authentic Anecdotes of 'Old Zack' "; "Ball's Bluff. A Reverie"; "Bartleby, the Scrivener"; *Battle-Pieces;* "The Bell-Tower"; "Benito Cereno"; *Billy Budd, Sailor;* "Burgundy Club Sketches"; "Chattanooga"; *Clarel;* "Cock-A-Doodle-Doo!"; "The College Colonel"; *The Confidence-Man;* "The Conflict of Convictions"; "The Cumberland"; "Donelson"; "Dupont's Round Fight"; "The Encantadas"; "The Fiddler"; "Fragments from a Writing Desk"; "The Frenzy in the Wake"; "The 'Gees"; "Gettysburg:—July, 1863"; "Greek Architecture"; "The Haglets"; "The Happy Failure"; "Hawthorne and His Mosses"; "House of the Tragic Poet"; "The House-top"; "I and My Chimney"; "In a Bye-Canal"; "Inscription for the Slain at Fredericksburgh"; "In the Turret"; *The Isle of the Cross* (lost); *Israel Potter;* "Jimmy Rose"; "John Marr"; *John Marr; Journal, 1856–57; Journal, 1860;* "Lee in the Capitol"; "The Lightning-Rod Man"; "The March to the Sea"; *Mardi; Moby-Dick;* "Montaigne and His Kitten"; "Morning in Naples"; "Mr. Parkman's Tour"; "Naples in the Time of Bomba"; *Narrative of a Four Months' Residence* (see *Typee);* "October Mountain" (unlocated); *Omoo;* "The Paradise of Bachelors and the Tartarus of Maids"; "The Parthenon"; "Pausilippo"; "Philip"; "The Piazza"; *The Piazza Tales; Pierre; Poems* (1860) (lost); "Poor Man's Pudding and Rich Man's Crumbs"; "The Portent"; "Rammon" (fragment); *Redburn;* "Rip Van Winkle's Lilacs"; "The River" (fragment); "The Scout toward Aldie"; "Shadow at the Feast"; "Sheridan at Cedar Creek" *(see* "Philip"); "Shiloh: A Requiem"; "Sketch of Major Thomas Melvill Junior by a Nephew"; "The South Seas"; "Statues in Rome"; "The Stone Fleet"; "A Symposium of Old Masters at Delmonico's" *(see* "At the Hostelry"); "The Temeraire"; "A Thought on Book-Binding"; *Timoleon;* "The Tortoise-Hunters" (lost fragment); "Travel"; "The Two Temples"; *Typee;* "A Utilitarian View of the Monitor's Fight"; "Venice"; "Weeds and Wildings Chiefly"; *The Whale* (see *Moby-Dick); White-Jacket; Works of Herman Melville* (Constable edition)

Melville, Jane Dempsey Randolph (1824–1890, Mrs. Allan; M's sister-in-law), 382–84, 414–15, 663, 825, 846; character, 415, 537, 564, 720, 853; death and funeral, 900; and George Dillaway, 825, 902; entertains, 704, 721; estate, 902; and stepdaughters, 538, 775, 868–69, 900; takes possession of Arrowhead, 536–37; visits Europe, 743, 748, 758–59, 853; will, 901–2

Melville, Julia (1854–1854; M's niece), 234

Melville, Lucy (1856–1885; M's niece), 280, 857, 868–69

Melville, Malcolm (Mackey or Mackie) (1849–1867; M's son), 681, 889; advice from M, 426, 432; character, 640, 642, 646; childhood, 174, 263, 344, 392, 516; death and funeral, 642–46; education, 510, 511; employment, 594; exposed to parents' marital problems, 600; gift from mother, 481; inscribes Bible, 583; photographs of, 646–47, 649, 742–43, 746; relations with M, 625; religious observations, 579–80; schooling, 482, 509; sees reviews of *Battle-Pieces*, 624; volunteer regiment, 641–42, 645, 742–43

Melville, Maria Gansevoort (1791–1872; M's mother), 525, 630–31; accident, 627; advice to children, 195–96, 198, 253–54; death and funeral, 740; fears for M's health, 152–53; finances, 596; illnesses, 559, 575, 594, 734, 737–38; move to Gansevoort, 269; reading, 591; religious views, 38–39, 40, 96, 195; urges political appointment for M, 152–54

Melville, Maria Gansevoort (Milie) (1849–1935; M's niece), 204, 262, 381–82, 392, 592, 649, 680; engagement, 763–64; role in family, 714; schooling, 533, 597, 605; "The Story of the Summer of 1869," 676–78, 681; "Thanksgiving-Day," 592; wedding, 774–75. *See also* Morewood, Maria Melville

Melville, Sophia Eliza Thurston (1827–1858; Mrs. Allan; M's sister-in-law), 70, 97–100, 262, 280; death, 382; health, 101, 144, 204, 381–82; visits Arrowhead, 121, 170

Melville, Stanwix (Stannie or Stanny) (1851–1886; M's son), 671, 681, 707–8; baptized, 549; and brothers and sisters, 509, 646; character, 702, 777–78, 782–83, 789; childhood, 474, 509, 511, 516; death, 888; education, 510; employment, 671, 673, 681, 702, 755, 758, 766, 773–74, 812, 815; finances, 812, 815, 839, 849; health, 671, 852; infancy, 31, 174; inheritance, 836, 900; religious views, 507; travels, 714, 738–39, 741, 743–44, 756, 758; visits to Gansevoort Mansion, 288, 291, 344, 478, 500, 707, 715

Melville, Thomas (1830–1884; M's brother), 121, 209; ambrotyped with M, 426; arrivals and departures, 9, 192, 244, 250, 252, 388, 396, 415, 482, 583, 627; career, 388, 484, 585, 589, 651, 787–88; character, 125–26, 196, 205; death and funeral, 858, 860; depicted, 754; and his family, 390, 393, 592, 596–97, 663; engagement and wedding, 656–60, 661; health, 852, 857; honeymoon, 660; obituary, 858–59; portrait, 860; *Redburn* dedicated to, 9; shore leaves, 112, 127, 137, 192–97, 250–51, 389–90, 483–84; voyage of 1860, 415; will, 483, 859. *See also* Sailors' Snug Harbor

Melville family: ancestry, 903; correspondence, 748; intimacy with Lemuel Shaw and family, 203; motto, 922

The Melville Log (ed. Leyda). *See* Documentation

Mermaid Series (of Elizabethan drama), 904

Messina, Sicily, M visits, 321–22

Metcalf, Eleanor Melville Thomas (1882–1964; M's granddaughter), 630, 658, 900. *See also* Thomas, Eleanor

Meteor (clipper ship), 196, 452–53, 483; captained by T. Melville, 388; voyage of 1860, 427–33, 442–43

Meucci, Antonio, 487, 656

Michelangelo Buonarroti (1475–1564), 328, 330, 734

Milan, Italy, M visits, 333–34

Miller, Joseph, 226–27

Miller & Curtis (publishers), 354–55

Milnes, Richard Monckton (1809–1885), "Memoir of" [Thomas Hood], 493

Milton, John (1608–1674), 404, 405; *Complete Poetical Works*, 31, 434; "Lycidas," 405, 690; *Paradise Lost*, 37, 162, 300–301, 359–60, 405, 607, 687, 689, 784; *Samson Agonistes*, 405, 438, 733

Milwaukee, Wisc., M lectures at, 394

Milwaukee, Wisc., periodicals: *Daily Free Democrat*, 394–95; *Daily Wisconsin*, 394–95, 442; *Sentinel*, 394

Minot, Kate Sedgwick (Mrs. William), 201

Mitchell, Donald G., 154

Mitchell, Maria (1818–1889), 116–17, 421–22

Mitchell, William (1791–1869), 116

Mitford, John, "Life of Milton," 405

Moby-Dick: American reception of *Moby-Dick*, 22–30, 38, 71–73, 110; binding of *The Whale*, 90–91; British and American reviews, 82, 134–35; British reception of *The Whale*, 17–22, 31–32, 101–6; British reviews quoted in U.S., 18–22, 32–33, 73, 99–100; composition, 12; criticism, 555; dedication, 1; Hawthorne offers to review, 3, 8; letter to Hawthorne about, 7–8, 15,

Moby-Dick (Cont.)
17; M's comments on, 15–16; models for characters in, 40, 151; presentation copies of *Moby-Dick*, 1, 74; presentation copies of *The Whale*, 90, 151, 191–92; as psychological novel, 12–15, 134–35; publication party, 1, 679; reception, 17–30, 33, 38, 72–73, 82, 99–100, 102–6, 134–35; recognition, 588, 710, 865; sales, 30, 106; "The Town-Ho's Story," 115, 163

Modern British Essayists, 402, 406, 428, 439–40, 496, 880

Mohawk (yacht), 807

"Montaigne and His Kitten," 874

Montégut, Emile, 250

Montgomery, Isaac, 772

Montreal, Que. (Canada), *Advertiser*, 368; M lectures at, 368

Moore, Thomas, *Poetical Works*, 494

Moredock, John, 257

Morewood, Allan (1875–1880), 825

Morewood, John Rowland (Rowland) (1821–1903), 5, 48, 173, 649

Morewood, Maria Melville (Milie) (1849–1935; Mrs. William; M's niece), 825, 840, 847, 849. *See also* Melville, Maria Gansevoort (Milie)

Morewood, Sarah Huyler (1824–1863; Mrs. John Rowland), 1, 2, 4, 50, 78, 169, 268, 480–81; burial, 554–55; death and funeral, 552–54; and George Duyckinck, 43, 45–48, 50, 52, 378, 477; and Alexander Gardiner, 42–43; "Greylock Thoughts," 45, 47; as hostess, 4, 41, 47–50, 262–64, 290, 421–22, 518, 549, 551–52; illnesses, 231–32, 384, 474, 480; and M, 48; visits Bash Bish, 552

Morewood, William Barlow (1847–1923), 50, 553, 554, 555, 677, 680, 762–63

Morgan, Edmund, 109

Morgan, Sen. Edwin Denison (1811–1883), 653

Mormonism, 742

"Morning in Naples," 419–21, 422, 489, 834, 879–80. *See also* "Naples in the Time of Bomba"

Morris, William (1834–1896), 898–99; *The Earthly Paradise*, 685

Morse, Samuel F. B. (1791–1872), 740

Mosby, John Singleton (1833–1916), 564–71, 581–83

Mosque of Omar (Jerusalem), 315

Mother Goose, 622

Mourning gifts, 717, 751–52, 799, 801, 825

"Mr. Parkman's Tour" (M's review of *The California and Oregon Trail*), 22

Mumford, Lewis, *Herman Melville*, 906

Munro, George F., 353

Murray, John, III (1808–1892), 100, 899

Murray's Home and Colonial Library, 876, 899

"My Chimney and I." *See* "I and My Chimney"

Mysseri (dragoman), 321

Nantucket, Mass., M visits, 112, 114–18

Nantucket, Mass., periodicals: *Inquirer*, 23, 113, 116, 357; *Weekly Mirror*, 116

"Naples in the Time of Bomba," 323, 420–21. *See also* "Morning in Naples"

Naples, Italy, M visits, 322–23

Napoleon I (1769–1821), 436

Narrative of a Four Months' Residence. *See Typee*

Nassau, the Bahamas, 708–9, 712–13

Nast, Thomas (1840–1902), 609–10

National Academy of Design (N.Y.C.), 588–89, 715

National Theatre (Cincinnati, Ohio), 373

Naushon Island, Mass., 118

Nelson Monument (Liverpool, Eng.), 298

Newark, N.J., *Daily Advertiser*, 349

New Bedford Copper Works (New Bedford, Mass.), 483, 526, 602

New Bedford, Mass., 113; M lectures at, 370, 373

New Bedford, Mass., periodicals: *Daily Mercury*, 248, 284; *Republican Standard*, 628; *Sunday Standard*, 794, 915

New Brighton, Staten Island, 652, 655

New Haven, Conn., M lectures at, 369

New Haven, Conn., periodicals: *Daily Palladium*, 29–30; *Journal and Courier*, 369; *New Englander*, 737

New Orleans, La., *Commercial Bulletin*, 11, 132–33

New South Church (Boston, Mass.), 467–71

New York Custom House, 336, 736; conditions, 756–57; M employed by, 603–5; M retires from, 877; M's duties, 693–95, 854, 871, 878; M's first post, 605; M's vulnerability, 667, 755, 757, 778, 818; office, 690,

691, 818, 821, 856; pay cut, 787; possible position for M, 346–47, 351, 355, 462; restores pay, 808
New-York Historical Society, 734
New York National Guard Second Volunteer Infantry Regiment, 641–42, 645, 742–43
New York, N.Y.: architecture, 414, 828–29; M lectures at, 390–91; M returns to, 555–56; M winters in, 480–81; waterfront, 690–93
New York, N.Y., periodicals: *Albion*, 25–26, 29, 128, 134, 248, 619, 620, 621–22; *American Machinist*, 172; *American Publishers' Circular*, 283; *American Review* (also called *American Whig Review* and *Whig Review*), 86, 142, 632; *Appletons' Journal*, 675, 707; *Arcturus*, 848; *Atlas*, 283; *Broadway Journal*, 176, 327; *Christian Inquirer*, 645; *Churchman*, 72, 82, 284–85; *Colophon*, 918; *Commercial Advertiser*, 82, 506, 617, 916–17; *Criterion*, 284; *Daily News*, 276–78, 283, 284, 587; *Day Book*, 132, 350, 632; *Democratic Review* (see *United States Magazine and Democratic Review*); *Dispatch*, 667; *Dollar Magazine* (see *Holden's Dollar Magazine*); *Eclectic Magazine*, 20–21, 163, 685; *Evangelist*, 82; *Evening Express*, 620; *Evening Mirror*, 129; *Evening Post*, 211, 248, 270, 272, 506, 619–20, 643–44, 667, 718; *Evening Telegram*, 775; *Figaro!* 277, 848; *Frank Leslie's Illustrated Newspaper*, 817; *Galaxy*, 807; *Harper's New Monthly Magazine*, 25, 27–28, 29, 57, 73, 99, 188, 208, 220, 223, 245, 269, 276, 375, 408, 592, 593, 604, 611, 622, 651, 685, 713, 744, 754, 756, 884; *Harper's Weekly*, 356, 408, 580–81, 591, 592, 610, 905; *Herald*, 54, 122, 123, 132, 183, 187, 192, 233, 238, 242, 411, 412, 447, 452–53, 506, 542, 558, 615–16, 617, 666–67, 679, 743, 805, 902; *Holden's Dollar Magazine*, 23; *Home Journal*, 25, 27, 29, 133, 412, 540; *Independent*, 25, 72, 82, 412, 605, 617–18, 622–23, 805; *International Magazine*, 21; *International Review*, 813; *Lantern*, 140; *Leader*, 621; *Library Table*, 807; *Literary Digest International Book Review*, 682–83; *Literary World*, 22–25, 38, 56, 77–78, 93, 107, 119–20, 128, 133, 179, 188, 403, 558–59, 848; *Mail and Express*, 896; *Methodist Quarterly Review*, 30, 73, 82; *Morning Courier and New-York Enquirer*, 233, 247; *Mrs. Stephens's Illustrated New Monthly*, 350; *Nation*, 619, 621, 771–72; *National Police Gazette*, 255; *National Quarterly Review*, 619, 620, 621; *Nautical Gazette*, 858; *North American Miscellany*, 21; *Norton's Literary Gazette*, 231, 247, 249; *Parker's Journal*, 30; *Press*, 921; *Putnam's Monthly Magazine*, 150, 166, 188, 210, 216, 246, 247, 249, 259, 269, 271, 276, 355, 650, 685; *Round Table*, 618, 620; *Scribner's Magazine*, 690–93, 801; *Spirit of the Times*, 25, 28, 29, 124; *Sun*, 807, 828–29, 902; *Times*, 138, 350, 382–83, 412, 447, 451, 452, 453, 487, 506, 558, 587, 616, 644, 655, 666, 667, 702, 736, 806, 813, 827, 837–38, 839, 917, 921–22, 923; *Tribune*, 25–26, 29, 82, 134, 153, 177, 284, 356, 411, 452, 480, 484, 487, 489, 506, 577, 587, 622, 644, 668, 717, 718, 724, 790, 791, 801, 802–3, 804, 806, 920–21; *United States Magazine and Democratic Review*, 72, 82, 110, 632; *World*, 397, 540, 604, 618, 620, 716, 745, 791, 804, 805, 921; *Yankee Doodle*, 757, 848
New York Society Library, 898
New York Thirteenth Cavalry Regiment, 539, 573, 575
Nichols, George Ward, *The Story of the Great March*, 609
Nichols, Thomas Low (1815–1901), 11
North, Christopher. *See* Wilson, John
North Adams, Mass., *News and Transcript*, 550
North Conway, N.H., 705–7
North Dutch Church (Albany, N.Y.), 658, 791
North Star (steamship), 452, 453
Nourse, Amos (1794–1877; M's uncle), 92, 268, 464–65, 825–26
Nourse, Lucy Melvill (1795–1877; Mrs. Amos; M's aunt), 125, 268, 280, 825

O'Brien, Fitz-James, 150, 349
Ocean House (Nantucket hotel), 114
O'Conor, Charles (1804–1884), 36, 154
"October Mountain" (unlocated), 223
Offley (whaleship), 238
Offley, Edward S., 309
Oken, Lorenz, *Elements of Physiophilosophy*, 191
Oliphant, Laurence (1829–1888), 917
Olmsted, Frederick Law, 250

Olsen-Smith, Steven, 710
Olson, Charles (1910–1970), 630
Olympus, Mount (Greece) 305
Omar Khayyám (12th c.), *Rubáiyát*, 885, 889, 909
Omoo, 9–10, 864; compared to later works, 129–30, 162, 215–16; reception, 16, 82
The Oregon Trail. *See* Parkman, Francis: *The California and Oregon Trail*
Orsay, Harriet, A. F., Comtesse d', *Clouded Happiness*, 408
Osborne, Frances Thomas (1883–1980; M's granddaughter), 845, 905–6, 910, 913–14. *See also* Thomas, Frances Cuthbert
Osgood, Samuel, 644, 645, 718
Ossian. *See* Macpherson, James
Oxford, Eng., M visits, 341–42

Pacific commerce, 375–78
Padua, Italy, M visits, 331–32
Page, William (1811–1885), 326–27
Paley, William, *Natural Theology*, 68
Palgrave, Francis (1788–1861), "Superstition and Knowledge," 15–16
Palmer, Erastus Dow (1817–1904), 560; *The White Captive*, 368, 560
Palmer, E. H., *The Desert of Exodus*, 687
Paltsits, Victor Hugo, 321, 790, 866
Panama, 375, 451–52
Panama Railroad, 262, 375
Panics (financial): *1857*: 355, 356, 363, 525; *1873*: 764–65
Panoramas, 257, 368
"The Paradise of Bachelors and the Tartarus of Maids," 212–13, 219, 245, 412; publication, 250
Paris, France, *Revue des deux mondes*, 249–50
Parker, Amasa J. (1807–1890), 153, 346–47, 653, 802
Parker, Cora Strong (1846–1883), 854
Parker, Harriet L. (1814–1889), 892, 895, 897
Parker, Hershel. *See* Higgins, Brian, and Hershel Parker
Parker, Theodore (1810–1860), 221
Parkman, Francis (1823–1893), 655–56; *The California and Oregon Trail*, 22
Parkman, George (1790–1849), 113
"The Parthenon," 419
Parvin, Rev. R. J., 180, 191

Pasquin, Antoine Claude, *Historical... Travels in Italy*, 490
Paul, Capt., 673, 674
"Pausilippo," 419
Paxton, William, 657
Peabody, Rev. Ephraim, 118
Peabody, George (1795–1869), 159, 413–14
Peabody, S. Endicott, 427
Peabody Institute (Danvers, Mass.), 411, 413
Pease, Capt. Valentine, 150, 915
Peck, George Washington (1817–1859), 142–43; reviews *Omoo*, 16, 82; reviews *Pierre*, 85–86, 142–43
Peebles, Anthony Augustus (1822–1905; M's second cousin "Augustus" or, among the Melvilles, "Lord of the Isle"), 182, 190, 265, 288, 736, 748, 891
Peebles, Maria Van Schaick (1782–1865; M's mother's first cousin), 264, 587
Peebles, Mary (Mrs. Augustus), 844, 859–60, 866
Pellico, Silvio (1789–1854), 421, 880
Pera, Turkey, M visits, 306
Periodicals (newspapers and magazines). *See under city of publication*
Perseverance (whaleship), 235
Peterson, T. B., & Bros. (publishers), 355, 587–88, 624, 791
Petra (now Jordan), 317
Petroleum, 583, 589
Phaeton, 58, 843
Philadelphia, Pa., periodicals: *American Literary Gazette*, 555, 618; *Daily Evening Bulletin*, 284, 350, 673, 808; *Dispatch*, 156; *Graham's Magazine*, 133; *Inquirer*, 620, 621; *Ledger*, 460; *Lippincott's*, 810; *North American*, 349; *Peterson's Magazine*, 30; *Press*, 805; *Sunday Dispatch*, 167; *Times*, 866
"Philip," 583, 593, 604, 620–21
Phillibrown, Thomas, 909
Phillips, Wendell (1811–1884), 221
"The Piazza," 273–74, 492, 648
The Piazza Tales: composition, 164; Constable edition, 899; offered to Dix, 271–72; publication, 271–72, 275, 276, 283; reception, 283–85; stereotype plates, 354–55
Picturesque, 490–91, 492–93
Pierce, Franklin (1804–1869), 128, 137, 154, 298, 576
Pierre, 30, 53–64; attacks Unitarian doctrine, 67–69; autobiographical elements, 404;

Berkshire County setting, 45–46, 58, 62, 87; biographical basis, 58–61; composition, 7, 8–9, 34–35, 49, 51; Constable edition, 899; dedication, 88; expansion, 79–88; family artifacts in, 58–59; offered to Bentley, 71, 99, 106–7, 108; plates melted, 892; presentation copy, 130; proofreading, 99; psychological novel, 13–15, 62–63, 135; publication, 70–71, 79, 93–94; reception, 54, 85–86, 123–25, 128–30, 131–34, 140; recognition, 711, 899–900; sales, 150; sources, 33, 54–58, 68, 69, 82, 406; style, 57, 61, 87; themes, 41–42, 61, 62–64

Piranesi, Giambattista (1720–1778), 660

Pirates, 238–39

Pittsfield, Mass., 520–21, 813; and Civil War, 473, 480–81, 545–46, 548–49; M lectures at, 388; M moves to, 520; M vacations at, 872; schools, 533. *See also* Arrowhead; Broadhall; Burbank's Hall; Melvill farm; St. Stephen's Protestant Episcopal Church

Pittsfield, Mass., periodicals: *Evening Journal*, 261; *Sun*, 66, 221, 244, 278, 285, 345, 354, 385, 386, 549, 678

Plaisted House (Jefferson, N.H.), 822

Plato, *Symposium*, 422

Poe, Edgar Allan (1809–1849), 99, 435, 436; "The Business Man," 176; M compared to, 188, 283, 285; *Works*, 456

Poems (1860) (lost or dispersed), 441; composition, 422–23; instructions for publication, 423–26, 443; offered to Charles Scribner, 443; offered to Rudd & Carleton, 444; poetic models, 422; probable contents, 418–23; remnants, 879. *See also individual poems:* "After the Pleasure Party"; "The Age of the Antonines"; "Greek Architecture"; "In a Bye-Canal"; "Morning in Naples"; "The Parthenon"; "Pausilippo"; "Venice"

Poetics, 404–7, 438–40, 606–7, 676

Poetry: American, 403, 437; audience for, 437–40, 497–500, 503–5, 685–86; British, 685–86; M studies, 433–39

Poets of the Nineteenth Century, 408

Pollard, Capt. George, 117

Polynesia, 882

Pompeii, Italy, M visits, 322

Pond, Frederick Eugene, *Life and Adventures of "Ned Buntline,"* 476

Pond, Rachel Turner, 677

Pontoosuc, Lake, 45–46

Pony Express, 431, 445

"Poor Man's Pudding and Rich Man's Crumbs," 165, 213, 220, 222–23

Pope, Alexander. *See* Homer

"The Portent," 611

Porter, George, 747

Porter, William T. (1809–1858), 124

Portland, Maine, *Transcript*, 617, 622

Potter, Henry L., 605

Poverty, 220, 304, 363

Powell, Thomas (1809–1887): "Ambrotype" of M, 277–78, 631; "Herman Melville—Romancist," 277; and *Pierre*, 123, 140; reviews *The Piazza Tales*, 283

Powers, Hiram (1805–1873), 330, 492, 675

Presidential campaigns: *1864*: 580–81, 582; *1872*: 748; *1876*: 811

Prince, Lebarron, 410

Prince, William R., 410

Proverbs, Book of, 192

Pruyn, John Van Schaick Lansing (1811–1877), 560, 573

Pruyn, Robert H. (1815–1882), 653, 791, 849

Pullan, Matilda M., *The Modern Housewife's Receipt Book*, 228

Putnam, George P. (1814–1872), 138, 668, 751; rejects "The Two Temples," 219; serializes "The Encantadas," 210

Putnam, G. P., & Co. (publishers), 179, 211, 246, 268, 271; and *Clarel*, 790, 839; publish *Israel Potter*, 232, 243, 247, 276; publish M's short stories, 188, 210, 216, 222, 271, 276; sales, 268. *See also* Dix & Edwards; New York, N.Y., periodicals: *Putnam's Monthly Magazine*

Pyramids (Egypt), 340; M visits, 311–13

Queequeg (fictional character), model for, 40

Quidor, John (1801–1881), 560

Quincy, Ill., M lectures at, 396

Quincy, Josiah (1772–1864), 195

Rabelais, François (ca. 1494–ca. 1553), M compared to, 349, 350

Race, 257, 377, 458, 615, 654; Melville family attitudes toward, 597; M's attitude toward, 614, 687

Radcliffe, Anne, *The Mysteries of Udolpho*, 54

"Rammon" (fragment), 883, 922

Randall, Robert Richard (d. 1801), 652, 821, 854
Randolph, Louisa Jane Dempsey. *See* Melville, Jane Dempsey Randolph
Rankin, Col. George Campbell, 295
Ranlett, William, 652
Rebellion Record, 610
Reconstruction. *See* Civil War (U.S.)
Redburn, 588; autobiographical basis for, 11; presentation copy, 90; proposed reissue, 901; psychological consequences to M, 9, 11–12
The Refugee. See *Israel Potter*
Reni, Guido, 769
Richards, William C., *Great in Goodness*, 479–80
Richmond County, Staten Island, *Gazette*, 667, 858
Richmond, Va., periodicals: *Semi-Weekly Examiner*, 129; *Southern Literary Messenger*, 129, 131
Richter, Johann Paul F. (1763–1825), *Titan*, 572, 574
Ripley, George (1802–1880), 25–26, 134
"Rip Van Winkle's Lilacs," 412, 886–87
Ristori, Adelaide (1822–1906), 626
"The River" (fragment), 286–87
Riverside Park (N.Y.C.), 916
Roanoke (U.S. ship), 539
Roberts, W., 271
Robertson (sailor), 114–15, 120
Rochester, N.Y., M lectures at, 370
Rochon, Alexis Marie de, *Voyage to Madagascar and the East Indies*, 143–44
Rockford, Ill., M lectures at, 395
Rockford, Ill., periodicals: *News*, 395; *Register*, 395–96; *Republican*, 395
Rockwell, Julius, 159, 164, 353, 463, 466
Rockwood (N.Y.C. photographer), 874
Rogers, Samuel (1763–1855), *Pleasures of Memory*, 495
Rolfe (fictional character), 684. See also *Clarel*
Root, Dr. O. S., 32, 48
Romans, Book of, 440
Rome, Italy, M visits, 324–27
Rosa, Salvator, 321
Rossetti, Dante Gabriel (1828–1882), 711
Rothenberg, Albert, *The Emerging Goddess*, 10
Rousse, Anna M. (b. 1825), 325, 328

Rousse, Peter Warren (1832–1887), 325, 328
Rudd & Carleton (publishers), 444
Ruins, Greek, 816
Russ, Oliver, 455
Russell, W. Clark (1844–1911), 865, 867, 889, 892, 893; dedicates *An Ocean Tragedy* to M, 892, 899; *Horatio Nelson*, 896; *In the Middle Watch*, 866; praises *John Marr*, 899; "Sea-Stories," 865

Saddleback Mountain (Mass.). *See* Greylock, Mt.
Sailors' Snug Harbor (Staten Island, N.Y.): administration and management, 664–67, 747, 752–53; description, 652–53, 654, 655; history, 651–52; improvements, 664, 747, 821–22, 827, 854; inmates, 654, 702, 744; news coverage, 666–67, 702, 713, 716–17, 754, 837–38, 843; T. Melville appointed governor, 653; trustees' entertainments, 663, 675, 745, 839
Salonica, Greece, M visits, 304–5
Salt, H. S., 898–99, 916
Saltus, Edgar Evertson, *Balzac*, 871–72
Sandberg, Robert A., 883–84
San Dominick (fictional slave ship), 239–40
Sands, Robert Charles, *Life and Correspondence of John Paul Jones*, 226
Sandusky, Ohio, *Register*, 243
Sandwich Islands (Hawaiian Islands), 459–60
Sanford, Edward, 271, 802
San Francisco, Calif., M visits, 443, 445–50
San Francisco, Calif., periodicals: *Daily Alta*, 446; *Daily Evening Bulletin*, 430, 445–46, 451, 619, 622; *Mercantile Gazette*, 450
Sankaty lighthouse (Nantucket, Mass.), 116
San Marco, cathedral of (Venice), 332
Santa Anna (or Ana), Antonio López de (1795?–1876), 655
Saratoga Lake, 600
Saratoga Springs, N.Y., 288, 823; M lectures at, 368
Saunders, Charles, 317–18
Savage, Samuel Hay (1827–1901), 109–10, 849
Savannah, Ga.: M visits, 897; *Republican*, 55
Schell, Augustus (1812–1884), 347
Schiller, J. C. F. (1759–1805): *Don Carlos*, 437; *Ghost-Seer*, 308; *Poems and Ballads*, 434
Scoonie, Scotland, 296

Scott, Sir Walter (1771–1832), 54, 296, 566, 614; *The Lady of the Lake*, 686; *The Lay of the Last Minstrel*, 686; *The Talisman*, 55, 726; *Waverley*, 55

"The Scout toward Aldie," 565, 566, 578

Scribner, Charles (publisher), 443

Sealts, Merton M., Jr. (1915–2000), *The Early Lives of Melville*, 845

Seaver, Chandler, 707

Secession crisis. *See* Civil War (U.S.)

Sedgwick, Catharine (1789–1867), 64–65, 201, 263; *The Poor Rich Man and the Rich Poor Man*, 220

Sedgwick, Charles (1791–1856), 31, 64, 288

Sedgwick, Elizabeth (1801–1864; Mrs. Charles), 31, 64

Seneca, Lucius Annaeus (ca. 4 B.C.–A.D. 65), *Morals*, 193

Serapis (British ship), 226

Sereno, Bonito. *See* "Benito Cereno"

Servants, 197–99, 455, 509, 541–43, 589–90, 596–97, 715, 782

Sewing machines, 543, 723

Sexual behavior, 42, 527

"Shadow at the Feast," 847

Shakers and Shaker settlements, 112, 537

Shakespeare, William (1564–1616), 56–57, 342, 404, 887. Works: *Coriolanus*, 56; *Hamlet*, 56; *Henry IV, Part 1*, 261, 574; *Julius Caesar*, 279, 440; *King Lear*, 56; *Macbeth*, 56, 404; *A Midsummer Night's Dream*, 361–62; *Pearls of Shakespeare*, 767; *Poetical Works*, 511; *Sonnets*, 722; *The Tempest*, 12–13; *Timon of Athens*, 502; *The Winter's Tale*, 56

Sharp, J. C., 109

Shaw, Caroline Cobb (1821–1884; Mrs. John Oakes; M's sister-in-law), 92, 146, 862

Shaw, Francis G., 655

Shaw, George Bernard, 899

Shaw, Hope Savage (1793–1879; Mrs. Lemuel; M's mother-in-law), 2, 32, 127; death and funeral, 841; estate, 841; hostility to M, 20, 109–10

Shaw, John Oakes (1820–1902; M's brother-in-law), 125, 127, 145–46; on *Pierre*, 128

Shaw, John Oakes, Jr. (1850–1909), 127, 533

Shaw, Josephine (1848–1933), 127, 343

Shaw, Lemuel (1781–1861; M's father-in-law), 38; alleged alcoholism, 217; attempts political appointment for M, 153–54; bust, 550; character, 281; death and funeral, 467–71; description, 158, 367, 470; financial assistance to M, 281–82, 285–86, 287, 385, 396–97, 417–18; illnesses, 127, 261, 344; judicial duties, 116, 418; political activities, 457–58; portrait, 145, 408, 550, 842; relationship with M, 116, 125, 144; visits Arrowhead, 181, 381; visits Europe, 147–48, 158–59; visits Nantucket with M, 113–18; will, 157, 472

Shaw, Lemuel, Jr. (1828–1884; M's brother-in-law), 20, 32, 100; career, 841–42; death, 860; encourages Melville marital separation, 600; estate, 861; hostility to M, 20, 32, 109–10, 125, 161; travels with father, 158–59; visits Bentley office, 109

Shaw, Oakes. *See* Shaw, John Oakes

Shaw, Samuel S. (1833–1915; M's brother-in-law), 112, 121, 169, 327–28; character, 630; encourages Melville marital separation, 599–600, 629–30; meets M in Rome, 327, 346

Shaw, Thomas Budd, *Outlines of English Literature*, 718

Shelley, Mary (1797–1851), *Frankenstein*, 134

Shelley, Percy Bysshe (1792–1822), 325; *The Cenci*, 325, 768; *The Poetical Works*, 472; *Prometheus Unbound*, 324

Shenstone, William, *Poetical Works*, 511

Shepherd, Daniel: M's verse epistle to, 401, 402; *Saratoga: A Story*, 288, 293

Sheridan, Philip, 582–83

"Sheridan at Cedar Creek." *See* "Philip"

"Shiloh: A Requiem," 621, 745

Siaconset, Mass., 116

Siddons, J. H. *See* Stocqueler, Joachim Hayward

Silver, 661

Silvio. *See* Pellico, Silvio

Simms, William Gilmore (1806–1870), reviews *Pierre*, 140

Sir Nathaniel. *See* Jacox, Francis

"Sketch of Major Thomas Melvill Junior by a Nephew," 5, 717, 813

Slavery, 35, 220–21, 241–42, 400

Smith, J. E. A. (1822–1896; Joseph), 48, 215, 262–63, 290, 522; "Herman Melville," 46, 261, 276, 522–23, 533, 872; *The History of Pittsfield (Berkshire County)*, 223, 717, 813; *Pontoosuc Lake*, 164, 384; *Taghconic*, 95, 139, 184

Smyrna, Turkey, M visits, 309, 320

Smythe, Henry A. (1817–1884), 336, 603, 605, 861
Somers (U.S. brig), mutiny on, 475, 514
Sorrento, Italy, M visits, 323
Souther, Helen Melvill (1798–1864; Mrs. Levitt; M's aunt), 200
Southgate, Horatio (1812–1894), 736–37
"The South Seas" (lecture): bookings, 385–87; composition, 374; content, 374–78; delivery, 386; reception, 386, 389, 391, 393–96; tour, 386, 388, 391, 393–96
Spenser, Edmund (ca. 1552–1599), 404, 434; "Colin Clout's Come Home Again," 295, 404, 406; *The Faerie Queene*, 111, 231, 404–5, 651, 726; *The Poetical Works*, 472, 510–11, 578–79
Sprague, William Buell, 658
Springfield, Mass., *Republican*, 17, 30, 129, 230, 255, 455, 520–21, 549, 550, 551, 552, 553, 577, 605, 618, 679, 803, 809–10, 921
Squier, Ephraim George: *Nicaragua: Its People*, 376; *Waikna: or, Adventures on the Mosquito Shore*, 262, 376, 451
Staël, A. L. G., Mme. de (1776–1817), *Germany*, 68, 499–500
Stanley, Arthur Penrhyn, *Sinai and Palestine*, 687
Stanton, Edwin, 528, 563
Starr, Alfred, 755
Staten Island, N.Y., 652, 655–56, 662–63. *See also* New Brighton, Staten Island; Sailors' Snug Harbor
"Staten Island Savages," 716–17
Statue of Liberty, 808, 833, 891
"Statues in Rome" (lecture): content, 356, 357, 358–62; delivery, 364, 370–71; profits and losses, 373; reception, 365, 366, 370–71, 373; tours, 363, 364, 366, 368–73
Stedman, Arthur, 893, 912, 920; "Introduction" to *Typee*, 493, 914, 918; " 'Marquesan' Melville," 397
Stedman, E. C., 443–44, 873, 896, 898, 918; *Library of American Literature*, 898; *Poets of America*, 893
Stephens, John Lloyd (1805–1852), 375; *Incidents of Travel in Central America*, 451; *Incidents of Travel in Egypt*, 178, 227, 317, 687
Stewart, Tertullus D., 6 ("Lansingburgh friend"), 33, 354; lends M money, 256; paid off, 285; presses M for repayment, 264, 278
St. Gaudens, Augustus, 821, 833, 854

Stirling, Scotland, 296
St. John, N.B. (Canada), *News*, 30
St. Johnstone, Charles, 894
St. Joseph's Cathedral (Albany, N.Y.), 460
Stocqueler, Joachim Hayward (pseud. J. H. Siddons), 477
Stoddard, Charles Warren, 650
Stoddard, Elizabeth Barstow (Mrs. Richard Henry), 125, 604
Stoddard, Richard Henry, 154, 443–44, 604, 618, 745; reviews *John Marr*, 896
"The Stone Fleet. An Old Sailor's Lament," 561; sources, 480
Storm King (clipper ship), 447
St. Peter's Cathedral (Rome), 324
Strain, Lt. Isaac, 375
Stratford-upon-Avon, Eng., M visits, 342
Stratton, Charles Sherwood (1838–1883; aka Tom Thumb), 527
Street, Alfred Billings, 139, 172, 817
St. Sophia, mosque of (Constantinople), 307
St. Stephen's Protestant Episcopal Church (Pittsfield, Mass.), 25, 94, 96, 180, 191, 554, 852
Stuart, Gilbert (1755–1828), 704, 910
Sumner, Charles (1811–1874), 462–66, 773, 829, 831
Swain, William, 118
Swift, Jonathan (1667–1745), 302; *Gulliver's Travels*, 257
Switzerland, M visits, 336
"A Symposium of Old Masters at Delmonico's." *See* "At the Hostelry"
Syra, Greece, M visits, 304

Taconic Dome. *See* Washington, Mt. (Mass.)
Taitt, Capt. Robert, 303, 309
Tarnmoor, Salvator R. (pseud. of M), 211
Tasso, Torquato (1544–1595), 435
Taunton, Mass., *Daily Gazette*, 619
Taylor, Bayard (1825–1878), 291–92, 393, 395, 491, 586–87; "National Ode," 805
Taylor, Benjamin Rush (b. 1820), 572
Taylor, Henry, *Notes from Life*, 480
Taylor, Tom, *Life of Taylor*, 217, 227
"The Temeraire," 561
Tennyson, Alfred, first baron (1809–1892), 283, 404, 876. Works: *Enoch Arden*, 625, 685; *The Holy Grail*, 625, 685, 709; *Idylls of the King*, 685; *In Memoriam*, 685, 722; *Maud*, 685; *The Princess*, 422; *Poetical Works*, 479

Terence (190?–159? B.C.), 572, 574
Thackeray, William Makepeace (1811–1863), *Newcomes*, 208
Thanksgiving (holiday), 144, 186, 234, 343, 454, 583, 777, 874–75
Thayer, Cornelia (Nilly) Paterson Van Rensselaer (1823–1897; Mrs. Nathaniel), 92, 190, 201, 203–4, 548
Thomas, Eleanor (1882–1964; M's granddaughter): birth, 849; birthday gift, 902; christening, 853. *See also* Metcalf, Eleanor Melville Thomas
Thomas, Frances Cuthbert (1883–1980; M's granddaughter), birth, 856. *See also* Osborne, Frances Thomas
Thomas, Frances Melville (1855–1938; M's daughter): children, 849, 856, 901; and M, 847; moves to New Jersey, 845. *See also* Melville, Frances
Thomas, Henry B. (1855–1935; M's son-in-law): courts Frances Melville, 824, 837, 838; engagement, 826–27; marriage, 837; remembers M, 824, 837, 850, 914, 915
Thomas, Katharine Gansevoort (1890–1968; M's granddaughter), 901. *See also* Binnian, Katharine G.
Thomson, James (1700–1748): *Poetical Works*, 476, 511; *Seasons*, 112
Thomson, James (1834–1882, pseud. B. V.), 863, 889; *The City of Dreadful Night*, 864; *Essays and Phantasies*, 877; *Satires and Profanities*, 877; *Shelley, a Poem*, 896; *Vane's Story*, 864; *A Voice from the Nile*, 897
Thomson, William McClure, *The Land and the Book*, 408
Thoreau, Henry David (1817–1862), 279; *Walden*, 876; *Week on the Concord and Merrimack Rivers*, 279
Thorp, Willard (1899–1990), 890
Thorpe, Thomas Bangs (1815–1878), "The Big Bear of Arkansas," 256
"A Thought on Book-Binding" (M's review of Cooper's *The Red Rover*), 22, 517
Thumb, Tom. *See* Stratton, Charles Sherwood
Thurston, Charles M., Jr. (1819–1878), 170, 826
Ticknor, William, 576
Tiffany & Co., 573, 574, 750, 751–52, 801, 818, 909
Tilden, Samuel J. (1814–1886), 819

Timoleon, 418, 423, 817, 879; dedication, 902–3; presentation copy, 903
Tivoli, Italy, M visits, 327
"Toby." *See* Greene, Richard Tobias
Todd, John (1800–1873), 386, 477; *The Student's Manual*, 712. *See also Index Rerum*
Toft, Peter (1825–1901), 889, 911, 914, 917
Toledo, Ohio, *Blade*, 243
Tombs (N.Y.C. prison), 178, 227
Tomes, Robert (1817–1882), 74, 293; *Panama in 1855*, 262, 376, 451, 756; *The War with the South*, 609
Toombs, Robert Augustus (1810–1885), 617–18
"The Tortoise-Hunters" (lost fragment), 186–87, 209–12, 216–17, 219, 223
"The Town-Ho's Story." *See Moby-Dick*
Townsend, Edward Davis, 743
Transcendentalism, 69, 260
Transportation, 201–2, 217–18, 599, 741–42
"Travel: Its Pleasures, Pains, and Profits" (lecture): bookings, 411; content, 409–10
The Travellers Club, 491, 587
Tropic (sailing ship), 450
Troy, N.Y., periodicals: *Budget*, 129; *Daily Whig*, 506
Trumbull, Henry, *Life and Remarkable Adventures of Israel R. Potter* (1824), 223–24. *See also Israel Potter*
Tryal (slave ship), 237
Tucker, Abraham, *An Abridgement of "The Light of Nature Pursued,"* 68, 170, 408, 477
Tuckerman, Henry T. (1813–1871), 246, 284, 461, 481, 655; character, 484–85; collects art, 485–86; collects books, 486; death, 718, 734; and Garibaldi, 487–89; library auctioned, 745; and M, 484–87, 593, 718–19; revises *Old New York*, 484, 593–94; studio, 485. Works: *American Artist Life*, 327; "Authors in Berkshire," 555; *Book of the Artists*, 487; *Isabel; or, Sicily*, 486; *Italian Sketch Book*, 487; *Life of Silas Talbot*, 487; "Sketches of American Literature," 718; *Thoughts on the Poets*, 496
Tupai Cupa (model for Queequeg), 40
Tupper, Martin Farquhar (1810–1889), 40, 132, 810
Turin, Italy, M visits, 334–35
Turnbull, John, *A Voyage Round the World*, 754
Turner, J. M. W. (1775–1851), 341; *The Fighting Temeraire*, 341

Tussaud, Madame. *See* Madame Tussaud's
Twenty-sixth St. home, M's (N.Y.C.), 205, 216, 234; art, 910–11; atmosphere, 906–7; contents, 907–12; description, 906–10; disrepair, 835–36; entertainments, 557, 672, 774; garden, 908; improvements, 836–37; move to, 555–56; purchase, 530–31, 580; visitors, 626–27, 649, 658–59
Twitchell, Asa (1820–1904), 802, 910
The Two Captains, 587–88
"The Two Temples," 218–19, 222, 879
Tyler, Robert O., 567, 572, 574, 578
Typee, 23, 207, 588, 716–17, 751, 754, 767–68, 864, 919; compared to later works, 129–30, 162, 215–16; cultural icon, 882; expurgated, 74, 82; presentation copy, 605; proposed new edition, 899, 901; reception, 16; rejected by Harpers, 73–74
Tytler, Sarah. *See* Keddie, Henrietta

"Umi: A Tale of Hawaii," 441–42
Unitarian church, 68–69, 176–77; doctrine, 65, 220, 501, 760, 795
United States (U.S. frigate), 9, 455, 473
U.S. Sanitary Commission, 540–41, 559–60
Unwin, T. Fisher (London publishers), 901
Utica, N.Y., *Daily Gazette*, 30
Utilitarian philosophy, 68–69
"A Utilitarian View of the Monitor's Fight," 561

Van Buren, John (1810–1866), 36, 85
Van Rensselaer, Stephen (1789–1868), 658
Van Rensselaer Manor House, 603, 889
Van Schaick, John (ca. 1820–1856; M's second cousin), 182
Vasari, Giorgio (1511–1574), *Lives of the . . . Painters*, 411, 433, 490, 495, 504–5, 734
Vatican City (Rome), M visits, 325–26
Vedder, Elihu (1836–1923): *Jane Jackson, Formerly a Slave*, 589; *Rubáiyát*, 885, 909; *Timoleon* dedicated to, 903
Venereal disease, 527, 529, 595
"Venice," 418
Venice, Italy, M visits, 332–33
Verdi, Giuseppe (1813–1901), *Macbeth*, 321
Vermilye, Rev. Thomas E. (1803–1893), 658, 740
Vesuvius, Mt. (Italy), 322
Vine (fictional character), 684. See also *Clarel*
Virgil, *The Aeneid*, trans. John Dryden, 435

Voltaire, François-Marie Arouet (1694–1778), 405

Wales, George W., 454, 716, 787, 818, 820
Wales, Henry, 850
Walker, George, *The Three Spaniards*, 54
Wallace, William, 296
Waller, John Francis, 103–4
Walpole, Horace (1717–1797): *Anecdotes of Painting*, 739; *Mysterious Mother*, 54
Wamsutta Club (New Bedford, Mass.), 113
Warburton, Bartholomew E. G., *Travels in Egypt*, 687
Ward, Capt. James H., 476
Ward, Thomas W., 158
Ware, William (1797–1852), 232
Warner, Dr., 920
Warren, Lavinia, 527
Warton, Thomas (1728–1790), *History of English Poetry*, 710
Washington, D.C., M visits, 464–66
Washington, D.C., periodicals: *National Era*, 12, 129, 133; *National Intelligencer*, 26, 28–29, 82, 134–35, 138, 403, 444, 460, 612, 782
Washington, Mt. (Mass.), 112, 174, 546, 547
Wayside (Concord, Mass., Hawthorne residence), 120, 145
Webster, John W. (1793–1850), 113
Weed, Thurlow (1797–1882), 464
"Weeds and Wildings Chiefly," 880, 884–85, 886–87; dedication, 904
Wegelin, Oscar, 918–19
Welles, Gideon (1802–1878), 519
West, Edward C., 154
West, William Edward (1788–1857), 472, 593
The Whale. See *Moby-Dick*
Whipple, Edwin Percy (1819–1886), 195, 448
White, Henry Kirke (1785–1806), *Poetical Works*, 502, 607–8
White, Richard Grant (1821–1885), 757, 821
White, Stanford (1853–1906), 821, 843, 854
White Bear (hotel, Liverpool, Eng.), 297–98
White-Jacket, 896, 911
Whitman, Walt (1819–1892), 621, 622, 872–73, 893; "Crossing Brooklyn Ferry," 741; *Leaves of Grass*, 135, 364; *Poems* (ed. W. M. Rossetti), 876
Whitmarsh, Caroline, 378, 549, 551; "A Rep-

resentative Woman" (tribute to Sarah Morewood), 552; "The Town in Gross," 520–21
Whittier, John Greenleaf (1807–1892): *The Chapel of the Hermits*, 172; *Snow-Bound*, 686
Whitwell, Lucy Cushing Scollay (1788–1883), 854
Wiley, John (1808–1891), 74
Willard, Mr., 297
Williams, Theodore Chickering, 863, 920
Willis, George S., 285, 396–97, 522
Willis, Nathaniel Parker (1806–1867), 336, 412; and Forrest divorce, 36, 85; reviews *Moby-Dick*, 26–27; reviews *Pierre*, 133
Willis, Samuel, 255
Willson, Forceythe (1837–1867), 621
Wilson, James, 387
Wilson, John (1785–1854; pseud. Christopher North), 406; "An Hour's Talk about Poetry," 402
Windsor, Vt., *Journal*, 1 (article by a "newcomer"), 44, 122
Winthrop, Guy (pseud. of M), 107
Winthrop, Theodore (1828–1861): *The Canoe and the Saddle*, 656; *John Brent*, 656; *Life in the Open Air*, 656
Winyah (New Rochelle, N.Y.; Lathers residence), 74, 184, 659–61, 853; M visits, 74, 156–57, 477, 681
Wolfe, Theodore F., 917; *Homes of American Authors*, 230–31; *Literary Haunts and Homes*, 906

Wood, Henry, 319
Woodbourne (Minot estate), 201
Worcester, Mass., *Palladium*, 82
Wordsworth, William (1770–1850), 57–58, 334, 360, 404, 434, 436, 585, 834; *The Excursion*, 57–58, 405, 784; "Immortality," 496; *Lyrical Ballads*, 334, 606–7, 609; *The Prelude*, 57; "Resolution and Independence," 328; "Vaudracour and Julia," 405–6; *The White Doe of Rylstone*, 136
The Works of Eminent Masters, 490, 719
Works of Herman Melville (Constable edition), 899
Worth, Francis S., 626
Worth, William J., 831–32; monument, 831–32
Wright, Jean Melvill (1788–1866; Mrs. Winslow; M's aunt), 199, 200, 594
Wyman, Morrill, *Autumnal Catarrh*, 747, 762

Yokohama (merchant ship), 674
Yonkers, N.Y.: *Examiner*, 377, 386; M lectures at, 386
York, Eng., M visits, 297
Young, Brigham (1801–1877), 741–42
Young, William, 26

Zenobia (character in *Blithedale Romance*), 119
Zion Church (N.Y.C.), 736, 751
Zummo (or Zumbo), Gaetano Giulio (1656–1701), 329–30, 340